SEMPER FIDELIS

SEMPER FIDELIS

*The History of the
United States Marine Corps*

Allan R. Millett

THE MACMILLAN WARS OF THE
UNITED STATES

Louis Morton, *General Editor*

Macmillan Publishing Co., Inc.
New York

Collier Macmillan Publishers
London

Copyright © 1980 by Allan R. Millett

The Free Press
A Division of Macmillan Publishing Co., Inc.
866 Third Avenue, New York, N.Y. 10022

Collier Macmillan Canada, Inc.

First Free Press Paperback Edition 1982

Library of Congress Catalog Card Number: 80-1059

Printed in the United States of America

printing number paperback
4 5 6 7 8 9 10

printing number hardcover
5 6 7 8 9 10

Library of Congress Cataloging in Publication Data

Millett, Allan Reed.
    Semper fidelis.

    (The Macmillan Wars of the United States)
    Bibliography: p.
    Includes index.
    1. United States. Marine Corps—History. I. Title.
II. Series: Macmillan Wars of the United States.
VE23.1154   359.9′6′0973   80-1059
ISBN 0-02-921590-3
ISBN 0-02-921570-6 pbk.

Contents

ACKNOWLEDGMENTS   vii

INTRODUCTION   xi

PART ONE: SOLDIERS AT SEA, 1775–1909

1   American Marines in the War for Independence, 1775–1783   3

2   The New Corps, 1798–1815   26

3   Archibald Henderson Preserves the Corps, 1815–1859   52

4   The Marine Corps Survives Its Doldrums, 1859–1889   87

5   The Marine Corps and the New Navy, 1889–1909   115

PART TWO: COLONIAL INFANTRY, 1899–1941

6   To Sunny Tropic Scenes, 1899–1914   147

7   Hispaniola, 1915–1934   178

8   The Marines in China, 1905–1941   212

9   Nicaragua: End of an Era, 1926–1933   236

PART THREE: AMPHIBIOUS ASSAULT
          FORCE, 1900–1945

10 The Creation of the Advanced Base Force, 1900–1916   267

11 The World War, 1917–1919   287

12 Amphibious Warfare and Fleet Marine Force, 1919–1939   319

13 World War II: Defeating Japan in the
    South Pacific, 1939–1944   344

14 World War II: Amphibious Drive Across the
    Central Pacific, 1943–1945   388

PART FOUR: FORCE IN READINESS, 1945–1970s

15 Winning the Right and Means to Fight, 1945–1950   445

16 The Korean War: Fighting on Two Fronts, 1950–1953   475

17 Building the Force in Readiness: Years of Trial and
    Accomplishment, 1953–1965   518

18 The Longest War: The Marines in Vietnam, 1965–1975   559

19 The Once and Future Corps, The 1970s   607

APPENDIX 1   COMMANDANTS OF THE CORPS   627

APPENDIX 2   STRENGTH OF THE MARINE CORPS   628

APPENDIX 3   UNITED STATES MARINE CORPS CASUALTIES   629

NOTES   631

ESSAY ON SOURCES   727

INDEX   754

Acknowledgments

Much like a Marine amphibious landing, the production of a scholarly history is the responsibility of one but represents the contributions of many. During the seven years I worked on this book, I enjoyed the assistance, encouragement, and support of many professional colleagues, acquaintances, and friends. I believe this book's strengths reflect their industry and concern. In no sense should any of them be held responsible for either errors in fact or misjudgments in interpretation, since I enjoyed final editorial control throughout this project. Nor does anything in this book represent the official position on history or current policy of the United States Marine Corps or any portion of it.

My primary debt is to the late Professor Louis Morton of Dartmouth College, the first editor and originator of this series. I hope that the final product comes close to matching the volume Professor Morton envisioned.

For both the research and editorial review of the book, I am indebted to Brigadier General Edwin H. Simmons, USMC (Ret.), the director of the Marine Corps History and Museums Division, and his staff at the Marine Corps Historical Center, Washington Navy Yard. I received critical assistance from two deputy directors of the division, Colonel Herbert M. Hart and Colonel John E. Greenwood, and their principal civilian associates, chief historian Henry I. Shaw, Jr., and the head of oral history, Benis M. Frank. All five read all or parts of the manuscript and made many suggestions for research and interpretation. Other current and former members of the History and Museums Division contributed their time as advisers and critics: Ralph W. Donnelly, Jack Shulimson, Dr. Graham A. Cosmas, Charles R. Smith, Lieutenant Colonel Gary W. Parker, USMC, and Major David N. Buckner, USMC.

I relied heavily upon the research suggestions of other members of the History and Museums Division, primarily reference historians Gabrielle M. Santelli and Dr. Martin K. Gordon, librarians Patricia E. Morgan and Evelyn A. Englander, operational records archivist Joyce E. Bonnett, personal papers curator Charles A. Wood, and still photograph archivist Gunnery Sergeant William K. Judge, USMC. I also appreciated the courtesy and friendship of all the other members of the division with whom I came in contact.

At the National Archives of the United States, I found the staff research advisers always patient, imaginative, and helpful. In the Military Archives Division I am indebted to Harry Schwartz, Dr. Gibson B. Smith, Dr. Timothy K. Nenninger, and Dr. William H. Cunliffe. I received equally competent assistance from another portion of the National Archives system, the staffs of the presidential libraries of Herbert Hoover (West Branch, Iowa), Franklin D. Roosevelt (Hyde Park, New York), Harry S. Truman (Independence, Missouri), Dwight D. Eisenhower (Abilene, Kansas), John F. Kennedy (Cambridge, Massachusetts), and Lyndon B. Johnson (Austin, Texas). I also appreciate the assistance I received from the staffs of the Manuscript Division of the Library of Congress and the Naval Historical Foundation.

As the scope of my research widened in the number and geographic location of sources, I profited from the assistance of many willing friends new and old. Among them are Dr. Dean C. Allard and Dr. William J. Morgan of the Naval History Division of the Department of the Navy; Dr. B. F. Cooling III and Dr. Richard T. Sommers of the U.S. Army Military History Institute; the staffs of the U.S. Army Center of Military History and the Naval War College; Karen L. Jackson and Harry McKown of the Southern Historical Collection, University of North Carolina Library; Charles G. Palm, deputy archivist for the Hoover Institution on War, Revolution, and Peace; and the staff of Breckinridge Library, Education Center, Marine Corps Development and Education Command. I want to acknowledge especially the research and advisory assistance of four of my former doctoral students, Dr. Peter Maslowski of the University of Nebraska-Lincoln; Lieutenant Colonel J. Frederick Shiner, USAF, of the U.S. Air Force Academy; Michael West of the staff of the House Committee on Armed Services; and Larry D. O'Brien. I also appreciate the assistance I received from those

Ohio State University students who served as my research assistants, especially Lauren Stevens, James Fehr, and V. Keith Fleming.

As I worked on this book I profited from the advice and often the critical reading of individual chapters from enough interested friends to form either a very distinguished platoon or a crack historical unit. For their encouragement and assistance I am indebted to Colonel Douglas T. Kane, USMC (Ret.); Colonel Kenneth J. Clifford, USMCR; Major Donald F. Bittner, USMCR; General Wallace M. Greene, Jr., USMC (Ret.); the late Colonel Robert D. Heinl, Jr., USMC (Ret.); the late Senator Paul H. Douglas; former Senator Mike Mansfield; Brigadier General James D. Hittle, USMC (Ret.); Robert Sherrod; Hanson W. Baldwin; General Charles L. Bolté, USA (Ret.); Dr. Richard H. Kohn of Rutgers University; Lieutenant General Victor H. Krulak, USMC (Ret.); Lieutenant General P. X. Kelley, USMC; Dr. Stephen M. Fuller of the University of Utah; Dr. Edward M. Coffman of the University of Wisconsin-Madison; Dr. Samuel Chu of Ohio State University; and Lieutenant Colonel Joseph A. Breen, USAF.

I also appreciate the permission to quote and cite from oral history memoirs that I received from Mrs. Julian C. Smith; Lieutenant General Alpha L. Bowser, USMC (Ret.); General Robert E. Hogaboom, USMC (Ret.); Lieutenant General Merwin H. Silverthorn, USMC (Ret.); Lieutenant General Charles H. Hayes, USMC (Ret.); and General Gerald C. Thomas, USMC (Ret.). I also received permission to cite and quote several Vietnam war studies from the RAND Corporation.

Like my earlier work on the U. S. Army, this study received the financial support of the Mershon Center for Research and Education in National Security and Leadership, The Ohio State University. During the conduct of this study Dr. Richard L. Snyder and Dr. Charles F. Hermann were directors of the center. I also want to thank Anne F. Trupp, the Center director of publications, for her editorial assistance, and Deborah L. Harper and Pamela S. Moots, my secretaries, for their patience and speed at the typewriter.

Support from a publisher is essential to a successful book, and I thank The Free Press, especially Charles E. Smith and Dr. Barbara Chernow, for their advice and assistance. The book's index was prepared by Benis M. Frank, who also proofread beyond the call of duty. In addition, I want to acknowledge the skill of Mrs. Yvonne Holsinger, Teaching Aids Laboratory, Ohio State University, who designed and drew the maps.

For any special insights into the U. S. Marine Corps that this book exhibits, I owe an immeasurable debt to more Marines than I can list in this acknowledgment. For their friendship and example in the performance of duty, I want to thank my former comrades of the regular 2d Battalion, 2d Marines, and 1st Battalion, 8th Marines (1960–1962); the dedicated Reservists of the 3d Battalion, 25th Marines (1963–1966, 1970–1971, 1978–   ), and the 3d Battalion, 24th Marines (1966–1969); and my officer-students and the faculty at the Marine Corps Command and Staff College (1973–1978). I owe special thanks to the Columbus Marines of Company L, 3d Battalion, 25th Marines, who gave a college professor turned company commander some of his most exhilarating experiences, including an unplanned double envelopment night attack that actually worked—at least in the absence of real bullets. To these Marines particularly—but to Marines everywhere past and present—this book is affectionately dedicated.

ALLAN R. MILLETT

Columbus, Ohio
January, 1980

Introduction

Bewildered by a traveler's incredible tales of magic oceans and flying fish, King Charles II of England dismissed the description with scornful disbelief: "Tell that to the marines! The sailors won't believe it!" One version of the story suggests that the King meant his marines had served in so many exotic places that only they could evaluate the traveler's claims. Another version, preferred by everyone but marines, implies just the opposite: The King wanted the traveler to know that his sailors were too smart to believe such lies, but the marines had a reputation for gullibility that might make them appreciate the traveler's fantasies. Even if apocryphal, this tale of King Charles might be turned on its head to teach an equally instructive lesson. How should the King have responded if his marines had told him incredible tales of their heroic performance in battle? Presumably, the answer would have been to "tell that" to gullible travelers.

Kings, flying fishes, and travelers' tales may appear to have little relevance to the history of the United States Marine Corps, but contemporary military historians have devoted about as much attention to the conceptual problems of analyzing military organizations as Charles II probably spent studying tropical fish. Given the importance of war to the development of modern nation-states, it is not surprising that the study of war has to a large degree conditioned most definitions of military history. To use Sir John W. Fortescue's phrasing, it is "the history of the strife of communities expressed through the conflict of organized bands of armed men." [1] Since Fortescue's 1914 description of military history as the study of war, other military historians have largely concentrated on defining just what the scope of the analysis of warfare should be. This debate has shaped the related question of what the history of military organizations should include.[2]

The writing of the history of military organizations divides roughly into two categories. Traditional authors view organizational history largely as an extension of describing wartime service. Such an approach may serve several purposes: to entertain, to educate civilians on the skill and dedication of a unit, to build organizational esprit, and to honor wartime heroes. Developed in American universities, the second approach or "new" military history treats armed forces as organizational expressions of the societies from which they come. Rather than focusing on their unique military functions—those related to war-making—the "new" military historians describe armed services in political, economic, social, and technological terms. In a sense one might write about General Motors and the Marine Corps in substantially the same terms. One deals with the military organization as a cultural artifact or case study, not a unique expression of collective social needs and experiences.[3]

The first large-scale attempt to combine traditional and "new" military organizational history came in the first volume in this series, a history of the Army.[4] Russell F. Weigley's examination of the land forces of the United States, however impressive, was the least difficult to conceive outside the mold of operational history, for the land forces of the United States have been sufficiently different in structure to affect military policy and wartime operations in significant ways. Although it was easy for Weigley to focus on the "two army" thesis in his book, no such convenient structural division will aid the historians of the Navy, Marine Corps, and Air Force. If sociologists of the military had provided pioneering studies, the synthesis might be easier, but this has not been the case. Influenced by research tasks defined by the armed forces and influenced by their political and professional concerns, sociologists see military organizations as complex "organized threat systems," but their work has been much like the work of many "new" military historians. Their interests are manpower recruitment, civil–military relations, leadership styles, group cohesion under stress, adjustment to military life, morale, discipline, and training.[5] The most appropriate research for the historian of military organizations has been the work on bureaucratization and professionalization, but these studies are incomplete models.

Examining the work of historians and social scientists, it is far easier to define what the history of a military service should not be than what it should include. It should not be strictly operational history with the stress on combat effectiveness and group and individual heroism, particularly if these concerns are used to make comparisons with other services. The conditions of combat are far too complex to allow a judgment about a service's fighting ability based on its casualties, its number of Medal of Honor winners, the enemy killed, and the hills taken. Pure administrative history often ignores the operational necessities that influence organizational management and the political environment in which administrators operate. Technical history, however valuable, has limited meaning by itself. Stressing the impact of great leaders often obscures the character of the organizations they command and probably attributes too much influence to individual actions and too little to the organizational setting. The task of the historian of a military service is to develop a model of organizational structure and behavior that blends the common characteristics of all organizations and the unique attributes of a military service.

Contemporary organizational theory provides such a framework. First of all, an organization should be seen as a set of relationships conditioned by three key variables: contextual, environmental, and sociocultural. The contextual variable deals with an organization's internal attributes and structure. The limitation of using contextual analysis alone is that it implies that an organization is a closed system. The other two variables stress the fact that no institution is isolated from other factors, which influence its character and behavior. The environmental variable identifies those influences that have the most direct and constant impact upon an organization. They include interorganizational relations, the state of the economy or fiscal policy for public institutions, technology outside the organization, and the relationship with immediate clients or customers. Sociocultural variables focus upon long-term, persistent, and powerful influences that shape an organization in an indirect but no less important way. Such variables include the character of an economic system, of an educational system, of political practices, and of the law. They would also consider class and ethnic make-up and the complex set of attitudes, beliefs, and values that shape a society and all its institutions.

As an organization forms and grows, it passes through three general stages that allow it to develop the subsystems necessary for survival and adaptation. Normally, some sort of environmental pressure or need brings the organization to life in a primitive form. The new organization provides rudimentary goods and services through fairly simple production units. Even the primitive organization, however, needs some sort of authority structure or managerial subsystem. As the organization moves to a higher degree of complexity—because of either size or differentiation of function—it requires supportive subsystems whose task it is to provide human and material resources.

When an organization reaches maturity—measured by its ability to expand in size and surmount external threats and internal strains—it has five basic types of subsystems. The first subsystem performs the organization's core function and is based on technical proficiency tested by actual performance. For a military service this subsystem would normally be its field combat units. The maintenance subsystem focuses upon providing stability by socializing people to the organization's goals and encouraging individual and group performance. For a military service, the maintenance system would include drill instructors, adjutants, judge-advocates, mess personnel, chaplains, medical staff, and noncommissioned officers in line units.

The third or resource subsystem works at the environmental boundary of the organization, and its function is to procure men, money, and matériel and to legitimize the call for resources by convincing suppliers that the organization's needs are worth filling. The procurement and legitimization subsystem might include recruiters, logisticians, fiscal officers, and public relations specialists.

The fourth or adaptive subsystem provides a hedge against both internal and external instability by monitoring those developments that will force the organization to change. The adaptive subsystem ensures survival by identifying threats and opportunities and by advocating internal reform. Its role is to keep the organization abreast of technology, more efficient operating procedures, shifts in the environment that may change function, and social trends that will affect the organization's membership. For a military service the adaptive subsystem might include colleges for officer education, research and development agencies, planning staffs, and civilian technical specialists in the service's employ.

Because none of these four basic subsystems can perform their roles without some conflict over resources and values, the organization requires a fifth or managerial subsystem. The managers provide the degree of control and coordination necessary to resolve internal conflict and soften outside pressures that might damage the other subsystems. It is the management subsystem's job to ensure long-term organizational survival.[6]

This history of the United States Marine Corps is essentially a story of institutional survival and adaptation in both peace and war. It describes how a primitive organization of some 1,000 officers and men in the early nineteenth century grew to a complex organization of 189,000 officers and men by 1979. It traces the Corps's transition from a one-function organization—supplying ships guards to warships—to a multi-function organization that combines ground and air combat units. The contemporary justification for the Marine Corps is that it provides a unique capability for amphibious assaults and a high degree of combat readiness. It would be, however, an error to make a history of the Marine Corps simply a history of the development of amphibious warfare.

Open-system organizational theory helps illuminate some fundamental facts about the history of the Marine Corps. The first is that the Marine Corps has never surrendered a major function or had one stripped from it. In 1979 some 600 Marines still served as detachments on Navy carriers and cruisers, and 6,600 more are security guards at naval shore installations. Yet the Corps has also shown its ability to change with American foreign and military policy, for more than half its strength serves in the Fleet Marine Force, the amphibious component of America's general purpose forces. The Corps's ability to create and preserve a Fleet Marine Force of three regular amphibious assault divisions and multipurpose wings of aircraft and helicopters is a political wonder, not an accident. Today, much to the consternation of its critics, the Marine Corps enjoys the special privilege of having its force structure written into law, the Douglas–Mansfield Act of 1952 (Public Law 416, 82d Congress). No other service has the same legitimization.

Another fact is that the Marine Corps, despite a "primitive ideology" holding that all its members are basically infantrymen, is a complex organization. Its size and physical resources alone would qualify it as such, and the fact that its primary "productive" units, the divisions and air wings of the Fleet Marine Force, deploy with the Fleet as Marine Air–Ground Task Forces of varying size creates even greater organizational complexity. In addition, 38 percent of Corps manpower in 1979 was serving not in operating units but in auxiliary, mission support, or central support roles that are austere only in comparison with similar systems in the other American armed services. To use the open-system organizational model, one finds Marines serving in maintenance, resource, adaptive, and managerial subsystems, including a service headquarters, schools, recruit depots, supply installations, ground and air bases, and many other specialized, technical activities. Supporting the active Marine Corps is a Ready Reserve of some 93,000 officers and men and a Navy Department civilian work force of 294,000. The Marine Corps spends more than $3 billion a year, and it has other expenditures that for historical reasons are absorbed in other portions of the Department of the Navy's budget, principally those funds devoted to aviation.

In its march from organizational simplicity to complexity, the Marine Corps passed through four function-related phases, all of which required adaptation. The first phase began with the service of the Continental Marines in the American Revolution and ended in the early part of the twentieth century. During it, the Marine Corps justified its existence by providing ships guards for the warships of the United States Navy. These guards' primary function was to provide internal security aboard ships; only secondarily were they to provide infantry for ship battles or landing operations. Since Marines needed some training ashore and could not be kept at sea constantly, the Corps established barracks at Navy yards and other facilities, which it rationalized by providing Marines for security duties ashore. Occasionally barracks Marines participated in land campaigns, but only when such service appeared essential to the Corps's reputation. As the Navy changed, however, the Corps's constabulary functions drew increased scrutiny, and in 1908 President Theodore Roosevelt ordered the ships guards ashore. Congress, however, restored the ships detachments in 1909, a clear victory for the Corps and a crucial test of its capability for survival.

The next significant phase of the Corps's development stemmed from the use of American naval forces in the Pacific and in Latin America for prolonged military interventions. The colonial infantry phase of Corps history began in the Philippines in 1899 and ended with the withdrawal of the 4th Marine Regiment from Shanghai in 1941. It required the Marine Corps to develop effective infantry and artillery units and all the support units required by an expeditionary force, however small. The colonial infantry mission also allowed the Corps to increase its reputation for "peacetime" utility and strengthened its claims for more manpower.

In the chronological sense, the colonial infantry period largely overlapped with the third major phase of the Corps's institutional development, its amphibious assault function. After the war with Spain in 1898, the Navy asked the Corps to provide forces to defend advanced naval bases, which eventually required the Corps to create units to seize advanced naval bases by amphibious assault. This mission brought about the creation of the Fleet Marine Force and the doctrinal guidelines for amphibious operations. Both received the ultimate test and legitimation in the Pacific campaigns of World War II.

Although the Marine Corps has not surrendered its claim to the amphibious assault, its role since World War II draws upon all the Corps's earlier missions. Since the United States adopted an activist foreign policy and a strategy of forward and collective defense in 1946–1947, the Marine Corps has argued that it is the nation's principal "force in readiness," particularly outside the European Continent. In this role it has fought in two major wars and participated in one-third of the 215 occasions when the United States has used military forces to respond to international crises.[7] Essentially, the Corps has used the amphibious assault mission as the foundation (but not the limit) for this function. Its greatest organizational challenge has been not only to preserve its amphibious warfare mission but also to create forces that will be adequate for duties other than a short-lived attack from the sea.

For all its contemporary complexity, the Marine Corps maintains an elitest image. In part, the image is a function of size. In comparative terms, the Corps has always been the smallest of the American armed forces. Even when it has taken part of its manpower from the wartime draft, the Corps has equated its elite character with the concept that every Marine is a volunteer. The elitest image developed initially in the nineteenth century, when Marine officers stressed military appearance, strict obedience to orders, and disciplined behavior in an effort to differentiate themselves and their men from the officers and sailors of the United States Navy. Only toward the end of the century did the question of combat effectiveness (favorably contrasted in Marine eyes to the Army) begin to reshape the concept of elitism. In many ways, Marine service in the American Expeditionary Forces in World War I fused the elitest strains of size (which implied selectivity), military discipline, and combat performance. Subsequent wars reinforced this elitest tradition. Just how the Marine Corps came to believe that it was an elite force and how it converted others to its vision of itself is an important consideration in the history of the Corps.[8]

Given the Corps's own stress on its heroic past and its contributions to America's wars, no history of the Marine Corps can exclude operations. In the history of a military service, however, as contrasted with the history of war, operations assume a different status. Essentially, operational history should be evaluated for its impact on the service and not solely its impact on the course of the war. For the Marine Corps, World War II provides a useful example of this concept. The campaign for Guadalcanal in 1942 was important to the Marine Corps primarily because it established an offensive role for the Corps in what became an offensive war. The assault on Tarawa in 1943 was invaluable to the Marine Corps as a test of amphibious warfare doctrine, and the lessons learned about the use of amphibian tractors, naval gunfire, and air support paid dividends in subsequent campaigns. The 1944 amphibious assaults on Guam and Saipan did not produce doctrinal changes, but they contributed significantly to the war against Japan and eventually shaped an important strategic mission for the Corps: the seizure of advanced bases for the strategic bombardment of an enemy. This mission enhanced the Corps's utility after World War II, when the possibility of a naval campaign virtually disappeared. Lastly, the capture of Iwo Jima in 1945 gave the Corps a heroic public image and doctrinal confidence that remain essential to understanding the Marine Corps as it exists today.

No American military organization can claim a history of placid progress and unalloyed success, but the Corps's history has been strikingly stormy. One senses that Marines would have it no other way. Battles with enemies foreign and domestic, battles fought with guns and words, have contributed to the Corps's folklore or "Marine tradition." [9] Yet survival and adaptation cannot be explained only by battles won in war and politics, for the Corps, like any other military organization, must win its battles with itself. In the continual struggle to match performance with elitest rhetoric, in the daily challenge to separate organizational mythology from relevant military doctrine, the Corps must understand its own past and appreciate it without excessive self-congratulation. Nor should the Corps's champions and detractors, civilian and military, assume that the Corps's past will invariably support their prejudices. It is my hope that this book will illuminate the history of the United States Marine Corps in ways that are always faithful to "Marine tradition," but not captive to it. The Marine Corps needs neither charity nor malice, only thoughtful examination of its accomplishments and character.

Part One

Soldiers at Sea
1775–1909

Sir, your particular Duty as Lieutenant of Marines on Board this ship, is to train . . . the Marines to the Use of small arms . . . to cause Centinels to be placed according to the Regulations of the Ship. . . . As it often happens, that Marines are sent on Shore on certain Enterprizes during an Expedition or Cruize, as well as cooperate with the Army on particular Occasions at Home, you should pay particular Attention to every Part of the Duty of a Soldier in all Situations . . .

Captain T. Truxton, USN, to Lieutenant of
Marines James Triplett, June 22, 1798

Visit the Navy-Yard, and behold a marine . . . —a mere shadow and reminiscence of humanity, a man laid out alive and standing and already, as one may say, buried under arms with funeral accompaniments.

Henry David Thoreau, "Civil Disobedience" (1848)

We are of the Navy; are governed by Naval Regulations on shore and afloat; have nothing in common with the Army . . .

Colonel Commandant John Harris, 1863

1. American Marines in the War for Independence, 1775–1783

The origin of marines as seagoing soldiers is lost in antiquity, but the modern genesis of marines dates from the European naval wars of the seventeenth century. As the Netherlands, France, and England vied for control of the waters of Western Europe, the contending monarchies increased their navies and gave them an organizational stability unknown in Europe since the decline of the Roman Empire. Although France and the Netherlands created marines by training seamen for infantry combat, England instead in 1664 formed a special regiment, the Duke of York and Albany's Maritime Regiment of Foot or the "Lord High Admiral's Regiment," to provide soldiers who would be clearly under the complete control of the Admiralty.[1]

Marines as a general military type appeared in the English service throughout the Dutch and French wars, but the majority of the infantry regiments that served with the Royal Navy were drawn from the British army. All the marine regiments had little permanence. In the throes of the Glorious Revolution of 1688 the "Lord High Admiral's Regiment" disbanded, but its functions were assumed two years later by the new 1st and 2d Regiments of Marines. After each war, however, the marine regiments, like the navy, rapidly dwindled and then had to be reestablished when war once more began. In 1702 the British government created six regiments of marines for service with the fleet against Spain. Unlike earlier campaigns in which English marines had fought as detachments aboard ship, the War of the Spanish

Succession (1702–1713) found marine regiments fighting ashore as part of landing forces sent by the British government to Gibraltar and Spain. The marine regiments again disbanded or returned to the army when the war ended.

In its next war with Spain (1739–1741) the British government formed ten regiments of marines for a naval campaign against the Spanish colonies in the Caribbean and the north coast of Latin America. The majority of the men, however, were drafted from the army. For this campaign, the British government asked its American colonies to form four regiments for service with Admiral Edward Vernon's fleet. Eventually raised under the command of the governor of Virginia, William Gooch, the American marines, some three thousand in strength, could hardly have given the name "marine" much distinction in the colonies. Raised in Virginia and the other middle colonies, "Gooch's Marines" were largely impressed men, commanded by amateur officers eager for a Crown commission. The colony of Virginia, in fact, used the regiment as a dumping ground for its debtors, criminals, vagrants, and wastrels. As an experiment in social purification, the regiment was a success, for only 10 percent of it survived the Cartagena expedition. Thinned by disease and near-mutinous from the conditions of its service, the regiment had only three hundred of its most trustworthy men serve ashore in Vernon's unsuccessful siege of Cartagena. Like their English counterparts, the colonial marines disappeared with the recall of the expedition.[2]

The War of the Austrian Succession (1744–1748) brought another set of ten British marine regiments into being for sea service against the French, but those regiments too were disbanded at the end of the war and their officers placed on half pay. The reputation of marines, established earlier in the eighteenth century, was reaffirmed in this war: The marines "acquired two reputations that clung to them for many generations—a reputation for good, honest, modest service and character, and a reputation among snobs for being socially less smart than the army."[3] The British system of purchasing commissions reflected the marines' lack of status, for a first commission as a marine officer cost half that of a lieutenant in the infantry.

Building upon Admiralty insistence for its own military force, the British government finally gave its marines some institutional permanence during the Seven Years War (1756–1763). In 1755 Parliament authorized the recruitment of five thousand marines in fifty independent companies, assigned as "divisions" to three large English naval bases. In the war against France, these marines once again provided detachments for Royal Navy warships and were assigned fairly distinct duties aboard ship. Their primary mission in ship-to-ship combat was to pick off officers and gun crews with musket fire, to repel boarders, and to serve as substitutes on gun crews. They were also to be part of a ships landing party for operations ashore. Under cruising conditions, the marines enforced ships regulations about fires, thievery, and unlawful conduct by sailors. Their ultimate function was to protect ships officers from a mutinous crew.

As the war with France developed, the ships detachments formed expeditionary battalions that fought ashore as part of the British army, seeing action in Canada, Cuba, and the Philippines. Now strictly under Admiralty control, the marines were used for the expeditions and raids so essential to the maritime strategy of William Pitt the Elder. By the end of the war 19,000 marines were in the British service, and even after the conflict ended, the British Corps of Marines remained an integral part of the ships companies of the Royal Navy. Despite friction with both the navy and the army over pay, billeting, rations, and command, the British marines were still in existence, numbering some 4,500 officers and men, on the eve of the American War of Independence. It was this tradition that influenced the American colonials when they decided to win their independence by arms in 1775.[4]

1

As the American War for Independence pulled the colonies into the conflict begun in Massachusetts in April 1775, the leaders of the rebellion soon recognized that they would have to fight a naval war to prevent the British army from restoring Crown rule by military occupation. This realization grew throughout 1775 until it engulfed the Second Continental Congress, which was reluctant to sponsor a naval campaign against the world's strongest fleet. Nevertheless, the Continental army's siege of Boston created a set of naval imperatives, complemented by the Royal Navy's successful efforts to support the Boston garrison. From the perspective of General George Washington, newly appointed commander of the Continental army, the effectiveness of the siege of Boston and the efficiency of his army depended on hampering the flow of men and supplies to the British army. Desperate for arms, powder, and supplies, Washington hoped to supply his own force from the holds of captured British military transports. In August 1775 Washington began to form his own fleet to interdict Massachusetts Bay, and by the end of the year he was directing a squadron of four warships against British transports and supply ships with some success. To man his fleet Washington turned to a unique regiment of the Massachusetts militia, subsequently mustered into the Continental army, the Marblehead Regiment. Composed of New England mariners, the Marblehead Regiment had little difficulty providing crews for Washington's navy.[5]

Washington's decision to create his own fleet did not exhaust the need for rebel naval forces, for the siege of Boston stirred the war along the entire coast of New England and spread the conflict to the strategic Lake Champlain area on the New York border. As the Royal Navy concentrated its vessels in New England waters, its smaller warships began raiding the coastal towns to capture foodstuffs, to destroy rebel military stores, and to punish the colonials for their rebellion. In response, the governments of Massachusetts and Connecticut commissioned several small vessels and authorized privateering against British government vessels in the summer of 1775. In the meantime, New England militia forces seized the strategic post of Fort Ticonderoga and temporarily eliminated British control of the Finger Lakes. To hold the lakes, Benedict Arnold organized a flotilla of shallow-draft craft armed with light artillery pieces.

In manning their infant fleets, the American commanders provided for marines as part of the ships crews. Although these 1775 marines left no description of their duties, their own activities suggest no break from English custom: Marines were basically soldiers detailed for sea service whose primary duties were to fight aboard but not to sail their ships. In the 1775 voyages of Washington's navy the ships crews were not divided distinctly into sailors and marines; the Marblehead Regiment's mariner-militia performed the full range of duties aboard a warship. Apparently the earliest privateers felt no need to distinguish between seamen and marines either. In Arnold's Lake Champlain flotilla, however, the distinction between marines and sailors appeared as early as May 1775. The payroll of the sloop *Interprise* carried eighteen men, presumably Massachusetts militiamen, as marines. When the Connecticut Committee of Public Safety sent £500 to Arnold later in the month, the specie shipment was "escorted with Eight marines . . . well spirited and equipped," although these men were actually seamen.[6] The Pennsylvania Committee on Safety, however, distinguished between sailors and marines when it decided to form a state navy to protect the Delaware River and its approaches.[7]

Prodded by an appeal for assistance from the Rhode Island assembly in August 1775, the Continental Congress addressed itself reluctantly to the problem of creating a national naval force to fight the Royal Navy. Acutely aware of British naval strength and its own financial limitations, Congress hesitated to form a force other than Washington's and Arnold's squadrons. One of the Congress's pet projects, however, forced it to consider the formation of a national force of marines: the invasion of Canada. Having launched two overland expeditions toward the St. Lawrence River, Congress planned in the autumn of 1775 to send a seaborne expedition to destroy the important British naval base of Halifax. Convinced that a force of marines could both fight at sea and mount military operations ashore, Congress decided on November 10, 1775, to raise two battalions at Continental expense not only for the Nova Scotia expedition but for subsequent service:

> *Resolved,* That two Battalions of marines be raised, consisting of one Colonel, two Lieutenant Colonels, two Majors, and other officers as usual in other regiments; and that they consist of an equal number of privates with other battalions; that particular care be taken, that no person appointed to office, or inlisted into said Battalions, but such as are good seamen, or so acquainted with maritime affairs as to be able to serve to advantage by sea when required: that they be inlisted and commissioned to serve for and during the present war between Great Britain and the colonies, unless dismissed by order of Congress: that they be distinguished by the names of the first and second battalions of American Marines, and that they be considered as part of the number which the continental Army before Boston is ordered to consist of.[8]

The Nova Scotia expedition, however, depended upon the cooperation of George Washington, who was extremely reluctant to lose any troops to the proposed marine battalions. Even before the two overland expeditions against Montreal and Quebec started to collapse, Washington convinced Congress that the two battalions could not be drawn from his army, because the enlistment terms were unrealistic and because he could not spare the men. He suggested instead that Congress form the battalions from unemployed seamen in New York and Philadelphia. Congress accepted his arguments. The United States Marine Corps still celebrates November 10, 1775, as its birthday, but the two battalions of American marines "resolved" by the Continental Congress were never formed.[9]

Although the Nova Scotia expedition collapsed, the Continental Congress debated the apparent need of a national navy, if only to provide its soldiers with captured British supplies. In early October 1775 Congress appointed a committee to examine the feasability of creating a Continental navy, however small. That Congress considered marines an integral part of any ships company was clear in its instructions that Washington should give "proper encouragement to the Marines and Seamen" in his fleet.[10] Pressed by such members as John Adams and pressured by colonial committees of public safety to help them fight Royal Navy raiders, Congress by November 1775 decided to enlarge its fleet and support it on a permanent basis.[11]

Despite reservations about its ability to finance a Continental navy, Congress authorized its Naval Committee to create a squadron of four converted Philadelphia merchantmen, to which were soon added two smaller vessels. Guided by expediency and tradition, the Naval Committee appointed captains and lieutenants for its ships and authorized them to recruit a crew. Presumably to safeguard its new vessels and to provide some discipline for the new crews, Congress created its own force of marines, issuing the first commission as captain of marines to Samuel Nicholas of Philadelphia on November 28, 1775. To Nicholas and the ten additional officers commissioned in December fell the task of raising men for the force eventually identified as Continental marines. Just what duties these marines would perform were not described in the "Rules for the Regulation of the Navy of the United Colonies," adopted on the same day Nicholas received his commission. It is likely that the Naval Committee, which borrowed freely from Royal Navy practices and printed instructions, intended that the American marines would provide the same services as British marines.[12]

The officers and men for the Continental marines came from among Philadelphia's small merchants and businessmen, skilled tradesmen and workers, and unskilled laborers. The officers were hardly prominent, at least in politics and business, but they probably had acquaintances in Congress or in the Pennsylvania Committee of Safety. The senior captain, Samuel Nicholas, was probably a tavernkeeper; certainly his minor prominence came not from his work but from his leadership in two local clubs for fox-hunters and sport fishermen. He and his officers might have had some maritime experience, but it is unlikely that they were skilled mariners. Since their primary duty was to persuade men to enlist as marines, the officers' most important qualification was probably some knowledge of the city's taverns and similar haunts of the working class. Accompanied by drummers, presumably borrowed from the Philadelphia Associators (city militia), the officers scoured the city for recruits during December 1775. To form five detachments, the recruiters gathered semiskilled and unskilled laborers in their mid-twenties, leavened with a handful of shopkeepers and skilled tradesmen. In Lieutenant Isaac Craig's company, the only one for which a muster roll exists, only eight of the forty-one recruits were native-born Americans, and none of the men claimed any prior experience at sea. Like their officers, the first Continental marines were ignorant of life at sea and naval warfare.[13]

Even though the Continental marine officers may not have immediately recognized it, the attractiveness of their infant corps was already limited by the conditions of service established by Congress for the Continental navy. As the war dragged on, recruiting conditions worsened.

The length of service was one year, also the term first established for the Continental army. The pay for a private was $6.66 a month, the same as for a common seaman, and the pay scale for officers and non-commissioned officers was comparable with that of the army and navy. The difficulty was that sailors and potential marines could find less onerous duty in the state navies for about equal pay. More important, service aboard a privateer was much more attractive. First, a privateer captain would be less likely to apply the discipline associated with the regular naval service. The potential for prize money was also much greater, as a privateer captain could divide the entire value of his prizes between the owners and the crew. On the other hand, state and Continental crews were allowed to divide no more than half their prize money, and the remainder went into the treasuries of the states or of the Continental Congress. Moreover, Continental service depended upon the financial health of Congress, whose paper currency was so valueless that it almost ceased to circulate by 1779.

The immediate problem of the Continental marines in December 1775 was not recruits but arms and equipment. Although they competed for scarce weapons with the Pennsylvania navy and the Philadelphia Associators, the marines eventually received adequate muskets and accessories for five small companies. It is unlikely, however, that they made their first cruise with uniforms, for the Continental army and the state forces (with greater need and credit) monopolized uniform receipts. Not until September 1776 did the committee managing naval affairs for Congress prescribe a uniform for the Continental marines. The standard uniform was a short green coat with white trim, complemented by a white waistcoat, white or buff short breeches, woolen stockings, and short black gaiters. Marine officers wore small cocked hats, and the enlisted men sported round black hats with the brim pinned on one side. The adoption of green coats and round hats probably reflects the constraints of availability, for both were also used by the Philadelphia Associators.[14] It is unlikely that the Marines appeared in uniform in any numbers until 1777. In any event, in January 1776 the companies of Continental marines, numbering about 230 officers and men, embarked on five vessels of the infant Continental navy for their first taste of war.[15]

Departing from American waters in February 1776, the small Continental squadron, commanded by Commodore Esek Hopkins, sailed south, not north, to engage the Royal Navy. Pressured by Southern congressmen (whose votes were essential to the navy's creation) and alarmed by the bombardment of Norfolk, Virginia, by British raiders, Congressional leaders ordered Hopkins to clear the southern American coast of British warships and then return north in better weather to perform similar services off New England.[16] Since rebel warships were already active off the New England coast and the middle states were forming their own coast defense navies, Hopkins's orders made strategic sense. Still restrained by Congressional conservatives, the Naval Committee could not yet declare war upon British merchantmen, so it limited Hopkins's operations to attacks on Crown vessels either supporting the British army or raiding American merchantmen and coastal towns.

For reasons that remain obscure, Hopkins, however, skirted the southern states and headed for the British-held Bahamas with a force that now numbered eight vessels, six of which carried marines. Surviving desertions before sailing and storms after putting to sea, the Continental squadron reached the Bahamas on March 1 and began operations against the sparse British forces guarding the islands. Hoping to capture British military stores, including some two hundred barrels of scarce gunpowder, Hopkins landed all his marines and some fifty seamen on New Providence Island on March 3. Although the landing resulted in the bloodless capture of two forts and New Providence Town, Hopkins's raiders inadvertently allowed a British merchantman to escape with all but twenty-four barrels of powder. The Americans, however, stripped the island of cannon and ordnance supplies before departing. For Samuel Nicholas's marines, the landing was not much of a military challenge. The island was defended by a handful of militia, who preferred capitulation to resistance. Nevertheless, the marines showed much ardor and a reasonable degree of discipline during their short occupation of New Providence and reembarked in high spirits from the first amphibious landing made by American marines.[17]

As Hopkins's squadron prepared for its cruise, the Continental Congress in December 1775 laid the foundation for an even more ambitious national naval force by establishing a permanent committee, the Marine Committee, to draft plans to expand the Continental navy. Only three days after its formation, the Marine Committee recommended that Congress build a force of thirteen frigates, armed with between twenty-four and thirty-six guns, at an estimated cost of nearly $900,000. Anxious to protect colonial merchant trade from British blockaders, Congress accepted the frigate program and the recommendation that construction of the vessels be decentralized. The vessels were apportioned to New Hampshire (one), Massachusetts (two), Rhode Island (two), Connecticut (one), New York (two), Maryland (one), and Pennsylvania (four).[18] In addition, Congress established a system of prize courts to handle captured British ships. Therefore, naval administration shifted from the Marine Committee to naval agents and to two naval boards, one for New England and another for the mid-Atlantic states.[19] This decentralization may have provided more attentive routine supervision of the navy, but it made it even more difficult for the Continental marines to become a cohesive organization and to establish uniform standards for recruitment and training.

Even more ominous for the future of the navy and marines was the fact that Congress expected its Continental naval forces to pay for themselves with the income from captured British ships. Although Congress might show occasional enthusiasm for specific naval expeditions to drive off British blockaders or to capture or transport military stores for the army, it did not design a consistent naval strategy, nor did it provide much institutional coherence for its ad hoc naval forces. In fact, Congress and the state assemblies were most enthusiastic about privateering, not only for its wartime utility but also because the patriot leaders wanted to preserve the colonial merchant fleet and its sailors for postwar commerce. Even though it no doubt bowed to local pressure and interests in not restricting privateering, Congress itself sincerely believed that the naval war could be best prosecuted by state navies and privateers while it used the Continental navy for missions of special urgency and importance.[20]

While Hopkins's squadron sailed back into the Atlantic, Congress purchased two more Continental vessels, the brigs *Lexington* and *Reprisal,* to supplement the efforts of the Pennsylvania navy in clearing the lower approaches of the Delaware River of raiders. It also appointed four new marine officers for each vessel, all of whom by March 1776 were recruiting enlisted men. For the rest of the year these marines either served with the Pennsylvania river defense forces or sailed with their Continental vessels on cruises along the American coast as far as the approaches to the Caribbean. Avoiding superior British vessels, the American brigs made several captures without combat. On April 7, 1776, however, the *Lexington* fought and defeated the sloop HMS *Edward,* the American navy's first victory over a British warship. Captain John Barry cited his seamen and marines for fighting "with much courage."[21] The Continental marines aboard the *Reprisal* had no sea battles but participated in a successful defense of the Delaware River in May, when two British frigates tried to run the system of forts, barriers, and small warships created by the Pennsylvania Committee of Safety.[22]

The main Continental naval force remained Hopkins's squadron, which reached the coast of Connecticut with six warships and six prizes in early April. Although the American squadron had suffered from disease since leaving the Caribbean, its officers were confident enough to tackle a British frigate, HMS *Glasgow,* on April 6. Despite superior numbers of guns and men, the four largest Continental warships found the *Glasgow* superior in gunnery and seamanship, and the British frigate eventually escaped after an hour and a half of close combat. The *Glasgow* lost much of its sails and rigging, but the American cannonade was too high to injure the British crew, which lost only four men, all to marine musketry. Among the Americans' twenty-five casualties (nine dead) were two marine lieutenants.[23]

Reduced by sickness and recruiting problems, Hopkins's squadron patrolled New England waters as far north as Nova Scotia for the rest of 1776. By winter only the brig *Alfred,* commanded by John Paul Jones, was still raiding British commerce, as the rest of the squadron awaited repairs or more crewmen. As the Continental squadron struggled to find crews, marine detachments shifted from vessel to vessel and were temporarily reinforced by detachments from the army and militia. Their ranks riddled by illness, the marines also lost several of their officers through resignation. Wisely running away from British frigates, the American warships took thirty-nine prizes, losing only four recaptures. But manning the prizes further reduced the crews of the American warships and scattered the sailors and marines along the Atlantic coast as far south as Virginia. In a sense, the very success of the Continental navy in 1776 diminished its efficiency, and by the end of the year Hopkins's squadron had ceased to operate as a cohesive force. Irritated by the commodore's liberal interpretation of its orders and dismayed by friction among the Continental captains over seniority and their assumed rights in command, Congress relieved Hopkins in early 1777 and thereafter laid few plans for squadron operations.[24]

While the makeshift Continental navy raided British supply vessels and merchantmen, the Marine Committee supervised the construction of its thirteen frigates, the first of which was commissioned in March. The last of the eleven actually completed went into service by the end of the year. During the year the Marine Committee asked its various agents and boards to recommend new marine officers for each frigate, provided that the prospective officer had already recruited from twenty-seven to forty enlisted men. Most of the new officers came from the state militia, although some had seen active service with short-term Continental regiments. In at least one case, a naval agent rejected one officer because he was too valuable to his state militia to go to sea.[25] Even though Congress liberalized the portion of prize money allowed ships crews, recruiting marines was difficult, for although officers' pay was increased, enlisted men's pay remained the same.[26]

If the Continental marines had a geographical base, it remained Philadelphia, to which Samuel Nicholas returned in the summer of 1776. Promoted to major for his service in the New Providence expedition, Nicholas assumed the responsibility of organizing the four marine companies for the frigates built in Philadelphia. During June 1776 Congress approved commissions for fourteen new officers, among them Robert Mullan, the owner of Tun Tavern, the legendary site of marine recruiting in 1775. Although recruiting went slowly, Nicholas had at least four small ships detachments by the autumn of 1776. Once more the Pennsylvania Committee of Safety armed the marines, which gave the state some cause for claiming their services. The four companies thus guarded both Continental and state vessels and stores while waiting for their frigates to sail. In November, however, Pennsylvania suddenly became open to invasion when Washington's army collapsed in the face of British assaults on its positions along the Hudson River. In the emergency Washington asked for the Philadelphia Associator brigade, a seamen's company, and Nicholas's four companies "if they came out resolved to act upon Land" instead of confining "their Services to the Water only." [27] For the first time American marines marched off to bolster an American army.

Leaving one company to man the Continental vessels, Nicholas led a battalion of 130 officers and men from Philadelphia in early December and joined Brigadier General John Cadwalader's brigade of Pennsylvania militia, a force of some 1,200 men. For two weeks the marines lived with their brigade in Bristol, Pennsylvania, while they awaited an attack, but the British army instead went into winter quarters along the New Jersey shore of the Delaware River. Gambling that foul weather and the Christmas season would lull the British into inactivity, Washington then attacked the German garrison at Trenton on Christmas day, but Cadwalader's brigade missed the victory because it could not cross the ice-choked Delaware. Washington, however, intended to exploit his success at Trenton with a similar attack on the British garrison at Princeton, but not without assistance. On his own initiative Cadwalader crossed the river on December 27. Advancing cautiously from the southeast, the Pennsylvania militia brigade marched into Trenton on January 2 as Washington concentrated his army. On the afternoon of the same day, the marines watched the cannonade between the Continental army and the British at Assunpink Creek and helped defend a crucial bridge.

The next day Cadwalader's brigade joined Washington's two-pronged attack on Princeton, following General Hugh Mercer's brigade of Continentals toward the village. Mercer's brigade ran into two British regiments well deployed in front of Princeton and soon collapsed in the face of heavy, disciplined musketry. Cadwalader's brigade came to the Continental's assistance, but it too stumbled into the British infantry and also fell back. Nicholas's small battalion was probably engaged, and it presumably retreated with the rest of the brigade. In any event, the second prong of Washington's attack caught the British on an open flank, scattered three British regiments, and took Princeton.[28]

After the Trenton–Princeton campaign, Nicholas's battalion disintegrated. Reduced by transfers, desertion, and disease to eighty men, the three marine companies joined Washington's army in its winter quarters at Morristown, New Jersey. In February 1777 Robert Mullan's company returned to Philadelphia as prisoner guards and found that it did not have a ship to man. Mullan's company disbanded in April. The marines of the other two companies either transferred into the Continental artillery, left the service altogether, or returned to Philadelphia in the spring to become part of the detachments of the frigates *Washington* and *Delaware*.[29]

2

Despite difficulties, the experience of the Continental navy and its marine detachments for the first two years of the War for Independence had not been discouraging, but the fortunes of the American naval force were to decline as Great Britain mobilized. Although Britain, facing a hostile Europe, could not deploy all its fleet to North American waters, the Royal Navy's strength increased enough to maintain control of the seas. In 1775 the Royal Navy numbered 268 vessels, and by the end of the war it grew to a force of 468 ships; its naval personnel increased during the war from 18,000 to 110,000. In contrast the Continental navy had 27 commissioned vessels in the winter of 1776–1777 and fell in numbers thereafter. Its manpower was probably never greater than 3,000 sailors and marines. Even with the state navies, whose total number of seagoing warships was no larger than the Continental navy's, and the hundreds of small privateers that cruised the North Atlantic, the American naval forces found it increasingly difficult to take prizes, let alone influence the outcome of the war.[30]

Nevertheless, the Continental Congress and the state assemblies attempted to mount a serious naval war between 1777 and 1780. In its main task, driving off the British warships blockading American harbors and capturing patriot merchantmen, the navy was none too successful. As commerce raiders the navy did somewhat better, especially when it shifted some of its cruises to European waters to use the ports of its new ally, France, as a base of operations. The few spectacular cruises mounted from France, however, could not compensate for the fact that American naval forces could not prevent the Royal Navy from going where it wanted in American waters. On inland waters American sailors and marines made some small contributions to the land campaign, but in the long run they did not make much difference in the war. Nevertheless, the Continental navy, the state navies, and the privateers helped prolong the war through 1777 to 1780, thus contributing to the eventual American victory by making it costly for Great Britain to maintain its army in America.[31]

The fortunes of the Continental marines from 1777 to 1780 were linked with those of the Continental navy. The hope of the navy as 1777 opened was the force of new frigates, the first of which, the *Randolph,* put to sea in early February. Joined by smaller Continental vessels, mostly from Hopkins's squadron, the frigates tried to breach the cordon of British vessels awaiting their departures. For many the task of reaching the open sea, in addition to the persistent manning problems, was too much. Those cruisers that reached the ocean found the Royal Navy combative. The ship *Cabot* was lost in March, the new frigate *Hancock* struck its colors in July, and the frigate *Delaware* was captured in action against the British on the Delaware River. American marines joined their sailor comrades in captivity.

The pattern of the cruises and sea battles that involved Continental warships left little opportunity for the marines to distinguish themselves. Ship captures were decided by naval gunfire, and outgunned vessels usually surrendered quickly. The marines seldom had much opportunity to contribute to their vessels' combat effectiveness, but they enforced ships regulations and furnished landing parties a bit more expert in land warfare than the sailors. In 1778, for example, an American squadron returned to New Providence and used its marines to seize the forts and haul away more supplies. In sea battles, the marines shared the navy's growing defeats. In 1778 the marine detachment of the frigate *Randolph,* commanded by the able and aggressive Nicholas Biddle, perished with most of their messmates in a desperate battle with the British ship-of-the-line *Yarmouth,* which literally blew the *Randolph* out of the waters off South Carolina. Another marine detachment disappeared (this time into prison) when a British squadron took the *Alfred* in the same year. To complete the series of disasters, two British warships chased and cannonaded the frigate *Raleigh* until they forced it aground off the coast of Maine. Most of the American crew and marines escaped, but the frigate was lost to the Royal Navy. In all, by 1780 seven marine detachments left the Continental service by death or capture, leaving only ten at sea with Continental vessels.[32]

Although Continental vessels found it progressively difficult to sortie from North American ports, the Americans shifted part of their operations to European waters in 1777 and for a time put new energy into their commerce raiding. The war around the British Isles, of course, depended upon French hospitality, for American warships and privateers depended upon France for ports, suppliers, some seamen and marines, and government money as well as the protection of the French navy. Although the French government did not become a belligerent until 1778, the foreign ministry of Louis XVI told the Continental Congress that if it declared the United States independent, it could depend upon French assistance in its war against the hated British. The assistance remained covert until 1778, but it included the use of French ports for naval operations as early as January 1777. Guided by commissioners Silas Deane, Benjamin Franklin, and John Adams, the naval war in European waters provided the American navy with much of its action during the war's middle stages.

Until France entered the war, Franklin was the driving force behind the campaign on British commerce, designed not only to finance American operations but also to arouse British shipowners against their own government. In 1777 Franklin purchased and outfitted three vessels, officered by Americans but manned by mixed crews, and sent the Continental brig *Reprisal* on successful cruises from Bordeaux and L'Orient. The *Reprisal* carried a full complement of American marines, but the new vessels and the *Lexington*, which joined Franklin's navy in May, carried marine detachments recruited in Europe, though the officers and some of the men were Americans. As Captain Lambert Wickes, captain of the *Reprisal*, learned, the marines were essential when the British resisted, for his marines had to fight well at close quarters to take a British mail packet, one of five prizes captured on the *Reprisal*'s first sortie. In a similar battle the *Lexington* lost eighteen men, including marines, before surrendering to a British warship in September 1777. In the meantime, Franklin's raiders found the British navy more formidable and British diplomacy influential. By the fall of 1777 the French government itself forced Franklin to stop the raids. The American squadron, which now included the *Alfred* and the frigate *Raleigh*, left French ports for home during November. Caught in an Atlantic storm, the *Reprisal* foundered, drowning most of its crew and all its marines.

Influenced by news of the American victory at Saratoga and its negotiations for an alliance with the United States, the French government soon allowed Franklin to resume his naval war. Early in 1778 Franklin's only available cruiser was the sloop *Ranger*, commanded by the audacious martinet John Paul Jones. Although he had no aversion to prize money, Jones was one of the few American captains who thought in strategic terms. His plan, which had Franklin's approval, was to assault both merchantmen and small British seaports. Such raids, he reasoned, would force the Royal Navy to withdraw some of its vessels from North American waters and thus strengthen the patriot campaign at home. Jones found to his dismay, however, that his campaign did not please his officers and men, who wanted prize money, not military victories. The first sign of trouble came when the *Ranger*'s crew demanded the removal of Marine Captain Matthew Parke because his share of the potential prize money was too large. Jones capitulated but kept Lieutenant Samuel Wallingford and his Marine detachment aboard. The *Ranger* then began an epic criuse, plagued by dissention among the crew and characterized by some hard fighting and sailing. Cruising the Irish Sea, Jones eventually landed his marines and seamen at Whitehaven and St. Mary's Isle in western England. The landing party tried to burn a fleet of colliers and fishing vessels, pillaged some forts, and confiscated the silver service of Lord Selkirk. On April 24, however, Jones's crew mutinied, and only the quick reaction of the marines helped stop the uprising. The next day, in spite of his crew's reluctance, Jones attacked the sloop HMS *Drake* and captured it in a stiff hour's fight. Among Jones's eight casualties was Wallingford, killed by musketry. With the *Drake* under a prize crew, Jones returned to France, only to have his crew protest to Franklin and insist that Joncs be relieved for imprisoning his first lieutenant for disobedience and incompetence. When the *Ranger* sailed for the United States, Jones remained in France to find another command and continue his raids.[33]

While Jones cruised, France drew other American vessels to its friendly ports and convenient raiding waters. The frigates *Boston* and *Providence* escaped the British cordon and reached France in the spring of 1778, but their stay was short. The *Boston*'s marine detachment was one of the few marine units that performed its duties—sentry duty on watch and musketry in battle—in accordance with written ships regulations.[34] The marines were observed by the *Boston*'s important passenger, Commissioner to France John Adams, who thought them undisciplined and ignorant of life at sea.[35] The *Boston* had its share of misfortune in France. Pressured by the American commissioners, its captain recruited French volunteers for his crew, only to have the Frenchmen refuse to work. The American marines kept order until the Frenchmen could be discharged. The *Providence* had no such trouble, because its sailors were all Americans and the vessel had come to France only to pick up military supplies. Both frigates returned to America with the *Ranger* in August, leaving Franklin with nothing with which to wage war.

Having exhausted Franklin's funds and some of his own, John Paul Jones persuaded the French government to buy him a merchantman, renamed the *Bonhomme Richard*, in January 1779, with which he intended to raid Liverpool. Although Jones abandoned that particular romantic plan, he recruited a crew and drew upon the French government for additional marines, a detachment of immigrant Irish infantry from the Regiment de Walsh-Serrant of the French army. John Adams inspected the unit and carped that their uniforms were red and white, not Continental green, but Jones was probably pleased to have a disciplined, trained force for his ship.[36] Before he sailed, Jones was joined by a Continental frigate, the *Alliance*. The national mix of the *Alliance's* company was uneasy. The captain, Pierre Landais, who was French, was mistrusted by his American lieutenants and marine officers. The crew was American but contained some British prisoners who had enlisted as sailors and marines. During the voyage the British planned to seize the ship but were stopped at the last minute by the ships officers and the American marines. A similar incident also occurred on the *Bonhomme Richard* before it sailed.

In August 1779 Jones's squadron, which included three smaller vessels contributed by the French, sortied to raid English merchantmen. After seizing several small prizes, Jones attempted to raid the port of Leith on the Firth of Forth but could not overcome a bad headwind. Sailing south, the squadron encountered the frigate HMS *Serapis* and a British sloop-of-war off Flamborough Head, and Jones, much to his command's consternation, decided to attack. In the subsequent action, the *Bonhomme Richard* did most of the fighting, closing to boarding range in order to cripple the *Serapis's* rigging and kill its crew with musketry. From the quarterdeck and fighting tops (platforms at the lower level of each mast) Jones's French marines grenaded and shot their British opponents, sweeping the frigate's main deck of gun crews and boarders. Although the *Bonhomme Richard* was so badly hulled by cannonfire that it eventually sank, the *Serapis* surrendered first despite the fact that half of Jones's crew were casualties. In the Continental navy's most celebrated victory, marines had proved indispensable.[37]

After Jones's victory naval operations from France came to a halt, but a detachment of marines was provided with a new tragicomic duty—dragging a Continental captain from his quarterdeck to be cashiered. After the squadron returned to France, Jones and Landais fought over command of the *Alliance*, a contest Landais won, to the dismay of his officers. Before the *Alliance* sailed for America with arms and uniforms, its marine detachment almost battled with Jones's crew, who claimed the ship was theirs. The senior marine officer, Captain Matthew Parke, was then confined for refusing to take an oath of personal loyalty to his unstable captain. Parke, however, had the grim satisfaction of having his marines forcibly carry Landais ashore in Boston when the neurotic captain refused to surrender his command.[38]

As Franklin organized his naval war from France, the heart of the Continental navy in 1779 was the eight frigates fitting out in New England ports, all of which carried marines. Two of these ships soon left for France, but the others, when they could find crews and supplies, patrolled off the American coast as far as the West Indies, usually accompanied by Continental sloops and brigs. Commanded by senior captains Abraham Whipple and John Burroughs Hopkins, the small squadrons preyed upon British supply vessels and avoided battle. During 1779 Continental vessels took thirty-four prizes and made four recaptures without a loss. Only the sloop *Providence* became engaged in heavy battle with a British brig, and once more marine musketry contributed to an American victory. As on other cruises, the marines did little else but stand guard. Ashore their officers resigned with regularity and argued with the ships captains about their duties and prize shares, while the enlisted men in two cases allowed the entire crews of two frigates to desert. But when the cruising was good, so too was the prize money; after Whipple's squadron took eight merchant vessels in July 1779, the common sailors and marines received more than $1,000 each in prize money.[39] Such windfalls, however, were a rarity in the Continental service.

3

The high seas adventures of the Continental navy did not alter the fact that much of the American naval effort was directed against British invaders in North American coastal waters. As a class of actions, the seaboard and fresh-water defense of the colonies was not successful and hastened the demise of the navy and marines. Nevertheless, the necessity of such a defense justified national and state naval forces—until these forces were defeated by British arms.

The most important early action occurred on Lake Champlain in 1776. After seizing Fort Ticonderoga in 1775, American commanders on the lake assembled a squadron of schooners and galleys manned by a handful of true sailors and numerous soldiers serving as marines. The next year the British attacked General Horatio Gates's northern army by the Lake Champlain route. To fill Benedict Arnold's squadron Gates drafted three hundred infantrymen for naval service. Arnold was not impressed with the marines, "the Refuse of every regiment." [40] In early October 1776 Arnold's squadron of fifteen vessels, still undermanned and weakly armed with cannon and swivel guns, met a larger and more effective British flotilla off Valcour Island. In a four-hour battle the Americans were soundly defeated, losing almost all their vessels and half their men. Arnold's stout defense, assisted by his erstwhile marines, did slow the British invasion sufficiently to postpone its continuation until 1777—and eventual defeat at Saratoga.

The next major coastal defense operation that involved American marines occurred in 1777, when Continental and Pennsylvania marines served both afloat and ashore in the defense of the Delaware River. The river defenses were impressive, including a series of island forts, water barriers, and warships deployed below Philadelphia. The British, however, landed at the head of Chesapeake Bay and captured Philadelphia from the west in late September. In the meantime, Continental and Pennsylvania vessels sparred with the Royal Navy along the river and lost the frigate *Delaware*, which ran aground. In early October British troops moved from the New Jersey shore and upriver to clear the river of the American defenses. Outgunned and outnumbered, the American militia hastily abandoned their forts, and Continental marines had to help save the garrisons and some of their precious munitions. The remnants of the Pennsylvania navy and four Continental vessels fled north of Philadelphia to a new base at Bordentown. From there Continental marines joined several waterborne raids on British supply vessels during the winter of 1777–1778. Provoked, the British sent a punitive expedition against Bordentown in May 1778, dispersed the American marines, and captured or destroyed nearly forty vessels. With the exception of one major warship commissioned in 1779, the Pennsylvania navy and marines all but disappeared. [41]

As soldiers under naval authority, other American marines saw service as far from the war's central theaters as the Mississippi River and the western coast of Florida. In 1777 James Willing, a bankrupt Natchez merchant, used his family connections in Philadelphia to receive a navy captain's commission and permission to raid Loyalist plantations and towns along the Mississippi. Drawing his marines from the Fort Pitt garrison, Willing and his band of freebooters started down the Ohio River in January 1778. They quickly demonstrated that their definition of Loyalist included virtually anyone with transportable property, and their river barge *Rattletrap* quickly filled with loot. In February Willing's company took defenseless Natchez and then raided plantations south of the town. Only rebel sympathizers (those who donated supplies or joined Willing's force) escaped the looting. The expedition received some legitimacy when the American agent in New Orleans raised additional forces to assist Willing. The river campaign, however, dwindled when the British sent troops from Florida to halt the raids and pressured the Spanish governor of New Orleans to prohibit the Americans from using his city as a base. With New Orleans closed as a market place for their loot, Willing's marines either left Natchez for private life or marched north to join the Virginia army then holding the Illinois country. By the end of 1778 the expedition had collapsed.[42]

Like Willing's piratical marine company and the more disciplined Continental marines that served on warships, the state marines found their service varied, although the common function of such forces was coastal defense. That the formation and use of marines was a common cultural heritage from British practice is certain, for every one of the eleven state navies designated part of its ships crews as marines. For the most part the state marines served on coast defense vessels and seldom sortied after the prizes whose sale made maritime service attractive. Generally recruited from the state militias, the marines played an important role in forcing state naval crews (which often wanted to join privateers) to stay aboard their small warships. Like the Continental marines, the state marines were highly informal organizations, plagued with poor pay and inferior recruits. Maryland, Virginia, and Massachusetts marines did, however, see combat and appear to have fought with some spirit, usually in a losing cause. One Virginia company had the unique task of patrolling the Ohio River against hostile Indians. On the other hand, marines aboard privateers saw service in virtually every part of the Atlantic and participated in some of the war's fiercest sea battles, further supporting the general conclusion that warships could not manage without some sort of infantry detachment.[43]

For both the Continental marines and the state navies, the coast defense mission in the later stages of the Revolution led to two major campaigns that contributed to the demise of the American naval war and to the existence of the American marines. The first incident, the Penobscot Expedition, occurred because of the very success of American commerce raiding, especially by New England privateers. In 1779 the British government ordered part of its Canadian forces south to seize a protected anchorage in Maine from which the Royal Navy could more effectively guard military convoys. Arriving at Penobscot Bay in June 1779, the British expedition established a base on Bagaduce Peninsula and garrisoned it with five hundred troops. Properly alarmed, the Massachusetts state government organized an expedition of Continental warships, Massachusetts navy vessels, privateers, and twenty-one transports to carry the expeditionary force of one thousand militiamen. Among the expeditionary troops were three companies of Continental marines. Under the hesitant direction of the expedition's commander, Continental naval captain Dudley Saltonstall, the Americans besieged the British position, a combination of hasty fortifications and warships, during July. On July 26 a landing force that included Continental and Massachusetts marines stormed Banks Island, upon which the British had emplaced several cannon. The outnumbered British withdrew. Two days later the Americans made their main effort against the British position on Bagaduce. Although disorganized by British fire, the landing force, which included practically all the American infantry and artillery, scaled the heights of Bagaduce but did not storm the British fort. In the forefront of the assault were the Continental marines, who lost their two ranking officers. Saltonstall's reluctance to engage the British warships, however, allowed the enemy to reorganize and continue its resistance. The assault degenerated into a desultory siege.

Plagued by dissention, disappointment, and command feuds, the American expedition was ripe for a counterattack, which the British mounted from the sea in August. A Royal Navy relief expedition engaged the American fleet and forced it to flee up the Penobscot River. All the American vessels were scuttled. The Americans, including the marines, fled overland back to Massachusetts. Not only had the expedition failed, but it had been a financial disaster for Massachusetts, which probably lost £11 million and its entire fleet in Maine. For the rest of the war there were no more amphibious operations mounted by any forces from New England.[44]

The Penobscot affair continued a series of patriot disasters along the American coast that reached a peak the next year at Charleston, South Carolina. Although Charleston's defenders had stopped one British naval expedition in 1776, the city became the focal point of the British effort to pacify the South in the war's late stages. Knowing that the British would make a maximum effort to capture Charleston, the Board of Admiralty (the executive committee that had replaced the Marine Committee in 1779) ordered Abraham Whipple's four-ship squadron from New England to South Carolina, which it reached in December 1779. Each Continental warship carried a marine detachment.

Working in pairs, the Continental warships sortied from Charleston in a vain effort to disrupt the concentration of British warships and transports gathering in Carolina waters, but after several troopship captures, the American vessels found they could not penetrate the British cordon. By the end of January Whipple's fleet was penned in the inner harbor, and its crews moved to the smaller vessels of the South Carolina navy, which seemed more suitable for shallow water operations. Under Whipple's command, the joint fleet prepared for battle by destroying navigational aids and those fortifications which the Americans could not man. Continental marines helped in these tasks. Nevertheless, the British fleet penetrated Charleston's inner harbor, forcing Whipple's Continental vessels up the Cooper River. The marine detachments then joined the artillery batteries defending the city proper. Their efforts were in vain, for the British army landed, marched around the city to the south, crossed the Ashley River, and besieged Charleston from the rear. When the Royal Navy ran the batteries at the harbor's mouth, General Benjamin Lincoln surrendered the American garrison of 3,400 Continentals and Carolina militiamen. With them into captivity went the 200 marines of Whipple's squadron. The Continental marines shrank to five detachments aboard four frigates and one sloop.[45]

4

Although the American need for a navy had not diminished, the twin catastrophes of Penobscot and Charleston dealt the Continental navy blows from which it did not recover. The American Board of Admiralty and its successor as executive agent for naval affairs, Superintendent of Finance Robert Morris, were keenly aware that Congress did not have sufficient taxing power or credit to continue the naval war, and the lure of privateering still denied navy captains adequate crews. Congress spent $1 million on the navy in 1780 alone and wanted two more ships completed, a frigate and the first American ship-of-the-line, but the money was quickly spent on the remnants of the navy, and the ship-of-the-line was eventually given to France. Upon the high seas the war against the Royal Navy and its military convoys (as well as British merchantmen) depended largely after 1780 upon American privateers and the French navy.[46]

For the Continental Marines the last three years of the War for Independence became a sequence of forlorn voyages, increased administrative difficulty, some fighting, and diminished opportunity for service. The marine captain of the frigate *Confederacy* summarized his men's deplorable condition:

> Some time ago Captain Harding [captain of The *Confederacy*] presented you my Ident of Marine Cloathing, which has then much wanting and be assured it now increases . . . the Marines in general not having Cloaths sufficient to cover their nakedness. Notwithstanding in the miserable condition, they are obliged to go thro' their Duty, Day and Night, in all the changes & inclemencies of the Weather, in this Country [Martinique] which has thrown the greatest part of them into Fevers, and now I have not Men enough, capable of going thro' the necessary ships duty.[47]

Since American waters were alive with British privateers and armed merchantmen, the Continental vessels found it difficult to take large prizes without a battle. In June 1780 the frigate *Trumbull* fought a severe but inconclusive battle with the British ship *Watt* and in one of the hardest battles of the war lost thirteen dead and thirty wounded. The fighting occurred at close range, and cannon fire and musketry swept both ships' decks and masts. The *Trumbull*'s marine detachment fired some 1,200 rounds during the battle. Among the frigate's killed were its three marine lieutenants and a sergeant. In May 1781 the frigate *Alliance*, then completing a successful cruise to France and back, fought and defeated two Royal Navy sloops-of-war under similar conditions. Once again the marines contributed to the close fighting with musketry and bore their share of the *Alliance*'s twenty-seven casualties.[48] Such victories were, however, scant reassurance for the American cause, for in 1781 two more Continental frigates struck their colors to superior Royal Navy forces. Their capture left only the frigates *Alliance* and *Deane* as the Continental navy's fighting core.

The American frigates' last cruises were marked by supply shortages and unrest among their crews, which now included an unhealthy mix of impressed seamen, foreigners, and former British prisoners. Insubordinate crews had already contributed to the inefficiency and capture of the frigates *Confederacy* and *Trumbull,* and Captain John Barry of the *Alliance* found that his marines were crucial in crushing two mutinies aboard his frigate.[49] Both the *Alliance* and the *Deane* had similar problems with their officers, demoralized by the lack of prize money and the hopeless condition of their crews, and at one point Barry court-martialed all his officers but two for leaving the ship without permission. Among those eventually tried and cashiered was Captain Matthew Parke, one of the Continental marines' longest-serving officers.[50]

After making several cruises to and from France with emissaries and supplies, the two remaining frigates ended the war in port. When a peace treaty with Britain was negotiated in 1783, only the *Alliance* still had a crew, which Captain Barry immediately discharged. The last marines held in the Continental service were the guards that stayed with the frigate until Congress decided to sell the vessel in September 1783. The same month the last marine, the *Alliance*'s lieutenant, left the Continental service, and the Continental marines disappeared.

If the Continental marines had little opportunity to establish themselves as an elite force during the War for Independence, their shortcomings were shared with the entire American naval effort. Like much of the patriot military effort, the naval war depended on the cooperation of the state governments and the collaboration of local authorities. In the land war that collaboration often existed (however inefficiently), but in the naval war it seldom did. By acquiescing to the existence of state navies and a fleet of probably two thousand privateers, Congress limited its ability to fight a national naval war with national forces like the Continental marines. Given its lack of legitimacy, the Continental Congress probably had no choice in the matter. In addition, Continental naval administration was dictated by the decentralized location of American ports and shipbuilders as well as its chronic lack of money. The focal point of the Continental naval war rested with individual ships captains.

This localized pattern of management held true for the Continental marines as well, whose senior officer, Major Samuel Nicholas, gave only one known order that applied to marines outside Philadelphia. In fact, after 1777 Nicholas served only short periods of active duty for recruiting purposes, and he ended his own service in 1781. Like the navy, the marines had chronic manpower problems. Marine officers came and went, many serving for only one cruise, and the enlisted men had little reason to build much *esprit*, given the shortages of pay, food, and clothing they faced. At the root of the Continental marines' lack of institutional stability was a basic assumption held by most of the American leaders: that the army and navy that fought the War for Independence would be unnecessary once the war was won.

At the same time, the War for Independence did nothing to discredit the belief that warships at sea needed detachments of marines, and Congress provided for marines as long as it had one vessel at sea. Discipline aboard American vessels was not especially good, and on more than one occasion marines supported ships officers in the face of hostile crews. Desertion and theft were chronic problems, thus justifying ships sentinels. The marines provided other essential services. For example, marines often became part of prize crews in order to guard captured seamen. The marines also gave a ships captain a landing party somewhat better trained than the ships crew. There is no evidence, however, that the "amphibious" mission was of primary significance in forming the Continental marines. The marines' primary combat role was close combat at sea. Since marksmanship with naval guns was notoriously poor, those sea battles that developed into serious engagements were almost always fought at ranges measured in yards. Under such conditions, marine musketry became an important element in a ship's combat effectiveness. As the Royal Navy had learned in the eighteenth century, there were excellent reasons to have soldiers at sea. The War for Independence taught American naval organizers the same lesson.

2. The New Corps
1798—1815

Although the Continental navy and its marines disappeared after the Revolution, the end of the war released the merchant vessels of the new United States to trade with the ports of Europe, Russia, the Mediterranean, the East Indies, and the Caribbean. The expansion of American maritime trade was inhibited by Great Britain, which limited legal trade with the West Indies, and by the constant threat of piracy. Some of the nation's political elite recognized the need for a navy. Articulate Federalists like Alexander Hamilton and John Adams, strong advocates of centralized government and national economic growth through manufacturing and trade, argued that a navy was crucial to the national government and private enterprise, for both depended upon the revenues from overseas trade. The first Congress under the new Constitution, having assembled in Philadelphia in 1789, quickly voted legislation favorable for the maritime trade but did not provide a navy. The merchant vessels would have to arm themselves for their own protection or, in a war, change their role to that of privateersmen. The Congress initially thought of a navy as a complement to the state militias as the first line of defense against invasion, not for commerce protection, and there was a solid core of Jeffersonian Congressmen who equated a navy with oppressive taxation at home and adventurism abroad. Faced with more pressing problems, the Washington administration and Congress chose to protect the merchant fleet with diplomacy, subsidies, trade embargoes, and cash payments to the Barbary pirate states of Morocco, Algiers, Tunis, and Tripoli.[1]

The outbreak of war in Europe in 1793 between Revolutionary France and a coalition of European powers increased the demand for American staples but also further increased the dangers to American merchantmen. In the Caribbean the French and British fought a naval guerrilla war against all vessels they thought were trading illegally. Seizures of American vessels in 1793 numbered in the hundreds. The European war also encouraged the Barbary powers to make more aggressive demands for protection money, gifts, and ransoms for enslaved seamen, an additional annoyance that troubled even the Jeffersonians. Faced with an increased demand for seamen, the Royal Navy began to impress men from American merchant vessels. Federalist or Jeffersonian, Congressmen became increasingly convinced that a more substantial fleet than the Treasury Department's revenue cutters might be needed to handle the complex set of national maritime problems.

Although Congress could do little to threaten either Great Britain or France with naval retaliation, it could presumably do something about the Barbary pirates. In 1794 Congress voted to build a merchant fleet protection force of six frigates. As Thomas Jefferson had written in 1784, "we cannot begin in a better cause nor against a weaker foe." [2] Three-masted, square-rigged warships bearing forty-four or thirty-six guns on the spar deck and gun deck, the six vessels were to be built in six separate ports under contract to private shipbuilders.

The Frigate Act of 1794 also established the organizational structure for each frigate's crew. Each crew would include a marine detachment of one officer and between forty-four and fifty-four enlisted men. The provision for marines was not a matter of great dispute; marines were a standard fixture on warships of the Royal Navy, the naval force for which Congressional naval experts had the most respect. In any event the marines, like most of the ships company, would not be needed until a frigate went to sea. In fact, except perhaps for a handful of guards, the marines would have no function until the crew was assembled, since their primary duty was to be police at sea.[3]

The Act of 1794 contained a hedge in favor of a negotiated settlement with the Barbary states, and in 1796 the Washington administration decided that the immediate solution to its Mediterranean problem was another treaty with Algiers. Frigate construction was going slowly, primarily because of material shortages, and the vessels' construction costs made a $2 million payment to Algiers a bargain. Congress, after a bitter partisan debate, authorized continued work on only three frigates, the

Constellation, the *Constitution,* and the *United States.* None of the vessels yet needed sailors or marines.

Although Washington and Secretary of the Treasury Alexander Hamilton preached the immediate need for a navy, Congress did not respond until French privateering in the Caribbean and along the American coast reached epidemic proportions in 1798. Relations with France had deteriorated steadily since Jay's Treaty with Great Britain in 1794, which had in effect made the "neutral" American merchant marine an adjunct of the British war effort against France. In retaliation, the government of the Directory demanded in 1797 that American vessels carry special papers and authorized French warships and privateers to confiscate those that did not. The Adams administration responded with diplomacy, but the French demands were more costly than the naval building program and far less palatable to the increasingly belligerent Federalists than a naval war, however undeclared.

To fight a "quasi-war" with France, President Adams, as staunch a supporter of a navy as he had been in the Revolution, and Congress provided funds to complete the three frigates and to renew construction on the three others authorized in 1794. Congress again provided for a marine guard for the frigates. Dismayed by the effectiveness of the French privateers, Congress passed a series of administration-sponsored naval acts between April and July 1798. In sum, the legislation created a United States Navy of six government-built frigates and thirty other warships either purchased or rented by the government or purchased by the patriotic citizens of America's port cities. This fleet would no longer be managed by the War Department but by the newly created Department of the Navy, headed by Benjamin Stoddert. The legislation, as in 1794, dictated the organization of ships crews, which included a marine guard on the rough scale of the Royal Navy's one marine for each gun. Concerned about the administrative problems and cost implications of creating a force of marines that might run to more than a thousand men, Congress on July 11, 1798, passed a law organizing the Navy's marines as a Corps of Marines.* Since the issue of marines had been discussed intermittently throughout the spring of 1798 without much opposition, "An Act for Establishing a Marine Corps" was not an occasion for much soul-searching and passed easily, supported by an effective Federalist majority.[4]

The Act of 1798 embodied the experience of Secretary of War James McHenry, who had been responsible for building and manning the first

---

* The word "Marines" designates members of the U.S. Marine Corps, and "marines" members of any military force performing marine functions.

frigates, and Congressman Samuel Sewall, who headed the committee drafting naval legislation. McHenry initially provided marines for the *Constellation* from the Army garrison at Fort Mifflin but soon decided to recruit a separate force in the spring of 1798. He directed that the marines be true (sober) volunteers, preferably native Americans between the ages of eighteen and forty, at least 5 feet, 6 inches in height, and "healthy robust and sound in . . . Limbs and Body," to serve a period of one year.[5] Recognizing the problems of recruiting, training, and clothing the marines, McHenry borrowed heavily from Army regulations and ultimately proposed the creation of an additional infantry regiment to provide marines for sea service and shore duty "to defend the coast, work upon fortifications, or in dockyards, and guard the public property from thefts and embezzlement." [6]

Sewall's committee accepted the view that sea service as guard detachments on naval vessels was the marines' primary function but authorized the President to use marines ashore as McHenry suggested. To allow shore service, it lengthened the enlistment to three years (like the Army), but did not provide for an organizational system for service ashore. The Corps of Marines structure was to provide a maximum of thirty-two ships guards: one Major Commandant to administer the Corps, 32 captains and lieutenants, 48 sergeants and corporals, 720 privates, 32 fifers, and 32 drummers. The Major Commandant was authorized to appoint a staff like that of an Army regiment (adjutant, paymaster, quartermaster, sergeant-major, quartermaster sergeant, and drum-and-fife major) for shore service. The officers' monthly pay scale (pay and ration allowance) was that of the Army; the Commandant received $50 and four rations; a captain $40 and three rations; a first lieutenant $30 and three rations; and a second lieutenant $25 and two rations. Enlisted men's pay was also Army scale, ranging from $9 for sergeants down to $6 for privates. Musicians received $7.

The Act of 1798 also provided for the internal governance of the Corps of Marines. When ashore the Marines would follow the Articles of War (the regulations for the Army), but at sea they were subject to Naval Regulations, as yet not written and in effect shaped by individual ships captains. This provision was to cause the Marine Corps considerable difficulty until it was modified in 1834, for many military and naval officers and civilian policy-makers assumed it meant the Marine Corps was either part of the Army or part of the Navy, when in fact it was neither. The Marine Corps, however, especially when blessed with a generous Secretary of the Navy and an effective Commandant, could and did exploit the ambiguity to improve its pay, allowances, rank structure, uniforms, disciplinary system, rations, clothing, and equipment by citing either the Articles of War or Navy Regulations as a justification for the desired reform.

The Act of 1798 did not give the Marine Corps an organizational existence or mission independent of the Navy, for the legislation authorized the President to discharge Marines whenever there were changes in the numbers of vessels in commission—if he did not want to use the Marines in other duties ashore. Nor did it specifically state that service ashore meant that the Marine Corps was to come automatically under the control of the Army, as some Army officers later assumed. In essence, the law allowed the President as Commander-in-Chief and the Secretary of the Navy by implication to use the Corps of Marines as they saw fit.[7]

1

Because the first of the Navy's frigates, the *Constellation,* was ready for sea before Congress created the Department of the Navy, Secretary of War McHenry organized the first marine guard, which he set at one lieutenant, six noncommissioned officers, fifty privates, a drummer, and a fifer.[8] To recruit the guard, McHenry appointed a bankrupt Baltimore newspaper editor, but he had to assign an Army artillery officer to the post when the first candidate refused to go to sea. McHenry quickly recognized the problems that would plague the Marine Corps throughout its infancy: There were no experienced officers available and few suitable recruits. Men who went to sea shipped as sailors because the pay was better; the Army's artillery regiments, which also recruited in East Coast cities, offered an enlistment bounty and better working conditions than the Marine Corps; and few citizens cared about military service of any kind.

Although Secretary Stoddert and President Adams remained active in selecting Marine officers, they were delighted to turn the Corps over to its first Commandant, a Philadelphia lawyer-merchant and staunch Federalist, William Ward Burrows (1758–1805). Raised in South Carolina and educated in England, Burrows was well known in Philadelphia for his civic activities, urbane manners, and close ties to such powerful Federalists as Robert Morris, Hamilton, and the South Carolina Pinckneys. Adams knew him well and probably appointed him for his organizing skill, not his military experience, for Burrows had seen scant service in the Revolution. When Burrows took his post in July 1798, the task of organizing the Corps had scarcely begun, but the difficulties were already obvious.[9]

Because the Navy was commissioning vessels and raising crews more rapidly than the Marine Corps could recruit and train ships guards, Burrows's tasks during the Quasi-War with France were burdensome. He was especially disappointed by his recruiting problems. His officers were an inexperienced mix of Federalist office-seekers, adventurers, and solid young men who probably saw their service as a patriotic interlude fighting the French, a chance for some prize money, and a secure job. Most came from Northern port cities or the Mid-Atlantic and Southern tidewater areas.[10]

Throughout the war the Marine Corps had recruiting difficulties. It never approached its authorized numbers and may have had no more than five hundred men at peak strength. Recruiting officers visited port cities and towns in New England, the Mid-Atlantic states, Virginia, and Charleston, South Carolina, but found few men of "sobriety and fidelity" who would enlist. There were no enlistment bounties for Marines, although a $2 advance in pay was soon authorized. Soldiers received $12 for enlisting and skilled sailors up to $50. Like the Army, the Marine Corps offered a generous clothing allowance worth $25, but without an effective supply system, Marine uniforms were slow to reach recruiting officers and were often shoddy. Burrows also had to allow his officers to recruit aliens (mostly Irishmen) up to one-quarter of the Corps's strength and reduce the height requirement to 5 feet, 4 inches, although he prohibited the enlistment of blacks, Indians, and mulattoes. Many recruits were physically defective, and Burrows finally had to force his officers to pay for such rejects' expenses from their own pockets. Marine officers often marched their recruits to their camps under armed guard and tried to get them aboard ship as quickly as possible, especially if warm weather was approaching, for desertions increased with temperature and the availability of unskilled jobs. Burrows offered bounties to his officers for both recruits and apprehended deserters. He despaired when his officers themselves got into trouble with civil authorities, shirked their duties, offered sergeants' rank to recruits, and mishandled money and supplies, as they often did. Burrows was especially concerned about the Corps's lack of fifers and drummers and eventually asked each Marine officer to donate $10 to a fund to offer musicians bounties. There was little about the new Corps that marked it as an elite military unit.[11]

Conscious that some members of Congress had opposed the creation of a Marine Corps headquarters, Major Burrows, both in Philadelphia and in Washington after 1800, attempted to make his Marine guards the epitome of military decorum. It was an impossible task, given the time and human material. Part of Burrows's problem was created by the "military" character of a unit in the Navy Department. The Marine Corps depended upon War Department agents and contractors for muskets, its blue-and-red uniforms, infantry equipment, and much of its underclothing and field equipment. The Army proved an undependable source, and its bookkeeping was confused. The Navy Department clerks and agents had comparable problems since they were supposed to pay, feed, equip, and transport Marines on scales designed for the Army, not the Navy. Ideally, Marine officers had to know both the existing regulations of the Army and the Navy—if they could find them. Under such conditions, the Marine Corps quickly became an administrative problem for both departments and Congress. Burrows tried to burnish the Marine Corps's image by making his Philadelphia headquarters a model camp, moving his recruits and staff outside the city in warm weather in order to escape the fleshpots and fevers as well as to find room to drill. Although plagued by drunkenness and petty thievery among his troops and handicapped by unskilled officers and sergeants, Burrows succeeded in staging a few parades and dispatching details to guard both Army and Navy stores and French prisoners. His biggest public relations success was the Marine band. Established to train fifers and drummers for sea duty, the band, reequipped by Burrows with wind instruments, gave public concerts in Philadelphia and Washington and became the President's ceremonial band.[12]

Burrows was able to translate his personal popularity with the President, the Secretary of the Navy, and the Federalist members of Congress into favorable legislation, but the Marine Corps did not prosper. In 1799 the Congress raised the Corps's statutory strength by 8 officers and 196 enlisted men, putting the Corps's paper strength over 1,000. Its actual strength was half that. Congress in the next year raised the rank of the Commandant to lieutenant colonel, partially in recognition of the Corps's regimental size, partially to reward Burrows, who badly needed the extra income. Yet, for all Burrows's efforts, the fate of his organization rested with the Marine guards at sea with the new Navy and its war with the French.

The Navy–Marine Corps love-hate relationship at sea began as the first frigates slid into the Atlantic's swells. The basic problem was whether the Marines should be aboard at all and what their duties should be. Only the oldest of the Navy's captains had served with the Continental marines during the Revolution; most of the Navy's officers came from privateersmen and the merchant fleet.[13] In a general way, the Marines' duties were inherited from the Continental marines and their immediate model, Britain's marines. They were aboard ship to protect the ships officers and the vessel from the crew, many of whom were or might be drunkards, malcontents, thieves, arsonists, thugs, and mutineers. In battle the Marines were to provide musket fire from the quarterdeck and fighting tops. Yet, in the absence of specific regulations from the Secretary of the Navy, each ships captain could use or abuse his

Marine guard much as he wanted, and his officers and midshipmen generally followed his lead. Few naval officers knew the customs of the Royal Navy in the handling of marines; some probably saw the Marines' presence as an insult to their crews' loyalty and their own capacity to handle their crews without bayonets behind them.

The Marine officers themselves were little help. Only rare individuals like Lieutenant Daniel Carmick of the *Ganges* and Lieutenant Bartholomew Clinch of the *Constellation* seemed to have grasped their duties. More typical was the plea of the Marine officer of the *Baltimore:* "When I came on board, this ship was entirely at a loss to know what the Marines duty on board a ship of war nor did I know who to apply to for information on this subject." [14] Burrows himself was not much help. Knowing something of British customs, he warned his officers not to let their men go aloft to handle the sails, inasmuch as this dangerous and skilled task was the sailors' business. Marines might go aloft voluntarily, and eventually Burrows even suggested that they be persuaded to perform such duties "for the good of the service." [15] Otherwise he assumed that the Marines would drill, care for their clothes and equipment, and occasionally do a little pulling and hauling on lines from the deck.

Of the Navy's captains, Thomas Truxton of the *Constellation* issued the clearest, most detailed orders for his Marines. The Marines were to drill under arms twice daily and practice musketry and tactics when possible, because, "as it often happens, that Marines are sent ashore on certain Enterprizes during an Expedition or Cruize." The Marines should muster on the quarterdeck when the crew went to "general quarters." Their daily tasks were to keep their arms, uniforms, equipment, and clothing clean; the Marine officer would inspect them daily. Marine sentries, working with the master-at-arms, would prevent unauthorized fires, lights, and movements about the ship by the sailors. The only work they should do around the ship was to clean their living spaces and pull and haul at the capstan.[16] From the Marine officers aboard the *Constellation*, Truxton expected perfection. At first he thought his Marines "would disgrace the most common and meanest of Privateers," but he was eventually satisfied with his guard.[17]

Truxton's outline of the Marines' duties was apparently followed on other naval vessels, but ships captains assumed that they had full authority to use the Marines as they wished—even when Marine officers protested that the duties were inappropriate and incompatible with the Marines' primary responsibilities as guards and marksmen. One duty was not resisted: If a ships crew was reduced by disease, desertion, and the use of prize crews, Marines were assigned to the main guns.[18] On the *Essex,* however, the captain used Marines to man the ships boats, run errands ashore, and to help the sailors with their housekeeping duties.[19] Although using Marines on work details satisfied Navy officers who saw the Marines as lazy passengers, doing ships work ruined the Marines' uniforms and made it difficult for the guard (chronically short of replacement clothing and funds) to appear military as sentinels and ceremonial detachments. Plagued by their men's proclivity for losing their hats and selling clothes to sailors, Marine officers found it virtually impossible to match British standards of appearance. Their administrative problems were complicated when ships captains swapped Marines, discharged men, or ordered their pursers not to advance the Marines money.

Most captains treated their Marine guards well, but some permitted their officers and midshipmen to order Marines about, interrupt their training, send them on personal errands, order them aloft, and on at least two occasions beat them. If ships officers abused and ridiculed the Marines, the crew followed their lead, knocking their hats off, stealing their belongings, and occasionally throwing the Marines' clothes overboard under the pretext of clearing the deck for general quarters. Feuds among Marine officers and Navy officers brewed to the point of duels on several vessels over the Marines' status, although the Marine officers themselves sometimes made their lot more difficult by insisting that they ranked Navy lieutenants in wardroom privileges and command responsibilities. The substantial pay differences between Marines and sailors of all ranks was another irritant. One captain applied the Navy regulation that all hands must pay for being cured of venereal disease; the rate for seamen was $5 and for Marines $3, despite the fact that most sailors' wages were triple those of Marines. Even though there were many "happy" ships, there were also vessels where the amount of flogging of Marines and the degree of abuse almost guaranteed friction at sea and desertions ashore.[20]

Braving death by disease and accident, bearing up under the sailors' ridicule for being "tin soldiers," coping with their anachronistic queued and powdered hair and defective muskets, Burrows's Marines endured and served. Whether their presence aboard the Navy's warships was crucial to the Navy's performance in the Quasi-War with France is doubtful, but there were enough indications of utility to allow the Marine Corps to survive. Because the Navy was putting to sea at the same time that the Royal Navy became plagued with mutinies, the Americans were conscious of the possibility of upheaval among their crews, even though American sailors were not impressed. In the American service the crucial factor was the leadership and seamanship of its captains and lieutenants and the living conditions aboard ship. Although discipline aboard American vessels was generally good, there were at least three occasions during the Quasi-War when American officers feared conspiracies among their crews, and six men were flogged aboard the *Congress* for "mutinous assembly." Perhaps those bayonets on the quarterdeck were necessary.

The importance of Marines in naval battle was inconclusive. Generally, naval encounters were decided by the relative size, armament, speed, and maneuverability of the combatant vessels. Only if a vessel was not clearly outgunned and could not escape was there a serious sea fight, and these battles were decided by the accuracy and the weight of each vessel's broadsides. The nature of the Navy's mission in the Caribbean produced little opportunity for combat during the Quasi-War. The Navy was to protect American merchantmen by convoying them or by patrolling the critical passages in and out of the Caribbean. The Navy's foes were more than a hundred French privateers and assorted pirate vessels that hovered about Santo Domingo, Cuba, and Puerto Rico. Between 1798 and 1801 American naval vessels captured or liberated some sixty vessels, sank one, and fought inconclusive engagements with perhaps fifteen others. Although Marines were aboard the vessels that made these captures and shared the prize money, it is doubtful that they were more than spectators, since the captures were generally made by American frigates, brigs, and schooners that outclassed the privateers and forced a quick surrender. When there was a fight, American gunnery carried the day without boarding or close-in fighting within effective musket range.

In the two most publicized engagements of the war, the *Constellation's* victories over the French frigates *L'Insurgente* (February 9, 1799) and *Vengeance* (February 7, 1800), Batholomew Clinch's Marines played a conspicuous if indecisive role. In Thomas Truxton's capture of *L'Insurgente* the fighting was close enough to make musketry a factor. The five-hour battle with the *Vengeance*, however, was at night, and the Marines' main contribution was beating back a boarding attempt at the battle's close. Clinch's guard lost six men in both battles. Truxton inadvertently forgot to praise the Marines in his first victory dispatch but later cited them for their steadfastness.[21] In several minor engagements Marines played a significant role. The guard aboard the brig *Enterprise* produced enough musketry to silence one French privateer; the guard of the *Constitution* under Daniel Carmick helped recapture a British merchantman from the harbor of Puerto Plata in a "cutting out" raid; the Marine guard of the schooner *Experiment* helped defeat a fleet of Haitian pirate barges; and twenty Marines from the *Patapsco* and the *Merrimack* helped save Dutch Curaçao from a French raid.[22]

The Quasi-War did not fade away in 1801 without the Marine Corps's performance becoming an issue in the Navy Department. Irritable about matters of rank and assignment, Thomas Truxton wanted to take Lieutenant Clinch with him to a new vessel. Angered when Burrows assigned another officer, Truxton challenged Burrows's authority to limit a captain's right to choose all his own officers. Truxton's anger at Burrows grew to include the very existence of the Marine Corps. He was convinced that the Corps was a unit without a future.[23] Believing that the friction between Navy and Marine officers aboard the frigate *President* was ruining the crew, Truxton told Burrows that he must educate his officers in the ways of the naval service. He also argued that no Marine officer had any power of command or seniority over any naval officer. To believe otherwise was to ignore "old and general custom" and encourage fights, duels, courts-martial, and ill will in the wardroom. Truxton warned the Commandant that he would lead a movement to eliminate the Marine Corps, since sailors could handle muskets and sentry duty if trained. The Marines, in fact, should be assigned to gun crews, serve aloft, and do other sailor duties to justify their presence on board.[24] Sending a copy of his letter to Burrows to Acting Secretary of the Navy Henry Dearborn, Truxton accused the Commandant of encouraging his officers to defend their honor and stir up friction with his officers. Although Truxton thought that Marines were useful and liked Burrows personally, he would "report the Marine Corps in time of peace unnecessary" and lobby for the abolition of Marine Corps headquarters unless the Marine officers were disciplined.[25]

Both Burrows and Dearborn admitted that Truxton's instructions for his Marine guard were the best in the service and that the irascible commodore had a complaint, but they said he had wrongly assumed that Navy captains could dictate to both the Secretary and the Commandant. They worked out a compromise policy statement, published shortly after the end of the Quasi-War. The Secretary's circular to all Navy captains was designed to clear up the confusion about the relationships and duties of sailors and Marines. The circular stated that all the ships company, including Marines, owed the captain "respectful subordination" and "unqualified submission." In establishing ships regulations, however, the captain could not order Marines aloft "or to perform Acts of more seamanship." No sailors would be assigned sentry duty, a Marine task. The commander of the Marine guard must be given specific duties for his men, and the captain was responsible for the guard's well-being, including adequate berthing and storage space. The captain could not transfer a Marine from his ship without the Secretary's approval, although he could transfer any Marine who volunteered to become a seaman to the Navy with the Secretary's consent. No Marine officer aboard had any rank over Navy officers, even those with later dates of commission.[26] Perhaps the Navy Department thought it had ended the controversy over the Marines' shipboard duties with this circular. If so, it was mistaken.

2

The closing stages of the Quasi-War with France coincided with several events that shaped the Marine Corps's institutional development for the next decade and, in some ways, for the rest of the century. The first was the move of the Commandant's headquarters to Washington in the summer of 1800. Although Major Burrows was unenthusiastic about leaving Philadelphia for the swampy bottoms and scattered houses of the new capital, he brought his staff, family, recruits, and bandsmen to Washington and put them in a tent camp near Georgetown. While the Navy Department dickered for lots for a Marine barracks and the Commandant's home, the Marines amused themselves and the District's socialites with concerts. The band quickly became a fixture of Washington's official and private social life and was adopted as "the President's Own." Its appearances were good publicity, although its Marines could hardly have been more different from the "old sweats" standing guard on America's storm-tossed frigates. Burrows and his staff (three lieutenants serving as adjutant, quartermaster, and paymaster) ran the Corps's business from his home and temporary quarters near the Executive Mansion. In 1801 Burrows, in consultation with President Thomas Jefferson and Secretary of the Navy Robert Smith, settled on a permanent site. The government purchased a block in the southeast quadrant of the city, bounded by Eighth and Ninth streets and G and I, streets for $6,000 and gave the Commandant $20,000 to start construction. The location of the Marine barracks was dictated by its closeness to both the Capitol and the new Navy Yard, where Marines were guarding public property. By 1804 enough of the new barracks was completed to allow occupancy, while in the interim the Marines lived in rented buildings nearby and helped with the construction.[27]

The move to Washington put Corps affairs into the mysterious web of party politics, personal feuds, gossip, newspaper stories, boarding house associations, and land speculation that shaped the new capital's culture.[28] The political environment in Washington was made even more complicated by the election of 1800, which put Jefferson and his Democratic Republicans in control of the government. Hostile to Federalist shipbuilding plans and taxes, the Jeffersonians came to office determined to cut naval spending. For the Marine Corps that meant a reduction in strength (particularly officers) and the possibility of eliminating much of the Commandant's headquarters and perhaps the Commandant himself. Jefferson's victory also implied additional power for Congressman

John Randolph of Roanoke. Randolph had already called the Marines an
evil group of would-be praetorians and had been roughed up in a theater
by two officers in retaliation. Although his predominately Federalist
officers railed about the Jeffersonians, Burrows adjusted quickly and
successfully.[29]

The Jeffersonians proved less hostile to the Navy than expected. Although the administration laid up all but fourteen vessels and considered
cutting the Navy Department's budget by two-thirds, the warring world
would not disappear, and naval power looked increasingly useful. In
1801 the Bashaw of Tripoli declared war on the United States, and the
next year Congress reciprocated, beginning a series of Barbary wars that
did not end until 1815. More important, the French Empire and its coalition of foes were once more at war by 1803. For the United States this
raised again the vexing question of impressment and trade restrictions
on the merchant fleet. Given the strength of the Royal Navy, the administration decided that an American battle fleet was too small to be
effective and too expensive and provocative, but it maintained its
cruising squadrons and supplemented the coast defenses with a fleet of
gunboats.

The Navy Department under Jefferson and Madison did not seriously
question the need for Marines on its naval vessels and extended the
Marines' assignment to its gunboat fleet. In addition, the department
decided to establish a guard detachment at each of its Navy yards:
Boston, Brooklyn, Philadelphia, Washington, and Norfolk. When it
considered its need for Marines, the department requested and received
an increase of 874 men for the Marine Corps, bringing its authorized
strength to more than 1,800 officers and men. In reality, however, the
Marine Corps never had more than thirty-five officers and a thousand
men on duty from 1801 to 1812.[30]

Even with the end of the Quasi-War and the reduction of the fleet,
Major Burrows addressed the persistent but postponed problems in the
Marine Corps's internal management. When he left Philadelphia he left
behind Captain Franklin Wharton, an old friend and Philadelphia so-
cialite, to begin a more systematic way of buying good uniforms and
equipment. In Washington, the Commandant tightened up discipline
and emphasized drill for both his officers and his men. In 1804, however,
Burrows, in ill health and financial difficulty, resigned. After Congress
considered abolishing the post of Commandant, Jefferson appointed
Wharton, the Corps's senior officer, to continue Burrows's reform program. Although he shared his friend's taste for socializing and real
estate speculation, Wharton was neither a strong leader nor a skilled
politician like Burrows. But, despite difficulties with his fractious staff

and his lack of force in arguing with the Secretaries of the Navy, Wharton contributed to raising the Corps's military standing. He made the Washington barracks a school for recruits and new officers ("It is hoped this Institution being particularly for their improvement, they will not neglect it"); tightened up the capricious disciplinary system; adopted the hand salute; and worried about the troops' health and quarters. Under his supervision, the Marine Corps adopted its own distinctive uniform: a leather shako with a brass plate with eagle and anchor, blue coat trimmed in red, white pantaloons, and black gaiters that reached the knee. The Corps also adopted a white fatigue uniform and issued more clothing. Like Burrows, the Commandant was able to persuade the Secretary of the Navy to authorize the Marine Corps to follow Army customs and regulations on such matters as pay and allowances, mustering-out bonuses, the abolition of flogging, staff practices, courts-martial, and clothing and equipment issues.[31]

The Marines Corps's critical problem was men, both quality and numbers. Officers continued to enter the Corps through patronage with little consideration except to their general character, personal influence, social connections, and physical condition. The enlisted men were unemployed laborers, runaway boys, teenage apprentices, and a smattering of farmers, skilled craftsmen, itinerant schoolteachers, and clerks. In 1809 enlistees were offered a $10 bonus, but the term of service was increased to five years. Officers recruited men from the countryside around the East Coast's cities. Wharton had to warn one of them to guard the recruits carefully: "I must request you to admit no Irregularities by our Men to the Citizens—the Articles of War forbid it—our true Policy at all time to cherish a good understanding with them."[32] Sometime between 1803 and 1808 the Commandant allowed his recruiters to take boys as young as twelve as apprentices for the Marine Band. Some of these boys eventually volunteered to serve as line Marines, and many were appointed noncommissioned officers, thus ensuring exemplars in obedience, appearance, and knowledge of drill.[33]

The most crucial development during Wharton's early years as Commandant was the establishment of Marine barracks at the Navy's five oldest yards. Serious discussion of establishing permanent Navy yards began under the Federalists when Congress authorized the construction of five ships-of-the-line in 1799. Although it put much of the fleet in ordinary, Jefferson's Navy Department not only detailed Marines to watch the tied-up ships (each frigate rated ten Marine watchmen) but wanted a minimum yard guard of seventeen men.[34] Inasmuch as the Marines in transit from recruiting rendezvous to ship and back already were being housed ashore near their vessels' berths, it seemed economical to provide a permanent barracks for both the yard guard and ships detachments. The barracks would be an admirable place to gather both groups for drill, especially since shipboard Marines developed "habits unfavorable to discipline." [35] The barracks assignment was also attractive to officers sick of sea duty who wanted to marry and live in a city, and barracks posts became hotly contested, although seniority and time-at-sea generally settled such matters in the Commandant's mind. In all, the creation of Marine barracks probably increased the attractiveness and self-esteem of the service.

Creating Marine barracks within or near the Navy yards, however, opened the question of the Marines' duties ashore and their relationship to the Navy yard commandants, who were the Navy's senior captains. Since the sentry duty depended on each yard's needs, the Commandant avoided giving the barracks commanders specific instructions, although he did think they might help defend the yard if it was attacked: "Injustice would be done the officer, & men to suppose they would remain inactive." [36] The Navy Department's position was that the Marine barracks commander had command of all Marines ashore at his station and reported to and received orders from the Commandant, but the yard commandants protested that they had to have complete authority, including assigning Marine officers to stand watch or sit on courts-martial. Wharton's position was that his authority over shore Marines would be rigorously defended, even if he had to compromise on shipboard jurisdictional disputes. Marine officers coming ashore upheld Wharton's position by refusing to report to the yard commandant. As long as the Secretary of the Navy supported Wharton, his position was strong. The matter also depended upon the degree of cooperativeness between Marine barracks commanders and Navy Yard commandants and their perceptions about their command prerogatives, the guard's duties and discipline, and their relationships with the Navy Department. Like the question of command of the ships guards, the Navy yard jurisdictional dispute poisoned the relationship of Navy and Marine officers for the rest of the century. [37]

With its Navy yard assignments, the Marine Corps accepted expanded duties along America's southern frontier, an area of great interest to the Jeffersonians. In 1804 the President had Secretary Smith send Captain Daniel Carmick, 3 officers, and 102 enlisted men to New Orleans. Although Carmick's mission was unclear and his detachment moved in and out of New Orleans for the next eight years, the Marines' duties suggest that Jefferson saw them as all-purpose federal troops for the principal city of the Louisiana Purchase. Carmick's initial orders were to report to Major General James Wilkinson, the territorial governor, who then assigned the Marines to the forts along the mouth of the Mississippi. When the Navy created a naval station at New Orleans, Carmick's detachment assumed sentry and gunboat duty. By 1810 Carmick was directly under the orders of Louisiana's territorial governor, who subsequently had the Marines prepare to suppress any slave or Creole rebellions that might occur.[38]

The Navy Department in 1811 also sent Captain John Williams, another officer, and forty-seven enlisted men to the extemporized naval station on Cumberland Island in the St. Mary's River between Georgia and Florida. They were to defend the station and help man the Navy's gunboats, which were patrolling the river against smugglers and Indian-Negro raiders. In 1812 Williams's detachment joined the small Army and Navy detachments supporting an American-inspired revolt in Spanish East Florida. While convoying supplies, Williams and a group of Marines were ambushed. Williams and another Marine died, and seven others fell wounded. The survivors later manned a cannon during several Army raids on Indian camps.[39] Although Carmick's and Williams's detachments served creditably, their main contribution seems to have been to confuse the question of Army–Marine Corps relations. The Navy Department's orders gave both officers some discretion about using their units and never relinquished Navy Department control, but local Army officers of higher (and sometimes lower) rank insisted they had every right to give Marines orders. Like the disputes with the Navy officer corps, the Marines' difficulties with the Army were an omen.

For all the new duties required by the Jeffersonians, the Marine Corps's primary mission continued to be as ships guards on the Navy's sailing ships. As Marine Corps administration and discipline improved and Navy captains applied the guidance of the circular of 1801, Marine Corps–Navy friction at sea abated but never disappeared. Marine officers still complained about captains' discriminatory practices and the ships pursers' failure to supply them adequately from Navy stores. Marine officers shot one another and Navy officers in duels over insults, real and implied, to their gentlemanly honor.[40]

The ships guards served primarily as seagoing constables. Aboard the frigate *Constitution*, Marine sentries manned the door to the cabin to prevent unauthorized traffic into "officer country," stood watch at both gangways, guarded the spirits room, stopped unauthorized movement in the forecastle at night, and patrolled the galley and gundeck to stop illegal fires and to keep sailors from jumping ship. The Marines drilled twice daily on the quarterdeck; those not on watch were to work on their uniforms and arms under their own officers.[41] The drill was occasionally supplemented by musketry and tactics instruction ashore, sometimes with other ships guards.[42] As they had been since their creation, the Marines were assigned to gun crews when a ship became short-handed.[43]

Part of the reason for the improved understanding between ships captains and their Marine officers was the Navy officers' desire to have well-turned-out ceremonial guards for the appearance-conscious European fleets in the Mediterranean. The Americans especially envied the splendor and precision of the British marines. Colonel Wharton urged his officers to ask their captains to allow them to save their uniforms by reducing the Marines' housekeeping: "The Commanding Officer on board, I am sure, if he is desirous that the detachment should appear military, exact of you and your command, no duty unpleasant or severe, as being unmilitary for you to perform." [44] Wharton did not challenge the captains' powers, but he demanded that his officers defend their men and draw their due rations, pay, and clothing.[45]

Just how much policing the Navy's crews needed is debatable. Since the sailors shipped for only one year, were well paid, and (even with flogging) were decently treated, the United States Navy had no troubles on the scale the Royal Navy experienced during the Napoleonic Wars. Only if a ship stayed overlong on station and did not return within a year was the crew likely to get edgy. One such incident occurred in 1807, when Captain Hugh Campbell of the *Constitution*, fearing a war with England after the *Chesapeake* affair, held his ship in Syracuse harbor. There his crew's enlistment expired. Despite the crew's mutterings, one officer-of-the-deck ordered a sailor flogged for swimming with his jacket on. The boatswain refused to administer the punishment. The ship's first lieutenant ordered him and four others into irons. The crew sullenly jeered him, then rushed the captain's cabin in protest, jostling several ships officers. The first lieutenant called out the Marines, whose appearance on the quarterdeck helped restore order without fighting.[46] Captain Campbell was incensed by the indiscipline but was unsure about the legality and wisdom of disciplining time-expired men, and none were tried. Although Colonel Wharton was pleased that his men had stood firm, he did not consider the episode important.[47] Another Marine officer did. Commissioned a year before the "mutiny" on the *Constitution* and later to serve on that frigate, Lieutenant Archibald Henderson, a punctilious, dour Scot from Dumfries, Virginia, remembered the episode for years. Since he served as Commandant of the Marine Corps for thirty-eight years, Henderson was in a position to remind the Navy how the Marines had saved the reputation of its finest frigate—when it served the Marine Corps's purpose.[48]

For the Marines of the Jeffersonian era, sea duty meant the Mediterranean and the sporadic war with Tripoli and Morocco, and the Marine

Corps made a small contribution to the Navy's operations against the Barbary pirates. The Marines' primary duties and the small numbers of the ships guards (there were seldom more than two hundred Marines in the whole Mediterranean squadron) prevented a more impressive role. The Corps profited, however, from the Navy's well-publicized exploits and the heroism of some individual Marines. By sharing the Navy's trials, frustrations, and occasional victories, the Marines probably lessened Navy criticism of their utility and fostered sentimental bonds with the naval service, which had not been strong in the Quasi-War with France.

Reacting to Tripoli's declaration of war in 1801, President Jefferson sent a four-vessel squadron to the Mediterranean to protect American merchantmen from Barbary raiders and, in August, to blockade Tripoli itself.[49] In the first serious naval clash of the war, the duel between the American sloop-of-war *Enterprise* and the Tripolitan vessel *Tripoli*, the Navy won a one-sided victory, killing two-thirds of the crew. The Marines played an important role in the three-hour battle, since the principal Barbary tactic was to close and board an enemy. The Marine guard of the *Enterprise* smashed each boarding attempt with effective musketry and shared the crew's extra month's pay bonus after the fighting.

Not until June 1803 did Marines get another chance to close with the Tripolitans. In the interim the blockading squadron had made little impression on Tripoli. Commodore Richard V. Morris's squadron moved closer to Tripoli harbor and on June 2, a Navy force of fifty sailors and a small Marine detachment attacked a fleet of Tripolitan grain ships near shore and burned several of them after fighting their way aboard in hand-to-hand combat. The blockade, however, was still not effective, but the Navy received greater incentive to punish the Tripolitans. In October the frigate *Philadelphia* ran aground off Tripoli and was captured; its crew of 409, including the 41-man Marine guard, entered the Bashaw's prison where they waited for ransom or liberation. The newly arrived squadron commodore, Edward Preble, having made peace with Morocco with a show of force, attacked the Tripolitans with new determination. He authorized a raid on the *Philadelphia*, which destroyed the vessel underneath the Bashaw's guns; a detachment of Marine enlisted men was part of Lieutenant Stephen Decatur's raiding party. In July–September, 1804, the squadron's Marines took part in the fighting around Tripoli harbor, serving ships guns and participating in gunboat battles and boardings. Of the Navy's fifty-four casualties in the fighting, the Marines lost five dead and nine wounded. When Commodore Preble praised his entire squadron, however, citing many Navy officers by name, he did not single out any Marines either by name or by organization.[50]

In the autumn of 1804 one Marine officer got a chance for the glory that had escaped the Marines thus far in the war. Lieutenant Presley N. O'Bannon, a high-spirited Virginian, tied his fortune to another American, former consul to Tunis William H. Eaton. O'Bannon, commissioned in 1801, was well known for his military ardor, thirst for glory, womanizing, and fiddle-playing; he was a free spirit in search of desperate ventures.[51] Eaton was a kindred soul. Connecticut-born, he had served in the Revolution as a sergeant and in the 1790s as an army captain in the Ohio territory. Linguist, marksman, horseman, and charismatic leader, Eaton had persuaded the Jefferson administration to allow him to organize a revolt against the incumbent Bashaw of Tripoli. The focal point of the revolt was to be the Bashaw's exiled older brother, Hamet Karamanli. The Navy was lukewarm about the project. Although Eaton talked about a landing force of Marines of between two hundred and a thousand, Commodore Samuel Barron gave him only a personal bodyguard of Lieutenant O'Bannon and seven enlisted men. Since Eaton was headed for darkest Egypt with $1,000 and wanted $20,000 more to finance Hamet's army, it was a reasonable precaution. There was little expectation (except, perhaps, in O'Bannon's mind) that the Marines would serve as the "Old Guard" of an army commanded by William Eaton.

After an odyssey up the Nile and numerous brushes with disaster in Egypt, Eaton and O'Bannon pulled together an "army" for a trek across the Libyan desert to the Tripolitan port of Derna, some 600 miles from Eaton's rendezvous west of Alexandria.[52] Under the putative command of Hamet but led by Eaton, the force consisted of the eight Marines, perhaps a hundred Mediterranean mercenaries, Hamet's personal entourage of seventy, two bedouin bands, and some Arab camel- and muledrivers. In all, it was a force of four hundred men. From March 6 until April 15, 1805, Eaton's army struggled across the desert, plagued more by internal dissension and short rations than the terrain and weather. On at least four different occasions O'Bannon's Marines helped Eaton stop mutinies in his army, thus performing their most important service of the epic march.

After regrouping and reprovisioning in the Gulf of Bomba and drawing munitions from the brig *Argus,* Eaton's army assaulted and took Derna on April 24. Again the Marines were conspicuous. O'Bannon's squad and the Mediterranean mercenaries with one cannon led the assault on Derna's outer fortifications while three Navy vessels shelled the city. Among the fourteen who fell were three Marines, two of whom died. With luck, pluck, and naval gunfire, O'Bannon raised an American flag over the Tripolitans' citadel. Eaton's force then held Derna against a

Tripolitan army until June 1805, with further glory for his Marine detachment. The expedition, however heroic, proved a fool's errand, for even before the epic capture and defense of Derna, another American had negotiated a peace treaty with the Bashaw of Tripoli. On June 12 Eaton, the incensed O'Bannon and his Marines, and the pathetic Hamet and his "army" embarked on the Navy's vessels and sailed off into the Mediterranean sunset.

The expedition on Derna was praised in the American press and commemorated in poetry by John Greenleaf Whittier. That the expedition was a diplomatic fiasco did not dim its significance as the Marine Corps's finest hour in its first decade of existence. Like the "mutiny" on the *Constitution*, O'Bannon's seven and the capture of Derna became a standard answer to the Marine Corps critics. Eaton and O'Bannon, both frustrated by lack of reward and acclaim, afterward argued that with two hundred Marines they could have taken Derna by storm without a desert march and that the Navy had betrayed both Hamet and the Marine Corps. Eaton also pointed out an uncomfortable truth: "In a bombardment or a cruise marines are of little more use in a man of war than cavalry or Pioneers, and while the vessels are laying in port they are used only as badges of Rank and machines of ceremony." [53] It remained to be seen whether the Marine Corps could fashion a more compelling rationale for its existence than it had by 1805—or 1812.

3

In the spring of 1812 the United States went to war with Great Britain after ten years of tension on the high seas and the trans-Appalachian frontier. Like the wars with France and the Barbary pirates, the War of 1812 was a corollary to the Napoleonic wars. Several factors persuaded Congress to declare war, but the primary grievances were maritime: the restriction of "neutral" American maritime trade, the impressment of American sailors for the Royal Navy, and two actual battles between American and British warships in 1807 and 1811. The American government attempted to apply economic sanctions after 1807, but the embargo and nonintercourse acts did little more than ruin American trade, increase smuggling, and cut the government's tax income. Of military preparations there were none of consequence, since Congress was divided on the wisdom of war. Insofar as the Royal Navy, even with its Continental commitments, could deploy more than a hundred of its six hundred warships into American waters, the sixteen-ship U.S. Navy hardly seemed strong enough to carry the fight to the British. [54]

As the critics of war with Great Britain prophesied, the war at sea was an uneven contest that the British won with ease once they dispatched more vessels to North American waters. Basically, the Royal Navy was able to give the British command of the seas. British commerce was adequately (if not completely) protected from American cruisers; American ports were blockaded; and British expeditionary forces were put ashore whenever their commanders saw some purpose for doing so. Only on Lake Champlain, Lake Ontario, and Lake Erie was the Royal Navy stymied. There the decisions won by the Americans were crucial to the land campaigns, which ended in Anglo-American stalemate but broke the strength of the Indian tribes of the Northwest Territory. That the United States Navy could not and did not win the war did not mean that its role was unappreciated. Since "national honor" was part of the cause of the war, single military victories or even stubbornly fought defeats against the British brought great emotional satisfaction to the American public and ringing acclaim from the government. There is little doubt that the Navy emerged from the war with a set of popular heroes, a new respect from Congress, and a fund of goodwill with the public. The Marine Corps shared this experience, and by 1815 its officers believed they had forever silenced Congressional critics like John Randolph, who charged that Marines were fancy palace guards who never fought.[55]

The Marine Corps entered the war with about a thousand officers and men, a bit more than half its authorized strength. Although the Secretary of the Navy authorized a $20 enlistment bounty and delivered new Army muskets and equipment to Colonel Wharton, the Marines had difficulty throughout the war meeting all the Navy's requirements for ships guards, Navy yard and station security guards, and flotilla duty along the approaches to Chesapeake Bay and New Orleans.[56] Army bounties remained higher, and even when Wharton authorized three months' advance pay for men going immediately to sea, Marine recruiting did not improve. In 1814 Congress authorized another manpower increase of forty-seven officers and nearly eight hundred enlisted men, but it was too late to help. The Marine Corps ended the war with little more manpower than it began it with. Wharton fretted about recruiting throughout the war. He pushed his officers to recruit men and get them to sea before they could desert: "I could spare you a *few men* if I knew how to convey them in safety—*they* have been rather irregular in their habits—not being of the first quality here but I think with you, your Enemy at hand they would improve, and most probably very soon become of the first class."[57] Under such circumstance there was little time for training and some doubt that the Marine Corps could add much to the Navy's desperate efforts.

In terms of real combat effectiveness, the Marines' contribution to the

Navy's battles on the high seas was problematic. During the war American and Royal Navy warships fought sixteen engagements that ended in one belligerent's vessels captured or sunk. In only six did Marine musketry play any role, and in all of these fights the victors won because of crew training, the weight of their broadsides, the type of naval ordnance, and seamanship. These six battles, however, proved the Marines' willingness to fight and die, a quality much appreciated by the Navy and the public. In the Navy's first famous naval duel, the *Constitution*'s victory over HMS *Guerriere* (August 19, 1812), the two frigates came close enough for each captain to consider boarding the other's ship in the last stages of the battle, but heavy seas prevented their doing so. For ten minutes, however, the frigates were close enough for musketry to be effective, and the *Constitution*'s Marines swept the *Guerriere*'s spar deck with fire, probably contributing significantly to the enemy's eighty casualties. The Marines, however, lost their commander when Lieutenant William Bush leaped to the taffrail, crying, "Shall I board her, Sir?" A Royal Marine answered him with a musketball through the head. Most of the Americans' fourteen casualties occurred at this stage of the battle, indicating the dangers of closing to musketry and boarding range when an enemy was not thoroughly pounded by cannon fire.[58] In the *Constitution*'s second battle, its victory over HMS *Java* (December 19, 1812), the Marines helped smash a British attempt to board at the end of a three-hour battle decided by the *Constitution*'s broadsides. Of the twelve Americans killed, one was a Marine.[59] In the *Constitution*'s twin victory over the outmatched *Cyane* and *Levant* (February 20, 1815), Captain Charles Stewart complimented Captain Archibald Henderson's Marines for their "lively and well-directed" fire, but again gunnery decided the engagement.[60] In two battles between American and British sloops-of-war (*Wasp*–HMS *Reindeer* and *Hornet*–HMS *Penguin*), Marine musketry caused British casualties at close range.[61] In fact, the Marines' finest hour came in an American defeat, the loss of the frigate *Chesapeake* to HMS *Shannon* (June 1, 1813). The *Chesapeake*, out of control, its raw crew demoralized by the *Shannon*'s gunnery, was boarded by the British. Only the Marines put up a stubborn resistance before the surrender, losing thirty-four of forty-four men. The guard's commander, Lieutenant James Broome, died in the desperate action.[62]

Of the two important inland lakes actions, Marines contributed to Oliver Hazard Perry's victory on Lake Erie (September 10, 1813) but did not in the battle of Lake Champlain the following year. Perry's squadron had ships guards from Lieutenant John Brooks's thirty-four-man detachment from the barracks at Sacketts Harbor, reinforced aboard Perry's vessels by Army troops. In Perry's fight, carried primarily by his flagship *Lawrence* and the *Niagara,* the Marines lost four dead (including Brooks) and fourteen wounded. The fighting was close enough for musketry to have been effective, but the Marines' contribution to the British losses is uncertain.

Although the Royal Navy menaced America's ports and Navy yards, Colonel Wharton viewed the Marine Corps's mission as sea duty with the Navy, not defense of its shore establishments. He was especially concerned that the Army would assume control over his shore detachments and that his own officers would forget that they were a naval service, not a glory-hunting adjunct of the Army. In any event, Wharton did not have enough men to add much to the coast defense forces, and he was unwilling to pull men off the some sixty Navy vessels that had ships guards.[63]

Service ashore, however, fortuitously provided the Marine Corps with several opportunities to enhance its reputation as a combat force. Although detachments of Marines occasionally joined Army operations along the Great Lakes and successfully defended the Navy yards at Norfolk and Baltimore from British raids in 1813 and 1814, the Corps's two most auspicious engagements were at Bladensburg in August 1814 and the battle for New Orleans at the war's end. Colonel Wharton's headquarters detachment (varying between 150 and 200 men) would not have been large enough to guard more than Navy property in the capital, but there is no evidence that the Army and militia officers of the District wanted Marine help. In 1813, however, the Commandant created a battalion of one hundred men, commanded by Adjutant Samuel Miller, to cooperate with the Navy's Chesapeake gunboat flotilla under Captain Joshua Barney. Barney gave the Marines little to do, assigning them as rear guard and baggage train sentries whenever his flotillamen took the field.[64] Miller's battalion, however, had time to train and, reinforced with additional experienced men from Captain Alexander Sevier's East Florida detachment, became as expert a force as the Marines had yet fielded ashore or at sea.

In the late summer of 1814 a British raiding force of Royal Navy vessels and Major General Robert Ross's army of four thousand regulars invaded Chesapeake waters. Confused about the British forces' ultimate destination, Brigadier General William H. Winder ordered his defense force of regulars and militia from Virginia, Maryland, and the District into the Maryland countryside. Unmolested, the British expedition landed and marched toward Washington on August 21. When the British turned north instead of forcing their way directly into Washington across the East Branch of the Potomac, Winder's regulars had to withdraw quickly to the capital and march north to Bladensburg. Included in this force were Barney's four hundred flotillamen and Miller's Marine battalion, still guarding baggage and ammunition wagons—much to Miller's disgust. On August 24 Winder's army met the British at Bladensburg. After a gesture of resistance characterized by occasional serious fighting on the part of some Maryland militia and by uninspired leadership, Winder's force disintegrated. Barney's force, late arrivals on the battlefield, formed a line with five heavy guns across the Bladensburg–Washington turnpike. Three times in heavy fighting the sailors and Marines threw back the British light infantry brigade leading the attack and inflicted more than two hundred casualties. Tired and footsore, short of ammunition, and crippled by having a quarter of its men casualties, Barney's force withdrew when the soldiers on both flanks gave way. The wounded Barney ordered the command back to Washington. Captain Sevier took the Marines out of the fight, for Miller was down with a serious arm wound. There was little doubt, however, that Barney's flotillamen and the Marine battalion had distinguished themselves on a dark day for American arms.[65]

Back in Washington, where the government and population had been evacuating the city for three days, Colonel Wharton gathered his headquarters remnant, the band, and the clerks with their records and marched to the Navy yard. Although instructed by Secretary of the Navy Jones to rally with the rest of the government at Frederick, Maryland, Wharton asked the yard commandant if he wanted the Marines to help either defend or destroy the yard. Captain Thomas Tingey, however, told him to leave, because the British were near the city and the yard was ready to be burned. Wharton, confused by the disaster, left by small boat. When the Marines returned home in a couple of days, the city was a charred wreck, plagued by looters and further ruined by a severe storm. Tired, wounded, and demoralized, the Marine battalion did not realize they were heroes until the Washington newspapers resumed publication. Unfortunately, however, some Marine officers far from the scene, such as Archibald Henderson, thought that Colonel Wharton had damaged the Corps's new fame for fighting by not taking the field himself.[66]

The battle of New Orleans added more luster to the Corps's reputation, but not because Marines played a large part in the action. Major Daniel Carmick's fifty-six-man company (actually commanded by Lieutenant F. B. DeBellevue) was an inconsequential adjunct to General Andrew Jackson's five-thousand-man army. Simply by being in the campaign, the most impressive American military victory of the war, the Marines shared the glory, however reflected. Part of the success was Major Carmick's, for he was wounded by a British shell on December

28 and was the senior American officer to fall in the campaign. At the time, he was not with his Marines but was serving with a New Orleans militia battalion as a volunteer. His Marines were busy elsewhere. On December 23 they participated in Jackson's night attack on the British position at Villere plantation, losing four men in a brief, confused fight. At one point the Marines began to fade away from a battery they were supporting; Jackson himself rallied them. During the major British assault of January 8, 1815, the Marines fought with a New Orleans volunteer battalion in a redoubt at the extreme right flank of the Rodriquez Canal line. Although they were pushed out of the redoubt by a British assault, they rallied and held the canal position. The British attack, crushed with heavy losses, hit Jackson's line elsewhere.[67]

As the nation entered its first long period of peace since the Revolution, the Marine Corps could count on a legacy of respect and affection from Congress and the Navy that it had not held before 1812. The Marines had received Congress's thanks in the form of extra pay and prize money for sea service. Congress sent special silver medals to the families of Lieutenant Brooks and Lieutenant Bush and praised Major Carmick and his men at New Orleans. Washingtonians knew all about Samuel Miller's battalion at Bladensburg. Legislation passed in 1814 also provided that Marine officers (like their Army counterparts) could receive brevet rank for their accomplishments; a Marine officer could wear honorary rank and even draw the pay of that rank (if serving in a position appropriate for brevet rank) for distinguished service or ten years in grade. Miller, Sevier, and two other officers were immediately breveted. Congress also allowed the Commandant to appoint captains to his headquarters staff with $30 extra pay a month, making staff billets very attractive.

Far more sympathetic to the Marines than they had been before 1812, Navy officers praised the fidelity and skill of their ships guard commanders, especially Lieutenant John M. Gamble of the frigate *Essex*. During the *Essex*'s epic cruise against the British whaling fleet in the Pacific, Gamble had actually commanded a prize vessel in combat with a British privateer. He and a handful of Marines protected Captain David Porter from hostile natives, rebellious prisoners, and mutinous crewmen, and eventually survived capture by mutinous sailors and an ocean trip to safety in an open boat. Of such heroics are the legends of elite military forces made.

Even though the Marine Corps had no impact on the course of the war or much influence in the battles it fought at sea or on shore, its officers felt that its faithful service and bravery more than justified the Marine Corps's existence. Inasmuch as the end of the European war would free American merchantmen to roam the world, with the Navy's frigates along as protection, the Marines would continue to serve as ships guards. Congress was also embarked on a large-scale shipbuilding program to give the Navy ships-of-the-line equal to the best in the world; in the Royal Navy, such vessels carried Marine detachments of three officers and nearly a hundred men. Even though Congress cut its authorized strength of 2,700 men, the Marine Corps prepared for a "Golden Age" of respect for its past services and new military reputation.

3. Archibald Henderson Preserves the Corps
1815–1859

The end of the war with Great Britain and the return of peace to Europe ushered in a golden era of American maritime expansion. Freed from the threat of capture, merchantmen carried cargoes of food, raw materials, and manufactured goods wherever the winds and the port authorities allowed. The United States Navy deployed its small squadrons around the world to protect the merchantmen from piracy, to carry diplomatic representatives abroad, to explore and chart unknown seas, to suppress the African slave trade, and to persuade hermit kingdoms like China and Japan that the American flag was to be taken seriously in matters of personal safety and commerce. The Navy's squadrons patrolled the world's maritime highways: the coasts of Asia, the Atlantic waters off Latin America, the islands of the eastern Pacific and the western coast of Latin America, the west coast of Africa, the Caribbean, the waters of northern Europe, and the Mediterranean.

The Navy emerged from the War of 1812 with an image of utility great enough to inspire several ambitious building programs. In 1816 Congress voted $8 million to build nine ships-of-the-line and twelve frigates. In 1825 it approved a program to build ten sloops-of-war, and it occasionally provided additional funds to purchase vessels and repair those already commissioned. From 1816 until 1842 the number of commissioned vessels grew from forty-one (1,178 guns) to fifty-six (2,002 guns), although only about half of the vessels on the naval register were normally manned and equipped for sea. In addition, by the late

1830s the Navy Department began to build steam-powered warships for the defense of the nation's coast line. The evolution of steam propulsion also coincided with improvements in naval ordnance; although the guns remained muzzle-loaders, they were increasingly heavy and sophisticated to operate, especially when they were rifled for greater range and accuracy and fired explosive shells. Although the technological revolution that was to reshape the Navy by the end of the nineteenth century was slow and uneven, the increased complexity of naval vessels was a reality by 1860.[1]

The Navy's expanded geographical responsibilities and the size and character of its building program had important administrative implications. In 1814 Congress and Secretary of the Navy William Jones concluded that more expertise was essential in planning and supervising naval programs and created a Board of Navy Commissioners composed of three Navy captains. Until the Board of Navy Commissioners was replaced in 1842 by six functional bureaus, it influenced the department's management and legislative programs. The board's power rested on its close relationship with the Secretaries of the Navy, most of whom had no knowledge of naval affairs. The board and Congress also displayed concern about the cost of running the Navy Department and demanded that the department rationalize its building programs and its personnel policies, both of which were touched with political favoritism, some corruption, and personal whim.

The postwar Navy also had serious personnel problems that limited its efficiency: an irregular system of officer promotions; the lack of an educational system for midshipmen; fondness for dueling and courts-martial for "affairs of honor" among its officers; and desertion, drunkenness, and chronic insubordination among its crews. Naval reformers proposed that flogging be eliminated, the grog ration ended, and recruiting practices changed to attract landsmen and apprentice boys into the naval service. By upgrading the service, the reformers hoped to create a Navy manned by sober, industrious, native-born Americans rather than degraded "old salts." [2]

In the immediate postwar period, Congress also considered the state of the Marine Corps, primarily to cut personnel budgets and align the strength of the Corps to the number of vessels kept in service after 1815. Secretary of the Navy Benjamin Crowninshield ably defended the Corps, pointing out that the Corps already had less than a thousand men and only two-thirds of its statutory ninety-three officers. He then established a table of organization that would allow the strength of the Marine Corps to slide with the number of vessels in service: Each ship-of-the-line would rate three officers and sixty-eight men; frigates two officers and between fifty-eight and forty-six men; sloops a sergeants guard of twenty-two; and small vessels a sergeants guard "proportionately diminished." [3] Crowninshield accepted the Marine Corps position that its total strength should be at least double its ships guards. When Congress finally passed a Peace Establishment Act for the Marine Corps in 1817, it did not particularly damage the Corps: Officer strength was set at 50 and enlisted strength at 865, which was later increased to 924. Eleven officers were released, and recruiting stopped, but the Marine Corps emerged from the postwar trimming in good condition. [4]

Most of the Marine Corps's postwar wounds were self-inflicted and, although not fatal, diminished the modest reputation the Corps had won in the War of 1812. Some problems persisted from the prewar period: the ambiguity over the governance of the Corps under the Articles of War and the Navy Regulations, pay and supply accounting irregularities, and the generally poor quality of the enlisted men. But the main problem was the conflict within the officer corps, primarily between Commandant Wharton, joined by Brevet Major Samuel Miller and Brevet Major Richard Smith, and another group led by Brevet Major Archibald Henderson. Angered by Wharton's alleged faint-heartedness in 1814, Henderson charged the Commandant with neglect of duty and dishonorable behavior in failing to answer criticism of his courage. Henderson argued that Wharton's conduct demeaned the Marine Corps's military reputation and encouraged other officers to ignore their duties in preference for their social lives and business ventures. After six months of furor, in 1817 a court-martial of senior Army officers and Marines acquitted Wharton, but the episode created permanent ill feeling among the Corps's officers. [5]

Wharton's authority was further eroded by his senior officers, who served as barracks commanders at the navy yards. After the war these officers assumed their seagoing days were over and settled into their shore stations determined to command without interference from either the Commandant or the Navy yard commandants. When new Navy Regulations in 1818 gave the Navy yard commandants more authority over the Marine guards, the barracks commanders protested that their guards were well disciplined and their detractors ignorant of military matters. One decided that the Corps had *"lost all"* and had entered "a *degenerated,* and *deplorable* state. . . . The word *Amphibious* may now, very justly, be applied to us; as neither the Army or Navy will acknowledge or aid us; and we are, as it *were,* a set of *outcasts, literally nothing.*" [6] The barracks commanders looked to Henderson and Miller, who often held the posts of either acting Commandant or Adjutant, to argue their case in Washington. Discredited and in ill health, Wharton had little influence but accommodated his critics by dying in September 1818. The Board of Navy Commissioners moved into the political vacuum while Henderson and Miller vied for the post of Commandant. In the meantime, the barracks commanders consolidated their own empires by cultivating the Secretary of the Navy and their political friends.[7]

Brevet Major Anthony Gale, the Corps's senior officer, replaced Wharton as Commandant and inherited all his problems. Gale was ill prepared for Washington politics. Born in Ireland, he had immigrated to Philadelphia and joined the Marine Corps in 1798. Except for a couple of short voyages, he had commanded the barracks and recruiting rendezvous in Philadelphia, where he had shown little aptitude for administration. But Gale was intelligent, and he recognized that the Marine Corps could not prosper unless the Commandant's authority was restored. Unfortunately, he was not the man to do it. He protested without success to Secretary of the Navy Smith Thompson that he and President James Monroe should quit granting officers furloughs, transferring Marines on personal whim, and interfering with Corps policies aimed at sharing sea duty equitably. His authority further damaged by Thompson's apathy, Gale went on a binge of public drunkenness and whoring near his headquarters; one evening he screamed at his own officers that they were disloyal malcontents and that "he did not care a damn for the President, Jesus Christ, and God Almighty!"[8] Court-martialed and convicted for conduct unbecoming to an officer, Gale was cashiered in October 1820.

President Monroe again followed strict seniority in appointing Gale's successor. Much to Samuel Miller's disappointment, the President selected Archibald Henderson to be Commandant. At thirty-seven, Henderson was seven years younger than Miller but had been commissioned two years before him. Henderson returned to Washington from New Orleans to take the command he held for the next thirty-eight years. He was no stranger to the politics of the period. Henderson's father, a Scots merchant-planter and member of the Virginia legislature, had been a business partner and agent for the elite of Fairfax and Prince William counties. A handsome, slight man of medium height, Henderson was politically astute, stubborn, intelligent, and a polished gentleman of considerable charm. He was also a bit of a martinet. Proud of his own service in the War of 1812, he would not let Samuel Miller forget that Miller had never been to sea and was viewed by "real" Marines as a headquarters toady. No slouch as a bureaucratic infighter and schemer,

Henderson moderated his capacity for dissimulation and his burning ambition with equally real moral probity, devotion to his Corps, and love of soldiering.[9]

The new Commandant quickly restored order at Headquarters. Before Thompson or anyone else could have second thoughts, he appointed a new Adjutant, Paymaster, and Quartermaster. He ordered all commanders of ships guards and barracks to send their reports directly to Headquarters, not directly to the Secretary of the Navy or through the yard commandants. He ordered all new officers to report to his Headquarters for instruction and tried to improve enlisted morale by abolishing flogging ashore, making Sunday a nonduty day, improving pay and clothing, and limiting the liquor ration. He encouraged the increased use of his Headquarters detachment and the Marine band for ceremonial purposes. And he demanded strict accounting for public funds, frugal use of uniforms and equipment, and obedience to the chain of command. Few Marine officers could doubt that Henderson meant to command the Marine Corps in ways his predecessors had not. If determination and intelligence could hold Congress and the Navy at bay, Archibald Henderson could supply both.[10]

1

Archibald Henderson had no doubt that the Marine Corps mission was to serve "on board the Ships of War in distant seas for the protection of our widely extended commerce," and he shaped his policies to provide fully manned and trained ships guards for outward bound naval vessels.[11] He never seriously thought that the ships guards might be an anachronism in a peacetime, all-volunteer Navy. His most immediate concern was that his senior captains (the rank of major was not provided in the Act of 1817) were not eager to go to sea and did not hesitate to use their influence to avoid sea duty. The most conspicuous case was Samuel Miller, who used his friendship with President Monroe to escape service with the West India Squadron. Although Henderson threatened to resign, he could not persuade the Secretary of the Navy that Miller was overdue for sea duty. Encouraged, those captains senior enough to be brevet majors (and eventually brevet lieutenant colonels) watched the orders to sea duty carefully and protested if they considered themselves wronged. For his first decade as Commandant, Henderson fought for control of officer assignments. Eventually he avoided the problem by sending the most junior captain to sea and letting the others stay in their shore billets at Headquarters and the Marine barracks.[12]

There were substantial reasons for Marine officers to find sea service disagreeable. Although death in action was not much of a threat, the mortality rate of Marine officers from illness, suicide, drownings, accidents, and duels was substantial.[13] The main difficulty, however, remained the acrimony between Navy and Marine officers over such matters as pay, messing and berthing privileges, and authority over the ships guard. In 1818 Commodore Oliver Hazard Perry and the Marine captain on the *Java* exchanged blows over the condition of the ships guard, and both were court-martialed and reprimanded. There were still clashes over the question of whether an officer-of-the-deck could give orders to a Marine captain senior to him and whether Marine lieutenants ought to mess in the wardroom. Marine officers like Richard Smith, who insisted that he deserved authority equal to his brevet rank of lieutenant colonel, did not improve relations. Relieved by his exasperated commander, Smith complained, "I was looked upon as a mere passenger." [14] Another irritation was the financial penalties Marine officers paid by going to sea. Not only were they paid less than Navy lieutenants but lost between $13 and $15 a month in allowances granted their shore-based peers even though expenses for uniforms and food increased aboard ship.[15]

Although the conditions for the ships guards in matters of berthing improved after the War of 1812 and many Navy captains worked harmoniously with their Marines, reciprocal contempt between the ships guards and crew persisted. Since Marine officers did not stand watch, they were viewed as "idlers" along with the purser, surgeon, chaplain, and schoolmaster. The sailors thought "the mizzenroyal and the captain of Marines are the two most worthless things aboard ship" and that the Marines, whose duty was to "spy out and bring to punishment all offenders against the laws of the vessel," ranked below a dog.[16] The schoolmaster on the *Constellation* in 1829–1830 remarked that "the lieutenant of Marines has few duties of any kind to perform. His office, thought necessary as long as the Marine Corps is continued, is nearly a sinecure." He added this definition: "A marine is a sort of ambidextrous animal—half horse, half alligator. His duties alternate between those of a sailor and soldier. He is a being for whom the genuine tar entertains very little respect, and on the other hand, his contempt is repaid . . ." [17] Other observers reported the same attitudes. Herman Melville, a seaman on the *United States* (1843–1844), found that the crew especially despised the Marine sergeants, "generally tall fellows with unyielding spines and stiff upper lips, and very exclusive in their tastes and predilections," and the other Marine enlisted men, who successfully smuggled liquor past their brethren on post and did little but promenade in their dress uniforms.[18] Marine officers recognized the tension below decks but viewed it as an inescapable condition of their service.[19]

Life for the ships guard depended upon amicable relations between the captain and the senior Marine officer, but there were too many points of dispute to make Marine–Navy relations easy. Urged by Henderson to champion their men at all costs, Marine officers protested when their guards ruined their uniforms in menial tasks. Insofar as the Commandant had declared that Marines, as a military force, were governed by the Articles of War even at sea, Marine officers protested when their men were flogged because flogging was illegal in the Army. They also complained that they had too few men for too many sentry posts, which left no time for the upkeep of uniforms, arms, and equipment. There were arguments over just what duties the ships guard could be required to perform and what ones it could not, and military training was virtually impossible aboard ship.[20]

Occasionally the Marines themselves exacerbated their situation through excessive zeal in enforcing ships regulations. On the *Brooklyn* in 1859, two noncommissioned officers bound and gagged a rowdy sailor, who subsequently died. Although the captain of the ship quieted the outraged crew by promising justice and turned the Marines over to civil authorities for indictment for murder, both the Navy captain and Marine Corps officers were publicly criticized by the New York press when the two Marines escaped punishment by fleeing.[21] A problem of another sort was Marines who went "native," accepting positions as members of the crew for extra pay. Some captains allowed Marines to serve as masters-at-arms, clerks, mechanics, armorers, and cooks, thus taking them off sentry duty. For at least one Marine lieutenant the result was a horror: "It is impossible for those who take but a lukewarm interest in the honor and efficiency of the Corps, to see or understand how humiliating it is, for the Officer who feels pride in his profession, when called upon to head a Guard of Swaggering fellows, who ape the manner and dress of the Sailor."[22]

For all the trials of shipboard life, Archibald Henderson never doubted that the ships guard was essential to the Navy's discipline, for he could see no evidence that sailors were any more trustworthy than they had been when he was first commissioned. His memory of the mutiny on the *Constitution* in 1807 was sharp. He attempted to collect evidence of similar incidents but found there were none except for a couple of occasions when time-expired crews had left ship illegally when they reached an American port, leaving the Marines to put the vessels in ordinary. When a time-expired Marine guard on the *Constitution* in 1838 joined the crew in refusing to work the ship, Henderson blacklisted the Marines.[23] He was pleased when his friend Captain Samuel E. Watson wrote him:

A sailor is the same character, whether he is forced aboard or come [sic] voluntarily. His love of drink is the same, and all the arts he can practice to gratify it one [sic] the same and the mutinous disposition consequent upon it the same. The hostility between the Marines and Sailors constitute in my judgment the strongest argument in favour of their great utility on board ships of war, and it should be the policy of Navy officers to promote that hostility in order to more effectively guard against mutiny of sailors.[24]

He found some evidence for his position. In 1842 the Navy was embarrassed when Commander Alexander Slidell MacKenzie hanged three mutineers, one of them the midshipman son of the Secretary of War, during a cruise of the training brig *Somers*. For Henderson the significant fact was that the *Somers* had no Marine guard. He made sure the House Committee on Naval Affairs did not overlook the lesson of the *Somers* affair: The Navy could not do without a Marine guard.[25]

Although Henderson did not dramatize the issue, his ships guards were showing increased usefulness as landing parties, thus offsetting some Navy criticism of their limited utility at sea. Even though part of the rationale for marines was their participation in landing parties, the Marine Corps had not seized upon the mission with much vigor. With American merchantmen, however, turning up in odd corners of the world and finding the natives often hostile, the Navy found itself committed to being waterborne constables. During the 1820s Marines participated in the operations of the West India Squadron in suppressing piracy in the Caribbean. Although most of the action was between the Navy's ships and pirate coasters, the West India Squadron did chase the pirates ashore and occasionally destroy their camps—with the Marines participating. The largest such landing (two hundred sailors and Marines from three ships) occurred at Fajardo, Puerto Rico, in 1824. Angered by the Spanish governor's assumed patronage of the pirates, Commodore David Porter sent his men ashore to spike the guns of a fort and to obtain an apology for detaining an American officer. The naval patrols off the coast of Latin America had similar experiences, and in the 1830s landing parties of sailors and Marines went ashore on the Falkland Islands; Callao and Lima, Peru; and Buenos Aires, Argentina, either to free detained American vessels or to protect American lives, property, and consulates. There was no fighting in these episodes, and the parties seldom stayed more than a day.[26]

In the Pacific the Navy was equally busy and more involved in actual fighting, in which the Marines took part. The most persistent foe was the pirate kingdoms of Malaya and the East Indies. In 1832 Commodore John Downes sent 250 sailors and Marines from the *Potomac* ashore to chastise the population of Quallah Battoo, Sumatra. In an all-day fight the landing party destroyed two forts, burned the town, and killed perhaps a hundred Malays with musketry at a cost of eleven American casualties, four of whom were Marines. The Marine performance was creditable, although the Malays were badly outmatched.[27] Similar incidents occurred during the next ten years. The landing party of the *John Adams* burned a town on Sumatra. The sloops *Peacock* and *Vincennes,* which were part of the Wilkes Expedition to explore the Pacific and Antarctic, put landing parties ashore on the Fiji Islands, Drummond's Island, and Samoa to rescue American citizens, enforce treaties, and burn villages in retaliation for grievances both real and imagined. In 1843 Matthew C. Perry's West Africa Squadron, enforcing the ban on the slave trade, performed similar duties, and the commodore's guard broke a conspiracy against Perry, killing the African king who planned the affair and burning his village. The Navy handled its punitive expeditions easily, exploiting its superiority in troop discipline and weaponry. These landings were small affairs in which sailors made up the bulk of the landing parties, commanded by Navy officers. Although the Marines did their duty, they showed little more aptitude for such operations than the sailors. But the landing operations were at least a way to demonstrate that Marines had their uses and never shied from a fight, however inconsequential.

Whether Archibald Henderson's ships guards were disciplining unruly sailors or burning thatched huts, the Commandant was certain his Marine detachments and his Corps were not large enough. On the other hand, a series of Secretaries of the Navy and Navy officers thought the Marine Corps was too large and too self-important. Henderson's performance in the battle over the Corps's size was dazzling. His first success was to have the Board of Navy Commissioners under the presidency of Commodore William Bainbridge draw up a manning table for ships guards in 1825. The "Bainbridge scale," which accepted the Royal Navy standard of one gun–one Marine, provided Henderson with an ideal argument against the force limitations in the Peace Establishment Act of 1817. The "Bainbridge scale" suggested that ships-of-the-line have as many as 4 officers and 112 enlisted men and no fewer than 3 officers and 81 enlisted men. The standard for frigates was 2 officers and 38 to 55 enlisted men, with the guards of small ships scaled down by the number of guns to sergeants guards of 14 to 26. Using this scale and the number of Navy ships in active service, Henderson in 1826 persuaded both Secretary of the Navy Samuel L. Southard and the House Naval Affairs Committee to admit that the Marine Corps needed at least two hundred more privates. Congress did not agree, but the Commandant was not easily dissuaded.[28]

Part of the Navy officer corps was hostile to the idea of more Marines at sea. Much of the criticism came from those reformers who viewed the ships guards as anachronistic as flogging and grog. Under pressure from these officers and from the Jackson administration to save money, Secretary of the Navy John Branch in 1830 asked his senior officers whether the service could do without ships guards. At least eight officers thought they could command without Marines. The most adamant reformers saw the Marines as "objects of mere pageantry" and wondered "why such an absurdity had been so long tolerated." [29] Anything the Marines could do, sailors could be trained to do equally well. The reformers pointed out that one of their number, David Conner, was at that moment at sea on the brig *Erie* without Marines as an experiment in disciplinary reform. Their position, summarized by Alexander Slidell MacKenzie in the *North American Review,* was that "we consider the abolition of the Marine Corps absolutely necessary to the efficiency and harmony of our ships." No Navy officer needed a "bulwark of bayonets" at his back, and the Marines did nothing to make Navy men-of-war more orderly or combat effective. Rather, the opposite was true, for the Marines were a disruptive influence who prevented the reform of the Navy's crews.[30] Other Navy officers were not so sure that the ships guards should be abolished. They thought the Marines did contribute as sentries, temporary gunners, musketmen in sea battles, and landing party infantry. Several argued that having a voluntary crew was no absolute barrier against mutiny, because disorder came from oppression, not impressment. Secretary Branch concurred, and in the face of such divided opinion Congress dropped the issue of abolition.[31]

In 1834 Congress responded to Henderson's pleas for more men and increased Corps strength by 13 officers, 97 noncommissioned officers, and 250 privates. Henderson was still not satisfied and asked for more men, but the Board of Navy Commissioners advised Secretary of the Navy Mahlon Dickerson that the size of ships guards could easily be half of what the Commandant considered ideal and that the Marine Corps had too many men ashore in any event.[32] Restating its position in 1839, the board observed that the Navy had gotten along nicely with smaller ships guards and assumed that the reduction was purposeful, so that more landsmen could be enlisted. Large ships guards were superfluous: "The Board has no apprehension from mutiny in our service so long as seamen are procured by voluntary enlistment." The only problems the

Navy had had came from time-expired crews, and time-expired Marines were of little use against such shipmates. To mollify Henderson and stop wild charges that the Marines were overworked aboard ship, the board suggested that the number of privates in the Marine Corps be increased by two hundred.[33]

Henderson would not surrender the "Bainbridge scale" and argued that the Marine Corps should have almost eight hundred men at sea and twice that number ashore for training and sentry duty at the Navy yards. Having collected testimonials from Navy officers, he pushed again for more men. The Board of Navy Commissioners accepted his argument that the ships guards should be larger but doubted that Marines should replace landsmen in ships crews, an idea Henderson had championed. The Board in 1839 rejected the idea that sailors should be "militarized" to perform Marine duties, because it felt that sailors' enlistments were too short for infantry drill and because the existing landing parties were effective enough. Sensing a chance for a substantial political victory, Henderson pressed his argument. He stated to Secretary of the Navy James K. Paulding that his requests were really quite modest, considering that the Corps would number 3,500 men if one used the Royal Navy's scale for the Royal Marines and nearly 3,000 if one used the "Bainbridge scale." All the Commandant wanted was a mere increase of twenty-seven officers and a thousand enlisted men, both for sea duty and for more "efficiency" ashore.[34]

The Navy's slow conversion to steam in the 1840s gave the Commandant a new rationale, although he never surrendered any of the old ones. Since steam-powered vessels would be used to either attack or defend harbors, their crews should be "a military force, regularly instructed in the Artillery and Infantry drills" and ready for "operations on land." England had increased the Royal Marines for such reasons, and "the experience of the greatest Naval Power in the world should not be disregarded by us." Experienced Marines were more useful than inexperienced landsmen in any situation, whether it was running a ship, fighting, or maintaining order. Service in the merchant marine might make decent sailors, but "none but good Soldiers should ever be sent on board ships-of-war." Obviously the Marine Corps needed at least a thousand more men—for the Navy's own good. Without them the Navy's new steam warships could not function, nor were the Navy's new bases for their maintenance safe without Marine sentries.[35] By the mid-1840s Henderson had no more men than he had been authorized in 1834, but he was confident enough to state that "a military guard is either useful and ought to be efficient in strength, or it is useless and should be abolished entirely." In any event, the Marine Corps's duties were "permanently fixed" aboard ship. Only its manpower shortages (one hundred men below its 1834 strength) kept the Marine Corps from peak efficiency at sea. Although the Commandant was concerned that the Navy Department had ordered more barracks Marines to sea and had taken the guards off brigs and schooners to increase the guards on larger vessels, he noted with satisfaction that this action ratified the absolute necessity of ships guards. A warship without Marines was unthinkable.[36]

2

The political battles ashore to keep the Marines at sea did not exhaust the challenges Archibald Henderson faced. Throughout his service as Commandant he fought to preserve a Marine Corps with such serious internal problems that honest men could wonder whether the Corps was worth saving. But Henderson never lost his own faith, and his political wisdom and long tenure allowed him to cope with his difficulties. One of Henderson's pressing problems was the character of the Marine officer corps. The combination of sea duty, low pay, inadequate military training and professional socialization, and the personal flaws of many officers combined to make the officership an unattractive career. Between 1798 and 1846 the Marine Corps commissioned 289 officers, but only 69 of them served more than fifteen years (reaching the rank of captain) and 170 served less than five years. Although 113 officers died in the service (7 in battle), 143 resigned, 25 were cashiered, 11 were dropped in 1817, and 6 were transferred to the Army or Navy.[37] The Commandant was well aware of the turnover among his officers. In 1824 he complained to the Secretary of the Navy that political patronage and social connections played too great a part in both winning commissions and making assignments; since the end of the War of 1812 half the new lieutenants had been dismissed or forced to resign. As he was to do the rest of his career, Henderson urged Congress to pass laws sending West Point graduates to the Marine Corps, but his plea was ignored.[38] One alternative was for Henderson to use his personal influence in attracting trustworthy officers and to hound the unfit from the Corps. One indicator that Henderson exercised his power is the change in the geographic origins of Marine officers. Partially defying population shifts and the distribution of strength of the national political parties, Henderson's officers came from Virginia (his home state) and the Mid-Atlantic region.[39]

The few officers Henderson did have gave him trouble. The barracks commanders often skirted Henderson's orders on recruiting, discipline, accounting, and drill. Henderson also became so incensed with the inefficiencies of his staff that he relieved the quartermaster and paymaster, only to find himself charged with conduct unbefitting an officer. Although acquitted, he lost his power to appoint his own staff. In 1828 President John Quincy Adams, encouraged by his Secretary of the Navy, decided that Marine Corps staff appointments, like those of the Army, could be made only by the President with the advice and consent of the Senate. For once the Marine Corps's habit of selectively using the Articles of War for its internal governance backfired.[40]

The condition of the Marine Corps enlisted ranks was equally distressing. Although Henderson was imperious with his officers, he attempted to play the kind father to his men. The enlisted ranks needed much fatherly attention. So unappealing was the Marine Corps that it could not recruit up to its legal strength, however inadequate Henderson thought that strength was. By law and Navy Department policy, the Corps was to enlist only native Americans between the ages of twenty-one and forty, but throughout Henderson's tenure the Corps enlisted aliens and minors, much to the periodic dismay of the government. With parents' consent and masters' permission, the Corps took both boys and indentured servants; one officer argued that minors made excellent sergeants and privates as well as musicians.[41] On the *Brandywine* in 1845 only eighteen of a ships guard of forty-nine were native-born; the Marine lieutenant thought the aliens could be good soldiers, but most were not, "particularly the Irish, there being several of whom the fear of punishment only will keep but respectably clean." [42]

The illiteracy, social and emotional immaturity, and lack of useful skills that marked Marine recruits combined with the hardships of sea service to send desertion soaring in the 1820s. In one three-year period (1821–1824) 607 Marines deserted 696 times, and only 265 were recaptured and 151 tried by court-martial. In the same period 191 Marines were court-martialed for offenses other than desertion and shipboard crimes. In other words about a third of the Marine Corps enlisted strength was probably in some sort of disciplinary status.[43]

The Commandant's immediate response to the discipline problem was to allow early discharges for the discontented, a practice that the Army had already tried and abandoned. The letters from enlisted men flooded his office and that of the Navy Department, for men who had fled unemployment, family quarrels, drunkenness, debts, and civil authorities found the Marine Corps no escape. As one wrote:

In 1825, while on a visit to the City of New York, through the influence of misfortune, in a desperate moment, I entered the United States Marine Corps. Previous to my enlistment, I was the printer of a public journal in Albany and had the reputation of an honest and industrious citizen. Upon serious reflection, I thought it best to keep my situation a secret from my friends, and more particularly from my wife, a young lady whom I had married but a few months previous; and an opportunity offering, I immediately set sail for the West Indies where I have continued from that time to the present.

After nearly two years service on a pestilential, contagious and sickly station, and under the conviction that the United States, in a time of profound peace would not wish to retain her citizens in the service, when assured that it is their wish to leave it, and that they are willing and capable of living out of it with honour and reputation to themselves, I have ventured to make this application for a discharge from the Marine Corps.[44]

Even though he increased clothing allowances, cut the liquor ration, improved training, granted discharges, improved ration and fuel allowances, and persuaded Congress to build better barracks, Henderson made little progress in making the Marine Corps attractive.[45]

Although the Commandant never denied that sea service was the Marine Corps's reason for being, he wanted to enlarge the Corps's barracks detachments to make the service more bearable and to improve his men's training and morale. He justified the size of Headquarters because it served as a school for both officers and men, and he wanted the other barracks to play the same role. He also believed that the barracks detachments played an essential role as Navy yard sentries and complained that he did not have enough men for his shore activities, both privates for guard reliefs and senior officers for command duties. Henderson's officers supported him, because they wanted better promotion opportunities and a chance to add artillery training to Marine Corps skills. Neither the Commandant nor his officers could believe that their services at the Navy yards were not essential or that the government would ignore the needs of the Corps, which had "for more than twenty years, performed its duties faithfully and effectively." [46] The Board of Navy Commissioners, listening to the complaints of Navy yard commandants, thought the Marine guards were "worse than useless."[47] The Navy Department's clerks could not understand why the Marine Corps ran up twice the costs of an Army infantry regiment and needed a headquarters in Washington of a "civil character." The Marine Corps budget, plagued with overruns in travel expenses, allowances, and court-martial costs, ran between $185,000 and $220,000 a year, whereas an Army regiment of similar size cost less than $75,000. Moreover, fully three-quarters of the Marine officers served ashore, an expensive place for them to be. The Navy Department knew there must be some economies somewhere, perhaps by eliminating the Marine Head-quarters and cutting the Corps's strength.[48]

Convinced that the federal government was far too costly, Andrew Jackson's administration conducted a careful study of the Navy Department's expenditures in 1829. Amos Kendall, the President's close friend and fourth auditor of the Treasury, found the Marine Corps budget a horror of illegal expenditures, particularly in officer pay and allowances. Kendall reported that the Marine Corps had persuaded a series of Secretaries of the Navy to apply Army pay and allowances to it illegally and that Henderson, his staff, and his senior officers were all overpaid. The nine most senior officers were getting $22,000 a year; "there is generally the greatest pay when there is the least service." Sea service Marine officers were badly discriminated against and resented the shore-based "drones." The pay situation was, moreover, symptomatic of Henderson's efforts to escape Navy Department control by invoking the Articles of War for his shore establishment's management, thus bluffing the department into giving the Corps unjustified autonomy to mismanage its own affairs. Kendall urged new legislation to integrate the Corps clearly into the Navy Department.[49]

Although Henderson insisted that his shore establishment was essential and improving, Kendall's report set off a crisis that did not abate until 1834. The House Committee on Military Affairs thought the Marine Corps was anomalous and should be merged with the Army. The Navy Department's position, adopted by the House Committee on Naval Affairs, was that ships guards might be justified, but yard guards were not and should be replaced with old or disabled sailors serving as watchmen. Henderson pleaded with Congress that he and his officers knew reform was necessary and wanted the government's help, but he could not stop the Treasury Department from getting their allowances reduced.

The reform impulse, however, was not anti–Marine Corps, for an act in 1833 designed to reduce desertion and improve the enlisted ranks raised enlisted men's pay $1 a month above Army pay for each rank and provided a reenlistment bonus. Enlistments were reduced from five to four years. Responding to a presidential order to return to its Revolutionary War colors, the Marine Corps adopted a new green-and-buff uniform that distinguished it from the Army. (This uniform was changed back to blue-and-red in 1840.) In 1834 Congress made many of the changes Henderson had wanted for more than a decade. It increased his rank to colonel, created the ranks of lieutenant colonel and major for five Line officers, and appointed the Commandant's four staff officers either majors or captains. The number of line captains was increased from nine to thirteen, although the number of lieutenants remained the same. The number of noncommissioned officers was more than doubled, and the number of privates increased by 250 men. Officers received pay at Army scale, and they were later given Army allowances as well, which especially helped lieutenants and captains.[50]

The favorable legislation of 1833 and 1834 was not without cost to the Marine Corps. The Board of Navy Commissioners had long argued that the Marine Corps should be more integrated into "the discipline and laws" of the Navy Department ashore and that the Commandant's ability to invoke his authority under the Articles of War be checked, if not eliminated. The board was particularly critical that yard commandants did not have full authority over the Marine barracks. By eliminating a dual administrative system the board thought the Department could save the cost of Marine Corps Headquarters and improve the Corps's military effectiveness by concentrating the Marines at three large naval stations for training purposes. The board thought that the scattered Marine detachments ashore were too small and undisciplined either to guard naval property or to prepare for shipboard duty.[51] Henderson did not deny that his sentries were too few in number, but he believed that they had done their duties well and should be maintained. Although he admitted that consolidating the detachments might mean better training, "it can hardly be said that the Corps is deficient in Military efficiency, at least not so much as to impair its utility." [52]

The board, however, was not dissuaded, and in 1833 it drafted a new set of Navy Regulations, which were adopted the next year. In addition, some of its recommendations were written into the Marine Corps Act of 1834. Essentially, the reforms specified that no Marine officer would have any authority over Navy officers unless the Marine was the senior officer of a landing party; Marines could command Marines ashore, but not afloat on watch. Regardless of date-of-rank, Marine officers were junior to Navy officers of equal rank. No Marine officer could command a naval station or ship. More important, Marine barracks commanders were under the control of yard commandants. The Marine Corps itself was clearly part of the Navy Department and subject to Navy Regulations both at sea and ashore, unless it was specifically ordered by the President to do duty with the Army. Congress rejected the board's recommendations to abolish Headquarters and concentrate the Marines under Navy officer command ashore. Henderson and his officers accepted the compromise, probably because of the rank, pay, and manpower increases of the Act of 1834 and because the new Navy Regulations also guaranteed ships guards equal treatment with sailors.[53]

If Congress thought it had solved the Marine Corps's problems, it was sadly mistaken. The question of the utility of having Marines guard Navy yards did not die. From Henderson's point of view, the question was not arguable, as the barracks were essential for training and organizing ships guards. In addition to insisting that the Navy yards would be picked clean without Marine sentries, Henderson stressed other Marine roles ashore. One was that the Marine barracks provided trained troops in domestic emergencies. In two decades (1820–1840) there were only five such episodes, but the Marine Corps forgot none of them. At least one was remembered by virtue of becoming a story in one of William Holmes McGuffey's readers. In 1824, at the request of civil authorities, Captain Robert D. Wainwright and his guard from Boston stopped a riot at the Massachusetts State Prison. The prisoners' revolt, worse than anything Marines had seen at sea, paralyzed the warden's staff until the Marines arrived. At Wainwright's command, thirty Marines marched into the mess hall, where the rioters had assembled, and leveled their muskets at the prisoners. When Wainwright convinced the rioters that he had given the last warning and that his men would shoot them without hesitation, the mob dispersed. The other incidents were less dramatic, but because they happened in the 1830s they gave the Marines much-needed visibility. In 1831 President Jackson ordered the Headquarters battalion to riot duty in Washington when he feared a mob might attack some public buildings. The same year ships guards patrolled Southampton county, Virginia, after Nat Turner's Rebellion. In 1833 the President again ordered the Marines to protect a wing of the Treasury Building that had been destroyed by fire. Marines performed similar sentry duties in New York after a fire had ruined part of the city.[54]

Despite his skilled defense of the Corps, Henderson recognized that his barracks were still troubled. The Act of 1834 did not fill the ranks, and he himself stopped giving easy discharges. Until the depression of 1836, recruits were hard to find, native or immigrant. Continually stripped for ships guards and full of noneffectives, the shore detachments were too small for unit training, and sentries were forced to stand long tours. Moreover, the barracks were not in very hospitable condition. One Secretary of the Navy said he had seen oxen better housed, and the Brooklyn yard guard rejoiced when it moved to an abandoned alms house.[55]

The most vexing problem remained the question of command authority. Henderson did not think the Act of 1834 prevented him from issuing orders to his barracks commanders, but yard commandants did. The Navy Department solution was to have Marine commanders forward their correspondence to Henderson through the yard commandants and for Marine officers to report daily on their guards' activities.[56] Henderson asked the Board of Navy Commissioners to draft a set of regulations for Navy–Marine Corps relations ashore, but the board supported the concept of unlimited authority for yard commandants. It continued to recommend that the Marine Corps be limited to the four largest yards and that watchmen be used elsewhere. Wrapping his rhetoric in the misty glories of the War of 1812, Henderson argued that such proposals were unnecessary, wasteful, and an insult to the memory of the Corps's courageous dead. Wherever the Navy flew a flag ashore, Archibald Henderson was convinced that Marines should guard it. Again the Navy Department wavered, and most yards had both Marine sentries and watchmen.[57]

Like Janus, Henderson watched the Navy Department with one face and his barracks with another. Conciliatory and diplomatic in Washington, the Commandant was a stickler in Marine Corps matters large and small. One of his captains wrote to complain: "Some of the officers have cut their hair short behind and shave the face all clean, others leave their hair long behind, and have large whiskers extending round the throat, others in addition wear a mustachio, and others again do not shave any part of the face, and you may suppose they are when together a motley looking group." The Commandant, therefore, decreed that Marines would have cropped hair in back, no hair below the ear, and no mustaches or beards—no matter what civilian styles were.[58] He also continued to command the Corps, although one Secretary of the Navy and Samuel Miller thought he violated the Act of 1834 and the Navy Regulations with impunity.[59] Henderson endured and persisted, and his critics in and out of the Marine Corps left office or died. The Commandant preserved the delicate balance with the Navy in executing the Act of 1834. He did nothing to encourage direct challenges to the Act, but one of his barracks commanders protested that the Act demeaned the Commandant and Marine officers by stripping them of their "military" authority, even going to the Supreme Court to challenge the law and losing in *U.S.* v. *Freeman*.[60] In continual conflict with yard commandants over his authority, Henderson collected evidence on the expense and ineptness of civilian watchmen. In 1842 the Board of Navy Commissioners dissolved, giving Henderson freer access to Congress and the Secretary of the Navy. Two years later Congress was asking the Navy Department why the Marine Corps should not have more men for Navy yard duties since they were clearly so essential. Archibald Henderson had won another battle.[61]

3

For all his insistence that the Marine Corps perform its traditional missions as ships guards and Navy yard sentries, Archibald Henderson did not overlook opportunities to enhance the Marine Corps's reputation as a military force prepared for active field service. Having successfully exploited Marine Corps bravery in the War of 1812 for twenty years, Henderson knew that the most impressive argument for his Corps's survival was that Marines could fight. Twice during his service as Commandant, Henderson committed the Marine Corps to battle—in the Indian wars in the Southeast, 1836–1842, and the Mexican War, 1846–1848. In both cases the Marine Corps participation had a dual character. The ships guards on Navy vessels on patrol and blockade duty participated in landing operations, a function already well developed and not unique to these two conflicts. The second type of Marine Corps participation was more novel—extended land service as a temporary part of the Army. Although such service was provided for in the Act of 1798 and reiterated in the Act of 1834, the Marine Corps had seldom sought such service until its very existence was challenged in the 1830s. But in 1836, shortly after his trials with the Navy Department and Congress, the Commandant decided that even field service in the Indian wars might enhance the Corps's reputation.

President Jackson, the Army, Southern settlers, and the Creek and Seminole Indian tribes combined to give the Marine Corps its first opportunity for field service since the War of 1812. The cause of conflict in the Southeast was the government's policy of resettling the Indians in order to open their lands to settlement. Although some of the tribes capitulated without much resistance, the Seminoles of Florida balked, and in December 1835 the Seminoles under Osceola attacked the Army posts northwest of Tampa Bay.[62] For the next six months, the Army unsuccessfully tried to seize the initiative from the Seminoles. To compound the War Department's problems, in April 1836 the Creeks and the Georgia settlers along the Chattahoochee River began raids upon one another. Heeding the Georgians' cries to crush the Creeks, but already saddled with the war in Florida, the War Department looked for more troops. Archibald Henderson made sure it did not overlook the Marine Corps.

On May 21, 1836, Henderson volunteered his barracks Marines for service with the Army in Georgia, arguing that the use of a Marine regimen would save the government money. This argument proved persuasive with Andrew Jackson, who ordered the Marines to join Brigadier General Thomas Jesup's army at Fort Mitchell, Alabama. Henderson's offer, graciously received by the Jackson administration, was enthusiastically approved by most of Henderson's officers. The Commandant assigned himself to command the regiment, no doubt remembering his criticisms of Franklin Wharton. Leaving only a sergeants guard at each Navy yard, Henderson assembled thirty-six officers and about four hundred men in Georgia by late June.[63]

Dressed in their white fatigue uniforms, Henderson's regiment spent the rest of the summer patrolling the Alabama–Georgia border by foot and steamboat. They had little contact with the elusive Creeks and no battles. Much of their time was spent guarding supply convoys and stagecoach way stations. They had, in fact, arrived too late to join the Army's roundup of the refractory Creeks. Having made his *beau geste* and finding no war, Henderson, in fact, was ready to return home and assign his regiment to "its legitimate duties." [64]

Having received the Marine regiment, the Army of the South was reluctant to let it go home, for there was another war in Florida in which Marine ships guards were already fighting. Henderson's men had proved capable of field service; their camp discipline was excellent and their disease problems minimal. When General Jesup went to Florida in September, he took Henderson's regiment with him. Assembled at Fort Brooke on Tampa Bay, the Marine regiment again served as road patrols and post and convoy guards. Like the ships guards from Commodore Alexander J. Dallas's squadron, the Marines found their duties largely passive and the Florida Indians elusive. In January 1837 Henderson's Marines got into one serious battle with the Seminoles near the "Great Cyprus Swamp" along the Hatchee-Lustee river, some eighty miles northeast of Fort Brooke. Having learned that a band of Seminoles was encamped in the swamp, Jesup sent part of his army to attack it. The force included a composite brigade of Army regulars, Marines, Georgia volunteers, and Indians commanded by Archibald Henderson. On January 27 Henderson assaulted the camp, capturing some women, Negro slaves and children, and Seminole supplies. The warriors, however, faded into the swamps. Henderson's Marines pursued the Indians across two streams but lost them in another swamp. Henderson's own conduct eventually won him a brevet promotion to brigadier general, and his men fought with skill and enthusiasm. The Marines lost six men.[65]

After the Battle of Hatchee-Lustee the Marines continued their patrols and their base and supply line security duties, but they saw little of the elusive Seminoles. In March 1837, when Jesup arranged some Indian surrenders, the Army thought the war was ending, although more than a thousand Indians remained at large. Henderson allowed the strength of his regiment to dwindle through discharges and disease instead of reinforcing it from his barracks troops. In June 1837, believing he had been too long from the Washington bureaucratic wars, the Commandant and part of his staff returned to Headquarters. Brevet Lieutenant Colonel Samuel Miller remained in Florida with a small battalion. After spending another year in Florida, primarily as depot guards and mounted patrols, Miller's force left the Army of the South and returned to its barracks. There were no more battles, but the Marines suffered twenty-two deaths from disease before their departure in 1838.[66] The ships guards, however, remained in the war until its official conclusion in 1842. The Navy, having formed a special Florida Squadron, or "Mosquito Fleet," of shallow-draft vessels, assisted the Army by patrolling the coastal waterways and rivers running into the Everglades. There were few skirmishes but many long and frustrating boat patrols by the "Mosquito Fleet" Marines, who lost sixteen men to disease and only one to wounds. Although they had seen limited action, the ships guards and Henderson's regiment had at least participated in one of America's most difficult Indian campaigns.

As the Marines were marching to Georgia to fight the Creeks, their countrymen in Texas were winning independence from Mexico, an event that would draw the Marine Corps into another campaign ten years later. When American sentiment shifted to favoring the annexation of Texas in the early 1840s, the federal government carried on a series of negotiations both to annex Texas without war and to purchase California and the Southwest in the bargain. Elected on an expansionist platform in 1844, President James K. Polk found the Mexican government stubborn on real estate matters and belligerent about both the annexation of Texas (by Congressional resolution in 1845) and the U.S. definition of the nations' common boundary. Both countries deployed small armies to the Rio Grande valley, and the Navy's Home Squadron under Commodore David Conner hovered about Mexico's Gulf Coast ports. Warships of the Pacific Squadron did the same along the coast of California. Both squadrons received orders in 1845 to blockade Mexico should war occur and to seize whatever ports the commodores thought essential to the further conduct of both Navy and Army operations and the Polk administration's diplomatic aims. For the Pacific Squadron this meant taking San Francisco, and for the Home Squadron the ports of Tampico and Veracruz. Thus when the war began in April 1846, the Navy's strategic tasks were clear, and its chief problems became the concentration of an adequate number of men and vessels to carry out its missions.[67]

With the outbreak of war, Archibald Henderson asked that the statutory strength of the Marine Corps be augmented by 27 officers and

1,740 enlisted men. Although the Commandant foresaw the use of Marines in landing operations, his primary concern was to increase the ships guards of the Home Squadron and the Pacific Squadron to the ideal strength of 1,334 enlisted men. Secretary of the Navy George Bancroft wondered how the Marine Corps was going to recruit the extra men, for it could not even find enough men to meet its peacetime strength of 1,000 privates. In 1847, however, the Congress authorized the Commandant to add 1,112 officers and men; although there were enough officer applicants to swell the officer corps from forty to seventy, the Marine Corps enlisted strength peaked at 1,700 men. The Navy had similar recruiting problems. However ambitious Henderson's plans became, the Marine Corps could not find enough men to play a major role in the conflict, even if it had had the opportunity.[68]

Having won control of the Gulf of Mexico and the Pacific approaches to Mexico by default from the minuscule Mexican navy, the Home and Pacific Squadrons concentrated on blockading enemy ports. The Home Squadron found itself handicapped by a lack of anchorages and bases and a shortage of shallow-draft steamers and sailing craft for coastal and riverine operations. Nevertheless, Conner's squadron (subsequently commanded by Matthew C. Perry) successfully supported the Army's operations and blockaded the Mexican Gulf coast from the Rio Grande to Yucatán. Its activities included landing operations by both sailors and ships guards. In May 1846 Conner's landing party of five hundred sailors and Marines reinforced the Army supply depot at Port Isabel near the mouth of the Rio Grande but did not see combat.

The squadron's Marines then participated in a series of expeditions that eventually closed Mexico's six largest Gulf ports. The pattern of these expeditions with one exception was much the same. If the Navy's vessels could conquer the problems of tides, sand bars, weather, and the Mexican shore batteries, they found the towns undefended or quick to surrender under the threat of the Navy's guns. The landing parties played a minor part in these operations, usually going ashore for a brief period while the Navy burned Mexican supplies and rounded up prize vessels. In the raids on Tuxpan (April 17, 1847) and Tabasco (October 23–25, 1846) the landing party had a skirmish or two, but the only casualties were sailors. The biggest operation the Marines joined was the Second Tabasco Expedition (June 14–July 21, 1847). Under Commodore Perry's command a force of steamers and towed gunboats chugged up the Tabasco River and landed a naval brigade of 1,175 men and six cannon on the river's bank. A small battalion of perhaps 200 Marines was part of the brigade's advance guard, which found the Mexican resistance negligible. The Marines then helped garrison Tabasco and fought several small battles with the Mexicans before Perry ordered the town abandoned. The Marines' performance as infantry was skilled, but they were not hard pressed by the Mexicans and had only one wounded.

In the one large-scale amphibious operation of the war, the landing and capture of Veracruz in March 1847, the Marines played a minor role. On March 9 soldiers of Major General Winfield Scott's army plunged ashore from surfboats and lighters against no resistance; in five hours 8,600 men were ashore under the Navy's protecting guns. Appreciating the Navy's contribution to the operation and understanding the Navy's urge to join the siege, Scott allowed Commodore Conner to set up a naval battery manned by sailors and to attach a Marine battalion to the 3d Artillery Regiment. Although the Marines proved as skilled as the Army's regulars in camp life, they did little during their two weeks ashore. The ships guards, however, were important enough for Commodore Perry to view them as crucial to his squadron's operations, and he resisted any detachment of his Marines for service with Scott's army, arguing that the Marines were essential garrison troops for those few coastal towns he permanently occupied.[69]

The ships guards of the Pacific Squadron had a more glamorous part in the Mexican War than their brethren with the Home Squadron. The basic difference in their experience was that the federal government wanted Commodore John D. Sloat, his successor Robert F. Stockton, and Consul Thomas O. Larkin to assist American dissidents in California. Annexation of California was clearly a possibility, a development that meant that the Navy's landing parties might become part of an American occupying force. In addition to the ships guards, the Marine Corps contributed First Lieutenant Archibald H. Gillespie, a thirty-three-year-old, Spanish-speaking adventurer who arrived in California as Polk's personal secret agent. An ardent Democrat of the "Manifest Destiny" persuasion, Gillespie delivered his messages and cast his lot with the "Bear Flag" rebels and Army Lieutenant John C. Frémont's mounted battalion.[70]

With the outbreak of war the operations of the Pacific Squadron began smoothly enough, for in one four-week period (July 7–August 6, 1846) naval landing parties (including Marines) took possession of Monterey, Yerba Buena, Sonoma, San Diego, Santa Barbara, and San Pedro in the name of the United States. Commodore Sloat assumed responsibility for the occupied towns from the cooperative "Bear Flag" rebels and set out to organize his land forces against either the Mexican army or Spanish Californians. Although Sloat was reluctant to use his small force for further operations, his successor, Commodore Stockton, was not. The Marines, however, stayed either aboard ship or in the coastal cities, while the "war of conquest" was assumed by the California Battalion of volunteers, local militia, and a column of Army dragoons sent overland from Missouri. In the meantime, ships of the Pacific Squadron cruised the coast of Lower California and Mexico proper in search of prizes and privateers.

In August 1846 Commodore Stockton, who had made himself civil governor of California, organized an expedition against the stronghold of Mexican-Californian resistance, Los Angeles. He ordered Frémont's battalion to march north from San Diego while he led a naval landing party of 360 men (90 of them Marines) from San Pedro. On August 13 the two forces marched into Los Angeles unopposed. Gillespie, now serving as a California Battalion captain and Frémont's civil deputy, remained in the city with a scratch garrison of unruly volunteers, and Stockton's force returned to their vessels for blockade duty against Mexico. The American victory, however, was short-lived. In September the Californians reorganized and rebelled in Los Angeles, forcing Gillespie's garrison to withdraw to vessels in San Pedro harbor. To Captain William Mervine of the *Savannah* fell the task of crushing the revolt. Throwing together a landing party of sailors and Marines from three ships and attaching Gillespie's troops to his force, Mervine marched toward Los Angeles without cannon, supplies, or adequate transport. For two miserable days (October 7–8, 1846) Mervine's force plodded along, plagued by the heat and harried by the Californians. When the Californians threatened to launch mounted charges against them, the sailors and Marines formed a square; the Californians then raked them with artillery fire. When the Americans charged, the Californians briskly rode off. With ten casualties, Mervine's landing party struggled back to their vessels.

Commodore Stockton reorganized his forces at San Diego for another campaign against the Californians, but his first task was to rescue Colonel Stephen Kearny's dragoon column, which had been badly mauled at San Pasqual on December 6. By December 23 the joint Navy–Army of some six hundred men was well enough organized to start again for Los Angeles; this time the army had adequate cannon, horses, wagons, and supplies, as well as some hard-earned experience in land warfare. The Marines from the *Congress,* the *Cyane,* and the *Portsmouth* formed one battalion under the command of First Lieutenant Jacob Zeilin, a future Commandant. Marching northward, the Americans defeated the Californians in two battles, at San Gabriel and La Mesa (January 8–9, 1847), and reoccupied Los Angeles. In Northern California another landing party of sailors and Marines helped crush another, smaller revolt. Having endured cannon fire and cavalry charges, the victorious landing parties once again boarded their vessels to return to the blockade of Lower California.

With Upper California safely under American control, the Pacific Squadron intensified its operations against the Mexican ports of Mazatlán, La Paz, and San José. Throughout the rest of the war, the Navy harried Mexico's Pacific coastline, and landing parties went ashore as both raiders and occupiers. The Marines defended Guaymas and Mazatlán, holding both towns against Mexican attacks. When the war ended in 1848, the ships guards of the Pacific Squadron had seen more fighting than any other portion of the Marine Corps.[71]

However useful the ships guards of the Home and Pacific Squadrons were in the Navy's landing operations, Archibald Henderson was not satisfied that the Marine Corps was distinguishing itself in the Mexican War, and he looked for opportunities for more visible service. In May 1847 the Commandant saw a new chance to win recognition for the Corps by attaching a Marine regiment to Winfield Scott's army, then marching on Mexico City in the war's epic campaign. In May the War Department was scraping together reinforcements to replace Scott's time-expired Volunteers. As he had done in the Seminole War, Henderson argued that the Marine Corps could with more speed and less cost add a "regular" regiment to Scott's army by recruiting new Marines in the United States and leavening them with the veterans of the Home Squadron. Henderson made his case directly with President Polk and Secretary of War William L. Marcy, much to the Navy Department's dismay, for the Pacific and Home Squadrons wanted more Marines for landing operations. Polk accepted Henderson's plan, and the Commandant set about forming a new six-company regiment. The result of the recruiting was not impressive. Except for the officers and a handful of noncommissioned officers, the Marine regiment was as green as the rawest Volunteers. Nine-tenths of the enlisted men were recruits, and they left the United States without much training. Yet the regiment was clearly Henderson's pride. Its commander was his old friend and fellow Virginian, Brevet Lieutenant Colonel Samuel E. Watson. Among its officers were Major Levi Twiggs, another hero of the War of 1812 and Seminole War and nephew of an Army general; the Commandant's teenage son Charles; and Adjutant A. S. Nicholson's two sons. Two of the company commanders were Marine hotspurs, Captain George H. Terrett and Captain John G. Reynolds, both favorites of the Commandant. Seldom have so few represented so much hope for military glory.[72]

Watson's regiment, subsequently reorganized as a battalion of 22 officers and 324 men, sailed three days after its formation and arrived at Veracruz on July 1. Reinforced by a small detachment from the Home Squadron, it joined 2,500 Army troops for the march overland to Scott's army. After a three-week march, much dysentery, and six minor brushes with Mexican guerrillas, the Marines joined Scott's army at Puebla on August 6. The battalion was then assigned to Brigadier General John A. Quitman's division, the smallest of Scott's four divisions, composed of Volunteer regiments from New York, Pennsylvania, and South Carolina. Quitman's division, however, did not figure prominently in Scott's plans to sweep south of Mexico City; much to Quitman's disgust, Scott assigned his troops to protect the army's supply trains. Scott tried to soothe Quitman with a polite dispatch to the effect that his division was in a "place of honor"—if the Mexicans attacked. A Mississippi politician who understood the popular benefits of military glory, Quitman was not happy, and neither were his Marines. When Scott's army fought at Cherubusco and Contreras (August 19 and 20, 1847), the Marines missed the action. As the army slid around Mexico City to the southwest, the Marines plodded along in the rear.[78]

After an ill-conceived truce expired in early September, Scott attacked the Mexican position at Molino del Rey, southwest of the city, and allowed the Mexicans to ruin Brigadier General William J. Worth's division. Scott, his generals, and his engineer officer-advisers then debated their next attack. Against the majority's opinion, Scott decided to follow the Molino del Rey attack with an assault on Chapultepec Castle, the Mexican military academy, which presumably controlled the roads to the San Cosme and Belén gates to the city. This time Scott's scheme of maneuver included Quitman's division, for the general was running short of battle-worthy infantry. The castle would be no easy prize. Defended by about a thousand Mexican soldiers and cadets, Chapultepec was on a steep hill surrounded by walls and newly constructed redoubts. Only its western face was easily climbed. Scott planned for Brigadier General Gideon Pillow's division to make the main assault from the southwest, with Quitman's division assaulting the steeper southern slope from the Tacubaya highway, which ran northeast to the roads to the Belén and San Cosme gates. The road junction was defended by two Mexican batteries and entrenched infantry and was covered by fire from Chapultepec itself. Scott did not think Quitman's attack would be much more than a diversion for Pillow and the subsequent advance by Worth's division on the San Cosme gate. There was little doubt from Quitman's perspective that his division had a difficult task, for during a reconnaissance on September 12 he and his party were peppered by the Mexicans, and seven Marines were wounded.

Quitman's plan of attack and organization was an invitation to confusion. His plan called for his division to advance in column down the Tacubaya causeway, then pivot to the left (thus exposing a flank to raking fire from the Mexican batteries at the junction of the Veronica and Chapultepec causeways) for an assault on the lower walls of Chapultepec Castle. To lead the assault, Quitman created a force with no overall commander: a "storming party" commanded by Levi Twiggs composed of 120 volunteers from the Marine battalion and Quitman's three Volunteer regiments; another "storming party" commanded by an Army captain composed of 250 men from six different Army regiments; a 40-man "pioneer" party from Quitman's division equipped with ladders, tools, and fascines and commanded by Marine Captain John G. Reynolds; and Watson's Marine battalion to provide covering fire for both storming parties and the pioneers. Quitman assigned his three Volunteer regiments to follow up the assault on the lower wall while an attached brigade under General P. F. Smith guarded Quitman's flank east of the Tacubaya causeway. As the American artillery pounded the castle, this force formed for the attack on the evening of September 12–13 and began their advance the next morning as Pillow's division began its assault up Chapultepec's southwestern slope.[74]

Two hundred yards from the Mexican position astride the junction of the Veronica and Chapultepec causeways, Quitman's advance party of storming parties, pioneers, and Marine battalion came under heavy Mexican fire. Forced to take cover in the ditches on the left side of the road and amid some ruined buildings, Watson's battalion deployed to fire both north toward the Mexican position and west toward the castle grounds and lower wall, also heavily defended. Since Watson's orders were to establish his firing position short of the Mexican ditch across the road, the Marines were near their prescribed position. In the fighting, however, all four units of the advance party became thoroughly scrambled, and their casualties mounted despite their own return fire. Levi Twiggs, walking along the ditches with his favorite fowling piece, met John Reynolds and exclaimed, "My God, I'm tired. . . . Are those your men or mine? . . . Where is my command?"[75] A bullet smashed into his chest, and he soon died. Reynolds carried Twiggs behind a low wall, where he found Watson and Major William Dulaney confused and awaiting orders and more ammunition. Having halted on orders, Watson was reluctant to move without word from Quitman.

In the meantime, seeing Pillow's men finally carry the lower wall and

Smith's brigade attacking the Mexicans along the Chapultepec causeway, Quitman ordered his Volunteer regiments to assault the lower
wall without the advance party's assistance. With considerable confusion, the Volunteers struggled through gaps in the wall and climbed
the hill to carry the castle with Pillow's division. Part of one Marine
company may have gone along with this force. As this assault began,
Quitman put the whole advance party under the command of an Army
officer and ordered it to capture the Mexican batteries to its front, which
it did. In the general confusion, most of the Marine battalion stayed in
its position and covered the two assaults with musketry. As the Mexicans began to break, however, Watson's battalion moved toward the
Mexican positions at the castle gate at the extreme eastern corner of the
lower wall and toward the batteries at the road junction. After penetrating the wall and capturing some Mexicans and some abandoned guns,
the Marines halted.

Captain George H. Terrett, however, took his own company and part
of another and joined the pursuit up the Veronica causeway. Having
been in the van in the rush for the castle gate and capturing one manned
battery, Terrett had no intention of stopping until he found more
fighting. Terrett's force of six officers (including Charles Henderson)
and perhaps twenty-five men attached itself to an Army battery in the
advance up the causeway. This force had a brush with a party of lancers
before reaching the buildings clustered around the point where the
causeway and aqueduct turned eastward toward San Cosme gate. Here
they, along with an ad hoc Army force, fought for and captured a
Mexican barricade. The Marines were the first troops to reach these
buildings, but they may not have reached the San Cosme gate itself,
which was heavily defended. In any event, Worth's division took over
the attack and eventually captured the gate after heavy fighting. During
this assault, Terrett's party was attached to the 11th Infantry. Having
lost six men wounded, Terrett's orphans rejoined the rest of the Marine
battalion three days later.

In the meantime, Watson reorganized the rest of his battalion and
joined Quitman's rush down the Chapultepec causeway to the Belén
gate. The regulars of Smith's brigade, Army batteries, and the South
Carolina regiment led the attack, again a melee. Penetrating the city
before Worth took the San Cosme gate, Quitman's division held on
to the buildings it seized around the Belén gate and fought off several
Mexican attacks. At this point (early afternoon), the Marine battalion
joined the fighting, losing two wounded and six dead, the only Marines
to die besides Twiggs. (In addition to Twiggs's and Terrett's casualties,
the battalion had two officers and fourteen men wounded at Chapulte-

pec; total casualties for September 13 were seven dead and twenty-four wounded.) The next day Quitman's ragged, exhausted division marched to the center of the city, which had been abandoned by Santa Anna's army.

Once inside the city, Quitman placed the Marine battalion on provost guard duty, and a Marine detachment cleared the central plaza and the Palacio Nacional of snipers and looters. This assignment was not a special honor but simply work someone had to do, and the Marines, not quite as soiled and worn as the soldiers, were presumably skilled at sentry duty. Distinguished by their high shakos and crossed white belts, the Marines served military governor Quitman until the battalion left Mexico City in January 1848. The waiting period was not entirely happy for the Marine battalion, for Colonel Watson died of illness, and the battalion officers fell into warring cliques over who had done what on September 13. William Dulaney, the senior surviving officer, did not help matters by being court-martialed for drunkenness on duty and looting, while his protégé, First Lieutenant John S. Devlin, accused some of the other officers, including Reynolds, of cowardice. Devlin, the battalion quartermaster, had joined the assault on Chapultepec castle and had been slightly wounded; convinced of his own heroism, he railed at the other officers for their timidity.

Archibald Henderson struggled to find something exceptional about the Marine battalion's performance. He corresponded with the battalion adjutant, First Lieutenant D. D. Baker, the only living Marine officer cited for heroism by Quitman, about the circumstances of the Chapultepec fight and Terrett's race for the San Cosme gate. Presumably he discussed the episode with his son Charles. Baker and other officers convinced the Commandant that Terrett had shown as much bravery and initiative as any officer in the field, although none argued that he had acted under orders. Henderson also convinced himself that Terrett's force had captured the San Cosme gate before the Army arrived and that Watson's battalion stormed Chapultepec castle. The report that a Marine lieutenant had raised the American flag over the Palacio Nacional pleased Henderson, who saw great significance in the act. He urged his officers to send him letters and documents so he could write a history of the battalion's great feats. "Justice alone to the Corps, particularly that part of it engaged in arduous service, would require a record of this nature." He eventually arranged brevet promotions for fourteen officers of the battalion and later court-martialed and cashiered Lieutenant Devlin for slandering these officers in a newspaper article in 1852. Although Henderson's effort to rewrite the battalion's experience did not immediately influence the histories of Scott's campaign, the Commandant's version eventually worked its way into histories of the Marine Corps. Whatever actually happened on September 13, the Marine Corps, a military organization in search of an elite reputation, was not going to let anyone forget that it had fought for "the halls of Montezuma." [76]

4

As it neared its fiftieth anniversary, uplifted by its real and imagined valor in the Mexican War, Archibald Henderson's Marine Corps had not changed significantly during the Commandant's twenty-seven-year tenure. Most of the changes after the Act of 1834 were superficial matters of uniform modifications, minor regulations, and equipment changes. On the other hand, the Marine Corps's existence was no longer challenged, despite the fact that the arguments against the necessity of ships guards and yard guards were just as reasonable as they had been in the 1830s. From 1847 to the Civil War, the Congress treated the Marine Corps well. The Commandant's Headquarters staff increased in rank and independent status; Marines who had served with the Army in Mexico were rewarded with land bounties and pensions like soldiers; all Marine wartime veterans since 1790 were granted 160 acres of land in 1855; and in 1849 the President was authorized to substitute Marines for landsmen aboard Navy vessels. The Navy Department once more increased Marine officers' pay by doubling the ration allowance of every officer who held a command position afloat and ashore. By reinterpreting legislation on the awarding of brevets in the Army, the Navy Department also granted brevet rank to eleven ships guard officers who had served in landing parties in the Mexican War. But the one thing Congress would not give the Marine Corps was the most crucial: It would not give the Corps more men. Despite Henderson's now-customary arguments, the Corps returned to its prewar size. Even with increases in the 1850s, the Corps's strength until the Civil War varied from only 46 to 63 officers and 1,200 to 1,700 enlisted men. The Marines' duties as ships guards and yard guards did not change, despite their increasingly ceremonial function.[77]

The Commandant's problems were not especially novel, nor were his policies any more imaginative. To reduce desertion among the enlisted men, he returned to granting easy discharges upon request. To soothe his officers, he pried increased allowances from the Navy Department. Worrying about the Marine Corps's reputation in Washington, Henderson in 1850 launched a short-lived program of moral reform aimed at his noncommissioned officers. Invoking the Articles of War, he outlawed swearing: "The Commandant fears that there is too much cause for issuing this order, and hopes it may prevent in future so bad a habit." [78]

In his own hand he scribbled out a similar injunction against drunkenness:

> Drunkenness disgraces the Soldier and degrades the Man; to see a Soldier in the undress [uniform] of his Corps staggering about the streets, a sad spectacle to the community, is indeed most disgraceful, not only to himself, but to the Corps of which he is a member.
>
> The Commandant himself has had the mortification, within a few days, personally to see both a non-commissioned officer and a private Soldier in this shameful condition. He now warns the Soldiers of all ranks against a repetition of this offense, with a full determination to reduce to the Ranks every non-commissioned officer who shall be guilty of it hereafter.[79]

Throughout his declining years, Henderson struggled to return the Marine Corps to its Mexican War authorized strength of 2,400 officers and men, and he continued to refine the arguments he had used since 1821. He stressed that the Marine Corps was a military organization that demanded discipline and "the steadiness of military drill" uniquely different from life in the Navy. Although the Act of 1834 had been expedient, it had made the management of Marine barracks difficult, because Navy yard commandants knew so little about military matters. *U.S.* v. *Freeman* had clearly established the military character of the Corps, but the Navy Department and Congress had failed either to provide definitive legislation for the Marine Corps's governance or to provide adequate strength for the ships guards and barracks detachments. Henderson saw no reason to undervalue the Corps. He thought Terrett's achievement at Mexico City showed the Marines' military utility, which should be no less useful on steamships or Southern naval bases menaced by slave insurrections and sectional rebellion. Although he admitted that yard commandants and Marine officers were still fighting over the command of the barracks Marines, the Commandant argued that "the protection of the public property of yards is not the main object for which the guards are maintained," for the barracks were actually training bases for ships guards. He had no doubts that ships guards were still essential, because American sailors were no more trustworthy than they had been in the War of 1812. If the Royal Navy needed marines, so did the U.S. Navy—at British manning levels. Marines could easily replace landsmen in crews, thus increasing the combat effectiveness and discipline of every large warship.[80]

In 1852 Congress obliged civilian social reformers, part of the Navy officer corps, and the Marine Corps by abolishing flogging on American warships. Until the Navy established an alternative set of procedures and punishments for shipboard offenders in 1855, indiscipline increased on some naval vessels. Henderson was certain the abolition of flogging demanded an increase in the size of the Marine Corps, and with the Navy Department's permission he canvassed Navy officers for their opinion on the subject. The response was overwhelmingly in favor of increasing the Marine Corps. The consensus of the twenty-six Navy officers who replied was that the Marines were increasingly useful on warships as sentinels, brig guards, emergency gun crews, and landing party infantry. What problems they had had with ships guards came from the guards' inadequate numbers and training, which could be remedied only by increasing the enlisted strength of the Marine Corps. The Navy officers thought the Marines could assume more landsmen's duties aboard ship, although they were satisfied that the Marines did their share of the housekeeping and ship-running, particularly in emergencies. Most thought that the Navy could not blame the Marines for crew indiscipline, which was a Navy recruiting problem. One captain praised the Marines as "steady, gallant and *firm,* under the most pressing circumstances, and may be emphatically regarded as the *minute men.*" Commander David Glasgow Farragut wrote that Marines were essential not only for shipboard discipline but also

> . . . for the important duty of landing to act against the enemy, when they become the *nucleus*: and in fact, the chief reliance of the Commanding Officer for the formation of landing forces, when an efficient guard, commanded by a *good drilled officer,* would prove a most substantial comfort to the commander in chief.[81]

The Navy Department responded by authorizing the Marine Corps to recruit two hundred more men, who would replace landsmen in ships crews, a program approved by the Congress in 1849. Henderson countered with a series of plans to make such recruiting and manning possible: The enlistment bounty was increased from $7 to $11 to match the Army's; new barracks were authorized; the Navy Department provided both ships guns and light field pieces for the Washington Barracks to train Marine gun crews. In 1859 the Department authorized two hundred more Marines to replace landsmen. The Marine Corps, however, could not respond to the Department's plans and Henderson's expectations. Many of the new recruits were new immigrants from Eastern cities, who became confused aboard ship; other Marines resented being assigned landsmen's duties at sea. Henderson recognized that pre-embarkation training of from two to eight weeks was not sufficient with inferior recruits, but he could not stop a wave of unhappy episodes at sea. Marine ships guards, plagued by increased duties, "broke" on the

Columbia (1853), the *Cyane* (1855), the *Vandalia* (1856), and the *Constellation* (1858). Embarrassed by the refusals to serve, Henderson decided to compensate for inferior recruits with more men, better training, and more professional officers. He once more advocated assigning West Point graduates to the Marine Corps and proposed that new officer candidates be subjected to strict examinations of their educational and moral fitness for commissions. Henderson also proposed that the Corps's senior officers be retired for physical and professional unfitness, but his reforms were still too dramatic for Congress and the officer corps to accept.[82]

As the Navy officers who wrote to Henderson in 1852 pointed out, the Marine ships guards were most valuable as part of their naval landing parties, and in the 1850s the Marines found increased service ashore.[83] Although Navy vessels continued to suppress piracy and the slave trade, and to quell occasional mutinies on merchant vessels, the Navy's patrolling squadrons saw their landing parties go ashore most often to protect American lives and property from Latin American insurrectionary armies, American Indians, and xenophobic Chinese and Japanese. In one decade American landing parties went ashore twice in Buenos Aires, twice in Montevideo, and five times in the coastal cities of Nicaragua to guard the consulates and private property against mobs. There was no fighting, and the stay ashore was seldom more than a few days. In 1856 the landing party of the sloop *Levant* beat back an Indian attack on Seattle with shellfire and musketry. Navy vessels put landing parties ashore across the reaches of the Pacific. Twice (1855 and 1858) American sloops sent sailors and Marines ashore for punitive expeditions against the Fiji islanders with the usual results: a few natives shot and a village or two burned in retaliation for the murder or harrassment of American mariners. Marines also participated in all the ceremonies that accompanied Commodore Matthew C. Perry's historic voyage to Japan in 1853–1854.

The landing parties met their greatest challenge in the five treaty ports of southern China, the European commercial and religious toehold in the sprawling Central Kingdom of the Manchu dynasty. Racked by the upheaval of the Taiping Rebellion, China was not a safe place for Europeans in the 1850s. In 1854 the landing party of the *Plymouth* joined a party of Royal Navy sailors and Royal Marines in an attack on Imperial troops in Canton who were threatening foreigners and seizing European property. The same year two Marines died in a successful boat attack on pirate junks in Kowloon harbor.

The East India Squadron's most ambitious operation occurred in Canton and along the Pearl River, which led to the city. In 1856 the landing parties of the *Portsmouth,* reinforced soon by the parties from the *Levant* and the *San Jacinto,* occupied the foreign compound in Canton to protect it from anti-European mobs. Brevet Captain John D. Simms commanded the combined force of some sixty Marines and sixty sailors, one of the first instances of a Marine officer commanding a landing party. Although fighting and upheaval swirled about the city in October, the landing party did not have to fight for the European compound. Despite the local officials' promise to respect foreign interests, however, a garrison of one of the four forts (the "Barrier Forts") along the Pearl River fired on the American vessels just as the landing party was returning on November 15. One sailor died. After an ineffectual exchange of cannon fire, Commander Andrew H. Foote organized a joint land attack and naval bombardment for November 20. Foote himself led the force of 287 sailors and Marines; the fifty squadron Marines, commanded by Brevet Captain Simms, served as the advance party and successfully assaulted and destroyed one fort. They learned, however, that Chinese were numerous (perhaps two thousand) and well armed enough to stand and fight. Marine musketry and Navy cannon fire, however, smashed three Chinese counterattacks with heavy losses before the landing party withdrew.

The next two days the landing party braved Chinese gunfire to assault and hold the other three forts. All three assaults were made from open boats into the face of Chinese cannon fire, however inaccurate. The squadrons' own guns pounded the forts and kept the Chinese infantry at a respectful distance, and the landing party demolished the forts before withdrawing on December 6. At a cost of forty-two casualties (six Marines wounded) the squadron landing party had ruined the "Barrier Forts" in an impressive proto-amphibious operation. They also learned that fighting the Chinese, who had not rejected European weapons, was a far more serious matter than chasing Fiji islanders.[84]

Although Commandant Henderson made no great issue of the matter, his Marines also became involved in four incidents of domestic peacekeeping between 1851 and 1858. None of the incidents was of any historic moment, but they gave the Commandant additional occasions for praising his barracks detachments. In 1851 the Philadelphia detachment lent a squad to police officials who wanted to capture some murder suspects in Cristiana, Pennsylvania. In 1858 Marine guards helped put down a riot in the Washington jail and helped protect a quarantine camp on Staten Island from an angry mob. The most dramatic incident involved Henderson himself. In 1857 the "Know-Nothing" faction of Washington imported a Baltimore mob to intimidate District voters. When the police admitted they could not stop violence, the mayor of

Washington asked President James Buchanan for a company of Marines. Buchanan sent two companies (mostly recruits, as usual) and General Henderson. At City Hall the mobs and Marines confronted one another, the Marines with muskets, the mob with pistols and a small brass cannon. Henderson asked the mob to disperse and warned it not to fire on the Marines. Convinced that the mob would open fire, Henderson walked back to his men as scattered pistol shots began. A platoon of Marines ran across the street and captured the gun, but the pistol fire increased. When one Marine was shot in the face and others were struck by stones, the enlisted men opened fire without orders and swept the street, but the officers quickly halted the firing. Although some sniping followed, the two companies stood their ground as the mob dispersed. After a short tour of guard duty at the railroad station, the battalion returned to the Marine barracks.[85]

The rout of the "Pug Uglies" was Archibald Henderson's last gift to the Marine Corps that he had protected and nourished for thirty-eight years. On January 6, 1859, Henderson returned from his office for his afternoon nap. Falling asleep on his favorite sofa, he never awakened. Vain, ambitious, and inclined to play favorites, Archibald Henderson had preserved an anomalous military force that had outlived most of its original functions. Through his opportunistic commitments of Marines in Army campaigns in 1836 and 1847, Henderson had built a modest public reputation for the Marine Corps as infantry, a reputation enhanced by the performance of Marine landing parties in the Mexican War and the 1850s. He had successfully convinced the senior officers of the Navy that they could not do without ships guards or Navy yard sentries. And while he lived, he disciplined the Marine officer corps. Whether Archibald Henderson's legacy would survive his death remained to be seen.

4. The Marine Corps Survives Its Doldrums
1859–1889

The Marine Corps that Archibald Henderson left behind was little different from the force that he had commanded for the first time in 1820. The officer corps still tended to be divided between young office-seekers, middle-aged company grade officers who performed their duties with a minimum of enthusiasm, and the handful of field grade officers who occupied sinecures as barracks commanders or Headquarters officers. In 1860 the most junior captain had eighteen years' service, and the most senior captain thirty-nine. The officer turnover in 1859 and through the rest of the nineteenth century remained high but was not as serious a problem as in the Corps's earliest years. Of the 220 men commissioned between 1846 and 1890, 97 survived long enough to make captain. Nearly half of the 1846–1890 officers either retired (45), a possibility after 1861, or died in the service (43). Geographically, the Marine Corps drew officers from its traditional recruiting areas along the Atlantic Seaboard. In 1860 Marine officers came predominately from New York–New Jersey (10), Pennsylvania (8), Delaware–Maryland (6), the District of Columbia (8), and Virginia (7). Only four officers came from the deep South, five from New England, four from the Midwest, and five from beyond the Mississippi.[1]

The competence of Marine officers in 1860 is difficult to judge, but it could not have increased much during the Henderson years, for there was little incentive or opportunity to improve performance. Most duties at sea and ashore were routine and demanded little more than a knowledge of close-order drill and Marine Corps regulations. With the exception of increased allowances and a command-at-sea bonus, officers' pay had not changed since 1798. Commissions came to men whose primary qualifications were family ties to the Corps, kinship with Navy officers, and political connections in the federal government; unlike the Army and Navy, there were no Marine graduates of the service academies, although some Marine officers were former cadets or midshipmen dropped by West Point or Annapolis.

Henderson's death removed an important force for efficiency in the officer corps, and the barracks commanders soon exploited the leadership vacuum at Headquarters to increase their own autonomy. Henderson's successor, John Harris, was one of their own. Commissioned during the War of 1812, Harris had served ably in the Seminole War but for the most part had been an archetypal barracks officer in New York and Philadelphia. A bearded, heavy, lethargic man over sixty, Harris had difficulty dealing with his officers. With Henderson gone, some Marine Corps officers took a holiday from duty, and there was little internal pressure to increase Marine Corps discipline and efficiency.[2]

The Marine Corps's enlisted men, some 1,800 in 1859, had also changed little in forty years. Drawn from Eastern cities and towns, they had few skills, little education, and no political ties of benefit to the Marine Corps. The ranks included almost everything except middle-class youths and blacks: runaway farm boys, fifty-year-old veteran privates, Irish and German immigrants, unemployed city workers, drunkards, fugitives, debtors, apprenticed bandsmen, and career sergeants and corporals in their thirties and forties. The pay was not especially good ($16 for an orderly sergeant, $6 for a private), but barracks life was tolerable. In addition to tours of guard duty at Navy yards, the barracks Marines also began to receive serious marksmanship training in 1859, and Lieutenant Israel Greene, an artillery enthusiast, conducted gun drill with field pieces and ships guns at Headquarters. The Marine Corps, however, was not free of its traditional personnel problems; Harris recognized that the Corps desertion rate was a scandal and worried about the number of Marines who missed sailings.

On the eve of the Civil War the Marine Corps again changed its uniform. Although the 1859 changes made Marines look more like soldiers, the Corps retained distinctive uniform characteristics. Its field service kepi was like the Army's, but its dress cap was stiff leather with a red pompom and a heavy brass plate. Both caps carried the special Marine Corps insignia, a light infantry hunting horn with an "M" in the center. The dress coat was blue with skirts halfway to the knee; it had a high-standing collar of gold trimmed with red, and heavy gold epaulets and scales; the field service coat retained only the red trim. With both coats Marines wore a black leather stock beneath the collar, a vestige of earlier uniforms. The blue trousers bore a thin red stripe. Unlike the Army, Marine noncommissioned officers wore their gold stripes with points upward in the French style, and officers wore gold shoulder knots rather than shoulder straps on service coats. The Marine officers, however, abandoned the traditional sword with Mameluke hilt in favor of the standard Army officer sword. The most distinctive items remained the Marine Corps black leather field equipment and double crossed white belts for bullet pouch and bayonet scabbard.[3]

John Harris's Marines performed the same duties as Archibald Henderson's. In 1859 and 1860 ships guards helped capture two slavers off the mouth of the Congo River and went ashore to protect American lives and property in Portuguese West Africa and on the Isthmus of Panama. In Washington the barracks Marines went about their tranquil duties—a ceremonial detachment to welcome the first Japanese envoys in 1860 and band concerts at the Executive Mansion and the Capitol grounds.

Only in October 1859 did the Marine Corps see hints of the coming national war. On October 16–17 the abolitionist John Brown led twenty-two followers into the arsenal town of Harper's Ferry, Virginia. After Brown's raiders captured the arsenal and killed, wounded, or seized several townspeople, they were cornered in the armory's firehouse by enraged citizens and Maryland and Virginia militiamen. The nearest regular Army troops were at Fort Monroe, Virginia, so the War Department asked the Navy Department for Marines, and by midafternoon on October 17 First Lieutenant Israel Greene and eighty-six men were on a train for Harper's Ferry. Joined there by the War Department's personal representative, Brevet Colonel Robert E. Lee, the Marines relieved the militiamen and assessed the situation. Lee decided that if Brown's men did not surrender, someone would have to storm the firehouse. When the militia declined the opportunity, Greene organized twenty-seven of his men for the attack. Brown refused to surrender, and the Marines rushed the door, battered it down with sledges, and poured inside the firehouse. Greene dropped Brown with his sword, but the raiders shot down two Marine privates, killing one. The Marines bayoneted two men to death but discovered that Brown's raiders had already been almost wiped out by the militia's wild fusillade the previous day. Of Brown's force eight were dead before the Marine assault, and most of the rest were wounded. After a short patrol to look for other insurrectionists, the Marines returned to Washington, having spent $62 for rations and one coffin. The coffin was a fateful omen for both the Corps and the country.[4]

1

The Civil War brought the United States Navy and Marine Corps their greatest challenge since their formation in the 1790s.[5] Like the land forces of the Union, the Navy and Marine Corps faced problems of institutional adaptation that carried with them the seeds of organizational disaster: the defection of Southern officers, the loss of Southern bases, the chaos of rapid manpower expansion and amateurish civilian management, the confusion of assimilating new technology, and the disconcerting experience of fighting a type of war for which neither the Navy nor the Marine Corps was prepared. Although there were some precedents for the Navy's shallow-water operations in the Civil War in the Barbary wars and the Mexican War, the scope and complexity of the Navy's operations against the Confederacy made this war a unique experience.

The Navy's Civil War tasks were threefold: protecting commerce from confederate raiders; blockading the Confederacy; and supporting the Army. The Navy's main role was the economic strangulation of the Confederacy by blockading its ports along the Atlantic Ocean and the Gulf of Mexico. The blockade was far more complex than the blockades the Royal Navy had maintained in North American waters or those the United States Navy had applied against Mexico. The introduction of steam power on naval vessels meant that Confederate blockade-runners were less constricted than sailing ships in their choice of time and place for running into the protected maze of bays, inlets, rivers, and harbors of the Confederacy. Moreover, the Confederacy created a good system of coast defense, both to protect its inner waterways and to discourage seaborne invasions of its coastal cities. To supplement the system of fixed coastal fortifications, the Confederate Navy developed its own shallow-water fleet to disrupt the Union blockading fleets. The backbone of the Confederate Navy was the steam-powered ram, which also carried main batteries easily capable of destroying Union wooden-hulled vessels. The rams were supported by shallow-draft armored gunboats, converted steamers, fixed underwater barriers, and both fixed and floating mines.

The Navy's response to the Confederate defenses emphasized three types of combat vessels: (1) steam-powered seagoing frigates and sloops-of-war with main batteries strong enough to reduce forts and cripple the rams; (2) shallow-draft, fully armored, turret-gunned, steam-powered monitors to fight the forts and rams at closer ranges in shallow water; and (3) armorclad steam gunboats for riverine operations. These vessels, most of which were built after the war began, were complemented by the Navy's older sailing vessels of all classes and by converted merchantmen.

The Navy also supported the Union Army's campaigns to destroy the Confederacy's armies and reoccupy the South in order to break the will of the Southern population. Although the Navy ably assisted the Army of the Potomac in the Eastern theater, its most dramatic and important actions were along the Tennessee and Mississippi rivers, where the naval forces (eventually commanded by Rear Admiral David Dixon Porter) contributed to the capture of the principal Confederate positions along both rivers. The inland fleet was an improvised mix of ships under both War Department and Navy Department control. It was this force that eventually defeated the Confederates' river defense fleets and neutralized its fortified positions.

The salient feature of the Navy's war against the Confederacy was not the size or fighting capacity of the Confederate Navy but the expanse of ocean coast line and "river frontier" the Navy had to blockade. To control adequately more than 3,000 miles of seashore and river valleys, the Navy had to expand. In 1861 it had ninety vessels in varying conditions of readiness and serviceability. By the time the war ended the Navy Department had built 179 vessels and purchased or assumed control of nearly 500 more ships. In 1861 the Navy had forty-two vessels in commission; by December 1864 it had 671 ships, 559 of which were steam vessels. To man this expanded fleet, the Navy increased from eleven thousand in 1861 to more than fifty thousand officers and men by 1865.[6]

Given the character of the naval war against the Confederacy, the Navy Department might have developed its own amphibious assault force to capture and occupy Confederate coastal and river fortifications rather than depend on the Union Army. From hindsight, this mission might seem the "natural" function of the Marine Corps, and at least two Navy officers, Rear Admiral Samuel F. DuPont and Rear Admiral S. P. Lee, proposed that Marine regiments be formed for such duties. With a couple of exceptions, however, the Marine Corps did not provide battalions of adequate strength, training, and organization for amphibious assaults. The basic reason was simply a failure of imagination within the Navy Department and Headquarters. John Harris and his successor, Jacob Zeilin, simply did not recognize the amphibious assault mission or else rejected it for being too much like the Army's tasks. Secretary of the Navy Gideon Welles and Assistant Secretary Gustavus V. Fox did not push the Commandants to develop such forces, nor was there any interest in doing so in either the War Department or Congress.

The Marine Corps position was that its purpose remained what it had always been: to furnish ships guards for Navy vessels in order to enforce shipboard discipline, man guns, and join landing parties for very limited operations ashore.[7] To assume any other mission would be to risk amalgamation with the Army, which actually was considered by Congress in 1863 and 1864. Colonel Harris, censuring a Marine major for not working harmoniously with a Navy yard commandant, warned that no officer should create the impression that the Marine Corps was not part of the Navy's ships crews: "This cannot be, and it is this very idea which has in some way gained ground, and is now giving us so much trouble here, and induced the recommendation that we be transferred to the Army. . . . We are of the Navy; are governed by Naval Regulations on shore and afloat; have nothing in common with the Army . . ." [8]

Despite the fact that Harris and Zeilin never asked for more Marines than they thought necessary to provide the expanded Navy with ships guards, they were unable to meet the Navy's demands in numbers until the closing months of the war. When compared with the Army and Navy, the Marine Corps's crucial problem was the quality of its officer corps, a problem aggravated by the defection of its Southern officers. Like the other regular services, the Marine Corps lost one-third (twenty of sixty-three) of its officers. Among the defectors were Adjutant and Inspector Henry B. Tyler and some of the Corps's most promising field commanders. The defections did little for the Marine Corps's status with the Lincoln administration or with social Washington. The Navy Department and Congress provided the Marine Corps with thirty-eight new lieutenants in 1861, but until these officers learned their duties, the Corps was plagued with a leadership vacuum in its ships guards. The new officers were actually no worse, and probably better, given the surge of pro-Union patriotism, than those the Corps recruited in peacetime. The majority were patronage appointments, but the group included the kin of military officers and government employees, including the sons of Gideon Welles and David Dixon Porter as well as a Breese, a Goldsborough, a Collum, a Hitchcock, a Humphrey, a Meade, and a Pope. Although the Marine Corps tightened up its commissioning requirements during the war by administering examinations and screening applicants with a board of officers, the new junior officers did not immediately improve the Corps's performance or reputation.[9]

The Marine Corps senior officers were an even greater problem. Although Congress increased the number of field grade officers in 1861, these officers had learned too much and forgotten too little to be of much value in a new war. All were in their sixties, old for field service, but there were both Army and Navy officers of similar age who served with great valor and imagination. The problem with the senior Marine officers was that they saw their role as that of administrators; of this group only John G. Reynolds and Jacob Zeilin, both combat veterans of the Mexican War, served as battalion commanders in the field. The others did little beyond their routine duties and retained such habits as court-martialing one another on petty charges. When Harris died in 1864, Secretary of the Navy Welles, in despair, selected Zeilin, a junior major at fifty-nine, as Commandant and retired the rest, although they actually remained on active duty in their sinecures throughout the war. Zeilin was an improvement over Harris, but neither the new Commandant nor his senior officers had much influence in the Navy Department.[10]

The quality of officers was not the only Marine Corps deficiency during the Civil War; it also could not recruit enough men for its ships guards. Accepting Harris's definition of the Corps's needs, the President twice in 1861 increased Corps enlisted strength, and in July 1861 Congress authorized a Marine Corps of 93 officers and 3,074 men, virtually twice the Corps's prewar strength. Without money for bounties and handicapped by terms of enlistment longer than those of the Volunteer Army, the Marine Corps could not attract recruits. In June 1862 it had only 2,355 men in its ranks.[11]

Harris continued to ask for more men as the Union Navy expanded, and in 1863 the Corps paper strength had climbed to 3,600 men, but its actual strength was still short of 3,000. Even though it dropped its minimum age to eighteen and sought apprentices as young as fourteen, the Corps made little headway with its manpower problems until 1864. Essentially it shared the Navy's even more severe manpower shortages, also caused by the War Department's bounty system and flaws in the conscription acts of 1862 and 1863, which did not count Navy and Marine Corps enlistments toward draft quotas. When Congress remedied this situation in February 1864, recruiting for both the Marine Corps and Navy improved.[12] In addition to bounty money provided by Philadelphia, Brooklyn, and New York City, as well as by the federal government, the Marine Corps was probably assisted by the massive casualties in the Army of the Potomac in 1863 and 1864. Both organizations drew recruits from the same region, and by the war's end service in the Marine Corps was a good deal safer than joining the Union Army. When the war ended, the Marine Corps was at full strength, with 87 officers and 3,773 enlisted men.

The Marine Corps began the Civil War on the defensive both tactically and institutionally, and it never recovered. Even before the rebel batteries of South Carolina fired on Fort Sumter, Marine detachments did their best to protect Washington and several Navy yards from mob capture. In Washington, Marines stood ready to halt pro-Southern mob violence in January 1861, and detachments from the Washington Barracks reinforced the Army posts at Fort Washington on the Potomac and Fort McHenry in Baltimore. The Brooklyn Barracks detachment was alerted to mob violence. In Florida, however, the Marine detachment at the Pensacola Navy yard surrendered on orders. Three months later Marine ships guards helped reinforce nearby Fort Pickens, which was still in Army hands. The Marines' first significant job after the formal outbreak of war in April 1861 was to help destroy the Navy yard at Norfolk, Virginia. When two timid Navy captains decided the yard could not be defended, Marines from the yard, the ships guards of vessels tied up in Norfolk, and a company of reinforcements from the *Pawnee* assisted in destroying it. Eight vessels were destroyed along with stores, buildings, equipment, and ordnance, but the destruction was so botched that Congress later investigated the incident. The Confederates recovered enough equipment and ordnance to equip both their gunboats and their coastal fortifications.[13]

The Marine Corps's next effort to assist the Union cause was a disaster, an omen for most of its battalion-size operations for the rest of the war. When Major General Irvin McDowell's extemporized Union Army marched south from Washington to attack the Confederate army concentrated around Manassas, Virginia, Secretary of the Navy Welles volunteered a Marine battalion for service with the Army. Colonel Harris's role in this assignment is uncertain, but given the legacy of the Henderson years the Marines could hardly have lagged in the rear of the first "On-to-Richmond" campaign. Although the Marine battalion looked disciplined and smart, it was a pitiable group of raw recruits. Of the 12 officers and 336 enlisted men, only the commander, Major John G. Reynolds, Captain Jacob Zeilin, and four other officers had any prewar experience, and the battalion had only nine experienced noncommissioned officers. All the others were new recruits of three weeks' service, and some had just been issued weapons. Attached to the 1st Brigade (Colonel Andrew Porter) of the 2d Division, the Marines joined the Army columns hiking south in the late afternoon of July 16, 1861. Porter assigned the Marines to follow Captain Charles Griffin's Battery D, 5th Artillery, an all-mounted regular Army unit. For the next two days the Marines jogged and stumbled after the guns as the Union Army struggled toward the enemy.

On the morning of July 21, the 2d and 3d Divisions of McDowell's army enveloped the Confederate positions northwest of Manassas and attacked the three Confederate brigades deployed on either side of the Warrenton turnpike. Porter's brigade was not heavily involved in the early fighting, but the Marines had problems finding Griffin's battery, which Porter ordered Reynolds to support. Reynolds found the guns on a hill north of the turnpike, where Griffin's battery was shelling the Confederates to the south. The reunion was not altogether happy, for the Marines, hovering to Griffin's rear, caught part of the Confederate counter-battery fire, and their casualties climbed. By 11 A.M., however, the 2d Division had driven the Confederates back across the turnpike to a new position on Henry House hill. It is unlikely that the Marines had yet fired a shot.

Erroneously believing the Confederates were on the verge of collapse, McDowell ordered a full assault by four brigades on Henry House hill, with Griffin's guns and another regular Army battery in the van. The Marines dutifully tagged along after the artillery, which went into action again on the western edge of the hill. The Marines and two New York regiments tried to form a battle line with the two Union batteries but were hammered with musketry and artillery at less than four hundred yards' range. Three times the Marines started to panic, but their few veteran officers and sergeants pushed them back into the firing line. Disaster beckoned. When a Confederate light cavalry charge disorganized the 11th New York, the brigade collapsed. Shortly thereafter, a Confederate infantry attack silenced the two Union batteries, the turning point of the battle. The Marines were already fleeing to the rear, some three hours before the general disintegration of McDowell's army. The battalion, less forty-four killed, wounded, and missing, straggled back to Washington minus its packs and some of its weapons, despite Reynolds's valiant efforts to rally it. Reynolds had to reclaim seventy of his recruits from the provost guard outside Washington before he marched his survivors back to their barracks. Much to its commander's chagrin, the Marine battalion had suffered as severe a defeat as any of the Army's amateur regiments.[14]

The rout of the Marine battalion at Bull Run (Manassas) did not end the Marine Corps's battalion-size operations, for at the request of Flag Officer Samuel F. DuPont, commander of the South Atlantic Blockading Squadron, Reynold's battalion was trained and refitted for fleet operations along the Atlantic coast. DuPont's objective was to capture a sheltered deep-water base at Port Royal, South Carolina, for his blockading fleet. Although the War Department sent 13,000 Army troops with DuPont's expedition, DuPont wanted the additional Marines, which, unlike the Army troops, would be under his direct control. Reynold's battalion left Hampton Roads with DuPont's fleet in late October aboard the chartered side-wheeler *Governor*. Two days out of port the fleet was lashed by a severe storm, and the *Governor* began to sink in spite of the Marines' desperate efforts at the bilge pumps. For two days the *Governor* wallowed in the troughs until the sloop *Sabine* arrived to take off the crew and Marines. Although seven Marines drowned, the troops' discipline in the escape was superior. The *Governor* remained afloat for another day, and Reynolds's men went back to recover most of their weapons and half their equipment. The disaster, however, prevented the battalion from participating in the capture of the Port Royal forts on November 7.[15]

Rejoining DuPont's fleet after the capture of Port Royal Sound, Reynolds's battalion spent the next five months cruising along the coast as far south as northern Florida. DuPont had little use for it; the Confederates either abandoned their coastal fortifications or surrendered after a brief naval bombardment. The Marine battalion was now a well-drilled and disciplined force, but DuPont could find little for them to do but temporarily hold the coastal towns and forts until the Army arrived. The Marines were a supply burden to his fleet, and although DuPont preferred using Marine landing parties to either sailors or soldiers, the battalion became "impossible to fit in" in joint operations. At the end of March 1862 the battalion returned north and was disbanded.[16]

Marine Corps battalion operations for the rest of the war were marked by minimal success. The low point was the capture of a battalion, bound via Panama for the new naval station at Mare Island, California, by the Confederate raider *Alabama*. When the captain of the steamer *Ariel* prudently decided to surrender without resistance, the Marines had to endure the humiliation of surrender and parole.[17] In 1863 Major Jacob Zeilin formed another battalion to assist the South Atlantic Blockading Squadron's operations against Charleston, South Carolina. Marines from this battalion joined a mixed force of sailors and ships guards in an ill-conceived boat attack on Fort Sumter on September 8, 1863. Led by Captain Charles G. McCawley, who had his doubts about the operation, the Marines joined the force of 34 officers and 413 men that were supposed to storm the fortress at night. The attack was a debacle. Most of the boats strayed some distance from the fort, and those that landed found the rebels alert and well fortified behind an unscalable wall. In the subsequent melee, the battalion quartermaster was mortally wounded, three Marines were wounded, and forty-one officers and men fell into Confederate hands.[18]

Serving ashore, Marine battalions had better luck and performed effectively. In 1864 a Marine battalion from Philadelphia prepared the defenses of the rail terminal at Havre de Grace, Maryland, against Confederate raiders, and another battalion from the Brooklyn Navy Yard helped restore order in New York City after the draft riot of 1863. Although Marine battalions formed at shore stations did not see serious action, they did develop a reputation for military efficiency, discipline, and appearance.

If the experiences of the Marine battalions did little to advance the prestige of the Marine Corps, the ships guards demonstrated their valor and usefulness. The shipboard Marines made their greatest contribution as permanent crews on their vessels' great guns. Although Marines had manned portions of main batteries before the war, it became common practice during the Civil War for Navy captains, chronically short of sailors, to assign their ships guards to one or two guns rather than have them muster on the quarterdeck as riflemen. Colonel Harris fully approved of the spreading custom and censured one Marine captain who did not want to form gun crews: "It should have been your pride to have made the men handle *those* guns, better than those manned by the Sailors." [19] As Harris recognized, the Navy might accept the ships guards as full partners if Marines manned ships guns in battle. Of the seventeen Marines awarded the new Medal of Honor during the Civil War, thirteen were sergeants and corporals serving as gun captains and gun division commanders.[20] Ships captains consistently cited their Marines for valor and high efficiency. Inasmuch as between ninety and one hundred Navy vessels carried Marine guards during the war, the guards' performance was a particular tribute to the professional skill of the lieutenants and sergeants who commanded most of the detachments.

Marine gun crews participated in some of the Navy's finest hours in the Civil War. One of the *Kearsarge*'s heaviest guns was manned by Marines when that sloop-of-war sank the raider *Alabama* off the coast of France in 1864. Marine gun crews fought and died when Rear Admiral David Farragut ran the forts at the mouth of the Mississippi and captured New Orleans in 1862, and other Marine gunners blasted away at the ram *Tennessee* and Confederate gunboats when Farragut damned the torpedoes and plunged into Mobile Bay in 1864. Eight Marines won Medals of Honor for their conduct in this single battle. Even in disaster Marine gun crews fought with distinction. When the Confederate *Virginia* sortied out against the Union fleet in Hampton Roads on March 8, 1862, Marine gun crews on the *Cumberland* and the *Congress* fought its guns until they died or the vessels sunk. On the *Minnesota*, run aground in the shallows to escape the *Virginia*, the gun crews hammered away at both the *Virginia* and her consort gunboats until the Confederate force withdrew. All three Union vessels took serious casualties in sailors and Marines but inflicted damage on the *Virginia* that made the *Monitor*'s task easier the next day when the new Union monitor forced the *Virginia* temporarily from Hampton Roads. In many other engagements, Marine ships guards fought with distinction in gunboat attacks on Drewry's

Bluff on the approaches to Richmond (1862) and at Vicksburg (1862), Charleston (1863), Port Hudson (1863), and Fort Fisher (1864).[21]

In their traditional role as part of landing parties, the Marine guards also enhanced their reputation for élan and efficiency. These operations fell into several categories: boat raids to capture Confederate blockade-runners, privateers, and gunboats; the temporary occupation of forts and towns captured by the Navy's blockading squadrons; inland riverine raids on Confederate supply depots and military outposts; and (on two occasions) naval brigade support for Army operations close to the coast. In all but the last category, the Marine ships guards performed admirably and began to prove that a Marine ashore was probably more useful than a sailor.[22]

If the landing party operation, however, became a full-scale engagement with sizable Confederate forces, the Marines and sailors had their problems, for they did not have the training, organizational cohesiveness, or supply support for sustained land combat. Two incidents illustrate the landing force's limitations. In late 1864 a naval brigade from the South Atlantic Blockading Squadron (including 250 Marines commanded by a first lieutenant) joined a small Army brigade on an expedition to cut a railroad line to Savannah, then being approached by Major General William T. Sherman's army. Carried by gunboat up the Broad River, the naval brigade fought the Confederate defenders over a period of four weeks (November 30–December 26, 1864) without much success. Although the men's behavior was more than adequate, the brigade did not have sufficient artillery support or numbers to overwhelm the Confederate defenses. Actually the "battles" of Honey Hill, Tulifinny Cross-roads, and Derang's Neck were little more than desultory cannonades, long-range musketry, and feeble Union attacks. At one point in the fighting the Marine battalion did not receive orders to withdraw and had to infiltrate the Confederate outposts to return to the Union positions. The Marines lost twenty-two men in the campaign.[23]

The Navy's most ambitious landing party operation was also its most dramatic failure, and Marines shared the debacle. The objective was Fort Fisher, guarding the entrance to the Cape Fear river and the port of Wilmington. Disappointed that an earlier bombardment and a weak Army attempt against the fort had not taken it, Rear Admiral David Dixon Porter not only promised the Army's XXIV Corps that the navy would give it gunfire support but also added a naval brigade of 1,600 sailors and 400 Marines to the assault. While the Army attacked the fort's northwest corner, the naval brigade would "board" the northeast corner in a simultaneous attack. The fleet would shell the rest of the fort. The naval brigade, led by Commander K. R. Breese, had problems. Few of the sailors were armed with anything more than cutlasses and pistols, and both the Marine and the seamen's companies had to be organized when the thirty-five landing parties came ashore on January 13, 1865. The next day the naval brigade marched toward the fort with the Marines leading. But before all the Marines could deploy to support the attack with rifle fire, Breese ordered both the Marines and the sailors toward the fort. In the confusion, some Marines joined the charge while others moved from rifle pit to rifle pit to fire on the defenders. At the base of the fort the naval brigade went to ground under the Confederates' musketry. After several minutes of punishing fire and unit dissolution, the exposed sailors broke for the rear, taking all but small parties of Marines and sailors with them.

In the meantime the Union Army regiments had begun the assault that eventually took the fort after a day's heavy fighting. Although fewer than five hundred of the two thousand Confederate defenders broke the naval brigade's attack, Admiral Porter argued that his "diversion" had opened Fort Fisher's doors for the Army, a questionable conclusion. For the "honor" of attacking Fort Fisher, the naval brigade lost 386 officers and men, 61 of them Marines. For both the Marines and sailors, individual gallantry and collective ardor could not overcome inept tactical leadership and romantic planning by both Porter and Breese. A posturing commander even in victory, Porter blamed the Marines for not clearing the rebel breastworks of infantry for his "boarders." For once the Marines were more sinned against than sinning in the war of words that followed every unsuccessful Civil War attack.[24]

If from Bull Run to Fort Fisher the United States Marine Corps had its misfortunes, its sister service, the Confederate States Marine Corps, suffered not only the institutional weaknesses of its parent organization but the ravages of national defeat. Formed in 1861 and modeled on the U.S. Marines, the Confederate Marines were doomed to serve through the war with diminished usefulness and growing anonymity. Its missions and fortunes rose and fell with the activity of the small Confederate States Navy. Small Marine detachments (six to twenty men) served on five Confederate raiders and twenty-five rams and gunboats; other Marines guarded Confederate naval stations. There is some suggestion that the Confederate Marines attempted to break with some of the U.S. Marines' traditions, for they organized themselves into permanent companies, scrapped the fife for the light infantry bugle, and changed their uniforms to resemble those of the Royal Marines. The Confederate Marines' assignment as coast defense artillery crews may also indicate some effort to copy the Royal Marine Artillery, since British Marines manned batteries both afloat and ashore. Confederate Marines served heavy guns aboard the rams *Virginia* and *Tennessee* and at Fort Fisher and the Drewry's Bluff defenses near Richmond. Marine infantry conducted raids on the Union blockaders and eventually, as part of a forlorn Confederate naval brigade, surrendered after the battle of Saylor's Creek in April 1865.

Whatever its potential effectiveness, the Confederate States Marine Corps had fewer political roots in the Confederacy than the U.S. Marines had in the Northern population. Its field grade officers and company commanders were largely former U.S. Marine officers with little political influence. As a result the Confederate Marines did not have bounty money for recruiting and only late in the war were allowed to have Army conscripts. Even though its authorized organization called for one thousand men, the CSMC seldom had more than six hundred men on duty at any time during the war, and the majority of its recruits were either Irish or German immigrants or native-born conscripts. It had close to its full complement of forty-six officers, but the officer corps squabbled over rank, shore duty, and administrative assignments. The enlisted ranks were beset with desertions and near-mutinies, the step-children of defeat. Like the U.S. Marines, the CSMC had an excessive administrative headquarters for its size. The CSMC died with the Confederate Navy in 1865.[25]

For all the heroism of the Marine naval gunners and landing party infantry during the Civil War, much of the U.S. Marine Corps's service was related only to the unique demands of the war itself, and its functions were not entirely unambiguous. For one thing, ships captains assigned Marines as gun crews as a matter of expediency, not as Navy Department policy. Many vessels survived without Marine gunners. Moreover, the vast majority of Navy vessels that participated in the war did not carry ships guards at all, and others had only a sergeants guard of ten to twenty men. Few if any Navy crews dissolved in mutiny and indiscipline in the absence of Marines. When Marine guards were not in combat, they still performed minimal duties aboard ship and had little opportunity to train. Nor had the Marine Corps as an organization assumed any new missions. When guerrillas ashore and afloat harassed Union river traffic in the Mississippi river valley, the War Department had its own "Marine Brigade" of Volunteer infantry, cavalry, and artillery created. Nevertheless, the Marine ships guards had become such a fixture on American men-of-war that influential Navy officers urged their continued presence aboard ship in terms that would have gladdened Archibald Henderson. Despite its uneven wartime record, the Marine Corps emerged in 1865 in a relatively strong political position. Buoyed by its shared experience with the Navy and sustained by postwar sentiment, the Marine Corps claimed enough friends in the Navy Department and Congress to continue to survive.[26]

2

In most important respects the U.S. Navy sailed on into the last third of the nineteenth century as if the Civil War had not happened. The Navy Department demobilized its wartime fleet as quickly as it had formed it; by 1868 the Navy had but eighty-one vessels in commission. The vessels that stayed at sea were the better-built steam frigates and sloops-of-war, which were most suitable for long deployments on foreign stations. The Navy yards were jammed with millions of dollars' worth of unused naval guns, monitors, ordnance supplies, and equipment left from the war.

After the war the Navy Department reorganized its commerce-protecting foreign squadrons: the European Squadron for the North Atlantic, Mediterranean, and the west coast of Africa; the South Atlantic Squadron for the eastern coast of Latin America; the North Altantic and Gulf squadrons for the Caribbean and the Atlantic; and the Asiatic and Pacific squadrons for eastern Asia to the western coasts of North and South America. The need for such squadrons for commerce protection was debatable. The bulk of America's growing foreign trade was with Europe, and the Navy could have done little to threaten any major European navy. Yet American entrepreneurs were increasingly active in the Pacific islands, Latin America, and East Asia, where they found more hostility than new markets. In essence the main activity of the Navy became the protection of a minuscule trade with areas of the world plagued by chronic instability and violence in an era in which a government's ability to protect the lives and property of citizens in obscure corners of the world was a measure of that government's authority.[27]

Congress, however, could not avoid scrutinizing the Navy Department, for the Civil War had saddled the federal government with a national debt of nearly $3 billion. Having defined its most important functions as protecting the stability of the dollar, halting inflation, and balancing the federal budget, Congress pruned the budget dramatically. From its wartime high in 1865 of $122 million, the postwar Navy Department spent no more than $43 million (1866) and as little as $13.5 million (1880) in the fifteen years after the war. In only ten of these years did the Navy Department budget go over $20 million, and only twice did it exceed $30 million.

With promotions stagnant and too many officers for its vessels, the

Navy officer corps fought over retirement plans, the relative pay and status of its line officers in comparison with the staff and bureau specialists, and commissioning policies. The older line officers, led by David Dixon Porter, won their battle to keep the junior officers, steam engineers, and staff specialists subservient. Thus, in the absence of strong leadership from the Secretary of the Navy, the professional voice of the Navy Department harked back to the halcyon days of iron men, wooden ships, and long cruises to mysterious isles. The postwar Navy was still more the "Old Navy" of Porter and Farragut than the "New Navy" of steam engineers like Benjamin Isherwood. And the Marine Corps was a part of that "Old Navy."

Commandant Colonel Jacob Zeilin's Marine Corps differed little from the service of 1861. The Commandant and his small staff in Washington processed the papers, made the reports, and kept the books on the Corps's expenses; the Commandant, the Adjutant and Inspector, the Paymaster, and the Quartermaster made their annual inspection trips and managed their little fiefdoms of officers, sergeants, civilian clerks, and the barracks on Eighth and I streets. The Commandant's greatest concern, as always, was the size of the Marine Corps. Even with the dramatic decline in the Navy's vessels, Zeilin and his successor, Charles McCawley, argued consistently for twenty-five years that the Marine Corps could not adequately man its ships guards and Navy yard sentry posts and conduct training ashore.

Unlike the Army and the Navy, the Marine Corps did not have a rapid demobilization. Its officers were all regulars, and its enlisted men, who had signed for four years and not the duration of the war, were not allowed to leave the service after the war unless they found a substitute. Zeilin also took pride in the fact that President Andrew Johnson's postwar amnesty for draft-dodgers and deserters did not apply to the Marine Corps. The Commandant did not want Union Army veterans or deserters in the Corps. For the Marine Corps the postwar period was to be one of traditional duties at sea and shore, an opportunity for better shore training for those duties, and a respite from the organizational turmoil of war.[28]

For a brief period in 1867 and 1868, Congress threatened to abolish the Corps or at least cut its strength. Those favoring abolition were a distinct minority, and even the economizers did not particularly ravage the service's ranks. In fact, Zeilin was promoted to brigadier general in 1867 as a symbolic reward for the Corps's wartime services; Secretary Welles regretted he could not move Marine Corps officers up the promotion list for wartime service (as he could for Navy officers) but argued that such a policy required special legislation, because the Marine Corps was a separate service.[29] At the height of the crisis, however small, Vice Admiral Porter testified that "if the Marines were abolished, half the efficiency of the Navy would be destroyed" and subsequently added that "we have had a hard time in the Navy to get a Marine Corps and are very anxious to hold onto what we have." [30]

The arguments then dissolved into a twenty-year debate over whether the Marine Corps should be a force of 3,000 or 1,800 men; not unexpectedly, the lower and less expensive figure was more palatable in Congress. In 1874 Congress reduced the Corps's enlisted strength from the wartime authorization of 2,500 privates to 1,500 privates, and in 1876 and 1885 it tried to get the Corps's officer strength down to seventy-five. From 1878 until 1889 the Congress annually provided funds for between 85 and 75 officers and 2,000 enlisted men. Occasionally individual or small groups of Congressmen raised questions about the Corps's cost and utility, but the Navy Department, the naval affairs committees, and Headquarters beat back the critics easily with ploys that included lectures on the Corps's martial past, calculations that showed that Marines were each $.25 cheaper a month than soldiers, and an offer to fight the Sioux in 1876. Although the Commandant lost the rank of brigadier general in 1874 and recruiting and commissioning were periodically curtailed, the government did not treat the Marine Corps badly during the Navy's doldrum epoch. The Commandants wanted a Corps one-third larger than the one they commanded, but with the Navy so small such an increase to perform traditional missions was difficult to justify.[31]

The Marine Corps was essentially a stable organization after the Civil War.[32] Like the Army, even its instability was stable, for it could count on having between a quarter and a third of its enlisted men desert every year. Neither Zeilin nor McCawley was pleased with their authorized strengths, but their proposals suggested a modest increase of from eight to ten second lieutenants and five hundred men in order to man the ships guards and barracks to their satisfaction. Not until 1885 and 1889 did Headquarters suggest different reasons for expanding the Corps. After a regimental-size intervention along the cross-isthmian route in Panama in 1885, McCawley argued that the manpower increase was imperative if more expeditionary duty was to follow. In 1889, with the Navy's new building program well under way, McCawley proposed more men to meet the demand for increased numbers of ships guards for the "New Navy." Even with arguments well developed by Archibald Henderson and the sympathetic if mild support of the Navy Department, Zeilin and McCawley could not evoke enough sense of urgency in Congress to produce the increases. On the other hand, they successfully fought off the weak attempts to reduce the Corps even further.[33]

If the post–Civil War Commandants were concerned about their authorized strength, they cared still more about the quality of enlisted Marine recruits, but they had little success in improving it. Zeilin thought that the Corps was getting its share of "young and robust men, of good appearance, and whose bearing gives promise of making good soldiers" in the social confusion after the war, but by 1872 he had concluded that the Marine Corps was still getting too many uneducated urban drifters from places like Philadelphia and Brooklyn.[34] He admonished one barracks commander who met his quota with poor recruits: "A few good men are preferable to a number of recruits of inferior material." [35] Secretary of the Navy George M. Robeson and Zeilin centralized recruiting under Lieutenant Colonel Charles G. McCawley, the next Commandant, earmarked more money for newspaper advertising and recruiter travel, and provided more Navy surgeons to administer physical examinations.[36] Their reforms were not altogether successful for the desertion rates were high. One Navy chaplain complained that the Marine Corps had recruited too many men characterized by their "desire to roam, being out of employment because of depression and because they find themselves without friends or home"—as well as plain criminals.[37]

The recruiters' problems were simple to analyze but difficult to overcome. Recruit pay of $13 increased for privates to only $15 after four years' service; scant travel funds prohibited recruiters from traveling far from their barracks for men; and the four-year enlistment (increased like the Army's to five years in 1870) discouraged many prospects. Yet the Marine Corps's small and stable size allowed some selectivity, and in 1882 it took only 10 percent of the men who applied for enlistment. Still, no Commandant was satisfied with his recruits, and both Zeilin and McCawley admitted that too many new men went to sea without adequate training and discipline, because they needed so much of both to be fit Marines.[38]

At sea the duties of the ships guards had changed little in fifty years, although there was less talk of stopping mutinies and more about serving the great guns. The Navy Department still expected the Marines to add military tone to ships companies, since a ships crew might include more than twenty different nationalities and every type of sailor from apprentice boys and landsmen to aged "salts." Generally, the Navy Department gave Marine officers greater authority over their detachments; the detachment commander was responsible for all the guard's administrative needs and training. No naval officer except the ships captain could interfere with Marine sentries or discipline Marines, although Navy officers could give Marines orders when not on guard. Marines were not required to coal the ship (an unpleasant task) or perform mechanical chores. Even the ships captain could not reduce a Marine's rank or coerce a Marine into becoming the master-at-arms or transferring to the Navy. The Navy Department thought Marines should be assigned to gun crews as units but allowed captains the right to make such assignments. After the Civil War the ships guards manned the great guns as standard practice, which increased the Marines' work load.[39]

For Marine officers sea duty was a mix of military duties, much leisure, socializing in port, and paper work. "How fearfully tiresome this is!" one officer wrote.[40] For the enlisted men, sea duty depended on the strength of the detachment and the attitude and competence of their officers and the Navy officers and sailors. Conditions varied widely from ship to ship. Because most ships guards were undermanned in relation to the number of sentry posts, duty on a smaller vessel could be an unrelenting schedule of guard duty; painting; caring for small arms, uniforms, and equipment; maintaining great guns; and rudimentary musketry and gunnery practice. On larger steam frigates and steam sloops, the duty was less pressing. Burdened with poor uniforms and equipment, as well as questionable recruits, the ships guards were not especially impressive in the 1870s but seemed to have improved in smartness in the 1880s.[41]

The Navy's ships carried the Marine guards to obscure corners of the world as seagoing constables. The ships guards helped stop a mutiny on a mail vessel in the Caribbean (1866); fought Mexican pirates (1870); put out fires in Shanghai (1866) and Callao, Peru (1873); accompanied exploring expeditions to Alaska (1867), the Arctic (1881, 1883), and Panama (1870); and went ashore twenty-four times between 1866 and 1889 to protect American lives and property or to punish "unenlightened" people who either had mistreated Americans or didn't want them ashore at all. Naval landing parties including Marines appeared around consulates and American business houses in Japan (five times), Formosa (once), Nicaragua (once), Mexico (once), China (twice), Korea (twice), Panama (twice), Hawaii (four times), Samoa (once), Uruguay (twice), Egypt (once), and Haiti (once). The landings in Hawaii helped save the Hawaiian monarchy from American intriguers, and the landing in Alexandria, Egypt, in 1882 in the wake of a British intervention allowed the ships guards, in collaboration with the Royal Marines, to stop fires and looting.[42]

The most publicized landing party operations occurred in Korea in 1871 and in Panama in 1885, and both revealed the strengths and limitations of landing party operations and the usefulness of the Marines. Designed to coerce the Hermit Kingdom into treaty relations and trade with the United States and to punish the Koreans for mistreating an American merchant crew, Commodore John Rodgers's expedition of five vessels steamed up the Han River in the spring of 1871. Rodgers and his diplomatic counterpart, Consul Frederick Low, were impatient with the Koreans' failure to negotiate. When two boats exploring the channel (against Korean warnings) were fired upon by nearby forts, Rodgers decided to destroy the offending forts. On June 10, 1871, under covering fire from two gunboats, the landing party of 542 sailors, 109 Marines, and seven cannon were dumped ashore in a broad mud flat but managed to struggle ashore unchallenged. The landing site was chosen simply because it was out of range of the main Korean position, the Kwang Fort, which returned the gunboats' fire with enthusiasm if not accuracy. Organized as a battalion under a Navy commander, the landing party set out the next day to take the Kwang Fort. With the Marine company leading, the landing party struggled in the oppressive heat two miles across a series of gullies, beating off some tentative Korean attacks with its field pieces. About 200 yards from the fort the landing party rested and set up its guns and skirmish line. Easily establishing fire superiority over the Koreans' small brass cannon and ancient muskets, the Americans stormed the fort and seized it in hard but brief hand-to-hand combat against the chanting, sword-wielding, rock-throwing Koreans. Captain McLane Tilton and two other Marines fought their way to the Koreans' flag and cut it down. The inside of the fort was strewn with mangled Korean bodies when the fighting stopped, but most had been killed by the shelling. Having lost three dead and ten wounded (two Marines), the landing party withdrew after blowing up the fort.

After the Fort Fisher episode the landing was a welcome success, but the Koreans thought they had again beaten back the Europeans, because the Americans had returned to their vessels. Tilton doubted that the expedition had accomplished much and thought the Navy's claims that it had killed 250 Koreans were exaggerated. He put the number closer to fifty. He himself learned that being shot at "was a caution to all those innocents engaged in war." [43] Tactically the operation had been modest enough and did little to test the staying power of the landing party. Diplomatically, it only increased antiforeign feeling in Korea and postponed treaty relations eleven more years. [44]

When secessionists in Panama rebelled in 1885, the Navy intervened to protect American lives and property and to reopen a railroad across the isthmus. The mission was too large an assignment for the landing parties of the American vessels hovering off Colon and Panama City. By stripping the barracks in the United States, the Navy Department gathered a Marine brigade of nearly seven hundred officers and men and added them to the naval landing parties. The two Marine battalions paraded from Brooklyn to their waiting transports through cheering crowds but landed in the face of angry mobs between April 3 and April 15 in Panama. Ashore the Marines joined the seamen's battalions and artillery batteries commanded by Commander Bowman McCalla. The Marines then patrolled the towns along the railroad, guarded the railway, and discouraged mob violence and looting. Brevet Lieutenant Colonel Charles Heywood, a Civil War combat veteran, was pleased by their discipline and appearance, but nonetheless closed the saloons. He also knew that his regiment could not have functioned without the tents and equipment given it by the War Department. Heywood and the Navy officers ashore were impressed with the Marine officers' enthusiasm for their duties; one lieutenant left his dying mother to go to Panama, which made news in the New York and Philadelphia newspapers. By the end of April Colonel Heywood was commanding the entire naval brigade, an unusual arrangement, inasmuch as the brigade included substantial Navy units. In any event, Colombia pacified Panama without the Americans' involvement in any of the fighting on the isthmus. The Marines were gone by the end of May.[45]

After a certain amount of self-congratulation within the Navy and Marine Corps about the expedition there were some sober afterthoughts, most raised by Commander McCalla. The commander, something of an expert on landing force operations, admitted that the Marines had performed their security duties well but doubted that they would be very successful in battle, since they used Civil War tactics. He also criticized the Marines for their ignorance of Gatling guns and Navy howitzers. Commandant McCawley, incensed by the criticism, pointed out that his men were ships guards first and lacked the equipment, personnel, and money for field training. He doubted that the better-equipped sailors were really more proficient infantrymen. The argument faded without a serious test of either McCalla's or McCawley's claims, but the Marines' shortcomings for extended operations ashore remained.[46]

For the Marines stationed in barracks in the United States, expeditionary duty was a relief from the monotony of guard duty and drill, but the Navy Department was now convinced that its yards were best and most cheaply patrolled by Marine sentries. Commandant McCawley urged that the barracks be allowed to have more men, so that his officers could give recruits a year's training before going to sea in addition to providing sentries. McCawley was not successful in getting more men, but he did strengthen the authority of his barracks commanders, for by 1876 the Navy Department had decided that yard commandants had no authority to interfere with the internal administration of the barracks Marines or countermand the Commandant's orders.[47] For Marine officers, barracks duty was a welcome relief from the boredom of sea duty. As one captain wrote a friend: "I notice Meade [Captain R. W. Meade] has been ashore *Nine* years. Not bad, is it?" [48] But duty ashore was little relief from routine: standing tours as officer-of-the-day, drill, parades, boards, courts-martial, inspections, and paperwork, all made even more onerous by an occasional martinet commander.[49] No one thought they had enough troops to man all the posts with *"vigilance, zeal and fidelity."* [50] The guards' duties included sentry duty, guarding prisoners, checking for fires, manning gates, watching Navy recruits, stopping smuggled liquor, enforcing curfews, and driving dogs, cattle, and vagabonds from the posts.[51]

Occasionally the barracks Marines received an opportunity to enhance their reputation for military discipline and efficiency. Because they were usually the only federal units (except for Army coast artillery companies) living in Northern cities, they were drawn into the turbulent urban life of the post–Civil War period. Barracks Marines fought fires in Portland, Maine (1866) and Boston (1873); stopped Cuban filibusters outside New York City (1869); and helped quell an election riot in Philadelphia (1870). Between 1867 and 1871 the Marines from the Brooklyn Barracks sortied into Brooklyn's "Irishtown" on nine separate occasions to help federal revenue officers break up illegal distilleries. The Marines' most conspicuous service came during the Railroad Strike of 1877. Marine battalions formed in Washington and Norfolk joined Army and militia units in Baltimore, Philadelphia, and Reading to clear the streets of mobs, stop looting and arson, and guard trains. The Marines rose to the occasion and performed their duties with restraint and composure in the face of mob violence. As always, their own supply system broke down, but local officials and ordinary citizens contributed to their hasty encampments and messes. When the Marines withdrew they were cheered by crowds of relieved civilians and praised by the Army. It was one of the Corps's most successful public appearances.[52]

3

Although the post–Civil War Marine Corps performed traditional duties, the Corps was not immune to pressures for change, and some of the reforms and reform ideas of the 1870s and 1880s influenced the Corps's future development. Part of the impulse for reform came from within the Corps, part from outside. But all the pressures for change eventually focused on the office of Commandant. Whereas Jacob Zeilin showed some awareness of the Corps's need for change, his successor, Charles G. McCawley, was both an active reformer in some areas and a dogged conservative in others. No one could doubt McCawley's ability and experience. The son of a former Marine officer, McCawley had been at Chapultepec in 1847 as a new second lieutenant and had served with distinction in the Civil War. When Zeilin at seventy voluntarily retired in 1876, McCawley was the next senior officer, a happy circumstance. A large, handsome man with a mustache, he was not only "Old Corps" but willing to carry on Henderson's plan to make the Corps an elite military organization.[53]

The Marine Corps's greatest barrier to elite military status was its officer corps—as McCawley and others acknowledged. Many of the officers were part of an elite, but their status had nothing to do with their military abilities. The Civil War had cemented the officers corps's ties with Eastern society, the Congressional Republicans, and the high command of the armed forces. Of the eighty-two active officers in 1880, sixty-five came from traditional sources, the cities from New England to Norfolk.[54]

A Marine Corps commission required passing an academic examination, but Marine officers were not noted for ambition or intellect. This public impression was especially acute in Washington, where the officers were part of a naval service–political social whirl that emphasized the Corps's exclusive, but not meritocratic, character. In 1886 the Corps's two most important officers (the Commandant and the Adjutant and Inspector) were sons of Marine officers. Three other officers were admirals' kin, and another was the grandson of a senator. Among their wives were the daughters of three senators and a general.[55] Their working hours were short and social engagements long and elegant. One critical observer noted that "the Marine officer wears corsets and parts his hair in the middle. He also has a pedigree and a sword. He carves out his career with his pedigree." [56] Marine officers seemed to have all the liabilities of military officers without any of the academic and intellectual attainments that at least some Army and Navy officers had by virtue of their academy educations and technical and administrative experience.[57]

In a service in which it took nearly twenty years to make captain, it is unsurprising that some of the more ambitious lieutenants and captains were concerned about the Corps's stature and their own careers. In the 1870s some officers found allies in Congress and advocated compulsory promotion examinations and mandatory retirement at sixty-two or after forty-five years service. Congress was particularly interested in keeping academy dropouts out of the Corps and democratizing the social origins of the officer corps, which, at least in theory, was what the academies did for the Army and Navy through the geographic patronage appointment process. When the Washington *Chronicle* ran a story critical of the Marine Corps in 1875, the junior officers praised its perceptiveness. First

Lieutenant Henry Clay Cochrane followed it up with a private pamphlet that called the Corps "a parasite on the body of government" and "a barnacle on the hull of the Navy." Cochrane's charges and his proposal that the Marine Corps purge its incompetents and become naval artillery was too much for most reformers, but his views were not completely ignored.[58]

The Marine Corps reformers already knew what they wanted, for in 1873 the Navy Department had sent Captain James Forney to Europe to study foreign marines. Forney found an admirable model abroad—the Royal Marines of Great Britain. Even though he recognized that the Marine Corps was not likely to be as large as the Royal Marines, Forney urged adoption of British standards for officer selection and training.[59] Forney's ideas were formally endorsed by a meeting of Marine officers organized by Cochrane in 1876. Cochrane's conferees, who included future Commandant Charles Heywood, urged permanent organization of the Corps into companies, more tactical training, promotion examinations, discharges for incompetence and disability, compulsory retirement and a pension system, and speedier promotions. Although their ideas were favorably reported by the Senate Naval Affairs Committee, the reformers were disappointed when Congress eventually rejected their plan in 1881, probably because of the cost implications and conservative opposition from within the Corps itself.[60]

Sensitive to the restiveness in the officer corps, Commandant Mc-Cawley curbed assignments based on personal convenience, made the precommissioning examinations more rigorous, and avoided appointing academy dropouts. He also tried to apply the Navy's regulations on compulsory physical examinations for promotion, but the Attorney General ruled that this was illegal, given the Corps's status as a separate service. McCawley ran into the same problems in holding retiring boards, but he was at least able to get longevity pay for Marine officers when the War Department made such pay provisions in 1882. The Army's compulsory retirement law (age sixty-four), passed the same year, was not applied to the Marine Corps, although McCawley himself set a personal example by retiring on his sixty-fourth birthday in 1891.[61]

McCawley's greatest success was in changing the source of new Marine lieutenants, for between 1882 and 1898 nearly all the new lieutenants were graduates of the Naval Academy. The change was fortuitous, despite the Commandant's longtime advocacy of such a measure. The problem was the number of officers in the Navy and the lack of billets for Annapolis graduates. Although Congress rejected promotion by selection and lengthened the Annapolis graduates' precommissioning service from four to six years, it ordered that officer vacancies in the

Marine Corps be filled with academy graduates. Not all the vacancies could be filled with volunteers from Annapolis, but at least the general quality of Marine lieutenants improved, and Congressional criticism of the officer corps subsided. Among the new officers was John A. Lejeune (USNA, 1888), who became the Corps's most important Commandant. Lejeune, who had served with distinction as a naval cadet aboard the *Vandalia* when it sank in a typhoon in Samoa in 1889, had to use Congressional influence to get his Marine Corps commission, an indication that the Navy Department did not want the best Annapolis graduates in the Marine Corps. Yet after 1882 the Marine Corps recruited a more intellectually alert group of officers than it had yet received from other sources.[62]

McCawley and some of his officers also took a heightened interest in the Marines' military training. The Commandant, a friend of the Army's Colonel Emory Upton, worked with Upton on his reform manual *Infantry Tactics* (1867) and adopted Upton's manual for the Marines when he became Commandant.[63] He also emphasized better marksmanship training, which the limited evidence suggests the Marines needed. In 1876 Captain James Forney's Philadelphia Barracks Marines hit the target only 152 times with 366 shots at distances of 100 and 200 yards.[64] Other Marine officers urged more battalion drill, more assignments to the Navy's ordnance and "torpedo" (mine warfare) schools, a revision of Marine Corps regulations for sea duty, and even the construction of Marine-manned rams for harbor defense. There were continued complaints that using Army rifles and Navy field equipment saddled Marines with the worst collection of fighting gear in the American service.[65]

The greatest internal barrier to increased military efficiency, however, was the character of barracks life for enlisted Marines. McCawley, in addition to asking for more men, did what he could to improve conditions for the troops. One of his first measures was to centralize the promotion of all noncommissioned officers at Headquarters; although local boards of officers screened the candidates, McCawley made the final selections.[66] He also persuaded Congress to apply the Army's new retirement pension system for enlisted men to the Marine Corps in 1885, thus assuring retirees of enough pay to keep them out of the Sailor's Home.[67]

McCawley's greatest battle, however, was over on-post drinking. In 1879, two years before President Rutherford B. Hayes forced the War Department to end liquor sales on Army posts, McCawley ordered the sale of alcohol stopped at Marine barracks. He wanted not only to curb the political power of post sutlers but to reduce Marine intake, which he thought caused both desertion and misbehavior on duty. The reform was a mixed blessing. The barracks commanders thought the experiment only increased off-post drinking, abetted by McCawley's decision to have more frequent paydays. There was one mass payday riot in the barracks at Brooklyn.[68] When one commander suggested cutting down the troops' work load and restoring beer and ale sales, McCawley lashed back: "The Marine Corps has never yet been considered as composed of holiday soldiers, and, while I have the honor to command it, I trust, may never merit that appellation." [69] Much to his dismay, however, the Navy Department restored the sale of beer and light wines in 1883, adopting Army regulations.[70]

The liquor issue was only one of several irritants to the troops, however, and McCawley continuously asked for more money to improve the barracks and provide Marines ashore with the Navy ration. Marine Corps food, even compared with the Spartan diet of the Army and Navy, was notoriously poor. The Commandant recognized the problem but argued that he could do nothing about it despite petitions from his men. He did admit that the Marine Corps desertion rate was as much a product of life within the Corps as the poor quality of recruits.[71] The changes in both were slow in coming.

Another matter of internal concern for the Marine Corps was the distinctiveness and quality of its uniforms, which were related to Marine reformers' desire to create a greater sense of corporateness and elitism in the Corps. Jacob Zeilin made the first contribution by designing a more distinctive and dramatic cap insignia: an eagle perched on a globe (showing the Western Hemisphere) superimposed over an anchor. After some modification and officer resistance, the insignia was adopted in 1868 and became common on all uniforms after 1875. The eagle, globe, and anchor became synonymous with the Marine Corps.[72] Zeilin also stole the Royal Marines' motto, "Par Mare, Par Terrum," but McCawley changed the motto to the more original "Semper Fidelis" in the 1880s. Of greater short-term importance were the design and quality of Marine uniforms, which were criticized by Marine officers and civilians. After some dreary parade performances in the early 1870s, Marine officers (among them the gadfly Henry Clay Cochrane) persuaded Zeilin to establish a board to revise the uniform regulations. The new uniforms, approved finally in 1875, were long on splendor but short on practicality. The most dramatic changes were the readoption of the Mameluke sword, the adoption of plumed dress caps, and the flowering of gold and mohair braid on the sleeves, chests, and shoulders of officers' tunics. Other than a shorter coat, the enlisted men's uniform changed little, and the pressing problem of finding some substitute for its expensive and shoddy wool fabric escaped solution.[73] McCawley continued to tinker with the uniform, and some of his reforms did deal with practical matters. Between

1878 and 1881 the Commandant adopted Army cartridge belts and boxes, bayonet scabbards, and accessories. The Marines also adopted the Army's Prussian-style dress helmets in both black and white. More important, McCawley in 1880 ordered the Marine Corps to start making its own uniforms in Philadelphia in order to eliminate the fraud, waste, and poor-quality goods customary in civilian contracting.[74]

Headquarters made sure the public saw the new uniforms, the improved drill, and the U.S. Marine Band, for McCawley and the reformers were beginning to realize that if they could cultivate public support, it might be transformed into more appropriations. Marine battalions drawn from the barracks and ships guards became consistent performers in presidential inaugural parades as well as at patriotic holiday celebrations in Washington and other Eastern cities.[75] The *pièce de resistance* was the performance of a Marine detachment commanded by Henry Clay Cochrane at the Paris Exposition of 1889. For nearly six months Cochrane's detachment guarded the American exposition. But, more important, the Marines paraded—to the general admiration of the Americans in Paris and the French government. Feted and praised in the name of Franco-American solidarity, Cochrane's detachment got almost as much publicity as the U.S. Marine Band.[76]

Although the quality of its music varied with the ability of its director and musicians, the U. S. Marine Band remained an important asset to Headquarters. Its appearances at Washington ceremonial functions, as well as private affairs, were an established tradition. After one pinnacle of success under Francis Marie Scala, the band deteriorated under two inept directors in the 1870s and was threatened with extinction by Congress in 1876. Part of the problem was recruiting accomplished musicians, for skilled bandsmen in Washington received twice the pay of Marine musicians. Nor did the Marine bandsmen like their military duties, however scanty, and they abhorred marching. Under pressure to improve the band's military appearance and playing, McCawley in 1880 hired young John Philip Sousa, son of a former bandsman and a former bandsman himself. An aggressive publicist as well as a brilliant composer and organizer, Sousa obtained permission to hire the band out for private engagements, thus making the bandsmen's wages competitive. He also broadened the band's repertoire by composing his own marches (dedicating one, in a stroke of genius, to the newspaper *Washington Post*), adding light operatic and concert pieces from Europe, and adapting traditional American folk songs for the band. He also drilled his men hard and sharpened their military performance, which pleased Marine Corps officers. He increased the band's engagements, although McCawley would not let it tour outside Washington. The next Commandant did, much to the glorification of the Marine Corps. However unrepresentative of the Marine Corps, the band played on, to the benefit of the Corps's standing with the public.[77]

The parades, uniforms, and band helped build the Marine Corps's reputation, but the officer reformers and their supporters in Congress also believed that the Marine Corps needed a history that would describe the absolute necessity of marines as a military unit and refresh people's memories about the glorious combat record and public services performed by the United States Marine Corps. Captain Richard S. Collum, a Naval Academy dropout commissioned during the Civil War, collected historical documents and gave them (as well as a draft history) to a Boston journalist, M. Almy Aldrich, in 1874. Aldrich's history, published in 1875, appeared too late to provide information for the Congressional debate over the Corps's status in that year but became a standard reference for the Corps's supporters. Aldrich's errors were numerous and obvious, so Collum continued to work on his own history, which finally appeared (still with errors) in 1890. In fifteen years, the Marine Corps acquired two histories where for nearly a hundred years it had had none.[78]

Thirty years after the death of Archibald Henderson and the frustrations of the Civil War, the Marine Corps was not only still in existence but even improving slowly as a military organization. Its institutional permanence was great enough to counteract its diminished usefulness in the tasks it had been established to perform: ship security and musketry in sea battles. Instead, Marines were more likely to justify their existence as landing party infantry and naval gunners, their primary roles after the Civil War. Moreover, the Marine Corps could survive without the autocratic rule of an Archibald Henderson. Its ties with the Navy, cemented by Civil War sentiment and kinship, appeared firm. As soon as the Navy built more ships, presumably there would be more Marines. As the Navy began to emerge from its doldrums of neglect in the 1880s, the Marine Corps was prepared to see that Congress and the American people would not forget that the U.S. Navy could not manage without Marines.

5. The Marine Corps and the New Navy
1889–1909

Only the most visionary reformer could have argued that the United States had begun a maritime renaissance in 1881, but by the end of the decade the United States Navy had launched a revolution in doctrine, weaponry, and organization. Just what impact these changes would have upon the Marine Corps could not be predicted, for the reformers themselves would not be able for several years to see what the shape of the "new" Navy would be. By 1889, however, the changes could be felt throughout the Navy Department, and they set off two decades of crisis for the Marine Corps.

A combination of circumstances pushed the Navy Department into the naval arms race brewing in Europe. Although the State Department advocated a stronger Navy for commerce expansion, the main thrust for reform came from the Congressional naval affairs committees and the junior officers of the Navy itself. Both groups had sincere if not selfless motives for advocating a new Navy. Congress was properly concerned about the cost and wastefulness of repairing cruisers and monitors that were rapidly disintegrating; in 1882 Congress prohibited repairing vessels that could be replaced at only three or four times the repair costs, thus ensuring the imminent retirement of most of the Navy's active warships.

Reading the storm signals, the Navy Department's First Naval Advisory Board recommended a $29-million building program in 1881. Although the board urged that the United States build a new fleet of steel vessels capable of higher speeds and carrying heavier guns, its proposals assumed that the traditional mission of commerce protection and coast defense had not changed. Its new fleet was built around thirty-eight cruisers, more than half built of wood and unarmored and all carrying full sail, and a mixed force of rams and torpedo boats. After another advisory board reviewed this program in 1882, Congress in the following year authorized the construction of three small steel cruisers (the *Atlanta,* the *Boston,* and the *Chicago*), the dispatch boat *Dolphin,* and five coast defense monitors. Although the building program was slowed by contract disputes, by the primitive condition of the American steel and munitions industries, and by design confusion, the new Navy was under way. From 1885 until 1896 three successive administrations authorized building programs totaling more than 200,000 tons and emphasizing vessels of ever greater tonnage, armament, speed, and range. The United States was committed to having a battleship navy.[1]

In 1889 Secretary of the Navy Benjamin F. Tracy explicitly stated in his annual report that the United States Navy was now on a new course in both naval strategy and warship design. Coached by the theoretician of the new Navy, Captain Alfred Thayer Mahan, Tracy called for a substantial expansion of the fleet and the adoption of a new strategy of naval defense. He argued that the planned fleet of eleven armored vessels and thirty-one unarmored vessels would not make the United States a first-rate naval power. Instead, the nation needed twenty first-class battleships organized as a concentrated fighting fleet that would be the first line of defense against invasion and the protector of maritime commerce. The following year another policy board of Navy officers proposed an even larger battleship fleet with sufficient range (15,000 miles) to extend American naval power well across the Atlantic and Pacific. Both Tracy and Congress recoiled from the cost and foreign policy implications of such a fleet but did agree to build three battleships (the *Indiana,* the *Massachusetts,* and the *Oregon*) that in everything but range were comparable to the best European battleships.[2]

By 1895 the new fleet was well enough developed to suggest that the Navy had serious organizational problems beyond the arguments about ship design and armament that dominated the dialogue about the new Navy. The strategic justification for the battle fleet was the least of the Navy's worries, for the promises of security, expanding trade, and "national greatness" trumpeted in the lectures and writings of Alfred Thayer Mahan were already generally accepted in the Navy officer corps by 1890.[3] Rather the chief issue, at least as line officers saw it, was adapting the officer corps and enlisted ranks to a Navy of technologically complex vessels operating not as single cruisers but as tactical squadrons for warfare with other battleships. The new vessels were a world of steam boilers, complex engines, electrical systems, water distillers, ammunition hoists, and mechanical turrets. They carried not muzzle-loaders but main batteries of guns as large as 12 inches and rapid-fire secondary batteries to ward off attacking torpedo boats. In an era in which the number of ships in commission was slowly growing and the size of ships companies was increasing, the Navy was still hampered by disputes within the officer corps and a serious shortage of intelligent, mechanically inclined enlisted men. In some ways, it was easier to win appropriations for the ships of the new Navy than it was to reshape the organization of the crews that would man the new ships.[4]

Like many of the nation's established institutions in the 1890s, the Navy Department was awash in reform. At the Naval War College, in the pages of the U.S. Naval Institute *Proceedings,* in the halls of Congress and the Navy Department, and in the wardrooms of cruisers on foreign stations, the Navy was alive with schemes for rapid, fundamental changes in virtually every phase of its institutional life. Fed by the frustrations and ambitions of line officers demoralized by stagnated promotions and limited opportunities for meaningful service afloat, the Navy reform movement pushed like an angry sea against the wooden practices of the old Navy of frigates and fighting tops. Among those anachronisms marked for change by the Navy's reformers was the United States Marine Corps.

1

Whether there would be a new Marine Corps as well as a new Navy largely depended upon the forcefulness and political skill of the Colonel Commandant. As Colonel McCawley's health began to fail, many of his responsibilities fell to a new lieutenant colonel, Charles Heywood, who was only fifty in 1889. Despite his relative youthfulness in his grade, Heywood had already been a Marine officer for thirty-one years and had had a distinguished career at sea and ashore. Commissioned in 1858, Heywood served with ships guards before and during the Civil War, ending the war as a captain and brevet lieutenant colonel. The "boy colonel" had survived the sinking of the *Cumberland* and the Battle of Mobile Bay to serve later as senior Marine officer in several squadrons and as a barracks commander. He had seen riot duty in 1877 and had served in Panama in 1885. His acknowledged energy and intelligence made him McCawley's logical successor in 1891 when McCawley retired.[5]

McCawley and Heywood believed that the Marine Corps suffered most from deficient numbers and quality of enlisted manpower. Both considered excessive guard duty ashore to be the main cause of Marine desertions, which averaged about one-quarter of the Corp's total strength every year. Whereas the officer corps was stable at its authorized strength of seventy-five, the enlisted appropriated strength of the Corps (two thousand) was inadequate, a condition aggravated by turnover rates of between 40 and 50 percent a year. An increase of one hundred privates in 1890 helped some, but Heywood continued McCawley's pleas for five hundred more men, even when it meant taking money from John Philip Sousa's ambitious band appropriation request. The Commandant argued that he could not man the existing barracks and ships guards, let alone provide men for the thirteen new battleships and cruisers, without more money for recruits. If Congress would only fund the Corps to its statutory strength of 3,167 officers and men, the Commandant promised he could man his ships guards and fifteen shore posts and save money on chasing deserters and recruits and shuttling Marines from one short-handed post to another.[6]

Undeterred by Congressional apathy, Heywood kept up his requests and collected evidence supporting his plea for more men. He polled the yard commandants and found that they wanted 300 more men than he could provide; he calculated that the new ships entering service would require 450 additional men as ships guards; and he speculated that the Depression of 1894 would improve the quantity and quality of recruits, a prediction proved correct. In 1896 Congress finally appropriated money for 500 more privates, and by the end of the year Heywood reported that 410 of the new men were already in uniform. With lighter barracks guard duty now a reality, he promised that the ships guards could be better trained before going to sea.[7]

While Headquarters grappled with its numbers problem, it simultaneously continued the reforms of the 1880s that sought to improve the Corps's attractiveness. The focus was primarily upon the quality of life for barracks Marines. Touring the barracks at Portsmouth in 1895, a reporter for the Manchester, New Hampshire, *Union* remarked that the average citizen knew little more about a Marine except that he had a pretty uniform and was "a hard character." The reporter did meet some toughs and many new immigrants in the ranks (at least a quarter of the enlisted men were aliens), but he found the men respectable, their barracks neat and clean, and their discipline and drill flawless.[8]

If the barracks Marines were to be the Marine Corps to the public, Heywood wanted them convinced that the Corps was fighting to improve their lot. In 1890 he had the Corps shift from straw-filled ticks to real mattresses and increased the ration. Arguing that an 1890 act to prevent desertion in the Army applied also to the Marine Corps,

Heywood was disappointed when the Attorney General ruled otherwise. He was further distressed when Secretary of the Navy Tracy then ordered that the increased Navy ration be given to Marines ashore; as Heywood suspected, the Congress would not authorize for the Marines the additional $31,000 to $56,000 the Navy ration would cost each year. When new legislation in 1892 extended all the provisions of the Army Reform Act to the Marine Corps, Heywood reported that he thought the new bunks and rations had cut desertion 20 percent.[9] There is little question where Heywood's priorities rested, for in 1891 alone he requested $50,000 to improve barracks life and only $500 for field supplies.

Drawing selectively from legislation that affected both the Army and the Navy, Heywood attempted to make the Marine Corps the most attractive of America's military forces. He adopted, for example, a savings plan initiated for sailors but rejected the argument that another Army reform of 1892, which prevented the enlistment or reenlistment of privates over thirty and thirty-five, applied to the Marine Corps. Army legislation that required promotion examinations for officers *did* apply. Heywood adopted the Army legislation providing for good conduct medals for enlisted men and the awarding of Medals of Honor for post–Civil War heroism. He also kept boards of officers busy with the Marine Corps uniform regulations, eventually adopting better-quality material for dress and undress uniforms, a comfortable dark blue billed cap, better shoes, and red trouser stripes for corporals.[10]

The reforms were not an end in themselves, for Heywood was consciously establishing a better institutional base for improved onshore training for shipboard duty. Although he recognized that barracks Marines still performed essential service as sentries and emergency infantry in civil disorders, he thought Marines would be most useful at sea, as they had always been. "It is as Artillerymen aboard our new floating batteries that their importance must be felt and acknowledged in the future." [11] Shortly after becoming Commandant, Heywood organized a School of Application at Headquarters for new lieutenants and selected enlisted men. Although the school taught infantry drill, tactics, and general field service subjects, it stressed training in naval gunnery, mine warfare, electricity, and high explosives. The ten-month course eventually included instruction at the Navy's Washington gun factory and the Torpedo School at Newport, Rhode Island. Barracks commanders complained that the school diminished the number of officers available for duty, but Heywood believed it would allow the Marine Corps to keep pace with the new Navy. He also knew that its success strengthened his argument that the Navy Department should order ships captains to assign Marines to their vessels' secondary batteries rather than rely on custom and convenience for such assignments. By increasing the technical, formal educational requirements for his officers, he could argue that he needed not only an increased number of lieutenants but a grade structure and retirement system that would bring captains in their fifties home from the fleet and allow the younger officers—especially the Annapolis graduates—to command the ships guards on the new battleships and cruisers.[12]

To supplement the training at the School of Application, Heywood persuaded Secretary of the Navy Hillary A. Herbert to order the Bureau of Ordnance to transfer eighteen rapid-fire guns to the Marine barracks for training purposes. When the Bureau of Ordnance responded slowly, Heywood complained to the Secretary and got his guns.[13] Without hesitation the Commandant adopted the revised *Instructions for Infantry and Artillery, U.S.N.* (1892) and made it the foundation of Marine Corps training. The Commandant also ordered his barracks commanders to deemphasize drill and increase rifle marksmanship. All officers would become expert riflemen so they could teach the enlisted men. Using Army regulations, Heywood declared that April through November would be the shooting season and that Marines would have to qualify by Army standards at ranges from 200 to 1,000 yards, a more rigorous test than the Navy's.[14] When the Navy adopted the bolt-action 6 mm. Lee magazine rifle in 1897, Heywood refused to accept it until he had money for three thousand Lees and adequate ammunition to continue his marksmanship program. Instead, the Marines held on to their single-shot Springfields until they could get ample rifles, ammunition, and better ranges for the entire Corps.[15]

For all the reforms, the primary mission of the Marine Corps remained service afloat as security forces and landing party light infantry. Only in the latter role did Marines see any action in the 1890s. Between 1889 and the War with Spain ships captains, responding to pleas of American consuls and businessmen, sent their ships guards ashore in Hawaii (1889 and 1893), Argentina (1890), Chile (1891), a guano island off Haiti (1891), Nicaragua (1894, 1896, and 1898), Colombia (1895), and Trinidad (1895). In all these cases the circumstances were substantially the same. There would be an outbreak of violence, ranging from labor unrest and threats against foreign property to civil war. Marine guards would arrive ashore and establish sentries around American holdings and legations, and in a few days to four weeks the danger would pass. In only one of these incidents did the Marines have to fight, and in only one (the *Baltimore* affair in Valparaiso, Chile) did the violence draw American naval forces near a shooting war. Since the landing parties (both Marines and sailors) seldom numbered so much as fifty, they would have been hard pressed in actual fighting.

In Asia the ships guards landed to perform a variety of duties. In 1890 the guard of the *Omaha* fought a fire in Japan but left after one day. From 1894 to 1896 the ships guards of the Asiatic Squadron found themselves doing guard duty in Tientsin, China, and Seoul, Korea, during the upheaval of the Sino-Japanese War. These landings were more serious affairs than the usual gunboat diplomacy, for they required that the landing parties march miles inland amid a potentially hostile population and protect American lives and property for several months.[16]

In one instance Marines served as seagoing policemen protecting the Bering Sea seals from international poachers. A joint American–British patrol, established in 1891 to halt the slaughter of the seals, included a small steamer carrying forty-three Marines commanded by the ubiquitous Henry Clay Cochrane. Cochrane's force accompanied four Navy vessels and two revenue cutters into Arctic waters, where it spent six months rounding up poachers and confiscating their vessels. Surviving slim rations, mutinous civilian crews, unhappy seal hunters, and ugly weather, Cochrane's detachment performed with efficiency, tight discipline, and restraint, for which it won the praise of the Secretary of the Navy.[17]

Ashore the barracks Marines assisted both civilian officials and the Army in crisis situations and enhanced the Corps's reputation by making public appearances. In 1892 Navy yard and ships guards from New York patrolled a quarantine camp at Sandy Hook, New Jersey, established to treat cholera victims on incoming ships. Marines from the Mare Island barracks joined an Army regiment guarding the yards and trains of the Southern Pacific railroad from Sacramento to San Francisco during the railroad strike of 1894. In addition, Marine detachments participated in Columbian Exposition parades and fairs in New York and Chicago, marched in the dedication of Grant's Tomb, and appeared in the inaugural parade in Washington.[18]

2

The Marine Corps's institutional health was not, however, as sound as most of its officers assumed, for the waves of reform pounded upon Headquarters Marine Corps throughout the 1890s. If the Corps's very existence was not in question, its primary function in the 1890s certainly was: Should the battleships of the new Navy carry Marine guards? The issue was far more complicated than a mere question of the strict utility of the ships guards. Navy officers were already embroiled among themselves over how to attract and keep more responsible sailor-mechanics as well as how to organize the ships companies of the new battleships. For all practical purposes, all these issues came to a head in 1889, when Secretary Tracy appointed a Board of Organization, Tactics, and Drill to examine the question of shipboard organization and landing party practices. Warned that the board would probably deliberate about the ships guard, Colonel McCawley asked Tracy to direct the board to "consider the Marine Corps in connection with the new Navy and that its duties on board ship be well defined as well as endorse his request for 400 more men." [19] Board president Commodore James A. Greer agreed to add a Marine officer to the board to present the Commandant's views. Captain Daniel A. Mannix, an experienced officer who headed Heywood's School of Application, joined the board and argued that Navy Regulations should specifically assign Marines to secondary batteries, not only for training but on a permanent basis. The Marine Corps's official position was predictable: No vessel could get along without its ships guard for security duty, as marksmen, and as the core of the landing party. The only thing that remained was to institutionalize the guards' roles as gunners on the secondary batteries. [20]

The Greer Board, however, came to conclusions that augured poorly for the ships guards. The majority of the board wanted to integrate the entire ships crew as an all-purpose force organized both to handle all the ships guns and to make up the entire landing party. In essence the board saw the modern battleship as an all-purpose weapons system manned entirely by a new breed of American sailor—native-born, mature, self-reliant, versatile, and loyal to country and service. The board may even have been convinced by the radical arguments of one of its members, Lieutenant William F. Fullam, USN, that the ships guard prevented the improvement of the ships crew: Marines infantilized the sailors and prevented the development of responsible petty officers. In any event, the board not only rejected the mandatory stationing of Marines at the secondary batteries but recommended their total removal from the warships of the Navy. Although it accepted the view of Major James Forney that the Marine Corps could benefit from permanent tactical organization and training ashore, it was not sure what the Marine Corps should do and almost by afterthought suggested that the Corps be reserved for large expeditions like the Panama landing of 1885. [21] Chagrined by the board's recommendations, McCawley could not believe that the Navy would reduce the "combative force" of its warships by one-fifth and leave "an essentially military Corps in the position of non-combatants." [22] But that is exactly what many line officers, with Fullam as their most articulate spokesman, had in mind.

Although Tracy did not accept the recommendation to abolish the ships guards, the issue did not die with the Greer Board's report. In 1890 Fullam took his argument to the Navy officer corps in the *Proceedings*, which was followed by extensive comments from other officers. The debate hardly reassured Marine officers. Fullam's argument was that modern naval vessels needed a better-educated, better-motivated crew and that the presence of the ships guard prevented both the recruitment and the development of first-rate petty officers and seamen. Fullam was convinced that the Marines gave a ship a penal colony atmosphere, did not do their share in running the ship, and contributed nothing to the landing party that could not be provided by sailors properly trained as infantry. Fullam had graduated first in his class at Annapolis (1877) and had later taught drill and tactics there, so he was credible on the subject of landing party matters. In sum, Fullam was a staunch believer in the efficacy of "military" training (drill, tactics, marksmanship) for instilling "exactness, care, and trustworthiness" in sailors; the presence of the Marines discouraged Navy officers and men from taking their own military training seriously. In addition, depending upon the guard to enforce ships regulations degraded the authority of line officers and petty officers.[23]

Uneasy about their own status and alarmed by McCawley's proposal for the mandatory assignment of Marines to secondary batteries (might not the main batteries be next?), other line officers rallied to Fullam's side. Of the nineteen Navy officers who commented upon his paper, eleven favored removing the Marines, four thought the benefits of removal were exaggerated or that the Marines were still useful, and four were noncommittal on the issue. Commodore Greer gave his blessing: "I can only say that I fully agree with the views and suggestions so admirably expressed by the writer." The other supporters argued that ships crews would only become more disciplined when the Marines departed, although few felt as strongly about the issue as Fullam. Several suggested that gun crews could be drilled to military standards with or without the ships guard. The four Navy officers and three Marines who challenged Fullam supported the ships guard because the Marines *did* provide special skills as sentries and infantry that the crew was unlikely to provide. No one made a case that the Marine Corps would be more useful to the fleet as an expeditionary force, although Fullam had raised this possibility.[24]

With his Greer Board service, *Proceedings* essay, and subsequent rewriting of the Navy's drill regulations, Fullam became the leader of a growing group of line officers who advocated abolition of the ships guards. Certainly Marine officers saw him as the evil genius behind all their subsequent troubles. Without doubt Fullam was hostile to the ships guards, a prejudice reinforced by his service on the cruiser *Chicago* in 1891–1892. During a call at La Guaya, Venezuela, part of the *Chicago*'s Marine guard looted and consumed some liquor while on guard at the American consulate, for which their captain was court-martialed and convicted for inattention to duty. When the captain's conviction was remitted, Fullam was incensed. Yet he and his friends were not persuasive enough to win over such influentials as Rear Admiral Stephen B. Luce or to alter the description of the ships guards' duties in the 1893 revision of the Navy Regulations. On the other hand, their opposition stopped Heywood's plan to have Marines assigned permanently to either the main or the secondary batteries.[25]

The anti–ships guards reformers had no official backing until 1892, when Commodore Frank M. Ramsay, chief of the Bureau of Navigation, ordered all-Marine gun crews abolished. Henceforth, gun crews would be mixtures of sailors and Marines under junior line officers. The captain of the *Newark* interpreted Ramsay's order to mean he might remove the Marines entirely from the secondary batteries, a move Heywood protested.[26] The Commandant began to suspect a pattern of harassment when Ramsay in the same year denied that the coast-defense monitor *Monterey* needed a Marine guard despite Navy Department policy. Heywood wanted Marines on both main and secondary batteries on the *Monterey*: "There is no duty on board this vessel that a Marine cannot perform . . . as well as a sailor." [27] The Commandant reluctantly concluded that the Bureau of Navigation and the junior line officers were embarked on a concerted campaign to remove the ships guards. He hoped that senior line officers would come to the defense of the Corps.[28]

The Bureau of Navigation's sympathetic acts for the Fullamites had thus far been blocked by the Secretary of the Navy, so the reformers decided to apply pressure to Congress and the Secretary by mounting a petition campaign against the Marines among the sailors of the fleet. Heywood learned of the campaign in July 1894 and appealed to Secretary of the Navy Hilary A. Herbert to stop the "conspiracy." The petitions, which included arguments suspiciously similar to Fullam's essay of 1890, reached Congress in August; two Senators responded by introducing a bill that would have merged the Army's coast artillery batteries and the Marine Corps into a European-style Corps of Marine Artillery. The naval affairs committees and Herbert, however, again rose to the Marine Corps's defense. The reform bill was tabled, and Herbert ordered his ships captains to stop the petition campaign. However, he placated the Navy line by also ordering ships guard correspondence to go from the captain to the Bureau of Navigation before reaching the Commandant, and he ordered Heywood to delete a portion of his annual report for 1894 that again called for the mandatory assignment of Marines to the secondary batteries. Neither side was yet strong enough to force a decision, but neither was yet convinced it would not eventually win.[29]

The next salvo against the ships guards came from Captain Robley D. Evans, USN, who was assigned in 1895 to command the new battleship *Indiana*. A convert to the school of shipboard reform and an experienced seagoing officer, "Fighting Bob" Evans asked to be exempted from carrying ships guards on the grounds that his ship had insufficient berthing space for Marines and that, in any event, the ships guards were an anachronism. Secretary Herbert, prompted by Heywood, rejected Evan's request. He conceded, however, that the Marines would be considered "in all respects" full members of the ships company, liable to the full range of shipboard duties. This meant that Marines would henceforth scrub decks, coal the ship, and perform the same dirty work as the sailors. Heywood was satisfied with Herbert's response, but argued that the Marine complement should be increased from sixty to one hundred so that the Marines could man not only the secondary batteries but the main ones as well. The Commandant argued that the Marines were better gunners, served longer enlistments, received less pay, and were better disciplined than sailors. He reminded Herbert that twenty-three of the Navy's highest-ranking officers had testified to the need of the ships guards during the petition controversy the previous year. Heywood and "the progressive men of the Navy" could foresee a day when sailors would be like Marines in discipline and Marines would do all the ship's fighting, whether with big guns at 4,000 yards or with rifles ashore.[30]

Again the end of the *Indiana* episode did not mean an end to the ships guard controversy. Reacting perhaps to Heywood's known plans and an essay by Major H. B. Lowry, a member of Heywood's staff, outlining the Marine Corps's intention to man more naval guns, Fullam in 1896 renewed his attack on the ships guards. Fullam's views had not changed since 1890 but had been reinforced by his own recent sea duty. He also probably hoped to capitalize on the petition and *Indiana* controversies. He observed that Marines had made no meaningful contribution to shipboard discipline in a hundred years and did nothing in landing parties that could not be done by sailors. The same thing could be said about manning the ships guns. The Marines should be grouped ashore in six battalions and provided with supplies and transports to prepare them for expeditionary duty aboard, a plan even some Marine officers advocated.[31]

The discussion that followed Fullam's paper again went against the ships guards; sixteen of the twenty Navy officers who responded essentially agreed with Fullam's views. With the exception of Admiral Luce, all concurred that the Marines were unnecessary in keeping order and were much too eager to seize the secondary and main batteries. There was division on the wisdom of emphasizing landing party training for the ships crews: The officers thought the battleship's complement should be kept aboard ship to man the vessel rather than protect Americans ashore. The Marine Corps might very well perform that function but should do it in expeditionary battalions, not as a collection of ships guards. Most of the Navy officers thought that the Marine officers and men of the guard did not do enough work, a charge with which two Marine lieutenants agreed. The Marines, however, argued that current Navy Regulations and the ships captains prevented the Marines from doing the full range of duties aboard ship. The Marine lieutenants did not respond to the proposal about the expeditionary battalion, and they did not deny that some Navy ships had managed without ships guards.[32]

As Heywood correctly surmised, Fullam's latest paper stirred great sympathy among Navy officers and won new converts, among them such influential officers as French E. Chadwick, Harry S. Knapp, Casper F. Goodrich, and Bradley A. Fiske. Heywood asked Herbert to censure Fullam for insubordination since his paper implicitly criticized the Secretary's decision in the *Indiana* case. Of critical concern was the fact that the Fullamites were now talking about transferring the Marine Corps to the Army, which was anathema to Heywood and his officers.[33] The Navy Department's official position, expressed in Article 999 of the Navy Regulations of 1896, remained unchanged. Large combat vessels would carry Marine guards, but whether or not they served guns remained a captain's prerogative. The captain's only responsibility was to train the Marines, not permanently assign them. If a gun crew was made up entirely of Marines, they should be commanded by a Marine officer, but Marines could be used in mixed crews under line officers if the captains so desired. The ships guards' other duties remained essentially the same.[34]

The ships guard controversy did not die with the publication of the revised Navy Regulations of 1896 or with the change in administrations in 1897. Early in his term Secretary of the Navy John D. Long responded to an inquiry from Captain J. J. Read, USN, as to whether Read had to assign Marines to guns on his ship, the cruiser *Olympia*, under the provisions of Article 999. Long replied that the captain's only responsibility was to train the Marines, but the final decision on how to use the Marines remained the captain's.[35] As Long pointed out to Read, there was still considerable ambiguity over the ships guards' status, an ambiguity that interested Assistant Secretary of the Navy Theodore Roosevelt. Author on naval warfare and a friend of many reformist line officers, Roosevelt was responsible both for direct contact with Heywood's headquarters and for a personnel board formed in 1897 to merge the line with the Navy engineers. During its deliberations Roosevelt's board also considered the amalgamation of the line with the Marine Corps and the removal of the ships guards.

Alarmed by the renaissance of the controversy, Heywood queried his officers by circular letter and found to his dismay that there was divided opinion as to whether the ships guards were worth staking the Corps's future on. His respondents, however, did agree on some crucial points: that the lack of Navy support for the Corps was alarming and that separation from the Navy Department would mean the Corps's eventual abolition. Although the officers preferred to retain the ships guards and widen their role as gunners and landing party artillery, they could also see merit in duty as colonial light infantry and coast defense artillery. None of them could accept the thought that the Marine Corps did not deserve to survive because of its past glories, nor did they think the Navy would be better off without the ships guards.[36]

Such was essentially the view Heywood sent to Roosevelt. The Commandant opposed any substantial change in the existence of the ships guards, citing the history of the Corps, the wisdom of the ages, Alfred Thayer Mahan, and the experience of the Royal Marines. Heywood argued that rivalry bred excellence aboard ship; that the Marines performed special functions as infantry and sentries that the sailors could not perform and run the ship as well; that the Marines were now full working members of the crew; and that their potential usefulness as gunners had not yet been exploited. "The Marines have always formed part of the ship's complement, and now, since the passing away of sail power, they are certainly more useful than ever." The Commandant mentioned no new missions nor, in fact, did he offer any arguments that had not been presented by Archibald Henderson. Essentially, he told Roosevelt that the new Navy was not so changed that it could afford to eliminate the ships guards as sentries or landing party infantry and that the real way to improve American battleships' efficiency was to give the Marines more guns to man.[37]

The deliberations of Roosevelt's board and the ships guard controversy were soon lost in the rush to prepare the fleet for a possible war with Spain. But the persistence of the controversy for a decade was ominous for the Marine Corps. In past controversies the Navy officer corps had supported the Marine Corps against attacks from civilian economizers and the War Department, but their support was no longer certain. Since 1889 only the conservatism of three Secretaries of the Navy had blunted the reformers; what might happen if a President or future Secretary declined to help the Corps was worrisome. Even more troublesome was the fact that the Marine Corps had done little since the Civil War to prove that ships guards were absolutely essential to the functioning of American warships. Yet to sever its ties with the fleet might very well be the first step toward amalgamation with the Army and abolition. Only if the Corps could refurbish its image as an elite part of America's naval forces could it feel confident about its survival. The War with Spain could not have come at a more opportune time.

3

From the time the Department of the Navy first considered a war with Spain, it concluded that the new Navy would be the primary instrument with which the United States would end Spanish colonialism in the Caribbean. After the renewal of the Cuban insurrection in 1895, officers of the Navy War College and the Office of Naval Intelligence drew up and then revised a series of war plans for the fleet in case the United States and Spain went to war. All three major parties endorsed freedom for Cuba during the election campaign of 1896, and the Spanish government would not end its pacification campaign or negotiate away its colonies, hence this planning was prudent. While President William McKinley and the State Department attempted to come to terms with Spain, a Navy War Board of five senior officers reviewed and revised the basic plan drafted in 1896. Essentially, the Navy War Board envisioned offensive operations against the Spanish fleet in the Caribbean and in the western Pacific near another Spanish colony, the Philippine Islands. A defeat in the Caribbean would isolate Cuba and blockade the Spanish armies in Cuba and Puerto Rico, while a victory in the Philippines would allow the American government to hold Manila hostage until a peace was negotiated. However sound the strategic concept, it assumed that the Navy could quickly enlarge its auxiliary fleet in order to support its warships with water, coal, stores, ammunition, spare parts, and maintenance work ships. The Navy War Board recognized that without adequate bases near the theaters of operations (which the Navy did not have) the Navy was more endangered by breakdowns and shortages than by the Spanish navy, which the Office of Naval Intelligence knew was not a first-rate force. Although the Navy War Board did not plan any specific operations to seize temporary bases, its plan implied that such actions might be necessary. In any event, by the end of 1897 the Navy Department had a fairly accurate vision of its responsibilities in 1898.[38]

The events that preceded the actual declaration of war on April 21, 1898, worked to the Marine Corps's advantage. When the battleship *Maine* blew up in Havana harbor on the night of February 15, one of the heroes was a Marine orderly, William Anthony, who escorted Captain Charles D. Sigsbee, USN, to safety from his smoke-filled cabin. Twenty-eight other members of the ships guard perished with their Navy shipmates and became martyrs in the pages of the American press. Since the *Maine* had been sent to Havana to protect American lives and property from Spanish anti-American riots, most Americans assumed that Spanish saboteurs had sunk the *Maine* and killed 266 of the crew. Thus the *Maine* became a popular *casus belli* and exceptionally good copy for the bellicose "yellow press."

The subsequent Congressional demand for action centered on the Navy Department, and Colonel Heywood suddenly found he could recruit the Marine Corps up to its full strength of 3,073 enlisted men. Moreover, Secretary Long wanted to know how much of an emergency defense appropriation of $50 million might be spent on the Marine Corps.[39] With the formal outbreak of war, Heywood asked for more officers and men and received almost all he requested in legislation passed on May 4, 1898. True, the Commandant wanted a permanent enlargement of the officer corps by 103 billets but received permission to commission forty-three second lieutenants for the war only. Heywood, however, was allowed to recruit 1,640 more enlisted men for the war, the exact number he had requested from the naval affairs committees. The Commandant was sure he now had enough men to protect Navy yards, man ships guards, and carry out any other missions the Navy Department might assign. The manpower drought was over, ended by war, Congressional funding, and new public interest in the Marine Corps. The Commandant dared hope that the Marine Corps might have as many as four thousand men even after the war ended. And Congress, in martial good feeling, raised the Commandant to the rank of brigadier general.[40]

Whether or not the Marine Corps would eventually profit from its honeymoon with Congress and its rediscovery by the American people rested as much with Heywood's scattered ships guards and barracks detachments as it did with the Commandant in Washington. After three decades of Marine promises that the Corps needed only a war to prove its military efficiency, it would have been awkward if the War with Spain had not provided new glories to be paraded for the benefit of Congress and the Navy Department.

If the Commandant's claims in the ships guards controversy was anything more than anachronistic rhetoric, the Marines of the Asiatic and North Atlantic squadrons would bear the heaviest responsibility in proving their essential value to the battle fleet. In two major and decisive sea engagements—at Manila Bay, May 1, 1898, and off Santiago de Cuba, July 3—the ships guards had no opportunity to prove their superiority as gunners, simply because both engagements were decided by the fire of the American main batteries. Despite the gross inaccuracy of the Navy's gunners, Commodore George Dewey's squadron and Rear Admiral William T. Sampson's combined squadrons pounded nine Spanish ships into flaming junk with their heavy guns. Although the secondary batteries blasted away with enthusiasm in both engagements, not all of the rapid-fire guns came into action and not all of those that did were manned by Marines. Disappointed when the initial reports of both fleet engagements did not mention the Marine guards, Heywood queried the ships captains and Marine officers about what exactly the Marines had contributed to the stunning American victories. The results of the Commandant's investigation and subsequent studies showed that the Marines had behaved with coolness under fire and had carried out all their duties with efficiency. Marines had committed acts of individual heroism, both at the secondary batteries and as messengers and ammunition-passers. As for the effect of the secondary batteries, it was difficult to find many hits on the Spanish hulks, and the investigators had only the word of the Spaniards that the rapid fire guns had disrupted some of their exposed gun crews and messengers. As it turned out, the Marines aboard Sampson's battleships and cruisers were more often posted as riflemen, signalmen, messengers, orderlies, medical aides, and ammunition-passers than as gunners. Although Heywood later claimed that the Marine gunners played a crucial role in destroying the Spanish squadrons, the testimony of his own officers showed that such was not the case.[41]

Yet the ships guards had, after all, been *there* during the debut of the new Navy, and Marines also participated in other naval actions during the summer of 1898. Marine landing parties from American vessels destroyed cable stations and cut cables in Cuba, captured a lighthouse, raised the flag in the Spanish naval yard at Cavite on Manila Bay, and claimed Apra, Guam, and Ponce, Puerto Rico, as conquests of the United States. They fired their guns in the bombardments of San Juan, Puerto Rico, and Santiago, Cuba. In a "splendid" and almost bloodless war for the United States Navy, the ships guards shared the Navy's public acclaim. That they had done anything special is not so clear.

As it developed, however, a single expeditionary battalion of barracks Marines commanded by a bearded ancient of the Civil War, Lieutenant Colonel Robert W. Huntington, made the greatest contribution to the Marine Corps's reputation for combat valor and readiness. No other unit of comparable size (with the possible exception of the "Rough Rider" cavalry regiment) received as much newspaper coverage during the Cuban campaign. And the experience of Huntington's battalion suggested to some Navy and Marine officers that the Corps might indeed have an important role to play in the new Navy.

On April 16, five days before the war formally began, Secretary Long ordered Colonel Heywood to organize one battalion for expeditionary duty with the North Atlantic Squadron in Caribbean waters. What Long had in mind is unclear, but he or the Naval War Board or Admiral Sampson must have contemplated extemporizing a base in Cuba, for Marine quartermasters purchased three months' supplies and wheelbarrows, pushcarts, pickaxes, shovels, wagons (but no mules), and barbed wire cutters for the expedition. Heywood rushed to the Brooklyn Marine Barracks (commanded by Huntington) to supervise the mobilization, the purchasing of supplies, and the outfitting of a newly purchased Navy transport, the *Panther*. Drawing Marines from East Coast barracks, Heywood created a six-company battalion of 24 officers and 633 enlisted men. One of the companies was armed with four 3-inch landing guns, while the others were infantry. Although the battalion's initial drills were a muddle, the troops (about 40 percent new recruits) were enthusiastic and the officers experienced, if more than a trifle superannuated. After a rousing parade, the officers' wives gave the battalion new flags, the troops cheered "Remember the *Maine*," and the battalion marched to the *Panther* on April 22. As the Marines departed, a Navy yard crowd roared with enthusiasm and the New York newspapers hailed the departing heroes. Colonel Heywood himself was pleased with the battalion's prospects, although he knew the *Panther* would be overcrowded. No one had the slightest idea what the battalion was expected to do, but it was ready for action.[42]

The odyssey of Huntington's battalion became progressively less romantic as the *Panther* plowed south for the Caribbean. While Huntington and the ships captain argued whether Navy Regulations for a Marine ships guard applied to an embarked battalion, the troops ate in continuous shifts, sweated in the packed compartments, listened to lectures, and fired ten rounds each from their new Lee rifles. Miffed by the Marines' reluctance to do chores and anxious to change his ship into an auxiliary cruiser, the ships captain persuaded a commodore at Key West to order the battalion ashore. Shoved ashore without all their supplies on May 24, the Marines continued training and fought the bugs in their hot, dusty tent camp.[43]

Finally the battalion received a mission. By May 28 the Navy had located and blockaded the Spanish squadron in Santiago harbor in southeastern Cuba. Looking for a temporary harbor for coaling his vessels, Admiral Sampson asked that the Marine battalion support his naval expedition into Guantanamo Bay east of Santiago. As Huntington's battalion reloaded on the *Panther* on June 7, Sampson sent the cruiser *Marblehead* and two small auxiliary cruisers into Guantanamo Bay, where they shelled and destroyed the Spanish shore positions and chased a gunboat up the bay. This force was then joined by the battleship *Oregon*, worn by a 12,000-mile cruise around South America. Worried by reports of seven thousand Spanish troops in the Guantanamo area, Commander Bowman McCalla, captain of the *Marblehead* and the expedition commander, had the Marines from his cruiser and the *Oregon* conduct a reconnaissance of a hilly point just inside the bay's mouth. The ships guards found the Spanish gone, and McCalla decided the position was defensible.

On June 10 Huntington's battalion started unloading their supplies, screened by one company. For the next twenty-four hours the Marines wrestled their gear ashore in the heavy heat. While they toiled, the *Marblehead* fired occasional shells in the neighboring hills to discourage any lurking Spanish patrols.[44] The position ashore, named Camp McCalla, was not well organized, but McCalla thought that it could be protected by naval gunfire. Essentially the battalion was supposed to prevent the Spanish from harassing the ships in the harbor with rifle or artillery fire, which could be done with active patrolling and by garrisoning the hill. But until they received some Cuban guides and established their base camp, the Marines were chained to their hill and three outposts beyond it in the heavy brush. The basic defensive position atop the hill close to the beach (selected by the Marine captain on the *Oregon*) was not wide enough to accommodate a tent camp for more than six hundred men, but Huntington raised his tents anyway along the hill's crest above the main trenches and the outposts.

In the early evening of June 11 the battalion began what Major Henry Clay Cochrane, Huntington's second in command, called "its one hundred hours of fighting." As the Marines unloaded, Spanish infantry closed about the weary camp, killed an unwary two-man outpost, and opened night-long harassing fire on the camp. Scurrying to their trenches, the Marines replied with a blind barrage of rifle and Colt machine gun fire, supplemented by a thunderous naval bombardment. For the sleepless Marines the next two nights were much the same, a storm of naval shelling, the whiz of Mauser bullets, signal lamps blinking in the darkness, constant alarms, and wild riflery into the heavy brush. Although the Spanish never closed, their fire killed the battalion's Navy surgeon and two sergeants and wounded three others. Much of the battalion, especially Huntington and the older officers, was soon in a state of near collapse.[45]

Obviously the tactical situation had to be reversed, and there was some question as to who was protecting whom from the Spanish, since the *Marblehead* and the auxiliary cruisers had just spent three nights at general quarters. For a start Huntington, at McCalla's suggestion, moved his camp to the beach area in order to protect it from direct fire and ease his resupply problems. A newly arrived Cuban colonel had a better idea: send an expedition to destroy the only nearby drinking water and the Spanish camp at Cuzco Well, some two miles away. On June 14 Captain George F. Elliott led two infantry companies and a detachment of fifty Cuban scouts on a circular six-mile march toward Cuzco Well. Although the Marines did not surprise the Spanish garrison of battalion strength, they won the foot race to the hill that dominated the Spanish camp and caught the enemy in the valley. At ranges up to 1,000 yards the Marines peppered the Spaniards with rifle and machine gun fire. During the fighting another Marine platoon on outpost duty on its own initiative closed off the head of the valley and caught the enemy in a crossfire, while the dispatch ship *Dolphin* added its shells to the general firing. The *Dolphin*'s shells, fired without much direction, also drove the Marine platoon from its position until the shelling was stopped by a wigwag message from Sergeant John H. Quick. After four hours of fighting the Spaniards withdrew from their cul-de-sac, having suffered at least 160 casualties. A Marine platoon went into the valley to count bodies, destroy the well, and burn the camp, and the action was over. By early evening the Marines were back in their jubilant camp. At the cost of four Cubans and three Marines dead and wounded and twenty heat casualties, the expedition had captured eighteen Spaniards, routed the rest, and ended the attacks on their own camp.[46]

Compared with the fighting soon to follow in the Army's campaign against Santiago, the action at Guantanamo Bay was a minor skirmish of no consequence to the course of the war, but it took on incalculable importance for the Marine Corps. As the first serious fighting by American troops on Cuban soil, it drew a squad of newspaper correspondents, whose reports made it sound as if Huntington's battalion had been on the edge of annihilation. The reporters, among them Stephen Crane, reported the Cuzco Well battle as an epic of bravery and professional skill that proved the military superiority of the Marines. When veteran Marine officers treated their situation with aplomb, the reporters waxed rhapsodic. By the time the skirmish ended, American readers of three big New York dailies (*World, Herald,* and *Tribune*), the Chicago *Tribune, Harper's Weekly,* and the papers served by the Associated Press knew who the Marines were and that they had won a magnificent victory against overwhelming odds. If the Commandant had staged the campaign for public effect, it could not have been more successful.[47]

Having languished at Guantanamo Bay through June and July 1898, Huntington's battalion embarked on the Navy transport *Resolute* and sailed for Manzanillo, Cuba, for another landing. But before the battalion could storm ashore, Spain agreed to an armistice, and as quickly as the war had started it was over. By the end of August the battalion was back in Portsmouth, New Hampshire, to be disbanded and sent to its home barracks for duty.

Huntington's battalion was not allowed to fade away, for its conduct at Guantanamo Bay and its light sick list (only 2 percent) at a time when soldiers were dying in droves in both Cuba and the United States made it a national sensation. Secretary of the Navy Long, with Heywood's prompting, announced that 1898 was the centenary of the Marine Corps's founding and that Huntington's battalion had performed admirably as a dramatic reminder of one hundred years of service. The battalion paraded especially for President McKinley on September 22, and Heywood received requests for more parades from Omaha, Boston, Philadelphia, and New York. By the time the battalion disbanded it had spent as much time parading as it had fighting, but it had been enormously successful at both. After the War with Spain the American public and, by implication, Congress would never again have to ask what a Marine did. Instead the word "Marine" now evoked an image of bravery, discipline, competence, and devotion to duty.[48]

4

The War with Spain was a historic watershed for the Marine Corps. The expansion of American naval power into the western Pacific and the Caribbean and the annexation of the Philippines, Guam, Hawaii, and Puerto Rico created a diplomatic and military environment that increased the importance of the Navy and the Marine Corps. The war accelerated pressure to create overseas bases and build a canal across the Isthmus of Panama. It also created an effective political consensus within Congress to enlarge the battleship fleet and fund a supporting establishment for it. And it propelled Theodore Roosevelt, popular hero of the

Battle of San Juan Hill, from lieutenant colonel of the "Rough Riders" to President of the United States. Given Roosevelt's fascination with the Navy and battle fleet diplomacy, the twentieth century began with both the Navy and the Marine Corps in a state of high institutional prosperity.

Brigadier General Commandant Charles Heywood was quick to capatalize on the Marine Corps's wartime heroics and the creation of an American overseas empire. Even before the final peace treaty with Spain, he appealed for a permanent Marine Corps of six thousand men, which was double the prewar authorized strength. Arguing that the expanded fleet and new bases, plus the apparent need for expeditionary battalions for the Philippines, demanded an enlarged Corps, Heywood pressed the Navy Department to revitalize the Marine Corps. However, he did not argue for any substantial change in the Marines' duties, for he still saw the Corp's chief role as providing ships guards and naval base security forces.[49]

For the next nine years the Marine Corps and Congress enjoyed an untroubled honeymoon. As part of a general enlargement and reorganization of the Navy Department in March 1899, the Marine Corps was increased to 211 officers and 6,062 enlisted men. Pressed by Heywood and his successor, George F. Elliott, Congress continued to expand the Corps. In 1902 it authorized the enlistment of 750 more men; the following year it provided for another increase of 67 officers and 280 men; in 1905 the Corps received 1,239 more enlisted men. After another review of the Corps's needs in 1908 the House Naval Affairs Committee recommended, and Congress accepted, another increase of 55 officers and 750 men, bringing the Marine Corps to an authorized strength of 332 officers and 9,521 enlisted men, or more than three times its size before the War with Spain. Although Congress by 1908 had cooled to all the Commandant's requested numbers, it accepted his argument that dollar for dollar the Marine Corps was a better buy than the Army (it had a higher officer–enlisted ratio) and that it was doing yeomen service aboard ships and on the frontiers of America's new Pacific empire.[50]

The Corps's rapid enlargement was accompanied by internal changes that dramatized the Marines' new popularity. Despite its hurried expansion, the Marine Corps had no difficulty finding new officers, for it was deluged with applications for commissions. Most of the new lieutenants came from civilian life, and although political patronage influenced the process, the new officers pleased the Commandant and brought into the Corps lieutenants who were already experienced in the War with Spain and the Philippine Insurrection or were college-educated—and sometimes both.[51] The recruiting of enlisted men went equally well. In the decade after the war the Corps had little difficulty meeting its authorized strength; when it fell short, it was because of rejecting enlistees on qualitative grounds. At a time when both the Army and the Navy (also enlarged in the same decade) were having trouble filling their ranks, the Marine Corps was not only finding men but extending its system of recruiting stations inland from both coasts and turning itself into a truly national institution.[52]

Despite overlong tours on Guam and in the Philippines, the enlisted men of the new Marine Corps shared their service's good fortune. In 1899, at the Commandant's request, Congress approved the new enlisted rank of "gunnery sergeant," thus creating 72 billets for specialists in handling naval ordnance; at the time gunnery sergeants were the highest-paid ($35 monthly) noncommissioned officers in the Corps. Additional sergeants-major and quartermaster sergeants were authorized, and the entire enlisted ranks received a 20 percent pay increase. In 1908 gun-pointers, signalmen, and marksmen received additional pay.[53]

Headquarters also prospered during the decade of expansion. Heywood was promoted by special act to major general just before his retirement, and Congress made the post of Commandant a permanent major general's billet in 1903. The Commandant's staff was enlarged and its ranks were increased as well; the Adjutant and Inspector, the Quartermaster, and the Paymaster became full colonels, while most of their immediate assistants were promoted to field grade. Headquarters moved to an office building near the White House, and Major Charles McCawley, the former Commandant's son, became one of Roosevelt's naval aides. When the General Board, an advisory committee dominated by Navy line officers, was created in 1900, Colonel George C. Reid was added to represent the Corps in the board's deliberations.[54] Not since the days of Archibald Henderson had the Marine Corps enjoyed as much popularity and influence in social and official Washington, and it would have been unusual if the officers around the Commandant had not succumbed to a case of hubris.

As the Marine Corps expanded and the Civil War veterans reached mandatory retirement age, the senior officers changed rapidly. In 1903 Colonel George F. Elliott, who had been a fifty-one-year-old captain when he led the attack on Cuzco Well, became Major General Commandant. Commissioned in 1870 after he had been expelled from West Point, Elliott had had an undistinguished career. He had, however, shown a stiffness of purpose and devotion to duty in Panama and Seoul that anticipated his heroics at Guantanamo Bay and subsequent service in the Philippines as a battalion commander. As Commandant, however, he had difficulty coping with the politicians in Congress, the Navy Department, and his own staff. Blunt, abrasive, hard-drinking, and a dogmatic loyalist to the Marine Corps of the nineteenth centry, Elliott sought to continue Heywood's policies without Heywood's skill. His divisive leadership, abetted by virtual anarchy in his staff, became a clear threat to the Corps in 1909.[55]

For all the Marine Corps's expansion, its functions remained virtually the same after the War with Spain. Although it provided expeditionary regiments for infantry service in the Philippines and in China during the Boxer Rebellion (1900), the Marine Corps remained in the hearts and minds of its senior officers a seagoing military service, equally adept at naval gunnery and landing party service, and a security force for Navy yards and stations. The revised Navy Regulations of 1900 and 1905 repeated the prewar functions and duties, although the 1900 revision did mention that the President retained the constitutional power to assign the Marines as he saw fit, which might include duty in seacoast forts.[56] But pressures were building from within the Navy Department to reorganize the Marine Corps into permanent expeditionary battalions that could develop and defend temporary advanced naval bases for the battle fleet. Yet General Heywood showed no special interest in the new tasks, and Elliott, his staff, and the senior members of the Corps did not surrender their attachment to the Corps's traditional duties.[57]

Despite the fact that Headquarters faced the necessity of manning barracks at new naval stations in the Caribbean and Pacific and of forming expeditionary battalions for land campaigns in China and the Philippines, the Marine Corps had no intention of deemphasizing the importance of the ships guards aboard the warships of the new Navy. During the decade after the War with Spain the ships guards did indeed find employment with the Navy. In 1898 ships guards patrolled the legations in Peking and Tientsin as civil war and antiforeign revolts racked the Manchu Dynasty. In 1900 the guards from two cruisers reached Peking to help defend the foreign community during the Boxer Rebellion. In 1899 a joint American–British expedition to crush a revolt on the protectorate of Samoa included ships guards; three Marines were awarded Medals of Honor for bravery when their landing party was ambushed and four Navy officers and sailors were killed. During the Philippine Insurrection, ships guards from Navy gunboats often landed in search of *insurrectos*. Ships guards also went ashore in Honduras (1903 and 1907), Nicaragua (1899), the Dominican Republic (1903 and 1904), Korea (1904 and 1905), Morocco (1904) and Beirut, Lebanon (1903). In two cases Marine ships guards became the spearhead of more substantial expeditions, which reached regimental and brigade strength, in Panama (1901–1903) and Cuba (1906–1909). Smaller detachments escorted American diplomats into Abyssinia (1903 and 1904), brought John Paul Jones's body home from Europe, and guarded the legation in Russia.[58]

Yet the more the need for ships guards appeared unchanging to Heywood and Elliott, the more the development of the Navy and the expansionist thrust of American diplomacy were modifying the very foundation of the Marine Corps's existence. After the War with Spain the Navy found that the general quality of its recruits improved substantially. The threat of serious crew indiscipline (let alone a mutiny) was long past, and the masters-at-arms were more than adequate to handle the enforcement of ships regulations. No one could argue that rifle fire would play any role in future sea battles, and it was a debatable point whether secondary batteries were useful for anything but chasing off torpedo boats. The thrust, in fact, in warship armament was away from radically mixed ordnance to fewer guns of larger caliber manned entirely by sailors. Even the sole reliance upon ships landing parties for interventions ashore was proving more questionable, for European weapons and some semblance of military discipline were rapidly making even the irregulars of the "uncivilized" world more formidable opponents than they had been in the nineteenth century. Wherever any actual fighting either occurred or appeared imminent or American intervention carried greater significance than the emergency protection of lives and property, the emerging pattern was to rush a Marine expeditionary battalion (or more) ashore behind the ships landing parties. Such was the context in which the Marine Corps fought its next political battle in Washington.

5

Already hard pressed by line officer reformers on the issues of battleship design and the creation of a Navy general staff, the Bureau of Navigation in 1906 resurrected one of the reformer's cherished programs: eliminating the Marine ships guards from the Navy's warships. The timing could not have been more propitious to placate the reformers and convince the President and Congress, for the Fullamites of the 1890s were now both the senior commanders of the Navy and its most influential politicians in Washington. Fullam himself was a fixture in the Navy Department's policy-making circles, and his friend Commander William S. Sims was Roosevelt's naval aide. Recently retired Robley D. Evans, a longtime critic of the ships guards, was enjoying great prestige after having commanded the "Great White Fleet" on its global cruise of 1907–1908. One of his successors, Seaton Schroeder, was also a Fullamite. The President himself was already sympathetic to the Fullamites and had conferred with his old friend, Major General Leonard Wood, about the Corps's status. The two Rough Riders agreed that both the Army and the Navy would profit if the Marine Corps were absorbed into the Army. Both felt that the Corps had inordinate influence on policy-making, an influence heightened by the patronage appointment of new officers since 1898. Although the Fullamites agreed with the President about the Corps's proclivity for institutional self-aggrandizement, they were not enthusiastic about losing the Marine Corps, for their basic interest was in putting the some two thousand seagoing Marines into new advanced base force battalions. This division of purpose between the Fullamites and the President eventually worked to the Corps's vast benefit.[59]

On October 16, 1908, Rear Admiral J. E. Pillsbury, chief of the Bureau of Navigation, requested that the Secretary of the Navy withdraw the ships guards. He asked the President to redefine the Marine Corps's duties and offered three reasons: The Marines should be grouped and trained ashore for expeditionary duty; ships crews were no longer so undisciplined that they required Marine sentries or "military" examples; and the absence of the Marine landing party for duty ashore weakened ships gun crews. Secretary of the Navy Victor Metcalf, who supported Pillsbury's position, approached Roosevelt with the proposal. General Elliott argued with Metcalf and Roosevelt but found the President firm for removal. Elliott then volunteered to draft a new Executive Order on the Corps's duties for Roosevelt's approval. Roosevelt also told Elliott that he wanted no post hoc attack on removal from the Corps. Convinced that he had made the best of a bad situation, Elliott accepted removal.[60]

On November 12 Roosevelt signed and published Executive Order 969, which listed the duties of the Marine Corps:

1. To garrison the different navy yards and naval stations, both within and beyond the continental limits of the United States.
2. To furnish the first line of the mobile defense of naval bases and naval stations beyond the continental limits of the United States.
3. To man such naval defenses, and to aid in the manning, if necessary, of such other defenses, as may be erected for the defense of naval bases and naval stations beyond the continental limits of the United States.
4. To garrison the Isthmian Canal Zone, Panama.
5. To furnish such garrisons and expeditionary forces for duties beyond the seas as may be necessary in time of peace.

With Roosevelt's decision now public, Secretary Metcalf ordered the fleet commanders to start sending their Marines ashore to the nearest barracks; within a week the Pacific Fleet had dropped its guards at Bremerton, Olongapo, and Mare Island, and the Atlantic Fleet commander announced he would have his vessels clear of Marines within a month. Except for Marine officers who were convinced that Executive Order 969 was a prelude to abolition, the first reaction to Roosevelt's decision was approval, for the order meant that some two thousand more Marines would be available for the missions outlined in the order and that the Navy reformers could prove their promises that the removal of ships guards would contribute to improvement of the naval service for enlisted men.[61]

Had the matter ended with the simple redefinition of duties in Executive Order 969, the Marine Corps guards would have remained off American warships, but Roosevelt's decision was immediately followed by speculation in Washington that the Marine Corps would shortly be merged with the Army and thus disappear as a separate service. Shortly after issuing Order 969, the President told one of his military aides that the Marine Corps's "downfall" was largely its own fault, for its political influence was abnormally great for the Corp's size and significance. "I do not hesitate to say that they [the Marines] should be absorbed into the army and no vestige of their organization should be allowed to remain. They cannot get along with the navy, and as a separate command with the army the conditions would be intolerable." [62] There were rumors that members of the War Department General Staff and the chairman of the House Military Affairs Committee were consulting about drafting appropriate legislation, for amalgamation would require a new law.[63]

Cultivated by officers at Headquarters who thought the abolition threat released them from vows of silence, a movement to repeal Executive Order 969 began to grow. Even the Navy Department became alarmed enough for Secretary Metcalf to speak against amalgamation and for Admiral Pillsbury to hold interviews to deny that the Navy wanted the Marine Corps abolished. Pillsbury told reporters: "I think it will be a very great mistake to put them in the Army. We want them in the Navy. We do not want them on board ship." He then went on to explain the advanced base force concept and emphasized that the duties outlined in Executive Order 969 were crucial to the future of naval strategy.[64] There were other pressures that assisted the repealers. Elliott, hectored by his staff, now announced that Roosevelt's decision was a mistake that demonstrated the President's ignorance of the importance of ships guards. The Navy Department also admitted that it would need funds for some two thousand more sailors to replace the Marines.[65]

It is unlikely that Congress was in any mood to abolish the Marine Corps. It was already irritated by Roosevelt's attacks on Congressional policy-making prerogatives, and the Senate was unhappy about Leonard Wood's promotion to major general and his ties with the President. Moreover, the Congressional naval affairs committees were miffed by the reformers' attacks on the Navy Department bureaus and were increasingly reluctant to accept the policies of a lame duck President who had discomfited many Congressmen for seven years. Some Congressmen, in fact, convinced that Roosevelt was on a personal vendetta against the Marine Corps, took the abolition rumors seriously. One Congressman wrote Fullam that no one doubted that sailors did not need guards and that the Marine detachment did nothing aboard ship that sailors could not do as well. Yet Congress feared that removal might be the prelude to abolition and was unconvinced that the Marine Corps was dispensable as either landing party infantry or expeditionary battalions. "It [the Marine Corps] is, and has been for many years, a better organization for certain purposes than the Infantry of the Army, and, I think, better for certain purposes [landing parties] than would be the Blue Jacket of the Navy." [66]

It is doubtful that any plan for amalgamation had any support. When the Senate passed a resolution to investigate the Marine Corps question in December, Senator Francis Warren, a powerful member of the Senate Military Affairs Committee, offhandedly suggested that the Naval Affairs Committee handle the problem, for his committee had no special interest in the matter. He also recommended that the investigation be confined to reviewing Roosevelt's authority to remove the Marines and the impact of the removal.[67] By January 1909 Congressional sentiment in the removal controversy favored not only halting any amalgamation schemes but legislating the Marines back aboard warships.

The repealers made their counterattack during the House of Representatives' study of the Naval Appropriations Bill of 1909. The House Naval Affairs Committee set up a special investigating committee to review the removal order; the subcommittee was chaired by Thomas Butler, the father of Marine Captain Smedley Darlington Butler. Between January 7 and January 15, 1909, Butler's subcommittee heard Secretary of the Navy Truman Newberry, Admirals Pillsbury and Evans, Commanders Sims and Fullam, and assorted active and retired admirals and ships captains. The Marine Corps position was presented by General Elliott and the most aggressive members of his staff, Adjutant and Inspector Charles Lauchheimer, Quartermaster Frank L. Denny,

Assistant Paymaster George Richards, and Lieutenant Colonel Charles McCawley. The committee also heard several well-known Marine line officers, among them Colonel L. W. T. Waller and Major Wendell C. Neville, recently returned from expeditionary duty in Cuba.

The Butler subcommittee heard the Navy officers repeat the classic arguments for removal and considered memoranda prepared by Admiral Luce and Commander Fullam. Fullam and Sims made the most dogmatic case for removal, and their position was generally supported by all the Navy witnesses, except for some retired ships captains. In essence, the Fullam position was that the Marines were no longer needed for shipboard discipline and that there was no evidence that Marine gun crews or landing parties had skills sailors did not have or could not develop. The Marine Corps should concentrate on training and organizing battalions for expeditionary and advanced base force duty rather than expend any time, men, and money for nonessential ships guards. Fullam charged that Elliott and his staff had not responded adequately to the General Board's request that the Marine Corps develop advanced base force battalions, a criticism supported in more diplomatic fashion by the president of the General Board, Admiral George Dewey. Fullam also pointed out that the money spent on replacing Marines with sailors would be offset by reducing the need to increase the Marine Corps for all the other duties outlined in Executive Order 969.[68]

Already sympathetic to the Marine Corps repealers, Butler's committee challenged every argument presented by the Navy reformers and allowed Marine officers in the audience to bully witnesses. Members of Elliott's staff fed questions to the committee, and a Marine captain served as committee secretary. When the Marines eventually testified, they argued that removal was the first step toward abolition and that the ships guards were an essential part of a warship's company. They showed no special interest in the advanced base force concept and argued that Marines were all so well trained that battalions and regiments needed no special training or permanent organization. In fact, they thought it more efficient (as well as cheaper) to build large landing parties around the ships guards on warships rather than put expeditionary battalions on Navy transports. They argued that the Marine Corps had no peer as a military organization and that its service from 1798 justified not only retention of all its traditional functions but an expansion of its duties aboard ship. They also talked much of "honor" and Navy perfidy.

In a dramatic presentation near the end of the hearings, Colonel Richards convinced the committee that removal would be an economic disaster. To replace a Marine guard with sixty sailors of comparable ranks would cost the Navy $211,447 more a year for each ship in pay alone. In addition, someone would have to expand Marine Corps shore facilities to accommodate two thousand more men and fund the increased housekeeping costs they would create. Richards estimated that these additional costs would reach $2 million a year. To provide three more transports for the new battalions would cost $6 million. By the time the Marines finished, the Butler subcommittee was ready to recommend that Congress legislate the return of the ships guards.[69]

The House Naval Affairs Committee submitted its findings and recommendation in House Resolution 26394: that no money should be authorized for the Marine Corps unless Marine guards were placed on all battleships, armored cruisers, and any other vessels the President designated, at a strength of no less than 8 percent of the ship's complement. The resolution became a rider on the Naval Appropriations Act, which virtually assured its acceptance, but the full House was confused by the issue and reluctant to act. The Senate, however, voted 51–12 to return the ships guards, an act urged by its naval affairs committee. The House then deferred to the Senate, and the Naval Appropriations Act went to Roosevelt with the Butler rider intact.[70]

Roosevelt signed the Naval Appropriation Act without hesitation, because it approved his shipbuilding plans and some other Navy Department reforms. Roosevelt himself was untroubled by the Butler rider and claimed he had never been interested in anything but increasing the Marine Corps expeditionary battalions. In any event, the Marine Corps ships guards question was of little significance to the departing President and his naval policy. "But the damage is not serious, and tho [sic] the bill is passed the Senate will . . . do a little damage, it does not do very much, and this damage will be limited chiefly to creating the belief that the Marines are kept aboard ship for nonmilitary reasons." [71]

Notwithstanding a study requested by President William Howard Taft on whether the Butler rider was constitutional, the Navy Department accepted the repealers' victory, and twenty-eight ships guards began to return to the fleet. Flushed with victory, Headquarters pressed the Secretary of the Navy to require that the ships guards train on the main battery, but this assault was beaten back by the Navy Regulations of 1909. Instead, the new regulations listed the missions of both Executive Order 969 and the Butler rider but increased the authority of Navy line officers over the Marine guard. The Bureau of Navigation also tried to prevent the reissue of instruction manuals on secondary batteries when the guards returned to their ships, but Taft ordered the Marines restored to all their pre-969 duties. Taft, however, believed that the Marine Corps was far too powerful politically in Congress and hoped someone someday would remove the guards forever. Like many of Taft's political assessments, the view that "the marines would have to leave the ships; that as a distinct body the Corps had become almost useless, and as far as the Navy was concerned it was an actual detriment" was flawed.[72] Without any serious change in their status, the ships guards were back aboard the Navy's largest men-of-war by the end of June 1909. The removal controversy had ended in victory for the Marine Corps.[73]

The ships guards removal controversy marked a political milestone in the Marine Corps's history, for the Corps had by now so developed its own popular constituency in the public and the federal government that it could survive an assault on its least defensible function. Although it is moot whether removal would have improved recruiting and crew discipline, the ships guards did nothing at sea that could not have been handled by masters-at-arms and seamen-gunners. As Admiral Luce pointed out in a 1909 memorandum for the Butler subcommittee, the real purpose of having Marines aboard warships was to provide a trained nucleus for the ships landing party. Yet sailors could and did serve as infantry ashore. How effective they were and how long they could be spared from the ships company were other matters, for few if any captains would sacrifice gunnery training time for infantry drill or were enthusiastic about having their crews ashore in some intervention. So Fullam's position had its flaws, but it was at least as objective as the Marine Corps position on the utility of the ships guards.

The issue was not settled on rational criteria anyway. It was decided by the power of the alliance between Headquarters and Congress, an alliance powerful enough to defeat the most influential anti-Corps coalition in 110 years. In 1908–1909 the removal advocates included two Presidents, an influential part of the Navy line, and one very political Army major general, all of whom were skilled in manipulating public opinion. In spite of the fact that Elliott's staff defended the Marine Corps with arguments that were irrelevant and even specious, they were successful in repealing Executive Order 969. When a military service can defend itself on grounds other than its present and future utility, it has clearly reached a point of high institutional autonomy and stability. Such was the case of the Marine Corps in 1909.

Part Two

Colonial Infantry
1899–1941

The people of every creed and class,
Of every country and clime
Have paid their respects to the Stars
  and Stripes
At one or another time
At times they raise trouble among themselves,
And someone must intervene,
Then the best man to send, so the President
  says
Is a United States Marine.

> *Private C. Hundertmark, "The United States*
> *Marine," Recruiter's Bulletin,*
> *April 1915*

6. To Sunny Tropic Scenes
1899—1914

With the end of the War with Spain the United States government embarked on a redefinition of the nation's relationship with the rest of the world, and the principal thrust of American foreign policy outside Europe slipped from nonintervention to active, conscious influence upon the affairs of other nations. This was particularly true with respect to China, the Pacific, the Caribbean, Mexico, and Central America. Although it is still difficult to sort out the various components of this new "Manifest Destiny," there were several motives for America's emergence as a quasi-imperial power. Part of the thrust was encouraged by substantial elements of American business: bankers with money to lend, entrepreneurs with plantations and mines to develop and protect, corporations with manufactured products to sell to new foreign consumers, and companies with dreams of railroads and canals to be built across trackless jungles and plains. Yet the search for new markets and natural resources does not exhaust the reasons for American intervention.

What made American foreign policy distinctive after 1898 was a blossoming of other interests that were equally imperialistic. One such influence was missionary, both religious and secular. The turn of the century found the overseas work of the Protestant churches at a new level of activity, especially in China, but in the Caribbean as well. Supported by congregations that tended to be elitist and political, the missionaries were a considerable force in American diplomacy. There were also other types of missionaries, whose interest was not necessarily in the propagation of the Gospel of Christ but in the gospel of Progressive reform. Although their rhetoric smacked of religious conviction, such men were secular modernizers whose interest was in transplanting American democratic political institutions, modern technology and managerial techniques, and business practices in underdeveloped nations. By occupation, these cultural imperialists were economic entrepreneurs, military and naval officers, politicians, newspaper and magazine writers, engineers, diplomats, and pure adventurers. Their point, expressed in varying language, was that the United States had a duty to spread the advantages of its own civilization to other states in order to provide a safer, healthier, and richer life for ordinary people.

Economic advantage and missionary reform mixed with other concerns to broaden the support for intervention abroad. American public officials and naval officers were concerned that European powers might preempt American interests and establish foreign bases too close to North America. The government was also interested in bases of its own to support its cruising squadrons and the battle fleet in war. Such bases would also encourage the rebirth of the American merchant marine and offer immediate assistance to Americans whose lives and property abroad were endangered. In the Caribbean the bases issue focused upon the protection of key passages into the Gulf of Mexico and the approaches to the isthmian canal, which Americans assumed would soon be built. In the Western Pacific the issue centered on deterring further European expansion in China (the "Open Door" policy) and the protection of American trade. The annexations of 1898–1899 also created a system of American insular possessions to protect: the Philippines, Guam, Hawaii, and Puerto Rico.

For the Navy and the Marine Corps, imperialism brought not only a geographic extension of ships and men but a redefinition of function as a military arm of American expansion. The protection of American lives and property abroad had been an important function of naval forces, but the practice of "interposition" now broadened to become intervention. In legal terms interposition meant simply protecting one's nationals from harm during a temporary crisis. Once the danger had passed, the troops withdrew. Intervention, however, meant that military forces were used to alter the political behavior and even the institutions of another country, an act of far greater significance than interposition. Although intervention was not war or military reprisal, it was a serious international action. It might be a long-term act to change a dangerous environment to one more hospitable to foreign economic interests; it might forestall intervention by another nation;

it might determine who would govern the host country; it might provide substantial military advantages in the form of new bases or annexed territory; or it might destroy armed forces that threatened some interest of the interventionist state.[1]

For the Marine Corps the changing nature of military intervention could not have been more dramatic. After 1898 Marine ships guards continued to go ashore to protect American lives and property in the traditional manner and to perform symbolic duties. Marines landed four times in Honduras for a week at a time; other detachments served in Abyssinia, Syria, Tangier, and Russia. But some landings after 1898 were not routine affairs. The Marines who protected the legations and consulates in China in 1899–1900 became two battalions, then in the 1920s an entire brigade of thousands. The ships guards that came ashore four different times in Panama in 1901–1904 stayed at battalion strength until 1914. A Marine regiment served in Cuba nearly three years during the Second Intervention (1906–1909), and other Marine regiments returned in 1912 for six months and in 1917 for eighteen months. In Nicaragua, ships guards landed in 1910, and a regiment in 1912, which remained six months; in the next intervention a brigade came for six years. The Marine Corps occupied Haiti and Santo Domingo for years with brigades of several thousand men. Similar forces landed in Mexico in 1913 and 1914, although their stay was measured only in months.[2] Such interventions were clearly more ambitious undertakings than sending a landing party to do sentry duty around a church or a warehouse.

The size and length of American military interventions reflected not only the more ambitious goals of those interventions but also some revolutionary changes in the conduct of war. For the Marine Corps the most significant development was the internationalization of military expertise and ordnance. Part of the thrust of European expansion was the sale of modern weapons to non-Western states. Whereas a century before European forces had faced undisciplined tribesmen with primitive weapons, they now often faced weapons as modern as their own and, sometimes, men who knew how to fire them as well as they did. In Peking in 1900 German marines were killed with Mauser bullets and Krupp artillery. In Nicaragua in 1927–1934 Marines were shot with submachine guns like those they themselves carried. One comparison dramatizes this development. In 1841 an American landing party came ashore in Samoa and killed uncounted natives and burned three villages in retaliation for cruelties to American missionaries. The seventy-man force faced inconsequential opposition and had no losses. But in 1899 a joint American–British landing force of sailors and Marines twice as large as the 1841 expedition was routed by the Samoans. Even though the Americans had a Colt machine gun, the Samoans ambushed the landing party and drove it back to the beach. Only naval gunfire saved the landing party. The cause of the rout, the senior American officer reported, was the volume and accuracy of the natives' rifle fire.[3]

Although the Marine Corps was not singled out for colonial service, the government in 1899 began to provide the Corps with the necessary men to assume new tasks in "sunny tropic scenes." The Naval Personnel Act of 1899, which increased the Corps's authorized strength to 211 officers and 6,062 enlisted men, was a Magna Carta for further expansion and additional duties. The lure of Asiatic service brought 100 new lieutenants and 1,500 recruits into the ranks in 1899 alone. Commandant Charles Heywood was convinced that both groups represented important qualitative improvements in Corps personnel. The new lieutenants provided the Marine Corps with a generation of officers whose entire careers, with the exception of World War I, were bound to colonial service. The most famous of the group was Smedley D. Butler, who rose from teenage lieutenant to major general, but Butler was only the most flamboyant of a host of Corps characters who saw themselves as American foreign legionnaires on the fringes of their nation's tropic empire. Pleased with his new officers, Heywood was similarly enthusiastic about his increased personnel budget (up from $1.3 million to $2.5 million), the Marine marksmanship program, and better field equipment. The Commandant knew that the Corps would need all the improvements it could manage, for its men had just been committed to a new type of American military duty: "foreign service." [4]

1

Across thousands of miles of sunswept ocean and green islands, the Philippines beckoned the Marine Corps. Actually, it was the less romantic Commodore George Dewey who wanted more Marines for his fleet, for the commodore had found that his problems in Manila Bay had only started with the defeat of the Spanish squadron on May 1, 1898. After some soul-searching regarding the possibility that other nations might take the islands, the McKinley administration decided to annex the entire archipelago, an act accomplished by the Treaty of Paris (1898) with Spain. The problem was that a substantial portion of the native Filipinos did not want to exchange one colonial master for another, however well-meaning. While Dewey's squadron lay at anchor awaiting an Army expeditionary force, the Filipino insurgents seized control of the countryside, set up their own government, replaced colonial officials, dispossessed Catholic religious orders, formed a militia army, and encircled Manila and those cities still occupied by Spanish troops.

The eventual surrender of Manila to the American VIII Corps solved nothing, because the insurgents refused to disband while they awaited the outcome of American–Spanish diplomacy. Led by Emilio Aguinaldo, the insurgent generals planned to attack the Americans if the Philippines did not receive its independence. The war both armies regarded as inevitable began by accident on February 4, 1899, when two patrols clashed. During the next four days VIII Corps and Filipino militiamen fought stubbornly for control of Manila, with the Americans victorious through more firepower and better discipline. The Philippine Insurrection had begun, and it would last four years.[5]

The outbreak of war prompted Dewey to ask for reinforcements for his squadron; his earliest request was for the battleship *Oregon* and a battalion of Marines. The request represented his fear that the Navy faced a double peril from insurgent attacks on its temporary base in the old Spanish naval station at Cavite and from attack by a foreign fleet, presumably German or Japanese.[6] The Cavite base had been in the hands of ships guards since May 1898 and had served as a valuable storage place, anchorage, and refuge for foreigners fleeing the Spanish and Filipinos. Worried because Cavite province was an insurgent stronghold, Dewey asked for a stronger garrison for his base. Aware that the Naval War Board wanted permanent bases in Manila Bay and sympathetic to Dewey's request, Secretary of the Navy John D. Long ordered a Marine battalion to the islands. Composed of 15 officers and 260 men and armed with rifles, two Colt machine guns, and four 3-inch cannons, the battalion arrived in Manila in May. Before the end of the year, two more Marine battalions reached Cavite, where the force was reorganized as a two-battalion regiment of Marines. It was the first time the Marine Corps had fielded a force large enough to be considered a real regiment. It was a foretaste of things to come.[7]

The Marine regiment, however, did not become immediately involved in the fighting on Luzon, for its chief problems in 1899 were establishing a comfortable base at Cavite and overcoming sickness and supply problems. The Cavite regiment, anxious for action, was restrained by the admiral in charge of the Asiatic Station, who did not want the Marines committed to land campaigns when there were naval bases to guard. In October 1899, however, the regiment was allowed to send one 400-man battalion with an Army expedition to clear Cavite province as far south as the Imus River. Cooperating with a Navy gunboat, the battalion attacked the coastal town of Novaleta from its land side on October 8. Although suffering from heat and thirst the Marines attacked the Filipino trenches with enthusiasm and skirmished their way into the town through rice paddies, marshes, and thick grass. Men fired without orders, young lieutenants raced madly about, companies became mixed, and some wounded were temporarily abandoned. But the weight of the joint attack drove the insurgents from their positions, and the battalion, with eleven wounded, returned to Cavite without further action. Although the Novaleta attack was less than professional, the Marines had at last gotten into the war and had done something more dramatic than post guards, drill, and do "setting-up" exercises.[8]

By December 1899 the conventional war with the Filipino insurgents was dwindling, and another war, one of classic guerrilla action and population control, was beginning. Faced with growing demands to garrison towns and mount combat patrols against the insurgents' mountain bases, VIII Corps headquarters surrendered the responsibility of garrisoning most of northern Cavite province to the Marines. In addition, a Marine company took control of the town of Olongapo, northwest of Manila at Subic Bay. At both positions the Marines became involved in the military pacification of Luzon. During the next year and a half they chased small bands of guerrillas, set ambushes, controlled the flow of rice and supplies, supervised public works projects, held elections, established schools, and guarded Navy facilities and lighthouses. With the arrival of additional battalions, the force was reorganized as a two-regiment brigade of nearly 1,600 officers and men. Although the Marines suffered few casualties and endured more boredom than anything else, they contributed to the Army's successful campaign against the insurrection on Luzon.[9]

Back in Washington the Commandant worried that the Corps could not maintain a force (counting Marines in China and ships guards) numbering more than two thousand, and Heywood argued that the authorized strength of the Corps should be raised from six thousand to ten thousand men. Heywood saw clearly that the Corps had not yet adjusted to colonial service. Enlistments dragged because of the long enlistment terms, the lack of recruiting funds, and the legal ambiguities of foreign service pay. What made the situation more distressing was that tropical illness had increased the normal attrition of manpower; in 1900 the Corps lost 1,900 men from all causes (including expired enlistments), which was nearly 40 percent of its actual strength. Inasmuch as Heywood had not given up any of the Corps's nineteenth-century missions, he wondered how long he could maintain the Philippine brigade and whether his Marines were being useful enough.[10]

The insurgents on the island of Samar provided the Marines with one last opportunity for field service when they wiped out a company of the 9th Infantry at Balangiga in September 1901. Determined to avenge this massacre, Army headquarters in Manila gave the job of pacifying and punishing the Visayans to the 6th Separate Brigade, commanded by Brigadier General Jacob H. Smith. The admiral in charge of the Asiatic Station provided the expedition with gunboat support and volunteered a Marine battalion to assist both the Army and his squadron commander at Samar. The Marine brigade assembled a battalion of volunteers commanded by Major Littleton W. T. Waller, a short, pugnacious, hard-drinking, and very energetic Virginian. Waller's battalion of fifteen officers and three hundred men included some of the brigade's most aggressive officers and veteran Marines. Arriving on Samar, the battalion garrisoned Balangiga and Basey on the island's southwestern coast and conducted expeditions against the insurgents, who had fled to their fortified base camps in the interior. Convinced that they had come to save the Army, the Marines immediately combed the coastal towns for insurgents and rebel supplies as well as the arms captured from the 9th Infantry. General Smith adamantly insisted on harshness in the conduct of the campaign. In one meeting he told Waller that all Visayans were to be considered the enemy and that the execution of all Filipinos over ten years old was justified. Waller did not take him seriously (such instructions were contrary to Army regulations), but the Marines plunged into the fray determined to turn Samar into a "howling wilderness," as Smith ordered.[11]

The Marine battalion in its first three weeks of operations followed Waller's own orders to destroy or confiscate all rice, hemp, animals, boats, and huts not under American control and to kill all Filipinos who resisted or who possessed captured Army equipment. The patrols and landing parties met scattered resistance but found the enemy elusive. Nevertheless, by November 12 Waller's expeditions had burnèd 255 huts and destroyed a ton of rice, half a ton of hemp, thirteen water buffalo, and fifty native boats. They had also killed thirty-nine insurgents and taken eighteen prisoners while losing only two killed in action. Waller, however, recognized that the insurgents would not surrender until the Marines penetrated the interior and destroyed their base camps, a formidable task in the mountainous jungles of Samar. It was rumored, however, that one camp was reachable from the Sohoton River, although supposedly impregnable among volcanic cliffs. Waller decided to attack this camp. On November 16 part of Waller's force assaulted a series of entrenchments on both sides of the river by scaling the cliffs and drove the insurgents off in a brief skirmish. The

Filipinos escaped, but not before losing perhaps thirty men to rifle and machine gun fire, and their precious camp and supplies were destroyed before the Marines withdrew. Ragged, and out of rations, the Marines returned to Basey convinced that they had broken the insurrection in southern Samar.[12]

Waller's battalion had made good progress in ending organized guerrilla warfare in its area, but its tasks were not completed. While part of his battalion continued its patrols, Waller himself led a reconnaisance of fifty-four Marines and thirty-five Filipino scouts and bearers across the interior in order to map southern Samar and locate a route for a telegraph line. The march became a disaster, for the terrain was much worse than Waller had expected and heavy rains slowed the column. On the verge of exhaustion and starvation, the force divided. One group tried to return to its base, and the other plunged ahead to the Sohoton River. Before the Marines finished marching to safety or were rescued, eleven had died of starvation and exhaustion. The survivors, including Waller, were close to collapse, and most had to be hospitalized.[13]

A monument to human endurance and poor planning, Waller's march had an epilogue that poisoned his own and his battalion's reputation. In the struggle to survive, some of the native bearers had attacked one of Waller's lieutenants. Convinced that the natives were mutineers, the outraged and bedridden Waller ordered eleven of them summarily executed by Marines at Basey. Another hostage was executed for different reasons by Waller's adjutant. When Major General Adna R. Chaffee, the senior commander in the Philippines, learned of the incident, Waller and the lieutenant were court-martialed for murder. There is no doubt that Chaffee was under great pressure from the War Department to punish violations of the laws of land warfare, for the United States in 1902 was abuzz with stories of atrocities in the Philippines committed by American troops. Waller, however, was not convicted by an Army court-martial, although Chaffee and his judge advocate agreed that the evidence of a crime was persuasive. Waller's battalion approved of its commander's acts, and the Marine Corps did nothing to discipline him, but neither he nor the Marine Corps gained anything from his intemperate act.[14]

Waller's battalion did not return to Cavite until March 1902, and during the rest of its stay on Samar it avoided the interior. One thing that Waller's march had proved was that the insurgents were bound by their food needs and families to the coastal *barrios*. The Marines continued their patrolling. Gradually resistance in Samar diminished as the Army forced the natives to "reconcentrate" in American-controlled towns. A smallpox epidemic further depleted and demoralized the Visayans. When the Marines departed, the insurrection on Samar was over.

The Samar affair was one of the last episodes of the Philippine Insurrection, and by the end of 1902 the Marines at Cavite and Olongapo had reverted to peacetime routine. Guarding fifteen separate naval facilities in the Manila Bay area, the Marines drilled and worried about being sent home to the United States. Some of them had been two and a half years in the Pacific. As one bit of doggerel suggested, the experience was not enchanting:

> When I came to the Philippines in 1899
> I didn't think they'd keep me here till the
>   sun had ceased to shine
> But it seems that they've forgotten that they
>   sent us here at all
> So I guess we'll have to stay until General Recall
> But when my time expires, and I am once more free
> I'll turn my back upon the mob, my face
>   no more 'twill see
> For I'm tired of boot-leg coffee and the
>   commissary bean
> Oh! may the devil take me if again
>   I become a Marine.[15]

General Heywood did not have to listen to barracks rhymes to know that Corps reenlistment rates were minuscule. Colonial service might be romantic for recruits and a way to increase the Corps's utility, but it did not keep men in the ranks.[16]

2

The deployment of Marine battalions to the Philippines gave the Corps an opportunity to participate in one of the best-publicized episodes in the extension of foreign influence in Asia. The location was northern China, the episode the Boxer Uprising of 1900. The Boxer Uprising was not a rebellion against the Manchu dynasty but a war to rid China of foreign missionaries and Christian Chinese. Rooted in religious traditionalism and peasant unrest and exacerbated by floods and famine, the antiforeign, anti-Christian hostility of the northern Chinese peasantry began to take organized form in 1899. A fusion of several secret societies, the "Society of Righteous and Harmonious Fists" or "Boxers" was an organization that trained its members in the martial arts, conducted secret rituals, and preached immunity from death in the battle against Christians and foreigners. When the Chinese government demobilized one-third of its army in 1898, many of the veterans joined the Boxers. Despite the movement's potential for subversion, the government of the Dowager Empress Tzu Hsi vacillated in suppressing the Boxers, for the Empress and some of her advisers sympathized with the Boxers' antiforeign activity.[17]

Although one provincial governor suppressed the Boxers, the movement flourished in Chihli province near Peking and Tientsin when the government did not support its local commanders in breaking up Boxer bands. In the spring of 1900 the Boxers in Chihli province began concerted attacks upon Christian Chinese and European missionaries in remote villages; when imperial troops attempted to stop the burnings and murders, their officers were censured by the Court. Emboldened, the Boxers turned their attacks against railway and telegraph lines and communications stations. By May 1900 Boxer bands began to appear openly in the streets of the capital city of Peking.

From their enclave within the walls of Peking's Tartar City, diplomats from Europe, Japan, and the United States watched the Boxer depredations spread. Although the diplomats suspected that each other's nations had territorial designs on China, they agreed that the safety of all foreigners and Christian Chinese in Peking depended on the protection of their own troops, not those of the Empress. On May 28 the diplomats requested that the Imperial foreign ministry provide railway transportation for foreign troops; these troops would land at the mouth of the Pei Ho River at Tangku and come overland through the city of Tientsin, a trip of about 115 miles. Reluctantly the foreign ministry cooperated, and on May 31 an international force of some 337 officers and men arrived: Royal Marines, German marines, Japanese marines, Russian sailors, Austrian marines, Italian sailors, and an American detachment of fifty Marines, five sailors, and a Navy doctor. This small force, short on ammunition and armed only with rifles and three antique machine guns, was supposed to protect a Legation Quarter housing more than a thousand Europeans and swelling daily with Christian refugees.

The Marine detachment was no better or worse than any group of ships guards, but in Captain John T. Myers it had a commander of style and force. "Handsome Jack" Myers led a force drawn from his own guard from the *Oregon* and the cruiser *Newark*. Myers made wise initial decisions. His men marched without baggage in order to carry nearly 20,000 rounds of ammunition for their rifles and 8,000 rounds for the Colt machine gun, which was manned by the sailors. When the detachment arrived in Peking, Myers quickly sensed how critical the situation was; the Europeans were nearly hysterical with relief, while the watching Chinese crowded in upon the line of march in sullen silence.[18]

As the Boxers swarmed into the city to burn buildings and murder those Christians they found outside the Legation Quarter, the Marines for the next three weeks patrolled the quarter and mounted occasional raids to rescue refugees and catch small bands of Boxers. In this first phase of the seige of Peking (May 31–June 20), the Allied defense force did what it could to keep the Boxers out of the enclave. Fortunately the location and character of the enclave allowed the defenders to cut off traffic with barricades and patrols; the legations and other European offices were tightly bounded by the Tartar Wall to the south, the road to the Imperial and Forbidden cities to the west, the wall of the Imperial City to the north, and another wide street to the east. The Marines' position in the extemporized defense plan was in the southwest quadrant around the American legation and on the Tartar Wall some 400 yards from the Chien Men gate, which was the main entrance to both the Tartar City and the inner Imperial and Forbidden cities. They shared this sector with the Russian sailors. To the Marines' rear was the German–Austrian position to the southeast; from this corner the defenses were manned by the French and Italians on the east, the Japanese and civilian volunteers on the northeast around a Chinese prince's palace, and by the Royal Marines and more volunteers around the British legation in the northwest quadrant. The only problem was that the area was too large to be easily defended by the small Allied force if the Chinese launched a full-scale assault.

While the Europeans fretted, the Boxers closed in around the Legation Quarter. The European ministers continued to demand more Chinese army protection and sent out desperate requests for relief to the Allied naval forces hovering off the mouth of the Pei Ho River. There were several incidents in which Allied defenders shot and killed Boxers around the quarter, but there was no full-scale fighting. The Chinese Court, however, was becoming increasingly belligerent, especially when it learned that an unauthorized two-thousand-man force was coming by rail from Tientsin. The fires in Peking swept closer to the legations, burning missionary churches, stores, hundreds of homes, and even gate towers on the Tartar Wall. Outside the city the Boxers destroyed the railway and continued their attacks on foreigners and Christians.

The siege of the legations began in earnest on June 20, after a series of incidents. The German minister was killed by an Imperial soldier, and on June 17 the Allied naval forces fired upon and captured the forts at Taku on the coast. The Manchu Court broke relations and offered the foreigners safe passage, which was wisely refused. After a twenty-four-hour grace period, the Court declared war and ordered its regular soldiers to join the Boxers in a full-scale attack on the Legation Quarter itself. The fifty-five-day siege of Peking opened with a barrage of artillery and rifle fire on the legation barricades.

For the Marines the siege quickly became an endurance contest for control of the Tartar Wall, one of the key points in the defense. About half the detachment manned the barricades on the wall, with the rest positioned below; reliefs were changed every forty-eight hours, which made the duty grueling. Like the rest of the defenders, the Marines faced only sporadic charges. The Chinese preferred to keep them under continuous artillery and rifle fire as they burned and burrowed their way closer to the legations. Against the wall the Chinese used several artillery pieces mounted near the Chien Men gate and built a series of barricades that put the attackers even closer to the Marine position. Moving to and from the wall was especially dangerous for the Marines and their own Chinese barricade-builders, as they had to use a ramp exposed to fire. The first four Marines to die were all shot through the head by snipers. The American riflemen and the Colt machine gun also forced the Chinese to stay under cover. Nevertheless, the Marines were not happy about the exclusiveness of their exposed position and twice withdrew without verified orders. Although the American civilians praised its heroism, the other Europeans deemed the detachment too skittish, undisciplined, and given to drunkenness. It was said that only Captain Myers's presence kept them on the wall. Nonetheless, most of the defenders admitted that the Marines were expert marksmen in the antisniper war around the legations.[19]

The crisis for the Marines came during the first days of July. After attempting one charge on June 27, the Chinese built a series of barricades, which by July 1 closed to within a few feet of the Marines' redoubt on the wall. The Chinese were close enough to lob rocks at the defenders. They then bombarded both the Marines and the Germans to the east, and both detachments quickly abandoned the wall. American Minister Edwin H. Conger and First Secretary Herbert G. Squires (both former Army officers) ordered Myers to retake the position; their orders were supported by Sir Claude MacDonald, the British minister and defense force commander. Myers asked for reinforcements and received a detachment of Russians and Royal Marines. The wall was reoccupied without incident, but the Chinese still held their barricade and, in fact, extended it during the next two nights. The defenders again conferred and decided that the wall position would have to be widened and strengthened, especially as the Germans had not retaken their position. Early in the morning of July 3, Myers led a mixed force of Marines, Royal Marines, and Russians in a desperate attack on the Chinese positions. Taking the Chinese by surprise, the attackers killed thirty men and captured the offending stone tower and several other barricades, which they then held. At a cost of two more Marines killed and several wounded, including Myers, the wall position was once more secure.

After the July 3 attack the Marines held their position with decreasing difficulty until the city was relieved. With the Chien Men part of the defense saved, the Marines strengthened the eastern or Hata Men gate approaches. During this move Private Dan Daly covered the builders with rifle fire during one long night and won his first Medal of Honor by alone stopping several Chinese sorties along the wall.[20] By July 16 the Tartar Wall was no longer in danger. Although the Marines had to endure more shelling, sniping, fatigue, sickness, and unappetizing meals of horsemeat and dirty rice, they were not hard pressed by the Chinese, who were applying the greatest pressure upon the northern perimeter, defended by the Japanese and British. After July 3 only one other Marine died. As an Allied relief force approached the city, the Chinese Court and military high command fell into disarray, and the defenders enjoyed the privilege of one truce and of buying food from their attackers. The Marines were still guarding the wall with ease when the first British and American units arrived below the Tartar Wall on August 14. At a cost of seven dead and ten wounded, the Marine detachment had served creditably, if erratically, in one of the most dramatic and most publicized sieges of the colonial epoch.[21]

All the time they were besieged, the Europeans in Peking prayed for relief from the coast, for the massacres in the Sepoy Rebellion in India and in China in 1860 were still vivid in their memories. The help was coming, but the relief of Peking was complicated by inter-Allied bickering, a lack of troops, and the fighting ability of the Chinese regular army that opposed the relief force. The first Allied effort, which began before the legations were directly attacked, was a muddle. On June 10 a force of two thousand men (half British) entrained for Peking from Tientsin. Commanded by British Vice Admiral Edward Seymour and including 112 American sailors and Marines, this force was surrounded and badly mauled by the Chinese in a week of fighting along the railroad. With over 20 percent casualties, Seymour's column struggled back toward Tientsin and finally found safe haven in a Chinese arsenal eight miles north of the city on June 22. There it found sufficient arms, ammunition, and food to outlast its attackers, but it brought no relief for Peking. Tientsin, defended by some 2,400 men (mostly Russian), was able to feed and defend itself under intense artillery fire, but it could not lift its own siege or help the Seymour force. More Allied troops would be necessary.[22]

As the situation in northern China became more alarming, ministries all over Europe, in Tokyo, and in Washington scoured their armed forces for more troops. The American admiral off Taku reported that he thought an American brigade of five thousand might both assist the Allies and adequately protect the "Open Door" policy in the face of European and Japanese aspirations. The Navy Department offered the War Department a force of two thousand Marines, although upon close study it found that it could provide no more than eight hundred men. In fact, the Marine Corps initially provided only eight officers and 130 men. This battalion, commanded by Major L. W. T. Waller, landed at Tangku on June 20, only to find that the rest of the relief force had not yet appeared. Waller, however, vowed he would march to the aid of the legations, and the Navy found him a train. Joined by four hundred Russians, Waller's battalion (supported by one machine gun and an antique field gun) rode north to a point twelve miles short of Tientsin.

Although Waller now recognized the strength of the Chinese resistance, he bowed to the demands of a Russian colonel that the force continue the march to Tientsin on June 22. In an all-day battle in which the Marines lost thirteen men, Waller's battalion not only did not penetrate the Chinese defenses but had to make a desperate fighting retreat in order to save itself. The next day, however, another expedition of British and Russian troops joined the Marines, and this combined force fought its way into the foreign settlement of Tientsin on June 24. Two days later Seymour's force was rescued, and the combined expeditions returned to the Tientsin foreign settlement to consider the next move. Worn and depressed by his losses, Waller requested more men and more whisky for himself. He reported that his men had marched 97 miles in five days with virtually no rest and one meal a day. Although his battalion was reduced to eighty-nine effectives and looked like "Falstaff's army," it marched with "brave hearts and bright weapons." [23]

The Allied expedition at Tientsin swelled with the arrival of more troops, including more Marines from the Philippines and two battalions of the Army's 9th Infantry. The situation in Tientsin was still perilous, for the walled city was held by the Chinese army. Unless the entire city was taken, no relief expedition could safely advance toward Peking. Therefore, the Allied force planned a full-scale assault on the walled

Native City for July 13. The Marines, now organized as a regiment of 22 officers and 326 men, were assigned to an extemporaneous brigade that included a battalion of the Royal Welsh Fusiliers, a Royal Navy battalion, and the 9th Infantry. With the Marines on the left flank and the 9th Infantry on the right, this force was supposed to assault the city's south wall while the Japanese and Russians enveloped the city from the east.

The plans were not well conceived, but the Marines found their place on the extreme flank of the Allied attack in the predawn hours. With the support of Allied artillery, which included a Marine-served battery of landing guns, the infantry plunged across a mud wall about a mile from the city and struggled across a series of mud flats and ditches until they were stopped by a canal 200 yards from the wall. The attack was a debacle, although no one could fault the individual courage of the attackers. The protected Chinese defenders shot the assault force to pieces, for the Marines, the Royal Welsh Fusiliers, and the 9th Infantry were unable to advance. For the rest of the day the attackers and defenders exchanged rifle fire and shells to the Europeans' disadvantage. Although the Marines were able to prevent the Chinese from turning the Allied flank, they were incapable of doing more than holding their position until nightfall. In the meantime, however, the Japanese had breached the wall and secured a foothold in the city. By the next morning the Boxers and the Chinese army had retreated, leaving the city to looters, foreign and domestic. The Marines did a bit of souvenir hunting themselves, although their officers kept them under fair discipline and turned over most of the booty to Navy authorities for safekeeping. As the city of Tientsin burned, the Allies fiddled with plans to continue the march on Peking.[24]

After much wrangling about rank, the order of march, and the need for more troops, the International Relief Expedition left for Peking on August 4 and relieved the legations nine days later. Commanded by Major General Adna R. Chaffee, the American contingent included two infantry regiments, a cavalry regiment, a field artillery battery, and a regiment of Marines numbering 29 officers and 482 men. For the Marines, as for the other Americans, the march was a nightmare of heat, bad water, low rations, and little fighting. In fact, the Marine regiment wasted away until it was an under-strength battalion, for nearly half the original force remained behind as guards or as casualties from heat and illness. Of those Marines who marched on, one-third fell out from heat prostration, a rate greater than the infantry regiments' and much greater than that of the other nations' forces.

Chinese resistance to the march was not great, and the Marines saw even less fighting than other units. At the battle of Yang-Tsun (August 6) the Marines served as supports to the Army's field artillery battery and lost one man wounded. Moving into line, however, the Marines had to struggle through several cornfields and lost 40 percent of one battalion to heat exhaustion. For the rest of the march the Marines guarded the wagon train and served with the rear guard.[25]

When the column reached Peking, the Marine regiment was reduced to 24 officers and 267 men and played no special role in the relief of the legations. As the Boxers faded away, the Chinese army retreated, and the Manchu Court fled, the Allies battered their way into the devastated city without much plan. The Marines marched in with the Army field artillery and on the next day (August 15) supported the infantry attack upon the Imperial City with long-range rifle fire from the Tartar Wall. The Marines played a restrained role (as did all the American troops) in the subsequent looting of the Imperial City, and then assumed provost duties in the American-occupied portions of Peking. As the war petered out and the diplomats began to negotiate the terms of the Chinese defeat, the Marines patrolled Peking until their withdrawal to the Philippines in late September 1900.

The China adventure, however, had been a superb opportunity to polish the Marine Corps's image as a combat-ready infantry force for colonial warfare. Myers's detachment had been available to guard the legations in their hour of crisis, and the Marine battalions from the Philippines had been available at a time when Army troops were committed to the pacification of the Philippines or had to be sent from the United States. In terms of military performance, the Marines (like the other American troops) were probably less effective than the British and Japanese but more effective than the other Europeans. The officers of the International Relief Force thought the Americans were conspicuous for their careless dress, casual discipline, and lack of skill in small-unit tactics. As one Japanese officer observed, the Americans individually were probably the best fighters in the entire force, but the worst when not on the firing line. Essentially, the Marine regiment that participated in the relief of Peking was too small to have made any difference in a force that numbered more than eighteen thousand. The same might be said for Myers's detachment, which made up only 15 percent of the legation defense force, but for the fact that its defense of the Tartar Wall was crucial to the defense of the legations.

The point was that the Marines had been *there*. They had done *something*. Waller, the youthful Smedley Butler, and the urbane John T. Myers had shown heroism and had been wounded before the eyes of all the civilized world. Forgotten Marine enlisted men had fought, died, endured, and shared the conquest of an enemy despised throughout the West. Even if the Marine Corps could not claim that its men were superior soldiers to the Allied regiments or even to the men of the Army's infantry regiments, it could congratulate itself that once again it had turned an opportunity for useful service to its advantage. It eventually placed 1,200 Marines in China, and the part of this force that actually faced the Chinese had defeated the Asian "hordes." [26] The 9th Infantry initially assumed the protection of the legation after the uprising, but a Marine detachment eventually replaced the soldiers as the security force for the Americans in Peking. For the next forty years the Marine Corps and service in exotic China were to be synonymous in the public mind. The fifty-five days at Peking and the adventure of the International Relief Force became another great epic for the new colonial infantry.

3

For all the drama of the Boxer Uprising and the subsequent diplomatic efforts to prevent the partition of China, the focus of United States intervention remained the Caribbean for thirty years after the War with Spain. Serving as the instruments of American foreign policy in the Caribbean was not a new experience for the Navy and Marine Corps; they had protected American merchantmen and business in the area for one hundred years. In the early years of the twentieth century, however, there were forces at work that changed military intervention. From small-scale, short-term landings for such limited goals as protecting property, military occupations became much longer-lasting affairs for more ambitious political goals, like the support of an incumbent government against insurgents.

The purposes of military intervention were nearly as numerous as the Caribbean republics. One justification, stated in 1904 as the Roosevelt Corollary to the Monroe Doctrine, was that the United States had the responsibility to force Latin governments to protect foreign lives and pay foreign debts, thereby preventing intervention by the European powers. Another purpose of intervention was to separate the parties in a civil war in order to save native and foreign lives and property, which might contribute to the Latins' chances for economic development and democratic political growth. This policy, for example, was expressed in the Platt Amendment (1902), which gave the United States the right to intervene in Cuba. There were also strong reasons for military intervention that had little to do with the internal affairs of the Caribbean republics. The most compelling was the need to protect trade routes across the Isthmus of Panama and, eventually, the canal built through the isthmus. Linked to the trade patterns was the American concern for establishing naval bases and preventing the creation of bases for the use of European navies. Lastly, there were the impulses of three Presidents, the State Department, and the commanders of the armed forces. They were convinced that they had a duty to be active and influential in a part of the world they regarded as an American pond and military playground. Theirs was neither a conspiratorial nor a minority position, for public opinion was equally interventionist.[27]

The Marine Corps was not eager to assume the mission of colonial infantry in the Caribbean, but it found that it could not avoid the duty. In a sense it was the cutting edge of the nation's most interventionist institutions, the State Department and the Navy Department. Even after the Philippine Insurrection and the Boxer Uprising, the Commandant's policy was that the Marine Corps existed primarily to provide ships guards and naval base security forces. Heywood was not loath to capitalize on the Corps's Asian adventures, but he was most concerned about the traditional problems of recruiting and housekeeping. Although he did not undervalue tactical training for expeditionary duty, Heywood found it difficult to find the men necessary to fill his small School of Application, let alone form a permanent expeditionary battalion as ordered in 1902 by the Navy Department. The difficulty was that the Marine ships guards were the first troops ashore in the Caribbean. From a managerial standpoint, it was then far easier to reinforce them with other Marines than to send Army troops. In any event, after the Philippine Insurrection the War Department was not eager to participate in other military occupations. Thus, the Commandant accepted the reality that his Corps would provide expeditionary forces, even though the Navy Department expected them to be trained and equipped either to defend advanced naval bases or to serve as colonial infantry. As the Marine Corps regrouped after the Boxer Uprising, it began to conduct more battalion-size maneuvers and to improve its ability to serve ashore in larger numbers and for longer periods of time.[28]

The first test of the new Marine Corps expeditionary battalions came in Panama. This province of Colombia was not a new locale for landings, for ships guards had often gone ashore at Colon and Panama City to protect lives and property and to guard the American-owned railway that linked the cities. When a civil war in Colombia spread to the isthmus in 1901 and 1902, ships guards again landed to perform these duties. In the meantime American naval officers negotiated with both warring factions and produced a temporary disengagement. When this arrangement broke down in 1902, the landing parties returned, this time reinforced by a Marine battalion from the United States. In both cases the American forces were ashore only several weeks. Their presence curbed the fighting and resultant damage but did not prevent the Colombian government from restoring its control over Panama. For the Marine Corps the intervention was much like the one in 1885. It had formed its battalion by drawing men from East Coast barracks and had sent them south in four days by Navy transport; an additional battalion was scraped up from twelve separate posts and placed in readiness at Norfolk but did not deploy. Both forces together numbered about five hundred officers and men.[29]

In the meantime, the American government had been negotiating intensely for conditions suitable to allow it to build an isthmian canal. First it secured from Great Britain the sole right to build, defend, and control the canal. The Roosevelt administration then decided that it preferred the Panamanian route to one in Nicaragua. In negotiations with the Colombian government the administration agreed to pay for canal rights and to assume the holdings and debts of the French company that had started a canal and then had gone bankrupt. After delicate negotiations, the Hay–Herran Treaty was signed in January 1903, but in the meantime the Colombian legislature attempted to increase its demands for money. An impasse developed, and Colombia refused to ratify the treaty. This sudden collapse of the canal negotiations outraged the Roosevelt administration, the agents of the French canal company, and the Panamanians, who anticipated enormous economic benefits from the canal. Representatives of the latter two groups in 1903 visited Washington and properly divined that another insurrection might result in American intervention, this time not to the benefit of the Colombian government.[30]

In the autumn of 1903 the Panamanian impasse broke when officials of the Panama Railroad refused to carry Colombian reinforcements across the isthmus. Encouraged by what they interpreted as American approval, a rebel cabal and mutinous Colombian troops seized Panama City and declared Panama independent. The next day, November 4, the landing party of the *Nashville* went ashore to perform its traditional lives-and-property mission. This intervention, however, was to be quite different, for the next day the transport *Dixie* dropped anchor off Colon (still in Colombian hands) with an embarked Marine battalion commanded by Major John A. Lejeune. This battalion, originally scheduled to go to the Caribbean to participate in fleet maneuvers off Puerto Rico, had sailed for Panama a week before the insurrection actually started. Someone in Washington (perhaps Roosevelt himself) had decided that the Marines would have an important mission on the isthmus.

On November 6 the United States recognized the Panamanian government and negotiated a new canal treaty on far more favorable terms than the earlier Hay–Herran Treaty. With the Navy controlling both Panama City and Colon, the Colombians capitulated. The Navy Department then ordered Lejeune to land his Marines to protect the new country against Colombian troops. Lejeune recognized the implication of his orders and the supplies he received to build a camp near Colon: There would be no withdrawal even if there were no fighting. But, as Lejeune wrote his sister, "there is no telling what will happen next with such a strenuous President in the chair. It keeps the Marine Corps busy at any rate and I hope it will result in giving us another increase so I can get my next promotion quickly." [31]

As the United States established control over its new Canal Zone and defended Panama from Colombia, Lejeune's battalion and ships guards deployed throughout Panama. They were joined by three other Marine battalions by January 3, 1904, and the Panama Marine force became a two-regiment brigade personally commanded by Commandant George F. Elliott. The Marines then reconnoitered Panama and set up a permanent barracks near Panama City. Although the brigade was reduced in February, one battalion remained behind and garrisoned the Canal Zone until 1914. As early as the autumn of 1904 General Elliott knew that the Marine Corps would remain in Panama to ensure that neither the Panamanians nor the Colombians would interfere with the canal. The Marine battalion ensured that the Canal Zone, which Theodore Roosevelt boasted he "took," remained taken.[32]

Hardly had the Canal Zone been secured when Roosevelt committed Marine Corps expeditionary forces to a two-and-a-half-year military occupation of Cuba. As Major Lejeune guessed, the "strenuous" President would keep not only the Marine Corps but the Navy and Army as well busy in Cuba in 1906. The cause of the intervention was a civil war between the government of Tomás Estrada Palma and the Liberal Party. Both sides maneuvered to attract American intervention under the Platt Amendment. The Cuban government wanted American troops to crush the rebels, while the rebels asked that the United States stop the war, take over the government, and hold new elections. As a device to hurry the Americans along, the rebels threatened the destruction of the sugar plantations, mines, and railroads belonging to American, British, and Spanish owners. Roosevelt, however, was not eager to intervene, for the War Department General Staff advised him that a pacification campaign against the rebels might produce a repetition of the Philippine Insurrection without saving the foreign property anyway. On the other hand, intervention to stop the war on the rebels' terms meant helping overthrow a constitutional government. In a quandary, Roosevelt sent a peace mission to Havana to negotiate with both sides. The Palma government, however, foiled Roosevelt's emissaries by resigning and turning the government over to them on September 28, 1906.[33]

As Roosevelt and the State Department groped for a way to keep Estrada Palma in office without fighting for him, the President ordered the Navy to rush part of the fleet to Cuban waters. Roosevelt wanted an impressive display of force without being clear as to what it might accomplish. The American legation in Havana, however, kept warning that the rebels would soon seize Havana and the city would dissolve into anarchy. Roosevelt reluctantly reacted: "We should have a large force of Marines in Havana at the earliest moment on any ship able to carry them. . . . We will send ships and Marines as soon as possible for the protection of American life and property." [34] One battalion aboard the transport *Dixie* was already on hand, cruising off Hispaniola. This unit reinforced the ships guards guarding plantations around Cienfuegos. The Havana force arrived between September 21 and October 1; it included ten warships with 2,866 Marines aboard. Although there was considerable confusion among the Americans as to what the force should do and when it should land, the head of the peace mission, Secretary of War William H. Taft, after he assumed control of the island, ordered it to disarm all the combatants. Since the Liberals had already promised not to fight, the task was peaceful.[35]

Until the end of the occupation in 1909, Marines served as part of the Army of Cuban Pacification, the Army's five-thousand-man expeditionary force. In the early stages of the occupation the Marines alone supervised disarming the Cubans and curbed pillaging by the dissolving armies. The experience was exhilarating for at least one lieutenant, who wrote his father:

> The whole thing is exactly like Richard Harding Davises [*sic*] description of a revolution. We have the dirty rabble of Negroes armed with every type of antiquated weapon (a general for about 8 men) the palms and other tropical vegetation, the queer houses and of course the palace . . . . You needn't worry . . . the people are harmless . . . our detachment could clear the island of them in a jiffy." [36]

As the Cubans disarmed, the Marine expeditionary brigade, commanded by the ubiquitous Colonel Waller, deployed. One regiment remained near Havana to welcome the Army, while the other occupied the towns of western and central Cuba. In November two-thirds of the brigade returned to its ships or home posts. For those Marines who stayed the occupation was routine. The elections that Roosevelt ordered in 1908 were held without incident, although the American program of institutional reform did not make much progress. For the Marines it was enough that the Corps had responded rapidly in 1906 (that is, more quickly than the Army) and had been praised in the American press for its readiness.[37]

The Marine Corps returned twice more to Cuba in succeeding years, for the prospect of American intervention had become an important factor in Cuban domestic politics. In 1912 a disgruntled group of black political leaders aroused the black peasants of Oriente province in rebellion; like the Liberals they threatened to burn foreign property if the United States did not intervene. Again Navy warships hovered about Cuban ports. This time, however, the State Department had no intention of allowing the Cuban government to fall. Although he demanded that the Cubans protect American lives and property, President William H. Taft provided another Marine expeditionary brigade as well as ships guards for the same purpose. Entering Cuba through the new naval base at Guantanamo Bay, the expeditionary brigade relieved Cuban army detachments guarding American-owned mines and plantations. This relief allowed the Cuban army to increase its field forces, which then crushed the revolt. Similarly, another expeditionary brigade occupied much of eastern Cuba in 1917, when the Liberals started a civil war against an incumbent Conservative regime. Again, the American response was to support the government by sending Marines to relieve Cuban troops guarding foreign property, which included the Cuban transportation system, and to protect the sugar crop. Although the brigade was reduced to a single small regiment in 1919, at least one battalion remained in western Cuba until 1922. As in the interventions of 1906 and 1912, the Marines saw no significant combat and used most of their time for sentry duty and field training, which increased their efficiency and presumably cowed any ambitious rebels.[38]

While the Marines were peacefully patrolling Cuba in 1906–1909 and 1912, the United States government was having increasing difficulty with the Republic of Nicaragua. The difficulties arose from long-standing tension between the United States and the dictatorship of José Santos Zelaya. The State Department believed that Zelaya fomented revolts throughout Central America, endangered American business ventures on Nicaragua's Caribbean coast through government monopolies, and perpetuated his regime through police-state methods. In all his acts Zelaya expressed open contempt for the United States and for his political rivals. In 1909 one of his own governors conspired with an exiled political faction of the Liberal party and started a rebellion in the Caribbean city of Bluefields, a bastion of foreign-owned businesses. When Zelaya executed two Americans serving with the rebels, the State Department added another grievance to its list.

Under pressure from the United States, Zelaya resigned in December 1909 but turned the government over to a colleague, who continued to fight the rebels. In fact, the insurgents did not make much headway until American warships and the Marine battalion from Panama, commanded by Major Smedley D. Butler, occupied Bluefields in May 1910. Although American warships had protected lives and property since February, this military concentration had wider political implications, for it prevented the *zelayista* army and navy from crushing the remnants of the rebel force. Correctly interpreting the American intervention as open sympathy with the rebels, other dissidents took up arms throughout Nicaragua and drove the *zelayistas* from the field in August.[39]

For the next two years the State Department did what it could to shore up a stable government in Nicaragua, working with American banks to provide new loans and with non-*zelayista* politicians to provide some sort of peaceful political process. In 1911 a new Conservative president, Adolfo Díaz, took office with the Department's blessing. Díaz, however, could not control his own army or several political factions that included both Liberals and Conservatives. Díaz was especially vulnerable to charges that he was an American puppet, because he accepted State Department proposals for loans, a customs-collectorship, claims settlements, and new laws that benefited foreign businesses. Díaz soon found himself seriously challenged by one faction led by Luis Mena, commanding general of the Nicaraguan army, and another under Emiliano Chamorro, the most influential Conservative in the country. Mena and Chamorro were rivals as well, and each feared that the other would depose Díaz first.

In 1912 General Mena struck first, and Nicaragua again split into warring factions. Although Mena's coup in Managua in July was crushed by a force led by Chamorro, whom Díaz named as the new commander-in-chief of the army, the Mena faction still controlled part of the army and rallied dissident Liberals to its ranks. Immediately Americans and other foreigners cried for protection. Advancing from their nearby base at Granada, the rebels attacked Managua with artillery but were driven off. Nevertheless, they surrounded the capital and cut the railroad that ran from Managua through Leon to Corinto on the Pacific coast. The city of Leon became the stronghold of the most militant Liberal faction, led by Benjamin Zeledón. The State Department's assessment was that only open American military intervention could save Díaz and restore American influence over Nicaraguan politics.

The forces for intervention were already at hand. On August 14 Butler's battalion from Panama arrived in Corinto and landed to save lives and property. The next day Butler took most of his force of 354 officers and men by train to Managua to reinforce the sailors guarding the legation. The analogy to the relief of Peking in the Boxer Uprising was as strongly imprinted in Butler's mind as it was in those at the State Department. Although his force reached Managua without incident, Butler found he could not restore communications with Corinto easily, for the rebels were preventing smaller detachments from using the railroad. Anxious to establish contact with the Navy commander in Corinto, Butler lost one train to the rebels and then had to bluff his way with 190 men through a hostile mob at Leon before reaching Corinto. A return trip to Managua was unopposed except for damage to the right-of-way.[40]

Help arrived for Butler's battalion on September 4, when two more Marine battalions from the United States arrived and also took trains to Managua. Organized into a provisional regiment commanded by Colonel Joseph H. Pendleton, the Marine expeditionary force gave the Americans sufficient forces to end the civil war. The Mena forces were already disintegrating from a lack of leadership and a shortage of converts and arms. The Liberals, however, were still armed and unrepentant in Masaya and Granada, east of the capital. Pendleton ordered Butler's battalion to clear the railway as the first step in dispersing the rebels in Masaya and Granada. Butler and Pendleton tried to persuade the rebels to disperse, and Zeledón agreed to let Butler's train pass, but some of his troops attacked the Marines as the train crept slowly through Masaya. In a running battle with rooftop snipers, the Marines cleared Masaya at a cost of five wounded and three missing. Butler was incensed at the rebels' treachery. His force roared on to Granada and threatened to annihilate Mena's army. Mena promptly surrendered and went into exile. His army scattered.

The remaining threat was Zeledón's fortified camp atop Coyotepe Hill near Masaya, which was already surrounded by government troops. The Nicaraguans could shell the camp, assisted by Marine artillery, but could not carry it by assault. Tiring of the operation, Pendleton and Butler gave Zeledón one last ultimatum, which he refused. A joint Marine–Navy assault force of three battalions, supported by artillery and machine guns, then stormed the position early on October 4. The rebels were completely routed in a forty-minute battle, losing some sixty dead. The survivors fled. Another Marine battalion occupied Leon, which was in anarchy, at a cost of six casualties, while killing some fifty rebels who refused to surrender. With the exception of some skirmishing with Marines who occupied several other northern towns, the rebels were successfully crushed.[41] In following weeks most of the Marine regiment withdrew, but the State Department had one company kept at Managua as a legation guard and a thinly veiled threat to other insurgents. President Díaz was shortly reelected to another term, and the State Department went on with its negotiations about loans and trade agreements. The intervention, however, had made its point: The Marine Corps had for the first time fought and died to keep a pro-American government in power in Central America.

The next intervention the Marine Corps participated in—the landing in Veracruz, Mexico, in April 1914—was designed to unseat an incumbent government, not protect it. This episode stemmed from years of tangled relations between the United States and Mexico, which had been deep in a revolutionary war since 1910. The administration of Woodrow Wilson, which took office in early 1913, faced a difficult situation when the first revolutionary president, Francisco I. Madero, was murdered by a group of conspirators led by General Victoriano Huerta. Idealist and missionary democrat, Wilson took the coup personally and convinced himself that the cause of humanity and constitutionalism demanded that he unseat Huerta. He refused to recognize the Huerta government and then lifted an embargo on arms, which assisted the Constitutionalist rebel forces. Huerta, however, refused to capitulate, although he ordered his army to protect American lives and property, especially in the oil-rich, foreign-dominated Gulf port of Tampico. American and European vessels also kept watch. Part of the force that the Navy kept near Mexico was a Marine expeditionary brigade either stationed in camps in Cuba, in Puerto Rico, or along the Gulf Coast or deployed on transports.[42]

Distressed that Huerta showed no intention of resigning, Wilson decided to take more open action to topple the Mexican government in the early months of 1914. His opportunity came when a small party of American sailors was accidentally detained in Tampico; this and earlier incidents the President chose to interpret as an affront to American honor. The admiral in Tampico was of a like mind and demanded a full apology and gunfire salute to an American flag. Both the local commander and Huerta balked at such a display over such a trivial incident. At Wilson's direction, however, the demands stood, and the Navy began to deploy its warships and Marine battalions along the west and east coasts of Mexico. It appeared that the anticipated intervention would occur at Tampico, not only the scene of the incident but a port crowded with foreign residents and property. But the Wilson administration disavowed the mission of interposition and stressed that it was interested in defending such lofty concepts as honor, democracy, peace, and justice. The War Department, in the meantime, alerted an expeditionary division then stationed near Galveston, Texas, and dusted off its war plans for an overland invasion of Mexico from Veracruz to Mexico City. Secretary of War Lindley Garrison and Chief of Staff Leonard Wood drew the President's attention to Veracruz rather than Tampico as the proper site for major military action against Mexico.[43]

As the Navy prepared for possible action at Tampico with an embarked regiment of Marines commanded by Colonel John A. Lejeune, Wilson's attention shifted to Veracruz. On April 18 the consul there reported that a German freighter would shortly arrive with munitions for Huerta's army. Wilson seized upon this news and manufactured another crisis with which to rationalize his crusade against Huerta. In three days of soul-searching the President convinced himself, his Cabinet, and much of Congress that the time for intervention had arrived, even if it meant war. The President, however, believed that the Mexicans would not defend Veracruz because the temporary occupation would so obviously be to Mexico's benefit.

On April 20 the Navy Department sent a series of messages to the scattered units of the Atlantic Fleet: The bulk of the battle fleet should go to Veracruz instead of Tampico; the Tampico force should steam for Veracruz, and the Veracruz force of Rear Admiral Frank F. Fletcher should the next day send its landing parties to occupy the port and customs house and stop the German arms shipment. To perform his unexpected mission Fletcher had two seamen's battalions from his battleships, his Marine ships guards, and a Marine battalion embarked on the transport *Prairie*. The composite expeditionary force of six hundred Marines was commanded by Lieutenant Colonel Wendell C. Neville, one of the Corps's most competent officers.

Like President Wilson, the Marines and sailors of Fletcher's force were confident that the landing would not be opposed and, even if it were, that they would have little trouble with the contemptible Mexicans. Admiral Fletcher encouraged this impression by suggesting to the local Mexican general that his two infantry regiments depart quickly. Before he received instructions from Mexico City not to defend the city, however, General Octavo Maass armed the local militia, released and armed more than a hundred convicts, and sent small parties of his soldiers toward the waterfront with rifles and machine guns. These defenders did not attempt to stop the initial landing, but as the Marines and sailors deployed from their launches and fanned out toward their objectives, the Mexicans opened fire.

The street fighting started around noon and went on into the night as the Americans fought back. For the Marine battalion, which had been assigned to occupy the wharves, warehouses, power station, office buildings, and railroad terminal on the north edge of the port area, the action was desultory. Unlike the seamen's battalions, the Marines quickly occupied nearby rooftops and went into action against the snipers. Other groups cleared the area house by house, block by block, while machine gun crews swept the streets of the Mexican irregulars. By nightfall the Marines were at the edge of the city but had to withdraw when they learned that the seamen's battalions had been pinned down along the streets to the south.[44]

Reinforced by an additional battalion from Lejeune's regiment and the ships guards of the Atlantic Fleet, the Marine force continued the battle the next day alongside the seamen's brigade, also reinforced. For the Marines the fighting was slow but routine against the amateurish Mexicans. One naval regiment, however, walked into an ambush near the Mexican naval academy, and the Navy's casualties soared to thirteen killed. The weight of the American landing force, supported by naval gunfire, was too much for the Mexicans, and resistance crumbled to occasional sniping by the end of April 22. For the next several days the Marines cleared buildings, patrolled the streets, and outposted the city limits. Within four days the Marine landing force had become a brigade of 2,469 officers and men. (The Navy force was 200 officers and 3,760 sailors.) The Marine casualties had been light—four dead and thirteen wounded—and Colonel Neville did not pretend that the Mexicans had put up much resistance.[45]

Although the Marine ships guards returned quickly to their ships, the Marine Corps (at Army request) stationed a brigade in Veracruz for the next eight months while the Wilson administration negotiated with Mexico. The brigade, commanded first by John A. Lejeune and then by L. W. T. Waller, trained and manned the city's outpost line, leaving the problems of military government to their Army commander, Brigadier General Frederick Funston. There was much talk of continuing the invasion, but the officers soon realized that Wilson had lost his taste for military intervention.[46] In any event, the Veracruz landing had helped accomplish Wilson's goal, for Huerta resigned and fled in July 1914. For the Marine Corps, however, the entire episode was quite satisfactory. Marine expeditionary forces had arrived much more quickly than the Army's brigade from Texas and had fought ashore with more skill and fewer casualties than the seamen's regiments of the Atlantic Fleet. Even though there were far more sailors ashore at Veracruz by the second day's fighting, the American press gave the impression that only the Marines had landed and "had the situation well in hand." It further solidified the impression in Washington and in the public mind that a Marine expeditionary force was an excellent antidote for Latin hostility.

4

By 1914 the Marine Corps had already been reshaped by its role as colonial infantry, and its image within the American military establishment had altered. The changes were substantial and persistent until the Corps's colonial mission began to fade in 1934. For the officer corps, colonial service ended the sharp division of function between field grade and company grade officers. As the Corps fielded units of battalion, regiment, and brigade strength, field grade officers could no longer relax in barracks sinecures and avoid field duty; in 1907, for example, 15 of 32 field grade line officers were on sea or foreign duty, along with 156 of 219 captains and lieutenants.[47] The demands of sea and foreign duty, however, prevented the Marine Corps from filling its quotas to Navy and Army schools, a condition that probably retarded the development of technological and managerial skills within the officer corps and perpetuated Marine Corps anti-intellectualism at a time when the other services were emphasizing formal midcareer training.[48] On the other hand, for the first time the names of Marine Corps officers became household words, as a generation of newspaper readers came to know L. W. T. Waller, John T. Myers, John A. Lejeune, and Smedley D. Butler.

Expeditionary duty and the increased strength of the Marine Corps for such duty also affected the organization of the Headquarters staff. The first development was an increase in the offices of the Adjutant and Inspector, the Quartermaster, and the Paymaster by eleven billets in 1903. In 1908 staff officers were increasingly assigned from Washington to such distant posts as San Francisco and Manila. More important developments lay ahead. In 1911 the office of assistant to the Commandant was created to give Headquarters a field grade line officer to manage such matters as training, equipping, and planning for expeditionary duty. With Colonel Eli K. Cole and Colonel John A. Lejeune filling this billet, line officers had powerful voices beside the Commandant. This influence on Headquarters policy-making was widened in 1913 when, in response to an economy drive by the Taft administration, the Marine Corps accepted the principle of interchangeability of assignment between the line and the office of the Adjutant and Inspector.

Advocates of further change argued that limiting staff assignments would provide fresh expertise from the field at Headquarters, an argument accepted in the Army twelve years before. In legislation in 1916 all the staff departments were opened for line officers on limited four-year tours. The gap between the perspectives of the staff and the concerns of the line began to close.[49]

Foreign service and expeditionary duty also influenced enlisted recruiting and retention. During the 1907–1911 period the Marine Corps reoriented its recruiting poster appeals to take advantage of its recent service abroad by embellishing the traditional appeals of pay, job security, good food and clothes, and travel with the fleet. The new posters urged men to become Marines and serve from "The Spanish Main to the Orient." The posters often showed photographs of Peking. But being a Marine now meant being a warrior. A new series of posters challenged potential recruits: "If You Want to Fight! Join the Marines." The posters featured khaki-clad infantry wading ashore or charging through tropical jungles. Other advertisements boasted that the Marines were now "The First to Fight." [50]

The new recruiting appeals must have had some impact, for despite the threefold increase after 1898 the Corps was filling its ranks to near-capacity after 1903. Recruiters turned away many applicants, and Headquarters even allowed enlisted men to purchase their release after one year's honorable service. Presumably, others waited to take their place. By 1908 the editor of the authoritative *Army and Navy Journal* thought that the Marines were the best dressed and best equipped of the American armed forces, which he attributed to their cosmopolitan service, probably their association with British troops in China. The paper also praised the Marine Corps in 1907 for having the highest reenlistment rate in the armed forces—35 percent.[51] Recruiting went so well that the Commandant cracked down on the enlisting of immigrants. He warned one recruiter in Chicago to stop putting advertisements in Polish-language newspapers—"it is not desired to enlist Poles in the Marine Corps as long as Americans are available." [52] During the first six months of 1908 a recruiting officer in Pittsburgh accepted only nine men in one group of five hundred and twenty-eight in another group of four hundred. Even when there was not substantial national unemployment, the Marine Corps found more than a few good men.

The recruiting campaign fostered a supporting effort at public relations when recruiters in Buffalo and Chicago decided to regale reporters with sea stories or to write articles on the Corps for the urban dailies. The earliest stories stressed Marine Corps heroism and action in the war with Spain and in colonial service. In 1911 the Commandant established a recruiting publicity bureau in New York City; three years later this bureau was publishing *The Recruiters' Bulletin,* a magazine full of adventure stories designed to lure prospective recruits and entertain enlisted men. Run by a small staff of enlisted men, the recruiting publicity bureau turned out handouts on the Veracruz landing, published a pamphlet on the Marine Corps, and impressed the big dailies of New York and Washington with its skilled appeals on the Corps's behalf. One of the bureau's biggest accomplishments was a motion picture, "The Peacemakers: An Educational Pictorial Showing the United States Marines in Barracks, at Sea, and on the Field of Battle." The field footage showed Marines landing and fighting in the Caribbean.[53]

The increased emphasis on expeditionary duty was reflected in new policies and plans issued from the Commandant's office. One suggestion was that the Marine Corps own and man its own fleet of transports so that it would not have to depend on the Navy for shipping. The proposal was not as ambitious as it might sound, for the Army already had its own transports to take troops to the Canal Zone, Hawaii, and the Philippines. The principal development, however, was probably in the Marine Corps marksmanship program. As soon as the Army adopted the .30 caliber Springfield rifle Model 1903, the Marine Corps clamored for funds to outfit itself with the new rifle and to stockpile a million rounds of ammunition. Headquarters persuaded the Navy Department to grant Marines marksmanship badges and extra pay for superior shooting and adopted the more rigorous Army course, which emphasized long-distance shooting. In national matches Marine team shooters were increasingly successful. In 1909 the *Army and Navy Journal* noted that the ratio of skilled marksmen in the Marine Corps made it the best unit of shooters in the world.[54]

Even in song and poetry the American Marine found redefinition as the jack-of-all-trades in America's global policing. One anonymous author praised the Marine as the fearless protector of consuls, missionaries, and the flag:

> With a hitch to his trouserloons, and a seaman roll in his gait,
> His handiest tool a Lee straight-pull; his home of armor plate
> Cavalry, guns and foot, he one and all combines
> As he charges the foe ashore or fights the water mines.
> No gay parade for him, his world a watery sheen,
> A rootin', tootin',
> Cuttin', shootin',
> Uncle Sam Marine.[55]

During the struggle with Roosevelt and the Navy over the removal of ships guards in 1908–1909, another author responded to the charge that shipboard Marines were "always in the way." After a long recital of the Corps's epic service since 1899, the poem ended:

> We've answered the call to Quarters,
> And helped make the big guns roar
> We've hit the pike on a drivin' hike
> With the doughboys on shore,
> And takin' our licks with the jackies [Royal Navy]
> Or the boys of the U.S.A.
> There's been many a time in a far-off clime
> When we wasn't much in the way.[56]

America's popular magazines echoed the barracks doggerel. The Marine was the nation's expert in tropical service and was capable of landing without confusion to support American diplomacy—even unto death. Springfield rifle in hand, globe-and-anchor fixed at the front of his peaked campaign hat, sleeves rolled above tanned arms, and khaki uniform bleached and stained by sweat and the tropic sun, "Uncle Sam Marine" in 1914 awaited new challenges. He had no intention of ever being "in the way" again.[57]

7. Hispaniola
1915—1934

The island of Hispaniola climbs from the Caribbean, its green-purple mountains ringed with brown coastal plains and surf. The island is 400 miles long and 170 miles wide at its widest part; its area is 28,000 square miles. When the Marine Corps became acquainted with Hispaniola in the early part of the twentieth century, the island was divided into two countries, Haiti and the Dominican Republic. Claiming the western third of the island, Haiti was a nation of some 2 million mulattoes and blacks descended from the plantation slaves who had thrown off French colonial rule early in the nineteenth century. Haitian society was divided into two very distinct groups. The mulatto *élite*, no more than 5 percent of the population, preserved French society in the capital, Port-au-Prince, and the few large towns. Raised in the Catholic Church and the tradition of Parisian polite society, the *élite* was an overeducated, underemployed minority that depended economically on business, professional work, and—primarily—officeholding in the national government. For the vast majority of Haitians, life was not far removed from slavery. Illiterate, plagued by malnutrition and infectious diseases, and living in a world dominated by the malevolent spirits of *vodun* (voodoo), the Haitian peasantry scratched out an existence on mountain farms or in unskilled urban jobs. Many, especially in the northeastern mountains, turned to banditry. Called *cacos* after a Haitian bird of prey, the mountain bandits became a political force as mercenaries to any Haitian politician who aspired to the presidency. Theo-

178

retically a constitutional republic, Haiti vacillated between dictatorship and anarchy.

Although its population was smaller and its land richer, the Dominican Republic was, by American standards, no less confused. Occupying two-thirds of Hispaniola, the Dominicans were the descendants of Spanish colonists and their slaves. The population of more than a million included an elite of white Dominicans and a mulatto majority of urban workers and peasant farmers. Economically, the majority of the people lived on subsistence farms, but the Dominicans exported enough sugar, coffee, and cacao to make the customs service attractive to office-seekers. Politically the Dominicans had had the worst of several possible worlds. They had been alternately occupied and governed by the Spanish, the French, and the Haitians through the nineteenth century. At those times when the Dominican Republic was independent, it was ruled by *caudillos*, strongmen who depended on their personal armies.

Topographically, the western half of the Dominican Republic was mountainous and underpopulated. The political and economic life of the country centered on two other regions. The northern region ran from the ports of Monte Cristi and Puerto Plata through the Cibao Valley and its principal city of Santiago to Samana Bay in the northeast. The island's only sizable railroad ran from Puerto Plata to Samana Bay, a center of foreign investment in sugar with a large bay suitable for a naval base. The other populous region was the southeastern coastal area around the capital city of Santo Domingo. A coastal road linked the capital with the heavily populated farming provinces to the east, a territory traditionally plagued by banditry.

For all their differences, Haiti and the Dominican Republic shared important similarities. Both had a political tradition that dictated office-holding as a political right and an economic necessity for the political class (the *élite* and the *caudillos*); to support the habits acquired in this tradition, both governments had accumulated substantial foreign debts by the early part of the twentieth century. Between 1875 and 1910 Haiti had borrowed $24 million from French investors, and between 1912 and 1915 the government had floated three more loans for $2.9 million, had borrowed $1.7 million more from the foreign-controlled Bank of Haiti, and had defaulted on $1.1 million in salary payments. The Dominican situation was no better. The Dominican government had defaulted and refinanced with such dizzying romanticism and corruption that no one was sure just what it owed, but the sum was estimated at between $20 million and $32 million. Its creditors included an array of European banks and the American-owned San Domingo Improvement Company. As income leaked from the government's coffers to the

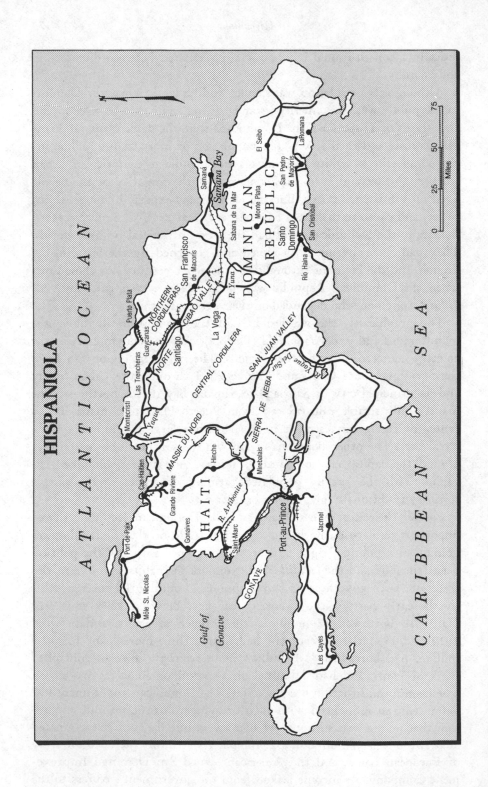

políticos, the Dominican government had difficulty making debt payments, a condition that made foreign intervention an increasing likelihood.

Another similarity was the Haitian and Dominican propensity to change governments by violence. Lacking a modern, dependable army or police force, the presidents of both governments were especially vulnerable to coups and civil wars. From 1908 until 1915 Haiti had seven presidents, none of whom served a full term and three of whom were killed by insurgents. The Dominican Republic experienced an equally rapid turnover of national leaders. The two most important *caudillos,* Horacio Vásquez and Juan Isidro Jiménez, either vied themselves for the presidency or sponsored supporters or weak third parties. A succession of Dominican presidents, penurious and harried, came and went in a whirl of coups and civil wars.[1]

American interest in Hispaniola dated back to the early nineteenth century, but the United States government took a more active interest in Haiti and the Dominican Republic after the War with Spain and the creation of the Canal Zone. The forces that shaped American policy were complex. Initially, the Roosevelt and Taft administrations were most concerned with the traditional tasks of protecting American lives and property, but as the State and Navy departments practiced gunboat diplomacy, they became increasingly concerned with strategic and economic concerns. Navy planners recognized the utility of naval bases at Mole St. Nicolas on Haiti's north coast and the Dominican Republic's Samana Bay. Naval forces operating from either could control the Windward and Mona Passages into the Caribbean Sea and access to the Panama Canal. The possibility that either France or Germany might attempt to establish bases was tied to the question of foreign loans. These European nations had already demonstrated that they might collect their debts with naval gunfire and might conceivably extend their influence into the internal management of weak Latin republics, so the American government might preempt European intervention with intervention of its own. Whether the policy was described as the Roosevelt Corollary to the Monroe Doctrine, "preventive intervention," or "dollar diplomacy," the purpose was the same. To deter European intervention in an American sphere of interest and to protect foreign investment in both the investors' and hosts' economic interest, the United States would protect Haiti and the Dominican Republic. This policy was applied to both countries between 1905 and 1913 as Navy warships and embarked Marines hovered offshore to protect foreigners and support American negotiators.

The policy was developed most completely first in the Dominican

Republic. At the request of a provisional president, the State Department between 1905 and 1907 worked out a set of agreements that gave the United States control of the Dominican customs service. Under American management the revenues would go to foreign bondholders and claimants and to the incumbent regime; to assist the Dominican government the State Department also helped negotiate a new $20 million loan in the United States. Although this agreement angered many Dominicans and failed to curb civil war, it pacified the foreign creditors and their governments. It also committed the United States to protecting Dominican sovereignty and made the United States in Dominican and European eyes the decisive actor in Dominican domestic politics.

The State Department took a similar approach in 1910 when the Haitian government began new loan negotiations with French and German agents. Although there were few American investments in Haiti, the State Department objected to a plan to reorganize the National Bank of Haiti and to finance a new foreign bond issue without American participation. After intrigue that involved the mulatto *élite*, European businessmen in Haiti, and a few American entrepreneurs, the State Department allowed American and European financiers to reorganize the national bank and the railways with increased American interest and further loans to the Haitian government. The American government, however, would not accept responsibility for another customs receivership, a proposal even more unattractive to the Haitian government. But the concept of American involvement in managing Haiti's finances was still alive in 1913.[2]

While the State Department was exploring the possibility of managing Haiti's finances, it was learning about the drawbacks of such responsibilities in the Dominican Republic. After the assassination of another president in late 1911, the Dominican *políticos* again went to war to decide upon a successor. Sporadic fighting dragged on into 1913, with no single faction able to consolidate its power. American naval officers and legation officials negotiated truces and urged compromise, while the State Department wondered whether it would have to defend the customs houses with Marines. The American role in dampening the rebellion consisted mostly in pouring money on the fires of insurgency; since the Dominican government could neither pay its bills nor borrow money without American approval, the State Department was able to influence the selection of a new provisional president and negotiate for greater control of Dominican fiscal policy. Early in 1913 the National City Bank of New York loaned the Dominican government $1.5 million dollars to pay its ragtag army and accommodate its opponents.

Into the diplomatic quagmire stepped President Woodrow Wilson. Convinced that American foreign policy was the instrument of greedy capitalists, Wilson promised that foreign-owned banks and railroads would no longer exploit either the State Department or Hispaniola. The United States would refuse to deal with governments that took power through violence or other unconstitutional means. Instead, it would negotiate the end of civil wars, the establishment of acceptable provisional governments, and free elections—under American supervision if necessary. The United States might also reorganize the island's armed forces in order to bolster the legitimate government against rebels. As the President told a visitor: "I am going to teach the South American Republics to elect good men!" [3] The substance of the "Wilson Plan" was communicated to the governments of Haiti and the Dominican Republic during 1913.[4]

The nations of Hispaniola ignored the sermon from Washington and continued to change governments with dispatch and bloodshed. In the Dominican Republic civil war simmered on until an American-supervised election produced a new president, the aging *caudillo* Juan Isidro Jiménez, in 1914. Jiménez immediately complained that the customs receivership was not providing him with enough money to buy off his enemies or to prevent his followers from joining a new coalition of oppositionists. Of particular concern was his Minister of War, Desiderio Arias, a popular *caudillo* from the northern Cibao region. Having played a prominent role in unseating one president in 1914, Arias was unhappy about the "Wilson Plan" and successfully organized opposition to increased American control of the Dominican treasury. The State Department itself was burdened with maladroit negotiators, but the basic problem was that the Dominican *politicos* would not surrender power to the *norteamericano* reformers, regardless of the treaty of 1907 or the "Wilson Plan."

The situation was no more promising in Haiti. From 1913 to 1915 the Haitians rotated presidents through civil war and conspiracy. Whoever was president now bore the additional burden of being tagged a tool of foreign imperialism, as the State Department continued to urge an American-managed financial protectorate. In 1914 and 1915 the State Department offered to protect incumbent presidents with Marines if they and the Haitian congress would accept a treaty like the one in effect with the Dominican Republic. Before the negotiations could progress, rebels led by General Vilbrun Guillaume Sam occupied Port-au-Prince with a *caco* army and sent the *élite* politicians scurrying. In the meantime, the State Department concluded that French and German financiers were subsidizing the rebels in order to curb American economic penetration; some Americans, like Secretary of State Robert Lansing, were convinced that the Europeans were seriously interested in a Mole St. Nicolas naval base. The Sam government, however, would not negotiate either the Mole St. Nicolas issue or the question of making the National Bank of Haiti a completely American-managed institution. The government would accept American troops on a temporary basis to restore order but would not accept long-term foreign intervention.[5]

1

The Navy Department, an active participant in the effort to pacify Hispaniola, had little inkling that its role would soon expand beyond providing landing parties to protect foreign lives and property or to bolster some administration the State Department thought worth saving. By 1913 American landing parties had been ashore thirteen times in Haiti alone. In 1914 Marine ships guards had landed three times, once to escort a National Bank gold shipment to a waiting gunboat. Twice between August 1914 and January 1915, Marine expeditionary regiments had sailed into Port-au-Prince harbor in response to State Department fears that a *caco* army was threatening the capital. Neither regiment landed, but their officers reconnoitered the city, knowing that their mission someday might be to occupy the capital.

The Navy plans, however, were confined to the occupation of Port-au-Prince, not a long-term, nationwide military occupation to enforce the "Wilson Plan." The State Department had started to think seriously about such action, but the Navy was not planning beyond stopping a *caco* bacchanalia. The Navy contingency plans assumed that landing parties, backed if necessary by Marine expeditionary battalions, would be adequate for Port-au-Prince and any other coastal town. The force would have to be large enough to protect *all* foreigners since the State Department did not want European forces ashore. Such forces had landed at Cap Haïtien in 1914, and the State Department wanted no recurrence of the temptation to intervene.[6]

In the spring of 1915 another uprising in Haiti gave President Wilson and the State Department a dramatic opportunity to put their reform plans into operation. Protesting that President Sam was about to sell the customs service to the United States, Ronsalvo Bobo raised a *caco* army along the northern border and took Cap Haïtien. A Marine guard landed on July 9 to guard foreign property, which was not harmed. The war simmered on until July 27, when a sudden coup in Port-au-Prince sent Sam and his henchmen running for sanctuary in the foreign legations. In the chaos the local military prison commander ordered all political prisoners executed; 167 members of the *élite* died in the eleventh-hour massacre. Outraged, the *élite* and a mob of urban workers stormed the French and Dominican legations and slaughtered Sam and the erring prison commander. Shredding Sam for a bloody torchlight parade, the Port-au-Prince mob made the Bobo rebels victors.

Learning of the rising, the State Department requested that the Navy protect all foreign lives and property. On July 28, 1915, the afternoon after Sam's death, Rear Admiral William B. Caperton landed a party from the battleship *Washington* to patrol the city. Believing that the intervention was temporary, the Port-au-Prince officials agreed to disarm the Haitian soldiers in the city, but the Americans were met with scattered shots. During the first night ashore two sailors were killed, probably shot accidentally by other members of the landing party.[7]

In reality, President Wilson worried about the wisdom and legality of extending the intervention to bring peace to Haiti. While the administration debated, Secretary of State Lansing asked the Navy to send sufficient troops to control Port-au-Prince and the surrounding countryside. One Marine company from Guantanamo Bay was joined by August 15 by the 1st Marine Brigade, composed of the 1st and 2d Marines Regiments, which had been organized in the United States. The brigade commander was that expeditionary veteran Colonel L. W. T. Waller, assisted by the irrepressible Major Smedley D. Butler.

In the meantime, the Wilson administration had decided to apply its reform program to Haiti, but not directly through an American military government. Instead, the Navy Department ordered Admiral Caperton to encourage the Haitian congress to elect a new president, preferably senate president Sudre Dartiguenave, who agreed to cooperate with the Americans. The chief obstacle to the plan was Ronsalvo Bobo and his *caco* force of perhaps 1,500 in the Port-au-Prince area. As the Haitian congress tried to avoid an election and persuade the Americans to leave, Marine patrols occupied key points around the city and disarmed the Haitian militia. During the sweeps two Haitians were killed, but there was no serious resistance to the occupation. With the Bobo forces neutralized and Caperton uncompromising, the Haitian congress elected Dartiguenave on August 12. The same day the American chargé d'affaires in Port-au-Prince presented the new president with a draft treaty that in effect made Haiti an American protectorate. The treaty provided for American control of Haiti's finances, the creation of an American-officered national constabulary, and the use of American engineers and public health officials to reform the public works and sanitation systems. The treaty also provided that Haiti would not sell any land to any other foreign power except the United States, but foreigners as individuals could buy Haitian land. More important, it provided for American intervention to preserve Haitian independence, to enforce the treaty's other provisions, and to maintain a Haitian government "adequate for the protection of life, property, and individual liberty." Designed to be in force ten years, with the possibility of a ten-year extension, the treaty was accepted by the Dartiguenave government on September 12 and later was ratified by the Haitian and American congresses. The great American reform of Haiti had officially begun.[8]

For the Marine expeditionary brigade, the first phase of the intervention had gone fairly smoothly. As Admiral Caperton and the State Department reconstructed the Haitian government, the Marines held Port-au-Prince and Cap Haïtien without difficulty. The greatest danger came from wild shots at night, slipping on street garbage, or a chamberpot bath from a hostile Haitian housewife. As Colonel Waller recognized, the Wilson administration did not want any open fighting, especially not before the occupation treaty was arranged. Waller's principal duty, in fact, was to negotiate for Haitian firearms, for which his officers could pay between $6 and $10. His other responsibility was to send small detachments to the other coastal towns to keep the peace and prepare for American control of the customs houses.[9]

Despite the compliance of the Dartiguenave government and the acquiescence of most of the Haitian *élite,* hostility to the occupation among Bobo's followers and the undisciplined *caco* bands in the north soon forced the Marines into combat operations. Disgusted at the primitiveness of Haitian life and no more immune to racial prejudice than their fellow Americans, the Marines had no reluctance to fight the *cacos.* They considered their feelings of military superiority justified: The Haitian peasant-mercenaries used their antique firearms with little skill and favored surprise charges from ambush with machetes. Such tactics in the Philippines had allowed the Army to kill twenty-five *insurrectos* for each American lost, and the Marine Corps of 1915 was even better armed than the Army of 1899. Analyzing the situation after the first patrol clash with the *cacos* on September 18, Colonel Waller decided that a full-scale campaign against the insurgents would take but a short time. Admiral Caperton agreed and supported the Marines with a declaration of martial law and press censorship. Waller saw the campaign as a combination of arms-buying, amnesty-granting, and selective attacks against only the most militant leaders and their bands. Much of the Marine effort would go into securing the coastal towns and opening roads to the interior. The most difficult problem would be finding the *cacos* in their trackless northern mountain strongholds.[10]

With a force of more than two thousand Marines, Waller felt confident that his brigade could pacify northern Haiti, break up the *caco* roadblocks that were hindering rural commerce, and disarm the Haitian peasantry. With his bases secure, he ordered company-size patrols into the interior in October. He was satisfied with the results, for he found most *caco* leaders willing to accept amnesty and money rather than face death or imprisonment with manual labor. In dealing with the Haitians, Waller developed sympathy for the impoverished peasantry and contempt for the *caco* leaders. His distaste for the urban *élite* was boundless: "You can never trust a nigger with a gun. . . . These people are niggers in spite of the varnish of education and refinement. Down in their hearts they are just the same happy, idle irresponsible people we know of." [11] Executed primarily by the 2d Regiment, the pacification of northern Haiti proceeded with little bloodshed and quick results. Marine losses in 1915–1916 were three killed, eighteen wounded; Haitian losses were larger but probably numbered only two hundred. As the Marine patrols converged on the mountain areas, they worked primarily to destroy *caco* camps, supplies, and arms. The most difficult task was finding the *caco* bases, but by the end of the year the Marines had dispersed most of *caco* bands and killed or captured the chiefs. [12]

The most dramatic combat patrols against the *cacos* were led by Smedley Butler. Working from the inland town of Grande Rivière, Butler's patrols repeatedly clashed with the *cacos* as they pushed into the mountains. Locating the supposedly impregnable *caco* camp in the ruins of ancient Fort Rivière, Butler surrounded the camp with four companies and assaulted it on November 17. In a dawn brawl, Butler and a handful of Marines plunged into the fort and took it in close fighting. As the *cacos* fled, the Marines slaughtered them with rifle and automatic rifle fire, later counting fifty-one dead Haitians. There were no Marine casualties. Butler's force then blew up the fort and withdrew. [13] The destruction of Fort Rivière and nearby Fort Capois brought an end to *caco* resistance. In December there were only six skirmishes with small bands, and the first months of 1916 produced no greater action.

By 1916 the Marine brigade had garrisoned sixteen Haitian towns and had settled into routine occupation duties. The Marines quickly learned that Haiti was no tropical paradise. Distressed by malaria and general ennui, the garrisons found little opportunity for relaxation. The officers were so scattered that commanders had to perform staff duties and supervise civil administration in their towns along with their command functions. One commander reported that his men were "listless and unenergetic," that they wanted to use a nearby beach for swimming but found that the Haitians already used it for a dump and sewer. [14] The language and cultural barrier prevented much contact with the Haitians outside of saloons and bordellos. Although the incidence of American troop misbehavior was slight (six cases in the first fifteen months of the occupation), public drunkenness and rowdyism provided newspaper copy for anti-occupation editors and grist for politicians. Another problem was Haitian insistence that the Marines were subject to Haitian law, as opposed to the American position that the troops were subject only to their own military regulations. Concerned about the impact of the climate and sanitary conditions upon his men and distressed by Haitian antipathy, Waller recommended that his brigade be replaced by a fresh, smaller force before the tension between the Marines and Haitians caused serious problems.[15]

The condition of his brigade and Secretary of the Navy Josephus Daniel's horror at the number of Haitian casualties in the 1915 *caco* campaign accelerated Waller's interest in creating a Haitian constabulary. The treaty of 1915 provided that a native constabulary would be one of the five "treaty services" that the United States would organize and manage. Although the Marine Corps had no prior experience in forming a native police force, it drew upon the Army's experience with the Philippine Constabulary, the Cuban *Guardia Rural*, and the Puerto Rican insular police. As early as September 1915, Headquarters provided organizational plans and cost estimates for a Haitian constabulary, and within Haiti the Marines had already begun to organize local police. The protocol establishing the *Gendarmerie d'Haiti* was not to be signed until 1916, but Waller assigned Smedley Butler as the *Gendarmerie* commandant in December 1915 and told him to move rapidly in organizing his force. Taking the rank of Haitian major general (which his fellow Marine officers ridiculed), Butler tackled the problem of abolishing the inefficient Haitian army and consolidating the five Haitian police forces into a single national constabulary.[16]

Butler threw himself into the assignment with characteristic enthusiasm. From an initial force of fewer than 500 local policemen, Butler started raising a constabulary of 120 American officers and 2,600 Haitian enlisted men. To attract dependable Marine officers and enlisted men (especially ones who spoke French), the Navy Department arranged for the Americans to draw both Marine Corps and Haitian pay. By becoming a *Gendarmerie* officer, a Marine noncommissioned officer could double his annual pay; on the other hand, the frustrations and squalor the officer faced probably discouraged many qualified Marines. It was also difficult to find Americans free of substantial prejudice against blacks, although the *Gendarmerie*'s officers tried to find such Marines. The problem of finding promising Haitian enlisted men was no less distressing. Members of the *élite* refused to join the *Gendarmerie*. Most of the gendarmes, therefore, were recruited from the urban unskilled masses; as a group the recruits were illiterate, undisciplined, irresponsible, and infected with a number of diseases, predominantly hookworm and syphillis. The basic appeal of the *Gendarmerie* was the steady pay, food, and clothes.

Using "monkey see, monkey do" instruction, the *Gendarmerie* officers first taught their recruits drill and found arms, equipment, and uniforms for them. The gendarmes were equipped first with obsolete French rifles and then American Krags and were outfitted in Marine uniforms with Haitian buttons and rank insignia. The gendarmes performed routine city police patrols and garrison housekeeping but received little field training, law enforcement education, or rifle instruction until their American instructors learned some Creole (or found a dependable interpreter) and trusted their dependability. In 1916, however, the gendarmes proved their willingness to fight *cacos* in a few scattered skirmishes, and Butler increased the pace of training and deployment to interior posts. He also placed *Gendarmerie* detachments in charge of the national penitentiary as well as local jails and linked the posts with telephone lines. As the *Gendarmerie* improved, it assumed many of the patrol routes that had been handled by the Marines and created its own administrative and logistical organization.

As the *Gendarmerie* grew, Waller and Butler increasingly saw it as a viable political force in Haiti and the chief instrument of American reform. So did the Haitian government, and for that reason the *Gendarmerie* was soon the target of *élite* critics of the occupation. Waller wanted the gendarmes to remember that "they are to preserve order, protect the rich and poor alike, fear God, and serve their Government and country," but the brigade commander was irritated at the uncooperative attitude of the *élite* and its criticism of the *Gendarmerie's* incorruptibility. He and Butler wanted to use the *Gendarmerie* free of Haitian influence and State Department supervision. They also believed that the *Gendarmerie* should assume not only police functions but also those of supervising sanitation, communications, and public works programs. In the absence of definitive guidance from either the State Department or their nominal Navy superior, they gradually expanded the *Gendarmerie's* functions into all phases of occupation administration except the customs service. By the time Butler left Haiti in 1918, the *Gendarmerie* was the principal agent of the occupation in its routine contact with the Haitian people.[17]

The *Gendarmerie's* rise to political influence was more rapid than the growth of its professionalism, and its ascent was soon to cause problems for the occupation. The *Gendarmerie* continued to have internal personnel problems. Especially after the Dominican intervention of 1916 and American entry in World War I the next year, it was difficult to find promising American officers, and the supervision of those who remained declined. Since *Gendarmerie* officers were recruited from the 1st Brigade, and since the brigade's strength fell after 1916, there were fewer Marines to choose from. Despite indoctrination, some of the Haitian gendarmes could not resist using their status to exploit the common people or settle personal scores by arrest or even murder. Relations with the *élite* remained especially strained. Few Haitians appreciated the *Gendarmerie*'s enforcement of laws governing gambling, tax collection, licensing practices, firearms control, and criminal activities. Haitian politicians continued to badger the *Gendarmerie* for favors. In addition, the *Gendarmerie* became responsible for supervising sanitation and public works projects, because the Navy provided few officers for the "treaty services," and Haitian revenues were not large enough to provide an adequate civil service even if the talent had been available in the Haitian population—which it was not. For roadbuilding, for example, the American officials invoked the ancient French law of the *corvée*, which required all Haitians to donate their labor in lieu of taxes. Supervised by the *Gendarmerie*, the *corvée* worked well enough when the laborers were well cared for and not used outside their own communes and when local Haitian officials did not misuse local funds. But the *Gendarmerie* also bore the onus when the *corvée* law was violated. In some cases this was deserved, for some *Gendarmerie* officers thought that their careers depended upon the number of miles of road they built and sometimes drove their workers beyond the time and geographic limits set by the law.[18]

In fact, the *Gendarmerie* became the occupation, for both the State Department and the Navy did little to supervise the occupation, leaving this task largely to the Marine brigade commander and the commandant of the *Gendarmerie*. Without a greater infusion of American money and skilled specialists, the occupation became a pale imitation of the great reform promises of the treaty of 1915. The Marines were left to explain why the dream of modernizing Haiti did not become reality.

2

While the 1st Brigade and the *Gendarmerie d'Haiti* struggled with the complexities of Haiti, the State Department closely followed the follies of the Jiménez regime in the Dominican Republic and considered the possibility of an occupation there. Although the State Department agreed to support the Dominican president with military forces, it did little else to improve the stability of the incumbent regime. President Jiménez's problem was factionalism within his own government, not American meddling. Knowing that Jiménez was old and ailing, one faction under presidential aspirant Federico Velásquez urged the president to crush Minister of War Desiderio Arias, the other important contender. When Jiménez attempted to arrest Arias's military supporters, the Minister of War commanded loyal troops in Santo Domingo to seize the city. In the meantime his supporters in the Dominican house of representatives began impeachment proceedings against the president. Jiménez retaliated by raising troops in the provinces and laying siege to the city barracks and fortresses held by Arias. As May 1916 opened, Santo Domingo was steeling itself for war, and foreigners fled to the American and Haitian legations and prayed for Marines.[19]

When reports of chaos in Santo Domingo city flooded the State Department, Secretary Lansing authorized American Minister W. W. Russell and Admiral Caperton to take whatever action they thought appropriate. That action was to call for two Marine companies from Haiti. These units appeared aboard the transport *Prairie* in Santo Domingo harbor along with the gunboat *Castine*, which also carried a Marine guard. Called ashore, the Marines defended the American and Haitian legations and waited as the American negotiators, who included Marine Captain Frederic M. Wise, tried to get Arias and Jiménez to come to terms. Arias would not surrender, and Jiménez's army was not strong enough to defeat him. Initially the Marines thought their mission was to defend the legations, but Russell and Caperton (with the State Department's approval) began to plan to attack Arias's six-hundred-man army. Wise's force had only four cannon, and the captains of the *Prairie* and the *Castine* were reluctant to challenge the port coastal guns, so Caperton sent for more Marines and an artillery battery from Haiti. The Marine attack was planned for May 15, but Jiménez, who had been impeached, refused to participate in shelling the city and withdrew to the interior. Arias still refused to surrender but left the city for his regional base at Santiago in the Cibao valley. In the face of some rooftop sniping from the Dominicans, the Marine battalion and the seamen's battalion occupied the city. The occupiers found the rum and cigars excellent but the people definitely unhappy about the intervention.[20]

Because the Dominican Republic had no constitutional government and the American Minister and Caperton were afraid that the Dominican congress would select Arias if pressed to form one, the State Department asked the Navy to take full control of the country while it negotiated for a compliant new regime. American policy was to arrange a new treaty with many of the same provisions as the Haitian treaty of 1915. To make this policy viable, the Marine Corps would have to disperse Arias's army in the Cibao valley. Marine units also would garrison Santo Domingo and the port towns on the southern coast. The first stage in the northern campaign was to seize the port cities of Monte Cristi and Puerto Plata. Under naval gunfire a sailor–Marine landing party took Puerto Plata against light resistance on June 1 after another landing party seized Monte Cristi on May 26 without opposition. The rebel forces were still intact, and the landing parties were too small for extended operations, so Caperton asked for reinforcements. After arriving by train from its base at San Diego, California, Colonel Joseph H. Pendleton's 4th Regiment sailed from New Orleans and reached Dominican waters in June. Caperton then sent the regiment to the north coast, where Pendleton organized his own regiment and Marine companies from Haiti, Cuba, and Caperton's warships into an expeditionary force. Pendleton's operation was easy to conceive. The main portion of his expedition (about 850 men) would march up the road from Monte Cristi toward Santiago, while another battalion would cross the mountains between Puerto Plata and Santiago along the railroad right of way. The only imponderables were the degree of rebel resistance and the efficiency of the Marines' jury-rigged supply train of primitive trucks, wagons, mule trains, and oxcarts. That the Marines outgunned the Dominicans was unquestioned; in addition to the reliable Springfields, the Marines brought with them three field artillery batteries and plenty of machine guns.

Leaving Monte Cristi on June 26, the main expedition easily routed two entrenched Dominican forces at Las Trencheras and Guayacanas and scattered two roadblocks. The Marines' firepower was too much for Arias's militiamen, and the only tense moment of the campaign came when a group of Dominican horsemen attacked the wagon train. With fewer than twenty-five casualties (four killed) the expedition joined the Puerto Plata battalion on July 5, having been delayed more by destroyed bridges and breakdowns than by fighting. The next day Arias surrendered Santiago rather than face full-scale Marine assault. Some of the Dominicans kept their arms and fled to their villages, but most of Arias's followers surrendered their weapons. Admiral Caperton warned Pendleton to avoid dealing with Arias but did not think it necessary to jail him, for he had been discredited as a military hero. Instead the Marines were to garrison the rest of the towns along the route to Samana Bay and await further orders.[21]

During the northern campaign Russell and Caperton attempted to find a Dominican government with which to work out the details of expanded American control of the nation's internal affairs. The Dominican congress elected a provisional president in July, but there was not much flexibility in either side's position. The United States insisted that Americans control both the national revenue system and a new national constabulary. Having no taste for American management, the *políticos* would not cooperate. After several months of impasse, the State Department asked Wilson to allow it to govern through an American military government. The President agreed, and on November 29, 1916, Rear Admiral Harry S. Knapp proclaimed himself military governor of the Dominican Republic. Knapp assured the Dominicans that the occupation was temporary and for the good of the country. Citing Article III of the 1907 treaty as the legal basis of the occupation, he announced that the United States would withdraw when the unauthorized war debts incurred in violation of Article III were cleared up and when the affairs of government could be carried on without violence and corruption.[22]

In legal theory if not political reality, the creation of a military government in the Dominican Republic gave the American occupiers complete freedom to work their reforms. As military governor, Admiral Knapp could rule by decree, subject only to the guidance of his superiors and his own judgment as to what the Dominicans would accept and his Marines could enforce. When no Dominicans chose to serve in his cabinet, Knapp appointed Navy and Marine officers to ministerial posts, with Dominican civil servants manning the lower posts. Colonel Joseph H. Pendleton became Minister of War, Navy, Interior, and Police as well as 2d Brigade commander. Colonel Rufus H. Lane was appointed Minister of Foreign Relations, Justice, and Public Instruction. Navy officers held the portfolios for public works and agriculture, while the American general receiver took control of the entire revenue system. By resuming payment of government salaries, Knapp was able to retain the Dominican minor functionaries, and the court system was preserved.

The military government, however, consciously changed the structure of government in the Dominican Republic. One of its primary goals was to reduce the ability of provincial governors and local officials to disrupt the peace and frustrate national programs. Therefore, the Marine officers serving as district commanders throughout the country were made responsible for the performance of local officials. They were also to see that the military government's decrees were obeyed; the most important of these imposed censorship of the press, mails, and telegraph and outlawed the possession of firearms and explosives. To assist the Marines the military government proclaimed a state of martial law, which allowed the Americans to establish a system of provost marshals and provost courts. This parallel system of law enforcement protected the Marines from Dominican court action and, more important, allowed them to try Dominicans for violations of the laws of the military government.[23]

Without much direction from Washington, the military government attempted to make the "Wilson Plan" a reality, despite the opposition of the Dominican political elite and the passive hostility of much of the population. The general receiver managed the revenue system with efficiency. But even honestly administered, the Dominican republic was not a wealthy country, and funds for internal reform were limited. The problem of unsettled claims was tackled by a claims commission that settled six thousand claims for $4.2 million but needed a 1918 bond issue to finance its judgments. The military government passed laws that modernized land taxes and cleared up disputed land titles, a process that benefited large-scale agricultural companies. On the other hand, the government rebuffed many foreign companies seeking special concessions in public works and commercial ventures. Under Colonel Lane's supervision, the Dominican school system grew from 84 primary schools to 489 and from 18,000 students to more than 100,000. Navy engineer officers designed and supervised substantial improvements in roads, public buildings, public sanitation, the postal system, telephone and telegraph communications, and port facilities.[24]

With the Marine brigade as the primary bulwark against armed opposition and with the provost court system to process Dominican dissidents, the military government presumably did not have to worry about effective obstructionism. Admiral Knapp, however, was too intelligent to believe that Dominican opinion was not a factor, and throughout his tour as governor he regularly took unofficial advice from Dominican notables. His successor, Rear Admiral Thomas Snowden, did not and further alienated the Dominicans by announcing that the occupation was indefinite. He also tightened up the censorship laws. When Dominican protests reached the State Department, Secretary Bainbridge Colby ordered Snowden to create a council of Dominican notables in 1919; the next year this group resigned when the admiral refused to modify his censorship decrees or accept the Dominicans' advice. The State Department then ordered Snowden to liberalize his press regulations. Because of such difficulties and the lack of money for modernizing the Dominican Republic, the State Department began to think about withdrawal in 1920. Influenced by Latin American criticism of the occupation, the State Department pressed the military government to plan a program for turning over the national administration to the Dominicans.

The main responsibility of the 2d Brigade within the reform program was to disarm the population and break up any bands of armed Dominicans, whether political dissidents or plain bandits. For the first eighteen months of the occupation, the Marines conducted searches and confiscated arms. Only in the early stages of the operation did they meet serious trouble. When the governor of San Francisco de Macoris refused to surrender his arms and dissolve his private army of two hundred men, a Marine lieutenant and a squad stormed the governor's fort and captured half the Dominican force; the rest were finally run down in a wild railroad chase as Marine patrols converged on the area. Two months later, in January 1917, Marine patrols operating in the region around San Pedro de Marcoris on the southern coast had several skirmishes with two large bandit gangs, but this threat to the occupation was largely eliminated by April 1917. Marine casualties in these operations were minimal (four dead, fifteen wounded), and most of the losses occurred in November 1916–January 1917. Dominican deaths probably were less than a hundred. The response to the campaign was as the military government had hoped: Most Dominicans surrendered their arms. By October 1917 the Marines had confiscated nearly 30,000 pistols, 10,000 rifles, 2,000 shotguns, 200,000 bullets, and thousands of machetes and knives. So successful was the disarmament program that the Commandant assured the Navy Department that organized political violence and banditry had been eliminated from the Dominican Republic. It was an unduly optimistic assessment.[25]

While the 2d Brigade was settling into its garrisons and chasing bandits, it also organized a new constabulary, the *Guardia Nacional Dominicana*. The *Guardia*, hastily formed to assist in the disarmament campaign, was hampered from the first by lack of funds and a shortage of able officers and recruits. When the *Guardia* was officially formed in April 1917, only one of its first thirteen American officers was a Marine commissioned officer, and no members of the Dominican elite would take a commission. The recruits, as in Haiti, were drawn from the lower class, and some were probably former bandits. Unlike *Gendarmerie* officers, the American *Guardia* officers did not initially draw double pay; the lack of special pay and the lure of battle with the Marine brigade in France limited the 2d Brigade's ability to provide competent noncommissioned officers to the *Guardia*. Although the *Guardia* mustered 691 men by the end of 1917, it was neither large enough nor well enough trained to be of much help in policing the interior of the country, especially in patrolling against the bandits. Pressed by the military governor to eliminate the bandits and collect arms, the 2d Brigade commander (who also commanded the *Guardia*) relied on his own Marines. The result was that the *Guardia*, despised by the Dominican *políticos* and neglected by the Americans, did not improve. Nevertheless, as in

Haiti, the Marine presence in 1917 ensured that the military government's version of the "Wilson Plan" did not meet with much violent resistance.[26]

3

Hardly had the treaty services in Haiti and the military government in the Dominican Republic begun their plan to regenerate Hispaniola when the American occupation was challenged by peasant uprisings in both countries. The causes of the risings were varied and complex, but the result was only too clear. Between 1918 and 1922 the two Marine brigades and their stepchildren, the *Gendarmerie d'Haiti* and the *Guardia Nacional Dominicana,* fought a tiring, brutal antiguerrilla war against the *cacos* and the Dominican bandits. The precipitating cause of the revolt in Haiti was rural antipathy to the *corvée.* Administration of the *corvée* was haphazard at best, and the gendarmes who supervised the laborers sometimes treated them like prisoners. There were incidents when road workers, forced to serve away from their homes and held beyond their obligated time, attempted to desert and were shot; in retaliation several road gangs rebelled against their guards, with loss of life on both sides. Reacting to these incidents, the chief of the *Gendarmerie* suspended the *corvée* in mid-1918, but one *Gendarmerie* colonel in the interior refused to obey the order for two months. Incidents in mountainous northeastern and north central Haiti increased. In the Dominican Republic the center of the revolt was in the impoverished eastern provinces of Seibo and Macoris. Conditions in these provinces worsened in 1918, when World War I disrupted the country's export trade; in addition, a progressively larger portion of the rural work force was switching to work on sugar plantations. As cane cutters, however, they became seasonally employed wage earners and lost their ability and will to farm. Such men were candidates for a bandit life.

Confronted with these seeds of rebellion, the Marine brigades and the native constabularies were not well prepared to react with effectiveness. Both brigades were devastated by the Corps's participation in the fighting in France. Experienced officers and men were transferred, and their replacements were often hastily commissioned officers and callow enlisted men who thought they had joined the Marine Corps to fight the Hun. Both brigades shrank to less than half their original size, which meant that Marine patrols were smaller and had to stay in the field for longer times. The Marines' mobility was limited to their shoes and their determination, both of which wore thin in the tropic heat. In the Dominican Republic, where the 2d Brigade had created mounted companies, there were only enough ponies to mount one-fifth of the patrols.

Nor did the Marines get much help from the native constabularies. Both the *Gendarmerie* and the *Guardia* had the same officer problems as the Marine brigades, and the native enlisted men were neither well trained nor totally dependable. Both the Haitian and Dominican gendarmes still had a tendency to use their official positions to settle grudges and were too eager to brutalize or shoot prisoners. Neither constabulary was prepared for hard field service. In Haiti, for example, the *Gendarmerie*'s marksmanship was so bad that the range for executions had to be reduced from thirty to fifteen feet. Even if the rebels were ill equipped and poor tacticians, their initial advantage in mobility and use of the inhospitable terrain was substantial, and their ability to fade into the population gave them an anonymity that frustrated the Marines. Such guerrilla warfare conditions would have confounded an elite colonial infantry, which neither the Marine brigades nor native constabularies were in 1918.

Playing upon native fears that the Americans would reintroduce slavery, and offering a return to the old life of mercenary soldiering, the *caco* chiefs organized active guerrilla bands, numbering perhaps 5,500 men, with a network of supporters twice as large. The principal leader was Charlemagne Peralte, a *caco* chieftain from a prominent Hinche family, who had just walked away from a *Gendarmerie* prison. A clever and charismatic leader, Peralte attacked *Gendarmerie* posts at Hinche and Maissade in the fall of 1918 and extorted supplies and money from the peasants for his army. His *cacos* ambushed small *Gendarmerie* patrols, blockaded roads, and disrupted the occupation's roadbuilding and sanitation programs. Although the *Gendarmerie* fought back, especially when led by American officers, the revolt spread. In March 1919 the chief of the *Gendarmerie* asked for the total commitment of the 1st Brigade. Reinforced with four additional companies, the brigade sent six companies to interior posts to reinforce the *Gendarmerie* and to begin more aggressive patrolling.[27]

The counterguerrilla campaign in the back country was carried on with considerable aggressiveness but not much success. The Marine-*Gendarmerie* forces occupied thirty towns and sent patrols to clear the roads and locate the *caco* base camps. It was a war of *caco* ambush met with heavy Marine rifle and machine gun fire; fortunately the *caco's* weapons were old and few in number, so large patrols risked little in such skirmishes. Nevertheless, the *cacos* drew blood and retained enough confidence to stay in the field. From fewer than forty contacts in January through June 1919, the number of jungle battles soared to more than eighty in July through September. Despite their own catastrophic losses, the *cacos* continued the war. Their casualties (probably about five hundred during this period) were heavy enough, however, to convince the 1st Brigade commander and Admiral Snowden that the war was going well for their forces. Their optimism was shattered in October, when Peralte attacked Port-au-Prince with some three hundred men. Fortunately the garrison had been warned of the attack and drove the *cacos* off with ease. At the same time it broke up a city mob that had formed in Peralte's support. The attack on Port-au-Prince jarred the Navy Department and focused public attention in the United States upon the war for the first time.

The first break in the war came in October 1919. It was accomplished by *Gendarmerie* Captain Herman H. Hanneken, who commanded the post at Grande Rivière. Infiltrating his own Haitian agents into Peralte's personal band, Hanneken lured Peralte's army toward his post. Smarting from his defeat at Port-au-Prince, Peralte needed a victory, and Grande Rivière looked vulnerable. Learning that Peralte would not personally lead the attack, Hanneken and his second in command, William R. Button, called for Marine reinforcements and took to the hills with a *Gendarmerie* patrol disguised as *cacos*. After a suspense-filled march, the patrol bluffed its way through Peralte's outer guards and found itself in the *caco* headquarters. Giving the order to open fire, Hanneken dropped Peralte with his Colt automatic while Button sprayed the bodyguards with a Browning automatic rifle. The patrol then fought off *caco* attacks for the rest of the night. In the meantime the attack on Grande Rivière was easily defeated, and Peralte's band dissolved. The next day the patrol returned with Peralte's body, which was photographed. Marine patrols and observation aircraft flooded the country with prints, which presumably demoralized the *cacos*. Certainly Peralte's death had removed the revolt's foremost leader.[28]

Under a new commander, Colonel John H. Russell, the 1st Brigade was reorganized and strengthened late in 1919 and gradually shifted to more effective offensive operations. Russell appointed the capable Louis McCarty Little to command all Marine and *Gendarmerie* operations against the *cacos*, thus giving the campaign more coordinated planning. The brigade also exchanged its short-service enlisted men and officers for veteran officers from France and regular Marines. In the face of rumors of urban revolt, continued disruption of the economy, and lack of cooperation from the Haitian government, the brigade stepped up its patrolling and soon penetrated the mountains to find the *caco* camps.[29]

In January 1920 the Marine brigade (about 1,300 men) and the *Gendarmerie* (2,700 men) mounted a coordinated campaign of military and political action. Relays of patrols operating in carefully mapped and identified sectors chased the *cacos* with increasing effectiveness; in addition, the *cacos* received offers of amnesty, and in the next six months nearly 12,000 gave up voluntarily. Russell's plan was not especially novel, but it worked. His Marines tracked down the most important *caco* leaders and in May killed the last remaining major chieftain. The patrols also destroyed *caco* camps and supplies and rounded up rural villagers who supported the guerrillas.

While the campaign was not organized to spread general death and destruction, some atrocities were inevitable. The combination of racism and revenge, fueled by stories of mutilation and cannibalism performed on two captured Marines, affected some of the Marines. The *Gendarmerie* too was still inclined to shoot prisoners. A Marine colonel recently arrived from France thought there was entirely too much shooting of "fleeing prisoners," and an officer saw Lieutenant Louis Cukela personally execute one group of prisoners in the middle of a Marine camp.[30] (Cukela, a Medal of Honor winner as a sergeant in France, was transferred but not court-martialed.) The majority of incidents, however, involved enlisted men in off-duty hours prowling for liquor and women and were not part of the pacification. When witnesses would testify, Russell had offenders court-martialed, and he cautioned his commanders not to allow violations of the rules of warfare. He also eventually restricted the use of provost courts and reminded his brigade that its purpose in being there was "the maintenance of Law and Order and the establishment and cementing of friendly relations with the inhabitants" so that the people could "carry on their vocation unmolested."[31]

Under unrelenting military pressure, the *caco* movement finally flickered out in the late summer of 1920. By the time it had ended, the occupation forces had killed at least two thousand Haitians at a cost to the Marines and *Gendarmerie* of one hundred dead and wounded. It was a costly reminder of the perils of military occupation.

The Marines' situation in the Dominican Republic was less dramatic, but it was no better. In 1918 the 2d Brigade was stripped of troops for France, and the green recruits did not match the regulars of 1916 in numbers or quality. In the northern occupation district, the 4th Regiment had fewer than 500 men to police 8,350 square miles and 500,000 people. In the southern district, which included Santo Domingo and the bandit provinces of Macoris and Seibo, the 3d Regiment's officers were spread thin over the Dominican constabulary, the regiment, and civil positions with the military government. Their men's greatest concerns (judging by brigade orders) were obtaining transfers, prostitutes, and rum. The more restricted recreation facilities in the eastern provinces limited the men to routine complaints about living conditions and wearisome patrols. The brigade was not in a very healthy condition to fight guerrillas, and the *Guardia Nacional Dominicana* was in even worse shape.[32]

Despite the antibandit campaign of 1917, the 2d Brigade had not eliminated all the bands in the eastern provinces but had left the mopping-up to the *Guardia*. The Marine sergeants and corporals serving as *Guardia* officers tried to survive on raw courage and hard governing, which did not always work. *Guardia* Captain William R. Knox, a champion of civic improvement in his district, was assassinated in January 1918. Following Knox's prior orders, his *guardias* then executed eleven prisoners, an act that incensed the district. Tried for manslaughter, a *Guardia* lieutenant was acquitted by a Marine court-martial, an act that angered Governor Knapp.[33] Following Knox's death, the Marines and *Guardia* increased their patrolling but seldom found the bandits except when they themselves were ambushed. Because of Marine firepower and unit discipline the ambushes usually ended with more Dominicans down than Marines.

The northern district remained peaceful, but the eastern provinces collapsed into a vicious guerrilla war that continued into 1919. Marine tactics did little to crush the war and much to create new guerrillas. Patrols, not well planned or coordinated, often abused the native population. One company commander was eventually court-martialed for murdering and mutilating suspects; he committed suicide before his trial. A lieutenant reporting to a company at La Romana found the men surly with the officers and natives and loading their rifles with dum-dum bullets. Another lieutenant in the same area found the Marines too enthusiastic about confiscating horses to ride and cattle to eat. Operating in the eastern area was a patrol of Mexican and Puerto Rican Marines led by Louis Cukela after his transfer from Haiti; this group, disguised as bandits, was the terror of Seibo province. Although no one could fault the Marines' marksmanship, the level of violence did not decline.[34]

The guerrilla war in the Dominican Republic dragged on despite the dogged patrolling and the bravery of small Marine detachments under fire. In 1919 alone there were two hundred skirmishes, usually sudden firefights at point-blank range or attacks upon abandoned bandit camps. After an abortive attempt to round up some of the rural population in Seibo province, the brigade commander called for reinforcements. The Commandant provided the 15th Regiment and an observation squadron, which brought the brigade strength to nearly three thousand men. Every one of them was needed, especially in the newly created eastern district, which was assigned to the 15th Regiment. While the Marines pursued the bandits (estimated at six hundred to one thousand men), the military government curbed its use of provost courts and press censorship in a successful effort to contain the population's disaffection. The senior officers in the eastern district also realized that their own troops were antagonizing the Dominicans and started serious indoctrination programs for their men and the *Guardia*. Despite continued personnel turnover, the Marines chipped away at the bandits' strength in one firefight after another. At the same time the Marine officers conciliated the villagers by enforcing troop discipline and supporting local leaders who preached nonresistance. The basic message was that the Marines were there to protect the common folk (the foreign plantations had their own guards) and to expand the government's public works and sanitation programs. The banditry began to subside.[35]

From the beginning of their attacks in 1918 the Dominican guerrillas had occasionally talked as if their objective was not just loot but the defeat of the military occupation. At one point the military government thought some of them were German-sponsored. After World War I the military government concluded that some of the bandits were motivated by their poverty and their fear of Marine retaliation. Lack of money and imagination limited Marine operations to patrolling and reaction raids until the brigade was jarred by the Wilson administration's announcement in 1920 that the occupation forces would soon withdraw. Pressed by articulate *políticos* and simply exhausted by the Dominican situation, the State Department ordered the military government to plan its own liquidation. To dramatize the change, nearly a third of the Marine brigade was withdrawn with the bandits still undefeated. Although the patrolling continued, the military government announced full pardons for those guerrillas who surrendered, curbed the excesses of the provost courts, and seriously reformed the *Guardia*. It also created small units of civil guards officered by Marines, patrols that proved extremely valuable for scouting and ambushes. To check *Guardia* excesses further, the military government made the guards subject to civilian law. Responding to Navy Department pressure, the military government also drew in the Marine garrisons of the northern and southern districts to larger towns.

In the eastern district, however, the military governor authorized one last effort by the 2d Brigade to eliminate the guerrillas. This the 15th Regiment did in a vigorous campaign in late 1921 and early 1922. In a five-month period the regiment conducted nine well-planned, skillfully run cordon operations to seal off and screen entire village populations for guerrillas. In part, the cordon operations were designed to allow Marine officers to supervise their men more closely, a difficult task when small patrols carried the fight to the bandits. Marines would surround a town in the early morning; then a mounted company accompanied by

Cukela's special unit would gallop into the village and question all the villagers, usually assisted by the local prostitutes, who seemed to know most of the guerillas. With no casualties the 15th Regiment screened more than two thousand people, holding about one-fourth of them for the provost courts. Most of those held were later convicted. The cordon operations and more patrolling finally brought the campaign to an end as the remaining bandits surrendered or were tracked down. By 1922 the war in the eastern provinces had finally ended. When the Marine brigade at last turned over its duties to the *Guardia,* it had lost nearly one hundred men, but had killed or wounded more than a thousand guerrillas since 1916. As in Haiti, the costs of humanitarian reform had run it heavily into the red.[36]

The guerrilla wars in Haiti and Santo Domingo brought substantial changes in American policy toward Hispaniola and damaged the Marine Corps's reputation for discipline and forthright leadership. The political ripples started with two investigations initiated in late 1919 by a new 1st Brigade commander, Brigadier General Albertus W. Catlin, into the causes of the *caco* war and into reports of *Gendarmerie* brutality. The results of the inquiries were damaging: A *Gendarmerie* colonel had known about, if not encouraged, the execution and brutalization of *caco* prisoners and *corvée* laborers. Catlin relieved the colonel (a Marine major) but reported that he could not gather evidence and witnesses for courts-martial. Instead he stopped *Gendarmerie* patrolling in the Hinche–Maissade area and had the new commander of the *Gendarmerie* issue a general order prohibiting summary executions and the oppression of the Haitians. A similar order was published and read to the Marines of the 1st Brigade.[37]

The atrocity stories could not be quieted. Returning Marines talked to other Americans, and the Haitian *élite* (showing new-found concern for the illiterate masses) arranged for civil rights groups to receive information on all the allegations against the occupation forces. Sympathetic to American liberals' claims, Secretary of the Navy Josephus Daniels early in 1920 ordered Commandant George Barnett to conduct a thorough investigation of the occupation. Barnett and his staff, however, mishandled the matter, either by design or through incompetence. Outraged, Daniels sent a new Commandant, John A. Lejeune, and Brigadier General Smedley Butler to Haiti in the late summer of 1920.

Upon its return the Lejeune-Butler mission reported that it had found General Catlin's earlier impressions correct. More disturbing, they found indications of continued atrocities in defiance of orders by Barnett and the brigade commanders. They admitted, however, that witnesses and evidence were in short supply and that many of the suspects had left

Haiti. General Barnett, still on active duty, attempted to exonerate himself by showing that he and Assistant Secretary of the Navy Franklin Roosevelt (now the Democratic vice-presidential candidate) had investigated the atrocity charges and found them exaggerated. At Barnett's urging, Headquarters released the various reports that were supposed to show how well affairs in Haiti really had gone, but the stratagem backfired. Among the documents was a 1919 letter from Barnett to Russell in which Barnett told the brigade commander that he was convinced from court-martial testimony that the Marines *were* committing untold atrocities. Barnett's conclusions had been extreme, but his letter gave the press the impression that the Marine Corps had been practicing genocide. Thrust into the middle of a presidential election in which Wilsonian foreign policy was a major issue, this interpretation made the occupation of Hispaniola a national cause célèbre.[38]

The Navy Department tried without success to stop the Republican accusations, and the charges against the occupation government continued for two years. The eventual winners in the dispute were the Haitians and Dominicans who wanted the occupations ended. The Haitian situation remained the more dramatic. Although a Navy board of inquiry headed by Rear Admiral Henry T. Mayo reported that Haiti was now calm and that the atrocities had ended, the American liberal press, the National Association for the Advancement of Colored People, and their Haitian allies of the *Union Patriotique* prevailed upon the new Congress to conduct its own investigation.

For a period of several months in 1921 and 1922 a special Senate committee heard testimony on occupation policies and concluded that American administration had indeed been ineffective. The committee, however, also concluded that neither Caribbean country was fit for self-government and urged the State Department to assume more responsibility and to reorganize the American agencies on the island. It approved President Wilson's order to prepare the withdrawal from the Dominican Republic but concluded that Haiti needed a long period of supervision, perhaps the full twenty years decreed by the State Department in 1916. To the frustration of American anti-imperialistic liberals, the *Union Nacional Dominicana*, and the *Union Patriotique*, the Senate committee decided that the initial intervention had been justified and that the occupation had suffered from poor administration, not evil intentions and unconstitutional action. These conclusions were supported by Professor Carl Kelsey, sent to Hispaniola by the American Academy of the Political and Social Sciences.[39] Immediate withdrawal was not palatable to the State Department and even less so to the occupation authorities, but it was clear that new negotiations and reorganizations were necessary.

The State Department also agreed with Kelsey that "the Marine Corps is intended to be a fighting body and we should not ask it to assume all sorts of civil and political responsibilities unless we develop within it a group of especially trained men." [40] The implication was that the Marines would now play a reduced role in the occupation.

The immediate changes in Haiti differed from those in the Dominican Republic. In Haiti the chief reform was to appoint a high commissioner of ambassadorial rank to coordinate civil and military agents of the treaty services and the Marine brigade. The State Department would not accept Smedley Butler, the Navy Department's choice, for this role. It considered John H. Russell, a former brigade commander, an excellent choice, because Russell favored creating a better life for the Haitian masses. The 1st Brigade was to be withdrawn from the countryside and replaced by a reformed and enlarged *Gendarmerie,* an ironic change in view of the fact that the gendarmes had been the worst culprits in mistreating the Haitians. In the Dominican Republic the Navy replaced the much-disliked Admiral Snowden. The State Department also ordered the new military governor to form a commission of notable Dominicans to draft constitutional amendments and new laws that would lay the groundwork for elections and the creation of a provisional government. In exchange the State Department would not block new foreign loans, which the military government wanted for its public works program. After a series of negotiations in Santo Domingo City in which the Dominicans and the military government proved uncooperative, the occupation was unilaterally extended until 1924. Thus the military government continued, but part of the price of compromise was that the 2d Brigade would be reduced and concentrated in central camps in the capital and in the northern cities. As in Haiti, the Marines would have to put more effort into improving the *Guardia Nacional Dominicana* as the primary peace-keeper. [41]

4

Largely as the State Department had planned, the withdrawal progressed more rapidly in the Dominican Republic. Despite the complaints by Admiral S. S. Robison, the military governor, that the public works and sanitation programs needed completing, the State Department listened more attentively to the Latin American diplomats and Dominican *políticos* who argued that the occupation had accomplished all it could. Another important factor was that the Dominican Republic, unlike Haiti, had organized political factions (still led by Vásquez, Velásquez, and lesser aspirants) that could fill government posts and organize elections. To work with the *políticos,* the State Department sent Sumner

Welles, author of the withdrawal plan, to the Dominican Republic. By September 1922 Welles and the Dominican leaders had agreed on the first steps for withdrawal and selected a provisional president to supervise the transfer of administrative duties and to plan for national elections as well as to continue negotiations with the United States.

Among the items Welles and the Dominican commission dealt with was the issue of the *Guardia* and the Marine brigade. Renamed the *Policia Nacional Dominicana,* the constabulary was placed under the command of a Dominican, Buenaventura Cabral, a regional *caudillo* and governor, who was acceptable to Admiral Robison. Marine officers, however, remained responsible for *Policia* training, which would be accelerated. At the same time the *Policia* would replace the Marine outposts in the countryside, and the brigade would retire to large garrison camps near the principal cities. If there were serious outbreaks of violence, the Marines would still be available to reinforce the *Policia.*[42]

The burden for supervising the military provisions of the withdrawal fell upon Brigadier General Harry Lee, a genial, intelligent veteran of twenty-four years' service. Acting as both brigade commander and military governor, Lee set his priorities: (1) develop the *Policia*; (2) promote good relations with the Dominican people by insisting on exemplary behavior by the police and Marines; and (3) keep order. His most important mission was to train and enlarge the *Policia,* the first time a brigade commander assigned the highest priority to this responsibility. The focal point of *Policia* reform was the constabulary training center at Haina, which had been opened in late 1921 to train enlisted men. Lee's 1922 plan was to bring in the twenty-four native officers and all the enlisted men for formal training and to start an officer candidate school. All the classes would have six months of training at Haina and six months of supervised field work before they left probationary status. Lee thought it would be possible to replace the *Policia's* forty-four American officers, adequately train an enlisted force of 1,200, and replace all the Marine outposts by the end of 1923.[43]

Under the direction of Colonel Presley M. Rixey, Jr., and Colonel Richard M. Cutts, the Haina training program worked as planned, despite persistent difficulty in finding literate, responsible Dominican officers and noncommissioned officers. The Marine instructors found the officers and cadets reluctant students, unwilling to do manual labor of any kind. The Dominicans balked at the classroom instruction on administration, law, map-reading, field sanitation, and elementary agriculture but took to riflery, tactics, and close-order drill. Both instructors and students emphasized personal appearance, but the Marine instructors found it difficult to create a service ethic other than loyalty to the

Policia. Despite their frustrations, the Marines kept standards high; of the first cadet class only thirty of sixty graduated, and some Dominican officers in the Haina program lost their commissions for incompetence. By the end of 1923, however, the *Policia* reform program had progressed enough to relieve the Marines of police duties and to create a four-hundred-man motorized *Policia* reserve force designed to respond to riots or uprisings. The Dominican government was satisfied enough to ask Colonel Cutts and his military assistants to remain beyond 1924, but the implied restrictions upon Cutts's autonomy and the probable politicization of the *Policia* persuaded the American instructors to leave along with the 2d Brigade.[44]

Lee's second task was to ensure that the behavior of the brigade Marines did nothing to interrupt the withdrawal plan. This was not an easy task. After the Dominican provisional government took office, it was deluged with complaints about Marine enlisted men who were rowdy in the *cantinas,* harassed police officers, refused to pay debts, fought with bootblacks and taxi drivers, and drove recklessly. Although discipline in the brigade had improved since 1919, there was still some truth in the observation of a former American Minister: "Many Marines are recruited from a low class of the population. In many cases they are the very worst type of young men who may be found in our country." [45] Lee could not improve the human material in his brigade, but he could and did investigate all charges (justified or not) against his men and make sure that the culprits were tried. He also established strong military police patrols to stop rowdyism by off-duty Marines. He won a concession from the State Department, however, that protected his men from the Dominicans: The provost courts continued to try Dominicans who abused Marines, and the military government still censored the most inflammatory Dominican newspapers.

Lee also started a vigorous indoctrination program for his troops. Its aim was to convince the men that the Dominicans were not "the enemy" and that the mission of the brigade was to make the withdrawal plan work. "There is no doubt as to what our mission is. It is—to help this Republic and its people." [46] Lee also made sure his subordinate commanders followed rigorous training plans. Within a year the brigade impressed both an inspector from Headquarters and a group of fifty congressmen with its discipline and military efficiency. As the brigade redeployed in 1924, Lee and the Navy Department were satisfied that the brigade had indeed contributed to the transfer of power to the newly elected Dominican government and that the Marines had accomplished their mission of bringing new order to the country through the brigade's antibandit campaign and the creation of the *Policia.*[47]

As the occupation of the Dominican Republic waned, the American effort to modernize Haiti increased under the direction of the State Department, which had replaced the Navy Department as the occupation's supervisor. Under High Commissioner John H. Russell's direction, the American government sent two hundred American civilians to staff the treaty services. Navy officers continued to hold positions in the public works and sanitation services. In 1924 the American effort increased when a civilian was appointed to administer the collection of Haiti's internal revenues and the State Department created the *Service Technique de l'Agriculture et l'Enseignment Professionel,* a system of agricultural and vocational schools, which numbered sixty-five by 1930. The older program to refinance Haiti's complex accumulated debts and unsettled claims was resuscitated with a $40 million loan, and additional Haitian revenues were pumped into sanitation and public works. A number of American treaty officials who were anathema to the Haitians were replaced.

The new vigor of the occupation, however, further alienated the Haitian *élite.* The *élite*'s complaints were numerous and loud: The Americans practiced racial discrimination; they censored the press; they had forced a new constitution upon the country in 1918; they had dissolved the congress in 1917; and they would not set a withdrawal date earlier than 1936. The Americans in Haiti responded, with reason, that the *élite* could not be trusted to spend public monies for the common good and that they wanted nothing but patronage when they insisted upon Haitianization of the treaty services. Although the treaty officials never reduced their reforms into a coherent plan, they hoped that the treaty services, especially the *Service Technique,* might eventually create a new Haitian middle class that would displace the *élite* and lead the rural poor into an era of economic improvement and village democracy.[48]

American relations with the Haitian client government were difficult and frustrating. Although the State Department would have preferred to hold elections in Haiti, it recognized that elections were meaningless to the masses and only served to legitimize the *élite* politicians. Yet it was also concerned that President Dartiguenave wanted to remain in office beyond his legal term. This concern was shared by Dartiguenave's political rivals, and in 1922 the State Department allowed the anti-Dartiguenave faction in the council of state, a rump legislature, to elect Louis Borno president. Borno proved as difficult to remove as Dartiguenave, but at least he was not as hostile to the treaty services as his predecessor and worked reasonably well with General Russell. Like Dartiguenave, Borno was sensitive to *élite* criticism of his press censorship and his reluctance to obstruct Russell and other treaty officials. The

Americans, on the other hand, found that Borno was no less interested in patronage appointments for Haitians in the treaty services than any other Haitian politician.

For the 1st Brigade the end of the *caco* war and the rejuvenation of the American occupation meant a reduction of responsibility. The brigade dropped below one thousand men and went into comfortable barracks in Port-au-Prince and in Cap Haïtien. The Marines normally trained about half a day and played sports the rest of the time. Occasionally Marine patrols went into the countryside to remind the Haitians they still stood behind the *Gendarmerie*. Although there were sporadic incidents in which off-duty Marines became involved in fights with Haitians and their military police and a predictable amount of drunkenness, the brigade officers kept their men under close rein. Limited provost courts continued to operate to protect the Marines and to try the most obnoxious Haitian agitators, but the State Department ordered Russell to diminish their activity, which he did. Commandant Lejeune eased the brigade's problems by putting the enlisted men on a set eighteen-month tour and by providing adequate funds for recreation facilities. Duty in Haiti tended to be boring, but it was no longer a matter of public controversy—at least not in the United States.[49]

The *Gendarmerie d'Haiti* prospered by necessity during the 1920s as the State Department and Russell depended upon it to assume total responsibility for day-to-day law enforcement. The end of *caco* resistance allowed the *Gendarmerie* officers to concentrate on troop training and indoctrination in nonpartisan law enforcement. The increase of American civilians in the other treaty services also allowed the *Gendarmerie* to free itself from some of its nonpolice duties. Its officers, however, were still supposed to serve as communal advisers and tax collection supervisors, and the *Gendarmerie* also created its own coast guard patrol squadron and assisted urban fire departments. Internally, the constabulary gradually improved its administrative system, health-care and supply facilities, telephone communications, and troop training. It built new, standardized buildings for its rural posts. The newly formed *Ecole Militaire* trained Haitian officer candidates, and recruit training in marksmanship and law enforcement improved under American instructors. In 1928 the constabulary changed its name to *Garde d'Haiti* in recognition of its nonpolice duties and to remove the stigma of the *caco* war–era *Gendarmerie* and earlier French rural police. By 1929 the *Garde* numbered 199 officers (71 of whom were Haitians) and 2,622 men. In addition, the *Garde* appointed and controlled more than 500 rural policemen. Although there were occasional incidents of *Garde* misbehavior in the field, the Haitian constabulary showed promise in fulfilling the occupation's goal of creating a disciplined, nonpartisan police force to enforce the law and stop revolts.[50]

For the *Garde*'s American officers, service in Haiti remained challenging, profitable, and exhausting. The Marines, often called "papa blanc" by the peasants, were often the sole government representatives in the back country, and even more often the only Americans. Generally their relations with the Haitian peasantry were good, especially as they mastered the Creole dialect, protected the people from unscrupulous Haitian officials, helped block land sales to foreign companies, and refused to interrupt local culture, including the practice of voodoo. The Marines, although annoyed by the peasants' penchant for petty thievery, found the masses more admirable than the *élite*. *Garde* officers, for example, served as unofficial justices of the peace to prevent the peasants from being victimized by the notoriously corrupt Haitian court system. When they returned to the cities, usually exhausted and ill, the Marines enjoyed the creature comforts of the urban posts but generally disliked having to deal with the *élite*. A laugh at the expense of the Haitian politicians was always welcome; one of the officers' favorite stories was about the time the *Garde* band sent President Borno off on a sea voyage with a stirring rendition of "Bye Bye Blackbird." Such small victories did not happen often. Instead the *Garde* officers tackled their routine duties: training troops, writing reports, collecting intelligence, and struggling to keep their posts clean and healthy. Some officers collapsed under the strain and died of suicide or disease. The majority were glad to return to Marine units in the United States.[51]

The *Garde d'Haiti*'s new efficiency received a stern test in 1929, when a wave of strikes and riots swept Haiti. Angered by President Borno's reluctance to hold elections and by the increasing influence of the *Service Technique*, agitators organized a series of student strikes, which then spread to Haiti's urban commonfolk. The anti-occupation movement in October 1929 started a general strike beyond the *Garde*'s capacity to crush, and General Russell wondered whether the *Garde* might not be either in sympathy with the strikers or cowed by the *élite* agitators. Although Russell sent Marine detachments to all the strike-affected towns and invoked curfews, martial law, and heavy censorship, he was unable to break the movement. The State Department warned him to keep his poise and denied his request for Marine reinforcements.

The State Department's hope that the strike would just fade away burst on December 6, when a Marine detachment outside Cayes tried to stop an armed mob of 1,500. Efforts to persuade the peasants to disband did not succeed, and the Marines could not stop the march. As the leaders reached the Marine lines, there was a scuffle, and the Marines opened fire without orders. Some of the Marines fired over the mob's heads, but others fired into it, killing and wounding more than fifty Haitians. The Cayes incident shocked Washington, and the next day President Herbert Hoover requested funds for another investigating commission. In the meantime Marine officers' homes had been fire-bombed and stoned. The strike, however, had begun to falter as the Marines and *gardes* pushed people from the streets, arrested leaders, and enforced the curfew. Many workers returned to their jobs; others were fired. By the end of December uneasy peace had returned.[52]

The 1929 uprising shortened the time allowed for the treaty officials to prepare for withdrawal and brought Russell's administration under criticism. In 1930 a presidential investigating committee visited Haiti, talked to the dissidents, and returned to recommend that the State Department quickly Haitianize the treaty agencies, including the *Garde*. Without much consultation with the State Department, President Hoover, who personally disliked both the armed forces and the idea of military occupation, ordered Haitianization to proceed more rapidly. Hoover also replaced General Russell with Dr. Dana G. Munro from the State Department's Latin American Division. Secretary of State Henry Stimson thought the general had done well under trying circumstances, but he also knew that Russell did not approve of the hasty withdrawal and the abandonment of his public works, educational, and sanitation programs. Nor was Russell happy about the prospect of national elections, which were also held in 1930. The elections resulted in a victory for the black nationalist leadership of the Haitian congress, but the shocked *élite* co-opted enough congressmen to elect one of their own, Stenio Vincent, the new president.

For the *Garde* the events of 1929 and 1930 forced a quickened pace in the appointment and promotion of Haitian officers and the rapid strengthening of the *Garde*'s supply of equipment and ordnance. The *Ecole Militaire* was enlarged and reformed, and its faculty was changed from Americans to Haitians. At the recommendation of the *Garde*'s senior officers, the Marine Corps also sold the constabulary more submachine guns and new mortars and machine guns. These arms went to the *Garde*'s mobile company in Port-au-Prince and to the presidential guard, which made up the *Garde*'s counterinsurgency force. Although its Marine officers had reservations about the *Garde*'s professionalism, they followed their instructions to turn over their duties to Haitian officers when the occupation ended in 1934.[53]

For the Marine Corps the occupation of Hispaniola had been long, difficult, and expensive. In a military sense, the experience had been of some value. A generation of Marine officers had gained experience in counterguerrilla warfare and in organizing native constabularies. Those who had served as constabulary officers had gained some painful insights into the problems of colonial administration, and others recognized the importance of close supervision of both American and native enlisted men during field operations among an alien population. Eventually, some of these lessons were applied in Nicaragua, but by 1934 that intervention, too, had ended. There had been some high costs as well. Whereas the American government generally approved of the Marine Corps's performance in Hispaniola, other articulate Americans became convinced that the Marine Corps was the tool of American overseas corporations and a bloodthirsty collection of sociopathic misfits who derived great satisfaction from gunning down helpless Dominicans and Haitians. This view was a caricature, but the Marine Corps was saddled with it until World War II.

Contrary to the critics' accusations, the Marine Corps was not enthusiastic about performing its duties in Hispaniola. In fact, it found itself mired in a misguided Wilsonian effort to reform two incorrigible Caribbean republics, and by the time the two Marine brigades departed, their officers were convinced that neither country could be governed except by dictatorship. They did nothing, however, to pave the way consciously for the future dictatorships of Rafael Leonidas Trujillo in the Dominican Republic and Paul Magloire and François Duvalier in Haiti. None of those strongmen, two of whom emerged from the ranks of the native constabularies, needed any instruction in the techniques of tyrannical power. The greatest lesson, which was eventually learned by the American government, was that American interests in the Caribbean could not be secured by any military occupation of acceptable duration and cost. It was an expensive education, and the Marine Corps became a scapegoat for those who either opposed intervention in principle or were disappointed that the occupation had not civilized Hispaniola. The political costs for the Marine Corps, then, could not be precisely calculated, but they existed nevertheless.

8. The Marines in China
1905—1941

The end of the Boxer Uprising and the humiliation of the Manchu dynasty intensified European and Japanese interest in the exploitation of China. The United States joined the rush as an ambivalent participant, acting as much to restrain the other imperialistic powers as to widen its own commercial and missionary interests. The tenor of American foreign policy in China for the next forty years was set by 1901. When the Powers forced the Manchu dynasty to sign the punitive Boxer Protocol, the United States did not ask for full indemnification for its public and private expenses. Yet the United States did agree that it and the other foreign powers should enjoy extraterritorial status in Peking and would share the responsibility for keeping communications open from the coast to the capital with military forces if necessary. The basic American position, in fact, was shaped by two State Department notes to the other major world nations before the end of the Boxer Uprising. Collectively, the "Open Door" notes of 1899 and 1900 announced that the United States supported the territorial integrity of China as a sovereign state and asked the other nations to accept the principle of equal trading and personal rights throughout China, even within their established spheres of interest. Although the Chinese government should honor all its earlier treaty concessions to foreign governments and businesses, it could assume some diplomatic assistance from the United States, whose policy would be

. . . to seek a solution which may bring about permanent safety and peace to China, preserve China's territorial and administrative entity, protect all rights granted to friendly powers by treaty and international law, and safeguard for the world the principle of equal and impartial trade with all parts of the Chinese Empire.[1]

A mixture of political and religious idealism and commercial self-seeking, the "Open Door" policy shaped American relations with China and eventually led to conflict with Japan. Its inherent problem was that it committed the United States to protecting the rights of its own nationals in China, preserving with joint military action if necessary the extraterritorial status of the Peking Legation Quarter as well as the foreign concessions in China's principal cities, and at the same time protecting China against further loss of control over its own soil to imperialistic exploiters. Had the Manchu dynasty recovered and reformed itself after the Boxer Uprising, the American commitment to a stable *status quo* might have survived the inherent contradictions in the "Open Door" policy. The problem, however, was that Chinese reform nationalists and regional warlords would not accept either foreign exploitation or Manchu rule, and in 1911 China entered what became more than a generation of revolutionary upheaval.[2]

The Chinese Revolution succeeded in displacing the last Manchu emperor but did not produce any lasting successor government. Instead, power passed to a limited national government in Peking under a politician-general, Yuan Shih-kai, and to a host of regional warlords. Jealous of their feifdoms, the warlords made China from the Yangtze Valley to Manchuria a battleground for their rapacious armies. Although most of the Chinese armies avoided harming foreigners and their property for fear of retaliation, the general threat of war and its periodic outbreak menaced aliens not only in the countryside but within the urban foreign concessions as well. Constantly fearing that the revolution would become violently antiforeign, the Powers' diplomats insisted upon increased military protection.

For the United States government, which had no intention of using military forces against either the Chinese armies or the other Powers, the pleas for military protection offered a unique opportunity. By maintaining a military presence in China, the government met its responsibilities to protect American lives and property. At the same time, the American military commitment gave the United States some influence upon the behavior of the other foreign forces in China and, presumably, checked their military adventures under the guise of occupying China in the name of peace and stability. Eventually, Japan would make a mockery of this policy, but for almost thirty years one Army infantry regiment, the antique vessels of the Asiatic Fleet, and units of the U.S. Marine Corps gave the United States a modicum of influence over events in China.[3]

Largely dictated by the State Department and modified by the recommendations of the American Minister in Peking and the admiral commanding the Asiatic Fleet, the American military presence in China from 1905 to 1941 was established in three ways. In north China, in accordance with the Boxer Protocol, the United States maintained a legation guard at Peking. From 1900 until 1905 the legation guard was a company of the 9th Infantry, but in 1905 the soldiers were for obscure reasons replaced by one hundred Marines. Apparently Minister W. W. Rockhill thought the Marines would provide a more prestigious guard, insofar as they had defended the Legation Quarter in 1900, were noted for their smartness, and could be reinforced without command squabbles from the ships guards of the Asiatic Fleet or from the yard guards in the Philippines. If simplifying the chain of command was a goal in replacing the soldiers, it was violated in 1912, when a battalion of the 15th Infantry arrived in Tientsin with the dual mission of guarding the international settlement and keeping the railroad open to Peking. From 1923 until its departure in 1938 the entire 15th Infantry became the main American contribution to the Tientsin defense force.[4]

The second American military concentration was primarily naval. After the war with Spain, the U.S. Navy maintained a flotilla of shallow-draft gunboats along central China's Yangtze River and its tributaries. Based at the great port of Shanghai near the East China Sea, the Yangtze gunboats patrolled the river through the large cities of Nanking, Hankow, and Chungking. In times of trouble, they could be reinforced with overage destroyers and cruisers from the Asiatic Fleet. Marines from the Asiatic Fleet could and did sail with the Yangtze gunboats as well as their cruisers.[5]

The Yangtze River patrol did not exhaust the Navy's ability to intervene locally, for other vessels of the Asiatic Fleet prowled the ports of the China coast, as they had done for years. Essentially the U.S. Navy made the Boxer Protocol garrisons in north China and the Yangtze Patrol credible, because it could dispatch both additional warships and Marines from the Philippines and Guam to the Peking-Tientsin garrisons and the Yangtze Patrol as well as steam into the harbor of any Chinese coastal city threatened with urban violence. Despite some problems with the Army over control of the north China forces, the Navy's representative in China, the admiral commanding the Asiatic Fleet, became an important voice in determining

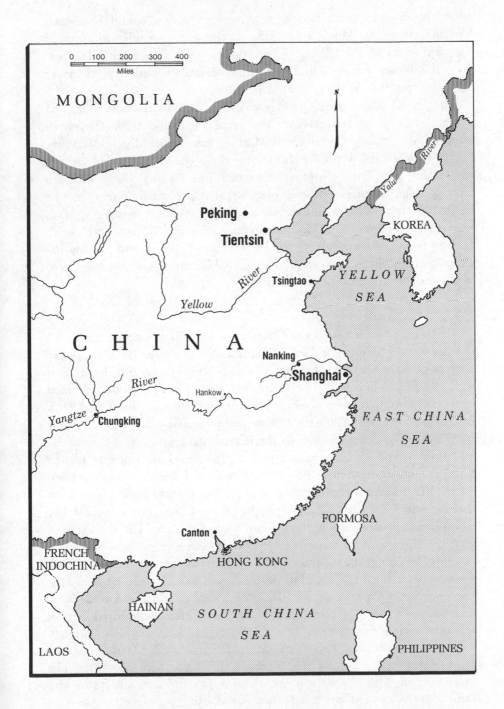

what the military contribution to American policy would be. Much like the American Minister in Peking, the admirals who interpreted the confusions of the Chinese Revolution usually recommended an increased military presence and preferred Marines to soldiers whenever they thought that presence should be ashore.[6]

The use of Marines in China grew from the same conditions that made the Corps so attractive to the State Department for Caribbean interventions. Fundamentally, the Marines were politically safe, having for years performed similar functions throughout the world at the cost of few casualties. Moreover, they could be sent by Navy warships from foreign stations without causing any particular flurry in the United States. With the exception of the Peking legation guard, Marines were not bound by the Boxer Protocol to cooperate with foreign troops. As a result of the "Open Door" policy and the Marine Corps's availability, American policy in China drew the Marine Corps into a long relationship with the Middle Kingdom.[7]

1

For the Marine Corps the China experience began and ended with the legation guard in Peking. Sporadically increased and decreased with the alarms caused by the Chinese Revolution and local civil wars, the legation guard grew from two officers and one hundred men to a small battalion of more than five hundred men by the early 1920s. Life in the Legation Quarter was busy and interesting by Marine Corps's standards. The legation guard specialized in hiking, marksmanship, and dress parades and remained one of the social adornments of the international community. For the officers and men of the legation guard, life was most comfortable. The Marine Corps's mess had at least three servants for each officer, and the enlisted men hired coolie labor to do laundry, clean the barracks, and cook for them. For the legation guard, military duty narrowed to the interesting essentials: field training, shooting, dress parades, and athletic contests against the other foreign detachments. The Marines' energies were largely absorbed in the Legation Quarter's social life. The daughter of the guard commander in 1911–1914 remembered that her parents employed fifteen servants and once went out thirty-six nights in succession.[8] Money was no problem, for American currency and credit were honored; most Marines signed chits for expenses and paid them monthly. The Marines vied with the British detachment for military smartness and athletic prowess and provided their band for social functions. One American Minister was sure the Marines were the best soldiers in Peking: "It was a delight to see the fine-looking companies of American marines, who among all the troops at Peking are noted for their well-groomed, smart, and soldierly appearance." [9] Despite the relative primitiveness of the barracks, the legation guard lived and trained with a high sense of well-being. Only occasionally would a member of the guard reflect on the incongruity of the American presence in China: "People always had an eye on you. It was just as if you were in a small boat on a big sea. You could be submerged and nobody would ever know what happened to you." [10] Despite feeling like Caucasian fish in a sea of Asians, the legation guard maintained itself as a critical component of the quarter defense force and an exemplary military unit.[11]

The upheavals of the early phase of the Chinese Revolution largely spared the Peking guard and placed the responsibility for military action on the ships guards of the Asiatic Fleet. On three occasions in 1911–1913 ships guards went ashore in or near Shanghai for a few days to guard American property and symbolize the State Department's dedication to international rights in China. In addition, Navy gunboats steamed up the Yangtze with Marine detachments embarked to cope with antiforeign riots in Wuchang, Hanyang, and Hankow, but the rival Chinese warlords generally restrained their troops from threatening foreigners or their property. Nevertheless, Marine battalions shuttled to and from the Philippines to provide extra muscle behind the Asiatic Fleet admiral's pronouncements on the sanctity of foreign property. As the soldiers of Yuan Shih-kai defeated the armies of Sun Yat-sen's military allies, the Yangtze Valley lapsed into an uneasy peace by the beginning of World War I.

The coming of the World War momentarily distracted the Navy from China and fundamentally changed the balance of power in the area by eliminating the Germans, by encouraging the Japanese to increase their pressure on Manchuria as revolution weakened Russia, and by reducing the European Powers' will to use military force in China to preserve their privileges. Only the Japanese improved their position during the war. The Americans, on the other hand, concentrated on a series of loan and railroad schemes, none of which either profited the investors or altered the balance of power in China. What military presence the United States maintained on the littoral of Asia was siphoned off from China to Asiatic Russia in 1918, when American Marines and soldiers participated in the intervention at Vladivostok to restrain the Japanese and aid the anti-Bolshevik armies in Siberia.

In the meantime, the Chinese Revolution became more radical, primarily because of internal unrest and resistance to Japanese imperialism. In May 1919 Chinese intellectuals and university students set off a series of national urban strikes that emphasized mass resistance to all foreign influences. Coalescing in Sun Yat-sen's reorganized Kuomintang party, the revolutionary movement turned away from the Western powers to pursue a strategy of civil war and closer relations with revolutionary Russia. While the revolutionaries were trying to unify south China through military campaigns and urban revolts, the warlords of the north fought among themselves to succeed the recently deceased Yuan Shih-kai. The military challenge to the Powers in China steadily increased.

As the war for China intensified, the Americans in Peking and Shanghai watched with dismay. Fearing radical urban mobs and undisciplined soldiers, American diplomats called for reinforcements. During a 1922 war between General Wu Pei-fu, the warlord ruler of north China, and General Chang Tso-lin, the generalissimo of all Manchuria, the Peking legation requested and received additional Marines. One ships detachment went to Peking, and a small Asiatic Fleet battalion occupied Tientsin to support the 15th Infantry and prepare for an overland dash to Peking. At Tientsin the Marines guarded American business installations and missions without incident.[12] Two years later the Kuomintang, bolstered by Russian advisers and military aid, once again challenged the warlords, who were themselves still fighting one another. Initially, the International Settlement at Shanghai, the most important foreign enclave in the Yangtze Valley, seemed in most danger from antiforeign mobs. In October 1924 the ships guard of the *Asheville* joined the settlement defense, soon to be reinforced by a hundred-man expeditionary force from the Philippines. The latter force was later sent to Tientsin to support the legation guard, which had already been expanded by 225 more Marines. Although the legation guard and the Tientsin force were reduced in 1925, additional Marines rotated in and out of Shanghai during most of that year.[13]

The pattern of Marine interposition to protect lives and property remained much the same through 1925, as the antiforeign agitation of the Kuomintang spread in the Yangtze Valley and the northern warlords conspired and fought for control of Peking. Early in the year the small expeditionary force at Tientsin withdrew, but another ships guard went ashore in Shanghai, where it was reinforced by an expeditionary force from the Philippines until February 9. In May, after the British-commanded police of the International Settlement had killed twelve student demonstrators, a company of Marines returned to Shanghai to guard American property during a mass boycott of foreign trade directed primarily at the British. Although the ships guards and expeditionary company reembarked by August, other detachments shuttled ashore at Shanghai and Tientsin until the end of the year. Vessels of the Asiatic Fleet hovered off the coast with additional Marine guards. The legation guard in Peking was equally busy. In both 1924 and 1925 the legation defense forces manned their positions to force warlord soldiers to abandon the Tartar Wall, to curb the flow of refugees, and to halt mobs of antiforeign student demonstrators who harried the Legation Quarter. Fearing another Boxer Rising, the Marines patrolled the quarter, organized caches of precious food and supplies, and kept in contact with outlying American missions and businesses. In performing their security duties, the Marines paraded with maximum spit and polish and self-restraint. At no time did the Marines jeopardize the American policy of avoiding combat with the Chinese and maintaining friendly (if distant) cooperation with other foreign armed forces.[14]

As the Marines patrolled Shanghai, Tientsin, and Peking, the Chinese Revolution deepened in its radicalism and violence, although the foreign communities were not yet seriously touched by either. The Kuomintang, fragmented after Sun's death in 1925, first rejected even nominal control from Peking and established its own national government in Canton, but then fell to fighting within itself. After a series of purges, the more radical wing of the Kuomintang (an uneasy alliance of reformist generals led by Chiang Kai-shek and the Communists) took control of most of the southern provinces and extended its influence into the cities of the Yangtze Valley. Aware of Soviet influence upon the Kuomintang, the Western nations and Japan braced for a "Red" assault upon their extraterritorial privileges and commercial concessions. The first priority of the Kuomintang, however, was to end warlordism in south China, a task accomplished by 1926. Hardly had this task been assumed when Chiang Kai-shek started a purge against the Communists, which added to the disorder in south China and impaired Chiang's ability to wrest control of the Yangtze Valley from the northern coalition of warlords led by Chang Tso-lin.

Still too small to influence events in China with the possible exception of restraining the other Powers, the Marine units ashore or afloat stood ready throughout 1926 to stop urban violence and preserve the bases of the Yangtze Patrol. Although the special guards at Tientsin and Shanghai were back aboard ship by June 1926, Rear Admiral C. S. Williams, commanding the Asiatic Fleet, kept his warships near the coast. In July 1926 the armies of Chiang Kai-shek began to probe north into the Yangtze Valley. The Nationalist advance resurrected the threat of violence against foreigners and galvanized the Asiatic Fleet into action. Admiral Williams ordered Marine units from his ships and the barracks at Cavite and Guam to stand ready for China duty, and in November the Guam detachment actually went ashore at Chinwangtao.

American policy, however, had not shifted to military intervention, for the State Department's position was that military expeditions would neither stop the Nationalists nor bring any special stability to central China. The "Old China hands" in the department generally favored an end to the foreign concessions, but they also feared that an end of extraterritoriality would finish European influence in China and increase the dangers to American lives and property. On the other hand, they thought no Chinese government could protect foreigners or withstand the pressures of the Russians and Japanese without American assistance. Adhering to the Nine Power Treaty (1922), which pledged the powers to respect Chinese sovereignty, the State Department did not want a military confrontation with the Chinese, because it suspected such a confrontation would give the Japanese and Russians a pretext for intervention. At the same time, it recognized that the American military presence might not only save lives but allow the United States to curb the Russian and Japanese imperialists until such time as some stable regime could govern all of China and renegotiate the unequal treaties to China's satisfaction. The Marines were needed in China not only to protect foreign lives and property but to prevent foreign military intervention in the Chinese civil war—without actually fighting. It was a difficult assignment and certainly beyond the capacity of the small detachments with which the Marine Corps had thus far provided the Asiatic Fleet.[15]

2

By early 1927 the Nationalist movement had mustered sufficient military strength and popular support to begin Chiang Kai-shek's long-planned offensive against the northern warlord alliance led by Chang Tso-lin. Fanning the emotions of the peasantry and urban workers with antiforeign propaganda against the unequal treaties, revolutionary organizers and political cadres moved ahead of the Nationalist armies into the Yangtze Valley, while the forces of two warlord allies moved cautiously toward Peking from their northwestern strongholds. Although their policy was not to harm foreign lives and property, Nationalist officials and army officers could not curb all inflammatory calls to attack foreigners or control all their soldiers, let alone the urban workers, who were often led by the Communists. Besides, the administrative apparatus of the northern warlord coalition along the Yangtze was rapidly dissolving in the face of the Nationalist advance, and there were few police or disciplined troops to face the urban mobs, bandits, and rowdy soldiers floating between the two warring factions. Under these conditions, the safety of foreigners became increasingly problematic.[16]

Faced with reports of increased violations of foreign property rights and threats to American citizens, the State Department once again reexamined its position on the Chinese Revolution. Although its protests failed to satisfy its own representatives in China and some American businessmen, the State Department refrained from suggesting that military intervention was likely and, in addition, placed limits on Navy cooperation with other foreign gunboats in order to reduce the exposure to incidents sparked by the more militant British and French. The American position was that the unequal treaties were negotiable, but not until one of the Chinese factions had established a stable national government. In the meantime, the State Department wanted to avoid incidents that might inflame American domestic demands for punitive military action against the Chinese. Military protection of a limited sort seemed to serve this purpose. Military forces would not be used to enforce treaty rights, which meant dissociation from the other Powers, even though other nations' military units might help protect American lives and property. The State Department's position, shaped by Secretary of State Frank Kellogg and endorsed by President Calvin Coolidge, was intricate and in an operational sense full of inherent contradictions. It was a diplomatic position designed to make the most sophisticated military commander more than a trifle bilious.[17]

The United States met the first threats to its nationals in the Yangtze Valley by increasing its naval presence on the river. Two destroyers joined the gunboat flotilla of seven in the autumn of 1926, and armed guards were placed on American-flag vessels, some of which had received sniper fire. American diplomats attempted to move their nationals out of the interior to the valley's larger cities, where foreign settlements offered some protection. In early 1927 the situation worsened when one of these enclaves, the British concession in Hankow, was racked with rioting and then surrendered to the Nationalists. This blow to the legitimacy of the treaty system lead to further disorders in central China, followed by the flight of many Americans to Shanghai and the movement of much of the Asiatic Fleet to Chinese waters. Although Nationalist leaders emphasized that the Americans were not to be harmed, they could not curb the anarchy spreading along the Yangtze Valley.

The foreign position in central China ultimately rested on control of Shanghai, near the mouth of the Yangtze. Established at the end of the First Opium War in 1842, the International Settlement of Shanghai had grown into a state within a state. Nearly one-third of the city's 3 million inhabitants lived in the International Settlement, and its 5,500 acres covered half the city. In addition, the French maintained their own concession south of the International Settlement. The Settlement itself was a unique mix of an Asian and a European city, although in appearance it was Western and modern. From a military standpoint, it had both advantages and drawbacks. Its chief advantage was that it was bordered on the south by the Whangpoo River, which served both as an avenue for supplies and reinforcements and as a barrier. The geographic disadvantages were more numerous. First, a large creek to the west, the Soochow, broke the Settlement into two subdivisions. Moreover, the Settlement was surrounded by thickly populated Chinese suburbs on three sides, and the city's main railroad system and much of its industrial area lay outside its boundaries. Politically, the Settlement had its own government and police force as well as a volunteer militia, but it could not have functioned without its Chinese inhabitants—even if they also were a potentially hostile mob.

As the center of foreign trade in China and cultural center of European China, Shanghai could not be abandoned without serious diplomatic repercussions. From December 1926 to January 1927, consular officials and military commanders in the Settlement discussed defense plans and concluded that they needed reinforcements, a conclusion endorsed by John V. A. MacMurray, the American Minister in Peking. Although Great Britain agreed to send a full division to Shanghai, Coolidge announced that the United States would not send troops, as it had no concessions to defend. The State Department and Admiral Williams, however, advised the President that the sanctity of the Settlement and the protection of American lives and property were indivisible. As a precautionary measure and a possible restraint against European excesses, Coolidge approved the assembly of the 4th Marine Regiment at San Diego on January 25, and three days later the regiment was ordered to sail for China. Although the State Department asked both Chinese factions to neutralize Shanghai and insisted that the Americans were not intervening, the Chinese interpreted the act as hostile military intervention.[18]

Fresh from guarding the mails west of the Missouri River from bandits, the headquarters and two battalions of the 4th Regiment sailed westward on the transport *Chaumont* on February 3. Arriving at an anchorage at the Standard Oil compound five miles from Shanghai on February 24, the regiment learned that President Coolidge had rejected Minister MacMurray's recommendation that the

Marines join the Settlement defense force. Instead the Marines would remain aboard the *Chaumont* until there was a direct threat to American lives and property. MacMurray continued to insist that one mission could not be divorced from another, and the State Department compromised by transferring responsibility for landing the regiment to Admiral Williams. When the regiment's commander, Colonel Charles S. Hill, conferred with the British major general commanding the Settlement defense force and Admiral Williams, he learned that the Settlement regulars (primarily a British division of 13,000 men) and the Shanghai Volunteer Corps (SVC) wanted a perimeter defense, but that Williams would only allow the Marines (should they land) to perform internal security duty. Following his scant guidance from Washington, Williams judged that Marine patrols would help the Settlement yet would avoid fighting with Chinese troops.[19]

Penned aboard their transport by the caution of Admiral Williams and the American consul in Shanghai, the Marines waited, watched, and stewed both physically and mentally in their hot, crowded compartments. The only contact with Shanghai came for those officers and sergeants who reconnoitered the Settlement and for small liberty parties. Finally, the whole regiment made a march through the Settlement on March 5 for exercise and psychological effect. In the meantime, the regimental staff planned in an emergency to send one battalion to the Settlement's northeastern section and the other to the western section. The Marines' area would cover two-thirds of the Settlement, but they would be prohibited from manning the sandbagged, barricaded perimeter defenses, which were manned by the British, Japanese, other European regulars, and the SVC. The Marines would share the internal security mission with the multinational Settlement police.

As the Nationalist armies slowly closed on Shanghai and tension in the city mounted during March, the 4th Regiment finally landed to stay in the afternoon of March 21. That same day the Shanghai municipal council declared a state of emergency and requested assistance from all foreign troops to preserve order in the Settlement. Persuaded that the emergency was real, Admiral Williams and the American consul ordered the regiment, which had just returned from another practice march, to land immediately. As the Marines ran to their posts during the next five hours, fighting broke out in the Chinese sections of the city between the Communist workers' militia and the warlord soldiery guarding the city's suburbs. The fighting raged for two days until the Nationalists arrived, and the British at one moment actually opened fire and killed warlord troops attempting to storm the Settlement in search of a refuge. The Marines did not join the perimeter defense (much to the disappointment of both the Marines and the British defense commander) and experienced little trouble with their internal patrol duties. The Shanghai situation, however, had not improved from the Western viewpoint. The Communists and radical Nationalist troops controlled the Chinese city, and the Settlement government feared attack.[20]

The long-feared antiforeign incident occurred in Nanking, not Shanghai, and its effect was to bring more Marines to China. On March 24, 1927, uncontrolled Nationalist troops pillaged foreign property, including several consulates, in Nanking and killed and wounded some foreigners. British, American, and Japanese warships off Nanking put landing parties ashore, and two American destroyers shelled a Chinese mob closing upon American refugees on Standard Oil Hill. The sailors themselves took casualties, and the foreign businessmen, missionaries, and diplomatic officials fled to their warships. The local naval commanders planned to bombard the city but were restrained at the last minute by their superiors. The incident alarmed European commanders in China. In Shanghai Admiral Williams conferred with newly arrived Brigadier General Smedley D. Butler, who had been sent to command all Marine forces in China, and learned that more Marines were available for foreign duty. Butler was dismayed that the Peking legation wanted an Army brigade to replace the Marines and insisted that Williams request Marine reinforcements immediately. As Butler wrote his old comrade, Commandant John A. Lejeune: "You surely agree with me that it would have been suicide for our Corps, had the Army come to Shanghai and we be put on a ship and sent home." [21] With Butler's prodding, Williams on March 25 requested and received Marine reinforcements: two battalions of the 6th Regiment, an artillery battery, two aircraft squadrons, and a brigade headquarters and service company for China duty.

Although the Nationalists were more energetic in controlling their troops and soothing the Powers after the Nanking Incident, the flow of American troops to China mounted, buoyed up by temporary Congressional and public enthusiasm for intervention. There was, however, little taste for punitive action in Washington, and the State Department did not modify Admiral Williams's orders. In fact, in the next year, it made sure that Commander Asiatic Fleet understood that he was to protect American lives by evacuating Americans from the interior of China and was to guard property only when necessary as part of the lifesaving mission. In fact and practice, the American intervention was designed not only to protect American lives but to increase American influence among the foreign diplomatic community. That influence was used to curb European and Japanese plans for joint military action. To amplify its voice in diplomatic counsels, the United States increased its military strength in China by dispatching a brigade of Marines. By preparing to fight but not fighting, this brigade was supposed to win Chinese respect through good troop discipline and prevent other Powers from waging war by refusing to cooperate with them.[22]

As the remainder of the 3d Brigade sailed for China in early April 1927, the 4th Regiment established a garrison in Shanghai that was to last nearly fifteen years. To save his worn troops, Butler changed the foot patrols to small but heavily armed motorized patrols and, as the threat of Chinese action waned in April, persuaded Williams to allow the Marines to hand over their patrol duties to the Settlement police and the SVC. By the time the rest of the 3d Brigade arrived, the Marines were settled into leased barracks and had assumed the role of emergency reserve force. Although the 3d Brigade had sailed without rations and ammunition, but afire with the mission "to keep the Communists out of Shanghai," the Marines soon learned that their daily problems were reduced to standing rigorous inspections, training, finding Chinese and White Russian girlfriends, and supervising the coolies who did all the routine garrison labor for a pittance. Duty in Shanghai rapidly assumed a quaint imperial character: athletic contests, shooting matches, much leisure time, spit and polish parades, friendly rivalry with the British troops in sports and band concerts, and a good deal of free time to explore the city's many sensory fascinations.[23]

No sooner, however, had the situation at Shanghai stabilized than the American legation in Peking, watching the Nationalist armies advance toward north China, requested more troops for duty in Tientsin. Encouraged by Admiral Williams and Brigadier General Joseph Castner, the senior Army commander in China, MacMurray asked that an Army brigade be sent to Tientsin. The War Department turned down a request to activate War Plan YELLOW, the contingency plan for the relief of Peking and the defense of Shanghai. Rebuffed by the Army, the State Department asked the Navy Department for more Marines and a build-up of the number of warships in Chinese waters, which reached fifty in May 1927. Secretary of State Kellogg agreed to reinforce the 15th Infantry at Tientsin, but only as an enclave to which the legation could retreat. There would not be another march on Peking unless the legation was directly attacked, which seemed unlikely.

A third Marine force sailed for China to join the 3d Brigade and allow Butler to divide his force between Shanghai and Tientsin in

June 1927. The reinforcements included a full artillery battalion of the 10th Regiment (less the battery already in Shanghai), a tank platoon, an engineer company, aviation support troops, and the two missing battalions of the two infantry regiments already in China. Formed as a provisional regiment and held in the Philippines, the infantry did not join the brigade in Shanghai like the other troops, but its men were eventually sent to China and absorbed into the 4th and 6th Regiments or used to form (along with ships guards and other detachments) an additional unit, the 12th Regiment. Leaving the 4th Regiment in Shanghai, Butler concentrated the rest of the 3d Brigade in Tientsin. With the legation guard and the reinforced 15th Infantry, the American troops in northern China soon numbered more than 5,000 in a force of 16,000 foreign troops.

When Butler arrived in Tientsin he found that his brigade's mission had not been simplified by the redeployment or the reinforcements. His troops were to protect American lives only, but to do so by preventing foreign intervention through noncooperation and by cultivating good relations with Chinese military commanders and the general populace. Under State Department interpretations, the 3d Brigade, unlike the 15th Infantry and the Peking legation guard, had no obligation to cooperate with other foreign forces under the terms of the Boxer Protocol. Butler, for example, told other commanders that his Marines might save the Americans in Peking, but they would not guard the Tientsin–Peking railroad or join any integrated defense command for the Tientsin concessions. Attempting to simplify his complex mission, Butler encouraged Minister MacMurray to move to the Tientsin enclave, but the stubborn diplomat would not leave Peking, thus leaving the Marines with the problem of planning to relieve the legation through unilateral action. At the same time, Butler did not say that he would categorically refuse cooperation or combat, and he sent staff representatives to foreign commanders' conferences.[24]

Throughout the rest of 1927 and all of 1928, Butler's 3d Brigade supported American foreign policy in China by its mere presence and through delicate negotiations with the Nationalists in the Yangtze Valley and with the warlord armies still holding north China. In Shanghai the 4th Regiment found that the worst enemies were boredom, drunkenness, and venereal disease, but the successive regimental commanders countered the lack of action with a rigorous schedule of military training, athletics, and social events. Heartened by the cheapness of coolie labor and entertainment, the troops remained exemplary garrison Marines and enjoyed contact with the British battalions in martial competitions and formal parades. Whether in forest green or khaki uniforms, the regiment became a showpiece in appearance and won the affection of the International Settlement. The regimental staff collected intelligence, made defense plans, and sent out small detachments to ride shotgun for the Yangtze Patrol, but the 4th Regiment found Shanghai routine if exotic garrison duty.[25]

In Tientsin the rest of the 3d Brigade found China service more demanding, if only because of Smedley Butler's presence and the requirement that the Marines stand ready to relieve Peking. Butler divided much of his time negotiating with the Japanese, who were taking an increasingly militant attitude toward the Chinese, and with the local Army commanders, who wanted the Marines firmly integrated into the Protocol defense system. The Chinese population and warlord forces were the least of Butler's problems, for good troop behavior and careful liaison removed most antagonistic issues. Butler kept his men busy with military training, athletics, and organized entertainment. He also held periodic exercises to test the brigade's readiness to move by truck to Peking. By preloading vehicles and building emergency benches and supply pallets that could be mounted on flatbed trucks, Butler organized a relief force of two thousand men and eighteen aircraft capable of getting on the road to Peking in two hours. His Marines were equally prepared to defend Tientsin if necessary. As one commander of the Asiatic Fleet remarked, Butler and his men showed unexpected restraint in performing duties "very unusual and quite different from anything the Marines usually are called upon to perform." [26] By the end of 1928 the Tientsin force reached a peak strength of 3,372 Marines even though the Navy Department wanted to begin reducing both the Shanghai and Tientsin forces. The State Department balked at withdrawal, believing that the brigade restrained the Japanese and encouraged the Chinese to respect foreign treaty rights. As with other interventions, it was often easier to commit troops than to withdraw them.[27]

Butler fully appreciated the delicacy of the brigade's position, both in its relationships with other military units in China and in American domestic politics. Even after the Nationalists finally occupied north China in the summer of 1928, Butler thought the brigade's presence in Shanghai and Peking was crucial to maintaining American influence (however benign) on events in China—as long as there was no fighting. He also thought that the 15th Infantry should be withdrawn in order to break any ties to the Protocol forces. He was not, however, as enthusiastic as the State Department about keeping the Marines in

Tientsin, primarily because he recognized that the ambiguities in American foreign policy might eventually force the Marines into unpopular pacification operations, even to save American lives:

> I can plainly see that the foreign policy of our administration with regard to occupations of weaker . . . countries is endangered. As long as we occupy these countries without great uproar and particularly, without the loss of our men, little attention is paid to our movements by the public at large. We may even kill a lot of the natives of such countries without much comment on the part of the press and state but, as soon as our losses begin to grow there is a big "hubbub," as you no doubt know, . . . and the Corps comes in for unfavorable criticism and the finger of accusation is inevitably pointed at the head of the administration for trusting us to quiet the disturbances, using our own judgment as to the numbers and disposal of troops necessary to make the job a good one.[28]

To ensure that there was no fighting with the Chinese, Butler's staff announced Marine Corps training flights, did not buy permanent barracks, worked closely with local Chinese commanders, and checked Japanese plans to expand the areas controlled by foreign troops.

Even though Nationalist control of north China was tenuous, the commander of the Asiatic Fleet proposed that the 3d Brigade be withdrawn from Tientsin since to support it would be difficult in case of war and because the 15th Infantry was adequate to maintain a refuge for American citizens. The State Department finally concurred, and throughout the last half of 1928 the Tientsin force returned to the United States or the Philippines. The 4th Regiment, however, was left in Shanghai to preserve the base of the Yangtze Patrol and reinforce the Settlement defense force. MacMurray wanted both Marine contingents withdrawn; Butler recommended that both remain on reduced status and be rotated to and from the Philippines. The Navy compromised and left the 4th Regiment in place, arguing that it could be hurriedly reinforced or evacuated by sea if necessary. Although the 3d Brigade disbanded in 1929 as the threat to foreigners waned, the Marine Corps added Shanghai to its list of permanent stations.[29]

3

The continued fighting in China did not again menace the international settlements until 1931. The Nationalists continued to preach an end to the unequal treaties and new tariff and administrative arrangements with the West, but the direct military threat to foreigners subsided except in rural areas infested with banditry. Of the Western nations, the United States was most willing to end the unequal treaties, and the Nationalist leaders fully appreciated the American lead in their behalf. Of all the Powers only Russia, Japan, and Great Britain sought to preserve their economic concessions and legal privileges unaltered. Even though the Soviet Union and Japan were still deeply antagonistic, they worked together in inadvertent harmony to stop the Nationalists from controlling Manchuria. American diplomacy, on the other hand, reinforced by sympathetic newspaper reports and Pearl Buck's novels about the "new" China, supported the Nationalists' legitimacy and the "Open Door." Unable to hold north China, the Kuomintang established a new capital in Nanking. Nevertheless, the United States kept its diplomatic mission in Peking and dealt with a succession of warlord-governors as if they were as legitimate as the Nanking government. The Marine guard remained with the legation.

For the legation guard, three companies of some five hundred officers and men, the rhythm of garrison life was seldom troubled by China's turmoil. The Marines drilled with their weapons—which included machine guns, mortars, and light artillery—took practice marches, shot the rifle qualification course near the ocean each year, and spent half of each day in athletics. Coolies did all the heavy, messy work. The guard's primary duty remained the defense of the Legation Quarter and scattered American missions and businesses in the city. To assist them the Marines in 1907 had created a small mounted detachment (the "Horse Marines") for use in crowd control and for warning the Americans living in the hinterlands. Mounted originally on cast-off Mongolian ponies from the Peking racetrack, the "Horse Marines" became an elite unit noted for their smart appearance, élan in mounted drill, and arrogance. The general attraction to service in the mounted detachment was quite practical. The detachment invariably played the "enemy" in field problems and was allowed to gallop back to the city at their conclusion, thus putting "Horse Marines" into the best bars and brothels long before their comrades afoot got liberty. Such privileges compensated for the chore of grooming the unfriendly ponies the Marines rode.[30]

The legation guard had a series of scares when the city changed hands among the Chinese generals, and the Marines had to tolerate an increasingly unfriendly Japanese detachment, but life in Peking was still cheap, entertaining, and exotic. In addition to military training, the guard challenged the 15th Infantry and the foreign detachments to virtually every game anyone could play, maintained fancy clubs, and scheduled an unending round of dances, smokers, and dinners. Even Japanese occupation of the rest of Peking in 1937 did not halt the social life of the isolated legation community. For the Marines who served in Peking and others who went there only in their imaginations, the curious ambience of the city was captured in the short stories of Captain John W. Thomason, Jr., who served in Peking in the 1930s. An accomplished illustrator and author, Thomason wrote for the *Saturday Evening Post, Harper's,* and *The New Yorker.* His tales of simple Marines in the confusing Orient, collected in *Salt Winds and Gobi Dust* (1934), linked China and the Marine Corps together in the minds of Americans who had never heard of the 4th Regiment. Yet the legation guard became an anachronism even though it provided at least a symbolic presence. In 1938 the Army finally received State Department permission to withdraw the 15th Infantry; a detachment of two hundred Marines from Peking took up the watch in Tientsin and helped fight a massive flood there in 1939. Two years later both detachments, stranded by diplomatic indecision, surrendered in the early days of the war with Japan.[31]

For the 4th Regiment in Shanghai, duty in China was as comfortable as it was for the legation guard. Quarters were roomy and cheap; servants were plentiful; the food and drink were delicious and cheap; the women friendly and cheap. All the enlisted men paid a "boy" to maintain their uniforms and equipment. Dodging the Settlement's Sikh police, the Marines roared off from their training and group athletics into Shanghai's night life, signing chits to be honored on paydays and arguing about baseball, beer, and their companies' prowess. Many a Marine boarded the Navy transport *Henderson* (so decrepit that it was nicknamed *Henny Maru*) for home with reluctance.[32]

The Japanese army interrupted the 4th Marines'* Asian idyll in 1931. Concerned over the Nationalists' growing military strength and Chiang Kai-shek's pledge to bring Manchuria under complete Chinese control, Japanese officers launched a campaign of conquest with Tokyo's permission. The United States responded by condemning the act and refused to recognize the Japanese successor state of Manchukuo. Unable to mount a successful military reaction to the Mukden Incident, the Nationalist regime advocated nonresistance, but it could not stop anti-Japanese riots in central China; one such mob in Shanghai killed five Japanese monks, and many Chinese boycotted Japanese businesses throughout China. In retaliation a Japanese mob in Shanghai destroyed Chinese shops and killed several Chinese. While the local Japanese commander, an admiral of the Special Naval Landing Force, negotiated for an apology and reparations, the Chinese general commanding the 19th Route Army moved his troops into the city's northern suburbs. Fearing

* After 1930 all USMC regiments were called "Marines," without adding the word "Regiment."

a Chinese attack, the Settlement defense force rushed to the barricades. The 4th Marines, flanked by a British brigade and the SVC, held the middle sector of the Settlements, with its front lines on Soochow Creek. The Japanese held all of the Settlement east of the creek and north of the Whangpoo River, but instead of waiting on the defense, they attacked the Chinese on January 28, 1932.

For the next three months the 4th Marines tried to keep their portion of the Settlement neutral. The regiment had two problems: preventing the Japanese from using their sector for attacks on the Chinese and stopping mobs of Japanese civilians from massacring Chinese within the Settlement. Through firmness, restraint, and military preparedness, the Marines curbed the rioters and turned back Japanese units that had come into the sector to "protect" Japanese property from enviable firing positions along the Chinese flank on Soochow Creek. The American position was strengthened by reinforcements. Although the Hoover administration had no taste for direct military action against Japan (the Army–Navy Joint Board thought a war with Japan would last ten years), Secretary of State Henry L. Stimson wanted the Shanghai garrison increased in order to deter the Japanese and passively to assist the 19th Route Army, which was fighting well. In early February the 4th Marines received four hundred additional men and the 31st U.S. Infantry to strengthen their lines. The additional troops settled into the sandbagged machine gun nests and infantry strongpoints. Although stray shells and bombs hit the Settlement, there were no further encroachments into the neutralized portion guarded by the Americans. The Japanese, however, flanked the 19th Route Army from the north and forced its withdrawal. The fighting ended in early March with the withdrawal of the Chinese army. After international negotiations, the Japanese also returned to their Settlement positions, and the crisis passed. Without a casualty, the 4th Marines had again not only protected the Settlement but probably also contributed to the Japanese decision to halt the fighting.[33]

The 4th Marines' success in defending the Settlement in 1932 and the constabulary naval actions of the Yangtze Patrol convinced the State Department that the continued military presence in China was a useful adjunct of American diplomacy with both the Chinese and the Japanese. At a minimum the Shanghai enclave served as a refuge for the ten thousand Americans left in China, but the Marines and Navy also supported "by peaceful means influences contributory to [the] preservation and encouragement of orderly processes" and demonstrated America's willingness to back commitments like the "Open Door."[34] Even though the 4th Marines' presence was largely symbolic, the regiment took seriously its new responsibilities for defending the Soochow Creek line in the Settlement's southern portion. After the 1932 crisis the 4th Marines grew to three battalions of 1,600 men, a strength the commanding officer considered essential for his sector's defense. Two years later, however, the force fell again to a thousand men when the State Department (then engaged in disarmament talks) requested a reduction in American troops overseas.[35]

Far from the Shanghai Racecourse, where the 4th Marines paraded in tailored uniforms to the music of their own fife and drum corps, the struggle for the mastery of China continued. Although by 1935 Chiang Kai-shek had managed to establish dictatorial control over the Kuomintang and the Nanking government, he would not free his armies from a bitter antiguerrilla campaign against the Communists. Taking advantage of the Nationalists' internal squabbles, the Japanese through puppet warlords extended their hegemony south from Manchuria. Chiang's efforts to appease Japan met with little success, and the Japanese government itself slid under the control of Army factions committed to the conquest of China for economic and ideological reasons. In July 1937 Japanese and Chinese troops clashed in several incidents around Peking; on August 8 the ancient capital fell to a Japanese column, and the second Sino-Japanese war had begun.

The war came to Shanghai as quickly as it spread throughout northern China. During July Chinese troops moved into the northern suburb of Chapei across Soochow Creek from the International Settlement, a position that confronted the Japanese-defended portion of the Settlement. Thousands of civilians fled into the western portion of the Settlement and the French Concession to the south. As the British and American troops went on alert, the Japanese moved warships and Special Naval Landing Force units into Shanghai. After two Japanese were killed by Chinese militia on August 9, the Japanese attacked Chinese positions in Chapei and north of the city on August 13. Since the Nationalists were preparing their main defenses along the Yangtze Valley, which Shanghai anchored near the sea, the Japanese offensive was not a retaliatory raid but the beginning of a full-scale attack.

For the 4th Marines the paramount concern was preventing the Japanese from using their sector to flank Chapei and preserving order in the Settlement. The Marines had orders not to fight the Japanese, and the first mission rested on diplomacy and bluff. The Chinese army was fighting well around Shanghai, so the Japanese did not try to flank it from the south but instead landed reinforcements from the Yangtze north of the city. A Japanese tactical decision thus made the Marines' duties somewhat easier. Unlike the 1932 engagement, however, the second battle of Shanghai did not spare the International Settlement, for Chinese airplanes attacking Japanese positions and warships mistakenly bombed the European sectors, causing more than a thousand casualties, mostly Chinese. In the chaos the Marines evacuated Americans living northeast of Soochow Creek and fully manned their perimeter defenses. With fifty-eight fortified positions to man, the regiment was hard pressed for troops, and even support troops performed infantry duties. As the fighting north of the creek continued unabated, Admiral Harry E. Yarnell, commander of the Asiatic Fleet, asked for reinforcements. Even though the 4th Marines had managed to negotiate neutrality with the Japanese, the Settlement was far from secure.[36]

Reluctant to confuse his command structure by asking the Army for an infantry regiment from the Philippines, Yarnell requested more Marines, and at San Diego the Marine Corps ordered a brigade headquarters (the 2d) and the 6th Marines to prepare for expeditionary duty. The mobilization was not an entirely happy event for Headquarters, for it stripped the Pacific Fleet of its only Marine regiment. In addition, the 6th Marines lost nearly a third of its strength when men with less than a year to serve refused to extend their enlistments for foreign duty; unlike 1927 China duty was no longer novel and promised little action. Nevertheless, within six weeks of being alerted the 2d Brigade headquarters had arrived in Shanghai and the 6th Marines were replacing the exhausted 4th Marines along the perimeter defenses. The two regiments, which had been supplemented by two ships guards in August, gave the American sector a sturdy defense.[37]

Until the Japanese tore open the Chinese lines north of the city in late October 1937, the 2d Brigade manned its outposts and patrolled its sector. Only three Marines were slightly wounded by stray bullets. After the Chinese army withdrew, the Settlement defense force found itself more concerned about Japanese intentions than ever before. Although he was certain that the immediate threat to the Settlement had passed, Brigadier General John C. Beaumont, the brigade commander, thought that the Japanese would not allow the International Settlement to live peacefully. The Japanese now controlled the lower Yangtze with a fleet and 200,000 troops. The European position was perilous.[38]

The collapse of the Nationalist position on the Yangtze in late 1937 eliminated what little influence the American military presence in China might have had upon the Japanese, but in Washington's eyes it did not yet justify the Marines' complete withdrawal. Basically sympathetic to the Chinese and hostile to Japan, the Roosevelt administration struggled to find some way to restrain the Japanese without actually fighting. This position assumed even more importance after Japanese aircraft bombed the gunboat *Panay* in December 1937, and the Japanese by word and deed demonstrated their hostility to the European gunboats on the Yangtze. Maintaining the International Settlement was one way to preserve a Western presence in China as well as save foreign lives; the city also still served as a principal base for the Yangtze Patrol. As the city slipped into the quiet of the moribund in early 1938, all of the Brigade but the 4th Marines left Shanghai, although the 6th Marines remained alerted for China duty.[39] The immediate American policy, however, was to avoid conflict with Japan and evacuate those citizens who wanted to leave China. A European island in the sea of the Japanese army, the International Settlement struggled along with fake gaiety and growing grimness as the Japanese officers and their puppet Chinese officials harried the remaining Europeans.[40]

Frustrated by his inability to halt Japanese aggression and restrained by Congressional and public opinion, Franklin Roosevelt could not use the Marine Corps for military purposes, but he could and did use one Marine officer to educate himself and stir pro-Chinese public opinion. That officer was Captain Evans F. Carlson, whom the President had met and had come to admire in 1937, when Carlson had commanded the Marine guard at White Sulphur Springs, Georgia. Carlson was equally impressed with the President's philanthropy toward fellow polio sufferers and admired the humanitarian programs of the New Deal. Carlson himself was an idealistic, romantic military adventurer. He had served nearly seven years in the Army as an enlisted man and officer before enlisting as a Marine private in 1922. Commissioned the next year, he served with distinction in Nicaragua and spent two long tours in China, where he learned the language and made many acquaintances. In late 1937 Roosevelt sent Carlson back to Shanghai, ostensibly to study Chinese, but in reality for informal political and military reporting on the Chinese capacity to wage war. For nearly a year Carlson wandered about the Chinese hinterland, visiting both Nationalist and Communist armies. Impressed by both forces, Carlson reported Chinese patriotism and valor in glowing terms. He especially admired the egalitarianism of the Communist armies and their programs of social reform, and he suggested to Roosevelt that the American armed forces needed more social democracy. Upon his return in 1938, however, Carlson chose to leave the Marine Corps and the cause of military reform in order to speak and write in favor of pro-Chinese intervention. The Marine Corps, however, had not seen the last of Carlson and his "Red" concepts of leadership.[41]

In Shanghai the 4th Marines watched the twilight of European imperialism in China. The Marine regiment and a small British brigade were all that remained to stiffen the Settlement's government and its municipal police, both of which were harassed by the Japanese. Colonel Charles F. B. Price and his subordinates found themselves in continuing negotiations with the Japanese commanders over jurisdictional disputes and foreign rights. At stake were the autonomous Settlement government, its police force, and the SVC, as well as foreign access to facilities outside the Settlement. In essence, the Japanese argued that the Settlement no longer needed any military forces or police, because the Japanese would now protect everyone from the Chinese. The British and Americans rejected this position, and the 4th Marines helped stop Japanese agitation within the Settlement. From 1938 through 1941 the Marines mounted internal security patrols to eject Japanese agitators, break up mobs, guard buildings against terrorist bombings, and man the perimeter defenses. After 1940 they performed these tasks alone, for the British brigade withdrew. For all its discipline and expertise, the 4th Marines' position was untenable. By the end of 1940 the Commander Asiatic Fleet was urging the regiment's withdrawal, and the Yangtze Patrol itself began to abandon the river. Marine dependents were sent home, and the regiment prepared desperate breakout plans. Finally, as diplomatic relations with Japan worsened in 1941, the State Department consented to the 4th Marines' departure. At the end of November 1941 the regiment's last echelon marched to its awaiting transport, the cheers of the Settlement inhabitants evoking sorrow and some sense of guilt for its eleventh-hour escape. The Shanghai adventure had ended, and with it a phase of Chinese history, American diplomacy, and Marine Corps service in the Orient.[42]

The 4th Marines' destination: Corregidor.

9. Nicaragua: End of an Era
1926—1933

The military occupation of Hispaniola and the "Open Door" policy in China did not exhaust the State Department's use of Marines as an instrument of American foreign policy. As neighbors to the Panama Canal and laboratories for missionary diplomacy, the five republics of Central America drew the attention of the State Department and the few Americans with economic interests in the area. American diplomacy in Central America followed the broad lines established between 1901 and 1921: The United States would use its influence to prevent wars between the republics and civil war within them and thus to encourage democratic government based on popular elections. Peace would provide conditions in which economic development and social progress might flourish, aided by foreign investment and foreign loans to stabilize governments. Such development would bring greater social stability, which in turn would reduce the possibility of political violence and the likelihood of intervention by either the European powers or the area's newest agitator, revolutionary Mexico. Although the State Department doubted that it could really create a utopian Central America or establish U.S. hegemony in the area, it did seek an influence there that would go beyond protecting American lives and property.[1]

The State Department expressed its position in a series of international agreements that affected the area. In 1907 the five republics, encouraged by the United States and Mexico, pledged to submit their disputes to an international tribunal, agreed not to interfere in one another's internal politics, and promised not to let revolutionaries mount military operations from their territory against their neighbors. Although the 1907 treaties did not work well in practice, the State Department in 1922 resuscitated them in another series of Central American agreements. In the General Treaty of Peace and Amity and a group of supporting conventions, the State Department made its own position clear, even if it did not persuade the Central American republics to share its views wholeheartedly. The new agreements reaffirmed the principles of nonaggression and the peaceful settlement of regional disputes as well as the continued pledge not to assist insurgents. The signatory states also promised not to recognize a government that came to power by coup or civil war and even not to recognize the election of a head of state who had participated in a successful revolt or was disqualified by constitutional requirements. At the State Department's urging, the signatories agreed to eliminate all standing armed forces and to replace them with constabularies trained by foreign instructors, meaning Americans. Although the Central American republics accepted this convention, they insisted on maintaining their own armies, however expensive and unreliable.

All five Central American republics caused concern to the State Department, but Nicaragua became its most exasperating problem. Nicaragua was a land of four peoples and three regions. In the 1920s it had a population of perhaps 700,000, divided into four general racial categories: 17 percent of the population was pure Spanish, 70 percent Spanish-Indian or *mestizo,* 9 percent Caribbean black, and 4 percent pure Indian. The bulk of the white and *mestizo* population lived in the cities and farm villages on the western coastal plain that ran along the Pacific Ocean and encircled Lake Managua and Lake Nicaragua. Although volcanoes and earthquakes made the western area a precarious place to live, its soil and rainfall supported farms and cattle ranches as well as a net of regional trade centers from Corinto on the coast through Leon and Managua, the capital, to Granada on Lake Nicaragua.

A minority of the population, largely *mestizo,* Indian, and black, lived in the two other areas, which made up the larger portion of Nicaragua. Running like a wedge from the Honduran border, the mountainous central highlands supported poor subsistence farms and occasional mines, some foreign-owned. Most of the land outside the river valley towns of Ocotal, Quilali, and Jicaro was pine forest and scrub. At the western edge of the highlands rested the region's largest towns, Jinotega and Matagalpa. Beyond them the mountains blended into the lowland jungles that dominated Nicaragua's third region, the Mosquito coast. Running from the Coco River on the Honduran

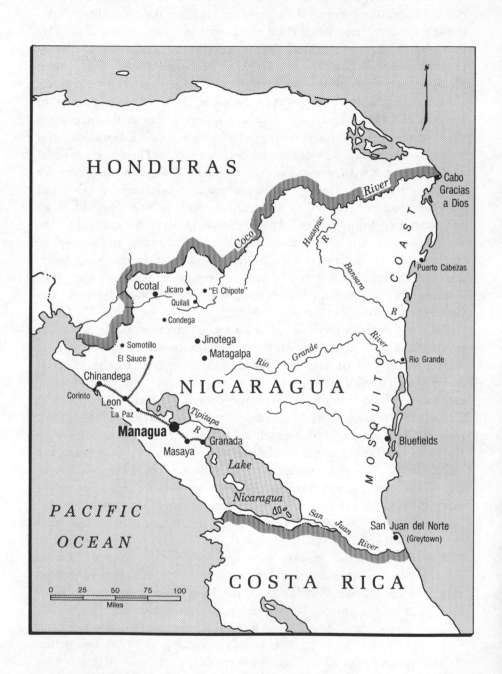

HONDURAS

Cabo
Gracias
a Dios

Coco River

Huaspuc R

Bansara R

COAST

Puerto Cabezas

Ocotal
Jicaro "El Chipote"
Quilali

Condega

Somotillo
Jinotega
El Sauce
Matagalpa

Chinandega
Rio Grande

NICARAGUA

Corinto
Leon
La Paz
Tipitapa
River

MOSQUITO

Managua
R

Masaya
Granada
Bluefields

Lake
Nicaragua

PACIFIC
OCEAN

San Juan River

San Juan del Norte
(Greytown)

COSTA RICA

0   25   50   75   100
Miles

Top: Father of the Old Corps: Archibald Henderson, Commandant, 1820–1859. Middle: Navy Yard Security Guards, 1861. Bottom: Marine Gun Crew, U.S.S. *Massachusetts,* 1890

Marine Guard, U.S.S. *Portsmouth,* 1885

Marines in the Philippines, 1900

Marine and Sailor Landing Party, 1918

Marines All: General Smedley D. Butler and Marine private on the march,
1924

Top: China Marines: The Legation Guard stands inspection, circa 1910. Middle: China Marines: Yangtze River armed guards, 1933. Bottom: Marines and *caco* captive, Haiti, 1916

The Palace Guard of the *Gendarmerie d'Haiti,* 1921

Counterinsurgency: Marine patrol, Nicaragua, 1927

Top: Marine Recruits, Parris Island, 1918. Middle: Veterans of the 4th Marine Brigade examine a captured German trench mortar, France, 1918. Bottom: Father of the amphibious assault Corps: Major General John A. Lejeune in France, 1918, Commandant of the Marine Corps, 1920–1929

Amphibious Development: Marines land a King armored car, 1916

Amphibious Development: Marines storm Culebra beaches, 1924

Birth of Marine Aviation: Lieutenant Alfred A. Cunningham learns to fly a Wright seaplane, 1912

Marine Aviation in Development: Vought 03U-6 observation planes and Curtiss-Wright R4C-1 transports at Naval Air Station, San Diego, Calif., 1934

border to the San Juan River on the Costa Rican border, the Caribbean coast was shaped by the jungles and the trading cities that grew at the mouths of the region's principal rivers. Draining the central highlands, these rivers were the region's only access to the interior. The Mosquito coast was the site of mining and lumbering (largely foreign-owned and foreign-staffed), with commercial centers in the coastal towns of Cabo Gracias a Dios at the mouth of the Rio Grande River, Bluefields near the mouth of the Escondido River, and San Juan del Norte or Greytown at the mouth of the San Juan. Marines had often landed at these cities to protect Americans and other foreigners during periods of internal unrest. The eastern coast was especially vulnerable to upheaval because it was accessible to waterborne filibusters yet difficult to reach for government troops stationed in the western cities.

Nicaragua's political life was ruled by two parties, the Liberals and the Conservatives. Dominated by alliances of families and regional *caudillos* who drew their strength from the western region, the parties were like big-city American political machines without discipline or rudimentary social services. They provided the cadre for the rebel armies that vied for control of the country in times of weak government and military impotence. The Liberals, whose geographic base was the city of Leon, and the Conservatives, concentrated in the city of Granada and the farmlands around Lake Nicaragua, had become hereditary enemies, forgetting and forgiving nothing from their years of political warfare.

After the intervention of 1912 the Marine Corps remained part of the State Department's plan to dampen the worst excesses of Nicaraguan politics. Although the Marine brigade that had disbanded the Liberal armies of 1912 then itself withdrew, the State Department asked for a permanent legation guard of one hundred men for Managua. This legation guard was supposed to serve as a warning to would-be rebels that the United States might again land Marines to stop a civil war; its practical effect was to preserve twelve years of uninterrupted Conservative rule. The legation guard was only part of the American effort to influence Nicaraguan politics. The State Department cooperated with the Managua government in obtaining a loan of $12 million from two New York banks, which deepened the U.S. commitment to Nicaragua. By the 1920s Americans were managing the customs service, the national bank, and the country's main railroad. After 1917 a high commission dominated by an American majority supervised Nicaraguan government spending and bond payments.[2]

The Marine legation guard proved to be a destabilizing influence, for its presence made it a target for Liberal dissidents and Managua rowdies. As on Hispaniola in the early 1920s, the Marines were largely ill-trained recruits, and the legation guard's service was blighted by bad quarters, poor leadership, little space for training and athletics, and sickness. When the Marines sortied from their miserable barracks to sample Managua's *cantina* nightlife, they often brawled with local thugs and the hostile police. After such fights, the Managua press would attack the Marines as barbarian oppressors. Outraged by newspaper insults, which included the charge that they had brought venereal disease to Managua, twenty-two Marines destroyed the press and sacked the offices of *La Tribuna* in February 1921. The culprits were court-martialed, but the incidents did not stop. In December 1921 some forty Marines assembled in a *cantina* in order to mount an attack on the police station. Before they could form their assault force, they were attacked by the Managua police. In the ensuing brawl the Marines killed four policemen and wounded three. When the detachment commander arrested suspected participants, four noncommissioned officers deserted and killed two more policemen before they were shot or captured. With anti-Americanism sweeping Managua, the American Minister called for more Marines from the naval vessels at Corinto. The unrest waned after the Marine vigilantes were court-martialed and the entire guard was replaced. The State Department, however, decided that the legation guard should be discontinued.[3]

The State Department was worried that the American Minister and the guard commander might involve the Marines in political acts that the department was unwilling to support. In 1920 the guard commander threatened to use his guard to stop a coup in Managua, a threat initiated by the American Minister. Aware that the U.S. government would not wage a war of pacification, the State Department pressured the Nicaraguan government to hold fair elections in 1924. The legation guard would then be replaced by a Nicaraguan national constabulary modeled after the *Gendarmerie d'Haiti* and the *Guardia Nacional Dominicana*, which the State Department thought would be an improvement over the expensive, ineffective Nicaraguan army. As a result of these conclusions, the department arranged for the electoral code to be rewritten by an American political scientist, Dr. Harold W. Dodds, who later monitored both the registration of voters and the election itself.

In the meantime the leading Liberal and Conservative *políticos* jockeyed for advantage in the forthcoming election. The political situation was unstable, for the incumbent Conservative president had died in office and had left the position to a vice president who did not represent the most influential wing of the Conservative party, which was dominated by General Emiliano Chamorro. When both the State Department and his own party disputed his fitness for office, the new president, Bartolomé Martínez, arranged a coalition ticket of Conservative Carlos Solórzano and Liberal Juan Maria Sacasa. The coalition ticket won the election of 1924 and organized a government of Liberals and anti-Chamorro Conservatives. Satisfied that the election was the best Nicaragua could manage without intense American supervision, the State Department recognized the new regime.

Although the new government wanted the Marines to stay, the State Department pressed it to accept a plan for a national constabulary drawn up by the commander of the legation guard. In anticipation of the creation of the *Guardia Nacional de Nicaragua*, several Spanish-speaking Marines with previous experience on Hispaniola were transferred to Managua, but the Nicaraguan government procrastinated until June 1925, when it finally came to terms with the State Department on the constabulary issue. Since no American officers on active duty could accept a Nicaraguan appointment without special Congressional approval, the Solórzano regime signed a one-year contract with Calvin B. Carter, a retired Army major and former officer in the Philippine Constabulary, and a group of American reserve officers and veterans to be instructors for the constabulary. The Nicaraguan army, however, was not disbanded. Despite severe recruiting problems and the hostility of the Conservative-dominated regular army, Carter formed the *Guardia* during the summer of 1925, and by August the Marine legation guard was gone.[4]

If the State Department believed that the *Guardia's* creation had ended its Nicaraguan trouble, it was quickly disillusioned. In September 1925 a Conservative army officer who commanded the key Managua garrison at La Loma fortress interrupted a state dinner and arrested Solórzano's Liberal allies. Although the prisoners were released, the president was afraid to punish the dissidents and followed their instructions to purge some prominent Liberal officeholders. Solórzano's vacillation encouraged the Conservative *caudillo* Emiliano Chamorro to assault the coalition government. In October 1925 Chamorro and army dissidents seized La Loma and demanded that Solórzano replace all the Liberals with Conservatives. The *Guardia* stood by the president and fought the insurgents, but Solórzano again capitulated. Chamorro would not let Solórzano resign until he had forced Sacasa to flee the country, purged the Congress, and arranged his own selection as the new president by the rump Congress. Chamorro tried to come as close as he could to constitutional legitimacy, apparently because he wanted American recognition. If so, he was quickly disappointed, for the

United States, invoking the 1923 convention on succession by force, refused to extend diplomatic recognition, an act that encouraged the Liberals to fight their way back into power. In May 1926 a band of Liberals seized Bluefields on the east coast but were defeated by government forces. During the fighting a landing party from the *Cleveland* protected Bluefields's foreign section.

Despite the urging of the American legation and the threat of another Liberal uprising, Chamorro decided to stay in office until he could arrange for his own candidacy in the next election, a plan for which he needed both State Department and Conservative concurrence. In the meantime, the Liberals, rallied by Sacasa and General José Maria Moncada, organized their forces for war. With the active assistance of the Mexican government, Moncada landed from ships on the Caribbean coast and captured Puerto Cabezas and Rio Grande in August 1926, but another Liberal uprising in the west was defeated. Reinforced from Mexico, Moncada then moved on Bluefields to the south, only to find that the U.S. Navy's Special Service Squadron had landed a ships guard there and had established a neutral zone to protect foreigners. Throughout the autumn of 1926 landing parties performed similar duties in the other eastern port towns, but their presence did not materially aid either side or bring the war to a halt.

In the meantime the State Department sponsored a conference between the warring leaders, but they were unable to work out a compromise peace. The meeting revealed the degree of Mexican aid the Liberals were receiving and made the State Department more enthusiastic about supporting an incumbent Conservative president—as long as he was not Chamorro and had been selected constitutionally. In November 1925 the Nicaraguan congress assembled with some of its purged Liberals returned and selected Adolfo Díaz to replace Chamorro. In rapid succession, Chamorro resigned, Díaz took office, and the United States recognized the new government. As part of the price of recognition and assistance Díaz promised to hold fair elections in 1928, pay off the Liberal army, bring Liberals back into the government, and negotiate a compromise peace with the Liberals. The State Department's promise of assistance did not include armed support. But it was disturbed to learn meanwhile that the exiled vice president, Juan Maria Sacasa, had returned to Nicaragua and established a Liberal government on the east coast. Even more distressing, the Mexican government immediately recognized Sacasa as president of Nicaragua and increased arms shipments to the Liberals. The State Department and the Navy Department began to recognize that more aggressive policies and more

Marines might be necessary if the United States intended to stop the Nicaraguan civil war and return that nation to peaceful politics.[5]

1

As it had turned interposition into military occupation in Hispaniola, the State Department found itself caught on the path to a widened military role in Nicaragua, a role that would again involve the Marine Corps in a pacification campaign. The most immediate problem was protecting foreign lives and property, which by December 1926 was becoming increasingly difficult. As the Liberal armies established control over eastern Nicaragua, their least disciplined units and bandits looted American-owned supplies and equipment and killed one American. Other nations asked the United States to protect their citizens. President Díaz informed the American Minister that he would surrender to the rebels if the United States did not stop Mexican aid to the Liberals. Rumors flooded Managua that a Mexican-based invasion of the western ports was imminent.

Distressed by the Liberal military victories in December, the U.S. government decided to enlarge its military role in Nicaragua. On January 6 a new legation guard from the *Galveston* reached Managua. The State Department also authorized the commander of the Special Service Squadron to create neutral zones in all the major eastern ports and to seize any arms declared "unauthorized" by Díaz. The Navy Department also dispatched six more ships, with six hundred Marines embarked, for Nicaragua. Responding to Latin American and Congressional criticism, the State Department explained that it was supporting a constitutional government in a country in which the United States had considerable interests. On January 10, in a special message to Congress, President Calvin Coolidge broadened the commitment in the name of protecting American lives, loans, foreign investments, and canal rights. He announced that he had authorized the sale of arms to the Nicaraguan army and would enlarge the Marine landing force. The President justified his action in terms that satisfied American interventionists: The intervention was necessary to stop the spread of Mexican-inspired "communism" and to protect foreign lives and economic interests. Despite testimony before the Senate Foreign Relations Committee by Secretary of State Frank B. Kellogg, Congressional criticism of the intervention did not abate even as the Marines sailed for Nicaragua. Although Kellogg stressed that the United States was interested only in preserving peace and constitutional government, the State Department saw that its influence in Nicaragua was already constrained by domestic criticism. This realization limited the role the Marines might play both to stop the war and to restore the Nicaraguan government.[6]

Marine deployments in Nicaragua clearly demonstrated the hardened commitment to the Díaz government—short of actually fighting the Liberals. During the next two months the Marine force ashore grew to brigade strength (two thousand) with the arrival of the 5th Regiment and additional landing parties. On February 1 a Marine battalion at Díaz's request took over the defense of Managua, and smaller detachments garrisoned the cities along the crucial railroad from Corinto to the capital. One detachment patrolled Chinandega, which had been ruined by fire and street fighting in February, while other Americans provided emergency food and supplies to its citizens. The Marine Corps also sent a six-plane observation squadron (VO-1M), commanded by Major Ross E. Rowell, to provide the ground forces with aerial reconnaissance of the Liberal armies. Late in March some Liberal troops fired on Rowell's aircraft, which they might have mistaken for Díaz's own hired air force. Although the Marine Corps disclaimed any effort to bolster Díaz's army, the January–March 1927 occupation placed Marine detachments and neutral zones around most of Nicaragua's large cities, including those in the interior, and put the Liberal armies between Marine units on both coasts. The Marine brigade, commanded by Brigadier General Logan Feland, was probably too small to guard lives and property and at the same time to campaign against the Liberals, but it was a force sufficient to encourage further negotiations.[7]

Despite the Marine intervention, the Liberals continued to best the government forces, and by March 1927 General Moncada's columns had marched across the central highlands to threaten Matagalpa and the lowland cities around the Nicaraguan lakes. Although Díaz's forces continued to fight with some skill and had not collapsed, the Liberals seemed near victory, which would embarrass the United States and increase Mexico's prestige. As a desperate attempt at a negotiated settlement, Coolidge appointed former Secretary of War Henry L. Stimson as his personal representative to talk with the Conservatives and Liberals. Stimson's mission was to assure the warring factions of American interest in a truce, amnesty, disarmament, and free elections and to see if some peace agreement might be reached.

With State Department assurance that the United States would leave a Marine expeditionary force in Nicaragua, Stimson and the two Nicaraguan parties worked out a peace settlement along the banks of the Tipitapa River by mid-May 1927. As the negotiators met, Marine detachments took positions between the two armies in order to prevent incidents. Both the Díaz regime and the Liberals now welcomed American intervention, for they were convinced that neither side was strong enough to win a decisive victory and that each would find political advantage in the peace. And neither could be sure of the future role of the Marine brigade.

In essence the Tipitapa agreement reflected the State Department's preferences, altered to fit Nicaraguan political realities. President Díaz was allowed to continue in office until new presidential elections, supervised by Americans, could be held in 1928, but Díaz would have to reappoint the Liberal congressmen, judges, and provincial governors removed by Chamorro. In addition, both parties would disband their armies. These forces, including the Nicaraguan regular army, would turn in their arms for money bounties and disperse. They would be replaced before the 1928 elections by a new *Guardia Nacional de Nicaragua,* which would be officered by Marines and supported by the Marine brigade. By the time Stimson left Nicaragua, the fighting had stopped and the native soldiers were turning in their arms and heading home for the spring planting. The State Department and the Marine Corps were now left with the task of making the Peace of Tipitapa work.[8]

Reinforced by another infantry regiment (the 11th) and aviation squadron (VO-4M), the 2d Brigade tightened its occupation of Nicaragua's major towns and collected some twenty-five thousand rifles and machine guns from the federal and rebel forces. Twice in May Marine detachments clashed with Liberal bands that would not surrender their arms or stop looting. Killed in the brief skirmishes were a Marine captain and private and a Liberal general. There were other occasional skirmishes, but the disarmament policy and the lack of resistance to the occupation allowed the Navy Department to reduce the brigade from 3,300 to 1,500 men less than two months after the Peace of Tipitapa. As they promised, the thirteen Liberal generals who signed the peace agreement cooperated with the Marines, as did the Díaz regime. Díaz disbanded the Nicaraguan army and the old *Guardia.* Even before Congress passed emergency legislation authorizing American military personnel to serve in the Nicaraguan armed forces, a Marine colonel had taken command of the new *Guardia* and was recruiting officers and men in Managua. In July Díaz appointed Colonel Elias R. Beadle as *Jefe Director* of the *Guardia* with the rank of brigadier general. Even without clear statutory authority in Nicaraguan law, the new *Guardia* received authorization to organize a force of six hundred officers and men and to take up posts in the interior. Stiffened by recruits from the old *Guardia,* the new Nicaraguan constabulary worked with the Marines in what appeared to be an increasingly peaceful occupation.[9]

Among the bands of the Liberal army, however, was Augusto César Sandino, the only one of Moncada's generals who had not signed the Tipitapa agreement. Denouncing the Marine occupation as *Yanqui* imperialism, the slight, thirty-two-year-old *mestizo* led a band of perhaps fifty men back to the area of the northern highlands, where they had joined the Liberal revolt the year before. Sandino was a complex man of intense passions and determination who burned with hostility toward the Nicaraguan elite, foreigners, and capitalism. The bastard son of a well-to-do white landowner and an Indian serving girl, Sandino grew up in his father's household near Granada. With some education and family influence, he had held various white-collar jobs until he fled his home after a gun battle with another man. He then traveled through Central America and Mexico, working as a clerk, mechanic, and minor supervisor. For two years in Tampico, Mexico, he watched *Yanqui* oil interests drain Mexico and learned something of the socialist-nationalist ideology of the Mexican Revolution. He began to envision himself as the leader of the emerging mixed-blood masses who would rid Central America of foreign economic exploitation. Returning home at his father's urging in 1926, he briefly held a job as a clerk in an American-owned gold mine in the department of Nueva Segovia near the Honduran border. With his own savings he armed a band of twenty-nine men and attacked a government outpost in November 1926. He then marched overland to take the port of Puerto Cabezas, where he became a Liberal general even though Sacasa and Moncada had never heard of him. Sandino was not close to the Liberal high commanders, not being an established Liberal *caudillo*. Nevertheless, he enlarged his band with pilfered arms and fought well in several battles with government troops. The Peace of Tipitapa found his column on the edge of the central highlands. Fading back into the mountains, Sandino vowed he would continue his battle against the forces of oppression—meaning the Díaz regime and the 2d Brigade.[10]

Although Sandino's intransigence irritated General Feland, the brigade commander viewed his band as only one of several groups of "bandits" hovering along the Honduran border, and Feland did not see these bands as a substantial barrier to peace and the elections of 1928. The Marine general's chief concern was disarmament and occupation duties on the populated west and east coasts. The challenge was to pacify the Liberals and Conservatives with government appointments and to replace the partisan urban police forces with the new *Guardia*. The Marines did not ignore Sandino since his band did represent the most important rebel unit still at large, but Feland had no desire for an open clash if Sandino could be persuaded to surrender. General Moncada and Sandino's father, in fact, corresponded with the guerrilla chief, but in vain.

In the meantime, Feland ordered the 5th Regiment to extend its garrisons into the northern departments (including Nueva Segovia) in order to disarm all bands in the area, and in early June a Marine patrol reached the department capital of Ocotal, the largest town near Sandino's mountain base. Commanded by Captain Gilbert D. Hatfield, the Ocotal garrison grew to a force of forty-eight *guardias* and forty-one Marines in early July, but Hatfield confined its activities to disarming cooperative Nicaraguans and collecting information on Sandino. What he learned was sketchy but suggested that Sandino was expropriating money, arms, supplies, and dynamite and gathering more men on a hilltop known as "El Chipote." Although no one was sure where "El Chipote" was, General Feland gathered 225 more Marines and *guardias* at Jinotega, for Admiral Sellers had on July 2 ordered him to disarm Sandino even if it meant fighting. Tired of exchanging insulting messages with Hatfield and worried that his band might disintegrate without action, Sandino did not wait for the Marines to find him. Instead he struck first and opened what was to be a five-year war.[11]

In the early morning darkness of July 16, Sandino's force of perhaps six hundred infiltrated Ocotal but were quickly discovered by Hatfield's alert sentries. Surprise lost, Sandino threw his guerrillas and peasant levies against the Marine and *Guardia* barracks, only to be greeted by a curtain of rifle and automatic rifle fire. Repulsed three times with serious losses, the guerrillas besieged the defenders as daylight broke, but Hatfield's force held fast and awaited relief. The first assistance came from the sky. From midmorning to midafternoon, the biplanes of VO-1M strafed and dive-bombed the *sandinistas*. When Hatfield's force sortied from its barracks, the last of the attackers fled, leaving behind some fifty-six bodies and carrying off perhaps twice as many dead and wounded. The garrison's loss was one dead and five wounded. With the help of what might have been history's first dive-bombing attack, the Ocotal garrison had so punished the *sandinistas* that the Marines announced the destruction of the last armed challenge to the occupation.[12]

2

Although Sandino threatened the success of the Tipitapa agreement, the American legation in Managua and the 2d Brigade could not concentrate all its energies solely on running down the messianic guerrilla leader and his followers. Instead the State Department worried most about conciliating the Conservatives and Liberals, who feuded over cabinet appointments, positions in the local police and revenue service, and control of the national judicial system. President Díaz and General Moncada conducted a running war between themselves over the former's legitimacy and the latter's eligibility to run in 1928. At stake in this bickering was control of the nation's election machinery. The American position was strengthened in late 1927 with the appointment of Brigadier General Frank R. McCoy, USA, to be chief election supervisor. Long experienced in colonial administration, McCoy proved a demanding partner, and he drew heavily upon the Marine brigade for supervisory assistance and police duties. In the meantime the legation pushed the Nicaraguan congress to adopt a new election law, which depended on American supervision to be effective. In the autumn of 1927 the election machinery was tested in a series of local and congressional elections, which were marred by irregularities like ballot-destroying and voter coercion. Only the active intervention of Marine garrisons ensured an honest count. With Congressional criticism in the United States still a worry, the State Department could not afford to allow the 2d Brigade to deploy just to fight Sandino. Instead the brigade was needed to continue to protect foreign lives and property from urban unrest and to deter political violence between the Liberals and Conservatives.[18]

Even after the battle of Ocotal, Sandino embarrassed the occupation. Not only was his guerrilla army a threat to the forthcoming elections and the country's general well-being, but his cause made him an instant celebrity and hero to both North Americans and *latinos* who wanted to hector the American government. Latin American radicals praised his heroic resistance, and American communists and anti-imperialists pledged their support in the press and mass meetings. *The Nation* sent a reporter, Carleton Beals, to join the *sandinistas,* and during several months with the rebels Beals wrote nine articles critical of American policy and the Marines.

The 2d Brigade attempted to deliver a coup de grâce after Ocotal, but its main instrument was slow and blunt—the horseback and bull-cart column of 225 Marines and *guardias* organized to reinforce the patrols in Nueva Segovia. Commanded by Major Oliver Floyd, the mounted Marines fanned out into the countryside around Ocotal and fought two successful skirmishes with the *sandinistas* in late July. Ill prepared and outgunned, the guerrillas fell back to their stronghold, "El Chipote," fifty miles northeast of Ocotal. Floyd established outposts along the Jicaro River at Jicaro and Quilali and on the Coco

River below Ocotal; these posts screened the Coco River valley from the *sandinistas* and served as patrol bases for operations into the mountains. In the meantime, Sandino reorganized his own forces, dividing them into four columns to conduct operations in Nueva Segovia. He also concluded that he could not fight the Marines except when surprise and numbers were in his favor, and he subsequently designed his operations for quick raids and ambushes. Although the 2d Brigade headquarters thought the *sandinistas* were disintegrating, the opposite was the truth.

Sandino made September and October a bad period for the optimists at brigade headquarters. First, a column led by one of his lieutenants, Carlos Salgado, attacked the garrison at Telpaneca. Although the Marine–*Guardia* defenders repulsed the assault, the boldness of the attack worried brigade headquarters. Next, Sandino mauled three patrols looking for a downed Marine plane crew in the hills west of the Jicaro River. Having already captured and executed the two Marine airmen, Sandino trapped the rescue columns and shot seven Marines and *guardias*. The Marines claimed to have inflicted much heavier casualties on the guerrillas, but there were no bodies left behind to count. The patrol actions did, however, suggest where "El Chipote" might be located, and in November patrol planes located Sandino's base. Major Rowell's squadron began to bomb and strafe the mountain with great ferocity and uncertain results; while the Marines certainly killed many animals and destroyed scarce supplies, the aerial attack did not inflict many casualties among the dug-in guerrillas.[14]

With "El Chipote" located, the 5th Regiment sent two large combat patrols totalling two hundred Marines and *guardias* against the stronghold, supported by aerial attacks. Near Quilali the *sandinistas* ambushed the larger of the two patrols and in a sharp exchange of fire downed thirty-two Marines and *guardias* before the Marines could get air support. Another guerrilla group harassed the other patrol with long-range fire. Two days later, January 1, 1928, the guerrillas struck the second patrol six miles north of Quilali and shot its two officers. The survivors rallied but had to await rescue by a patrol from Quilali. Falling back on Quilali and joining the other patrol, the combined force was then besieged by nearly four hundred *sandinistas*. The Marine situation was not good. The patrols' officers were nearly all casualties, supplies and ammunition were low, and thirty-one wounded needed immediate medical aide. Help came from the sky. Flying a Vought 02U-1 "Corsair" biplane, Lieutenant Christian F. Schilt made ten landings and takeoffs on Quilali's main street, bringing in supplies and taking out the wounded. Schilt's feat, for which he received a Medal of Honor, was made under fire, and his plane had to be brought to a stop on each landing by a squad of Marines, because it had no brakes. Schilt's heroism did not conceal the fact that the offensive against "El Chipote" had ended in failure.

Later in January the Marines again moved against Sandino's stronghold with an aerial attack and ground patrol. The Marine aviators bombed and strafed the base with such determination that Sandino decided to abandon the camp and wage a war of greater maneuver. As his rear guard skirmished with the oncoming Marine patrol, Sandino withdrew to the south. At his rear the Marines took three days to go 6 miles, clearing the trail with mortar and rifle-grenade fire. The Marines found "El Chipote" deserted when they arrived. Once again the elusive Sandino had faded into the mountains. This time the 2d Brigade, having no reason to think he had been defeated, asked for reinforcements in order to continue the pursuit.[15]

Despite an official Navy Department announcement that Sandino was "finished, and is simply trying to escape," Commandant John A. Lejeune agreed that the brigade needed assistance. Early in 1928 he ordered the 11th Regiment, commanded by the able Colonel Robert H. Dunlap, back to Nicaragua. The regiment was assigned to the newly organized Northern Area (the northern Nicaraguan departments), and Dunlap assumed responsibility for directing all Marine–*Guardia* operations against the guerrillas. At the same time General Feland returned to Managua to command the brigade, with instructions to suppress Sandino before the 1928 elections. Although he doubled the strength of the brigade to 2,500 officers and men, Lejeune agreed with his local commanders that the Marine force was probably still too small to fight an organized enemy like the mounted and popularly supported *sandinistas*.[16]

Under increased Marine pressure, Sandino kept his movement alive during 1928, but his activities—so frustrating to the 2d Brigade—did little to put pressure on the Díaz regime or the State Department's electoral plans. By early February Sandino was on the move in Jinotega department, left underdefended by the campaign on "El Chipote." He then sent one column doubling back to the northwest while he led two columns with the majority of his guerrillas on a raid toward the Mosquito coast. The western column ambushed one Marine supply convoy but lost men fighting the rescue patrols and faded back into the mountains. The 11th Regiment's patrols had made Nueva Segovia less hospitable than it had been six months before, and during the summer of 1928 some 1,600 *sandinistas* sought amnesty. These guerrillas, however, were only local militia of dubious value. Sandino did not miss them.

In the meantime, he was leading his best fighters on a quixotic raid against foreign-owned mines and lumber companies. The flaw in his plan was that it took the *sandinistas* away from the political heart of Nicaragua and pitted them against the very targets most likely to harden the resolve of the American government. The campaign to the east did little to disrupt the forthcoming elections and scarcely more to damage the Díaz government. Nevertheless, Sandino's columns did take and sack three mines in April and then established camps for further raids. Marine aircraft occasionally strafed the guerrillas, but Sandino's columns successfully fought off the Marine patrols that trailed them from the west.

Sandino's movement to the east was not entirely unexpected by the area commander, Major Harold H. Utley, and he had already taken steps to push his outposts into the interior. Working from a base camp at Cabo Gracias a Dios, Utley sent patrols up the Coco River to reconnoiter the river system and to plant bases in the interior. Led by Captain Merritt A. Edson, an aggressive and jungle-wise commander, the Marine patrols overcame their ignorance of the river, floods, jungle, and weather to establish a series of rough camps along the Coco River and its tributaries. When he learned of the raids on the mines, Utley ordered patrols inland from the south with the hope that the guerrillas would turn north toward the border and into ambushes set by Edson's patrols. Instead the guerrillas faded back westward, but not without having to fight Marine patrols moving into the foothills west of the Mosquito coast. One ambush the *sandinistas* set for Edson's river patrols ended with the Nicaraguans losing thirteen men, the Marines four. By the end of the summer Marine boat patrols were ranging up the Coco River almost to Quilali. In the process they had mauled several *sandinista* bands and captured both men and supplies. The 11th Regiment and the Coco River patrols could not corner the *sandinistas*, but together they had demoralized the guerrillas, cut their effectiveness, and pinned them down in the wildest part of Nicaragua as the elections approached.[17]

Certain patterns in Marine operations had emerged by the end of 1928 and continued to shape the Nicaraguan occupation and the campaign against Sandino for the next four years. The greatest difficulty was that there were too few Marines to guard fixed posts and patrol against Sandino in strength. Marine–*Guardia* patrols were often too small and too brief to be effective; moreover, Marine training in patrol methods and march discipline was deficient. To complicate operations, brigade headquarters tended to overcontrol local operations and to badger subordinate commanders. Life on the trail was tiring. Supplies and equipment had to be carried by mule, as did fodder for the mounted patrols, for the countryside was too poor for foraging. Skilled patrol leaders were also in short supply, and many of the Marines did not take the war seriously—until they were ambushed by *sandinistas*.

On the other hand, the Marines were better armed and better trained in tactics and marksmanship than the *sandinistas*. Even when ambushed, a patrol could fight back with Springfield rifles, Thompson submachine guns, Browning automatic rifles, Lewis light machine guns, mortars, and rifle grenades and hand grenades. *Sandinista* fire superiority was usually short-lived, and as the Marines grew trail-wise, they habitually mortared any suspicious hill or turn in the trail before advancing. Under a demanding commander like Colonel Dunlap, the Marines could be formidable foes. Faced by a hostile population and difficult terrain, the patrols in the Northern Area made their rounds in soiled uniforms, wilting campaign hats, and ragged shoes, but their weapons were clean and always loaded.[18]

One decided advantage in the campaign was the availability of Marine aircraft for reconnaissance, close air support, communications, and supply. Small Marine squadrons had assisted the Marine brigades in Hispaniola with all of these services in the most primitive and limited form, but Marine aviation came of age in its support of ground troops in Nicaragua. So valuable was air support that Rowell's original squadron of six obsolete DeHavilland scout-bombers grew to a composite squadron of twenty-six aircraft by 1933. Before the occupation ended, Marine aviators were flying modern scout-bombers, amphibians, and Ford and Fokker transports in support of brigade operations. In the early days of the occupation Marine aircraft ferried 60,000 pounds of supplies for the brigade. At a cost of eight dead, the Marine squadron often provided the combat and supply edge the short-handed brigade and *Guardia* needed to stay in the field on equal terms with the *sandinistas*. Sandino's soldiers showed their respect for the Marine aircraft. They often moved at night, refrained from firing at aircraft to avoid detection, and became proficient in camp camouflage.[19]

The other auxiliary of the Marines' campaign, the *Guardia Nacional de Nicaragua*, was not of as much immediate utility, but by the end of 1928 the *Guardia* was an increasingly important factor in occupation policies. Like the constabularies on Hispaniola, the *Guardia* was easier to conceive than to organize. Not until December 1927 did the Nicaraguan government sign a constabulary agreement with the United States, and even then the Díaz government was unhappy about the Guardia's cost—estimated at $689,132 annually. Officers could be recruited from the 2d Brigade by the allure of action and double pay, but suitable enlisted men were difficult to find. Few Nicaraguans believed that they would be clothed, fed, and paid as promised; as on Hispaniola the recruits tended to come from the urban unemployed and the peasantry. Although the Nicaraguans knew a great deal about guns and killing, they did not easily take to military discipline, obedience to regulations, and manual labor. As a consequence, the *Guardia* soon had 82 of its authorized 93 officers but only 574 of its enlisted strength of 1,136 at the end of 1927.[20]

There were also serious disagreements about how the *Guardia* should be used. The State Department wanted the *Guardia* to assume quickly the law enforcement duties of a national police force, which included the supervision of elections, firearms control, prison management, and the enforcement of the nation's civil and criminal codes and its laws on sanitation and smuggling. The Liberals and Conservatives supported these functions, but each party was concerned that its rival might control the *Guardia*. The 2d Brigade wanted the *Guardia* committed to the campaign against Sandino as soon as possible, and two of the *Guardia's* first three companies were in fact sent to the Segovias in 1927. Although President Díaz was supposed to be the *Jefe Director's* only superior, the fact that Colonel Beadle was a Marine officer and his subordinates were Marine and Navy officers and enlisted men meant that they were still subject to informal pressures from the 2d Brigade. Thus the *Jefe Director* found himself importuned by the brigade commander and Admiral David F. Sellers, commander of the Special Service Squadron, to provide more troops for the war against Sandino while at the same time he was pushed by Díaz and the American legation to emphasize police duties in Nicaragua's urban centers, the hotbeds of party rivalries.

The only answer to the *Guardia's* dilemma was to make it larger. By the eve of the 1928 elections it numbered 173 officers and 1,637 men, manning posts not only in the northern departments but throughout the rest of the nation as well. This pattern of growth came from the American legation's concern with electoral supervision. The rapid expansion put heavy burdens on the *Guardia's* budget, supply system, and training capacity. As in Hispaniola, troop training became the responsibility of local commanders, which produced uneven results and inordinate loyalties or hatreds toward individual officers. The *Guardia* also divided along functional lines, with one part of each company assigned permanently to police work and the other for patrol duty against the *sandinistas,* which added to the classic problems of personal and regional rivalries.

The *Guardia's* internal problems meant that it could be used only sparingly in serious combat, and then it was usually incorporated with Marine units for patrols. Between July 1927 and March 1929 all-*Guardia* patrols made only thirteen contacts with the *sandinistas,* while all-Marine patrols made fifty-nine. Mixed Marine–*Guardia* patrols made thirty-two contacts. In the same period the Marines suffered seventy casualties, the *Guardia* twenty-six. Marines claimed 113 *sandinistas* killed, the *Guardia* only twelve. Although the disparity in active combat could be explained by the *Guardia*'s many duties and its growing pains, it did not make the *Jefe Director*'s relations with the Marine brigade any easier.[21]

Ready or not, both the Marine brigade and the *Guardia* played the most important role in ensuring that the Nicaraguan national elections of 1928 took place without party violence and *sandinista* interference. By any reasonable measure, the Marines and *guardias* contributed to the success of General McCoy's efforts. Under their protection, Nicaraguan voters registered at a rate 28 percent higher than in 1924. Despite sporadic violence (including one *sandinista* raid near Jinotega) and some corruption, the election turnout in November was impressive: 90 percent of the registered voters went to the polls and elected the first Liberal president in years, General José Maria Moncada, by a margin of nearly 20,000 votes. Even in troubled Nueva Segovia 82 percent of the voters appeared on election day. During the election nearly 5,500 Marines and sailors and 1,600 *guardias* saturated the country with 239 posts and monitored the election to General McCoy's satisfaction. Even though Sandino was still at large, the election seemed to vindicate American intervention and proved that a Liberal president could take office with the State Department's blessing. It did not mean, however, that the occupation was over or that the fighting had ended.[22]

3

Notwithstanding the successful election of 1928, the State Department suspected that the military occupation had not yet accomplished all the goals of the Tipitapa agreement, a view articulated by Secretary of State Henry L. Stimson. Conceding that military intervention was futile and expensive, Secretary of State Stimson nonetheless believed that the settlement he had negotiated in 1927 could not be considered secure until another Nicaraguan presidential election could be held in 1932. This position, shared by American policy-makers, was reinforced by Sandino's guerrilla war and the slow progress in building the *Guardia Nacional*. Until some combination of military success and *Guardia* effectiveness against Sandino emerged, the Marine brigade would have to stay in Nicaragua. The State Department was especially concerned that the Nicaraguan congress had not yet ratified the *Guardia* agreement. It also knew that President Moncada, who faced a Conservative majority in his congress, did not feel secure and depended upon the brigade not only to fight Sandino but to protect him from what he perceived as a pro-Conservative *Guardia.* Moncada's position was encouraged by Admiral Sellers and General Feland, much to the consternation of the American Minister and *Jefe Director* Beadle. On the other hand, the defeated Conservatives saw that only continued American occupation would preserve their chances in the elections of 1930 and 1932 and save their officeholders from Liberal reprisals. When the State Department analyzed resistance to the occupation, that resistance (with Sandino's considerable exception) seemed to come from outside Nicaragua, not from within. Convinced that electoral reform and the growth of the *Guardia* justified the war against Sandino and continued occupation, the State Department held fast to its original goals.[23]

The continued occupation did not mean, however, that the 2d Brigade would step up its fight against Sandino. On the contrary, to reduce criticism at home and the cost of the occupation, the Navy Department ordered the 11th Regiment home in 1929, which decreased the brigade strength to about 1,500 officers and men. Correctly believing that General Feland saw himself as Moncada's personal adviser and prospective director of all American activities in Nicaragua, the State Department requested and obtained the brigade commander's relief. At the same time the small brigade (the 5th Regiment and supporting units) gradually withdrew its combat patrols from the Northern Area and deployed to defend the large towns threatened by the guerrillas and to protect foreign properties in the central highlands and the Mosquito coast. Portions of the brigade concentrated in Managua and the cities along the western railroad for the unspoken purpose of protecting the government and the Conservatives from the *Guardia.* The move was welcome, for the Marine officers saw that without the use of provost courts and more aggressive patrols the campaign against Sandino was at a stalemate. Although garrisoning the larger towns called for greater troop discipline, the brigade commander preferred the thankless but safe role of supervising the elections of 1930 to the thankless and hazardous mission of fighting Sandino with inadequate numbers and inadequate authority.[24]

Although the 5th Regiment could disengage from the counterguerrilla campaign, the brigade's aviation squadron could not, for the *Guardia Nacional* and the small Marine outposts guarding mines and coffee plantations depended on aircraft for supplies, communications, and occasional air strikes against suspected guerrillas bases. In four months in 1929 and 1930 the squadron's sixteen aircraft flew 1,001 missions to haul 250,000 pounds of freight, take aerial photographs, move personnel, deliver messages, and support combat patrols. Although it never inflicted the number of casualties its pilots reported, the squadron did inhibit the *sandinistas'* movement and their use of large mountain base camps. Ordered not to risk civilian casualties, the squadron could not bomb the guerrillas out of villages, an enormous frustration for the pilots. Nevertheless, Marine air support helped ensure that the campaign against Sandino did not collapse during the period when the brigade was disengaging and the *Guardia* was struggling toward greater combat effectiveness.[25]

Despite the policy to reduce casualties and to turn the counterguerrilla war over to the *Guardia*, the 2d Brigade could not entirely disengage from the pacification campaign. Its reduced posts in the Northern Area still sent out small local patrols to check telephone and telegraph lines. When one such patrol in 1931 lost eight Marines killed in an ambush near the Honduran border, the incident caused a newspaper furor in the United States. Other patrols were more successful. One in 1929 captured the *sandinista* general Manuel Giron, later executed by Nicaraguan volunteers. Throughout the period 1929–1932 the Marines still skirmished with small guerrilla bands, but the brigade's contributions were minimal, restricted to providing occasional reinforcements to the hard-pressed *Guardia* and protecting Marine *Guardia* officers from their own unreliable enlisted men.

After the election of 1928 the *Guardia Nacional* inherited the war against Sandino. Its ability to suppress the guerrillas was hampered by disagreement about its character and missions and by the nature of the campaign itself. In the departments of Nueva Segovia, Esteli, and Jinotega, the *Guardia* faced the same problems that had confronted the 2d Brigade: the open border with Honduras, the unfavorable balance of numbers and terrain to be patrolled, the uncooperativeness and hostility of the local population. The basic numbers were unpromising. The *Guardia* had roughly one thousand men to confront a nearly equal number of guerrillas who had more than 4,000 square miles of terrain and 73,000 people to hide them, with a sanctuary in Honduras at their backs.[26]

The other serious restraint upon the *Guardia*'s effectiveness was its relationship with the Moncada government. The Liberal president needed the *Guardia* to fight Sandino and was not loath to use it to harass the Conservatives, but he was suspicious of its loyalty and distressed by its cost. One of Moncada's first acts was to request the removal of *Jefe Director* Beadle, who was replaced by Douglas C. Mc-

Dougal, a Marine colonel who had commanded the *Gendarmerie d'Haiti*. McDougal's relations with Moncada were also strained; the president spied on McDougal's staff and tapped its phones.[27] Moncada and the American legation also bickered constantly about the *Guardia*'s size. In early 1930 the constabulary was increased to 2,256 officers and men (annual cost $1.1 million), but Moncada insisted that his depression-ravaged treasury could not support such a force, and by the end of the year it was cut to 1,800 officers and men. The press of the war against Sandino, however, forced Moncada to increase the *Guardia* to 200 officers and 2,150 men in 1932.

Part of Moncada's foot-dragging, however, had nothing to do with budgets. The Nicaraguan president did not trust the *Guardia* and did not want it to be the sole armed force in the country. Arguing that the *Guardia* was inadequate to fight Sandino, Moncada created a force of several hundred Liberal *volontarios* in 1929 and sent them into the Northern Area. After an abortive campaign in which the *volontarios* abused peasants and shot suspects and prisoners, the American legation and the Marine commanders insisted that the force be dissolved. Moncada held firm and persuaded the Americans to accept the creation of locally financed urban policemen (*guardias municipales*) and rural militia (*civicos* and *auxiliares*). Both groups were under *Guardia* supervision, but both were also subject to Moncada's influence.[28]

Caught between the *sandinistas* and the Moncada regime and only partially supported by the State Department, the Marine officers of the *Guardia* served with skill and patience. As they struggled to learn Spanish and understand the whims of both the guerrillas and their own enlisted men, the *Guardia* officers soon learned that only vigor and personal leadership could compensate for their men's uncertain performance. On patrol they quickly adopted the 2d Brigade's standard practice of meeting ambushes with overwhelming automatic weapons fire. Few officers were ever satisfied that they had adequate numbers, intelligence, or dependable noncommissioned officers. Moreover, they also had to perform many demanding civil functions, such as making the villagers use privies and supervising local officials. There were insufficient funds to improve the primitive upland and eastern posts, and the *Guardia* officers worried constantly about the poor condition of their men's weapons and uniforms. As in Hispaniola, the *guardias* needed constant supervision lest they sell their equipment, rob the peasantry, and align themselves with local *políticos* for personal favors. Yet for all the frustrations, the *Guardia* did provide some security in the rural areas and did fight the *sandinistas* with occasional success. It is unlikely that the *Guardia* inflicted nearly two thousand casualties on the *sandinistas* by 1933, as it claimed, but it did harry the guerrillas with enough effectiveness, and with limited losses (197 killed and wounded), to justify the 2d Brigade's eventual withdrawal.[29]

In contrast with duty in Haiti and Santo Domingo, the *Guardia* officers faced a more adept enemy and did so with less manpower, material resources, and less political control. Although they themselves were protected by *Guardia* courts from irresponsible civilian prosecution, the suspects they captured went unpunished; in one twelve-month period Nicaraguan courts convicted six and released 556 *Guardia* captives. Although Moncada insisted on declaring martial law in the *sandinista* areas, the State Department ordered Marine officers not to participate in military trials, for the trials' political partisanship and irregularities might make the occupation more unpopular with American noninterventionists. Within the *Guardia* there was justified concern about the troops' loyalty. Although the *Jefe Director* could and did remove unsatisfactory American officers, he could not prevent a series of disturbing mutinies. During the period in which Americans officered the *Guardia,* there were ten mutinies in which seven Marines died at the hands of their own men. Three of the mutinies were caused by *sandinista* subversion.[30]

The greatest frustration remained Sandino. Although Sandino left Nicaragua in 1929 to spend nearly a year in Mexico enlisting support and recruiting experienced Central American rebels, his remaining bands, led by such chieftains as Pedron Altimirano and Angel Ortez, raided the northern departments, ambushed patrols, and avoided the larger Marine, *Guardia,* and *volontario* columns. The Nicaraguan government responded with a modest roadbuilding program for unemployed peasants on the theory that the bandits might take to honest work; the program was not successful. A more promising tactic was the creation of an elite *Guardia* mobile battalion organized for extended company-size patrols. The most successful of these companies (Company M) was commanded by Captain (GNN) Lewis B. "Chesty" Puller, a short, barrel-chested Virginian with Haitian experience, and Lieutenant (GNN) William Lee. Trail-wise, aggressive, and ruthless, Company M became the *sandinistas'* nemesis in Jinotega department, but there were too few similar units to crush the insurgency.[31]

In 1930 Sandino returned from Mexico, reorganized his army into eight independent columns of seventy-five to one hundred men, and ordered his guerrillas to step up the campaign of extortion, terrorism, and raids. The *Guardia* responded by sweeping the countryside between Ocotal and Jinotega with nine combat patrols, began to take hostages, and resettled part of the rural population. The campaign was ill managed and unsuccessful; it also raised questions in the United States about the morality of "reconcentration." Later in the year, the *Guardia* saturated the area between the Honduran border and the Coco River with patrols but had little more success. In both campaigns the *sandinistas* avoided pitched battles and either ambushed the flank patrols or raided towns behind or outside the area of *Guardia* operations. The *Guardia* nevertheless inflicted some casualties in ground contacts and aerial attacks, captured supplies and base camps, and kept the guerrillas on the move. But it did not seriously disrupt Sandino's army.[32]

Sandino demonstrated just how formidable he had become in 1931 by sending his columns on his most ambitious campaign. Three columns once more invaded the Eastern Area, where leagued with local *sandinista* sympathizers, they ravaged the foreign-owned mines and sawmills and the property of the Standard Fruit Company and actually occupied the Coco River towns all the way to Cabo Gracias a Dios. Ships of the Special Service Squadron landed Marines to protect the coastal towns, and the *Guardia* struck back, but the invasion reinforced the Hoover administration's conviction that it should end the occupation soon and that it could no longer protect foreign property without starting a revolt in Congress.

The eastern invasion did not exhaust Sandino's opportunities. While three columns pinned down the *Guardia* in the northern departments, two others struck westward toward the towns at the western edge of the central highlands, and another marched as far south as the jungles west of Bluefields to rob a mine and support a *sandinista* uprising in the town of Rama. By the end of the year *sandinista* guerrillas were fighting the *Guardia* in towns perilously close to the heavily populated areas along the Corinto–Granada railroad. Although the *Guardia* was hard pressed and some of its units collapsed when attacked, the constabulary managed to contain the guerrillas, who by the end of the year had retreated to their mountain strongholds. It had not been a good year for the occupation, exacerbated by an earthquake that ruined Managua. In sum, the Hoover administration strongly reaffirmed its intention to withdraw the Marines and further reduced the brigade to only six hundred men, most of them stationed in the capital.[33]

For the *Guardia* and the State Department the next year was crucial, for 1932 brought another presidential election. After several disheartening ambushes and two mutinies, the *Guardia*, led by Puller's Company M, increased its pressure on the *sandinistas* in a series of successful patrols. From April to September the *Guardia* whittled away at Sandino's columns in 104 contacts, never quite destroying them but taking a toll in men and supplies. The most dramatic success came in

September, when Puller's company surprised a *sandinista* column that
had planned to disrupt a railroad dedication by President Moncada. In a
ninety-minute fight along the railroad, the *Guardia* killed thirty guerrillas, the heaviest casualties Sandino had suffered since the attack on
Ocotal. Sandino still had a force of probably one thousand men in the
field, but the *Guardia* kept the guerrillas in the northern departments
and allowed the voting to go on without major interruption. In November the Liberals again won the presidency with Dr. Juan B. Sacasa,
the deposed vice president of 1926, and the State Department ordered
the Marine brigade and the *Guardia* to prepare for an American withdrawal early in 1933.

For the *Guardia* high command the greatest problem was replacing
the American officers with Nicaraguans, for even at the end of 1930,
during which the *Guardia* had opened a military academy, there were
only fifteen Nicaraguan officers. The number had grown to thirty-nine
in mid-1932. The *Guardia* academy, therefore, increased its classes and
turned out enough lieutenants from its short training program to fill
the company-grade billets. There remained the question of the *Guardia*'s
high command. Neither the Liberals nor the Conservatives accepted
the idea of a nonpartisan constabulary, and the American legation and
Jefe Director Calvin B. Matthews had to work out a scheme in which
each presidential candidate selected both Liberal and Conservative candidates for the field-grade billets. After the election, Sacasa's list was
used to appoint new officers, who then worked several months with
their American counterparts. Among this group was the new *Jefe
Director*, a burly extrovert named Anastasio Somoza, whose principal
recommendations were that he spoke English, had been a Liberal general in 1926, and was related to Sacasa by marriage.[34]

Leaving the undefeated Sandino to negotiate a peace with the Sacasa
administration, the last of the Marines sailed without regrets early in
1933. Although the occupation had ended the civil war of 1926, created
the *Guardia Nacional*, and supervised a series of elections, its lasting
effectiveness was questionable even at the time of the withdrawal. Nicaraguan politics remained Nicaraguan. Within two years, however, the
Guardia Nacional solved the problems of *sandinismo* and electoral
violence—in ways that Americans had not anticipated. After extended
negotiations during 1933, Sandino agreed to disband and disarm in
return for amnesty and land along the Coco River for some of his men.
The officers of the *Guardia*, whose patrols continued to clash with the
guerrillas, were unenthusiastic about the peace, as they made clear by
assassinating Sandino and some of his officers early in 1934. Their
troops then attacked and massacred the remaining *sandinistas*. In the
ensuing political chaos, General Somoza deposed Sacasa and established

a family dictatorship, backed by the *Guardia*, that lasted forty-five years.

4

Although the 4th Regiment remained in Shanghai to protect the International Settlement until 1941, the withdrawal of the 2d Brigade from Nicaragua in 1933 and the return of the 1st Brigade from Haiti the next year ended the Marine Corps's experience in reform military occupations and large-scale expeditions into Asia and the Caribbean. Service as "State Department troops" (a term used by Marine officers themselves) left the Marine Corps a mixed heritage.

The most important result of the Corps's colonial service was the tendency of Congress, the Navy Department, and some Marine officers to view military intervention as the Corps's primary mission. With two-thirds of the Corps's total manpower (18,000) serving at sea or abroad in the late 1920s, it was hard to avoid such a conclusion. Even though Commandant John A. Lejeune insisted that sea duty and advanced base force duty justified the Corps's existence, he found that the Bureau of the Budget and Congress thought the Corps could be reduced in size when the occupations ended. Headquarters Marine Corps spokesmen argued that such reductions jeopardized the Corps's ability to protect American lives and property. This argument was attacked by pro-interventionists, who knew that the State Department was not really fighting for American economic interests abroad. Anti-interventionists, on the other hand, attacked the Corps as the willing tool of American businesses in underdeveloped lands. The result was such a close identification between the Marine Corps and State Department activism in the Caribbean and China that in 1932 the Navy Department actually categorized two-thirds of the Marine Corps as part of the "land forces" of the United States, that is, performing the same mission as the Army and its reserves.[35]

Another result of the occupations in the 1920s was that they retarded the Corps's development of units, doctrine, and equipment for the defense and seizure of advanced naval bases. With so much of the Marine Corps deployed abroad, it was impossible to provide fleet maneuvers with adequate expeditionary battalions, and in the late 1920s the Marine Corps could not provide even token advanced base forces for training purposes, let alone the force proposed in Navy war plans. By the time the expeditionary brigades had returned from Haiti, Nicaragua, and China, the Depression had forced the Marine Corps to reduce its strength and its ambitious plans to reconstitute itself as an amphibious assault force.[36]

Although the long-term ineffectiveness of the reform occupations in the Caribbean make any costs questionable, the Marine Corps built its reputation as the nation's peacetime fighting force at minimum costs. In terms of casualties, the Marine Corps lost only seventy-nine officers and men killed in action or dead of wounds in Haiti, the Dominican Republic, and Nicaragua.[37] The number of Marines who died abroad from other causes was more than twice as great. In terms of dollar costs, Headquarters estimated that additional foreign-service pay had added more than $2 million to the Corps's personnel budget since 1919 and that the total cost of the Caribbean occupations since 1920 had been about $7 million.[38] Whether the costs were justified by the success of the State Department's policies is moot, but Congress by the 1930s clearly thought the outlays were excessive.

Within the Marine Corps the mission of colonial occupation and pacification was viewed as a mixed blessing. From the Boxer Uprising to World War I most officers seem to have relished the chance for combat and adventure abroad, and enlisted recruiting certainly emphasized the lures of tropical campaigning. After the Senate investigations and furor over the occupations in Hispaniola in the early 1920s, the risks of such missions were clearer. Writing in 1921, Major Earl H. Ellis, an intimate of Commandant Lejeune and a key Headquarters planner, recognized that military pacification was a difficult proposition, even if American motives were altruistic. It was especially difficult to exercise any control over a hostile or apathetic native population and to make any lasting institutional change, but Ellis dodged the political issue by saying that the Marines were simply following orders: "Yes, the Marines are down in jungleland and they did kill a man in a war, and a great many people did not know anything about it. This is most unfortunate, but—the Marines are only doing their job as ordered by the people of the United States." [39] Six years later Headquarters warned Marines that service in China and Nicaragua would be "devoid of the thrills and glory of actual combat" but maintained that military occupation was necessary to protect lives and property and to further American diplomatic interests. Such duty was necessary, but Marines should not expect that they would escape boredom or criticism for an essentially thankless task.[40] By the time the Hoover and Roosevelt administrations had renounced military occupation as a tool of American foreign policy, there is little evidence that Marine Corps officers opposed the renunciation of intervention. Few agreed, however, with Major General Smedley D. Butler, who announced from retirement that he had spent his life making the world safe for American investors and corporations.[41]

At a level less metaphysical than American foreign policy, the Marine Corps did its best to profit from its Caribbean experiences. From writings in the *Marine Corps Gazette* to the syllabi of the officers' courses at the Marine Corps Schools at Quantico, Marine officers wove their experiences into a doctrinal guide to the problems and tactics of counterguerrilla warfare and population control. Many of the hard-learned lessons from the Caribbean had little immediate utility for the Corps, but the military occupations, especially in Nicaragua, gave a generation of company-grade officers valuable experience in leading troops in combat. Some, like "Chesty" Puller and Merritt Edson, developed reputations that would make them appealing combat leaders in World War II, but the most useful lessons had less to do with personal careers. The Nicaraguan occupation particularly had given the Marine Corps some appreciation of the value of automatic weapons in infantry combat and emphasized the importance of close air support, effective communications in poor terrain, proper supply planning, troop training, and patrolling and ambush tactics. All of these lessons, however, were on a scale and against an enemy that limited their utility in World War II. Nevertheless, the "small wars" experience provided an intellectual challenge to such officers as Major Samuel M. Harrington and Major Harold H. Utley, whose writings eventually helped shape the *Small Wars Manual* (1935), an official guide to pacification operations.[42] Although the political assumptions of the *Small Wars Manual* were dated when the book was published, the experiences that shaped the manual provided Marine Corps officers with political and tactical challenges that helped awaken the Corps from the somnambulance of sea duty.

The ultimate impact of the era of intervention upon the Marine Corps is elusive. On the plus side, the Corps's tropic adventures aided recruiting, kept the Corps in the popular press, probably increased its effectiveness as infantry in small units, trained a generation of officers in combat leadership, and provided a mission a bit more important (if transitory) than sea duty. On the other hand, the growing Congressional distaste for reform occupations threatened the Corps's fiscal requests and retarded the development of the advanced base force. The counterguerrilla campaigns also brought the Corps unfavorable publicity and demythologized the Marine Corps enlisted man. As the U.S. Army had learned in an earlier era, pacification campaigns were not popular in the United States. By the time the last troops came home from Haiti and Nicaragua, the Marine Corps was glad to accept the verdict that it had more useful things to do.

Part Three

Amphibious Assault Force 1900–1945

If . . . the Marine Corps be utilized as an Advance Base organization, it would have the opportunity to share with the Navy the glory always resting on those who strike the first blows at the enemy, and it also would have the satisfaction of feeling that it had an important, semi-independent duty to perform and that on the manner of its performance would largely depend the success or failure of the Fleet.

Colonel John A. Lejeune,
Marine Corps Gazette (1916)

This means there will be a Marine Corps for the next 500 years.

Secretary of the Navy James V. Forrestal,
commenting upon the flag-raising on Mount
Suribachi, Iwo Jima, February 23, 1945

10. The Creation of the Advanced Base Force, 1900–1916

A year after the war with Spain the United States Navy assumed strategic duties unimagined before 1898. By the time the Treaty of Paris was ratified in 1899, America's overseas empire, the legacy of its victory over Spain and contemporaneous diplomacy, was well established. In the western Pacific the United States had annexed the Philippines and was attempting to influence events in China and Korea, primarily through the presence of the Asiatic Squadron. In the vastness of the central Pacific the McKinley administration had added Guam and the Hawaiian Islands to the south Pacific protectorate of Samoa. In the Caribbean the government annexed Puerto Rico, agreed to protect newly independent Cuba from foreign attack, and negotiated with Nicaragua and Colombia for the right to build and defend an isthmian canal. The new possessions represented a frontier for American idealism and commercial expansion, but they also represented a series of strategic outposts from which the Navy might defend the continental United States against an invader. They were vulnerable targets for the European powers and Japan, especially in the Pacific. Flushed with its quick victory over Spain and championed by President Theodore Roosevelt, who preferred wielding battleships to big sticks, the Navy began to consider the full implications of defending the nation's maritime domain.[1]

Established in 1900 to make recommendations on naval policy, the General Board, a committee of nine officers, assumed the task of assessing the nation's strategic challenges. Although the General Board shared the duty of strategic analysis with the President, the State Department, and the War Department General Staff, its studies in cooperation with the Naval War College provided the Navy Department with its only institutionalized war planning. Its influence, though limited in shaping actual naval legislation and appropriations, was enhanced by the prestige of its president for fourteen years, Admiral George Dewey. Much of the board's actual work fell to the younger officers of the Bureau of Navigation and the Office of Naval Intelligence, most of whom were true believers in Mahan's "Sea Power" doctrines. Convinced that international affairs were dominated by economic rivalries and the grasp for territory, and viewing great-power relations—with some justification— as close to war, the General Board planners urged Roosevelt and his Secretaries of the Navy to persuade Congress to authorize more ships, men, and bases.[2]

The strategic rationale for the expansion and improvement of the American battle fleet was complex and unduly alarmist but in its time persuasive. Although they often disagreed on details, Roosevelt and the Navy Department believed that the Atlantic maritime frontier was the most important. The most dangerous potential foe, the Royal Navy, was fortunately the least likely enemy, for the United States and Great Britain were already committed to a growing rapprochement, influenced by the British decision to strengthen its fleet in European waters. American planners agreed with the Admiralty that their most likely foe had become the Imperial German Navy, a burgeoning force of battleships designed to support Wilhelm II's adventuristic diplomacy. The General Board did consider a war with Britain in its RED war plans, but it concentrated on studying a feasible response to the German seizure of a Caribbean base, a conceivable prelude to attack on America proper. In its BLACK plans, the General Board concluded that it would have to meet the German fleet outside the Lesser Antilles if it were to defend the Caribbean and the isthmian canal. Such a campaign would require some sort of base structure in the eastern Caribbean.[3]

The situation in the Pacific was less menacing if concern was restricted solely to an invasion of the West Coast, but the General Board had to plan for the defense of the Philippines, Guam, and Hawaii. In the western Pacific the strategic environment was especially complex in the early years of the Roosevelt administration. Japan and Russia appeared to neutralize each other in their competition for control of Manchuria, with France a potential Russian ally and Great Britain linked to Japan by an alliance in 1902. Germany, having established a leasehold and naval base in China in 1900 and having purchased Spain's remaining central Pacific island colonies, including the Marianas and the Carolines, was a possible threat, for its new holdings sat astride the direct route to the Philippines and menaced Guam and Hawaii. Only after the Russo-Japanese War (1904–1905) did the situation become clearer, and then not to America's advantage. Navy planners assumed that victorious Japan was now free to expand its influence south and west into the Pacific, which it might do at America's expense. Given the vast distance between the Navy's West Coast ports and the Philippines and the limited cruising radius of the coal-burning, mechanically delicate American battle fleet, the General Board concluded that its contingency plan for a war with Japan (ORANGE) was meaningless without a system of Pacific naval bases.[4]

The Roosevelt administration persuaded Congress to add fourteen new battleships and armored cruisers to the fleet and to increase the size of the Navy from 25,000 to 44,500 men. But Congress and the State Department combined to frustrate the General Board's recommendations for a system of fixed overseas bases like those maintained by Great Britain. At one time or another, the Navy Department proposed that the government purchase base rights on China's southern coast, near Korea, and on Hispaniola, Cuba, and the Danish West Indies in the Caribbean. Of all these proposals the only one eventually approved was a training base at Guantanamo Bay, Cuba; the rest of the government had misgivings about the costs of further expansion. The Navy was scarcely more successful in winning appropriations to build bases on those islands already in American hands. Congress was generous in funding bases and navy yards in the United States, where such funds went directly into voters' pockets, but the Navy Department struggled for four years to get its first appropriation for the Philippines, and it received virtually nothing for Guam and Hawaii. The Navy Department did its cause no good when it changed its mind about base locations and about whether a base should have dry-dock and full overhaul facilities, but Congress was ultimately responsible for not allowing some progress on the Navy's fixed overseas bases.[5]

The General Board's proposals about bases were complicated by a series of strategic and jurisdictional disputes with the War Department, particularly on the location of a fixed base in the Philippines. Navy–Army cooperation had never been impressive at either the planning or the operational level in the nineteenth century, and it had been particularly strained in 1898 by disagreements over the Caribbean campaign. In 1903 Army–Navy friction was institutionalized when Roosevelt created the Joint Board, an advisory committee staffed by representatives from the General Board and the General Staff. Joint Board conflict over the fixed base issue was especially acute because the Army had progressively assumed responsibility for fixed base defense while the new Navy focused on fleet action rather than close-in coast defense.

The General Board soon found to its dismay that the General Staff, the Coast Artillery Corps, and the Corps of Engineers were formidable foes, a lesson it learned during the Subic Bay base dispute of 1900–1909. Essentially, the Navy Department lost presidential and Congressional support for a large Philippine base at Subic Bay when the Army argued that the base, situated on Luzon's western coast, could not be defended against a land attack. Moreover, the Army considered it more important to defend Manila Bay and Manila, the political and economic heart of the Philippines. The Navy could, of course, take advantage of such an Army defense system by expanding its Cavite naval station and using other sites within Manila Bay. Analyzing the strategic, operational, and fiscal implications of this alternative, the Navy Department chose instead to build its principal Pacific base at Pearl Harbor, Oahu, the Hawaiian Islands.[6]

The Navy Department's frustrations over fixed bases were not the full extent of the General Board's war planning problems, for the Navy also learned that Congress would not provide money for a balanced fleet. If the Navy was not to have an adequate fixed base system, especially in the Pacific, the battle fleet would have to depend on a large fleet of auxiliary vessels. When it came to funding, however, the General Board found Congress more enthusiastic about battleships than auxiliaries. Knowing that the Navy would have to operate from temporary bases in wartime, the General Board between 1900 and 1914 estimated that its war plans called for a force of 340 vessels. The Navy Department requested only 186 vessels, and Congress appropriated funds for 181 of them. Among the critical shortages were auxiliary vessels, including colliers, stores ships, and transports.[7] Therefore it was especially crucial that such auxiliaries as did exist, especially at the beginning of war, be protected both by cruisers and destroyers at sea and at those temporary bases where they would have to carry on their crucial support service for the fleet.

In sum, the Navy's war planning after 1900 assumed that maritime attacks on the United States were possible in both the Pacific and the Caribbean and that the American battle fleet would have to meet these attacks without fixed bases or an adequate number of auxiliaries. Given the thousands of miles the fleet would have to steam to save the Philippines, for example, the General Board became convinced that the Navy would have to depend on hastily developed advanced bases and that it could not depend upon the small, overextended, and uncooperative U.S. Army to defend those bases.

1

Analyzing the lessons of the war with Spain, Marine Commandant Charles Heywood did not see the relationship of advanced bases to the postwar Navy strategic plans, but he was certain that the Marine Corps would need more men to serve at sea and meet "the requirements of our colonial possessions." Explaining the Navy's need for a larger Marine Corps, Heywood pointed out the utility of Huntington's battalion in securing the temporary base at Guantanamo Bay in 1898. Although the Commandant thought a ten-thousand-man Marine Corps would suffice, he knew that some Navy and Marine officers thought "there should be a force of 20,000 well drilled and well equipped Marines who should be placed on naval transports at very short notice and sent to the many possessions recently acquired by the Government without the necessity for calling on the Army." [8] Admiral Dewey came to a similar conclusion, testifying in 1909 that an expeditionary force of Marines in 1898 would have enabled him to seize Manila without having to enter a disastrous collaboration with the Filipino insurgents.[9] But not until the General Board began to consider its base problem did a new mission for the Marine Corps emerge, and even then it was confused with expeditionary duty in support of the State Department's diplomacy in Asia and the Caribbean.

Supported by studies from the Naval War College, the General Board in 1900 concluded that defense of a temporary base against raiding cruisers and a landing force was both possible and desirable.[10] At an early meeting the board asked its Marine Corps member, Adjutant and Inspector George C. Reid, who had been appointed at Dewey's request, to report on the size and organization of a Marine force adequate to defend Culebra Island off the east coast of Puerto Rico, a base on Samana Bay, and Guantanamo Bay. The board also requested of the Navy Department two transports for two Marine expeditionary battalions for the Far East, although the mission of these battalions was obscure. In any case, the board was certain about two things: It was dealing with "naval campaigns" and "advanced bases," and the Army could not be expected to provide the necessary troops to support the Navy's needs.[11]

The official Marine Corps response to the General Board's request, which Secretary of the Navy John D. Long had made an order, was positive but restrained. Heywood agreed to train his Marines in building hasty fortifications, mounting and manning fixed defense artillery, setting up searchlights and telephone-telegraph systems, and laying mines, but he warned that it would take time to create a thousand-man regiment capable of defending an advanced base. He also thought that many unanswered questions remained about the organization, equipment, and transportation for the advanced base force.[12] Almost a year later, the General Board, seeing no sign that the Commandant was creating an advanced base force, again asked the Secretary of the Navy to order the creation of "a military organization of sufficient strength in numbers and efficiency, to enable the Navy to meet all demands upon it for services within its own sphere of operations, without dependence upon the cooperation of the Army for troops and military supplies, for such a force of the Army may not always be available." [13]

Pressed by both the General Board and Secretary Long, Heywood agreed to form a four-company battalion for "emergency" duty but stressed that he did not have enough men to create such a unit immediately. Unwilling to discard any traditional Marine Corps missions, the Commandant refused to create permanent tactical units and argued that Marines were adequately trained for both artillery and infantry duties. Nor did the Marine Corps have any funds for expeditionary supplies or advanced base force equipment. Unless the Navy Department provided more funds and men, the Corps could not assume the advanced base mission.[14]

Heywood's position was not obdurate. He agreed to form a battalion at Annapolis and Newport for expeditionary duty and advanced base training. The battalion, however, did not have sufficient strength or a clear mission until the summer of 1902, when Secretary of the Navy William H. Moody ordered it to prepare for fleet exercises in the Caribbean the next winter.[15] Only then did the battalion seriously train in the problems of transporting naval guns ashore and setting them up for base defense. Other detachments had begun such training in 1901. In the Philippines, the expeditionary battalion stationed at Cavite had already held an exercise at Subic Bay and had planted eight heavy guns at the bay's entrance. In five days the battalion had set up battery positions, a camp, roads, and communications and had learned how hard it was to wrestle naval guns and their platforms into position. A similar experiment at Culebra proved exhausting: Twenty-seven Marines needed nearly four days to move a single 5-inch gun 1,300 feet over broken terrain. The job required·moving thirteen tons of equipment, which did not include ammunition.[16]

At the theoretical level, a few Marine officers recognized that the advanced base force served a real need and offered the Corps an important future role in the nation's defenses. One of the earliest prophets was Captain Dion Williams, then serving in the Office of Naval Intelligence, who wrote in 1902 that America's safety rested on the Navy's ability to coal its vessels in wartime. Since any conceivable war for the United States would begin as a naval war, Williams argued, the Navy should have forces adequate to defend *all* its bases, permanent and advanced beyond the territorial United States. He proposed that all defense forces "should be entirely controlled by the Navy, and not as in the case of forts and shore stations of the continental territory, by the Army." The new colonies should be policed by native constabularies, but the new bases should be defended by Marines to ensure unity of command under the Navy in wartime. Williams recognized that the Marine Corps would also have to set up and defend temporary bases, but he did not clearly differentiate between advanced base defense in the geographical sense and advanced base duty in the temporary-base sense. Such a confusion was bound to excite the Army, especially when advanced base duty became a rationale for nearly doubling the size of the Marine Corps.[17]

The first real advanced base force exercises in 1903 and 1904 proved just how far the Marines were from becoming the General Board's ideal force and just how poisonous the new mission was to interservice relations. In the Culebra maneuvers of 1903 the advanced base battalion was subjected to constant harassment from its transport commander over its duties both ashore and afloat. The captain of the *Panther* insisted that the Marines perform the same duties as a ships detachment, thus forcing them to neglect their own training and preparations. Ashore, naval officers interfered with the battalion's defense plans and work schedules and showed little understanding of the problems caused by the terrain and equipment.[18] The 1904 exercises at Subic Bay proved that the Navy and Marine Corps could work together cordially but antagonized Major General Leonard Wood, the commander of the Philippine department; Wood thought the Marines were building permanent defenses for the Subic Bay base, an Army function. He saw the exercise as the first step in transferring "the defense of our insular possessions entirely to the Navy and the Marine Corps." [19] To add to the confusion, the commander of the Asiatic fleet, assuming that an advanced base force and an expeditionary battalion were interchangeable, recommended withdrawing half the Marines in the Philippines, a proposal that distressed the General Board and Commandant Heywood.[20]

With the East Coast Marines deployed to Panama and Cuba between 1903 and 1906, the creation of the advanced base force languished until the war scare with Japan in 1907, and then only the Marines in the Philippines were directly affected. Although the General Board in

1906 conceded that the Army should handle expeditionary duty in the Pacific, it insisted that Marines be prepared to defend Subic Bay, especially during the winter of 1906–1907, when diplomatic relations with Japan were strained by San Francisco's segregation of its school system. The Navy deemed war unlikely, but the General Board nonetheless planned the most ambitious advanced base exercise to date in the Philippines. During a ten-week period a battalion commanded by Major Eli K. Cole emplaced forty-four heavy guns at Subic Bay, an operation that further convinced the Army that the Navy was encroaching upon its coast defense mission. The exercise also convinced the Navy Department that it should organize the matériel for an advanced base force in the Philippines and at Philadelphia. Because Marine Corps strength had increased by two thousand men since 1903, the General Board also thought that the Marines had enough men for advanced base force duty, thus making further cooperation with the Army unnecessary.[21] The 1907 exercises also clarified the advanced base force's needs. Analyzing the exercises through 1907, Major Dion Williams urged the organization of a force "ready at instant notice to embark and proceed with the fleet on a campaign requiring an advance base; and their training would enable them to quickly establish such a base and defend it." Williams, however, differentiated between fixed and mobile defense forces, both of which were needed. The fixed defense force should be a permanent regiment of 1,312 Marines to man fixed artillery and to establish the necessary minefields and barriers. The mobile defense force should be a regiment of two infantry battalions and one field artillery battalion, which could be formed quickly from Marine navy base detachments. He also urged stockpiling equipment and weapons, assigning transports permanently to the force, and holding annual maneuvers.[22]

The slow development of the advanced base force played a significant role in the controversy over the removal of the ships guards in 1908–1909 and provided an opportunity for Navy officers to criticize Commandant George F. Elliott and his staff for not carrying out Heywood's agreements. Admiral Dewey himself said he was disappointed in the Marine Corps's failure to form a fixed defense regiment, and more vocal critics, like Commander William F. Fullam, denounced Elliott for failing to use his additional men for advanced base duty. To naval reformers it seemed as if the only hope for creating an advanced base force was to assign to it the two thousand Marines on sea duty.[23]

Disappointed by the Marine Corps's lack of aggressiveness in assuming the advanced base mission, the General Board in 1909 reviewed the scant progress since 1900 and concluded that neither the Navy Department nor the Marine Corps had done much to make the advanced base force a reality. Conceptually, there had been some progress. Aided by studies by Lieutenant Colonel Eli K. Cole and Major John H. Russell, the General Board concluded that a force of one to two regiments could adequately defend a base against a cruiser raid and a landing with thirty emplaced naval guns, high-angle-fire field artillery, machine guns, infantry, and water and land minefields. The optimum force would be supported by torpedo boats and perhaps a coast defense monitor or two.[24]

Probably discounting resistance to the mission within the Navy, the General Board considered the main obstacles to creating the advanced base force to be Headquarters Marine Corps and Congress. The first would not provide the men, the latter the necessary appropriations for equipment and contingency supplies. In both cases the criticism appears justified. With the exception of a handful of Marine officers like Williams, Cole, and Russell, the Marine Corps did not show much official interest in the advanced base force. It certainly did not try to reorder its many functions in order to carry out the Navy Department's instructions on the advanced base force. Although the need for advanced bases was far more obvious in 1909 than it had been in 1900, the Navy and the Marine Corps had not yet done much to provide the men and arms to make the advanced base force an operational reality.

2

The advanced base force moved rapidly from concept to permanent tactical unit between 1910 and 1914, but its progress owed more to the persistence of the General Board than to the innovativeness of Headquarters Marine Corps. Several factors help explain renewed Navy Department interest in the advanced base force. Probably the most important was that Navy war planners gained new strength from the appointment of George von L. Meyer as Secretary of the Navy in 1909 and Meyer's subsequent creation of the naval aid system. Meyer's aids were four line officers with direct responsibilities for policy in four functional areas: operations, inspections, personnel, and matériel. Moreover, the Secretary staffed these posts with aggressive line officers like Bradley A. Fiske and the Marine Corps's nemesis, William F. Fullam. Usually allied with the General Board in policy matters, the aids were a powerful influence in behalf of war preparedness and the balanced fleet.

Another factor consisted of changes within the Marine Corps. With Corps manpower steadily creeping toward ten thousand, and with more men available for advanced base force training between the Nicaraguan expedition of 1912 and the Veracruz landing in 1914, Headquarters could not argue that it was unable to provide troops. In addition, one particular bulwark against change, Commandant George F. Elliott, re-tired in 1910 and was replaced by Colonel William P. Biddle, an un-controversial, lethargic product of Philadelphia high society and years of sea duty. Biddle approved at least three important reforms that strengthened the Corps's ability to respond to the advanced base mission. These changes were the creation of an assistant to the Commandant with important responsibilities for military training and preparedness, the creation of permanent expeditionary companies at each Marine bar-racks, and the institution of mandatory three months' recruit training. In addition, Biddle continued Elliott's policy of assigning a few Marine officers to Navy and Army advanced officer schools, where they might learn the niceties of large unit maneuvers, artillery, communications, and contingency planning.

The main impetus, however, once again came from the General Board. Reviewing the slow progress of the advanced base force, the board asked Secretary Meyer to order the Commandant to assume responsibility for the advanced base equipment assembled at Philadelphia and Subic Bay. In March 1910 Assistant Secretary of the Navy Beekman Winthrop sent a direct order to the Commandant: "You will prepare for the care and custody of advanced base material and take necessary steps to in-struct the officers and men under your command in the use of this ma-terial." [25] In response, Headquarters established an Advanced Base School at New London, Connecticut, and assembled a handful of officers and men to begin the formal study of advanced base defense. The next sum-mer the school moved to the Philadelphia Navy Yard in order to work with the force's actual equipment; in essence the school and the force became the same, as more than 250 officers and men trained during 1911. The training, however, had little continuity, because the Philadelphia Marines were transferred often and were used for expeditionary duty in the Caribbean. [26]

Even the modicum of training at Philadelphia, however, was useful, for it revealed how little Marines knew about fixed defense and how much more training they needed. Assessing the experience to 1911, Major Henry C. Davis argued that the advanced base force was the Corps's "true" mission and should be embraced as such. He urged more practical work, including regimental maneuvers with the fleet. Davis clearly outlined the Corps's needs: more doctrinal development and practical work with artillery, electronic communications, mines, mech-anized transportation, bulk supply handling, and staff functioning. Thus far neither the Navy nor the Marine Corps had provided the necessary ingredients for a real unit: transports, arms, equipment, supplies, and men. "We have work to do and no tools with which to do it," Davis noted, "because the tools have not been fashioned from the rough material at hand." [27]

In the meantime, two quiet revolts within the Marine officer corps improved the advanced base force's legitimacy. The first was the formation of the Marine Corps Association in 1911. Angered by Headquarter's handling of the ships guard issue in 1908–1909 and disappointed by President Taft's appointment of Biddle as Commandant, the officers of a provisional brigade training at Guantanamo Bay for possible intervention in Cuba or Mexico decided to form their own lobby and self-education forum. With the approval of the brigade commander, Colonel L. W. T. Waller, a disappointed candidate for Commandant, and led by such seasoned line officers as George Barnett, Ben H. Fuller, Franklin J. Moses, and John A. Lejeune, the officers of the brigade pledged to oppose any efforts to curb Marine missions and to educate the officer corps on the Corps's naval value, including advanced base work. The brigade officers, nearly a quarter of the Corps's total officer strength, immediately raised funds for the association, money that by 1916 allowed the association to found its own journal, the *Marine Corps Gazette*. For Marine officers the *Gazette* soon became the primary vehicle for discussing Corps policy and new military training, techniques, and equipment. [28]

The second revolution took place in the sky. One of the Marine officers assigned to the Philadelphia Navy Yard in 1911, Lieutenant Alfred A. Cunningham, thought he saw a role for aircraft in the advanced base force. He successfully requested assignment to the Navy's nascent flying school at Annapolis in 1912. A teenage Volunteer in 1898 and later a bored realtor in Georgia, Cunningham had developed an intense interest in club flying and ballooning. He returned to military life at the age of twenty-seven, in part because he thought it would give him an opportunity to fly. Joined at Annapolis by Lieutenant Bernard L. Smith, Cunningham learned to fly a primitive Curtis seaplane from civilian instructors. Cunningham became Naval Aviator No. 5 and Smith Naval Aviator No. 6. More important, the Navy Department returned Cunningham and Smith to the advanced base force in 1913 with the understanding that they would create an aviation section for the force. Flying seaplanes, the Marine pilots would perform an important reconnaissance role for the force, a function they were prepared for by 1914. The fortunes of Marine aviation from its infancy were associated with the advanced base mission. [29]

Despite the creation of the Advanced Base School, the General Board was not satisfied that the Marine Corps and the Navy Department bureaus had done enough to make the advanced base force a reality.

There had been "spasmodic attempts" to assemble men and materiel, but the Navy had neither the trained units nor modern equipment for advanced base duty. Too much energy had been spent on academic arguments about the force. The time had come for a full test of the concept in fleet maneuvers in the Caribbean, after which the results could be analyzed and a second force created on the West Coast. On February 5, 1913, Secretary Meyer ordered the maneuvers. Having approved of the maneuvers in the earliest stages of their planning, Commandant Biddle pledged to provide an expeditionary force of 1,797 officers and men for the exercise.[30]

The planned maneuvers assumed even greater importance when the United States and Japan again clashed diplomatically in April 1913. Angered by discriminatory California legislation against its nationals, the Japanese government allowed anti-American demonstrations in Tokyo and ordered diplomatic protests in Washington. The Army and Navy responded by reexamining their plans and requesting a redeployment of the fleet to the Pacific.[31] At the height of the crisis, the Aid for Inspections, Captain William F. Fullam, renewed his criticism of the Marine Corps. Using an inspection report on the advanced base force, Fullam charged that the Marine Corps had shirked its "true field" of expeditionary duty and advanced base force training for thirteen years and had demonstrated its lack of interest by "its failure or inability" to form permanent battalions and to surrender its anachronistic ships guard and Navy yard security functions. Except for the Subic Bay problem of 1907, the Corps had done little to support Navy war planning, and it was sadly unprepared for the maneuvers.[32]

Although much of Fullam's criticism was justified, the Aid for Inspections set off another round of charges and countercharges about the Marine Corps's duties, a dispute exacerbated by a companion essay by Commander W. W. Phelps in the *Proceedings of the U.S. Naval Institute*. Like Fullam's earlier articles, Phelps argued that the Marine Corps was not fulfilling its responsibilities to the Navy. Phelps thought that the Marine Corps could not accept the fact that the Navy did *not* want it abolished or transferred to the Army, only that it perform its primary mission, "its proper field . . . that of the naval advanced base." To show its good faith, the Marine Corps should withdraw its two thousand ships guards and use them to form two advanced base force regiments.[33] In response, Colonel George Richards, a Headquarters stalwart, accused Phelps of reopening the 1908–1909 battle against the wishes of the Navy Department and Congress. Calling advanced base duty "the most important auxiliary service" performed by the Corps, Richards argued that the Marine Corps was a seagoing service and would not transform itself into another Army; he feared that creating permanent Marine battalions was the first step in another Fullamite plot to ruin the Corps. Sea duty, on the other hand, was excellent training for both expeditionary and advanced base force service, a view that Fullam rejected.[34]

As plans for the Caribbean maneuvers progressed and the Marines at Philadelphia worked with their guns and equipment, Commandant Biddle and Fullam clashed over the readiness of the advanced base force. Biddle admitted that the Marine Corps was ill prepared but denied that it was responsible. The Corps was still short of men and could not escape expeditionary duty, which limited technical and unit training. Moreover, the Navy had not supplied transports and equipment for the advanced base force.[35]

The General Board attempted to halt the dispute by assuring Secretary of the Navy Josephus Daniels that it was convinced that Biddle was sincere about conducting meaningful maneuvers in 1914 and that Fullam's criticisms were extreme. With a curtailment of expeditionary duty and some reorganization, the Corps should be able to form two advanced base force regiments without surrendering any of its other duties. Moreover, the removal issue once more made the Marine Corps defensive about its existence and encouraged those who thought it should be transferred to the Army, a development the General Board regarded with horror.[36] The board, however, could not silence Fullam, and the Aid for Inspections made his argument directly to Daniels, repeating his charge that the Marine Corps was unable and unwilling to perform advanced base force duties.[37] Pressed by Daniels's personal intervention, Biddle outlined all the Marines' duties for the Secretary, emphasizing the demands of sea duty and expeditionary service. In ideal circumstances, the Corps might have nearly three thousand men in the United States for advanced base force duty, but the reality was that barracks duty, recruit training, security functions, and personnel turnover for administrative and disciplinary reasons reduced this pool to virtually nothing. The Corps needed more men.[38]

The controversy peaked in September 1913, when the General Board held formal hearings on the Marine Corps's inability to form a permanent advanced base force. It heard Captain Fullam once more outline his plans to reform the Corps. It agreed that the advanced base force was not yet a reality but disagreed that an assault on the Corps's other functions offered a solution. Major Eli K. Cole, assistant to the Commandant, argued that permanent battalions would prevent the Corps from performing its other duties and that the villain in the advanced base force problem was the Navy, which had not provided transports and equipment. Cole, however, pledged that Headquarters fully supported the advanced base force concept and was working to make the 1914 maneuvers a success. The one thing the board and its witnesses agreed upon was that they did not want the Marine Corps lost to the Army, and the War Department General Staff, watching the dispute with amusement, was pleased that the Marine Corps was being pushed away from expeditionary and permanent coast defense duties back to its naval functions. The hearings ended with the controversy defused but not forgotten, especially for Fullam, who wanted Daniels to order the formation of permanent advanced base force regiments and troop transports for duty in the Caribbean.[39]

The controversy over functions in 1913 stirred Headquarters in a way that it had not been moved since General Heywood had retired, and for the first time Biddle's small staff, directed by Major Cole, provided concrete recommendations for the advanced base force. Working with students from the Advanced Base School and collaborating closely with the General Board, Headquarters argued that the advanced base force needed more and heavier field guns and fewer fixed, vulnerable naval guns; the force should have three transports instead of two; the Marine Corps needed more specialist training; and machines must replace men in moving guns and equipment. The General Board responded that manpower was crucial: Could the Corps provide troops for two permanent fixed defense regiments of 2,500? Headquarters thought not, without stripping its other units. The board told Daniels it thought this was a good idea, and Biddle shortly announced plans to cut the size of his shore detachments and recommended that the Navy Department develop one large base on each coast to house the new, larger units. By December 1913 the Marine Corps had done more to make the advanced base force a reality in one year than it had in the preceding twelve.[40]

The proof of the Commandant's promises rested with the single advanced base unit forming at Philadelphia, and the Marines of the 1st Regiment (Fixed Defense) found their training in 1913 more demanding than any they had ever experienced. Laboring by day and studying by night, the regiment's officers trained their men to assemble and aim a confusing melange of 3-inch and 5-inch naval guns, Army field guns, mines, searchlights, and primitive automatic weapons.[41] At Pensacola, Florida, Biddle assembled a second, mobile defense regiment from the expeditionary battalions in Mexican waters; concentrated on the transport *Prairie* and commanded by Lieutenant Colonel John A. Lejeune, the 2d Advanced Base Regiment sailed for the rendezvous in late November. Commanded by Colonel Charles G. Long, the Philadelphia regiment departed on January 3, 1914 to join the Marine Corps's first operational advanced base force brigade. Led by Colonel George Barnett, who commanded the Philadelphia Barracks and the Advanced Base School, the brigade prepared to demonstrate that the Marine Corps was now serious about its new mission.

For the senior officers of the 1st Advanced Base Brigade, the exercises on Culebra island were especially significant, for they knew that their brigade's performance was crucial to the Marine Corps's future and their own careers. Commandant Biddle was about to retire. Because the Congress in 1913 had extended a Commandant's tenure to four years, plus an additional four if requested, succession appeared to be open to any energetic, reform-minded colonel who impressed Secretary Daniels. In fact, Daniels already favored two candidates, Colonel Barnett and Lieutenant Colonel Lejeune, both of whom were particularly satisfactory as being Naval Academy graduates (which pleased the Navy) and having connections with several powerful Southern Democrats in Congress. Neither Barnett nor Lejeune felt confident about their chances, for they would not be able to lobby in Washington; they would have to take their chances at Culebra by demonstrating the Corps's commitment to the advanced base force.[42]

Acting according to general instructions prepared by the General Board and Naval War College, Barnett's brigade landed in mid-January and spent a week preparing Culebra's defenses. The transports had been loaded to allow the first-needed supplies and guns to be unloaded first, so the disembarkation went smoothly, although unloading was handicapped by unsuitable booms and hatches and by high seas. The Marines also discovered that their landing craft, both experimental lighters and ships boats, were not easily loaded or landed. Ashore the Marines found shortages of engineering tools and transportation, even with the use of a portable railroad. Nevertheless, the brigade was in position on time with its guns manned, its infantry entrenched, and its counterattack forces hidden in the hills. Most of the crucial work had been done by sheer manpower. The attacking force, simulating a raid by cruisers and a large landing party, found the brigade defenses stubborn—at least so the umpires ruled. Although the Navy observers thought the Marines were wrong to engage the "enemy" warships in an artillery duel, thus risking exposure and destruction, they agreed that high-angle artillery and flat-trajectory naval gunfire would make fixed defenses very dangerous to ships. The chief umpire, William S. Sims, ruled that the landing force of 1,200 sailors and Marines could not have breached the island's defenses. As a barrage of blanks and a battery of searchlights splashed the Caribbean night with smoke and light, the Advanced Base Brigade proved to its own and the umpires' satisfaction that it had successfully defended Culebra. Assessing the exercise reports during 1914, the General Board congratulated the Marine Corps for the soundness of its recommendations on armament and equipment and for its cooperativeness. For the first time since 1900 it appeared that the General Board and the Marine Corps could work together to refine the advanced base force concepts and to organize the operational units required by the board's war plans.[43]

3

In the years between the Culebra exercise and America's entry into World War I, the advanced base force prospered both as a concept and, to a lesser degree, as an operational component of the Marine Corps. Like other naval programs in the developmental stage, the advanced base force followed like a cockboat in the wake of the naval preparedness movement of 1915–1916. As the Wilson administration, prodded by the General Board and its Republican critics, contemplated the meaning of the World War and growing Japanese ambitions in the Pacific, the Marine Corps began to relate its manpower requests and internal reforms more explicitly to the advanced base mission. In no small way, the Marine Corps's intensified interest in its new duty reflected the priorities of its new Commandant, Major General George Barnett, selected for the post while he commanded the advanced base brigade on Culebra. The first Naval Academy graduate (Class of 1881) to serve as Commandant and a veteran of both sea duty and expeditionary service, Barnett was a compromise candidate, selected by Secretary Daniels over L. W. T. Waller and John A. Lejeune.[44] Barnett proved a persuasive advocate for the Marine Corps's interests, especially the advanced base force, and his effectiveness was enhanced in late 1914 when he asked Colonel Lejeune to be his assistant. He also worked harmoniously with Adjutant and Inspector Charles H. Lauchheimer, the most powerful influence at Headquarters and Barnett's Annapolis classmate. The Marine Corps also had a friend at the Navy Department, Assistant Secretary of the Navy Franklin D. Roosevelt. This adroit group assured that the Marine Corps would profit from Congress's mounting interest in naval preparedness.

Continuing its studies of the requirements for a war with Japan in the Pacific and Germany in the Caribbean, the General Board clarified the Marine Corps's probable war role. Pleased with the Culebra exercise, the board thought that the Marine Corps should form only one advanced force brigade, assuming that (1) the Navy's main Pacific base at Pearl Harbor would be adequately defended by the Army and (2) the isthmian canal would be open. After 1914 these assumptions became realities, thus reducing the uncertainties about the Marines' mission and manpower needs.[45] Responding to the Navy Department's intention to hold annual advanced base force exercises, Headquarters eliminated some of its smaller security forces and brought its Panama battalion back to a continental station. Its plans were to form regiments at Philadelphia, Norfolk, and San Francisco and to use these units for a 2,500-man brigade during the 1915 maneuvers. The return of two infantry regiments from Veracruz in late 1914 would provide the rest of the troops. As it planned, Headquarters worried about other nagging problems: the need for about one thousand more men, the lack of adequate transports, the scant funds available for contingency supplies and modern arms, and the lack of training space at the Navy's crowded yards. Nevertheless, in the year after Culebra the Marine Corps made significant progress on the advanced base force.[46]

Commandant Barnett, while showing no readiness to abandon any of the Corps's traditional duties, gave the advanced base force more structure in 1915. He could not reassemble his units from Mexico soon enough for exercises in early 1915, but he reopened the Advanced Base School at Philadelphia and organized the 1st Regiment (Fixed Defense) at the same station. This regiment had a headquarters, which included communications units, and eight companies, four of which were equipped with 5-inch fixed naval guns. The others were a minelaying company, a searchlight company, an engineer company, and an "aero-defense" company. For the force's mobile defense component, Headquarters wanted to station mixed regiments of infantry and artillery on both coasts, with 3,500 men on the East Coast and 1,500 on the West. These units would also serve as expeditionary forces. To make these plans a reality the Commandant requested an increase of 7,200 men, of which 3,000 would be assigned to advanced base force duty.[47]

The Commandant's plans fell victim to the pressures of Caribbean expeditionary duty. His mobile defense regiments spent their time either training at Guantanamo Bay or aboard transports and then went ashore to pacify Haiti in 1915 and the Dominican Republic in 1916. The manpower problem on Hispaniola became so acute in 1916 that the fixed defense regiment packed its heavy weapons and shouldered rifles to become infantry in the Caribbean. Still referring to the advanced base force as one of the Corps's "chief missions," Barnett found that he could not man the Advanced Base School or train with the $189,000 worth of new arms and equipment provided by the Bureau of Ordnance.

Nevertheless, the Marine Corps prospered in 1916, in part because of the advanced base force mission. In the ambitious, generous wave of naval legislation in that year, Congress accepted the Wilson administration's argument that the United States needed a naval establishment "second to none" to ensure American neutrality in the World War and to protect the United States in the postwar world. For the Marine Corps this meant more men—the increase of the Corps by 255 officers (including, for the first time, five brigadier generals) and 5,034 men. In addition, Congress authorized the Corps to create its own federal reserve force as well as to encourage the training of the marine companies of the various state naval militias already under Navy Department patronage. Congress also accepted the proposition that the Marine Corps's strength should be maintained at one-fifth that of the Navy, a formula dear to Corps planners. The first transport designed from the keel up to carry Marines, the *Archibald Henderson,* was commissioned in 1916, and Congress appropriated funds to build an additional transport of the same design. The Corps also received naval aviation funds adequate to form an advanced base force aviation company of ten officers and forty men. To relieve the problem of stationing and training Marine regiments at urban Navy bases, the Corps received money to develop its new base at San Diego to house advanced base/expeditionary units, and it would soon purchase a similar training area at Quantico in the Virginia woodlands some 35 miles south of Washington.[48] Even though expeditionary duty prevented the Corps from focusing on the advanced base force mission in 1915 and 1916, the new naval role was reshaping the Marine Corps in fundamental ways.

As important for the future was the fact that the advanced base force concept provided the Marine Corps with a wartime mission important to the Navy and a function that encouraged Marine officer reformers and planners. Between 1900 and 1917 the advanced base force mission was legitimized by the General Board and the Navy War College by providing Marine officers with an opportunity to participate in war planning and to proselytize for a larger Corps. After Barnett became Commandant, Headquarters became equally encouraging, adding the Advanced Base School to the Naval War College as a center of advanced base force indoctrination. The earliest missionaries were Dion Williams, Eli K. Cole, John H. Russell, and Robert H. Dunlap, all of whom became generals. All used the Naval War College to spread the advanced base force gospel: The mission was essential to fleet operation, and the Marine Corps, with more men and proper organization and training, could perform it. They also insisted that the mission required close Marine Corps–Navy cooperation at every level of planning and execution.[49] Their lectures and writings for the Naval War College were ably supported by another officer, Captain Earl H. Ellis, a slight, brilliant, and erratic Kansan commissioned after the war with Spain. A student at the Naval War College in 1912–1913, Ellis participated in drafting war plans against Japan, a task that became his lifelong obsession. Unlike his peers, who considered only base defense, Ellis pondered the conceivable requirement that the Marine Corps first might have to seize a defended island before it could become an advanced base. He also became convinced that the Marine Corps was not responding to the new mission, and he argued forcefully with other Marines that the Corps's future rested upon the advanced base force, both for defense and for assault. As a planner for the Culebra maneuvers, Ellis had an opportunity to impress John A. Lejeune, who became his patron as well as a co-advocate of the new faith.[50]

The Culebra experience set off a wave of interest that penetrated the thinking of Marine officers through Advanced Base School lectures and articles in the *Marine Corps Gazette*. As school commandant and commander of the 1st Regiment (Fixed Defense), Eli K. Cole in 1915 continued his own advocacy, emphasizing the need for technical training and the development of new weapons and equipment.[51] More important, Marine officers at Philadelphia heard Colonel Lejeune, speaking for the Commandant, stress in 1915 that advanced base duty was the Corps's *"true mission."* Whether the foe was a strong or a weak naval power, any foreseeable campaign would require advanced bases for the Navy, and the Marines "would be the first to set foot on hostile soil in order to seize, fortify, and hold a port from which, as a base, the Army would prosecute the campaign." Lejeune also thought that the Marines should not only prepare for base defense but join the subsequent land warfare in cooperation with the Army. The advanced base mission, therefore, provided "the true soldier's Elysian state," preparedness for war.[52] Lejeune's argument was supported in a subsequent article in the *Marine Corps Gazette* by Major John H. Russell, who as a Naval War College student had drafted one of the earliest advanced base force studies. Russell, like Lejeune, an Annapolis graduate and a future Commandant, went so far as to urge the Marine Corps to surrender some of its traditional duties and to embrace its new naval mission with unqualified enthusiasm. He argued that the Marine Corps needed reorganization as "one *organic whole*" to make the advanced base force its primary mission.[53]

Although Headquarters hesitated to surrender any missions, Barnett and his staff agreed that the Marine Corps's function in wartime was now quite clear: "The fortification and defense of naval advance or temporary bases for the use of the fleet has been made the principal war mission of the Marine Corps."[54] Only expeditionary duty in the Caribbean prevented the Corps from forming advanced base units on a permanent basis. Even as Headquarters struggled to support the occupations on Hispaniola, it was requesting additional funds in 1916 for tractor-drawn howitzers, trucks, and armored cars for the advanced base force. The Culebra maneuvers had shown that the advanced base force was a more sophisticated organization than many Marines had appreciated, and Headquarters knew that the technical and artillery companies were not as well equipped and well trained as they should be. As always, Barnett stated, the Marine Corps had too much to do and not enough men to do it. Nevertheless, he did not question the proposition that the Marine Corps should assign the highest priority to its advanced base mission.[55] What would have been heresy within the Marine Corps in 1900 had become by 1916 a new creed. In an organizational and technical sense, the Marine Corps had entered the world of twentieth-century warfare. All that remained was the test of actual combat.

II. The World War

1917–1919

Like the nation it served, the Marine Corps was too absorbed with its own problems to believe that it would someday fight in France. When the German and Austrian armies plunged into battle against the coalition of Great Britain, France, and Russia in August 1914, the Corps had no reason to suspect that the war would pull the United States into its red whirlpool and draw American troops, including the Marine Corps, to the trenches of Western Europe. Commandant George Barnett, however, was interested enough in the European war to send Marine officers to France to observe the fighting in 1914 and 1915, and his staff, directed by Colonel John A. Lejeune, studied the impact of the war on military organization, weapons, and tactics. By the autumn of 1915, Headquarters fully appreciated the importance of machine guns, aviation, heavy artillery, trucks, and the techniques of trench warfare. Given American neutrality, this knowledge did little to influence Corps policy.[1]

As the Wilson administration, harried by German submarines and American interventionists, drifted toward war in early 1917, the Marine Corps was ready to capitalize on the growing interest in military preparedness. Although its four expeditionary regiments were deployed in the Caribbean and its remaining men were scattered on warships and on Navy shore stations, the Marine Corps stood ready to swell its ranks and fulfill its boast that it was "First to Fight." Since the Naval Appropriations Act of 1916 the Corps had had an authorized war strength of

17,400 enlisted men, presumably to bring the advanced base force up to strength for a naval campaign. In fact, an increase to 17,400 men required only presidential action, not Congressional approval. In addition to its favorable legislative position, the Corps's recruiting officers and Recruiting Publicity Bureau in New York had already cultivated the public with material stressing the Corps's ardor to do battle. From the Commandant down to the recruiting sergeants, the Corps waited for the first sign that American policy would force some military preparedness. The Corps did not intend to let the opportunity for service and expansion pass.[2]

Dismayed by the Germans' unrestricted assault on Allied and neutral shipping, the Wilson administration broke diplomatic relations with Germany in February 1917. Although Wilson wanted to avoid intervention, he and his Cabinet became convinced by mid-March that war was inevitable. The President's first military act was to order the Navy's strength increased from 68,700 to 87,000 to man the fleet at war strength. His executive order of March 26, 1917, meant that the Marine Corps could recruit 7,000 more men. The increase enabled the Corps to reconstitute the advanced base regiments that it had deployed to the Caribbean as well as provide more ships guards and security detachments. Even though fleet action against the German navy was highly unlikely, the administration saw the Navy and the Marine Corps as its most immediately useful and important military tool. Insisting, with exaggeration, that "We Are Ready Now," the Navy Department thus began to mobilize even before the formal declaration of war on April 6, 1917. In America's big cities the doors of Marine recruiting stations swung open, and the Recruiting Publicity Bureau flooded the newspapers with Marine Corps stories and recruiting appeals.[3]

Buoyed by their faith in their Corps and the paralysis of the War Department, Marine recruiters enjoyed their finest hour in 1917. With no assurances that Marines would actually go to Europe to fight the Germans, the recruiters nevertheless stressed the Corps's heritage of combat valor and emphasized that the new men were enlisting for wartime service only. The latter point, legally correct, gave the Corps an advantage over the regular Army and the National Guard, which were bound to fixed terms of enlistment. So overwhelming was the public response that even before the Corps was authorized to exceed its 17,400-man ceiling, Headquarters announced that it would probably recruit 30,000 officers and men. When Congress authorized the Corps to go as high as 30,000 in May, there were already 21,864 Marines. The passage of the Selective Service Act in the same month worked to the Corps's advantage, for the recruiters stressed that the Corps was still an all-volunteer, elite service, an appeal that spared the Corps the residual contempt for conscripts and allowed it to attract the most adventurous, physically fit men while the War Department was toiling to create the Selective Service System.

Although the Marine Corps did not reach 30,000 men until October, the recruiting drive drew into its ranks the cream of the 1917 volunteers. The Corps became for the first time a national force, drawing as many men from such states as Montana and Colorado as from New Jersey and Massachusetts. Ohio, Illinois, and Missouri sent more men into the Corps than New York and Virginia. Aided by an enthusiastic Secretary of the Navy, whose son became a Marine officer, and by citizens' groups and newspapers, the Corps had no need to compromise its recruiting standards. Before the war ended, it had taken only 60,189 of the 239,274 men who had tried to join the Marines. It was especially successful in attracting new officers by democratizing its commissioning policies, a decision that pleased the egalitarian Josephus Daniels. Whether regulars, temporary officers, or Reserves, the Corps wanted the best junior officers and found them on college campuses (especially on athletic teams) and in the ranks of the new recruits. It commissioned military college graduates, university cadet corps veterans, noncommissioned officers, and former members of the Army's prewar Plattsburg-type summer training camps. In special cases it waived age and other requirements to attract prominent patriotic citizens, the most conspicuous being Detroit businessman and former Congressman Edwin Denby, who at forty-seven became a private (later major) and the inspirational leader of recruit indoctrination at Parris Island.[4]

With his recruiting program in full cry, General Barnett had no intention of using his expanded Corps for naval service only. The Wilson administration and the War Department inadvertently gave Barnett the opportunity to commit the Marine Corps to the ground war in France, thus allowing the Corps to make good its boast that it was the "First to Fight." Barnett himself was aware that the Corps had to send troops to France if it was to justify its expansion, its recruiting appeals, and its claims to elitism. Although the Wilson administration, reflecting Congressional and public reservations, was reluctant to send Americans to the fatal Western Front, the War Department General Staff believed the United States had no other choice. The General Staff, however, was not enthusiastic about sending an expeditionary force until it could organize a national army of millions. In April 1917 the British and French sent special missions to Washington to plead for at least a token commitment to bolster flagging Allied morale. While Congress toiled with conscription legislation, the General Staff planned to send one regular

Army division to France. By the end of May 1917 the President had approved the commitment and had selected Major General John J. Pershing, the most competent, reliable, and energetic officer of his rank in the army, to command the expedition.[5]

In the confusion, Barnett persuaded the War Department to include a Marine regiment in the first expeditionary force. Aided by Secretary Daniels and Chief of Naval Operations William S. Benson, Barnett cajoled the War Department to accept his offer of one Marine regiment immediately and another to follow, thus forming a full infantry brigade of more than six thousand men organized like the Army. Pershing had no choice in the matter, which was decided by Secretary of War Newton D. Baker and Army Chief of Staff Tasker H. Bliss. The War Department promised to provide any weapons and equipment the Marines needed to bring the regiments up to Army tables of equipment if the Marine Corps would furnish both the original regiments and adequate replacements, to which Barnett agreed. Pershing himself promised to treat the Marines equally in all supply and personnel matters, and Secretary of War Baker went so far as to pledge that the Marine brigade would be assigned to a combat division. The only thing the Army could not provide was transports, but the Navy Department agreed to send the Marines to France aboard American warships. As Pershing's division assembled for the voyage to France, the New York newspapers announced that the Marines would indeed be the "First to Fight," having provided a "seasoned regiment" of Caribbean veterans for the American Expeditionary Forces. The Marine Corps was on its way to the Western Front.[6]

1

For most of the young men who rushed to the Marine recruiters in 1917 and 1918, the road to France began on an obscure, flat 10-square-mile island of sandy marshland struggling to remain above the tides of Port Royal Sound in South Carolina. For these recruits and the generations that followed them the raw Marine base in South Carolina, a sometime Navy disciplinary barracks, quickly became memorable. It was known as Parris Island, and it was so special that one Marine thought Parris Island (or "PI") was as important to the Corps as parochial schools were to the Catholic Church.[7] Before World War I ended, the recruit depot at Parris Island had trained and indoctrinated 46,202 of the 61,000 enlistees and had provided specialist training for other enlisted men. The rigor and standardization of Marine recruit training at the depot assured the Corps of better-trained enlisted men than the Army could provide for the American Expeditionary Forces.

Recruits, some of them still thinking they had been promised dress blue uniforms for enlisting, shambled into the depot, herded by sergeants barking commands through megaphones. The first trauma came when the recruits stripped off their civilian clothes and donned white pajamas, which made them look like convicts. The next event was Edwin Denby's standard oration on patriotism, the heroic past of the Marine Corps, and the evils of drink, desertion, and venereal disease. Then the men lost all their hair to the sheep-shearers in the post barbershop. With iodine numbers painted on their heads, the recruits worked their way past the series of doctors and corpsmen and completed their physical examinations. After receiving field uniforms, the men marched to their tents or barracks and started eight to twelve weeks of intense drill, physical training, forced marches, and marksmanship, whipped on by the sharp tongues of the drill instructors. When the men were not training —broiled by the sun and blasted by the wind and sand—they built more barracks and hauled tons of crushed oyster shells to pave the depot's streets. The Marine Corps allowed little time for individual anguish; the only officially approved thoughts of home were supposed to be the evening letters to the recruits' families. The high point of the experience was usually the two or three weeks of marksmanship training; the Marine Corps, unlike the Army, was willing to take the time to keep its qualification standards high. By the time the recruits escaped the sand-fleas and palmettos, Parris Island had done its job: "The first day I was at camp I was afraid I was going die. The next two weeks my sole fear was that I wasn't going to die. And after that I knew I'd never die because I'd become so hard that nothing could kill me." [8]

Up the coast at Quantico, Virginia, the new Marine barracks along the Potomac, which was to have been the home of the advanced base force, swelled with new officers and men from Parris Island and the small groups of recruits who had trained at other posts. Aided by Allied officers, the Quantico staff hurriedly established a series of courses in troop leading and all the techniques of trench warfare. By 1918 the advanced training schools at Quantico had become the Marine Corps Overseas Depot, sending replacements to France and additional troops to the Caribbean. But in May 1917, when the first large detachments of men began to arrive, Quantico was a morass of red mud and raw lumber for new barracks and buildings. The training at Quantico was enthusiastic and physically demanding, but amateurish and oriented to individual and platoon-level skills. The living conditions were so poor that the post commander, upon receiving a well-deserved commendation, reflected that he should have been given a general court-martial. [9]

Headquarters could not wait for quarters and training areas to be built, and it assembled the new 5th Regiment at Philadelphia. Commanded by Colonel Charles A. Doyen, the regiment was hurriedly formed by merging barracks companies, ships detachments, small companies drawn from the Caribbean, and recruit drafts. In each company only the commander and senior lieutenant were prewar officers; the rest were new officers from military schools like Virginia Military Institute, land-grant universities, and Eastern colleges. The enlisted men were about half prewar veterans, half new recruits, mostly city toughs and farm boys. Among the noncommissioned officers and older privates, there were

. . . a number of diverse people who ran curiously to type, with drilled shoulders and bone-deep sunburn, and a tolerant scorn of nearly everything on earth. Their speech was flavored with navy words, and words culled from all the folk who live on the seas and the ports where our warships go. . . . Rifles were high and holy things to them, and they knew five-inch broadside guns. They talked patronizingly of war, and were concerned about rations. They were the Leathernecks, the Old Timers . . .[10]

In size the new companies of 6 officers and 250 men were an anomaly for the Corps. The arabic numbering of companies in Marine fashion, on the other hand, probably confused all Army officers who dealt with Marines. The regiment had three infantry battalions of Army size, more than 1,000 officers and men, but the companies retained their Marine Corps designations; in the First Battalion the companies were the 17th, 49th, 66th, and 67th. However puzzling the size and composition of the 5th Regiment, it was composed of the finest junior officers and enlisted men yet to serve in the Corps, leavened by hardened majors, captains, and sergeants. Although the regiment had had little time to train before sailing in June 1917, it was a high-spirited, self-confident organization deeply imbued with Marine Corps *esprit* and very conscious that its mission was to enhance the Corps's reputation for valor.[11]

Attached to the 1st Division, the symbolic American reinforcement of early 1917, the 5th Regiment landed in France ready to begin serious training. Its expectations were frustrated by General Pershing, whose foremost problem was creating a system of training camps and logistical installations to support the rest of the divisions of the American Expeditionary Forces then training in the United States. Like the General Staff, Pershing's GHQ staff had underestimated the AEF's need for support troops. Since the 5th Regiment was excess in the 1st Division, Pershing assigned the Marines as security detachments and labor troops. His decision was based not on any lack of confidence in the Marines, whose discipline and smart appearance Pershing admired, but on the urgent need to provide men for the AEF's support system. Pershing's decision was supported by the General Staff, which thought the Marines would make perfect provost guards.[12] As a result, seldom did more than a battalion participate in the 1st Division's training in the summer and autumn of 1917. The Marines assumed the security assignments with ill-concealed displeasure. One sentry told Pershing's press officer that his duty would at least prepare him for a postwar job: "I can wear a striped waistcoat and brass buttons and open cab doors in front of a New York hotel." [13] Other Marines composed a new verse for the Marine Corps Hymn:

> So here we are at St. Nazaire
> Our guns have rusty bores,
> We are working side by side with Huns
> And nigger stevedores.
> But if the Army and the Navy
> Ever gaze on Heaven's scenes
> They will find the roads are graded
> By United States Marines.[14]

The assignment angered Commandant Barnett, who vigorously stated in American newspapers that the Marines would soon see action and was barely mollified by Pershing's praise of the Marines' discipline.[15] Pershing's staff had labored against War Department and Navy Department meddling to provide the regiment with adequate supplies, rations, and uniforms, but the 5th Regiment and Headquarters nevertheless began to suspect an Army conspiracy to deny the Marine Corps a combat role. In fact, AEF headquarters planned to release the Marines for training as soon as it had enough units to create another full division.[16]

In the meantime General Barnett organized another regiment, the 6th, and the 6th Machine Gun Battalion at Quantico in order to complete the full Marine brigade for the AEF. Barnett pressed Secretary Daniels to provide shipping and to ensure that Secretary of War Baker would order Pershing to include the brigade in one of his divisions.[17] Trained hard by its commander, Colonel Albertus W. Catlin, the 6th Regiment included only a handful of veteran officers and sergeants but the pick of the wartime lieutenants and new recruits. Catlin claimed that some 60 percent of the troops were college men. Even though not completely trained, the regiment soon satisfied Catlin and General Barnett. By February 1918 the entire regiment had landed in France, where it trained and shared security duties.[18]

Even before the 6th Regiment arrived Pershing assigned the Marine brigade to the newly assembled 2d Division, which, like the 1st Division, was designated a "Regular" division because its units were built upon the prewar Army's regiments. Inasmuch as the Army was still identifying its units as "Regular," "National Guard," and "National Army," Barnett asked Pershing if the Marine brigade could be officially called the 4th Brigade (U.S. Marines), for it had become the fourth Marine brigade then serving in 1917. The brigade was already the 4th Infantry Brigade of the AEF, so Pershing's staff saw no objection to the special designation, thus assuring that the brigade would retain its Marine Corps identity not only in official reports but in the newspapers as well.[19] This casual decision, routinely made, eventually created jealousy of the Marines in the AEF when Pershing's censors in 1918 decided that newsmen could not identify AEF units by number but could refer to the Marine brigade by name. The enlisted Marines themselves saw to it that no one confused them with the AEF's soldiers. As their distinctive forest green uniforms unraveled, they sewed their Marine buttons onto their army khakis and wore their cap insignia on their overseas caps, helmets, and breast pockets. Someone sent the brigade literally hundreds of extra Marine insignia, so the men blossomed with the hallowed globe and anchor.[20]

Through the bitterly cold, muddy winter of 1917–1918 the 4th Brigade trained with their French instructors and their Army comrades of the 2d Division. While recruiters in the United States told gullible youths that the Marines spent many happy hours drinking and singing in French cafés, joined by girls "red lipped and of fair delicate complexion," [21] the brigade threw grenades, dug trenches, fired weapons, and went on backbreaking hikes in the sleet and snow. Billeted among the French peasantry, the Marines huddled in their chill barns and homes, fought lice and colds, and griped about the food. One sergeant remarked that his company had become "so damn mean they would have fought their own grandmothers." [22] There were continuous irritants. The Marines learned army drill, which they despised. They also turned in their trusted Lewis machine guns in exchange for French Chauchat automatic rifles and Hotchkiss machine guns, both heavy, unreliable weapons that used different ammunition from the Marines' Springfields and thus complicated supply problems. Nevertheless, the brigade's morale remained high. The men played football with such abandon that the brigade commander, Brigadier General Doyen, had it banned as too dangerous. Often in formation the men chanted "G-A-B! G-A-B!" or "Get a Boche!" [23] As the brigade lost its slackers to rear echelon billets and saw some Marines killed or injured in traffic accidents and training mishaps, the Marines toiled with their weapons, steel helmets, and suffocating gas masks and waited for Pershing to send them to the Front.[24]

Back in Washington, General Barnett saw to it that the brigade's labors did not go unnoticed and worked to the Corps's benefit. Convinced that the Corps in 1917 had established the nation's most efficient training system, Barnett argued that the Corps should again be expanded, both to serve in France and to fulfill all its naval responsibilities. Testifying before Congress in January 1918, Barnett reported that the Corps was at full strength at 1,230 officers and 36,334 men but contended that Congress should enlarge it by 38,260 more men. Barnett wanted sufficient men to replace the two regiments sent to Cuba in 1917 in order to reinforce the three regiments left for the advanced base force. The Commandant, however, stated that what he really wanted was to send another infantry brigade to France and perhaps include the artillery regiments of the advanced base force as well. It would then be possible to create an entire Marine division in the AEF. Such a plan would exploit the Marine training facilities at Quantico, San Diego, and Parris Island, all of which required additional funds for development as wartime bases and postwar advanced base force installations. Barnett also pointed out that the 4th Brigade would probably soon need replacements after it went to the front. In sum, the Commandant wanted the Corps increased not only for wartime service but permanently, justifying the expansion by citing the AEF's presumed needs and the Navy's continued demands for advanced base and expeditionary regiments.[25]

Barnett's plans for an enlarged Corps ran straight into a wall of governmental skepticism. Congress was sympathetic, and one of its investigative subcommittees reported that the Corps had mobilized with matchless efficiency: "There are today on the firing lines of France no better trained, no braver, no more effective force than our own Marines now serving there, and we hope their numbers may soon be increased." [26] A permanent increase, however, did not seem appropriate unless the War Department asked for more Marines for the AEF. This was a request Pershing would not make.[27] Encouraged by an anti-Barnett cabal in the Corps and Congress, Secretary Daniels equivocated in his support, and the naval affairs committees also divided over Barnett's request for more generals and more rank for his staff.[28] Undismayed by his failure to receive an authorization for more men, Barnett pressed Daniels to persuade Baker to accept another infantry brigade for the AEF. In April 1918, despite Pershing's known reluctance to accept more Marines, the War Department relented. Startled by the massive German offensives that had begun in March, the General Staff accepted another brigade, assuming that the Navy would provide shipping. Barnett immediately asked Congress to increase the Corps to 62,000 men, assuring it that the AEF needed more Marines. Both the House and the Senate approved a 75,000-man Corps, but the authorization stalled on the issue of increased rank for Barnett and his staff.[29]

The War Department's capitulation on the issue of a second Marine infantry brigade raised again the question of organizing a full Marine division for the AEF. Distressed by the departure of their infantrymen (but not artillerymen and other specialists) for France, the senior officers of the advanced base regiments training at Quantico pressed Barnett to approach Pershing directly. The Commandant responded by sending two of the Corps's most persuasive officers, Brigadier General John A. Lejeune and Major Earl H. Ellis, to France in May 1918. Their first assignment was to change Pershing's mind about the Marine division. Pershing and his staff were adamant. Sensitive to any challenge from either the Allies or Washington on the management of the AEF, they argued that an entire Marine division meant increased Navy Department interference in France. Moreover, a Marine division would create unnecessary administrative problems during a period of the AEF's growth. Despite Lejeune's forceful argument that the Marine Corps needed the combat service to develop the advanced base force, Pershing remained firm in his decision: There could be Marine replacements for the 4th Brigade, and individual Marine officers could command Army units, but there would be no Marine division in the AEF.[30]

2

For the Allied high command the winter of 1917–1918 was a time of despair, and the Allies' pessimism swept across AEF headquarters, giving new urgency to Pershing's plans to create an independent American army. The Allied gloom was well founded, for what had been a three-front war against the Central Powers twelve months before was now a one-front war. First, revolution in Russia had brought an end to the fighting in Eastern Europe, and in the autumn of 1917 a German–Austrian offensive had almost destroyed the Italian army. Consequently the German high command of Field Marshal Paul von Hindenburg and General Erich Ludendorff redeployed the bulk of their forces to the Western Front, massing 191 divisions for the 1918 offensive that they hoped would win the war. The Allies appeared ready for the coup de grâce. During 1917 the British economy had staggered under the on slaught of unrestricted submarine warfare; the British Expeditionary Force had once again gamely but futilely attacked in Belgium and northern France; and the French army had collapsed in mutiny. With fewer divisions than the Central Powers, the Allies defended their trenches and called for American troops.

AEF headquarters was as aware as the Allies that the Germans were likely to attack in 1918, but Pershing's plans were not shaped by that realization. Pressed hard by the Allied generals to incorporate his divisions into the Allied command structure, Pershing would not compromise his plan to create an independent American field army, with which he intended to crush the Germans in the Metz-Saar region in 1919. Pershing would allow his four divisions to train with the Allies, and he eventually agreed that in return for Allied shipping he would bring more of his army to France in early 1918. In the meantime he attached his divisions (the 1st, 2d, 26th, and 42d) to French corps in Lorraine, the sector in which he intended to deploy his own independent army.[31]

In mid-March 1918 the 2d Division moved from its training areas to a quiet sector along the northern edge of the St. Mihiel salient southeast of Verdun and started its final examination on trench warfare. Pershing wanted the Americans trained for "open" warfare assaults, but he recognized the value of actual combat experience and was anxious to move his divisions into his own sector before they were drawn elsewhere by the Allies. For the next two months the 4th Brigade learned the perils and discomforts of life in the trenches. As battalions and attached machine gunners rotated to and from the front, the Marines dug trenches, weathered bombardments in their dugouts, went on raids, stood watch, worried about trench foot and cold food, and found that even in a quiet sector the Germans could be dangerous adversaries. On April 1 the brigade lost its first killed in action, a private caught by a shell burst while carrying supplies to the front. Two weeks later an entire company of the 6th Regiment fell in a gas barrage on a reserve billet, and forty men died. As spring brought green life to the scarred farmlands, the Marines waged war with increased skill and determination.[32]

There was much urgency to the 2d Division's training, for on March 21, 1918, the long-awaited German offensive struck in the Somme region and sent two British armies reeling back toward the city of Amiens. In the crisis the French army hurried reserves north and asked Pershing for reinforcements. Reluctant to place new divisions under commanders who had demonstrated little skill in three years of war, Pershing at first equivocated, then pledged that "all he had" could be used temporarily in the crisis. For practical purposes, "all" meant the 1st Division, which hurried north in April as part of the French First Army. The 2d Division then left the front in mid-May to complete its training in open warfare in order to prepare to join the French army, which was then desperately containing the German breakthrough in Picardy. Before it too went north, the division conducted several attack maneuvers under the watchful eye of Pershing's staff. The AEF inspectors watched the 4th Brigade and reported that it was "probably the best" American unit in France for appearance and discipline. Like its Army brethren, however, the brigade was poor in tactics and in its use of machine gun and artillery fire support. Its communications were deplorable. There was no question about the brigade's zeal, but its skill in the attack left much to be desired.[33]

Trench duty and open warfare exercises brought the 4th Brigade an unwelcome change in its command, the relief for illness of Brigadier General Charles A. Doyen. Pershing was equally demanding and unforgiving with elderly, ill officers of the Army, but Doyen's relief nonetheless was taken as another sign that AEF headquarters thought the Marine brigade was more trouble than it was worth. This impression was strengthened by Pershing's message to the War Department that he would assign his own chief of staff, Brigadier General James G. Harbord, to command the brigade and that the Marine Corps need not send another general to France.[34] In assigning Harbord, Pershing increased the pressure on the brigade to perform wonders in combat. A college graduate, Harbord was a former enlisted man who had made his reputation as an officer in the Philippine Constabulary and on the General Staff. Pershing, who viewed the Marine brigade as the most military in the AEF, told him that he had no excuse for failure. Harbord himself knew that the brigade was "a fine body of officers and men" who were not hostile to him, but not enthusiastic either. "If I make good I shall probably never know anything more about it than I do now." [35] When he assumed command on May 6, Harbord met with the regimental commanders, Colonel Wendell C. Neville and Colonel Albertus W. Catlin. They reminded him that the Corps's motto, "Semper Fidelis," meant that the brigade would be loyal even to an Army cavalry officer.[36] The change of command, though amicable, heightened the tension between the brigade and Pershing's staff.

While the 2d Division waited for the call to combat in northern France, the Germans launched a third offensive against the French Sixth Army. Ill deployed along the Chemin des Dames ridge north of the Aisne River, the French Sixth Army, a weak force of seven worn French and British divisions, was no match for the devastating artillery bombardment and eighteen German divisions thrown against it. In the first day of their attack, May 27, the German Seventh and First Armies drove 12 miles and crossed the Aisne River. Ahead of them lay the

Marne River, the Paris–Metz highway, and less than 100 miles of easy terrain to Paris. Despite the fact that Ludendorff had intended the attack only to draw French reserves away from Flanders, the prospect of a spectacular victory lured the German armies past Soissons to Château-Thierry on the Marne and to the open farmlands north of the river. Deflected by the Allies' stiffening resistance to the east around Rheims and the barrier of the Marne, the German advance slid southwest toward Château-Thierry and the open countryside to the west. All that faced them were the remnants of the French Sixth Army and local reserves, although French headquarters was hurrying troops to hold the western side of the salient in the Allied front. To the apex of the salient at Château-Thierry hurried one American machine gun battalion, which helped stop an attack across the Marne on June 1. Weakened by casualties, supply problems, and straggling, the Germans were already close to exhaustion, and Ludendorff ordered the offensive halted. Nevertheless, the German army commanders could and did launch local attacks to improve their defense of the salient. To the Allies it still appeared as if the Germans intended to march into Paris.[37]

Having finished its last open warfare maneuver, the 2d Division was spending a leisurely Sunday, May 30, when it received orders to prepare for a hurried ride south. Its assignment was to join the French Sixth Army, at that moment fighting a desperate rear-guard action northwest of Château-Thierry. For the Marines of the 4th Brigade the next forty-eight hours were crowded with confused images: French staff officers squabbling over orders, Americans trying to decipher their instructions, long lines of French trucks, and a stream of refugees buffeting the convoys as they pressed toward the front. Struggling forward without definite orders and marching without its artillery and supply trains, the 2d Division on June 1 finally deployed along either side of the Paris–Metz highway northwest of Château-Thierry. Although the arriving battalions of the 4th Brigade were mixed with the soldiers of the 3d Brigade, the division staff eventually organized the Marines north of the highway in support of the scattered French units still fighting to their front. Attached to General Jean Degoutte's French XXI Corps, the 2d Division approached the Germans. Now afoot, the long columns of infantry pushed through the French stragglers and the frightened villagers. Tired and dusty, without food for two days, the Americans were too anxious to feel like saviors, but their presence heartened the French high command and delighted Pershing's headquarters.[38]

The expected German attack came in corps strength on June 2 and rolled the French outposts back toward the 2d Division. In front of the Marine brigade two German divisions pushed into the towns of Torcy

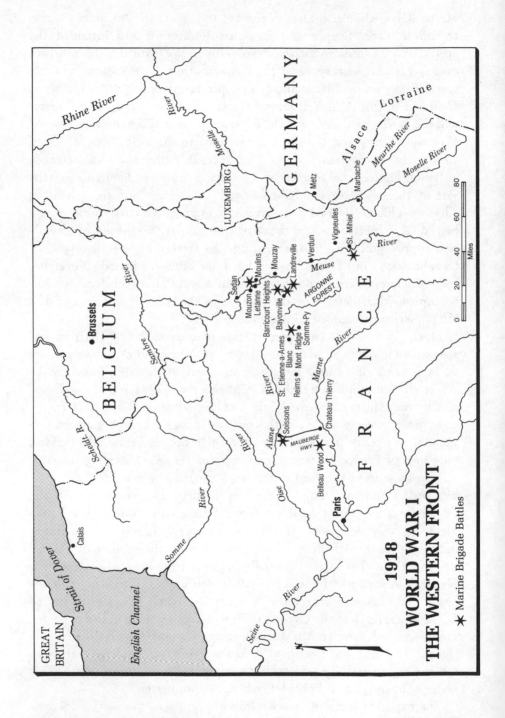

GREAT BRITAIN

Strait of Dover

English Channel

Calais

Rhine River

River

Moselle

LUXEMBURG

GERMANY

Lorraine

Alsace

Meurthe River

Moselle River

Metz

Marbache

Vigneulles

St. Mihiel

Verdun

Meuse

River

Mouzay

Landreville

Moulins

Letanne

Mouzon

Sedan

Barricourt Heights

Bayonville

ARGONNE FOREST

St. Etienne-a-Arnes

Blanc

Reims

Mont Ridge

Somme-Py

River

BELGIUM

Brussels

River

Sambre

Marne

FRANCE

Scheldt. R.

River

Aisne

Oise

River

River

Soissons

MAUBERGE HWY

Belleau Wood

Chateau Thierry

Somme

Paris

Seine

River

80

60

40

20

0

Miles

N

1918
WORLD WAR I
THE WESTERN FRONT

★ Marine Brigade Battles

300

to the north and Bouresches to the south and soon occupied a dark wood in between, the Bois de Belleau. The French flooded back through the Marine positions. When one French officer advised Captain Lloyd Williams that he too should withdraw, Williams replied with disgust: "Retreat, hell! We just got here." [39] The next day the Germans continued the advance as infantry battalions in *feldgrau*, backs bowed under their weapons and faces hidden in their deep helmets, stepped out in dense columns across the woodlots and wheatfields. Well trained and backed by superior artillery fire, the 4th Brigade defended its line with skill, blasting the German columns apart with long-range rifle and machine gun fire. Fighting from prepared positions, the Marines proved that their weeks on the marksmanship ranges and in trench warfare training had made them spirited, effective defenders. The German advance, designed for only limited objectives, halted, and the Germans shifted to the tactical defense along their front. [40]

When it became apparent on June 5 that the Germans had given up their attacks, General Degoutte, an apostle of the unrelenting attack, decided to seize the initiative and use the 2d Division for a series of counterattacks designed to deprive the Germans of the property between Torcy and Bouresches, which they might use to mount another attack of their own. Reinforced by the French 167th Division, Degoutte ordered the 2d Division to shift to the attack on June 6. [41] While the plans involved a French regiment to its left and the 23d U.S. Infantry to its right, the 4th Brigade assumed the responsibility for the main attack. Degoutte's plans were reasonable, but his timetable was badly flawed: The 4th Brigade and the assault battalions received their orders only hours before they were supposed to attack. Artillery support and reconnaissance were inadequate, fatal conditions for infantry schooled in tactics that by 1918 were bloody anachronisms.

The month-long action remembered as the battle of Belleau Wood began at dawn on June 6, when one battalion of the 5th Regiment assaulted Hill 142, which commanded the terrain around Torcy. Because of inadequate time to organize the attack, only two Marine companies made the first assault. The Marines eventually swarmed over the hill, but first German machine guns ravaged the lines of skirmishers as they plowed through the fields of wheat and poppies. Throughout the rest of the day, Marines and German infantry struggled around Hill 142. At one point the Marines almost took Torcy, at another they almost lost Hill 142. Before the fighting died down, almost half of the original assault battalion had become casualties, and part of another battalion had to join the fight to hold the position. Supporting units on the flanks of the attack had equal difficulty, thus subjecting the 5th Regiment to devastating enfilade fire. Rifles and raw courage against machine guns and experience, the Marines and Germans shot and grenaded in hot fury until the survivors collapsed with exhaustion. The Marines, however, still held Hill 142.[42]

The attack on Hill 142 had proved that the Germans were determined to hold the front. Nevertheless, the large-scale assault on Belleau Wood and Bouresches began as planned late in the afternoon of June 6. The only uncommitted battalion of the 5th Regiment was supposed to take the woods from the west, while two battalions of the 6th Regiment attacked the woods and Bouresches from the southwest. Again begun without adequate artillery, the three-battalion attack, directed by Colonel Catlin but designed by Harbord, flirted with disaster from the first. Crossing an open field west of Belleau Wood, its lines dressed with parade-ground discipline, the 5th Regiment battalion was nearly annihilated, and few of its men actually reached the trees. Aided by the less open terrain, the two 6th Regiment battalions had more success. Four companies stormed into the wood's southern edge and fell upon the machine gun nests and supporting infantry. The remnants of two other companies finally cleared Bouresches that night in desperate street fighting; reinforced and resupplied during a night of terror and death, the Marines held the town against repeated counterattacks. Like the fighting around Hill 142, the attack cost the Marines about 60 percent of the men in its infantry companies and an even higher percentage of officers and sergeants. Even Colonel Catlin, observing the attack, fell with a rifle bullet in the chest. One veteran sergeant said it all as he plunged ahead toward the next machine gun nest: "Come on, you sons-ofbitches! Do you want to live forever?" Shocked and maddened, his men apparently did not. By the time the late twilight fell, the Marine Corps had suffered more casualties (one thousand officers and men) than it had lost in its entire history.[43]

Although AEF headquarters refused to call the battle of Belleau Wood anything more than a minor local engagement, Pershing's press officers allowed American newspapermen covering the battle to identify the Marines as the attacking American troops. Much to the amazement of the 4th Brigade and the consternation of the 3d Brigade and the U.S. 3d Division, in the newspapers the entire fight around Château-Thierry became a Marine Corps affair. Banner headlines throughout the United States hailed the Marines' combat skill and the great German losses, both exaggerated impressions. In addition to the Associated Press's bulletins, the papers circulated the particularly vivid, adulatory story of the attack on Hill 142 written by Floyd Gibbons of the *Chicago Tribune*. Having filed his story of the morning attack, Gibbons had accompanied the late afternoon assault and had been gravely wounded. Having heard rumors of his death, Gibbons's censor friends passed his "last" story through unaltered to the United States. Belleau Wood thus was a dearly bought but stunningly successful public relations coup for the Corps.[44]

Unaffected by any opinion other than that of German and American generals, the battle of Belleau Wood went on. Harbord, although uncertain about the Marines' positions and casualties, ordered the attacks on the wood renewed on June 8. Thinking that he had sealed the wood's entire western edge with two battalions of the 5th Regiment, Harbord ordered a battalion of the 6th Regiment to drive north through the tangled woods, rocks, and ravines that made the woods a defender's dream. The attacks again gained little ground, for the Germans could reinforce easily from the north and east and did so. When the assault ended, Major Burton Sibley's battalion, which had made one of the June 6 attacks, was a wreck. Harbord then had his artillery rake the entire wood, but the barrage did not break the German resistance.

Nevertheless, on June 10 Harbord sent two relatively fresh battalions against the Germans in a complex converging attack mounted from both the west and the south. The southern attack by a battalion of the 6th Regiment struggled through the wood taking heavy casualties and making small gains. Frederic M. Wise's battalion of the 5th Regiment once more swept across the deadly wheatfield and was ruined by German artillery and machine guns, but it reached the wood and linked up with the 6th Regiment. Fatigued and harried, Wise reported that he thought the Marines had taken the wood, which Harbord then reported to division. Wise was wrong: The brigade held only the lower third. When the situation became clearer, Harbord continued the attacks north along the wood's long axis. It was a battle of companies and platoons, all reduced to a handful and losing raw replacements in each assault. Sniping, grenading, machine gunning, and shelling the Marines with high explosives and gas, the Germans bent but did not break. On June 18 Harbord and the 2d Division commander both conceded that the 4th Brigade was no longer battle-worthy and needed complete relief. Colonel Wise, who had seen his beloved battalion reduced from 1,000 men to 6 officers and 350 men in two weeks, summed up the situation with little exaggeration. Asked by his wife how the Marines were, he responded: "There aren't any more Marines." [45] Courage and *esprit* had reached their limits, and the 4th Brigade left the battle.[46]

Having punished three German divisions, the 4th Brigade surrendered its front to the U.S. 7th Infantry, which had scant success in assaulting the German-held northern third of the wood while the Marines regrouped. The Marine brigade's courage awed those who observed the struggle, since the battle was viewed as the acid test of American determination. Pershing's observers at French army headquarters reported that the French high command was clearly heartened by the brigade's performance and anticipated with relish the commitment of other fresh American divisions.[47] On the other hand, the Germans were dismayed by the Americans' disdain for losses:

> The Second American Division must be considered a very good one and may even perhaps be reckoned as a storm troop. The different attacks on Belleau Wood were carried out with bravery and dash. The moral effect of our gunfire cannot seriously impede the advance of the American infantry. The Americans' nerves are not yet worn out.
>
> The qualities of the men individually may be described as remarkable. They are physically well set up, their attitude is good, and they range in age from eighteen to twenty-eight years. They lack at present only training and experience to make formidable adversaries. The men are in fine spirits and are filled with naive assurance; the words of a prisoner are characteristic—"WE KILL OR WE GET KILLED." [48]

Returning to the wood, still reeking with gas and the dead, the 4th Brigade completed Belleau Wood's capture with a two-battalion assault on June 25–26. Assisted by more cautious tactics and better artillery fire, the 5th Regiment drove the last German battalion from its positions. In the early morning of June 26, Harbord finally received the long-awaited news: "Belleau Woods now U.S. Marine Corps entirely." To complete the division's action the 3d Brigade shortly thereafter assaulted and took the town of Vaux to the south, thus ending the French XXI Corps counterattack. Measured against the assaults of early June, the last advances were relatively easy; the division probably killed and captured more Germans than it itself lost. Nevertheless, the entire operation had cost the division 170 officers and 8,793 men. The 4th brigade alone had lost 112 officers and 4,598 men. More than 1,000 Marines had died. If nothing else, the 2d Division had proved its fighting heart. The ecstatic French subsequently awarded the division's infantry brigades unit citations for gallantry and renamed Belleau Wood the Bois de la Brigade de Marine. For the 4th Brigade it was enough that it at last could leave the ruined wood, a charnal house of blasted stumps, and turn its attention to such healing things as food, rest, mail, and baths. The war along the approaches to Paris appeared truly *finie*.[49]

Reassured by the diminished strength of the German attacks, the French high command planned to shift to the attack, and its plans included Pershing's available divisions. Neither another German offensive in Picardy on June 9 nor a last desperate attempt to cross the Marne on July 15 altered these plans. Even as French and American divisions were blunting these last German offensives, French headquarters began to shift its reserves to encircle the German troops left in the Aisne-Marne salient. The main effort was to strike the western edge of the salient and drive toward the German supply lines running from Soissons to Château-Thierry. The spearhead of the attack, the French Tenth Army, would include an American corps composed of the 1st and the 2d Divisions. Ignorant that they would soon return to the front and not go on liberty to Paris, the Marines of the 4th Brigade manned a quiet sector and waited.

Bewildered by rapid changes of orders and transportation mismanagement, the 4th Brigade once more rode French *camions* to war, dismounting west of the Forêt de Retz on July 17. The Marines were no more confused about their mission than Major General James G. Harbord, now the 2d Division commander. (Colonel Wendell C. Neville led the brigade.) Passed from one headquarters to another, Harbord finally learned that his division was to attack at dawn on July 18 on the right flank of a three-division spearhead aimed at the Soissons–Château-Thierry highway some eight miles to the east. Having no idea how the French Tenth Army would bring his troops to the line of departure, Harbord drafted an attack order placing the two regiments of the 3d Brigade on line on the right and the 5th Regiment on the left, linking the division with the 1st Moroccan Division. The 6th Regiment was assigned by the French to corps reserve.[50]

Planned as an unpleasant surprise for the Germans, the Soissons attack depended on the rapid movement of the assault divisions through the Forêt de Retz and a slashing first day's assault. The deployment was chaotic, hampered by rain, serious traffic jams, and poor regulation. The Marines remembered the march with distaste, for it was a nightmare of darkness, horse-drawn wagons, mud, and vast confusion. With little sleep and no hot food for two days, the brigade reached the line of departure barely a half-hour before the attack. Most of the machine gun units did not arrive at all, and one company reached its position only by running. With little more than a general objective and a direction of attack, the 5th Regiment stepped out at 4:30 A.M. behind a rolling barrage. The early fighting, still within the forest, was bitter and costly, but the regiment reached the farmlands beyond. Attempting to eliminate fortified farms and to maintain contact with the Moroccans, the two assault battalions of the 5th Regiment became scattered and disorganized by early afternoon. The Germans contributed to the confusion with shelling and machine gun fire, and the lines of Marines toppled as at Belleau Wood. Heat exhaustion and sheer fatigue felled others.

When the attack crumbled along a large ravine outside Vierzy, Harbord attached the remnants of the 5th Regiment to the 3d Brigade, which then successfully took the town that evening in hard fighting in which the Marines participated. By nightfall all of the 2d Division except the 6th Regiment was unfit for an organized attack.[51]

Although the July 18 attack had covered nearly 6 miles, the 2d Division was still short of the final objective, and the next day the 6th Regiment joined the assault. Despite the use of tanks and artillery, the attack did not reach the highway but did carry the ridges above it. Swept by shrapnel and machine gun bullets, the Marines also fell prey to lack of food and water. When the 2d Division halted the assault after the second day, the 6th Regiment had lost 40 percent of its strength, and the entire brigade had shrunk by nearly two thousand new casualties. On July 20 the 2d Division was once again allowed to return to a rest area and fill its thin ranks with replacements. In the infantry companies of the 4th Brigade the survivors of Belleau Wood and Soissons were an elite handful.[52]

Whether the Marines of the 4th Brigade realized it or not, their heroics at Belleau Wood and Soissons had helped breathe new life into Commandant Barnett's plans to expand the Corps. On July 1, 1918, Congress finally authorized a wartime increase of the Marine Corps to 3,017 officers and 75,500 men, a force large enough to perform every naval mission and provide more than a brigade for the AEF. Riding the euphoria of Belleau Wood, which grew in a direct ratio to the distance from that stricken field, Marine recruiters in July 1918 accepted 8,500 new men, the war's largest one-month total. In August, however, the Wilson administration halted voluntary enlistments. It took a month for the Navy Department to work out a new agreement: The Marine Corps would receive 5,000 inductees a month for four months and 1,500 a month thereafter. The Corps controlled quality by insisting successfully that the draftees volunteer for the Marines and meet its standards. Although Barnett still had strong critics in Congress and the War Department, public opinion carried the Corps to dazzling manpower strengths and quality in both its officers and its enlisted men.[53]

The increased Corps did not mean that Barnett's dream of seeing another Marine brigade in combat would be fulfilled. For one thing, Barnett had difficulty providing replacements for the 4th Brigade. AEF headquarters reported that it needed more than twenty thousand men in the replacement system to support the brigade. The seven replacement battalions Barnett sent to France between February and August did not even match the brigade's total casualties. Barnett asked General Lejeune, the senior Marine in France, to persuade Pershing to relieve

Marine security detachments for front-line service. Nevertheless, Barnett on his own initiative created the 5th Marine Brigade at Quantico and shipped it to France on September 5 with the War Department's approval. The War Department, however, knew that Pershing, probably miffed by the 4th Brigade's publicity and mindful of its personnel shortages, would not incorporate the new brigade into a combat division. The War Department would not face criticism at home for keeping the Marines away from France, but neither would it order the AEF's commander to use them in combat. Pershing's stubbornness closed the question of adding more Marine units to the AEF.[54]

3

Far from the splintered trees and shell-plowed wheatfields of France, and closer to the land of the recruiting posters of Howard Chandler Christy and James Montgomery Flagg, the Marine Corps by 1918 had secured a safe place for itself in the American war effort. While maintaining the 4th Brigade, the Corps continued to perform all its traditional missions for the Navy Department. Of the nearly 73,000 Marines in service when the war ended, only 24,555 were with the American Expeditionary Forces. Nearly 8,000 more were overseas manning naval stations in the American territories or serving in the occupations of Cuba, Haiti, and the Dominican Republic. The legation guards in Peking and Managua stood firm on State Department orders. In November 1918 there were still some 37,000 Marines in the United States, most of them either part of the advanced base force or training for overseas deployment. The Marine Corps provided security detachments for seventy-five Navy installations during the war and at the same time expanded its own base and training establishment. In addition, the war did nothing to alter the Marines' service as ships guards. At the end of the war, more than two thousand Marines still paced the decks of twenty-nine American battleships and cruisers, which were deployed for service with the Royal Navy at Scapa Flow and for the intervention at Vladivostok during the Russian Revolution. George Barnett's Marine Corps did not surrender any of its traditional tasks.[55]

The World War marked the true beginning of three eventually significant parts of the Marine Corps: the Marine Corps Reserve, Women Marines, and Marine Corps aviation. There was no Marine Corps Reserve in any real sense during the World War; the "Reserve" designation was simply a legal category provided by the Navy Appropriations Act of 1916 that allowed the Marine Corps to exceed its regular and wartime manpower ceilings. The only difference between a "Reserve" and a "temporary" officer or "duration" enlisted man was that the former status implied some sort of postwar obligation. The mere use of the Reserve category, however, had the result that some 6,773 officers and men in November 1918 were "Reserves." The wartime use of the Reserve designation preserved the category to accommodate "duration" Marines and former members of the state naval militia marine companies (merged with the Reserve in July 1918) who wanted to continue their Corps affiliation after the war.[56]

The use of the Reserve category for wartime service also opened the door for women to serve in the Marine Corps, a bastion of the masculine ethic. Although it trailed the Navy in enlisting women for clerical duties, the Marine Corps did recruit women in August 1918, and the War Department did not. By the end of the war 305 Marine Reserves (Female) were hard at work at their typewriters and files, primarily at Headquarters. Although their purpose was to release men for combat duties by taking their office jobs, the Reserves (F) received instruction in drill and ceremonies, served under military discipline, and wore an austere, long-skirted version of the enlisted green service uniform. The women Marines scoffed at their Navy yeoman sisters, who sported open collars and feminine lace. Patriotic, hard-working, and quick to take offense at slights to their Corps service, the women Marines impressed at least the magazine *Leatherneck,* spokesman for male enlisted men: "Everyone is proud of the Marine girls. They carried themselves like real soldiers . . . and proved they were ready to go anywhere and conduct themselves with honor to the Marine Corps."[57] As the women Marines were mustered out after the end of the war, Secretary of the Navy Daniels paid them an inadvertently hilarious tribute: "We will not forget you. As we embrace you in uniform today, we will embrace you without uniform tomorrow."[58]

Of all the widely deployed elements of the Marine Corps, none prospered more than Marine aviation. When the war began, the Marines attached to the Navy's infant aviation force numbered only five officers and thirty men, divided between the aeronautical company assigned to the advanced base force at Philadelphia and the Navy's aeronautical station at Pensacola. But the Navy was at the threshold of expanding its aviation force. The Naval Appropriations Act of 1916 had provided $3.5 million for aviation and had established a separate naval flying corps. When the United States entered the war, the government, seized with aviation mania, deluged the Army and Navy with more money for planes and men than the services could effectively use until late 1918. The Navy Department, prodded by Admiral William S. Sims, launched an ambitious expansion program, directed primarily toward the use of naval aviation against German submarines. General Barnett preferred forming a Marine squadron to support the 4th Brigade. Captain Alfred A. Cunningham, the senior Marine aviator, arranged for his pilots to use Army planes and facilities and designed a composite squadron of pursuit planes and observation balloons that would be useful only in a land warfare role.[59]

Growing with naval aviation, the Marine aviation force in October 1917 numbered 34 officers and 330 men and was still organized either for advanced base work or support of the 4th Brigade. Barnett and Cunningham apparently did not realize that the Navy did not want its pilots to fly in a land campaign when their precious skills could be used for naval missions or that the Army was unenthusiastic about including a Marine squadron in the AEF. In the meantime Naval aviators were already at work designing a force to aid the Royal Navy in combating the submarine menace and had deployed several aviation units (without planes) to France. Reflecting the division in the Navy over the utility of seaplanes and land-based aircraft in the antisubmarine war, the Marine Corps reorganized its one aviation company into two distinct units: the 1st Marine Aeronautic Company, equipped and trained for seaplane operations, and the 1st Marine Aviation Squadron, organized to fly land-based bombers. After limited training the 1st Marine Aeronautic Company deployed to a base in the Azores, from which it flew antisubmarine patrols until its recall to the United States in March 1919. The bulk of the Marine aviators (24 officers and 237 men) moved to a training field on Long Island to learn to fly land-based aircraft, primarily the Army JN-4B, for Barnett still hoped to send a squadron to the AEF.

In the meantime, Captain Cunningham persuaded General Barnett to send him to Europe to assess the potential Marine role in the air war, for both now had doubts that the Army would accept a Marine squadron. Cunningham returned in January 1918 convinced that the Marine Corps should add squadrons of its own to the Navy's planned twelve-squadron force, with which Admiral Sims intended to bomb the German submarine bases along the Belgian coast. Cunningham argued persuasively that the Naval Appropriations Act of 1916 intended that Marine aviation units (like the total Marine Corps) be 20 percent of naval aviation, but that Marine aviation must "be . . . for the Navy," not to support ground operations. In 1918 this meant the bombing campaign against German submarines, which, Cunningham argued, neither the Royal Flying Corps nor the Army Air Service was willing to undertake. Barnett agreed to the General Board's plan to attack the submarine bases, thus ensuring both Marine Corps participation in the Navy's air war and the subsequent belief that Marine squadrons were primarily the Navy's to use as it saw fit.[60]

If the Marine Corps was to join the Navy's war against the German submarine bases, its instrument would be the 1st Aviation Squadron, which in January 1918 had moved to Louisiana to continue its training at a warm-weather Army field. In April, when it was reasonably certain that the Marine aviators would go to France, the squadron moved to Miami to join another Marine detachment already training there under the command of Captain Roy S. Geiger. Having survived their exciting instruction with civilian pilots, the Marine flyers, a mix of prewar regulars and enthusiastic wartime volunteers, finally had the opportunity to fly the DH-4, the British designed two-seater bomber they would fly in France. They quickly learned that the DH-4, a heavy biplane of uncertain flying characteristics, was a dangerous weapon—at least for its pilots. The plane's gas tank rested between the pilot and the observer, and its fuel-transfer pipes ran perilously close to the hot exhaust manifolds, all of which placed a high premium on avoiding German pursuit planes and making very soft landings. Nevertheless, the zeal of the Marine aviators was undiminished, and the training of the 1st Marine Aviation Force of four flying squadrons continued.[61]

Despite Cunningham's reservations about the 1st Marine Aviation Force's training, the unit deployed to France under his command in July 1918 and established itself (without airplanes) at bases in northern France. Cunningham's force of 149 officers and 842 men went right to work. While their senior officers scoured Britain and the United States for aircraft, the Marine flyers borrowed fighters and bombers from the Royal Flying Corps for their indoctrination flights. Constituted as the Day Wing of the Northern Bombing Group, the Marines in October 1918 finally found themselves an operational unit with four squadrons of DH-4s. Although individual pilots and observers had made earlier combat patrols with the Royal Flying Corps, the 1st Marine Aviation Force did not make its first organized bombing raid until October 14, by which time the submarine menace had disappeared. Consequently, the Marines bombed inland targets in support of the British and French armies then driving the Germans back toward the Rhine. When the armistice came, the Marines had flown fourteen raids and dropped 27,000 pounds of bombs on the enemy. Their kills in the air numbered somewhere between four and twelve, and four Marines had died in action. Even before the 1st Marine Aviation Force returned to the United States in December 1918, the Commandant was convinced that Marine aviation had proved it should be an integral part of the advanced base force as well as a part of naval aviation. Marine aviation had come of age in the World War.[62]

4

Although it had shared some of its glory with its flying brethren, the 4th Marine Brigade of the 2d Division remained the Corps's centerpiece. After its second major bloodletting at Soissons, the brigade went into a rest area to refit and absorb replacements. During its short period in reserve and its subsequent service in the quiet Marbache sector, the brigade received a replacement battalion from the United States and culled 2,500 more Marines from posts and stations in England and France. In addition to the replacements, the Marine brigade found itself with a new division commander, none other than Marine Major General John A. Lejeune. Having proved he could serve the AEF loyally as a brigade commander in two Army divisions, Lejeune came to the 2d Division to command the Marine brigade, then moved to division headquarters when Pershing assigned General Harbord to the AEF's Services of Supply. An experienced field commander, respected by the officers with whom he attended Army schools, Lejeune led the 2d Division through the end of the war. Wendell C. Neville, promoted to brigadier general, retained command of the 4th Brigade, assisted by a new brigade adjutant, Lieutenant Colonel Earl H. Ellis, who brought the brigade's planning to a new peak of efficiency. Logan Feland and Harry Lee, who had led the 5th and 6th Regiments at Soissons, continued in command of their regiments. From division headquarters to the Marine battalions, the brigade enjoyed firm, experienced leadership throughout the rest of the war. When it left its quiet sector on September 2, it was again fit for battle and marched to a new front highly self-conscious of its elite reputation in the AEF.[63]

Marching north, the 2d Division first intensively trained its new men, then joined the I Corps of the new U.S. First Army, which was assembling for its maiden offensive along both sides of the St. Mihiel salient. The summer crisis having passed, General Pershing had finally begun his own strategic plan for the offensive toward Metz. Pershing, however, compromised with the Allied high command and agreed to reduce only the salient in a limited attack. He promised then to redeploy the U.S. First Army west of Verdun, from whence he would drive north toward Sedan between the Meuse River and the Argonne Forest. Knowing that he would soon provide the southern arm of a great Allied offensive on the bulk of the German army, Pershing wanted a quick victory with minimum casualties in the St. Mihiel operation.

Showing hard-won expertise in moving troops and coordinating artillery fire, the 2d Division went over the top on September 12 with the 3d Brigade in the attack and the 4th Brigade in reserve. Catching the Germans already withdrawing from the salient, the division captured its first day's objectives by early afternoon. Except for two battalions that had maintained liaison on the division's flank, the 4th Brigade was not heavily engaged. For the next three days, however, the 4th Brigade assumed the division's attack role as the Americans pushed the Germans back toward their new defenses, the "Michel" position. The Germans counterattacked several times to slow the American advance, but the 4th Brigade was not hard pressed. Only the 6th Regiment, battling through a thick wood on the division's left flank, faced stiff resistance; it suffered two-thirds of the brigade's casualties of 12 officers and 862 men. Compared with Belleau Wood and Soissons, St. Mihiel was a holiday. When the division was relieved on September 16, it had once again proved its solid fighting qualities and had demonstrated that it not only could take casualties but could kill and capture Germans with reduced losses to its own infantry.[64]

Not assigned to the opening attacks of the Meuse–Argonne offensive, the 2d Division left its training area near Toul on September 25 for a reserve position behind the U.S. First Army. The movement soon brought the division its hardest fighting since Soissons. Pressed by the French to use some of his reserve divisions in the French Army of the Center, whose Fourth Army was responsible for the attacks west of the Argonne Forest, Pershing released the 2d Division and the new 36th Division. Conferring with General Henri Gouraud, the Fourth Army commander, before the initial assault on September 26, General Lejeune was impressed with the obstacles the French divisions faced in the Champagne region. He was especially concerned about the long Mont Blanc ridge, which dominated the countryside between Sommepy and St. Etienne-à-Arnes. The main German trenches, a maze of concrete bunkers and machine gun positions, lay along Mont Blanc, and German control of the ridge assured accurate artillery fire and observation along the whole Fourth Army front. Discussing the situation with the French, Lejeune was disturbed to learn that the Fourth Army wanted to use the American infantry brigades separately. When the French attack on the German "Essen" position in front of Mont Blanc stalled, Lejeune volunteered to attack the German bastion, provided the 2d Division was used as a whole unit. Having lost the better part of three divisions just to approach the "Essen" position, General Gouraud accepted Lejeune's proposal. As the trains began delivering the 2d Division to the Suippes-Souain area, long lines of American troops marched toward the Champagne front.[65]

Coming to a battlefield that had borne hard fighting for four years, the Marines drew no comfort from their first observations of the front. A land of scrub pines and farmlands, the Champagne was no longer pastoral:

> . . . [T]he battalion looked out on desolation where the once grassy, rolling slopes of the Champagne stretched away like a great white sea that had been dead and accursed through all time. . . . Areas that had once been forested showed only blackened, branchless stumps, upthrust through the churned earth. What was left was naked, leprous chalk. It was a wilderness of craters, large and small, wherein no yard of earth lay untouched. Interminable mazes of trench work threaded this waste, discernible from a distance by belts of rusty wire. . . . Through glasses one could make out bits of blue and bits of greengray, flung casually between the trenches. These, the only touches of color in the waste, were the unburied bodies of French and German dead. . . . A long grayish hill lay against the gray sky at the horizon, and over it a good glass showed, very far and faint, the spires of the great cathedral [of Rheims], with a cloud of shell-fire hanging over them.[66]

Having first relieved the French troops in the "Essen" position trenches, the 2d Division assaulted Mont Blanc along a 3-mile front on October 3 and entered four days of bitter fighting and heavy losses. The initial attack, well supported by artillery, was novel, for the 4th and 3d Brigades attacked on a converging axis with a mile of open front between them. This plan allowed both brigades to deploy troops to protect their vulnerable flanks where French divisions failed to keep pace. The 4th Brigade went over the top at 5:50 A.M., with the 6th Regiment leading and the 5th Regiment in reserve. There was nothing novel about the brigade's tactics. With companies on line, with six battalions leaving the trenches one after the other, it was again rifles, bayonets, and grenades against artillery and machine guns. Winnowed by German shelling, the 6th Regiment plunged through the trenches and up Mont Blanc's slopes. In its wake the 5th Regiment diverted parts of two battalions to clean up German machine gunners and snipers in the "Essen Hook," a switch-trench on the brigade's left flank. The Marine attack bludgeoned its way up Mont Blanc. The lead battalion died punching through the German outposts, but its remnants and two other battalions were astride Mont Blanc two hours after the attack began. Even though much of the ridge remained in German hands, the 6th Marines had clearly taken a position the French had called impregnable.[67]

The capture of Mont Blanc did not end the fighting, for the Germans were determined to hold their line in front of St. Etienne, and the 2d Division's attack had left it vulnerable to shelling and infantry counter-attacks. For a moment in the afternoon of October 3 it seemed as if the two weak German divisions holding the front would collapse, but the 5th Regiment could not reorganize rapidly enough to push the attack that evening. When the 5th Regiment plunged down Mont Blanc toward St. Etienne the next day, the Marines faced the troops and artillery of a fresh German division, and the attack stopped well short of the town. In the bitter, close fighting along Mount Blanc's reverse slope the battalions of the 5th Regiment again lost half their men; one battalion after a charge mustered fewer than three hundred men of the thousand who had left Somme-py the day before. On October 4 the brigade lost more than 1,100 men, the worst single day's casualties for the Marines in the war. In the meantime, however, the 6th Regiment cleared Mont Blanc and linked up with the 3d Brigade, thus giving the division increased security.

The 4th Brigade's losses had so crippled it that its subsequent attacks, even though artillery-supported, did not reach St. Etienne, but the brigade did its best. On October 5 the 6th Regiment tried to advance a mile but was halted by severe flanking machine gun fire and shells. The next day one battalion captured a crucial knoll bristling with German machine guns but could go no farther. On the night of October 6–7 the brigade, less 90 officers and 2,228 men, left the front, relieved by a brigade of the U.S. 36th Division. One 6th Regiment battalion remained behind with the 36th Division, and on October 8 it captured St. Etienne as part of a general attack. The Marine brigade once again marched to the rear to rest and absorb replacements as the Meuse–Argonne campaign flamed on.

In the World War's waning days, the 2d Division rejoined the U.S. First Army in time to play a significant role in the last two weeks of the Meuse–Argonne offensive. Although his army had not advanced as quickly as he had hoped, by the end of October Pershing had captured half of the German main position, the *Kriemhilde Stellung,* and his three corps held the ground that would enable them to breach the position with one more grand assault. Pershing's staff gathered fresh divisions for the attack. After several weeks of reorganization the 2d Division joined the First Army's V Corps. As the center corps of the First Army, the V Corps assumed the mission of leading the attack that would finally breach the German defenses south of Sedan and clear all the territory west and south of the Meuse River. A successful attack would not only ruin the German holding action south of the Meuse but compromise the German defenses from the Ardennes to the Rhine and sever the railroad line of communications serving the entire German center of the Western Front. Acutely aware of Allied criticism of his First Army's performance, General Pershing would accept no excuses for failure against the crumbling but dangerous German defenders. Conscious of its elite reputation, the 2d Division marched toward the front through chill rains and heavy mud to pace the V Corps's attack.

Brought once more to full strength by replacements, the 4th Brigade moved from its rest area to the front lines. In terms of martial glory, the brigade had nothing left to prove. For the Mont Blanc battle, the 2d Division had received its third unit Croix de Guerre, which entitled its members to wear a green and red *fourragère* in honor of the division's heroism, (Members of the 5th and 6th Regiments still wear the *fourragère*, derisively called "pogey ropes" by other Marines.) The division's most serious problem was reclaiming all its units, for its artillery brigade, engineer regiment, and service units had remained in the Champagne to support the 36th Division. General Lejeune persuaded First Army headquarters to postpone the division's attack until he could gather all his units. The delay allowed the 2d Division to prepare its attack plans carefully, coordinate the support of three artillery brigades, and reconnoiter its sector.

Supported by a heavy artillery barrage, the 2d Division went over the top on November 1, with the 4th Brigade on the division's and corps's left flank. With both Marine regiments abreast and battalions in column, the brigade smashed through the German defenders and gained five miles in one day, a spectacular advance. The assault carried the *Kriemhilde Stellung* and the German reserve fortifications, the *Freya Stellung*. Advancing close to the corps's ambitious schedule, the 2d Division secured its objectives with minimum casualties and then spent four days securing the flanks of the salient it had pushed forward from the First Army's line. Although the two weak German divisions to its front were destroyed by the attack, the division found German shelling and long-range machine gun fire still dangerous. But compared to Soissons and Mont Blanc the attack had been cheap in American lives. Only the open left flank, uncovered by the weak advance of the 80th Division, complicated the division's situation, but the Germans could not exploit the gap in the face of American artillery and well-placed infantry supports. So confident was the division that it began a series of successful night advances to exploit its breakthrough. The results were more ground gained, more Germans captured, and fewer casualties. Probably for the first time in its history, the division inflicted more casualties than it suffered.[68]

Jubilant over the V Corps's advance and aware that the Germans

were streaming across the Meuse, First Army headquarters ordered the
V Corps to cross the Meuse and establish a bridgehead southeast of
Sedan. The task fell to the 2d Division, which marched obliquely left
behind the front and occupied positions along the river on November
7. The 4th Brigade, assigned to cross the river on pontoons and seize
the heights on the east bank, prepared for the assault, which General
Lejeune personally believed was unnecessary and risky in the face of a
still determined German defense. No doubt rumors of an imminent armistice made the attack unappealing, but First Army headquarters
insisted that the offensive continue. The attack on November 10–11
was neither well conceived nor well executed. The pontoon bridges in
the 2d Division sector were pounded with artillery fire and were not
completed. Fortunately, the four Marine battalions that were supposed
to make the assault remained in covered positions, and when news
of the armistice came during the morning of November 11, the battalion commanders wisely called the attack off. In another division's
sector, however, two Marine battalions suffered heavy casualties crossing the Meuse and taking the heights, where they learned of the armistice near noon on November 11.

So, incredulously, the Marines learned that the war was over. As the
firing died, the men simply collasped, stunned by the silence. Worn,
thinned by illness and fatigue, the 4th Brigade celebrated with caution
and little comment. Slowly, small groups of men collected and built
warming fires. Even though it had performed with an admirable combination of ardor, skill, and caution in the Meuse–Argonne, the Marine
brigade had suffered the further loss of 41 officers and 1,114 men. But
the killing and dying had finally ended.

The Armistice did not immediately finish the Marines' service in
France. As part of the 2d Division, the 4th Brigade marched in chilling
rain through Luxembourg into occupation areas along the Rhine. The
marching men trod along in silence, burdened by their equipment and
their memories. In the 96th Company, for example, only 21 men remained of the 250 who had entered Belleau Wood in June. Only when
the brigade reached the Rhine was there some celebration; the officers
of one battalion marched to the bank and urinated into the historic
river.[69] The 4th Brigade participated in the American *Wacht am Rhine*
from December 1918 until July 1919, when the Germans finally signed
a peace treaty. Behind them in France other Marines, principally from
the uncommitted 5th Brigade, carried on security duties. Much of the
Marines' energy, communicated by the irrepressible Smedley D. Butler,
went into managing the AEF's primary reembarkation camp at Brest.[70]
Finally, in 1919, all the Marines returned to the United States, the reg-

ulars to be reassigned and the "duration" and Reserve Marines to return to civilian life. Efficiently processed at Quantico, the 4th Brigade disbanded. Even though they were officially civilians, the Marine veterans formed into companies and marched to the trains that waited to take them home.[71]

5

For the Marine Corps the World War marked an important watershed in a century-long search for military respectability and public approval. As part of one of the AEF's most distinguished divisions, the 4th Brigade had proved that the Marine Corps's claims for valor and skill were not simply recruiting publicity or organizational hubris. Even if the majority of the brigade's officers and enlisted men were only "duration" Marines, they had drawn strength from their conviction that the Marine Corps was the nonpareil of American military units and from their pride in the Corps's legends and symbols. More practically, the Marine Corps had ensured that the 4th Brigade and its replacements had entered battle better trained than many of their soldier contemporaries, primarily because the AEF would not allow more than one Marine brigade into combat and because Headquarters created a training system in the United States and France that did not collapse in the rush to build an independent American army in 1918. In this case smallness had truly made elitism possible. Moreover, the Corps's wartime recruiting effort had made "Marine Corps" virtually a household word throughout the United States and had captivated the public not only for the length of the war but afterward. How could the Marine Corps be forgotten when its wartime exploits were recorded in new popular histories?[72] Even Laurence Stallings's message that the World War was hell, a vision captured in the Broadway play *What Price Glory?*, changed to a hymn to the Marine Corps when Hollywood made a movie of Stallings's play in 1926. With the birth of "Captain Flagg" and "Sergeant Quirt," the Marine Corps image of battlefield bravery and boisterous camaraderie was sanctified in celluloid, an act reinforced by the officially produced film *Tell It to the Marines,* another World War epic.

The World War provided two generations of Marine officers with an expensive education in the intricacies of modern warfare. Among the lessons to be learned (and many were learned) was that infantry tactics should provide for fire superiority as well as maneuver, that artillery support was essential against a determined enemy, that careful operational planning paid dividends in lives saved and objectives taken, that combat units down to battalion level needed effective staffs, that success in battle required continuous logistical support, and that battlefield communications needed vast improvement.[73] Subjected to German bombing and air-directed artillery fire, the 4th Brigade's officers also appreciated the necessity of air superiority over the battlefield. In sum, six months of extensive combat in France gave the Marine Corps enough practical experience to sustain two decades of serious study on the problems of attacking an entrenched enemy, problems particularly appropriate for an amphibious assault force.

The war also exacted some costs. The principal loss was the chance for harmony with the United States Army, for some of the Army's senior officers returned from the war convinced that the Marine Corps would do anything it could to belittle the regular Army's reputation. Part of the friction developed in Washington, where Josephus Daniels had been too effusive about the Marine Corps's performance for the War Department's taste. General Barnett had been no less vocal, and when the war ended, the War Department was tired of hearing about Belleau Wood (which the Marine recruiting posters called "Château-Thierry") and the 4th Brigade's prowess.[74] In 1919 the American press, perhaps prodded by the War Department, revealed that the 4th Brigade had *not* saved Château-Thierry, a disclosure that brought countercharges from the Navy Department. Miffed that the War Department had not listed Belleau Wood as a major engagement, Headquarters charged the War Department with misrepresenting the 4th Brigade's accomplishments. The press crisis passed when the War Department admitted that Belleau Wood was part of the Château-Thierry operation, but some Army generals remained convinced that the Marine Corps ("Useless Sonsofbitches Made Comfortable") should be merged with the Army. One influential AEF general suggested as much in a plan drafted for General Pershing. Although Lejeune and others took pains to honor Pershing and Harbord, Marine officers looked with distrust at the War Department General Staff.[75]

Accustomed to insults from both the Army and the Navy, the Marine Corps, uplifted by the undeniable heroism of the 4th Brigade, was in no mood to accept an inferior role in the nation's defense in the postwar era.

12. Amphibious Warfare and the Fleet Marine Force, 1919–1939

I n early 1919 the German High Seas Fleet steamed into captivity at the chill British anchorage at Scapa Flow, symbolizing the World War's dramatic influence on the global maritime balance. For the next three years, the United States, Great Britain, and Japan cajoled and bullied one another until a new set of naval and political relationships was adopted at the Washington Conference on Naval Disarmament, 1921–1922. The focus of world naval affairs swung to the Pacific Ocean, where the victors of the World War faced one another. From the American point of view, the sources of potential conflict included Japanese territorial ambitions in Manchuria and China and the security of the Philippines. The results of the war had weakened the American position in the western Pacific, for the Japanese had seized Germany's central Pacific islands just north of the Equator. Lying along the main route to China and the Philippines, the island groups of Micronesia— the Marshalls, the Carolines, and the Marianas—potentially threatened the American way stations of Guam, Midway, and Wake by providing the Japanese navy with forward airfields and fleet operating bases. The United States Navy reviewed its strategic responsibilities and concluded that it needed a fleet "second to none" to check British influence and deter its most likely enemy, Japan, in the Pacific.[1]

The postwar negotiations on naval building and Pacific security ended with three treaties that would shape American naval policy until the mid-1930s and influence the development of the postwar Marine

Corps. The Five Power Treaty (1922) established Great Britain and the United States at parity in capital ship tonnage (500,000 tons each), with Japan accepting a 300,000-ton limit, an inferiority softened by a provision that the signatories would not construct permanent fortifications around their naval bases in the western Pacific. For the United States the nonfortification pledge meant that neither the Philippines nor Guam could be developed as a major base. This agreement, anathema to the Navy, was simply a recognition of domestic political realities and the hope that Japan would not develop its Micronesian islands into naval bases. The other two treaties signed at the Washington Conference justified the naval limitations, for they pledged the conferees to respect each other's Pacific holdings and to preserve the territorial integrity of China.

Already bedeviled by Congressional budget cuts and by a public conviction that naval armaments had helped cause the World War, the Navy Department adapted its long-range fleet development program to the results of the war and the Washington treaties. As early as 1919 the General Board of the Navy Department, the Naval War College, and the Office of Operations reviewed the Navy's War Plan ORANGE, the basic study for a war with Japan. The Navy Department by 1921 had drafted a new war plan that assumed Japan would challenge the U.S. fleet in the central Pacific, using its Micronesian islands as bases to support the Japanese navy. The Navy and the Army continued to debate the defensibility of the Philippines in the deliberations of the Joint Army and Navy Board, but contingency planners agreed that the fleet would have to fight its way across the central Pacific before it could relieve the Philippines or defeat Japan by blockading the home islands. Such a campaign would require forces both to capture Japanese bases and to defend advanced bases established to support American fleet operations.[2]

In January 1920 Chief of Naval Operations Robert E. Coontz warned Marine Commandant George Barnett that War Plan ORANGE would henceforth determine all the Navy's plans and programs and recommended that the Marine Corps plan to provide a West Coast expeditionary force of between six thousand and eight thousand men ready to embark in forty-eight hours for a campaign against the Marshall and Caroline islands. A similar force should be organized on the East Coast for Atlantic and Caribbean contingencies, Admiral Coontz said, but the Pacific should receive first priority. The expeditionary forces, built around the prewar advanced base force concept, should exist independently of Marines committed to traditional naval duties and the Caribbean occupation forces. Coontz recognized that the expeditionary forces would require additional men and money, which did not appear plentiful, but War Plan ORANGE did "furnish a definite point of aim, which will permit of the logical development of the Marine Corps for the duties it will be called upon to perform under the War Plans." [3]

Even if the seizure of defended advanced naval bases seemed essential to War Plan ORANGE, the British experience at Gallipoli in 1915 suggested that such an operation would be a tactical nightmare, if not impossible. The Marine Corps thought otherwise. Fortunately, the British attempt to open a supply route to Russia through Turkey was exhaustively studied. The studies of Gallipoli emphasized the inherent strength of the defenders, based on the presumed advantage of prepared fortifications and firepower. But at least one Marine Corps analyst thought as early as 1921 that the flaws in the Gallipoli operations were correctable by proper planning and appropriate doctrine on the use of naval gunfire and the deployment of the landing force. The Marine Corps was also aware that the Germans had made successful opposed landings against the Russians in the Gulf of Riga in 1917. Even if other military forces doubted that an amphibious assault could succeed, American plans for a Pacific war made such operations essential, and the Marine Corps thought it could make an amphibious assault a tactical reality. [4]

Some Marine officers knew that the balance between a defender and an attacker was a dynamic relationship based on relative strength and tactical doctrine, not an absolute advantage to the defender. Colonel Robert H. Dunlap, an amphibious planner on Admiral William S. Sim's staff, concluded from his studies of a proposed Adriatic landing in 1918 that shore defenses could be overcome. Major Alfred A. Cunningham, the father of Marine Corps aviation, agreed that a successful amphibious assault was a real possibility. Both argued that aviation and artillery were essential elements in the seizure of advanced bases. They agreed that the Marine Corps should stress base defense and seizure as part of a naval campaign under Navy control. Smarting from the Army's rejection of Marine aviation and artillery units in the World War, Cunningham and Dunlap encouraged Headquarters to embrace the base-seizure mission. Their views received official sanction in 1920, when the Joint Army and Navy Board approved the Marine Corps's mission as an advanced base force and implicitly agreed that nothing that had happened in the World War had made an amphibious assault inconceivable. [5]

Despite the General Board's increased interest in amphibious operations, Headquarters was as slow to respond to the new mission as it had been to the original concept of the advanced base force. General Barnett argued rightly that the postwar Marine Corps did not have enough men for expeditionary duty of any sort but stressed that providing ships guards, security detachments at home and abroad, and occupation forces in the Caribbean still took higher priority than organizing for war. If he could have the authorized 27,200 officers and men rather than the 14,849 for which he had funds, Barnett agreed that advanced base missions should receive first priority. The Joint Board and Secretary of the Navy Josephus Daniels accepted Barnett's position that amphibious assault missions did not supersede the Corps's traditional peacetime functions. The result was that by 1920 the advanced base force, whether for base defense or for seizure, had virtually ceased to exist.[6] War Plan ORANGE might represent a new concept for the Marine Corps, but it remained to be seen whether the Corps would respond to the amphibious assault role.

1

Whether or not the Marine Corps would accept the additional mission of amphibious assaults in the Pacific depended largely upon the Corps's internal stability and cohesiveness. The years 1919 and 1920 were not propitious. In addition to the turmoil of postwar demobilization and reorganization and the press of duties in Haiti and Santo Domingo, the Corps faced substantial political and institutional challenges in the United States, to which it did not fully adapt until 1922. Among the most significant difficulties was that General Barnett had by 1919 antagonized Secretary of the Navy Daniels and Congressman Thomas Butler, chairman of the House Naval Affairs Committee and father of Brigadier General Smedley D. Butler. Irritated by Barnett's pursuit of honors and promotions for the Headquarters staff in recognition of its wartime service, Daniels and Butler pressured Barnett into resigning as Commandant in June 1920, two full years before the expiration of his second term. To replace Barnett, Daniels appointed John A. Lejeune as Commandant, which made way for Smedley Butler to be promoted to major general and to assume command at Quantico, the Corps's most important post. Discomfited by the circumstances of his promotion but ambitious to bring the Corps closer to modern military practices, Lejeune took office determined to improve the Corps's relations with Congress, the Navy Department, and the American public. Although a traditionalist, the new Commandant also recognized the importance of the amphibious assault role to the Corps's future.[7]

In his nearly nine years as Commandant, John A. Lejeune became the most important Corps leader since Archibald Henderson, for he guided the Corps toward the amphibious assault role while wooing three Presidents, Congress, the Navy, the public, and the apathetic, conservative officers within the Corps itself. A stocky man of average height with a square, leathery face and jug ears, the fifty-three-year-old Lejeune charmed people with his Southern manners and sharp intelligence. In view of his service with distinction in the Caribbean and France, there was little question about his ability as a commander. More important, he was a student of warfare and a shrewd practitioner of bureaucratic politics. He was equally at home with troops or at Headquarters, and he quickly showed a knack for combining the best traditions of the "old" Corps with the pressing need for reform. Among his first acts was to convene a board to reconsider the appointment and rank of the Corps's postwar junior officers. An earlier board appointed by Barnett to select permanent officers had given little weight to combat performance in France. The second board, headed by Brigadier General Wendell C. Neville, favored officers who had served in the 4th Brigade. The result was an officer corps balanced between proven troop leaders and staff specialists.[8]

No happier than Barnett with the Corps's enlisted strength of 16,085 men, Lejeune persuaded Congress to increase this force to 20,596 by 1922 and convinced the legislators that the Corps would not only train its men but uplift them with basic educational and vocational skills. As a postwar commander at Quantico, Lejeune had established a general education program for his troops. As Commandant he converted the program into the Marine Corps Institute, a correspondence school that offered both military and basic education. This reform pleased Secretary Daniels, who viewed naval service as a great classroom for America's youth.[9]

Lejeune also recognized that the Headquarters organization of 1920 could not cope with the Corps's diverse peacetime missions and wartime duties, and in late 1920 he reorganized the staff. The Paymaster, Quartermaster, and Adjutant and Inspector departments continued to perform their traditional administrative functions, but Lejeune supplemented them with a new Operations and Training Division, which quickly developed into the heart of Marine Corps efforts to contend with its wartime functions. In addition, the Commandant completed the reorganization of the Marine Corps's officer educational system by centralizing officer training at the new Marine Corps Schools (MCS) at Quantico. By 1922 the Company Officers School and the Field Grade Officers School could not only provide adequate professional training but also serve as a reservoir of faculty and student talent to study the Corps's new amphibious warfare role. The Marine Corps Schools gave the Commandant an important vehicle for propelling his officers to new professional heights and indoctrinating them in Headquarters policy.[10]

General Lejeune did not confine his educational reforms to Marines alone. Sophisticated in public relations, the Commandant in 1925 removed publicity matters from his recruiting section and increased public awareness of the Corps through the commercial newspapers, magazines, and movies. Under the skilled management of Major Joseph C. Fegan, Marine publicity specialists interested the media in maneuvers, athletic events, marksmanship contests, and the history of the World War. Stressing that "we seek good publicity," Lejeune helped organize the Marine Corps League, a veterans association, in 1923 and sent Marines to state fairs and national expositions. When Marines guarded the U.S. mail in 1921 and 1926, Headquarters made sure the media knew that the Marines were more than a match for mail robbers. Marine recruiters began to cultivate local businessmen, and Headquarters ordered post commanders as well to put public relations high on their list of duties. Convinced that the Corps's good health depended upon public acceptance—expressed in influence upon Congress—Lejeune systematically organized and developed a public relations program envied by the other services and noted for big achievements and a small staff.[11]

At the base at Quantico the Commandant had two incomparable public relations attractions, General Smedley Butler and the East Coast Expeditionary Force. Even more enthusiastic about enlisted education than Lejeune, Butler envisioned turning Quantico into a great Marine Corps school in which enlisted men would train half the time and learn trades the other half. With their remaining time, they would become great athletes or at least build a stadium for great Marine athletes. Under Butler's guidance the Quantico Marines started to build a 25,000-seat stadium and fielded a football squad that scheduled college teams. Butler served as head cheerleader. More significantly, Lejeune reorganized the advanced base force in 1920 and renamed it the East Coast Expeditionary Force. Built around the infantry of the 5th and 6th Regiments and the artillery of the 10th Regiment and supplemented by technical units and aviation squadrons also stationed at Quantico, the force in 1921–1923 staged annual maneuvers that were attended by Washington politicians, Army and Navy representatives, and the public. A history buff, Lejeune had Butler's force reenact famous Civil War battles using modern arms in order to demonstrate the greater complexity of twentieth-century warfare. Although the maneuvers gave Marine officers much-needed training in handling long marches and tactical problems, the field exercises were designed to show that the Marine Corps was as alive as it had been in 1918.[12]

For all of Lejeune's flair for public relations, he never lost sight of the fact that the Marine Corps existed to perform missions with the fleet. His position was not shared by all other senior Marine officers, particularly Smedley Butler; the Caribbean occupations and the war in France had convinced some officers that the Corps flourished in direct relation to its distance from the Navy. Lejeune did not agree. Although he did not abandon any of the Corps's traditional missions, including service in a land war with the Army, Lejeune stressed that the wartime mission of the Corps was "to accompany the Fleet for operations ashore in support of the Fleet" and termed this wartime role "the real justification for the continued existence of the Marine Corps." [13] He correctly argued that the Washington treaties on naval limitations had placed no limitation on mobile forces for the seizure and defense of extemporized advanced bases. Lejeune knew that peacetime expeditionary duty might be necessary and that ships detachments and shore security duties drew men from his two expeditionary forces, but the Commandant repeatedly stressed that the Corps must concentrate on training for its wartime assignment. His view was the official Headquarters position.[14]

John A. Lejeune's commitment was more than rhetoric, and under his direction the Marine Corps slowly steered toward the amphibious assault mission. Unable to place a Marine representative on the Joint Board, in 1921 he sent Major Holland M. Smith to the Navy War Plans Division and Colonel Ben H. Fuller to the planning staff of the Naval War College. (By the beginning of World War II nearly sixty Marine officers had served in significant billets in Navy intelligence and war planning agencies.) Both Smith and Fuller warned Lejeune that the Navy was making detailed versions of War Plan ORANGE and urged the Commandant to have his Operations and Training Division develop a Marine Corps plan for a naval campaign in the central and western Pacific.[15] Lejeune did not need prompting, for he had already assigned the brilliant former adjutant of the 4th Brigade, Earl H. Ellis, to study the problems of a war with Japan. Even more obsessed with the Japanese threat than before the World War, Ellis went into monastic isolation at Headquarters, surrounded by maps and intelligence reports. His first study focused primarily upon base defense in the Pacific. Predicting that a Pacific war would be determined by base seizure and defense, Ellis decided that defended bases would be difficult to capture but that the Marine Corps should be prepared to "execute opposed landings and attacks on denial positions . . . with the greatest rapidity." [16]

Fueled by his mania, Ellis by early 1921 had produced several versions of Operation Plan 712, "Advanced Base Force Operations in Micronesia." [17] Even though Ellis's plan drew its strategic inspiration from the well-developed War Plan ORANGE, it outlined with prophetic insight the fundamental problems of assaults on the Marshalls and Carolines and established the rudiments of amphibious assault doctrine. Having no doubt that his plan would "serve as a guide for the co-ordination of all peace activities and training of the Marine Corps," Ellis argued that the success of an opposed landing depended on a rapid ship-to-shore movement of waves of assault craft covered by over-whelming naval gunfire and aerial attacks. Given the strength of the tactical defense, "the landing will entirely succeed or fail practically on the beach." Preceded by a naval version of the World War "box barrage," the assault regiments would require not only infantry but also machine gun units, artillery, engineers, and light tanks to penetrate beach defenses and obstacles. These units would require special landing craft or vehicles armed with machine guns and light cannon. Unlike other contemporary planners, Ellis stressed that landings should occur in daylight to avoid confusion among the landing craft and assault forces. Close-in naval gunfire would have to neutralize the defenders. In any event, Ellis insisted, an amphibious assault depended on detailed planning, much peacetime training, and careful tactical and logistical organization. He knew that the Marine Corps, despite the obstacles, could take a defended beachhead.[18]

While the Operations and Training Division pondered his study, Ellis with Lejeune's collusion took an extended leave in May 1921 to visit the Marshalls and Carolines. Officially, he was an American businessman; unofficially, he made a quixotic personal reconnaissance of the islands. Ellis died under still mysterious circumstances in the Palau island group in May 1923. His disappearance made him a martyr in the eyes of World War II Marines and gave his studies the heroic glow of prophecy. Ellis's credentials as a seer may be suspect, given the advanced state of the Navy's own work on War Plan ORANGE, but Operation Plan 712 had the intended effect. On July 23, 1921, John A. Lejeune approved Ellis's study in its entirety and ordered that henceforth the Marine Corps would use it to guide war planning, field exercises, equipment development, and officer education.

The Commandant could, of course, decree that amphibious warfare would shape Marine Corps training, but that did not mean he could immediately change both the Corps and the Navy. Initial progress in landing operations was slow. At the Marine Corps Schools, for example, the curriculum stressed land combat, and in 1924–1925 the advanced students spent only two hours on landing operations. But in 1926 the curriculum included forty-nine hours of instruction, and in 1927 the number of hours had soared to more than a hundred. Behind the changes lay hard-earned experience, for in 1924 and 1925 the Marines and the Navy had conducted their first full-scale beach assaults.

The first landing problem in 1922 differed little from advanced base problems before the war, but the landings of 1924 and 1925 were large enough to provide valuable tests of the new doctrine. In the 1922 problem two companies practiced unloading and loading field guns of up to 155-mm. along with their 5-ton and 10-ton tractors at Culebra and Guantanamo Bay. The exercise proved that heavy artillery could be brought ashore—provided the weather was ideal, the surf low, and the enemy passive. The exercise commander and Headquarters agreed that the Marine Corps and Navy had just barely examined the problems of an amphibious assault.[19] The next test came in December 1923–February 1924, when General Lejeune sent the East Coast Expeditionary Force of 3,300 officers and men to the Caribbean for the annual winter fleet exercises. Commanded by two pioneers of the advanced base force, Brigadier General Eli K. Cole and Colonel Dion Williams, the force was divided in half for a series of problems. While Williams's force prepared to defend Culebra, Cole's reinforced infantry regiment landed against Army defenders in the Canal Zone and "won" the mock battle. At Culebra, on the other hand, the attackers were defeated by Williams's defense force, built around the 10th Regiment. The night assault landing, testing not only tactics but an armored troop barge and a primitive amphibious tank, was a fiasco. The Navy coxswains did not reach the right beach at the proper time; the unloading of supplies was chaotic; the naval bombardment was inadequate; and the Navy's landing boats were clearly unsuitable for both troops and equipment. The exercise, however, identified enough errors to keep the Corps busy for fifteen years.[20]

In April 1925 the Marines tried again, this time against the Army on the island of Oahu. The problem resulted in a clear improvement in staff work, for Lejeune sent the faculty and students of the Field Officers School to Hawaii to manage the landing. Using 1,500 San Diego and Quantico Marines to simulate a landing by two full divisions (42,000 men), the Marines poured ashore despite heavy first-wave "losses." Again, the exercise dramatized the need for better boats, improved communications, and more training on debarking troops and equipment.[21] Before additional exercises could be held, however, the Marines deployed first to guard the U.S. mail and then to China and Nicaragua. The exercises of 1926 involved only a small detachment from Quantico, which tested two lighters for surf landings. Neither was satisfactory: Having no engines, they could not retract from the beach. At this point the landing exercises ended, not to be resumed until 1934.

While the Marines were wading ashore in Hawaii, the Joint Board was reexamining the missions of the Army and Navy, a task arising in 1925 from controversies over coast defense and the employment of Army and Navy aviation. Asked for his opinion on revising a 1920 pamphlet on coast defense doctrine, General Lejeune encouraged the Navy Department to make the revision a comprehensive statement of all the responsibilities of the armed forces, a suggestion the Joint Board adopted. In describing the duties of the Marine Corps in war and peace, Lejeune argued that the Corps should be entrusted with sole responsibility for "the initial seizure and defense" of advanced bases until relieved by the Army.[22] In the final version of *Joint Action of the Army and Navy* (1927), the Marine Corps not only retained its traditional missions (including service with the Army) but assumed responsibility for "land operations in support of the fleet for the initial seizure and defense of advanced bases and for such limited auxiliary land operations as are essential to the prosecution of the naval campaign."[23] The Army might also "conduct land operations in support of the Navy for the establishment and defense of naval bases." *Joint Action* did not resolve the question of who would command a joint expedition overseas, leaving the question to the discretion of the President. Given the Navy's traditional position that only naval officers should conduct naval campaigns, the unity-of-command issue prejudiced operations with the Army and made the Marine Corps a more attractive instrument for naval operations. A subsequent Joint Board study in 1933 did not resolve the unity-of-command issue.[24] At the tactical level, the Joint Board agreed that "landing attacks against shore objectives" would be conducted the same way, whether done by Marines or by soldiers, for the exercises of 1924 and 1925 had given all the services a basic understanding of amphibious operations.[25] That did not mean that all the problems—conceptual or practical—were near solution.

The difficulty with the principles expressed in *Joint Action* was that the Joint Board could not order the Marine Corps or the Navy to assign priorities to their various missions, and precedent favored every duty but amphibious warfare. Given the funding limitations of the 1920s, the Marine Corps could not do everything, and so amphibious warfare languished. The Navy was even less interested. Even though virtually every Joint Board war plan in effect in 1930 anticipated an amphibious operation in either the Pacific or the Caribbean, the Marine Corps barely kept the study of landing operations alive, primarily in the Marine Corps Schools. Even there the defense of naval bases, the conduct of land operations by a Marine division, and counterguerrilla operations competed for the students' attention. For all the real progress of the 1920s in defining the Corps's wartime role, amphibious warfare doctrine

remained primitive, and the Marine units available to develop the doctrine were by 1927 committed to other duties.[26]

2

Just as the expeditions to China and Nicaragua stripped the fleet of
amphibious exercise units, the politics of defense spending forced the
Marine Corps to scrutinize its missions and structure. The beginning
of the Great Depression made the Hoover administration reduce Marine
Corps enlisted strength from 17,586 to 15,355 men. The impact of the
manpower cut was clear to Headquarters: It was "impossible for the
corps to carry out its primary mission of supporting the United States
Fleet by maintaining a force in readiness to operate with the fleet . . . .
The Marine Corps is not prepared to perform its allotted task in the
event of a national emergency." [27] Despite the Manchurian incident of
1931, Hoover did not regard Japan as a threat and thought only of
nonintervention and hemispheric defense. Preoccupied with the collapse
of the economy, which he proposed to rebuild by reducing federal
spending, Hoover forced the Army and Navy to review their most
cherished programs. Interservice rivalry over missions heightened as each
service searched for reasons to preserve both manpower and weapons
purchases. As in the 1920s, the conflict was sharpest in areas of joint
operations: coast defense and overseas expeditionary duty.[28]

Pressed by the Army to consider the transfer of Marine aviation to
the Army Air Corps and to have the Marine Corps assume all base
defense missions while relinquishing expeditionary duty, the Navy's
General Board in 1931 scrutinized the Corps with unusual thorough-
ness. The board's initial response to the Army challenge was to defend
the Corps, but it pressed Commandant Ben H. Fuller, a methodical
but uninspiring officer, to justify the Corps's many missions and to
assign them some priority. Fuller answered the challenge: The Marines
were primarily a wartime force to seize and defend naval bases. The
Corps did not need weapons (like heavy artillery) for an extended land
campaign, because its attacks would begin and end within the range
of naval gunfire. Fuller also argued that the objectives of amphibious
assault would be not only enemy naval bases but also air bases that
menaced fleet operations. Fuller's greatest concern, however, was making
the two expeditionary forces an integral part of the fleet, and he asked
the General Board to support his recommendation that the Corps's
association with the Navy be strengthened. The War Plans Division of
the Office of the Chief of Naval Operations supported Fuller's response
that the Corps's primary duty was to prepare for wartime amphibious
operations, particularly against Japan. The division also thought the

time had come to reform the Corps and commit it to the base seizure mission.[29]

The General Board's review of Marine missions supported the Corps, a position shared by Chief of Naval Operations William V. Pratt. Both the General Board and Pratt urged greater attention to Marine aviation and ground units for base seizure and defense. The Marine Corps was too small to train for its wartime duties, they contended, and should again be one-fifth the size of the Navy, not just 56 percent of its authorized peacetime strength. Concluding its study, the General Board recommended that the Marine Corps be "organized to provide forces for the execution of its war-time missions; primarily, assisting the fleet in the seizure and initial defense of advanced bases, and secondarily, guarding naval shore stations." [30] These 1932 reports, approved by Secretary of the Navy Charles Francis Adams, were reviewed again in 1934 by the General Board with similar conclusions: The Marine Corps should exist as a separate service, should reform its officer corps through promotion-by-selection, and should have a minimum of 17,000 enlisted men in order to develop the cadre of a wartime Corps of nearly 40,000 men. Again, the board stressed the amphibious assault role for a war in the Pacific.[31]

As Marine units returned from China and Nicaragua, General Fuller saw an opportunity to integrate the old expeditionary forces into the fleet's organizational structure, which might help the Corps to obtain more funds and encourage the Navy operating forces to train for amphibious warfare. At the urging of his assistant, Major General John H. Russell, Fuller asked the Chief of Naval Operations to approve a name change for Marine expeditionary units. Heartened by a successful fight in Congress to stop another manpower cut, Russell suggested that the expeditionary forces be renamed the Fleet Marine Force, a title that would cover both base defense and amphibious assault units. Approved by Admiral Pratt, the Fleet Marine Force (FMF) became a conceptual reality with Navy Department Order 241 of December 7, 1933. Despite the fact that Fuller could assign only two thousand men to the new force, the Commandant explained to all his senior commanders that developing the FMF would henceforth be the Corps's first priority. Even if it appeared that the Corps had surrendered its autonomy to the Navy, a development that nettled many Marine officers, the Commandant found that his officers generally approved of the FMF concept. As General Russell realized, the Marine Corps had decided that amphibious operations were the first order of business.[32]

As Headquarters fought the bureaucratic wars that eventually produced the Fleet Marine Force, the faculty and staff at the Field Officers

School studied amphibious operations and began to draft a basic doctrinal manual for future landings. The work on the *Tentative Manual for Landing Operations,* which began in 1931 and ended in 1934, not only produced a sound body of operating principles but also indoctrinated many of the officers who passed through the MCS in the 1930s.[33] Sponsored by Brigadier General Randolph C. Berkeley and Brigadier General James C. Breckinridge and largely directed by Lieutenant Colonel Ellis B. Miller and Major Charles D. Barrett, the study group identified the crucial elements of an amphibious operation: command relationships, naval gunfire and aerial support, the ship-to-shore movement, the tactics of securing a beachhead, and logistics. Although many of the basic concepts of a landing already existed, the study group brought greater specificity to the principles of amphibious operations and described in much greater detail the actual problems and techniques of attacking a hostile shore. Even though the officers who worked on the *Tentative Manual* changed often and their research was interrupted by other duties, the study group profited not only from open debate within its own ranks but also from exchanges with officers from Headquarters and the Naval War College. The participants often found the study the most exciting work they had ever done—outside of field operations—and recognized that they were shaping the future of the Corps. Most agreed with Colonel Miller that the study was too theoretical, but they knew they were designing operational concepts unique in warfare. They also recognized that the *Tentative Manual* would influence the Navy's planning by stressing the Navy's amphibious warfare responsibilities.[34] Only operational testing remained to verify or modify the *Tentative Manual*'s guidelines.

Subsequently revised and adopted by the Navy in 1938 as *Fleet Training Publication 167,* the *Tentative Manual* stressed the peculiar problems of an amphibious operation. As for command relationships, it assigned overall command of the landing to the naval commander, since the landing force was only one element of a complex naval task organization designed to protect the landing force from enemy sea and air attacks. Unanswered was the question of transfer of command ashore to the landing force commander once the campaign developed, but because the planners were thinking of short operations to secure the beachhead only, their silence on this question is understandable. Like earlier studies, the *Tentative Manual* emphasized the importance of fire superiority established by naval guns and aircraft that were not part of the landing force. Recognizing the inherent limitations of both weapons, the manual nevertheless expressed the hope that adequate bombardment planning and fire direction from spotting parties ashore would solve the fire superiority problem. Drawing upon conventional infantry tactics, the concept of the ship-to-shore movement stressed dispersion and speed and the landing of units in accordance with the objectives ashore. The small boats would rendezvous some 2,500 to 4,000 yards off the beach and advance in various formations (the line abreast eventually was preferred) to the assigned beaches, where they would disembark task-organized Marine units of infantry, light artillery, tanks, and engineers. A crucial problem was organizing special groups to move landing craft back to sea and supplies off the beach as successive waves landed. As for logistics, the manual stressed the basic principle that transports should be combat loaded—that is, the first-needed supplies of ammunition, water, food, and special equipment should be the last loaded and the most accessible.[35]

What the *Tentative Manual* did not describe was the serious limitations of both the Navy and the Marine Corps in testing amphibious warfare doctrine and preparing the Fleet Marine Force for war. First, the Navy maintained only two transports, the *Henderson* and the *Chaumont,* until the eve of World War II. In 1934 the Naval Transportation Service had only seven vessels to service a fleet of 149 surface combatants, and of the 70 vessels under construction in 1938 and 105 vessels in 1939, not one was a transport or cargo ship. A transport authorized back in 1916 was never built. Neither the Navy nor Congress was sympathetic to Marine Corps pleas for more shipping, probably assuming that such vessels could be quickly drawn from the merchant and passenger services in wartime. Peacetime training suffered accordingly.[36] The low priority for transports extended to landing craft, which, according to the Bureau of Construction and Repair, had to be suitable for storage and handling aboard the Navy's most likely amphibious vessels—the two transports, overage battleships, and destroyers. Between 1935 and 1938 the Navy tested a set of surf boats modeled on fishing boats; all the designs tested were difficult to maneuver, difficult to disembark troops from, and impossible to retract from a beach. The search for a landing craft continued, as did the quest for a suitable lighter for tanks and artillery.[37]

The naval gunfire problem remained intractable, partially because the Navy was not seriously interested in it. The basic difficulty was that the application of naval gunfire was transposed too exactly from World War artillery concepts, while using weapons not designed for high-angle-fire barrages. Naval guns were flat-trajectory, high-velocity weapons designed to penetrate the armor of enemy vessels. Naval guns could not fire registration rounds; the ammunition was limited and unsuitable for shore bombardment; long periods of firing destroyed the guns' rifling; and the ships themselves were vulnerable to shore batteries. These limitations, coupled with a lack of money for practice firings, made the naval gunfire doctrine of the 1930s faulty. Instead of slow, pinpoint, carefully controlled prelanding bombardment, the prevailing doctrine stressed short, intense area barrages designed to "neutralize" exposed enemy infantry and machine guns. The naval vessels that provided these fires would move along the shore at high speed in order to avoid counterbattery fire. Such conditions would preclude accurate artillery fire any closer to friendly troops than 1,500–2,000 yards.[38] As World War II was to prove, this doctrine was a prescription for trouble.

The status of Marine Corps aviation after the World War heartened amphibious warfare planners. First, Marine aviation moved closer to the main currents of Headquarters when General Lejeune placed the aviation section in the Operations and Training Division in 1920 and replaced Major Alfred A. Cunningham with Lieutenant Colonel Thomas C. Turner. As fanatical in his own way about naval aviation as General Billy Mitchell was about an air force independent of the Army, Cunningham had exhausted his usefulness at Headquarters. His successor, Colonel Turner, was a maverick but also a favorite of Lejeune's, probably because of his military strictness with aviation personnel. Turner had learned to fly during the World War with the Army and had actually taught Army pilots. A superb pilot and a skilled politician, Turner ran Marine aviation from 1921–1925 and from 1929 to his death in an accident in 1931. Turner and his disciple, Major E. H. Brainard, who managed the aviation section in 1925–1929, built a force of more than one hundred pilots, one thousand men, and twelve squadrons by the early 1930s. Co-located with the two expeditionary forces at Quantico and San Diego, these squadrons supplied air support of all types to the Corps.[39]

Sharing the perils and thrills of flying biplanes with their Army and Navy comrades, Marine pilots had the added advantage of actual combat operations in Haiti, the Dominican Republic, and Nicaragua, which they used to develop techniques for supporting ground troops. Among those techniques was dive-bombing, first attempted by Lieutenant L. H. M. Sanderson in 1919, which may be a unique Marine contribution to aerial warfare. There was little question among Marine aviators that their function was to support ground operations. Along with the experience of actual combat flying, close air support enthusiasts in the 1920s had several advantages. Their aircraft flew low and slow enough to make visual communication with the infantry and sightings of the enemy possible, and those same flying characteristics permitted bombing and strafing with some accuracy despite primitive aiming systems. In addition, Marine pilots profited not only as members of the naval aviation establishment but also by training at the Army Air Corps Tactical School, an advanced air war center. Not yet an aerie of strategic bombing disciples, the Tactical School gave Marines an opportunity to test Army planes and concepts. Headed in the field by such strong leaders as Major Roy S. Geiger and Major Ross E. Rowell, regular Marine pilots, backed by some six hundred enthusiastic Reserves, stood ready to support Marine land forces wherever they went—including against a defended beach.[40]

The Marine pilots who drafted the aviation sections of the *Tentative Manual* recognized the special importance of aviation in an amphibious landing. The first priority was to gain air superiority over both the objective and the fleet operating areas, thus protecting both the fleet and the landing force from enemy air attack. Navy and Marine fighters together, it was hoped, flying from carriers and land bases, could provide air superiority. Under the fighters' protective umbrella, other aircraft would reconnoiter the objective to provide photographs and visual reports of the enemy defenses; these scouts could also direct naval gunfire. Navy and Marine attack aircraft would also bomb and strafe shore targets, especially enemy defenses (for example, on the rear slopes of hills) that could not be easily shelled by naval guns. When the landing force's artillery came ashore, the attack aircraft would continue operations against targets beyond artillery range, but Marine Corps doctrine also recognized that aircraft could be used close to attacking infantry in emergencies or against any targets that naval guns and artillery could not hit.[41]

Although the aviation doctrine in the *Tentative Manual* was fundamentally sound, Marine air support for landings grew more complicated in the 1930s for several organizational and technical reasons. Basically, Marine aviation depended on Navy funding and facilities. To get access to the Navy's best planes and to cement its alliance with the powerful Bureau of Aeronautics and the fleet, the Marine Corps accepted a secondary mission of providing squadrons for carrier operations and the defense of naval bases. Just as the Marine ground troops performed many "naval" missions, so too did Marine aviation. The amphibious assault mission was only one of them, and it often suffered from inattention while Marine squadrons went to sea in the 1930s or deployed to defend Guam and Pearl Harbor. Close air support became more difficult technically when the Navy adopted faster high-performance single-wing aircraft in the 1930s, such as the SB2U "Vindicator" scout bomber and the F2A "Buffalo" fighter. Designed primarily for carrier operations, these aircraft made the already difficult problems of communicating with friendly infantry and spotting ground targets nearly impossible, as the development of air–ground radios did not keep pace with aircraft design. Although the *Tentative Manual* and the accompanying *Text for the Employment of Marine Corps Aviation* (1935) stressed the critical nature of the coordination of air operations with ground attacks, the Marine Corps and Navy made only marginal progress in close air support techniques during the 1930s. The admirals who controlled naval aviation concentrated on building the Navy's carrier force and slighted the less crucial amphibious mission. Caught between a Marine high command dominated by ground officers and a naval aviation hierarchy that regarded them as poor relations, Marine aviators took their place in the Fleet Marine Force and waited for better times.[42]

3

The development of the Fleet Marine Force (FMF) in the 1930s depended upon several factors, only one of which was increased concern about Japan.[43] The political chances for increasing the FMF were not promising. Still Depression-anxious, Congress avoided financing military modernization with the exception of some shipbuilding. With isolationism at high tide, Congress saw the FMF as provocative and interventionist. At the White House, however, Franklin D. Roosevelt, long-time friend of the Marine Corps, made one critical decision that strengthened the future of the FMF: He appointed John H. Russell as Commandant in 1934. Although he was already sixty-two and had alienated many Marine officers with his advocacy of promotion by selection and his long service for the State Department in Haiti, Russell as Fuller's assistant had brought the FMF to life. A personal friend of Roosevelt since 1915, Russell was reformer enough to impress retired General Lejeune, who refused to support Smedley D. Butler's anti-Russell lobbying. Outraged at missing the Commandant's office for a second time, Butler retired, to the relief of official Washington and much of the Navy. His departure eased Russell's task. A Naval Academy graduate and polished spokesman for Marine Corps–Navy harmony, Russell cultivated his close relationship with FDR. These sentimental ties were further strengthened when Russell arranged for the President's son James to be commissioned (without prior service) as a lieutenant colonel in the Marine Corps Reserve. Headquarters then used "Colonel" Roosevelt as a direct spokesman for Corps policies in the Oval Office. Among his assignments was to advocate the FMF.[44]

Russell and his successor, Thomas Holcomb, gave the FMF their highest priority and repulsed challenges to the amphibious warfare mission from inside and outside the Corps. Unable to prevent the Army from assuming amphibious roles (it even had its own transports), Russell nonetheless blocked any change in the Corps's mission in revisions of *Joint Army and Navy Action*.[45] He also banned the use of the word "expeditionary" for Marine units: "It is desired that the service be alive to the significance of the authorized designation [Fleet Marine Force] and avoid obsolete, less-inclusive terms."[46] Russell argued in 1936 that he had only 2,805 men of the 7,500 he needed in FMF ground units, and when Congress finally authorized him to recruit one thousand additional men, he promptly assigned six hundred more Marines to FMF artillery and technical units.[47] Viewing the FMF as the crucial training organization in the Corps, Russell and Holcomb tried to shift as many Marines as possible into the FMF, even when it meant a 50 percent turnover each year.[48] Paradoxically, the Navy's own expansion after the Vinson–Trammell Act of 1934 did not benefit the FMF, for as new warships readied for sea and new naval facilities opened, the demand for ships guards and security detachments soared, and Headquarters had to plan to strip its shore stations to fill the FMF in wartime. Even though the FMF of 1939 was at less than one-third its planned wartime strength of 25,000, Holcomb agreed with Chief of Naval Operations William D. Leahy that it was politically wiser to stress the FMF's base defense role for American possessions rather than the seizing of enemy bases, for Congress would not fund "interventionist" forces.[49] Despite the Commandants' best efforts, the Marine Corps of 19,367 officers and men in June 1939 was smaller than the Corps of 1922 and fewer than half the Marines belonged to the FMF.

Even within the Marine Corps the FMF concept and the focus on amphibious warfare did not immediately convert an officer corps raised on the World War and the Caribbean pacifications. First as assistant to the Commandant and then as commanding general of the FMF, Major General Louis McCarty Little, a sagacious officer with family ties to the Navy, found that some Marine officers were no more converted to the FMF than the most traditionalist admirals. As a circuit rider for amphibious warfare, Little preached Marine Corps–Navy cooperation and the use of landing exercises to refine the *Tentative Manual*.[50] At the Marine Corps Schools the indoctrination continued with increasing enthusiasm as class after class of Marine officers studied revisions for the *Tentative Manual* and drafted war plans for campaigns in the central Pacific. Their awareness that the Army had little interest in amphibious operations gave the MCS students and faculty a unique sense of purpose. Equally important, as they studied maps of Guam, Saipan, Truk, and the Palaus, the student officers knew that Navy plans gave their study undeniable realism. The MCS faculty, moreover, was first-rate and included many of the Corps's future division and regimental commanders and staff officers. Their work had an urgency that the students carried to the fleet and to the FMF, where they converted Navy admirals and their own peers to the importance of the amphibious assault.[51]

The final legitimation of the Fleet Marine Force occurred not in the classrooms of Quantico but on the beaches of Culebra and California. The FMF resumed landing exercises in 1934.[52] To guide the landings and assist in writing contingency plans, Headquarters established FMF headquarters, first at Quantico and after 1935 at San Diego. The basic units for the FMF were the 1st Brigade at Quantico, comprising the 5th Marines, an artillery battalion of the 10th Marines, small engineer and service units, and several aviation squadrons. On the West Coast the 2d Brigade, built around the 6th Marines, assumed the same structure but was badly understrength, so the 1st Brigade was the only force able to deploy. When the San Diego Marines took to the field, they had to be reinforced from Quantico. Both brigades could be (and were) reinforced by ships guards, but this expedient complicated the planning and execution of landings.

The first large-scale landing lasted only five days (May 5–10) during the 1934 Caribbean fleet exercises and was little better than the 1920s landings; there was no naval gunfire practice and little serious effort to analyze the problems of debarkation and the ship-to-shore movement. Freed from the possibility of an intervention in Cuba, which had complicated planning in 1933–1934, the 1st Brigade conducted extensive operations with the fleet off Culebra, Puerto Rico, from January 15 to March 15, 1935. The series of problems, called Fleet Landing Exercise (FLEX) 1, tested the doctrine in the *Tentative Manual* and included extensive landings, naval gunfire experiments, and aviation operations. The brigade used the ship-to-shore movement to test the possibility of firing all its organic weapons—from rifles through machine guns and 81-mm. mortars to the new 75-mm. pack howitzers—against beach targets. The results were mixed but convinced the planners that better boat guns were needed and should be developed. In one exercise the landing craft were covered with a protective smoke screen, but they immediately slowed, the waves broke, and many of the boats lost their way. The results, one Marine officer reported, "gave us a lot to think about." [53] While the brigade conducted maneuvers ashore, the Navy held naval gunfire tests, primarily to assess the effect of different shells and fuzes. In addition to demonstrating again the limitations of naval gunfire, the tests further convinced gunnery experts that area fire rather than pinpoint bombardment was best. The need for armor-piercing shells against bunkers was ignored, because the shore targets were only rough wooden silhouettes. The aviation bombing and strafing practices were, like the shore bombardments, so restricted by safety precautions that their utility was limited. The participants once more agreed that the standard Navy boats and lighters, some still towed to shore, were inadequate. They also found that Marine Corps and Navy communications techniques and equipment were too primitive to control the boat waves and supporting fires. More landings were clearly needed.[54]

The next year the under-strength 1st Brigade returned to Culebra for FLEX 2 (January 4–February 24, 1936) and relearned the 1935 lessons. The question of transports for the landing force remained worrisome. The brigade embarked on battleships, then transferred to four destroyers, which brought the assault units near the beach. The troops then disembarked (still using gangways) into the battleships' boats. The obvious solution, based on the need for close naval gunfire support and planning simplicity, was to load the troops on special destroyer-transports (APDs), a conclusion the Navy accepted in order to free its battleships for more pressing missions. Given the restricted carrying capacity of the destroyers and their limited ability to carry landing craft and heavy equipment, it was an unsatisfactory solution. The landing boats remained a problem, being slow and vulnerable. In several tests ships boats proved unstable gun platforms, dangerous to disembarking troops, and unable to cross coral reefs. The use of smoke and darkness to conceal the landing only added to the confusion. As for naval gunfire, the artificial tests continued; the doctrine of rapid area fire made aerial spotting difficult. Several Army officer-observers approved of the barrage-type bombardment, simply reinforcing a fundamentally unsound doctrine. Communications remained a knotty problem. The brigade gained valuable tactical experience ashore, but otherwise FLEX 2 provided no special breakthroughs.[55]

For FLEX 3 the 1st Brigade moved to San Diego and absorbed both the small FMF units in California and a provisional Army expeditionary brigade. During the exercises (January 26–March 3, 1937) the landing force assaulted the beaches of San Clemente Island. The problems identified during FLEXes 1 and 2 reemerged with a vengeance. The heavy California surf convinced the Navy and Marine exercise commanders that ships boats were amphibious disasters, as coxswains dumped their troops far from the beach, broached their boats, or scattered for safer landing spots. Using smoke or making the landings at night only worsened the problem. The naval gunfire and aviation bombardment exercises were extensive, but the ordnance, communications, and spotting techniques remained imperfect with the available equipment. For the landing force there were three significant improvements: For the first time the troops used cargo nets to disembark over the side of their destroyer-transports; new Army radios provided better communications; and Marine pack howitzer batteries showed they could quickly go into action ashore. The Marines also had learned that aerial attacks in support of the landing force had to be made at right angles to the direction of the attack to avoid hitting friendly troops; the aviators argued, however, that they needed special attack aircraft and better air–ground communications before their bombing and strafing could gain precision. In addition, FLEX 3 showed that the Navy and Marine Corps had hardly begun to tackle the problems of evacuating casualties and moving supplies ashore. Nevertheless, the landings convinced the Navy participants that the Marine Corps was doing its best within its resources to make an amphibious assault workable. More landing exercises and much more research and development on landing craft and radios were clearly warranted.[56]

As the world situation worsened, the fleet landing exercises assumed a new urgency, and FLEXes 4 and 5, conducted in January–March of 1938 and 1939, pressed the Fleet Marine Force to new heights of performance. To avoid assumed Japanese spying, the FMF returned to the Caribbean and made landings on both Vieques and the main island of Puerto Rico. During FLEX 4 the 1st Brigade (a meager force of 1,857 Marines) for the first time made landings against three Army and National Guard regiments and "fought" ashore under umpired rules. The competition gave the landings new zest, particularly when the Marines made a successful night landing. The height of one problem came when Marine aviators ruined an Army cocktail party with molasses bombs.[57] The Marines also learned new lessons about the digestive effects of riding small boats in a heavy sea and about tropical insects, which were so bad that the warring regiments made a truce to avoid the mosquitoes. Nevertheless, the landings gave the Navy–Marine Corps task force valuable practice in handling supplies and casualties (which it did not do well) and in managing the ship-to-shore movement. The ships boats again proved inadequate for landing troops, but a new Navy lighter for carrying tanks and vehicles performed well. The Navy boat handlers also showed unexpected skill. As for gunfire support, the Navy emphasized point-target counterbattery fire in its independent drills and for the first time began to consider modifying its area bombardment doctrine. It also recognized, with Marine Corps approval, the wisdom of assigning special warships to shore bombardment missions in order to improve training and ordnance problems. In all, the FMF emerged from FLEXes 4 and 5 with new confidence and enthusiasm.[58]

Of all the difficulties dramatized by the FLEXes, none became more obsessive than the search for better landing craft, and throughout the 1930s the Marine Corps struggled to find substitutes for the Navy's ships boats. The search was frustrating, for the ultimate approval and funding for landing craft came not from the Corps but from the Navy's Bureau of Construction and Repair. Nevertheless, Headquarters in 1933 established a Marine Corps Equipment Board at Quantico with the primary task of lobbying for better landing craft.[59] The first experiments with modified fishing craft disappointed the board, but tests on bureau boats continued until 1941. The first hopeful alternative came from a civilian designer, Andrew Higgins of New Orleans. Having tried unsuccessfully in 1926 to interest the Navy in one of his boats, Higgins remained convinced that his "Eureka" boat was the answer to the beach assault. Developed for use in bayou waters, the "Eureka" provided critical improvements: a shallow draft, a broad, flat bow for landing and retracting, and a protected propeller. In 1938 tests the "Eureka" impressed the Navy and Marine Corps observers, and the Navy provided Higgins with additional development money. When its length, troop compartment, and engine were modified, the "Eureka" became Marine Corps's choice, and the Equipment Board pushed hard for its adoption. The Marines had one reservation: The "Eureka" was still unsuitable for troop disembarkation. The answer was obvious but novel. Drawing on research on Japanese landing craft done by Lieutenant Victor H. Krulak in 1937, the Equipment Board persuaded Higgins to redesign "Eureka" with a retractable bow ramp. Finally built and tested in 1941, the modified "Eureka" soon became the Navy's Landing Craft Vehicle Personnel (LCVP)—the much-loved and much-hated "Papa" boat that took thousands of Marines to beaches for the next thirty years.[60]

Higgins's emergence as the premier designer of landing craft also influenced the development of larger lighters for transporting tanks, wheeled artillery, and vehicles to the beach. Drawing upon the Navy's experiments and his own "Eureka" design, Higgins built a series of lighters whose basic developmental problem was size, not design. Marine Corps planners knew from the FLEXes that the landing force needed immediate assistance from tanks to overcome beach defenses. When they finally gave up the burden of designing their own tank, they found that Army tanks (which finally included the 30-ton Sherman) were too heavy for Navy lighters. Higgins, therefore, had to design and build a 50-foot lighter, which became the standard Landing Craft Mechanized (LCM) or "Mike" boat, another sturdy fixture in amphibious landings.

The concern about the early arrival of tanks on a hostile beach also made the Marine Corps sensitive to the development of an amphibian tank. Its early experiments with a Christie model were disappointing, but in 1937 Headquarters learned that the inventor Donald Roebling had created an amphibian tractor for rescue missions in the Florida swamps. Alerted by a magazine article on Roebling's "alligator," Headquarters and the Equipment Board grew ecstatic when they examined the tractor. Although the vehicle was too complicated and underpowered for military use, Roebling and the Corps planners redesigned and tested improved models after 1938 until they had a vehicle that was reliable and seaworthy enough for combat operations. Often the enthusiasm of the developers outdistanced the "alligator's" performance, and several Navy admirals and Marine generals got short, wet rides during the early tests. But the vehicle's potential was so obvious that development never slowed. Using its tracks to drive it through water and over reefs, the "alligator" had begun its life in the Marine Corps as a troop carrier. Even though it was not adopted until 1941, the "alligator," or Landing Vehicle Tracked (LVT), grew from the demonstrated needs of the FMF in the FLEXes of the 1930s.[61]

Although fully able to tackle the doctrinal problems of the amphibious assault, the Fleet Marine Force was too deficient in strength to be taken seriously as a war-ready force. Headquarters therefore paid increasing attention to the Marine Corps Reserve. Reorganized under legislation passed in 1925, the Reserve fell into two categories, companies of the Fleet Marine Corps Reserve and individuals of the Volunteer Marine Corps Reserve. All Reserves were assigned to some unit for administrative purposes, but only the FMCR companies drilled and went to summer camp according to an enlistment contract; they were paid only for summer camp. Plagued by equipment, facility, and uniform shortages and with few incentives beyond patriotism and some social elitism, the Reserves managed to stay alive into the 1930s through the determination of many politically adept officers (including U.S. Representative Melvin J. Maas) and its loyal enlisted men, most of whom were service veterans. Recognizing the potential of the Reserve, a recognition encouraged by the Marine Corps Reserve Officers' Association (1926), the Marine Corps took several important steps to improve it. A Reserve section appeared in the Headquarters organization after the 1925 law. Directed by Reserve Lieutenant Colonel J. J. Staley, a zealous promoter, the section lobbied for more money and training opportunities. Through gradual growth, the Reserve units eventually organized as seventeen infantry battalions, one artillery battalion, and twelve aviation squadrons and moved closer to the training standards of the FMF units. In 1935 Headquarters established a twelve-week Platoon Leaders Course for college students in order to provide the Reserve with trained junior officers. In addition, regular officers inspected and trained Reserve units in inspector-instructor billets, and Reservists often served with FMF units during summer camp. The Naval Reserve Act of 1938 completed the process of institutionalization by dividing the Reserve into an Organized Marine Corps Reserve of units with training responsibilities and a Fleet Marine Corps Reserve and Volunteer Marine Corps Reserve of individuals with reduced service obligations. In 1939 the total Reserve numbered 850 officers and 14,000 men with some training. Although not all the Reserves were fit for combat service, they outnumbered the FMF, and Headquarters viewed them both as essential fillers for FMF units and as replacements for regular Marines assigned to the FMF for emergency service.[62]

4

In the summer of 1939 Secretary of the Navy Claude Swanson asked the General Board to assess the Navy's readiness for war. Only one day before the German invasion of Poland the General Board made its final assessment of the Navy's ability to fight a major war. Its report was not optimistic, and among the "critical deficiencies" it identified was the lack of Pacific bases west of Hawaii. The Navy, the board reported, did not have the forces to defend or seize bases. The Fleet Marine Force lacked modern arms in adequate numbers and types, and the Navy could not support it with transports, lighters, and landing craft. Yet the board did not stress the amphibious warfare mission among the imperative steps it recommended for immediate action. Of its twenty recommendations, only one—to arm the existing FMF—dealt with Marine Corps problems. Not a single measure the board identified as "urgent" or "immediate" in assigning priorities affected the FMF. Despite the successes of the Marine Corps in developing a doctrine for amphibious warfare and the Fleet Marine Force's useful FLEXes, the amphibious warfare mission remained distinctly secondary to the problems of fleet action on the high seas and the defense of fixed naval bases.[63] Only the trauma of another war would provide a sufficient sense of urgency for the further development of the Fleet Marine Force.

Yet when weighed against the primitive concepts and pessimism that characterized amphibious warfare doctrine in the 1920s, the Corps's accomplishments by 1939 cannot be overstated. Alone among the American armed forces, it had embraced the amphibious assault mission and had created through trial and error an invaluable body of knowledge and experience. The Marine Corps had established an essential role in American naval strategic plans and had responded to the challenges of War Plan ORANGE by writing the *Tentative Manual* and creating the Fleet Marine Force. Taking nothing away from its gallant service in the Pacific in World War II, the Marine Corps made its most important contribution to American military history during those frustrating, threadbare days when far-sighted Commandants, Quantico planners, and small FMF units pieced together the essential concepts for a successful amphibious assault.

13. World War II: Defeating Japan
in the South Pacific, 1939–1944

A week after German tanks in Poland ignited World War II, and three days after the United States declared itself neutral, President Franklin D. Roosevelt on September 8, 1939, announced a "limited national emergency" and authorized the Marine Corps to increase its enlisted ranks to 25,000 men, its statutory wartime strength. Neither the President nor the Commandant could have foreseen that this announcement was the first step toward a Corps of nearly 500,000 men and an amphibious war to recapture the Pacific from Japan. In 1939 military unpreparedness and public apathy limited Roosevelt to a minimum program of continental and hemispheric defense. For the Marine Corps the beginning of World War II in Europe brought no dramatic change in its amphibious forces. Instead, responding to a 1938 Navy Department study, the Marine Corps formed four defense battalions to prepare the anti-aircraft and antiship defenses of America's central Pacific island outposts—Wake, Midway, Johnston, and Palmyra islands. The formation of the defense battalions was an omen. Even as war flamed in Europe, the dictates of American strategy and the preferences of the Navy drew the Marine Corps to the Pacific.

With Great Britain and France at war with Germany, the Army–Navy Joint Board, the collective voice of American strategic planning, reasoned that the Allies would control the Atlantic and would soon mount an effective offensive against Germany's Rhine frontier. Scrapping the color-coded war plans, the strategists drafted a series of RAIN-

BOW plans based on the possibility of simultaneous wars with Japan and Germany. During the winter of 1939–1940 the strategic situation seemed to justify RAINBOW 2, which assumed a successful Anglo-French war against Germany, as the basis for enlarging and deploying the American armed forces. RAINBOW 2 mirrored the old ORANGE war plan, for it foresaw a war against Japan in the Pacific waged primarily by the Navy.

In the war posited in RAINBOW 2 the Marine Corps would play an important role. While its defense battalions held off the Japanese, the Fleet Marine Force would form two divisions for amphibious assaults upon Pacific advanced bases. If the Allies could not defeat Germany, a contingency studied in RAINBOW 1, the same Marine units would be used with the Army to hold America's possessions in the Western Hemisphere. Such a situation, however, seemed implausible as the "phony war" in Western Europe dragged on during the winter of 1939–1940. Lulled by its assumption of Allied superiority, the American government watched without making any serious improvement in its military posture.[1]

In the late spring of 1940 all the assumptions of RAINBOW 2 crumbled as the Germans launched a series of invasions that occupied Denmark and Norway, drove the British Expeditionary Force to Dunkirk, and crushed France. In less than three months, Great Britain faced Germany alone, and the United States found itself protected only by its own small regular armed forces and the scattered units of the wounded but defiant British Commonwealth. Galvanized to action by the Allied defeat, Congress voted in June 1940 to increase taxes by almost $1 billion a year, and the next month it approved a naval building program designed to give the United States a "two-ocean" navy and a naval aviation force of 15,000 aircraft. Good intentions and realistic alarm could not, however, provide adequate naval forces. The Navy's General Board urged a sweeping program to put the fleet and the shore establishment on a war footing to defend the hemisphere. Its program proposed to "fully equip [a] Marine Expeditionary Force, especially as to armament, landing equipment, and suitable transports."[2] What made the increase and modernization of the Fleet Marine Force so essential was the planners' fear that the Germans would occupy France's Caribbean islands and use them for air and naval operations against America's munitions trade with Britain. In the same month that Congress passed the "Two Ocean Navy" Act, the Joint War Planning Committee of the Joint Board assigned to the 1st Marine Brigade the mission of seizing Martinique. The Marine Corps now faced a two-ocean amphibious mission with inadequate resources.[3]

The accelerated naval mobilization of 1940, supported by the Roosevelt administration in the name of hemispheric defense, worked in confusing cross-currents upon the Marine Corps. Headquarters found itself hard pressed to handle all its accumulated missions. Amphibious warfare was not the Navy's highest priority, but increased spending provided almost 1,400 new landing craft by the eve of Pearl Harbor. Nearly five hundred amphibian tractors were under construction or authorized. In the same period the Navy created an amphibious force of thirty large transports and eleven amphibious supply ships. Formed to carry three amphibious divisions, the new ships and landing craft hardly met the nation's wartime needs, but their appearance in 1941 lent a new reality to amphibious training and provided a limited amphibious capability in 1942.[4] The general fleet building program would provide additional cruisers and destroyers for naval gunfire support—if their crews were trained for such duties and they were not employed on other missions.

The mobilization also benefited Marine aviation, although naval aviation policies were a mixed blessing for the Fleet Marine Force. Supported by Roosevelt's obsession with military aviation as both a diplomatic signal and a strategic panacea, the Navy Department asked for and received authorization for a 15,000-aircraft force in the legislation of 1940. Because one-tenth of the force (thirty-two squadrons) would go to the Marines, the naval aviation program meant the Corps would have to provide thousands of pilots and aviation support personnel. At the end of 1940 the Marine Corps had only 425 pilots and fewer than 3,000 enlisted men in its two small Marine Aircraft Groups 1 and 2.[5] Men for the expanded aviation force would have to come from the most intelligent recruits, for aviation duty seemed to require special mental ability. That meant the Fleet Marine Force ground units would have to do with fewer skilled officers and noncommissioned officers. The FMF's losses were not matched by increased capability, because the Marine squadrons could be used aboard carriers and as base defense forces, not solely for amphibious assaults.

The Marine Corps was also plagued by military faddists, both outside and inside the Corps, who mined an inexhaustible fund of lessons from the European war and the possibility of a war with Japan. The result was the creation of special units that required scarce skilled personnel. The special units' demands for manpower became most onerous in 1942, but even before Pearl Harbor the Marine Corps created seven defense battalions (each with about a thousand officers and men) and was ready to organize more. In addition, the Corps, pushed by Roosevelt, was about to form raider battalions to ape the British Commandos and parachute battalions to ape the Germans. More men went into training to fly assault gliders and operate barrage balloon squadrons to defend naval bases. Ever responsive to its civilian and Navy masters, the Marine Corps prepared itself for virtually every duty anyone could imagine for it.[6]

While Commandant Thomas Holcomb and Chief of Naval Operations Harold R. Stark argued for more Marines, Roosevelt would not approve an increase to 50,000 men until he was safely reelected and inaugurated.[7] Under pressure from Secretary of the Navy Frank Knox, Roosevelt did authorize the Marine Corps to recall its retirees and mobilize the Reserve in the autumn of 1940. The members of the Organized Reserve added only 5,000 men to the Fleet Marine Force. When all the elements of the Marine Corps Reserve reported for active duty by the summer of 1941, the Corps had a welcome addition of 15,000 troops. And Roosevelt approved a total force of 50,000 officers and men by mid-1941, as promised.[8]

By the time the Corps had reached nearly 50,000 men, its troop strength was again inadequate, for the Navy war plans for an active defense of America's Pacific and Atlantic frontiers now required two amphibious divisions, thirteen defense battalions, two Marine aircraft wings, a full supporting establishment, and thousands of base security guards. General Holcomb's planners found a minimum peacetime strength of 75,000 officers and men essential. They estimated that if the United States entered the war, the Corps should expand to more than 150,000 in order to provide three divisions. The administration and Congress responded favorably, and when war came in December 1941, Marine Corps strength had climbed to 65,881. Less than half of this force was in the Fleet Marine Force, which included two divisions, the defense battalions, and two Marine Aircraft Wings (MAWs). For the Fleet Marine Force to field two full divisions, it needed not only modern equipment but more men.[9]

The mobilization of 1940 and 1941 sent waves of urgency throughout the Marine Corps. At Headquarters the adjustment was minimal. The Divisions of Operations and Training changed to the Division of Plans and Policies in 1939, but not until after 1941 did separate staff fiefdoms for aviation, gunnery, and communications splinter staff coordination. For the moment Headquarters, suitably reinforced with more officers, functioned without serious confusion or haste. The greatest organizational concession to the mobilization was the creation of a public relations division of five Marines to coordinate recruiting publicity.[10] At the two recruit depots the mobilization strained the physical plants and staffs, and the training cycle was trimmed from ten weeks to twenty-four days to save both. At Parris Island the monthly average number of trainees jumped from 190 to 1,600. Recruit training hardened into four basic methods for hammering civilian youths into novice Marines. From their drill instructors (DIs) the recruits learned to drill, to exercise, to obey all sorts of mystifying orders, and to shoot a rifle. When the "boots" of 1940 failed to qualify with the rifle in alarming numbers, the training cycle was increased to seven weeks, with three weeks devoted to marksmanship training. Field skills and tactics had to be learned when the recruits reported to FMF units. The new Marines had been physically and mentally toughened by childhoods spent on the farms and in the modest homes of a nation racked by an economic depression. One in five recruits had a minor police record. Many of the 1940 and 1941 recruits were nearly as hard as their DIs.[11]

The crucial priority was manning the Fleet Marine Force. The two expanded brigades became the 1st and 2d Marine Divisions (activated in February 1941). The 1st and 2d Marine Aircraft Wings (activated in the summer of 1941) and the defense battalions completed the FMF. On the Atlantic coast the 1st Division began as a "crotchety, cantankerous, prideful, and intolerant" organization that took pride in being "raggedy-assed Marines," shunted from one inadequate base to another.[12] When it was not at sea, the division wandered from Florida to Norfolk, from Culebra to Guantanamo Bay for training. Finally, in the spring of 1941, the Marine Corps purchased and leased a reservation of scrub pines and sand flats along the New River in North Carolina. The new base's only recommendation—other than the fact that the land was cheap—was its proximity to the new port at Morehead City, a prize PWA project the Democrats wanted to publicize.[13] The new camp, a raw complex of huts and tents, eventually became Camp Lejeune, but in 1941 the 1st Division found its new home a Southern wasteland. As the division trained, at least one officer complained about the terrain: "This division . . . won't be fit for anything but jungle warfare." [14] Its mission was amphibious assaults, not small unit actions in thick underbrush. The assumption was logical but not prophetic.

On the West Coast, the 2d Division or "the Hollywood Marines" (they made war movies as part of their training) expanded beyond the confines of the San Diego base but found a new home at Camp Elliott at Kearny Mesa, 12 miles northeast of the city. In March 1942 the Navy Department acquired more adequate terrain by buying the 132,000-acre Rancho Santa Margarita y Las Flores, 48 miles north of San Diego. Camp Pendleton, the new base, became a training ground for FMF divisions and other units, while Camp Elliott was used to train replacements.[15] The MAWs, still only two groups in December 1941, made their homes at Quantico and San Diego but dispatched squadrons and detachments to the Pacific island garrisons, the Navy's Caribbean bases, and two Pacific Fleet carriers.

For the divisions the process of organization was speedy and painful; no sooner had a regiment formed and trained than it had to relinquish at least a third of its strength to form new units. The 1st Division built outward from the 5th Marines and the rest of the 1st Brigade, forming the 7th Marines (January 1941) and then the 1st Marines (February 1941). The 11th Marines expanded from one artillery battalion to four in a year. The 2d Division went through the same metamorphosis, expanding to three infantry regiments (2d, 6th, and 8th Marines) and a full artillery regiment (12th Marines). In addition to the expansion and internal reorganization of its basic combat regiments, each Marine division formed a novel assortment of supporting units. In 1941 the divisions included headquarters, service, medical, and engineer battalions and transportation, service, tank, signal, chemical, and anti-aircraft companies. Within a year the divisions had a full engineer regiment (including a Navy construction battalion) and full battalions of special weapons (halftrack-mounted cannon and anti-aircraft guns), tanks, amphibian tractors, raiders, parachutists, Navy medical personnel, and service troops. Organizational structure notwithstanding, neither Marine division mustered more than nine thousand men in 1941, a manning level barely 60 percent of full strength. Neither division could be considered ready, in equipment and training terms, for serious combat.[16]

Within its personnel and equipment limitations—some uncontrollable, some self-inflicted—the Marine Corps accelerated its amphibious training of 1941. The first wartime exercise, FLEX 6, differed little from the earlier FLEXes, for the Navy still could not provide a single amphibious transport larger than a destroyer, and the 1st Brigade could send barely two thousand Marines to land in the Caribbean. The basic accomplishment of the exercise was to test experimental landing craft.[17] FLEX 7 in early 1941 showed some improvement, as five large transports were available for the 1st Division, but the shortage of ships and landing craft still made the exercises unrealistic, and there was little naval gunfire or aviation support.[18]

Amphibious training became more complicated in 1941, for American and British military planners feared German thrusts against the Allies' island bases in the Atlantic. The endangered areas ranged from Iceland to the Azores to the Caribbean. Reflecting the shift of American strategic interest to the European war, the Army–Navy Joint Board (soon to become the Joint Chiefs of Staff) urged the formation of an amphibious corps for the Atlantic Fleet. This corps, built around the 1st Marine Division and the Army's 1st Infantry Division, became the 1st Joint Training Force (June 1941) and then (August 1941) the Amphibious Force Atlantic Fleet. Although the Army tended to view the force as a training organization, the Atlantic Fleet commander, Admiral Ernest J. King, and the corps commander, Marine Major General Holland M. Smith, regarded it as a tactical organization preparing for contingency deployments. The orders from Washington suggest that their position was the correct one. In any event, the Army–Marine Corps unit made practice landings off New River, North Carolina, in the summer of 1941 and inside Chesapeake Bay in January 1942. The landings were marred by the lack of adequate transports and assault craft and by Navy inexperience in ship-to-shore movement. In neither exercise did the whole corps land, and the movement of supplies and vehicles over the beach showed gross mismanagement. Similar exercises on the West Coast, organized by Major General Clayton B. Vogel's 2d Joint Training Force (later the Amphibious Force Pacific Fleet) and mounted by the 2d Marine Division and the 3d Infantry Division, were even less satisfactory. The Pacific Coast forces also suffered a severe manpower leak when Roosevelt sent the 6th Marines, reinforced to brigade strength, to Iceland in the summer of 1941 to augment the British garrison there. Some progress had been made, but the United States did not possess much amphibious capability as it faced the possibility of a two-ocean world war in the autumn of 1941.[19]

The amphibious training of 1941, however, had one important result: It convinced the War Department General Staff that the Army should have as little to do with the Navy–Marine Corps amphibious force as possible and that the Army should assume all amphibious duties for the Atlantic and the Marine Corps for the Pacific. Assessing the Army's amphibious experience in 1941, the General Staff concluded that the use of a Marine Corps–Army amphibious corps in cooperation with a Navy amphibious force was an organizational nightmare. The Army's primary complaint was that the Navy could not provide ships and landing craft for a real division landing and that Navy landing techniques were too timid. The Army was also unhappy about placing troops under a corps commander who was a Marine and a Marine–Navy corps staff. It protested Marine criticism of the number of artillery pieces and vehicles in Army divisions. Arguing that Atlantic Ocean amphibious operations were simply preludes to the Army's reconquest of Europe and that Pacific landings would be small and part of a distinctly naval campaign, Army planners recommended that the Fleet Marine Force shift all its units to the Pacific. In 1942 this proposal delighted Chief of Naval Operations and Commander-in-Chief U.S. Fleet Ernest J. King, who wanted the war against Japan to be a Navy-dominated campaign. American strategic planning proceeded accordingly, and the Marine Corps eventually stormed Iwo Jima but not Normandy.[20] From an institutional standpoint, the geographic division favored the Corps, much to the Army's eventual dismay.

The disputes over joint training in 1941 and early 1942 continued Army–Marine Corps tension from World War I, which persisted through World War II. Part of the problem was logistical, for President Roosevelt decided in 1941 that the Fleet Marine Force (which could be deployed outside the United States because it contained no draftees) should take priority in the distribution of scarce weapons. Army Chief of Staff George C. Marshall, no friend of the Marines since his service in France, lamented: "My main battle is equipping the Marines. Whether we have anything left after the British and Marines get theirs, I do not know." [21] There was no improvement of relations at the amphibious corps level. The General Staff was not happy to have even one Army division commanded by Holland M. "Howling Mad" Smith. Smith, the ultimate Marine loyalist, was a bigger Navy-hater than Army-hater but had little patience with what he considered Army inefficiency. Having suffered Army insults in the AEF and at Army schools in the interwar period, Smith, a combative perfectionist, made no secret of his contempt for Army commanders. Smith's outspokenness on the Army's amphibious inadequacies and apathy did not win the Marine Corps friends.[22] On the Pacific Coast the same sort of problems emerged. The Navy would not adjust to real division-size operations or shift the landings nearer to the Army's major base at Fort Lewis, Washington. The Marines, represented by General Vogel, did little to help organize serious landing exercises. The result on both coasts was that the Army decided to run its own amphibious training and even form its own landing craft crews within its new amphibious engineer brigades, of which it eventually formed eight.[23]

While the Fleet Marine Force expanded, the United States and Japan moved closer to war. On tense diplomatic terms since Japan's invasion of China in 1937, the two Pacific antagonists found themselves on the brink of conflict after the outbreak of war in Europe. For Japan, whose government was dominated by the military, the European war provided an exciting opportunity for expansionism. The German conquest of Western Europe and campaigns in North Africa sent the British Commonwealth into a crisis so severe that British and Commonwealth forces could not be spared for Asia and the Pacific. The position of the other

European colonial powers in Asia was even less strong. The Netherlands East Indies were virtually undefended, and the French possessions (Indo-China and some islands in the South Pacific) were equally vulnerable. Aware of its opportunity, the Japanese government in 1940 put diplomatic pressure upon all its possible victims and won base rights from the Vichy French administration of Indo-China; all the other governments stood firm except Thailand. By default the United States, not yet involved in the European war, became the leader of the Allied coalition against Japan. Concerned not only for the safety of the Philippines but also for the military potential of the British Commonwealth's Asian domain for the war with Germany, the Roosevelt administration increased its assistance to China and began a series of economic countermeasures to deprive Japan of raw materials for military production.

The last significant barrier to Japanese expansion fell in the summer of 1941 when Germany attacked the Soviet Union, thus removing the threat to Japan's northern flank. Japan immediately increased its diplomatic pressure on the Allies, extended its control of Indo-China, and stepped up its military mobilization. The United States responded with a broader program of economic sanctions, mobilized and reinforced its Philippine forces, and held the Pacific Fleet at Pearl Harbor. American planners recognized that the central Pacific route to the Philippines, given Japanese strength in Micronesia, would fall with war but pushed the defense of Wake, Midway, and Johnston islands as outposts for Pearl Harbor. A more secure way to Australia and then north to the Philippines grew along a route that ran southwesterly through Palmyra to American Samoa, then through the British Fiji Islands to the French New Hebrides and New Caledonia. Conceived before December 1941, this route, so essential to the defense of Australia, the Philippines, and the Malay Barrier of the Netherlands East Indies, dictated the first important campaigns of America's war against Japan.

The Japanese government, stung by America's economic sanctions and aid to China, made one last faint effort to negotiate a capitulation from Roosevelt while the Japanese army and navy deployed for a grand assault. For Admiral Isoroku Yamamoto's Combined Fleet the crucial objective was the Pacific Fleet at Pearl Harbor; quick destruction of America's battleships and carriers would end any serious Allied counteroffensive threat. At the same time, Japanese forces from Japan proper, Micronesia, and Indo-China would sweep as far east as Wake Island and the British Gilbert Islands and would seize a southern frontier that would run from the Bismarck Archipelago and New Guinea (under Australian control) through the Netherlands East Indies to Burma. This new Japanese empire, the "Greater East Asia Co-prosperity Sphere," would then be held until the Allies sued for peace. Knowing that the Allies' first priority was to free Europe, the Tojo government thought that the Allies would sue for peace in less than a year.[24]

The dual threat of Germany and Japan had spread the Marine Corps thinly, like the rest of the armed forces, along America's military frontiers in the Pacific and the Atlantic. During those tense days of early December 1941, as the carriers of the Combined Fleet pitched toward Pearl Harbor across the stormy northern Pacific, Marines from Iceland to the Philippines watched peace disappear. More than 18,000 men of the 65,881-man Corps were already overseas. The 1st Provisional Brigade (nearly 4,000 men) patrolled Iceland, while more than 1,500 men of the 4th Marines and a separate battalion prepared defenses around Manila. To the Navy's island bases and stations abroad the Marine Corps had sent 3,400 security guards and 5,600 FMF Marines in five defense battalions and units of the 2d Division and 2d MAW. Nearly 4,000 more Marines were serving in ships detachments, many walking posts aboard the battleships anchored at Pearl Harbor. Almost 20,000 more FMF Marines huddled around portable stoves in their tents in North Carolina or hiked through the dust of Southern California, waiting for war or the next amphibious exercise. About 27,000 other Marines manned supply bases, recruiting stations, the recruit depots, and forty-three posts and stations of the Navy's shore establishment. This Marine Corps, more than twice the size of the 1939 organization, was already a "new" Corps, jammed with Reservists, new lieutenants, and eager recruits. Just how soon even this Corps would disappear in the throes of war was beyond the ken of most Marines as they faced a rare day of rest on Sunday, December 7, 1941.[25]

1

The first Japanese bombs that smashed American aircraft and battleships at Pearl Harbor began as grim a six-month period of war as the United States had ever faced. Too small and too weakly armed for a real world war, the American armed forces suffered defeat after defeat, all of them foreordained by the nation's lack of preparedness and by its preoccupation with the war in Europe. Like their Army and Navy comrades, Marines from Hawaii to China faced a Japanese onslaught characterized by strategic daring and tactical skill. For the Marine Corps, the first six months of the World War II were heart-rending, as scattered detachments fell before the Japanese offensive. But never did so few do so much to enhance the reputation of a military organization for endurance and bravery. From the time the first Marines died with their battleships until the last member of the 4th Marines dropped his rifle on Corregidor, Marines faced the Japanese with a desperate courage that has survived wartime exaggeration and postwar romanticism. If the first six months of the war in the Pacific embarrassed the United States, it also demonstrated that the Marine Corps of 1942 was as tough as the Corps of 1918. It needed only training, better weapons in adequate numbers, and more men to demonstrate its superiority to the Japanese. Along the perimeter of America's Pacific frontier, Marines fought to buy time.

At Pearl Harbor, 4,500 Marines scrambled to their posts on December 7 to find that the Japanese aircraft that had struck about 8 A.M. had done their work only too well. At the air station at Ewa, MAG-21 lost nearly all of its forty-seven planes in the first attack. Nevertheless, the aviation personnel fought back with machine guns stripped from the rows of smoldering planes. The men of the 1st and 3d Defense Battalions set up their anti-aircraft machine guns throughout the Navy Yard and added their fire to the defense of the Pacific Fleet. Those ships guards not caught below by bombs and torpedoes manned their posts and took the full fury of the aerial assault. Of the 112 Marines who died at Pearl Harbor, 108 were ships guards. As the numbed, furious Americans of the Hawaii defense forces and the Pacific Fleet fought fires and gathered their nearly 3,500 casualties, the Marines of the defense battalions and MAG-21 manned their Hawaii posts and organized reinforcements for the Pacific outposts to the south and west. The Japanese carriers had left Hawaiian waters, but other portions of the Combined Fleet and Imperial army were already hammering at other American garrisons.[26]

In China and on the island of Guam, the Marine detachments manned defensive positions, but their commanders correctly concluded that more than a token defense would serve no useful purpose and surrendered. Some two hundred China Marines scattered from Tientsin to Peking went into captivity without a fight (although the troops were willing to stage an Asiatic Alamo) on December 8. On Guam, fewer than two hundred Marines, reinforced by Guamanian police and volunteers, faced a Japanese brigade of 5,500 troops, which landed after American naval installations were bombed and shelled for three days. With fewer than five hundred combatants armed only with infantry weapons, the Navy governor surrendered on December 10 after a spirited but token resistance that killed four Marines and 15 Guamanians.

Although Japanese naval units and aircraft crossed the International Date Line to attack the garrisons at Midway, Johnston, and Palmyra islands in early December, only Wake Island faced a determined invasion. Still in the process of being developed as a base for Navy patrol planes, the three small islands of Wake atoll were defended by 449 Marines from the 1st Defense Battalion and a Marine fighter squadron, VMF-211, which had brought twelve Grumman F4F Wildcats to Wake's airfield. The rest of Wake's population included fewer than fifty Navy and Army specialists and some 1,200 civilians of the atoll construction force. The Marine defenders faced insurmountable personnel and equipment shortages. The defense battalion had only a third of the men necessary to man its 3-inch and 5-inch dual purpose guns and machine guns. Its fire direction equipment and early-warning radars were insufficient. VMF-211 had only four days to start operations before the Japanese arrived, and its ground detachment was short-handed even before it suffered irreplaceable casualties.[27]

The Japanese naval forces based to the south in the Marshall Islands had no intention of allowing the Americans to reinforce Wake, and on December 8 (December 7 at Pearl Harbor) Japanese aircraft blasted the Marine airstrip, destroying all but one aircraft on the ground and the four-plane patrol. Nearly half of the aviation maintenance personnel perished in the rain of bombs, and VMF-211 lost scarce parts and equipment. Their morale lifted by the news that reinforcements were on the way from Hawaii, the Wake garrison dug in to meet the amphibious assault it was sure would soon follow. On December 11 a Japanese fleet of nine cruisers and destroyers and four transports approached the island and quickly learned that the Marines were both combative and skilled. Under the direction of Major James P. S. Devereux and VMF-211's Major Paul S. Putnam, the Marines greeted the Japanese invasion fleet with accurate gunfire and desperate aerial assaults. Before the Japanese retired in disarray, the invaders lost two destroyers sunk and seven other vessels damaged. Only four Marines were wounded. Clearly Wake required more aerial pounding before the invaders returned.

From December 12 until Wake fell on December 23, the Japanese bombed the beleaguered garrison until VMF-211 could no longer put a plane in the air and the defense battalion dwindled from casualties and equipment damage. In the meantime the relief convoy plowed westward from Hawaii, but, much to the frustration of its Marines, the expedition turned back, its commander fearing a Japanese naval ambush. The decision suggested to some Marine officers that the Navy would sacrifice Marines but not its own ships. Devereux's defenders could not indulge in interservice second-guessing; they had the Japanese to fight. Early in the dark morning of December 23 the Marines faced an amphibious assault of eight hundred Japanese, backed by twelve cruisers and destroyers. Meeting the Marines' heroic resistance, reinforced with Navy and civilian volunteers, the landing force nevertheless seized several lodgements by daylight, even though the Marines wiped out one landing party. With communications broken, counterattack forces limited, and ammunition in short supply, the Navy officer commanding the island surrendered to spare the surviving Marines and the civilian workers. After eleven hours of desperate resistance, the Marines, having lost 20 percent of their strength, joined their China and Guam comrades in captivity, leaving behind a legend of courage that heartened a generation of Marines.

As the Wake garrison turned back the first Japanese invasion, the Marines in the Philippines joined General Douglas MacArthur's forlorn defense of Luzon, which to Japan's embarrassment went on until May 1942. Although American planners considered the Philippines indefensible, Roosevelt ordered the islands held as long as possible. The Army and Navy did their best, hoping that American aviation and submarines, in cooperation with the Army's defense force and the raw Philippine army, might hold on long enough to allow reinforcements to reach the islands from Australia. On December 8 MacArthur's defense was handicapped when much of its air force was destroyed on the ground. After some hopeless forays, the weak Asiatic Fleet fell back as planned to join an Allied fleet based in the Netherlands East Indies. The Philippine defense then became an uneven contest of Filipino-American ground forces against a balanced Japanese invasion force of experienced (though numerically inferior) army divisions, airplanes, and naval forces. Faced with successful multiple landings, MacArthur withdrew to Bataan Peninsula on the northwest flank of Manila harbor. In the redeployment the 4th Marines, fresh from China, passed from Navy control to MacArthur, who in late December ordered the regiment to fortify Corregidor Island. Augmented by other Marine detachments, sailors from Cavite and Olongapo, and stray American and Filipino soldiers, the regiment became the backbone of the island's defense force. Other Marines joined a naval battalion sent to Bataan to protect the Army's flanks against amphibious assaults.[28]

Until Bataan fell in early April, the Corregidor garrison was spared direct attack except from the air. Having wiped out one Japanese amphibious assault, most of the Bataan naval battalion joined the 4th Marines on Corregidor for one last stand. For Colonel Samuel L. Howard's regiment, an interservice conglomerate of four battalions, the defense of Corregidor was an ordeal without hope. Ringed by Japanese heavy artillery and open to air attack, the defenders could survive in the island's tunnels, but their heavy weapons and defensive positions could not be saved. In the night of May 5–6 the Japanese mounted a full-scale invasion of the pulverized fortress and, despite desperate positional defense and infantry counterattacks by two 4th Marines battalions, held a third of the island at daybreak. Knowing that he had lost about half his active defenders and that the Japanese had landed tanks, General Jonathan Wainwright, MacArthur's successor, surrendered the island and all the rest of the Philippine defense force. With nearly seven hundred Marines dead or wounded, Colonel Howard burned the 4th Marines' colors and led his still combative regiment into the prison camps. As at Wake Island, the Marines could not stop the enemy, but they could add to the Corps's reputation for valor.

While the American armed forces in the western Pacific fought their gallant delaying action, the Joint Chiefs of Staff adjusted to a war with both Japan and the German–Italian Axis. With a commitment to emphasizing the war with Germany, General Marshall and Admiral King nonetheless acted to support MacArthur's forces and secure the outposts to Hawaii and the shipping routes to Australia. Army planners saw Australia as a "second Britain," an island bastion from which to mount air and naval attacks on the Japanese forces thrusting into the Netherlands East Indies. Admiral King was also interested in the South Pacific as the last refuge for the remnants of the Asiatic Fleet, which was staunchly but ineffectively trying to halt the Japanese along the Malay Barrier. On December 31 King ordered Admiral Chester A. Nimitz, the new commander of the Pacific Fleet, to defend the Hawaiian Islands and the routes to the United States with forward outposts at Midway, Johnston, and Palmyra and to guard the routes from the United States and Hawaii to Australia through Samoa and the Fiji Islands. Early in 1942 King envisioned a South Pacific base system for air and naval units that included the New Hebrides and New Caledonia. With the Navy too weak to challenge the Japanese in the central Pacific in 1942, the South Pacific theater for the moment seemed the only place to mount even the most limited counteroffensive. Despite the immense distances involved and the absence of existing bases, the South Pacific became the frontier of the war with Japan. The Japanese dramatized the southeast corner of their new empire by pushing naval units and naval landing forces into the area along an arc that ran from the British Gilberts into the Solomon Islands and the Bismarck Archipelago to the north coast of New Guinea. The growing threat to northern Australia was perceived by Admiral King and General MacArthur, who arrived in Australia in April under Roosevelt's orders to mount a new effort to halt the Japanese. The Joint Chiefs of Staff gave MacArthur his own theater, the Southwest Pacific Area, and assigned the rest of

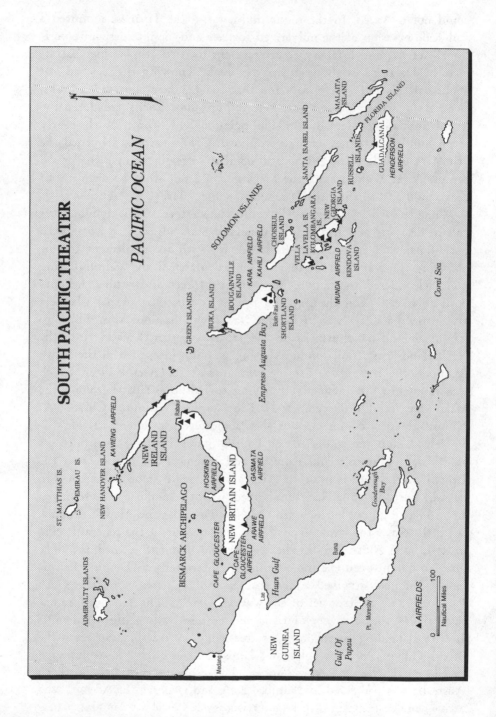

SOUTH PACIFIC THEATER

PACIFIC OCEAN

ST. MATTHIAS IS.

ADMIRALTY ISLANDS

MUSSAU IS.

NEW HANOVER ISLAND

KAVIENG AIRFIELD

NEW IRELAND ISLAND

BISMARCK ARCHIPELAGO

Rabaul

HOSKINS AIRFIELD

GASMATA AIRFIELD

NEW BRITAIN ISLAND

CAPE GLOUCESTER

CAPE GLOUCESTER AIRFIELD

ARAWE AIRFIELD

GREEN ISLANDS

BUKA ISLAND

BOUGAINVILLE ISLAND

Empress Augusta Bay

Buin-Faisi

SHORTLAND ISLAND

KARA AIRFIELD

KAHILI AIRFIELD

CHOISEUL ISLAND

SOLOMON ISLANDS

VELLA LAVELLA IS.

NEW GEORGIA IS.

MUNDA AIRFIELD

KOLOMBANGARA

RENDOVA ISLAND

SANTA ISABEL ISLAND

MALAITA ISLAND

FLORIDA ISLAND

RUSSELL ISLANDS

GUADALCANAL

HENDERSON AIRFIELD

Coral Sea

Medang

NEW GUINEA ISLAND

Lae

Huon Gulf

Bina

Gulf Of Papua

Pt. Moresby

Goodenough Bay

▲ AIRFIELDS

0   100
Nautical Miles

358

the Pacific theater (Pacific Ocean Areas) to Admiral Nimitz. American Army ground forces, Air Corps, Navy warships and land-based aircraft, and much of the Fleet Marine Force began to move into the South Pacific despite limited shipping and scarce base equipment.[29]

The Joint Chiefs' design for the war against Japan drew the Marine Corps far from the atolls of the central Pacific. Across thousands of miles Marine units, formed before Pearl Harbor or hurriedly assembled from continental stations, shifted westward. In December the 1st MAW moved from Quantico to San Diego, while units of the 4th Defense Battalion and a fighter squadron reinforced Midway and additional defense units joined the garrisons on Palmyra and Johnston islands. From the 2d Division the Corps formed a brigade around the 8th Marines, an artillery battalion of the 10th Marines, and the 2d Defense Battalion and sent it to Samoa. By March the 1st Marine Brigade had returned from Iceland, and the 6th Marines soon rejoined the 2d Marine Division. Two more squadrons arrived at Midway, giving the island commander a complete air group, MAG-22. Army ground units and AAF squadrons reached New Caledonia and the New Hebrides by April. MAG-13 flew into Samoa the same month. The 3d Marine Brigade, formed from the 1st Division's 7th Marines and the 7th Defense Battalion, reinforced Samoa's defenses, and the 4th Defense Battalion and VMF-212 moved into Efate in the New Hebrides by the end of April. On April 29 Admiral King designated the 1st Marine Division (still based at New River, North Carolina) as the amphibious force for the South Pacific theater. Even as he shored up the defense of the route to Australia, King pondered the possibility of a limited offensive against the Japanese. But first the Navy would have to halt the Japanese fleet, and the Marine Corps would have to provide adequate forces for its defensive and offensive missions.[30]

Instant Marines were not to be had and in fact, by Corps definition, were an impossibility, but at any rate the Japanese bombs that fell on Pearl Harbor, Wake Island, and Corregidor blew away the Corps's manpower ceilings. Before the end of February 1942 Roosevelt had ordered Commandant Holcomb to form a Corps of more than 160,000 officers and men as the pool from which to form a third division, seven more defense battalions, and another aircraft wing and bring the existing units to full strength. This strength was to be reached by June 1943. The Marine Corps, however, did not wait that long and soon received authorization to speed its enlistments. By June 30, 1942, the Corps had swollen to 143,388 officers and men. The recruiters hardly had to look for prospects. Before Pearl Harbor the Marine Corps had hired an advertising firm, J. Walter Thompson Inc., to recommend ways to improve recruiting, but after December 7 the lines in front of recruiting stations formed quickly. From a pre–Pearl Harbor one-week high of 552, the weekly enlistments soon ran as high as 6,000. Nearly 45,000 men joined in the first three months after Pearl Harbor. The quality of the recruits improved; rejection rates dropped from 40 percent to 15 percent. Recruiters offered "Japanese hunting licenses," promising the recruits unlimited rifles and ammunition; in Detroit the first showing of the Hollywood epic *Wake Island* in September brought 350 recruits in one night and $1.3 million in war bond purchases. Marine Corps recruiting posters urged the nation's toughest, most physically fit, and most patriotic youths to wear the "Globe and Anchor." For the Marine Corps 1942 was a special year, for it brought into the Corps some of the finest men it had seen since World War I.[31]

Hard pressed to handle the patriotic, naive, but eager hordes, the recruit depots concentrated on creating Marines, not combat-ready infantrymen. Lashed by drill instructors' (DI) tongues (physical violence seems to have been rare), the "boots" drilled, hiked, exercised, and learned the rudiments of Marine Corps traditions and customs. Significantly, the vast majority of World War II Marines passed through the recruit depots or similar officer-candidate courses at Quantico, and the same majority received basic infantry training, at least in handling weapons. As agencies of socialization the recruit depots were superb. Clad in loose green twill dungarees and pith helmets, the recruits labored, sweat running from their shaved skulls, and soon learned the unique behaviors and attitudes that made them Marines. They also learned a new language, the naval dialect that made lavatories "heads," floors "decks," and rumors and drinking fountains "scuttlebutt." [32] If they had not already added the word to their vocabulary, they were introduced to the Corps's all-purpose rhetorical curiosity:

> Always there was the word. Always there was that four-letter ugly sound that men in uniform have expanded into the single substance of the linguistic world. It was a handle, a hyphen, a hyperbole; verb, noun, modifier. . . . It described food, fatigue, metaphysics. It stood for everything and meant nothing; an insulting word, it was never used to insult; crudely descriptive of the sexual act, it was never used to describe it . . . one could only surmise that if a visitor unacquainted with English were to overhear our conversations he would, in the way of Higher Criticism, demonstrate . . . that this little word must assuredly be the thing for which we were fighting.[33]

The heart of the training was marksmanship. To have been a Marine and not be a rifleman was unthinkable to veteran Marines, from the

Commandant (himself a crack shot) down to the DIs. In addition to the careful marksmanship training at boot camp, the young Marines memorized a new creed, "My Rifle":

> This is my rifle. There are many like it but this one is mine. My rifle is my best friend. . . . Without my rifle, I am useless. I must fire my rifle true. I must shoot straighter than my enemy who is trying to kill me. I must shoot him before he shoots me. I will . . . . We will hit . . . . Before God I swear this creed. My rifle and myself are the defenders of my country. We are the saviors of my life. So be it until victory is America's and there is no enemy . . .[34]

Tactical and specialist training depended on the ability of the armed forces specialist schools and the FMF units, and the Marine Corps as early as 1942 found it difficult to ensure adequate access to schools run by the hard-pressed Army and Navy. Not until December 1942 did the Corps use the Army's classification tests to identify those men best suited for technical training. Because the Marine Corps before World War II had required so few proficient technical specialists, it could not easily create its own schooling system, and FMF units other than infantry battalions soon found themselves attempting to conduct rudimentary training in individual military jobs while they also attempted unit training. The recruit depots and specialist schools did their jobs well, but the Marine Corps could not overnight become a large, technologically sophisticated force ready for battle. Most of the Corps's early World War II specialists learned their skills in the field, often under fire.[35]

The training for Marine pilots provided the same skills learned by their Naval Aviation comrades but taught them precious little about the Marine Corps, because their precommissioning and postcommissioning training was in the Navy's hands. Only the presence of a few prewar Marine aviation officers and enlisted men gave Marine aviation some veneer of Corps character and exposure to the doctrine of close air support. Given the rapid expansion of Marine Corps aviation (from thirteen squadrons on December 7, 1941, to eighty-seven in 1943) and the integration of Marine aviation units into the Navy's land-based air organization, the wonder is not that Marine pilots learned the air superiority and fleet-destroying doctrines of the Navy but that they retained any Marine Corps character at all. Yet the indoctrination doggedly provided by senior officers gave Marine aviation a special flavor and an interest in the close support of ground troops. World War II may have created two different Marine Corps—one on the ground, one in the air—but they were not so different as to menace seriously the tradition that the Marine Corps should be an air-ground fighting force.[36]

The mobilization of 1942, however rapid and chaotic, soon brought the Fleet Marine Force to three full divisions by August 1942, but the process of filling the ranks of the scattered 1st and 2d Divisions and forming the 3d Marine Division inhibited stateside training at the unit level. The basic problems were not equipment shortages or a lack of semiskilled recruits, but the constant turnover of skilled officers and NCOs. The experience of the regiments that formed the nucleus of the 3d Marine Division is illustrative. The infantry regiments (3d Marines, 9th Marines, 21st Marines) were built around cadres provided by the 1st and 2d Divisions at the training camps in California and North Carolina, but no sooner were the new regiments formed than they had to provide more than half their strength as drafts for three more new regiments; the same process affected the artillery regiment (12th Marines) and engineer regiment (19th Marines). Although quick infusions of new officers and men soon brought the regiments back to full strength, unit training had to be repeated. In addition, the Headquarters and FMF staffs thought in 1942 that amphibious combat teams, each a reinforced infantry regiment, should train together in order to allow close personal liaison by the commanders and their staffs. This well-meaning policy meant that the training of specialized units (artillery, engineers, communications units) was too decentralized to use efficiently the few trained officers and NCOs and training facilities these units needed. Often regiments had to deploy overseas before their subordinate units reached a common high level of training and personnel stability. The 2d and 3d Marine Divisions found more time to train in New Zealand and Samoa. The 1st Division (with the exception of the 7th Marines) did not have this opportunity, for it suddenly received orders in early May to prepare for deployment to the South Pacific. Events in the Pacific war had overtaken the Fleet Marine Force.[37]

2

The Japanese conquest of the Netherlands East Indies was the most dramatic assault on the Malay Barrier, but Japanese army and navy units also brushed aside small Australian and native Melanesian units and occupied the islands of the Bismarck Archipelago and the northern and central Solomons. The Japanese quickly developed a base system anchored on the harbors and airfields of Rabaul on the northeast tip of New Britain island and Kavieng on New Ireland. The base system soon spread through New Britain to the north coast of New Guinea and through the Solomons from Bougainville to the islands of Vella Lavella,

Kolombangara, and New Georgia. The Japanese advance alarmed General MacArthur and Admiral King, the most ardent advocate on the JCS for a Pacific offensive. Both realized that the advances in the southeast corner of the Japanese "Southern Strategic Area" menaced the Allied bases in Australia, New Zealand, and the South Pacific. By March 1942 both MacArthur and King were urging limited offensive operations against the spreading Japanese base system. While still giving top priority to the war with Germany, Roosevelt approved such operations the same month, provided they would not jeopardize the American build-up in England. American planning then received a welcome boost from the American naval victories in the Coral Sea (May 4–8) and at Midway (June 3–6), and King and MacArthur pressured the JCS to approve a South Pacific offensive immediately.

Interservice differences on objectives and timing complicated American strategic planning, and no final decision came until July 2. In the meantime, Admiral King ordered Nimitz to prepare for an offensive using only naval forces. The CNO wanted to do something more than send carrier raids into the central Pacific, and he wanted to force the Army to divert more forces to the Pacific. King was also dubious about MacArthur's proposal to strike directly at Rabaul, a plan that underestimated Japanese strength and the dangers to naval forces in restricted waters. Instead, King advocated an essentially naval campaign against the Solomons, built around elements of the Pacific Fleet, a South Pacific amphibious force of Marine and Army divisions, and Army and Navy land-based air forces.

After considerable debate on who would exercise control of the campaign against Rabaul, the JCS approved a three-phase offensive. There was some urgency in their decision, because the Japanese were moving to new bases in southern New Guinea, Tulagi, and Guadalcanal in the southern Solomons. The JCS chose to meet the latter threat first. The initial offensive would be a naval thrust into the southern Solomons commanded by Nimitz, with his subordinate, Vice Admiral Robert L. Ghormley, CINC South Pacific, in immediate command. The next two phases of the offensive—clearing the rest of the Solomons and the northern coast of New Guinea and then assaulting Rabaul—would fall under General MacArthur's strategic direction. Neither Nimitz nor MacArthur had complete authority, hence the final decisions on force commitments, objectives, and timing remained in the hands of the JCS.[38]

The planning for the campaign in the Solomons continued under Admiral Nimitz and Admiral Ghormley. During July 1942 they selected the objectives and assembled the forces for Operation WATCHTOWER. Basically, the forces had to come from the naval forces in Nimitz's command, although MacArthur promised air strikes against Rabaul and sent his own cruiser forces to Ghormley. The planners learned that the tactical units, shipping, and supplies for WATCHTOWER were so limited that they dubbed the campaign "Operation Shoestring." The command system for WATCHTOWER was complicated by interservice sensitivities and the shortage of precious air cover. At least two of the senior commanders involved, Admiral Ghormley and Admiral Frank Jack Fletcher, were pessimistic to the point of defeatism about the operation. Ghormley, moreover, remained unsure about his authority over the Army air and ground units in his theater, and Nimitz compounded his problems by retaining control over Admiral Fletcher's carrier task force, the combat heart of the Pacific Fleet. None of the principals had any experience in amphibious operations, and the Solomons campaign gave them ample opportunity to demonstrate their ignorance.[39]

The selection of objectives was fairly simple, but Ghormley, in collaboration with Rear Admiral Richmond Kelly Turner, commander of the South Pacific amphibious force, made WATCHTOWER unnecessarily complex. Because the planners thought the critical question was air superiority, the principal objective would be the new Japanese airstrip near the Lunga River on Guadalcanal's north coast. If the Marines captured the air base, the Americans would control the southern Solomons and their adjacent waters. The planners, however, added other objectives to assault: the small islands of Tulagi and Gavutu-Tanambogo off the coast of Florida Island, some twenty miles from Guadalcanal. These small islands provided good anchorages for small craft and ships and were occupied by Japanese naval infantry and supply personnel. The Navy wanted the harbors for its own ships.

From the planning viewpoint, the critical problem was air cover for the landings: Japanese land-based aircraft were numerous in the Solomons and within range of Guadalcanal, and American land-based combat aircraft were not. To prevent Japanese air and surface attack on Turner's amphibious force, Nimitz provided three carriers commanded by Admiral Fletcher, who by virtue of seniority became the tactical commander afloat. Fletcher then announced that his carriers would cover the landing for four days at a maximum. Nimitz did not countermand him, and Ghormley did not appeal the decision. The airfield on Guadalcanal assumed new importance. Fletcher's decision also put a heavy burden on Turner's cruisers and destroyers, which would have to protect the troop and cargo ships against surface and air attack as well as guard against submarines.

Under pressure to start the operation, Ghormley and Turner obtained a postponement until August 7. For the amphibious force and the 1st

Marine Division the short delay did not solve all the problems. Turner's seventy-six ships were scattered from Australia to Pearl Harbor, and some vessels did not join the expedition until the run for Guadalcanal. The shortage of time and the lack of adequate transports and cargo ships, plus the task of organizing two simultaneous landings, presented Major General Alexander Archer Vandegrift, commander of the 1st Marine Division, with incredible difficulties. The organization of his landing force added to Vandegrift's problems, and only his optimistic disposition and professional skill, supported by an able division staff, gave the 1st Marine Division a sense of hope. Knowing little of the Japanese forces or the terrain at Guadalcanal (code-named "Cactus") and unable to assemble adequate maps and aerial photographs, Vandegrift shaped the landing to the available troops. The 1st Division lacked one infantry regiment, the 7th Marines of the Samoa garrison, which was replaced by the 2d Marines from the 2d Marine Division. Admiral Turner, however, declared that this regiment was his reserve and would be used to occupy Ndeni in the nearby Santa Cruz islands. The regiment was not Vandegrift's to use. Its loss was partially offset by the addition of the 1st Parachute Battalion and the 1st Raider Battalion, which Vandegrift assigned to the Tulagi and Gavutu-Tanambogo landings along with one of his own infantry battalions and supporting units. The Guadalcanal landings on beaches five miles west of the Lunga River would be made by the five remaining battalions of the 1st and 5th Marines, the rest of the division, and the 3d Defense Battalion.[40]

WATCHTOWER quickly became a logistical nightmare for the 1st Division, because the Navy could not provide adequate sealift for all the troops and all the division's supplies and vehicles. Thus the success of the invasion depended upon uninterrupted resupply after the landing, particularly in engineering and aviation equipment. Nor was the Navy's South Pacific base system ready yet to support an operation as ambitious as WATCHTOWER. When Turner's amphibious ships finally put to sea, they carried only sixty days' general supplies, enough ammunition for ten days' serious fighting, the minimum of personal baggage, and less than half the division's vehicles, essentially the lighter ones. The loading was complicated by the fact that the division had sailed to New Zealand loaded not for operations but for the most economical use of space. The division had to unload and reload its ships in New Zealand. The process was complicated by heavy rains, a dock workers' strike, and the poor boxing of the division's supplies. The 1st Division Marines long remembered the chaos on Wellington's lone quay: lines of wet, hungry, tired Marines manhandling supplies, trudging ankle deep in ruined food and cardboard boxes, their work running night and day under flickering lights—and all for what they thought was a mere training exercise.[41]

After a limited rehearsal in the Fiji Islands, useful only in exercising the Navy's landing craft in the ship-to-shore movement, Turner's amphibious force sailed for the Solomons on July 31. From Admiral Turner to the 1st Division's youngest private, the chief concern was whether the division would get ashore the first day. Blessed by bad weather and Japanese inattention, the amphibious task force slipped safely into the waters between Guadalcanal and Florida islands during the night of 6–7 August. As dawn broke, the 1st Division took its first look at Guadalcanal, "an island of striking beauty. Blue-green mountains, towering into a brilliant tropical sky. . . dominate the island. The dark green of jungle growth blends into the softer greens and browns of coconut groves and grassy plains and ridges." [42] Not entirely clear from the troop ships were the heavily forested rivers and open ridges that were to play an important role in the campaign. As Turner's cruisers and destroyers opened fire on the coastline and Navy planes darted along the shore to strafe and bomb, all eyes were on the beaches.

To everyone's immense relief the landings on August 7 went largely as planned, and by nightfall most of the landing force was ashore. On Tulagi and Gavutu-Tanambogo, the Marines met stubborn resistance from eight hundred Japanese, and it took three days of close fighting to secure the islands. The three assault battalions found the Japanese in caves, using machine guns to riddle the Marines, who had to dynamite and grenade the enemy to extinction. The landings had one advantage, for Vandegrift persuaded Turner to return most of the 2d Marines, whose added weight ensured a speedy victory. The main landing was an unexpected success, as the surprised Japanese abandoned their camps and headed for the mountains. The 1st and 5th Marines secured the beach area and swung west to take the airfield. The Marines, however, found that their primitive maps (prepared from Australian interviews) were inaccurate; they did not learn until much later that they had misidentified both the rivers and the high ground in their area. Nevertheless, the infantry established a perimeter and prepared to take the airfield the next day, even though the men were gasping with heat exhaustion and units had become scrambled in the thick jungle. On the beaches, the unloading of artillery, engineering equipment, and supplies slowed. The Marines and sailors assigned to stevedore duties could not move the supplies without more men and vehicles. The landings proved that infantry units could get ashore with commendable speed but also demonstrated that Navy–Marine logistical arrangements left much to be desired. The ability of the 1st Division to establish itself ashore for extended operations depended upon Japanese lethargy. Since air attacks on Turner's task force had been beaten back by Fletcher's fighters and anti-aircraft fire without serious loss on August 7, Turner was confident that the unloading could continue as planned and the carriers could leave without undue risk. At the moment of victory, however, WATCH-TOWER went to pieces, and the 1st Division found itself in a situation it compared with Wake Island.[43]

The fate of the campaign on Guadalcanal depended on the Navy's ability to stop Japanese reinforcements from overwhelming the 1st Division, to protect the division from air and naval attack, and to keep the flow of men and supplies coming to Vandegrift's command. Until the end of November 1942 victory hung in balance. In six major engagements with the Japanese navy, the Navy lost twenty-four warships and thousands of men. It did not really secure victory until a series of naval engagements off Guadalcanal on November 12–15. The first engagement set the tone of the bitter struggle. Early in the morning of August 9 a Japanese cruiser force eluded the inadequate American patrol planes and destroyer pickets and sank four cruisers and a destroyer off Savo Island. Coupled with the hurried departure of Fletcher's carriers, the destruction of Turner's surface screen forced the transports to hurry off with only half their cargoes unloaded. The 1st Division was left with no air cover and scant supplies. Within a week fast destroyer-transports were shuttling in scarce supplies, but the resupply effort was at best sporadic. At night Japanese warships—"the Tokyo Express"—drove down "The Slot" to bombard the Marines and to convoy troop ships to the island, landing 30,000 men with artillery and tanks. The cautious Admiral Ghormley and his welcome successor, Vice Admiral William F. Halsey, fought back with surface units and carrier air. In the daytime naval air battles the Navy hurt the Japanese fleet (but lost two carriers), but in night surface actions the American battleships and cruisers took heavy punishment from Japanese guns and long-range torpedoes. Only when Halsey replaced Ghormley in October and threw his fleet, reinforced under direct orders from Roosevelt, at the Japanese with greater skill and urgency did the naval battle turn, and with it the campaign.[44]

While the fleets battered each other, the air battle roared on in the skies above Guadalcanal. For Marine aviation it was probably the war's finest moment. On August 20 the first two of fifteen Marine fighter and dive-bomber squadrons flew to Guadalcanal's Henderson Field. Vandegrift's air units, which included Navy, AAF, and New Zealand squadrons, waged a six-month campaign to stop air attacks on the Marine position and destroy incoming Japanese troop ships. At a loss of more than one hundred aircraft and nearly three hundred pilots (about one hundred killed), the "Cactus Air Force" downed at least four hundred Japanese planes and destroyed ten transports. For the Marine airmen, the campaign redeemed a reputation partially tarnished by the ineffectiveness of the two land-based Marine squadrons that had been virtually wiped out during the battle of Midway. At Guadalcanal the Marines now flew first-rate aircraft and proved their ability to down every kind of Japanese aircraft, from the elusive "Zero" to twin-engine bombers. Directed from the ground by Brigadier General Roy Geiger and Colonel Louis Woods, who established a forward headquarters of the 1st MAW on Guadalcanal, the Marine pilots survived naval shelling and almost daily bombings of Henderson Field and eventually won control of the air in the southern Solomons. Flying F4Fs, the pilots, lead by aces like John Smith, Joe Bauer, Joe Foss, and Marion Carl, splashed Japanese aircraft while the dive-bomber squadrons punished the convoys. Operating on scarce supplies, the Marine ground crews patched, fueled, and armed aircraft by hand so that their overworked, underfed pilots could meet each Japanese assault. Marine and Navy "Seabee" engineer battalions patched Henderson Field and carved another strip from the jungle. Although close air support for the 1st Division was impaired by poor communications, the 1st MAW proved decisive in holding "Cactus." [45]

The ground battle for Guadalcanal proved as difficult and uncertain as the naval and air campaigns, and the fight did not shift decisively until November. Worried by short supplies and the possibility of a Japanese counterlanding, General Vandegrift concentrated his three infantry regiments, artillery regiment, defense battalion, and supporting units along the coast on both sides of the Lunga River. He covered the interior with patrols, which soon proved that the Marines had much to learn about jungle warfare. The Marines (aided by British-led native scouts) found out that the Japanese army was approaching their perimeter from the interior. To meet this threat Vandegrift drew the raiders, the parachutists, and two infantry battalions from Tulagi. When the Japanese struck, the Marines met them with punishing tank and artillery fire and desperate infantry defense. At the Battles of the Tenaru River (August 21) and Raider Ridge (September 12–14), the 1st Division virtually wiped out three Japanese regiments. Correctly deciding that the Japanese would put more pressure on his western flank along the Matanikau River, Vandegrift received vital reinforcements in mid-September, his wayward 7th Marines, and shifted to the offensive in order to enlarge his perimeter. On the offensive the 1st Division proved less proficient, failing to drive off the Japanese in a series of punishing fights along the Matanikau in late September and early October. While continuing minor operations and heavy combat patrolling, Vandegrift husbanded his troops, requested more reinforcements, and awaited the major Japanese attack he felt certain would still be launched at Henderson Field.[46]

For the Marines of the 1st Division the campaign for Guadalcanal became an ordeal in which death and wounds were only part of the dangers endured. They had entered the battle convinced they would be soon relieved by the Army and confident of their mission: "War was killing. Seeking out the enemy and killing . . . without mercy. . . . It was something like being a Boy Scout. You camped out. You killed for God and Country. There was no plan to die." [47] Their resolve to kill Japanese hardened early in the campaign, when a patrol led by the division intelligence officer was annihilated under circumstances that suggested treachery; thereafter, the division intelligence section experienced difficulty in finding Japanese prisoners. The Marines respected the skill and tenacity of the Japanese in the defense but viewed their suicidal assaults with contempt. Their fear of the Japanese as a superman vanished. But there were other enemies. Japanese bombing and shelling, especially a punishing battleship bombardment on October 14, tore at the nerves. The short rations and limited rest eventually pared an average of thirty pounds from each man, and in October a malaria epidemic hospitalized two thousand men. Other assorted fevers and infections put more Marines out of commission than did bullets. The troops also developed a gnawing suspicion that the rest of the American armed forces had forgotten them, that their ordeal was a secret in the United States. Bearded, thin, clad in ragged dungarees, they longed for relief and sang of their contempt for the Navy, General MacArthur, and anyone not part of the 1st Marine Division:

> For we're saying goodbye to them all
> As back to our foxholes we crawl
> There'll be no promotion
> This side of the ocean
> So cheer up, my lads,
> Fuck 'em all.

Disgruntled and cynical, the 1st Division Marines watched their ranks thin but continued to fight the jungle and Japanese with grim fatalism.[48]

By early November the land battle slowly shifted in the 1st Division's favor, but not before the Japanese army made one last major assault on Henderson Field. With some twenty thousand troops on the island, the Japanese commander, Lieutenant General Haruyoshi Hyakutake, could throw more than a division, backed by ample artillery and tanks, against the perimeter. In a series of ill-coordinated attacks on October 21–28, the Japanese assaulted Vandegrift's lines at the mouth of the Matanikau and along the ridges east of the Lunga River. Again the Marines broke the attacks with determined infantry defense and supporting weapons and with timely counterattacks, which included the Army's newly arrived 164th Infantry Regiment. At a cost of two hundred Marines and soldiers, the 1st Division killed nearly three thousand Japanese and broke Hyakutake's will to attack the perimeter. As the Japanese again faded into the jungles, Vandegrift prepared to take the offense and stay on the attack. The difference now was that he knew that Roosevelt had approved, at the urging of Admirals King, Nimitz, and Halsey, a general redeployment of the Pacific forces. The 1st Division was close to exhaustion, but it would soon be reinforced by the 2d Marine Division and the Army's Americal Division and 25th Infantry Division. In addition, Vandegrift had finally managed to halt Admiral Turner's questionable schemes to send troops to other enclaves on Guadalcanal and to other parts of the southern Solomons. The battle for Guadalcanal was to be won first.[49]

In November Vandegrift's force, which soon grew to the equivalent of two divisions, started large-scale attacks along the western coast, while other battalions pushed eastward against scattered resistance. An epic long patrol by the 2d Raider Battalion disclosed that the majority of the Japanese garrison remained west of the perimeter, so Vandegrift committed the bulk of his force to the Matanikau front. Despite stubborn Japanese resistance and occasional Marine setbacks, the offensive continued into December and January against lessening resistance, for the Japanese high command had decided to fight a delaying action and to withdraw its survivors when further resistance was clearly futile. In the middle of the campaign the 1st Division finally left Guadalcanal, and Vandegrift turned his command over to Major General Alexander M. Patch, USA. Fighting alongside two Army divisions, the 2d Marine Division participated in the drive toward the island's northwestern capes. When the Japanese evacuated the last survivors in early February 1943, the struggle for Guadalcanal ended as an American victory, for which the Marine Corps paid with 1,152 dead and 2,799 wounded.[50]

The Guadalcanal campaign produced ample "lessons learned" in jungle warfare for the 1st and 2d Marine Divisions and in air superiority operations for Marine aviation. The principal influence on future amphibious operations, however, came in the area of Marine Corps–Navy command relations. From the beginning Admiral Turner and General Vandegrift had waged a war of words over control of the landing force of the South Pacific amphibious force. Turner's orders gave him clear authority over Vandegrift's command, but the extended nature of the land campaign produced problems unforeseen in prewar amphibious doctrine. Essentially, Turner wanted to influence Vandegrift's operations by controlling his access to reinforcements, which Turner often assigned to missions Vandegrift thought peripheral to the main battle on Guadalcanal. Besides, Turner toyed with the organization of Marine forces outside Vandegrift's immediate control. For example, he organized a provisional raider battalion from elements of the 2d Marine Division and urged his superiors to press the Marine Corps to create more small, raider-type landing teams. The long-suffering Vandegrift finally enlisted the help of Commandant Holcomb, who visited Guadalcanal. Holcomb persuaded Admirals Halsey, Nimitz, and King to accept an important modification of FTP-167, the doctrinal manual for amphibious operations. Henceforth, the Navy agreed, the landing force commander would be subordinate to the amphibious task force commander only during the actual movement to the objective area and the initial landings. During the planning stages and the land campaign, the Navy and Marine commanders would be coequals; they would submit their disagreements to the common superior (presumably a Navy theater commander) for resolution. In addition, Holcomb, who nursed this reform through channels, established a Marine Corps headquarters—I Marine Amphibious Corps—in the South Pacific in order to coordinate all Marine ground units, principally in the areas of logistics and administration. This additional echelon of Marine Corps command would presumably protect Marine tactical commanders from Navy interference and lighten the worries of division commanders. Whereas Turner was miffed by the change, the senior Marine and Navy commanders in the Pacific believed they had eliminated an important barrier to future Navy–Marine Corps cooperation. Their optimism was not totally justified, but in the euphoria that followed Guadalcanal the reform looked ironclad.[51]

3

As the campaign to capture Rabaul progressed on New Guinea and in the Solomons, operations against the Japanese developed into a protracted war of attrition waged over thousands of miles of ocean. The Marine Corps continued to adjust and expand to meet its growing role in the Pacific conflict. As they did throughout the war, the Joint Chiefs of Staff and the JCS planning arm, the Joint United States Strategic Committee, set the guidelines for Marine Corps expansion and deployment. In a study concluded while the Guadalcanal campaign raged, the

JCS ratified the earlier decisions that had sent the Marines to the Pacific. Army divisions would make up the landing force in the European-Mediterranean area and the Southwest Pacific. Three Marine divisions would comprise the landing forces for the South Pacific. Although the Central Pacific corps might include Marine and Army divisions, the Army planners agreed it should have a Marine general as commander.[52] As for Marine Corps strength, the JCS approved a Corps of 22,661 officers and 285,000 enlisted men by July 1943. (Actual strength on June 30, 1943, was 21,938 and 287,621.) Army planners wondered why the Corps needed so many men for only three divisions and wings, but the Navy convinced President Roosevelt that the Corps was sending its men into combat in commendable percentages, estimating that in 1943 70 percent of the Corps would be serving in the Fleet Marine Force, and 50 percent would be deployed abroad.[53] Roosevelt approved the plans in September 1942. In fact, Commandant Holcomb soon found that he had enough men to activate a fourth division and air wing, a decision accepted by the JCS.

The increasing scope of amphibious operations in the Pacific forced Headquarters to reorganize and expand the FMF. As the Solomons campaign developed, it activated the 3d Marine Division (September 1942), 3d Marine Aircraft Wing (November 1942), 4th Marine Division (August 1943), and 4th Marine Base Defense Aircraft Wing (August 1943). All four organizations absorbed tactical units already in training.

Headquarters also realized that Marine operations had become far too large and geographically dispersed to be managed only at the division and air wing level. Ground units in the South Pacific were assigned to the I Marine Amphibious Corps (I MAC), while other units passed to the control of the Amphibious Corps Pacific Fleet, a headquarters colocated with CINCPAC in Hawaii. The latter corps also supervised landing force training in Hawaii and California. Ground organization continued to be complicated by the proliferation of special units, primarily additional defense and raider battalions. Acknowledging the rapid expansion and complex logistical problems of Marine aviation, Holcomb in 1943 made the director of aviation an assistant commandant after appointing a pilot-general commander of Marine Aircraft Wings, Pacific, in 1942.

In the final analysis, the Marine command structure in the Pacific was only as good as the senior officers who ran the new headquarters, and in 1943 the Commandant found himself short of generals who could grasp the scope of the Pacific campaign. On the verge of his own retirement, General Holcomb did his best to leave a Corps strong at the top. Holcomb's choice for his successor was no surprise: General Vandegrift.

Given Vandegrift's high repute in the Corps, enhanced by the Guadalcanal campaign and his new public acclaim, Holcomb safely assumed his appointment would be both wise and popular. Although dubious as to whether Holland M. Smith's temper could survive the stresses of interservice relations, Holcomb confirmed the fiery Alabaman's position as commander of the Amphibious Corps Pacific Fleet. The South Pacific post, commander of I MAC, proved the most bothersome. Major General Clayton B. Vogel, the first incumbent, proved unsuited to the post and returned to the States to train troops. Vandegrift assumed the command temporarily before returning to Headquarters but soon (September 1943) relinquished the job to Major General Charles D. Barrett, an amphibious pioneer and much-liked officer. Within a month, however, Barrett died of injuries received in an accidental fall. Vandegrift again took over I MAC but then turned the post over to Major General Roy S. Geiger, an aviator with an infantryman's grasp of ground operations. With his appointment, the South Pacific Marines found a commander worthy of their mettle.[54]

Whereas establishing a system of command for the amphibious war was challenging, Headquarters found that meeting its expanded manpower requirements after the early 1942 flood of enlistments had abated was still more troublesome. Headquarters preferred to recruit officers from colleges and process them through the Marine Corps Schools candidates program, but recruiters could not find adequate numbers of volunteers in 1942, and the Marine Corps shifted to other programs. The substitute was to commission enlisted men with college education (a requirement soon dropped to high school level), meritorious noncommissioned officers, and men with some prior service or military training. More than half the 5,618 officers commissioned in 1942 received direct commissions. The results were mixed. The 1942 programs, though they democratized entry into the officer ranks, also allowed uneven screening and insufficient training, a condition FMF commanders complained about in 1943. Aided by the threat of the draft and the creation of the Navy's V-12 program, which kept officer candidates in college, Headquarters cut down direct commissioning and successfully depended upon the officer candidate courses at Quantico and the V-12 program for officers after 1942.[55]

Enlisted recruiting went through equally complex structural changes. For all the recruiting hoopla and its supposed love affair with American youth after Pearl Harbor, the Marine Corps had difficulty meeting all its 1942 goals with volunteers. In April 1942 the physical and moral standards of recruits were lowered in order to meet quotas. Three months later the upper age limit rose from thirty-three to thirty-six.

But in December Roosevelt ended volunteering and placed all man-power in the eighteen to thirty-six age group under Selective Service. In 1943, therefore, the Marine Corps had to adjust to recruiting within the general structure of the draft while attempting to retain its elitest, volunteer image. It did so in two basic ways. The first was to identify draftees who preferred serving in the Marine Corps, to steer these men (through the use of Marine liaison personnel at induction centers) into the Corps, and then to change their status to regulars or Reserves. Of the 224,323 draftees who entered the Corps, only some 70,000 remained in an inductee status. To make this program work, the Corps needed the cooperation of civilian authorities, which it won with much friendly persuasion. Selective Service, however, did not fill the Corps's quotas. To meet its enlisted needs, Headquarters urged its recruiters to enlist seventeen-year-olds, who were true volunteers, in the Marine Corps Reserve. Headquarters could then call these youths to active duty to meet its quotas. Between 1943 and 1945 nearly 60,000 youths entered active duty under this program, giving the replacement drafts and new divisions a definite adolescent tinge.[56]

In the throes of war the Marine Corps's social character changed, for in the rapid expansion of 1942 and 1943 the Corps enlisted both women and Negroes. Neither group (enlisted as Reservists) was particularly welcome, and neither appeared to be any more than a wartime expedient largely forced upon the Corps for domestic political reasons. From General Holcomb down to the ranks, there was considerable unhappiness about making the Corps anything but a club for white men. Women joined the Corps with more enthusiasm than many of their male peers, for they were unaffected by the draft, and the Women's Reserve easily met its quotas ahead of schedule. More than twenty thousand women joined the Corps for wartime service. The Division of Reserve at Headquarters contributed to the program's success by insisting that women Marines were not auxiliaries and did not form a unique all-women's branch like the WACS or the WAVES. The Corps's policy in assigning women, however, demonstrated that it had not suddenly marched to the front of the feminist movement. Despite some rhetoric about a sexless Marine Corps and pressure from Mrs. Roosevelt, the Marine Corps did not provide field and weapons training for its women, assigning them to administrative, clerical, and a limited number of technical jobs. The variety of assignments available to women Marines was much greater than it had been in World War I, but women never moved very close to the Corps's basic functions of ground and air combat, even by World War II standards. Essentially, the women Marines did what Headquarters expected them to do—meet Marine Corps standards in appearance and discipline and replace men in rear-area jobs, thus freeing male Marines for FMF assignments in the Pacific.[57]

Blacks were even less welcome than women in the Corps, the Marine Corps having been (unlike the Army and Navy) an absolutely segregated organization. Headquarters had no taste for social experiments in the midst of war. At the insistence of the Roosevelt administration, which was worried about black cooperation in the war effort and later elections, the Marine Corps agreed to form a few all-black units (officered by whites) in 1942. Reluctant to put blacks into combat units for fear of their supposed ineffectiveness, Headquarters at least recognized the right of blacks to fight and even acknowledged that they might have some technical skills. Thus it organized its first black recruits into a defense battalion. Matching carefully screened black recruits with select officers and NCOs and placing them in a separate training base at Montford Point, North Carolina, Headquarters made the Corps' first black unit a success—even if they had been treated with a care unknown in the "real" Corps. As training progressed, black NCOs assumed the responsibility of driving their eager men to Marine Corps proficiency with their base defense artillery and machine guns. A second all-black defense battalion was organized in 1943, and both battalions soon deployed to the Pacific, but neither saw combat. Still pressed to enlist blacks, the Corps responded by creating sixty-three black depot and ammunition companies, a designation that meant essentially labor units. Because the Corps was chronically short-handed for beach labor troops, however, some of these companies made combat landings in the Pacific and occasionally served as infantrymen, suffering nearly one hundred combat casualties. By the end of the war more than 15,000 blacks were in green, a figure considerably less than 10 percent of Corps total strength, the quota set in 1943. The black Marines served well, although in the Pacific they faced frustration and racial discrimination, mostly in their relations with enlisted Marines and sailors. There was, however, no intention at Headquarters to continue the units after the war ended.[58]

Besides bringing the Marine Corps to a size and a social composition never before experienced, the war in the Pacific required the Corps to cope with logistical problems of unprecedented size and complexity. Because matériel requirements were computed to fit the Corps's manpower strength and the types of units it formed, logistical planning remained in flux well into 1944. Logistical planning, however, shared by the Quartermaster Department, the Aviation Division, and the Division of Plans and Policies, was not the heart of the Corps's supply problems. Basically, the Corps had to create a system for procuring, storing, and distributing matériel virtually from scratch. It did so by attaching its own supply activities to those of the Navy and Army and extemporizing its own system only when absolutely necessary. In the United States this policy generally worked well. Even when it was convinced that it had equipment and weapons superior to Army and Navy models, Headquarters accepted standardization for the sake of efficiency and to limit the numbers of men soaked up by the supply system. During World War II 65 percent of Marine Corps equipment and supplies (measured by numbers of types) came from Army sources; 5 percent came from the Navy; 5 percent were manufactured only for or by the Marine Corps; and 25 percent came directly from commercial sources. For classification purposes the Corps adopted the Army's five-class system but never did establish a uniform system during the war.

The distribution of supplies presented more serious problems. The Corps simplified distribution by using both Army and Navy rail and maritime shipping systems, but it had to establish a complex depot system in California. The Corps's depot in San Francisco proved inadequate to handle the volume of shipments, so the Corps established a new depot in Barstow, California, and a series of smaller installations in the San Diego–Camp Pendleton area to service outward-bound FMF units. The sheer volume of aviation and heavy equipment matériel and ordnance (one hundred amphibian tractors required twenty boxcars of spare parts) and military shipping congestion on the West Coast in 1943 forced Headquarters to create an alternative system. The solution was to send matériel destined for the Pacific forces to underutilized Gulf Coast ports and ship them through the Panama Canal. This expedient put an additional strain on the supply facilities at Philadelphia and Camp Lejeune.[59]

In the Pacific the Marine Corps logistical effort was hampered by shipping shortages, overused and underdeveloped supply bases, and dependence on the Army and Navy. The Marine Corps also had to learn much of its logistical wisdom on the job. Supply duty had never attracted the Corps's best officers, and logistical administration proved less imaginative than tactical operations. Marine ground forces and aviation seldom lacked supplies when shipping was available, but the Corps could not claim that it had established an optimum system of shipping and storing supplies from the United States to the Pacific beachheads. The structure of American military logistics in the Pacific placed a high premium on interservice harmony, particularly for the dependent Marine Corps. This was a lesson some senior Marine commanders did not fully appreciate, but it was a situation thoroughly understood at Headquarters.[60]

4

As the campaigns for Buna on New Guinea and for the southern Solomons ended in early 1943, the Joint Chiefs of Staff and MacArthur, Nimitz, and Halsey reexamined their directives of 1942 and the prospects for further action in the South Pacific. At the global level the JCS won the approval of Roosevelt and the British at the Casablanca conference (January 1943) for increasing the forces in the Pacific as long as such reinforcements did not endanger operations in the Mediterranean and the build-up in England for the invasion of France. The American planners, especially Admiral King, having reservations about the conduct of the war against the Germans in 1943, pressed successfully for a continuation of the drive towards Rabaul.[61] The strategic implementation of the war against the Japanese in the South Pacific remained, however, a delicate exercise in interservice diplomacy as well as strategic analysis. Not until the end of March 1943 did the JCS, MacArthur, and Nimitz hammer out a satisfactory arrangement.

The essential outline of the plan was to continue a two-axis approach to Rabaul under MacArthur's general direction, but with Admiral Nimitz still in control of the area's two naval forces, the 7th Fleet with MacArthur and the 3d Fleet under Halsey. MacArthur's forces would work their way up New Guinea's north coast until they had freed the straits between New Guinea and New Britain. They would then seize western New Britain. Halsey's forces would advance northwestward through the Solomons until they gained a base on Bougainville and neutralized the Japanese positions east of Rabaul. In early 1944 the two theater forces would converge on Rabaul. Because part of this plan, Operation CARTWHEEL, included the continued bombardment of Rabaul and Kavieng, the objectives in the campaign would be determined largely by air warfare considerations. The American advance required that naval and ground forces operate within the range of land-based AAF, Navy, and Marine air and that the American landings be designed to capture or isolate Japanese airfields. Neither MacArthur nor Halsey felt that they had adequate air strength, particularly heavy bombers, so they chose a conservative, step-by-step approach toward Rabaul. Their ground strength, which they also believed marginal, reinforced their caution, as did Admiral Nimitz, who did not want to risk his carrier task forces in restricted waters. The result was a campaign characterized not by strategic surprise but by careful timing on the part of MacArthur and Halsey, so that the Japanese would have to defend their positions simultaneously (and weakly) on New Guinea and in the Solomons.[62]

In addition to their growing naval and air superiority (Allied air outnumbered the Japanese by about 2:1), the American amphibious forces gave MacArthur and Halsey a tactical flexibility that compensated for their strategic conservatism. In early 1943 the amphibious forces in the South Pacific began to receive welcome reinforcements to their groups of transports, cargo ships, and destroyer-transports. The new arrivals, largely the product of British designers and efficient American shipyards, were ungainly looking, unseaworthy, and absolutely necessary for future landings. The new vessels were landing ships and craft—the Landing Ship Tank (LST), Landing Ship Dock (LSD), Landing Ship Medium (LSM), Landing Craft Infantry (LCI), and Landing Craft Tank (LCT). The common feature of all these vessels, except the LCI, was that they could load and unload vehicles directly on a beach. All but the LSD could actually beach and discharge troops and vehicles from bow ramps and doors. The LSD, however, could carry preloaded smaller landing craft in its flooded well deck and launch these beaching craft without additional handling. The LCI, which came in several versions, was designed to carry more than two hundred infantrymen, who disembarked from the beached craft on ramps. The addition of the landing ships and craft to the South Pacific amphibious forces meant the speed and military weight of the ship-to-shore movement increased and that essential tanks, artillery, engineering vehicles, and truck-borne supplies would join the infantry more quickly than they had at Guadalcanal. Their use also meant that amphibious planners could choose beaches that were hardly beaches at all, which complicated Japanese defense planning.[63]

With the exception of the 1st Marine Division, which was assigned to MacArthur's theater for retraining and eventual use on New Britain, Marine Corps participation in CARTWHEEL focused on the Solomons. For Admiral Halsey's ground forces, I MAC provided the 2d and 3d Marine Divisions and raider and defense battalions. The force represented about one-third of Halsey's ground forces, while the Army provided four infantry divisions and assorted smaller units. In the summer of 1943, however, I MAC could provide only raider and defense battalions; the 2d Division was recuperating from Guadalcanal, and the 3d Division was still training. The Marine Corps also provided around one-third of the nearly eight hundred aircraft committed by COMAIR-SOPAC to operations in the Solomons. Like their Navy and AAF brethren, Marine squadrons rotated to and from bases in the Solomons, where their operations were directed by COMAIRSOLS, an all-service air command headquarters. In 1943 more than thirty Marine squadrons of all varieties supported Halsey's forces. For Marine aviators, the most welcome development was the arrival of a truly superior fighter, the Chance-Vought F4U "Corsair." The gull-winged fighter had the range, armament, and handling characteristics necessary to match the Japanese Zero in aerial combat. Technically unsuited for carrier service, the Corsair was perfect for land-based Marine squadrons, which could use it for both air superiority and close-support missions. Because Marine ground and air units were leavened with Guadalcanal veterans and new equipment—from Corsairs to Sherman tanks to camouflaged jungle uniforms —was flowing to Marine units, the Marines in the South Pacific entered the renewed offensive with confidence.[64]

Along with other American and Allied units, the Marines faced a Japanese defense force in the Solomons that was already waning in strength and quality, but not in fighting spirit. By mid-1943, when CARTWHEEL began, the Japanese had shifted to both strategic and tactical defense. Their last great effort, an air offensive against MacArthur's and Halsey's bases in April 1943, did little to slow American preparations. In the Solomons, an area generally dominated by Japanese naval commanders, the Americans faced the equivalent of two Japanese army divisions, a navy special landing brigade, some six hundred land-based army and navy aircraft, and the cruisers and destroyers of the 8th Fleet. The Japanese surface units and land-based naval aviation could be reinforced by ships and planes from the Combined Fleet, based at Truk, but Japanese naval commanders were reluctant to strip their central Pacific forces to fight a war of attrition in the South Pacific. Instead they hoped that poor weather, rugged terrain, and thick jungles, exploited by air and naval raiders and suicidal ground defenders, would stop the Americans.[65]

Even before MacArthur and Halsey massed their forces for the opening of CARTWHEEL in June 1943, Halsey and his immediate tactical commander, the demanding, difficult Richmond Kelly Turner, started their amphibious march up the Solomons by sending most of an Army division and a Marine raider battalion to seize the Russell Islands northwest of Guadalcanal. The islands would be used for fighter bases to cover the assault on the central Solomons. This force occupied the undefended Russells in February 1943. The sortie was only a prelude to the attack on the New Georgia island group, principally the islands of New Georgia and Rendova, in June. Halsey's and Turner's planners computed air distances and forces and cast covetous eyes on the Japanese airfield at Munda on the southwest shore of New Georgia. They designed a complex operation of six landings to seize Munda, using two Army divisions assisted by two Marine defense and two raider battalions. The role of the Marines was to capture several small-boat anchorages on the southern New Georgia coast, to isolate Munda by capturing the Japanese way stations on the northern coast of New Georgia, and to establish a heavy artillery position on Rendova that would cover the Army attack on Munda.

Impeded by rain and the inexperience of the Army divisions in jungle warfare, the Munda campaign lasted far longer than the planners had anticipated and did not end until late August 1943. The landings on Rendova and along New Georgia's south coast in early July went largely as planned, and the Navy ensured that Japanese air and naval units did not seriously disturb the operation. For the Marines, playing a supporting role, the campaign was arduous enough. The raider battalion that landed on the south coast secured its objectives against scattered resistance but found the terrain and weather a trial. Along the north coast, Colonel Harry B. Liversedge's 1st Raider Regiment, which controlled two Marine raider battalions and two Army battalions, fought hard to cut the Japanese resupply routes but, having insufficient men and firepower, did not completely disrupt Japanese reinforcements sent to Munda. Battling thick jungle and heavy rains, the raider assaults gutted Liversedge's force and did not—for all the raiders' undeniable courage—affect the battle for Munda. The Army assault on the Japanese airstrip went so poorly that the senior Army commander was relieved by Halsey and Turner, an act that strained interservice relations. For the Marines, the slogging attack on Munda provided an opportunity for the defense battalions to prove their value. In the attacks that eventually breached the Japanese defenses west of the airstrip, three Marine tank platoons provided essential fire support for the Army infantry, for only tanks could penetrate the system of pillboxes the Japanese manned in the jungle. At the same time Marine heavy artillery pounded Munda from Rendova, and Marine anti-aircraft batteries protected the artillery positions. Marine units also assisted the Army's XIV Corps in its landings on Vella Lavella in late August, an operation that concluded the central Solomons phase of CARTWHEEL.[66]

The central Solomons campaign once again demonstrated the critical importance of providing effective air support for an amphibious operation, and COMAIRSOLS, operating from Guadalcanal and the Russells, provided this support with some thirty-two fighter and bomber squadrons, six of which were Marines. In addition to continuing their raids on Rabaul, American pilots attacked Japanese air bases throughout the Solomons and flew cover for Turner's amphibious force and its escorts. In two weeks of intense operations in July American fighters prevented the Japanese from disrupting the operations, while Navy cruisers and destroyers battled Japanese naval units in a series of night battles north of New Georgia. The result was that Turner's fleet lost only one transport and suffered minimal damage to other vessels, and the Japanese found they could reinforce only at night and with prohibitive losses from American antishipping strikes. American aircraft also bombed and strafed ground targets on New Georgia, primarily around heavily defended Munda, but true ground-controlled close-air support did not yet exist.[67]

While the offensives on New Guinea and New Georgia progressed, Admiral Halsey's staff examined objectives for the next phase of the campaign, a landing in the northern Solomons. The obvious target, the island of Bougainville, was not particularly attractive. The largest of the Solomons, Bougainville had hills carpeted with thick rain forest; inland mountains limited movement, and swamps along the coast restricted land travel to a series of muddy trails that meandered through the jungle. The Japanese already held the island's largest habitable areas on the northern and southern tips of the island, with three airfields and some 35,000 men. Assessing this situation, Halsey considered landings on other islands, primarily on Choiseul and the Shortlands, but MacArthur insisted that Bougainville be the objective and that the landing coincide with his attack on western New Britain. The decision to attack Bougainville accelerated American aerial and ground reconnaissance of the island; special patrols landing from submarines searched the coasts for adequate beaches and landing field sites. In September 1943 Halsey and the planners for the III Amphibious Force and I MAC selected the landing area: the northern portion of Empress Augusta Bay on the island's western coast. Landing in early November, I MAC would establish an enclave between the Laruma and Torokina rivers that could be developed as an air base and be defended by two divisions. The immediate landing beaches would be along the coast north of Cape Torokina.[68]

The Bougainville landing, like other amphibious assaults, depended on the Navy's ability to isolate the objective area from air and surface attack. This task became doubly important because the amphibious force had only twelve large transports and cargo ships, eight short of I MAC's requirements. Simultaneous operations in the central Pacific had produced this shortage. Rear Admiral Theodore S. Wilkinson's III Amphibious Force could ill afford casualties as it shuttled additional supplies and troops from the southern Solomons to Bougainville. Fortunately, American air cover prevented serious losses to Japanese bombers, and a Navy cruiser-destroyer task force drove off a similar Japanese force in a spirited night engagement in Empress Augusta Bay on November 1–2 during the landing phase of the operation. Even with scarce resources, the American amphibious forces had so improved in a year that the ship-to-shore movement produced few anxious moments. The focus of the tactical problem moved from the protection of the amphibious force to the ground action ashore. At Bougainville I MAC first complicated the Japanese defense planning by landing a New Zealand brigade group in the Shortlands off the island's south coast and a Marine parachute battalion on Choiseul; neither diversion proved particularly effective, although the Marine parachutists waged an epic series of combat patrols. The decisive action remained at Cape Torokina, where two raider battalions and six infantry battalions of the well-trained but inexperienced 3d Marine Division stormed ashore on November 1, 1943.[69]

The Bougainville landings clearly surprised the Japanese, and only one Marine battalion on the extreme right flank at Cape Torokina met heavy resistance. A raider battalion erased the defenders on nearby Puruata Island in a day and a half of fighting. Before the Japanese could respond, two-thirds of the 3d Marine Division was ashore with adequate heavy weapons and supplies to hold the beachhead. Bothered more by swamps and hot weather than by resistance, the 3d Division had no particular difficulty destroying a battalion-size Japanese counterlanding on the perimeter's western flank on November 7–8. The Bougainville battle then became a contest to see how long it would take and what it would cost the Marines to expand the perimeter as far east as the Torokina River, some 10 miles from the landing beaches.[70]

Until it was relieved in late December by two Army divisions, the 3d Division (reinforced by a defense battalion, raiders, and paramarines) pushed north and east through the jungles until it had captured a series of important hills west of the Torokina. The jungle and the rain produced as many hardships as the Japanese, slowing supplies and casualty evacuation and making reconnaissance, unit coordination, and fire support a nightmare. A veteran artillery officer recalled that "the oppressive heat, the continuous rain, the knee-deep mud, the dark overgrown tangled forest with the nauseous smell of the black earth and rotting vegetation, all combined to make this one of the most physically miserable operations that our troops were engaged in during the war." A corporal suggested that "what we ought to do when the war is over is to give Bougainville to the Japs—and make 'em live on the damned place forever!"[71] For the 3d Marine Division infantry, clad in drenched camouflaged dungarees and snaking their way along muddy jungle trails, the campaign was not soon forgotten.[72]

The first phase of the campaign to expand the beachhead to the east drew the 3d Marines, reinforced by a raider battalion, into a series of jungle actions along the Piva Trail, the main path northward west of the Piva River. The Marines forced their way north to the crucial junction of the Piva Trail, the Numa Numa Trail, and the East-West Trail and in a series of sharp fights at the "Piva Forks" took control of the trails by the end of November. The key battle was the successful attack and defense of Cibik's Ridge, which commanded the East-West Trail. Impressed by the skill and determination of the Japanese regiment facing the Marines, the 3d Division commander, Major General Allen H. Turnage, redeployed his division by sending the late-arriving 21st Marines against the East-West Trail defenses and placing the 9th Marines to its left and the 3d Marines on its right. Half the perimeter was defended by the Army's 37th Infantry Division.

During December the 3d Division struggled to capture four hill masses—Hill 1000, "Hellzapoppin Ridge," Hill 600A and Hill 600—on either side of the East-West Trail, a task that was not completed until December 27. The Japanese defenders made the most of the terrain, fighting from hidden bunkers and covering their infantry with accurate artillery fire. Having suffered serious casualties in their frontal assaults, Marine commanders relied on true close air support and massive artillery fire to dislodge the Japanese. The December attacks proved that observed artillery fire and ground-controlled air strikes were essential if the infantry was to close with the enemy still in any condition for a final assault. Some senior infantry commanders had trouble learning this lesson, but their troops proved quick converts to supporting fire tactics. In any event, the seizure of the Torokina River region showed the importance of combined arms action, unrelenting supply efforts, and Marine valor.[73]

Although the Bougainville campaign ended for the 3d Division before the dawn of 1944, neither the battle for Bougainville nor the Marine role in the capture of the northern Solomons ended there. On Bougainville itself the Army's XIV Corps assumed the responsibility for the perimeter's defense and spent the next six months expanding the enclave and beating back additional Japanese attacks before relinquishing the island's conquest to the Australians. Marine defense battalion artillery and anti-aircraft units also participated in the campaign after the 3d Marine Division withdrew. Marine units served in the final stages of the isolation of Rabaul: The new 4th Marines, constituted from the raider battalions, captured Emirau Island north of New Ireland in March 1944. Marine aviation, staging northward through the Solomons, continued to attack the remaining Japanese bases.

Across the Solomon Sea the other Allied advance on Rabaul had by late 1943 worked its way to the straits between New Guinea and New Britain, but even as MacArthur's advance progressed, the importance of

CARTWHEEL diminished. In August–September 1943 both the Allies and the Japanese reconsidered the importance of the South Pacific theater and decided to shift their efforts elsewhere, thus reducing Rabaul's importance. Stung by their aircraft losses and the attrition to the Combined Fleet, Japanese planners decided to fall back to a new defense perimeter anchored upon western New Guinea, Truk, and the Marianas. American planners doubted that it would be necessary to attack Rabaul and Kavieng, which could be isolated by air and naval forces. For the Navy, supported by the JCS, the main effort should come in the central Pacific, the most direct route to Japan. MacArthur urged the continuation of CARTWHEEL, but even he was busily drafting plans for moving northwestward toward the Philippines rather than making an all-out effort against New Britain and New Ireland. Nevertheless, MacArthur believed that the isolation of Rabaul and the advance along the New Guinea coast required operations on New Britain to neutralize the three Japanese air bases on the western half of the island and to disrupt the system of coastal shipping points used by the Japanese to reinforce their New Guinea positions. For operations on New Britain MacArthur assigned an orphaned unit in his U.S. Sixth Army—the veteran 1st Marine Division.[74]

Hampered by a lack of amphibious shipping and plagued by the Army planners' fascination with dispersed, undersupported multiple landings, the 1st Division commander, Major General William H. Rupertus, and his staff finally succeeded in focusing the New Britain operation on Cape Gloucester, the site of a Japanese air base and several coastal stations on the island's northwest tip. The Japanese had only ten thousand men dispersed throughout western New Britain, so the planners did not anticipate massive resistance at the beaches. The terrain, they knew, was troublesome, for New Britain's north coast was, if anything, a worse morass of rain forest, deep streams, and swamps than Bougainville. The landings would have to be made right into the jungle, because the beaches were narrow and their approaches shallow. Fortunately the bulk of the amphibious shipping was LSTs, LCIs, and similar craft with beaching abilities. Moving supplies and vehicles inland would be an enormous task. Tactically, the 1st Division planned to seize a beach on the eastern edge of the landing area with the 7th Marines, then land the 1st Marines, who would then drive westward down the coast and capture the Cape Gloucester airfield. The 5th Marines and the rest of the division would then land and consolidate an enclave sufficient in depth to defeat any Japanese counterattack. One battalion of the 1st Marines would also land west of the airfield to disrupt reinforcements moving along the shore trails.[75]

Staging northward for final rehearsals, the 1st Division, retrained and recovered from malaria and fatigue, faced the Cape Gloucester landing with supreme self-confidence and contempt for the Japanese. More than half the division had served on Guadalcanal. One transport of Marines leaving Australia saluted their hosts; they filled the air behind their ship with inflated prophylactics, which drifted back to their waving Australian sweethearts.[76] Although it had not made a shore-to-shore movement in the new beaching ships and craft, the division's rehearsals and final training went smoothly. Throughout the division the basic concern was not beating the Japanese but beating the jungle and the mud.[77]

Preceded by Army air strikes and uninterrupted by serious Japanese air or naval attacks, the 1st Division waded ashore on December 26, 1943, and began a three-week campaign to secure the Cape Gloucester enclave. While the 7th Marines drove off small Japanese attacks in some of the worst jungle in the South Pacific, the 1st and 5th Marines worked their way up the coast, battling torrential rains and approximately two battalions of Japanese defenders. On December 31 the airstrip and the commanding terrain around it were in Marine hands. In the 7th Marines' sector, however, the fighting increased in intensity as the sector commander, Brigadier General Lemuel C. Shepherd, the assistant division commander, pushed southward into the hills dominating the enclave's southeastern flank. For the 7th Marines, supported by three artillery and special weapons battalions and reinforced by a 5th Marines battalion, the three weeks after D-Day were a grueling battle against the Japanese and the jungle. In some of the fiercest fighting in the South Pacific, the Marines fought for and held such memorable landmarks as Suicide Creek, Target Hill, Aogiri Ridge, and Hill 660. When they were not throwing themselves at the Marines in hopeless assaults, the Japanese used their concealed bunker systems with great skill, forcing the Marines to mount overwhelming fire superiority in order to cover infantry assaults. Tanks, half-tracks, and tractor-drawn howitzers wallowed slowly to the front to provide this support. The movement of supplies and casualties produced new ordeals for the Marines, who despised the mud and vegetation more than they did the Japanese. Their rage was not misplaced, for some men were killed by falling trees, and dysentery and trench foot racked the troops. Yet by mid-January 1944 Japanese resistance in western New Britain had collapsed, and the 1st Division had accomplished its mission.[78]

General MacArthur, professing a fondness for the 1st Division that it did not reciprocate, refused to return it to Navy control and used it until April 1944 to consolidate the Sixth Army's hold on New Britain.

For the 1st Marine Division, this campaign of exploitation was not especially arduous. Units of the division patrolled the western end of the island, then headed east overland after the fleeing Japanese while other battalions moved by landing craft along the north coast. Neither group fought more than a few small actions with the Japanese rear guards. The very speed of the Marine movements prevented the Japanese from regrouping, so the thrust east was little more than a mopping-up operation. Even the terrain and weather proved more hospitable, and the Marines enjoyed the assistance of native Melanesian scouts and bearers. When MacArthur finally released the division, the operation, at a cost of 1,393 combat casualties, was a clear success. It also ended the Marine Corps's last significant operation in the South Pacific.[79]

Although in retrospect the South Pacific campaign probably went on a year too long for the American amphibious forces, it contributed to Japan's eventual defeat. The operations that began with Guadalcanal and ended with New Britain also prepared the Marine Corps and Navy for the drive across the central Pacific. By 1943 Halsey's III Amphibious Force, MacArthur's VII Amphibious Force, the I Marine Amphibious Corps, and Marine aviation in the area had developed a clear understanding of the problems of amphibious operations, particularly the ship-to-shore movement. The campaign had clearly proved the need to isolate the landing area from air and naval attacks, essentially a Navy function. The Navy, in fact, had lost 10,195 men in the South Pacific by December 1943, while the Marines had suffered 8,485 combat casualties, figures that reflect the intensity of the sea and air war. Marine dead in the same period numbered 2,271, far fewer than Navy dead and a figure that made Marine amphibious landings look less bloody than originally feared.[80] The keys were the successful protection of the amphibious forces and the wise selection of weakly defended beaches, taking advantage of the size of the large South Pacific islands and the dispersed Japanese defenses. Three Marine divisions, supported by defense battalions, raider and parachute battalions, and other corps troops, had mastered jungle warfare and destroyed the myth of Japanese invincibility. Even Army observers admitted that the Marine divisions had become crack organizations by the end of 1943, and MacArthur for one wanted more, not fewer, Marines in his theater.

The very character of the amphibious war in the South Pacific, however, obscured some important latent problems for future operations. Air attacks and naval gunfire covering the ship-to-shore movement had not been especially crucial. Close air support had not played much of a role, because it, too, had not been critical to success. The only aviation squadrons that believed in close air support—Marine fighter and dive-bomber squadrons—had been used primarily for air superiority and interdiction operations. Moreover, the Marine squadrons operated from land bases, a situation that could work in the tightly clustered islands of the South Pacific but not elsewhere. In addition, the Marine planners had not yet faced the fact that their arrangements for the movement of supplies ashore and then forward to the combat units had been tested by the jungle environment, not the enemy. Logistical support from the beach to the front lines remained a problem, primarily because of the insufficient personnel permanently assigned to supply duties. Tactically, the Marine infantry regiments were spoiled by Japanese ineptness in the South Pacific. The Japanese had committed scarce units in piecemeal counterattacks, which American firepower turned into disasters. When the Japanese contented themselves with a tactical defense based on prepared positions, they proved difficult foes; but such actions on Guadalcanal, New Georgia, Bougainville, and New Britain were of such small scale that they never really tested Marine infantry-artillery-air coordination or inflicted shocking casualties.[81] In essence the Marine Corps learned a great deal about jungle warfare in the South Pacific, but the lessons would not always apply in the central Pacific. The Corps by late 1943 had survived the throes of expansion and the trials of first combat against the Japanese, but its largest challenges lay ahead.

14. World War II: Amphibious Drive
Across the Central Pacific, 1943—1945

W hile Allied forces struggled to control the South Pacific, the Joint Chiefs of Staff debated whether or not to expand the war to the vast, island-dotted waters of the central Pacific. For the Marine Corps the stakes in the plans for defeating Japan could not have been higher, for a central Pacific campaign would provide the ultimate test of amphibious warfare doctrine. With little influence on planning, the Corps watched the deliberations until the autumn of 1943, when an outline of the Pacific strategy emerged. American planners, spurred by Admiral Ernest J. King, won their first victory from the British in January 1943, when the Combined Chiefs of Staff approved an increased effort in the Pacific. Assured of Allied strategic blessing, King in February 1943 directed his planners to examine not only operations in the South Pacific but an offensive across the central Pacific as well.[1]

In a series of conferences from March until May 1943, American planners hammered out the broad design for an offensive in the central Pacific. The result of decisions designed to placate General MacArthur and adjust both objectives and timing to the available American forces, the Pacific plans reflected the results of the South Pacific campaigns in 1942–1943 and the Navy's preference for a naval campaign that used its rapidly growing fleet of fast carriers, fast battleships, and numerous supporting ships. In geographic terms, the goal of the two-axis advance remained the Philippines, with eventual lodgment in Formosa and China. The purpose of the offensive was to cut Japan off from the economic resources of Southeast Asia and the Dutch East Indies. If economic strangulation did not force a Japanese surrender, the Allied offensive would include long-range air bombardment from China and the Pacific islands against Japan. The ultimate act, when the Japanese had lost their air and naval forces, might be invasion of the home islands.[2]

Just how and when the Allies would reach the western Pacific caused American planners considerable problems. Admiral King's planners focused their attention on the Japanese-held Marshall and Caroline islands. Covering an ocean area the size of the continental United States and including more than a thousand islands, the Mandates provided an optimum arena for naval power and amphibious forces. In their most optimistic moments, Navy planners hoped they might lure the Japanese fleet into a truly decisive fleet engagement. The campaign would present problems even so, for the Marshalls appeared too strong to take in 1943, with scarce amphibious forces, amphibious troops, and land-based air already committed to South Pacific operations. After much debate, American planners postponed an assault on the Marshalls until 1944 but added an offensive on the Gilberts for late 1943. The selection of the Gilberts reflected a strategic compromise. An offensive on the former British islands, which lay northeast of the Solomons and south of the Marshalls, might contribute to the MacArthur–Halsey drive on Rabaul and might also provide useful bases for the aerial reconnaissance and bombardment of the Marshalls. Moreover, the Gilberts landings could be made with the available landing forces (the 2d Marine Division and the 27th U.S. Infantry Division) and could be covered by land-based air.[3]

By the end of 1943 the planners had also included the Marianas as part of the central Pacific campaign. Northwest of the Mandates, the Marianas formed an important part of the Japanese Pacific defense perimeter. Whereas the Japanese regarded the Gilberts, Marshalls, and eastern Carolines as expendable outposts, they knew that the Marianas could not be lost, for they provided naval and air bases within striking distance of the home islands. Admiral King and H. H. Arnold, commanding general of the Army Air Forces and a strategic bombing enthusiast, came to similar conclusions. The Marianas joined the list of objectives in the drive into the central Pacific. Knowing that the U.S. Navy would outnumber the Japanese Navy by 2:1 in every important class of warship and carrier aircraft by January 1944, Admiral King pressed Admiral Chester Nimitz to open the central Pacific campaign as soon as possible.[4]

With its historic commitment to a naval campaign in the central Pacific, the Marine Corps unsurprisingly encouraged King's enthusiasm for an offensive in the new theater. Working through a handful of planners on the CNO's staff and the Joint Staff, Headquarters Marine Corps in 1943 estimated that the expanded war would require six divisions, seven aircraft wings, and thirty-eight defense and anti-aircraft battalions in addition to more corps troops, primarily artillery and amphibian tractor (amtrac) battalions. With King's firm support, Headquarters Marine Corps, despite Army reluctance, pressed the JCS successfully to concentrate the air and ground units of the Fleet Marine Force directly under Nimitz. The JCS allowed MacArthur and Halsey to retain the 1st and 3d Marine Divisions for the last phases of the isolation of Rabaul, while the veteran 2d Marine Division and the new 4th Marine Division joined the new V Amphibious Corps for the attacks on the Gilberts and Marshalls. At least three more Marine divisions, both veteran and newly formed, would join Nimitz's campaign as soon as they were available. At last the Marine Corps was on its way to its special war.[5]

With a confidence based on its performance in the South Pacific, the Marine Corps prepared for the central Pacific war with justifiable pride. At Headquarters the transition in Commandants from General Holcomb to General Vandegrift went smoothly, and Vandegrift soon gathered a close group of trusted officers, primarily veterans of Guadalcanal, on his staff. Having made some minor reorganizations of the Headquarters staff structure, Vandegrift concentrated on executing Holcomb's expansion plans, which, approved by the JCS, provided for a 478,000-man Corps by the middle of 1944. The Army objected to a sixth Marine division, but Vandegrift inherited the new 4th Marine Division (activated in August 1943) and the nucleus of the 5th Marine Division, created around a cadre of veterans from the parachute regiment and other units. In addition, Vandegrift had two independent regiments, the 4th Marines and 22d Marines, to use first as a brigade and eventually as the core of a sixth division. Additional troops could come from the excess defense and anti-aircraft battalions and other specialist units languishing in continental camps or the South Pacific. The aircraft wings presented difficult deployment and supply problems, but they were adequately manned with pilots and support personnel. In addition, by the autumn of 1943 the Corps training system in the United States had reached peak efficiency. Despite continued worries about recruiting and sluggishness in the supply system, Headquarters radiated confidence as the central Pacific campaign approached.[6]

Nowhere was Corps pride more dramatically displayed than by Brigadier General Robert L. Denig, the reactivated retiree who directed the Division of Public Relations. A sign on his wall declared: "If the public becomes apathetic about the Marine Corps, the Marine Corps will cease to exist." By 1943 Denig's personal inspiration—to train newspapermen as combat Marines and deploy them with FMF combat units to report the Pacific battles—had matured and flourished. Denig's enthusiastic reporters and cameramen numbered no more than 268 officers and men at the height of the war, but the Marine combat correspondents, which included such journalistic "names" as Earl Wilson, Keyes Beech, Murrey Marder, Jim Lucas, and David Douglas Duncan, flooded American newspapers and magazines with taut copy. By 1944 the correspondents' output reached more than three thousand stories a month. Their work, supplemented by the reporting of civilian journalists, soon was accompanied by photographs, sound transcriptions, film, and art done by other Marines. Overcoming the conservatism of some veteran officers, the correspondents found their way into the early waves of each landing, bled and died beside infantry in the front lines, and wrote wartime prose reminiscent of Stephen Crane and Ernest Hemingway. With Jesuitical loyalty to the Corps, the correspondents carried Denig's motto to its ultimate limits, much to the Marines' pleasure and the discomfort of the Army and Navy. If the central Pacific campaign was the supreme test of amphibious doctrine, it was also a media event of unparalleled drama for American war reporting. And it was the Marine version of that war that largely dominated the press.[7]

In addition to exciting copy, the central Pacific campaign produced a web of Byzantine interservice relations that made the MacArthur–Navy stresses in the South Pacific pale by comparison. Caught in the middle of complex Army–Navy disputes about the control of land-based aviation and logistical management, the Marine Corps found itself both the victim and the agitator of interservice disputes. The problem began in Washington at the JCS level. Admiral King irritated the Army by suggesting that CINCPAC, Admiral Nimitz, should run the entire Pacific war, making MacArthur his subordinate. This idea found little sympathy with General Marshall. Thus Nimitz and MacArthur worked as coequals, coordinating the timing and objectives of their campaigns. The basic issue became Nimitz's dual status as a theater commander and commander of naval forces in the theater, a status Admiral King demanded. As such, Nimitz could and did deal with King as part of the Navy chain of command outside of JCS jurisdiction. Neither wanted to alter this relationship. To placate the Army, which argued that Nimitz should surrender his role as commander of the Pacific fleet and create a true joint staff, CINCPAC requested that Lieutenant General Robert C. Richardson, Jr., USA, the senior Army commander in Hawaii, control Army ground and air forces in the theater for administration, training, and logistical purposes, but not for operational command. This arrangement was modified to give an AAF general control of Army air units in the central Pacific, although these units worked for a Navy air admiral. Army ground units remained under the operational control of the Amphibious Corps Pacific Fleet, a Marine headquarters. Because the Army provided much-needed logistical support to the central Pacific theater as well as ground and air combat units in equal strength to the Marines, Nimitz's concern for harmonious relations with Richardson was understandable. The Navy wanted to run the campaign, but it could not ignore the Army contribution, even if mollifying the Army meant upsetting the senior amphibious commanders.[8]

The tension in Army–Navy relations colored Navy–Marine Corps coordination, which was none too stable before the Gilberts operation. With some reluctance, Admiral Nimitz appointed Major General Holland M. Smith, USMC, commander of the Amphibious Corps Pacific Fleet, to head a successor command, V Amphibious Corps (V AC), and to work with the new commander of the V Amphibious Force, Rear Admiral Richmond Kelly Turner. Stubborn and argumentative, Smith and Turner proved difficult subordinates, particularly during operational planning. Despite experiences to the contrary in the South Pacific, Turner still thought he could dictate operations ashore. Smith challenged Turner's judgment: "I don't try to run your ships and you'd better by a goddam sight lay off my troops." [9] Ever the Marine loyalist, Smith saw his duty as making the Navy plan its operations in order to preserve Marine lives. Smarting from the near denial of his command of the central Pacific Marines and concerned about his own reputation, Smith was in no mood to be an interservice diplomat and team player, particularly when Marine lives hung in the balance. The Turner–Smith arguments reached sharp peaks, because their common superior, Vice Admiral Raymond A. Spruance, commander of the Central Pacific Force (later 5th Fleet), did not stop his subordinates' squabbling during the planning phase of amphibious operations.[10]

Already concerned about Army criticism of Marine–Navy logistical arrangements, Headquarters cautioned Smith to work harmoniously with both the Army and the Navy.[11] Smith was not disposed to do so if it meant compromising his standards for a successful amphibious operation. No fan of the Navy, Smith had ample opportunity to develop an equal aversion for Army methods. On this point he and the Navy agreed: Army divisions did not assault defended islands with the proper élan. The Army's tactics unnecessarily subjected the Navy's forces to attack by enemy air and submarines. In any amphibious operation, speed was of the essence, even if infantry casualties in the early stages of the operation were heavy. Smith was certain "his" Marines understood the reason for such sacrifices but doubted that the Army appreciated the problem. Only actual operations, meaning the Gilberts invasion, would test the Marine concept of the amphibious assault and its relation to a naval campaign.[12]

1

Even before the first Marine plunged ashore in the Gilberts and the Marshalls, Navy and Marine planners recognized that the American amphibious forces were entering a new kind of war. In a series of conferences that began in July 1943 and stretched into October, Nimitz's planners, working with Admiral Spruance, Admiral Turner, and General Smith, finally selected the three objectives of the Gilberts operation. These were Tarawa, Makin, and Apamama atolls. As military objectives, they all had a common characteristic: They were air base sites and potential anchorages. The prevailing wind patterns and the size of the islands determined which islands the Japanese defended in strength. At Tarawa it was Betio and at Makin the island of Butaritari. The three atolls had other common characteristics. Each was a two-sided necklace of small, level islands or islets linked by a great barrier reef, which formed a lagoon. Each island in each atoll was also ringed by a coral reef, over which tides moved unpredictably. As defensive positions the islands were formidable. Their flatness provided fine fields of fire for antiboat guns and machine guns, and the reefs and tides could be supplemented by mines and barbed wire. If the defenders were determined and well armed—and the Japanese were both—an amphibious assault might very well be a slaughter. To make a landing the Marines needed massive air and naval gunfire support and infantry, reinforced with tanks and demolition teams, steeled for vicious close combat.[13]

Awakened to the Gilberts' vulnerability by carrier raids and an abortive attack on Makin in August 1942 by the 2d Marine Raider Battalion, the Japanese naval commander in the Gilberts quickly strengthened his positional defenses. The Japanese concept of defense included land-based air and submarine counterattacks on any invasion force, and it was possible that the Combined Fleet might even sortie from Truk, its base in the eastern Carolines, to engage the Americans. Unaware that the Japanese naval air arm and surface ships had suffered so in the South Pacific that the Japanese would not risk them for the Gilberts and Marshalls, American planners had to assume that any invasion might face a surface engagement as well as air attacks from the Marshalls. For the Marines, however, the island defenses were the main

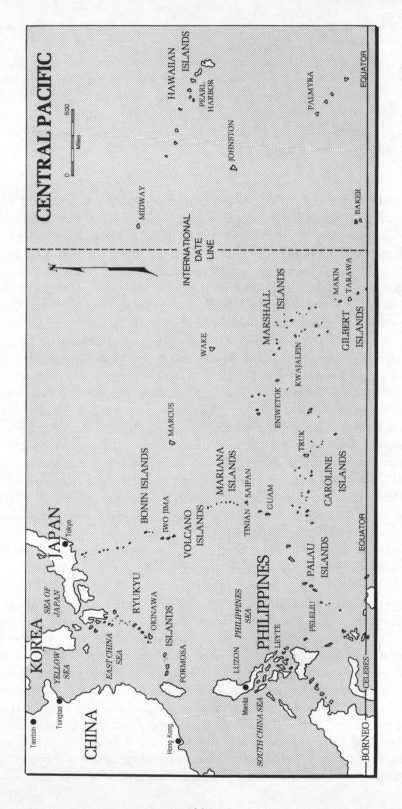

worry, and early aerial reconnaissance proved that Betio would be no pushover. The island bristled with some 200 guns and machine guns, manned by 2,600 crack naval landing infantry and base defense troops, supported by 2,000 labor troops. Betio, an island only three miles long and 800 yards wide at its widest point, was one massive fortified position.[14]

As American planning progressed for Operation GALVANIC—the simultaneous assaults on Tarawa and Makin—V AC and 2d Marine Division planners, working with their Navy counterparts, isolated the worst problems Betio presented. In retrospect, it is hard to fault their reasoning. To avoid the most formidable beach defenses, the planners chose to attack Betio from inside the lagoon. This decision meant that the assault craft would have to move from the transports outside the lagoon and maneuver inside the lagoon through 6 miles of water. This circumstance meant that air and naval gunfire support had to be carefully controlled and timed. There remained the problem of the Betio reef, which ran from 600 to 1,000 yards from the beach. At high tide there should have been enough water over the reef to float the LCVPs and LCMs that carried vital artillery, tanks, and reinforcements. If, however, the Marines caught a "dodging" or erratic tide, there might be far less than the 4 feet needed to float an LCVP. The only answer was to use amphibian tractors (LVTs) to cross the reef. The 2d Marine Division, backed by General Holland M. Smith, scratched together 125 LVTs from its own tractor battalion and new tractors sent from California. Still, when the landing plan was decided, there were only enough LVTs to land the first three waves of the three assault battalions. This meant that subsequent waves would depend on a high tide; otherwise the troops would have to transfer to the LVTs at the reef—or they would have to wade ashore.[15]

Without overwhelming fire support, the 2d Marine Division faced potential disaster, but in both the planning and the execution of fire support for the Tarawa landing the Marines were shortchanged. From the Navy point of view, which placed a premium on speed, the risk was acceptable. Concerned about potential Japanese air and sea counterattacks, Admiral Spruance and Admiral Turner limited the prelanding air and naval gunfire bombardment to four hours and denied a Marine request to seize lightly defended neighboring islets as artillery bases. With seventeen fire support ships and carrier planes saturating Betio, Navy planners thought a short, violent bombardment would smash the defenses; Holland M. Smith and Julian C. Smith, the 2d Division commander, were not so sure. Their concern was justified. The Navy aviators had not trained for attacks on fortified positions, and air control was weak at best. Besides, the fire support ships would be firing from outside the lagoon along the island's long axis, which meant that the flat-trajectory fire would be difficult to adjust on inland targets. The Navy planned, moreover, to mix pinpoint destruction fire on the heaviest Japanese emplacements with area neutralization fire, a combination that would make aerial spotting and adjustment very difficult. Yet such was the confidence of the naval gunfire planners and the lack of practical experience that several Navy officers promised the Marines that they would walk safely ashore upon a devastated objective.[16]

The 2d Division's problems did not end with the fire support plan. Because the Gilberts operation included two simultaneous landings, Admiral Turner and General Holland Smith stripped the division of one regiment, the 6th Marines, and made it the corps reserve. Fortunately, the regiment went to Tarawa, but Julian Smith could not plan to use it for the landing. Therefore, the 2d Division planned to use four reinforced battalions landing on a broad front to seize a quick victory. The actual assault, led by the 2d Marines' Colonel David M. Shoup, included three battalion landing teams (infantry reinforced with a pack artillery battalion, engineers, and a tank company) with one in reserve. Again, the emphasis was upon speed, shock, and rapid reinforcement to exploit success ashore, all of which depended on accurate communications. This condition, however, was endangered by the ineffectiveness of the landing force radios and the dependence of the headquarters afloat on the radios of their ships. For the 2d Division the flagship was an old battleship whose radios balked when shaken by gunfire. The Tarawa operation proved decisively that amphibious commanders needed special command ships. Such vessels were on their way but did not reach the Pacific in time for GALVANIC.[17]

In a violent four-day struggle that left the 2d Marine Division staggered but glorious, the Marines seized Betio and annihilated the entire Japanese garrison in one of the Pacific war's most desperate battles. Despite many obvious defects, the landing of November 20–24 proved that the amphibious assault worked. Yet the battle for Betio reached such levels of ferocity that American leaders reacted almost as if the Marines had lost. They communicated some of their horror to their superiors and gave others, particularly Army generals, the impression that the battle had been mismanaged and Marine losses excessive. In view of the unique circumstances of the Tarawa landing, this impression was inaccurate.[18]

The reason the battle for Betio hung in the balance for a day and a half was that the character of the naval bombardment, the unpredictability of the tides over the reef, and the shortage of LVTs combined to deprive the initial assault of adequate reinforcements during the critical hours when the assault companies were punching through the Japanese waterline positions. Despite vast confusion in the early hours of November 20 on the coordination of naval air and gunfire, the initial three waves of LVTs plunged ashore with acceptable losses even though they reached their objectives almost an hour late. In addition, it took longer than expected to transfer the Marines from their transports to the LVTs, which had been carried in LSTs. But the most serious problem was the tide. There was insufficient water over the reef to float the critical LCVP-borne infantry and LCM-borne tanks and artillery. Because the LVTs had brought ashore only half of Shoup's three assault battalions, reinforcements were critical. Ashore the first waves of Marines found the Japanese ready to die in place inside a maze of heavy fortifications. Although the naval gunfire and bombing had destroyed Japanese communications and silenced most of the heavy guns, the Japanese naval infantry had suffered minimal losses in personnel and automatic weapons. In many ways the battle ashore mirrored the worst trench warfare of World War I: infantry against machine guns. In the first day Shoup's three battalions all lost about half their men and most of their unit cohesion; two reserve battalions suffered similar losses when their troops tried to wade ashore from the reef through a hail of machine gun fire. Punching against the Japanese pillboxes with flamethrowers, demolition charges, hand grenades, and the fire of a few tanks, the 2d Marines and two 8th Marines battalions held only two shallow enclaves along Betio's northwestern shore at the end of the first day.

On the second day of the battle, the landing hung in the balance, but by the end of the day it swung toward the Marines. The scene around the island sickened the most hardened veterans. Along the beaches LVTs burned, and dead Marines by the score bobbed in lagoon water turned milky by gunfire-blasted coral dust. Smoke and flame blanketed the island. Ruined small craft, broken supplies, and bodies swept along the reef, swirled around the long pier that ran from the shore toward the reef, and littered the beach. The smell of powder, flame, and burnt flesh reached even the amphibious transports. Into this inferno General Julian Smith sent the last battalion of the 8th Marines, but it too took heavy losses while wading ashore. Having received the 6th Marines back from Holland Smith, Julian Smith sent two of its battalions to the relatively clear western tip of the island, where they joined an isolated battalion of the 2d Marines.

Bunker by bunker, the eight Marine battalions converged, assisted by tank reinforcements and 10th Marines pack howitzers. By the afternoon of the second day, Shoup reassured Smith that the battle had turned: "Casualties many; percentage dead not known; combat efficiency: We are winning." [19] Because the Japanese interior defenses were not well organized and the defenders did not mount a serious night counterattack, which the Marines feared most, Shoup's assessment proved accurate. The third day's attacks closed the gap between the Marines' two beaches, and for the first time the Marines were sure they were inflicting more casualties than they were taking. On the fourth day the 6th Marines swept to the island's eastern tip, and the rest of the force mopped up the survivors. When the casualties were tallied, the Marines had killed all but 146 defenders at a cost of 3,318 Americans, of whom 1,085 died. Amid the smoldering bunkers, bloating dead, and shattered palm trees, the 2d Division faced the reality:

> Death is a quire of red tape.
> It is posting a name in the MIA column.
> It is dropping a name from the OD roster.
>
> It is listing the contents of a field trunk
> And sunning the blankets.
> It is a routine call for replacements
> and the curse of a corporal.
>
> It is a good word said in silence
> And an extra bottle of warm beer.[20]

The lessons of Betio escaped no one, from the lowliest private to Admiral Spruance. Obviously the air and naval gunfire to crush beach defenses had to be methodical, accurate destruction fire if the assault waves, reinforcements, and supplies were to reach the beach as planned. If possible, supporting artillery should be landed on nearby islands to assist the attack. The landing force would need many more LVTs to cross the reefs; an alternative was to blow passages in the coral for landing craft. (This mission became a task of the Navy's Underwater Demolition Teams, or UDTs.) Communications at all levels of command begged for improvement. Tactically, the Marines would have to perfect the coordination of infantry attacks with tanks and artillery, so that flamethrower operators and demolition men might approach pillboxes with some hope of success. Yet for all their anguish over Marine casualties, Spruance, Turner, Holland Smith, and Julian Smith believed they had proved the effectiveness of Navy–Marine amphibious doctrine.[21]

The Navy and Marine leaders' appreciation for the 2d Division's gallant assault rose when they contrasted it with the Army's slow seizure of Makin. Against weak opposition a reinforced regiment of the 27th Division took four days to capture Makin and performed with such caution that even Army observers felt the division needed more aggressive leadership. To make the Makin operation even more painful, on the fourth day a Japanese submarine sank the carrier *Liscome Bay*, which carried more than 750 officers and men with it to the bottom, including a rear admiral. Even if the "hurry-up" Marine tactical approach to atoll warfare cost lives in its early phases, it seemed preferable to the Army emphasis on careful attacks.[22]

As Marines and soldiers of the V AC cleared the weak Japanese posts from the other islands of Tarawa and Makin atolls, the Marine Corps appraised the public impact of the Betio landing. General Vandegrift found that the press coverage, most dramatically stories by *Time*'s Robert Sherrod and Marine correspondent Jim Lucas, had so emphasized the valor and sacrifice of the Marines that many civilian and military leaders thought the battle was a disaster. Only through rapid lobbying did Vandegrift stop a Congressional investigation of the battle. The lessons of Tarawa had to be quickly learned and new expertise demonstrated if the central Pacific campaign was to continue under Navy–Marine Corps leadership.[23]

The recapture of the Gilberts was only a prelude to the offensive against the Marshalls. CINCPAC planners debated the basic concepts for Operation FLINTLOCK (the Marshalls operation) even as the Gilberts operation progressed. The final choice of objectives, made by Nimitz over the protests of his immediate subordinates, reflected CINCPAC's new confidence in the 5th Fleet's ability to isolate the objective area from serious Japanese air and naval attacks. Given its access to Japanese radio traffic, CINCPAC may have been aware, too, that Imperial Headquarters had decided to defend a main line through the Marianas and the western Carolines, thus leaving the Marshalls as expendable outposts. Without heavy air and naval support, the 30,000 Japanese troops in the Marshalls invited isolation and annihilation. The Marshalls included some thirty-two atolls of 2,000 islands scattered across 800 square miles of ocean, but only six of the atolls had become important Japanese bases. In the easternmost tier were Mille, Maloelap, and Wotje; the central tier included Jaluit to the south and Kwajalein to the north; and at the northwestern edge of the Marshalls, Eniwetok atoll anchored the system. Rejecting an obvious attack on the eastern atolls, Nimitz decided to strike Majuro and Kwajalein at the center of the island group and then use air and naval forces to reduce the other atolls. He also marked Eniwetok as an additional objective to be taken after the fall of Kwajalein.[24]

From strategy to detailed operational plans, the attack on Kwajalein atoll demonstrated that Nimitz, Spruance, Turner, Holland Smith, and their subordinate amphibious and landing force commanders had learned well from the Gilberts landings. With the first landings scheduled for January 31, 1944, land-based Navy and AAF air pounded all the occupied atolls for a month, supplemented by carrier air strikes and surface bombardment. Japanese vessels and aircraft soon disappeared from the Marshalls, and the island defenses shuddered under the pounding. Of the major Japanese bases, Kwajalein, primarily a support base, was the least defended, but it did not escape the bombardment. The atoll contained two main islands at its northern and southern rims. The twin islands of Roi-Namur on the north, shaped like a pair of waterwings joined by a sand spit and causeway, held an airstrip (Roi) and a supply and administrative complex (Namur) garrisoned by some five thousand Japanese sailors and soldiers. Forty miles away a similar force held Kwajalein island. Neither objective was heavily fortified or armed with more than a few coast defense and anti-aircraft guns. Against these islands, none of them more than a few square miles in size, the Americans were ready to hurl a V Amphibious Force of 300 ships and an assault force of 53,000 soldiers and Marines.[25]

Working in relative harmony with General Smith, Admiral Turner designed the Marshalls landings with a new emphasis on massive fire support, a continuous and accelerated ship-to-shore movement, and rapid operations ashore. The inexperienced but enthusiastic 4th Marine Division drew Roi-Namur, and the 7th U.S. Infantry Division, a veteran of the Aleutians campaign, took Kwajalein. In addition to the usual nondivisional reinforcements, the expeditionary force included a reserve of two regiments from the 27th Infantry Division and the 22d Marines, a fresh, well-trained regiment that had defended Samoa for more than a year. Major General Harry Schmidt's 4th Marine Division landing could be supported by two reinforced battalions of 285 troop-carrying LVTs and a battalion of 85 new armored LVT(A)s carrying 37-mm. guns and machine guns. The 7th Division had similar but smaller numbers of LVTs to traverse the reefs. The Navy also added a new assault LCI(G), a gunboat armed with rockets and 40-mm. guns, to lead the LVTs to the reef.

The key to a quick victory and minimum casualties, the planners agreed, rested in the pre-landing bombardment, and the Marshalls operation clearly demonstrated what careful preparation meant in atoll warfare: victory. After the preliminary bombardments, Turner's fire support ships, firing methodically from ranges down to 1,800 yards, pulverized Roi-Namur's defenses for two whole days. Assisted by air strikes and airborne spotters, the ships smashed nearly all of the important Japanese strongpoints and buildings. As a welcome preliminary to the main landing on Roi-Namur, the 25th Marines and two artillery battalions landed on nearby islets on January 31 and added their fire to the surface ships'. The Kwajalein landings followed the same approach.

Although less than orderly in the tactical sense, the main landings on February 1 by the 23d and 24th Marines justified the planners' hopes. The 23d Marines piled ashore on flat Roi and raced across the airstrip along with tanks and LVT(A)s. So weak was the opposition and so effective the fire support that the green Marine regiment actually complicated the fire support by advancing too rapidly. With great aggressiveness and minimal coordination, the 23d Marines secured the island by nightfall, although wild firing and bypassed Japanese pockets made the night dangerous for anyone moving above ground. Still, the attack was a stunning success. The 24th Marines' assault on Namur, however, started late and did not clear the island until the second day. The 24th Marines' problem was that the regiment's LVTs had lifted the 25th Marines the preceding day, and many of the amtracs, hindered by fuel shortages and uncooperative Navy officers, did not reach the assigned transports carrying their assault teams. Switching units and commandeering stray amtracs and LCVPs, the 24th Marines pieced together an assault force that finally seized half the island by nightfall. The attack ashore suffered from the mixing of units and the accidental explosion of a blockhouse full of torpedo warheads, which made Namur look as if it had disappeared. The 24th Marines' confusion, however, slackened to manageable proportions on the second day, and Marine tank-infantry teams eliminated the remaining pockets of Japanese resistance with increasing efficiency. At a cost of fewer than eight hundred casualties, the 4th Marine Division secured Roi-Namur, while to the south the 7th Infantry Division, moving more cautiously, captured Kwajalein in four days.[26]

While battalion-size and company-size expeditions cleared the rest of Kwajalein's islets, Navy and Marine planners decided to attack Eniwetok (Operation CATCHPOLE) before the Japanese could respond, thus securing the Marshalls without a pause. Having already plunged the fleet 2,000 miles into the Mandates, the Navy thought another expedition 326 more miles to the west possible. The first test was whether the fast carriers could isolate the objective area, this time without land-based aerial assistance. The early Marshalls operations indicated likely success, and Spruance's fast carriers proved their power by striking the principal Japanese base at Truk and hitting airfields on the Marianas. Again the Japanese did not respond, hoarding their undestroyed aircraft for later operations. Behind the Navy air cover steamed Rear Admiral Harry Hill's amphibious task force, carrying the 22d Marines and the

106th Infantry. Marine Brigadier General Thomas E. Watson commanded the expeditionary troops.[27]

Again protected by heavy naval gunfire and prelanded artillery, Watson's force seized the three defended islands of Eniwetok atoll (Engebi, Eniwetok, and Parry islands) in four days, February 18–22, 1944. Enjoying only a 3:1 superiority in numbers over the some 3,500 Japanese defenders, the Americans assaulted the islands one at a time. The regiment had not had adequate amphibious training, but the 22d Marines demonstrated considerable tactical skill in overrunning Engebi and Parry in one day cach. On Eniwetok, however, the 27th Infantry Division troops again showed that they could not or would not close with the enemy. Nevertheless, the Eniwetok operation ended in early March with the atoll cleared for use as an air base and anchorage at a cost of only 1,200 American casualties. With the completion of the operation, the United States had regained control of almost 60,000 square miles of the central Pacific.[28]

When contrasted with the Gilberts operation, FLINTLOCK-CATCHPOLE was an exhilarating success, but it too provided more lessons. Certainly, methodical pre-H-Hour bombardment proved itself against clearly identifiable positions. In the Eniwetok operation, however, the Japanese use of camouflaged trenches and tunnels made naval gunfire and aerial bombing less useful until the Americans switched to ordnance with high fragmentation and burning effect. The implication was clear: Japanese fortified positions at the waterline could be overcome, but other types of defenses might not, without serious casualties. In the ship-to-shore movement, the Americans had made significant advances, primarily by using LVTs and LVT(A)s, in keeping the landing waves moving. Pre-H-Hour reconnaissance and barrier clearance by Navy UDTs assisted the landings. The biggest lesson, however, was to keep the landing plans simple and to join the assault troops with their amtracs before the actual assault. This could be done by transferring the troops from their transports to the amtrac-carrying LSTs before the final approach to the objective area instead of waiting for a pre-H-Hour transfer at the objective. Such a policy would have simplified the Roi-Namur attack. Another lesson from FLINTLOCK was the utility of the Army's amphibious truck, the DUKW. Although unsuited for assaults, preloaded DUKWs could free amtracs for tactical missions by carrying artillery, ammunition, and supplies ashore. In addition, the ship-to-shore movement could still benefit by more adequate communications for both the assault waves and the fire support elements.[29]

Perfecting the ship-to-shore movement was something all the participants could agree upon, but the questions of command and tactics ashore opened acute interservice differences. The problem of command now focused essentially on the authority of the expeditionary force commander to influence operations when the landings themselves were division-size or less. At the center of the controversy were, as always, Admiral Turner and General Smith. In the Marshalls operation Smith remained at Turner's mercy; Admiral Spruance gave Turner the right to change ground operations if for some reason the amphibious force was endangered. Turner remained in tactical command throughout the operation, since the landings took so little time, whereas Smith's authority over his subordinates eroded. The circumstance strengthened the Army's argument that Smith and his staff were superfluous and should be eliminated, a position stimulated by Smith's criticism of the 7th and 27th Divisions' cautious tactics.

The command relationships deteriorated further because of honest differences of opinion about infantry tactics. Both the Army and the Marines recognized the need to perfect tank–infantry coordination and to use supporting arms in abundance, but the Marines tended to be less methodical or thorough in mopping up pockets of resistance. By pressing forward instead, Marine officers argued, the Marines eventually reduced casualties by disrupting the enemy's organized defenses and spared the amphibious ships the danger of air and submarine attack. The Army, on the other hand, stressed methodical advances. Many Marines regarded such tactics as inept, especially in the 27th Infantry Division. That division, blooded at Makin and Eniwetok, suffered not so much from cowardice as from uninspired leadership and inadequate training, but many Marines could not see the difference. Marine disgust with the 27th Infantry Division, in fact, hit a new high when the Army regimental commander on Eniwetok received a Navy Cross for heroism. The undeserved award to the Army officer struck Marines as a gesture by Admiral Nimitz to foster interservice harmony.[30]

The amphibious assaults in the Marshalls did not end Marine Corps operations in the island group. Aviation units of the 4th Marine Base Defense Aircraft Wing moved onto the newly liberated atolls to complete the isolation of the remaining Japanese bases. Flying from bases on Kwajalein, Majuro, and Eniwetok, fourteen Marine fighter and dive bomber squadrons pounded the Japanese bases on Wotje, Jaluit, Maloelap, and Mille until the war's end. It was not an especially dangerous or glorious campaign, for Army and Navy air had already driven off most of the Japanese aircraft in the islands, and after a few Japanese raids in February 1944 the Marines found their sorties routine. When the Army and Navy land-based air staged to the west in the spring of 1944, the 4th MBDAW assumed the burden of stopping the flow of supplies to the Japanese atolls and of punishing the remaining 13,701 Japanese troops. By August 1945 the Marines had dropped 7,000 tons of bombs on the pitiful atolls and had killed or helped starve half of the defenders at a cost of 22 American lives. For more than a year the Marine strikes at the Marshalls resembled little more than training missions. Marine squadrons used their stay in the Marshalls to perfect their dive-bombing and strafing techniques, hoping they would use them against more important targets in the western Pacific. Marine air had not yet caught up with the rest of the Fleet Marine Force, but not because it was unwilling or unskilled.[31]

2

As Marines in the Marshalls and the South Pacific eliminated or isolated the remaining Japanese garrisons and prepared to assault the main Japanese defenses in the Marianas and the Carolines, Commandant A. A. Vandegrift assured his predecessor, General Holcomb, that the Marine Corps in the Pacific stood ready for stiffer challenges. Vandegrift promised to fight "to retain what we have." [32] The Commandant did not mean islands. Vandegrift could see that the Corps' expansion to five divisions (with enough separate units to create a sixth), five aircraft wings, twenty-nine separate artillery battalions, twelve amtrac battalions, and numerous logistical units disturbed the Army. Prodded by Army studies of postwar defense organization, which stressed the need for a single military commander and armed forces staff, a select committee of the House of Representatives (the Woodrum Committee) investigated military organization in the spring of 1944. Vandegrift helped Admiral King defuse the hearings, but he warned Holland Smith that the Army wanted the Corps reduced after the war and might press to absorb Marine aviation even before the war ended. Vandegrift was satisfied that Marine representation in the Navy contingent on the Joint Staff and in King's headquarters adequately cemented Navy–Marine Corps cooperation and would best the Army planners, but the Commandant worried about interservice relations in the Pacific and the efficiency of his own Marine Corps organization in the field. With the Corps shifted to the amphibious assault role in the central Pacific, reorganization appeared overdue.[33]

The approach of the Marianas campaign and the declining American ground role in the South Pacific set off a flurry of reorganization in early 1944 that went on through the rest of the year. The results were mixed. Marine Corps ground combat and service units came under almost exclusive control of Marine generals, whereas Army units remained outside the Marine-commanded amphibious corps structure except for specific operations, and the Navy continued to dominate the use of Marine aviation. Both of the latter decisions—interservice compromises dictated by Admiral Nimitz—displeased General Smith. In March 1944 Smith, newly promoted to lieutenant general, proposed an integrated Army–Marine Corps amphibious field army under his command. The chief Marine components would be his own V Amphibious Corps and Roy Geiger's III Amphibious Corps, which would join the central Pacific amphibious forces for the Marianas and subsequent operations. Nimitz, with Vandegrift's approval, rejected the plan but approved the creation of a consolidated all-Marine logistical and administrative system under Smith's command. By July 1944 Smith's headquarters had become Fleet Marine Force Pacific, which controlled all Marine ground units in Nimitz's theater. The reorganization centralized support functions under Administrative Command FMF Pacific. In the autumn of 1944 the consolidation finally included Marine aviation with the creation of Aircraft, Fleet Marine Force Pacific. This headquarters, subordinate to Smith's FMF Pacific command, dealt with Marine aviation units for administrative and supply purposes only, for Nimitz insisted that the operational control of Marine aviation remain in the hands of the Commander, Air Force, Pacific Fleet, who was a Navy admiral.[34]

For the Marine Corps the emergence of FMF Pacific headquarters improved administrative and logistical planning and service to Marine units, and it gave Smith improved flexibility in organizing his complex amphibious forces. The reorganization may have helped tie Marine ground and aviation into a closer association, but the split between the two in the Pacific could not be solved by organizational reform. The air–ground division remained a problem of doctrine and of the absence of carriers from which Marine squadrons could operate. And the use of Marine air in combat remained not Smith's responsibility but the Navy's. Moreover, Smith found himself progressively immersed in administrative duties, not operational planning and active tactical control. This development appears in retrospect to have pleased the Army and certainly did not distress Nimitz. With the creation of FMF Pacific the Marine Corps gained more control over its scattered divisions and air wings, but the reorganization did not alter the Navy's operational domination and did not provide any significant influence over General Richardson's Army command.

With firmer control over its own forces and now rich in operational experience, Headquarters reorganized the FMF units for more efficient future action. In one set of changes, Marine divisions fell in strength from almost 20,000 to 17,465 men. Special weapons battalions, scout companies, amtrac battalions, and Navy construction battalions disappeared from the divisions, most becoming corps troops. The divisional artillery fell from five battalions to four. Army Sherman medium tanks replaced the light tanks in the divisions. Within the infantry battalions, the separate weapons companies disappeared, leaving each battalion with a headquarters and service company (which included mortars and machine guns) and three rifle companies. In a major development in 1944, Marine rifle squads drew three Browning automatic rifles (BARs) for each squad instead of one. Marine planners approved a change that had already occurred simultaneously and slowly in many combat units: dividing the rifle squad into three fire teams. This change gave each squad more positive leadership in combat, for the fire team leaders could maneuver their teams separately, locate targets, and direct the BAR fire more effectively than one squad leader. The reorganized squad was also easier to organize for assaulting fortified positions.[35]

Streamlining the divisions in 1944 did not end reorganization, for the emerging amphibious war suggested radical change in the Corps's policy toward special units. The two raider regiments and one parachute regiment became conventional infantry, while the defense battalions changed to eleven heavy artillery battalions and eighteen anti-aircraft artillery battalions. FMF Pacific headquarters also controlled twelve amtrac battalions, two engineer battalions, twelve logistical battalions, and assorted other headquarters and service troops. The trend meant that specialized units were pooled and allocated to the amphibious corps as needed and that the emphasis in support had clearly shifted to heavier fire support and more mechanized landings. Support activities proliferated and service units multiplied, until FMF Pacific could call itself an amphibious army in all but name.[36]

Reorganizations and reinforcements—both of which reshaped FMF Pacific in 1944—could not alone assure victory, and the Marine Corps and Navy cooperated to ensure that the naval gunfire and air support of future landings improved. Late in 1943 Smith's headquarters created the V Corps Naval Gunfire Section, which in 1944 became the principal agency for training supporting arms coordinators and the ships and planes delivering the ordnance. The key unit for fire support coordination was the Joint Assault Signal Company (JASCO), a triservice creation responsible for communications for air coordinators, naval gunfire spotters, and shore party commanders. The joint nature of the JASCOs made training and administration difficult, but the JASCO concept survived.

The JASCO (with the "Joint" and many sailors dropped) became an integral part of the Marine division and specialized in naval gunfire.

To work out doctrine and train the JASCOs, the Naval Gunfire Section turned Kahoolawe Island, Hawaii, into a ship gunnery school and eventually supervised the qualification firing for 532 Pacific Fleet warships. The training exercises dramatized the need for intelligent gunfire spotting. The NGF Section first stressed putting trained Marine ground officers into spotting aircraft but then shifted to training Navy and Marine officer spotting teams for ground employment. It took time and much practice to create spotting teams that understood tactics and naval gunfire, but by mid-1944 the NGF Section had improved both naval gunfire doctrine and practice.[37] The quality of naval gunfire support, however, continued to vary because of conditions over which the Marine Corps had little control: the state of training of ships crews, fleet operating plans, and the terrain and defense of the amphibious objective area. The uncertainties of naval gunfire further dramatized the need for better close air support.

If improving naval gunfire support was difficult, increasing the effectiveness of close air support taxed Marine Corps ingenuity and persistence to their limits. Geography and Navy policies in 1944 at first looked insurmountable, and the reluctance of some senior Marine air officers to change Marine air's role complicated reform. Essentially, Marine aviation had integrated itself into the Navy's land-based aviation force. In the South Pacific this force had contributed by providing air superiority, interdicting supply lines, and bombing bases. By using Marine squadrons for these missions, Navy air commanders freed Navy squadrons for carrier operations, so they were reluctant to see Marine air shift its efforts to the direct support of amphibious landings or campaigns ashore. In any event, Marine land-based dive bombers and fighters could not reach the objectives in the Gilberts and Marshalls, and the Marianas were even beyond the reach of Marine medium bombers. Air support for the landings and for the ensuing ground campaigns would have to come from Navy carrier air—unless, of course, the Marines could put some of their own squadrons aboard carriers. Another option was to improve Navy close air support techniques and to wrest some control of the air operations from the amphibious task force commander and place it in the headquarters of the landing force commander. The Marine Corps tried both options with only modest success.

At first glance the problem of getting Marine aviation back into the Fleet Marine Force appeared minimal, for the Corps in 1944 had plenty of air: about 10,000 pilots and 126 squadrons with more than 100,000 Marines in support. With the isolation of Rabaul complete and the Marshalls neutralized, Marine air was conspicuously underemployed. In addition, the Navy had thirty-five escort carriers to man, and one important role of the escort carriers was to provide air support for amphibious task forces. Yet Marine air could not seize the opportunity easily, for in 1943 the Navy (with the approval of Major General Ross E. Rowell, the senior Marine Air commander in the Pacific) had stopped qualifying Marine pilots for carrier landings. In addition, Rowell had convinced his Navy superiors in Hawaii that the Marines did not want to go to sea to support amphibious landings. Vandegrift, ably supported by Brigadier General Louis E. Woods and Brigadier General Field Harris, the directors of Marine aviation in 1944, convinced King and Nimitz that this was not so and made his point by relieving Rowell. In a complicated reform plan negotiated with the Navy in October 1944, Vandegrift obtained a promise from King that four new escort carriers could be manned with eight Marine squadrons—provided the Marines learned how to operate from carriers. Vandegrift established a training command in California to do just that, but it was early 1945 before the first Marine squadrons went aboard an escort carrier. Eight squadrons out of a 1944 high of 145 was not exactly a massive commitment, but it was all the Navy would accept. It exacted a further price: When pressed by a shortage of Navy fighter squadrons in late 1944, the Navy asked for Marine assistance and received ten fighter squadrons for its fast carriers. King and Nimitz also demanded that Vandegrift reduce the number of Marine squadrons, increase the number of planes per squadron, and consolidate Marine aviation support activities. All these changes were justified and long overdue. In return, the Navy accepted Vandegrift's recommendation that Marine air rejoin the FMF by becoming a subordinate part of Holland Smith's FMF Pacific—at least for administrative purposes. This part of the October 1944 agreement did something to bridge the schism between Marine air and ground and restored some of the influence of ground operations upon Marine air doctrine.[38]

Marine commanders in the Pacific recognized that regaining the support of Marine air for amphibious operations would be a slow process, and they sought to improve the quality of the Navy's close air support. As part of the October 1944 reform, General Smith created a Marine Air Support Control Unit, headed by Colonel Vernon E. Megee, a close air support enthusiast. Megee's command provided close air support training, but its main effort focused upon wresting some control of air operations from amphibious force commanders and providing the landing force commander with the ability to plan and direct air strikes, particularly during extended operations ashore. Over Admiral Turner's objections, the Marine close air support advocates organized four Landing Force Air Support Control Units (LFASCUs) to coordinate air strikes with ground operations. This change, first tested at Iwo Jima, gave Marine ground commanders greater influence over air operations, much to the delight of the Marine divisions.

The final step in improving close air support—actually directing the strikes from the front lines against targets close to friendly troops— also originated with Megee's command. Equipped with improved jeep-mounted radios, Marine air controllers argued, they could direct strikes against ground targets within hundreds (rather than thousands) of yards of American troops by communicating directly with the aircraft. This technique, which ran counter to Navy and Army doctrine, required air strike controllers well versed in ground tactics and aircraft capabilities. At first the forward air controllers were air-indoctrinated ground officers, but the Air Liaison Parties (ALPs) soon became the instrument of pilots-turned-infantrymen. This reform proved successful for the Army in the Philippines and the Marine Corps on Okinawa.[39]

The Marine Corps still had much to learn from its future campaigns, but the development of the FMF suggested that the Corps, working closely with the Navy's amphibious forces, had mastered the basic problems of the amphibious assault. The final test, of course, was whether the Japanese would cooperate in their own defeat. As the Marine Corps soon learned, the Japanese had no such disposition.

3

Far from the clamor of battle and the burning islands of the Gilberts and Marshalls, the Joint Chiefs of Staff weighed the relative importance of MacArthur's drive toward the southern Philippines and Nimitz's sweep across the central Pacific. There was no disagreement about the immediate objective of the Pacific campaign: It was to establish a firm Allied position in the triangle formed by Formosa, the Chinese mainland, and Luzon. Control of this area would strangle Japan's economy and open the home islands to direct attack. To move American forces toward the Formosa–China–Luzon triangle, Admiral King throughout 1943 had urged a 1,000-mile leap from the Marshalls to the Marianas, a key position in Japan's "National Defense Area." King's enthusiasm for the Marianas was based on several factors. First, the large islands of the Marianas (Saipan, Tinian, and Guam) would provide bases for operations against Luzon, Formosa, and the Japanese home islands, all of which were less than 1,500 miles distant. Second, an assault on the Marianas would outflank the Japanese bases in the Carolines to the south, especially the bastion of Truk. Third, a Marianas thrust might force the Japanese fleet to engage in a decisive battle at the limits of range from its southwest Pacific bases and land-based air cover, a prospect that gladdened the Navy. Army Air Forces planners shared the Navy's enthusiasm for different reasons. Dubious about the prospects of developing China as a base area, the AAF wanted alternate airfields for its new long range bomber, the B-29, which could reach Japan from the Marianas. After much discussion among themselves and the British, the JCS directed in December 1943 that the Marianas be Nimitz's next major objective.

The JCS had not reckoned with General MacArthur's opposition to the Marianas campaign. Four more months of interservice negotiation were needed to work out the next phase of the dual drive across the Pacific. While MacArthur would continue his return to the Philippines—with appropriate Navy support—the JCS again ordered Nimitz in March 1944 to invade the Marianas. The advance was to come in June. Carrier strikes and landings had discovered the weakness of the Japanese positions on the islands outside the "National Defense Area." Still shaped by interservice rivalry within and between theaters, the dual advance across the Pacific continued.[40]

As the planners in Washington and Honolulu recognized, the Marianas campaign would test the skill and fighting heart of the 5th Fleet and the Marine and Army divisions of the landing forces, for the islands' size and Japanese strength meant the days of atoll warfare were over. The three objectives—Saipan, Tinian, and Guam—were elongated islands that dwarfed the atolls. Saipan was 72 square miles, Tinian about 50 square miles, and Guam 225 square miles. Tinian, heavily cultivated, was relatively flat, but Saipan and Guam mixed sugar cane fields with rugged, wooded hills and deep ravines that ran along their spines. All three islands had substantial civilian populations. Coral reefs surrounded them, and sharp bluffs near the water's edge limited access from the beaches and provided the defenders with excellent positions. Moreover, peninsulas on Saipan and Guam provided fields of fire along the beaches.

Although subjected to American submarine operations and carrier strikes in the western Pacific, the Japanese by the summer of 1944 had built a formidable defense for the Marianas. Having husbanded scarce planes and pilots, the Japanese fleet and land-based army and navy air stood ready to attack the 5th Fleet in the Philippine Sea west of the Marianas. Mixed forces of the Japanese naval base defense units and balanced army forces of infantry, tanks, and artillery hurried the defensive preparations on Saipan, Tinian, and Guam. Thirty thousand Japanese troops awaited an invasion on Saipan, while 9,000 men on Tinian and 18,500 on Guam dug in and sited their weapons. The Japanese might have planned a mobile defense of the islands, but a lack of construction materials, time, and vehicles for moving artillery forced the Japanese commanders to emphasize the immediate defense of possible invasion beaches. The beach defense forces could count on tank-infantry counterattacks and abundant artillery positioned in well-camouflaged reverse slope positions, where they were relatively immune to naval gunfire. Unlike the atolls of the Gilberts and Marshalls, Saipan, Tinian, and Guam offered some room for mobile defense and for the use of hasty fortifications in the mountains. This pattern of defense meant that the Americans would be challenged both at the beaches and inland.[41]

Covered by 5th Fleet air strikes against Japanese land-based air, Admiral Turner's amphibious force approached Saipan for a June 15 landing. The Saipan landing force of 71,000 men, commanded by Holland M. Smith, was designated the Northern Troops and Landing Force (NTLF). The 2d and 4th Marine Divisions and the Army's 27th Infantry Division and XXIV Corps artillery, supplemented by specialized units and garrison troops, composed the NTLF. Also operating under Smith's command, the Southern Troops and Landing Force (STLF) waited to invade Guam. Built around the 3d Marine Division and the new 1st Provisional Brigade (the reinforced 4th and 22d Marines), Major General Roy Geiger's STLF numbered 55,000 men and included corps troops and the Army's untested 77th Infantry Division. As commander of the 5th Fleet, Admiral Spruance coordinated the actions of the fast carrier task forces responsible for isolating the Marianas from air and naval counterattack, and Turner's amphibious force, while Turner retained overall responsibility for all three landings of Operation FORAGER and direct command of the Saipan invasion.

Designed to overwhelm the Japanese with crushing supporting fires and a massive ship-to-shore movement, the NTLF landing across Saipan's southwest beaches quickly developed into a disappointing, bloody slugging match for the 2d and 4th Marine Divisions. Instead of one day, it took three to secure a solid beachhead. Overoptimistic American planning assisted the stubborn Japanese defenders. Instead of depending upon a methodical bombardment by trained slow battleships and old cruisers, Turner had carrier planes and fast battleships provide most of the four days' preliminary fires. While they scourged many buildings and supply dumps and disrupted Japanese communications, the Navy planes and fast battleships missed many artillery positions and infantry strongpoints. A short methodical bombardment on June 14 did not eliminate the remaining defenses. Moreover, the bombing and shelling, as well as the activities of the Navy's UDTs, tipped off the exact location of the landing, and the Japanese moved up reinforcing artillery, tanks, and infantry. The ship-to-shore movement itself in the early morning hours of June 15 provided a stunning demonstration of American power. Covered by tons of naval shells and hammering gunboats, more than seven hundred armored and troop-carrying amtracs plunged across the reefs and landed eight thousand Marines along a 4,000-yard front in twenty minutes. The landing plan called for the amtracs to continue inland for more than a mile and, covered by the guns of the LVTAs, debark the troops at the base of the low ridges that marked the NTLF's first objective. The Japanese did not cooperate. As the amtracs ground onto the beaches, they ran into a hail of artillery and machine gun fire, and only a few managed to proceed inland. Marine infantry scrambled for cover as the shells poured in. Before the day was over, more than two thousand Marines were down, and at least one-fourth of the amtracs were junk. Although twenty thousand men came ashore the first day, along with artillery and tanks, the two Marine Divisions found themselves struggling to clear the beachhead in the face of heavy Japanese shelling, fanatical tank-infantry counter-attacks, and suicidal infantry strongpoints. With casualties reaching 30 percent in some infantry battalions and losses high among officers, the Marines finally cleared the beachhead by June 17.[42]

Aware that the 5th Fleet faced a major naval engagement to the west, Holland Smith hurried the attacks and the unloading; he rushed the 27th Infantry Division ashore to take Aslito airfield (a prime objective) and to isolate the Japanese defenders on the island's southeast corner. In the meantime, the 2d and 4th Divisions pivoted to the northwest to divide the island and face the Japanese mountain defenses in central Saipan. The 2d Division pushed forward slowly against moderate opposition on the left, while the 4th Division punched into the rugged hills and came abreast on the right. Despite beach congestion and the disorganized unloading of Turner's amphibious ships, the NTLF consolidated its positions, pushed tanks and heavy weapons to the front, and organized its artillery support for the next phase of the fighting. In the meantime, the 5th Fleet met the Japanese Mobile Fleet in the Battle of the Philippine Sea (June 19–21) and destroyed Japanese carrier aviation for the rest of the war. Having already lost half of its first line troops and equipment at the beachhead, the Saipan defense force could expect no further assistance. The NTLF forces and the Japanese would fight it out on the ground, and the American victory became an issue not of "if" but of when and at what cost.[43]

The campaign to destroy the Japanese defense across central Saipan took more than a week of heavy fighting and tested the Marines and soldiers of the NTLF to the limits of their endurance. Casualties on both sides soared as the American and Japanese infantry tore at each other from the outskirts of Garapan Town, around Mount Tipe Pale, and in the struggle for Mount Tapotchau, the island's highest point. The bulk of the 2d Marine Division, reinforced by an attached battalion of the new 29th Marines and occasional reinforcements from the 4th Division, fought for and eventually captured the mountain itself, while most of the 27th Infantry Division tried to punch past a rugged plateau and hill line east of the mountain. On the right the 4th Division battered away at the Japanese defenses on the Kagman Peninsula and its covering hills. American artillery and tanks could do only so much in the jungle-choked, broken terrain, so the fighting became a match of American grenades, demolition teams, and infantry weapons against mortars and machine guns. Close air support could have contributed more, but the Navy pilots were too heavily involved with the Mobile Fleet and often not skilled enough to knock out well-concealed ground targets. Against the numerous Japanese caves only direct fire and small-unit assaults could end resistance. With battalions that often looked more like exhausted companies, the Americans slowly pushed forward.[44]

The central Saipan campaign also produced a crisis in interservice relations that poisoned Marine Corps–Army relations for the rest of the war, made Holland Smith a controversial commander, and even fueled postwar interservice controversies. At issue was the performance of the 27th Infantry Division, a New York National Guard division noted for its uncertain leadership. Already irritated by the division's performance at Makin and Eniwetok, Holland Smith had no patience with the 27th Division or its senior officers. After the soldiers had shown a disturbing inability to attack on time, press their assaults, or hold the ground they gained west of Aslito field and east of Mount Tapotchau, Holland Smith, upon conferring with Spruance and Turner, relieved the division commander, Major General Ralph C. Smith, on June 24. Holland Smith accused Ralph Smith of not following NTLF orders, but his actual purpose was to coerce a greater show of determination on the division's part. In this the relief was a failure. The 27th Division, demoralized by high and largely futile casualties in central Saipan, did not respond to new leadership. The division never recovered from the low esteem in which it was held, even by ranking Army officers, but Ralph Smith's relief gave the Army added determination to embarrass Holland Smith and prevent him from ever commanding soldiers again.[45]

As the "Smith versus Smith" controversy ripened, the NTLF by July 4 had ripped the heart from the Japanese defense and was working its way north against scattered but occasionally fierce resistance. The 2d Marine Division captured Garapan and with the 27th Division survived a *banzai* attack by three thousand Japanese on July 7. Plunging down Tanapag Plain on the western coast, the Japanese overran two Army battalions, pushed two other Army battalions aside, fell upon two Marine artillery battalions, and died in a furious battle in which desperate courage was shown by both Marines and soldiers. Two days later the Americans reached the northern tip of Saipan in a mopping-up operation, and Holland Smith declared Saipan secure. Since American patrols hunted down Japanese survivors (and lost men doing so) until the end of the war, "secure" was a relative term, but organized Japanese resistance had ended. At a cost of nearly 12,000 Marines and almost 4,000 soldiers, Saipan fell, and with it the Japanese government of Premier Hideki Tojo. The inner defense of Japan had been irreparably breached.[46]

Lessons abounded from the Saipan campaign. Once again, naval gunfire and aerial support needed far greater attention. Artillery–infantry coordination suffered from careless computations in the fire direction centers and inadequate centralized control as well as the inability of some infantry commanders to identify correctly their own and the enemy's positions. Accidental friendly shellings marred the operation. Although tank–infantry coordination was good, infantry assaults too often began well after the supporting fire had lifted, allowing the cave-dwelling Japanese to return to their positions. Close air support, delivered by either carrier air or Army fighters, lacked precision and timeliness. The management of supplies on the beachhead suffered from a lack of labor troops and vehicles (not enough shipping had been available for many trucks) and general disorganization. Although the campaign did not experience fundamental supply problems, some obvious defects in Smith's logistical arrangements further encouraged Army criticism. In addition, Smith's headquarters often did not allow subordinate commanders enough time to organize their attacks and on several occasions underestimated the Japanese defenses and strength. The commanders of the two Marine divisions complained through channels and obeyed, even when they knew they would take excessive casualties. The 27th Division, on the other hand, sulked and asked for more understanding than Holland Smith had to give. The concept of the unremitting assault, developed in atoll warfare, still survived on Saipan, where its assumptions were more questionable.[47] Pressed by their superiors, Marine regimental commanders viewed the 27th Division leaders with contempt. When one Army colonel complained to the Marine counterpart on his flank that his men were being hit with friendly fire, the Marine's response was typical: "Goddam you, in order to shoot at you, I'd have to reverse every weapon 180 degrees, and you'd still be out of range."[48]

Although organizational reforms built on the Saipan campaign could be made, the first phase of FORAGER produced a lasting schism in Army–Marine relations. Spruance and Turner backed Holland Smith's decision to relieve Ralph Smith, but Nimitz and Lieutenant General Robert C. Richardson, USA, questioned Holland Smith's competence and judgment. Richardson fueled the controversy by flying to Saipan to decorate men of the 27th Division and to snub Spruance, Turner, and Smith. He then convened an Army investigating board, which concluded that Ralph Smith's relief was legal but unjustified. Holland Smith, the board reported, was so biased against the Army that he should never again command soldiers. Even members of Holland Smith's staff thought he had been too impatient with Ralph Smith, a view shared by Nimitz. As the controversy developed, Nimitz became a key figure. Ever sensitive to Army–Navy relations, Nimitz did not restrain Richardson, censured the Marine Corps for a film on the Saipan campaign that he believed glorified the Marines and denigrated the Army, and threatened to revoke the press credentials of Robert Sherrod, who had reported the 27th Division's shortcomings for *Time* and *Life*. The tempest blew its way east to Washington. Just what sort of compromises Admiral King, General Marshall, and General Vandegrift made remains obscure, but Army–Navy–Marine Corps relations were patched up. By moving Holland Smith up to the command of FMF Pacific, Vandegrift could minimize the chances for further friction. As it turned out, Smith never again directly commanded Army troops, although Roy Geiger did. Smith had become a liability to the Corps, which he never could accept or forget.[49]

Impassioned interservice rivalries aside, the Marine Corps–Army expeditionary forces in the Marianas still had the Japanese to defeat, and in the Tinian campaign (July 24–August 1, 1944) the American amphibious forces conducted a bravura demonstration of their hard-earned skills. Only 4 miles from Saipan and defended by a small but dedicated Japanese force of nine thousand, Tinian had to be taken because its relatively flat terrain offered exceptional air base sites. With total naval and air superiority, the NTLF planners, directed now by a new commander, Major General Harry Schmidt, USMC, had one critical decision: where to land. Tinian offered three possibilities, two of them heavily defended by the Japanese. After extensive reconnaissance, the planners persuaded Turner and Smith, still in charge of the whole Marianas campaign, to approve a landing on two narrow beaches on Tinian's northwest coast. Knowing that the landing force (the 4th Marine Division) could come ashore only two companies at a time, the planners stressed prelanding deception, overwhelming supporting fires, and a rapid build-up ashore. All three conditions were met. As early as June 27, naval and air strikes pummeled Tinian, and these attacks were soon reinforced by long-range artillery fire. As Saipan operations waned, naval gunfire ships pounded Tinian's defenses with methodical fire while both carrier and AAF planes tore up inland positions. To cover the landing Schmidt massed thirteen Marine and Army artillery battalions on southern Saipan, and their fire blanketed northern Tinian targets with ease. The preliminary fires could be adjusted and evaluated by airborne spotters and photo reconnaissance planes, and thus the fire support met the most exacting standards. What supporting fire did not provide, deception did. On the day of the landing one task group menaced the most likely beach off Tinian Town, and recon teams and navy forces also appeared off the other possible landing sites. When the 4th Division struck on July 24, it put three infantry regiments, tanks, two artillery battalions, and adequate supplies ashore with fewer than three hundred casualties.[50]

Despite desperate but uncoordinated Japanese counterattacks during its first night ashore, the 4th Division expanded the beachhead while the 2d Marine Division came ashore and joined the attack. Supported by a logistical system designed to shift supplies ashore by preloaded amtracs, DUKWs, and trucks, the two Marine divisions moved methodically down the island, supported by artillery fires and close air strikes. Objectives fell and phase lines went by with a smoothness unseen on Saipan. Even when a tropical storm disrupted the beach unloading on July 28, the operation did not pause, for the build-up ashore had reached adequate proportions to support two divisions. The attack continued, clearing the scattered hills of central Tinian, all the airfields, and Tinian Town itself. Not until July 30 did the Marines find firm resistance in the broken ridges of Tinian's southern tip. The Marine infantry-tank teams, still opposed by about half the Japanese defenders, met the challenge. As the 4th Division progressed through the hills, breaking Japanese *banzai* attacks and taking strongpoints, the 2d Division worked its way up a sheer cliff and punctured the Japanese main defense position. In Tinian's heaviest fighting, two 2d Division regiments smashed a series of desperate *banzai* attacks and held a road up the cliff. From this penetration the Marines fanned out and cleared the island of organized resistance on August 1. With fewer than two thousand casualties, the 4th and 2d Divisions had taken Tinian. The Navy's ships and planes, Army artillery and planes, and triservice logistical and engineering support assured that the Marine divisions met the Japanese on highly unequal terms. Tinian represented a high point in amphibious warfare.[51]

Even before the NTLF captured Tinian, the assault on Guam, the second major campaign of Operation FORAGER, had finally begun. Postponed until the need for reinforcements for Saipan had passed and the 77th Infantry Division could join the operation from Hawaii, the Guam landings fell to Rear Admiral Richard L. Connolly's naval task force and Major General Roy Geiger's Southern Troops and Landing Force. The major elements of STLF were the veteran 3d Marine Division and the 1st Provisional Brigade, commanded by Brigadier General Lemuel C. Shepherd, Jr. The new but well-led and well-trained 77th Division became the corps reserve. Again, the vulnerability of the ship-to-shore movement shaped STLF planning. Rejecting two ideal beaches as too well defended, Geiger's staff selected two widely separated beaches on either side of the strategic Orote Peninsula on Guam's western coast. A beachhead at this location would give the Americans access to Apra harbor, a good anchorage for unloading, and the airfield on the peninsula, but steep hills dominated both landing sites. The key to the campaign, then, became control of the hills dominating the beaches. Even though the defenders had concentrated on the wrong beaches, the Japanese senior officers could also read a map, and the Asan beach to the north of the peninsula and the Agat beach to the south were not left undefended. With the Saipan battle already raging, real surprise was gone, but Admiral Connolly compensated for the delay by conducting a model thirteen-day preliminary air and naval bombardment. By moving his fire support ships in to close range, Connolly arranged for the ships and airplanes to conduct their missions simultaneously and with careful attention to damage assessment and target assignment. To the degree that supporting fires could reduce the risks to the ship-to-shore movement, the Navy did its job. The final success, however, still rested with the Marine infantry, tanks, and artillery that would flood ashore under the bombardment.[52]

Having lived for a month aboard hot, crowded transports, the surly Marines of the 3d Division and 1st Brigade finally plunged ashore in their amtracs on July 21 and struggled up into hills above the beaches. Despite the ever present reefs and normal confusion in crossing them, both the 3d Division and the 1st Brigade placed all their infantry regiments and most of their artillery ashore without crisis. The struggle for the hills was quite another matter. For four days the STLF had to fight with the highest degree of skill and courage to secure the beachhead, and the 77th Division landed and entered the battle on the second day of the operation. At the southern beach (Agat) the soldiers widened the southern and eastern edges of the front, while the 1st Brigade pushed north against stubborn resistance to take the Orote Peninsula and link up with the 3d Division. At the northern (Asan) beach, the 3d Division pushed the 9th Marines south to meet the 1st Brigade, but the 21st Marines in the center and the 3d Marines on the northern flank measured their gains in yards and soaring casualties as they pushed the Japanese off a series of cliff and hill positions. In four days of fighting the 3d Marines virtually disappeared as an infantry regiment and had to get help from the 9th Marines. Despite excellent artillery and tank assistance, two 3d Marines battalions mustered at about company strength after several daytime assaults and night defenses against Japanese counterattacks.[53]

The crisis of the Guam campaign came during the night of July 25–26, when the Japanese launched one of their few effective night counterattacks. Using his best infantry troops and hoping to reach and destroy the Marine artillery with human demolition squads, the Japanese commander threw five thousand men against the STLF. The heaviest attack struck the 3d Division and penetrated into the Marine positions to such depth that the division hospital, artillery, engineers, and service troops had to join the fighting. In a night of vicious combat at close quarters, the 3d Division crushed the attack and killed probably 3,500 Japanese. At those points where the attack made the first contact, Marine infantrymen fought and died in place; one 21st Marines company mustered nineteen survivors at daylight. The battle raged on into the next day, but by the end of July 26 the 3d Division counterattacked and captured the last commanding heights above the beaches. Moving carefully across hilltops thick with Japanese dead, the Marines consolidated the front lines and took a much-needed day's rest to reequip, reorganize, and absorb replacements. Having lost half of its first line troops, the Japanese defense force fell back into the heavy jungles and hill country of northern Guam to sell its remaining lives as dearly as possible.[54]

In a ten-day sweep to Guam's northern tip, the STLF crushed the last organized resistance on the island in the face of heavy rains, transportation problems, water shortages, heat, and occasionally heavy resistance. Operating side by side with admirable cooperation, the 3d Marine Division and 77th Infantry Division carried the main burden, with the 1st Brigade joining the push in its final stages. To General Geiger's credit, STLF headquarters coordinated the northern offensive with an attention to supporting arms and time-space factors absent on Saipan. The push ended on August 10 with minimal casualties and without a last *banzai* attack. Instead, disorganized and nearly weaponless, some eight thousand Japanese survivors took to the hills for guerrilla warfare, where they had to be hunted down for the rest of the war (and years afterward) by the island defense command. With casualties of seven thousand Marines and nine hundred soldiers, STLF completed the conquest of the Marianas and turned over the island to the Navy and AAF to develop as a major naval and air base.[55]

The Marianas campaign provided the ultimate test for American amphibious operations in the Pacific and the fighting qualities of the Marine divisions. Although every landing brought refinements to amphibious doctrine, primarily in the use of supporting arms and logistical support, Operation FORAGER demonstrated that the Japanese could not destroy the American amphibious task forces by ordinary aerial and naval attacks or halt the American landing forces on the beaches with a conventional defense. Backed by tanks and artillery, the Marine infantry proved that it could clear caves with hand-carried demolitions, stand firm against human-wave attacks, capture hills against the most stubborn resistance even if it left bodies along the barren, blasted slopes, and endure all the numbing rigors of warfare amid coral cliffs and entangling jungles. As both the Marines and the Japanese learned, naval gunfire, air support, massed artillery, and tanks gave the Americans the tactical initiative, but in the end the last Japanese defenders had to be beaten by Marine infantry. The hero of FORAGER was the individual rifleman. Barely out of boyhood, often scared and sometimes blindly heroic, he fought and conquered—and created the image of the modern Marine Corps. On his head rests a helmet covered with camouflaged cloth; his light green cotton dungarees with the black USMC globe and anchor on the left pocket are stained and often bloody; his M-1 is scratched but clean; his leggings (if he still has them) cover soft brown work shoes; around his waist hangs a cartridge belt carrying two canteens, a first aid packet, and a K-Bar knife. Burned by the tropic sun, numbed by the loss of comrades, sure of his loyalty to the Corps and his platoon, scornful of the Japanese but wary of their suicidal tactics, he squints into the western sun and wonders what island awaits him. Ahead lie Peleliu, Iwo Jima, and Okinawa.

4

Despite the Marianas campaign and Admiral King's gaze upon new targets nearer Japan, General MacArthur's advance drew elements of the Fleet Marine Force into the western Pacific and eventually the Philippines themselves. Responding to an appeal for greater naval support, the JCS and Admiral Nimitz in early 1944 decided to support MacArthur with a campaign against the western Carolines. From MacArthur's perspective, this operation (STALEMATE) secured the northern approaches to Mindanao by neutralizing the Japanese bases at Yap and

Babelthuap. From the Navy's viewpoint, the prize was Ulithi atoll, an anchorage without peer, and the isolation of Truk. As planning progressed throughout 1944, CINCPAC narrowed the number of objectives, because MacArthur's forces were making accelerated advances along New Guinea and the Marianas campaign was taking more time and forces than anticipated. What was at first designed as a two-corps expeditionary force (commanded by Major General Julian C. Smith, USMC) shrank to a two-division corps (Western Troops and Landing Force, or WTLF), directed by Major General Roy Geiger and his staff. While Geiger participated in the Guam campaign, Smith's staff handled the planning with its naval counterpart, III Amphibious Force. In these meetings, the planners selected the specific objectives: Peleliu and Angaur islands in the Palau chain and Ulithi atoll. Geiger's WTLF, composed of the 1st Marine Division, the 81st Infantry Division, and corps troops, would take Peleliu and Angaur, from which American air could neutralize heavily defended Babelthuap and other Caroline bases. The logic of STALEMATE was impeccable—except that Japanese air and naval forces had already left the western Carolines and MacArthur invaded Leyte, not Mindanao. Nevertheless, once ordered, STALEMATE moved forward on its own momentum, in part because Nimitz wanted no more confrontations with MacArthur.[56]

Peleliu's terrain and the Japanese defense forces combined to make the 1st Marine Division's campaign one of the most trying of the Pacific war. In size Peleliu Island, 6 miles long and 2 miles wide, resembled the atolls of the Marshalls; in shape it looked like a lobster claw, having a long peninsula to the north and shorter one to the south, with swamps and a bay in between. Peleliu's terrain, however, was lunar. A volcanic island of limestone and coral, Peleliu provided the Japanese with a trackless maze of small hills, cliffs, caves, and pinnacles from which to cover the flat south end of the island with fire. Swamps, thick jungle, and heavy scrub made movement difficult for attacking troops. The ground was so hard that foxholes could not be dug, and the heat and humidity hovered around the 100° mark. To defend this paradise the Japanese had sent a crack infantry regiment with tanks and light artillery. Including naval base troops and service units, the Peleliu garrison numbered ten thousand and could draw reinforcements from neighboring islands. With almost a year's warning that Peleliu might be an American objective, the Japanese had built hundreds of cave and bunker positions with connecting tunnels and multiple firing positions. These defenses extended from the beaches into the massive Umurbrogol Ridge, which dominated the northern peninsula. The Japanese defense plan, moreover, did not anticipate massive counterattacks or a decisive struggle at the beaches; knowing he could no longer count on air and naval relief, the Japanese commander decided to wage a war of attrition against the Marines from the caves. Such tactics would nullify much of the advantages of American supporting arms and make the battle infantry against infantry.[57]

Having survived the mud, falling coconuts, rats, land crabs, and ennui of its primitive base camp on Pavuvu Island in the Solomons, the veteran 1st Marine Division prepared to join the central Pacific campaign for the first time. As it entered its third campaign, the division retained more than half of its veterans, mostly specialists and troop leaders. It was a self-confident division, and no one was more sure of its prowess than its commander, Major General William H. Rupertus, who had been with the division since Guadalcanal. Absent during much of his division's planning for Peleliu and hobbled physically and temperamentally by a broken ankle, Rupertus set much of the tone of the operation: It would require stiff fighting to get ashore, but the division would overrun the island in two to four days. Rupertus made this prediction to his troops and to the press. More pessimistic assessments from Brigadier General O. P. Smith, the assistant division commander, and Geiger's WTLF staff went unheeded.

The landing plan reflected Rupertus's optimism, which was shared by his Navy counterparts. The operation provided for only two days' preliminary bombardment, and even that limited shelling was not carefully managed. The landing itself was designed to overwhelm the Japanese defenses and airfield complex on Peleliu's southwest coast. All three of the division's infantry regiments would land abreast, with only one battalion in division reserve; Rupertus showed little interest in arranging for an additional reserve from the 81st Infantry Division, although a regiment was available. Having focused on the problems of the ship-to-shore movement and having loaded supplies on scattered amphibious ships, the 1st Division left Pavuvu convinced that it would roll over the Japanese in its first central Pacific assault.[58]

On September 15, 1944, covered by air and naval bombardment, wave after wave of 1st Marine Division infantry churned toward Peleliu's beaches in amtracs, followed to the reef by small boats and DUKWs. The Japanese response was devastating. Artillery and mortars punished the amtracs from the reef to the beach, and the Marines scrambled from their vehicles into the face of heavy machine gun fire and more shelling. Losses in the 1st Marines on the left flank and among the 7th Marines on the right mounted. Although the 5th Marines in the center reached portions of the airfield, the Japanese held the attack to a 4,000-yard arc along the beaches. As the beachhead thickened with succeeding waves of Marines and equipment, the Japanese pounded the position with mortar fire, scourged its front with more fire, and threw tanks against the most advanced positions. By the time the first day ended, the division was barely holding and had lost nearly 1,300 men, or more than twice as many as its staff had predicted. This was not a happy omen.[59]

In a week of severe fighting, the 1st Marine Division finally cleared all of Peleliu except Umurbrogol Ridge and most of the northern peninsula, but the cost of the Marine success was staggering. To eliminate probably six thousand Japanese defenders, the division lost nearly four thousand of its own men, and the 1st Marines ceased to exist as a combat regiment. Having fought its way into the nearest hills of the Umurbrogol, the 1st Marines, led by the dynamic Colonel "Chesty" Puller, left the battle with fewer than half the troops it brought ashore. Its mission against the Umurbrogol shifted to the Army's 321st Infantry Regiment, ordered into the battle by General Geiger. Not well informed of his own losses and motivated by stubborn pride, Rupertus had not wanted reinforcements. His division suffered accordingly. Clearing the rest of the island, the 5th and 7th Marines had a trying battle against the entrenched Japanese. Punished by long-range observed fire from the northern ridges and ravaged by heat exhaustion and fatigue, the Marines struggled from one pillbox to another. Behind the front the number of crumpled bodies and smoking ruins grew. When the 1st Marine Division could shift its entire attention against the Umurbrogol, it was questionable how much longer the division could last, as both the 1st Marines and the 7th Marines had already made scant headway against the cave positions.[60]

The remnants of the 1st Division, assisted by the 81st Division, finally reduced the Japanese defense of the Umurbrogol by October 12, but not before the division had thrown practically all its troops into the infantry battles for the caves. Filling its ranks with artillerymen, service troops, stragglers, and virtually anyone who could hold a rifle, the 5th and 7th Marines gradually encircled and isolated the Japanese defenders on the Umurbrogol. At the same time, units of the 5th Marines bypassed the pocket, cleared the rest of the northern peninsula, and captured nearby Ngesebus Island. Amtrac and naval patrols cut off Japanese reinforcements. Against the Umurbrogol caves, there were no easy approaches. When tanks and artillery could reach a cave, they were used with effect, and Marine Corsairs and dive bombers of MAG-11, flying from Peleliu's airfield, pounded the caves with bombs and napalm. Nevertheless, the final battles fell to the Marine infantry, which sealed the caves with demolitions and flamethrowers. Amid the shattered scrub trees and crumbling coral cliffs, bitter small-unit battles eroded both American and Japanese strength and endurance. When the 1st Marine Division finally left the fight, leaving the mopping-up to the 81st Division, the division had lost 6,336 Marines and spent nearly 1,600 rounds of infantry and artillery ammunition to kill each Japanese soldier. Overshadowed by MacArthur's Leyte landings and fought outside the boundaries of both military and public awareness, the battle for Peleliu introduced a new level of savagery to the Pacific war and a new type of Japanese defense that would provide the ultimate test for the Marine Corps.[61]

The American offensive into the western Pacific not only thrust the 1st Marine Division back into the main Pacific war but brought the Solomons-based 1st Marine Aircraft Wing under MacArthur's command and added Marine aviation to the reconquest of the Philippines. Operating under JCS instructions of March 1944, MacArthur assumed control of many of the forces previously commanded by Admiral Halsey in the South Pacific area. Still pounding Rabaul and its outposts, the 1st MAW was among these units. Learning of the forthcoming operations, the 1st MAW commander, Major General Ralph J. Mitchell, requested and received from MacArthur's senior air commander, Lieutenant General George C. Kenney, a close air support mission for MacArthur's Sixth Army. Training with Army units in the Solomons throughout the summer of 1944, the 1st MAW prepared for its role.[62]

Based on reports of weak Japanese air resistance to American carrier strikes in September 1944 and other intelligence, the JCS canceled the Mindanao landings and directed MacArthur to invade Leyte in the central Philippines in October. A prelude to the main attack on Luzon, the Leyte operation would give the Americans land-based air superiority and a base for further operations against the Japanese lines of communications in the western Pacific. Although no Marine aviation was initially assigned to the Leyte operation, Kenney ordered Mitchell to prepare seven dive-bomber squadrons (MAGs 24 and 32) for service on Luzon. Under the direction of Colonel Clayton C. Jerome and Lieutenant Colonel Keith B. McCutcheon, a pioneer in close air support techniques, the Marine dive bombers in the Solomons continued to perfect their skills while MacArthur mounted the invasion of Leyte.

The Leyte landings of October 20 went well, but the Japanese response so threatened the success of the campaign that Kenney asked the Marine Corps for unscheduled aviation reinforcements. In addition, two Marine heavy artillery battalions joined the campaign as part of the XXIV Corps artillery. But it was aircraft that Kenney needed. Stunned by the massive, suicidal Japanese air and naval attacks in the Battle of Leyte Gulf (October 23–26) and Japanese resistance on the ground, MacArthur and Admiral Halsey agreed that the American land-based air effort needed stiffening. Kenney doubted that his primitive fields on Leyte could handle more aircraft, but he recognized that his AAF pilots needed help in cutting off Japanese reinforcements from the other islands and in supporting the Sixth Army. Japanese *kamikaze* attacks on the invasion shipping had also complicated air superiority operations. By early December the Marines had arrived on Leyte. First to appear were the radar-equipped Grumman F6F "Hellcats" of VMF(N)-541, a 2d MAW squadron based in the Palaus. Right behind the nightfighters landed four Corsair squadrons of MAG-12, based in the Solomons. The Marine aviators joined both AAF and Navy squadrons in the mud of Tacloban and immediately entered the air war.[63]

For the rest of December 1944, when the campaign for Leyte closed, the Marine squadrons performed with skill and enthusiasm under the most primitive conditions. Flying primarily against Japanese waterborne reinforcements, MAG-12 destroyed twenty-two ships and shot down forty aircraft at a cost of thirty-four planes and nine pilots. Some of MAG-12's 264 missions were also flown against ground targets. In its attacks against both ships and ground positions, MAG-12 demonstrated its ability to fly "down on the deck" and hit targets with greater accuracy than most AAF pilots. This fact was not lost on Army ground commanders. As the campaign on Leyte dwindled, MAG-12 launched strikes against Japanese targets on Luzon and prepared to support the Luzon landings. In the meantime, the nightfighters of VMF(N)-541 had been equally busy. Before it returned to Peleliu in mid-January, 1945, the squadron flew 312 missions and nearly 1,000 hours. It destroyed twenty-two Japanese aircraft in aerial combat and smashed others on the ground; its nighttime patrols over the VII Amphibious Force in Leyte Gulf helped spare the Navy from serious damage.[64]

With the remaining Japanese on Leyte isolated by the newly arrived U.S. Eighth Army, MacArthur's Sixth Army launched the principal Philippine campaign upon Luzon in early January 1945. From its beginning, the Luzon operation included Marine aviation. As the invasion fleet struggled northward against serious *kamikaze* attacks, MAG-12 Corsairs flew air cover while other carrier-based Marine fighters in the 3d Fleet struck Japanese air bases on Luzon and Formosa. With so much of his ground-based aviation committed to the Luzon campaign, General Kenney sought additional reinforcements to support the Eighth Army's simultaneous operations in the central Philippines. Responding to Kenney's orders, the 1st MAW sent the four Corsair squadrons of

MAG-14 from the Solomons, and in early January the Marines began flying missions from another rude strip on Samar. The chief Marine contribution, however, particularly for the development of Marine aviation doctrine, came after the Sixth Army's successful landings at Lingayen Gulf, Luzon, on January 9, 1945. Building upon a three-man advance party that included Colonel Jerome and Colonel McCutcheon, the 1st MAW scratched an airstrip together in the rice paddies near Dagupan and dispatched the dive bombers of MAGs 24 and 32 to perform their preassigned close air support role. By the end of January, Colonel Jerome was commanding seven squadrons of obsolescent Douglas SBDs and nearly five hundred Marines on Luzon, as well as coordinating all American air efforts from Dagupan.[65]

The Luzon operation gave Marine aviators an opportunity to demonstrate the soundness of their special approach to close air support, and they responded to the challenge. The essential difference between Marine close air support for ground troops and the types of missions flown by the Navy and AAF was simple enough in concept: The air liaison parties (ALPs) attached to ground units would not only request air strikes but would direct them as well. This technique ensured greater accuracy, quicker response time, fewer chances for friendly casualties, and much greater flexibility of employment near friendly troops. The Marines received their first important chance to show how close air support should be handled when the 1st Cavalry Division made a three-day dash to Manila to save three thousand Filipino internees. Receiving their directions from the radio-jeeps of the ALPs with the 1st Cavalry Division, the SBDs of MAGSDAGUPAN pounded Japanese positions as the Army's mobile columns swept toward Manila. In actual operation, the concept of ground–directed air strikes proved as feasible as it had looked in rehearsals and converted many senior Army officers to Marine close air support doctrine. Throughout the rest of the Luzon campaign, Marine dive bombers gave effective close air support to both the Sixth Army and Filipino guerrilla groups, who desperately needed air support in their operations in northern Luzon. More important, the concept of ground-directed strikes spread throughout the Sixth Army, so that by the end of the campaign AAF fighter-bombers, directed by Army ALPs, were providing effective support for the ground troops. The Marines continued to carry the bulk of the close air support role. The seven Marine squadrons on Luzon provided only 13 percent of the American aircraft on the island, but MAGSDAGUPAN flew almost half of the total American sorties on Luzon between January 27 and April 14, 1945. The high sortie rate reflected Marine specialization in close air support, ground forces enthusiasm for air support, and the high efficiency of Marine service units at Dagupan. By the end of the Luzon campaign, MAGs 24 and 32 had proved that close air support could save American lives and give ground operations a new flexibility.[66]

As the Luzon operation changed to a hunt for small bands of Japanese soldiers, Marine aviation operations in the Philippines shifted to the southern islands, where Army divisions of the Eighth Army and Filipino guerrilla units were fighting against the scattered but numerous Japanese garrisons. MAG-14 continued to fly missions from Samar, but the other three MAGs shifted south in March and April 1945. The foremost site of Marine air activities became Moret Field on the extreme western tip of Mindanao near the town of Zamboanga. From Moret Field, the squadrons of MAGs 12, 24, and 32, reinforced with ground units and some separate squadrons, flew virtually every type of mission, from air cover for American invasion forces to close air support for Army and guerrilla units. Their reputation for skill firmly established on Luzon, the Marine squadrons supported all phases of MacArthur's liberation of the southern Philippines. Using ALPs and advanced auxiliary strips, the Marine pilots continued to provide devastating close air support, aided by a much greater freedom from centralized AAF control over air operations. If anything, the Army's enthusiasm for close air support became excessive, and many ground units saw Marine aviation as a solution for every tactical problem. In some cases, for example the assault on Bud Dajo Mountain on Jolo Island, close air support by itself won battles. In any event, MAGSZAMBOANGA sorties gave the Americans a decisive tactical advantage. On Mindanao alone the Marines flew more than ten thousand sorties and contributed to killing more than ten thousand Japanese at a cost of fewer than four thousand American and Filipino casualties. By the time the Philippine operations had neared their close in July 1945, the 1st MAW had proved that Marine air could handle all aspects of tactical air war and that Marine close air support was a dependable instrument for inflicting maximum destruction on the Japanese.[67]

5

Committed to the liberation of the Philippines by the autumn of 1944, the JCS and the Navy's planners at CINCPAC turned their attention to additional operations in the western Pacific. With the Philippines in American hands, Formosa declined in strategic importance. Rejecting Formosa as an objective, the JCS looked northwest from the Marianas toward the Bonin Islands, the Ryukyus, and the Japanese home islands themselves. After conferences with Nimitz, the JCS on October 3, 1944, ordered Nimitz to mount an invasion of Iwo Jima in the Bonins and Okinawa in the Ryukyus in the first quarter of 1945. The assault on Iwo Jima, code-named DETACHMENT, would deny the Japanese two airfields and provide the AAF with fighter bases from which it could escort the B-29s already pounding Japan from the Marianas. Almost equidistant (650 miles) between Japan and the Marianas, Iwo Jima would also provide an emergency landing site for AAF aircraft crippled over Japan. None of the planners thought DETACHMENT would be a cheap operation for the landing force, the V Amphibious Corps, but the value of the island to both the naval and the air campaigns appeared self-evident.[68]

Of all the unpleasant islands the Marines saw in World War II, Iwo Jima was the nastiest, prepared by nature and the Japanese armed forces as a death trap for any attacker. Shaped like a porkchop with its narrow tip to the south, the island's 7.5 square miles held a mixture of black volcanic ash, scrub vegetation, sulphur springs, and hills that resembled rock quarries. At Iwo's southern tip, Mount Suribachi loomed almost 600 feet above the 3 miles of soft, terraced beaches. From the low ground of the southern third of the island, the terrain climbed and became the Motoyama Plateau, where the Japanese had built two airfields and had begun another. The Pacific surf, unbroken by a barrier reef, surged against the plateau's coastline of cliffs, which prevented any alternate landing sites. Even though harassed by American submarines and aircraft, Iwo's commander, Lieutenant General Tadamichi Kuribayashi, had had eight months to fortify the island and gather at least 21,000 troops. Almost half of them were tank, artillery, and anti-aircraft units amply supplied with guns and ammunition. Kuribayashi's defense organization demonstrated the ultimate in Japanese cave warfare. Conceding American air and naval superiority, Kuribayashi hoped to destroy the American landing force by positional defense. Prohibiting anything but small, local counterattacks and infiltration, he ordered his troops to build two major defense systems across the Motoyama Plateau and to fortify Mount Suribachi. To protect their tanks, artillery, mortars, and machine guns, the Japanese built hundreds of concrete blockhouses and thousands of smaller emplacements. They developed Iwo's thousand caves as defense positions and linked many of them with tunnels. Ammunition and supplies were distributed widely to protect them from American supporting fires. Kuribayashi wanted his men to die in place and kill as many Marines as they could.[69]

Photographing Iwo Jima even as they pounded it with AAF bombers in early 1945, Navy and Marine commanders recognized that DETACHMENT would test the American amphibious team, and they committed their best units. Postponing the landing until February 19 in order to assemble a task force of almost eight hundred ships and landing craft, Admiral Spruance and Admiral Turner, once more putting to sea as the commanders of the 5th Fleet and V Amphibious Force, insisted that Holland M. Smith join them for the operation as commander of the expeditionary troops. Because the landing force was all-Marine with the exception of small Army support units, Nimitz and the Army did not object. The direct responsibility for the land campaign rested with Harry Schmidt's veteran V Amphibious Corps, built around the 3d, 4th, and 5th Marine Divisions. The 3d and 4th Marine Divisions were veterans of the Pacific war. The 5th Division, formed in late 1943, contained a strong cadre of veteran officers and NCOs and had trained hard for more than a year. The corps artillery, amphibian tractor battalions, and service units were equally experienced. Moreover, after the Marianas campaign and Peleliu, the Marines understood the perils of cave warfare and had reorganized accordingly. The infantry battalions that landed at Iwo now included an assault platoon equipped with bazookas, flamethrowers, and demolitions, and the tank battalions had increased their number of flamethrower tanks. Prelanding training stressed assaults on fortified positions. For the first time, the V AC organized Fire Support Coordination Centers (FSCCs) at the corps and division levels to ensure the most efficient use of close air support, naval gunfire, and artillery. Smith worried about the short (two-day) preliminary naval bombardment, but Turner's planners thought the main question was not the success of the ship-to-shore movement but the momentum of the ground attack against the most massive and dangerous Japanese defenses the Marine Corps had yet faced. Against Iwo's caves supporting arms could do only so much, and victory rested with the fighting heart of the seventy thousand men of three Marine reinforced divisions.

Given the nature of the terrain and the Japanese defenses, the V AC scheme of manuever for the landing and subsequent campaign could not be—and was not—subtle. Landing with eight battalions across the eastern beaches between Mount Suribachi and the Motoyama Plateau, the 4th and 5th Marine Divisions, commanded by Major General Clifton B. Cates and Major General Keller E. Rockey, would seize the beaches and then wheel northward with the 5th Division on the left and the 4th Division on the right. The 3d Division (Major General Graves B. Erskine) would join the attack when and where needed. One regiment of the 5th Division, the 28th Marines, had the task of eliminating the defenses of Mount Suribachi while the rest of the landing force attacked the defenses of the Motoyama Plateau, seizing both airfields. To take a beachhead and breach Kuribayashi's first defense line, the

V AC needed at least two divisions, but the landing plan also meant that there would be incredible congestion in the operation's earliest stages, with nearly fifty thousand Marines packed into only 2 or 3 square miles of volcanic ash. Under such circumstances, Japanese gunners, firing preregistered fires, could hardly miss the Marines.[70]

Preceded by the planned preliminary air and naval bombardment, which destroyed most of the identifiable heavy Japanese guns, and heavy prelanding fires on the beaches, the 4th and 5th Marine Divisions swept toward Iwo in amtracs and landing craft as scheduled in the early morning of February 19, 1945. The ship-to-shore movement did not meet serious resistance. Under a pale blue sky flecked with clouds, and cooled by a strong, salty breeze, the invading Marines might have thought the landing was a painless maneuver. As the amtracs struggled to climb the terraces of dark ash, the landing quickly became a nightmare. Having held their fire until the first waves were ashore, Japanese gunners soon deluged the beaches with artillery and mortars. By the time the third wave hit Iwo, it was clear that the fight would be even worse than anticipated. A veteran sergeant of the 25th Marines was appalled by the Marine body fragments and entrails littering the ashes: "The exact word that told all that was happening on this morning at this miserable place . . . was *carnage*." [71] Suffering almost 2,300 casualties, the two assault divisions by nightfall had seized a beachhead about 3,000 yards long and between 1,500 and 700 yards in depth; into this enclave V AC packed almost thirty thousand men, hundreds of guns and vehicles, and tons of supplies, all under heavy artillery fire. Well short of the first day's objectives, the two divisions scooped holes in the earth and awaited the counterattacks that never came. Few Marines had yet seen a live Japanese, but around them rested their own poncho-covered dead. In the darkness supplies burned, ammunition dumps exploded, and wounded died under the shellfire. Along the beaches wrecked landing craft and LVTs mingled with the bodies pounded by the heavy surf. It was inconceivable that more horrible days lay ahead, but they did.[72]

In four more days of fighting of ever increasing intensity, the V AC captured Mount Suribachi, overran the first Japanese airfield, and reached its landing-day objectives, which were at the edge of Kuribayashi's main defensive position across the Motoyama Plateau. The most dramatic success was the capture of Suribachi, which dominated the Marines' left flank. Capturing the hill's approaches in heavy fighting, the 28th Marines on February 23 sent a series of patrols to the summit. Against scattered resistance, the patrols reached the extinct volcano's crater and raised a small American flag to announce their success. Seeing the small flag go up on Suribachi, Secretary of the Navy James V. Forrestal, observing the operation, turned to Holland Smith and said: "The raising of that flag on Suribachi means there will be a Marine Corps for the next 500 years." [73] The Marines must also have sensed the historic importance of the capture of Suribachi, for another patrol reached the crest with a larger flag from an LST. The second flag-raising, captured in a still photograph by Associated Press photographer Joe Rosenthal, matched Forrestal's sense of history. The picture of six ordinary Americans, half of them doomed to become casualties on Iwo, came to symbolize the Corps of World War II and served as an inspiration to Marines and their fellow citizens ever since.[74] The photograph also ensured that later Marines would seldom be without a flag to raise over their conquests.

In the meantime, seven battalions of the 4th and 5th Divisions, reinforced by tanks and supported by naval gunfire and artillery, struggled northward against the defenses of the Motoyama Plateau. As the casualties mounted, Schmidt committed two regiments of the 3d Marine Division against the strong defenses in the center of Kuribayashi's position. Slowly, painfully, measuring their gains in yards, the three Marine divisions advanced abreast into a maze of cliffs, caves, and pillboxes. The American losses, particularly in officers and NCOs, were appalling. (Of the twenty-four original infantry battalion commanders, nineteen fell.) As the rifle companies dwindled, commanders consolidated the survivors and drew replacements both from the normal replacement drafts and from the division's supporting units. In one battalion of the 25th Marines, fewer than 150 of the battalion's more than 900 Marines survived the battle unhurt.[75]

For the Marine infantry there was little hope of survival: "They send you up to a place. . . and you get shot to hell and maybe they pull you back. But then they send you right up again and then you get murdered. God, you stay there until you get killed or until you can't stand it any more." [76] Seldom seeing their tormentors, the Marines knocked out one position after another, all the while ravaged by mortar and machine gun fire. From shore to shore the Motoyama Plateau seethed like a cauldron as flamethrower fires and demolitions mixed their smoke with natural sulphur springs and volcanic dust. Not until D-plus-19 (March 10) did the V AC finally work its way through the Japanese main defenses, seize the high ground along the crest of the Motoyama Plateau, and penetrate the second defense line to the sea. In the process, the three Marine divisions suffered nearly 13,000 casualties, but they had also destroyed the vast majority of the Japanese defenders.[77]

The fighting continued with a numbing, horrible sameness. Marine

World War II: Jungle War. Gunners of the 1st Marine Division manhandle a 105-mm. howitzer, Cape Gloucester, 1944

World War II: Atoll War. The beachhead on Betio Island, Tarawa, 1943

World War II: The price of victory

World War II: Marine Aviation in the Pacific. Chance-Vought F4U "Corsairs" on a bombing mission, 1944

World War II: The beachhead at Iwo Jima, 1945

World War II: For all the ships ... dead Marine, Iwo Jima, 1945

Top: World War II: Cave Warfare. Marines destroy a Japanese position, Iwo Jima, 1945. Middle: Major General O. P. Smith USMC, commanding general, 1st Marine Division, confers with Major General Edward M. Almond, USA, CG X Corps, about the liberation of Seoul, Korea, 1950. Bottom: Winners, Losers, All Cold: Marines guard Chinese prisoners on the march out from the Chosin Reservoir, Korea, 1950

Top: Marines outpost the Main
Line of Resistance, the JAMESTOWN
Line, Korea, 1952. Middle: Marine
Aviation at War: Grumman F9F
"Panthers" begin a mission,
Korea, 1953. Bottom: Harry and
His "Police Chief": President
Truman and General Clifton B.
Cates, Commandant of the
Marine Corps, circa 1950

The New Amphibious Assault: Marines of the 2d Division and 2d Marine Aircraft Wing practice landings at Camp Lejeune, N. C., 1964

Vietnam: Marines and the pacification war, 1967

Top: Vietnam: The DMZ War. Marine machinegunners defend Khe Sanh, 1968. Middle: Vietnam: A Combined Action Platoon Marine explains the M-16 to a Popular Forces soldier, 1967. Bottom: Vietnam: Vertical Assault. Marines leave a HUS helo in operations near Da Nang, 1966

United States Marine Corps

Top: Vietnam: Marine aviation goes to war. The first A-4B "Skyhawk" arrives
at the SATS airfield, Chu Lai, 1965. Bottom: Recruiting Poster, the 1970s

United States Marine Corps

artillery and air strikes pounded the Japanese cave systems and pill-boxes, and then tanks and infantry, moving cautiously across the broken ground, would advance on the cliffs. Met with withering anti-tank and machine gun fire, Marine tanks burned and infantry sprawled, some already dead. The Marines would creep forward using whatever cover they could find. If enough men survived, they might eventually reach a position where they could scorch the cave with a flamethrower and blast it with dynamite. Tanks and halftracks pressed forward to provide direct fire and fell to mines and artillery, but others pressed the attack. Bulldozers pushed forward to seal the caves. Stretcher bearers staggered to the rear with casualties, often under fire, and carrying parties struggled to the front with scarce water, food, and ammunition. Behind the infantry, artillery battalions positioned nearly hub to hub fired missions around the clock and endured sporadic Japanese counter-battery fire. Along the beaches the Navy beachmaster party and the shore party manhandled supplies ashore and dragged mired vehicles onto wire mats laid from the beaches. Thousands of foxholes, draped with ponchos and shelter-halves, pocked the island, and telephone wire criss-crossed the ground in bizarre patterns. Chilled by sudden rains, harassed by heavy surf, the support and service units doggedly per-formed their tasks under the constant threat of artillery fire. On Iwo every place seemed like the front.

For two more weeks the exhausted Marine divisions slowly eliminated Japanese pockets of resistance in northern Iwo Jima. On March 16 the V AC declared the island secure and turned the mopping-up over to an Army regiment and other garrison troops. Except for small *banzai* attacks, Kuribayashi's 21,000-man garrison died in place as ordered. In the process the Japanese inflicted almost 26,000 casualties on the Marines, 2,798 on the Navy, and 37 on the Army. For the first time in the central Pacific campaign, the Japanese, without much air and naval support, had inflicted more casualties on an American invasion force than they had taken. Marine dead alone reached almost 6,000 men, and all three Marine divisions would need fundamental rebuilding be-fore another operation.

Particularly well reported by Marine and civilian correspondents, the battle inspired and distressed the American public. The Hearst news-paper chain criticized Marine tactics, only to be rebutted by *Time* and *Newsweek*. An outraged party of Marines stormed the offices of the *San Francisco Examiner* and demanded an apology for the paper's slurs on Marine skill.[78] Even at the top of the command structure, the cam-paign caused concern. Holland Smith, as always a defender of his troops, remained convinced that more naval gunfire could have saved lives, but his Navy colleagues argued that naval guns could not hit what they could not see or reach. Commandant Vandegrift had to soothe important members of the government by explaining the perils of cave warfare. Yet, as an epic of human endurance, the battle awed even its participants. Admiral Nimitz announced that on Iwo "uncommon valor was a common virtue," and twenty-seven Marines and sailors received Medals of Honor for heroism, a new high for one operation. And, justifying DETACHMENT in part, more than 25,000 AAF airmen eventually used Iwo Jima for emergency landings in 1945. Controversial and awesome, Iwo Jima represented the pinnacle of the amphibious assault in skill and cost.[79]

While Army patrols rooted out Iwo's stragglers, the Central Pacific forces gathered at bases from the Philippines to Hawaii for the most ambitious and largest amphibious assault of the Pacific war—the invasion of Okinawa. The seizure of the largest of the Ryukyus would put the Americans on Japan's doorstep: Okinawa is but 360 miles from the island of Kyushu; the distance to Formosa and mainland China is about the same. With Okinawa as a base, the Americans could cut the last supply routes from China and Southeast Asia, reach Japan with medium bombers, and invade the home islands under land-based air cover. Conversely, an American invasion fleet would be in range of more than one hundred air bases from which the Japanese might launch as many as four thousand aircraft. How many of these attackers might be *kamikazes* was unpredictable, but after the Philippine experience Navy planners had little doubt that Admiral Spruance's 5th Fleet would see the *kamikazes* again. After Iwo Jima, too, American planners expected a fierce defense of Okinawa itself by the some 100,000 Japanese soldiers and sailors of General Mitsuru Ushijima's Thirty-second Army, a force well supplied with artillery and automatic weapons and built around two crack divisions and an independent brigade. Okinawa itself was made for a stiff defense. Some 60 miles long and from 2 to 18 miles wide, Okinawa is mountainous to the north and hilly in the southern third of the island. Strategically, the southern third of the island was most important, for it held four airbases and the port of Naha as well as the best beaches and anchorages.[80]

In planning the invasion of Okinawa (Operation ICEBERG), Nimitz's planners amassed a joint expeditionary force designed to overwhelm the anticipated Japanese aerial assault and the expected defense of the beaches. To isolate Okinawa from air and naval attack, the Navy's fast carrier task forces pounded the airfields and harbors of Formosa, Japan, and the Ryukyus themselves. At Nimitz's insistence, the AAF's B-29s also joined the airfield bombardment. In the meantime Spruance formed an invasion fleet that totaled more than 1,200 vessels; Admiral Turner once again commanded the amphibious force, which was supported as usual by escort carriers, gunfire support ships, and specialized logistical vessels. Numbering 183,000 men, the landing force was organized as the U.S. Tenth Army (Lieutenant General Simon B. Buckner, Jr., USA, commander), composed of the Army XXIV Corps and the all-Marine III Amphibious Corps. The Army contribution to ICEBERG totaled four infantry divisions, while Roy Geiger's III AC included corps troops and the 1st, 2d, and 6th Marine Divisions. The veteran 1st Division had recovered from Peleliu, and the 2d Division from Saipan. The new 6th Division faced its first operation as a division, but most of its units were already veteran. To help protect the invasion fleet and support the Tenth Army, the planners organized an AAF–Marine Tactical Air Force (TAF), which eventually included four Marine air groups, several separate squadrons, and air control and ground support elements. The commander of TAF throughout the campaign was a Marine major general, first F. P. Mulcahy and then Louis E. Woods. In all, the Okinawa landing force included nearly 90,000 ground and aviation Marines.[81]

Anticipating a battle at the beaches and around the two airfields (Yontan and Kadena) they had selected as the first important objectives, the American commanders began ICEBERG by pounding Okinawa with a week of intense aerial attack and naval gunfire and by seizing the Kerama Retto island group, which menaced the western invasion beaches. By seizing the Keramas, the 77th Infantry Division eliminated a Japanese flotilla of suicide boats and secured an anchorage for the American fleet. In the meantime the amphibious force massed for the main landing. Selected for their width, the mild surf and reef conditions, and proximity to the airfields, the Hagushi beaches provided the Tenth Army with a front of more than 5 miles. While a transport group carrying the 2d Marine Division, the landing force reserve, demonstrated off a southeastern beach to fix Japanese reserves, the Tenth Army landed two infantry divisions and the 1st and 6th Marine Divisions on April 1 in an almost flawless ship-to-shore movement. Much to the amazement of the Americans, Japanese resistance ashore and attacks against the invasion fleet were minimal. In four days the Tenth Army had split the island and seized objectives the planners had thought it would take two weeks to reach. As the III AC shifted northward and the XXIV Corps moved south, supplies and supporting units, including the first elements of the TAF, flowed onto Okinawa. For a few breathtaking days, it looked as if the rest of the campaign would be much like the first day; the Americans would advance "standing up." It was a forlorn hope.[82]

The Japanese, predicting the American invasion with precision, defended Okinawa to the upper limits of their will and resources. Conceding American superiority in naval surface warfare, conventional air warfare, and the amphibious assault, the Japanese hoped to weaken and demoralize the Americans in a campaign of attrition against both the invasion fleet and the Tenth Army. Even if Okinawa eventually fell (as the Japanese planners anticipated), the campaign would delay and perhaps stop an American invasion of the home islands. The brunt of the attack against the 5th Fleet would come from the air in a mix of *kamikaze* and conventional air assaults, supplemented by equally suicidal surface and submarine attacks. (Eventually the Japanese launched ten large-scale *kamikaze* attacks on the 5th Fleet with almost 1,500 planes; these attacks, along with conventional bombing, sank 30 Navy ships and craft, damaged 368 others, and killed or wounded nearly 10,000 American sailors.) On the island itself, the Japanese Thirty-second Army conceded the beachhead. Ushijima's defense concept was simple and brilliant. Rejecting senseless mass counterattacks, he established a series of defensive positions across the southern portion of Okinawa. The main position was anchored in front of Naha on the west, on the heights of Shuri town and castle in the center, and in the hills around Yonabaru on the east coast. Tactically, the Japanese resorted to cave warfare to minimize the effects of American supporting fires. By tunneling and building fortified positions on both the forward and reverse slopes of the island's important ridges and hills, the Japanese could confine the Americans to the open farmlands and narrow roads, where their tanks and infantry would be vulnerable to artillery, mortars, and machine guns. Southern Okinawa, with ample limestone caves and cliffs, deep draws, and broken ridges, offered the perfect terrain for a positional, diehard defense.[83]

For the Marines the Okinawa campaign began with a euphoric rush across Kadena airfield to the island's east coast, despite occasional bitter fighting at the company level with Japanese delaying units. According to plan, the 1st Marine Division held its ground and stayed in reserve, as Spruance anticipated its use in landings elsewhere in the Ryukyus. To the 6th Marine Division fell the task of clearing the Japanese defenders from the mountainous northern part of the island. As small Marine units cleared the northern offshore islands and the 77th Infantry Division seized the important northern island of Ie Shima, the 6th Marine Division moved north. It found the Japanese defenders concentrated on the extremely hilly Motobu Peninsula on the island's western coast. Moving against stiffening resistance, the 6th Division found some 1,500 Japanese defending a hill complex known as Yae Take. The 29th Marines tested the position and took heavy casualties in fighting poorly organized by the regiment, the only really new unit in the division. The division commander, Major General Lemuel C. Shepherd, Jr., held two regiments along the base of Yae Take and sent the 4th Marines against the hill mass from its rear (western) approaches. With assistance from the 29th Marines, the 4th Marines overran the position in sharp fighting. By April 20, at a cost of nearly a thousand casualties, the 6th Division had broken the only organized defense of northern Okinawa. For the rest of the month the Marines swept north until they had covered the island with patrols and scattered the Japanese remnants in a series of small actions.[84]

In the meantime, the XXIV Corps, with the 7th and 96th Divisions on line, had met the first of Ushijima's defensive positions and had taken serious casualties while making scant gains. General Buckner added the 27th Infantry Division to the attack, but the Japanese not only blunted the American three-division offensive but counterattacked on April 12–14. The product of internal division among Ushijima's staff and division commanders, the counterattack failed, but its ferocity convinced General Buckner and his planners that the campaign needed reanalysis. This conclusion was shared by Navy commanders, for the 5th Fleet and its air umbrella had already felt the force of the Japanese *kamikaze* assault. During the last two weeks of April the American commanders considered bypassing the Naha-Shuri-Yonabaru line with another amphibious assault. Such an attack might land on either coast and involve the uncommitted 77th Infantry Division, the two Marine divisions already on the island, or the 2d Marine Division, held in theater reserve on Saipan. General Geiger and his division commanders favored another amphibious attack, as did several of General Buckner's Army subordinates, but Buckner and his staff decided that the tactical risks, supply problems, and shortage of shipping made another landing unattractive. The senior Navy officers supported Buckner, much to the Marines' dismay. At the same time, Nimitz concluded that the III AC would not be needed elsewhere in the Ryukyus, thus releasing the 1st and 6th Marine Divisions for Buckner's bludgeoning of Ushijima's defensive belt. In late April and early May 1945 the 1st and 6th Divisions moved into the western half of the Tenth Army's front and joined the XXIV Corps's slow and costly advance.[85]

Through the entire month of May the 1st and 6th Marine Divisions launched attack after attack against the western half of the Naha-Shuri-Yonabaru line and felt the full effect of the determined Japanese defense. The 1st Division joined the offensive under XXIV Corps direction but reverted to III AC control within a week when the 6th Division moved into the line on the 1st Division's right flank. In a week of heavy fighting the 1st Division crossed the Asa River, thus clearing the approaches to Naha for the 6th Division, and then reoriented its advance to the east in order to envelop the western approaches of the main Japanese position at Shuri. The fighting was as bitter as the struggle for Iwo Jima. Although the Americans employed massive artillery barrages, continuous naval gunfire, and close air support, the conquest of each successive Japanese position depended on the "blowtorch" (flamethrowers) and "corkscrew" (demolitions) tactics of the American tank-infantry teams. Hindered by heavy rains, the two Marine divisions fought slowly forward against stubborn Japanese resistance. Marine infantry battalions took, lost, and retook hill after hill as rifle companies shrank until they reached platoon-size remnants of dazed survivors. Marine infantry fought its way up hills only to find the Japanese waiting in ingenious reverse-slope defenses. Every hill became a battleground of flying grenades and raking machine gun fire, and movement forward or backward for the Marines sent casualties soaring. On many days progress was measured in yards, and on some there was no advance at all. For the 6th Division the battle for Sugar Loaf Hill ruined the 22d and 29th Marines, while the 1st Division spent the fighting strength of the 7th Marines and 5th Marines to capture Dakeshi Ridge and Wana Ridge.[86]

The battle of attrition along the Naha-Shuri-Yonabaru line began to shift in favor of the Americans in the third week of May, and at the end of the month General Ushijima, having lost fifty thousand men, broke off the defense. From the Marines' viewpoint, however, it was difficult to tell that the Americans were winning. In heavy fighting the 6th Division finally captured Naha during the last week of May, and the 1st Division enveloped the last Japanese bastions around Shuri's west flank. To the east the XXIV Corps also advanced with heavy casualties and slow progress. Then on May 26 the Japanese suddenly emerged from their positions and retreated south under heavy American fire, for Ushijima had decided to regroup for another prolonged defense of Okinawa's southern tip. At the front the resistance, however, did not collapse, for the withdrawal was covered by strong forces around Shuri. After two more days of heavy fighting, patrols from the 5th Marines penetrated the walls of Shuri castle to raise an American flag. Even then a Marine battalion was cut off in Shuri until American soldiers reduced the last defenses. On May 31 the Tenth Army had taken the Naha-Shuri-Yonabaru line, but it had not yet taken Okinawa, because the Japanese withdrawal had been more disciplined than the Americans imagined. Ushijima's soldiers dug in again to the south and awaited the Americans.[87]

As the Tenth Army fought southward, Marine aviation fought its own battle for Okinawa as part of the TAF. Although the four MAGs sent to Okinawa expected to devote most of their attention to close air support for the Tenth Army, the Marine pilots flew fewer than 1,000 of their nearly 5,000 sorties from April 7 to May 3 against ground targets. Because most of the Marine squadrons were Corsairs or Grumman F6F nightfighters, they were drawn into the Navy's desperate effort to stop the *kamikazes*. In the course of the Okinawan campaign, Marine pilots shot down 500 Japanese aircraft, while Marine radar and air control units helped the Navy. The land-based squadrons were assisted by all-Marine carrier air groups aboard two escort carriers. Even though Marine air (and AAF squadrons as well) concentrated on the battle to protect the fleet, the TAF also conducted 10,000 sorties in support of the Tenth Army. In addition, Marine aircraft made emergency aerial resupply drops, and four Marine observation squadrons provided aerial artillery spotting for the Tenth Army. The TAF effort against the Japanese, however, was limited not only by the *kamikaze* problem but by the terrain and the character of the fighting. The ground troops wanted as much air support as TAF could provide, but the abundance of artillery fire and the closeness of the fighting made the control of air strikes difficult. Instead of allowing the air liaison parties to control strikes at the front, the commander of air support operations, Colonel Vernon E. Megee, decided to restrict control to the three rear-area Landing Force Air Support Control Units, where the strikes could be carefully coordinated. This decision slowed response time but was probably unavoidable in an intense battle waged along only a 10-mile front.[88]

Until the final collapse of organized Japanese resistance in late June 1945, the III AC continued to push south in the Tenth Army's western zone of action. To the 6th Division fell the task of clearing the Oroku Peninsula, which was defended by some 2,000 Japanese naval base defense troops. On June 4 the 4th Marines made a shore-to-shore amphibious assault on the peninsula and, joined by the 29th Marines, spent the next week in stiff fighting eliminating the Japanese on the peninsula. In the meantime, the 1st Marine Division marched south in the face of increasing resistance until it faced a major battle for Kunishi Ridge. Losing 1,150 more men in a week's fighting, the 1st Division finally captured the ridge, the last major stronghold in the division's zone. Joined by the 6th Division and reinforced by the 8th Marines of the 2d Marine Division, the 1st Division finally reached Okinawa's southern coast on June 19, but the fighting continued inland against the last holdouts for several more days. Nevertheless, the campaign for

Okinawa—the Marine Corps's last in World War II—was finally over. In eighty-two days of sustained combat, the III AC had helped kill more than 110,000 Japanese defenders at a cost of 19,231 casualties, of whom 3,277 died. The Tenth Army's total losses numbered 65,631, which, added to the Navy's 10,000 casualties, made Okinawa the most costly single campaign of America's Pacific war.[89]

The campaign's slowness and cost also strained interservice relations in Admiral Nimitz's theater and further deepened Army–Marine Corps tensions. Marine generals in the western Pacific and Commandant Vandegrift, who visited Okinawa, questioned General Buckner's decision not to make a second landing. Their opinion was shared by some Navy admirals, although not by Nimitz. The question of the second landing found its way into the American press through civilian correspondents on Okinawa and was exploited by pro-Marine Corps columnists like David Lawrence. Only unprecedented statements by Secretary of the Navy Forrestal and Admiral Nimitz supporting General Buckner (who not long afterward was killed in action and succeeded by Roy Geiger) mollified the Army. But the impression persisted that the Marine Corps had once again pulled a public relations coup at the Army's expense.[90]

With Okinawa and Iwo Jima fresh in their minds, the six divisions of FMF Pacific, supported by four MAWs and assorted corps troops, welcomed the Japanese surrender in August 1945 with enthusiasm. From the muddy fields of Okinawa to the training areas of Hawaii and California, Marines celebrated V-J Day with special happiness, for already three divisions had begun training for the invasion of Kyushu, and the remaining three would have landed on Honshu early in 1946 if the war had continued. Immediately Marine plans shifted from invasion to occupation tasks, principally accepting Japanese surrenders in China, the home islands, and the bypassed islands of the Pacific and then disarming and repatriating the Japanese armed forces. As the guns fell silent, Marines must have wondered with awe at what their Corps had become and what it had accomplished in the nation's greatest war.[91]

6

Although uncommon valor may characterize the Marine Corps's role in World War II, common statistics also illuminate the Corps's contribution to the Axis defeat. Numerically, the Corps was within its own experience huge. On August 15, 1945, it had 458,053 officers, men, and women, with more than half of them serving overseas. During the entire course of the war some 669,000 men and women were United States Marines, a figure that exceeds the total of all Marines who had served before 1941. For all its expansion, however, the Corps remained a numerical elite. It made up less than 5 percent of the 16.3 million Americans who served in the armed forces in World War II, and it expanded in size to only twenty-five times its prewar strength, whereas the Navy expanded thirty times and the Army sixty. Compared with its own history, the Marine Corps bled as never before, losing 19,733 killed in action or died of wounds and 67,207 wounded in action of an American total of 291,557 and 670,846 in the two categories. That being a Marine in World War II was dangerous is obvious: With less than 5 percent of the American armed forces, the Corps suffered nearly 10 percent of all American battlefield casualties. The reason for Corps casualties lies in not only the nature of the Pacific war but also the fact that the Marine Corps, relying upon the Navy and Army for much of its continental logistical support, sent more of its troops overseas. By V-J Day 98 percent of Marine officers and 89 percent of Marine enlisted men had served in the Pacific; the all-armed-forces average for service abroad in World War II was 73 percent.[92]

As even its detractors acknowledged, the Marine Corps provided a valuable body of prewar thought and experience in amphibious operations that was priceless in World War II. But in the actual war the Marine Corps had no monopoly on amphibious operations. In the war against Japan, eighteen different Army divisions made twenty-six landings, while the six Marine divisions made fifteen landings. The Marine divisions, however, made more landings in proportion to their numbers. The question as to whether the Army or the Marine Corps faced the toughest fights or battled best in the Pacific is unanswerable—though certainly soldiers and Marines of 1945 and veterans since have tried to answer it. In the only campaign in which Army and Marine divisions fought in equal strength for equal duration under similar conditions— Okinawa—there was little difference in battlefield performance and casualties. Unfortunately, Marines tend to remember the hapless 27th Infantry Division and not the efficient 7th, 77th, 81st, and 96th Infantry Divisions.

It is understandable, however, that the Marine Corps emerged from World War II with an institutionalized sense of self-importance that affected its highest generals and its greenest privates. The Corps had made a major contribution (perhaps *the* major contribution) to creating an essential Allied military specialty, the amphibious assault against a hostile shore. At the same time, the Corps's ability to grow and adapt to the Pacific war remains impressive. When Pearl Harbor came, Navy and Marine planners envisioned a Corps balanced between FMF assault divisions and base defense forces, made up of infantry, coastal and anti-aircraft artillery, and aviation. By V-J Day the ground elements of the FMF were an amphibious assault force without peer, and the Marine divisions had gone through four basic organizational changes to find the right mix of men and weapons for each succeeding campaign. The FMF also had created corps troops of heavy artillery, tanks, amtracs, reconnaissance units, and varied service units where none had existed in 1942. The changes represented rapid organizational responses not only to the tactical and logistical challenges of the ship-to-shore movement but to the shifting character of the fighting ashore. Essentially, the Corps fought four different ground wars against the Japanese: the jungle warfare of the South Pacific, the atoll warfare of the Gilberts and Marshalls, the mobile warfare of the Marianas, and the cave warfare of Peleliu, Iwo Jima, and Okinawa. Each war made its special demands, and the Corps met them. It did so by adjusting its infantry training, increasing the firepower of its infantry and artillery regiments, using tanks and armored amphibians not only as mobile artillery but as flamethrowers, and stressing the coordination of supporting fires. By 1945 the Corps had made important conceptual and practical advances in using artillery, naval gunfire, and close air support against ground targets, but it was also aware that it needed further experience in fire support coordination.

Although prewar Marine planners foresaw the creation of the ground divisions of the FMF, they could not have predicted that the unique circumstances of the Pacific war would create the Marine aviation forces of World War II. By the end of the war Marine aviation constituted almost a separate Corps of more than 100,000 officers and men, of which 61,000 were serving overseas with four Marine aircraft wings, four Marine carrier groups, and a variety of ground support and headquarters squadrons. Conceived as a close air support force for amphibious operations and land campaigns, Marine aviation had instead flown ground attack missions only when its land bases were within range of the front lines. Only the South Pacific campaigns and the battles for Peleliu and Okinawa met this condition as far as the Marine Corps was concerned. Even when bases were available and the land campaigns went on long enough to permit forward displacement, Marine aviation fought its own war largely as a part of the Navy's land-based air force. From the attack on Pearl Harbor to the battle against the *kamikazes*, Marine fighter pilots fought the Japanese for air superiority. Other Marine pilots, flying everything from dive bombers to Mitchell medium bombers, pounded Japanese airfields, shipping, and bases from the Solomons to the western Pacific. Marine pilots flew nightfighters, reconnaissance aircraft, transports, observation planes, antisubmarine aircraft, and long-range patrol planes, but they did so more in support of the general naval campaign rather than in support of amphibious operations. Even when Marine squadrons went to sea aboard carriers in the war's closing stages, they flew proportionately few close support sorties. After the Philippine experience, there was no question that Marine pilots could deliver close air support with unmatched effectiveness. Whether they wanted to or whether the ascendant admirals of naval aviation would allow them to was quite another matter.[93]

A larger question persisted: what remained for a Marine Corps that had met and conquered an enemy it had planned to fight for twenty years? Even without the advent of nuclear weapons, would the United States need a force designed for amphibious operations as part of a "naval campaign" when the only possible hostile fleet was now gone and the Pacific Ocean had become an American lake?

Part Four

Force in Readiness
1945–1970s

In Asia, in a vast area stretching from Afghanistan to Korea, free countries are struggling to meet Communist aggression in all its many forms. Some of these countries are battling the Communist armies of Soviet satellites; some are engaged in bitter civil strife against Communist-led guerrillas; all of them face the immediate danger of Communist subversion. . . . this campaign threatens to absorb the manpower and vital resources of the East in the Soviet design of world conquest . . . the continued independence of these nations is vital to the future of the free world.

President Harry S. Truman May 24, 1951

Bless 'em all, bless 'em all,
The Commies, the U.N. and all:
Those slant-eyed Chink soldiers
Struck Hagaru-ri
And now know the meaning of U.S.M.C.
But we're saying goodbye to them all
We're Harry's police force on call.
So put back your pack on,
The next stop is Saigon
Cheer up, my lads, bless 'em all.

Marine song, Korea, 1950

15. Winning the Right and Means to Fight, 1945–1950

Despite the efforts of Army and Navy planners to prescribe postwar military police, the surrenders of Germany and Japan left American diplomacy and defense planning with many questions and virtually no answers. Outside of North America, the world north of the Equator was in physical, political, economic, and spiritual collapse. In Europe, Great Britain and France, ruined by war, struggled to restore democratic governments and sound economies while attempting at the same time to hold their colonial empires. To the east of ravaged Germany and prostrate Italy, resistance movements vied for control of Eastern Europe, with the United States a distant onlooker and Russia an active participant in the struggle for power. The Soviet Union remained the only substantial military power other than the United States. There had been suggestions during the war that Russia intended to create a band of client states around its borders and tighten its own system of internal controls, but Russian policies in the autumn of 1945 were not yet belligerent enough to alarm America's political leadership. The most pressing problems for the United States appeared to be the occupation of Germany and Japan, disarming Japanese forces in China and Korea, and demobilizing the armed forces. As Soviet forces closed their grip on Eastern Europe and Communist guerrillas from Greece to Indochina waged war against the vestiges of colonial rule, American policy-makers peered into the military future with little success, for the nation's world role was imperfectly defined.

From a peculiar mix of domestic politics and international events, some vague outlines of a new American international security policy emerged. To the administration of a new President, Harry S. Truman, and an assertive Congress, it appeared that the peace of the world was indivisible and that such traditional American goals as national self-determination, economic progress, and democratic institutions could not be fostered throughout the world without active American participation. For the United States international security seemed best assured by the creation of the United Nations Organization and a complementary set of financial and trading associations. For Europe the original policies stressed bilateral arrangements, primarily for economic rehabilitation, with the nation's former allies. In Asia, American diplomacy sought the peaceful reform of occupied Japan, the reunification of Korea, support of Chiang Kai-shek's Nationalist government in China, independence for the Philippines, and the peaceful creation of new nations from India eastward along the arc of European colonies that reached to the Dutch East Indies. Too firmly wedded to American notions of political and economic development, the postwar policies of the United States could not avoid conflict with the other messianic political movement that had been resurrected by World War II. In all its national and ideological variants, this movement was Communism.[1]

Military planners for the Joint Chiefs of Staff and for the War and Navy departments found American internationalism difficult to transform into military programs. With a public outcry, accepted by both the Truman administration and Congress, to "bring the boys home" and slash military spending, the armed forces divided and took policy positions that rested as much on traditional service philosophies as on current circumstances. The Army chose to return to the concept of cadre-conscript ground forces, led by professionals but manned by trainees recruited through universal military training, or UMT. The strategic bombing enthusiasts of the Army Air Forces, recognizing that organizational independence was near, stressed that American defense rested first upon a deterrent force of long-range bombers armed with nuclear weapons; AAF generals argued that nuclear weapons made traditional ground and naval forces marginally useful, especially when budgets were meager. The only imaginable war the nation might fight should deterrence fail would involve nuclear strikes against the enemy's cities and bases, not great land and sea campaigns. For the Navy this strategic concept was anathema. Even in the absence of a naval enemy, the Navy argued, Sea Power provided deterrence, international influence, and a war-fighting capability through the use of carrier-based aviation and the Fleet Marine Force. Although military planners recognized that the Soviet Union might be America's next enemy and that the American nuclear monopoly might be short-lived, the JCS could not produce a coherent national strategy.[2]

For the Marine Corps the post–World War II era began with the rapid demobilization of the FMF and much of its supporting establishment and the redeployment of the remaining units to bases in the eastern Pacific and the United States. The Corps's ultimate goal was to reestablish an FMF of two divisions and two aircraft wings, a plan that assumed a peacetime Corps of 7,000 to 8,000 officers and 100,000 enlisted men. From a V-J Day high of 485,053, the Corps dropped to 155,592 in less than a year; by the end of 1946 FMF Pacific numbered only 15,300 officers and men. Using the same point system for length of service and combat experience adopted by the Army, Commandant A. A. Vandegrift insisted that his subordinates release men in order to please Congress and to avoid any hint of the indiscipline that plagued the Army's units abroad. The latter point was emphasized by Lieutenant General Roy S. Geiger, who reduced and jailed nine NCOs in Hawaii for petitioning Congress for their immediate release.[3]

As the demobilization progressed into 1946, Headquarters grappled with some severe internal problems. Aware that military funding would plunge, Headquarters insisted that Marine equipment and supplies return from the Pacific, be rehabilitated, and then be stored at the supply depots. (Tradition holds that many Army weapons and vehicles made the trip back, too, and ended up with a new coat of forest green paint.) Serious shortages of skilled supply, maintenance, and aviation personnel, however, impeded the heroic salvage effort. The other sizable challenge was the character of the officer corps. Instead of reducing the superfluous generals and colonels, Vandegrift insisted that half of them retire; no active duty general lost his stars, but some colonels reverted to lieutenant colonel and lieutenant colonels to major. Among the retirees were the Corps's more conspicuous wartime failures. A related problem involved the large number of high-ranking pilots who wanted to remain Marines. With limited civilian and military education but impressive service records, the wartime pilots were a worry to the ground officers who dominated policy-making at Headquarters, for the pilots had little common bond with the ground Fleet Marine Force. Vandegrift's solution was decisive but hard for the aviators to accept: A special board reviewed the records of many pilots and reassigned them to ground duty with no other option but resignation. However harsh, the reassignment policy did much to integrate the ground and air tribes in the officer corps and saved many technical specialists for support units. (No new aviator lieutenants were trained in 1946–1950 without first serving as ground officers.)

At the enlisted level, the manpower problems were less severe. Voluntary long-term enlistments kept Corps strength close to the 100,000 mark, but the Corps could not replace many of its experienced specialists and had to institute a special program in 1946 to attract men skilled in electronics, aviation, vehicle maintenance, ordnance, and supply.[4]

Amid the personnel confusion of demobilization, General Vandegrift wanted the Marine Corps to remain in the field, "occupied for the best advantage of the Corps." The occupations of Japan and China provided such an opportunity.[5] The first Marines to reach defeated Japan, a 5,400-man force built around the 4th Marines, occupied Yokosuka naval base and other facilities as part of a joint American operation to seize control of Tokyo prior to Japan's formal surrender. Anticipating Japanese resistance, the Marines found instead cooperation and poised dignity, a pattern that characterized the Japanese military the Marines met in Japan and China. So well did the occupation of Honshu develop that Marine air and ground units, with the exception of a security battalion, left the island by the spring of 1946. Farther to the south, the 2d and 5th Marine Divisions of the V Amphibious Corps performed similar duties on the island of Kyushu. Landing at Sasebo and Nagasaki, the two Marine divisions fanned out across the island to battalion-size posts. Troop reductions and shifts kept the Marines on the move. The main task of the two divisions, providing a military presence behind the establishment of occupation rule, proved relatively easy, as the Japanese authorities cooperated. Much of the Marine labor on Kyushu involved collecting and destroying Japanese military matériel, processing released Allied prisoners and internees, repatriating Chinese and Korean laborers, protecting government property, and providing some relief foods and engineering equipment for clearing away rubble. The occupation went so smoothly that the 5th Division left Kyushu in the autumn of 1945 for demobilization, and the 2d Division, also reduced by discharges, turned over its billets to the Army and left Japan in the spring of 1946.[6]

The 1st and 6th Marine Divisions of the III Amphibious Corps found their simultaneous occupation of North China (Operation BELEAGUER) anything but peaceful and uncomplicated, and it was 1947 before the bulk of the Marines left China. The initial mission of III AC appeared simple enough: occupy the key cities of Hopeh province and the Shantung peninsula and disarm and repatriate the some 500,000 Japanese troops in the area. Major General Keller E. Rockey's Marines were to keep order until the Chinese Nationalist government could assume control of North China. From the outset, General Rockey knew that the mission would be difficult, for Chinese Communist forces controlled much of the countryside in Hopeh and Shantung. Rockey's orders, however, cautioned him to avoid conflict with the Communists and not to take sides in the brewing civil war; early in the occupation Rockey and his naval superiors demonstrated their grasp of their mission by not landing at Communist-occupied Chefoo, much to the Nationalists' unhappiness. Elsewhere the Chinese and Japanese welcomed the Marines with enthusiasm. By November 1945 all of III AC had arrived in China and had begun its repatriation duties. In Hopeh province the 1st Division and elements of the 1st Marine Aircraft Wing spread out along the railroads connecting Peking in the northwest, Tientsin and Taku in the south near the Gulf of Chihli, and Chinwangtao up the coast to the northeast. The larger garrisons took stations at Peking, Tientsin, Taku, Tangshan, and Chinwangtao. To the south in Shantung, the 6th Division (less the 4th Marines) established a substantial enclave around the coastal city of Tsingtao. Mounting air and ground patrols from its new posts, the China Marines found Nationalist military units widely dispersed, and Marines and armed Japanese assumed security duties in the large towns and along the lines of transportation. In the meantime, the repatriation of the Japanese and Koreans in North China went fairly smoothly, slowed only by the lack of shipping and Chinese reluctance to relieve Japanese security forces. By the summer of 1946 more than 500,000 Japanese and Koreans had been processed by III AC, and the repatriation phase of its mission ended.[7]

In the meantime, the Marines found themselves caught in the web of Chinese politics and Sino-American relations, a circumstance that made the China occupation both trying and dangerous. The difficulty began when Chiang Kai-shek and Mao Tse-tung spurned American advice and maneuvered for advantage for their renewed civil war. Instead of relieving the Marines, Chiang sent his scarce troops north to Manchuria, thus leaving III AC and Nationalist militia to face the Communists in Hopeh and Shantung provinces. Unwilling to concede control of the two provinces to the Americans or the Nationalists without at least the propaganda advantage of "incidents," the Communists harassed low-flying Marine aircraft with rifle fire and sniped at patrols, train guards, and other small parties. Between October 1945 and January 1946, in ten incidents, one Marine died and ten were wounded. Whether or not the Communists initiated all the incidents remains uncertain, but the tension, especially in the 1st Marine Division's sector, mounted.[8]

As they endured the cold winter of 1945–1946, the Marines of III AC found themselves supporting America's last serious effort to prevent a full-scale Chinese civil war and a Communist conquest of North China. In December 1945 President Truman sent General George C. Marshall to China to arrange a truce and conduct negotiations with the Nationalists and Communists. Unwilling to commit American troops directly to the weak Nationalist cause, Truman and Marshall were equally reluctant to surrender whatever political advantage the Marine presence provided. In addition to controlling the key cities in Hopeh and Shantung, the Marines also ensured that the critical coal supplies from Hopeh reached the ports for shipment to southern China. Chiang Kai-shek, of course, was eager to have the Marines, who strengthened his political and military position. The Communists, on the other hand, did not want a military confrontation with III AC that might bring direct American intervention. As the Chiang–Marshall–Mao negotiations dragged on and Americans tried to supervise the truce and furnish relief supplies to the North Chinese, the Marines patrolled and rode coal trains in Hopeh. For the city garrisons, the occupation was a pale reflection of "old" China service, but in the countryside the Communists lay in wait for the unwary.

For the China Marines, remaining aloof from the Chinese civil war proved impossible. Moreover, the press of Corps demobilization eventually reached China, and the 6th Division in Shantung decreased to little more than a reinforced battalion guarding American naval property in Tsingtao. In crucial Hopeh, the 1st Division–1st Aircraft Wing expeditionary force, periodically reorganized and reduced in strength, remained on the "front lines." Nationalist army reinforcements allowed the Marines to curtail some of their security patrols but not to avoid the Communists completely. As the truce dissolved in the summer of 1946, the Communists renewed their attacks on small American units. Between April 1946 and April 1947, Marine bridge guards, motor convoys, and ammunition dump and train guards fought Chinese raiders and suffered nine dead and thirty wounded. The most serious incidents occurred at Anping on the Peking–Tientsin highway, where a convoy drove into an ambush, and at the Hsin-Ho supply dump near Tangku, where Communist raiders struck four times. Allowed to fire back when fired upon, the Marines fought back and may have downed as many as seventy Communists, but American policy prevented any active punitive operations.[9]

As Nationalist–Communist fighting grew in early 1947, the Truman administration conceded the failure of the Marshall mission and ordered the China Marines to redefine their duties. Troop strength in China, influenced by demobilization and redeployment, fell from a high of nearly 46,000 men in early 1946 to only about 5,000 a year later. The remnants of III AC became a three-battalion force designated FMF Western Pacific and restricted its activities to guarding American naval facilities in the Tsingtao area. From this enclave the Marines helped evacuate American nationals caught in the Chinese civil war. Until the final collapse of the Nationalist government in 1949, battalion- and company-size Marine expeditions helped the Navy evacuate Americans from North China, the Yangzte Valley, and Shanghai. Performing their security duties with restraint and effectiveness, the last China Marines watched a new era dawn in China with no inkling that other Marines would face the victorious People's Liberation Army again in Korea in less than two years.[10]

The Chinese occupation eventually ended in disappointment and slowed the postwar reorganization of the FMF, but Headquarters viewed the China experience as a sample of the service the Corps might provide for American diplomacy. The Marine Corps had no intention of surrendering its principal wartime function as a naval base seizure force, but it recognized that a global war involving a sizable naval campaign might not occur. On the other hand, American national interest dictated control of the Pacific, the Western Atlantic, and the Western Hemisphere, interests that might require ready forces with an amphibious capability. To support either the United Nations or the United States, Marine planners wanted a Fleet Marine Force of "minute men . . . held in readiness to be moved instantly with the Fleet to any part of the world to strike hard and promptly to forestall at its beginning any attempt to disrupt the peace of the world." The force should also be ready to expand to 500,000 in wartime, but Marine planners thought the most likely contingency was a conflict that would not bring a formal declaration of war, so they chose to stress the readiness of the standing forces. At least until 1946 the new FMF appeared to be not only an optimal national force but a United Nations peacekeeping force as well.[11]

Already concerned that the Soviet Union would be its next adversary, the Navy supported the Marine Corps's concept of an air-ground FMF built upon divisions and air wings as arguments on postwar force structure grew in the JCS. The planners working for the new Chief of Naval Operations, Fleet Admiral Chester A. Nimitz, saw a specific need for the FMF that was not linked to the concept of the naval campaign. The key strategic problem in containing the Soviet Union, the planners thought, was control of the Middle East's oil. Whichever side lost control of the oil reserves of Iran and Saudi Arabia would not be able to wage a protracted conflict. Dismayed by the Army's emphasis on Europe and the AAF's faith in nuclear bombs, the Navy argued that the FMF should be prepared to intervene in the Persian Gulf region in order to control the region's oilfields. The Navy reassured the Army that the FMF would not duplicate the ground Army and that its size was tied by tradition to the Navy's as a fixed percentage of total strength. With the Marine Corps deployed for duty in the western Pacific and the eastern Mediterranean, it would not encroach upon those missions and places the Army held most dear.[12]

The Army rejected any need for the type of Marine Corps that had fought World War II without denying the Navy's strategic logic. Mixing strategic and functional arguments, including the tri-elemental concept of the separation of air, sea, and land operations, Army planners questioned the idea that future ground operations would be part of a "naval campaign." Instead, they argued, if such operations were necessary, they should be performed by the ground and air Army. Essentially, the Marine Corps had no significant wartime mission. It should be organized as regiments, "small, readily available and lightly armed units to protect United States interests ashore in foreign countries," or a reversion to the role of colonial infantry.[13] Vandegrift responded that the Army did not appreciate the Corps's competence in amphibious operations (for whatever purpose) and underestimated the unique combat potential of an integrated air-ground force. World War II had proved the efficacy of Sea Power, which included the FMF as an instrument of a national maritime strategy.[14]

So the arguments developed as the United States entered the postwar era. For the Navy and the Marine Corps, the nation's postwar security needs included a Corps still based on the FMF. The FMF should include a division and an air wing for Mediterranean duty and a division, a brigade, an air wing, and an air group for duty in the Western Pacific. The Navy would provide amphibious shipping for two divisions and six escort carriers for Marine close air support squadrons. There was no need to change the Corps's amphibious, base-seizure mission. If this deployment concept was altered, it would be only by financial stringency, not a change of mission. The Army, on the other hand, thought that any land-based air, whatever its function, should be AAF. The Army also proposed that it dominate the use of the Navy's amphibious shipping for training. Vandegrift suggested that the Navy use its limited shipping only for FMF training, inasmuch as the Marines were already best prepared for amphibious landings.[15]

1.

With a thunderous roar the nuclear device detonated beneath the center of Bikini lagoon pushed a tower of water into the clouds, sent shock waves across the lagoon, and bathed the anchored fleet in radiation. It also cast doubt on the Marine Corps's main function, the amphibious operation. The shock waves of Operation CROSSROADS, a series of Navy-directed nuclear tests in the summer of 1946, reached Headquarters Marine Corps and stimulated General Vandegrift to call for a reanalysis of amphibious doctrine. Already pressed by the Army to reorganize the FMF as light infantry, Vandegrift faced similar pressures from Rear Admiral Forrest Sherman, a key planner for the Chief of Naval Operations, and from Lieutenant General Roy S. Geiger, one of the Corps's most respected senior officers and commanding general of FMF Pacific. An eyewitness at the Bikini tests, Geiger warned the Commandant that nuclear weapons made it difficult to envision World War II–type amphibious operations with their emphasis on mass and concentration of forces. Both Sherman and Geiger suggested that Vandegrift reexamine current doctrine, paying attention to the possibility of using smaller dispersed units that would reach the beach more quickly than Marines had in World War II. The reevaluation was crucial to preserving the FMF.[16]

Vandegrift reacted quickly. Appointing a board composed of Major General Lemuel C. Shepherd, Jr., Major General Field Harris, and Brigadier General O. P. Smith, the Commandant instructed the Special Board to make a thorough examination of the relationship between nuclear weapons and amphibious operations. In turn the Special Board drew upon the staff of the Marine Corps Schools for research and formed a secretariat directed and inspired by Colonel Merrill B. Twining, an officer whose dedication to the Corps and brilliance as a planner had become legendary in the World War II FMF. The planner next to Twining in importance was Colonel E. Colston Dyer, a pilot with a respected background in research and development and important contacts among naval aviators, especially those working on a new craft designed for vertical flight. This craft, in the early stages of experimentation, was called the helicopter.

After the Special Board had examined the Navy's data on nuclear effects and examined the studies of its secretariat, it reported to Vandegrift in December 1946 that the Marine Corps would have to make radical changes in the ship-to-shore movement if amphibious operations were to be successful against an enemy armed with nuclear weapons. The board believed that the amphibious task force, if well dispersed on the high seas, could reach an objective area without crippling losses. It also reasoned that once ashore the landing force would be too close to the enemy for nuclear weapons to be used. The most vulnerable target would be the waves of amtracs and landing craft plowing slowly toward the beaches. The board concluded that a Japanese nuclear weapon would have destroyed the two divisions that assaulted Iwo Jima before they reached the beaches. But it believed it saw a solution to the ship-to-shore problem: The initial assault waves would land behind the beach defenses, dropped into weak points in the enemy positions by helicopters. Flying from well-dispersed carriers, the helicopter forces would both close with the enemy rapidly (thus preventing nuclear strikes) and open the beaches for reinforcements and heavy equipment, which could be brought to the beaches by landing craft or large seaplanes. Such a landing would deprive an enemy of a decisive nuclear target and yet retain the proper combination of speed and concentration that would prevent the landing force from being defeated in detail. Both the board and Vandegrift quickly concluded that the "vertical envelopment" assault (the term was not yet used in 1946) gave new life to the amphibious operation, although neither the troop-carrying helicopters nor the seaplanes yet existed. They concluded that a vigorous development effort could produce both in five to seven years. Examining their new concepts, Marine planners concluded that, at least in theory, the helicopter assault was the only answer to the nuclear threat. All the Marine Corps needed were the proper helicopters and the carriers from which to fly them.[17]

The concept of the helicopter assault reflected the same boldness that characterized the Corps's commitment to the amphibious assault in the early 1920s, for in 1946 the Corps did not own a single helicopter. The light helos then in the hands of the Navy could not carry a reinforced squad of Marines. The studies of the Special Board, however, seized the imagination of many officers at the Marine Corps Schools, and they threw themselves into the further study of helicopter operations with an abandon that approached fanaticism. Following Vandegrift's approval of the conclusions of the Special Board, the staff of the MCS formed additional study groups to examine all the implications of the vertical assault. Twining and Dyer continued as study leaders and recruited additional helicopter enthusiasts, including Lieutenant Colonel Victor H. Krulak, whose intellectual grasp, boundless energy, and combat record marked him as a gifted shaper of Corps policy.

For all the new interest in helicopters, neither the Navy nor the Marine Corps was a stranger to vertical flight aircraft. Both services had experimented with various types of experimental "autogyros" in the 1920s and 1930s, but the uncertain handling characteristics of these craft and their limited payloads made them a dubious investment. Nevertheless, the Department of the Navy had already formed working relationships with two pioneer helicopter entrepreneurs, the Russian-exile aeronautical engineer Igor Sikorsky and the young, self-taught Frank N. Piasecki. Piasecki's work especially caught the Corps's attention, because he promised to produce a helicopter that could carry a 14,000-pound payload, whereas Sikorsky thought he could develop only a 5,000-pound-payload craft. Working with these helo developers, as well as the Bell Aircraft Corporation, the Marine planners plunged into the task of drawing up the specifications for an assault helicopter.[18]

Drawing upon the assumptions of the Special Board, the MCS theorists imagined the sort of craft the Corps required. At a minimum the helo should be able to carry 5,000 pounds for 200 to 300 miles at a speed of 100 knots at altitudes of 4,000 to 15,000 feet. These characteristics would enable the assault helo to carry from fifteen to twenty combat troops at a speed and distance that matched the requirements of dispersion, relative safety, and rapid concentration on the objective. The Navy's Bureau of Aeronautics, Sikorsky, and Piasecki thought such a helo could be built. For the developers the problem appeared to be essentially an engineering one: Could they build engines and rotor systems that would give the helo the adequate power and pitch to carry heavy loads? The Bureau of Aeronautics thought Sikorsky and Piasecki could do so but doubted that the helo would be small enough to use the elevators and hanger decks of escort carriers. Would the Navy provide its larger attack carriers for Marine helicopters? It seemed doubtful.[19]

Impelled by their concern for the Corps's future, the MCS planners continued their studies. By November 1948 they produced a tentative manual for the employment of helicopters in the amphibious assault. This manual, PHIB 31, was part of a general reexamination of amphibious techniques and was largely the work of Twining, Dyer, Krulak, and Colonel Robert E. Hogaboom. The doctrine did not rest upon any substantial amount of experience, but it reflected the Corps's first use of helicopters. In January 1948 Vandegrift activated the Corps's first helicopter squadron, HMX-1, based at Quantico to make it accessible to the planners. Under Dyer's command, HMX-1 formed around Marine pilots recruited from the MCS student body and Marine test pilots who had been working with the Navy's helicopter program. HMX-1's early flying, an exciting experience in "on-the-job training," came in Sikorsky HO3S-1s and Piasecki HRPs, a heavy-lift helo nicknamed "the flying banana." Pushed by Twining and Krulak, HMX-1 made its troop-carrying debut in May 1948, when five helos of HMX-1 carried sixty-six Marines from the decks of the escort carrier *Palau* to the piney woods of Camp Lejeune during PACKARD II, a command post exercise for MCS students. Because each helo could carry only three Marines, the exercise demonstrated only the Corps's faith in the future of the vertical assault, not a real combat capability. Nevertheless, PACKARD II heartened the helo enthusiasts and gave them the modicum of real experience they needed to write PHIB 31. The planners at Quantico continued to take their gospel of salvation to other Marine officers and anyone else who could see the potential of the helicopter as an assault craft.[20]

For all their enthusiasm, the helicopter advocates faced serious opposition within the Marine Corps and the Navy to the bold concepts incorporated in PHIB 31. Other influential Marine planners, both aviators and ground officers, had serious reservations about helicopter operations. Within Marine aviation, the helicopter menaced the plans of the close air support champions, who worried that the number of helicopters would count against the fixed quota of aircraft allowed the Marine Corps by the Navy's aviation planners. When Twining and Krulak tried to reassure close air support advocates like Brigadier General Vernon Megee that close air support operations and the vertical assault were inseparable, the critics of close air support itself thought they saw a conspiracy that would eventually rob the Marine Corps of its field artillery. These critics questioned whether either helos or fighter-bombers could operate over a battlefield in which an enemy utilized increasingly potent anti-aircraft guns and missiles. Of more immediate effect, Navy aviation planners recognized the enormous cost of a heavy-lift assault helicopter. Marine Corps planners wanted two helicopter squadrons for the FMF by 1953, but the likely craft, the Piasecki HRP, would cost almost $1 million each. To save development costs, the Bureau of Aeronautics decided to share the HRP project with the Air Force, which was developing a similar heavy-lift helo for the Army. The problem was that the HRP grew larger and larger as it went through development, so that the Piasecki helo was too large for the elevators and hanger decks of escort carriers, while the alternative, the Sikorsky HO3S-1, could not carry a satisfactory number of troops. As a consequence, in a period of diminishing defense budgets, in 1948 the Marine Corps did not have a helicopter even in the development stage that could meet its requirements.[21]

2.

As it worked to change the Fleet Marine Force for operations in the nuclear age, the Marine Corps began a seven-year struggle to save the FMF and, by implication, its own existence. Caught in the complex political currents that characterized the unification of the American armed forces, the Marine Corps found itself pitted against a strong War Department–executive branch–Congressional coalition that wanted to strip the Corps of its wartime amphibious assault mission, transfer Marine aviation to the newly independent Air Force, and so constrain Marine combat functions that the Corps could have been a "force in readiness" only if its opponents had been Pacific islanders. In a sense, the Corps's critics wanted a nineteenth-century Marine Corps while the Corps wanted its World War II capabilities and missions written into law. By 1952 the Corps, exploiting its traditional identification with Congress and its public appeal, had saved itself, but the contest was a near-run thing, particularly in the period between the end of World War II and the passage of the National Security Act in the summer of 1947.[22]

The battle lines over armed forces reorganization solidified in 1945. A committee of the Joint Chiefs of Staff proposed the creation of a single department of defense guided by a single civilian secretary and a single chief of the armed forces, both of whom would have substantial power to decide service roles and missions and the defense budget. Many of the traditional functions performed by the War and Navy departments would go to a series of civilian secretaries, and the JCS would continue as an advisory body divorced from the command of the military forces. The services would grow from three to four, as the Army Air Forces would become the Air Force, built around the mission of strategic bombardment but incorporating all land-based air activities. This approach to unification, strongly backed by General George C. Marshall and General H. H. Arnold, commander of the Army Air Forces, stirred a concerned response from the Navy Department, led by Secretary of the Navy James V. Forrestal and Fleet Admiral Chester A. Nimitz. Forrestal recognized the inherent dangers to the Navy in the plan and countered with an alternative approach developed by Ferdinand Eberstadt, an experienced defense manager and consultant. The Eberstadt Plan urged greater civilian–military coordination of national security policy through new agencies and boards like the Central Intelligence Agency, but it proposed that the JCS and separate departments be continued on the World War II model. It recommended no substantial change in service roles and missions, even if the Air Force became independent.[23]

Ever vigilant to threats, Headquarters followed the development of the unification controversy, primarily through the few Marine officers serving the JCS and the Chief of Naval Operations. Determined to save the FMF as a team of divisions and aircraft wings, Vandegrift quickly developed the Corps position of unification. Coached by two intimates from Guadalcanal days, Brigadier General Gerald C. Thomas and Brigadier General Merritt A. Edson, the Commandant set the Corps stand.

The air-ground FMF must be preserved as the amphibious element of the Navy's "naval campaign" fleet organization; the Marine Corps must be recognized as an independent service; and defense decision-making must not be centralized under either a single, powerful civilian secretary or a single chief of all the armed forces. Instead, the 1945 pattern should continue, for "the greatest advantage of the current organization from a national point of view is that it is responsive to the control of Congress and the people." [24] To cooperate with Forrestal and Nimitz—and to preserve the Corps independent of Navy advocacy—Vandegrift approved the creation in early 1946 of two groups of Marine officers, coordinated by Thomas and Edson, to prepare position papers for the Corps, to monitor developments in both the executive branch and Congress, to brief friendly newspapermen, to review legislative proposals, and to perform research on roles and missions. Much of the work load fell upon the same group of Marine Corps Schools colonels, led by Twining and Krulak, who had been drafting the conceptual papers on vertical envelopment. The MCS group, nicknamed "The Chowder Society," soon developed into the Corps's political action arm, and its agents prowled the Pentagon and Congress arguing the Marine Corps case. [25]

The first test of the Navy–Marine Corps position came in the autumn of 1945, when the Senate Military Affairs Committee considered legislation based on Army concepts of defense organization. The Navy fought a successful legislative holding action against reorganization and against centralized decision-making on roles and missions, and the Truman administration decided to postpone further action until it had conducted further studies and had drafted a law that would satisfy the Navy and its Congressional supporters. Within the executive branch the reappraisal fell to the JCS, which gathered opinions from leading service spokesmen labeled the JCS Series 1478 papers, and to Secretary of War Robert Patterson and Forrestal. At the service level the chief negotiators were Lieutenant General J. Lawton Collins, USA, a deputy chief of the War Department General Staff; Major General Lauris Norstad, USAAF; and Vice Admiral Arthur W. Radford, a deputy CNO and forceful champion of both naval aviation and the FMF. For the Navy the negotiations had a particular urgency, for President Truman, who preferred the Army proposals (labeled the Collins Plan), announced in December 1945 that he wanted a single military department with a civilian secretary and single military commander with control over service roles and missions. Truman tried to placate the Navy by saying that he wanted no change in the World War II roles and mission, including the functions of the Marine Corps. Convinced that the President had been captured by his own pro-Army biases and the baleful influence of George C. Marshall and Dwight D. Eisenhower, the new Army Chief of Staff, the Navy Department girded for new hearings in the spring of 1946.[26]

The Marine Corps doubted the constancy of Truman's commitment to the FMF, being aware that Eisenhower (a likely candidate to be the first head of all the armed forces) and General Carl W. Spaatz, the new chief of the AAF and likely chief of staff of the new Air Force, had filed opinions in the JCS 1478 studies that would have reduced the FMF to light infantry regiments without aviation. Provided with an unauthorized set of the 1478 papers by General Edson, the Corps planners prepared Vandegrift for the 1946 hearings. With executive branch, Congressional, and public opinion swinging toward the Collins Plan, the Corps faced a crisis of substantial proportions.[27]

In April 1946 the Senate Military Affairs Committee held hearings on S. 2044, a unification bill that appeared to satisfy both the Army and the Navy. The product of intense negotiations between its Congressional sponsors and the Truman administration, S. 2044 still so resembled the Collins Plan that the Marine Corps viewed it with alarm. The proposed powers of the single chief of the armed forces had been reduced to advisory duties, and the JCS had returned to share those duties, but it appeared nonetheless that the single civilian secretary and his associates, who would head a single department, could use their control of the budget process to assign service roles and missions without Congressional approval. In addition, Truman had ordered Forrestal to prohibit his admirals and generals from criticizing S. 2044 in public, a "gag" that threatened the Navy's political position. When S. 2044 cleared the Senate Military Affairs Committee without substantial alteration, the alarmed Forrestal arranged supplementary hearings on the bill by the friendly Senate Naval Affairs Committee. The additional hearings gave the Navy and Marine Corps what appeared to be a last opportunity to stop unification on the Army's terms.[28]

The Senate Naval Affairs Committee hearings produced the desired result, a postponement of action on S. 2044 and a complete airing of Navy–Marine Corps criticism of unification. For the Marine Corps the high point of the hearings was General Vandegrift's testimony on May 6. Reading a statement drafted largely by Twining and Krulak and based on the Army positions revealed in the JCS 1478 papers, Vandegrift made a quiet but impassioned case for the FMF. Reviewing the history of amphibious warfare in doctrine and execution in World War II, Vandegrift urged the Congress not to eliminate the positive benefits of interservice rivalry in designing military techniques. He also testified that the Army had shown little interest in amphibious operations and would continue to stress instead conventional land operations. Yet even with nuclear weapons, he believed, the nation and the Navy would still need the FMF in order to prosecute naval campaigns incident to a general war. Still more passionately, Vandegrift argued that the Marine Corps was the nation's force in readiness: "*The Marines are ready*, and if it came to a fight today I do not know who could replace them." Supported by the Fleet, the Corps provided a military instrument adequate for limited intervention and general war, nuclear or not, but only if it retained an air-ground FMF. As it had in the past, the Corps embodied standards of bravery, success, and economy not found in the Army. In any event, the Corps's future should not be decided by executive fiat. Concluding his statement with an appeal designed to stir the Congress against the administration's proposals, Vandegrift summed up the Corps's position:

> The Marine Corps, then, believes that it has earned this right—to have its future decided by the legislative body which created it—nothing more. Sentiment is not a valid consideration in determining questions of national security. We have pride in ourselves and in our past but we do not rest our case on any presumed gratitude owing us from the nation. The bended knee is not a tradition of our Corps. If the Marine as a fighting man has not made a case for himself after 170 years of service, he must go. But I think you will agree with me he has earned the right to depart with dignity and honor, not by subjugation to the status of uselessness and servility planned for him by the War Department.[29]

As Headquarters basked in the favorable public response to the "bended knee" speech, Truman again met with Patterson and Forrestal in order to draft a compromise version of S. 2044 before the Congress rejected unification legislation altogether. Once again the President said he favored maintaining the FMF but also confirmed his commitment to an independent Air Force that would control all land-based aviation. This position not only incensed naval aviators but contained the implication that much of Marine tactical air might also go to the Air Force. Truman's public statements were ambiguous enough to allow almost any interpretation, but it appeared as if he had agreed that a powerful single civilian secretary and even a titular military commander of all the armed forces were politically unacceptable. The revised S. 2044 reflected additional movement toward the Navy Department's position that the World War II roles and missions were sacrosanct and that department autonomy was not negotiable. When the Senate Naval Affairs Committee heard additional testimony against the limiting of naval aviation, the administration finally conceded in the summer of 1946 that Congress would not pass a unification law that year. Convinced that the Russians had clearly emerged as an adversary and pressed by the Bureau of the Budget to cut defense costs in order to stabilize the economy, Truman had no intention of surrendering to the Navy and its champions, but he recognized that the Navy and Marine Corps had won another delaying action.[30]

Anticipating another round of unification hearings after the 80th Congress convened in early 1947, the Marine officers of the "Chowder Society" and the Thomas–Edson group at Headquarters reassessed the Corps's political position and found that, despite the "bended knee" speech and Truman's statement, the Corps was still in a battle. Truman's commitment to the Corps remained suspect, and the Army, incensed by Navy intransigence, appeared unwilling to surrender the Eisenhower concept of a small, limited Corps. This view gained further strength when an AAF general publicly called the Corps "a small bitched-up Army talking Navy lingo. We are going to put those Marines in the Regular Army and make efficient soldiers out of them."[31] Even more worrisome to some Marine planners was their feeling that Forrestal and his admirals, and perhaps even General Vandegrift, would not continue to fight for the FMF with sufficient ardor. Under intense pressure from Truman and the War Department to agree to a new unification bill, Forrestal replaced Admiral Radford as the department's principal negotiator with Vice Admiral Forrest P. Sherman, a zealous naval aviator. Sherman, the Marines thought, might very well trade Corps interests in order to save naval aviation. Other dangers emerged. The hearings of 1946 had revealed that most important civilian and military witnesses, including the Navy's judge advocate, did not regard the Marine Corps as a separate service. Because the FMF fell under the operational control of the CNO and other Marines served Navy masters, the confusion (despite legislative precedents) was understandable but alarming since the bulk of opinion implied that the Corps's roles and missions could be changed unless the Corps received specific protection.

Therefore, the Marine planners believed that only legislative protection would save the FMF, and they made that the goal of the 1947 campaign. This position ran up against Truman's dogged defense of his presidential powers, hardened by the election of a Republican Congress in 1946. In addition, Forrestal and his advisers seemed cowed by the President's insistence on a consensus administration position for 1947. The diminished militancy in the highest echelons of the Navy and Marine Corps coincided with another alarming development in Congress itself. In an attempt to handle its business more efficiently, Congress in 1946 had passed legislation reorganizing its committee system. Among the victims of reform were the Senate and House naval affairs committees, key strongholds of pro-Marine sentiment. In the 80th Congress, these committees (and their Army counterparts) would reappear as merged committees on the armed services. Although it seemed certain that Congressman Carl Vinson, an ardent navalist, would dominate the new House committee, the Senate committee appeared to be a bastion of pro-Army sentiment at worst and unlikely to specify service roles and missions at best.[32]

The earliest acts of the 80th Congress confirmed Marine fears. After a bitter referral fight, the Senate gave the new Armed Services Committee the opportunity to review the latest administration proposal, labeled S. 758. Although S. 758 resembled the Forrestal–Eberstadt proposals more than it did the original Collins Plan, it contained no legislative protection for the Marine Corps. The hearings on S. 758 brought no joy to the Marine advocates. Despite passionate testimony from Marine champions like Senators Edward V. Robertson and Joseph R. McCarthy (an erstwhile Marine officer), S. 758 sailed through the committee and the floor vote without having service roles and missions written into the legislation. The militants of the "Chowder Society" worried, for Navy Department witnesses, including Vandegrift, had not made a strong case for legislating service roles and missions. Instead, the administration witnesses urged S. 758 as the military's and the nation's best hope for unification. Because the bill included the Forrestal–Eberstadt system of civilian–military agencies, a weak secretary of defense, the JCS system of military planning, and broad autonomy for the military departments, the Navy Department's performance was defensible but disturbing to Marine militants.[33]

The final battlefield became the hearings on H. 2319, the House version of the administration's unification bill. Hoping to avoid the pro-Navy House Armed Services Committee, the administration's unification managers urged the House leadership to have Congressman Clare E. Hoffman of Michigan introduce H. 2319 and then have Hoffman's Committee on Expenditures in the Executive Department hold hearings. The House leadership agreed, and Hoffman assumed responsibility for H. 2319. That pleased the pro-Army advocates, who assumed that Hoffman, with no interest or experience in military matters, would turn the bill over to a subcommittee headed by Representative James W. Wadsworth, a longtime pro-Army expert on defense matters. The strategy failed dramatically. Learning that Hoffman and Lieutenant Colonel James D. Hittle's father were friends, the "Chowder Society" urged Hittle to persuade Hoffman to handle the hearings himself before the full committee. Quickly educating Hoffman on the issues as Marines saw them, Hittle persuaded Hoffman to manage the hearings, which soon became a pro-Marine testimonial, much to the chagrin of the administration.[34]

The Hoffman Committee hearings produced just the effect the Edson–Thomas group and the "Chowder Society" had hoped for, a thorough exposure of Army anti-Marine hostility and a convincing argument that service roles and missions should be included in the final version of the National Security Act. Alerted by Hittle to the existence of the JCS 1478 studies, Hoffman announced he could not report out H. 2319 until his committee had examined those papers. Truman and the JCS, desperate for passage of unification legislation, allowed the release of the papers, which immediately compromised Eisenhower's testimony that he meant the Corps no ill and gave pro-Marine reporters exciting copy. The testimony mounted against the Army and its "militaristic" plans to dominate defense planning. In addition to Vandegrift, committed by both principle and circumstance to supporting his militants, the Committee heard protectionist advocates from the Marine Corps Reserve Officers Association, the Veterans of Foreign Wars, the National Guard Association, and the National Rifle Association, as well as such ardent champions of the Corps as General Edson and retired Rear Admiral Ellis M. Zacharias, the Navy's intelligence genius.

The hearings became such a menace to any unification law (including the independence of the Air Force) that the Truman administration finally accepted the fact that it would have no law at all unless the Marine Corps and naval aviation received legislative protection. Administration opposition to the Hoffman Committee dwindled, and the chairman finally drafted and submitted to the full House a new act, H. 4214, which included a section on service roles and missions and further diminished the powers of any executive official to modify those missions through the budget process. Section 206(c) of H. 4214, drafted largely by Colonel Twining, Lieutenant Colonel Krulak, and Lieutenant Colonel Hittle, gave the Marine Corps primary responsibility for developing amphibious warfare doctrine and equipment, reaffirmed all the Corps's traditional duties, asserted the Corps's wartime utility and right to expand, and provided that the Corps, a separate service within the Navy Department,

. . . shall include land combat and service forces and such aviation as may be organic therein. The primary mission of the Marine Corps shall be to provide fleet marine forces of combined arms, together

with supporting air components, for service with the fleet in the seizure or defense of advanced naval bases and for the conduct of such
land operations as may be essential to the prosecution of a naval campaign.[35]

Although H. 4214 underwent modification during the floor debate
in the House and in the final conference committee negotiations with
the Senate, the Corps had won a singular legislative victory. The House
version of Section 206 (c) survived the additional rewrites of the National Security Act despite a last-ditch effort by pro-Army advocates
to exclude the roles-and-missions provisions of the law. When the National Security Act of 1947 finally passed both houses and went to
Truman for signature, the Marine Corps believed it had won the ultimate legislative sanction for its role as both amphibious assault specialist
and force in readiness.[36]

3.

As it fought its political battles to keep the Fleet Marine Force alive,
Headquarters did its best with diminishing funds to provide ready forces
to support Fleet Cold War activities and to save the framework of a
wartime FMF. Given its buffetings by the Army, Headquarters might
have been unduly apprehensive about the Corps's future, for neither the
JCS nor the Navy Department had really consigned the Corps to the
military scrap heap. In its first comprehensive contingency plan for a
war with Russia, the JCS assigned the Marine Corps two missions. The
first was to seize air and naval bases in Iceland, the Azores, and the Persian Gulf from which Air Force B-29s would pound the Soviet Union
with nuclear weapons. In the second phase of this global war, two Marine divisions would join an American expedition that would seize the
Middle East in order to secure oil resources and develop bases for operations against Russia.[37] In similar studies of both global and regional
conflict, the Navy's General Board predicted that the skillful integration of vertical envelopment, close air support, naval gunfire, and a
more rapid surface ship-to-shore movement would make the Marine
Corps amphibious landing a useful tool for both nuclear and conventional war.[38] Even if some of the more visible service spokesmen seemed
to have given up on the Corps, other planners had not. The Marine
Corps of 1948 did not lack missions. It lacked the men and modern
equipment to perform them.

The supposed obsolescence of the Corps notwithstanding, the Marines of 1948 found themselves spread too thin. The only partially
ready forces in 1947 had been a brigade in Guam and part of the 2d

Marine Division, stationed at Camp Lejeune, North Carolina. Further concentrated by 1948 with the 1st Division at Camp Pendleton and the 2d Division at Camp Lejeune, the FMF could field only eleven battalion landing teams (BLTs) from both divisions. (Two divisions should have had eighteen BLTs.) To provide men for the BLTs, the Corps in 1947 had temporarily eliminated infantry and artillery regimental headquarters and concentrated combat support and combat service support units at the divisional or corps level. Even though this concept was reversed in 1949 to allow skeleton tactical headquarters at the regimental level, none of the infantry and artillery regiments had the World War II number of subordinate battalions and companies. Responding to JCS contingency plans and commitments, the Corps in early 1948 had only four BLTs not preassigned or deployed. Two BLTs were still in China, two were assigned on a rotating basis as the landing force of the 6th Fleet in the Mediterranean, two were assigned to missions in the Persian Gulf, and another was stationed at Quantico to test new tactical concepts and equipment. Amphibious training in the United States and the Caribbean, plagued by personnel and equipment shortages, continued on a shoestring level despite Vandegrift's understanding that the Corps needed much more experience in antitank warfare, night operations, and fire support coordination.[39]

The fate of the FMF passed in 1948 to a new commandant, Clifton B. Cates, who was no less committed than Vandegrift to keeping the Corps amphibious and ready. Having interviewed Cates and the other leading contender, Major General Lemuel C. Shepherd, Jr., Truman found them both qualified and their records identical. Both Cates and Shepherd had fought in World War I as lieutenants in the 4th Brigade and bore decorations for gallantry and wounds; both became distinguished division commanders in World War II. Truman chose Cates because he was slightly older and senior but promised Shepherd he would succeed Cates as commandant; fortunately, the surprise election victory of 1948 made his promise viable. If Truman thought, however, that he had anointed two generals who would accept a diminished role for the Marine Corps, he was badly mistaken.[40]

Cates's Corps shrank to fit federal budgets rather than expanding to fit contingency plans. Whereas Headquarters thought it needed at least 114,200 Marines to meet its peacetime duties, its funded manpower fell from 92,222 to 83,609 men in 1948 and dropped again to 74,279 by the spring of 1950. About 50,000 men were assigned to the operating forces, but the FMF had only about 35,000 men in the two divisions and aircraft wings, while nearly 15,000 men served in shore security detachments and ships guards. The Corps supporting establishment was so small and its tasks for maintaining Corps bases so extensive that many FMF troops spent more time housekeeping than training. With the Truman administration committed to holding down spending to about one-third of the total federal budget and the JCS dividing the defense budget of $11 billion to $14 billion almost equally among the three military departments, the Marine Corps share fell in the $300 million—350 million range. It was not enough to buy adequate manpower, training, or new equipment; the Marine Corps lived on skeletonized units, World War II surplus, and dwindling amounts of Navy amphibious shipping of World War II vintage. (The Navy's amphibious force fell from 151 vessels to 91 between 1948 and 1950.) Headquarters saw little chance to improve its readiness except by performing limited air-ground exercises and testing prototype weapons for antitank warfare (the 3.5-inch rocket launcher and 75-mm. recoilless rifle) and close air support (the Navy Douglas AD propeller-driven attack aircraft and the first jets). Torn between ambitious concepts for its future deployment and scant funds, the Corps limped along on attitudes that ranged from pure faith to utter demoralization.[41]

Assaulted by Truman's budget-cutters, especially Secretary of Defense Louis H. Johnson, the Corps faced an even more dismal future in 1949–1950. The Corps ran a series of vertical envelopment demonstrations at Quantico but then found that Truman nevertheless wanted the number of BLTs cut to six by FY 1951 and the number of aviation squadrons reduced to twelve by the same time. In view of the Corps's contingency missions in the Mediterranean, two-thirds of the FMF's BLTs and squadrons would be stationed on the East Coast at the air station at Cherry Point and at Camp Lejeune. The 1st Division at Camp Pendleton would have one regiment of two skeletonized battalions and the 1st MAW of only three squadrons. The Corps would be hard pressed to meet any crisis in Asia, but the State Department had ruled out the defense of either non-Communist South Korea or the Nationalist Chinese regime on Taiwan, so the deployment pattern at least reflected American diplomacy.[42]

Nowhere in the Corps were hopes higher and disappointments greater than in Marine aviation. Having gained the ascendancy over the air superiority fighter pilots in the fixed-wing community, the close air support enthusiasts found themselves saddled with the aging if reliable Corsair and challenged by the militants of HMX-1, the helicopter heretics. Moreover, in the battle for funds, the helo pilots had staunch allies in the MCS ground officer elite, which had considerable influence at Headquarters. In the two skeletal MAWS, equipment was scarce and flying time curtailed. If anyone prospered in Marine aviation in the

1948–1950 doldrums, it was HMX-1 and the helo planners. The only concession to the fixed-wing leaders was a Navy decision not to count helicopters as part of the Corps's set number of aircraft; since there were seldom more than twenty operational helos in the period, it was not much of a concession. The fixed-wing community also profited from the fact that flying helos was considered dangerous and low-status work among flyers, hence few pilots sought helicopter assignments. At the developmental level, the picture brightened for the helo advocates. While HMX-1 pilots proved the versatility of their craft in exercises in 1949 and 1950, aviation planners in the Navy Department assigned a higher priority than helos had yet enjoyed to two Sikorsky projects, one to develop a better light troop carrier (the HRS) that relied on existing systems and the other to build a true heavy troop carrier powered by multiple engines (the HR2S). With more funding, both helos might arrive in the FMF in the early 1950s. To ensure the proper appreciation of the Corps's helo projects, HMX-1 spent much of its flying time performing for important observers from the Truman administration and Congress.[43]

For both the aviation and the ground units of the FMF, the only real hope (as Headquarters recognized) rested with the Marine Corps Reserve, for the Corps would need almost fifty thousand Reserves to fill out two full-strength divisions and aircraft wings in the event of war. In 1946 Headquarters, spurred by oldtime enthusiasts like Clark W. Thompson and Melvin J. Maas, revived the Division of Reserve, gave it special staff status, and ordered the division to form eighteen infantry battlions, ten supporting arms battalions, and twenty-four fighter-bomber squadrons. The initial membership of the Organized Reserve (unit members) started at approximately 32,000 men and gradually climbed to more than 50,000 by 1950. Other Reservists, usually officers, could join the new, nonpaying Volunteer Training Units (VTUs) or agree to be Volunteer Reservists, who seldom trained but were subject to call-up. Thanks to hardsell recruiting and a great deal of public relations promotion (including collecting Christmas toys for underprivileged children or "Toys for Tots"), the Marine Corps Reserve by early 1950 mustered about 127,475 men of its ceiling of 150,000. The Reserve organization, however, had its special characteristics, some of which prevented real readiness. At the leadership levels the situation provided some cause for enthusiasm, for 98 percent of the officers and about 25 percent of the enlisted men were veterans. In addition, more than one hundred American communities had Marine Reserve units, which gave the Corps a solid recruiting base. The enlisted Reserves, however, were largely untrained, and many had joined for social and athletic reasons. Once-a-week nighttime drills inhibited training, and summer camps were not well attended. More significantly, new recruits did not attend boot camp or receive advanced training except in their units, which were hard pressed to find the money and time for field training. The result was a Reserve largely unprepared for war.[44]

Outside of the FMF and the Reserves recruited to join it in a national emergency, the Corps experienced little change in its duties and composition, but two social groups, women and Negroes, gained their first toehold in the regular establishment between 1945 and 1950. Neither group, however, was welcome, and neither was allowed to make a significant contribution to Corps readiness. Women Marines could and did join Reserve units after World War II but did not become a part of the regular Corps until the passage of the Women's Armed Services Integration Act of 1948, a law largely forced upon the services by Congress. As amplified by executive orders, the law provided a place for 1,110 regular Women Marines but limited their assignments to administrative and clerical positions, which did little to advance sexual equality in a Corps unsympathetic to feminism.

For Negroes the Corps was no more hospitable. Under pressure from the Truman administration to enlist Negroes after the war, the Corps set its quota at 2,800 black Marines but insisted that they serve in all-black service or security companies or continue in the segregated Steward's Branch. As Corps strength dropped, so did the ceiling on black troop strength, and the Corps found civilian communities and Navy commanders unenthusiastic about having all-black Marine companies at posts and stations. Nor was the Corps very attractive to the kind of patriotic, motivated black men who had joined the Corps during World War II. In July 1948 President Truman complicated the problem in the short run by ordering the integration of the armed forces. In November 1949 Headquarters bowed to the inevitable and ordered the assignment of black Marines on the basis of occupational specialty, making official a policy of integration that had already been tested on athletic teams and at recruit training depots. The policy of integration did not disrupt the Corps, with fewer than 1,500 black Marines (and only one regular officer), but it did not occur very quickly or happily either.[45]

More bedeviled by the complexities of postwar contraction than it had been by wartime expansion, Headquarters sought some relief from its woes in the time-honored tradition of reorganization. As serious problems emerged, so too did special Headquarters agencies to cope with them. So great had the proliferation of special HQMC divisions become by 1948 that Cates had his staff study the creation of a more centralized

HQMC based on concentrated, functional general staff lines. As Cates learned, the reorganization effort came too late. On one hand stood the bastion of the supply/financial community, led by the indomitable Major General William P. T. Hill. A seasoned performer for Congress and adept bureaucratic infighter, Hill had profited from a 1946 reorganization that had merged the Quartermaster and Paymaster Departments into a single Supply Department. He dominated all Marine Corps budgeting and fiscal management from this power base. Although a pioneer in supply accounting and the use of computers, Hill would brook no alteration of his power, and he rallied his Congressional friends. Allied with the directors of Reserve and Aviation and logistics planners, he mustered such opposition to a Corps general staff that Cates abandoned the reform movement.[46] The implications of the failure of the general staff reform movement remain indistinct, but it is plausible to conclude that Cates entered another round in the battle to preserve the FMF with a Headquarters divided over Corps policy and unlikely to provide the Commandant with adequate facts and coordinated policies with which to meet the Corps's critics.

4.

Despite the legislative protection of the National Security Act of 1947, Headquarters remained convinced that civilian budget-makers and the JCS might destroy the FMF, and between 1948 and 1950 the Corps and its champions mounted another effort to increase the Corps's power within the national military establishment. At issue was the Commandant's access to the Secretary of Defense, the Secretary of the Navy, and the JCS, all of whom, Marines feared, might alter Corps roles and missions and destroy the Corps as a force in readiness. As the unification controversy passed into its second stage in 1948 and units of the FMF disappeared in Truman's economy drive, the pro-Corps political coalition focused on a single legislative cure-all: to make the Commandant a statutory member of the Joint Chiefs of Staff. Such a law, its advocates stressed, would further identify the Corps as a separate service and give the Commandant direct access to the men drawing up the military budget. To provide the Commandant with enhanced power, pro-Corps reformers faced complex battles within the Navy Department, within the Department of Defense, and in Congress. Although unsuccessful by June 1950, the reformers at least kept the Corps's status alive as a public issue and built the political basis for a final victory in 1952.[47]

The Corps's potential difficulty within the Navy Department hinged on the Navy Reorganization Act of 1947, which so increased the power of the Chief of Naval Operations that a CNO might conclude that he commanded the Marine Corps and represented its interests not only on the JCS but before the Secretary of the Navy as well. Such an interpretation rested on the belief that the FMF and other Corps operating forces were Navy type commands and Headquarters was a bureau. The Commandant did not have the privileges of a head of service. When Executive Order 9877 strengthened this impression, Vandegrift in December 1947 asked for a decision on his status. Secretary of the Navy John L. Sullivan and CNO Chester Nimitz reassured him that neither the new law nor the executive order altered the Commandant's direct access to the Secretary, but this "gentlemen's agreement" might (and did) come apart when a new Secretary and a new CNO took office in 1949.[48]

Pressed by Secretary of Defense Forrestal to make the National Security Act of 1947 effective and to prepare the bare-bones FY 1950 defense budget, the JCS in 1948 studied service roles and missions and strengthened the impression that it would scrap the FMF. The conflict over roles and missions centered primarily upon increasing the Air Force budget and setting the future role of naval aviation, but the JCS continued to deal with the Corps as if it were a part of the Navy and stressed that its wartime role and size hinged on the need to conduct a naval campaign. Neither Army nor Air Force planners thought such a campaign likely, certainly not one that would require large amphibious assaults.[49] When Forrestal and the JCS hammered out the "Key West Agreement" on roles and missions in March 1948, they further refined this position by limiting the FMF to a wartime strength of four divisions and agreeing that the FMF should have no headquarters or forces beyond the corps level.[50] Not present at Key West and distressed by the JCS action, General Cates protested that the agreement violated the Congressional intent of the National Security Act of 1947, diminished the Corps's ability to perform its amphibious missions, and endangered the nation's security.[51]

Attempting to reconcile a war plan–based budget of $30 billion with a presidential decision to spend only $14 billion for defense, Forrestal and the JCS paid Cates's position little attention and made further agreements on roles and missions that suggested little need for a peacetime FMF larger than six BLTs and a wartime FMF not much larger. Again, the basic problem, Army and Air Force planners asserted, was that there seemed to be little need for amphibious operations exclusively designed to prosecute a naval campaign. The most likely amphibious operations would probably come in Europe and be part of a land and air war against Russia. Such a war was Army and Air Force business, not the Marine Corps's. Distracted by similar attacks upon naval aviation and the number of attack carriers in the fleet, CNO Louis E. Denfeld and his planners seemed to agree with the positions argued so forcefully by the Army and the Air Force.[52]

Although Headquarters would have preferred to work out its functions and budgets within the executive branch, the Corps's status became part of a series of public controversies in 1949 that wracked the armed forces. Headquarters drew little comfort from a wave of bitter disputes that engulfed it. Two retired generals caused special problems. Still smarting from slights real and imagined, Holland M. Smith in retirement published his memoirs first in the *Saturday Evening Post* and then as a book, *Coral and Brass*. So bitter and slanted were Smith's attacks on the Navy that an old Corps friend, the reporter Robert Sherrod, tried to persuade Smith not to publish. Lieutenant Colonel Robert D. Heinl, Jr., a member of the "Chowder Society" and Corps historian, offered to rewrite the manuscript, but, impatient as ever, Smith approved publication before Heinl could complete his revisions. The final version remained a pro-Corps polemic and irritated several admirals as well as the Army.[53] Equally bitter toward the other services, Merritt A. Edson, who had retired to protest the National Security Act of 1947, mounted another counterattack on the Air Force, the JCS, and anyone else who wanted to give the Secretary of Defense and the JCS more power. The determined Medal of Honor winner, collaborating with old Guadalcanal friend Richard Tregaskis and his former colleagues, orchestrated a public attack against Truman and the JCS, largely by publishing an insider's account of the unification battles of 1946–1947. Convinced that the President and Secretary of Defense Johnson meant to use the defense budget to destroy the FMF, Edson aroused a pro-Corps coalition of veterans groups, the Marine Corps Reserve Officers Association, and sympathetic Congressmen. Concerned over the sharpness of Edson's attacks upon the Air Force and Army, particularly upon General Eisenhower and General Bradley, Headquarters nonetheless mildly encouraged Edson, for Cates recognized that the Corps faced another deep cut in the FY 1951 budget.[54]

Headquarters had both ample opportunity and reason in 1949 to argue for strengthened legal protection, and Congress again heard Corps champions attack the Truman administration as interservice rivalry swelled. In addition to hearings on the FY 1951 budget, Congress found itself embroiled in conflict over the further reorganization of the national military establishment and Air Force–Navy disputes over aviation policy and the use of nuclear weapons. At the root of all the disputes rested the questions of service functions and Truman's determination to cut defense spending. Having replaced the ailing Forrestal with Johnson, an American Legion comrade and political fund-raiser,

Truman ordered Johnson to make more defense cuts and to stifle service protests. The President was also convinced that Congress should strengthen the powers of the Secretary of Defense and the JCS in order to curb independent lobbying by the Air Force and Navy. Using a study of governmental organization drafted by the Hoover Commission, the administration and its Congressional supporters managed to amend the National Security Act of 1947 in 1949, creating the Department of Defense as a single executive department and establishing a chairman for the JCS who presumably would enforce budget discipline. Initially the Navy Department opposed further centralization, but when Francis Matthews succeeded Secretary of the Navy Sullivan and Forrest P. Sherman replaced Denfeld as CNO (both incumbents having quit in the dispute over aviation policy), the Navy Department fell into line. Although it had tried to state its case against centralization with restraint, Headquarters recognized that both the 1949 amendments and the change of personalities in the Department of Defense could hardly have been worse. Louis Johnson and Francis Matthews were the President's men in ways Forrestal and Sullivan had not been; CNO Sherman was suspect; and the new chairman of the JCS, Omar N. Bradley, was Eisenhower's crony and anti-Corps in his own right. All had clear records against admitting the Commandant to the JCS or providing additional legal protection for the FMF.[55]

General Cates and his subordinates received an additional opportunity to educate Congress on the depth of the "conspiracy" to ruin the Corps during the 1949 hearings on unification and strategy sparked by the "revolt of the admirals." Caught in a bitter dispute caused by added funding for the B–36 strategic bomber and Johnson's cancellation of the building of the supercarrier U.S.S. *United States,* Headquarters supported the "mutiny" of Secretary of the Navy Sullivan and the aviation admirals—but did so with caution. Marine witnesses focused upon the Air Force's interest in absorbing Marine tactical aviation and the Corps's lack of adequate representation in JCS planning. Before the sympathetic House Armed Services Committee, Cates recommended that Congress limit the powers of the JCS, place the Commandant on the JCS, and establish by law that the FMF should be no smaller than two divisions of six BLTs each and two air wings with twelve squadrons each. Cates also pointed out that Johnson and Bradley did not think the Corps was a separate service or had a wartime role, a position Bradley himself admitted. Bradley insisted that the CNO spoke for the Corps and included Marines on his own staff and among the Navy representatives on the Joint Staff. Bradley recognized that Congress might protect the Corps for "sentimental reasons," but he saw no need for

FMF divisions and combined supporting arms. Other administration witnesses made similar points. By the time the Congressional investigation of "the revolt of the admirals" had concluded, the Corps had made a strong case that it needed further Congressional protection.[56]

The controversies of 1949 allowed the Corps again to take its case directly to Congress, but the results disappointed Headquarters and did nothing to arrest the erosion of manpower in the FMF, for Truman and Johnson insisted that the main threat to the nation came from inflation and unbalanced budgets, not the Soviet armed forces. The 1949 hearings and press coverage of the interservice rivalry over roles and missions, however, stirred Corps champions in Congress, particularly Carl Vinson, the powerful chairman of the House Armed Services Committee. As he had promised the Marines in the unification and strategy hearings, Vinson introduced legislation to curb the JCS powers over roles and missions and to put the Commandant on the JCS. Similar proposals would also have set the Corps's strength at 6 percent of America's uniformed manpower and created an assistant secretary of the Navy to represent the Corps. Such congressional advocates as Donald L. Jackson, Paul H. Douglas, Mike Mansfield, George A. Smathers (all ex-Marines), and the ever faithful Clare Hoffman filled the *Congressional Record* with pro-Marine testimonials and released the suspect JCS 1478 papers to public view. Fifty-five members of the House endorsed legislation protecting the Corps. The difficulty, however, was that the Congressional appropriations committees and the Senate Armed Services Committee saw no urgent reason to protect the Corps and feared increasing the defense budget and angering the Truman administration. Exhausted and bewildered by all the controversy over defense spending and unification, Congress in early 1950 refused to intervene in the administration's defense budgeting and policy-making process in any way that benefited the Corps.[57]

Ironically, while Truman and Johnson cut funds for conventional war forces from the defense budget, foreign policy planners from the Defense and State departments, including JCS representatives, concluded that the United States needed massive rearmament. Buffeted by Communist victories and near-successes from Europe to Asia since 1947, the planners argued in NSC-68, their final report, that the United States should, and could afford to, rearm to make "containment" militarily viable. They believed the nation should spend $30 billion a year on the armed forces, for the Soviet development of nuclear weapons, an established fact after the first Russian A-bomb exploded in 1949, placed greater importance on nonnuclear defense. Instead of the Cold War ending in some cataclysmic nuclear exchange, the analysts predicted a series of military confrontations that would fall short of global war but that might extend indefinitely over time and might include not only Europe but other parts of the world as well. To meet such a Communist challenge at the military and psychological level, the United States needed more conventional military strength. Privately, Truman agreed with the reasoning of NSC-68, but he allowed Johnson to reduce military manpower, including the FMF. With no real knowledge of NSC-68, the Marine Corps could only conclude that it had lost another battle to Johnson and the JCS. With no Congressional protection, the FMF seemed doomed to fall to six BLTs and twelve squadrons in 1950. Little did Headquarters guess that the North Korean People's Army would save the FMF and, indeed, the nation's commitment to collective security from extinction.[58]

16. The Korean War:
Fighting on Two Fronts, 1950–1953

Eight divisions of the North Korean People's Army (NKPA), plunging south across the 38th Parallel on June 25, 1950, brushed aside patrols of the army of the Republic of Korea (ROK) and began a blitzkrieg campaign to unify Korea as a Communist state. Frustrated by its inability to subvert the anticommunist government of Syngman Rhee, Kim Il Sung's regime, presumably with Soviet approval, finally chose direct attack as its final solution to the problem of a divided Korea. By June 1950 the NKPA was ready. A force of 135,000 men built around veterans of the Russian and Chinese Communist armed forces, it had sufficient Russian training and T-34 medium tanks, mobile artillery, and supporting aircraft to more than match the eight ROK divisions of South Korea. The ROK army of 95,000 men, trained and equipped for internal security duties by its American sponsor, lacked heavy weapons and aircraft. Enjoying both matériel and manpower superiority at the point of attack, the NKPA headed south for Seoul, South Korea's nearby capital, and a victorious *coup de main*.[1]

The North Korean attack found the Truman administration unprepared for a military challenge; the United States had not considered the defense of Korea solely its responsibility. Distressed by the fall of China and by the Communist insurgencies in Malaya, the Philippines, and Indo-China, the Truman administration had not yet formed a policy toward mainland Asia that accepted the emergence of Communist movements. Unlike its European allies, the United States would not recognize the Mao Tse-tung regime, but neither would it commit itself to protecting Chiang Kai-shek's government on Taiwan. In January 1950 Secretary of State Dean Acheson attempted to clarify American policy toward Asia in a major speech. Acheson's position, which reflected the thinking of the Joint Chiefs of Staff, committed the United States to acting unilaterally only to defend Japan. Nevertheless, the United States did not rule out a wide range of assistance to countries outside its sphere of strategic interest, provided such support came multilaterally under the aegis of the United Nations. In sum, the United States did not say it would not defend Korea, only that it would not do so without international support. Even many Americans thought Acheson was writing off Korea to Communism, so the Russians and North Koreans probably expected no American intervention to save South Korea. If so, they were wrong.[2]

Having first served as South Korea's patron and then backing United Nations supervision of the creation of a non-Communist regime in 1948, the United States government confounded Communist planners by deciding in less than a week to defend South Korea. In a series of complex decisions, the Truman administration and its commander in the Far East, General Douglas MacArthur, shaped the American commitment to Korea. Truman and his civilian and military advisers recognized a historical (if weak) American commitment to a free Korea and respected Rhee's militant anticommunism, but the American government was most concerned about dramatizing the United Nations's ability to halt territorial aggression by military action and showing the Soviet Union that it could not wage proxy war on the Eurasian land mass. At the same time, the American government feared that the Korean conflict was a diversion to pin America's scarce military forces in Asia rather than allow them to remain in strategic reserve in the United States or join the newly formed North Atlantic Treaty Organization (NATO) military alliance. General MacArthur argued that Asia was the critical battleground on which to defeat Communism, but the Truman administration remained convinced that a war in Korea must not obscure its more important mission: to defend Japan and Western Europe. Fearing a global war rather than a conflict limited to Korea, the Truman administration tried to defend South Korea while it preserved America's military ability to act elsewhere if necessary.[3]

Having withdrawn its troops from South Korea in 1948 and allowed its forces in Japan to shrink to marginal effectiveness, the United States began its Korean intervention, properly sanctioned by United Nations resolutions, in abysmal military condition. To rescue the ROK armed forces, MacArthur had four poorly equipped Army infantry divisions in Japan, each at less than 60 percent of its wartime strength. The Far East Air Forces (FEAF) were no more impressive. Although it had air units on Okinawa and the Philippines, the FEAF had only three weak wings of fighters and one of light bombers, augmented by three separate squadrons of fighters, in Japan. Vice Admiral C. Turner Joy's Naval Forces, Far East (NFFE) provided a 7th Fleet of one carrier, one cruiser, and eight destroyers, all of which Truman ordered to protect Taiwan when the Korean War began. In Japanese waters the NFFE maintained a small amphibious force of five vessels to train MacArthur's soldiers and a support force of one cruiser, four destroyers, and six minesweepers. Although the United States retained a substantial residual military potential in its World War II veterans and mothballed equipment, its strategic reserve in the United States was inadequate in numbers, training, and equipment.[4]

MacArthur's unified command in early July 1950 began air, sea, and ground operations against the NKPA in cooperation with the shattered but game ROK forces. Despite air superiority and interdiction operations against the NKPA supply lines by both air and sea forces, the American and ROK ground units, merged as United Nations Command (UNC), could not stop the NKPA offensive south of Seoul. One after another, the key towns along the rail and highway network of South Korea fell, until the U.S. Eighth Army found itself forced into the southeastern corner of Korea with its back to Pusan, the last major port under UNC control. The Eighth Army, commanded by the combative Lieutenant General Walton H. Walker, took its final positions along a 50-mile front defended by four American infantry divisions and five ROK divisions. Running along the Nam-Naktong River line on the west and anchored on the south coast at Chindongni, the Eighth Army front turned above the crucial city of Taegu and ran eastward to the Sea of Japan south of the port of Pohang. At the end of August 1950, while MacArthur's staff and the JCS still considered the possibility of evacuating Korea, the Eighth Army steeled itself for one more full-scale attack by the thirteen NKPA divisions it faced. The American portion of the front, which ran roughly from Taegu south to the coast, was the longest and was held by only three weak infantry divisions backed by the battle-worn 24th Infantry Division. Although MacArthur remained optimistic that the Eighth Army could hold, the military situation by August 1950 was desperate.[5]

Even before President Truman made the final decision to commit American ground troops to Korea, Commandant Clifton B. Cates on June 29 urged Chief of Naval Operations Forrest Sherman to tell MacArthur that the Marine Corps could send at least one regiment to

Korea. Frustrated at being excluded from both JCS and Navy Department deliberations during the first week of the war, Cates pressed Sherman to volunteer the Marines immediately, but the CNO waited until July 1, the day after Truman decided to commit ground troops, to cable MacArthur (through Admiral Joy) that the Marine Corps wanted to send him a reinforced regiment. In Tokyo, Admiral Joy found MacArthur delighted to make the request, for the general was already considering an amphibious attack behind the NKPA's lines. MacArthur cabled the JCS, which had not collectively ruled the Marines available or approved Sherman's cable to Joy, and requested a Marine regiment on July 3. On a hunch, Cates the day before had alerted the 1st Marine Division at Camp Pendleton that a deployment was imminent. The JCS and Truman approved the commitment of a Marine brigade on July 3. On July 4, even before he was certain he would receive Marine reinforcements, MacArthur conferred with Rear Admiral James H. Doyle, the NFFE's amphibious group commander, and the officers of a Marine amphibious troop training unit to start detailed planning for an amphibious landing.* On July 7 the 1st Marine Division ordered the formation of the 1st Provisional Marine Brigade, composed primarily of the reinforced 5th Marines and Marine Aircraft Group (MAG) 33. Admiral Arthur W. Radford, CINCPAC, informed Mac-Arthur two days later that he would have the Marine brigade for employment early in August. The Marine Corps was on its way to the Korean War.[6]

General Cates had no intention of allowing either the JCS or Admiral Sherman to limit Marine Corps participation in the war. On July 4 he ordered Lieutenant General Lemuel C. Shepherd, Jr., commanding general of FMF Pacific, to Tokyo to confer with MacArthur and Admiral Joy. Shepherd found MacArthur desperate for troops for an amphibious attack, for MacArthur had just ordered the 1st Cavalry Division to join the Eighth Army, thus committing the only division that might conceivably make a landing. On July 10, at Shepherd's urging (and somewhat to Cates's surprise), MacArthur asked the JCS to send him an entire Marine division with supporting aircraft. MacArthur told the JCS he still intended to make an amphibious counterstroke somewhere on Korea's western coast. He admitted he had made no decision yet upon the date or site of a landing, although he personally favored Inchon, port for the city of Seoul and close to both the 38th Parallel and the NKPA's supply lines. Much depended on the fighting in the Pusan perimeter and the availability of more American troops. Although

* There are fourteen-hours' difference and an international date line between Washington and Tokyo; the dates cited here are according to the local calendar.

pressed by MacArthur, Cates, Joy, and Radford, the JCS took almost four weeks to decide to send the 1st Marine Division to Korea, and even then the JCS wanted the division to deploy without a third infantry regiment and, perhaps, without a companion Marine air wing. As a group the JCS approved bringing the 1st Marine Division to war strength, but they wanted to hold it in strategic reserve, because the Army was stripping its stateside units for replacements and fillers for MacArthur's skeletonized divisions as well as sending two more full divisions to the Far East. Even with mobilization of the Marine air and ground reserves, a two-regiment 1st Marine Division would leave only three Marine battalions for European contingencies.[7]

MacArthur insisted that he wanted a full Marine division and wing for an amphibious assault in mid-September, and he pressed the JCS to commit the 1st Marine Division and 1st Marine Aircraft Wing. Admiral Sherman finally supported MacArthur's request, but the JCS Chairman, General Omar N. Bradley, and the Air Force Chief of Staff, General Hoyt Vandenberg, questioned whether the Marines could make the September deadline even with a two-regiment division. The Air Force position, additionally, reflected Vandenberg's and the FEAF's reluctance to turn much of the air war over to Navy and Marine Corps aviation outside Air Force control. A heated discussion over the use of air power further delayed a JCS decision. The Air Force wanted to use American aviation against NKPA lines of communication, not in direct support of UNC ground troops. Close air support, the Air Force argued, was wasteful and too dangerous to friendly troops. Although willing to fly interdiction missions, which the Navy was already doing with carrier-based air, Navy and Marine aviators argued that ground-controlled air strikes orchestrated with ground action would prove the Eighth Army's immediate salvation. The Marine Corps had no intention of sending a division to Korea without an accompanying wing. The argument spilled from the Pentagon into the Washington press and Congressional hearing rooms, much to Bradley's and Sherman's embarrassment. Rather than risk either MacArthur's or Congress's ire, the JCS on August 10 authorized not only the full-strength 1st Marine Division to go to Korea but a full-strength 1st MAW to join it there. Fearful that a larger Marine Corps would upset the Navy's own mobilization, Sherman, however, would not approve an FMF of more than two divisions and wings.[8]

In less than two weeks (July 2–12) the 1st Marine Brigade, commanded by Brigadier General Edward A. Craig, performed miracles in gathering men and equipment. Built around the skeletonized 5th Marines (Lieutenant Colonel Raymond L. Murray), the brigade included not only FMF Marines but men ordered west from Marine posts and stations throughout the United States. Reconditioned arms and equipment flowed to Camp Pendleton, the embarkation docks at San Diego, and the El Toro air station from the depot at Barstow and other supply points. By July 12 the brigade numbered 6,600 Marines, air and ground. For the first time the FMF went to war as a truly integrated air-ground team. Only MAG-33's observation squadron of light helicopters and observation planes, however, would actually serve ashore with the reinforced 5th Marines; its three Corsair squadrons would fly from two escort carriers and an FEAF base in Japan. Even with prodigious efforts to find men for the 1st Marine Division (which began the war with one-quarter of its wartime strength), Headquarters sent the 1st Brigade to war without its full complement of tactical units. Each of the 5th Marines' three infantry battalions deployed without its third rifle company, and the attached artillery battalion of the 11th Marines lacked two howitzers in each of its three firing batteries. Although blessed with World War II veterans in both its officer and its NCO ranks, the brigade sailed without further individual training, unit exercises, adequate weapons firing, or physical conditioning.[9]

Having reduced the 1st Division to a handful of cadres and stripping regulars from posts and stations for the brigade, Headquarters had to draw upon the 2d Marine Division (only one-third of wartime strength) and the Reserves to build the rest of a wartime division and air wing. In fact, Cates and Shepherd assumed that the Marine Corps Reserve would be mobilized immediately when they urged the Marine deployment to Korea, and both were chagrined when Truman and the JCS postponed the ground Reserve mobilization until July 20 and the air Reserve mobilization until July 23 in order to clear up some legal complications. Since World War II, Headquarters had planned on using Reserves and had stockpiled nearly all the matériel necessary for the 1st Marine Division and the 1st MAW. Now the Reserves would be tested to see whether they would respond. Despite predictable administrative errors and the problem of granting delays, the Reserves put the FMF on a wartime footing. Exceeding Headquarters' expectations, nearly 90 percent of the 33,258 Marines of the Organized Reserve were available for active duty. Half of this group proved sufficiently trained to be considered combat-ready, and nearly three thousand joined the 1st Marine Division. The others reported to the 2d Marine Division and to posts and stations, replacing regulars destined for Korea. The non–combat-ready Reservists received additional training, and many reached Korea in the autumn of 1950 as replacements. When the 1st Division's third infantry regiment, the 7th Marines, was formed in late August, 1,809 of its 3,836 men were Reservists. The mobilization of Reserve aviation units proceeded more slowly, but by September one-quarter of the 1st MAW was mobilized Reservists, and eventually twenty of thirty fighter squadrons and all ten ground-control squadrons in the Reserve became integrated in the regular aircraft wings.[10]

The Volunteer Reserve (individuals not belonging to units) provided a pool of 88,000 more Marines for mobilization. The Volunteer Reserve was an especially important source, for 99 percent of its officers and 75 percent of its enlisted men were World War II veterans. Called to active duty between August and December 1950, Volunteer Reserves filled the training and support establishment, provided almost the total strength of the reorganized 2d Marine Division, and went to Korea as replacements for the 1st Marine Division. By December 1950 there were 43,940 Volunteer Reserves, primarily company grade officers and enlisted men, on active duty; 80 percent of the Volunteer Reserve reported as ordered, and 15 percent of the remainder were not physically qualified for active duty. Like their comrades in the Organized Reserve, the Volunteer Reserves provided the margin of ardor and skill that made the rapidly expanding FMF a combat organization.

The final test for the Marines, whether career officers and NCOs, trained regulars from the FMF, or Reservists only a few weeks removed from civilian life, waited in Korea. Following the 1st Brigade to the San Diego docks, the columns of 1st Division Marines, distinctive in camouflaged helmet covers and leggings, boarded transports and sailed for Japan between mid-August and early September. From its station in the Mediterranean a battalion of the 2d Marine Division sailed for Japan to become a battalion of the 7th Marines. Transports and escort carriers brought the division's equipment and ferried another air group for the 1st MAW. Ahead of the gathering division-wing team, the 1st Brigade was already at war.

1.

For the Marine Corps the last five months of 1950 brought combat in Korea that for sheer drama, valor, and hardship matched the amphibious assaults of World War II—except, fortunately, in casualties. In that short period Marines helped the Eighth Army stop the NKPA along the Pusan perimeter; landed at Inchon and, in a dramatic two-week campaign, liberated Seoul; landed on the east coast of North Korea and drove as far north as the Chosin Reservoir; and then destroyed seven divisions of the Chinese Communist army as the 1st Marine Division "attacked in a different direction" and escaped by sea at Hungnam. Even if they had been designed at Headquarters, Marine operations in Korea from August through December could not have been better calculated to dramatize key elements of Corps doctrine and institutional values. As a force in readiness, the 1st Marine Brigade mounted out for the Far East less than a week after it was created. It did so with trained personnel and ample equipment and accompanied by its own close air support squadrons. In four weeks of heavy combat in the Pusan perimeter, the brigade proved its fighting heart and effectiveness. With the brigade then rejoined, the 1st Marine Division proved at Inchon that amphibious landings had not disappeared from the American military repertoire. With the 1st MAW providing close air support, the division captured Seoul and then fought a two-month mountain warfare campaign in biting cold, once more proving the importance of Marine *esprit*, individual combat training, and close air support. Even stripped of Corps legend and media myth-making, the Korean campaigns of the 1st Marine Division in 1950 retain an epic quality.

For the 1st Marine Brigade, the Korean War began not with amphibious training in Japan but with active combat along the southwestern approaches of the Pusan Perimeter. Unaware that July's fighting had reduced the front line NKPA troops to 70,000 men (or less than his own American and Korean force of 92,000), General Walker pressed MacArthur for more reinforcements. Walker's concern was understandable since his battle-worn and under-strength divisions held frontages of between 20 and 40 miles, or more than twice the ground normally assigned a full-strength division. Air Force interdiction strikes and American ground firepower could not alone redress the situation, for the NKPA could strike along any one of four major approaches to the perimeter with locally superior force. Therefore, MacArthur committed the 1st Marine Brigade, the lead regiments of the U.S. 2d Infantry Division, and the U.S. 5th Infantry Regiment in early August, along with new tank and artillery battalions. Having lost vital ground along the southern coast at the Chinju–Masan corridor, Walker assigned the Marine brigade and the 5th Infantry to the U.S. 25th Infantry Division's "Task Force Kean" and ordered this task force to mount the first substantial American counterattack to retake the Chinju corridor and, perhaps, begin an envelopment of the NKPA front. The attack was to begin August 7, a scant four days after the Marine brigade landed at Pusan.[11]

"Task Force Kean" collided with a similar limited attack mounted by the NKPA 6th Division with the result that the drive toward Chinju began with heavy fighting and ended in frustration. Deployed on the extreme American left flank, the 1st Brigade for three days fought a series of hard small-unit actions among the dusty hills east and

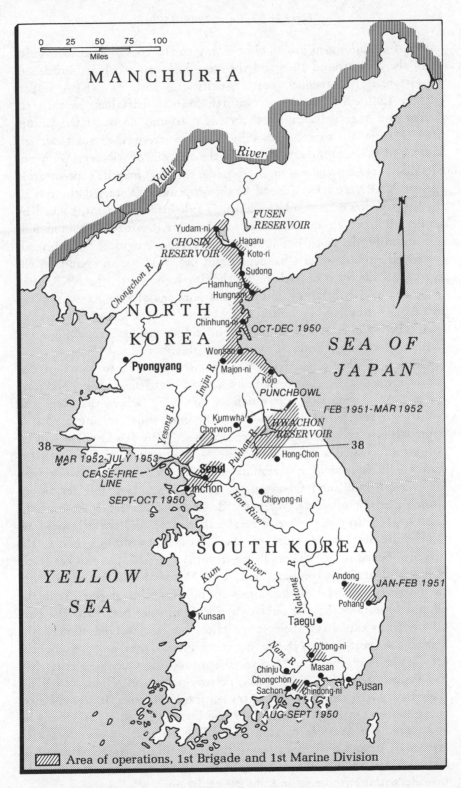

north of Chindong-ni just to clear a way to the coastal road to Chinju. With the heat around 100° and the steep hills too much for burdened, sea-softened infantrymen, heat casualties as well as NKPA bullets quickly thinned the ranks of two 5th Marines battalions as they attacked and eventually captured the high ground north of the Chinju road. Marine air strikes, flown by Corsairs from the escort carriers *Sicily* and *Badoeng Straits,* provided the margin of victory. With one battalion holding the northern shoulder of the brigade's penetration against NKPA attacks, General Craig on August 9 started the rest of the brigade down the road to Chinju. Tank-infantry teams, backed by artillery and air strikes, cleared a series of NKPA roadblocks and hillside ambushes in sharp but limited battles. On August 12 the brigade destroyed an ambush at Changchon and prepared for an assault on the key crossroads town of Sachon. To the north, however, the NKPA had bloodied the 5th Infantry and overrun portions of two Army artillery battalions, thus halting "Task Force Kean's" attack. After a week's hard fighting over 29 miles of roads and ridges, the 1st Brigade, less 315 casualties, withdrew to the Chindong-ni area.[12]

General Walker ordered the Chinju counterattack to halt and dispatched the 1st Brigade to a more crucial battlefield, the "Naktong Bulge." At a wide loop just north of the point where the Nam and Naktong rivers joined and flowed to the east, thus creating a natural approach into the Eighth Army sector, the NKPA 4th Division had by August 13 created a salient across the Naktong that the U.S. 24th Infantry Division could not eliminate. If the NKPA held two ridges, "Cloverleaf Hill" and Obong-ni, it commanded favorable terrain to launch a major offensive. Walker ordered the Marine brigade and the U.S. 9th Infantry Regiment to retake the ridges, and the brigade drew Obong-ni. Moving 75 miles to the north in twenty-six hours, the brigade opened its attack on Obong-ni on August 17. Despite heavy air strikes and artillery bombardment, two Marine battalions seized only the northernmost two of the ridge's six hilltops at great cost. As in the Chinju operations, having only two rifle companies prevented the battalions from exploiting their scant gains, but the toehold allowed the brigade to beat back NKPA night counterattacks and resume the attack the next day. The Marines also proved at Obong-ni that they had little to fear from T-34 tanks, destroying five in minutes with air, their own M-26 tanks, and infantry antitank weapons. It was a heartening lesson. On August 18 and 19 the brigade seized all of Obong-ni and joined the Army in driving the NKPA back across the river with American air and artillery ravaging the retreating Koreans. At a cost of 258 Marines, the brigade had helped seal Walker's perimeter, and the brigade withdrew to rest and absorb replacements.[13]

Although the 1st Brigade was already behind schedule for rejoining the 1st Marine Division for the Inchon landing, General Walker convinced MacArthur that the Eighth Army needed the Marines, for Walker saw indications that the NKPA was massing for another offensive against all of the perimeter's weak points. MacArthur reluctantly assented. Instead of leaving the perimeter, the brigade reassembled near Masan. It had less than a week's respite, for on September 1 the NKPA launched an offensive with all thirteen of its armor-supported divisions. Again the American troops along the Naktong gave ground, and Army counterattacks stalled. With additional Army troops, the Marines returned to the "Naktong Bulge." In three days of hard counterattacks (September 3–5) and taking 220 casualties, the Marines pushed the NKPA back toward the Naktong. With the attack still in progress but the issue decided, MacArthur ordered Walker to release the 1st Brigade from Eighth Army control and send it to Pusan for reembarkation. The Inchon operation could no longer do without the brigade. At the same time the squadrons of MAG-33, having become the heroes of Marines and soldiers alike for their low-level attacks, sailed away to join the invasion fleet. In four weeks of fighting, the 1st Brigade had inflicted an estimated total of ten thousand casualties on the NKPA at a cost of 903 Marines and Navy corpsmen, provided much-needed ardor to the Eighth Army's defense, and received welcome acclaim from its Army superiors and American war correspondents. If the Marines swaggered and boasted about how they "saved" the Army again as they piled into Pusan, the exaggerations were understandable.[14]

Far from the 1st Brigade's noble strife, General Douglas MacArthur dreamed of a dramatic blow that would crush the NKPA. Although the Eighth Army took his strategic reserves from him, MacArthur early in July decided he would launch an amphibious counterstroke on South Korea's western coast that would disrupt the NKPA supply system and demoralize the Communist invaders. MacArthur's attention focused upon Inchon, the port city for Seoul, 25 miles distant, and a portal to vital Kimpo airfield and the road and rail systems across the Han River. A joint plans group in UNC headquarters, working with Admiral Doyle's amphibious force staff, gathered information and made tentative plans throughout July. Studying Inchon as MacArthur's first choice, the planners found much about the objective area to dislike. Weather and hydrographic conditions headed the list of problems, followed by the possibility of Russian or Chinese intervention or determined NKPA defense. Korea's weather patterns meant that the landing had to come in September, before the winter monsoons struck. (In fact, the first typhoon of the season disturbed the invasion fleet.) The hydrographic problems Inchon presented were incredible. To reach the city the amphibious task force would have to navigate a narrow channel with swift currents while dodging islands and potential coast defense battery sites. Moreover, the channel was perfect for mining. (Although few mines actually appeared in the channel, the NKPA was about to begin extensive mining when the invasion occurred.) Potential anchorages for transports and gunfire-support ships were scarce. Worst of all, the tides of Inchon varied as much as 35 feet, flooding back and forth over 6,000 yards of mud flats with shallow gradients. The tides meant that any invasion would have to ride a high, flooding tide of between 23 and 29 feet in order to float landing craft and LSTs all the way to the seawalls (the "beaches") that ringed Inchon harbor. The draft of the LSTs was critical. Because no landing could be called an acceptable risk without the supplies and equipment provided by the LSTs, the highest flood tide set September 15 as the invasion date. As for the NKPA defenses, MacArthur's intelligence staff declared (in an act of faith) that the defense would be weak; in fact, Inchon was defended by only about 2,500 second-rate NKPA troops with inadequate artillery. MacArthur's staff discounted the possibility of Chinese or Russian intervention.[15]

Marine planners found little to recommend Inchon, particularly since they shared the Navy's concern about the technical details ("merely mechanical" said MacArthur) and the training deficiencies of both the amphibious and the landing forces. Representatives from a Marine training team worked on the early plans, joined shortly by the advance party of the 1st Marine Division staff and visitors from Headquarters FMF Pacific. The most telling criticisms came first from General Shepherd and then from Major General O. P. Smith, commander of the 1st Marine Division. Although both thought MacArthur's plan splendid in concept, they thought Inchon a poor objective, particularly when another site to the south seemed equally suitable as a base from which to take Seoul. As the 1st Division planners gathered in Japan between the first and third weeks of August, they found MacArthur's staff adamant for Inchon but also woefully ignorant of amphibious operations. A veteran of three major World War II operations in which he had served in positions from regimental commander to Tenth Army deputy chief of staff on Okinawa, O. P. Smith, a spare, thoughtful, highly skilled, and patient man of fifty-seven, thought MacArthur's staff patronizing and abrupt. The most irritating Army officer was his immediate commander, Major General Edward M. Almond, MacArthur's chief of staff and commander-designate of the Seoul expeditionary force, X Corps. Smith's objections to assaulting a defended city against uncertain odds and with reinforcements controlled by the tidal tables did not change

MacArthur's mind. The best Smith could do was to second Admiral Doyle's position: At best, Inchon was not impossible.[16]

Working concurrently with Navy planners, the 1st Division staff shaped the landing's basic character before either the 7th Fleet commander (redesignated Commander Joint Task Force 7 for the operation) or X Corps made their own plans. The first problem was to eliminate the NKPA defenses on the harbor island of Wolmi-do, which commanded the approaches to the inner harbor. The solution to time, tides, and defenses was to bombard the island for two days (the Marines insisted) and then take it with one reinforced battalion on the early morning flood tide. Since regular transports could not navigate the channel in the dark during flood tide, this force would have to reach Wolmi-do upon fast attack transports (converted destroyers) and a powerful radar-equipped LSD, which carried tanks and heavy equipment in the landing craft in its flooded well deck. Seizing Wolmi-do meant, however, that the main landing would come on the late afternoon flood tide, which meant that the 1st Division would have only two hours to seize the high ground dominating an industrial city of 250,000 inhabitants. Because the citizens of Inchon were South Koreans, heavy air and naval gunfire bombardment was precluded. The main landing, then, required a maximum effort. Two reinforced battalions of the veteran 5th Marines would land on RED Beach, the seawall at the foot of the city, and capture an enclave for the LSTs and reinforcements, while the raw 1st Marines, led by the irrepressible Colonel Lewis B. "Chesty" Puller, would land on BLUE Beach and capture the dominating terrain southeast of the city. If the NKPA defenders were not in strength, if Navy and Marine air stopped reinforcements, if reinforcements and supplies got ashore on schedule, if the assault regiments performed up to World War II standards, if naval gunfire and air supported the ground attack up to World War II standards—the "ifs" were many—the Inchon landing would succeed.

Even as the planning progressed and JTF-7 assembled its improvised invasion fleet (thirty of the forty-seven LSTs were drawn from Japanese coastal runs and largely remanned by scratch American crews flown from the U.S. and Japan), Douglas MacArthur persuaded his subordinates and superiors that Operation CHROMITE would work. It was a bravura performance. In a series of briefings for representatives of the JCS and all the top Pacific commanders, MacArthur crushed all objections. He told Navy and Marine commanders that he knew from their World War II performance that they could do the job. He added for Marine commanders that a successful attack on Inchon would ensure an important place for the Corps in the American defense establishment for the foreseeable future. He assured the JCS that the landing would win the Korean war: "We shall land at Inchon, and I will crush them." [17] The JCS weakly approved the operation on August 28, but President Truman and his military advisers did not give their final assent until September 8. Nevertheless, MacArthur in the meantime had all the elements of JTF-7 assemble at Pusan and at Japanese ports for CHROMITE. From the perspective of the 1st Marine Division, the operation was "go" on August 28, but two weeks seemed hardly enough time for adequate organization. MacArthur consoled General Smith. He knew the landing would succeed even if it proved "a little helter-skelter." [18]

A tribute to all the American, Korean, and British forces sent to Inchon with JTF-7, Operation CHROMITE succeeded beyond all but MacArthur's wildest hopes. After five days of aerial bombardment and two days of naval gunfire, the brunt delivered by a destroyer squadron that silenced Wolmi-do at close range, the landings on September 15 brought the reinforced 5th and 1st Marines to their objectives by nightfall with about two hundred casualties. The early morning landing at Wolmi-do went well as a 5th Marines battalion seized the island and eliminated the surviving NKPA troops. The lack of guide boats, the inexperienced boat crews, and heavy smoke impeded all but the early waves of the main landing, but the 5th Marines plunged up the seawall and captured the hills commanding the crucial LST landing sites at RED Beach. NKPA resistance did not disorganize the landing as much as did the search for ways off the waterfront; the worst moment for the 5th Marines came from American LSTs that, under fire and with two awash with gasoline, turned their guns indiscriminately on the landing area. A mile to the south the 1st Marines landing, spearheaded by Army amphibious howitzers, turned into a muddle as LVTs and landing craft lost direction. The first three waves, however, hit BLUE Beach more or less in order and, pushed by "Chesty" Puller, fought their way to the regiment's hilltop objectives along Inchon's southeastern fringes. Although hardly an artistic success, the Inchon landing caught the NKPA by surprise, and by early morning of September 16 there was no doubt that the 1st Division was ready to exploit the landing. With adequate tanks, artillery, and service units ashore and covered by carrier air, the 1st Division started down the highway for Seoul.[19]

In five days of textbook campaigning, the 1st Marine Division closed on the approaches of Seoul by September 20. The 1st Marines took the direct road toward the Seoul suburb of Yongdungpo west of the Han River, while the 5th Marines drove to the northwest to capture Kimpo airfield and the hills overlooking the Han north of Seoul. Behind the two leading Marine regiments, a regiment of the Korean Marine Corps

(KMC) and the lead regiment of the U.S. 7th Infantry Division guarded the advance's southern flank and rear. NKPA resistance to the Marines did not stiffen until the Americans reached the Han. Marine battles with the NKPA along the approaches to Seoul took many forms. When small NKPA tank and infantry columns mounted counterattacks, the Koreans wilted and burned under air strikes and massed infantry, tank, and antitank weapons fire. When the NKPA dug in to contest a hill or crossroads, the Marines brought in air strikes and artillery and crumpled the defenses with tank-infantry attacks, the crucial assaults normally delivered against exposed NKPA flanks. The advance was not bloodless, but the drive to the Han went so well that MacArthur and the battalion of newsmen watching the campaign waxed rhapsodic over the Marines' performance. Since X Corps was not exercising much direction or support, the campaign was O. P. Smith's, but the division commander did not need to push Murray or Puller. Both regimental commanders shared their troops' aggressiveness. Optimism close to euphoria, enhanced by the news that the NKPA was falling apart in front of the Eighth Army's offensive to the south, spread from the Marines through X Corps to MacArthur, a frequent battlefield observer.[20]

The 1st Marine Division, with help from the KMC regiment and the U.S. 32d Infantry Regiment, wrested Korea's capital from the NKPA after ten days of fighting. The battle left Seoul devastated and the Marines exhausted. After an abortive attempt by a reconnaissance company to cross the Han, the 5th Marines on September 20 punched across the river on LVTs, seized the commanding heights in stiff fighting, and turned south toward Seoul's northern edges. The defenders of Seoul, an NKPA reinforced division heavily armed with Russian weapons, contested every hill along the 5th Marines advance. Several 5th Marines companies shrank to platoon size as the Marines wrested the hills from the NKPA in bitter fighting. Fortunately, General Smith could give Murray some assistance, for the division's third infantry regiment, the 7th Marines (Colonel Homer L. Litzenberg), landed at Inchon on September 21 and was soon in action on the 5th Marines' northern flank, thus allowing Murray to narrow his frontage and attack with battalions in column toward Seoul.

The unrelenting Marine infantry pressure, backed by solid air support, bludgeoned the NKPA backward. In the meantime, the 1st Marines took Yongdungpo in three days of confused, occasionally sharp fighting that went on day and night. On September 24 the 5th Marines and the KMC regiment finally cracked the NKPA main defenses, and the 1st Marines crossed the Han on a bridge provided by Marine engineers. The fighting entered a new phase. Recognizing its desperate situation, the NKPA fought for Seoul block by block. With the 1st Marines bearing most of the burden of the street fighting, tanks dueled in the streets, neighborhoods disappeared in flames, and Koreans and Marines blasted away at each other from houses and barricades. X Corps did not make General Smith's task easier by declaring the city secure and ordering a pursuit at the very moment when the 1st Marines was throwing back a vicious night counterattack. Moreover, General Almond complicated the Marines' task by committing the 32d Infantry in a poorly coordinated attack. Nevertheless, the Marines methodically eliminated pockets of resistance, decorated the city with American flags (the Iwo Jima syndrome), and allowed Douglas MacArthur on September 29 to return the Korean government buildings to Syngman Rhee in an emotional ceremony. Although the 7th Marines went on to pursue the NKPA north to Uijongbu, the 1st Division had completed its mission. On October 7 X Corps announced that the Inchon–Seoul campaign had ended.[21]

Douglas MacArthur now saw additional missions for the 1st Marine Division, for, even before the Inchon–Seoul campaign ended, the UNC commander had received authority to continue the war north of the 38th Parallel. In a series of decisions fashioned in Washington, the Truman administration authorized MacArthur to destroy the NKPA as a threat to South Korea and to secure the military victory that would unify the two Koreas under UN supervision. Only if either China or Russia intervened would the mission be reconsidered. Flushed by victory, neither MacArthur's headquarters nor the JCS anticipated intervention, but the JCS cautioned MacArthur not to violate international borders or send American troops all the way to the Yalu. Nevertheless, MacArthur's planners committed the Eighth Army and X Corps, still a separate command, to an ambitious exploitation campaign into North Korea. X Corps's mission was to land at Wonsan on Korea's east coast and hurry the drive largely carried there by ROK troops.[22]

Even more hurriedly mounted than the Inchon landing, the Wonsan operation stalled when the advance elements of JTF-7 found the approaches to Wonsan harbor heavily mined. Even before the scheduled landing, ROK troops captured the city, and the 1st Marine Division did not land until October 25. In the meantime, elements of MAG-12, the newer of the 1st MAW's two air groups, flew from Kimpo airfield to a strip near Wonsan in order to reassume its mission of supporting X Corps. Marine airmen enjoyed a USO show and welcomed the division ashore with caustic comments. As service units established a base of operations at Wonsan for X Corps, the reinforced infantry regiments of the Marine division fanned out to the west and north, and the ROK divisions slid westward through the mountains to maintain contact with the Eighth Army or drove northeastward toward the Yalu. The Marines soon learned that the Korean war had not ended, and the "home by Christmas" vision that hypnotized American troops was a cruel delusion.[23]

Sharing his patron's optimistic estimate of the state of the UNC campaign, General Almond scattered X Corps for more than 100 miles along northeastern Korea's coast in November. Despite intelligence estimates that the NKPA was beaten, the 1st Marines fought a series of battalion actions south and west of Wonsan. The 7th Marines moved north to relieve ROK units in the Hungnam-Hamhung area and under corps's orders began to move north along the 78 miles of mountain road that led to the Chosin Reservoir. In the meantime, thousands of Chinese troops were marching across the Yalu to blunt the UNC offensive. Warned by a Chinese attack on the Eighth Army in early November, Colonel Litzenberg's Marines were not completely surprised when they encountered the 124th Division of the People's Liberation Army (PLA) at Sudong on November 2. The ferocity of the fighting, however, momentarily rocked the 7th Marines. Unlike their Korean brethren, the Chinese did not depend on Russian tanks and heavy artillery. Building upon its own guerrilla warfare experience and its respect for American airpower, the PLA fought largely at night and sought tactical penetrations into the command, logistical, and supporting arms system of the UN forces. At Sudong, the PLA enjoyed initial success because the Marines still used scattered company defensive positions rather than tightly formed battalion perimeters. Surviving desperate combat against the Chinese and attached NKPA tanks, the 7th Marines shifted to the offensive and, with ever present air support from MAG-12, virtually destroyed the Communist division in five days of fighting. The Chinese forces disappeared into the vastness of Korea's northern mountains. Followed by the 5th Marines, the 7th Marines edged up the road toward the Chosin Reservoir.[24]

The Sudong battle convinced General Smith that the 1st Marine Division must be concentrated, and the Marine commander persuaded General Almond to shift the rest of the division north to Hamhung. The 1st Marines and the division's support units moved north. A charter member of the MacArthur school of military romanticism, Almond then ordered Smith to push the Marine division rapidly to the northwest for a final drive toward the Chinese border. Smith, who had no confidence in Almond's strategy or prophetic gifts, moved his regiments cautiously up the road toward Chosin and paid particular attention to his logistical arrangements and security force (largely the 1st Marines) along the main supply route (MSR). The weather on November 11 turned miserable. The temperature fell from 32° to −8°, with gusting winds making the cold even more devastating. Provided with only about three-quarters of the cold weather clothing his division required, Smith ordered the protective clothes distributed to his combat units, but the first cold wave stupefied the troops. With its left flank unprotected by the Eighth Army and with only scattered ROK and 7th Infantry Division units to its right, the division edged up the MSR. Smith and his staff deflected X Corps demands for more speed and nursed their gnawing suspicion that the 1st Marine Division faced a new war.[25]

Struggling toward each other in the bitter cold, the 1st Marine Division and the PLA Ninth Army Group, a veteran force of 100,000 Chinese in ten divisions, deployed for four weeks of some of Korea's fiercest fighting as November ended. As part of their scheme to halt the UN offensive well short of the Yalu and to embarrass the UNC militarily, China's military leaders planned to smash the Eighth Army's right flank, isolate X Corps, and defeat both in detail. Although weak in artillery and lacking close air support, the Chinese proved worthy foes, specializing in rapid, determined night attacks to penetrate UNC lines and infiltrating supply lines in order to set up ambushes. The PLA, made up of disproportionate numbers of infantrymen, nonetheless had enough heavy mortars and machine guns to be lethal at long range as well as in the assault. The 1st Marine Division was no pushover, but its deployment presented the PLA with a tempting target. General Smith by November 26 had concentrated the reinforced 7th and 5th Marines at Yudam-ni west of the Chosin Reservoir, but the rest of the division huddled in enclaves along 45 miles of mountain road. Along the 14 miles from Yudam-ni to the forward division base at Hagaru-ri, only one rifle company at the critical Toktong Pass guarded the MSR. At Hagaru at the base of the reservoir, Smith's headquarters and the division's many service and supply elements depended on one 1st Marines battalion, some Army troops, and their own weapons for defense. Eleven more miles down the road, "Chesty" Puller held Koto-ri with one battalion of his regiment, 235 Royal Marines, some supporting arms, and service units. And 10 miles farther down the road Puller's last battalion garrisoned Chinhung-ni at the base of the mountains. Against these enclaves the PLA Ninth Army Group planned simultaneous attacks, with other units blocking the MSR between the Marine units. By annihilating MacArthur's crack division, the Chinese anticipated a stunning military and psychological victory.[26]

When the Ninth Army Group struck Yudam-ni on the cold night of November 27 and invested Hagaru and Koto-ri in the next two days, the Chinese found the Marines well deployed and full of fighting heart. The Marines lost some high ground in both the Yudam-ni and Hagaru perimeters, but the Chinese attacks failed decisively. Backed by artillery around the clock and air strikes in daylight, the 5th and 7th Marines stopped the attack at Yudam-ni, and the company in the Toktong Pass refused to be overrun in a five-day stand. At Hagaru extemporized infantry units made up of artillerymen, service troops, and Army stragglers held the critical supply base and primitive airstrip. Ravaged by the cold (which hurt the Chinese even more), the Marines fought with unmatched ferocity and determination. Some of the individual and small-unit heroics matched Greek and Nordic legends—except that they really happened. The only serious Marine defeat occurred when Smith sent a Marine–Royal Marine–Army motorized task force up the MSR to reinforce Hagaru; the PLA ambushed the column, and only half of it either reached Hagaru or fell back on Koto-ri. When General Smith on November 30 received the authority to fall back along the MSR and extract the 1st Division, the Marine position was precarious, but the division remained unbroken if bloodied.[27]

On December 1 the 1st Marine Division began one of history's epic retrograde movements, a fighting withdrawal that eventually ended with the amphibious evacuation of X Corps from Hungnam. Because the PLA invested the MSR all the way to Chinhung-ni, General Smith correctly called the operation "an attack in another direction" in tactical terms, but for the UNC, with the Eighth Army reeling back in eastern North Korea, the campaign was part of a major strategic defeat. For the Marines, the campaign was a victory, for the march out from Chosin saved X Corps and virtually destroyed seven PLA divisions. The 1st Division did so against heavy odds and at center stage for world military and press observers.

The first phase (the critical one) of the retrograde saw the 5th and 7th Marines fall back on Hagaru. Bringing their dead, their wounded, and their equipment, the 7th Marines attacked south along the high ground above the MSR while the 5th Marines held off the Chinese at the rear. One 7th Marines battalion in the meantime marched overland in incredible cold and with much suffering to relieve the Toktong Pass company. Despite persistent Chinese attacks against the motorized column on the road and desperate fighting for the critical hills, the two Marine regiments began to reach Hagaru on December 3. When the haggard, crippled, exhausted troops in the vanguard managed to march into the Hagaru perimeter, other Marines burst into tears. At a cost of over three thousand casualties (it inflicted four times as many on the Chinese), the 1st Marine Division survived its first test.

At Hagaru, General Smith regrouped and rested his command while planning the next phase of the withdrawal. The Marines buried their dead, flew out the wounded and frostbitten, brought in replacements, and reinforced the skeleton rifle companies with twenty-six platoons of Marine service troops and artillerymen. Smith's Marines also rescued the remnants of an Army task force east of the reservoir and integrated all the stragglers into the breakout force. Smith and his staff planned the next phase of the operation, the march down the road to Koto-ri, with the same governing assumptions that characterized the withdrawal from Yudam-ni. The infantry battalions would clear the hills above the MSR, supported by artillery that would displace in echelon along the MSR and by close air attacks. Only the minimum number of troops would be tied to the MSR to drive vehicles and provide close security; many of the vehicle defenders were the walking wounded and frostbite cases. The division would come out fighting and come out as Marines, or it would not come out at all. With the 7th Marines leading and the 5th Marines covering, the division fought its way forward at a cost of 1,600 casualties to Koto-ri by the evening of December 7. Oiling their weapons with hair tonic, eating PX candy and rations warmed by body heat, plodding forward on unfeeling feet, pulling triggers with numb fingers, and plagued by dysentery that fouled their clothing, the Marines blasted the PLA aside and reassembled for the final breakout.[28]

The last phase of the Division's Anabasis had no less drama than its earlier stages. The PLA had destroyed a crucial bridge at Funchilin Pass, so Marine and Army engineers, provided with air-dropped bridge sections, had to cover the abyss in order for the column to continue with its vehicles. In a masterpiece of engineering improvisation, the bridge was built. As the division marched, the 1st Marines battalion at Chinhung-ni attacked northward into the hills above the MSR and defeated the last PLA forces between the division and safety. The lead elements of the 1st Division, reached Hamhung late on December 10, entering X Corps defenses manned by the U.S. 3d Infantry Division and ROK troops. The march to the sea had ended, but the glory was only beginning.

Viewed in emotional terms—focusing on the endurance and heroism of the 1st Division's Marines—the Chosin Reservoir withdrawal remains one of those military masterpieces that occur when skill and bravery fuse to defy rational explanation. However, the campaign in retrospect dramatized the soundness of Marine training and doctrine. First, the division's Marines, regardless of their assignment, could and did function as infantrymen when the PLA attacks ravaged the regular rifle companies. At the same time, the supporting arms units, though stripped of personnel, continued to provide punishing fire support. The fighter squadrons of MAG-33 devastated the PLA, assisted by Navy pilots from the fast carriers of Task Force 77. (Disappointed by the Eighth Army's inability to direct close air strikes, TF-77 moved to support X Corps where it knew Marine air controllers would use its strikes well.) The 1st Division also managed its logistical problems with verve and confidence. Assisted by Navy and Air Force transports, the division flew in precious gasoline, rations, and ammunition in sufficient quantities to keep up the fight and the vehicle movement. In addition, despite occasional communications lapses, the division's senior officers, assisted by helicopter reconnaissance, never lost a firm grip on the tactical situation. General Smith and his regimental commanders fought the division with patience and skill; their decisions, however, found inspiration in the battalions, where officers, NCOs, and enlisted men seldom failed to show whatever initiative, courage, and sacrifice the tactical situation demanded. The fortitude of the division's Marines awed even the hardest veterans. In one representative incident, General Smith, laid low by exhaustion and heavy responsibilities, rallied when he heard a group of enlisted men in a nearby warming tent actually singing the Marine Corps Hymn.

As a capstone to the fighting in the Pusan Perimeter and in the Inchon–Seoul campaign, the 1st Marine Division's withdrawal from the Chosin Reservoir brought the Marine Corps unmatched public acclaim, which became increased political power. Marine officers knew that their troops made mistakes and had much to learn about tactics and cold-weather warfare. Nevertheless, such knowledgeable experts as S. L. A. Marshall, the Army's premier tactical analyst, and the experienced war correspondents who covered the latter phases of the March to Hungnam agreed that the 1st Marine Division shone during the Korean War's darkest hour. Fair-minded senior Army officers agreed. President Truman's personal observer in Korea, Major General Frank E. Lowe, U.S. Army Reserve, assured Truman that the 1st Marine Division deserved all the favorable publicity it was receiving for the Chosin withdrawal. At a cost of almost seven thousand casualties (about half from critical frostbite), the 1st Marine Division had polished the Corps's reputation for valor and skill at a time when Army divisons of the Eighth Army appeared infected with defeatism. Whether Headquarters Marine Corps could capitalize on the 1st Division's reputation remained to be seen, but the battles on the Korean War's "second front"—Washington, D.C.—would soon provide the test.[29]

2.

The mobilization in the late summer of 1950 provided the Marine Corps and its champions with a fresh opportunity to expand the Corps and to provide legislative protection to ensure that the expansion was permanent. As the 1st Marine Division moved into battle against the NKPA, the House Armed Services Committee examined the Truman administration's first of four requests to supplement the FY 1951 defense budget. In the course of the discussions, Representative Carl Vinson, committee chairman, announced that he favored an expanded Corps of four divisions and four wings. The Department of Defense first advocated a Corps of three divisions and twenty-four squadrons (General Cates's plan), but this proposal shrank at Admiral Sherman's insistence to two full-strength divisions and two wings of eighteen squadrons for a total of 166,155 Marines. Sherman privately censured Cates for not adhering to the official Truman administration—JCS position, which was that the Korean War would be quickly won. Benefiting by a pro-Corps publicity campaign organized before the war began, Cates resurrected the issue of Marine representation on the JCS and the size of the FMF, but the Commandant, under pressure from the JCS and Secretary of Defense Louis Johnson, softened his advocacy. Even though Congressional advocates wanted protective legislation, the issue drifted.[30]

In a public relations gaffe of the first magnitude, President Truman himself handed Corps champions a new opportunity. In response to a letter from Representative Gordon L. McDonough (R.—Calif.) about the Marine Corps legislation, Truman, perhaps in jest, called the Corps "the Navy's police force" and complained that it had "a propaganda machine that is almost equal to Stalin's." The President said he saw nothing wrong with the current arrangements, which made the CNO the Marine spokesman on the JCS. Truman implied that the Corps was not a separate service and existed only at the sufferance of the Navy and Army.[31] For presumably pro-Corps and partisan political purposes, McDonough released Truman's letter, much to the President's chagrin, for Truman thought he was only writing a fellow World War I Army officer on personal terms. The McDonough letter stirred up a wave of hostile letters to the White House, unfavorable press comment, and Congressional objections. (In Korea, Marines chalked "Harry's Police Force" on their trucks.) Private citizens, most of them ex-Marines or Marine relatives, swamped Truman with letters (unsolicited by any pro-Marine lobby) suggesting that the President retire or at least apologize. Convinced by his advisers that he had made a political error in the middle of a Congressional campaign and had maligned the Corps, Truman sent a public letter of apology to General Cates and later made a similar statement to the national convention of the Marine Corps League. The President avowed his high regard for the Corps's military contributions and *esprit*. He regretted his injudicious remarks. Truman, however, did not modify his position on the status of the Marine Corps within the defense establishment.[32]

Exploiting the public reaction to Truman's McDonough letter and the glowing accounts of the Marines in Korea, pro-Corps champions in Congress (particularly Senator Paul H. Douglas and Representatives Carl Vinson and Mike Mansfield) urged that the Marine Corps be expanded and the Commandant placed by law on the JCS. Headquarters assisted by admitting that it preferred a Corps of four divisions and two wings and a total strength of 326,000. In addition, David Lawrence, syndicated columnist of *U.S. News* and the *Washington Star*, published a series of strong articles describing the Marines as an air-ground force in readiness unlike any of the other armed forces. The Marine Corps Reserve Officers Association threw its lobbying weight into the controversy as well, supported by other veterans and military associations. On September 8, Senator Douglas, the Corps's foremost Congressional champion, introduced a bill (S. 677) that proposed a permanent FMF force structure of four divisions and four wings, full membership in the JCS for the Commandant, and an assistant secretary of the Navy to represent the Corps in the Navy Department. Even though he knew that much of the tempest over the McDonough letter was anti-Truman rather than pro-Corps, Douglas believed the time had come to give the Corps the statutory protection it needed. Serious legislative consideration would have to wait until the 82d Congress assembled in 1951, but pro-Corps advocates kept the issue alive. Events in Korea, which enhanced the Corps and damaged the reputations of Truman and the JCS, strengthened their hand. Seeking a third supplemental defense appropriation in January 1951, a request that finally accepted the need for serious rearmament and the probability of a long Korean War, the Defense Department urged substantial expansion of the armed forces but only one additional regiment for the Marines. Angered, Douglas collected forty-six co-sponsors for S.677, and Mike Mansfield introduced a similar bill in the House to force the issue.[33]

Stung by Congress's implied criticism of the JCS and the Army, which he attributed to a conspiracy orchestrated by Headquarters Marine Corps, General Omar N. Bradley counterattacked. Bradley had one of his aides brief four influential Washington columnists that the Corps planned a six-division/four-wing force of more than 400,000 men, which would make it a "second" Army. Bradley's agent implied, in addition, that Corps militancy endangered the war effort and Truman's rearmament plans. He argued that press reports from Korea unfairly condemned the Army's performance and glorified the 1st Marine Division. When the sympathetic columnists did special features critical of the Corps in *The Christian Science Monitor* and the *St. Louis Post-Dispatch,* General Cates momentarily worried about the momentum of the Douglas–Mansfield bills, but his advisers reassured him that pro-Corps articles in *The Saturday Evening Post, Look, Fortnight,* and many daily papers more than offset Bradley's efforts. Nevertheless, the Commandant warned his subordinates, including General Smith in Korea, that the pro-Corps media blitz (including a Hollywood feature film on the Chosin Reservoir campaign) must not come at the Army's expense. With the Corps's Congressional champions in full cry, Headquarters assumed a patient, background role. But it did not intend to let the springtime of glory pass without obtaining some sort of permanently expanded Corps, protected by law, and direct CMC access to the JCS.[34]

Bradley's inept ploy could not counteract the fact that the Eighth Army had not met the Chinese intervention well—and Truman knew it. Early in the war the President had sent Major General Lowe, who had served as Truman's military aide during World War II, to Korea to observe the fighting and make recommendations for further defense reorganization. Lowe had broadened his mission to include an examination of American combat effectiveness. Lowe's letters and final report praised American fighting heart at the small-unit level but criticized the Army's senior leadership and combat doctrine in scathing terms. By contrast, Lowe reassured the President that the Marine Corps was everything it claimed as a force in readiness. "The First Marine Division is the most efficient and courageous combat unit I have ever seen or heard of." Moreover, Marine use of helicopters and close air support suggested that the Corps not only was prepared for amphibious operations but had outrun the Army in doctrinal reform. All future amphibious operations should be strictly Navy–Marine, Lowe recommended, and the Corps should be expanded to a permanent three-division/three-wing force and "be assigned the mission of readiness for aggression against the United States."[35] Although Truman's reaction to Lowe's report remains unclear, the President's determination to stop the Douglas–Mansfield bills waned in 1951.

In April and May 1951 the Senate and House armed services committees of the 82d Congress, 1st Session, reviewed the arguments for and against legislative protection for the Marine Corps and persuaded their colleagues that such action was necessary. The hearings and floor debate produced no final legislation, for Defense Department opposition and Congressional confusion over the exact terms of the legislation prevented final passage. Nevertheless, pro-Corps champions impressed the Truman administration with their militancy, and final passage of a Marine Corps bill seemed certain by the summer of 1951. In the Senate hearings, with Douglas managing his own bill, the pro-Corps advocates made familiar arguments. The Marine Corps provided cheaper yet more effective combat power; the Corps was a separate service with such unique capabilities (including as a force in readiness) that the Commandant belonged on the JCS; the Marine Corps did not want to curb the Army, but vice versa; and the Navy Department did not adequately represent Marine Corps interests in designing budgets and force structure.

The Defense Department, opposing the bill, attempted to answer these arguments, with Admiral Sherman the most persuasive witness. Sherman made some tough points: The Marine Corps's "cheapness" depended on Navy and Army logistical support; the Navy could not provide amphibious shipping for a larger Corps unless Congress gave it more money; the CNO by law and custom represented the Corps on the JCS, and his authority should not be diminished. On the last point, Sherman slipped, for the committee examined earlier opinions indicating that the Corps was indeed a separate service. Nevertheless, the version of S.677 that the committee reported out unanimously disappointed most pro-Corps advocates. Revised S.677 provided a 400,000-man Corps (no second Army) but as a ceiling rather than a minimum strength; the Commandant would sit with the JCS, but not as a voting member and only on matters of direct concern to the Corps. The committee, however, reported that its purpose was to provide a four-division/four-wing Corps and make the Commandant a more important influence on defense planning. The full Senate approved the bill unanimously on May 5.[36]

The subsequent House hearings on Mansfield's version of S.677 (and many varieties of it) produced a Senate–House impasse, but one favorable to the Corps. Attacking the deficiencies of the revised S.677, Carl Vinson and his colleagues listened sympathetically to pro-Marine witnesses and concluded that a 400,000-man ceiling might not provide an adequate Marine Corps. Instead, the committee recommended legislation setting the minimum number of active duty Marines at 300,000. This figure, the committee believed, assured an adequate Fleet Marine Force and a satisfactory supporting establishment. Hoping to allay Army and Navy fears, it accepted a peacetime ceiling of 400,000 regulars but did not disallow further expansion in times of war or national emergency.

It rejected JCS and Navy proposals to fix the Corps at some percentage of the Navy or the total armed forces, because the committee, even more than the Senate, saw the Corps as the nation's force in readiness. In addition, the House committee wanted the Commandant to be a full-time voting member of the JCS. Once again, Admiral Sherman opposed the reforms. The CNO, however, admitted that JCS plans saw the need for a three-division/three-wing FMF in order to provide amphibious forces for both the Atlantic and the Pacific fleets, a concession that suggested a future compromise. The other members of the JCS insisted that Congress should not legislate force structure but admitted under stern questioning that Congress had already done so for both the Air Force and the Navy. Bradley, Collins, and Vandenberg also argued that the Commandant did not belong on the JCS, but the committee rejected this position. It accepted without question that the Corps was a separate service specializing in amphibious warfare; it was also the nation's force in readiness "to suppress or contain international disturbances short of war." Its commander belonged on the JCS. The House committee reported out a bill by a vote of 26–1 for a 300,000-man regular Marine Corps with the Commandant on the JCS, and this bill passed the full House, 253–30.[37]

Despite overwhelming Congressional support for legislative protection, the Congress produced no final action in 1951 for several reasons. First, some of the most important Congressional actors devoted much of their time to the exhausting hearings on Truman's Far East policy and MacArthur's relief; some Marine Corps champions in Congress were, indeed, MacArthur defenders eager to embarrass the administration. Other members of Congress had serious reservations about the cost and quality of an expanded Corps. The official estimate of a onetime increase of about $2 billion looked suspect when one calculated the need for more bases, aircraft, equipment, and amphibious shipping. Given Admiral Sherman's considerable influence in Congress and the JCS, even Headquarters recognized that too big a victory might poison relations with the JCS and the Navy Department. Cates himself thought that a three-division/three-wing FMF would suffice, although he testified that this force would require a 334,000-man Corps. In addition, the sheer number of bills on the Marines complicated compromise. The issue dragged on. So, too, did the war in Korea.[38]

3.

As X Corps redeployed to South Korea, the Chinese army turned its full attention to the American and ROK divisions falling back to the 38th Parallel. Once again crossing the border, the Communist forces drove the Eighth Army past Seoul and the critical Han River early in January 1951. Although MacArthur and the JCS discussed evacuating Korea, the Eighth Army rallied under the leadership of Lieutenant General Matthew B. Ridgway, USA. Replacing General Walker, who had died in a jeep accident, Ridgway traded ground for time and used his troops wisely, while American air punished the lengthening Communist supply line. When the PLA offensive dwindled in late January, Ridgway launched several limited counteroffensives. For the 1st Marine Division, built to near full strength with replacements and adequately reequipped, Ridgway's decision brought a new mission. From its camps near Masan, the division moved into an area west of the east coast port of Pohang and spent four weeks chasing scattered NKPA guerrillas. The division drove the Koreans back into the hills, cleared the coastal supply lines, and secured the UNC's right flank (manned by two ROK corps), while Ridgway counterattacked on the left and center of the front.[39]

On the eve of its return to heavy combat, the 1st Marine Division remained a crack organization. One great unknown—the division's ability to handle Communist tanks—had been answered; the regimental antitank companies, the division tank battalion, artillery, and close air support blunted every NKPA tank thrust without serious loss. The fire support for Marine infantry on the attack or defense benefited not only from tanks, artillery, and air but from an increase in the number and size of mortars in each infantry regiment. Marine artillery again proved its efficiency, but for sustained offensive operations the division's four battalions of towed 105-mm. and 155-mm. howitzers needed reinforcement, which came from attached Army self-propelled guns. In this case the organization for amphibious operations required changes for sustained warfare. The division required similar modifications in its logistical system for the same reasons. Although the division deployed to Korea with two (rather than the standard one) motor transport battalions, it campaigned without adequate vehicles. A bonus at Chosin, the vehicle shortage became a liability in 1951 and forced the division to rely on supplementary ways to transport supplies. The answer mixed the primitive and modern: Korean laborers backpacking supplies and helicopters overhead whirling to the front with critical loads. With its own service support group and medical, engineering, ordnance, and shore party battalions, the division could handle most of its own service requirements, and the Army provided additional support. Built upon its signal battalion and VMO-6 light aircraft and helicopters, the division's command and control system also proved adequate, although radio shortages and Korea's broken terrain sometimes made tactical contact difficult. Nevertheless, the Marine methods from World War II, modified by postwar reforms and 1950 experience, met the test of combat.[40]

As the Eighth Army renewed offensive operations in 1951, the 1st Marine Division found, however, that its close air support left much to be desired in timeliness and quantity. The problem had nothing to do with Marine doctrine or the 1st MAW's effectiveness, but rather was a matter of the character of the air campaign and the Air Force's system of managing close air support. Far East Air Force (FEAF) commanders and their subordinates at Fifth Air Force headquarters in Korea insisted that the Communists would suffer most from (even be defeated by, some thought) attacks on their transportation system. This interdiction campaign required an all-out air effort, including Marine and Navy aircraft. While the air campaign, labeled Operation STRANGLE, slowed Communist supply efforts, it also limited the Fifth Air Force's ability to provide close air support. With the number of close air support sorties reduced, the Fifth Air Force insisted that all air operations be arranged through its Joint Operations Center (JOC), which would allocate air strikes for all the Eighth Army. This procedure applied to the 1st MAW as well as to Air Force squadrons. Orbiting, on-station Marine aircraft disappeared from the air space along the front. From the 1st Division's perspective, moreover, what air strikes it received were not well run when Navy and Air Force fighters, rather than Marine Corsairs or the new F9F "Panther" jets, arrived. The JOC's procedures favored the use of airborne spotters rather than ground air-control parties; this practice meant that many strikes were inaccurate and not close enough to the front lines to please Marines. High-level Marine protests and occasional Air Force compromises increased air support, but the 1st Marine Division remained unhappy about the JOC's tendency to delay air strikes and send Marine air to support Army divisions, which, the Marines felt, did not adequately direct close air strikes.[41]

Weathering a limited Chinese attack in early February 1951, the Eighth Army opened a steady offensive (Operations KILLER and RIPPER) on February 21, and the 1st Marine Division returned to the front as part of Ridgway's drive. For six weeks the division fought methodically northward through the mountains of east-central Korea and in early April recrossed the 38th Parallel. Hampered as much by the terrain and cold, wet weather as by Communist resistance, the division demonstrated that it had left none of its valor or skill at Hungnam. When KILLER closed on March 4, the Marines had pushed the PLA defenders back almost 20 miles at a cost of 395 casualties. Recognizing that they faced only Communist delaying forces, the Marines resumed the offensive when Operation RIPPER began on March 7. Reinforced by four battalions of the KMC 1st Regiment, the division met stiffening resistance, but the Marines reached Phase Line Kansas north of the 38th Parallel on April 10 and, according to orders, halted while the Eighth Army prepared for another advance. As in Operation KILLER, the division followed Ridgway's sound guidance to emphasize supporting arms and minimize infantry casualties in order to kill Chinese and to keep the Eighth Army ready to meet an expected Communist major offensive. Operating on the IX Corps right flank, the division held the UN front just west of the Hwachon Reservoir with two regiments and the KMC regiment on line.[42]

On April 22 the Chinese opened their fifth major offensive, and for more than a week PLA commanders committed the better part of 500,000 men against the UNC. Because the main Communist effort fell upon I and IX Corps on the western half of the Eighth Army front, the 1st Marine Division felt the attack most on its left flank, where on April 24 the ROK 6th Division fell back rapidly in front of the Chinese attacks. Other Chinese penetrations also threatened I Corps, so Lieutenant General James Van Fleet, USA, the Eighth Army's new commander, ordered a general withdrawal. To prevent being cut off from his withdrawal routes, General Smith committed the reserve 1st Marines to a series of hard battles to refuse the division's left flank. As the division fell back in orderly fashion, additional battalions joined the defense until the entire division reached a new line south of the Pukhang-gang River north of Hongchon. In many ways, the fighting reassembled the Chosin campaign, as Chinese night attacks dented Marine defenses and sought vulnerable artillery and service units. The Chinese found few weak spots and fell by the thousands to infantry and artillery fire. When the Chinese offensive finally ended in mid-May, the 1st Division was ready to shift again to the offensive and exploit what was clearly a major Communist defeat.[43]

Shifting east into the zone of X Corps, the Marines fought northward past the eastern tip of the Hwachon Reservoir from May 23 until June 17 as part of the Eighth Army's renewed drive to crush the Communists. Initially the division faced light resistance, for the PLA was a broken, demoralized force, but as the division trudged north into some of Korea's worst mountains, it found ridge line defenses manned by units of the NKPA that had not been ruined by the Communist spring offensive. When the Eighth Army again reached the high ground along Phase Line Kansas, the division received a welcome relief in X Corps reserve. In the meantime, the Communists, desperate for time to regroup, called for truce talks. When the United Nations agreed to start negotiations, the fighting dwindled in July.

Having received reinforcements and restored their battered divisions, the Communists broke off negotiations, and the Eighth Army returned to the offensive in late August 1951. Now commanded by Major General Gerald C. Thomas, another division veteran from World War II, the 1st Marine Division returned to the front and found some of the year's hardest fighting. By now most of the 1950 veterans were gone, either evacuated as casualties or rotated back to the United States, but the division had lost nothing of its effectiveness. When not actually committed to the fighting, the division trained. The division's leadership, still drawing upon World War II veteran officers and NCOs, remained high in quality. In the fighting between August 27 and September 20, when the new offensive halted, the Marines needed all their skill, for their mission required them to take a series of high ridges north and east of "The Punchbowl," a deep valley in the Korean mountains. General Ridgway (now UNC commander after MacArthur's relief in April) and General Van Fleet, anticipating a shift to the strategic defense for the Eighth Army, wanted control of a line in Korea's mountains that would minimize UNC casualties and prevent another serious Chinese offensive. Bothered by rain and lack of roads, which made the movement of supplies extremely difficult, the division seized its objectives in the face of stubborn NKPA resistance. Even with adequate supporting fires and air support, Marine infantry had to pry the Koreans from well-dug ridge line positions often supported by fire from transverse ridge spurs. The fighting was often close, and some units suffered casualties that exceeded the fighting at Chosin. Nevertheless, the division was still attacking when X Corps suspended major offensive operations in late September. Eighth Army attacks in other sectors continued for another month, but the mobile phase of the Korean War had ended for the 1st Marine Division.[44]

While the division shared the varied fortunes of the Eighth Army throughout 1951, the 1st MAW found itself progressively integrated into the FEAF air campaign and committed to a variety of missions that had less and less relevance to the 1st Marine Division, the unit it was supposed to support. The year began with three Corsair squadrons flying from carriers, two all-weather squadrons patrolling the skies above the sea of Japan, and the one all-jet squadron flying interdiction missions from an Air Force field in Korea. In the general redeployment forced by the Chinese offensive, Marine air relocated temporarily on Japanese and southern Korean airfields, where fuel and facility inadequacies curtailed 1st MAW operations. Only VMF-212, flying from the light carrier *Bataan*, remained part of the FEAF effort to halt the Chinese armies in early 1951. Although most of the 1st MAW had returned to Korean fields by May, the wing's operations conformed to the Fifth Air Force's grandiose interdiction plans. Only a third of Marine air strikes went to support the Eighth Army's divisions, and response time climbed from fifteen to eighty minutes for close air support missions. The 1st Marine Division received only 65 percent of the strikes it requested, and only about half of those involved Marine fighter-bombers. In addition, the interdiction sorties and related "armed reconnaissance" strikes sent Marine air casualties soaring; in one two-month period, the 1st MAW lost fourteen pilots to intense Communist ground fire, a rate much higher than incurred in close air strikes. Conversely, in the heavy autumn fighting of 1951, the Fifth Air Force supplied only 96 strikes a day to the entire Eighth Army, and the 1st Marine Division received only its share. Further burdened by its responsibilities for air defense, supply flights for the division and its own bases, and its need for more sophisticated ground radar units for aircraft identification and control, the 1st MAW found itself heavily engaged but not to the particular benefit of the 1st Marine Division. [45]

The closing weeks of the mobile phase of the Korean War brought a "first" for Marine aviation and for the military use of aircraft—the deployment of transport helicopters in war. From their earliest use in the Pusan perimeter, the light helicopters of VMO-6 had reinforced the Marine conviction that helos had an important battlefield role, but VMO-6's craft were too small to carry troops. Instead, they carried out reconnaissance and liaison missions, rescued fliers, evacuated casualties, laid wire, and delivered small loads. The more ambitious use of helicopters awaited the arrival of HMR-161, which was equipped with Sikorsky HRS-1s, an interim transport helo adopted by the Corps in July 1950. (The initial order, not directly connected with the Korean War, was for forty helos for two squadrons with a delivery date in early 1951.) By the time HMR-161 had formed, received its helicopters, and prepared for deployment to Korea, the helo enthusiasts of the 1st Marine Division (which included General Thomas and his chief of staff, Colonel Victor H. Krulak) were ready to give the concepts of vertical envelopment a real test. [46]

The officers of HMR-161 and the division staff, aware of the HRS-1's substantial limitations, designed modest initial operations. The helo could carry only four to six combat troops or 1,750 pounds of supplies; its range and navigability were limited. Because the division was fighting in the rugged terrain northwest of "The Punchbowl" when HMR-161 moved close to the front in September 1951, the helo operations had some tactical value, but the initial operations were more experimental than operationally necessary. Working out operating techniques in two resupply missions, HMR-161 made its maiden troop-carrying mission in Operation SUMMIT on September 21, 1951. In a four-hour mission of sixty-five flights, HMR-161 carried 224 Marines of the division reconnaissance company and 17,772 pounds of cargo to an isolated hill-top at the edge of the division's front. The landing, as planned, was not opposed, for the Marines were replacing a KMC outpost. Heartened by SUMMIT, division planners and HMR-161's commander, Lieutenant Colonel George W. Herring, then launched increasingly ambitious oper-ations. By December HMR-161 was ferrying entire infantry battalions to the front to relieve other units. Shuttling troops and supplies across the division area became common for HMR-161, and the helos per-formed many of the same tasks assigned to VMO-6 as well. Although none of the operations included an opposed vertical envelopment, HMR-161's heavy workload proved the helo's durability and convinced Marine planners that the helicopter would eventually revolutionize Marine Corps operations. A new era for Marine air-ground cooperation had dawned.[47]

4.

While the tempo of the fighting in Korea slowed, the pressure to pass the Douglas-Mansfield Act intensified. Unwilling to spend more polit-ical capital in a minor battle to stop pro-Marine legislation, the Truman administration reduced its resistance, particularly after the death of Admiral Sherman in July 1951. Passage remained a matter of arrang-ing a compromise between the Senate and House bills passed in May 1951. When the House reconsidered S. 677 in May 1952, pro-Marine Congressmen again insisted that the Commandant be a full member of the JCS. This position was still unsatisfactory to the Senate. On Corps strength and structure, the House and Senate moved toward com-promise when House negotiators, working out a position to take to the conference committee on S. 677, fashioned a proposal for a three-division/three-wing FMF with a peacetime floor of 220,000 and a peacetime ceiling of 400,000. Since the Truman administration had al-ready authorized a Corps expansion to three divisions and three wings, this proposal appeared less controversial, and the 400,000-man ceiling presumably quieted fears of a "second land army." In the conference negotiations in June 1952, the manpower floor disappeared altogether, for even Marine Corps advocates feared that a peacetime Corps of more than three divisions and three air wings might lose its elite character. Headquarters heard this concern and accepted the compromise. As for the question of JCS representation, General Lemuel C. Shepherd, Jr., who had succeeded Cates on January 1, 1952, preferred full status, but this issue too was negotiable. The conference committee produced another reasonable solution: The Commandant could sit with the JCS and vote on all issues of direct interest to the Marine Corps, with the Commandant deciding what those issues were. Obviously, the defense budget and service roles and missions fell in this category. When the conference committee made its report, both the Senate and the House approved the Douglas-Mansfield Act by voice vote on June 20, 1952, and President Truman signed Public Law 416 (82d Congress, 2d Session) eight days later. The Marine Corps had reached through legislative protection a new "high ground" in American interservice politics.[48]

Headquarters, while satisfied with the three-division/three-wing structure of the FMF and the new relationship of the Commandant to the JCS, believed that the greatest contribution of PL 416 stemmed from its implications for Navy–Marine Corps relationships within the Navy Department. Because PL 416 clearly stated that the Marine Corps was a separate service with its own specified roles and missions, thus amending the National Security Act of 1947, the Commandant no longer had to worry about his access to the Secretary of Navy or the Secretary of Defense since he enjoyed coequal status with the Chief of Naval Operations. Unlike its supporters in the media, who saw PL 416 as a victory over the "militarism" and "despotism" of the JCS and the Secretary of Defense, Headquarters had no desire to join a congressional witch hunt against the JCS or the Truman administration as both had shown a new willingness to support Marine Corps expansion plans. After Secretary of the Navy Dan Kimball approved a revision of General Order 5, which defined command relationships in the Navy Department, Headquarters alerted its highest-level commanders that the Commandant was satisfied with his coequal status with the CNO and that the Marine Corps was still an amphibious force "intimately" linked to the United States Navy. Rather than exploit its political power, Headquarters wanted only a reassertion of traditional roles and missions.[49]

By the time PL 416 passed, the Marine Corps could not afford much gloating, for the pains of rapid expansion had given Headquarters more than enough problems. The Corps ballooned from 192,620 men in June 1951 to 231,967 a year later and 249,206 by June 1953. A little more than half the troops actually served in the operating forces, and the 1st Marine Division and 1st MAW were kept up to strength without Korean fillers, much to the Army's envy. By March 1953 the Corps had more than 35,000 Marines serving in Korea, the wartime high. In the meantime, the 2d Marine Division and 2d Marine Aircraft Wing reached full strength for their European contingencies. In June 1951 Headquarters activated the 3d Marine Brigade, built around the 3d Marines, at Camp Pendleton. In 1952 the brigade expanded to become the 3d Marine Division, and the same year the 3d MAW formed and occupied a new base in Miami. In another important reorganization, Headquarters in 1951 formed an organization known as Force Troops in order to provide the heavy artillery and service units necessary to sustain a Marine division in a land war. The first Force Troops units supported FMF Atlantic.

Such expansion was not without its costs. Despite a reactivation of officer candidate schools and enlargement of the summer platoon leaders course, the Corps remained 3,000 officers short in September 1952, and some suggested that officer quality had declined as well. As usual, voluntary enlistments waned as casualties grew and the war continued. In July 1951 the Marine Corps willingly accepted draftees for the first time in the Korean War. From initial monthly quotas of 7,000 the number of draftees entering the Corps each month grew to 11,650 by February 1952. By March 1952 the Corps had enlisted 73,430 draftees. The Corps manpower problems were complicated further by the release of veteran Reservists in increasing numbers in 1952. Accelerated promotions, broadened commissioning criteria, and shortened formal training for all Marines—all the price of rapidly expanding the FMF—worried Headquarters. In retrospect, it is hard to see how the Marine Corps could have reached even 300,000 men and retained its elitism, in view of the war's growing unpopularity. For Headquarters, 1951 and 1952 were years of consolidation, not exploitation.[50]

Other structural problems concerned Headquarters. When General Shepherd became Commandant in 1952, he attempted to simplify Headquarters organization and strengthen the planning agencies by creating a general staff like that of FMF units. The Policy and Plans Division separated into a four-section staff (G-1, G-2, G-3, and G-4) with many of the "Pots and Pans" special staff sections divided and subordinated to a series of new assistant chiefs of staff; the chief of staff/assistant commandant received a deputy and his own secretariat. Shepherd's reforms, however, stopped short of simplifying the Commandant's control over his own administrative agencies, for the important divisions of aviation, fiscal and supply, personnel, and Reserve affairs remained outside general staff supervision. Additional bureaucratic battles, particularly with aviation and fiscal/supply, loomed.[51]

At the troop level, the Marine Corps had to adjust to expanded, changed roles for women and blacks. For Women Marines, the war brought an increase of numbers to almost 3,000 but no redefinition of duties. For blacks, the war accelerated integration by rank and ability. From a June 1950 strength of 1,502 (2 percent of the Corps) the number of black Marines increased to 14,731 (6 percent) by 1953. Moreover, from the first security detachments and Reservists assigned to the 1st Division in 1950, blacks took their place in integrated units and for the first time commanded white troops. Generally, the Corps escaped the problems of integration the Army faced, for the Corps had no all-black tactical units to reorganize, and the quality of black Marines (and their relatively few numbers) made their integration fairly smooth.[52]

The expanded budgets and manpower of the Korean War period provided the Marine Corps with new opportunities to develop its concepts and equipment for future warfare. When the Department of Defense and the Atomic Energy Commission began tests of battlefield nuclear weapons in 1951, Marines joined the Army test units in the Nevada desert and witnessed their first tactical nuclear explosion in May 1952. After assessing radiation levels and distances, Marine planners published Landing Force Bulletin 2, an interim report on the conduct of operations on the nuclear battlefield and the first such study done by the armed forces. In additional Nevada tests in April 1953, two thousand Marines, protected by trenches some 2.3 miles from the explosion site, actually conducted a tactical exercise in the blast area, with two hundred men seizing one objective by helicopter.

Intimately linked to the force in readiness mission that Congress expected the Corps to play, amphibious warfare techniques and equipment absorbed much of the Corps's attention during the Korean War. Boards and study groups at Headquarters and the Marine Corps Schools continued to grapple with the problems identified in the late 1940s. To institutionalize doctrinal research and development in amphibious warfare, General Cates in 1950 established the Landing Force Development Center (LFDC) at Quantico and separated it from the schools system. A year later the JCS asked the LFDC to support a Joint Landing Forces Board with representatives from all the services, but this agency was not long-lived. Instead, the main developmental work remained in the hands of the LFDC's two boards, which evaluated tactics-techniques and equipment. As intended by the legislation of the 1947–1952 period, the Marine Corps remained the nation's expert in amphibious warfare.[53]

While battalion landing teams conducted World War II–style landings off California, in the Caribbean, and in the Mediterranean, Marine planners continued to evaluate the troop and equipment requirements for a successful amphibious assault in future (possibly nuclear) wars. The helicopter remained at the heart of Marine planning. Buoyed by the successful operations of HMR-161 and similar exercises in the United States, the Corps enlarged its requests for numbers of helicopters. It planned to have nine transport helicopter squadrons (one group of three squadrons in each wing) by 1954 and to equip its three observation squadrons with light helos. With modest cooperation from the Bureau of Aeronautics, Marine Corps helicopter numbers climbed from fewer than 20 on the eve of the Korean War to 202 in 1953. Of the 1953 helos, 141 were troop-carrying HRSs of the type flown by HMR-161 in Korea. The Corps still wanted an assault helicopter that could carry small vehicles and about thirty troops. After much testing, the Bureau of Aeronautics awarded a contract to Sikorsky to proceed with the engineering development of the HR2S-1, a two-engine helicopter whose virtue was its size and engineering simplicity, which meant an earlier delivery date. A design selection in 1952, however, meant the HR2S-1 would not appear in helicopter squadrons until 1956. To bridge the gap between the HRS-1 and the HR2S-1, the Navy and Marine Corps agreed to convert a Sikorsky utility helicopter designed for the Navy's antisubmarine warfare forces into a troop carrier. This model, the HUS, could carry twelve troops or 4,000 pounds of internal cargo. With double the capacity of the HRS, the HUS became the workhorse of Marine helicopter squadrons well into the 1960s.[54]

Although helicopter development—as well as the reequipment of Marine fixed-wing squadrons with advanced jet fighter-bombers—promised to make the vertical envelopment amphibious assault a reality, the question of Navy amphibious shipping for helicopter operations proved the greatest limitation upon Marine plans. Over and over boards and study groups associated with the LFDC pondered shipping requirements. The planners, assuming that a landing against a first-rate foe would require lifting 10,000 troops and 3,000 to 4,000 tons of supplies in the helicopters being developed in the 1950s, concluded in 1951 that the amphibious force might require as many as twenty-eight aircraft carriers. In 1953 another study group, chaired by Major General Field Harris, reduced the carrier requirements to sixteen on the assumption that the Navy would either build a special helicopter carrier (LPH) or convert escort carriers into LPHs. Caught in the budget reductions for FY 1954, which reflected an end to the Korean War rearmament boom, the Navy made no provisions for converting even a single carrier for helicopter use. Amphibious Marine plans for vertical envelopment ran aground on the realities of Navy shipbuilding priorities.[55]

Even if it did not convince Navy planners that its needs deserved first priority, the Corps continued its love affair with the American public in spite of diminished popular enthusiasm for the Korean War.

In addition to sympathetic press coverage of Marine activities, the reading public could weigh the Marine contribution to World War II and amphibious warfare doctrine by studying *The U.S. Marines and Amphibious War* (1951), a careful history written by two Princeton University professors, Jeter A. Isely and Philip A. Crowl. A companion piece, Robert Sherrod's *History of Marine Corps Aviation in World War II*, appeared in 1952, along with *The New Breed*, a popular book on the 1950 campaigns written by Andrew Geer, a Marine Reserve major. A 1954 book on Marine helicopter development, Lynn Montross's *Cavalry of the Sky*, also contributed to this high point in Marine historical literature. At a less sophisticated but still memorable level, Hollywood, with Marine cooperation, produced four war films of enduring appeal: *Retreat, Hell!*, *Halls of Montezuma*, the John Wayne epic *Sands of Iwo Jima*, and a remake of *What Price Glory*. At the same time, sculptor Felix de Weldon was working on a statue of the Iwo flag-raising (privately financed) for a Marine Corps memorial next to Arlington National Cemetery.

Even the unhappy experiences of American prisoners of war in Korea, which seemed a national disgrace in 1953, enhanced the Corps's image. In the hysterical recriminations over "brainwashing" and collaboration that followed the POWs' return in 1953, Marines emerged untainted, with the exception of one colonel and one enlisted man. Moreover, Marines survived captivity in higher percentages than did other American servicemen, and five were decorated for meritorious service as POWs. No Marine was among the 192 men convicted for misconduct or the 21 Americans who refused repatriation. When Defense Department and Senate investigating committees completed their examination of the POW "scandal," they praised the Marines for their exemplary performance in a captivity characterized by extreme psychological and physical cruelty.[56]

5.

As the chill breath of another Korean winter stiffened the scrub trees in the 1st Marine Division's sector, the war in Korea changed. The truce talks, which had temporarily lapsed, resumed in October 1951 just as the UNC forces moved against the final objectives along Phase Line Kansas. Aware that they would not receive either the additional units or the tactical freedom needed to smash the Communist forces, General Ridgway and General Van Fleet shifted to the defense. Because the UNC and the combined Chinese and North Korean armies mustered about the same number of men (600,000) in the battle area, the UNC change in strategy appeared overcautious. By the winter of 1951, however, the political context of the war had changed. Within the United Nations, even among nations providing troops to the UNC, sentiment now supported a negotiated settlement. Battered at home by rising defense costs, inflation, and public unhappiness with its "indecisive" war, the Truman administration accepted the same limited goals. With general military rearmament well under way and the defense of Western Europe accelerating under NATO's aegis, the administration wanted a settlement that appeared to accept the prewar *status quo*. Continuing the war, however, supported an important American goal in north Asia: ensuring the stability of South Korea and Japan by giving their non-communist governments time to build their armed forces and political legitimacy. These goals could be obtained with time, and time could be purchased at less cost on the defense than in the attack.[57]

For the 1st Marine Division the change in the fighting meant digging, patrolling, and observing along the mountains northwest of "The Punchbowl" in east-central Korea. In their second winter in Korea, the Marines spent much of their time fashioning a line of trenches and bunkered outposts, ringed with barbed wire and mines, along the hills they had seized in the autumn of 1951. Under orders to minimize casualties, the division occasionally raided the NKPA positions to its front, but the weather and the conservatism of both belligerents brought the combat and casualties down to new low levels. The division normally held the Main Line of Resistance (MLR) with seven infantry battalions (three of them KMC) with five in reserve. With fire support from the division's four artillery battalions and one tank battalion, assisted by X Corps artillery, the division front seemed safe enough from serious attack, although it was 14 miles long. At the troop level, where the digging was unwelcome, the second winter brought notable changes. In addition to the replacements who allowed the last 1950 veterans to return home, the 1st Division received two welcome items of equipment developed by Navy–Marine Corps research teams. The first was a thermal boot that used a vapor barrier to preserve body warmth; unless a Marine wore a punctured boot or remained inactive for hours, the "Mickey Mouse" boots prevented frostbite. Even more important, the 1st Division infantrymen began to wear an armored vest or "flak jacket" designed to stop shell and grenade fragments and low-velocity bullets. Made of a combination of laminated fiberglass plates and woven nylon, the vests provided critical protection to Marine chests and abdomens, thus reducing fatal wounds an estimated 30 percent and even preventing some lucky Marines from being wounded at all.[58]

As the war's third year approached in 1952, the UNC made significant adjustments to its pattern of deployment in order to improve the effectiveness of the ROK army and strengthen the United Nations military (and hence negotiating) position. With the truce talks slowed by disagreements on the repatriation of POWs and specifics of a ceasefire and military disengagement, the eighteen-division, multinational UNC army shifted along the MLR in order to put American divisions in the most critical sectors while opening new portions of the MLR to the expanding ROK army. No organization made a more dramatic move than the 1st Marine Division. In March 1952 the division redeployed by motor march and sealift to the extreme western portion of the UNC defense position, the JAMESTOWN line.

The division's new sector was no prize. Running 33 miles from the Kimpo Peninsula along the valley of the junction of the Imjin and Han rivers, the new sector guarded the approaches to Seoul and the corridors used by UN truce negotiators. With its back against the Imjin, sometimes only 6 miles behind the MLR, the division had little ground to give and depended upon only four bridges to support its logistical system. One advantage, however, came from the division's proximity to the logistics base at Munsan-ni and others in the Seoul–Inchon area. The chief difficulty of the sector was simply the relationship of infantry strength to frontage. Even with the 1st KMC Regiment attached and two of its own infantry regiments on the MLR, the division stretched thin along its trenches, and its artillery battalions were so scattered that massing fires became difficult, if not impossible. The sector defense depended essentially on counterattack forces in reserve and the effectiveness of the division's combat outpost line, established a mile or so in front of the MLR.[59]

With the 1st Division's movement to the western corner of the MLR, Marine operations in Korea assumed the characteristics they retained until the war's end in July 1953. The division's mission was to defend the JAMESTOWN line north of the Imjin while a Marine–KMC provisional regiment defended the Kimpo Peninsula. Other American Marines provided the leadership and technical personnel for the Korean Marine defense units that manned UNC island outposts off both east and west coasts. For the 1st MAW the war continued to focus on Fifth Air Force interdiction operations with close air support a secondary role. (For the rest of the war, only one-third of the 1st MAW's sorties were close air support, and they supported every Eighth Army division.) The 1st MAW's flying, air control, and supporting squadrons concentrated at Pyongtaek (MAG-12) on the west coast and Pohang (MAG-33) on the east coast, with HMR-161 and VMO-6 deployed forward at Munsan-ni under division control. Both the division and the air wing drew support from logistical units in Japan, which included part of a transport squadron and processing centers for the replacement and re-turnee drafts that moved to and from Korea. In addition, at least one Marine squadron flew from a TF 77 carrier. Marines helped train the Korean armed forces, supported the UN truce negotiators, and pro-vided planes and ground radar and anti-aircraft artillery units for the UNC air defense system. Although the Marines constituted in theory the Eighth Army's amphibious force (and, in fact, trained as such), the Marine ground-air team by 1952 had become separate parts of the Eighth Army and the Fifth Air Force.

As the 1st Marine Division learned in the spring of 1952, the war in Korea had moved to a diplomatic and strategic standoff, but along the MLR the Chinese still sought tactical gains that might lead to important propaganda and operational advantages. Against the Marine sector, the Chinese army deployed fifteen infantry and ten artillery battalions with a total strength of 50,000 men, or about twice the 1st Division's strength. Patience, time, and the fixed nature of the lines multiplied the PLA's threat, because the Chinese proved masters at digging gun positions and troop shelters that partially offset UNC heavy artillery and air superiority; the Chinese also specialized in camouflage and night operations with the same effect. In the face of Marine patrols and small raids, the Chinese dug forward ("creeping tactics," the Marines called it) to the division's line of outposts and launched a series of attacks along the left portion of the MLR in April. Despite a shortening of the lines and withdrawal from the most exposed positions, the division found the Chinese pressing its combat outpost line by July. Marine raids and heavy rains slowed the PLA "advance" during the summer of 1952, but the Chinese in late August launched a series of regimental night assaults that continued until October. The battle for the outposts reached a peak of ferocity in the successful Marine defense of outpost "Bunker Hill" in August and the equally successful defense of a salient in the MLR, "The Hook," in late October. After losing the "Bunker Hill" battle in the division's center, the Chinese concentrated their at-tacks against the KMC regiment on the division's left and upon the Marines defending the division's right sector west of the Samichon River.[60]

The 1952 outpost battles along the JAMESTOWN line uncovered some special problems for Marines in positional warfare. Tactically, the most worrisome developments were the volume and intensity of Chinese ar-tillery and mortar fire and the comparative vulnerability of Marine positions to that fire and to night infantry assaults. At first, the divi-sion created its own problems by building forward slope defenses open to artillery observation and fire registration; moreover, many Marine bunkers depended upon above-ground sandbagging rather than deep digging, and some Marines thought they should fight from the bunkers (which often they could not) rather than the more exposed trenches and fighting holes. Preplanned Marine artillery concentrations saved many outposts (when communications worked), but supplementary barbed wire and land mines around the outposts and the MLR made counterattacks (especially at night) particularly hazardous. As Marine rifle companies learned at "Bunker Hill" and "The Hook," night assaults through Chinese artillery fire provided horrors equal to Tarawa and Iwo Jima. Only the highest valor and the careful use of supporting arms kept the Chinese at bay. Although JAMESTOWN remained inviolate, the Chinese extracted an appreciable price, considering the manpower resources and 1952 war aims. In "The Hook" battle (October 26–28), the Marines suffered about five hundred casualties and POWs in holding the MLR, while the Chinese lost probably three times as many men. Nevertheless, the loss ratios were much closer than those of 1950 and 1951. One fact dramatizes the cost: 40 percent of Marine casualties in the Korean War occurred between April 1952 and July 1953, when the war was supposed to be a "stalemate." [61]

For Marine aviators as for Marine infantrymen, the war demanded that endurance become a common virtue. Assigned interdiction missions that they sensed were not worth the risks, Marine pilots (like their Air Force and Navy comrades) braved intensifying ground fire to bomb Communist supply routes until the Air Force planners, recognizing the limits of interdiction, shifted the main air effort to the limited industrial and economic targets in North Korea. In the realignment of air war missions, the fighter-bombers of the 1st MAW (particularly the slower, nonjet Corsairs and ADs) concentrated upon close air support missions for the Eighth Army. For the ground Marines, the quality and quantity of air support improved in late 1952 when Fifth Air Force returned most operational planning responsibilities to the 1st MAW. Reflecting the close air support convictions of two of its commanders, Major General Clayton C. Jerome and Major General Vernon E. Megee, the 1st MAW provided about 40 percent of all strikes along the entire Eighth Army front. Informally, once freed of close Fifth Air Force supervision, Jerome and Megee assured the 1st Marine Division that it would receive top priority in air strikes, not only because of service bonds but because Marine ground-control teams usually assured that strikes in the 1st Division sector would hit the intended targets. In addition, the Marine pilots had greater confidence that 1st Division artillery support would suppress Communist flak batteries and that air strikes would be run close to American troops where Communist flak was less intense.[62]

As the winter of 1952–1953 brought a cooling of the battles along the MLR and another breakdown in the truce negotiations, the 1st Marine Division manned its outposts and trenches and awaited events. On the political and diplomatic fronts, the war struggled toward an end. President-elect Dwight D. Eisenhower promised to end the war and made a perfunctory trip to Korea. More ominously, officials of the new administration hinted darkly at expanding the war to China, even with the use of nuclear weapons. When it took office, the Eisenhower administration also shifted additional military forces to the Far East, although not to Korea. On the Communist side, the death of Soviet premier Josef Stalin presumably caused some disarray in the Chinese–North Korean partnership; in addition, Communist propaganda, diplomatic, and subversive pressure against Syngman Rhee's regime in South Korea failed to undermine the fragile nation that the United Nations was trying to save. By 1953, in fact, South Korean intransigence toward a ceasefire became the chief political problem for the United Nations coalition, although the exchange of POWs remained the most intractable issue between the truce negotiators. When the Communists finally agreed that POWs who did not desire repatriation could be placed in the custody of a "neutral" agency, the truce talks assumed new life. So too did the fighting, as the Communists sought last-minute tactical and psychological victories over the UNC and the South Korean armed forces.

In March 1953 the Communist forces mounted a massive offensive on the UNC outpost line that in the 1st Marine Division's sector hit the outposts in the division's vulnerable right sector, manned by the 5th Marines. On March 26 the Chinese fell upon outposts "Reno," "Vegas," and "Carson" with the predictable combination of heavy shelling and night infantry assaults. Attack, desperate defense, counterattack, a deluge of shells from American and Chinese artillery falling upon all the infantry, flares sputtering and glaring above the bare hills, bunkers blasted, bodies in padded green and bleached herringbone twill piling up among trenches and rocky hills—the battle for the outposts raged for five days. When the fighting died down, with "Vegas" and "Carson" held but "Reno" gone, the Marines counted 1,015 casualties and missing, with Chinese losses at least twice as high. The Marines raised no flags on "Vegas," the critical position along the outpost line, but it was, as one Marine called it, "the highest damn beachhead in Korea." [63]

Patrol actions and outpost probes continued into the summer of 1953, but the only heavy action before the ceasefire of July 27 in the 1st Marine Division sector occurred around the 7th Marines outposts on the division right flank on July 24–26. Having reorganized its defenses in greater depth and knowing that its MLR would be part of a demilitarized zone if and when a ceasefire went into effect, the division did not fight for every outpost with unmitigated fury. Nevertheless, it did not concede any key terrain, and it took 1,611 casualties in the war's last month, which made July 1953 second only to October 1952 as the division's most costly month in the western sector. When the ceasefire finally went into effect, the 1st Marine Division, its artillery and machine guns still hot, could not quite believe that the war was really over. Three years and almost thirty thousand casualties after the 1st Brigade's defense of the Pusan perimeter, the Marine Corps had finished its second most expensive war. If the war was something less than victorious in Korea, it remains nearly as important as World War II for its impact on Corps self-esteem and public acceptance.

17. Building the Force in Readiness:
Years of Trial and Accomplishment
1953–1965

With the Korean War ended, the Marine Corps focused on developing the Fleet Marine Force as the force in readiness sanctioned by the passage of the Douglas–Mansfield Act. The three-division/three-wing force structure was now paired by law with its Cold War roles and missions, and so the Corps appeared to be assured of an important role in American defense planning. Corps advocates in Congress remained ardent, reassured by the Marines' performance in Korea. At the Pentagon and at Headquarters Marine Corps, officers worked to ensure that Corps interests would receive the attention of the Joint Chiefs of Staff and the Secretary of the Navy without interference from the office of the Chief of Naval Operations. Few planners thought the armistice in Korea reduced Communist threats elsewhere in the world; the Corps's importance seemed magnified by the confrontations short of war and the proxy conflicts the United States might face. Despite desperate budget battles and internal strains, the FMF was by 1965 as effective a force as the Corps had ever fielded in peacetime.

Given the defense assumptions and programs of the Eisenhower administration, which labeled its policies the "New Look," the Corps superficially had little reason for self-assurance. Concerned over the domestic economic implications of high defense costs and unbalanced federal budgets as well as the growing threat of Soviet nuclear attack, the President and his closest advisers emphasized the Air Force's strategic forces and cut Army, Navy, and Marine Corps conventional forces. The administration, convinced that the anticommunist nations of Asia and the Middle East should bear the human costs of limited wars, patched together two alliance systems for the Pacific and the Middle East, supplemented by bilateral defense pacts with Japan, South Korea, and Taiwan. The Eisenhower administration further committed the United States to providing a global nuclear umbrella for its allies ("massive retaliation") with the bombers of the Strategic Air Command while it increased research and development on both land-based and sea-based strategic missiles. It urged the Army and Navy to compensate for the diminished number of divisions and carrier task forces by adopting tactical nuclear weapons. Whether packaged for the public as "security with solvency" or as "more bang for the buck," the Eisenhower "New Look" did not offer much hope for manpower-intensive conventional forces like the Marine Corps.[1]

The first years of the "New Look" did not cut too deeply into the Corps's strength, padded by the Korean mobilization. In the review of the FY 1954 budget, the last submitted by the Truman administration, Congress and the Corps accepted an Eisenhower revision of Corps strength from 248,000 to 225,000 and a budget cut from the requested $1.4 billion to $1.097 billion. The cuts did not seriously disturb the FMF, for the Korean armistice had ended casualties and the high flow of replacements and trainees through the manpower pipeline. Adjusting to an administration mandate that the Corps plan for 215,000 men in FY 1955, the Corps still managed to increase the proportion of men in its operating forces to 60 percent, up from 47 percent during the Korean War. By squeezing additional men out of its training and support base, it managed to man all its FMF units at 94 percent of wartime strength and still assign nearly 13,000 Marines to naval base security forces, 3,000 more to ships detachments, and 700 to security duties with the State Department. The reductions made it difficult to keep both the 1st and 3d Marine Divisions, both deployed to the Far East, up to wartime strength, but Headquarters accepted the strength reductions. The Corps was most concerned with developing a permanent base structure to support its force in readiness mission and procuring supplies for a wide range of contingencies. Guided by the astute Lemuel C. Shepherd, Jr., the Corps preserved its newest bases: the cold-weather training center at Pickel Meadows and its desert warfare and supporting arms center at Twenty-nine Palms, both in California. On the East Coast, the critical new base was a supply depot at Albany, Georgia.[2]

Although concerned about the "New Look," Headquarters took comfort in its enhanced position within the defense policy-making structure. As provided by PL 416, the Commandant met with the Joint

Chiefs of Staff on matters of Marine Corps interest. General Shepherd used his powers sparingly and attended only one-fourth of the JCS meetings in order to reassure the JCS that Marines were "team players." The Commandant's entry into the JCS was eased by the fact that the new chairman, Admiral Arthur W. Radford, was sympathetic to the Corps. Shepherd also enjoyed cordial working relations with the Eisenhower Chiefs of Naval Operations, Admiral Robert B. Carney and Admiral Arleigh A. Burke, as well as a series of Secretaries of the Navy. Already assured that Congress protected the Corps's interests, Headquarters believed that its programs would receive a fair hearing in the executive branch as well and that interservice relations, fraught with tension over budget questions and issues of roles and missions, had reached a new degree of harmony. This view was well founded, but it wrongly assumed that defense policy would be made within the Department of Defense.[3]

At the borders of America's Cold War frontier, the FMF stood guard, ready for any post-Korea conflict. With the defense of South Korea, Indochina, Taiwan, and Japan still high on the Eisenhower administration's list of foreign-policy concerns, the weight of the Corps's deployment leaned toward the western Pacific. The 1st Marine Division patrolled the DMZ in South Korea, while the 3d Division and 1st Marine Aircraft Wing trained at bases in Japan. To support the Pacific deployment, the new 3d MAW shifted from Florida to new homes at MCAS El Toro and auxiliary bases in California. On the East Coast the 2d Marine Division at Camp Lejeune and the 2d MAW at other bases in North and South Carolina provided amphibious forces for the 2d and 6th Fleets, with one reinforced infantry battalion and one squadron normally deployed to the Mediterranean. To ensure the readiness of these FMF units, Headquarters marshaled its influence in Washington.

1.

As the Eisenhower administration pressed for further economies and reductions in defense spending in 1954 and 1955, the Corps sensed that the FMF would fall victim to the budget officers in ways it would not to defense planners. Headquarters turned to Congress and was again successful in minimizing the impact of the Eisenhower austerities. Having reduced personnel turnover largely by relying on reenlistments and shifting men from non-FMF assignments to the operating forces, which reached a high of 66 percent of Corps strength in 1955, Headquarters accepted another planned manpower reduction to 205,000. Although the Corps would accept modest cuts in its procurement and construction program, it drew the line at cutting personnel. In addition, as the possibility of intervention in Indochina* passed with the signing of the 1954 Geneva agreements, it sought further economies by returning the 1st Marine Division to Camp Pendleton and reducing the 3d Division, shifted to new bases on Okinawa, by one-third. Part of the 3d Division (a reinforced infantry regiment) and an air group moved to Hawaii. As the Corps budget slipped below $1 billion, Headquarters agreed to the cuts, as long as they went no further.

Once again Congress favored the Corps. Reassured that the Corps would cut its support base, Congress rejected the administration's proposal that Corps strength fall to 193,000 men. In a test of strength, the Senate rejected Corps manpower cuts by a vote of 40–39 and refused to approve the defense budget for FY 1956 until the administration assured it that the Defense Department would keep the Corps at 215,000 men for at least one more year. The House, after an inquiry about the development of vertical envelopment amphibious assaults and the level of Corps supplies, supported the Senate's position and stood firm until the administration agreed not to cut Corps strength. With the entire defense appropriation for FY 1956 at stake, the administration agreed to spend $46 million more on the Marines. In a defense review in which the Army and Navy had suffered serious cuts in their requests, the Corps had again triumphed.[4]

The Eisenhower administration made the victory short-lived, for it impounded the additional funds and forced the Corps to drop to near 200,000 men by the end of FY 1956. Nevertheless, Headquarters believed it had absorbed the cuts well by deactivating some supporting units. The manpower trends, however, were ominous. Total Corps strength fell by less than 5,000 men, but the operating forces lost 23,274, and the percentage of Corps strength in the operating forces dropped from 65 percent to 57 percent. The strength of the three divisions could be maintained only by taking men from Force Troops and Marine aviation. To persuade Congress to appropriate money for 205,000 men, the Corps reduced its procurement request by almost $100 million; Congress accepted the procurement cuts and then refused to approve the higher manning level. Again the budget fell below $1 billion. Both personnel and matériel readiness suffered.[5]

The budget cuts, which were to worsen during Eisenhower's second term, might have been more manageable had the Marine Corps been more structurally sound. The 1950s found the Corps with internal problems accumulated since World War II and deepened by both the Korean War itself and the reorganization of the Department of Defense before and after the war. The commitment to vertical envelopment

* Hereafter, this current spelling (having changed from Indo-China) will be used.

amphibious assaults created additional internal uncertainties from the research and development programs and procurement planning to the tactical organization of the FMF. The continued deployment of the FMF to the western Pacific, coupled with the force in readiness mission, put strains on married Marines, for Headquarters ruled in 1956 that families could not accompany Marines assigned to the 1st MAW in Japan or the 3d Marine Division on Okinawa. Readiness and cost-cutting precluded any other policy, so Marines in the western Pacific in the late 1950s served fourteen months away from their dependents. The ban on families, broken with regularity by the pilots of the 1st MAW, was symptomatic of a host of similar troubles that pitted Marines against Marines in the "New Look" era.

At Headquarters the most vexing challenges came from the Corps's successful effort to join the JCS planning process. Marines dedicated to resisting centralization in the Department of Defense followed the same policy at Headquarters, and Corps management suffered accordingly. General Shepherd had made a fundamental change by shifting Corps budgeting and fiscal accounting from Quartermaster General William P. T. Hill to a new fiscal division headed by troubleshooter Brigadier General David M. Shoup, the hero of Tarawa turned dogged efficiency expert. Even upon his retirement for age in 1955, Hill relinquished power grudgingly; while his successors served only two-year tours (he had served eleven), Hill badgered Headquarters from retirement by advising his Congressional friends on how to find the "fat" in the Corps budget.[6] Other problems were less troublesome but contributed to stress at Headquarters. The sheer demands for information for the JCS and the growing defense bureaucracy forced the detail of Marine officers throughout the Joint Staff committee system and the Office of the Secretary of Defense, as well as the Navy Department; to support both interservice planning and its internal management, Headquarters stressed the use of automated data processing and increased standardization of reports, orders, and operating procedures. The attempt to stretch precious dollars brought growing bureaucratic complexity and an enormous increase of effort.[7]

Postwar lethargy and "New Look" economizing dramatized the fact that many Corps senior leaders, officers and NCOs alike, had lost interest in meeting Corps standards in appearance, physical fitness, and personal responsibility. The Corps had little trouble recruiting lieutenants, most of whom were draft-inspired Reserves who served only two or three years, to meet the annual needs of about two thousand new officers. The problem was the age of and the maldistribution of regular officers commissioned from 1942 to 1946, who now crowded the ranks of major and captain; Reserves recalled during the Korean War further bloated these ranks when integrated into the regular Corps. When the Korean-era Corps demobilized, nearly five thousand of these officers had to be shifted from support billets to the FMF's tactical units. Such reassignments seldom brought rejoicing. Since the officers in the "hump" had sufficient rank to guarantee a twenty-year career, Headquarters had little hope of revitalizing the officer corps without additional compulsory retirement legislation, but Congress balked at severing World War II and Korea veterans. A similar difficulty arose from the thousands of NCOs who had received temporary commissions during the Korean War. With the cut in Corps strength, these officers were the first to revert to enlisted status, many unhappily. Unless the Corps increased the number of specialist billets ("Limited Duty Officer" or LDO) protected from automatic promotion-or-retirement laws or enlarged the number of warrant officers, it would lose much-needed specialists. Such legislation was difficult to draft, so complex were the organizational and personal equity implications, and it was not until the early 1960s that a new officer force structure reached maturity. The number of LDOs increased from 147 to 460, and the number of warrant officers from 100 to 1,300.[8]

The condition of the NCO ranks was even more troublesome. With many of the best NCOs shifted to officer status or assigned to technical specialties and security duties, the quality of troop leadership declined in the FMF. The manpower cuts, along with the growth of specialist billets, further reshaped the Corps along unsatisfactory lines. In 1954 nearly 40 percent of all Marine enlisted men were NCOs (corporal or above), twice the NCO percentage before World War II. Long on combat experience but short on professional maturity and training and leadership skills, the NCO ranks needed drastic reform. With automobiles, occupational specialization, better pay, and increased numbers of marriages eroding traditional barracks life, the obstacles to combat readiness at the troop level mounted. The principal Headquarters response was to change the enlisted rank structure. At the lower end of the rank structure, it created the rank of lance corporal at pay grade E-3 (formerly the corporal's pay grade), a non-NCO rank. In a similar set of changes, all of which demanded new legislation, the Corps reestablished the prestigious rank of gunnery sergeant at pay grade E-7 (abolishing the term "technical sergeant") and moved the grades of first sergeant, master sergeant, master gunnery sergeant, and sergeant major to the new grades of E-8 and E-9 to give senior NCOs more prestige and pay and encourage better leadership. Along with the reformed rank structure came new rank insignia, primarily the addition of crossed rifles below Marine

chevrons, a design that differentiated Marines from soldiers and reminded Marine NCOs that they were the leaders of combat troops, regardless of their jobs.[9]

Personnel problems hardly exhausted all the Corps's structural difficulties, for both the aviation and the ground elements of the division-
wing team moved into a period of organizational upheaval. At the
heart of the turmoil rested the challenge of adapting the helicopter to
amphibious warfare—and of doing so without minimizing the FMF's
force in readiness role. Alive to the unresolved conceptual and organizational problems of vertical envelopment, Shepherd appointed an Advanced Research Group (ARG) to examine the future marriage of the
helicopter and the FMF. After adventurous speculation, encouraged by
Assistant Commandant Gerald C. Thomas, the ARG recommended that
future Corps planning produce a division that could be entirely helo-
lifted ashore for combat and then be sustained largely by helo-lifted
supplies and reinforcements. The ARG made some breathtaking assumptions: that the Navy would supply sixteen helo-carriers or Landing
Platform Helicopter (LPH); that Navy–Marine aircraft could clear
landing zones and guarantee local air superiority for the helos; and that
the Sikorsky heavy HR2S could lift 12,500 pounds, which would allow
it to bring 155-mm. howitzers and 6 × 6 trucks ashore. Responding to
aviation opinion, the ARG rejected the armed helicopter, assuming
that fixed-wing aircraft, using either tactical nuclear weapons or conventional ordnance, would clear the way for massive helo-lifts. Aware
that it was requesting an increase in number of planned HR2S's (with
correspondingly high costs), the ARG recognized that Marine aviation
leaders, working with a ceiling of 1,425 aircraft set by the Navy, would
not accept a larger reallocation of aircraft from fixed-wing to helo
status. Already stung by Headquarters policies that gave the divisions
manpower priority over the wings, Marine aviators saw an extensive
HR2S program as a costly drain on scarce pilots and crewmen and a
menace to warm relations with Naval aviation, which furnished the
money for aircraft, operations, and maintenance. The all-helo assault
concept, then, worried not only close air support advocates, but also
the Navy, which wanted Marine air available for naval missions as well
as amphibious operations.[10]

Despite Marine aviation's reservations about the all-helo assault,
Shepherd and Admiral Burke approved the concept in 1955 and directed that future Marine–Navy programs reflect the goal of lifting
not only a division but also the ground support elements of a wing
ashore by helicopter. The concept, given official approval in Landing
Force Bulletin 17 (December 13, 1955), required both men and equip-

ment not then available or anticipated in the austere "New Look" era. Encouraged by the exercises of Marine Corps Test Unit 1, a reinforced infantry battalion formed for helo operations in 1954, and the optimistic reports of Sikorsky engineers, the Corps plunged into the vertical envelopment era despite the reluctance of its own aviators. Helicopter requirements ballooned with further studies of the all-helo assault. Another Commandant-appointed board examined logistical requirements and recommended that the Corps double its number of light transport (HUS) helicopters, again at the expense of fixed-wing craft. The Navy rejected the request for budgetary reasons. Almost simultaneously, Headquarters and the Bureau of Aeronautics began to receive reports that the HR2S was not meeting performance requirements and would require major engineering breakthroughs. After a series of aviation reviews, the Corps and the Navy decided to reduce HR2S procurement from 158 to 34, far too few for an all-helo assault. The only compensation came from a Navy agreement to procure 140 HUS helicopters for the Corps by 1959. If vertical envelopment was to remain a viable concept, the FMF's ground divisions would have to be organized to reduce their lift requirements and improve their ability to sustain themselves in combat, including tactical nuclear war. The doctrinal and organizational upheaval that had already upset aviation operations now spread to the FMF's ground divisions.[11]

For the three divisions and Force Troops of the FMF, the post-Korean War years had been turbulent enough without the reorganization that awaited them in 1957. Training and personnel turnover absorbed their attention, culminating in the massive redeployments of 1955. Headquarters struggled to squeeze more combat readiness from its support structure. One option was to place more tactical units into the existing organization, and the Corps experimented with four-battalion infantry regiments and four-company infantry battalions. Another experiment was to merge the service and support battalions of each division into a combined service regiment, a change that reduced manpower but did little else. With a growing awareness that the FMF's organization was inadequate for vertical envelopments, Headquarters awaited the results of further studies.

In 1956 another high-level board, chaired by Major General Robert E. Hogaboom, reexamined every aspect of FMF doctrine and organization. After nearly six months of study, the Hogaboom Board made its report—and set off a reorganizational wave unseen since the early days of World War II. The board found the basic concepts of amphibious warfare sound, including vertical envelopment, but its assessment of the Corps's future role and its prescriptions for reorganization were radical, particularly for ground units. Breaking with conventional wisdom, the board doubted that the Corps would fight in a nuclear war with Russia and stressed the greater likelihood of war with Communist proxies outside of Europe. The board also doubted that the Navy and Marines would ever find the ships and helicopters to mount a division-wing all-helo assault and stressed the need to maintain the ability to mount simultaneous vertical and over-the-beach assaults. Even as it resurrected the traditional amphibious assault, the board emphasized that the Corps's force in readiness mission required greater strategic mobility, a mobility not necessarily tied to the Navy's amphibious forces. Therefore, the Marine division of the future should be air-transportable, and its assault battalions helo-transportable.

To increase strategic and tactical mobility without sacrificing combat effectiveness required substantial changes in divisional organization. The infantry battalions and regiments lost their heaviest weapons and most of their supply and maintenance functions. The infantry battalions gained a fourth rifle company but lost their weapons company; their headquarters and service companies assumed control of the remaining 81-mm. mortars, 106-mm. recoilless antitank rifles, and flamethrowers. Regiments lost their heavy weapons and service units; regimental headquarters would serve tactical purposes only. For the artillery regiments the changes were even more radical. Instead of planning to deploy as battalions, the artillery was to reorganize for independent operations at the battery level. Each firing battery would have enough forward observers and fire direction center personnel to operate attached to infantry battlions; in fact, the battery commander would become the fire support coordinator for the infantry battalion and establish a fire support coordination center (FSCC) within the battalion operations center. Moreover, three of the four artillery battalions would switch from truck-drawn 105-mm. howitzers to 4.2-inch mortars, which could be carried in light vehicles and therefore could be transported by helicopter. To offset the loss of firepower in the infantry regiments and the artillery regiment, the number of artillery tubes grew from 72 to 92. (So radical was the switch to the 4.2-inch mortar, a weapon of limited range, that the artillery regiments retained most of their beloved 105-mm. howitzers.) The Hogaboom Board then shifted the Corps's heavy artillery—towed 105-mm. and 155-mm. howitzers, self-propelled 155-mm. guns and 8-inch howitzers, and Honest John surface-to-surface rockets—to a Force Troops artillery group. These batteries would engage only in protracted operations that could be supported from the sea.

The Hogaboom Board worked similar surgery throughout the rest of the existing divisional structure. To ensure air transportability, the tank battalions also went to Force Troops. To compensate for the dramatic loss of antitank capability in the division, the board recommended that the tanks be replaced by an antitank battalion armed with a tracked, lightly armored vehicle known as the "Ontos." Armed with six 106-mm. recoilless rifles, the Ontos had a reasonably high first-shot kill probability using 50-caliber spotting rounds, but its enormous backblast and thin armor made it a marginal weapon against enemy tanks and artillery. In another significant effort to increase combat effectiveness, the board increased each division reconnaissance company to a full battalion in recognition of the need for better intelligence and target acquisition.

The principles of austerity and mobility also determined the reorganization of the division service and support units. The main criterion was that each unit be able to support both helicopter and amphibious assaults. The division service regiment shrank to a service battalion, with the extraneous units shifted into an expanded Force Service Regiment, which would provide difficult and expensive services like major maintenance, ordnance care and disposal, and complicated supply operations. Other Force Troops would include topographical companies, specialized dental and medical companies, engineer bridging companies, and additional motor transport battalions.

Endorsed by the Commandant in 1957 and subsequently used as the basis for the "M" Series of Tables of Organization and Equipment, which remained relatively unchanged for the next twenty years, the Hogaboom Board studies threw the ground FMF into reorganizational turmoil. Although the board had examined aviation organization, it did not make proposals for extensive reform. For the future of the Marine Corps, however, the board's reorganizational proposals had substantial significance. Its conclusion that future amphibious assaults would combine both vertical envelopments and over-the-beach attacks was realistic, and the streamlining and reequipping of the divisions simplified both naval and air transportability. On the other hand, the board took substantial calculated risks with fire support and logistical capability. It assumed that Marine close air support and naval gunfire would offset the losses in artillery and tank fire in the early stages of an assault. It also so stripped Corps logistical organizations that sustained operations would require considerable improvisation in the face of the enemy. Confronting an uncertain future, the board made many correct guesses. Another war in Asia would confirm its predictions.[12]

To guide the Marine Corps through the "M" Series reorganization and to absorb the helicopter into all aspects of Corps operations were tasks that called for leadership of the highest order, but in General Randolph McCall Pate, its twenty-first Commandant, the Corps did not have such a leader. Sponsored for the commandancy by General Shepherd, a fellow VMI graduate and distant cousin, Pate had rich experience in staff jobs but little of the military stature and moral authority necessary to command the Corps. After Holcomb, Vandegrift, Cates, and Shepherd, the Corps fell heir to a Commandant who combined the worst habits of garrison traditionalism and the new managerial-bureaucratic style. Unlike his predecessors, Pate had not run the professional risks of command in extended combat. Through World War II he had done high-level staff work in the Pacific, although he had served as the G-4 of the 1st Marine Division on Guadalcanal until removed by illness. Being a part of the "1st Division club," which included his three predecessors and such other powerful generals as Gerald C. Thomas, Merrill Twining, and Edwin A. Pollock, gave Pate an aura of strength he did not fully deserve. The new Commandant disliked Washington and preferred to travel rather than stay at Headquarters; moreover, his closest associates suspected that he suffered from mental and physical lapses that affected his judgment.[13] Even without unanticipated crises, Pate's commandancy promised little gain for the Corps as the fiscal cuts of the "New Look" deepened.

2.

The new dangers to the Corps in 1956 came not from the Bureau of the Budget and the White House but from the dark waters of Ribbon Creek, a tidal estuary behind the rifle range at Parris Island. In the evening of April 8, Staff Sergeant Matthew C. McKeon, an inexperienced drill instructor, led seventy-four recruits of Platoon 71 from their barracks at the rifle range to Ribbon Creek. He plunged into the water, followed by the skylarking, straggling line of young Marines. When the column unexpectedly reached a pothole in the creek bottom, the mood changed to hysteria, particularly among those recruits who could not swim. All order disappeared in the panic that seized Platoon 71. When the recruits pulled themselves up the creek's steep bank, they found that six of their number were missing. They had drowned.[14]

Training accidents were hardly unheard-of in the Corps, but the Ribbon Creek tragedy struck right at the heart of the Corps's popularity and legitimacy.* The difficulty was that the Corps's most ardent champions differed on the causes of and cures for Ribbon Creek, and the conflict over how the incident should be handled divided Marines and

---

* Between 1951 and 1955, five officers and sixty-five enlisted men died in non-aviation training accidents. In the same period 192,000 recruits went through Parris Island without a death.

their civilian allies into warring camps—with all the bitter words spread over the pages of the nation's press. The six recruits had died swiftly; the uproar over the episode perished with agonizing slowness, poisoning relations inside the Corps and handicapping the Commandant's authority at a time when he could ill afford diminished influence.

General Pate made Ribbon Creek his personal business and quickly formed opinions that weakened his ability to manage the crisis, but his decision to fly to Parris Island the day after the drownings was not ill considered. Aware that the House Armed Services Committee had been interested in earlier reports of recruit abuse and might have to make a full-scale investigation of Marine recruit training practices, Pate consulted with committee chairman Carl Vinson. Vinson urged Pate to take immediate action, not only to prosecute McKeon and anyone else who seemed criminally involved but also to assume that something was wrong with the Marine Corps. Already distraught by the incident, Pate went to the depot and announced to the assembled reporters that he would root out DIs who abused recruits and would reform the recruit training system, so dear to Marine traditionalists. Outraged by early reports that McKeon had been drinking on duty, Pate also implied that the sergeant was guilty of serious crimes even before a court of inquiry convened by Major General Joseph C. Burger, the depot commander, had completed its hearings. The press had a field day with the story that McKeon had been drunk when he marched the recruits into Ribbon Creek, which hardly helped future recruiting or softened the despair of the dead youths' families.[15]

Although the court of inquiry, chaired by Brigadier General Wallace M. Greene, Jr. (Pate's personal selection), conducted a thorough investigation of the incident and found McKeon subject to prosecution for manslaughter and recruit abuse, Pate could not accept the court's findings or Burger's endorsement. Instead, he insisted that the Corps itself was "on trial" for the systemic flaws that brought about the incident, flaws that were real enough and the product of years of inattention. The difficulty was that McKeon could not be dealt with as an alcoholic sadist. His prior service of ten years as a sailor and Marine had been solid; he had led a squad in Korea; he was a good family man and a practicing Catholic; he had survived rigorous screening and training to become a DI and had finished high in his DI class; his performance until April 8 had been excellent. More perplexing, no one who dealt with McKeon in the harrowing hours of April 8–9 thought he behaved abnormally, although witnesses said and medical tests showed he had been drinking.

McKeon was probably trying too hard to be a good DI, for he was convinced that his platoon had become an undisciplined mob during its marksmanship training. (In fact, DIs try to reduce the recruits' high level of anxiety during firing in order to improve their scores.) On April 8 McKeon had already held two "field days" and disciplined several of the recruits. He thought his platoon, a typical mix of big-city and rural youths with limited education and work experience, needed "extra instruction of a constructive nature," the Parris Island euphemism (so DIs interpreted it) for mass punishment. In this case, McKeon, desperate to succeed as a DI and tormented by the pain of a bad back, decided to march the platoon into Ribbon Creek. Parris Island folklore suggested that such cold-water walks worked miracles on defiant recruits and, even though illegal and infrequent, had been used by other DIs. If McKeon was psychologically sound, then his lack of judgment (or luck, other DIs thought) must have had an institutional sanction.[16]

Convinced that he could not satisfy the Congress with only a McKeon trial, Pate shook the Corps by appointing two trusted brigadiers as commanders of independent Recruit Training Commands. They would report directly to the Commandant through a newly established Inspector General of Recruit Training, the driving David M. Shoup. Shoup's mission appeared simple: to end recruit abuse by increasing officer supervision of the DIs. The new policy struck straight at the DI practices of "thumping" or striking individual recruits and ordering mass labor or calisthenics in addition to regular training. The new policy outraged DIs, many other Marines of all ranks, and even recruits. The reorganization of the depots also antagonized senior officers and NCOs, because it implied culpability on the part of the major generals who commanded the depots and their principal subordinates, a guilt not justified—at least, not by the Ribbon Creek incident. Indeed, Pate fueled the discontent by relieving General Burger and Colonel William B. McKean, the commander of the weapons training battalion in whose area the drownings occurred. At the same time, the media pressed for more reliefs and inquiries, accepting Pate's comments that Marine recruit training had reached the point of barbarism.[17]

In his immediate purpose—allowing the Corps to police its own problems and blunting the chance of Congressional intervention—Pate succeeded. The House Armed Services Committee, guided by Vinson, complimented the Commandant on his reforms and promised no immediate inquiry—and there was none. The White House, following the crisis, remained passive.[18] Yet the incident would not fade away, for McKeon had yet to be tried. His case became a rallying point for Pate's critics, most of whom were not civil libertarians but Marine militants in and out of uniform. The Ribbon Creek case quickly degenerated into a struggle between contending parties who saw themselves as the "best"

Marines. For Headquarters, General Shoup insisted that extending recruit training two weeks and increasing physical training would eliminate the hazing. Shoup's own research, however, revealed that most officers and NCOs wanted Parris Island to remain unchanged, meaning the DIs could continue to slap recruits and scream obscenities at them. Out in the field, Marines held a permissive public and weak Commandant responsible for the Corps's troubles.[19]

While the training reforms took hold at the recruit depots, Corps and public attention shifted to the McKeon court-martial, which began at Parris Island on July 16. Postponed in order to give McKeon's defense team of civilian lawyers, led by Emile Zola Berman, a relentless and brilliant New York trial counsel, sufficient time, the court-martial lasted three hot, frustrating weeks. With General Pate still insisting that the whole Corps was on trial, Berman assured the court that Corps training was guilty of the recruits' deaths. Depite a tortuous prosecution and an equally wordy defense, Berman succeeded only in convincing the court of the obvious: that McKeon had not willfully killed the recruits. Even Berman's most dramatic stroke, calling retired General "Chesty" Puller to testify that night marches in creeks made tough Marines, failed to sway the court. On August 4 the court found McKeon guilty of negligent homicide and drinking on duty and sentenced him to be reduced to private, fined $270, confined for nine months, and separated from the service with a bad conduct discharge.[20]

The court's verdict and sentence, particularly the latter, set off a storm of protest that further anguished Headquarters, for the bulk of the protesters were Corps loyalists. Attempting to influence the mandatory review by Secretary of the Navy Charles S. Thomas, the 1st Marine Division Association, the Marine Corps League, the Veterans of Foreign Wars, and the Amvets called for a reduced sentence. Berman publicly denied that the Corps had made McKeon a scapegoat, so Secretary Thomas's decision to slash the sentence to the reduction to private and three months' confinement showed as much expediency as humanity. McKeon slipped into oblivion and left the Corps on a medical discharge as a corporal in 1959.[21]

After the McKeon settlement Headquarters found it still had a recruit training problem, related to both internal morale and public skepticism. General Shoup's continued investigations found that Parris Island recruits reported more "thumpings" but also more satisfaction with their training than recruits at San Diego. At both depots the loudest complaints were about the food, and barely 2 percent of recruits thought they were poorly treated or trained. Marines of all ranks favored tougher training and less drill and administrative processing.[22]

At Parris Island, General Greene uncovered a rash of incidents of DIs slapping recruits and extorting money from them; in one incident an overzealous lieutenant punched a recruit who had charged his DIs with abuse. More courts-martial received press attention. Greene thought subversive elements were ruining recruit training, while Pate and Congressman F. Edward Hébert charged that Defense Department officials encouraged the press to pillory the Corps. Recruits and their parents wrote their Congressmen, and the American Civil Liberties Union and parents of recruits who had died in Ribbon Creek started a series of damage suits against the Corps in the federal and civil courts and called for more investigations. For two more years Marine recruit training remained a subject of public concern—at least in the newspapers and magazines. Gradually, the tide of opinion shifted back to the Corps's side as publicized incidents diminished and the worst recruit problems disappeared into the platoons of the new Special Training Battalions. Nevertheless, the memory of Ribbon Creek cast a cloud over Corps popular favor and Pate's leadership.[23]

3.

Still deeply concerned about the health of the economy, the Eisenhower administration in 1956 increased its pressure on the Defense Department to hold its requests at or below $40 billion a year. Although the department's requests, largely shaped by the Office of the Secretary of Defense and the Bureau of the Budget, leveled off at around $38 billion a year for the next four fiscal years, actual defense spending edged upward from $40 to $45 billion by FY 1960. Harried by mild inflation, a sluggish economy, and the growing cost of modern weapons, the Eisenhower administration launched a "Second New Look" to hold the line on defense costs. International developments, meanwhile, were providing contradictory guidance to defense planners. On one hand, the Sino-Soviet split and unrest in Eastern Europe, as well as a leadership crisis in Russia, produced the first faint signs of a reduction of tension in Europe. At the same time, the Soviet Union in 1957 demonstrated its capacity to build intercontinental ballistic missiles ("the Sputnik crisis"), an assumed capability that escalated into a "missile gap." In addition, the anti-Communist position in the Middle East eroded badly with the Suez Crisis and the Arab–Israeli War of 1956 and the rise of radical Arab nationalism in Egypt, Syria, and Iraq. In Asia the Chinese Communists renewed their pressure on Quemoy, Matsu, and the Pescadores islands, offshore military positions manned by Nationalist troops.

In order to control defense spending and meet the Soviet strategic nuclear buildup, the Eisenhower administration reemphasized its commitment to strategic programs first and tactical nuclear war capability second. Weapons and forces for conventional war suffered, despite the growing conviction among defense analysts that "massive retaliation" would not meet the shifting nature of the Communist threat. In broad budget terms, the administration increased the funds for the Air Force and emphasized research and development and the adoption of modern weapons. To finance the Air Force, Navy, and Army strategic weapons programs, the administration cut military manpower in all the services except the Air Force and slowed the procurement of weapons and supplies for limited wars. Although the Army suffered most, the Marine Corps bore its share of the economizing. Its budgets dropped from an already austere $942 million in FY 1958 to $902 million in FY 1961. Its strength fell from 200,780 in June 1957 to 170,621 three years later. Despite two serious Congressional attempts to provide money for a 200,000-man Corps, the "Second New Look" forced the Corps to cut the operational capability of the FMF. Even more serious, the Navy Department and the administration assigned to the modernization of the Navy's amphibious forces, particularly the construction of new helicopter-carrying vessels, lowest priority, thus limiting the Marines' ability to be a force in readiness and to continue the development of the vertical assault from the sea.[24]

Of all its problems, Headquarters considered the manpower reductions the most serious, and it used the budget process, particularly Congressional hearings, to argue its case. Although Corps spokesmen were not so aggressive in their criticism of the nation's shrinking limited war forces as were senior Army officers and private critics of the "Second New Look," Pate and his staff insisted that a Corps of 175,000 men or less would be capable of handling only minor crises. Headquarters allowed the supporting establishment to bear the heaviest manpower cuts but decided in 1959 to deactivate six Battalion Landing Teams (two in each division) and six aircraft squadrons. Only such a decision, Pate believed, would allow the Corps to keep its active ground units at 90 percent of strength and air units at 80 percent. Even though Congress provided additional money for a larger Corps, the administration either used the funds to pay for the increased costs of operations or simply impounded the money. With Force Troops units at only 40 percent of full strength and the procurement of contingency supplies slowed by lack of funds, Headquarters doubted it could carry out any operations that required it to deploy the entire FMF. The only thing that made the manpower cuts palatable was Headquarters' faith that a conventional war with Russia was unlikely. Nevertheless, Pate warned Congress that 175,000 men was the absolute floor for the reductions the Corps could

bear and still remain close to providing the force structure dictated by
PL 416. Given Congressional disarray on defense matters and the stain
of the Ribbon Creek incident, it is probably well that Pate did not have
to mount the political campaign he promised if Corps troop strength
again fell.[25]

Only a set of internal personnel changes kept more than 60 percent
of the Corps in the operating forces. Some of the changes came from
policy decisions, some through circumstance. The basic challenge was to
reduce personnel turnover and to reenlist the best NCO troop leaders
and technical specialists. With the reduction in the Corps's size, the
number of recruits fell. The quality of the recruits, assisted by an economic recession and reformed training, improved. By reducing the number of recruits of marginal mental capacity from 25.6 percent to 9.7
percent by 1959, the Corps cut the number of men who left the service
without completing their enlistment and increased the number of potential first-class Marines. Lengthening enlistments to four years also
reduced turnover. Other personnel trends were equally heartening. First
reenlistments increased from 16.5 percent to 22 percent in 1955–1959,
and career reenlistments climbed from 33 percent to 77 percent in the
same period. The introduction of pay grades E-8 and E-9 and of proficiency pay in scarce skilled occupational specialties in 1958 also helped.
In the officer ranks additional stability came from increasing Reserve
lieutenants' initial obligated service from two to three years and
that for regular officers from three to four years. With the peacetime
draft still an incentive for volunteering, the Corps met its needs in
high-quality privates and lieutenants with relative ease. The internal
reforms were significant, for they allowed the Corps to cut the proportion of its strength in its training establishment from 23.5 percent in
1957 to 17.5 percent by 1961. The FMF profited from the changes.[26]

The difficulty of obtaining modern amphibious shipping ranked just
behind Headquarters' concern for manpower problems. Although Marines could still make Inchon-style landings with the Navy's World War
II vintage transports, the Corps awaited helicopter carriers (LPHs) to
make vertical envelopment a reality. The Corps would have preferred
a fleet of twelve new LPHs, supplemented by the new Landing Platform
Dock (LPD), which could launch helos and landing craft, but it was
willing to accept a much more modest program in 1956. Pate agreed to
a Navy proposal to begin a five-year LPH program in FY 1958 that
would provide for one new LPH each fiscal year and the conversion of
five escort carriers to LPHs in the same period. Because the earliest the
new LPHs could reach the fleet would be 1961, the Navy offered to convert several of its *Essex*-class carriers of World War II design, then be-

ing used for antisubmarine warfare duties, to LPHs. Having tested the *Thetis Bay* in helo operations, the Corps knew the limitations of escort carriers and preferred converted *Essex*-class carriers to nothing at all. While the four new LPHs that survived the budget process were being built (the *Iwo Jima*, the *Okinawa*, the *Guadalcanal*, and the *Guam*), the Corps tested the *Essex*-class carrier in landing operations in early 1958 and found it adequate as an "interim" LPH. Between 1959 and 1961, therefore, three converted carriers (the *Boxer*, the *Princeton*, the *Valley Forge*) joined the amphibious forces. The LPD program moved even more slowly, but the Navy partially compensated for the lack of troop lift by converting two commercial ships into high-speed amphibious transports, the *Francis Marion* and the *Paul Revere*. While both the "interim" LPHs and two transports provided improved troop capacity and living conditions, they had loading and operating limitations that made the new LPHs and LPDs even more attractive. The Marines entered the 1960s with only two operational LPHs, each capable of carrying one reinforced battalion and helicopter squadron.[27]

In addition to the shipping problem, the Corps's determination to use waterborne transportation for its force in readiness role forced continuous modifications of Marine aviation policy and force structure. Within a new ceiling of 1,050 aircraft, the Corps changed from a Korean War force of two-thirds fighter-attack aircraft to a force of half helicopters, half fixed-wing aircraft. Among its aircraft inventory, the Corps retired most of its transports, many of its observation planes, and its propeller-driven fighters. The number of estimated close air support sorties Marine aviators could provide the landing forces fell to half the Korean War rates. Increased ordnance loads per plane did not make up the difference, and the estimated ordnance that could be carried by Marine fighter-attack aircraft fell from 900 to 600 tons. The types of aircraft also imposed limitations. The Corps shifted with the Navy to the Chance-Vought F8U "Crusader" after 1960, but the Crusader was basically an air superiority fighter ill suited to close air support. Another newcomer, the Douglas A4 "Skyhawk," a light attack plane, could provide close air support but was not an air superiority fighter. Like the Navy, the Corps was enthusiastic about the McDonnell F4 "Phantom II" as a dual-purpose, all-weather fighter-bomber, but the Phantom was not available until 1962. Moreover, Marine aviation still required Navy attack carriers to move it into the zone of amphibious operations unless it used land bases along the way and had a place to land when it arrived.[28]

The Corps, however, worked on several programs designed to improve its close air support. One approach stressed improved bombing accuracy at night and in foul weather by adopting ground-based radar (MPQ-14) to guide air strikes; other radars, eventually linked up with computers, also brought greater efficiency to controlling all types of air missions. Another program focused on the early establishment of Marine squadrons within the beachhead area. Corps planners and engineers developed a "Short Airfield for Tactical Support" (SATS) from metal runway matting and carrier-like catapults and arresting gear. Tested first between 1958 and 1960, the SATS in more sophisticated versions proved workable. The SATS, however, would have been useless without some provision for rapidly bringing jet fuel and other POL (petroleum, oil, lubricants) supplies ashore. To provide both aviation and ground units with POL, the Corps designed a bulk fuel farm system of portable tanks, pipes, and pumps that could be maintained from pipelines that ran to amphibious ships. Eventually named the Amphibious Assault Fuel System (AAFS), the new expeditionary fuel farm, along with the SATS, meant some freedom from the Navy's fleet operations, but it increased the need for conventional amphibious shipping. And the SATS and AAFS were also expensive and had to be paid for with Marine Corps (not Navy) appropriations.[29]

In addition to aviation improvement, Marine planners plunged into the research, development, and procurement programs necessary to reshape the FMF in the image of the Hogaboom Board. Other requirements for modernization came from the increased demand for a ground-based air defense and the adoption of American weapons compatible with the standardized 7.62-mm. NATO ammunition. The programs—and spending—mounted. Marine Corps procurement rapidly climbed from $135 million in 1957 to nearly $190 million three years later; more than 80 percent of the dollars went to equipment modernization for the active forces and only 8 percent for stockpiling supplies for war. Ground force modernization brought the Corps into high-cost areas like the adoption of air defense missiles. After much testing and guessing, the Corps adopted the "Hawk" anti-aircraft missile and began forming the first of three missile battalions in 1960. The Corps also participated in Army programs to develop surface-to-surface tactical nuclear rockets and introduced the Honest John rocket to Force Troops. Tactical mobility, Corps planners decided, would rest not with the helicopter alone but with an air-transportable, light, jeeplike vehicle ("Mighty Mite") and a lightweight infantry weapons carrier ("Mechanical Mule").

In the ordnance field, Corps planners evaluated a bewildering array of guided antitank missiles, all in primitive but promising states. In the small arms field, the Corps examined several competing systems but eventually accepted the Army-developed M-14 rifle, a modified M-14 automatic rifle, and the M-60 machine gun as its standard small arms. All fired the 7.62-mm. NATO cartridge but distressed marksmanship purists, who valued accuracy above firepower. Yet the amount of money for modernization did not keep pace with the assumed requirements and technical possibilities, and procurement commitments stretched out for many fiscal years into the future. The results were great expectations, little discernable improvement in the FMF, and the adoption of some dubious equipment simply in the name of modernization and helo transportability. Like its sister services, the Corps sought "more bang for the buck" in order to appease the Defense Department and Congress, but its operational readiness remained only marginally better than it had been in the Korean War.[30]

With most of its budget committed to personnel costs and procurement, the Corps struggled to increase the effectiveness of the FMF. Although Headquarters wanted to hold one division/wing amphibious exercise a year and one or two regiment/air-group landings, it found that its budget for operations and maintenance permitted a far less ambitious program during the "Second New Look" era. In FY 1958 its largest exercise was LANTPHIBEX 1-58, a test of a vertical envelopment of regimental size. The following year the Corps reached a new high for post–World War II maneuvers when it conducted twenty-five separate landing exercises. Only one, however, approached a full division/wing problem while six were of regimental size. Eighteen landing exercises involved battalion landing teams (BLTs) and single helicopter squadrons; the BLTs deployed on a six-month rotating basis to the 6th Fleet in the Mediterranean made twelve additional landings. In FY 1960 the number of landings, influenced by increased deployments to the troubled Caribbean, increased to thirty-eight. Helicopter participation gave the landings a new dimension, but the basic exercises remained over-the-beach plunges in the World War II mode. The most unusual aspects of the landings were that they often included token forces provided by NATO or SEATO allies and provided tests of the "M" Series FMF units.[31]

To improve readiness in the Pacific, Headquarters accepted an FMF Pacific proposal to rotate infantry battalions between the 3d and 1st Divisions. Battalions would form and train in the 1st Division during a fifteen-month cycle, then deploy to Okinawa for fifteen months' additional service as a cohesive unit. Designed in 1957 and begun in 1959, the "transplacement" system ensured improved readiness in the 3d Division but turned much of the 1st Division into an undermanned, turbulent training command, ill prepared for its contingency missions in the

Pacific and Caribbean. In 1960 Headquarters applied a similar system—with similar drawbacks—to the 2d Marine Division. Called the "controlled input" program, the system put each infantry battalion through a year-long cycle of filling its ranks, training, deploying, and then transferring half its personnel. With each battalion manned by veterans who would serve two years in the same unit, the system provided some personnel stability and continuity, but it also guaranteed that several battalions in the division could not be easily deployed in a crisis. With BLTs rotating to and from both the Mediterranean and the Caribbean, the 2d Division seldom bothered to unpack its seabags and mount-out boxes.[32]

The rebuilt Marine Corps Reserve, which by 1959 numbered more than 300,000 ground and air Marines, stood by to reinforce the FMF in any major war contingency. The heart of the Reserve, the 230 units of the Organized Reserve, numbered fewer than 40,000, or about the same size of the OMCR in 1950, when the Marine Corps had only two divisions to reinforce. Limited by equipment shortages and training appropriations, the Reserve nevertheless benefited by a series of acts between 1951 and 1955 that increased readiness. For officers, the principal reforms set age and time-in-grade standards that ensured a more youthful, vigorous, competitive leadership in the Reserve. Armed Forces Reserve Acts in 1952 and 1955 strengthened the enlisted ranks by allowing potential draftees to serve in the reserve units for six years rather than spend two years on active duty, provided they first spent six months of active duty training and attended forty-eight drills a year. Complementary legislation established compulsory drill attendance, including two weeks of summer camp. In practice, training attendance, however, did not reach 90 percent, and personnel instability plagued reserve units. In addition, the reservists who were not members of drill-pay units found the opportunities for active duty training limited by lack of money. In the organized units one distinct improvement came with the increased adoption of one-a-month weekend drills rather than one-night-weekly meetings; this reform increased the likelihood of field training. Although the Corps could not create a Ready Reserve of 246,000 (its authorized size) without more money and the pressure of a larger draft to spur recruiting, the Reserve provided a welcome source of wartime reinforcements as both individual fillers and battalions and smaller units.[33]

While Marine planners toiled to improve combat readiness with limited modernization budgets and dropping manpower, the Corps found ample opportunity to demonstrate its usefulness in international crises that stopped short of war. The focal point of American interest during most of the "Second New Look" era was the Mediterranean and Middle East. With NATO's eastern flank, the security of Israel, and access to Middle East oil at stake, the United States feared that Soviet pressure and growing Arab nationalism endangered the pro-Western position in the area. The collapse of the Egyptian monarchy in 1952 set off a chain of events that produced a war between Egypt and Israel in 1956, complicated by an Anglo-French attack to regain control of the Suez Canal. As American and Soviet diplomats brought the crisis to a close before Egypt suffered a total defeat, a Marine BLT landed men at Alexandria (November 1–2, 1956) to evacuate 2,177 foreigners during the height of the attack on the canal area. Three additional BLTs (two from the 2d Division, one from the 3d Division) stood ready as reinforcements, and one company flew to a Navy communications station at Port Lyautey, Morocco, to provide extra security as tensions flared throughout the Mediterranean.[34]

Already linked to its Middle East clients by the Baghdad Pact (1955), the Eisenhower administration in 1957 pledged military assistance to any Middle Eastern nation that was invaded and incapable of repelling the aggressor with its own forces. The following year two pro-Western states, Lebanon and Jordan, both under pressure from the new radical alliance of Egypt and Syria, asked for assistance. American attention focused on Lebanon while the British assisted Jordan. Having committed himself to the pro-Western system in 1956, President Camille Chamoun upset the delicate balance of religious and regional politics in Lebanon by seeking a second term in 1958, an act that required a constitutional change and set off intercommunal strife in Lebanon's large cities. As urban violence increased in the spring of 1958, accompanied by the first signs of antigovernment guerrilla warfare in Lebanon's Moslem-dominated mountain areas, the Lebanese army showed no taste for suppressing the revolt by force. An uneasy amalgam of Christian and Moslem troops commanded by a general with political ambitions, Fuad Chehab, the Lebanese army watched and waited, thus prompting Chamoun to ask for American intervention. The American response was firm: It would not keep Chamoun in office by force, and Lebanon must establish foreign intervention through UN investigation. In the meantime, however, Eisenhower ordered the amphibious force of the 6th Fleet increased to an amphibious group, with three BLTs embarked. For the Marines this precaution meant changing a routine amphibious exercise for two BLTs (the 2d Provisional Marine Force, commanded by Brigadier General Sidney S. Wade) into a contingency deployment. Adding a third BLT from the 2d Marine Division, Wade's force concentrated in the Eastern Mediterranean and worked with the British on a series of plans, including BLUEBAT, a landing to secure Beirut, Lebanon's sea-coast capital, against an anticipated Syrian invasion.[35]

The actual order to land in Lebanon on July 15, 1958, caught the 6th Fleet unawares, and the subsequent operation reflected the hurried commitment. The final crisis occurred two weeks after the earlier contingency deployments had been canceled and found the amphibious forces scattered around the Mediterranean in the process of carrying out delayed shifts of ships and units. A rapid change in the Middle East's political balance created the emergency. On July 14 radical army officers destroyed the Iraqi government, thus depriving Lebanon and Jordan of their main Arab protector. Chamoun again requested intervention. After hurried discussions, Eisenhower ordered the 6th Fleet to put its landing force around Beirut, presumably to discourage a rebel coup and to protect the oil pipelines in Lebanon. The immediate tactical mission was to secure the Beirut airport in order to hold it for further U.S. Army reinforcements and deny it to possible invaders. Despite a serious lack of tanks, appropriate ammunition, and beach-party personnel and equipment, the Marine BLT closest to Beirut charged ashore amid soft drink vendors and bathers on the afternoon of July 15 and secured a beachhead area. Three companies moved inland to occupy the airport.[36]

Amid swelling political complications, the Marine expeditionary force grew as the two other BLTs arrived and another infantry battalion flew to Beirut from the United States. By July 19 Wade had almost 6,000 Marines ashore, soon to be joined by an Army expeditionary force of 8,500 men from Germany. An additional BLT from the 3d Division and a full RLT and MAG from FMF Atlantic deployed to provide further reinforcements if needed. The largest problem the American forces faced, however, was not the Syrians or the rebels but the Lebanese army. Only anxious negotiations with General Chehab and some of his fractious subordinates prevented clashes on the road to Beirut, but after American diplomats and senior officers reassured the Lebanese military that the Marines were not there to keep Chamoun in office or to occupy the country permanently, the Marines were able to move into Beirut for security duty. In the meantime, American diplomats encouraged the Lebanese political factions to settle their differences and select a new president through the normal constitutional processes. The reward for Lebanese moderation would be the withdrawal of American forces. As Marines manned outposts and patrolled carefully selected routes that menaced neither the rebel quarter of Beirut nor the Lebanese army and Christian paramilitary forces, the Lebanese parliament selected General Chehab to replace Chamoun. To demonstrate its good faith, the United

States started the phased withdrawal of its own forces. After a 102-day occupation, the last American forces left Lebanon in October. Disciplined restraint and the sufficient operational readiness and flexibility of the 2d Marine Provisional Force had helped temporarily to prevent Lebanon from being engulfed in the growing violence of inter-Arab politics.[37]

The Lebanon operation provided the FMF with its most dramatic opportunity to support American diplomacy, but crises in the western Pacific and the Caribbean put embarked Marine ground-air expeditionary forces off other trouble spots as well. Amphibious forces in the Pacific watched the partition of Vietnam by the Geneva Accords (1954) and assisted in the subsequent evacuation of 800,000 refugees from North Vietnam. During a civil war in Indonesia in 1957–1958 an RLT and helicopter squadron stood by to protect foreign nationals. During a Communist threat to the Nationalist regime on Taiwan in 1958, an entire air group deployed to strengthen the island's air defenses. Marine task forces sailing from Okinawa routinely made landings in the Philippines and British Borneo in cooperation with token SEATO forces.

In the Caribbean, Marines stood ready to evacuate American civilians during the U.S.-orchestrated overthrow of the Arbenz regime in Guatemala (1954) and to rescue Americans, including Vice President Richard M. Nixon, during upheavals in Caracas, Venezuela, in 1958. The point of growing concern, however, which required the 2d Marine Division to keep at least a BLT in the Caribbean at all times, was Cuba. In January 1959 Fidel Castro's guerrilla band, assisted by urban terrorists not under Castro's control, toppled the government of General Fulgencio Batista. After Castro announced six months later that he was a Communist, relations with the United States deteriorated rapidly. In response FMF Atlantic reinforced the marine security detachment at the American naval base at Guantanamo Bay ("Gitmo") and increased the deployments of FMF ground and air units to the Caribbean. Although FMF Atlantic mounted periodic brigade exercises on Vieques Island off Puerto Rico, standing procedure was to send Marine fighter and helicopter squadrons to the naval air station at Roosevelt Roads, Puerto Rico, while the BLT of the Caribbean ready force trained at Vieques or cruised with its amphibious squadron.

Buoyed by the growing number of landing exercises and crisis deployments, Headquarters resisted any alteration of Corps functions and legal status when the Eisenhower administration proposed further reorganization of the Department of Defense in 1958. Once again the Corps emerged victorious in all aspects of the reorganization important to it. The defense review uncovered some emerging problems, however, particularly rivalry with the Army in the force in readiness mission. For the administration the key issues concerned the relative power of defense decision-makers. Attempting to force efficiencies and check interservice rivalry, particularly in weapons programs, the administration proposed that the powers of the Secretary of Defense be increased to include the transfer of statutory roles and missions either from service to service or to the unified and specified commands. The same sort of proposal applied to service department administration in areas common to all the services. The implications of such a reform for the Corps were ominous, for it meant that the Corps would lose its hard-won foothold in the three agencies that would surrender power in the reorganization—the Navy Department, the JCS, and Congress. When the legislative coalitions formed, Pate lined up with the CNO and the House Armed Services Committee, which in its own bill proposed less centralization rather than more.[38]

Pate's Congressional testimony was something short of spellbinding, but Headquarters contributed its weight to the fight to preserve Section 206 (c) of the National Security Act of 1947. This section, which listed Corps roles and missions, escaped revision. Resorting to its traditional plea that defense centralization menaced civilian (that is, Congressional) control, Marine witnesses urged Congress to preserve its right to dictate service organization. When the revised version of the National Security Act amendments of 1958 passed, it contained provisions Eisenhower called "legalized insubordination" but which pleased the Corps. The amendments granted the Secretary of Defense substantial new powers to centralize research and development, procurement, and administration activities, but the law prevented the Secretary from transferring major "statutory" roles and missions without Congressional approval. The individual service chiefs could appeal directly to Congress when they thought a "major" mission endangered. Although Headquarters did not like the increased centralization of the reorganization act, it decided the Corps could best win its battles in the JCS and Navy Department as long as the service departments submitted separate budgets each year to the Congress, a practice unchanged by the 1958 law. Headquarters nevertheless vowed to resist any attempt by the Secretary of Defense to cut Corps functions through the budget process, contingency planning, and executive reorganization. This position, well known in Washington, did not endear the Corps's senior generals to the Eisenhower administration.[39]

In other aspects of the 1958 defense organization review, the Corps picked up clear signals that its force in readiness mission did not enjoy the same Congressional support it had in 1952. At issue was the question of strategic air mobility. In order to enhance its own responsiveness to international crises, the Army in 1958 designated two airborne divisions and two infantry divisions as its Strategic Army Corps (STRAC) and streamlined and modernized all four divisions for air transportability. Alarmed by STRAC's popularity in Congress, a Headquarters study group warned Pate that he and other Marine generals would have to alert the Navy to the importance of the limited war mission before the Army took it by default. Marine witnesses in the 1958 hearings took great pains to explain the freedom and staying power of amphibious ready forces and the logistical limitations of strategic air transportation. As with other aspects of the 1958 defense debate, Corps criticism of STRAC, though muted, aligned the Marines against both the Secretary of Defense and the Army, who otherwise might have been allies in the debate on conventional force preparedness. STRAC's existence, however, also stimulated Marine policy-makers to press for further FMF modernization, which required money the Corps did not have. When a presidential panel on limited-war capabilities examined the Corps in 1959, it found Marine officers frustrated by a lack of modern equipment and adequate manpower. With its developmental programs at the "takeoff" stage, the Corps awaited a change in the political environment that would consolidate its amphibious force in readiness mission.[40]

4.

In 1960 the Marine Corps began a five-year surge in its readiness that brought it to its highest level of peacetime effectiveness by the eve of the Vietnam War. Although the doctrinal studies and field research and development programs of the late 1950s provided an essential foundation for the surge, the critical changes began with a set of internal redirections in 1960 and a change of presidential administrations in 1961. The changes fortuitously complemented one another. The redirections within the Corps began with the appointment of General David M. Shoup as Commandant and Lieutenant General Wallace M. Greene, Jr., as chief of staff (and Shoup's eventual successor). Both major generals when selected, Shoup and Greene profited from the judgment of Secretary of Defense Thomas S. Gates, Secretary of the Navy William B. Franke, and the JCS that the Corps needed leaders with "the capacity for dealing objectively—without extreme service partisanship—with matters of the broadest significance to our national security."[41] Quite accurately, Eisenhower believed Shoup shared his own suspicions about the "military–industrial complex" and defense costs. The implication was that the Corps's senior officers in 1959, including Lieutenant General Merrill B. Twining, the generals' own choice for Commandant, would not accept the "Second New Look" and work harmoniously with the Office of the Secretary of Defense (OSD), the Department of the Navy, and the Joint Chiefs. At issue especially were Headquarters' repeated requests for 190,000 men rather than the budgeted 175,000. With Shoup's appointment, every lieutenant general in the Corps retired, much to Shoup's pleasure.[42]

The Shoup–Greene team gave the Corps two leaders who differed in temperament and style but not in energy, determination, and sharp political skills. Shoup impressed outsiders with his blunt talk, his Medal of Honor, his drive, and his identification with the FMF and the honor of the Corps. His subordinates found the new Commandant extremely demanding, impatient, brutal in his language and behavior toward slack senior officers, and contemptuous of Corps elitest affectations (like swagger sticks and eight-man squad drill) and the domination of policy by the "1st Division gang." Shoup quickly told his staff that he wanted more real readiness in the FMF, better fiscal and supply management, more honest cooperation with the other services and OSD, and fewer parochial arguments over roles and missions. Hardly insensitive to the Corps's need for new technology, especially data-processing equipment for communications and logistics, Shoup nonetheless stressed "people" issues like appearance, physical fitness, leadership, and training. Where Shoup's style annoyed his associates and constrained Corps negotiations on sensitive policies, the tireless, methodical Greene filled the gap. An accomplished staff officer for almost twenty years, Greene also drove the Headquarters staff but enjoyed better personal relations within and outside the Corps. A self-contained New Englander who had graduated from Annapolis in 1930, Greene provided an essential link between the Pate commandancy's modernization programs and Shoup's dogged pursuit of a more rugged, ready FMF. When Shoup's populist instincts, born in the Indiana farmlands, clashed with the Byzantine life of political-social Washington, the suave Greene moved smoothly through interservice and political intriguing. In combination the two generals, even though often uncomfortable with each other, worked to the Corps's decided benefit.[43]

As he recognized when he became Commandant, Shoup had to accept the 175,000 manpower ceiling at least through FY 1961, but he planned to strip Marines from the supporting establishment and reactivate five of the six cadred BLTs in the same eighteen-month period. He also wanted to shorten the tour of Okinawa infantry battalions from fifteen to thirteen months but preserve the ban on dependents at western Pacific FMF bases. In addition, the Commandant stressed that the Corps would fall into line with centralized Department of Defense policies on officer promotions and the assignment of promising officers to OSD and JCS billets in order to prepare them for flag rank. As 1960 passed, few could doubt that (as Shoup announced) a "strong hand" had taken "the plow" and that the new Commandant intended to have his way even if some senior Marine officers got plowed under.[44]

The presidential election of 1960 opened new opportunities for the Corps. The victor, Senator John F. Kennedy, had made the national unpreparedness for conventional war a campaign issue. Tutored by retired Army officers and civilian academics about the wisdom of a "Flexible Response" strategy that offered more military alternatives than nuclear war, the new President respected the Corps's primitive ardor and muscular approach to military problems. On the other hand, a victory by Vice President Richard M. Nixon would have been no disaster, for the Republican candidate had been carefully schooled in Marine doctrine by his close military assistant, Brigadier General Robert E. Cushman, Jr. Because both Kennedy and Nixon had promised to meet the Communist threat more aggressively, the Corps stood to profit by the 1960 election no matter who won. Nevertheless, the early days of the Kennedy administration showed that the Marine Corps had a new group of civilian masters in the White House and Pentagon who were impressed by the Corps's limited war capability and were, conversely, unimpressed by the wisdom of the senior officers of the three larger services. Outsiders in the political arena, the "New Frontiersmen" found allies in an outsider service that was as ready as they to question the conventional wisdom of the JCS and the civilian bureaucracy.[45]

As the new administration took office, Headquarters measured the Kennedy appointees and policies and found them basically congenial despite some concerns about the centralized management concepts of the new Secretary of Defense, Robert S. McNamara. At the strategic level, "Flexible Response" could hardly have been more attractive, for the new policy stressed conventional force improvements in manpower, equipment modernization, and strategic mobility. The administration had been in office less than six months when it recommended that the Marine Corps be increased to 190,000 and that its budget be raised by $67 million to pay for the new men and accelerated modernization. When the administration proposed supplements to the FY 1962 budget and submitted its own request for FY 1963, both budgets pushed defense spending up almost $10 billion. The Corps shared the new prosperity. Moreover, McNamara's new budgeting system, which grouped forces by function rather than service, probably benefited the Corps, for much of its support base and its cost fell in the "General Purpose Forces" category and there disappeared in the billions allocated to all four services.[46]

McNamara held Corps strength at 190,000 men when Shoup asked for 9,000 more in 1962, but generally the Secretary and his planners proved friendly to Corps requests in virtually every other area. Although the Headquarters staff staggered under the paperwork demanded by OSD and complained about the Navy's amateurish planning, the Corps budget for procurement and operations/maintenance climbed above the $200 million mark in the first category and neared $200 million in the second, both substantial improvements over the "New Look" era. While some of the new equipment, particularly the NATO-caliber small arms and communications equipment, went directly to the FMF, McNamara and Shoup agreed to emphasize the stockpiling of emergency equipment and supplies of all kinds. The basic goal dramatized that "Flexible Response" meant a Marine Corps capable of sustained combat ashore, not just short-lived amphibious operations. As McNamara told Congress, his objective was to provide supplies for four divisions and four wings that would allow them to fight "for a substantial period of time." [47] In specific terms, Headquarters brought its war reserves of organizational and special equipment up to more than a year's estimated needs for the whole FMF. In addition, it set aside a ninety-day allowance of equipment, POL, and ammunition in contingency supplies for each division and wing. Headquarters' goal, which it expected to reach in FY 1964, was eighteen months' war reserves and nine months' contingency supplies.[48]

The buying spree also revealed that the Corps did not know how to run a supply system, a disaster in the cost-effectiveness reign of Secretary McNamara. In effect, Shoup inherited a system developed during the liberal days of World War II and unchanged thereafter. A General Accounting Office study completed in 1960 found supply management an undiscovered art in the Corps. Instead of having a single automated inventory control agency, Headquarters and the Philadelphia supply facility shared the procurement and storage accounting of 270,000 different items valued at $1.78 billion. Headquarters controlled 1 percent of the items, essentially high-cost equipment, while Philadelphia managed some 267,000 items valued at $351 million. It was the latter category—basically equipment used in volume and replacement parts—that represented the largest problem area, for neither the principal supply depots at Albany and Barstow nor their satellite agencies serving the FMF had a good estimate on what they had or what they needed. Both depots had a discouraging record of ordering supplies they already had in abundance while at the same time refusing as many as 800 requisitions a month for material they couldn't find in their warehouses. The delays in repairing vehicles and heavy ordnance were equally discouraging because parts could not be located. Delays ran three times estimates, and costs double.[49] Despite Headquarters' heightened concern for supply matters and a crash program to computerize and reorganize procurement and inventory control, the GAO found serious irregularies in 3d Division maintenance in 1963 and ammunition overprocurement in 1964. Shoup insisted to Congress that the problem was in hand, however, and a 1964 GAO study of FMF Atlantic's supply readiness did indeed show substantial improvement.[50]

Although supply problems again surfaced in the Vietnam War, the FMF soon profited from the wide-scale adoption of sophisticated computers and better-trained personnel and the completion of the Marine Unified Material Management System (MUMMS) in 1967. A reform complicated by the simultaneous shift to a highly centralized DOD supply management system, MUMMS centralized all inventory control at Philadelphia. Instead of meandering through the depots in search of equipment, requisitions went directly to Philadelphia, where supply managers checked Corps-wide inventories and then ordered distribution from one of the four large supply points on each coast. Marines of the 1960s, however, remembered the period as one of feast or famine in the FMF and blamed everyone but the Corps for supply shortages, when in reality the money and even the supplies were normally always there—if they could be found.

If doubts arose about the efficiency of the supply system in the FMF, Headquarters left no confusion about what the supplies were for: amphibious operations associated with all conflicts from general war to limited Cold War interventions. "Flexible Response" could not have been a more congenial strategy for the Corps. Although Headquarters planners used JCS general war plans to define requirements, Corps policies by 1965 placed increasing emphasis on the use of amphibious forces for alliance support and crisis control in nonnuclear confrontations. Corps doctrine reaffirmed an institutional position: The United States depended upon a forward collective defense in Europe and Asia that, short of nuclear war, required maritime supremacy. Long-range Corps programs, designed for the 1970s and 1980s, stressed the need for improved strategic and tactical mobility and the combined use of Marine ground and air units. The latter concept became nonnegotiable in Corps doctrine despite persistent problems in getting aviation units to the area of amphibious operations. To emphasize the bond of ground and air operations, Corps doctrine stressed the "Marine Air-Ground Task Force" (MAGTF). Deployed FMF units with both ground and air components became Marine Expeditionary Units (MEU), Marine Expeditionary Brigades (MEB), and Marine Expeditionary Forces (MEF). Built around BLTs, tactical air and helicopter squadrons, and combat support and combat service support units of the FMF, the expeditionary forces provided, so the Corps preached, capabilities dear to military planners—"mobility," "flexibility," "versatility," and "readiness"—for combined vertical and surface amphibious assaults. [51]

Steering the straight course of doctrinal purity sometimes proved difficult for Headquarters. So it was with the counterinsurgency (CI) mission. Alarmed by what it interpreted as the growing incidence of Communist-inspired "wars of national liberation," the Kennedy administration made counterinsurgency a key element of its national security policy. Spurred by the President and his closest advisers, the "special warfare" movement swept through the civilian foreign-policy agencies and the armed forces. Although "special warfare" found enthusiastic supporters in the Army, especially officers associated with Special Forces and Army aviation, the counterinsurgency movement did not budge the Corps from its commitment to amphibious warfare. With the exception of Major General Victor H. Krulak, who became a special assistant to the JCS for counterinsurgency, no senior Marine general embraced the mission. Unwilling to antagonize Kennedy CI cultists, Headquarters met the "Third Challenge," as insurgency was labeled, in two ways. First, formal instruction in counterinsurgency increased at all levels of Marine Corps schooling. At the same time, tactical training in the FMF included counterguerrilla warfare problems but paid little attention to the subtleties of population control, psychological-political action, civil affairs, and special operations in counterterrorism and raiding. In fact, the Marines held only one large-scale exercise, SILVER LANCE in California in 1965, that was counterinsurgency to the core. At Headquarters, the planners took their cues from General Shoup, who considered CI a fad that appealed to the Army and should be Army business. The Corps position was that it had fought guerrillas before in Latin America and could do so again if required:

> Counterinsurgency is an attention-getting word these days and you may properly ask what the Marine Corps is doing in the field. We do not claim to be experts in the entire scope of actions required in counterinsurgency operations.
>
> We do stand ready to carry out the military portions of such operations and to contribute to such other aspects of the counterinsurgency effort as may be appropriate.
>
> The Marine Corps has long recognized that fighting guerrillas is an inherent part of landing force operations.
>
> Counterguerrilla warfare is essentially one of small units and we have traditionally emphasized individual leadership and small unit operations.
>
> I am convinced that the training properly equips our tactical units

to combat rabble, insurgents, guerrillas or an enemy equipped with modern conventional or nuclear weapons.[52]

Using its harmonious relations with the administration and its colonial infantry heritage, plus a flood of paper pronouncements, to sooth its potential critics, the Corps made no special concessions to special warfare.[53]

The biggest battles in the early 1960s occurred not against guerrillas but against Navy and OSD planners and Congressional critics. Once more the Corps won significant victories. Although Headquarters stressed the Corps's intimate ties with the Navy, it won more autonomy from the Chief of Naval Operations during a crisis over the CNO's authority within the Navy in 1964. When revisions of Navy Department General Orders 5 and 19, which governed command relations, appeared in 1965, the Commandant's control over both the operating forces and the Marine base system was clarified, as was his direct access to the Secretary of the Navy and his authority over the Chief of Naval Material in Corps-related logistics matters. Only those operating forces specifically assigned to the Fleet for special missions fell under the operational control of the CNO and the Navy's chain of command. All other relations remained negotiable and ultimately resolvable by the Secretary of the Navy. The Commandant's improved autonomy did not set off any sharp Navy–Marine conflicts, for Shoup avoided open bureaucratic warfare. Moreover, Marine and Navy planners had to work as allies in the face of increased demands by McNamara's staff for instant, highly quantified studies probing every weapons program and departmental plan dear to the heart of both the Navy and the Corps. Nevertheless, the Corps did very well in exploiting its political position within the Navy Department and the tension between the CNO and OSD to improve the future of the FMF.[54]

Enjoying harmonious relationships with the armed services committees and defense appropriations subcommittees of Congress, Headquarters had only one minor skirmish with Congress and again improved its image—and probably its funding. In 1961 staff members of a Senate special preparedness investigating subcommittee reported that the Corps was not indoctrinated on the perils of "International Communism." The furor arose over charges from anti-Communist ideologues, championed by Senator Strom Thurmond, that McNamara had "muzzled" the military chiefs and banned right-wing "hate Communism" indoctrination materials from military bases. Shoup replied hotly to the charges: "We're professional soldiers. We fight any enemy the President designates."[55] Two of Thurmond's staff members then cowed Headquarters officers into allowing them to administer an amateurish survey to a group of enlisted men, who did demonstrate some trouble in identifying Mao Tse-tung and the convolutions of Marxist-Leninist doctrine. Shoup again proclaimed the Corps an impartial combat force that found its strength in training, not hate. Buoyed by popular support for Shoup's stand, Congress, prompted again by Paul Douglas and Mike Mansfield, let the matter drop.[56]

Alert to its relative strength in Washington, Headquarters worked hard to improve its amphibious capability and scored impressive gains in two critical areas, amphibious shipping and aviation assets. It was less successful in curbing the Navy's shift from guns to missiles on its cruisers and destroyers. The switch reduced fire support, but air was supposed to fill the firepower gap. Headquarters set impressive goals for the Navy's amphibious force: 16 LPHs and 88 other vessels, or enough lift for two complete Marine Expeditionary Forces (division/wing teams). As Shoup put it: "If we don't get the ferry, we don't get the fight." [57] McNamara and the Navy responded with heartening agreement. Impressed by the need for more modern, fast amphibious shipping (particularly after the Missile Crisis of 1962), McNamara moved the shipping goals from 102 vessels to 143 by the early 1970s. OSD planned for 67 new vessels in FY 1965–1969 alone, a plan that would have provided lift for two MEFs with 75 percent of the Marines embarked on new 20-knot amphibians. For FY 1965 21 percent of the Navy's shipbuilding and modernization funds were tagged for the amphibious force, which pleased Corps champions in Congress. The LPH and LPD programs received fresh life, and the Navy began work on new command-communications ships and LSTs with higher speeds and front ramps rather than bow doors. It appeared that the Navy–Marine Corps amphibious team was en route to its brightest peacetime future.[58]

The aviation program prospered, too, in the flush fiscal days of the early "Flexible Response" era. McNamara, despite some doubts about the cost-effectiveness of Navy–Marine Corps aircraft adoptions, approved the plans to build a Marine fixed-wing air force around the Phantom II for both air superiority and attack missions, the Skyhawk for normal close air support, and the A-6A "Intruder" for night and bad-weather level-flight bombing. He also recommended additional funds to develop more sophisticated automated radar systems for coordinating air operations, provided the systems were compatible with Air Force and Army programs. OSD, however, refused to seek substantial research and development funds for a pet Marine project, the testing of vertical/short takeoff and landing (V/STOL) aircraft like the British Hawker-Siddeley "Harrier." Instead, McNamara offered the

Navy its own share of an Air Force–Army light attack/reconnaissance plane, the OV-10A "Bronco," which was neither a V/STOL aircraft nor an effective close air support weapon by Marine standards. Convinced that the Harrier offered the best prospects for both carrier operations, especially from the LPHs, and quick-response air operations ashore, the Corps persisted with the Harrier program until it was approved in the late 1960s.[59]

The helicopter program also fared well, but it was rocked slightly by McNamara's fascination with the Army's new "airmobile" concept and the creation of an Army air assault division to test helicopter tactics. The Marine programs for adopting new troop-carrying and heavy-lift logistical helos survived the usual close encounters with the Navy's aviation bureaucracy, now concentrated in the Bureau of Weapons, and emerged with the development, testing, and procurement of two large turbine-engine powered helos that met Corps requirements for payload, speed, and range. These two helos, the Boeing-Vertol CH-46A "Sea Knight" and the Sikorsky CH-53A "Sea Stallion," became the mainstay of Corps helicopter operations in the late 1960s. Both were designed for amphibious operations, which meant large payloads and high speeds but (because of high unit cost) reduced numbers. Since the Marine Corps anticipated supporting the helos with attack aviation, the new helos' vulnerability to ground fire did not look like an unacceptable risk.

McNamara's insistence on joint service development, however, complicated the development of a third, light helicopter for command and utility duties. The issue was further clouded by Headquarters' lack of interest in arming light helos for close air support, a concept dear to the Army. Over Marine objections, the Bureau of Weapons chose the Army's Bell UH-1 or "Huey" as the Corps assault support helicopter; procuring the UH-1 would speed adoption and reduce cost, it reasoned, because its procurement could coincide with a massive Army buy. The adoption of an Army helo, however, opened the door to questions about Marine doctrine. General Shoup assured Congressional doubters that armed helos, which meant the UH-1, could not replace attack aircraft in heavy combat, which meant the amphibious assault. He insisted that the Army's airmobile division, which would have more helos than all three Marine wings, was meant for one type of vertical envelopment, while the Corps helicopter program was designed for another. Defense analysts sometimes missed his point—as did some Marines.[60]

As the critical modernization programs for the FMF plunged ahead, the Corps also went forward with reorganizations and changes reaching all the way from Headquarters to the rifle squads. All the changes were made in the name of readiness, and most of them did indeed mean improved management and combat capability, even if they did not occur overnight. At Headquarters Shoup increased and centralized the supervision of critical programs by creating deputy chiefs of staff for air, plans and programs, and research and development. For the FMF, Headquarters squeezed men from the supporting establishment and cut Force Troops units in order to bring the strength of the FMF to 115,000 men in 1962, with the wings the special beneficiaries of the reallocated personnel. New weapons and equipment appeared in the operating forces and were generally welcomed, particularly communications equipment and the 7.62-mm. family of small arms and the M-79 grenade launcher. Marines less happily donned all-service utility uniforms (with globe-and-anchor quickly applied to the jacket pocket) and all-service combat boots. Artillery batteries dropped from eight to six guns in the name of mobility but retained the dependable 105-mm. howitzer. Weapons platoons shrank with the adoption of the M-60 machine gun, which reduced the need for ammunition bearers (in theory), but the rifle platoons increased with the addition of an M-79 gunner to each rifle squad. The M-79 or "blooper" fired 40-mm. shells from a shotgun-like grenade launcher, giving each squad its own miniature cannon.

The reforms reached even the Marine Corps Reserve, not only with equipment but with new doctrine. In 1962 Headquarters ordered the Organized Reserve to reform as a complete division and wing with appropriate supporting Force Troop components. Instead of envisioning reserve units as training commands for individual replacements for the regular divisions and wings, Headquarters formed the 4th Marine Division and 4th Marine Aircraft Wing, manned by 90 percent Reservists and 10 percent regulars. Although the redesignation and retraining of Reserve units took time, the reorganization improved the training and equipment status of Reserve units and encouraged a sense of mission and *esprit* based on both professionalism and local pride.[61]

For the tactical units of the FMF the early 1960s could hardly have been busier. The combination of increased amphibious exercises and contingency deployments kept the ready forces, particularly FMF Atlantic, on the move. One focus remained the Mediterranean, where at least a BLT (and often larger units) sailed with the 6th Fleet. Headquarters eyed an enlarged NATO role, especially on the northern Norwegian and Baltic flanks, and received JCS permission to conduct exercises there with an MEU in 1966. The size of the possible Marine role in Europe grew with the geographic extension. In 1964 II MEF conducted Operation STEEL PIKE I, an amphibious exercise that exceeded all earlier exercises in both the size of the Marine force deployed and the distance covered. Unlike QUICK KICK, a division-size maneuver off

North Carolina in 1962, STEEL PIKE I took II MEF all the way to Spain. An amphibious force of sixty vessels (seventeen of them commercial) carried 21,642 Marines, 5,174 vehicles, and almost a million cubic feet of cargo to Europe. Although II MEF did not take all its vehicles, and the vessels left much to be desired in numbers and condition, STEEL PIKE I represented a new plateau in readiness.[62]

By 1964 landing exercises worldwide numbered forty-five, with FMF Pacific about as heavily engaged as FMF Atlantic. While FMF Atlantic forces shuttled between Europe and North Carolina, with additional deployments to the Caribbean and Africa, FMF Pacific units trained along the littoral of Asia and conducted large-scale exercises in California. In 1965 FMF Pacific conducted its own less ambitious version of STEEL PIKE I by landing much of the 1st Division with supporting air in SILVER LANCE, an amphibious assault followed by a counterinsurgency problem. As in STEEL PIKE I, SILVER LANCE showed that the Corps could now helo-lift almost a full regiment in active operations. Although the large-scale exercises again revealed that the Navy's amphibious force was not keeping pace with the FMF's growing readiness, particularly in providing sustained air support and logistical services ashore, the FMF made satisfying steps toward reaching the effectiveness planned in the late 1950s.[63]

The FMF exercises had a special tinge of excitement and urgency, for units of both the III (western Pacific) and II (Atlantic) MEFs found themselves flirting with shooting wars. The crisis deployments also dramatized the Corps's force in readiness mission in ways that training exercises could not. For FMF Pacific the growing instability of the anti-Communist governments of Southeast Asia dominated contingency commitments. Inheriting two low-level civil wars in Laos and South Vietnam in 1961, the Kennedy administration chose to interpret both as proxy wars orchestrated by the Soviet Union through its agent, the Democratic Republic of Vietnam, which was Ho Chi Minh's Communist regime created in 1954. Behind the military missions, clandestine agents, and diplomatic and foreign aid officials dispatched to Southeast Asia stood the ready forces of III MEF. Initially, Marine planning centered on Laos. While international negotiations for a ceasefire and neutralization of Laos continued from 1961 into 1962, the Communist Pathet Lao forces, with North Vietnamese and Russian assistance, struck Laotian government forces along the border of Thailand and seized control of the Laotian panhandle, the key terrain along the Mekong River and the approaches to South Vietnam. To protect Thailand and stabilize the military situation, the Kennedy administration ordered a Marine expeditionary force into Thailand along with an Army brigade and Air Force units. Arriving in May, the 3d MEB established a base at the Thai airfield at Udorn. Although contingency plans provided for a full three-infantry-battalion component for the 3d MEB, the force contained only one battalion, two aviation squadrons of A-4s and helos, and supporting units, or about 3,500 men. Improvement in both the military situation and parallel diplomatic talks, however, stopped the deployment short of its full force goals, and in late July the Kennedy administration, confident that it had momentarily halted Communist pressure in Laos, withdrew the American task force.[64]

Like the rest of the American effort in South Vietnam, Marine participation in the counterinsurgency effort that swelled in 1961 focused on advisory and support missions with the armed forces of President Ngo Dinh Diem's regime. A small Marine detachment helped create a South Vietnamese marine brigade that specialized in riverine operations. In April 1962 the Corps sent its first tactical unit—a helicopter squadron and supporting service troops—to Vietnam as part of a desperate effort to give the South Vietnamese more air mobility. Along with Army helicopter companies, the Marines of Operation SHUFLY supported Vietnamese army (ARVN) operations against the Communist Viet Cong guerrillas in the Mekong delta before shifting to a new base in the autumn of 1962. Established at Danang, South Vietnam's largest northern city and the center of operations in Vietnam's five northern provinces or (in military usage) the I Corps area, the SHUFLY force conducted vertical assaults and resupply missions for the ARVN and American advisory teams for the next two years as the war worsened. Helicopter squadrons rotated to and from Okinawa, and the ground element of SHUFLY expanded as the months of inconclusive action dragged on. In the meantime, additional Marine advisers, service troops, communications teams that included security elements, and III MEF observation teams joined the American advisory effort. Often the 7th Fleet's Special Landing Force, a Marine MEU, hovered off Vietnam without going ashore. With the rest of the American armed forces, the Corps awaited long-postponed decisions about its Vietnam mission as 1964 ended.[65]

While the actual Marine deployments to Southeast Asia did not reach serious operational proportions, II MEF of FMF Atlantic saw more of the coastlines of Cuba and the Dominican Republic, once moved to the brink of war in 1962, and fought ashore during the Dominican civil war of 1965. At issue was the spread of Soviet influence in the Caribbean and the spread of a Latin variant of Communism, Castroism, within the hemisphere. After the abortive attempt at the Bay of Pigs in 1961 to overthrow Castro by means of CIA-conceived paramilitary operations (with American amphibious forces in the background), the Kennedy administration ordered the JCS to plan for direct American intervention. In the meantime, the Soviet Union increased its military and economic aid to Cuba and talked darkly of protecting Cuba from an American invasion. At the same time, the JCS planned and assigned U.S. units for possible operations in Cuba. At the heart of the plans was the Army's Strategic Army Corps and Air Force tactical units, merged as Strike Command for operational purposes in 1961, and the Navy–Marine Corps forces of the 2d Fleet and II MEF. In addition to testing its own plans in Caribbean exercises in 1961 and 1962, II MEF participated with Strike Command in the first of the QUICK KICK exercises in the spring of 1962.

During the summer of 1962, for reasons that still remain partially obscure, Soviet Premier Nikita S. Khrushchev ordered a dramatic change in the size and type of assistance to Cuba and moved toward a confrontation with the United States. Russia had already transferred significant quantities of military equipment to the Cuban armed forces of 75,000 regulars and 100,000 militia but had accompanied this aid with only about 500 advisers. After July 1962, however, Khrushchev sent almost 20,000 Soviet troops (including four armored battle groups) to Cuba along with some 40 intermediate-range ballistic missiles and 40 medium bombers, all nuclear-capable. This attempt at a shift in the strategic balance, which then heavily favored the United States, posed a serious threat to the cohesion of the NATO alliance, American hegemony in the Western Hemisphere, and the authority of the Kennedy administration. In addition, the Cuban missiles and bombers posed a threat to America's southern cities. When aerial reconnaissance over Cuba verified agent reports in early October, Kennedy decided he could not accept Khrushchev's *coup de main* and publicly ordered the Russians to remove their nuclear forces from Cuban soil or risk war.[66]

Alerted only forty-eight hours before Kennedy delivered his ultimatum to Khrushchev, the American armed forces went quickly to a war footing with an efficiency unseen since World War II. To secure the naval base at Guantanamo Bay, menaced by both ground assault and rocket attack, the Corps deployed two reinforced battalions by air from the United States and another from the Caribbean amphibious ready force; as Ground Forces Guantanamo Bay swelled to more than 5,000 men, air units deployed to Key West and Puerto Rico. Allied with Navy carrier task forces, nearly 400 Marine aircraft prepared to throw an aerial umbrella over Guantanamo Bay and fly cover for any amphibious operation against Cuba. Among the 400,000 American troops prepared to invade the island if war came, II MEF provided its own full available strength and assumed control of the 5th MEB, a 10,000-man task

force provided by the California-based I MEF. As the Kennedy administration hammered out its policy of quarantine and controlled escalation,
the Corps in eight days assembled over 40,000 troops for the joint task
forces encircling Cuba. Had the JCS invaded the island, II MEF would
have led the way across well-defended beaches west of Havana as Army
airborne divisions and armored divisions joined it in battle. Even if the
campaign had lasted only ten days, as the JCS predicted over General
Shoup's skepticism, the Corps would have lost 8,000 men, the planners
thought. As Kennedy and Khrushchev shaped a face-saving compromise
that avoided war, embarked II MEF Marines prepared for the largest
amphibious landing since Okinawa, while their "Gitmo" comrades patrolled the base fence line and prepared hasty minefields and bunkers
for a last-ditch defense of the installation.[67]

After the Russians declined to challenge the naval blockade of Cuba
and began to withdraw their missiles and most of their troops, the
crisis passed, and Headquarters assessed the FMF's performance. Although joint planning and logistical arrangements, particularly access
to the Navy's amphibious fleet, left considerable room for improvement,
Headquarters took great satisfaction from II MEF's performance under
extreme emergency conditions. Given the highly extemporaneous and
complex nature of the Cuban deployment, the Corps had matched (if
not surpassed) the operational responsiveness of Strike Command. As a
serious test of the FMF's ability to fulfill the force in readiness mission,
the Cuban Missile Crisis could not have ended more happily for the
Corps. The very readiness of the FMF (and the rest of American military) seemed to prove that the conventional war stress of "Flexible Response" had been a signal improvement in the nation's ability to deter
war.[68]

Influenced by a continuing fear of Castroism in the Caribbean, the
United States government kept amphibious ready forces shuttling from
the traditional training areas in Puerto Rico to the south coast of Hispaniola, for both Haiti and the Dominican Republic showed signs of
increasing radicalism and instability, some of it exported from Cuba.
Unlike Haiti, where François "Papa Doc" Duvalier passed his power
without war to his son, the Dominican Republic dissolved in political
confusion when embittered assassins finally shot Rafael Leonidas Trujillo
in 1961. In the power struggle that followed, provisional juntas of
military officers and civilians came and went until the first free election
in years brought a leftist reformer, Juan Bosch, to office in 1963. Before Bosch took power, American diplomacy and the presence of the
Caribbean ready force helped prevent the restoration of another military–police dictatorship by the Trujillo clan in 1961 and 1962. When

the Dominican military, however, drove out Bosch in September 1963, the United States did nothing to prevent or reverse the coup and accepted another series of juntas, eventually headed by a businessman, Donald Reid Cabral, but backed by the military. Reid Cabral could neither appease the Dominican military, itself divided into predatory factions, nor form a broad-based, civilian-supported government. Bosch's supporters in the meantime tried to organize their hero's return from exile and courted Dominican radicals, including some Communists, and more liberal officers in the army and national police. In April 1965 pro-Bosch military units drove Reid Cabral from office in the name of the Constitutionalist cause, and the remaining elements of the armed forces, concentrated around the city of Santo Domingo, did nothing to save the Reid Cabral government. Convinced that the Constitutionalists were pro-Bosch (which was certain) and Communist-dominated (much less clear), the Dominican armed forces, directed primarily by General Elias Wessin y Wessin, tried to crush the rebels. Street fighting engulfed the capital.[69]

The American response to the Dominican civil war reflected the Johnson administration's obsession with Castroism and the State Department's commitment to a negotiated solution to the latest Dominican crisis. Neither the President and his advisers nor the career diplomats wanted a Castroite succession, a category in which they included Bosch's return; they were almost equally fearful of open conflict with the right-wing military and the rebels. Into this complex political situation sailed the 6th MEU, the Caribbean ready force of a reinforced infantry battalion and LPH-based helo squadron, whose first mission was the protection and evacuation of foreign nationals caught in the fighting. Following long-established contingency plans, part of the 6th MEU flew ashore to establish an enclave around the Hotel Embajador on the western outskirts of Santo Domingo. During April 28–30 the Marines evacuated civilians and reinforced the security detachment at the American embassy, the scene of occasional sniping and frightening rumors of atrocities and Castroite plots.[70]

On April 30 the character of the American intervention shifted as the Johnson administration decided that the Constitutionalists represented a Castroite threat. Although it did not totally embrace the military junta, which could not crush the revolt but claimed its own political legitimacy, the administration decided to shape the conclusion of the civil war by separating the junta forces from the Constitutionalist rebels, a decision that in effect favored the military right-wingers. As the junta forces regrouped, Marines pushed eastward along the city's streets to link up with paratroopers of the 82d Airborne Division, who had flown into San Isidro airfield east of the city on April 29. On the same day the Marines exchanged fire for the first time with snipers, presumed to be rebels, but, as one Marine asked a reporter, "Which are the good guys here and which are the bad guys?" [71] In the narrow streets of Santo Domingo no one could tell. On May 1 the Marines met the paratroopers and established a cordon or "international security zone" (ISZ) that split the city and isolated the rebels. Marine and airborne patrols and outposts battled the rebels and lost men (for the Marines, nine killed and thirty wounded) without undertaking active operations to crush the Constitutionalists. In the meantime, more American troops poured into the Dominican Republic.

Before the Dominican civil war faded away in a series of complex international agreements and a wave of exiles, the United States concentrated more than 20,000 troops in Santo Domingo, of whom 8,000 were Marines. Before the intervention ended, FMF Atlantic had three BLTs ashore and another in reserve, and had committed two helo squadrons and two attack squadrons to the Marine command, redesignated the 4th MEB. As negotiations among American diplomats and special representatives, Dominican military and civilian politicians, and agents of the Organization of American States progressed with exquisite complexity, the Marines manned their ISZ posts and watched the Dominican military and rebels battle one another in a series of local clashes. Dangerous and frustrating, the occupation tested Marine discipline and restraint. After early orgies of night firing and incidents with Dominican civilians—divided from most Marines by language and race—the 4th MEB at least did nothing to complicate the negotiations and probably performed its constabulary duties as well as the conditions permitted. Nevertheless, few Marines mourned when the brigade withdrew in June to leave Santo Domingo to the 82d Airborne and a token OAS peacekeeping force. In a striking repetition of its duties during the colonial infantry era, the 4th MEB gave Headquarters another reason to laud FMF readiness. [72]

Weighing the FMF's experiences in Southeast Asia and the Caribbean since 1960 and the progress of Corps modernization and training programs, Commandant Wallace M. Greene, Jr., no Pollyanna, reported to Congress in 1965 that "the Marine Corps is in the best condition of readiness that I have seen in my thirty-seven years of naval service." [73] Despite a demanding training program and the crisis deployments that often complicated that program, Headquarters with justification assured the senior officers of the Corps and the public that the Fleet Marine Force, both regular and Reserve, by 1965 had reached a level of readiness that exceeded the hopes of the 1950s. [74]

18. The Longest War:
The Marines in Vietnam, 1965–1975

A ssessing the "strange war" in 1970, a Marine general remarked that

> . . . we had not only averted the expected disaster, but had also
> turned the course of the war against the enemy. . . . I was keenly
> aware that over four thousand men under my command had given
> their lives in that fight and that almost seventeen thousand had been
> wounded. I knew, however, that this was the price we paid to deci-
> mate the Viet Cong, to drive him away from the people into the
> Laotian hills, to fight off the divisions of regular North Vietnamese
> invaders, and to root out the "tax collectors" and terrorists who
> preyed upon the villagers.[1]

There were other prices levied upon the Marine Corps itself. Watching
his company of slightly crazed, rain-soaked youths struggle under their
loads of flak jackets and munitions, a veteran gunnery sergeant mused:
"First there was the Old Corps, then there was the New Corps. And
now there's this goddamned thing." More concerned about their safe
return to "the world" than about saving the Republic of Vietnam from
Communism, the troops sang:

> We're using a theory
> We've used it before
> If you ain't got no people,
> You ain't got no war.[2]

The Vietnam War became the ultimate test of the Corps's surviva-
bility. Statistics alone provide some index to the organizational strains

the Corps faced. Vietnam was the Corps's longest war (1965–1971), measured by the commitment of FMF ground and air elements to combat. During that era 794,000 Americans served as Marines, as against 669,100 in World War II. At peak strength in 1968, the III Marine Amphibious Force (III MAF) in Vietnam numbered 85,755, more troops than made the landings on Iwo Jima and Okinawa. This force, however, rested upon a narrower troop base than the World War II Corps. Peak strength for the Vietnam War (1969) reached only 314,917, short of the 485,053 peak in 1945. Although the intensity of the Vietnam War varied drastically over time and place, the war cost the Corps 101,574 killed and wounded, or almost 4,000 more casualties than World War II. Only in the numbers of dead (19,733 to 12,983) did World War II cost the Corps more. Of course, statistics are not the sole measure of the Corps's experience. Despite its generally admirable combat performance in Vietnam under conditions not fully appreciated by either its military superiors or the American public, the ordeal of III MAF extracted a high cost in professional skill and *esprit*. The war once again threw the Corps into an internal debate about its mission and military standards and opened it to unprecedented public criticism. It also delayed substantial modernization programs designed to keep the Corps's amphibious warfare mission alive in the 1970s. The war ended barely soon enough for the Corps to reconstruct itself as an elite force in readiness.

For the vast majority of Marines the war in Vietnam was the war for control of South Vietnam's five northern provinces, identified variously as the I Corps Tactical Zone or Military Region I but by Marines as simply "Eye Corps." The Marines could not have found a more difficult place in all South Vietnam to fight either a war for control of the rural population or a war of attrition against the invading North Vietnamese army (NVA). Terrain and weather conspired to make I Corps an unpleasant place to fight, despite the deceptive beauty of its mountains, rice lands, and beaches. From the flat, sandy coastal areas, carpeted with scrub vegetation, the terrain changes to delta rice lands along the rivers that flow to the South China Sea. This strip of arable land merges into the foothills and forested mountains of the Annamite mountain chain. The rice paddies, dikes, narrow village trails, and tree lines of the delta areas turn into bamboo thickets, roaring streams, and thick rain forests. In the delta lands there is enough topsoil to grow rice, but centuries of cultivation have turned much of it into a gluey, red clay subsoil called laterite, which grabs feet and wheels and slides from beneath buildings and runways. Everywhere there is water. I Corps has the heaviest rainfall in Vietnam; while Saigon receives 80 inches annually, Hue drowns in 128 inches. Unlike the rest of the country, the north has its monsoon rains in the chilly months of September–January, and the rains often last until March, sometimes in the form of the *crachin,* or cold drizzle and fog. The monsoons are amplified by typhoons that roar in from the South China Sea. While the winter monsoon brings numbing cold, the summers produce temperature-humidity indices near 100 and clouds of dust. Marines who thought they had seen bad conditions in Korea revised their thinking in Vietnam.

Whether committed against the Viet Cong (VC) political infrastructure and guerrilla bands or against the NVA, the Marines faced not only disheartening terrain and weather but also a demographic/political situation that taxed all of III MAF's ingenuity and resources. The five provinces of I Corps—from north to south: Quang Tri, Thua Thien, Quang Nam, Quang Tin, and Quang Ngai—had been a hotbed of Viet Minh political and military action during the First Indochina war. When that war ended in 1954, the new administrative and military organizations of South Vietnam controlled little more than the larger cities along Route 1, the national highway and railroad running parallel to the coastline. Optimistic estimates in the early 1960s might have placed only 500,000 people of I Corps's 2.5 million inhabitants under the influence of the government of South Vietnam (GVN). Viet Minh cadres, their name changed to the National Liberation Front (NLF), controlled most of the rural population. Of the estimated 150,000 VC faced by the South Vietnamese government, perhaps a third were doing political work and staging raids in I Corps in early 1965. To meet the Communist military challenge in I Corps, the GVN had deployed about 60,000 men, divided into two army (ARVN) divisions and one regiment of 25,000 troops, a Regional Force of 12,000, and a Popular Force (militia) of 23,000. Most of this GVN force defended the large cities and towns and the transportation system; limited mobility, arms, numbers, training, and morale restricted the GVN forces to a static defense posture. The VC, on the other hand, strengthened their control of the countryside through the twin "struggle" strategies of political organization and low-level guerrilla warfare and terrorism. Part of the VC's self-confidence stemmed from the knowledge that the NVA was massing across the Laotian border and north of the Demilitarized Zone (DMZ).

Although I Corps was uncomfortably close to the NVA base sanctuaries in Laos and North Vietnam, by 1965 the most important fact in I Corps was that the VC had cowed the region's rural population. I Corps bulged with Vietnamese peasants, the ocean in which the insurgents "swam" in Maoist doctrine. Quang Nam province, the site of continuous

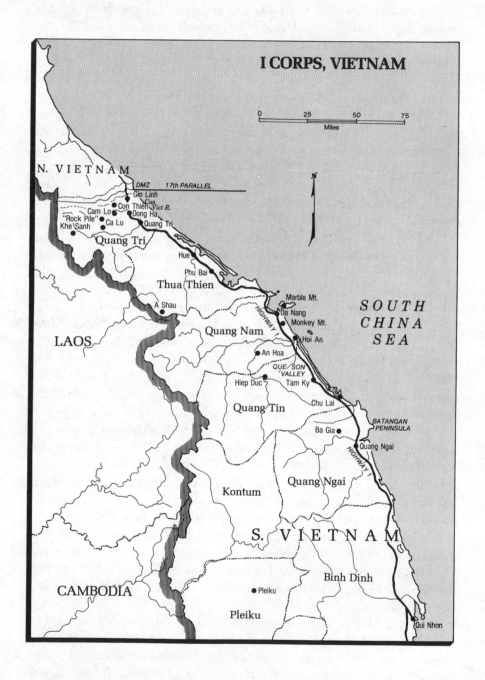

I CORPS, VIETNAM

0   25   50   75
Miles

N. VIETNAM

DMZ   17th PARALLEL

Gio Linh
Cua
Con Thien   Viet R.
Cam Lo   Dong Ha
"Rock Pile"   Ca Lu   Quang Tri
Khe Sanh

Quang Tri

Hue

Phu Bai

Thua Thien

A Shau

Marble Mt.
Da Nang
Monkey Mt.

Quang Nam

Hoi An

An Hoa

QUE SON
VALLEY
Hiep Duc   Tam Ky

Quang Tin

Chu Lai

Ba Gia

BATANGAN
PENINSULA

Quang Ngai

HIGHWAY 1

Quang Ngai

Kontum

S. VIETNAM

CAMBODIA

Pleiku

Pleiku

Binh Dinh

Qui Nhon

LAOS

SOUTH
CHINA
SEA

HIGHWAY 1

Marine operations until III MAF's withdrawal, had a population density of 2,000 people per square mile, in contrast with a national density of 210 per square mile and a density in the Mekong Delta, supposedly heavily populated, of 525 per square mile. No American state has a population density as great as Quang Nam province. In addition, Vietnamese culture—a primitive peasant society conditioned by family and village relationships and the cycle of rice growing—could hardly have been more foreign to Americans. Concepts of time and of interpersonal relationships and a language that defied American tongues separated Marines and the Vietnamese. In retrospect, the United States could hardly have chosen a less promising place to combat a Communist war of national liberation, and the Marine Corps drew the most difficult Vietnamese region to pacify.[3]

After ten years of supporting the anti-Communist regime of South Vietnam, American policy-makers in 1964 faced the most serious crisis thus far in the faltering war against the Viet Cong. Once again they examined the question of committing American ground troops to the battle. After 1960 the number of American military advisers and supporting units—which included a Marine helicopter squadron and its ground elements—had climbed from 3,200 to 17,000 without any lasting improvement in the situation. Following the fall of the Ngo Dinh Diem regime in late 1963, the NLF and its sponsor, the Ho Chi Minh government of the Democratic Republic of Vietnam, began a concerted drive to unify the two Vietnams through military action, including the use of the regular North Vietnamese army. Despite the American advisory effort and millions of dollars of military and economic assistance, the government of South Vietnam teetered on the verge of collapse. The central government rotated by coup or threat of coup between ARVN generals and ineffectual civilians, and province and district administrations remained hobbled by inaction, corruption, and collaboration with the NLF. Only elite units of the ARVN—airborne, ranger, and marine battalions—could be counted upon to fight effectively. All elements of the South Vietnamese armed forces were under heavy pressure from VC main force units, especially in the Central Highlands and around Saigon. As ARVN losses mounted, President Lyndon B. Johnson, in the heat of a presidential campaign, conferred with his civilian and military advisers to seek a course of action that offered some hope for Vietnam and had some chance of acceptance with the American electorate.[4]

Unwilling to jeopardize domestic support for his "Great Society" reforms by entering a declared war, and fearing overt Russian and Chinese intervention in Vietnam, Johnson could not bear the thought of either withdrawal or the commitment of American ground troops to the war. The only military escalation Johnson seriously considered was a bombing campaign against North Vietnam, a campaign some of his advisers believed would improve GVN morale and discourage the North Vietnamese from increasing the southward deployment of the NVA. Surreptitious ground and air operations had already begun against the Ho Chi Minh Trail through Laos and along the DRV's southern panhandle without appreciable success. In August 1964 these operations sparked the Gulf of Tonkin incident—an attack against two patrolling U.S. destroyers—after which Johnson extracted a resolution from Congress that gave him the equivalent of a declaration of war—or at least the impression that he could authorize bolder military operations. The air raids he approved against North Vietnam were limited in duration and targeting, but Johnson also examined plans to mount a serious air campaign against North Vietnam—Operation ROLLING THUNDER—and the implications of that campaign for the whole conduct of the war. The Joint Chiefs of Staff and General William C. Westmoreland, the commander of the U.S. Military Assistance Command, Vietnam (MACV), were understandably worried about the security of the bases the Air Force would use in ROLLING THUNDER. One of these key bases was Da Nang in Quang Nam province, already in use by Marine helicopters. Although Johnson once again avoided any hard decisions about committing ground troops, the plans he examined included a Marine Corps role at Da Nang.

As argued by the JCS, Westmoreland, and General Maxwell D. Taylor, the new Ambassador in Saigon, a Marine ground force at Da Nang would serve several purposes. Commandant Wallace M. Greene, Jr., and Lieutenant General Victor H. Krulak, CG FMF Pacific, agreed with Johnson's uniformed advisers and most of his civilian confidants as well. Deploying the Okinawa-based 9th Marine Expeditionary Brigade would not only secure the Da Nang airfield but would presumably release ARVN units for more aggressive operations in I Corps. Marine Hawk batteries would safeguard the base against possible DRV and Chinese air retaliation. In addition, the Marines could establish an American enclave that could be used either to escalate the war in South Vietnam or to protect an American withdrawal should Johnson decide to cut the commitment. Because Da Nang could be safely supplied only from the sea, a Navy–Marine operation there simplified command relationships. The only other immediately available American ground force—an Army airborne brigade on Okinawa—had a different role in Westmoreland's contingency planning. It became a foregone conclusion in 1964 that the American troops who would go to Da Nang, if necessary, would be Marines.[5]

American procrastination and political upheaval in South Vietnam forestalled a ground commitment, but Johnson approved limited punitive air raids on military installations in North Vietnam in late 1964. He then authorized a truncated version of ROLLING THUNDER in February 1965. VC and NVA ground operations correspondingly increased in the south. Among the Communists' prime targets for the first time were American installations, and scores of airmen and soldiers fell in rocket and mortar attacks in South Vietnam. The Air Force and Marine units at Da Nang were not bombarded, but VC movements in Quang Nam province suggested that the base might not be ignored for long. As the Johnson administration again discussed the wisdom of committing ground troops, the 9th MEB set sail for Da Nang.

1

On the morning of March 8, 1965, the assault companies of the 9th MEB plunged through the surf on Da Nang's elegant beach and met the heavy resistance of lei-bearing Vietnamese schoolgirls, ARVN officers, sightseers, and four American soldiers bearing a sign: "Welcome Gallant Marines." Brigadier General Frederick J. Karch's brigade—two reinforced Marine battalions—began its airfield defense mission by establishing a cordon of outposts close to the base, a pattern of deployment that the brigade knew could not guarantee safety from rocket attack. The ARVN commander in I Corps, General Nguyen Chanh Thi, however, had no desire to give the Marines an expanded mission, for he feared their effect upon the Da Nang population, a concern shared in Saigon by Ambassador Taylor and MACV. Taylor also worried about the political implications of the MEB's heavy weapons; he and Westmoreland insisted that the MEB change its name, because "expeditionary" sounded too French. (The change occurred two months later after the issue had gone to Washington for resolution, so the Marine organization in Vietnam became the III Marine Amphibious Force—III MAF.) Pressed into a hodgepodge of Air Force and Marine aviation installations and a dense Vietnamese shantytown, the Marine brigade awaited developments.[6]

As the result of a series of complex policy reviews by American civilian and military leaders in Saigon and Washington, the Marine force in I Corps grew to a full reinforced division/wing Marine Amphibious Force of 25,000 during the summer of 1965. Base security remained III MAF's primary mission, but the definition of that mission shifted in April to include offensives against the VC—if General Thi approved and the operations could be related to base security. Reflecting Johnson's gradual escalation and Westmoreland's conviction that only American offensive operations could save Vietnam in 1965 from a VC military victory, the Marine deployment moved in fits and starts. Problems within FMF Pacific—particularly the policy of infantry battalion rotation and the need to establish a logistical system ashore—also shaped the commitment.

As part of MACV's Phase I program, designed to forestall disaster in 1965, III MAF, commanded in turn by Major General William R. Collins and Major General Lewis W. Walt, occupied three enclaves in I Corps. Just south of Hue, one or two battalions occupied Phu Bai in order to secure an Army radio intelligence station and auxiliary airfield; the bulk of the 3d Marine Division and 1st Marine Aircraft Wing moved into III MAF's expanding Da Nang tactical area of responsibility (TAOR); and the 3d MAB, which had formed on Okinawa in March, opened a new enclave at Chu Lai in southern Quang Tin province in May with a reinforced infantry regiment and air group. A regiment and additional supporting units from the 1st Marine Division moved from Camp Pendleton to Okinawa to provide FMF Pacific with a strategic reserve, part of which was deployed as the 7th Fleet's Special Landing Force (SLF). Concerned about the worsening situation in the Central Highlands, where VC main force and NVA regiments were on the move, MACV requested that the Marines protect a fourth enclave at Qui Nhon. In July a reinforced battalion and helicopter squadron from Okinawa assumed this temporary mission.

The commitment of American ground troops to Vietnam set off a strategy debate in April–July 1965 that fixed American operational concepts for the next three years. The result of this debate was simple: President Johnson accepted the recommendation of General Westmoreland (supported by the JCS) that American ground troops be enlarged to more than 200,000 men and begin offensive operations to deny the enemy victory in 1965 and defeat him on the battlefield by 1968. Influenced by assessments of the limited effectiveness of ROLLING THUNDER and the ARVN, as well as Vietnam's lack of military mobilization, Westmoreland recommended that the United States and other nations (e.g. Australia, New Zealand, South Korea) deploy a minimum of forty-four maneuver (infantry) battalions to Vietnam for use against the NVA and VC regulars. While three division-equivalents should prevent a Communist triumph in 1965, decisive victory would have to await a more orderly buildup and the systematic destruction of Communist units within Vietnam, their base camps, and (perhaps) their sanctuaries in Cambodia and Laos. Westmoreland disagreed with Ambassador Taylor about the number of American troops needed to deny a Communist victory and the ultimate effectiveness of ARVN, but they agreed that military efficiency and politico-cultural considerations required that American troops abandon a base-defense, enclave strategy.

Shaped first by the realities of base defense at Da Nang and later by more comprehensive analysis, the Marine Corps strategy did not coincide with Westmoreland's recommendations. Instead the Marine Corps position, articulated by CG FMF Pacific Victor H. Krulak, was that an enclave, pacification strategy offered the best long-term chance of victory. Krulak, Major General Lewis W. Walt, and CINCPAC Admiral Ulysses S. G. Sharp, agreed that American troops should pursue a hold-and-pacify strategy from coastal enclaves. Krulak thought this strategy would be equally effective in denying an immediate Communist victory and more promising for improving GVN and ARVN performance. Such a strategy might take more time but offered the hope of fewer American casualties. It also implied a different relationship with the unstable, undependable South Vietnamese government and armed forces. Krulak thought that Westmoreland's failure to establish a combined U.S.–ARVN command made success in the field impossible. He also contended that great battlefield victories would not mean much if the GVN had no control over the rural population. Krulak did not believe, moreover, that the cultural differences between the Americans and Vietnamese peasantry were so great that pacification was impossible as long as the United States insisted upon land reform, economic development, physical security, and grassroots village democracy. While he did not deny the utility of opportunistic strikes against Communist main force units, Krulak argued for a "spreading ink blot" system of rural pacification rather than "search and destroy" operations in Vietnam's backlands.[7]

The system of command in Vietnam virtually assured disputes over operational concepts between American military commanders. Nowhere was the command system more complex than for III MAF in I Corps. By the end of 1965 General Walt commanded III MAF and his own 3d Marine Division. He also served as naval component commander, which gave him the responsibility for Navy shore-based activities, and as senior U.S. military adviser for I Corps, which gave Walt control of the largely Army advisory group with the ARVN. Yet Walt had no direct control over any GVN civilian or military organizations in the corps area, nor did he have control over American civilian activities in I Corps. On the other hand, Walt had more than enough military supervisors. His force fell under the operational control of Westmoreland at MACV, but III MAF still remained subordinate to CG FMF Pacific for administrative and logistical matters. General Krulak showed no reluctance to provide tactical guidance as well. Krulak's influence in the war's early stages was particularly significant, for he was the confidant of Admiral Sharp, technically MACV's superior. Westmoreland, however, often submitted his assessments through his own Army chain of command, through his Air Force component commander, through the JCS, and through the American Ambassador in Saigon. This system of command (or lack thereof) placed a high premium on interpersonal bargaining both with the Vietnamese and within the American military. For Walt, a bluff, blunt, impatient, and highly decorated veteran of World War II and Korea, the negotiations with Krulak, Westmoreland, and the ARVN proved time-consuming. None of his successors found the job any easier, even when the personalities changed.[8]

In addition to MACV and III MAF differences over the importance of offensive operations against the Communist regulars, the Marine deployment in I Corps strained relations with MACV. Not only did Westmoreland resent Krulak's pressure on Walt to emphasize pacification, he also disliked the Sharp–Krulak policy of waging a separate CINCPAC war from the sea. Besides his responsibility for ROLLING THUNDER, Admiral Sharp also controlled the Navy's blockade to interdict Communist maritime supply efforts. As part of this campaign— Operation MARKET TIME—Sharp deployed the 7th Fleet amphibious ships with the embarked Marine Special Landing Force (usually a battalion landing team and helicopter squadron) to conduct raids inside Vietnam. Although these raids were coordinated with MACV, they irritated Westmoreland, who saw them as a command aberration. In fact, the SLF concept had other than tactical purposes: It allowed battalions to leave Vietnam for retraining and refitting and kept Navy–Marine amphibious training alive.[9]

Another source of interservice difficulty proved to be Marine air operations. By the autumn of 1965 the 1st MAW, commanded by Brigadier General Keith B. McCutcheon, controlled two helicopter groups and two fighter-attack groups. Already aware of Air Force uneasiness about having no direct control of Marine fixed-wing aircraft, Krulak insisted on a rapid buildup and integration of Marine air operations in the III MAF pacification campaign. His main accomplishment—the creation of a base at Chu Lai—required a decision by Secretary of Defense Robert S. McNamara and engineering miracles. The decision to create a Marine enclave at Chu Lai, in fact, followed the decision to build an air base there. Krulak's plan to develop Chu Lai stemmed primarily from the need for close air support in southern I Corps and northern II Corps. Instead of waiting for a concrete strip, III MAF used an expeditionary Short Airfield for Tactical Support (SATS) constructed of steel matting and arresting equipment built upon a base of laterite over Chu Lai's shifting sands. The 1st MAW and Navy engineers produced an

8,000-foot strip close to Krulak's deadline, but only half the strip could be used at any one time, as the laterite base proved as shifting as the sands. Much to MACV's amazement, however, the Chu Lai strip worked. It also gave III MAF a rationale for extending its operations in Quang Tin and Quang Ngai provinces and for arguing that one of its chief goals should be the linkage—through pacification—of the Da Nang and Chu Lai TAORs.[10]

Like the rest of the American forces committed to Vietnam, III MAF faced the predictable difficulties of establishing a base system in a primitive, faraway country and adjusting to a long war. The Corps's amphibious mission and deployment policies also produced special problems that dominated much of III MAF decision-making in 1965–1966. HQMC approved of limiting individual tours in Vietnam to thirteen months (the same policy that had applied to service on Okinawa) and suspended the rotation of entire infantry battalions by the end of 1965, chosing instead to replace Marines individually. This policy required that the units deployed in 1965 be "mix-mastered" in order to stagger individual departures and preserve some sort of organizational integrity. However justified by events, the policy caused some unit instability in the war's early stages.

Logistical reorganization caused an even more serious problem. Although FMF Pacific could draw upon Navy–Marine facilities in Japan, Okinawa, and the Philippines, the shift to a war footing in the Pacific required a drastic change in the intensity of the logistical effort. The use of stockpiled contingency supplies could and did carry the war effort in its early stages, but III MAF was unprepared organizationally for a long stay ashore. (For example, as late as 1967 III MAF had only one computer to manage logistical operations.) After much experimentation and frustration, III MAF in March 1966 created a Force Logistics Command, with subordinate groups and units, by merging the logistical units of its divisions and wing with elements of FMF Pacific's Force Service Regiment. III MAF tried to keep its logistical base austere and actually reduced its percentage of support personnel to 40 percent, less than the World War II–Korean War average of 43 percent. Nevertheless, III MAF depended upon both Navy and Army assistance. For example, III MAF eventually included five Marine engineering battalions but required the support of eight Navy engineering battalions. With the assistance of the Naval Support Activity in I Corps, the Marines managed to jury-rig a logistical system that gave them considerable independence from MACV and compared favorably with the Army effort, which for three years was a model of generous chaos.[11]

The organizational turmoil of its Vietnam buildup notwithstanding,

III MAF in its first full year of combat developed all of the important pacification tactics it would employ throughout the rest of the war. The most telling weakness in III MAF's struggle for control of the rural population in I Corps was obvious to realistic observers: The GVN did not match the Marines in money, enthusiasm, and organization, so much of the pacification effort ultimately failed because of lack of continuity and rural security. For almost two years the pacification strategy absorbed III MAF's attention, and the concepts and techniques the Marines extemporized convinced them they had found a more appropriate approach to victory than MACV's big-unit battles. In geographic terms III MAF's pacification vision ran along the thin belt of coastal population from the Phu Bai enclave to the Da Nang TAOR into the great river basin that extended from An Hoa to Hoi An and then south along the coast to Tam Ky and the Chu Lai enclave. Effective control of this three-province area would have placed more than half I Corps's Vietnamese population under Marine supervision, destroying a major VC political base.

Under the direction of General Krulak and General Walt, III MAF developed its pacification campaign with considerable ingenuity in 1965. Because base security depended on continuous patrolling, the Marines had to move out among the villages, if only to look for VC raiders and to gather intelligence. The saturation patrolling in the TAORs opened the way for civic action or direct welfare work with the villagers. (Early in the war, "winning hearts and minds" gave civic action a high-minded tone, but the troops changed the slogan: "Grab them by the balls, and their hearts and minds will follow.") In addition to distributing American relief supplies, the most effective tactic (at least in turning out a crowd) was the MEDCAP patrol, which offered immediate medical assistance to the Vietnamese villagers. For Marine civic action planners, band-aids and soap assumed more importance than bullets. In areas actually occupied by Marine units the possibilities for civic action were endless: schools built, orphanages funded, wells dug, markets opened, hospitals supplied, food distributed. To supplement the supplies provided by American civil agencies and GVN sources, the Marines dug into their own pockets and then organized a special civic action fund supported by Marine Reservists and administered by CARE. Village visitations assumed a more concerted political effort with the development of COUNTY FAIR operations in early 1966. These operations, conducted by mixed Marine–Vietnamese task forces, combined civic action with population control techniques designed to eliminate the VC political cadre and village guerrillas.

Another civic action program benefited the villagers and confounded the VC. At the request of village councils south of Da Nang, the 9th Marines provided immediate security during the rice harvest of August 1965. This operation—named GOLDEN FLEECE—also became a standard technique for III MAF. In fact, III MAF civic action operations had become so aggressive that General Walt had sufficient power to create a Joint Coordinating Council of American and Vietnamese for pacification operations in I Corps. The American pacification effort in I Corps in 1965–1966 enjoyed a unity absent from the rest of Vietnam and gave III MAF the impression that it was making real progress.[12]

As III MAF pacification efforts spread into the countryside from the towns along Route 1, the Marines became increasingly aware that all their humanitarianism would have little lasting effect unless the villagers received permanent protection and honest government assistance. The thousands of patrols per month, the COUNTY FAIRS, and the GOLDEN FLEECE operations were transitory victories without effective hamlet-level security. In fact, civic action might be politically unproductive, for it raised the peasants' expectations and demanded pro-GVN commitments that might subject the peasants to VC counteraction, including terrorism. It also turned the villages into battlegrounds and the villagers into unintentional targets. As one observer noted of Marine operations among the peasantry: "They underestimate both our savagery and our compassion." [13]

Because the ARVN and other representatives of the GVN proved inconstant in providing rural security, the Marines developed their own answer: the Combined Action Program (CAP). First initiated in the Phu Bai enclave in 1965, the CAP spread to the Da Nang TAOR—especially its southern area—where rural control was of decisive importance to both the GVN and the VC. In principle, the CAP was simplicity itself. In execution, it demanded political and tactical sophistication. The program required that a specially selected and trained Marine rifle squad join a Popular Forces (militia) platoon and work in concert to provide continuous security from the VC. The Marines would live and work among the people and inspire the PF to conduct nighttime patrols and ambushes. Although theoretically coequal, the Marine squad leader tended to dominate the PF platoon commander; the Marine NCO had greater access to civic action assistance and military support. Again, in theory, the Marine element of the CAP platoon would eventually surrender its duties to some all-Vietnamese security force.[14]

The early successes of III MAF's pacification program—particularly COUNTY FAIR and the Combined Action Program—kept the issue of Marine strategy alive into 1966. Although it recognized the local effectiveness of Marine pacification, MACV thought the Marine approach too limited and too slow. III MAF, so MACV reasoned, controlled only 2 percent of the terrain and 13 percent of the population in I Corps; more important, ARVN and GVN "revolutionary development" and security units would not or could not consolidate Marine gains in the villages. MACV preferred battalion or larger unit operations against main force VC units along the coast of Quang Tin and Quang Ngai provinces or assaults on VC bases deep into the river valleys of Quang Nam province south of Da Nang.[15]

III MAF, on the other hand, stressed the war against the VC cadre and village guerrillas (estimated at 18,000 in 1966) rather than organized VC main force units (estimated at 11,700) in their mountainous base areas. Faced with occasional attacks upon support installations, which sent MACV into convulsions of concern, III MAF tried to integrate its base security and opportunistic offensive strategy into a coherent pattern of pacification. Aware that MACV either did not fully understand the war in I Corps or did not believe the Marines had the time or talent for a pacification campaign, III MAF insisted that pacification operations by small patrols killed almost as many VC as did larger operations and paid more significant dividends by destroying the Communists' access to manpower, food, and information. (In 1965 alone FMF Pacific estimated that the Marines had killed 3,600 VC in large operations and 2,500 in patrols and ambushes.) At the heart of debate about III MAF's strategy were two unanswerable questions: How much time did the Marines have, and how did III MAF's programs increase the effectiveness of the GVN?[16]

For all its commitment to pacification, III MAF did not avoid large-unit operations when such operations either promised special success or rescued hard-pressed ARVN units and U.S. Army Special Forces camps beyond the Marine TAORs. Whenever possible, III MAF attempted to follow its own "search-and-destroy" missions with pacification operations, but because the pacification follow-up usually depended upon GVN agencies, this effort was normally unsuccessful. Responding to the VC–NVA offensive across the Central Highlands in 1965, the first large-scale Marine operations occurred south of the Chu Lai enclave. In August–September 1965 a four-battalion force controlled by the 7th Marines mounted Operations STARLITE and PIRANHA against the 1st VC Regiment, an attack that eventually cost the Communists at least 700 dead with Marine killed-in-action less than 200. Fought near the coast, the first battles proved that vertical envelopment, naval gunfire, close air support, and aggressive infantry tactics more than matched VC tenacity. Despite the monsoons of late 1965, additional battalion operations outside the Da Nang and Phu Bai TAORs reinforced III MAF confidence that it could stop VC main force penetrations into its pacification areas. The most ominous aspect of the thrusts beyond the TAORs was the Marines' first contact with regular NVA units, who proved hard fighters willing to contest helicopter landing zones even in the face of devastating Marine close air support. Reacting to MACV's insistence on more big-unit operations and his own accelerated pacification program, General Walt made a critical change: He established "task force" head-quarters commanded by a brigadier general for operations beyond the Marine TAORs. Walt thought the latter reform would increase Marine–ARVN cooperation, which showed much room for improvement.[17]

As III MAF tried to orchestrate its task force operations against the VC main force units with the pacification programs within its own TAORs, the Johnson administration groped for some policy that prom-ised eventual victory, defined as the collapse of the NLF and the end of NVA infiltration. In a series of studies, conferences, and decisions in 1965 and 1966, the administration accepted MACV's recommendation that the commitment of ground troops should increase to between 400,000 and 500,000 by 1967. Approved by Johnson, MACV's Phase II program doubled the number of U.S. and Allied maneuver battalions as well as enlarging the ARVN. Although MACV anticipated that its field forces would be most effective against large Communist units (particularly the nine NVA regiments in the country by 1966), the American strategy did not deny the need for rural pacification. The American position on pacification was stressed in two high-level con-ferences with the GVN—now led by Nguyen Van Thieu and Nguyen Cao Ky—at Honolulu and Manila in 1966. The goal of American policy was to deny the Communists a military victory in South Vietnam while the GVN and ARVN improved their control over the rural population. Buffeted by the first antiwar demonstrations in the United States, grow-ing international concern, the scant results of ROLLING THUNDER, and the failure of its own ill-conceived peace feelers, the Johnson administra-tion still believed it could save South Vietnam by escalating the ground war. The greatest imponderables were the stability of the GVN, the willingness of the Communists to take high casualties and continue rein-forcing their own army, and the ability of the Vietnamese people and economy to bear an enlarged American force.[18]

For III MAF the increased commitment meant that it entered the post-monsoon campaigning season of 1966 with enlarged forces and re-sponsibilities, but General Krulak and General Walt saw no reason to change their emphasis from pacification to big-unit operations. Never-theless, the appearance of three NVA regiments in I Corps—plus the expanded VC strength of an estimated total of 30,000—required that

III MAF use its own fire power and mobility to assist the hard-pressed ARVN. For much of 1966 the big-unit war for III MAF occurred in Quang Tin and Quang Ngai provinces. Operating from the Chu Lai enclave, which came under the control of the 1st Marine Division in early 1966, the multibattalion Task Force Delta fought a series of on-again, off-again battles against the durable 1st VC Regiment and a companion regiment of NVA regulars from January through June. Within the Chu Lai TAOR the 1st Marine Division (normally short one of its regiments but reinforced for Task Force Delta operations from the SLF and the 3d Division) continued pacification operations along the coast.

In Thua Thien and Quang Nam provinces, the pattern of operations was much the same. While three reinforced regiments protected and pacified the Phu Bai and Da Nang enclaves and provided battalions for Task Force Delta, the 9th Marines expanded the TAOR south to Ky Lam and west toward the An Hoa basin, a high-priority pacification area because of its coal and rice production. From March until July the 9th Marines, drawing reinforcing battalions from the 3d and 1st Marines, pushed into An Hoa in the face of skilled, stubborn resistance by the VC *Doc Lap* battalion, which died and reappeared more times than the Marines cared to count. Although the GVN once again failed to provide adequate troops and rural cadres to reinforce Marine pacification efforts, III MAF had entered the An Hoa basin to stay, and the area quickly developed as the key battlefield of Quang Nam province, as the VC also recognized the region's importance.[19]

The expansion of the war in Quang Nam province placed new burdens upon the Marine pacification program. For one thing, the expansion of the III MAF TAOR required additional GVN support. Yet the GVN's ability to provide cadres and militiamen remained unequal to the challenge despite a rapid expansion of the Combined Action Program. (The number of CAP platoons increased from twelve to fifty-seven in 1966.) Political instability also plagued GVN operations in I Corps. From March until June the ARVN and some civilian groups split into warring factions and forced III MAF, particularly General Walt and his staff, to play negotiator when it preferred to wage war. Sparked by General Thi's removal by Saigon's ruling junta of generals, the "Struggle Movement" plunged both Hue and Da Nang into political conspiracy and street battles, which paralyzed the GVN effort throughout I Corps. The central government gradually regained control of its own troops in I Corps—to a large degree because General Walt threatened to use his own forces against both the rebels and pro-GVN forces—but the political turmoil damaged the ambitious pacification program and allowed the VC to regain control of some of the villages it had lost in 1965. An election in September for members of a new South Vietnamese assembly, whose task would be to write a new constitution, came and went without serious VC interruption; 80 percent of the potential electorate went to the polls, which heartened pacification planners. On the other hand, a more sophisticated system of evaluating hamlet security showed that much of the Marine civic action program had produced no lasting GVN control.[20]

The pacification war in 1966–1967 showed some signs of health, largely American-inspired. Reflecting greater coordination and emphasis on pacification at MACV—which now controlled all American programs through the new office of Civil Operations and Revolutionary Development Support (CORDS)—the flow of technical assistance and relief supplies improved. Most of the quantitative indicators of progress, which had become a fetish from III MAF all the way back to the Pentagon, showed bullish signs. Yet the persistence of VC terrorism (largely focused on the PFs and GVN cadres) and the low level of VC defections suggested that the Communists were far from defeated. Even more ominous, the increased violence of the big-unit war, particularly in the An Hoa basin, was turning the peasants of I Corps into a society of displaced persons. Of a population of 2.5 million, at least 300,000 Vietnamese in I Corps had become refugees in 1966, and this refugee population—living in squalid camps—absorbed much of the civic action assistance meant for the villagers still in the countryside.

III MAF might receive some comfort from the several thousand true defectors it processed (the "Hoi Chanh") and the few hundred it returned to action as friendly intelligence scouts, but it could not compensate for either GVN incompetence or the unfortunate cruelties its firepower visited upon the peasantry. General Walt also learned to his dismay in 1966 that many of his own troops had come to despise and distrust the Vietnamese people they had come to save, because of both their VC-inspired treachery and their unfamiliar living habits. The rise of unprovoked civilian casualties—largely from driving accidents and off-duty violence—persuaded Walt to introduce a "Personal Response" program for incoming Marines. This program, carried on with differing degrees of effectiveness, stressed the importance of showing understanding and compassion in dealing with the Vietnamese. Such conduct was often easier to understand in the classroom than in the field, but certainly III MAF did not condone criminal acts against the Vietnamese.[21]

The basic threat to pacification, however, became the regulars of the North Vietnamese army. In 1966 the Marines received their first unwelcome experiences with the hardened NVA, who were armed with such Russian weapons as the AK-47 assault rifle, heavy machine guns and mortars, and the effective B-40 rocket-propelled grenade (RPG). Task Force Delta had met an NVA regiment in Operation UTAH in Quang Ngai province in March and, although it had punished the NVA, Marine casualties (although not deaths) had come close to Communist losses. An NVA force had then overrun a Special Forces camp in the A Shau valley on the Laotian border. As in UTAH, the Marines lost aircraft to ground fire during the relief operations. In July the intelligence evidence of a major NVA effort in I Corps mounted as ARVN units and Marine recon patrols identified elements of a NVA division that had crossed the DMZ to challenge the ARVN 1st Division, the sole defender of Quang Tri province. The headquarters of Task Force Delta shifted north to Dong Ha and directed six Marine and five ARVN battalions against the North Vietnamese in Operation HASTINGS, a savage conventional battle that sent the NVA reeling with 1,000 dead and produced the heaviest Marine casualties of the war. Although HASTINGS officially ended on August 3, Task Force Delta and the SLF remained in Quang Tri into September to conduct Operations PRAIRIE and DECKHOUSE IV, which netted another 1,000 NVA. Again Marine casualties, despite profligate air and supporting arms fire, climbed to more than a thousand, primarily wounded.[22]

The NVA penetration across the DMZ sent strategic reverberations throughout III MAF and produced new concern at MACV with the pattern of operations in I Corps. Westmoreland was especially insistent that the Marines protect the Special Forces camps along the border, especially the one at Lang Vei. A Marine battalion heloed into a landing site at an obscure crossroads along Route 9 named Khe Sanh but found few NVA. With the main NVA threat centered along the DMZ in an area bounded by Cam Lo, Dong Ha, and Gio Linh, General Walt shifted the 3d Division headquarters, two full regiments, and most of a helo MAG to Quang Tri and Thua Thien provinces. With four reinforced regiments under its control, the 1st Marine Division headquarters moved to Da Nang and assumed responsibility for Marine operations in Quang Nam, Quang Tin, and Quang Ngai provinces. The change put particular stress upon the 9th Marines, which continued the taxing pacification of the An Hoa basin. Already stretched thin by operations inside and outside of its Chu Lai and Phu Bai–Da Nang TAORs, III MAF did not need another "front" or another type of Vietnam War, but it found both along the DMZ by the end of 1966.

As the first phase of the DMZ war dwindled with the coming of the winter monsoon, III MAF could clearly see the immensity of its commitment. In nearly a year and a half of fighting, it had killed an estimated total of 11,000 NVA and VC and had lost 1,700 dead and more than 9,000 wounded (80 percent of Marine wounded eventually returned to duty in Vietnam). III MAF now numbered nearly 70,000 Marines, who had assumed the defense of nearly 1,800 square miles and a million Vietnamese. The Marines had mounted 150 battalion or larger operations and more than 200,000 small-unit patrols, ambushes, and sweeps. Despite its early promise, the Marine pacification war had stalled because of GVN ineptness, MACV's insistence on big-unit operations, and the threat of NVA invasion from Laos and across the DMZ. The "light at the end of the tunnel" glowed only dimly.[23]

2

For the Marine Corps the first two years of war in Vietnam created severe expansion problems, but the Corps's approach to the war was "can do," and the Corps by and large did. Nevertheless, the expansion and readjustment programs exposed difficulties that would eventually tax Corps relationships with the Department of Defense and Congress. Uncertainties that characterized the entire American war effort fueled the Corps's emerging problems: How long would the war last, and to what degree could the armed forces fight a serious conflict and still retain programs and policies more appropriate to normal Cold War contingency planning? Like the rest of the government, the Marine Corps fought the war on a year-by-year basis. In terms of supplies and equipment, war and expansion created demands that could not be immediately met, and shortages and inefficiencies in deliveries and maintenance occurred. But by and large the Corps met the logistical challenge. The personnel problems, largely ones of quality rather than sheer numbers, proved more intractable. With national policy dictating a thirteen-month tour for Marines in the war zone—but with no relaxation of other commitments—the effectiveness of both III MAF and the rest of the FMF quickly became grave issues.

From the complex plans for ground force enlargement, the Marine Corps eventually received the authority to execute its plans for manpower expansion in order to support Westmoreland's Phase I and Phase II strategy. By January 1966 McNamara had approved plans to increase the Corps by 85,200 to a temporary wartime level of 278,000 by mid-1967. The increase allowed both an expansion of the training base and manpower "pipeline" serving III MAF and the activation of the 5th Marine Division at Camp Pendleton, as well as additional aviation units. With the 1st Division on its way to Vietnam, the 5th Division assumed reinforcing and strategic reserve missions that placed its units on Okinawa as the reconstituted 9th MAB and established others in Hawaii and California. (In fact, the division's first infantry regiment—the 26th

Marines—left for the western Pacific in June 1966.) For awhile in 1965 and 1966 it appeared that the Marine Corps Reserve—primarily the 4th Marine Division and the 4th Marine Aircraft Wing—would enter active service. Headquarters favored mobilization. Concerned about the one-time use of the Marine Reserve and the lack of a strategic reserve for Atlantic contingencies, McNamara disapproved the request, a decision supported by Johnson, who feared the political consequences of a Reserve mobilization. The lack of a Reserve call-up deprived the regular Corps of badly needed infantry. It also exempted officers and NCOs with critical technical skills from active duty except by individual request.

Wartime expansion forced the Corps to increase its officer corps by more than a third (from roughly 17,000 to 25,000), and this expansion proved difficult for many reasons. Headquarters temporarily suspended resignations and voluntary retirements for regulars, but it could not legally hold either career or Reserve officers on active duty after the emergency buildup of 1965–1966. Forced to double new officer accessions to nearly 5,000 a year, it expanded its college recruiting (assisted by increased draft calls) but could not meet its needs, especially in technical skills, without commissioning thousands of warrant officers and NCOs. By 1967 the Corps had more than 5,000 temporary officers, which meant that it had stripped its NCO ranks of many of its best leaders. While Headquarters shortened training for new officers in the combat arms, it found its requirements for technical specialists far outstripping its manpower pool, particularly if it allowed officers two years between Vietnam tours. As a result, some specialists did not receive two years between tours. And service in hard-pressed FMF Atlantic hardly qualified as stateside duty. Officer retention rates fell in consequence, and so did morale.[24]

Wartime expansion and service fell hardest upon Marine aviators, particularly helicopter pilots. Despite some fancy bookkeeping and intense DOD pressure to hide its problems, the pilot shortage was real. The Deputy Chief of Staff (Air) reported with scant humor: "Surely everyone knows that there is no pilot shortage; it is merely that requirements exceed resources." [25] Except by stripping pilots from nonflying billets (and thus endangering career advancement as well as air-ground training) and reducing both pilot training and stateside tours, the problem proved insoluble. Essentially, Headquarters needed to expand its peacetime pilot numbers from 4,000 to more than 5,000 in order to maintain an equitable Vietnam rotation policy and adequate skill. Neither DOD nor the Navy cooperated except under heavy pressure from HQMC and Congress. Handicapped by too-low training quotas,

Headquarters watched pilot losses from combat and the end of obligated service grow. Even by sending aviators to the Air Force for fixed-wing training and to the Army for helicopter training, Marine aviation still fought the war with 1,000 fewer pilots than it needed. Although Marine pilots flew in Vietnam with exceptional courage, they became a pocket of cynicism and frustration within the officer corps, thus once again opening the classic ground–air split.[26]

The difficulties in the enlisted ranks became almost as worrisome as officer programs. In terms of sheer numbers, the Corps met its expansion goals for 1967, but not without shortages of enlisted technicians and experienced troop leaders. The Corps continued to depend basically upon volunteer enlistments, which still proved reliable through 1966 even if draft-influenced. But to meet its goals, the Corps had to take 19,000 draftees in 1967, thus tarnishing its elite image. Reflecting Johnson's and McNamara's peculiar notion that wartime military service provided opportunities for social uplift, the Marine Corps had to accept 18 percent of its new recruits from Mental Group IV, a classification that meant not only subaverage intelligence but also higher rates of disciplinary and training problems. To meet its Project 100,000 goals the Corps had to reject more promising recruits. The personnel picture in the NCO ranks and among specialists proved even grimmer. At a time when experienced small-unit leadership became essential, expansion reduced the average length of service of sergeants from 10.9 to 5.7 years and the average length of service for corporals from 5 to 2.7 years. In critical-skill MOSs the personnel problems became even more difficult. Only a year into the war, Headquarters discovered that 90 of 210 MOSs did not have adequate numbers to support its Vietnam rotation policies. Although drastic retraining and reassignments cut the number of "deprived" MOSs in half by 1967, the Corps could not avoid sending NCOs with scarce skills (particularly in logistical and aviation billets) back to Vietnam with less than two years outside III MAF. Even with accelerated promotions and extensions and leave bonuses, the retention of NCOs fell. As with the officer corps, the war brought a critical weakening of the NCOs ranks.[27]

In personnel terms, the Vietnam war fell with devastating impact upon all Marine forces outside III MAF, particularly upon the air and ground units of FMF Atlantic. Although it lost none of its ninety-two contingency missions, FMF Atlantic by 1967 could field only one "austere" amphibious brigade. The 2d Marine Division could provide only three combat-ready infantry battalions even by cutting the infantry companies from four to three. The 2d MAW was in worse condition. Only four of its eleven fixed-wing squadrons were deployable, and only one of its six helo squadrons could meet combat readiness standards. Since II MAF had become little more than a haven for Marines on their way to and from Vietnam, the annual turnover in the 2d Marine Division soared to 123 percent. The same rate in the 2d MAW climbed to 92 percent. Like a cancer, the effects of the war spread throughout the Corps and weakened its cohesiveness.[28]

In a material sense the war in Vietnam offered little of lasting value to the Corps and created periodic crises that strained Corps managerial effectiveness and offered DOD and other military critics new opportunities to attack Marine force structure and missions. More seriously, the war began to tarnish Corps relations with Congress. As it did with personnel problems, Headquarters tried to be forthright in identifying its difficulties and requirements, but it found DOD particularly sensitive to Johnson's and McNamara's growing thirst for only good news. In addition, the growing experience of III MAF created all sorts of new requirements for weapons and equipment that were difficult to reconcile with the Corps's long-range plans for modernization, which were keyed to the amphibious force in readiness mission. In financial terms, the Johnson administration acted as if the war would end any moment, while at the same time DOD personnel and procurement policies seemed to assume it would last several years. During the initial buildup the Corps requested and received almost $2 billion in FY 1966, but then it actually reduced its requests for FY 1967. The Corps had no trouble obtaining money to fight the war—especially to satisfy emergency needs—but saw its modernization programs in aviation, transport, and communications progressively deferred. Early in the war the Corps thought that increased defense spending might bring some lasting benefit, particularly in the amount and quality of Navy gunfire support and amphibious shipping, but in 1967 the indications grew that the Navy would, in fact, cut its shipbuilding and retention plans.[29]

The war in Vietnam itself caused enough logistical difficulties to tax the Corps, whose supply system had not yet adjusted to many new management reforms. The Corps was not prepared for extended combat in a tropical country. Despite heroic efforts to meet III MAF's escalating requirements, Marine logistical problems also multiplied. The Corps's dependence on the same suppliers who served the Army did not help. By 1967 Headquarters had satisfied as best it could demands for tropical-weight utility uniforms, shotguns, tropical boots, barbed wire, sandbags, generators, and spare parts for virtually every kind of heavy ordnance and equipment. Field wear and the effects of sand and water placed discouraging demands upon both III MAF maintenance facilities and Corps procurement efforts. Even by dipping into contingency supplies and starving other FMF units, as well as the Reserve, Headquarters had great difficulty in keeping III MAF close to its material requirements, which soared as the war along the DMZ intensified.

In many ways the question of a new rifle dramatized the sort of problems, both operational and political, the Corps faced. Armed with the M-14 rifle when it arrived in Vietnam, the Corps soon learned that MACV wanted it to switch to the Armalite-manufactured M-16 rifle, which fired a 5.56-mm. cartridge. The new rifle had certain advantages: higher velocity and rates of fire that were devastating at close ranges, lighter ammunition that allowed infantrymen to carry twice as many bullets, and logistical commonality when all American and ARVN forces adopted the weapon. But Marines in Vietnam in 1967 had not trained with the rifle, and they preferred the long-range power and accuracy of the M-14. The M-16, moreover, came with ammunition that was too powerful for its extraction system; unless the weapon was constantly cleaned, it had a tendency to jam and become a plastic club. Over Marine objections to the M-16 (which eventually produced changes in the ammunition and the manufacturing of the chamber), MACV insisted that the Marines trade in their M-14s in order to encourage the M-16's adoption by the ARVN. The Marine Corps, which was testing a family of weapons with much the same characteristics as the M-16, had to adopt the M-16 for the entire FMF in order to please McNamara, who went to President Johnson for support for his M-16 policy.[30]

The M-16 issue paled beside the arguments over the effectiveness of Marine aviation. Unsympathetic to Marine requests for more pilot-training billets, DOD in June 1967 recommended that Marine aviation reduce its fixed-wing inventory by sixty-seven aircraft immediately and consider further cuts in its fighter-attack forces. The result of systems analysis studies, the DOD recommendation questioned whether III MAF needed twice as much close air support as the Air Force provided the Army in Vietnam. It also assumed that either the Air Force or the Navy could provide the Corps with reconnaissance, electronic warfare, air superiority, and long-range interdiction air support. Marine planners, who had already programmed the fixed-wing inventory to drop from 639 aircraft to 435 in the 1970s as more sophisticated fighter-attack planes became available, were stunned by the recommendation. Understandably skeptical about the dependability of either Air Force or Navy air support in Vietnam and in any future conflict, Headquarters insisted that Marine close air support missions were not excessive, given the character of Marine operations in Vietnam and the Corps's tradeoffs in air rather than heavy self-propelled artillery. Besides, nearly half of all Marine fixed-wing sorties in Vietnam in 1967 were not being flown as close air support for Marines. Headquarters thus regarded DOD's proposal as gratuitous.[31]

DOD and Army criticism of Marine helicopter operations did nothing to promote interservice harmony in Vietnam or Washington. Intoxicated by the early success of Army aviation battalions in Vietnam, especially in the operations of the 1st Cavalry Division (Airmobile) in late 1965, MACV criticized III MAF helicopter operations for their conservatism and lack of troop and equipment lift. Already committed to the adoption of the CH-46 and CH-53, which had been designed for amphibious operations, Headquarters could hardly fill the skies with the smaller, agile, and cheaper Bell UH-1 "Huey," which was the Army's workhorse. In fact, Marine planners worried that the Corps's few Hueys were flying too many fire-support missions as gunships rather than providing observation and utility support for III MAF. The shortage of helicopter pilots and crew members hardly improved the situation. Nevertheless, Marine Corps plans to make the CH-46 and CH-53 the standard helos for its Vietnam helicopter squadrons would have increased III MAF's lift capabilities from a low 130 tons to a high 450 tons by the end of 1967. Unfortunately, some flaws in the CH-46's performance limited its utility in 1966 and 1967. Deployed to Vietnam with inadequate operational testing, the CH-46 developed engine problems attributable to an excessive diet of sand. Just as Marine maintenance experts and Vertol engineers brought the engine problems in hand, the helicopter developed structural problems with its tail section that produced an alarming number of fatal crashes in Vietnam and the United States in 1967. Emergency grounding and rebuilding restored the CH-46 for III MAF use, but not before doubt had spread about the Corps's judgment.[32]

With all its difficulties in fighting the Vietnam War and assuring its own future, the Marine Corps did not need a leadership crisis as well, but it developed one in 1967. The basic difficulty was Lyndon Johnson's compulsive need to muster support for the war and to reward personal loyalty. Already dismayed by domestic criticism, the President had turned to the senior leadership of the armed forces to bolster his position that the war was worth fighting. The Marine Corps had done its best to sell the war. Its most enthusiastic public spokesman had been Lewis W. Walt, promoted to lieutenant general and brought back to the United States in 1967 for Congressional and public appearances. A tough rustic after Johnson's own heart, Walt had won the President's confidence as well as that of General Westmoreland. On the other hand, the heir apparent within the Marine Corps itself was Lieutenant General

Krulak, whose combat career had been less heroic than Walt's but whose contributions to Corps innovation had been more impressive. Krulak had the disadvantage of being a Kennedy man, in the White House's view, and too controversial for the Department of Defense. The result of the infighting was the appointment of another candidate as Commandant, Lieutenant General Leonard F. Chapman, Jr., the chief of staff. A perfectionist artilleryman with an exemplary record as both a commander and a staff officer since World War II, Chapman satisfied the President's loyalty criteria and General Greene's standards of excellence. The JCS also found Chapman more to its taste than Walt or Krulak. Agreeing to make Walt (raised to four stars) his Assistant Commandant, Chapman assumed the leadership of the Corps as it entered its most trying campaigns in both Vietnam and Washington.[33]

3

Amid monsoon rains, bombing halts, and holiday truces, III MAF faced a new Vietnam War as 1967 dawned. This phase of the war would throw the Marines against the best of the North Vietnamese army for almost two years. On the battlefield the phase ended in 1968 in an American victory, shared with the ARVN. But measured in diplomatic leverage and domestic political support, the cost of the victory in American lives and antiwar dissent in the United States convinced the Johnson administration that the nation could no longer afford the price of more military victories, no matter how decisive. In I Corps the "big" war against the NVA redirected Marine attention away from pacification, particularly in Quang Nam province, and brought large units of the U.S. Army into the region for the first time, which forced reorientations of command arrangements. The period also brought a heated dispute over the control of Marine aviation. The new war in I Corps, too, focused public attention not on III MAF's innovative, hard-learned pacification programs—which continued under great tactical stress—but on the battles along the DMZ, largely shaped by NVA initiatives and DOD–MACV responses. In a war of attrition and positional defense it neither sought nor favored, III MAF turned from a force of "ambassadors in green" protecting Vietnamese villagers to "the finest instrument ever devised for the killing of young Americans." [34]

Alarmed by the strength and persistence of the NVA's incursions across the DMZ in 1966, MACV assigned highest priority in its 1967 campaign plan to preventing any sizable Communist battlefield success in Quang Tri province. Although MACV had drafted various plans to send Army reinforcements to III MAF, the burden of the DMZ war fell upon the 3d Marine Division and the ARVN 1st Division, both periodically reinforced with other III MAF and I Corps units. From the III MAF point of view, the mission had many disadvantages, all of which were perfectly obvious to the NVA. For one thing, American policy prohibited ground and artillery strikes into the DMZ itself and limited air attacks in the same area. Sensing this policy, the NVA moved both ground divisions and heavy artillery and rockets south of the Ben Hai River (which bisected the DMZ) and set up extensive air defenses to protect them. This NVA movement dramatized another difficulty along the DMZ: logistical support for the expanded war. American aircraft could deliver some supplies to the Dong Ha airfield, itself occasionally under Communist fire, but the full supply burden of the DMZ war could be met only by bringing supplies by landing craft and LST up the Cua Viet River. Protection of the Cua Viet, an easy target for Communist interdiction, required extensive ground operations. Forced by the nonincursion policy to assume a posture of static defense and reaction, the 3d Marine Division established eight bases for artillery support, ground defense, and counterattacks. The bases became synonymous with frustration, discomfort, and casualties: Khe Sanh, The Rockpile, Ba Long, Ca Lu, Camp Carroll, Cam Lo, Cua Viet, and Gio Linh.

The defense of the DMZ produced other tactical headaches for III MAF. Reflecting McNamara's growing frustration with the war and Westmoreland's fixation with battlefield defeat in I Corps, DOD and MACV forced III MAF to assume responsibility for an ambitious barrier plan—Operation DYE MARKER—designed to block an NVA invasion by means of an exotic combination of electronic sensors, mines, barbed wire, aerial surveillance, and fixed ground bases. As III MAF predicted, DYE MARKER, which actually went into effect in 1967, did not free troops for mobile operations. It only increased the number of Allied troops exposed to NVA artillery fire and ambush-and-trap operations. Casualties increased accordingly. Already divided by their assessments of DYE MARKER, MACV and III MAF also differed on the question of the place where the NVA might flank the ARVN–Marine positions along the DMZ. Engrossed by superficial analogies with the Communists' operations against Dien Bien Phu in 1954, Westmoreland became fixated upon Khe Sanh as the place where the NVA would begin operations to drive eastward along Route 9. III MAF did not deny this possibility but argued that such an obvious move could be met with mobile counterattacks and air operations. It believed that the Communists might instead mount a deeper envelopment from the A Shau Valley, seized by the NVA in 1966 and developed into a dangerous network of bases fed from the Ho Chi Minh Trail in Laos. Such an offensive might overwhelm the thinly spread province defense forces and cut off the two northern provinces from the rest of I Corps if the Communists closed the Hai Van pass north of Da Nang.

One thing was indisputable: The Communists had turned I Corps into a critical theater. Although III MAF and GVN forces had grown in the region to almost 150,000 troops, the ratio of Allied to Communist forces had dropped to less than 4:1, the worst in Vietnam and ominous for a campaign that combined both conventional and pacification operations. Statistical evidence confirmed a feel of the war shared by all Marines: The combat was growing in intensity. From 1965 into 1967 the percentage of enemy-initiated attacks throughout Vietnam had grown in I Corps from 25 to 45 percent. In the same period the I Corps share of all enemy killed climbed from 13 to 44 percent, and its percentage of all U.S. battle deaths had grown from 20 to 57 percent. In terms of the ratio of enemy to American dead, the DMZ war brought dramatic changes. While the Marines had killed almost ten Communists for every Marine who died in the pacification war, the DMZ war closed this ratio to an unhappy 3:1. If these trends continued, the war in I Corps would pose serious problems for both the Marines and the United States.[35]

As the intensity of the war increased in 1967–1968, the role of Marine air operations assumed mounting importance. In 1967 the combat power of the 1st MAW reached a degree of effectiveness unknown in the history of Marine air operations. Ironically, the very absence of amphibious operations allowed Marine air and ground organizations, colocated in a sustained land campaign, to mature into an integrated team. To support the two ground divisions of III MAF, Marine aviation deployed more than half of its flying squadrons to Vietnam by 1967. The force, divided into five MAGs, included eleven fixed-wing squadrons and ten helicopter squadrons. The internal composition of both forces showed the 1st MAW's increased sophistication and flexibility. The three fixed-wing MAGs in 1967 included four squadrons of dual-purpose F-4s, four squadrons of A-4s, two squadrons of new all-weather A-6As, and a composite reconnaissance-electronic warfare squadron. A detachment of the wing's transport-refueler squadron completed the 1st MAW's fixed-wing component. The helicopter MAGs in 1967 had seven transport squadrons and three observation squadrons, which used their Hueys for a range of medical evacuation, resupply, transport, attack, and reconnaissance missions. While the adoption of new aircraft and helos increased Marine air capability, the 1st MAW also increased its number of sorties. In 1966, for example, the wing flew 61,457 fixed-wing sorties and 436,267 helo sorties. In 1967 the number of sorties increased 20 percent.

The pattern of III MAF air operations reflected Marine air doctrine and the command relationships developed since World War II. As a basic component of III MAF, the 1st MAW flew to support Marine ground operations within South Vietnam. In 1966 only one-quarter of its sorties served either other ground units or the Air Force's interdiction campaign into Laos and North Vietnam. Within South Vietnam on any given day in 1966–1967, Marine jets flew one-third of all missions in the entire war zone. To some degree this high level of activity reflected Marine doctrine, which assigned jets to on-station, on-call missions for battalion or larger-unit operations and kept other jets on quick-reaction ground alert ("hot-pad"). It also reflected a Marine all-weather capability not adopted by the Air Force; by 1967 the 1st MAW had deployed five Air Support Radar Teams (ASRTs), whose radars could put bombs from A-4s and A-6As on targets blanketed by rain clouds or invisible in the darkness. Even without ASRT-controls, the A-6A squadrons were so effective—especially when supported by ECM aircraft—that they drew missions against Communist positions in Laos and North Vietnam. In sum, Marine air had come of age, and III MAF ground commanders appreciated the critical role of close air support and helos in virtually all their operations.[36]

The effectiveness of Marine air operations, however, sparked controversy. At the heart of the matter were Air Force frustrations over virtually every aspect of the air war and Air Force doctrine that all air operations in a theater of war must be directed by a single commander. Although the Air Force effort escalated with the war, the control of air operations by the MACV Deputy for Air Operations/Commander Seventh Air Force did not keep pace. Denied complete authority for ROLLING THUNDER and the interdiction of the Ho Chi Minh Trail, the senior Air Force commander in Saigon, General William W. Momyer, chose to make the operational control of the 1st MAW the issue that would at least assert MACV's authority over fixed-wing operations within the area of the Vietnam land battle. To some degree, the issue turned on differing concepts of supporting ground operations. The Air Force contended that preplanned strikes were more economical than Marine Corps on-station sorties. More important, General Momyer wanted to concentrate on interdicting the Ho Chi Minh Trail, an effort that eventually enlarged his control over Air Force missions flown from Thailand and Guam. By expanding his control to include the 1st MAW, Momyer could increase the number of interdiction sorties by using more Marine air and releasing more Air Force sorties from close air support missions for the Army and ARVN. The 1st MAW would thus become responsible for all close air support missions in I Corps. Such an option looked particularly attractive since III MAF insisted that close air support was the 1st MAW's primary mission. Having lost earlier disputes on the single-theater-of-war air commander issue to CINCPAC, MACV at Momyer's urging turned upon III MAF to score at least one Air Force victory.[37]

The heavy fighting in I Corps in 1967 and early 1968 brought the single management issue to a dramatic peak in March 1968. In reality, the Air Force assumption of "mission control" of all fixed-wing sorties flown from South Vietnam did not produce any radical change for the 1st MAW, but it heightened the interservice debate over the role of Marine air, which persisted after the war. Worried that Air Force–directed strikes would determine ground operations rather than vice versa and that single management would set an unhappy precedent for future amphibious operations, III MAF and Headquarters chose to fight the issue, largely on the basis that single management in practice produced no real benefits that justified a change. III MAF protested that single management simply forced the 1st MAW to increase its staff, doubled the delay of preplanned strikes, and reduced its quick-response air attacks.

Two tactical developments created the single management crisis: the rise of Air Force strikes along the DMZ and the introduction of Army units into the battle for Quang Tri province. After Momyer convinced Westmoreland that the 1st MAW did not provide adequate support for the Army and the ARVN, Westmoreland pushed the issue all the way to Secretary of Defense Clark Clifford and President Johnson for resolution. Arguing that the Army relied primarily upon its abundant armed helicopters and that Momyer did not intend to merge the parallel Air Force–Marine air control systems, III MAF protested. Impressed by Momyer's argument that the air war in I Corps demanded single management, Johnson ruled in MACV's favor.[38]

Irritated by the continuation of single management, which was supposed to be only a temporary measure, Marine commanders challenged the system as soon as MACV created it. Arguing with Westmoreland and his successor, General Creighton W. Abrams, that Marine air could more effectively support all Allied units in I Corps if operational control was returned to it, III MAF persuaded MACV to return direction of 70 percent of Marine sorties as early as May 1968. The key change was Momyer's recognition of "Marine peculiar" air missions. In the meantime 1st MAW, with MACV's approval, flew missions in excess of Seventh Air Force programmed sorties and increased its number of "hot pads." In 1970 a revision of MACV's guidance on air operations reaffirmed the air-ground integrity of III MAF and gave the CG Seventh

Air Force only the broadest coordinating authority, a change that preserved single management in name but brought actual air operations back to pre-1968 practices. Although the Seventh Air Force might have assigned more than half of Marine sorties in 1970, the Air Force actually controlled no more than 20 percent of the actual missions flown. The Air Force kept its pale doctrinal victory, but III MAF received the best close air support ever provided Marines as it closed with the NVA in desperate battle.[39]

From the sea to Khe Sanh four NVA divisions pressed against the Marine positions along the DMZ, and much of III MAF's 1967 campaign focused on stopping NVA incursions across the border. At the center of many operations stood the low, muddy hill base of Con Thien, 14 miles from the coast and 2 miles below the DMZ. As Marine infantry battalions shuttled between Con Thien and other bases, they received heavy artillery and rocket fire and periodically met the NVA in regimental strength. On more than one occasion NVA assault forces hurled themselves against maneuvering Marine battalions and base camps, usually with disastrous results. But the Marines sometimes paid dearly, too, by American standards. (In one day the hard-luck 1st Battalion, 9th Marines lost almost 300 casualties near Con Thien.) To disrupt NVA movements, the 3d Marine Division mounted a continuing series of operations, the most notable of which was HICKORY, the first Allied incursion into the DMZ itself. Marine attacks prevented any lasting NVA advantage, but the effort for III MAF strained its resources. The tactical situation worsened when two NVA regiments appeared in the hills around Khe Sanh and had to be dislodged with hard uphill assaults in April–May 1967 by two Marine battalions and abundant air strikes. Although the 3d Division could utilize the Special Landing Force to gain some tactical surprise near the coast, its forward territorial defense mission and the ban against attacking NVA sanctuaries placed it in an unenviable position. It had to contain the NVA and construct the "McNamara Line" in the face of great logistical problems and disruptive NVA shellfire that reached all the way to Dong Ha. Recognizing the stress upon its infantry battalions along the DMZ, III MAF by the end of 1967 had shifted five of its seven infantry regiments and most of their organic battalions to 3d Division control. (Regimental headquarters normally assumed a territorial sector with infantry battalions shifting from regiment to regiment as the tactical situation dictated; organizational flexibility, however, often came at the cost of rapport between commanders.) The DMZ war also forced FMF Pacific to deploy its strategic reserve—the 9th MAB—and curtail the marginally useful operations of its two SLFs.[40]

The DMZ war in 1967 was more like World War I's Western Front than counterinsurgency. The strongpoints sprouted wire, mines, bunkers, and craters. The countryside turned into a moonscape as the NVA and Americans pounded each other. Half of all Marine casualties in the DMZ came in shell and rocket barrages, and cases of real "shell shock" began to appear at battalion aid stations. Although the gallantry and generally skilled tactics of Marine infantry took their toll among the NVA regulars, American supporting arms wrecked at least two NVA divisions. In September–December 1967 alone, tactical air dropped 21,000 tons of ordnance on the battlefield, and B-52s added 42,000 tons. American artillery—both Marine and Army howitzers and heavy self-propelled guns—fired almost 700,000 rounds, and Navy warships contributed 55,000 rounds. All the supporting fire, however, could not prevent the NVA from blowing up command bunkers, ammo dumps, fuel depots, truck convoys, supplies, and young Marines. Deprived of the necessary troops and the political will to attack the NVA across the DMZ, the 3d Marine Division endured and fought. But, as one PFC told a reporter, the "grunts" could hardly wait until 1968 to vote against Lyndon Johnson.[41]

For the thinly spread 1st Marine Division in I Corps's three southern provinces, the pacification war continued and spread against the NVA 2d Division and the persistent local VC battalions and village guerrillas. Although the Communists could not disrupt another series of elections in 1967, they rocketed the air base and logistical facilities at Da Nang, which forced the Marine battalions to patrol the "rocket belt" that extended 5,000 to 9,000 meters around Da Nang. The VC also raided Hoi An near the coast and freed nearly a thousand prisoners. To counter such dramatics, the 1st Division staged a series of operations along the Route 1 coast areas, once more using the SLF, and attacked VC bases in both the An Hoa and Nui Loc Son basins in Quang Nam and Quang Tin provinces. Such operations usually did not bring on the heavy fighting and casualties that characterized the DMZ war, but they took their toll of Marines and VC alike. For 1st Division Marines, the war created its own list of unhappy place names: "Antenna Valley," Go Noi Island, the "Arizona Territory," and the Que Son Mountains.

The population control, anti-VC war had its own deadly characteristics. Exhausted by sweeps and searches by day and patrols and ambushes at night, the Marines, even when assisted by friendly Vietnamese scouts, fell prey to snipers, mines, and booby traps, which inflicted half of all casualties in the 1st Division. The 1st Division's operations allowed the extension of GVN control, particularly in Quang Nam province, and provided new opportunities for CAP units and Revolutionary Development cadres, but the VC cadre and guerrilla units proved hardy survivors in the face of heavy losses. The best development of 1967 was simply that the 1st Division turned over all of Quang Tin and Quang Ngai provinces to the ARVN, a Korean marine brigade, and the Army's Americal Division.[42]

As probably anticipated by North Vietnamese strategists, the pressure of the Communist regulars all over I Corps forced III MAF to reduce emphasis on population control. Although American civic action improved under centralized direction, Westmoreland insisted that MACV's combat units assume the burden of the battle with the NVA and that ARVN support the GVN's new Revolutionary Development (RD) program for controlling the villages. In I Corps the change did not, however, end pacification Marine-style. Even though General Walt left Vietnam in mid-1967, his successor, Lieutenant General Robert E. Cushman, Jr., appreciated the need for pacification, if only for improved intelligence, base security, and recruit denial to the Communists. The CAP program, even in the face of intensified conventional war, grew during 1967, with the number of CAP platoons increasing from fifty-seven to seventy-nine. The odds that CAP Marines would become casualties were even greater than those for ordinary "grunts," but CAP Marines volunteered for extended Vietnam tours in greater percentages than their comrades. There were some signs of improved rural security: higher turnouts at elections, reduced terrorism, greater freedom of movement on rural roads, and improved security for GVN officials. But the refugee population had grown to half a million, and large areas of farmland had lost their inhabitants. In the territorial sense III MAF had brought more Vietnamese under its protection, but this security remained largely dependent on Marine efforts and was too tenuous for anyone's comfort.[43]

If the war in I Corps looked mildly hopeful to III MAF—though not decisive or pleasant—its course prompted a dramatic reassessment of strategy by the North Vietnamese high command. Concerned that its strategy of attrition would ruin it before American will collapsed, North Vietnam decided to attempt a dramatic politico-military victory in 1968 by hurling its own regulars and all the VC it could muster against South Vietnam's major cities, military installations, and symbolic targets like the American Embassy in Saigon. Although Hanoi's leadership knew that 1968 was an American presidential election year, its main target was not American public opinion but the morale of the GVN and ARVN and their urban supporters. Part of North Vietnamese revolutionary ideology stressed the possibility of "great risings" in people's wars; even so, the idea of urban infiltration and combat came in part from an uneasy compromise within the politburo over the relative merits of a prolonged war of terrorism and political erosion versus a war of military victory. In any event, the tactical situation in I Corps, not unlike that in the rest of South Vietnam, offered the Communists an opportunity to slip by the widely dispersed Americans and strike at the towns and cities. Having decided in the late summer of 1967 to attempt a countrywide attack in early 1968, eventually timed to coincide with the Tet holidays, the Communists began to organize and move their mixed VC/NVA forces toward their objectives. American and ARVN intelligence found signs of increased Communist activity, but the enemy's specific intentions remained unclear. In fact, MACV was most concerned about the DMZ war.

As the monsoon rains pelted the Marine combat base at Khe Sanh, American intelligence in late 1967 identified two NVA divisions closing upon the exposed and undermanned base. The 26th Marines headquarters had already outposted the critical hills north of the base, but the Khe Sanh perimeter—which encircled an airfield, supply dumps, and artillery positions—stretched beyond the capacity of its ground defenders. Although not so overwrought as President Johnson and MACV about Dien Bien Phu analogies, General Cushman and Major General Rathvon McC. Tompkins, 3d Division commander, reinforced the base. By January 1968 the 26th Marines had added an ARVN ranger battalion, a tank platoon, and five artillery batteries, in all about 6,000 men. The rain and the enemy had closed Route 9 to the base, but the Marine generals were not overly worried about resupply; the base defense force would probably require 185 tons a day, which could be air-delivered even under fire. Helicopter resupply of the hill outposts, which absorbed half of Khe Sanh's infantry, might be somewhat more difficult. As for fire support, Khe Sanh had ample help from Air Force and Marine air and Army long-range artillery positioned at Ca Lu.

From III MAF's perspective the basic question was not whether Khe Sanh could be held but whether it should be. Any attack down Route 9 could be stopped more efficiently at Ca Lu, and Tompkins suspected that a Khe Sanh attack might be only a diversion preceding another drive at Con Thien and Gio Linh. Cushman shared Tompkins's concern but, at MACV's insistence, promised to hold Khe Sanh because Westmoreland had concluded that he had a superb chance to destroy two NVA divisions and win his own psychological victory. Both he and the Marine generals were astounded to learn that Johnson so feared a defeat that he required the JCS to pledge personally that Khe Sanh would not fall. Such acts and a media thirst for dramatic news gave the battle undeserved importance.[44]

The siege of Khe Sanh (January 21–March 30, 1968) ended in an overwhelming American victory, brought about by the sturdy defense of the base and outposts by Marine infantry and massive air and artillery support. Although the NVA pounded the base with as many as a thousand shells and rockets a day, its infantry attacks on the hill posts and the perimeter itself did no lasting damage to the position. When the Americans took precautionary measures like curtailing patrols and using air drops and quick-release offloading techniques, they did so only to reduce unnecessary losses in men and transports. Despite the rain and some anti-aircraft fire, Khe Sanh did not suffer lasting supply difficulties. (Media misrepresentations notwithstanding, only four Air Force transports at Khe Sanh fell prey to enemy shells.) The most worrisome aspect of the siege became the coordination of American fire support. Using target information gathered from both ground and airborne sensors and photographs, American air pulverized NVA positions with 100,000 tons of bombs. Artillery and mortar expenditures may have gone as high as 200,000 rounds. On the ground, Marines and ARVN rangers beat back all assaults on the perimeter and outposts despite some sharp night fighting. In fact, the only small American defeat occurred when tank-supported NVA overran the Lang Vei Special Forces camp, which should have been abandoned earlier. Although the NVA attack was real enough, Khe Sanh came no closer to being a Dien Bien Phu than Iwo Jima was to a Wake Island. The relative casualties spoke volumes: 205 defenders dead and about 800 seriously wounded, as against probably 10,000 NVA killed in action.

With a breadth and ferocity unanticipated by MACV, the Communists threw some 80,000 NVA and VC regulars against the garrisons of 105 South Vietnamese cities and towns on January 29–31, 1968, in Vo Nguyen Giap's great Tet offensive. With equally unanticipated ferocity, the ARVN, although reduced by Tet furloughs, fought back. Alerted American units and other ARVN forces in the countryside came to the rescue of the beleaguered cities. In I Corps the Communist assault fell upon Quang Tri City, Hue, Phu Loc, Da Nang, Hoi An, Tam Ky, and Quang Ngai City, accompanied by rocket attacks at Phu Bai and Chu Lai. The main Communist effort was aimed at the area's two biggest cities, Da Nang and Hue. In I Corps the offensive found the Americans and ARVN in great strength (250,000 men) and decent alertness, but not deployed for heavy fighting along the coast. In addition, American command arrangements were in the process of rearrangement as MACV moved the 101st Airborne Division and the 1st Cavalry Division into Quang Tri province to enter the DMZ war. This commitment seemed to require a new corps headquarters for Quang Tri, so Westmoreland created MACV Forward (eventually XXIV Corps), with an Army general in command, for a corps that included the Army divisions and the 3d Marine Division. The new corps, however, still served as a component of III MAF, although some Marines were worried about an Army takeover of all Marine ground units. The unsettled command arrangements complicated operations, but the Marine response to Tet hinged primarily upon the fact that III MAF had only parts of two regiments to reinforce the embattled ARVN.[45]

The Communist attacks in Quang Nam province lasted about a week and failed dramatically. Two Marine infantry battalions, Marine artillery, an ARVN regiment, and an Army brigade threw the 2d NVA Division and its supporting VC battalions back into the countryside with serious losses. In a series of small melees, American and Vietnamese rear area security units eliminated the infiltrators while infantry battalions, air, and artillery stopped the main Communist units from penetrating Da Nang. Although NVA rocket fire damaged the air base and other installations, Da Nang escaped occupation. But at Hue, the ancient imperial capital, the Communists initiated I Corps's most difficult struggle.

In less than a day seven Communist battalions (supported by at least four others) seized virtually all of Hue and raised the Communist flag over the thick walls of the city's ancient Citadel. The ARVN defended its own headquarters, but the Communists held the city and its inhabitants, some 6,000 of whom died or disappeared in a subsequent orgy of terrorism. It took a month to recapture Hue. Essentially the battle for Hue evolved as a helter-skelter rush of ARVN and Marine reinforcements to the city, followed by a systematic street-by-street battle to crush the NVA defenders of the walled inner city. Marines had seen nothing like this battle since Seoul in 1950. While two Army brigades and the ARVN beat back Communist reinforcements trying to enter the city, other ARVN troops and three under-strength Marine battalions recaptured the Citadel. Because the close fighting and the fear of killing innocent civilians restricted the use of supporting arms, the Marine infantry had to root out the Communists with direct-fire weapons like 106-mm. recoilless rifles, tanks, rocket launchers, and LAAWs as well as grenades and satchel charges. The skilled NVA contested almost every building, every street. For the Marines, the battle for Hue became a wearing, horrible school of street-fighting, but the "grunts"—seized with the strange madness that only close combat produces—pressed forward against the Citadel's defenders. When the fighting finally ended, more than 5,000 NVA bodies lay among the rubble. American and ARVN casualties were hardly light, but only 142 Marines died in the battle, although media coverage suggested once again that Hue had been a slaughter pit for the Corps.[46]

Tet-related battles continued for four more months, but the Communists had suffered a stunning defeat and lost more than 80,000 precious NVA regulars and VC cadres, half in I Corps. Nonetheless, they had provoked a political crisis in the United States that changed the Vietnam War. At the urging of the JCS, Westmoreland requested 206,000 more troops in order to mount the massive counteroffensive he thought would drive the Communists from South Vietnam. Confused and shocked by the request, the Johnson administration chose instead to curb ROLLING THUNDER, halt reinforcements not required to stifle the Tet offensive, and begin truce talks with the Communists. The President himself announced his retirement from office, a decision not entirely dictated by domestic opposition to the war but certainly a free benefit to Hanoi. While the Democratic party spent 1968 in an orgy of self-destruction, the Republican party candidate for President, Richard M. Nixon, made indistinct promises to win the war and to reduce the American ground force commitment. The implications for MACV, however, particularly General Abrams, its new commander, were clear enough. The shift away from escalation required a rethinking of MACV's strategy of attrition, in execution if not in concept.[47]

For III MAF the shift in American policy did not have dramatic impact for almost a year, for the Tet offensive had left tactical problems that could not be decided in Washington or Paris. Instead the war in I Corps gave MACV a new opportunity to give the NVA a beating. With additional Army and Marine reinforcements, including the 27th Marines from Camp Pendleton and Hawaii, III MAF mounted a counteroffensive that not only threw back an NVA advance on Dong Ha in April but sent Army and Marine battalions into NVA mountain sanctuaries that had not been threatened before. As the monsoons ended, Operation PEGASUS—a joint Army–Marine offensive of massive proportions—"relieved" the relaxed garrison of Khe Sanh. Additional airmobile operations punished the dispirited NVA and destroyed base camps in the A Shau Valley and along the entire border of I Corps. While helicopter-rich Army units swept the mountains, Marine battalions pushed the NVA back into the DMZ and returned in force to the populated areas of Thua Thien and Quang Nam provinces. Assisted by the ARVN and an Army mechanized brigade, the 3d Marine Division reorganized its DMZ defenses for more mobile operations, which included the abandonment of Khe Sanh and the development of Ca Lu as a combat base that would serve as the anchor for its western flank. Taking advantage of the NVA's momentary confusion and the VC's Tet losses, MACV emphasized raids on Communist base camps and pacification operations throughout Vietnam. Both tactical options pleased III MAF, particularly because they finally brought an end to DYE MARKER. With ARVN and Army units assuming the principal burden for the defense of the DMZ, III MAF again returned to its preferred pacification operations. Although it had killed some 60,000 enemy at a cost of 4,500 Marines dead in 1968, III MAF did not complain about the changes in American operations.[48]

The start of another year of war and a new administration in Washington did not immediately bring dramatic changes for III MAF. Although the attrition of morale and skill among the Marines in Vietnam had grown, III MAF pursued its ambitious post-Tet campaign of pacification and base camp destruction. The Communists in I Corps, despite their losses, could still muster an estimated total of 63,000 combatants in-country or skulking in Laos. For the 3d Marine Division in Quang Tri province, the DMZ still needed policing, and the division used two of its regiments for limited operations designed to stop any further NVA incursions. The division commander, Major General Raymond G. Davis, a tough Medal of Honor winner in Korea, looked for more ambitious missions. In January 1969 Davis directed the 9th Marines to attack a series of NVA bases along the Laotian border. Despite the difficulties of the monsoon and an all-helo logistical effort, the 9th Marines in DEWEY CANYON I spent almost two sodden months in the mountains destroying NVA camps and killing 1,617 enemy at a cost of 121 Marine lives. For tactical sophistication, it was one of the Marines' best operations. In addition to tenacious helo flying by Marine pilots, DEWEY CANYON profited from the use of shifting artillery fire-support bases as Marine gunners in helos leapfrogged across the mountains to keep pace with the infantry sweeps.

Using similar techniques at the same time, TAYLOR COMMON, a 1st Division operation west of An Hoa, produced almost equal results. III MAF simultaneously stepped up its pacification operations, increasing its CAP units by thirteen platoons and mounting nearly six thousand patrols a month. Although the VC still proved combative in the An Hoa basin, FMF Pacific estimated that III MAF and the GVN had reasonable control over nearly 90 percent of the population in the Marines' TAORs. Then, after an extensive review of Vietnam policy by the Nixon administration, the Marines learned in June 1969 what many had anticipated: The United States would begin withdrawing units (if not individuals) from Vietnam and hand over the war, for better or worse, to the Vietnamese.[49]

4

As the American commitment to the Vietnam War waned, Headquarters assessed what damage the war had done to the Corps and found human and material wounds that would take much time and effort to heal. Essentially, the war had sucked much of the psychological and physical strength from the FMF. Acutely aware of the war's unhappy influence upon the Corps by 1969, Headquarters embraced the "Nixon Doctrine," announced in July 1969, which proclaimed an end to American ground force commitments to stop wars of national liberation. Headquarters interpreted the "Nixon Doctrine" as a national commitment to a maritime strategy of limited commitment outside of NATO, a strategy that suggested an increased need for a force in readiness like the FMF. With the United States already involved in delicate negotiations to support the People's Republic of China against Russia and protect South Korea and Japan, Headquarters thought the Pacific would remain the FMF's most likely theater for use. Yet the Corps had not yet lost its possible missions in the Caribbean and Mediterranean. Convinced that domestic political and economic pressures would determine American policy toward Vietnam, Headquarters pursued its own disengagement and rebuilding policy.[50]

Headquarters understood that the Corps faced a series of growing crises related to the Vietnam War. Overdue base construction and equipment modernization programs had been deferred; the Navy's ambitious shipbuilding program dropped in projected numbers and anticipated availability as the war and inflation ate into the defense budget. In addition, Headquarters acknowledged that the national television and newspaper networks had turned against the Corps in their rejection of the war. Although Headquarters cultivated local media outlets, it seemed doubtful that the Corps still enjoyed any special rapport with the public. In the face of governmental skepticism about its elitism, the Corps sought a postwar role much like its 1965-posture: an FMF of three division/wing teams supported by a manpower base of 243,000 men. It wanted an aviation component of 1,004 aircraft, about evenly divided between fixed-wing fighter-attack planes and helicopters. Headquarters also knew that its manpower and aircraft figures did not have DOD support. Regardless of how the budget battles developed, Headquarters had a clear idea of the sort of Corps it wanted in the 1970s: highly skilled, highly disciplined, smaller, uncivilianized, naval in character, physically fit, and traditionalist. The Corps senior officers hoped to increase Corps uniqueness, to make Marines Spartans among the Babylonians.[51]

Even while still supporting III MAF in Vietnam, the Marine Corps felt the postwar budget-cutting imposed by Nixon's DOD that, combined with inflation, put inordinate fiscal pressures upon the Corps. No one at Headquarters thought that Corps funding could produce an FMF adequate to the needs of the Nixon Doctrine, but it hedged by restructuring the FMF to provide one MAF for a high-intensity war in Europe and another for a low-intensity war in Asia. This assumption made cuts in Force Troops and Marine aviation more acceptable. The Corps's basic fiscal problem was that so much of its budget went into personnel. With Vietnam-era military pay raises and the new policy making military pay comparable with civil service pay, the Corps personnel budget dominated all other Marine Corps programs. The statistics were inexorable. Between FY 1964 and FY 1975 the Corps share of the defense budget climbed only 8 percent while the Corps contribution to military manpower climbed to 29 percent of the active duty forces. During the same period pay raises, war costs, and inflation drove up personnel costs 106 percent, operations and maintenance 51 percent, and procurement 35 percent. In order to support III MAF, the Corps had reduced the personnel and material readiness of the rest of the FMF training and support establishment to critical levels. While deactivations in aviation particularly helped preserve some semblance of readiness in the 2d and 3d MAWs, the total number of aircraft and aviation personnel fell dramatically by 1972. DOD-programmed manpower reductions relieved some fiscal pressures but did not improve real readiness, for compensatory modernization programs did not keep pace.[52]

Despite the phased reduction of III MAF after 1969, the personnel trends in the Corps spelled disaster in terms of readiness and public image. Reflecting a political decision to end the draft and still prosecute the war, DOD policies stressed quantity recruitment of marginal youths and the rapid release of Vietnam veterans in order to reduce political criticism. As Corps leaders anticipated with relative impotence, the Corps faced hard times. To maintain even a reduced III MAF, as well as rebuild part of the FMF, Headquarters had to recruit 8,000 to 10,000 new Marines a month in the early 1970s in the face of continued casualties and a reduced draft. New Marines went to Southeast Asia with a maximum of seventeen weeks' training. Those who survived were virtually guaranteed that their tours of service would be shortened, and early releases in the early 1970s ran close to 20,000 a year. In FY 1972 alone nearly 78 percent of the entire Marine Corps either joined or left the service. In the face of such turbulence, the Corps required quality recruits it did not have. In FY 1970 DOD still forced the Corps to make a quarter of its recruits marginal "New Standards" men. In less than two years (1970–1972) the percentage of Corps recruits who were not high school graduates (and thus high disciplinary risks) grew from 50 percent to 72 percent. At the same time, the retention rates for skilled officers and NCOs dropped, while a 1971 "reduction in force" action forced nearly 5,000 temporary officers to leave the Corps or revert to enlisted or warrant officer status. As recruit accessions fell to 3,700 a month and the Corps dropped back toward 200,000 men, Headquarters recognized that it would take several years to return the Corps to prewar professional standards.[53]

Part of a nation caught in political and social turmoil, the Corps faced substantial human problems in its search for postwar normality. Antiwar radicals harassed Marine recruiters, especially on college campuses. A Reserve center in Oregon was leveled by arson. California Reservists refused to have their hair cut to regulation length, and a federal judge voided their courts-martial. The main problems, however, were inside the barracks, not outside the gate. In a Corps infested with sociopathic recruits and led by too many cynical, demoralized NCOs and insensitive, apathetic officers, the signs of social disintegration grew. Although no worse than Korean war rates, unauthorized absences climbed from 270 a month in 1964 to 1,000 a month in 1972. Disciplinary action against Marines for drug use (primarily marijuana) mounted but did nothing to arrest drug use; an FMF Pacific survey of 7,000 Marines in 1971 found that one-third of them were smoking or had smoked "grass." What had been a minor problem in 1967, when the Corps separated 94 drug users, had become a legal epidemic by 1970, when the Corps separated 1,700. Between 1968 and 1970 the number of Marines investigated for drug use increased from about 3,000 to more than 7,000. Related to drug use, barracks thefts also increased. Whether drug use was a cause or a symptom of cultural alienation or service-induced or not, it spread demoralization. The FMF Pacific 1971 study found that fewer than half the command's junior enlisted men and no more than 60 percent of its officers and senior NCOs liked their work. Ominously, the generational gap (partially on different attitu ᵤₑ about the use of alcohol and drugs) between senior NCOs and young NCOs yawned.

Even more ominously, absenteeism and drug use problems paled beside the Corps's race relations difficulties. The integrated Marine Corps had experienced its share of racial tension before the waning days of the Vietnam War, but the Corps's official stance and general practices toward blacks stressed nondiscrimination. Off-duty customs and inadvertent discriminatory assignment and promotion policies, however, made the slogan "there are only green Marines" less than convincing to even the most loyal black Marines. Black officers, who stood with senior NCOs as the primary diplomats for racial harmony in the Corps, numbered only 155 in an officer corps of 23,000 in 1967. (Their number more than doubled by 1973.) The civil rights movement of the 1960s, particularly the rise of militant and sometimes violent black nationalism in urban ghettos, and the Vietnam-era manpower expansion ended Marine self-congratualtion on race relations as hostile black youths flooded into the ranks. In January 1970 32,403 of 301,675 Marines were black.[54]

In part alerted by the urban riots of 1968 and growing reports of black–white tensions in the ranks, Headquarters began to keep statistics and follow the investigations of incidents with racial overtones. The situation was particularly acute at Camp Lejeune, where the Corps sent many blacks so that they could be near their families on the Eastern seaboard. (Conversely, black officers went to California in order to avoid off-base housing discrimination.) Although the commanding general of the 2d Marine Division, beset by high personnel turnover and weak junior leadership, recognized the tension and issued guidance to his subordinates, the eleventh-hour effort did not prevent a major riot in July 1969. After a series of incidents at an enlisted club, gangs of black Marines terrorized the base, beating white Marines, one of whom died. Further violence so plagued Camp Lejeune that armed patrols and riot units became part of the base police force. Racial incidents broke out elsewhere. Within a year Marine enlisted men had fought each other in Hawaii, San Diego, and Camp Pendleton. For savagery, Vietnam won the prize, for in February 1970 a group of blacks threw a grenade into a crowded enlisted club at Da Nang. One Marine died and sixty-two were injured in the blast.

Jarred by the violence out of their complacency, the Corps senior commanders, led by General Chapman, prosecuted the violent blacks but also started programs designed to recognize legitimate black cultural symbols, strengthen interracial understanding, and eliminate discrimination in promotions, assignments, and disciplinary practices. Assisted by career black officers and NCOs as well as sympathetic black veterans and civilian leaders, the Corps human relations program made some headway despite deep-seated racial hostility in the ranks. The greatest difficulty proved to be convincing officers and NCOs that they would have to take positive action to stop interracial tension and allay the fears of black Marines that they would be victimized by "The Man."

White Marines had to be convinced that not all black Marines were potential thieves and muggers and that violence between Marines would not be tolerated. An incomplete and uneasy effort, the human relations–equal opportunity program within the Corps helped contain racial strife by 1972 and at least institutionalized Headquarters' genuine concern with black aspirations—within Corps definitions of discipline. The human relations campaign came none too soon, for the racial violence had drawn Congressional attention, including two investigations. As with its problems with deserters and drug-users, the Corps quickly learned that racial violence and discrimination damaged public confidence and endangered any real chance for postwar recovery.[55]

As the war dragged to a close, the Corps began to solve its acute human problems and move back toward prewar standards. Although it did not approve of DOD's deep manpower cuts, Headquarters recognized that a reduction in force of about 100,000 men gave the Corps an opportunity to recruit more selectively, extend training, and stabilize personnel in its FMF units. Recruit quotas dropped two-thirds, and the early-release program allowed underemployed and potentially unhappy Vietnam veterans to leave the ranks. In addition, General Chapman persuaded DOD to curb its demands that the Corps take marginal mental group recruits. Chapman also urged his subordinates to exploit DOD's permissiveness toward administrative discharges and purge unsuitable and unfit Marines quickly without disciplinary action; in about a year (1970–1971) the Corps separated about 15,000 Marines as administrative problems. Yet, despite Headquarters' campaign against its "people problems" and its effort to obtain funds for modernization and contingency supplies, the Corps's reconstruction program still fell hostage to the war and the demands of III MAF. And in Vietnam the war continued.

5

Between the summers of 1969 and 1971 III MAF left Vietnam in much the same way it entered—in increments, with caution, and stressing pacification operations in Quang Nam province. Headquarters questioned the likely success of MACV's cache-raiding strategy and the use of the ARVN in big-unit operations against the NVA, but the Marine Corps had had enough of saving Vietnam. Headquarters wanted a Marine presence in Vietnam as long as other American troops were engaged in combat, but it was more than willing to reduce III MAF in order to rebuild the 3d Marine Division and much of the 1st Marine Aircraft Wing for future Asian contingencies. Ironically, the American withdrawal from Vietnam found III MAF in some ways at the peak of its combat efficiency. Relieved of the mission of static defense of the DMZ, III MAF operations in 1969 showed new sophistication. In raids against NVA base areas, the Marines used mobile fire support bases, reconnaissance units to locate the NVA and attack them with supporting arms, and infantry battalions to maneuver the NVA into killing zones. With rebuilt CH-46s and growing numbers of CH-53s, the 1st MAW's helicopter support improved despite pilot shortages and diminishing pilot zeal. Marine helo operations added another dimension when the Bell AH-1G "Cobra," an armed helo with awesome rocket and cannon firepower, joined the 1st MAW in 1969 for escort duty. At the pacification level, the Combined Action Program reached its peak in Marine commitment (114 platoons with 1,700 Marines and Navy corpsmen) and skill. To reinforce pacification operations III MAF initiated the Combined Unit Pacification Program, which committed Marines from regular infantry battalions to joint duty with the Popular Forces and the new, growing village militias.[56]

With the departure of the 3d Marine Division in late 1969, the pattern of deployment for the remaining units of III MAF assumed the character it would retain until 1971. Essentially, III MAF surrendered its operating areas north and south of Quang Nam province to the ARVN and U.S. Army units, although it occasionally assumed responsibility for areas in southern Thua Thien and northern Quang Tin provinces. Reflecting the relative contributions of each serivce to I Corps, the Army's XXIV Corps became III MAF's superior headquarters. Marines turned over their installations to American soldiers or the ARVN and moved their reduced ground and air units to the Da Nang area and the combat bases that circled the city and stretched into the dark and bloody ground of the An Hoa basin. The difficulty was that the Communists showed few signs of real defeat. Both the NVA and the VC had suffered enormous losses in 1968–1969, but insurgent strength in I Corps held steady at approximately 50,000, with 15,000 in Quang Nam province alone. The Communists had simply shifted away from big-unit offensives to more limited sapper and rocket attacks on American installations and conventional guerrilla-terrorist operations against the ARVN and Vietnamese villagers. In the meantime, the regular NVA divisions fell back to Laos and north of the DMZ. Yet within northern South Vietnam, some indicators suggested success. More villages enjoyed relative security, and rural transportation improved. In Quang Nam province, however, the statistical indicators hid fundamental social instability. Although the GVN forces and the Marines could claim control of all the province's people, nearly half of the Vietnamese in the province (900,000) lived around Da Nang, and the vast majority of these new urbanites were refugees. In the depopulated countryside the balance still lay between the Communists and the GVN.

The "grunts" of the 1st Marine Division could hardly tell that the war had changed as they stumbled into booby traps and traded shots with the NVA in the hills around the An Hoa basin. Yet it had. The number of battalion-size operations declined, and both Communist and Marine casualties fell by half in 1969. For offensive operations against Communist regulars, III MAF preferred to use small recon teams (generically called STINGRAY) backed by quick-reaction forces built around infantry platoons and armed and transport helos. Reflecting increased caution and restraint, the number of Marine artillery and close air strikes in-country declined, and III MAF allowed most of its tanks and amtracs to redeploy. Operations in 1969 also brought an end to SLF forays into Vietnam's coastal areas. After nine landings of minimal success, the SLF did not reappear inside Vietnam, although the Okinawa-based I MAF kept combined helo-infantry teams at sea. With the significant exception of periodic hard fighting with NVA regulars and sapper-raiders in the An Hoa basin, the Marines in Vietnam sought no wider war and edged back toward Da Nang.[57]

Given the mind-set of the Vietnam era, it was fortunate that statistical evidence supported the Marines' disposition to stress pacification and small-unit patrolling. The statistics on both STINGRAY patrols and CAP operations suggested that both the NVA and the VC lost proportionately more troops to Marine small-unit operations than battalion-size sweeps. While the losses in small units might occasionally be dramatic, their successes were even more dramatic. In the heavy fighting of 1968, for example, CAP Marines (only 1.5 percent of III MAF) inflicted 7.6 percent of Communist dead and lost 3.2 percent of all Marines killed. With the 1969–1971 stress on reducing American casualties, III MAF reemphasized small-unit operations, but with mixed results. Although recon units and CAP platoons, characterized by superb leadership and tactical skill, could outmatch the VC, the regular infantry showed signs of slackened enthusiasm and professionalism. Marine operations, therefore, showed striking contrasts between very good and very bad.[58]

For III MAF the shift in tactics, combined with strained race relations and the prospects of withdrawal, produced alarming differences in discipline and field performance. Although units in combat proved valorous, the Marine base camps and rear areas (havens for slackers and drug-users) shared a MACV-wide phenomenon in 1969–1971—the attack upon officers and NCOs by alienated and disturbed American troops. During the withdrawal period Americans made more than 800 "fragging" attacks upon their superiors. In 1970 the U.S. Army reported 271 incidents or 0.91 attacks per 1,000 soldiers; the 1st Marine Division had 47 "fraggings" or .2 attacks per 1,000 Marines. Although two-thirds of the incidents occurred in rear areas, front line Marines were not immune, and overaggressive or incompetent officers and NCOs or those who challenged drug-users and racial militants ran special risks. Concerned that enlisted Marines would not testify against their peers, III MAF commanders developed quick-reaction forces to cordon off and question suspects after an incident, and "shakedowns" for unauthorized munitions became common. As successful prosecutions increased and the stand-down advanced into 1971, Marine "fraggings" declined while Army incidents increased to 1.8 assaults per 1,000 in 1971. It was a strange era for III MAF. On one hand skilled, dedicated Marines (now clad in jungle-camouflage uniforms) consistently bested the Communists, while other Marines shirked and killed one another. The "fragging" phenomenon made withdrawal even more attractive.[59]

Crimes against Vietnamese civilians, a by-product of pacification operations and reduced professionalism, also made withdrawal attractive. No Marine unit committed anything like the My Lai massacre, but 115 Marines faced courts-martial for the murder, manslaughter, and rape of Vietnamese, and 77 were convicted. With witnesses reluctant to testify for fear of retaliation or peer sympathy, an unknown number of incidents went unreported or unprosecuted. How many acts of violence were "war crimes" (acts against the international laws governing the treatment of prisoners and unarmed civilians) cannot be determined with any accuracy, but III MAF senior commanders believed that crimes against Vietnamese, like the "fraggings" and racial violence, made the withdrawal period especially difficult for the Corps.[60]

Following revised troop withdrawal plans, III MAF shrank in numbers and territory, largely unaffected by the Cambodian incursion of 1970 and ARVN's unhappy foray into Laos in Operation Lam Son 719 in 1971. Although Marine aviation contributed to the massive American air support of ARVN and Army operations against Communist sanctuary, the reduced ground forces of III MAF, only two reinforced infantry regiments by the end of 1970, fell back toward the "rocket belt" and security operations designed to minimize Communist disruptions within the Da Nang enclave. In 1970 only 403 Marines died in Vietnam, no less hard for the dead, but a substantial reduction of Corps losses. In return, the 1st Marine Division claimed more than 5,000 Communists killed in Quang Nam province. In reality, III MAF, which changed to an amphibious brigade of one regiment/one MAG in April 1971, spent most of its energy turning over villages and installations to the ARVN. Harassed by sapper and rocket attacks, the Marines reduced their

TAORs to the immediate Da Nang area in 1971. Following General Chapman's demanding guidance that the Marines not leave $5 worth of property in Vietnam, III MAF and its successor, 3d MAB, loaded tons of equipment and junk aboard Navy amphibious shipping, which took the war refuse to either Okinawa or Japan for further disposition. With the war still unresolved, the Marines left Vietnam in force in June 1971.[61]

The departure of large Marine units from Vietnam did not end Marine participation in the war. Like the United States, the Corps could not rid itself of its unhappy Southeast Asia intervention. When III MAB departed Vietnam, it left behind a Marine security guard for the embassy in Saigon, air–naval gunfire teams to support Army and ARVN units in I Corps, and some sixty advisers for the Vietnamese Marine Division, which moved into I Corps in 1972 to throw back a large-scale NVA invasion of Quang Tri province. As they had in Lam Son 719, Marine aviation units came to the rescue of ARVN in 1972 when the NVA launched a massive conventional offensive against the ARVN 1st and 3d Divisions. Supporting the ARVN with both close air support and armed helo strikes, Marine air assisted ARVN in recapturing most of its Quang Tri positions in heavy fighting in 1972. Working closely with their ARVN counterparts, Marine advisers stiffened the Vietnamese counteroffensive. The failure of the Communist efforts in 1972, combined with the retaliatory air raids of LINEBACKER and the successful ARVN counteroffensive, finally created the conditions that produced the Paris Peace Accords of 1973, a dramatic end of direct American military involvement in Southeast Asia, but only another significant turning point in an unfinished war.

Demoralized by the resignation of President Nixon and the Congressionally mandated reduction of military assistance, the South Vietnamese government went into a psychological and military funk by 1975 that provided the NVA with a new opportunity to win the war. Although the Communist high command did not anticipate a complete victory in 1975, its initial thrusts against the ARVN in both II and III Corps produced such impressive gains that the Communists pressed their attack throughout Vietnam. The guerrilla war was long gone. The Communists made their advances by fighting the kind of conventional war that had produced victory in 1954 and defeat every other time until 1975. Driving across the Central Highlands and down Route 1 from Quang Tri province, the NVA closed around Saigon in early April. In a simultaneous offensive, the Vietnamese-backed Khmer Rouge insurgents in Cambodia began a final drive on Phnom Penh, the capital. Embassy officials in Saigon and Phnom Penh did not request evacuation, but the senior American officer in Southeast Asia, the Air Force general serving as Commander United States Support Activities Group, Thailand, asked CINCPAC to order in the on-station Marine Amphibious Brigade for a complex set of evacuation contingencies. Moving more or less in accordance with prepared plans, the Marines were on their way to the final act of the Vietnam tragedy.

In a hectic month of vertical envelopments and extractions made under fire and in poor weather and lighting conditions, five Marine helicopter squadrons supported by security forces from two Marine infantry battalions rescued 276 people from Phnom Penh and nearly 7,000 from Saigon. Although Americans and other foreign nationals were the principal targets for evacuation, the bulk of the evacuees were Cambodians and Vietnamese. EAGLE PULL—the Cambodian rescue—went smoothly in two and one half hours on April 12, but the Saigon operation—FREQUENT WIND—had more than a few tense moments. The primary LZ near the American military compound at Tan Son Nhut air base came under sporadic artillery fire, which killed two Embassy Marines, and Communist anti-aircraft fire threatened the landings and takeoffs. Orbiting attack aircraft, however, discouraged the NVA gunners, and no helos fell to enemy fire. As the extractions neared a close, however, the Marines received orders to pluck nearly 2,000 people from the roof of the American Embassy, which had not been designated a prime evacuation point because of its limited helo landing sites. In the midst of pandemonium, Marine helos swooped in and out throughout the night of 29–30 April until the last boarders, a rear guard of Marine infantry, reached the roof. With the loss of only one helo in an accident, the 9th MAB had finally ended the Marine war in Vietnam.[62]

Yet the Corps was not free of fighting and dying in Southeast Asia, for on May 12, 1975, the Khmer Rouge seized the American container ship *Mayaguez* during a routine voyage to Thailand. Unhappily, all the Navy and Marine forces that had made EAGLE PULL and FREQUENT WIND well-organized operations were no longer on station. With President Gerald Ford edging toward military intervention to save the crew and the ship, the American commander in Thailand mustered eleven Air Force helos and a Marine battalion flown from Okinawa for the rescue. The May 15 boarding of the *Mayaguez* proved anticlimactic, for the Cambodians had abandoned the vessel. But the helo assault on Koh Tang island, where Communists were supposedly holding the crew, became a bloody botch. Hoping the Cambodians would see the error of their ways and not resist, the helos plunged in without prior air strikes. Immediately two helos crashed in flames with Marines aboard, and another plunged into the sea after dropping its helo team on the island. Scattered in three different LZs, the hundred or so Marines found themselves fighting for their lives against the enraged Cambodians. As the Marines fought the Communists, the crew of the *Mayaguez* returned safely to American custody from another island, which produced such command confusion and indecision that the Marines on Koh Tang did not receive reinforcements for half a day. In the meantime the three groups of Marines fought their way to one another, supported by Air Force fighters and an AC-130 gunship. With the reinforcements, which brought the total force to 240 Marines, the landing team could hold enough of an LZ to allow a relatively safe extraction during the early evening of May 15. With forty-one wounded and fourteen dead or missing (four Air Force and Navy participants also perished), the Kho Tang assault force finally brought the Marine war in Southeast Asia to a close. Marines throughout the world found a variety of ways to express their opinions about Vietnam in 1975. It is doubtful that many of them regretted that this particular war was finally over.[63]

19. The Once and Future Corps
The 1970s

Staggered by its Vietnam experience, the Marine Corps found little time for leisurely readjustment in the postwar 1970s. It faced serious external criticism and internal confusion about its missions, force structure, and personnel policies. Although some of the pressure to reduce and restructure the air and ground components of the Fleet Marine Force subsided by the end of the decade, no Marine could feel confident that the Corps had satisfied its critics. Instead of dwelling on its public relations honeymoon during World War II and the Korean War, the Corps recalled a longer history of adversity, perseverance, and adaptation. It was a historical lesson that took some relearning, but the 1970s provided Marines with ample opportunities to examine their most cherished assumptions. As the uncertain 1980s began, the Corps could claim that it had emerged from another period of testing with revived confidence and military capability.

The breakdown of a public consensus for global "containment" and the decline of NATO's readiness to deter the Warsaw Pact's larger and modernized ground and air units convinced defense policy-makers in the Nixon and Ford administrations that American general purpose forces should be designed for virtually no other mission but European defense. With the Air Force and Army racing to modernize their con-

The author acknowledges the review of this chapter provided by principal staff officers of Headquarters Marine Corps in September, 1979, coordinated by Maj. P. W. Chapman, Division of Public Affairs and Information.

ventional war forces for the only contingency that commanded any governmental consensus, the Navy and Marine Corps became hard pressed to maintain their position that global strategic flexibility still served American interests. Concerned over the diminished value of inflation-eroded defense dollars, civilian defense managers in the executive branch and influential Congressmen and their staffs focused upon the armed forces' most expensive investments—ground combat divisions, tactical aviation, and ships. In all three categories the Marine presence was small but visible. In all three categories persistent critics could find "duplication" of functions performed by the three larger services, especially if one assumed that amphibious assaults had become obsolete.

In the orgy of criticism that followed the Vietnam War, the most outspoken external assault on the Corps's amphibious mission came from civilian analysts in the Office of the Secretary of Defense, the Senate Armed Services Committee, and the Brookings Institution and centered on the assumed irrelevance of amphibious warfare to NATO's operational challenges. The critics argued in technical terms that the development of precision-guided munitions (PGMs) and the spread of Soviet armored warfare doctrine and equipment outside Europe posed unacceptable threats to the Navy's amphibious forces and the Marines' air-ground combat units. In assessing Corps force structure, the critics usually emphasized five points: (1) U.S. military commitments outside Europe and its surrounding waters were highly unlikely; (2) Marine ground forces did not possess adequate tanks and antitank weapons for European and Mideast warfare; (3) Marine Corps fixed-wing aviation duplicated Air Force and Navy tactical air and starved the ground FMF for funds and high-quality personnel; (4) the Corps's dependence on heavy-lift troop-carrying helicopters made its tactical mobility questionable on battlefields affected by bad weather and intense anti-air defenses; and (5) the Navy's diminished interest in gunfire support ships and amphibious lift would prevent the FMF from reaching the battlefield on time and then landing against serious opposition. Given the NATO-only assumptions of the critics, the "weaknesses" of the FMF's force structure had some theoretical basis, as even Marine planners recognized.[1]

Pressed by its critics and aware that some were middle-rank Marine officers turned skeptics by the Vietnam War, Headquarters defended the FMF's amphibious orientation and pressed forward with many ambitious weapons modernization programs. Commandant Robert E. Cushman, Jr., and his forceful assistant, General Earl E. Anderson, emphasized an accelerated improvement in the Corps's tank force (adopting the M-60A1 and increasing tank numbers), artillery, antitank units (rearmed with the TOW and "Dragon" missiles), and anti-aircraft missiles. Forced by fiscal constraints to make hard choices, Headquarters gave its greatest attention to reequipping and manning FMF Atlantic. Starved for resources during the Vietnam era, FMF Atlantic showed new signs of readiness by the Yom Kippur war of 1973. In 1975 it launched its first true NATO exercise outside the Mediterranean when a Marine Amphibious Unit (MAU) conducted maneuvers in Norway and northern Germany. These exercises, which became annual and expanded to brigade size, revealed that NATO warfare presented difficulties of mobility, firepower, and tactical coordination that the Corps had not yet overcome.[2]

Although the NATO orientation of the Corps's top-priority modernization programs dominated Marine procurement throughout the 1970s, the pressure upon the Corps to shape itself for only one theater of action diminished toward the end of the decade. As Marine strategists argued, American interests could not be defined only in terms of Western Europe. Amphibious ready forces, backed by the undeployed FMF units, gave the United States a unique instrument unaffected by the complexities of base rights, overflight rights, and inter-allied diplomacy. At issue were Soviet naval expansion and the reality of Russian intervention in the tumultuous new nations of Africa and the Middle East. The growing capacity of the Soviet navy for "blue water" operations—if only to restrict American reinforcement of Europe and to attack American ballistic missile submarines and carriers—opened the possibility of an extended naval campaign for the U.S. Navy for the first time since 1945. Once again the landfalls and islands that border the Atlantic took on the special significance they held in 1940–1943; the Soviet capacity for land-based air attack, submarine interdiction, and surface raiding made the seizure and defense of naval bases a strategic reality. In addition, anxiety over American access to imported oil heightened strategists' concern over control of the world's sea lanes, particularly the some twenty narrows and straits whose military exploitation would stop oil tankers and other raw material carriers.

The revolution in Iran and the Soviet intervention in Afghanistan in 1979 dramatized the range of contingencies short of general war that faced the United States. They also bolstered the Corps's argument that flexibility and strategic mobility should not be sacrificed for NATO-only reinforcement missions. As a variant to its amphibious ready forces, the Corps supported the creation of an all-service Rapid Deployment Force, built around prepositioned logistics and equipment-carrying ships and air-transportable Marine and Army units based in the United States. An initiative championed by Secretary of Defense Harold R. Brown, the new force widened the FMF's force in readiness role without compromising its amphibious mission.[3]

The amphibious mission itself became clouded by the Navy's doubts about the cost-effectiveness of its amphibious forces in the 1970s. Hard pressed by its own manning problems and the soaring cost of its ships, the Navy with the approval of OSD retired about half its active amphibious vessels, cut the procurement of the 40,000-ton, $300 million General Purpose Amphibious Assault ship (LHA) from nine vessels to five, and postponed the LSD-41 program. While the share of amphibious vessels in the fleet (65 of 439 in 1979) held at about 15 percent, the specter of block obsolescence in the 1990s haunted Corps planners. By conservative estimates about the service life of the present amphibious force, all but six vessels will end their service by the end of the century. The LHA program characterized Navy–Marine difficulties in keeping the amphibious art alive. Designed to carry a full MAU (reinforced infantry battalion, logistic support unit, and composite air squadron) and deliver it by helo, assault craft, and amphibian vehicles, the LHA was designed for the extended deployments of the Cold War period, thus requiring expensive investments in troop living quarters and working spaces. Its very size, comparable to a World War II attack carrier, may make it a vulnerable target to the jet aircraft and missile-firing patrol boats common throughout the world. Because the Navy and Marines do not yet have fast, long-distance surface assault vehicles or landing craft, the LHA is particularly vulnerable when it closes to launch its water-borne elements of the Marine assault echelon. Furthermore, Marine planners suspected that the Navy coveted the LHA and the older LPHs for sea control missions. In any event, the amphibious force is less than half the size endorsed by the Department of Defense before Vietnam as minimally acceptable for the assault echelons of the FMF.[4]

For all the incongruities between the Corps's missions and the Navy and Marine forces available in the 1970s to perform them, no Secretary of Defense or Congress relieved the Corps of any of its statutory missions. Nor did they provide the resources necessary to perform them all with equal skill. Although the Corps budget (including the "blue dollars" spent on aviation) climbed to $4.9 billion in FY 1980, the actual buying power of the Corps budget maintained the FMF tradition of doing its best with very little. From the Corps's perspective, it provides 15 percent of America's divisions and 12 percent of its tactical air forces on only 3.6 percent of the defense budget. Reasonable men differed on the likelihood of a successful amphibious assault against an enemy armed with modern weapons; hence the Corps stressed that amphibious assault might be its most unique mission but not its only one. Instead it insisted that it provided a global force in readiness that did not depend exclusively upon fixed land bases and strategic airlift to perform a range of military missions short of direct warfare with the Soviet Union. Ahistorical policy-makers questioned the Corps's roles and force structure with a false sense of novelty, but senior Marine officers understood that they were continuing the Corps's hallowed arguments for survival.

1

Of the post-Vietnam issues that jarred the Corps, few proved so difficult as the status of Marine aviation. For the Corps of the 1970s, aviation problems began with several doctrinal assumptions: (1) Amphibious operations require continuous air superiority; (2) Marine ground operations from the beginning of an amphibious assault through sustained land campaigns require lavish close air support, particularly in the absence of naval gunfire and heavy artillery; and (3) Marine landing forces require helicopters to lift troops and supplies and helo gunships and planes to protect them. Marine aviation planning and force structure, however, faced intractable realities. One was simply that Marine aviation was fiscally and operationally part of naval aviation, and the Navy was not eager to fund aircraft unable to operate from carriers. In addition, Navy planners saw Marine fixed-wing aircraft as naval air war assets, and Marine squadrons were, in fact, rotated to carrier assignments. Because carrier aircraft represented the surface fleet's primary offensive capability, Marine planners knew that the carriers could not linger long in an amphibious operations area, for they had other missions to perform. Therefore, the Marine Corps had to provide its own land-based air support, which meant seizing or building its own airfields. Such a requirement hardly promoted planning flexibility and tactical surprise. Nor did it make for an austere Marine aviation component in terms of either money or quality personnel.

The saga of the Corps and the F-14 dramatized the conceptual and political problems inherent in Marine aviation. A superb but very costly ($20 million each in 1979) air superiority fighter, the Grumman F-14 became the Navy's primary weapon for fleet protection in the 1970s. To reduce unit costs and expand the number of F-14 squadrons available for carrier deployment from fourteen to eighteen, the Navy pressed General Cushman in 1973 to accept sixty-eight F-14s instead of buying twice as many improved F-4 Phantoms. Marine aviation planners were themselves divided on the issue, and the influence of General Anderson, an F-14 advocate, probably swayed Cushman. Navy pressure, however, was decisive. Skeptics thought that the Navy never intended for the Corps to have the F-14 but would instead force it to accept a

McDonnell-Douglas fighter, the less capable F-18, as its dual-purpose aircraft of the 1980s and 1990s. Moreover, the F-14 program not only would have reduced the Marine fighter force but would have virtually dominated all other fixed-wing planning and manning. At the same time, it would have done nothing to solve the problem of reducing Marine dependence on carrier-based air. These considerations persuaded a new Commandant, General Louis H. Wilson, to cancel the F-14 program immediately upon assuming office in July 1975. Wilson chose to return to the F-4 program and to await data on the F-18. In the meantime, the Corps pressed on with its own revolutionary aircraft, the vertical-takeoff AV-8A, which entered the inventory in 1971.[5]

Although the British-built Harrier proved less capable and more difficult to fly and maintain than originally anticipated, the Corps saw VSTOL aircraft, either successors to the AV-8A or American-designed planes, as the ultimate solution to its fixed-wing basing problems. Building from the original purchase of four squadrons of Harriers, the Corps hoped to convert all its light attack (A-4) squadrons to VSTOL and then convert its dual-purpose force as well. Civilian, Navy, and Air Force planners, however, found little merit in the Harrier. Thirty-three Harrier crashes by 1979, though not excessive in terms of hours flown and takeoffs and landings attempted, gave the aircraft an unsavory public image. Whatever the original Harrier's defects, largely correctable in the follow-on version built by McDonnell-Douglas, the VSTOL concept is uniquely suited to amphibious, force in readiness aviation. At sea the Harrier can fly from LHAs or LPHs, assuring the Marines of close air support and freeing carrier aircraft for air superiority and interdiction missions for the fleet and landing force alike. In addition, a VSTOL aircraft can safely operate from paved roads and hardened pads, both of which are likely to be available before either a SATS strip can be built or an existing airfield seized.

Nevertheless, the Marine VSTOL program limped through the 1970s and remained only slightly alive at the end of the decade. First, the British manufacturer, Hawker-Siddeley, had difficulty providing parts, and in 1975 Great Britain ended its own participation in the joint development program to replace the AV-8A. McDonnell-Douglas negotiated licensing rights to build the next Harrier, the AV-8B, but the construction of the first four prototypes suggested that unit costs would be double the original aircraft's. Although the AV-8B finally met Marine performance standards and the proposed buy of more than three hundred new Harriers pleased the American aircraft industry, Department of Defense planners did not approve continued development and procurement in 1978. Instead, they forced the Corps to await the attack version of the F-18. Headquarters was willing to accept the F-18 as the F-4's replacement, but it still preferred the Harrier to either the A-18 or the A-4M, still the standard light attack aircraft. In the meantime, the Corps continued to improve its Phantoms and Skyhawks and to increase the power, range, and ordnance-carrying capacity of its existing Harrier force.

Fiscal pressures and mission disputes made other inroads into the Marine fixed-wing force. Although Headquarters succeeded in stalling DOD plans to cut the number of active Phantom squadrons from twelve to six, it could not prevent the immediate reduction of its all-weather attack (A-6) force from sixty to fifty planes. DOD also wanted to phase the Intruder out of the Marine inventory by preventing the replacement of older models with the "E" or later versions. Convinced by its Vietnam performance that the Intruder provides dependable close air support at night and in bad weather through its advanced guidance systems, Headquarters wanted the A-6 in larger numbers and with greater capability. Other planners argued that the Marine Corps did not need a deep interdiction aircraft, deep interdiction being an Air Force and Navy function. Once again, Marine planners doubted that the Corps could count on the other overburdened services to divert their Intruders to Marine missions when the historical evidence suggested that any diversion was likely to go in the opposite direction. In any event, despite the planned addition of 120 planes by FY 1987, the Marine fixed-wing force faced reduction in the same period from 380 to 300 aircraft.[6]

While they struggled to modernize and maintain their fixed-wing force, Marine aviators adjusted their close air support tactics to meet more dangerous enemy air defenses. Impressed by Soviet anti-air weapons and doctrine, dramatically demonstrated by the Egyptians in the Yom Kippur War of 1973, air tacticians worked with the Air Force to change mission profiles. Instead of leisurely, medium-altitude approaches to front line targets, Marine aircraft will orbit out of range of enemy defenses, then hurtle at 400 knots over friendly troops at tree-top levels before popping up to deliver their ordnance. In theory, they will make only one run. Such tactics place new burdens on controlling air strikes, and the Corps depends on complicated electronic data-processing equipment and radios in the air and on the ground to make close air support workable. The new tactics, of course, required high investments in pilot training, maintenance, and guidance technology.[7]

For Marine aviation, the modernization and maintenance of its helicopter force posed different and somewhat less difficult problems in the 1970s. Built around helos that joined the Corps in the 1960s and early

1970s, the helicopter component numbered three squadrons of Sea Cobra gunships, three squadrons of all-purpose Hueys, eleven squadrons of troop-carrying medium-lift Sea Knights, and six squadrons of heavy-lift Sea Stallions. The latter aircraft (CH-53 A-D) became the main focus of helo modernization; its manufacturer, Sikorsky, had developed an "E" model with three engines powerful enough to lift almost all the equipment of a Marine division and all aircraft but one. The Corps requested six CH-53E squadrons, but fiscal constraints slowed procurement. The other principal helo program focused on the gunship force of forty-eight AH-1Ts, all to be fitted with the TOW antitank missile. The remaining Sea Cobra squadron in the active forces, as well as the Reserve gunship squadron, would remain armed with 20-mm. cannon and rockets. (Reservists also provide two additional Huey squadrons.) Given the availability of amphibious flight decks, the Marine Corps is unlikely to increase its helicopter inventory or change its characteristics in the near future.[8]

Despite some doubt that helicopters can operate against intense air defenses, Marine planners believe that attack aircraft and gunships can provide adequate protection, and helo tacticians stress that landing zones should be selected away from defended objectives. In addition, the Corps hopes to exploit new guidance technology in order to improve its ability to fly helicopters in bad weather and at night, conditions that inhibit air defenses. Because the helicopter force remains the backbone of the Marines' tactical mobility and costs only about one-third of the fixed-wing force, the Corps is unlikely to surrender its hard-won expertise in the vertical envelopment assault. Except perhaps in the heavy firepower, mechanized war that might occur in Germany, the Marines predict that their helo-borne forces remain combat effective—if given appropriate artillery and close air support. Other military forces, especially the Russian and American armies, appear to agree, for they continue to develop vertical assault units.

2

For the ground combat and supporting organizations of the Fleet Marine Force, the post-Vietnam era brought significant changes in organization and training. Marines had far fewer new weapons, however, than anticipated in the early 1970s. Many of the new tools of war championed by the Cushman–Anderson administration did not meet the cost-effectiveness criteria applied by civilian planners and General Wilson. Ten years of hard decisions, however, produced several distinct trends in Marine Corps ground combat effectiveness. First, radical investments in new weapons, vehicles, and command/communications technology were deferred to the 1990s. Headquarters, particularly after General Wilson's succession, stressed more imaginative task organizing and training to improve Marine readiness rather than technological fixes. In the meantime, Headquarters focused its research and development interest on a few critical projects, primarily a new amphibian vehicle, a lightweight assault gun, and real-time computer systems for processing intelligence and controlling air-ground fire support.

Before operational difficulties and cost curtailed procurement, the Marine Corps appeared ready to win its future wars with electronic technology rather than firearms. Headquarters' strong interest in electronics, however, stemmed essentially from a conviction that manpower and massed firepower could no longer be used with liberality on the battlefield. Although the Corps's own austere R&D budget prevented independent projects outside of amphibious warfare, Marines monitored and supported many R&D projects of others, particularly those of the Army. By 1974 Headquarters had developed exotic tastes in electronic technology; it had made substantial investments in elaborate computer-based systems for controlling air operations, collecting and analyzing intelligence data, integrating air and ground fire support, and exercising a wide range of command functions. In real terms, the new systems worked best at the MAF level or at the division and wing level, the tactical headquarters least likely to be deployed except in extended land campaigns. At the MAU and MAB level the systems would have been less efficient. Nevertheless, the new electronic Corps not only placed improved radios in the hands of the FMF but increased the sensing devices available to both infantry and artillerymen. Night-vision and seismic sensing devices enhanced operations, but the early laser systems for target designation proved too awkward for field use. The same was true of early ground radars, and the addition of a surveillance and target acquisition platoon to every infantry battalion proved unrevolutionary.[9]

Although devices using every part of the electromagnetic spectrum promised to change Marine operations, improvements in Corps firepower for the 1980s and the FMF reorganizations to support the changes dominated ground warfare development. To counter Soviet doctrine and weapons, the Corps replaced its M-48 medium tanks with the M-60A1 with its better 105-mm. gun, sighting systems, and mobility. The precision-guided TOW and Dragon missiles began to join the FMF in 1977 to enhance infantry anti-armor capability. Night-firing devices enhanced the first-shot kill probability of all three weapons systems. In 1978 Headquarters made another overdue decision: to replace the aging 105-mm. howitzer with the towed M198 155-mm. howitzer as the Corps's direct support artillery weapon. Helo-transportable with the CH-53E, the M198 proved superior because of its range (three times the 105's) and the versatility of its ammunition, which is devastating as either a high explosive area weapon or as precision guided antitank ordnance. After much debate and testing, Marine infantry battalions retained their M-16s, M-60 machine guns, and 81-mm. and 60-mm. mortars, with the latter weapons benefiting from improved ammunition. The infantry battalion received three new weapons in the 1970s: the M203 combination M-16 and 40-mm. grenade launcher, the four-shot incendiary rocket launcher that allowed bunkers to be attacked from safe distances, and the Dragon antitank weapon. The next most dramatic procurement decision for the ground FMF will also be firepower-oriented: In the mid-1980s the Corps will decide whether it will buy a lightweight, highly mobile assault gun for anti-armor and beach attack operations.[10]

Ground force mobility, exclusive of helos, also received high-priority Marine attention, particularly the related problems of ship-to-shore movement and mechanized operations ashore. For transporting large cargoes and vehicles, the Corps supported Navy development of surface-effect hovercraft as replacements for its antique landing craft. In the meantime it sought a high-speed, long-range armored vehicle designed for beach assaults and mechanized operations. Although the Corps will improve its current LVTP-7 for operations in the 1980s, it definitely wants a new, vastly improved assault amphibian vehicle. To develop such a vehicle, the Corps must make delicate tradeoffs in the hull design and between water and land travel systems, armor and armament, and weight and speed.[11]

The logistics portion of FMF modernization became no less important, but even more difficult, than increasing Marine firepower and mobility. The sea-basing concept, which anticipated keeping logistics facilities at sea and depending primarily upon helo transportation, did not survive the shrinkage in the Navy's amphibious force and the characteristics of the newer amphibious vessels. If Marine logistics units must move ashore in strength and bulk, they prefer to move across the beach and inland with heavy-lift vehicles capable of moving preloaded containers of electronic command systems, ammunition, food and water, fuel, and equipment. The bulk and weight of containerized logistics facilities have thus far limited FMF modernization, for such "packaging" demands prime movers (wheeled and tracked) that the Corps does not yet have.

To some degree, reorganization as well as new technology can enhance the FMF's combat effectiveness, and Marine Corps planners in the 1970s searched with fervor for ways to save manpower and enhance firepower and logistics effectiveness. The first trend, which culminated in 1979, was to streamline the Marine division by moving many of its service units into a Force Service Support Group. While the divisions retained engineer battalions and truck companies, all landing support units joined the FSSG. The tactical elements of the division remained three infantry regiments of three battalions each, an artillery regiment of three to five battalions, and a reconnaissance battalion with a division headquarters battalion providing command capabilities. At the same time the infantry companies shrank when every rifle squad dropped from fourteen to thirteen with the introduction of the M203 grenade launcher. More radical changes followed in the late 1970s, largely to improve ground force firepower. Marine infantry battalions converted one of their four rifle companies to a weapons company armed with mortars and Dragon, and the division regained control of its own amtrac battalion and tank battalion, expanded by a fourth tank company and a TOW company. In a complementary move, the division artillery regiment gained control of the heavy self-propelled guns of the Force Field Artillery Group. In a novel departure, these reorganizations did not apply equally to all three Marine Amphibious Forces. In numbers of equipment and units, the II or Atlantic MAF "heavied up" for European warfare first, followed by select portions of the I MAF at Camp Pendleton, the Corps's global strategic reserve force. The Pacific-oriented III MAF remained "light."

Aware that neither technology nor reorganization would provide revolutionary changes during his "watch," General Wilson stressed enhanced operational readiness through intensified training. One of Wilson's first decisions upon becoming Commandant was to establish a combined arms training center at the Marine base at Twenty-nine Palms, California. Designed to give regular and Reserve battalions a taste of live-fire operations with air and artillery support, as well as develop mechanized forces of tanks and LVTPs, the annual "Palm Tree" exercises for ten to twelve battalions soon brought training a new degree of realism. The desert setting, however, persuaded amateur critics that the Corps was especially interested in Middle Eastern intervention, an analysis that ignored other contingency missions and the land requirements for live firing. In the meantime, more traditional amphibious exercises in the Caribbean and the Mediterranean tested new equipment and techniques. The most novel doctrinal development, however, stemmed from "Palm Tree" and a series of NATO exercises in northern Europe. For the first time, Marine MAU and MAB commanders used entire tank companies and battalions, supported by LVTP-mounted infantry, as independent maneuver elements. Marine tank officers, afflicted by Rommelesque dreams, finally found themselves the brides of field problems, not the bridesmaids. Nevertheless, the Corps resisted pressures to create permanent mechanized brigades, insisting that it could always task-organize such a force if it had to.[12]

For individual training, the Corps mixed specialization and centralization in ways that joined new demands with pre-Vietnam practices. Infantry training particularly received new emphasis under General Wilson. While shortening The Basic School course for second lieutenants, which sped noninfantry officers to their basic technical courses, the Commandant established a special course for infantry officers. In a similar move, each division established its own central infantry training school for new Marines instead of relying on FMF on-the-job training, habitually impeded by deployment schedules, leadership shortages, and conflicting unit training demands. Separate division and wing SNCO and NCO leadership courses also came under central management in order to ensure uniformity in doctrine and training standards. In the meantime, the Corps continued to rely on the other services' schools for a third of its skill training in order to keep its training base as austere as possible. In sum, the Marine Corps by 1980 had enhanced its ability to function as a modern force in readiness without abandoning its amphibious uniqueness.

3

Of all its post-Vietnam readjustments, none wrenched the Corps more than the Great Personnel Campaign, 1973–1977. Although the initial defeats came from the Nixon administration's political decision to end the draft in 1973, the campaign brought about its special trauma by virtue of the fact that some of the Marines' wounds were self-inflicted, the product of judgmental collapses from Headquarters to the drill fields of Parris Island and San Diego. Only a counteroffensive mounted by Commandant Louis H. Wilson, Lieutenant General Robert H. Barrow (the director of manpower and the Commandant's confidant), and thousands of other dedicated reformist officers and SNCOs assured success. Although the Corps shared all the armed forces' growing difficulty in securing volunteer recruits in quality and quantity in the 1970s, it had much to learn about the extent of the challenge.[13]

Although DOD-sponsored surveys in 1971–1972 indicated that all the armed forces would face a massive manpower and public relations problem without the draft, the Cushman–Anderson regime did not respond with special alarm when the all-volunteer force became a reality in 1973. Headquarters apparently took comfort in statistics that said that more Marine recruits (by percentage) than other new recruits were true volunteers. It ignored less promising factors. Survey research also determined that half of all new Marines (some 50,000 a year in the post-Vietnam Corps) were evading Army service. Furthermore, the Marine Corps had traditionally stressed its institutional uniqueness and the epic experience of recruit training to such a degree that by 1972 prospective recruits believed Marines received no useful occupational training, had no foreign travel opportunities, and received less pay than other servicemen. The image of the combat-ready infantry Marine, overendowed with muscles and machismo, attracted some teenagers but scared away most. To make the situation worse, Marine recruiting had slackened in conception and execution during the draft years. Recruiters were not specially selected or trained; for its estimated needs, the recruiting budget of $16 million was inadequate; Marine advertising had become limited by policy to public-service-only outlets; and Marine recruiters could not or would not reach out to identify and convince the young men most likely to serve well. All of the recruiting system's flaws became apparent in FY 1974 when non-prior-service enlistments fell nearly 10,000 men short of the Corps's needs.

Unwilling to accept less than its budgeted end-strength of 196,000 and smarting from its recruiting problems, Headquarters decided in 1973 that it would enlist "quality" Marines on the basis of intelligence test scores (which indicated trainability) rather than high school diplomas (which indicated adaptability to service life). Appalled by the performance of some high school graduates, who tested in the lowest acceptable mental group (IV) upon enlistment, Headquarters chose to underemphasize statistics that indicated high disciplinary problems with nongraduates and overemphasized the transformations produced by boot camp. In FY 1975 the Corps rebounded and enlisted 101 percent of its quota and reduced its Mental Group IV accessions from 20 percent (1972) to 5.7 percent (1975). The "progress" came at some institutional cost. Nongraduates made up 46 percent of new recruits in FY 1973 and 49 percent in FY 1974. Concerned, Congress in 1975 ordered all the services to enlist at least 55 percent high school graduates. The order affected only the Corps. In addition, critics charged that using mental group criteria discriminated against black prospects, although black accessions actually increased by 1975.

At the recruit depots and the units of the FMF, the recruiting policies of the true all-volunteer Corps proved an invitation to organizational disorder. In theory, the end of the Vietnam War and the draft should have reduced disciplinary problems. In the other services where job satisfaction, better leadership, and relaxed discipline had coalesced as "improved human resources management," morale indicators did, indeed, suggest that more servicemen would be on the job. In the Corps, however, the trends moved in other directions. Rates of courts-martial, nonjudicial punishments, confinement, unauthorized absence, and desertion climbed past the totals of the other services and in all but unauthorized absence exceeded their combined totals. For the FMF the reality was stark. Only units actively deployed for exercises could be maintained at anything close to combat effectiveness; such "gold plating" meant that other units survived only as administrative symbols, not real organizations. Widespread frustration throughout the FMF focused with accuracy upon recruiting policies that mocked Marine elitism.

Under intense pressure to meet their recruiting quotas in both high school graduate and mental group categories, the recruiters struggled to find "a few good men" and to understand the sophisticated media recruiting blitz Headquarters had begun in 1974. For Corps public relations specialists, suspect with many Marines, the "parity-plus" strategy shone with promise as it showed potential recruits that the Corps offered the same opportunities as all the other services with the added distinction of being a Marine. For the sergeants in storefront offices and federal broom closets, the temptations "to make quota" through extralegal methods proved attractive. Mental tests could be doctored more easily than high school diplomas; lack of access to juvenile records made it easier to process teenage criminals; physical defects might be missed or waived in the "warm body" environment of the average Armed Forces Entrance and Examining Station. A few recruiters, most of whom were not volunteers, buckled, but the basic difficulty was recruiting policy, not recruiter performance. As long as the mental group criteria held sway, the Corps doomed itself to being a way station for America's maladjusted male youths.

To their credit and eventual embarrassment, the DIs at the two recruit depots actually attempted to "build men" from too many boys beyond rehabilitation. Just as aware as the recruiters that the Marine Corps had strength figures to meet, the DIs held attrition at boot camp to around 10 percent through 1975. Resorting to what they believed to be time-honored practices of verbal harassment, physical abuse, and high-stress training, the DIs thought they were performing miracles. In reality, they secured temporary conformity; the Marines who were antisocial "time bombs" went off instead in the FMF. Reported and prosecuted cases of maltreatment (always fewer than the actual incidents) climbed to 151 in 1975 by Department of Defense count, a number three times higher than the combined incidents of the other services. Shunting off their worst problems to the recruit special training battalions, the DIs continued to bear down hard on the recruits in a desperate attempt to make Marine reality match rhetoric.[14]

In July 1975 the new Commandant, Louis H. Wilson, inherited a recruiting and recruit training problem that threatened the FMF's future as the national force in readiness. Benefiting unintentionally from a revolt among Marine generals against the Cushman–Anderson regime and Anderson's assumed succession, Wilson's credentials made him a perfect choice to bring the Corps back from the brink of disaster. A Medal of Honor winner in World War II and a successful officer in the FMF ever since, infantryman Wilson also had proved more than adept in the Corps's inner circles in Quantico and Washington. His integrity, rough wisdom, and ability to handle Congressmen, especially fellow Southerners, were known quantities. As commanding general of FMF Pacific, he certainly knew the Corps's problems. As Commandant he quickly set two clear goals: to make annual recruiting accessions 75 percent high school graduates and to bring all FMF units up to substantial combat effectiveness. If, in the meantime, Corps strength fell below authorized strength, so be it. Wilson urged Marine commanders to purge the ranks of malcontents and misfits through either disciplinary or administrative action. To assist him in the reformation, in some respects already under way in the recruiting service, Wilson brought Robert H. Barrow, an equally distinguished field officer, to Washington as the director of manpower. Under Wilson's and Barrow's direction, the Corps launched an all-out attack on its substandard Marines.[15]

At the recruit depots, the pent-up frustration and welcome license to purge the ranks produced rising attrition rates, even though the reformed recruiting service had begun to produce more trainable and adaptable Marines. When Headquarters informed the depots that the new quality of the recruits should make reduced attrition rates possible, the DIs sulked or struck back with added pressure on the recruits. The gap between Headquarters policies, which leaned toward reducing the stress in recruit training, and DI practice yawned in the winter of 1975–1976, when two recruits died and another was shot by a DI under dubious circumstances. All three recruits appeared to be examples of recruiting malpractice as well. Aware that Marine recruiting and recruit training would be matters of increased public and Congressional concern, Wilson accelerated the reform program and essentially challenged Marine officers and DIs to adapt to new recruit training or see their careers founder.

Wilson's most important changes linked recruiting with recruit training and reduced the stress of recruit training, at least the sort of verbal harassment and "thumping" that had passed for building men. Recruit depot commanders assumed direct control of recruiting, and recruiters, who finally reached the Commandant's goal for high school graduates in FY 1977, received no credit for accessions unless they finished recruit training. Armed with better training and a recruiting budget that more than doubled, the recruiters proved that the Corps could indeed enlist more stable youths, even in a progressively narrowing market. At the depots, the DIs had to adjust to having an additional officer assigned to each four-platoon serial and to allowing the recruits more free time and opportunity for self-discipline and leadership. Since no concessions came in the arduousness of recruit physical training or the demands for team-work and perfect performance, the new policy probably produced better Marines. It certainly reduced all the indices of indiscipline in the FMF and made it easier for recruiters to attract quality youths. Whether the Corps will attract enough able male youths to fill its labor-intensive structure and still hold female Marines to about 10,000 in the 1980s remains to be seen.

Fiscal pressures combined with other morale problems in the FMF to induce General Wilson to experiment with other personnel policy changes. Some reforms were uniform to all the services: more careful individual career management, fewer permanent changes of station, more attention to job satisfaction. The Corps, however, had a unique problem. With III MAF permanently stationed on Okinawa and Japan, 15 percent of all Marines were serving overseas without dependents for thirteen-month tours. The going and coming from "West Pac" con-tributed to unit instability and individual unhappiness. To reduce this burden, Headquarters developed a plan, initiated in 1977, to rotate in-fantry battalions and aviation squadrons for six-month periods to III MAF from Hawaii and California. When fully implemented in the early 1980s, this unit rotation plan will reduce by half the number of Marines serving unaccompanied tours with III MAF. (Even with unit rotation the Marine Corps requires unaccompanied overseas tours at rates twice those of the other services.) Combat readiness, not personal convenience, drives Corps policy, but at least some officers realized that such morale considerations may pay dividends in recruiting, retention, and job satisfaction without compromising efficiency and toughness.

4

Having survived—indeed, prospered—over more than two hundred years of existence, the once and future Marine Corps faced the 1980s with renewed confidence. The uncertainties of American foreign and defense policy will continue to defy rational defense planners, a condi-tion that favors the Corps–Congressional tie that lives on history and emotion. As long as the United States maintains any pretense of a for-ward defense that stresses alliance relationships, nuclear and conven-tional deterrence, and rapid military response, the Marine Corps will have an important defense role. In practical terms, this means that the Corps will emphasize the amphibious force in readiness role of its three active and one reserve division/wing teams. It also means that the Corps will insist that its air and ground elements be deployed as integrated units, a policy that has caused and will cause difficulties in dealing with the other services and allied forces. The Corps is well aware that its airground character rather than the uniqueness of its size (smallest of the American services, yet far larger than any other world marine corps) gives it a special organizational structure, functional effectiveness in amphibious operations, and "warrior" image. The Marine Corps is, after all, the only service in which the late John Wayne could portray a rifle squad leader and a fighter pilot.

In the fixed statistical portrait that Congress receives every year at budget time, the Marine Corps shows relatively the same characteristics it has maintained for the last twenty years—the Vietnam War excluded. At 18,135 officers and 171,675 enlisted men, its strength is short of wartime requirements but probably adequate for less-than-war contingencies. The Corps maintains three divisions, the Army sixteen. Its helicopter force of about 500 is minuscule compared to the Army's fleet of more than 8,000 helos, but Marine helos are designed and procured for amphibious operations, not airmobile land warfare. Even larger disparities in Army–Marine Corps inventories in tanks and armored personnel carriers reflect the substantial differences in service missions and geographic orientation.

To maintain the Fleet Marine Force, the Corps remains America's most youthful and labor-intensive service. The Corps needs far more than "a few good men." Instead, it must recruit about 40,000 new officers and enlisted men every year and 12,000 new Reserves. Given the amphibious assault mission and force structure of the FMF, retentions and promotions will not compensate for recruiting needs. While the Department of Defense average age is 24.4 years for enlisted men, the Corps average is 22.5; while only 39 percent of all American servicemen fall in the three lowest paygrades, 54 percent of all Marines serve in the ranks of private to lance corporal. Although retention rates improved in the late 1970s from 12 to 19 percent, intraservice transfers and discharges still gave the FMF more personnel instability (and less training) than Corps planners liked. After the Vietnam War the aviation personnel situation improved some, and the Corps entered the 1980s with 3,177 aviators and about 700 naval flight officers and navigators. Nevertheless, it must qualify nearly 550 such officers every year to man its aircraft wings, and it remains short of pilots.

To compensate for the conflicting demands of the FMF and the rest of the Corps's varied training and collateral missions, the Corps depends heavily upon its Reserve division/wing team for a wartime surge capability. Organized units of the Marine Corps Reserve had a budgeted strength of 33,600; actual membership is slightly below the fiscal authorization. In a crisis the Corps would, no doubt, welcome the troops of its three Reserve infantry regiments, but these regiments in the all-volunteer era are not fully manned. Instead, Headquarters recognizes that the attractions of technical training and the greater personnel stability that Reserve units enjoy, especially in the NCO ranks, make the Reserve an admirable source of combat and combat support units, excluding infantry. In FY 1980 Reserves provided one-third of all Marine light attack aircraft squadrons, one-third of all heavy artillery batteries, two-fifths of all tank battalions, and one-third of all Hawk and two-thirds of all Redeye anti-air batteries. Similar regular–Reserve unit ratios exist in truck companies, amphibian assault battalions, and combat service support elements. For the Marine Corps to meet any large, extended contingency without serious organizational disruption, it must mobilize its Reserves, which requires a presidential decision of potentially high political difficulty.

No officer is more sensitive to the Corps's special problems and uniqueness, as well as its global combat capability, than General Robert H. Barrow. An infantryman who wears medals from three wars, Barrow may be the last Commandant and member of the Joint Chiefs of Staff to have served in World War II. An adaptive traditionalist like General Wilson, Barrow is unlikely to make any revolutionary changes in Corps programs. Rather he stressed a forthright attack on the Corps's "people problems" and weapons modernization while maintaining the Corps's reputation for cost-effectiveness and readiness. The twenty-seventh Commandant believes the Corps is "a certain force in an uncertain world" and promises that "we will be prepared to fight anyone, anytime, anyplace. If not, who else?" [16]

Ultimately, the once and future Corps depends not upon the Commandant's words but on the labor and dedication of those obscure Americans who choose to serve their turn in the Fleet Marine Force. The real Marine Corps is far removed from the Corps tourists in Washington see when they attend the sunset parades on Tuesday in front of the Iwo Jima monument or on Friday at the Marine Barracks at "8th and Eye." Watching the ceremony of the Marine Corps band and the drill companies, sparkling in dress blues and shining equipment, the average American sees a gaudy incarnation of the Marine spirit. Little does he realize what price thousands of other Marines have paid or are paying to make these parades such splendid celebrations of the Corps's heritage. On any parade evening, as the rifles spin and the trumpets blare, other Marines prowl the piny woods of Camp Lejeune or the dusty ridges of Camp Pendleton as sweat pours into their camouflaged utilities. Radios squawk in the darkness, and compasses glow faintly as dark figures move cautiously forward. Perhaps the growls of tank and amtrac engines split the night, and to the rear humming lanterns and groaning generators mark the artillery positions.

The ground elements of the FMF have no monopoly on fatigue, frustration, labor, and occasional exultation, for on any given evening the pilots of the FMF thrust their aging fighters and helicopters into the darkening skies of the United States or, perhaps, into the sparkling clouds above the Mediterranean or the Sea of Japan. Whether their paths are marked by the roaring glow of jet engines or the blinking lights and whump-whump of flailing rotor blades, the Marines of the MAWs are on station to provide the firepower and mobility the ground units demand. The squeeze of G-suits and the smell of oil-stained flight coveralls, the discomfort of helmets and bother of flight documents, and the laconic mumbo-jumbo of flight communications push aside the memories of families, happy hours, and ready room banter. From their bases —whether they be the pads of air stations or pitching carrier decks— Marine ground crews watch the descendants of Alfred A. Cunningham, Christian Schilt, Roy Geiger, and Keith McCutcheon plunge into the heavens, men-boys of all ages bonded by their dedication to flight and the Corps.

For any Marine the Corps means many things and expresses itself in many half-forgotten moments that wring the heart and surprise the mind. Whether it is the feel of a rifle company pushing along on a forced march or a flight of F-4s tight and fast, the pull is inexorable. Perhaps one can best understand the Corps, however, not by seeing a Sunset Parade but by visiting a barracks late at night after a hard field problem. After the raucous confusion of cleaning gear fades, there may be one lone Marine, noteworthy only for his youth and very average appearance, who wanders late to the messy community shower. The lone bather pauses in the cascade of water—probably cold since the earlier crowd has used all the hot water—and begins to whistle. It is likely that the tune will be the Marine Corps Hymn. The Washington evening parades notwithstanding, the most moving sound is the evocation of the "halls of Montezuma" and the "shores of Tripoli" from a lonely shower-room whistler.

Whatever his role in threatening the Marine Corps in the early days of the twentieth century, Theodore Roosevelt understood the spirit that has sustained and nourished the Corps throughout its days of triumph and trial: "Far better it is to dare mighty things, to win glorious triumphs, even though checkered by failure, than to rank with those poor spirits who neither enjoy much nor suffer much, because they live in the gray twilight that knows not victory or defeat." As long as the United States maintains any martial tradition or tests its power on the field of battle, the Marine Corps will more than bear its share of the burden. Marines face the future unafraid. Semper Fidelis.

Appendix 1

Samuel Nicholas (Senior officer, Continental Marines)	1775–1781
William W. Burrows	1798–1804
Franklin Wharton	1804–1818
Anthony Gale	1819–1820
Archibald Henderson	1820–1859
John Harris	1859–1864
Jacob Zeilin	1864–1876
Charles G. McCawley	1876–1891
Charles Heywood	1891–1903
George F. Elliott	1903–1910
William P. Biddle	1911–1914
George Barnett	1914–1920
John A. Lejeune	1920–1929
Wendell C. Neville	1929–1930
Ben H. Fuller	1930–1934
John H. Russell	1934–1936
Thomas Holcomb	1936–1943
Alexander A. Vandegrift	1944–1947
Clifton B. Cates	1948–1951
Lemuel C. Shepherd, Jr.	1952–1955
Randolph McC. Pate	1956–1959
David M. Shoup	1960–1963
Wallace M. Greene, Jr.	1964–1967
Leonard F. Chapman, Jr.	1968–1971
Robert E. Cushman, Jr.	1972–1975
Louis H. Wilson	1975–1979
Robert H. Barrow	1979–

Appendix 2

STRENGTH OF THE MARINE CORPS

	Officers	Men
Continental Marines		
(1775–1783)	231	2,000 (est.)
1799	25	343
1803	23	501
1809	35	943
1812	37	1,294
1820	47	875
1836	58	1,086
1837	71	1,599
1855	63	1,340
1865	78	3,177
1876	92	1,871
1895	76	2,100
1898	116	4,700
1900	187	5,520
1910	334	9,267
1916	341	10,056
1918	2,462	72,639
1920	962	16,085
1926	1,177	17,976
1936	1,199	16,040
1940	1,556	26,369
1943	21,938	287,621
1945	37,664	447,389
1948	6,765	76,844
1950	7,254	67,025
1953	18,718	230,488
1958	16,741	172,754
1964	16,843	172,934
1967	23,592	261,677
1969	24,994	289,423
1971	22,000	190,000
1975	19,000	177,000
1979	18,325	171,675

SOURCE: Reference Section, Marine Corps History and Museums Division, Subject Files, "Strength and Distribution."

Appendix 3

U.S. Marine Corps Casualties

	Killed in action and died of wounds	Wounded in Action	Casualties All Causes *
Revolutionary War (1775–1783)	49	70	Unknown
Quasi-War with France (1797–1800)	6	11	Unknown
Barbary Expeditions (1801–1805)	4	10	Unknown
War of 1812	46	33	378
Creek-Seminole Wars (1836–1841)	8	1	65
Mexican War (1846–1848)	11	47	164
Civil War (Union only)	148	131	551
Spanish–American War (1898)	7	13	34
Philippine Insurrection (1899–1902)	7	19	41
Boxer Rebellion (1900)	9	17	187
Nicaragua (1912)	5	16	37
Veracruz Expedition (1914)	5	13	Unknown
Dominican Republic (1916–1920)	17	50	133
Haiti (1915–1934)	10	26	172
World War I (1917–1918)	2,457	8,894	12,179
Nicaragua (1926–1933)	47	66	202
World War II (1941–1945)	19,733	67,207	90,709
Korean War (1950–1953)	4,267	23,744	29,529
Southeast Asia (1961–1975)	12,983	88,591	103,255

* Includes KIA, DOW, WIA, and deaths from accidents and disease in area of combat operations.

SOURCES: Reference Section, Marine Corps History and Museums Division, Subject Files, "USMC Casualties and Strengths," 1976, and Annual Reports of the Commandant of the Marine Corps, 1899–1903.

Notes

INTRODUCTION

1. The Hon. J. W. Fortescue, *Military History: Its Scope and Definition,* lectures delivered at Trinity College, Cambridge (Cambridge: At the University Press, 1914).
2. Maurice Matloff, "The Nature and Scope of Military History," in Russell F. Weigley, ed., *New Dimensions in Military History* (San Rafael, Calif.: Presidio Press, 1975), pp. 387–409.
3. For statements of the "new" military history, see Pater Paret, "The History of War," *Daedalus* 100 (Spring 1971): 376–396; Jay Luvaas, "Military History: An Academic Historian's Point of View," and Theodore Ropp, "Armed Forces and Society: Some Hypotheses," in Weigley, *New Dimensions in Military History,* pp. 19–36 and 41–71.
4. Russell F. Weigley, *History of the United States Army* (New York: Macmillan, 1967).
5. Morris Janowitz, *Sociology and the Military Establishment,* 3d ed. (Beverly Hills, Calif.: Sage Publications, 1974), pp. 25–40; Kurt Lang, *Military Institutions and the Sociology of War* (Beverly Hills, Calif.: Sage Publications, 1972), pp. 53–82; and *idem,* "Military Organizations," in James G. March, ed., *Handbook of Organizations* (Chicago: Rand McNally, 1965), pp. 838–878.
6. Anant R. Negandhi, ed., *Modern Organizational Theory* (Kent, Ohio: Kent State University Press, 1973), pp. 2–4; Daniel Katz and Robert L. Kahn, *The Social Psychology of Organizations* (New York: Wiley, 1966), pp. 71–109; and Graham Allison, *The Essence of Decision* (Boston: Little, Brown, 1971), pp. 78–95.
7. Barry M. Blechman and Stephen S. Kaplan, *Force Without War* (Washington, D.C.: Brookings Institution, 1978), p. 45.
8. On this point, see especially Dennis E. Showalter, "Evolution of the U.S. Marine Corps as a Military Elite, *Marine Corps Gazette* 63 (November 1979): 44–58.
9. Bruce Catton, "The Marine Tradition," *American Heritage* 10 (February 1959): 24–25, 88–90.

CHAPTER 1. AMERICAN MARINES IN THE WAR FOR INDEPENDENCE, 1775–1783

1. Col. Cyril Field, RM, *Britain's Sea Soldiers,* 2 vols. (Liverpool: The Lyceum Press, 1924), I: 14–25.
2. Richard L. Morton, *Colonel Virginia,* 2 vols. (Chapel Hill: University of North Carolina Press, 1960), II: 526–532; E. Alfred Jones, "The American Regiment in the Cartaghena Expedition," *Virginia Magazine of History and Biography* 30 (January 1922): 1–20; Sir John W. Fortescue, *A History of the British Army,* 13 vols. (London: Macmillan, 1911–1935), II: 55–79.
3. G. M. Trevelyan, *England Under Queen Anne,* 3 vols. (London: Longmans, Green, 1932), II: 47.
4. Field, *Britain's Sea Soldiers,* I: 93–134.
5. For the naval history of the War for Independence, see Charles O. Paullin, *The Navy of the American Revolution* (Chicago: Burrows Brothers, 1906); and *idem,* "Classses of Operations of the Continental Navy," *U.S. Naval Institute Proceedings* (hereafter, *USNIP*), 21 (May 1905): 153–164; William M. Fowler, Jr., *Rebels Under Sail: The American Navy During the Revolution* (New York: Scribner's, 1976); and Frank C. Mevers III, "Congress and the

Navy: The Establishment and Administration of the American Revolutionary Navy by the Continental Congress, 1775–1784," unpublished Ph.D. dissertation, University of North Carolina–Chapel Hill, 1972. The basic source of documents is William Bell Clark and William J. Morgan, *Naval Documents of the American Revolution,* 7 vols. to date (Washington: Naval History Division, 1964–   ) (hereafter cited as *NDAR*).

For a description of ship types and characteristics, see Howard I. Chapelle, *The History of the American Sailing Navy* (New York: Bonanza Books, 1959), pp. 52–114.

6. Jesse Root to Silas Deane, May 25, 1775, *NDAR,* I: 528. The origins of marines in the American service was pursued most carefully by Major Edwin N. McClellan, "American Marines in the Revolution," *USNIP* 49 (June 1923): 957–963; *idem,* "The Birthday of the U.S. Marine Corps," *Daughters of the American Revolution Magazine* 58 (November 1924): 682–686; and *idem,* "Natal Day of the American Navy and Marines," *Daughters of the American Revolution Magazine* 68 (August 1934): 470–472.

McClellan eventually summarized his research on the Revolution in his "History of the United States Marine Corps," 2 vols., mss., Washington: Headquarters, U.S. Marine Corps, 1925–1932, Chapters 3–7, now superseded by Charles R. Smith, *Marines in the Revolution* (Washington: History and Museums Division, HQMC, 1975).

7. John W. Jackson, *The Pennsylvania Navy, 1775–1781* (New Brunswick, N.J.: Rutgers University Press, 1974), pp. 26–38.

8. Journal of the Continental Congress, November 10, 1775, and Committee on Nova Scotia, "Proposals," November 9, 1775, *NDAR,* II: 972, 957–958.

9. G. Washington to J. Hancock, November 19 and 28, 1775, and Journals of the Continental Congress, November 30, 1775, *NDAR,* II: 1071, 1168–1169, 1206–1207; J. Hancock to G. Washington, December 8, 1775, and G. Washington to J. Hancock, December 14, 1775, *NDAR,* III: 11, 94.

10. J. Hancock to G. Washington, October 5, 1775, *NDAR,* II: 311.

11. Mevers, "The American Revolutionary Navy," pp. 14–41.

12. Journal of the Continental Congress, "Rules for the Regulations of the Navy of the United Colonies," November 28, 1775, *NDAR, II:* 1174–1182; "First Commission in the Continental Marine Corps," November 28, 1775, *NDAR,* II: 1183.

13. Smith, *Marines in the Revolution,* pp. 12–16; "Muster Roll of Captain Craigs-Company of Mariens [sic] Philadelphia 19th December 1775," reprinted in Smith, *Marines in the Revolution,* p. 417. Genealogical data on Continental Marine officers are described in "Biographies of Continental Marine Officers" on pp. 429–478.

14. E. N. McClellan, *Uniforms of the American Marines, 1775 to 1829* (original ed. 1932; reprint, Washington: History and Museums Division, HQMC, 1974), pp. 2–4, and John R. Elting, ed., *Military Uniforms in America: The Era of the American Revolution, 1755–1795* (San Rafael, Calif.: The Company of Military Historians, 1974), pp. 98–99, 104–105.

15. Smith, *Marines in the Revolution,* pp. 17–18, 41–42.

16. Naval Committee to Commodore E. Hopkins, January 5, 1776, *NDAR,* III: 637–638.

17. Smith, *Marines in the Revolution,* pp. 41–57.

18. Journals of the Continental Congress, December 13, 1775, *NDAR,* III: 90.

19. Charles O. Paullin, *Paullin's History of Naval Administration, 1775–1911* (Annapolis: U.S. Naval Institute, 1968), pp. 3–53.

20. Mevers, "The American Revolutionary Navy, 1775–1784," pp. 42–66. See also John J. Kelly, Jr., "The Struggle for American Seaborne Independence as

Viewed by John Adams," unpublished Ph.D. dissertation, University of Maine, 1973, pp. 28–82.

21. Capt. J. Barry, CN, to Continental Marine Committee, April 7, 1776, *NDAR,* IV: 702.

22. Jackson, *The Pennsylvania Navy* (note 7 above), pp. 39–57, and Smith, *Marines in the Revolution,* pp. 64–68.

23. "Remarks on board His Majesty's Ship *Glasgow* Saturday the 6th day of April 1776" and "Extract of a Letter from the Captain of Marines [Samuel Nicholas] on board the Ship *Alfred . . .* April 10, 1776," *NDAR,* IV: 680–681, 748–751, and Smith, *Marines in the Revolution,* pp. 71–73.

24. Smith, *Marines in the Revolution,* pp. 73–79.

25. "Journal of the Committee Appointed to Build Two Continental Frigates in Rhode Island," June 20, 1776, and J. Langdon to W. Whipple, May 20, 1776, *NDAR,* IV: 637, 160.

26. Smith, *Marines in the Revolution,* pp. 79–83.

27. G. Washington to J. Cadwalader, December 7, 1776, quoted in Smith, *Marines in the Revolution,* p. 90.

28. William S. Stryker, *The Battles of Trenton and Princeton* (Boston: Houghton Mifflin, 1898), pp. 241–243, 253–274.

29. Smith, *Marines in the Revolution,* pp. 103–105.

30. Paullin, *The Navy of the American Revolution* (note 5 above), pp. 157–159.

31. For the operations of the Continental navy, see William Bell Clark, *Captain Dauntless: The Story of Nicholas Biddle of the Continental Navy* (Baton Rouge: Louisiana State University Press, 1949), and *idem, Gallant John Barry* (New York: Macmillan, 1938); Samuel Eliot Morison, *John Paul Jones* (Boston: Little, Brown, 1959); and William J. Morgan, *Captains to Northward: The New England Captains in the Continental Navy* (Barre, Mass.: Barre Gazette, 1959). The experience of the Continental marines is not well documented but can be sampled in "Diary of John Trevett, Captain of Marines," "Journal of William Jennison, Lieutenant of Marines," and "Journal of Joseph Hardy, Captain of Marines," reprinted in Smith, *Marines in the Revolution,* pp. 325–376.

32. Smith, *Marines in the Revolution,* pp. 109–122, 125–126, 155–172, 174–177.

33. Morison, *John Paul Jones,* pp. 103–181.

34. "Journal of William Jennison, Lieutenant of Marines," in Smith, *Marines in the Revolution,* pp. 346–347, 349.

35. Herbert Butterfield, ed., *Diary and Autobiography of John Adams,* 4 vols. (Cambridge, Mass.: The Belknap Press, 1961), II: 272.

36. *Ibid.,* II: 370–371.

37. Smith, *Marines in the Revolution,* pp. 232–234, and John S. Barnes, ed., *Fanning's Narrative: The Memoirs of Nathaniel Fanning, an Officer of the Revolutionary Navy* (New York: Naval History Society, 1912), pp. 37–38.

38. Smith, *Marines in the Revolution,* pp. 236–239.

39. *Ibid.,* pp. 199–204.

40. Brigadier General B. Arnold to Major General H. Gates, September 18, 1776, *NDAR,* IV: 884.

41. Jackson, *The Pennsylvania Navy* (note 7 above), pp. 205–305, and Smith, *Marines in the Revolution,* pp. 123–128, 172–173.

42. Smith, *Marines in the Revolution,* pp. 181–194.

43. Charles O. Paullin, "The Administration of the Massachusetts and Virginia Navies in the American Revolution," *USNIP,* 32 (March 1906): 131–164; George M. Brooke, "The Virginia Navy in the American Revolution," *Daughters of the American Revolution Magazine,* 44 (March 1960): 187–191;

Robert A. Stewart, *The History of Virginia's Navy of the Revolution* (Richmond, Va.: Mitchell and Hotchkiss, 1933); Gardner W. Allen, "State Navies and Privateers in the Revolution," *Proceedings of the Massachusetts Historical Society*, 46 (1913): 179–191; and Charles O. Paullin, "The Naval Administration of the Southern States During the Revolution," *Sewanee Review*, 10 (October 1902): 418–428.

44. Smith, *Marines in the Revolution*, pp. 204–214.
45. Morgan, *Captains to Northward* (note 31 above), pp. 189–207.
46. Mevers, "The American Revolutionary Navy (note 5 above), pp. 257–286. See also Stephen E. Powers, "The Decline and Extinction of American Naval Power, 1781–1787," unpublished Ph.D. dissertation, University of Notre Dame, 1965, pp. 1–37, 42–187.
47. Captain J. Hardy, CM, to W. Bingham, January 29, 1780, quoted in Smith, *Marines in the Revolution*, p. 252.
48. Smith, *Marines in the Revolution*, pp. 250–251, 258–259.
49. Clark, *Gallant John Barry* (note 31 above), pp. 211–213, 258–260.
50. "Matthew Parke," in Smith, *Marines in the Revolution*, pp. 463–464.

CHAPTER 2.   THE NEW CORPS, 1798–1815

1. Marshall Smelser, *The Congress Founds the Navy, 1787–1798* (Notre Dame, Ind.: University of Notre Dame Press, 1959), and Harold and Margaret Sprout, *The Rise of American Naval Power, 1776–1918* (Princeton, N.J.: Princeton University Press, 1944), pp. 16–49.
2. Quoted in Smelser, *The Congress Founds the Navy*, p. 38.
3. Naval Act of 1794 in U.S. Navy Department, *Laws of the United States in Relation to the Navy and Marine Corps* (Washington: J. and G. S. Gideon, 1843), pp. 31–32. See also E. N. McClellan, "From 1783 to 1798," *Marine Corps Gazette*, 7 (September 1922): 273–286.
4. Smelser, *The Congress Founds the Navy*, pp. 191–192. The Naval Act of 1797 is reprinted in U.S. Navy, Historical Division, *Naval Documents, Quasi-War with France*, 7 vols. (Washington: Government Printing Office, 1935–1938), I: 7–8 (hereafter cited as *ND/QWF*).
5. Secretary of War J. McHenry to Lieutenant of Marines, Frigate *Constellation*, March 16, 1798, *ND/QWF*, I: 40–42.
6. J. McHenry to S. Sewall, April 9, 1798, *ND/QWF*, I: 52–53.
7. "An Act for Establishing and Organizing a Marine Corps," U.S. Navy Department, *Laws of the United States in Relation to the Navy and Marine Corps*, pp. 42–44.
8. J. McHenry to House of Representatives, June 16, 1798, *American State Papers: Naval Affairs*, 4 vols. (Washington: Gales and Seaton, 1834–1861), I: 29–30 (hereafter cited as *ASP/NA*). See also Lucius C. Dunn, "The *Constellation's* First Marine Officer," *Maryland Historical Magazine*, 43 (September 1948): 210–219.
9. For the early days of the Navy Department, see Charles O. Paullin, *Paullin's History of Naval Administration, 1775–1911* (Annapolis, Md.: U.S. Naval Institute, 1968), pp. 89–118; John J. Carrigg, "Benjamin Stoddert and the Foundation of the American Navy," unpublished Ph.D. dissertation, Georgetown University, 1953; Leonard White, *The Federalists: A Study in Administrative History* (New York: Macmillan, 1948), pp. 156–163; Robert G. Albion, "Makers of Naval Policy, 1798–1947," mss. history for the Naval Historical Division, 1950, pp. 89–100, 140–141, 371–375; and William G. Anderson, "John Adams, the Navy, and the Quasi-War with France," *American Neptune*, 30 (April 1970): 117–132.

On Burrows and the early Marine Corps, see E. N. McClellan, "First Commandant of the Marine Corps, William Ward Burrows," *DAR Magazine,* 59 (March 1925): 155–159; *idem,* "History of the U.S. Marine Corps," 2 vols., mss., Washington: Headquarters, U.S. Marine Corps, 1925–1932, Vol. I, Chs. 10 and 11; and Lucius C. Dunn, "The U.S. Navy's First Sea-Going Marine Officer," *USNIP,* 75 (August 1949): 919–923.

10. Secretary of the Navy S. Stoddert to President J. Adams, August 3, 1798, *ND/QWF,* I: 269–270; Thomas Pinckney to Maj. Cmdt. W. W. Burrows, August 30, 1798, *ND/QWF,* I: 235; Maj. Cmdt. W. W. Burrows to Lt. M. Reynolds, August 23, 1799, General Records, HQMC, "Letters Sent, August 1798–June 1801 and March 1804–February 1884," Records of the United States Marine Corps, Record Group 127, National Archives of the United States (hereafter cited as HQMC "Letters Sent, 1798–1884," RG 127).

See also Bernard C. Nalty and Lieutenant Colonel Ralph F. Moody, *A Brief History of U.S. Marine Corps Officer Procurement, 1775–1969,* rev. ed., Marine Corps Historical Reference Pamphlet (Historical Division, HQMC, 1970).

11. Lt. D. S. Wynkoop to Maj. Cmdt. W. W. Burrows, August 5, 1798, Historical Division, HQMC, "Letters Received, 1798–1817," RG 127 (hereafter cited as HD/HQMC, "Letters Received, 1798–1817," RG 127); Lt. J. Tallman to Maj. Cmdt. W. W. Burrows, September 19, 1798, HD/HQMC, "Letters Received, 1798–1817," RG 127; Lt. J. Hall to Maj. Cmdt. W. W. Burrows, October 12, 1798, HD/HQMC, "Letters Received, 1798–1817," RG 127; Maj. Cmdt. W. W. Burrows to Lt. H. A. Williams, September 10, 1798, HQMC, "Letters Sent, 1798–1884," RG 127; Maj. Cmdt. W. W. Burrows to Lt. J. Weaver, September 29, 1798, HQMC "Letters Sent, 1798–1884," RG 127; Maj. Cmdt. W. W. Burrows to Lt. J. Church, November 9, 1798, HQMC "Letters Sent, 1798–1884," RG 127; Lt. R. Lilly to Maj. Cmdt. W. W. Burrows, November 2, 1798, HD/HQMC, "Letters Received, 1798–1817," RG 127; Maj. Cmdt. W. W. Burrows to Lt. R. Lilly, December 15, 1798, HQMC, "Letters Sent, 1798–1884," RG 127; Maj. Cmdt. W. W. Burrows to Lt. J. Church, March 6, 1799, HQMC, "Letters Sent, 1798–1884," RG 127; Maj. Cmdt. W. W. Burrows to Lt. J. Howard, June 7, 1799, HQMC, "Letters Sent, 1798–1884," RG 127; Lt. C. Church to Maj. Cmdt. W. W. Burrows, *ND/QWF,* III: 472; Lt. P. Edwards to Maj. Cmdt. W. W. Burrows, September 28, 1799, HD/HQMC, "Letters Received, 1798–1817," RG 127.

The recruiting program is described in McClellan, "History of the U.S. Marine Corps," Vol. I, Ch. 11.

12. Maj. Cmdt. W. W. Burrows to B. Stoddert, September 27, 1798, HQMC, "Letters Sent, 1798–1884," RG 127; Maj. Cmdt. W. W. Burrows to B. Stoddert, October 4, 1799, HQMC, "Letters Sent, 1798–1884," RG 127; "Summaries of Orders, 1798–1803," HQMC, RG 127; B. Stoddert to Maj. Cmdt. W. W. Burrows, April 1, 1799, *ND/QWF,* III: 1; B. Stoddert to W. Crafts, naval agent, Charleston, April 12, 1799, *ND/QWF,* III: 42; B. Stoddert to Maj. Cmdt. W. W. Burrows, June 23, 1800, *ND/QWF,* VI: 74; Carrigg, "Benjamin Stoddert and the Foundation of the American Navy," pp. 305–325; and Major E. N. McClellan, "How the Marine Corps Band Started," *USNIP,* 49 (April 1923): 581–586.

13. On the early Navy, see Dudley W. Knox, *A History of the United States Navy* (New York: G. P. Putnam's Sons, 1936), pp. 44–135, and Harold D. Langley, *Social Reform in the United States Navy, 1798–1862* (Urbana: University of Illinois Press, 1967). The best picture of the Navy, however, comes from the biographies of naval officers: David F. Long, *Nothing Too Daring: A Biography of Commodore David Porter, 1780–1843* (Annapolis: U. S. Naval In-

stitute, 1970); Thomas Harris, *The Life and Services of Commodore William Bainbridge* (Philadelphia: Carey Lea and Blanchard, 1837); H. A. S. Dearborn, *The Life of William Bainbridge,* ed. James Barnes (Princeton, N.J.: Princeton University Press, 1931); Christopher McKee, *Edward Preble: A Naval Biography, 1761–1807* (Annapolis: U. S. Naval Institute, 1972); Hulbert Footner, *Sailor of Fortune: The Life and Adventures of Commodore Barney, U.S.N.* (New York: Harper and Brothers, 1940); Allen W. Gardner, ed., *Papers of Isaac Hull* (Boston: Athenaeum, 1929); Bruce Grant, *Captain of Old Ironsides* [Issac Hull] (Chicago: Pellegrini and Cudahy, 1947); Charles O. Paullin, *Commodore John Rodgers, 1773–1838* (1909; reissue, Annapolis: U. S. Naval Institute, 1967); Charles Lee Lewis, *The Romantic Decatur* (Philadelphia: University of Pennsylvania Press, 1937); and Eugene S. Ferguson, *Truxton of the Constellation* (Baltimore: Johns Hopkins Press, 1956).

For the Quasi-War, see Gardner W. Allen, *Our Naval War with France* (Boston and New York: Houghton Mifflin, 1909), and Alexander DeConde, *The Quasi-War* (New York: Charles Scribner's Sons, 1966).

14. Lt. R. Harwood to Maj. Cmdt. W. W. Burrows, January 29, 1799, HD/HQMC, "Letters Received, 1798–1817," RG 127.

15. Maj. Cmdt. W. W. Burrows to Lt. J. W. Geddes, August 23, 1798, HQMC, "Letters Sent, 1798–1884," RG 127; Maj. Cmdt W. W. Burrows to Lt. J. Middleton, May 25, 1799, *ND/QWF,* III: 257; Maj. Cmdt. W. W. Burrows to Lt. R. Harwood, February 14, 1799, HQMC, "Letters Sent, 1798–1884," RG 127.

16. Capt. T. Truxton, USN, to Lt. J. Triplett, June 22, 1798, *ND/QWF,* I: 130–131; Capt. T. Truxton to Lt. (?) Saunders, August 21, 1798, *ND/QWF,* I: 362; Capt. T. Truxton, USN, to CO, USMC frigate *President,* July 28, 1800, *ND/QWF,* VI: 189–190.

17. Quoted in Carrigg, "Benjamin Stoddert and the Foundation of the American Navy," p. 62.

18. Capt. A. Murray, USN, to Lt. B. Clinch, July 1, 1800, *ND/QWF,* VI: 101.

19. McKee, *Edward Preble* pp. 80–81.

20. Lt. W. Cammack to Maj. Cmdt. W. W. Burrows, December 15, 1798, HD/HQMC, "Letters Received, 1798–1817," RG 127; B. Stoddert to Maj Cmdt. W. W. Burrows, December 4, 1798, *ND/QWF,* II: 64; Maj. Cmdt. W. W. Burrows to Lt. J. Hall, December 15, 1798, *ND/QWF,* II: 93; Lt. A. Gale to Maj. Cmdt. W. W. Burrows, February 22, 1799, *ND/QWF,* II: 386; Capt. D. Carmick to Maj. Cmdt. W. W. Burrows, July 9, 1799, *ND/QWF,* III: 480; Lt. H. A. Williams to Maj. Cmdt. W. W. Burrows, August 2, 1799, HD/HQMC, "Letters Received, 1798–1817," RG 127; Lt. J. Hall to Maj. Cmdt. W. W. Burrows, November 2, 1799, HD/HQMC, "Letters Received, 1798–1817," RG 127; Capt. D. Carmick to Maj. Cmdt. W. W. Burrows, August 18, 1799, *ND/QWF,* IV: 91–92; Lt. H. Caldwell to Maj. Cmdt. W. W. Burrows, October 19, 1799, *ND/QWF,* IV: 299; Lt. B. Strother to Maj. Cmdt. W. W. Burrows, February 26, 1800, HD/HQMC, "Letters Received, 1798–1817," RG 127; Lt. B. Strother to Maj. Cmdt. W. W. Burrows, January 11, 1800, *ND/QWF,* V: 64–65; Lt. S. Llewellin to Maj. Cmdt. W. W. Burrows, May 19, 1800, *ND/QWF,* V: 536; Lt. N. Keene to Maj. Cmdt. W. W. Burrows, June 18, 1800, *ND/QWF,* VI: 58; Maj. Cmdt. W. W. Burrows to B. Stoddert, July 31, 1800, *ND/QWF,* IV: 212; Maj. Cmdt. W. W. Burrows to B. Stoddert, November 25 and 27, 1800, *ND/QWF,* VI: 550; Lt. S. Llewellin to Maj. Cmdt. W. W. Burrows, December 28, 1800, *ND/QWF,* VII: 51; and Lt. J. L. Lewis to Maj. Cmdt. W. W. Burrows, February 23, 1801, *ND/QWF,* VII: 127–128.

See also N. R. [Edwin N. McClellan], "The Early Years of the Marine

Corps," *Marine Corps Gazette,* 4 (September 1919): 259–267 (hereafter cited as *MCG*).

21. Lt. B. Clinch to Maj. Cmdt. W. W. Burrows, June 8, 1799, HD/HQMC, "Letters Received, 1798–1817," RG 127; "Extract from a Letter on board the U.S. Frigate *Constellation. . . ,*" February 7, 1800, *ND/QWF,* V: 164–166; and Maj. Cmdt. W. W. Burrows to B. Stoddert, July 24, 1800, *ND/QWF,* VI, p. 175.

22. Colonel William M. Miller and Major John H. Johnstone, *A Chronology of the United States Marine Corps, 1775–1934,* Marine Corp Historical Reference Pamphlet (Washington: Historical Branch, HQMC, 1965), pp. 36–44, and Clyde H. Metcalf, *A History of the United States Marine Corps* (New York: G. P. Putnam's Sons, 1939), pp. 33–36.

23. Lt. J. Lewis to Maj. Cmdt. W. W. Burrows, August 11, 1800, *ND/QWF,* VI: 239–241; Cmdre. T. Truxton to Maj. Cmdt. W. W. Burrows, July 21, 1800, HD/HQMC, "Letters Received, 1798–1817," RG 127; Lt. J. Lewis to Lt. Col. Cmdt. W. W. Burrows, January 1, 1801, HD/HQMC, "Letters Received, 1798–1817," RG 127; Lt. J. R. Fenwick to Maj. Cmdt. W. W. Burrows, February 18, 1800, HD/HQMC, "Letters Received, 1798–1817," RG 127; Lt. N. Keene to Lt. Col. Cmdt. W. W. Burrows, April 11, 1801, HD/HQMC, "Letters Received, 1798–1817," RG 127; and Lt. J. R. Fenwick to Lt. Col. Cmdt. W. W. Burrows, April 15, 1801," HD/HQMC, "Letters Received, 1798–1817," RG 127.

24. Cmdre. T. Truxton to Lt. Col. Cmdt. W. W. Burrows, April 12, 1801, *ND/QWF,* VII: 187–189.

25. Cmdre. T. Truxton to the Secretary of the Navy, April 15, 1801, *ND/QWF,* VII: 195.

26. "Extracts from the Secretary of the Navy's Department Circular to the Captains," August 19, 1801, in "Marine Corps Orders, August, 1803–January 11, 1815," Orders Issued and Received, HQMC, RG 127, reprinted in Historical Division, U.S. Navy, *Naval Documents Related to the United States Wars with the Barbary Powers,* 7 vols. (Washington: Government Printing Office, 1939–1944), I: 556–558 (hereafter cited as *ND/BW*). See also Lt. Col. Cmdt. W. W. Burrows to Acting Secretary of the Navy H. A. Dearborn, June 28, 1801, *ND/BW,* I: 492.

27. Karl Schuon, *Home of the Commandants* (Washington: Leatherneck Association, Inc., 1966), pp. 49–59.

28. Constance McLaughlin Green, *Washington: Village and Capitol, 1800–1878* (Princeton, N.J.: Princeton University Press, 1962), pp. 23–55.

29. Lt. Col. Cmdt. W. W. Burrows to Lt. R. Greenleaf, April 3, 1801, *ND/QWF,* VII: 179; Capt. J. McKnight to Lt. Col. Cmdt. W. W. Burrows, April 6, 1801, and Lt. P. N. O'Bannon to Lt. Col. Cmdt. W. W. Burrows, April 7, 1801, HD/HQMC, "Letters Received, 1798–1817," RG 127; and McClellan, "History of the U. S. Marine Corps," (note 9 above), Vol. I, Ch. 16.

30. Paullin, *Paullin's History of Naval Administration* (note 9 above), pp. 122–148; Leonard D. White, *The Jeffersonians: A Study in Administrative History, 1801–1829* (New York: Macmillan, 1951), pp. 265–298; McClellan, "History of the U. S. Marine Corps," Vol. 1, Chs. 16–18; Secretary of the Navy R. T. Smith to the House of Representatives, February 14 and November 2 and 4, 1803, *ASP/NA,* I: 110–111; and R. T. Smith to the Senate, February 9, 1809 *ASP/NA,* I: 192.

31. R. T. Smith to T. Jefferson, March 27, 1804, *ND/BW,* III: 534; R. T. Smith to Lt. Col. Cmdt. F. Wharton, April 9, 1804, *ND/BW,* IV: 18; Lt. Col. F. Wharton to R. T. Smith, March 27, 1804, HQMC, "Letters Sent, 1798–1884," RG 127; Lt. Col. Cmdt. F. Wharton to Lt. J. Johnson, August 21, 1806,

HQMC, "Letters Sent, 1798–1884," RG 127; and HQMC, "Marine Corps Orders, August 22, 1803–January 11, 1815," RG 127.

32. Lt. Col. Cmdt. F. Wharton to Lt. W. L. Bush, June 10, 1811, HQMC, "Letters Sent, 1798–1884," RG 127.

33. Brig. Gen. A. Henderson to Secretary of the Navy J. C. Dobbin, May 27, 1854, HQMC, "Letters Sent, 1798–1884," RG 127.

34. R. T. Smith to Lt. Col. Cmdt. W. W. Burrows, May 21, 1802, *ND/BW,* II: 157, and R. T. Smith to Lt. Col. Cmdt. W. W. Burrows, May 6, 1903, *ND/ BW,* II: 400. For the development of two of the yards, see Henry B. Hibben, *Navy Yard, Washington: History from Organization, 1799, to Present Date,* 51st Congress, 1st Session, Senate Executive Doc. 22, (Washington, 1890), and George H. Preble, "History of the Boston Navy Yard, 1797–1874," 3 vols., Naval Records Collection of the Office of Naval Records and Library, Record Group 45, NA.

35. Secretary of the Navy Order, August 19, 1811, HQMC, "Marine Corps Orders, August 22, 1803–January 11, 1815," RG 127.

36. Lt. Col. F. Wharton to Lt. R. L. Wainwright, June 29, 1810, HQMC, "Letters Sent, 1798–1884," RG 127.

37. On the jurisdictional question: R. T. Smith to Capt. S. Nicholson, USN, July 20, 1802, *ND/BW,* II: 206; Lt. Col. Cmdt. F. Wharton to Capt. H. Caldwell, December 12, 1810, HQMC, "Letters Sent, 1798–1884," RG 127; Lt. Col. Cmdt. F. Wharton to R. T. Smith, January 26, 1808, HQMC, "Letters Sent, 1798–1884," RG 127; Lt. A. Henderson to Lt. J. Brooks and Lt. J. Johnson to Capt. I. Chauncey, USN, January 20, 1808, HD/HQMC, "Letters Received, 1798–1817," RG 127; and Lt. J. Johnson to Lt. Col. Cmdt. F. Wharton, January 20, 1808, HD/HQMC, "Letters Received, 1798–1817," RG 127.

38. Secretary of the Navy to Capt. D. Carmick, January 21, 1804, *ND/BW,* III: 350; Lt. Col. Cmdt. F. Wharton to Capt. D. Carmick, May 10, 1907, HQMC, "Letters Sent, 1798–1884," RG 127; Secretary of the Navy Paul Hamilton to Lt. Col. Cmdt. F. Wharton, December 18, 1810, Office of the Secretary of the Navy, "Letters to the Commandant and Other Officers of the Marine Corps, 1804–1886," General Records of the Navy Department, RG 80, NA; Major D. Carmick to Lt. Col. F. Wharton, January 30, 1811, HD/HQMC, "Letters Received, 1798–1817," RG 127; McClellan, "History of the U. S. Marine Corps," Vol. I, Ch. 17; and Major E. N. McClellan, "The Navy in New Orleans," *USNIP,* 50 (December 1924): 2041–2060.

39. P. Hamilton to Capt. R. Greenleaf, April 22, 1811, HD/HQMC, "Letters Received, 1798–1817," RG 127; Capt. J. Williams to Lt. Col. Cmdt. F. Wharton, September 15, 1818, HD/HQMC, "Letters Received, 1798–1817," RG 127; and McClellan, "History of the U.S. Marine Corps," Vol. I, Ch. 19.

40. Capt. D. Carmick to Lt. Col. Cmdt. W. W. Burrows, October 15, 1802, HD/ HQMC, "Letters Received, 1798–1817," RG 127.

41. Capt. E. Preble, USN, to Capt. J. Hall, July 25, 1803, *ND/BW,* II: 497, and Capt. E. Preble, USN, "Internal Rules and Regulations for U.S. Frigate *Constitution, 1803–1804,"* *ND/BW,* III: 32–41.

42. Capt. A. Gale to Lt. Col. Cmdt. F. Wharton, January 20, 1806, HD/HQMC, "Letters Received, 1798–1817," RG 127.

43. McKee, *Edward Preble* (note 13 above), p. 262.

44. Lt. Col. Cmdt. F. Wharton to Capt. J. Hall, March 14, 1807, HQMC, "Letters Sent, 1798–1884," RG 127. On the contrasts with the British, see Lt. N. Keene to Lt. Col. Cmdt. W. W. Burrows, July 9, 1801, and Lt. J. R. Fenwick to Lt. Col. W. W. Burrows, August 5, 1801, *ND/BW,* I: 506–507 and 542–543.

45. Lt. Col. Cmdt. F. Wharton to Capt. D. Carmick, February 5, 1808, HQMC, "Letters Sent, 1798–1884," RG 127.
46. Lt. C. Ludlow, USN, to Capt. H. Campbell, USN, June 9, 1807, and Capt. H. Campbell, USN, to the Secretary of the Navy, September 3, 1807, both in "Letters from Captains, January, 1805–December, 1861," Naval Records Collection of the Office of Naval Records and Library, RG 45, NA.
47. Lt. Col. Cmdt. F. Wharton to Lt. W. Amory, October 22, 1807, HQMC, "Letters Sent, 1798–1884," RG 127.
48. Lt. Col. Cmdt. A. Henderson to Secretary of the Navy S. L. Southard, November 28, 1828, HQMC, "Letters Sent, 1798–1884," RG 127.
49. For detailed accounts of the Barbary Wars, see Glen Tucker, *Dawn Like Thunder: The Barbary Wars and the Birth of the U.S. Navy* (Indianapolis: Bobbs-Merrill, 1963), and McClellan, "History of the U. S. Marine Corps," Vol. I, Ch. 15.
50. Cmdre. E. Preble to the Secretary of the Navy, September 18, 1804, *ND/BW*, IV: 293–309, and Cmdre. E. Preble, "General Orders," August 4, 1804, *ND/QWF*, IV: 361.
51. On O'Bannon, see Capt. H. Campbell, USN, to Lt. Col. Cmdt. W. W. Burrows, December 16, 1802, HQMC, "Letters Received, 1798–1884," RG 127, and Charles Lee Lewis, *Famous American Marines* (Boston: L. C. Page and Company, 1950), pp. 39–54.
52. On the Eaton expedition, see Tucker, *Dawn Like Thunder,* pp. 347–430; Samuel Edwards, *Barbary General: The Life of William H. Eaton* (Englewood Cliffs, N.J.: Prentice-Hall, 1968), pp. 1–15, 153–223; and Louis B. Wright and Julia H. Macleod, *The First Americans in North Africa* (Princeton, N.J.: Princeton University Press, 1945).
53. W. H. Eaton to the Secretary of the Navy, August 9, 1805, *ND/BW,* VI: 213–218.
54. For naval policy in the war of 1812, see Sprout and Sprout, *The Rise of American Naval Power* (note 1 above), pp. 73–85, and the classics: Alfred T. Mahan, *Sea Power in Its Relation to the War of 1812,* 2 vols. (Boston: Little, Brown, 1905), and Theodore Roosevelt, *The Naval War of 1812* (New York: G. P. Putnam's Sons, 1882). For the Navy's role, see Knox, *History of the United States Navy* (note 13 above), pp. 79–135. The most detailed account is McClellan, "History of the U. S. Marine Corps" (note 9 above), Vol. I, Chs. 20–24.
55. McClellan, "History of the U. S. Marine Corps," I, Ch. 18: 7–8.
56. P. Hamilton to Lt. Col. Cmdt. F. Wharton, June 19, 1812, HD/HQMC, "Letters Received, 1798–1817," RG 127.
57. Lt. Col. Cmdt. F. Wharton to Lt. T. R. Swift, January 6, 1814, HQMC, "Letters Sent, 1798–1884," RG 127.
58. Lt. J. Contee to Lt. Col. Cmdt. F. Wharton, August 30, 1812, HD/HQMC, "Letters Received, 1798–1817," RG 127, and Roosevelt, *Naval War of 1812,* p. 91.
59. Roosevelt, *Naval War of 1812,* pp. 121–122.
60. Capt. C. Stewart, USN, to Secretary of the Navy B. W. Crowninshield, May, 1815, *ASP/NA,* I: 406–407.
61. Lt. J. Blakely, USN, to W. Jones, July 8, 1814, *ASP/NA,* I: 315–318, and Roosevelt, *Naval War of 1812,* pp. 321–326, 431.
62. Roosevelt, *Naval War of 1812,* pp. 185–186.
63. Lt. R. D. Wainwright to Lt. Col. Cmdt. F. Wharton, July 10–17, 1812, and Maj. D. Carmick to Lt. Col. Cmdt. F. Wharton, August 31, 1812, HD/HQMC, "Letters Received, 1798–1817," RG 127, and Lt. Col. Cmdt. F. Wharton to

Capt. R. D. Wainwright, December 20, 1812, HQMC, "Letters Sent, 1798–1884," RG 127.

64. Lt. S. Miller to Lt. Col. Cmdt. F. Wharton, August 24 and 25, 1813, HD/ HQMC, "Letters Received, 1798–1817," RG 127.

65. Reports of Brigadier General W. Winder and Commodore Joshua Barney, August 27 and August 29, in U.S. Congress, House of Representatives, *Report of the Committee . . . to Inquire into the Causes and Particulars of the Invasion of the City of Washington by the British Forces in the Month of August, 1814* (Washington: A. and G. Way, 1814), and Lt. Col. S. Miller to Secretary of the Navy David Henshaw, December 24, 1843, Samuel Miller Papers, Marine Corps Personal Papers Collection (MCPPC).

66. Captain T. Tingey, USN, "Destruction of the Washington Navy Yard," August 27, 1814, in Hibben, *Navy Yard, Washington* (note 34 above), pp. 52–54; Lt. Col. Cmdt. F. Wharton to Capts. A. Henderson and J. Heath, both September 4, 1814, HQMC, "Letters Sent, 1798–1884," RG 127; and court-martial order, case of Cpl. T. Patterson, October 7, 1814, HQMC, "Marine Orders, August 22, 1803–January 11, 1815," RG 127.

67. Wilburt S. Brown, *The Amphibious Campaign for West Florida and Louisiana, 1814–1815* (University, Ala.: University of Alabama Press, 1969), pp. 101–162.

CHAPTER 3.   ARCHIBALD HENDERSON PRESERVES
THE CORPS, 1815–1859

1. Charles O. Paullin, *Paullin's History of Naval Administration, 1775–1911* (Annapolis, Md.: U.S. Naval Institute, 1960), pp. 159–247; Dudley W. Knox, *A History of the United States Navy* (New York: G. P. Putnam's Sons, 1936), pp. 149–190; Robert E. Johnson, *Thence Round Cape Horn: The Story of United States Naval Forces on Pacific Station, 1818–1923* (Annapolis, Md.: U.S. Naval Institute, 1963); *idem, Far China Station: The U.S. Navy in Asian Waters, 1800–1898* (Annapolis, Md.: U.S. Naval Institute Press, 1979); Edward B. Billingsley, *In Defense of Neutral Rights: The United States Navy and the Wars of Independence in Chile and Peru* (Chapel Hill: University of North Carolina Press, 1967); and Maury D. Baker, Jr., "The United States and Piracy during the Spanish–American Wars of Independence," unpublished Ph.D. dissertation, Duke University, 1946.

2. Harold D. Langley, *Social Reform in the United States Navy, 1798–1862* (Urbana: University of Illinois Press, 1967).

3. Secretary of the Navy B. W. Crowninshield to Lt. Col. Cmdt. F. Wharton, March 13, 1815, Office of the Secretary of the Navy, "Letters Sent to the Commandant and Other Officers of the Marine Corps, 1804–1886," General Records of the Navy Department, Record Group 80, National Archives (hereafter cited as SecNav Letters Sent USMC, 1804–1886," RG 80).

4. *Annals of Congress,* 14th Congress, 1st Session (1815–1816), pp. 1308, 1410, 1438; B. W. Crowninshield to Hon. James Pleasants, Jr., April 11 and 16, 1816, with appendices, *American State Papers: Naval Affairs,* 4 vols. (Washington: Gales and Seaton, 1834–1861), I: 427–29; and Navy Department, *Laws of the United States in Relation to the Navy and the Marine Corps* (Washington: J. and G. S. Gideon, 1843), p. 113.

5. Documents, "Trial of Franklin Wharton, Lieutenant Colonel of Marines," transmitted by B. W. Crowninshield to the House of Representatives, April 4, 1818, *ASP/NA,* I: 503–510, and Navy General Order, October 1, 1817, "SecNav Letters Sent USMC, 1804–1886," RG 80.

6. Bvt. Maj. R. Smith to Bvt. Maj. A. Henderson, November 19, 1818, Historical

Division, Office of the Commandant HQMC, "Letters Received, 1818–1915," Records of the United States Marine Corps, Record Group 127, National Archives (hereafter cited as HD/HQMC, "Letters Received, 1818–1915," RG 127).

7. Capt. R. D. Wainwright and Bvt. Maj. J. Gamble to Bvt. Maj. A. Henderson, November 20, 1818, HD/HQMC, "Letters Received, 1818–1915," RG 127; Bvt. Maj. S. Miller–Bvt. Maj. R. Smith correspondence, December 29, 1820–March 12, 1821, Miller Papers, and letters of eight members of Congress to President James Monroe on behalf of Bvt. Major S. Miller, 1818, Miller Papers, MCPPC.

8. Bvt. Maj. S. Miller to Lt. Col. Cmdt. A. Gale, September 11, 1820, General Records, HQMC, "Letters Sent, August 1798–June 1801 and March 1804–February 1884," 38 vols., Records of the United States Marine Corps, Record Group 127, National Archives (hereafter cited as HQMC, "Letters Sent, 1798–1884," RG 127).

    For Gale's position, see Lt. Col. Cmdt. A. Gale to Secretary of the Navy S. Thompson, August 8, 1820, HQMC, "Letters Sent, 1798–1884," RG 127, and report on the petition of Anthony Gale, Committee on Naval Affairs to the House of Representatives, January 27, 1829, *ASP/NA,* III: 284.

9. I have drawn my own conclusions about Henderson from reading his correspondence in the Marine Corps archives. For laudatory but detailed sketches, see Ralph W. Donnelly, "Archibald Henderson, Marine," *Virginia Cavalcade* 20 (Winter 1971): 39–47, and Charles Lee Lewis, *Famous American Marines* (Boston: L. C. Page and Company, 1950), pp. 75–79.

10. Commandant of the Marine Corps and Adjutant and Inspector to "All Officers on Foreign Service or Commanding Posts," November 1820–April 1822, "Marine Corps Orders, 1815–1822," Orders Issued and Received, HQMC, August 1798–February, 1886, Records of the United States Marine Corps, Record Group 127, National Archives.

    See Major E. N. McClellan, "History of the U. S. Marine Corps," 2 vols. (typescript manuscript, 1924–1935, Breckinridge Library, Education Center, MCDEC, Quantico, Virginia), Vol. II, Chapter 2, for Marine Corps affairs, 1816–1820.

11. Lt. Col. Cmdt. A. Henderson to S. Thompson, February 7, 1821, HQMC, "Letters Sent, 1798–1884," RG 127.

12. Lt. Col. Cmdt. A. Henderson to President J. Monroe, January 13, 1823, HQMC, "Letters Sent, 1798–1884," RG 127; Lt. Col. Cmdt. A. Henderson to Secretary of the Navy S. L. Southard, May 23, 1826, HQMC, "Letters Sent, 1798–1884," RG 127; S. L. Southard to Lt. Col. Cmdt. A. Henderson, October 19, 1827, HD/HQMC, "Letters Received, 1818–1915," RG 127; Lt. P. G. Howle to Col. Cmdt. A. Henderson, April 14, 1836, HD/HQMC, "Letters Received, 1818–1915," RG 127; and Bvt. Lt. Col. R. Smith to Lt. Col. Cmdt. A. Henderson, December 27, 1827, HD/HQMC, "Letters Received, 1818–1915," RG 127.

13. Appendix, "Register of Officers, U.S. Marine Corps, 1798 to 1903," in Richard S. Collum, *History of the United States Marine Corps,* rev. ed. (Philadelphia: L. R. Hamersly and Co., 1903), pp. 429–479.

14. Bvt. Lt. Col. R. Smith to Lt. Col. Cmdt. A. Henderson, July 3, 1828, HD/HQMC, "Letters Received, 1818–1915," RG 127. See also report of the Committee on Naval Affairs to the Senate, January 21, 1818, *ASP/NA,* I: 453–455; documents, "Trials of Captain Oliver H. Perry, of the Navy, and Captain John Heath, of the Marine Corps," B. W. Crowninshield to the House of Representatives, January 30, 1818, *ASP/NA,* I: 470–480; Board of Navy Commissioners to Secretary of the Navy M. Dickerson, July 2, 1835, "Letters Sent to the Secretary of the Navy," records of the Board of Navy Commissioners,

Naval Records Collection of the Office of Naval Records and Library, Record Group 45, National Archives (herafter cited as BNC "Letters Sent"); Lt. J. L. Broome to Cmdre. W. Mervine, USN, February 4, 1855, John L. Broome Papers, MCPPC; and Capt. A. Claxton, USN, to Lt. J. C. Rich, January 1 and 2, 1840, HD/HQMC, "Letters Received, 1818–1915," RG 127.

15. Lt. T. Linton et al. to the Congress, February 11, 1829, *ASP/NA,* III: 307 and pay voucher, Lt. T. Y. Field, February 1, 1855, Thomas Yardley Field Papers, MCPPC.

16. Charles Nordhoff, *Man-of-War Life* (Cincinnati: Moore, Wilstach, Keys and Co., 1856), pp. 57, 65.

17. E. C. Wines, *Two Years and a Half in the Navy,* 2 vols. (Philadelphia: Carey and Lea, 1832), I: p. 34.

18. Herman Melville, *White Jacket,* rev. ed. (London: J. Lehman, 1952), pp. 39, 169, 180–81. See also George Jones, *Sketches of Naval Life,* 2 vols. (New Haven: H. Howe, 1829), I: 26–27, 44.

19. Lt. Robert L. Browning, USMC, journal of cruise on USS *Savannah,* 1853, Browning Family Papers, Naval Historical Foundation Collection, Manuscript Division, Library of Congress, and Lt. A. H. Gillespie to Brig. Gen. Cmdt. A. Henderson, September 17, 1845, HD/HQMC, "Letters Received, 1818–1915," RG 127.

20. Capt. C. Tuppen to Col. Cmdt. A. Henderson, June 30, 1836; Lt. A. H. Gillispie to Col. Cmdt. A. Henderson, July 7, 1839; Lt. A. Garland to Col. Cmdt. A. Henderson, April 13, 1840, all in HD/HQMC, "Letters Received, 1818–1915," RG 127, and "Harry Gringo" [Lt. Henry A. Wise, USN], *Tales for the Marines* (Boston: Sampson and Company, 1855), pp. 115, 135–36.

21. Charles Lee Lewis, *David Glasgow Farragut* (Annapolis: U.S. Naval Institute, 1941), pp. 276–83.

22. Lt. H. N. Crabb to Col. Cmdt. A. Henderson, April 12, 1835, HD/HQMC, "Letters Received, 1818–1915," RG 127. See also S. L. Southard to Lt. Col. Cmdt. A. Henderson, November 8, 1826, HD/HQMC, "Letters Received, 1818–1915," RG 127.

23. Lt. Col. Cmdt. A. Henderson to S. L. Southard, November 28, 1828, and Lt. Col. Cmdt. A. Henderson to Bvt. Lt. Col. J. M. Gamble, October 30, 1828, HQMC, "Letters Sent, 1798–1884," RG 127; Bvt. Lt. Col. J. M. Gamble to Lt. Col. Cmdt. A. Henderson, November 11, 1828, HD/HQMC, "Letters Received, 1818–1915," RG 127; and Brig. Gen. A. Henderson, circular to commanding officers of Marine posts and rendezvous, September 18, 1828, "Orders and Circulars Issued by the Commandant, 1805–1860," RG 127.

24. Capt. S. E. Watson to Lt. Col. Cmdt. A. Henderson, March 17, 1830, HD/HQMC, "Letters Received, 1818–1915," RG 127.

25. Col. Cmdt. A. Henderson to the Hon. W. P. Fessenden, January 9, 1843, HQMC, "Letters Sent, 1798–1884," RG 127.

26. The section on landing party operations is based on Capt. Harry A. Ellsworth, USMC, "One Hundred Eighty Landings of United States Marines, 1800–1934," 2 vols., (typescript copy in Breckinridge Library, Education Center, MCDEC, Quantico, Virginia). See also McClellan, "History of the U.S. Marine Corps" (note 10 above), Vol. II, Ch. 3.

27. Collum, *History of the United States Marine Corps* (note 13 above), pp. 64–66, and David F. Long, " 'Martial Thunder': The First Official American Armed Intervention in Asia," *Pacific Historical Review,* 42 (May 1973): 143–162.

28. Office of the Commandant, "Exhibit Showing the Numbers of Commissioned, Non-Commissioned Officers, Musics and Privates required for the several classes of vessels in the U.S. Navy," 1825, copy in "Marine Corps Orders, 1822–1851,"

HQMC, Orders Issued and Received, RG 127; S. L. Southard to Lt. Col. Cmdt. A. Henderson, May 3, 1826, *ASP/NA,* II: 723; and Committee on Naval Affairs, House Report 196, "Increase Marine Corps," May 6, 1826, 19th Congress, 1st Session.

29. Capt. C. G. Ridgely, USN, to the Secretary of the Navy, March 6, 1830, and Lt. J. M. Keever, USN, to the Secretary of the Navy, March 9, 1830, appendixes to Secretary of the Navy John Branch to the U.S. Senate, March 23, 1830, "On the Expediency of Dispensing with the Marine Corps as Part of the Armed Equipment of a Vessel-of-War," *ASP/NA,* III: 560–69. Other "antis" who wrote the Secretary were Isaac Hull, L. Warrington, Daniel Patterson, W. M. Crane, and A. J. Dallas. John Rodgers and William Bainbridge were guarded in their response.

30. n. a. [A. S. Mackenzie], "Report of the Secretary of the Navy . . . December 1, 1829," *North American Review,* 30 (April 1830): 385–386.

31. Letters of Charles Stewart (March 8, 1830), J. Jones (March 6, 1830), J. Orde Creighton (March 6, 1830), E. P. Kennedy (March 6, 1830), J. J. Nicholson (March 7, 1830), B. F. Hoffman (March 5, 1830), and T. apC. Jones (March 5, 1830) to the Secretary of the Navy, appendixes to Branch to Senate, March 23, 1830, "On Expediency of Dispensing with the Marine Corps"; and Lt. H. H. R. Hodes USN and Lt. J. Williams USN to Lt. G. F. Lindsay, October 20, 1830, and Bvt. Lt. Col. J. M. Gamble to Lt. Col. Cmdt. A. Henderson, March 21, 1831, all HD/HQMC, "Letters Received, 1818–1915," RG 127.

32. Board of Navy Commissioners to M. Dickerson, June 11, 1836, and December 20, 1837, BNC "Letters Sent," RG 45.

33. Board of Navy Commissioners to Acting Secretary of the Navy Isaac Chauncey (Commodore, USN), September 24, 1839, copy in Subject File VR ("United States Marine Corps"), Records Collection of the Office of Naval Records and Library, RG 45.

34. Col. Cmdt. A. Henderson to Secretary of the Navy James K. Paulding, October 7, 1839, copy in Subject File VR ("United States Marine Corps"), RG 45; Board of Navy Commissioners to J. K. Paulding, October 8, 1839, BNC "Letters Sent," RG 45; and Col. Cmdt. A. Henderson to J. K. Paulding, October 17, 1839, HQMC, "Letters Sent, 1798–1884," RG 127.

35. Col. Cmdt. A. Henderson to Secretary of the Navy George E. Bader, May 11, 1841, Subject File VR ("United States Marine Corps"), RG 45; Col. Cmdt. A. Henderson to Secretary of the Navy Abel P. Upshur, November 9, 1841, HQMC, "Letters Sent, 1798–1884," RG 127; and Col. Cmdt. A. Henderson to the Hon. W. P. Fessenden, January 9, 1843, HQMC, "Letters Sent, 1798–1884," RG 127.

36. Col. Cmdt. A. Henderson to Secretary of the Navy John Y. Mason, April 18, 1844, and to Secretary of the Navy George Bancroft, October 13, 1845, both HQMC, "Letters Sent, 1798–1884," RG 127, and Navy Department Order, October 15, 1844, "Marine Corps Orders, 1822–1851," HQMC, Orders Issued and Received, RG 127.

37. Appendix, "Register of Officers US Marine Corps, 1798 to 1903," in Collum, *History of the United States Marine Corps,* rev. ed. (note 13 above), pp. 429–449.

38. Lt. Col. Cmdt. A. Henderson to S. L. Southard November 28, 1824, HQMC, "Letters Sent, 1798–1884," RG 127.

39. Charles W. Goldsborough, clerk of the Navy Department, *Naval Register 1820* (Washington: n.p., 1820), and *Naval Register 1840* (Washington: n.p., 1840).

40. Lt. Col. Cmdt. A. Henderson to S. L. Southard, April 5, 1827, HQMC, "Letters Sent, 1798–1884," RG 127; S. L. Southard to Lt. Col. Cmdt. A. Henderson, January 28 and April 9, 1828, HD/HQMC, "Letters Received, 1818–1915," RG 127; and Secretary of the Navy Isaac Toucey to Maj. H. B. Tyler, December 31, 1860, HD/HQMC, "Letters Received, 1818–1915," RG 127.

41. Bvt. Lt. Col. J. M. Gamble to Lt. Col. Cmdt. A. Henderson, April 15, 1831, HD/HQMC, "Letters Received, 1818–1915," RG 127.

42. Lt. A. H. Gillespie to Brig. Gen. Cmdt. A. Henderson, July 18, 1845, HD/HQMC, "Letters Received, 1818–1915," RG 127.

43. Headquarters Marine Corps, "Register of Desertions from the United States Marine Corps . . . ," November 18, 1824, Annex F to the opinion of the Secretary of the Navy to the Senate, January 1, 1825, *ASP/NA,* II: 59–78.

44. Pvt. Henry S. Donley to Lt. Col. Cmdt. A. Henderson, July 17, 1827, HD/HQMC, "Letters Received, 1818–1915," RG 127.

45. The enlistment problems are summarized in the following sources: Maj. S. Miller to Lt. P. G. Howle, September 28, 1817, HQMC, "Letters Sent, 1798–1884," RG 127; Lt. Col. Cmdt. A. Henderson to Maj. J. M. Gamble, September 25, 1823, HQMC, "Letters Sent, 1798–1884," RG 127; S. L. Southard to Lt. Col. Cmdt. A. Henderson, May 3 and August 7 1826, HD/HQMC, "Letters Received, 1818–1915," RG 127; Headquarters Marine Corps, Orders of April 26, 1824, May 10, 1825, November 8, 1826, November 11, 1826, and and March 23, 1835, "Marine Corps Orders, 1822–1851," in Orders Issued and Received, HQMC, RG 127; and Lt. Col. Cmdt. A. Henderson to Secretary of the Navy Levi Woodbury, September 10, 1833, HQMC, "Letters Sent, 1798–1884," RG 127.

46. Lt. Col. Cmdt. A. Henderson to S. Thompson, February 7, 1821, HQMC, "Letters Sent, 1798–1884," RG 127; Lt. Col. Cmdt. A. Henderson to S. L. Southard, November 18, 1823, and February 16, and November 22, 1824, HQMC, "Letters Sent, 1798–1884," RG 127; and Maj. R. Smith et al. to S. L. Southard, November 19, 1825, *ASP/NA,* II: 93–94.

47. Board of Navy Commissioners to S. Thompson, November 28, 1821, BNC "Letters Sent," RG 45.

48. Report of Mr. Stevenson Archer, committee on expenditures to the Navy Department, to the House of Representatives, February 28, 1821, with appendixes, *ASP/NA,* I: 739–743 and Annex E to the report of the Secretary of the Navy, 1828, *ASP/NA,* III: 228–230.

49. Fourth Auditor Amos Kendall to Secretary of the Navy J. Branch, May 28, 1829, communicated to the House of Representatives, May, 25, 1830, "Statement Relative to the Pay and Emoluments of the Officers of the Marine Corps," *ASP/NA,* III: 581–588.

50. Lt. Col. Cmdt. A. Henderson to J. Branch, August 15, 1829, HQMC, "Letters Sent, 1798–1884," RG 127; Lt. Col. Cmdt. A. Henderson to the Hon. W. Drayton, February 7, 1831, HQMC, "Letters Sent, 1798–1884," RG 127; House Committee on Military Affairs, "Alter Organization Marine Corps," February 5, 1830, House Report 158, 21st Congress, 1st Session; Branch to Senate, March 23, 1830, "On the Expediency of Dispensing with the Marine Corps" (note 29 above), *ASP/NA,* III: 560–569; corrspondence, "Recommendations that the Pay and Allowances of the Officers of the Marine Corps Be Increased, and that the Allowances from the Contingent Fund of the Navy Be Denied," *ASP/NA,* III: 873; and Marine Corps Acts of 1833 and 1834, Navy Department, *Laws of the United States in Relation to the Navy and Marine Corps* (Washington: J. and G. S. Gideon, 1843), pp. 154–159.
The implications for the cost of the Marine Corps was to increase its

budget from around $250,000 to $438,000 in 1836, although part of the latter expense came from service in the Indian wars in the South.

51. Board of Navy Commissioners to Secretary of the Navy Levi Woodbury, October 25, 1831; September 28, 1833; and January 23 and May 30, 1834, BNC "Letters Sent," RG 45.

52. Lt. Col. Cmdt. A. Henderson to L. Woodbury, October 22, 1831, and October 16, 1833, HQMC, "Letters Sent, 1798–1884," RG 127.

53. "Regulations for the Navy of the United States," *ASP/NA,* IV: 395–427.

54. Collum, *History of the United States Marine Corps* (note 13 above), pp. 61–64.

55. Col. Cmdt. A. Henderson to M. Dickerson, October 7, 1834, and October 6, 1835, HQMC, "Letters Sent, 1798–1884," RG 127; Bvt. Lt. Col. R. D. Wainwright to Lt. Col. Cmdt. A. Henderson, October 6, 1832, HD/HQMC, "Letters Received, 1818–1915," RG 127; Bvt. Lt. Col. S. Miller to Lt. Col. Cmdt. A. Henderson, November 11, 1832, HD/HQMC, "Letters Received, 1818–1915," RG 127; Lt. Col. S. Miller to Col. Cmdt. A. Henderson, December 10, 1834, HD/HQMC, "Letters Received, 1818–1915," RG 127; and Headquarters Marine Corps, Order, February 18, 1835, "Marine Corps Orders, 1822–1851, HQMC, Orders Issued and Received, RG 127.

56. Navy Department Order, M. Dickerson to Col. Cmdt. A. Henderson, December 11, 1835, "Marine Corps Orders, 1822–1851," HQMC, Orders Issued and Received, RG 127.

57. Col. Cmdt. A. Henderson to M. Dickerson, January 21, 1836, and to President A. Jackson, February 10, 1836, Office of the Secretary of the Navy, "Letters Received USMC Officers," RG 80; Col. Cmdt. A. Henderson to Cmdre. Charles Stewart, USN, March 14, 1836, HQMC, "Letters Sent, 1798–1884," RG 127; and Board of Navy Commissioners to M. Dickerson, May 27, 1836, June 11, 1836, and December 20, 1837, BNC "Letters Sent," RG 45.

58. Capt. J. Harris to Col. Cmdt. A. Henderson, August 20, 1840, HD/HQMC, "Letters Received, 1818–1915," RG 127, and Headquarters Marine Corps Order, August 24, 1840, "Marine Corps Orders, 1822–1851," HQMC, Orders Issued and Received, RG 127.

59. Secretary of the Navy J. K. Paulding to Col. Cmdt. A. Henderson, April 23, 1839, "Marine Corps Orders, 1822–1851," HQMC, Orders Issued and Received, RG 127, and Lt. Col. S. Miller to Secretary of the Navy M. Dickerson, May 7 and May 20, 1836, Office of the Secretary of the Navy, "Letters Received USMC," RG 80.

60. Memorial, Bvt. Lt. Col. W. H. Freeman to the U.S. Congress, February 15, 1836, *ASP/NA,* IV: 835–847, and *U.S.* v. *Freeman* (1845), U.S. Supreme Court *Reports* (3 Howard) pp. 557–568.

61. Congressional Resolution, 28th Congress, 1st Session, January 29, 1844, copy in HD/HQMC, "Letters Received, 1818–1915," RG 127.

62. Francis P. Prucha, *The Sword of the Republic: The United States Army on the Frontier, 1783–1846* (New York: Macmillan, 1969), pp. 258–261, 269–306.

63. Adjutant General's Office, U.S. Army, General Order 33, May 21, 1836, "Marine Corps Orders, 1822–1851," HQMC, Orders Issued and Received, RG 127; M. Dickerson to Bvt. Lt. Col. S. Miller, May 23, 1836, Office of the Secretary of the Navy, "Letters Sent USMC Officers," RG 80; Col. Cmdt. A. Henderson to Bvt. Lt. Col. W. H. Freeman, May 23, 1836, HQMC, "Letters Sent, 1798–1884," RG 127; Bvt. Lt. Col. S. Miller to Col. Cmdt. A. Henderson, May 24, 1836, HD/HQMC, "Letters Received, 1818–1915," RG 127; and Brig. Gen. Cmdt. A. Henderson to Secretary of the Navy J. Y. Mason, October 21, 1846, HQMC, "Letters Sent, 1798–1884," RG 127.

64. Col. Cmdt. A. Henderson to M. Dickerson, June 9 and July 1, 1836, Office of the Secretary of the Navy, "Letters Received USMC Officers," RG 80. For a detailed account, see Adjutant General's Office, U.S. Army, memorandum, "Marines on Duty with the Army in Alabama and Florida during the Years 1836 . . . 1842," November 3, 1842, HD/HQMC, "Letters Received, 1818–1915," RG 127.

65. Collum, *The History of the U.S. Marine Corps* (note 13 above), pp. 69–70.

66. Col. Cmdt. A. Henderson to M. Dickerson, September 11 and November 18, 1837, HQMC, "Letters Sent, 1798–1884," RG 127. The Marines' experience in Florida after Henderson's departure is described in personal correspondence and official orders of the Army of the South (1837–1838) in the Samuel Miller Papers and in George E. Buker, *Swamp Sailors: Riverine Warfare in the Everglades, 1835–1842* (Gainesville: University Presses of Florida, 1975).

67. K. Jack Bauer, *Surfboats and Horse Marines: U.S. Naval Operations in the Mexican War, 1846–48* (Annapolis: U.S. Naval Institute, 1969); Francis J. Manno, "History of United States Naval Operations, 1846–1848," unpublished Ph.D. dissertation, Georgetown University, 1954; John L. Betts, "The United States Navy in the Mexican War," unpublished Ph.D. dissertation, University of Chicago, 1955; Daniel J. O'Neil, "The United States Navy in the Californias, 1840–1850," unpublished Ph.D. dissertation, University of Southern California, 1969; and Knox, *History of the United States Navy* (note 1 above), pp. 169–179.

68. Bvt. Brig. Gen. Cmdt. A. Henderson to Secretary of the Navy G. Bancroft, May 28, 1846, HQMC, "Letters Sent, 1798–1884," RG 127; G. Bancroft to Bvt. Brig. Gen. Cmdt. A. Henderson, June 22, 1846, HD/HQMC, "Letters Received, 1818–1915," RG 127; Navy Department, *Laws Relating to the Navy and the Marine Corps, and the Navy Department* (Washington: Government Printing Office, 1865), p. 65; and Paullin, *Paullin's History of Naval Administration, 1775–1911* (note 1 above), pp. 227–228.

69. Bauer, *Surfboats and Horse Marines,* pp. 23–131, and Collum, *The History of the United States Marine Corps,* pp. 88–94.

70. Werner H. Marti, *Messenger of Destiny: The California Adventures, 1846–1847, of Archibald H. Gillespie* (San Francisco: John Howell, 1960).

71. Bauer, *Surfboats and Horse Marines,* pp. 149–233, and Collum, *The History of the United States Marine Corps,* pp. 81–88.

72. Bvt. Brig. Gen. A. Henderson to Secretary of the Navy J. Y. Mason, May 20, 1847, HQMC, "Letters Sent, 1798–1884," RG 127; Office of the Secretary of the Navy, Order, May 21, 1847, "Marine Corps Orders, 1822–1851," HQMC, Orders Issued and Received, RG 127; Brig. Gen. Cmdt. A. Henderson to J. Y. Mason, November 22, 1847, HQMC, "Letters Sent, 1798–1884," RG 127; and "General Size Roll of a Regiment of Marines, on Service in Mexico Under Bvt. Lieut. Col. Samuel E. Watson," June (?), 1847, File January–June, 1847, HD/HQMC, "Letters Received, 1818–1915," RG 127.

73. The experience of the Marine battalion on the march is described in Maj. L. Twiggs to George Twiggs, July 1, 1847, and to Mrs. L. Twiggs, July 5, July 14, August 1, and August 24, 1847, Levi Twiggs Papers, MCPPC, and in Lt. Richard McSherry, M.D., USN (battalion surgeon), *El Puchero: or A Mixed Dish from Mexico* (Philadelphia: Lippincott, Grambo, 1850), a collection of letters and diary entries.

    For dependable participant histories of Quitman's Division, see Cadmus Wilcox (Quitman's aide), *History of the Mexican War* (Washington: Church News Publishing Company, 1892), pp. 443–483, and J. F. H. Claiborne, *Life and Correspondence of John A. Quitman,* 2 vols. (New York: Harper and Brothers, 1860), I: 330–391.

74. The Marine battalions' fight on September 13 is based on the following sources: Capt. J. Reynolds to Mrs. L. Twiggs, February 29, 1848, Twiggs Papers; Bvt. Maj. John G. Reynolds, *A Conclusive Exculpation of the Marine Corps in Mexico* (New York: Stringer and Townsend, 1853); the testimony of Capt. J. G. Reynolds (pp. 15–19), Lt. D. D. Baker (pp. 114–116), Capt. G. H. Terrett (pp. 31–35), and Lt. J. C. Rich (pp. 27–31) in *The Marine Corps in Mexico; Setting Forth Its Conduct as Established by Testimony Before the General Court Martial, Convened at Brooklyn, N.Y., September, 1852, for the Trial of First Lieut. John S. Devlin* (Washington: Lemuel Towers, 1852); "Report of Maj. Gen. Scott," September 18, 1847, "Gen. Worth's Report," September 16, 1847, "Report of General Pillow," September 18, 1847, "Report of General Quitman," September 29, 1847, all in U.S. Senate, Senate Executive Document 1, Vol. I, Senate Executive Documents, 30th Congress, 1st Session (Washington: Government Printing Office, 1848), pp. 375–386, 391–395, 400–408, and 409–420; casualty returns, Scott's army, for September 13–14, 1847, in *ibid.*, pp. 465, 470; Lt. D. D. Baker to Bvt. Brig. Gen. Cmdt. A. Henderson, January 10, 1848, HD/HQMC, "Letters Received, 1818–1915," RG 127; and Lt. Col. S. Watson to Brig. Gen. Shields, September 16, 1848, and Capt. G. H. Terrett to (?), undated statement attached to Bvt. Brig. Gen. Cmdt. A. Henderson to J. Y. Mason, May 12, 1848, HQMC, "Letters Sent, 1798–1814," RG 127.

75. Capt. J. G. Reynolds to Mrs. L. Twiggs, February 29, 1848, Twiggs Papers, and testimony of Capt. J. G. Reynolds, *The Marine Corps in Mexico*, pp. 15–19.

76. Bvt. Brig. Gen. Cmdt. A. Henderson to Lt. D. D. Baker and to Maj. W. Dulany, both December 31, 1847, HQMC, "Letters Sent, 1798–1884," RG 127; Bvt. Brig. Gen. Cmdt. A. Henderson to Capt. D. D. Baker, April 20 and 21, 1848, HQMC, "Letters Sent, 1798–1884," RG 127; Bvt. Brig. Gen. Cmdt. A. Henderson to J. Y. Mason, January 13 and May 12, 1848, HQMC, "Letters Sent, 1798–1884," RG 127; Adjutant and Inspector's Office, HQMC, circular to the commissioned and noncommissioned officers of the Marine Corps, April 6, 1848, "Orders and Circulars Issued by the Commandant, 1805–1860," RG 127; and extracts from the court-martial proceedings of 1st Lt. John S. Devlin, September 20, 1852, "Marine Corps Orders, 1851–1886," HQMC, Orders Issued and Received, RG 127.

77. Navy Department, *Laws Relating to the Navy and the Marine Corps, and the Navy Department* (1865), pp. 65, 70, 96–97, and Secretary of the Navy, "Communication . . . in relation to the organization of the Marine Corps," August 4, 1848, Senate Executive Document No. 66, Senate Executive Documents. Vol. III, 30th Congress, 1st Session (1848).

78. HQMC, Order, March 18, 1850, "Marine Corps Orders, 1822–1851," HQMC, Orders Issued and Received, RG 127.

79. Brig. Gen. Cmdt. A. Henderson, circular, April 13, 1850, "Orders and Circulars Issued by the Commandant, 1805–1860," RG 127.

80. Bvt. Brig. Gen. Cmdt. A. Henderson to Rep. T. B. King, chairman of the House Naval Affairs Committee, February 14, 1848; Bvt. Brig. Gen. Cmdt. A. Henderson to J. Y. Mason, April 28, 1848; Bvt. Brig. Gen. Cmdt. A. Henderson to Secretary of the Navy P. Ballard, November 9, 1849; Bvt. Brig. Gen. A. Henderson to Secretary of the Navy W. A. Graham, November 19, 1850; and Bvt. Brig. Gen. Cmdt. A. Henderson to Secretary of the Navy J. P. Kennedy, November 11, 1852, all HQMC, "Letters Sent, 1798–1884," RG. 127.

81. Capt. C. W. Morgan, USN, to Bvt. Brig. Gen. Cmdt. A. Henderson, July 30, 1852, and Cmdr. D. G. Farragut, USN, to Bvt. Brig. Gen. Cmdt. A. Henderson, July 28, 1852, (emphasis in original), both HQMC. "Letters Sent, 1798–

1884," RG 127. The Navy officers' replies were attached and filed with Henderson's original circular of July 24, 1852, but were transmitted to the Congress as part of the annual report of the Secretary of the Navy, 1852, U.S. Senate, Senate Document 1, 32d Congress, 2d Session (1852), pp. 583–608.

82. Acting Secretary of the Navy T. Smith to Bvt. Brig. Gen. Cmdt. A. Henderson, November 1, 1852, "Marine Corps Orders, 1851–1884," HQMC, Orders Issued and Received, RG 127; Bvt. Brig. Gen. Cmdt. A. Henderson to Secretary of the Navy J. C. Dobbin, November 17, 1853; Bvt. Brig. Gen. Cmdt. A. Henderson to Cmdre. O. Paulding, USN, November 5, 1858; Bvt. Brig. Gen. Cmdt. A. Henderson to Capt. A. N. Brevoort, USN, May 19, 1858; and Bvt. Brig. Gen. A. Henderson to I. Toucey, June 12 and November 20, 1858, all HQMC, "Letters Sent, 1798–1884," RG 127.

83. Ellsworth, "One Hundred Eighty Landings of United States Marines, 1800–1934," 1934, ms., with landings listed by country.

84. Bvt. Capt. John D. Simms to Bvt. Brig. Gen. Cmdt. A. Henderson, December 7, 1856, "Marine Corps Orders, 1851–1884," HQMC, Orders Issued and Received, RG 127, and Bernard C. Nalty, *The Barrier Forts,* Marine Corps Historical Reference Series No. 6 (Washington: Headquarters Marine Corps, 1962).

85. Collum, *The History of the United States Marine Corps,* pp. 104–106, and Constance McLaughlin Green, *Washington: Village and Capitol, 1800–1878* (Princeton, N.J.: Princeton University Press, 1962), pp. 215–216.

CHAPTER 4. THE MARINE CORPS SURVIVES
ITS DOLDRUMS, 1859–1889

1. Appendix, "Register of Officers, U.S. Marine Corps, 1798 to 1903," in Richard S. Collum, *History of the United States Marine Corps,* rev. ed. (New York: L. R. Hamersly and Co., 1903), pp. 429–499, and Navy Department, *Naval Register 1860* (Washington: Government Printing Office, 1860).

   Legislation passed in 1861 provided pensions for officers, who could retire voluntarily after forty years' service or through disability and also provided that the President could involuntarily retire officers with more than forty-five years' service or over sixty-two years old.

2. Col. Cmdt. J. Harris to Bvt. Maj. J. Reynolds, July 25, 1859, HQMC, "Letters Sent, 1798–1884," RG 127; Col. Cmdt. J. Harris to Maj. W. Marston, December 20, 1859, HQMC, "Letters Sent, 1798–1884," RG 127; Col. Cmdt. J. Harris to Secretary of the Navy I. Toucey, December 24, 1859, HQMC, "Letters Sent, 1798–1884," RG 127; and Lt. J. R. F. Tattnall to Col. Cmdt. J. Harris, September 3, 1860, HD/HQMC, "Letters Received, 1818–1915," RG 127. There is a sketch of Harris in Karl Schuon, *Home of the Commandants* (Washington: Leatherneck Association, 1966), pp. 170–171.

3. *Regulations for the Uniform and Dress of the Marine Corps of the United States, October 1859* (Philadelphia: Charles Desilver, 1859); H. Charles McBarron, Jr., "U.S. Marine Corps, 1859–1875," *Military Collector and Historian,* 1 (December 1949): 1–2, plate 13, and *idem,* "U.S. Marine Corps, Field Service, 1859–1868," *Military Collector and Historian,* 5 (June 1953): 47, plate 71.

4. Bernard C. Nalty, *United States Marines at Harper's Ferry and in the Civil War* Marine Corps Historical Reference Pamphlet, rev. ed., (Washington: Historical Division, HQMC, 1966), pp. 1–8.

5. For the naval portion of the Civil War, see Charles O. Paullin, *Paullin's History of Naval Administration, 1775–1911* (Annapolis: U.S. Naval Institute,

1968), pp. 249–307; Dudley W. Knox, *History of the United States Navy* (New York: G. P. Putnam's Sons, 1936), pp. 191–316; Richard S. West, Jr., *Mr. Lincoln's Navy* (New York: Longman's, Green, 1957); and U.S. Office of Naval War Records, *Official Records of the Union and Confederate Navies in the War of the Rebellion,* 30 vols. (Washington: Government Printing Office, 1894–1922). Among the important biographical studies, see John Niven, *Gideon Welles* (New York: Oxford University Press, 1974); Howard K. Beale, ed., *Diary of Gideon Welles,* 3 vols. (New York: W. W. Norton, 1960); R. M. Thompson and R. Wainright, eds., *Confidential Correspondence of Gustavus V. Fox, Assistant Secretary of the Navy, 1861–1865,* 2 vols. (New York: Naval Historical Society, 1918–1919); John D. Hayes, ed., *Samuel Francis DuPont: A Selection from His Civil War Letters,* 3 vols. (Ithaca, N.Y.: Cornell University Press, 1969); Charles Lee Lewis, *David Glasgow Farragut: Our First Admiral* (Annapolis: U.S. Naval Institute, 1943); Richard S. West, Jr., *The Second Admiral: A Life of David Dixon Porter, 1813–1891* (New York: Coward-McCann, 1937); and Edward W. Sloan III, *Benjamin Franklin Isherwood, Naval Engineer* (Annapolis: U.S. Naval Institute, 1965).

6. Paullin, *Paullin's History of Naval Administration,* pp. 280, 298–299, 304.

7. Col. Cmdt. J. Harris to Secretary of the Navy G. Welles, November 23, 1861, HQMC, "Letters Sent, 1798–1884," RG 127; Col. Cmdt. J. Harris to G. Welles, October 28, 1863, HQMC, "Letters Sent, 1798–1884," RG 127; Col. Cmdt. J. Harris to Rep. A. H. Rice (chairman, House Naval Affairs Committee), April 6, 1864, HQMC, "Letters Sent, 1798–1884," RG 127; Capt. S. P. Lee, USN, to G. Welles, October 24, 1864, and G. Welles to RAdm. S. P. Lee, November 2, 1864, U.S. Office of Naval War Records, *Official Records of the Union and Confederate Navies in the War of the Rebellion,* Series 1, 26: 701 and 708; and Col. Cmdt. J. Zeilin to G. Welles, October 22, 1864, HQMC, "Letters Sent, 1798–1884," RG 127.

8. Col. Cmdt. J. Harris to Maj. A. Garland, December 23, 1863, HQMC, "Letters Sent, 1798–1884," RG 127.

9. Col. Cmdt. J. Harris to G. Welles, November 23, 1861, HQMC, "Letters Sent, 1798–1884," RG 127; Col. Cmdt. J. Harris to Lt. A. J. Hays and Lt. G. Holmes, March 2, 1861, HQMC, "Letters Sent, 1798–1884," RG 127; Col. Cmdt. J. Harris to Capt. G. W. Collier, Lt. W. Wallace, and Lt. H. C. Cochrane, February 5, 1864, HQMC, "Letters Sent, 1798–1884," RG 127; and Col. Cmdt. J. Harris to Lt. N. L. Nokes, September 23, 1862, HQMC, "Letters Sent, 1798–1884," RG 127.

10. August 20, 1862, May 14 and June 9, 1864, entries, Beale, ed., *The Diary of Gideon Welles,* I: 89 and II: 31, 47; G. Welles to Lt. Col. J. G. Reynolds, August 21, 1862, Office of the Secretary of the Navy, "Letters Sent USMC Officers," General Records of the Navy Department, RG 80; Col. Cmdt. C. G. McCawley to R. M. Thompson, December 14, 1877, HQMC, "Letters Sent, 1798–1884," RG 127.

11. Col. Cmdt. J. Harris to G. Welles, May 18 and November 23, 1861, HQMC, "Letters Sent, 1798–1884," RG 127; Act of July 25, 1861, Navy Department, *Laws Relating to the Navy and Marine Corps, and the Navy Department* (Washington: Government Printing Office, 1865), pp. 96–97; and Col. Cmdt. J. Harris to G. Welles, November 13, 1862, HQMC, "Letters Sent, 1798–1884," RG 127.

12. December 29, 1863, entry, Beale, ed., *The Diary of Gideon Welles,* I: 498–499; Col. Cmdt. J. Harris to G. Welles, October 8, 1863, HQMC, "Letters Sent, 1798–1884," RG 127; Provost Marshal General James B. Fry, USA, to Col. Cmdt. J. Harris, February 9, 1864, in HQMC, "Marine Corps Orders,

1851–1884," Orders Issued and Received, RG 127; Col. Cmdt. J. Harris to Capt. J. L. Broome and Maj. J. Zeilin, March 14 and 19, 1864, HQMC, "Letters Sent, 1798–1884," RG 127; and Col. Cmdt. J. Zeilin to G. Welles, October 22, 1864, HQMC, "Letters Sent, 1798–1884," RG 127.

For general accounts of the Marine Corps in the Civil War, see Nalty, *United States Marines at Harper's Ferry and in the Civil War,* pp. 8–26; Collum, *History of the United States Marine Corps* (note 1 above), pp. 111–173; and Marshall C. Miller, "A History of the U.S. Marine Corps During the Civil War Period," unpublished M.A. thesis, Colorado State College, 1936.

13. Nalty, *United States Marines at Harper's Ferry and in the Civil War,* pp. 8–9, and Knox, *A History of the United States Navy,* pp. 184–195.

14. G. Welles to Col. Cmdt. J. Harris, July 15, 1861, HD/HQMC, "Letters Received, 1818–1915," RG 127; Maj. J. G. Reynolds to Col. Cmdt. J. Harris, July 23, 1861, HD/HQMC, "Letters Received, 1818–1915," RG 127; Col. A. Porter, USA, "The Battle of Bull Run," July 25, 1861, copy in volume for 1860–1862, HD/HQMC, "Letters Received, 1818–1915," RG 127; and Bvt. Maj. Gen. James B. Fry, "McDowell's Advance to Bull Run," in Robert U. Johnson and Clarence C. Buel, eds., *Battles and Leaders of the Civil War,* 4 vols. (New York: The Century Company, 1884–1887), I: 183–195.

The Marine losses were one officer and eight men killed, two officers and seventeen men wounded, and sixteen men missing. Porter's brigade losses were 86 dead, 17 wounded, and 201 missing, the second largest brigade losses in McDowell's army.

15. Maj. J. G. Reynolds to Flag Off. S. F. DuPont, USN, November 8, 1861, reprinted in Collum, *History of the U.S. Marine Corps,* pp. 121–122.

16. Col. Cmdt. J. Harris to Maj. J. G. Reynolds, December 9, 1861, HQMC, "Letters Sent, 1798–1884," RG 127; Maj. J. G. Reynolds to Col. Cmdt. J. Harris, March 10, 1862, and Flag Off. S. F. DuPont, USN, to G. Welles, March 25, 1862, both HD/HQMC, "Letters Received, 1818–1915," RG 127; Flag Off. S. F. DuPont, USN, to G. V. Fox, November 9, 1861, in Thompson and Wainright, eds., *Confidential Correspondence of Gustavus V. Fox,* I: 65–67; Flag Off. S. F. DuPont, USN, to Mrs. S. F. DuPont, March 23, 1862; and editor's notes in Hayes, ed., *Samuel Francis DuPont* (note 5 above), I: 372–373, 377, 384.

17. Maj. A. Garland to Col. Cmdt. J. Harris, December 12, 1862, HD/HQMC, "Letters Received, 1818–1915," RG 127.

18. Collum, *History of the U.S. Marine Corps,* pp. 147–150, and Frederick Tomlinson Peet, *Personal Experiences in the Civil War* (New York: F. T. Peet, 1905), p. 85.

19. Col. Cmdt. J. Harris to Capt. D. M. Cohen, February 18, 1864, HQMC, "Letters Sent, 1798–1884," RG 127.

20. Jane Blakeney, *Heroes, U.S. Marine Corps, 1861–1955* (Washington: Jane Blakeney, 1957), pp. 5–6.

21. Collum, *History of the U.S. Marine Corps.* pp. 130–134, 138–143, 144–146, 153–159, 163–167, and Major E. N. McClellan, "The Capture of New Orleans, *MCG,* 5 (December 1920): 360–369.

22. John F. Cassidy, "Field Service in the Civil War: Squadron Marines in Combined Operations," *MCG,* 1 (September 1916): 290–297.

23. Collum, *History of the U.S. Marine Corps,* pp. 167–170, and Nalty, *United States Marines at Harper's Ferry and in the Civil War,* p. 19.

24. Major E. N. McClellan, "The Capture of Fort Fisher," *MCG,* March 1920, pp. 59–80; Capt. L. L. Dawson to Col. Cmdt. J. Zeilin, January 27, 1865, HD/HQMC, "Letters Received, 1818–1915," RG 127; Collum, *History of the U.S. Marine Corps,* pp. 171–177; and Captain Thomas O. Selfridge, Jr., USN,

"The Navy at Fort Fisher," in Johnson and Buel, eds., *Battles and Leaders of the Civil War,* IV: 642–661.

25. Ralph W. Donnelly, *The History of the Confederate States Marine Corps* (Washington, D.C.: Ralph W. Donnelly, 1976); J. Thomas Scharf, *History of the Conferedate States Navy* (Albany, N.Y.: Joseph McDonough, 1894), pp. 769–772; Richard Harwell, ed., *A Confederate Marine: A Sketch of Henry Lea Graves with Excerpts from the Graves Family Correspondence, 1861–1865* (Tuscaloosa, Ala.: Confederate Publishing Co., 1963); James C. Gasser, "Confederate Marines in the Civil War," unpublished M.A. thesis, Alabama Polytechnic Institute, 1956; and G. W. Van Hoose, "The Confederate States Marine Corps," *MCG,* 13 (September 1928): 166–177.

26. RAdm. J. A. Dahlgren, USN, to Col. Cmdt. J. Harris, December 20, 1863, Subject File VR (Marine Corps), Naval Records Collection of the Office of Naval Records and Library, RG 45, NA; Capt. S. C. Rowan, USN, to Col. Cmdt. J. Harris, December 23, 1863, Subject File VR (Marine Corps), RG 45; Col. Cmdt. J. Zeilin to G. Welles, October (?), 1865, HQMC, "Letters Sent, 1798–1884," RG 127; *Army and Navy Journal (ANJ),* June 30, 1866; and U.S. Congress, House Committee on Naval Affairs, "Marine Corps," February 21, 1867, House Report 22, 39th Congress, 2d Session.

    For Marine life aboard ship, see Peet, *Personal Experiences in the Civil War,* pp. 85–107; "The Journal of Private Charles Brother, USMC," appendix 4 to Navy Historical Division, *Civil War Chronology* (Washington, D.C.: Government Printing Office, 1971), pp. 47–83; and "Watch, Quarter & Station Bill of the U.S.S.S. Iroquois, 1864, East Indies, Cmdr. C. R. P. Rodgers, Commanding," Rodgers Family Papers, Manuscript Division, Library of Congress.

    Twenty-one Marine officers were breveted for Civil War service. Marine Corps wartime casualties from all causes were 551, a low ratio compared with volunteer infantry regiments.

27. For naval policy from 1865 to the 1890s, see Paullin, *Paullin's History of Naval Administration, 1775–1911* (note 5 above), pp. 309–385; Knox, *A History of the United States Navy* (note 5 above), pp. 317–328; Lance C. Buhl, "The Smooth Water Navy: American Naval Policy and Politics, 1865–1876," unpublished Ph.D. dissertation, Harvard University, 1968; and Kenneth J. Hagan, *American Gunboat Diplomacy and the Old Navy, 1877–1889* (Westport, Conn.: Greenwood Press, 1974).

28. Col. Cmdt. J. Zeilin to G. Welles, October (?), 1865, HQCM, "Letters Sent, 1798–1884," RG 127, and Col. Cmdt. J. Zeilin to Rep. A. H. Rice, June 22, 1866, HQMC, "Letters Sent, 1798–1884," RG 127.

29. *ANJ,* January 5, 12, and 26, and February 9, 1867.

30. Quoted in *ANJ,* May 23, 1868, and VAdm. D. D. Porter to Sen. C. D. Drake, January 21, 1869, David Dixon Porter Papers, Manuscript Division Library of Congress. See also Adm. D. D. Porter to Rep. W. C. Whitthorne, December 28, 1880, Porter Papers; Navy Department, *Report of the Secretary of the Navy, 1880* (Washington: Government Printing Office, 1880), pp. 19–20; *idem Report of the Secretary of the Navy, 1887–1888* (Washington: Government Printing Office, 1888), p. xliii; and Senate Report 931, Senate Naval Affairs Committee, April 11, 1888, 50th Congress, 1st Session.

31. *ANJ,* January 23, 1869; April 6, 1872; January 31, and December 12, 1874; November 20, 1875; June 3 and August 26, 1876; January 22, 1881; December, 24, 1887; and April 21, 1888.

32. Historical Division, HQMC, memo, "Strength of the Marine Corps," December 11, 1969, copy provided by the Reference Branch, HD/HQMC; HQMC, "Authorized Strength of the United States Marine Corps, 1798 to 1916," May 15,

1916, copy from Subject File VR (Marine Corps), RG 45; Col. Cmdt. J. Zeilin to A. H. Rice, June 22, 1866; Brig. Gen. Cmdt. J. Zeilin to G. Welles, October 19, 1868; Col. Cmdt. C. G. McCawley to R. W. Thompson, October 1, 1878; Col. Cmdt. C. G. McCawley to Secretary of the Navy W. C. Whitney, October 9, 1886; and Col. Cmdt. C. G. McCawley to Secretary of the Navy B. F. Tracy, October 1, 1889, all HQMC, "Letters Sent, 1798–1884," and "Press Copies of Letters, Endorsements, and Annual Reports to the Secretary of the Navy, February 1884–January 1904," RG 127 (the letter source cited hereafter as LSSN, RG 127).

33. Brig. Gen. Cmdt. J. Zeilin to G. Welles, May 18, 1868; Brig. Gen. Cmdt. J. Zeilin to Secretary of the Navy G. M. Robeson, February 1, 1870, and August 1, 1871; Brig. Gen. Cmdt. J. Zeilin to Lt. Col. C. G. McCawley, March 18, 1871; Col. Cmdt. C. G. McCawley to Secretary of the Navy W. G. Chandler, October 1, 1882; Col. Cmdt. C. G. McCawley to Secretary of the Navy R. W. Thompson, October 23, 1880; Col. Cmdt. C. G. McCawley to Secretary of the Navy W. C. Whitney, October 1, 1885, and October 1, 1888; and Col. Cmdt. C. G. McCawley to Secretary of the Navy B. F. Tracy, October 1, 1889, all HQMC, "Letters Sent, 1798–1884" and "LSSN," RG 127.

34. Col. Cmdt. J. Zeilin to Capt. D. M. Cohen, July 7, 1866; Col. Cmdt. J. Zeilin to G. Welles, October 15, 1866; Brig. Gen. Cmdt. J. Zeilin to G. Welles, October 15, 1866; and Brig. Gen. Cmdt. J. Zeilin to Capt. C. Heywood, January 17, 1873, all HQMC, "Letters Sent, 1798–1884," RG 127.

35. Brig. Gen. Cmdt. J. Zeilin to Maj. T. Y. Field, April 1, 1872, HQMC, "Letters Sent, 1798–1884," RG 127.

36. G. M. Robeson to Brig. Gen. Cmdt. J. Zeilin, January 5, 1872, Office of the Secretary of the Navy, "Letters Sent USMC Officers," RG 80.

37. Quoted in *ANJ,* April 19, 1873.

38. Brig. Gen. Cmdt. J. Zeilin to G. M. Robeson, May 6, 1873, and January 28, 1875, HQMC, "Letters Sent, 1798–1884," RG 127; Maj. A. S. Nicholson, A&I, to Lt. Col. T. Y. Field, August 14, 1878, HQMC, "Letters Sent, 1798–1884," RG 127; Col. Cmdt. C. G. McCawley to W. E. Hunt, November 1, 1881, HQMC, "Letters Sent, 1798–1884," RG 127; and *ANJ,* March 18, 1882, and August 27, 1887.

39. Navy Department, *Regulations for the Government of the United States Navy 1870* (Washington: Government Printing Office, 1870), pp. 201–203; *idem, Regulations for the Government of the Navy of the United States 1876* (Washington: Government Printing Office, 1876), pp. 89–91; Col. Cmdt. C. G. McCawley to Cmdr. J. H. Howell, USN, December 13, 1879, HQMC, "Letters Sent, 1798–1884," RG 127; and order book and guard reports, USS *Guerriere,* 2 vols., 1867–1869, Field Organization Records, RG 127.

40. 1st. Lt. H. C. Cochrane diary entry, May 19, 1869, Henry Clay Cochrane Papers, MCPPC. Officers' experiences at sea may be sampled in the Cochrane diaries, 1865–1879, and in the letters of Capt. McLane Tilton to his wife, 1870–1878, McLane Tilton Papers, MCPPC.

41. H. C. Cochrane, notes, memoranda on "Guard Duty," morning reports and rolls of the ships guard, USS *Lancaster,* 1884, Subject File "Marine, Naval and Military Miscellany," Cochrane Papers; Pvt. Walter Bronson, diary of cruise on USS *Alaska,* 1870–1873, Walter Bronson Papers, MCPPC; 1st Lt. C. F. Williams to Capt. W. H. Macomb, USN, March 31, 1869, Subject File NL (Naval Personnel), RG 45; Capt. P. R. Tindall to Brig. Gen. Cmdt. J. Zeilin, December 23 and 24, 1867, HD/HQMC, "Letters Received, 1818–1915," RG 127; and Adm. D. D. Porter to R. W. Thompson, November 25, 1878, Porter Papers.

42. Captain Harry A. Ellsworth, "One Hundred Eighty Landings of United States

Marines, 1800–1934," 1934, ms. in Breckinridge Library, Education Center, MCDEC, Quantico, Virginia. See also Albert P. Taylor, "The Storming of the U.S. Consulate at Honolulu in 1870," *USNIP,* 55 (April 1929): 313–314; Major E. N. McClellan, "Battles of the American Marines: Alexandria, Egypt, in 1882," *The Marines Magazine and Indian,* 5 (July 1920): 3–4, copy in Subject File OH (Landing Operations), RG 45.

43. Capt. McL. Tilton to Mrs. Tilton, June 21 and 27, 1871, Tilton Papers. The two Marine enlisted men later received Medals of Honor.
44. Capt. McL. Tilton to Brig. Gen. Cmdt. J. Zeilin, June 15 and 19, 1871, HD/ HQMC, "Letters Received, 1818–1915," RG 127; Robert E. Johnson, *Rear Admiral John Rodgers, 1812–1882* (Annapolis: U.S. Naval Institute, 1867), pp. 305–333; K. Jack Bauer, "The Korean Expedition of 1871," *USNIP,* 94 (June 1968): 46–53; and Albert Castel and Andrew C. Nahm, "Our Little War with the Heathen," *American Heritage,* 19 (April 1968): 18–23, 72–75.
45. Col. Cmdt. C. G. McCawley to W. C. Whitney, April 8, 1885," HQMC, "LSSN," RG 127; *ANJ,* May 2 and 16 and November 21, 1885; Philadelphia *Press,* April 4 and 25, 1885; New York *Herald,* April 3 and 28, 1885; New York *Times,* April 4, 1885; Brooklyn *Eagle,* April 25, 1885; Frank E. Evans, "The First Expedition to Panama," *MCG,* 1 (June 1916): 125–132; H. C. Reisinger, "On the Isthmus, 1885," *MCG,* 13 (December 1928): 230–239; and Collum, *History of the United States Marine Corps* (note 1 above), pp. 220–237.
46. Col. Cmdt. C. G. McCawley to W. C. Whitney, July 3, 1885, HQMC, "Letters Sent to Secretary of the Navy, 1884–1904," RG 127.
47. Navy Department, *Regulations for the Government of the Navy of the United States 1876,* pp. 161–62; *ANJ,* February 20, 1869, and May 3, 1879; Col. Cmdt. C. G. McCawley to W. C. Whitney, October 1, 1887, HQMC, "LSSN," RG 127; Col. Cmdt. C. G. McCawley to Cmdre. J. Guest, USN, December 26, 1878, HQMC, "Letters Sent, 1798–1884," RG 127; and Cmdre. P. Crosby, USN, to Lt. Col. T. Y. Field, December 31, 1878, Thomas Y. Field Papers, MCPPC.
48. Capt. H. C. Cochrane to Capt. L. E. Fagan, May 15, 1888, Cochrane Papers.
49. Henry Clay Cochrane, journal notes, "Marine," 1866–1883, Cochrane Papers.
50. Marine Barracks, Portsmouth, N.H., "Orders," March 27, 1876, Field Papers, and Col. Cmdt. C. G. McCawley to R. W. Thompson, April 10, 1882, HQMC, "Letters Sent, 1798–1884," RG 127.
51. Lieutenant Colonel J. G. Reynolds, "Internal Regulations" (n.d.), Cochrane Papers, and Captain McLane Tilton, *Internal Regulations of the U.S. Marine Barracks at Annapolis, Md.* (1875), Tilton Papers.
52. Col. Cmdt. C. G. McCawley to R. W. Thompson, July 22 and November 16, 1877, HQMC, "Letters Sent, 1798–1884," RG 127; R. W. Thompson to Col. Cmdt. C. G. McCawley, August 17, 1877, Office of the Secretary of the Navy, "Letters Sent USMC Officers," RG 80; and Collum, *History of the U.S. Marine Corps,* pp. 203–217.
53. *ANJ,* November 23, 1878; Schuon, *Home of the Commandants* (note 1 above), pp. 174–175, and Charles Lee Lewis, *Famous American Marines* (Boston: L. C. Page, 1950), pp. 109–120.
54. Navy Department, *Naval Register 1880* (Washington: Government Printing Office, 1880), pp. 130–135.
55. Philadelphia *Times,* December 5, 1886, HQMC Scrapbook, 1880–1889, RG 127.
56. Boston *Sunday Transcript,* January 15, 1882, HQMC Scrapbook, 1880–1889, RG 127.
57. *ANJ,* July 31, 1869; October 14, 1871; February 24, 1872; and July 17, 1875.

For an example of Washington life, see Charles M. Remey, *Reminiscent [sic] of Colonel William Butler Remey United States Marine Corps and Edward Wallace Remey United States Navy* (n.p., 1955), pp. 14–27, copy in Remey Records, University of Illinois library.

58. *ANJ,* October 18, 1873; December 20, 1873; January 9 and 24, 1874; September 4 and 11, 1875; and November 20, 1875, and First Lieutenant Henry Clay Cochrane, "The Status of the Marine Corps," pamphlet, October 1, 1875, copy in Cochrane Papers.

59. Report, Capt. J. Forney to G. M. Robeson, September 15, 1873, Subject File VR (Marine Corps), RG 45. Forney's report on the Royal Marines and his conclusions survived an ocean wreck, but his studies of Continental marines did not.

60. Minutes, meeting of Marine officers, North Atlantic Squadron and Norfolk station, February 12, 1876, copy in Cochrane Papers; House Report 762, Senate Naval Affairs Committee, January 18, 1881, 46th Congress, 3d Session, copy in Cochrane Papers; and *ANJ,* December 24, 1881.

61. Col. Cmdt. C. G. McCawley to Lt. F. D. Webster, March 26, 1877, and Col. Cmdt. C. G. McCawley to Maj. A. S. Nicholson, A&I, May 1, 1877, HQMC, "Letters Sent, 1798–1884," RG 127; and *ANJ,* October 2, 1875; January 22, 1876; August 14, 1880; April 30, 1881; June 11 and 18, 1881; December 24, 1881; February 25, 1882 and May 20, 1882.

62. Bernard C. Nalty and Lieutenant Colonel Ralph F. Moody, *A Brief History of U.S. Marine Corps Officer Procurement, 1775–1969,* rev. ed., Marine Corps Historical Reference Pamphlet (Washington: Historical Division, HQMC, 1970), p. 3; *ANJ,* January 1, 1887; Captain John E. Greenwood, "Seventy-Five Years of Academy Marines," *Shipmates,* November 1957, pp. 3–6; Peter Karsten, *The Naval Aristocracy: The Golden Age of Annapolis and the Emergence of Modern American Navalism* (New York: Free Press, 1972), pp. 277–289; Joe A. Simon, "The Life and Career of General John Archer Lejeune: The Greatest Leatherneck of Them All," unpublished M.A. thesis, Louisiana State University, 1967, pp. 37–69; and Hugh Rodman, *Yarns of a Kentucky Admiral* (Indianapolis: Bobbs-Merrill, 1928), pp. 79–81.

63. Col. Cmdt. C. G. McCawley to Col. J. H. Jones, USA, June 12, 1879, HQMC, "Letters Sent, 1798–1884," RG 127.

64. Capt. J. Forney to Brig. Gen. Cmdt. J. Zeilin, June 9, 1876, HD/HQMC, "Letters Received, 1818–1915," RG 127.

65. *ANJ,* March 1, 1873; June 7, 1879; August 14, 1880; December 17, 1881; March 22, 1884; May 2, 1885 and December 7, 1889.

66. Col. Cmdt. C. G. McCawley to R. W. Thompson, July 2, 1877, HQMC, "Letters Sent, 1798–1884," RG 127.

67. *ANJ,* August 29 and November 21, 1885.
    Retirement benefits began after thirty years service; in 1885 there were only fifty soldiers and Marines who qualified for retirement pay. The Navy had no system until 1899.

68. Maj. A. S. Nicholson, A&I, to Col Cmdt. C. G. McCawley, February 7, 1882, HD/HQMC, "Letters Received, 1818–1915," RG 127, and New York *Star,* October 23, 1887, and New York *Sun,* October 24, 1887, HQMC Scrapbook, RG 127.

69. Col. Cmdt. C. G. McCawley to Capt. J. Forney, May 21, 1883, HQMC, "Letters Sent, 1798–1884," RG 127.

70. Col. Cmdt. C. G. McCawley to W. E. Hunt, February 15, 1882, and Col. Cmdt. C. G. McCawley to Secretary of the Navy W. E. Chandler, October 12, 1883, HQMC, "Letters Sent, 1798–1884," RG 127.

71. *ANJ*, July 30, 1881; February 25, 1882; June 13, 1882; November 14, 1885; May 15 and 19, 1886; August 20, 1887; and December 21, 1889.

72. Richard A. Long and Don P. Wyckoff, "The Marine Corps Emblem," *USNIP*, 95 (November 1969): 49–55.

73. *ANJ*, September 21, 1872; December 21, 1872; February 22, 1873; March 15, 1873; May 17 and 24, 1873; September 5, 1874; April 3, 1875; June 5, 1875; October 16 and 23, 1875; and November 20, 1875, and Quartermaster Department, Headquarters Marine Corps, *Regulations for the Uniforms and Dress of the Marine Corps of the United States, May 1875* (Washington: Government Printing Office, 1875).

74. Col. Cmdt. C. G. McCawley to R. W. Thompson, May 19, 1877, HQMC, "Letters Sent, 1798–1884," RG 127, and *ANJ*, April 28, 1877; May 5, 1877; and March 5, 1881.

75. *ANJ*, December 11, 1869; March 1, 1873; February 26, 1881; March 12, 1881; March 21, 1885; and June 8, 1889.

76. *ANJ*, October 26 and December 26, 1889; January 18, 1890; Collum, *History of the U.S. Marine Corps*, pp. 260–66.

77. Kenneth W. Carpenter, "A History of the United States Marine Corps Band," unpublished Ph.D. dissertation, University of Iowa, 1970, pp. 74–100; David M. Ingalls, "Francis [Marie] Scala [1819–1903], Leader of the Marine Band from 1855–1871," unpublished M.A. thesis, Catholic University, 1957; John Philip Sousa, *Marching Along* (Boston: Hale, Cushman, and Flint, 1928), pp. 66–125; and *ANJ*, August 17, 1872; September 13, 1873; August 14, 1875; June 3, 1876; May 26, 1877; June 13, 1885; and July 24, 1886.

78. M. Almy Aldrich, *History of the U.S. Marine Corps* (Boston: H. L. Shepard, 1875); *ANJ*, September 26, 1874; March 6 and 13, 1875; and October 16, 1886; Ralph W. Donnelly, "Historians of the Corps: Richard Strader Collum," *Fortitudine* (newsletter of the Marine Corps historical program), 3 (Summer 1973): 10–12; and Capt. Richard S. Collum, *History of the United States Marine Corps* (Philadelphia: L. R. Hamersly, 1890).

CHAPTER 5. THE MARINE CORPS AND THE NEW NAVY, 1889–1909

1. For a general introduction to the new Navy, see Harold Sprout and Margaret Sprout, *The Rise of American Naval Power, 1776–1918* (Princeton, N.J.: Princeton University Press, 1944), pp. 183–222; Charles O. Paullin, *Paullin's History of Naval Administration, 1775–1911* (Annapolis: U.S. Naval Institute, 1968), pp. 387–426; and John D. Long, *The New American Navy*, 2 vols. (New York: Outlook Company, 1903).

2. Department of the Navy, *Report of the Secretary of the Navy, 1889* (Washington: Government Printing Office, 1889), pp. 3–6, 10–17; "Report of the Policy Board," January 20, 1890, *USNIP*, 16 (1890): 201–271; and B. Franklin Cooling, *Benjamin Franklin Tracy* (Hamden, Conn.: Archon Books, 1973), pp. 46–101.

3. Peter Karsten, *The Naval Aristocracy: The Golden Age of Annapolis and the Emergence of Modern American Navalism* (New York: Free Press, 1972), pp. 326–352.

4. Department of the Navy, "Report of the Secretary of the Navy," *Annual Reports of the Navy Department, 1894–1895* (Washington: Government Printing Office, 1895), pp. 3–10, 15, 27–28.

5. Karl Schuon, *Home of the Commandants* (Washington: Leatherneck Association, 1966), pp. 175–177, and *ANJ*, September 20, 1890.

6. Col. Cmdt. C. G. McCawley to Secretary of the Navy B. F. Tracy, March 28, 1890, and July 7, 1890, HQMC, "LSSN," RG 127; Col. E. D. Hebb to B. F. Tracy, October 1, 1890, HQMC, "LSSN," RG 127; Col. Cmdt. C. Heywood to B. F. Tracy, October 18, 1891, HQMC, "LSSN," RG 127; Col. Cmdt. C. Heywood to Secretary of the Navy H. A. Herbert, June 30, 1893, HQMC, "LSSN," RG 127; and *ANJ,* November 16, 1889; December 7, 1889; October 24, 1891; and November 21, 1891. The strength figures are from "Authorized Strengths of the United States Marine Corps, 1798 to 1916," memorandum, Subject File VR (USMC), RG 45, and "Strength of the Marine Corps," memorandum, December 11, 1969, HDR-1, Reference Section, H&MD, HQMC.

7. Col. Cmdt. C. Heywood to H. A. Herbert, September 28, 1893; October 11, 1895; and October 9, 1896, all HQMC, "LSSN," RG 127.

8. Manchester *Union,* March 18, 1895, clipping in HQMC Scrapbooks, RG 127. Marines were still recruited along the Eastern seaboard, as they had been since the 1790s. Col. Cmdt. C. Heywood to H. A. Herbert, June 26, 1896, HQMC, "LSSN," RG 127.

9. Col. Cmdt. C. G. McCawley to B. F. Tracy July 7, 1890; Col. Cmdt. C. Heywood to B. F. Tracy, May 13 and October 15, 1892, all HQMC, "LSSN," RG 127; and *ANJ,* September 20 and 27, 1890, and November 14, 1891.

10. Col. Cmdt. C. Heywood to B. F. Tracy, October 15, 1892, HQMC, "LSSN," RG 127; *ANJ,* May 14 and 28, 1892; November 14, 1896; and November 13, 1897.

11. Col. Cmdt. C. Heywood to B. F. Tracy, October 18, 1891, HQMC, "LSSN," RG 127.

12. Col. Cmdt. C. Heywood to B. F. Tracy, October 15, 1892, HQMC, "LSSN," RG 127; Col. Cmdt. C. Heywood to H. A. Herbert, October 9, 1896, HQMC, "LSSN," RG 127; and *ANJ,* April 4 and 25, 1891; May 20, 1893; and July, 22, 1893.

13. Col. Cmdt. C. Heywood to H. A. Herbert, September 28, 1893, HQMC, "LSSN," RG 127.

14. Col. Cmdt. C. Heywood, "Small Arms Firing Instructions," December 29, 1897, HQMC, "Letters Sent, 1884–1911," RG 127.

15. Col. Cmdt. C. Heywood to Secretary of the Navy J. D. Long, August 30, 1897, and October 1, 1897, HQMC, "LSSN," RG 127.

16. Capt. Harry A. Ellsworth, USMC, "One Hundred Eighty Landings of United States Marines, 1800–1934," 2 vols., ms., Breckinridge Library, MCDEC, Quantico, Virginia.

17. Capt. H. C. Cochrane to Mrs. E. L. Cochrane, June 24–July 19, 1891, and Capt. H. C. Cochrane to Col. Cmdt. C. Heywood, October 16, 1891, Henry Clay Cochrane Papers, MCPPC.

18. Clyde H. Metcalf, *A History of the United States Marine Corps* (New York: G. P. Putnam's Sons, 1939), pp. 248–250; Maj. P. C. Pope to Capt. H. L. Harrison, USN, August 22, 1894 (on strike duty), HD/HQMC, "Letters Received, 1818–1915," RG 127; and *ANJ,* November 5, 1892; May 20, 1893; and July 20 1893.

19. Col. Cmdt. C. G. McCawley to B. F. Tracy, October 1, 1889, Subject File NF ("Distributions and Transfers"), RG 45.

20. Cmdre. J. A. Greer, USN, to B. F. Tracy, October 12, 1889, Subject File NF, RG 45, and Col. Cmdt. C. G. McCawley to the Board of Organization, Tactics, and Drill, October 18, 1889, Subject File NF, RG 45.

21. The issue is best discussed in H. W. Russell, "The Genesis of FMF Doctrine: 1879–1899," *MCG,* 35 (April 1951): 52–59; (May 1951): 49–53; (June 1951): 50–56; and (July 1951): 52–59.

22. Col. Cmdt. C. G. McCawley to RAdm. S. B. Luce, December 18, 1889, Stephen B. Luce Papers, Naval Historical Foundation Collection, Manuscripts Division, Library of Congress.
23. Lieutenant William F. Fullam, USN, "The System of Naval Training and Discipline Required to Promote Efficiency and Attract Americans," *USNIP,* 16 (1890): 473–495.
24. "Discussion," *ibid.,* pp. 495–536, and *ANJ,* December 13, 1890.
25. Lt. J. F. Meigs, USN, to Lt. W. F. Fullam, USN, November 15, 1890, and RAdm. S. B. Luce, USN, to Lt. W. F. Fullam, USN, November 24, 1890, both William F. Fullam Papers, Naval Historical Foundation Collection, Manuscripts Division, Library of Congress; *ANJ,* January 24, 1891; and Department of the Navy, *Regulations for the Government of the Navy of the United States, 1893* (Washington: Government Printing Office, 1893), pp. 199–214. See also Lieutenant Colonel John G. Miller, "William Freeland Fullam's War with the Corps," *USNIP,* 101 (November 1975): 37–45.
26. Col. Cmdt. C. Heywood to B. F. Tracy, January 21, 1892, HQMC, "LSSN," RG 127.
27. Col. Cmdt. C. Heywood to B. F. Tracy, November 30, 1892, HQMC, "LSSN," RG 127.
28. Col. Cmdt. C. Heywood to Cmdre. F. M. Ramsay, USN, January 22, 1894, Subject File VR (USMC), RG 45.
29. Col. Cmdt. C. Heywood to H. A. Herbert, July 20, 1894, HQMC, "LSSN," RG 127; *New York Herald,* July 20, 1894, and *Washington Post,* July 2, 1894, HQMC Scrapbooks, RG 127; *ANJ,* August 4 and 5, 1894; and Col. Cmdt. C. Heywood to H. A. Herbert, October 1, 1894, and December 6, 1894, HQMC, "LSSN," RG 127.
30. Col. Cmdt. C. Heywood to H. A. Herbert, October 31, 1895, HQMC, "LSSN," RG 127; H. A. Herbert to Capt. R. D. Evans, USN, November 1, 1895, HD/HQMC, "Letters Received, 1818–1915," RG 127; and *ANJ,* November 2, 1895. See also Major H. B. Lowry, USMC, "The United States Marine Corps Considered as a Distinct Military Organization," *Journal of the Military Service Institution,* 16 (May 1895): 532–539.
31. Lieutenant W. F. Fullam, USN, "The Organization, Training, and Discipline of the Navy Personnel as Viewed from the Ship," *USNIP,* 22 (1896): 83–116.
32. "Discussion," *ibid.,* pp. 116–190.
33. Capt. W. C. Wise, USN, to Lt. W. F. Fullam, USN, April 18, 1896, Fullam Papers; Col. Cmdt. C. Heywood to H. A. Herbert, April 14, 1896, HQMC, "LSSN," RG 127; and *ANJ,* March 28, 1896, and April 11, 1896.
34. U.S. Navy Department, *Regulations for the Government of the Navy of the United States, 1896* (Washington: Government Printing Office, 1890), pp. 183–201. Article 999 is on p. 197.
35. Secretary of the Navy J. D. Long to Capt. J. J. Read, USN, May 24, 1897, HD/HQMC, "Letters Received, 1818–1915," RG 127.
36. Commandant Marine Corps circular letter, November 11, 1897, and replies from 1st Lt. G. Barnett (November 16, 1897), Capt. C. McCawley (November 16, 1897), 1st Lt. C. H. Lauchheimer (November 19, 1897), Capt. H. C. Cochrane (November 19, 1897), and Capt. A. K. White (December 12, 1897), all HD/HQMC, "Letters Received, 1818–1915," RG 127.
37. Col. Cmdt. C. Heywood to Assistant Secretary of the Navy T. Roosevelt, November 22, 1897, HQMC, "LSSN," RG 127.
38. John A. S. Grenville and George Berkeley Young, "The Influence of Strategy upon History: The Acquisition of the Philippines," in *Politics, Strategy, and American Diplomacy* (New Haven: Yale University Press, 1966), pp. 267–296.

For the naval campaigns against Spain in 1898, see Captain French E. Chadwick, USN, *The Relations of the United States and Spain: The Spanish American War,* 2 vols. (New York: Scribner's, 1911). The Marine Corps experience
is summarized in Bernard C. Nalty, *The United States Marines in the War
with Spain,* rev. ed., Marine Corps Historical Reference Pamphlet (Washington: Historical Branch, HQMC, 1967).

39. Col. Cmdt. C. Heywood to J. D. Long, March 12, 1898, HQMC, "LSSN," RG
    127. Throughout the war Headquarters Marine Corps kept extensive clippings
    on the Corps, preserved in HQMC Scrapbooks, 1880–1901, RG 127. The
    Marine Corps eventually spent $106,529 from the emergency fund.

40. Col. Cmdt. C. Heywood to J. D. Long, April 25, 1898, and September 24,
    1898, HQMC, "LSSN," RG 127.

41. Heywood's position is stated in Col. Cmdt. C. Heywood to J. D. Long, Septem-
    ber 24, 1898, HQMC, "LSSN," RG 127, and in "Report of the Commandant
    U.S. Marine Corps," U.S. Navy Department, *Annual Reports of the Navy De-
    partment, 1898* (Washington: Government Printing Office, 1898), pp. 854–
    862. Detailed analyses of Marine duties are in Lt. Col. R. L. Meade (Fleet
    Marine Officer) to Col. Cmdt. C. Heywood, August 29, 1898; Capt. L. W. T.
    Waller to Col. Cmdt. C. Heywood, September 1, 1898; and 1st Lt. R. H. Lane
    to Col. Cmdt. C. Heywood, August 27, 1898, all HD/HQMC, "Letters Re-
    ceived, 1818–1915," RG 127. The effects of American gunfire are assessed in
    Lieutenant John M. Ellicott, USN, *Effect of the Gun Fire of the United States
    Vessels in the Battle of Manila Bay,* Office of Naval Intelligence War Notes
    No. 5 (Washington: Government Printing Office, 1899), and Commander
    "J" (Imperial German Navy), *Sketches from the Spanish–American War,*
    Part II, Office of Naval Intelligence War Notes No. 4 (Washington: Govern-
    ment Printing Office, 1899), pp. 5–15.

42. Entries for April 17–22, 1898, journal of Marine battalion under Lt. Col.
    R. W. Huntington, 1898, Field Organization Records, RG 127; Col. Cmdt.
    C. Heywood to J. D. Long, April 23 and September 24, 1898, HQMC, "LSSN,"
    RG 127; Maj. Henry Clay Cochrane diaries, entries for April 19–23, 1898,
    Henry Clay Cochrane Papers; John H. Clifford, *History of the First Battalion
    of U.S. Marines* (Portsmouth, N.H.: the author, 1930); and Carolyn A. Tyson,
    ed., *The Journal of Frank Keeler* (Quantico, Va.: Marine Corps Museum,
    1967), pp. 3–4.

43. Lt. Col. R. W. Huntington to Col. Cmdt. C. Heywood, April 30, 1898, and
    May 25, 1898, and Maj. C. McCawley (battalion QM) to Col. Cmdt. C.
    Heywood, January 8, 1900, all HD/HQMC, "Letters Received, 1818–1915,"
    RG 127.

44. Lt. Col. R. W. Huntington to Col. Cmdt. C. Heywood, June 17, 1898, and
    Cmdr. Bowman McCalla, USN, to CINC, Atlantic Fleet, June 19, 1898, both
    HD/HQMC, "Letters Received, 1818–1915," RG 127, and Maj. Henry Clay
    Cochrane diaries, entries for June 10–11, 1898, Cochrane Papers.

45. Entries for June 10–14, 1898, journal of Huntington's battalion, RG 127;
    extracts from the manuscript autobiography of Admiral B. H. McCalla, File
    OH (Landing Operations), RG 45; Lt. Col. R. W. Huntington to Col.
    Cmdt. C. Heywood, June 17, 1898, and Cmdr. Bowman McCalla, USN, to
    CINC, Atlantic Fleet, June 19, 1898, both HD/HQMC, "Letters Received,
    1818–1915," RG 127; and Maj. H. C. Cochrane to Mrs. Cochrane, June 14,
    1898, Cochrane Papers.

46. Capt. G. F. Elliott to Lt. Col. R. W. Huntington, June 15, 1898, and Cmdr.
    H. W. Lyons (CO, *Dolphin*) to Secretary of the Navy, August 15, 1898, both
    HD/HQMC, "Letters Received, 1818–1915," RG 127; Maj. Henry Clay

Cochrane diaries, entries for June 14 and 15, 1898, Cochrane Papers; and Tyson, *The Journal of Frank Keeler,* pp. 16–18.

47. Charles H. Brown, *The Correspondents' War* (New York: Charles Scribner's Sons, 1967), pp. 279–289; New York *Herald,* June 16, 1898; *ANJ,* July 2, 1898; R. W. Stallman and E. R. Hagemann, eds., *The War Dispatches of Stephen Crane* (New York: New York University Press, 1964), pp. 140–154, 171–172, 267–274; and Maj. Henry Clay Cochrane diaries, entries for June 12–15, 1898, Cochrane Papers.

48. Col. Cmdt. C. Heywood to J. D. Long, September 24, 1898, HD/HQMC, "LSSN," RG 127, and *ANJ,* August 13, 1898; September 24, 1898; October 22, 1898; November 12, 1898; and May 23, 1903.

49. Brig. Gen. Cmdt. C. Heywood to J. D. Long, November 9, 1898, and December 12, 1898, HQMC, "LSSN," RG 127.

50. Maj. Gen. Cmdt. C. Heywood to Secretary of the Navy W. H. Moody, September 22, 1903, HQMC, "LSSN," RG 127; *ANJ,* October 22, 1898; January 14, 1899; March 11, 1899; April 8, 1899; May 26, 1900; January 11, 1902; November 14, 1903; December 5, 1903; January 21, 1905; April 21, 1906; February 23, 1907; February 15, 1908; and May 16, 1908; and House Committee on Naval Affairs, U.S. Congress, "Increase of Efficiency in the Marine Corps," House Report 1299, 60th Congress, 1st Session, 1908. The strength figures are from "Strength of the Marine Corps" (1969), and "Authorized Strength of the United States Marine Corps, 1798 to 1916" (1916) (both note 6 above).

51. Maj. Gen. Cmdt. C. Heywood to W. H. Moody, September 22, 1903, HQMC, "LSSN," RG 127, and *ANJ,* March 11, 1899; May 13, 1899; June 3 and 24, 1899; October 14, 1899; January 20, 1900; January 7, 1905; and October 31, 1908.

52. *ANJ,* January 11, 1902, and March 21, 1908.

53. Bernard C. Nalty et al., *United States Marine Corps Ranks and Grades,* rev. ed., Historical Reference Pamphlet (Washington: Historical Division, HQMC, 1970), pp. 20–24, and *ANJ,* July 15, 1899, and August 26, 1899.

54. Kenneth W. Condit and Major John H. Johnstone, USMC, *A Brief History of Marine Corps Staff Organization,* Historical Reference Series 25 (Washington: Historical Branch, HQMC, 1963), pp. 6–7.

55. Elliott is characterized with great charity in Schuon, *Home of the Commandants* (note 5 above), pp. 177–178, but less so in Acting Secretary of the Navy Beekman Winthrop to Maj. Gen. Cmdt. G. F. Elliott, July 15, 1910, copy in the Fullam Papers.

56. U.S. Navy Department, *Regulations for the Government of the Navy of the United States, 1900* (Washington: Government Printing Office, 1900), pp. 203–221, and idem, *Regulations for the Government of the Navy of the United States, 1905* (Washington: Government Printing Office, 1905), pp. 211–230.

57. Brig. Gen. Cmdt. C. Heywood to J. D. Long, October 1, 1901, and Maj. Gen. Cmdt. C. Heywood to W. H. Moody, September 22, 1903, both HQMC, "LSSN," RG 127, and *ANJ,* November 5, 1904. Even reorganization into permanent companies assumed the importance of the ships guards as the nucleus of expeditionary battalions. See Captain H. L. Roosevelt, USMC, "Permanent Company Organization for the United States Marine Corps," *USNIP,* 33 (September 1907): pp. 917–926.

58. Ellsworth, "One Hundred Eighty Landings of United States Marines, 1800–1934" (note 16 above).

59. The most inclusive sources for the 1908–1909 removal controversy are House

Committee on Naval Affairs, Hearings, "Status of the Marine Corps," January 7–15, 1909, 60th Congress, 2d Session (1909), which also includes many documents and correspondence; the contemporaneous newspaper clippings in the HQMC Scrapbooks, RG 127; and the correspondence and memoranda in the Fullam Papers. See also Senate Committee on Naval Affairs, "Methods of Conducting Business and Departmental Changes: Statement of Hon. Truman H. Newberry, Secretary of the Navy," February 1, 1909, Sen. Doc. 693, 60th Congress, 2d Session (1909); Elting E. Morison, *Admiral Sims and the Modern American Navy* (Boston: Houghton Mifflin, 1942), pp. 176–234; Maj. Gen. L. Wood to Capt. F. R. McCoy, USA, December 13, 1907, and to T. Roosevelt, November 26, 1908, Leonard Wood Papers, Manuscripts Divisions, Library of Congress; and T. Roosevelt to Maj. Gen. L. Wood, November 28, 1908, in Elting E. Morison, ed., *The Letters of Theodore Roosevelt,* 8 vols. (Cambridge: Harvard University Press, 1952), VI: 1389. The definitive account is Jack Shulimson and Graham A. Cosmas, "Theodore Roosevelt and the Removal of the Marines from Warships, 1908–1909," paper delivered at the Duquesne History Forum, 1979.

60. Chief, Bureau of Navigation, to Secretary of the Navy, October 16, 1908, House Naval Affairs Committee, Hearings, "Status of the Marine Corps," p. 402; Commandant of the Marine Corps, memorandum, November 6, 1908, Hearings, "Status of the Marine Corps," pp. 414–421; testimony of Maj. Gen. Cmdt. George F. Elliott, Hearings, "Status of the Marine Corps," pp. 608–611; and Cmdr. W. S. Sims, USN, to Cmdr. W. F. Fullam, USN, October 31, 1908, Fullam Papers.

61. Baltimore *American,* November 16, 1908; New York *Herald,* November 14, 1908; Oakland *Tribune,* November 22, 1908; Washington *Post,* November 15, 1908; New York *Evening Post,* November 12, 1908; "Putting the Marines Ashore," *The Nation,* 89 (November 19, 1908): 481–482; and *ANJ,* November 21, 1908.

62. Capt. A. W. Butt, USA, to Mrs. L. F. Butt, November 19, 1908, in Lawrence F. Abbott, ed., *The Letters of Archie Butt* (Garden City, N.Y.: Doubleday, Page, 1924), pp. 184–185.

63. Washington *Post,* November 15, 1908, and December 4, 1908; Washington *Evening Star,* December 4, 1908; Boston *Transcript,* December 2, 1908; and *ANJ,* November 28, 1908, and December 26, 1908.

64. *Army and Navy Register,* December 19, 1908.

65. Washington *Post,* November 22, 1908; *Army and Navy Register,* November 21, 1908, and December 19, 1908; and *ANJ,* December 19, 1908.

66. Rep. John W. Weeks to Cmdr. W. F. Fullam, USN, January 11, 1909, Fullam Papers. Other Congressional reactions are reported in the New York *Tribune,* December 12, 1908; New York *Sun,* December 11, 1908; Washington *Evening Star,* December 17, 1908; Baltimore *Sun,* December 17, 1908; and *ANJ,* January 2, 1909.

67. *Congressional Record,* 43 (60th Congress, 2nd Session): 361.

68. Testimony of Secretary of the Navy Newberry, Admirals Evans and Pillsbury, Commanders Fullam and Sims, and other Navy officers, House Naval Affairs Committee, Hearings, "Status of the Marine Corps," pp. 400–577; memorandum, "Summary of Evidence Concerning Withdrawal of Marines from Cruising Ships," 1909, Fullam Papers; memorandum, "The Executive Order Withdrawing Marines from Cruising Ships," 1909, Fullam Papers; memorandum, "Expense of Replacing Marines with Bluejackets on Board Ship," 1909, Fullam Papers; Washington *Evening Star,* January 15 and 16, 1908; New York *Sun,* January 11, 1909; Baltimore *Sun,* January 13, 1909; *ANJ,* January

2, 9, and 16, 1909; and RAdm. Stephen B. Luce, USN (Ret.), memorandum "The U.S. Marine Corps," 1909, Luce Papers.

69. Testimony of General Elliott; Colonels Waller, Lauchheimer, Richards, Mc-Cawley, and Denny; and other Marine officers, House Naval Affairs Committee, Hearings, "Status of the Marine Corps," pp. 608–727; Washington *Post,* January 8, 1909; *ANJ,* January 9, 1909; New York *Sun,* January 14, 1909; and Washington *Herald,* January 14, 1909.

70. *Congressional Record,* 43 (60th Congress, 2nd Session): 2276–2279, 2445–2454; Julius Caesar Burrows, "History of the Marine Corps," February 15, 1909, Sen. Doc. 719, 60th Congress, 2nd Session; Washington *Herald,* February 11 and 18, 1909; Washington *Evening Star,* January 20, 1909, and February 17, 1909; and *ANJ,* February 13 and 20, 1909.

71. T. Roosevelt to G. E. Foss, February 18, 1909, in Morison, ed., *The Letters of Theodore Roosevelt* (note 59 above), VI: 1525, and *ANJ,* March 13, 1909.

72. Capt. A. W. Butt, USA, to Mrs. L. F. Butt, July 25, 1909, Archibald W. Butt, *Taft and Roosevelt: The Intimate Letters of Archie Butt,* 2 vols. (New York: Doubleday, Doran, 1930), I: 156–158.

73. U.S. Navy Department, *Regulations for the Government of the Navy of the United States, 1909* (Washington: Government Printing Office, 1909), pp. 347–370; Maj. Gen. Cmdt. G. F. Elliott to the Secretary of the Navy, April 21, 1909, HQMC, "LSSN," RG 127; *ANJ,* March 6, 13, and 20, 1909; April 3 and 10, 1909; and June 26, 1909; RAdm. J. E. Pillsbury to Maj. Gen. Cmdt. G. F. Elliott, March 20, 1909, File 51295, HQMC Case Files, RG 127; and diary entry for March 22, 1909, George vonL. Meyer diaries, George vonL. Meyer Papers, Manuscripts Division, Library of Congress.

CHAPTER 6. TO SUNNY TROPIC SCENES, 1899–1914

1. D. A. Graber, *Crisis Diplomacy: A History of U.S. Intervention Policies and Practices* (Washington, D.C.: Public Affairs Press, 1959), pp. 1–18, 132–191, and Milton Offutt, "The Protection of Citizens Abroad by the Armed Forces of the United States," *Johns Hopkins University Studies in Historical and Political Science,* 46 (Baltimore: Johns Hopkins Press, 1928): 409–579.

2. Captain Harry A. Ellsworth, "One Hundred Eighty Landings of United States Marines, 1800–1934," ms., 1934, Breckinridge Library, MCDEC, Quantico, Virginia.

3. Capt. E. White, USN, to Commander-in-Chief, U.S. Naval Forces, Asiatic Station, April (?), 1899, *Annual Report of the Secretary of the Navy, 1899* (Washington, D.C.: Government Printing Office, 1899), pp. 935–936.

4. Brig. Gen. Cmdt. C. Heywood to Secretary of the Navy John D. Long, February 13, 1899; April 10, 1899; and September 30, 1899, all HQMC, "LSSN," RG 127. Among the officers commissioned in 1899 were such Corps influentials as George C. Reid, Jr., Hiram Bearss, Harry Lee, Robert H. Dunlap, Randolph C. Berkeley, Louis McCarty Little, and Logan Feland.

5. For American military operations in the Philippines, see William T. Sexton, *Soldiers in the Sun* (Harrisburg, Pa.: Military Service Publishing Co., 1939), and John M. Gates, *Schoolbooks and Krags: The United States Army in the Philippines, 1898–1902* (Westport, Conn.: Greenwood Press, 1973).

6. On naval operations in Philippine waters, 1898–1902, and naval policy for the Pacific, see William R. Braisted, *The United States Navy in the Pacific, 1897–1909* (Austin: University of Texas Press, 1958), pp. 3–74. The establishment of the Marine post at Cavite is described by a participant in Brigadier General Dion Williams, "Thirty Years Ago," *MCG,* 13 (March 1928): 3–24.

7. "Report of the Secretary of the Navy," *Annual Report of the Secretary of the Navy, 1899* (Washington, D.C.: Government Printing Office, 1899), pp. 32–33; "Report of the Commandant of the United States Marine Corps," *Annual Report of the Secretary of the Navy, 1899,* pp. 918–919; Major John H. S. Johnstone, *A Brief History of the 1st Marines,* rev. ed. (Washington, D.C.: Historical Branch, HQMC, 1968), pp. 1–2.

8. Lt. Col. G. F. Elliott to Brig. Gen. Cmdt. C. Heywood, October 12 and 13, 1899, Office of the Commandant, HQMC, "Reports Relating to Engagements of Marine Corps Personnel in the Philippines and China, 1899–1901," RG 127 (hereafter cited as "Philippine–China Reports"). See also Capt. H. C. Haines to CO, Marine Brigade, NS, Cavite, October 4, 1899, and Capt. B. H. Fuller, to CO, Marine Brigade, NS, Cavite, October 9, 1899, in "Philippine–China Reports," RG 127. The attack was also recalled by Smedley Butler in Lowell Thomas, *Old Gimlet Eye: The Adventures of Smedley D. Butler* (New York: Farrar and Rinehart, 1933), pp. 29–41. For conditions at the Cavite barracks, see Col. P. C. Pope to Brig. Gen. Cmdt. C. Heywood, May 27, 1899, and July 29, 1899, *Annual Report of the Secretary of the Navy, 1899,* pp. 930–931, 935, and *ANJ,* September 16 and 23, 1899.

9. "Report of the Commandant of the United States Marine Corps," *Annual Report of the Secretary of the Navy, 1901* (Washington, D.C.: Government Printing Office, 1901), pp. 1226–1231.

10. Brig. Gen. Cmdt C. Heywood to Secretary of the Navy J. D. Long, May 5, September 29, and October 13, 1900, HQMC, "LSSN," RG 127.

11. For the experiences of Waller's battalion, see Major L. W. T. Waller, "Operations of the First Battalion, First Regiment, United States Marines, in the Island of Samar . . . 1901 and . . . 1902," appendix 3 to *Report of the Secretary of the Navy, 1902* (Washington, D.C.: Government Printing Office, 1902); Joseph L. Schott, *The Ordeal of Samar* (Indianapolis: Bobbs Merrill, 1964); and Joel D. Thacker, "Stand, Gentlemen, He Served on Samar!" March 1945, ms., History and Museums Division, HQMC. There is a sketch of Waller in Charles L. Lewis, *Famous American Marines* (Boston: L. C. Page, 1950), pp. 155–171. For enlisted men's opinions by two participants, see John H. Clifford, *History of the Pioneer Marine Battalion at Guam, L.I., 1899 and the Campaign in Samar, P.I., 1901* (Porstmouth, N.H.: the author, 1914), and Sergeant Henry C. Adriance, USMC, "History of the Life of the Soldier in the Philippine Islands During the Spanish American War," ms., Wisconsin State Historical Society Library.

12. Maj. L. W. T. Waller to CG, 6th Separate Brigade, October 27 and 31, 1902; November 12 and 23, 1902; and December 1, 1902, and Cmdr. E. B. Barry, USN, to senior squadron commander, Southern Squadron, October and November 1901, in "Reports of Operations in the Sixth Separate Brigade," appendix F to "Annual Report of Maj. Gen. A. R. Chaffee, U.S. Army, Commanding, Division of the Philippines," *Annual Reports of the War Department, 1902,* 9 vols. (Washington, D.C.: Government Printing Office, 1902), IX: 438–441, 432–433.

13. Schott, *The Ordeal of Samar,* pp. 102–121.

14. *Ibid.,* pp. 122–284; Office of the Secretary of War, U.S. War Department, "Trials or Courts-Martial in the Philippine Islands in Consequence of Certain Instructions," Senate Document 213, 57th Congress, 2d Session (Washington, D.C.: Government Printing Office, 1903), pp. 2–17, 43–48; Richard E. Welch, Jr., "American Atrocities in the Philippines: The Indictment and Response," *Pacific Historical Review,* 43 (May 1974): 233–253; and *ANJ,* March 22 and 29, 1902.

15. Anonymous, "Lament of a Marine," Timothy Buckley papers, U.S. Army Military History Institute, Carlisle Barracks, Pa.

16. Brig. Gen. Cmdt. C. Heywood to Secretary of the Navy, September 22, 1902, HQMC, "LSSN," RG 127.

17. Chester C. Tan, *The Boxer Catastrophe* (New York: Columbia University Press, 1955), pp. 3–75, and Irwin J. Schulman, "The Emergence of the Boxers," December 12, 1974, seminar paper, Modern China Seminar, Columbia University.

18. This account of the siege is based on the following sources: Capt. J. T. Myers to commander-in-chief, U.S. Naval Force, Asiatic Station, September 26, 1900, File 6320, Office of the Secretary of the Navy, "General Correspondence, 1897–1926," RG 80; Captain Newt T. Hall, "Siege of the Legations—Summer of 1900," ms. (1932), Newt T. Hall Papers, MCPPC; and 1st Lt. J. R. Lindsey, USA, study for the Commanding General, U.S. Forces, China Relief Expedition, November 1900, "Reports of Military Operations in China for the Year Ending June 30, 1901," in "Report of the Lieutenant General Commanding the Army," *Annual Reports of the War Department, 1901,* 2 vols. (Washington, D.C.: Government Printing Office, 1901), I, Pt. 6: 454–459. See also Robert W. Glickert, "The Role of the United States Marine Corps in the Boxer Rebellion," unpublished M.A. thesis, American University, 1962.

19. The following observer accounts praise the Marines without reservation: W. A. P. Martin, *The Siege of Peking* (New York: Fleming H. Revell, 1900), pp. 83–84, 120; Robert Coltman, Jr., *Beleaguered in Peking* (Philadelphia: F. A. Davis, 1901), pp. 70, 72, 184–185; the Reverend Courtenay Hughes Fenn, "The American Marines in the Siege of Peking," *The Independent,* 52 (November 29, 1900): 2845–2849; M. S. Woodward, "The Personal Side of the Siege of Peking," *The Independent,* 52 (November 22, 1900): 2782–2891; and Sara Pike Conger, *Letters from China* (London: Hodder and Stoughton, 1909), pp. 101, 111, 157. Sympathetic but not uncritical are Mary Hooker [Polly Condit Smith], *Behind the Scenes in Peking* (New York: Brentano's, 1910), pp. 30–34, 64, 93, and A. H. Tuttle, comp., *Mary Porter Gamewell and Her Story of the Siege of Peking* (New York: Eaton and Mains, 1907), pp. 185–281.

British volunteers, however, thought the detachment was not as dependable as their own marines and the Japanese. See L. R. Marchant, ed., *The Siege of the Peking Legations: A Diary by Launcelot Giles* (Nedlands: University of Western Australia Press, 1970), pp. 107–178; Nigel Oliphant, *A Diary of the Siege of the Legations in Peking* (New York and Bombay: Longmans, Green, 1901), pp. 23–24, 57–90; B. L. Putnam Weale [Bertram L. Simpson], *Indiscreet Letters from Peking* (New York: Dodd, Mead, 1913), pp. 150–151, 173–174; and Dr. G. E. Morrison, "The Siege of the Peking Legations," *The Times* (London), October 13 and 15, 1900.

20. Capt. N. T. Hall to Capt. J. T. Myers, August 30, 1900, File 6320, Office of the Secretary of the Navy, "General Correspondence, 1897–1926," RG 80.

21. Lt. G. A. Lung, MC, USN, "Wounded and Killed," August 26, 1900, and memo, "Casualties During the Siege of Peking," both in File 6320, Office of the Secretary of the Navy, "General Correspondence, 1897–1926," RG 80.

22. D. W. Wurtzbaugh, "The Seymour Relief Expedition," *USNIP,* 28 (June 1902): 207–209, and Capt. J. K. Tausigg, USN, "Experience During the Boxer Rebellion," *USNIP,* 53 (April 1927): 403–410.

23. Maj. L. W. T. Waller to Maj. Gen. Cmdt., June 28, 1900, "Philippine–China Reports," RG 127. Three Marine officers recalled their experiences around Tientsin and Peking in Lowell Thomas, *Old Gimlet Eye: The Adventures of*

Smedley Butler, pp. 42–79; Frederic M. Wise, *A Marine Tells It to You* (New York: J. H. Sears, 1929), pp. 25–74; and Captain H. Leonard, "The Visit of the Allies to China in 1900," *Papers of the Military Historical Society of Massachusetts: Civil War and Miscellaneous Papers,* No. 14 (Boston: n.p., 1918), pp. 295–318.

24. Col. R. N. Meade to Brig. Gen. Cmdt., July 16, 1900, and March 19, 1901, and Capt. C. G. Long to CO, 1st Marine Regiment, July 16, 1900, both "Philippine–China Reports," RG 127.

25. Reports of Maj. W. P. Biddle, Maj. L. W. T. Waller, Lt. S. D. Butler, Lt. F. M. Wise, Capt. F. J. Moses, Lt. W. C. Neville, and Capt. C. G. Long, "Operations of the U.S. Marine Corps, Tientsin to Peking," in "Reports of Operations of the China Relief Expedition, July 29 to September 1, 1900, by Maj. Gen. Adna R. Chaffee, U.S.V., Commanding," *Annual Reports of the War Department, 1900,* 2 vols. (Washington, D.C.: Government Printing Office, 1900), I, Pt. 7: 79–86; extract reports, "China Relief Expedition," appendix D to "Report of the Lieutenant General Commanding the Army," *Annual Reports of the War Department, 1901,* 2 vols. (Washington, D.C.: Government Printing Office, 1901), I, Pt. 3: 198–204; Lt. Col. C. A. Coolidge, USA, to the Adj. Gen., USA, July 26, 1900, File 6320, Office of the Secretary of the Navy, "General Correspondence, 1897–1926," RG 80; Edwin L. Neville, Jr., ed., "The Diary of Pvt. Sullivan," *MCG,* 52 (November 1968): pp. 68–74; James D. Bevan, "With the U.S. Marines on the March to Peking, China—1900," *MCG,* 18 (June 1935): 5–7, 55–56 (July 1935): 14–15, 50; Brigadier General A. S. Daggett, USA, *America in the China Relief Expedition* (Kansas City, Mo.: Hudson-Kimberly, 1903); and Frederick Palmer, "With the Peking Relief Column," *The Century Magazine,* 61 (December 1900): 302–307.

26. "Report of the Commandant United States Marine Corps," *Annual Report of the Secretary of the Navy, 1900* (Washington, D.C.: Government Printing Office, 1900), pp. 1116–1132, and *ANJ,* November 24 and 30, 1900.

27. Dana G. Munro, *Intervention and Dollar Diplomacy in the Caribbean, 1900–1921* (Princeton, N.J.: Princeton University Press, 1964), pp. 3–23, and Richard D. Challener, *Admirals, Generals and American Foreign Policy, 1898–1914* (Princeton, N.J.: Princeton University Press, 1973), pp. 12–45, 81–119.

28. Maj. Gen. Cmdt. C. Heywood to Secretary of the Navy W. H. Moody, September 25, 1902, and September 22, 1903, HQMC, "LSSN," RG 127.

29. Brig. Gen. Cmdt. C. Heywood to Secretary of the Navy W. H. Moody, September 25, 1902, and Col. G. C. Reid to Secretary of the Navy W. H. Moody, September 22, 1902, both in HQMC, "LSSN," RG 127.

30. Munro, *Intervention and Dollar Diplomacy in the Caribbean,* pp. 37–60.

31. Maj. J. A. Lejeune to A. Lejeune, December 23, 1903, John A. Lejeune Papers, Manuscripts Division, Library of Congress. The intervention is described in detail in Maj. J. A. Lejeune to A. Lejeune, October 23–December 23, 1903; Maj. J. A. Lejeune to Brig. Gen. Cmdt., December 2, 1903; and RAdm. J. B. Coughlan, USN, to Maj. J. A. Lejeune, December 7, 1903, all Lejeune Papers.

32. Maj. J. A. Lejeune to CO, Caribbean Squadron, March 14, 1904; Maj. Gen. Cmdt. G. F. Elliott to Maj. J. A. Lejeune, October 21, 1904; Gov. G. W. Davis to Maj. J. A. Lejeune, November 2, 1904; and Maj. J. A. Lejeune to A. Lejeune, January 11–December 21, 1904, all in the Lejeune Papers. See also *ANJ,* January 2, 1904; October 22, 1904; November 4, 1904; January 14, 1905; March 25, 1905; and April 22, 1905.

33. Allan R. Millett, *The Politics of Intervention: The Military Occupation of Cuba, 1906–1909* (Columbus: Ohio State University Press, 1968), pp. 59–119.

34. T. Roosevelt to Acting Secretary of State R. Bacon, September 12, 1906, File

244, Numerical File, 1906–1910, General Records of the Department of State, RG 80, NA.

35. Capt. A. R. Couden, USN, to Secretary of the Navy, October 11, 1906, Area 8 File (Caribbean, 1775–1910), Naval Records Collection of the Office of Naval Records and Library, RG 45, NA; and "Report of the Commandant of United States Marine Corps," *Annual Report of the Secretary of the Navy, 1906* (Washington, D.C.: Government Printing Office, 1906), pp. 1097–1098.

36. Lt. William P. Upshur to Dr. J. N. Upshur, October 5, 1906, William P. Upshur Papers, Southern Historical Collection, University of North Carolina–Chapel Hill Library.

37. Brig. Gen. Cmdt. G. F. Elliott to Secretary of the Navy, October 12, 1906, File 24111, Office of the Secretary of the Navy, "General Correspondence, 1897–1926," RG 80, NA, and *ANJ,* September 22 and 29, 1906; October 20, 1906; and December 26, 1906. For detailed accounts of this intervention and others, see also Joel D. Thacker, "Interventions in Cuba Under the Platt Amendment," ms., no date, Cuba File, Reference Section library, History and Museums Division, HQMC.

38. Allan R. Millett, "The United States and Cuba: The Uncomfortable *Abrazo,* 1898–1968," in John Braeman, Robert H. Bremmer, and David Brody, eds., *Twentieth-Century American Foreign Policy* (Columbus: Ohio State University Press, 1971), pp. 433–438.

39. Munro, *Intervention and Dollar Diplomacy in the Caribbean,* pp. 160–186; Thomas, *Old Gimlet Eye* (note 23 above), pp. 125–137; and Bernard C. Nalty, *The United States Marines in Nicaragua,* rev. ed., Marine Corps Historical Reference Series No. 21 (Washington, D.C.: Historical Branch, HQMC, 1962), pp. 5–7.

40. Maj. S. D. Butler to Col. J. H. Pendleton, September 19, 1912, Joseph H. Pendleton Papers, MCPPC. See also Major E. N. McClellan, "Battles of the American Marines: Occupation of Managua, Nicaragua 1912," ms., 1920, copy in the Harold H. Utley Papers, MCPPC; Thomas, *Old Gimlet Eye,* pp. 138–168; and Nalty, *The United States Marines in Nicaragua,* pp. 7–9.

41. CO, 1st Prov. Regt. USMC, memo, "Report of Matagalpa Expedition," November 2, 1912; Lt. Col. C. G. Long, "Report of Operations," November 18, 1912; CO, 1st Prov. Regt. USMC, to Secretary of the Navy and Maj. Gen. Cmdt., "Report of Operations," November 28, 1912; Campaign Order 4, U.S. Pacific Fleet, September 4, 1912; Col. J. H. Pendleton to B. F. Zeledón, September 18, 1912—all in the Pendleton Papers. See also Lt. Col. C. G. Long to Secretary of the Navy, January 21, 1913, File 27827, Office of the Secretary of the Navy, "General Correspondence, 1897–1926," RG 80, NA. American losses in Coyotepe attack were four killed, fourteen wounded.

42. For the diplomatic background of the Veracruz intervention, see Arthur S. Link, *Wilson: The New Freedom,* (Princeton, N.J.: Princeton University Press, 1956), pp. 392–405; P. Edward Haley, *Revolution and Intervention: The Diplomacy of Taft and Wilson in Mexico, 1910–1917* (Cambridge, Mass.: Harvard University Press, 1970); and Robert E. Quirk, *An Affair of Honor: Woodrow Wilson and the Occupation of Veracruz* (Lexington: University of Kentucky Press, 1962).

43. Maj. Gen. L. Wood, USA, "Memorandum for the Secretary of War," April 15, 1914, and L. Garrison to W. Winslow, April 18, 1914, both appended to the Wood diary, 1914, Leonard Wood Papers, Manuscripts Division, Library of Congress.

44. Jack Sweetman, *The Landing at Veracruz: 1914* (Annapolis, Md.: U.S. Naval Institute, 1968), pp. 69–119.

45. Colonel Wendell C. Neville, report, "Operations of the Second Advance Base

Regiment from April 21, 1914 to 8 P.M. April 25, 1914," April 27, 1914, and Capt. F. H. Delano to Mrs. F. H. Delano, April 20 and 29, 1914, both in the Frederick H. Delano Papers, U.S. Army Military History Institute.

46. The Marine occupation is described in Col. J. A. Lejeune to A. Lejeune, April 24, 1914, and July 7, 1914, Lejeune Papers; Capt. F. H. Delano to Mrs. F. H. Delano, April 29–November 22, 1914, Delano Papers; and Thomas, *Old Gimlet Eye,* pp. 178–180.

47. *ANJ,* July 13, 1907.

48. On the problems of officer assignments, see Brig. Gen. Cmdt. G. F. Elliott to Rep. S. Mudd, February 21, 1908, and Maj. Gen. Cmdt. G. F. Elliott to Sen. B. R. Tillman, June 18, 1909, CMC, HQMC, "Letters Sent, 1884–1911," RG 127.

49. Kenneth W. Condit, Major John J. Johnstone, and Ella W. Nargele, *A Brief History of Marine Corps Staff Organization* (Washington, D.C.: Historical Branch, HQMC, 1971), pp. 6–10.

50. Lieutenant Colonel Gary L. Rutledge, "The Rhetoric of United States Marine Corps Enlisted Recruitment," unpublished M.A. thesis, University of Kansas, 1974, pp. 61–105.

51. *ANJ,* May 18, 1907, and May 16, 1908.

52. Maj. Gen. Cmdt. G. F. Elliott to OIC, Recruiting, Chicago, November 5, 1908, CMC HQMC "Letters Sent, 1884–1911," RG 127.

53. Robert Lindsay, *This High Name: Public Relations and the U.S. Marine Corps* (Madison: University of Wisconsin Press, 1956) pp. 8–17.

54. The development of Marine Corps marksmanship programs is outlined in the correspondence in File 14883, HQMC "Letters and Endorsements Received, 1904–1912," RG 127. The newspaper commentary is summarized in *ANJ,* November 14, 1908; May 8, 1909; August 7, 1909; and December 25, 1909.

55. *ANJ,* January 30, 1904.

56. New York *Sun,* January 31, 1909.

57. *Harper's Weekly,* 55 (June 24, 1911): 12; *Everybody's Magazine,* 30 (June 1914): 180–112; *Outlook,* 108 (November 24, 1914): 686–694; and *Overland Monthly,* 64 (September 1914): 233.

CHAPTER 7. HISPANIOLA, 1915–1934

1. Rayford W. Logan, *Haiti and the Dominican Republic* (New York and London: Oxford University Press, 1968); Sumner Welles, *Naboth's Vineyard: The Dominican Republic, 1844–1924,* 2 vols. (New York: Payson and Clarke, 1928); and Carl Kelsey, "The American Intervention in Haiti and the Dominican Republic," *The Annals of the American Academy of Political and Social Science,* 100 (March 1922): 109–199.

2. Dana G. Munro, *Intervention and Dollar Diplomacy in the Caribbean, 1900–1921* (Princeton, N.J.: Princeton University Press, 1964), pp. 78–111, 116–125, 245–268. The strategic question is described in Adm. G. Dewey to Secretary of the Navy, December 10, 1910, File 413, General Board Records, Operational Archives, Naval Historical Division, and summarized in Richard D. Challener, *Admirals, Generals, and American Foreign Policy, 1898–1914* (Princeton, N.J.: Princeton University Press, 1973), pp. 119–148, 323–344.

3. Burton J. Hendrick, ed., *Life and Letters of Walter Hines Page,* 3 vols. (Garden City, N.Y.: Doubleday, Page, 1922), I: 204.

4. Arthur S. Link, *Wilson: The Struggle for Neutrality, 1914–1915* (Princeton, N.J.: Princeton University Press, 1960), pp. 495–550.

5. Munro, *Dollar Diplomacy and Intervention in the Caribbean*, pp. 274–304, 333–351.
6. Office of Naval Intelligence, File 4801A, "Haiti and Santo Domingo—Plan of Occupation," October–December 1914, WA-7, Area 8 File (Caribbean), Naval Records Collection of the Office of Naval Records and Library, RG 45, NA. The Navy plans are discussed in Hans Schmidt, *The United States Occupation of Haiti, 1915–1934* (New Brunswick, N.J.: Rutgers University Press, 1971), pp. 64–65, with the implication that the Navy expected more than a lives-and-property operation. The plans show no such awareness. See also Lt. Col. B. H. Fuller to Maj. Gen. Cmdt., February 10, 1915, File 27827, "General Correspondence of the Secretary of the Navy, 1897–1926," RG 80, NA, and David Healy, *Gunboat Diplomacy in the Wilson Era: The U.S. Navy in Haiti, 1915–1916* (Madison: University of Wisconsin Press, 1976).
7. Munro, *Dollar Diplomacy and Intervention in the Caribbean*, pp. 351–352; Captain Edward L. Beach, USN, "Admiral Caperton in Haiti," ms. history, File ZWA-7, Subject File, 1911–1927, RG 45; testimony of RAdm. W. B. Caperton, U.S. Senate Select Committee, hearings, "Inquiry into Occupation and Administration of Haiti and Santo Domingo," 2 vols., 67th Congress, 2d Session, 1921–1922, I: 289–421 (hereafter cited as Senate Select Committee, "Inquiry into Occupation.")
8. Munro, *Intervention and Dollar Diplomacy in the Caribbean*, pp. 256–262.
9. Col. L. W. T. Waller to Col. J. A. Lejeune, August 21 and 18, 1915, John A. Lejeune Papers. The best accounts of Marine activities in Haiti in 1915 are Brig. Gen. G. Barnett to the Secretary of the Navy, "Report on Affairs in the Republic of Haiti, June 1915 to June 30, 1920," October 11, 1920, copy in the L. W. T. Waller, Jr., Papers, MCPPC; and the testimony of Brigadier General L. W. T. Waller and Brigadier General S. D. Butler, Senate Select Committee, "Inquiry into Occupation," pp. 607–647 and 511–542. See also Colonel Frederic M. Wise, *A Marine Tells It to You* (New York: J. H. Sears, 1929), pp. 130–156.
10. Col. L. W. T. Waller to Col. J. A. Lejeune, September 21 and 26, 1915; and October 26, 1915, Lejeune Papers, and Regt. Cmdr. 1st Regt. to Brig. Cmdr., "Operations Against Caco Forces Around Cap Haitien," September 30, 1915, WA-7, Subject File, 1911–1927, RG 45.
11. Col. L. W. T. Waller to Col. J. A. Lejeune, October 13, 1915, Lejeune Papers.
12. Col. L. W. T. Waller to Col. J. A. Lejeune, October 6 and 7, 1916, and November 1, 1916, Lejeune Papers, and Expedition Commander to Maj. Gen. Cmdt., "Operations in Northern Haiti," January 13, 1916, File 127, General Correspondence of the Expeditionary Commander and 1st Brigade, 1915–1920, Field Organization Records [FOR], RG 127.
13. Maj. S. D. Butler, memo, "Report of Operations, October 9th, 1915, to November 27th, 1915," December 7, 1915, copy in Smedley D. Butler Papers, MCPPC, Washington Navy Yard. The patrolling in northern Haiti is vividly described in "Diary of Capt. Chandler Campbell, 13th Company, 1915," and Capt. C. Campbell, "Military History of [13th] Company from Sept. 26, 1915, to Oct. 15, 1915," Chandler Campbell Papers, MCPPC.
14. CO, 12th Company, to Expeditionary Commander, U.S. Forces, Haiti, October 16, 1915, File 138, General Correspondence, Expeditionary Commander and 1st Brigade, 1915–1920, FOR, RG 127.
15. Expeditionary Commander to Maj. Gen. Cmdt., August 31, 1916, General Correspondence, Expeditionary Commander and 1st Brigade, 1915–1920, FOR, RG 127, and Captain Randolph Coyle, "Service in Haiti," *MCG*, 1 (December 1916): 343–348. Troop behavior is discussed in Col. L. W. T. Waller to the

President of Haiti, October 16, 1916, and in the reports in File 042 ("Complaints"), General Correspondence, Expeditionary Commander and 1st Brigade, 1915–1920, FOR, RG 127.

16. The best sources for the history of the *Gendarmerie* (later *Garde*) *d'Haiti* are Major Franklin A. Hart, "A Critical Analysis of the Initiation, Organization, Operations, and Policies of the Garde d'Haiti," 1935, Senior School thesis, copy in Breckinridge Library, MCDEC, and *idem,* Headquarters, Garde d'Haiti, "The History of the Garde d'Haiti," 1934, copy in Breckinridge Library. The archival records of the *Garde d'Haiti* are included in Field Organization Records, RG 127.

17. Hart, "The History of the Garde d'Haiti," pp. 1–40; Brig. Gen. L. W. T. Waller to Col. J. A. Lejeune, June 26, 1916, and August 20 and 31, 1916, Lejeune Papers; Col. L. W. T. Waller to Maj. S. D. Butler, May 19, 1916; Maj. S. D. Butler to Mr. (?) Mann, April 4, 1916, and to Rep. T. S. Butler, July 15, 1916, all Butler Papers; and Maj. S. D. Butler to Col. J. A. Lejeune, July 13, 1916, Lejeune Papers.

18. Hart, "The History of the Garde d'Haiti," pp. 40–45, and Chief of the *Gendarmerie* to the Maj. Gen. Cmdt., September 18, 1919, HQ *Gendarmerie d'Haiti,* "General Correspondence, 1916–1919," FOR, RG 127.

19. Welles, *Naboth's Vineyard* (note 1 above), pp. 744–796, and Munro, *Intervention and Dollar Diplomacy in the Caribbean* (note 2 above), pp. 305–307.

20. Captain Stephen M. Fuller and Graham A. Cosmas, *Marines in the Dominican Republic, 1916–1924* (Washington, D.C.: History and Museums Division, HQMC, 1974) pp. 7–10.

21. Wise, *A Marine Tells It to You* (note 9 above), pp. 138–139; Capt. P. A. del Valle, "Notes on the Landing at Santo Domingo, May, 1916," ms., 1925, Harold H. Utley Papers, MCPPC; and memoir of Lt. Gen. Julian C. Smith (1968), pp. 38–43, and memoir of Lt. Gen. Pedro A. del Valle (1966), pp. 24–37, Marine Corps Oral History Collection (hereafter cited as MCOHC).

22. Col. J. H. Pendleton, "Report of Provisional Detachment, U.S. Expeditionary Forces, U.S. Naval Forces operating ashore in Santo Domingo . . . June 26th to July 6, 1916," July 20, 1916, with appended battalion and company operations reports, copy in the Joseph H. Pendleton Papers, MCPPC; Sergeant John H. Nichols, "Hiking and Fighting," *Recruiter's Bulletin,* 3 (November 1916): 10; Kenneth W. Condit and Edwin T. Turnbladh, *Hold High the Torch: A History of the 4th Marines* (Washington, D.C.: Historical Branch, HQMC, 1960), pp. 37–67; and RAdm. W. B. Caperton to Col. J. H. Pendleton, July 11, 1916, Pendleton Papers.

23. Munro, *Intervention and Dollar Diplomacy in the Caribbean,* pp. 307–325.

24. Welles, *Naboth's Vineyard,* pp. 797–899, and Kelsey, "The American Intervention in Haiti and the Dominican Republic" (note 1 above), pp. 177–187.

25. Colonel R. H. Lane, "Civil Government in Santo Domingo in the Early Days of the Military Occupation," *MCG,* 7 (June 1922): 127–146; Commander C. C. Baughman, "United States Occupation of the Dominican Republic," *USNIP,* 51 (October 1925): 2306–2327; Department of the Navy, memo on the occupation of the Dominican Republic, August 5, 1921, in Senate Select Committee, "Inquiry into Occupation," I: 90–104; Office of the Military Governor, *Santo Domingo,* January 1, 1920, File ZWA-7, Subject File, 1911–1927, RG 45; Lieutenant Colonel Charles J. Miller, "Diplomatic Spurs, Our Experience in Santo Domingo," *MCG,* 19 (February 1935): 43–50, (May 1935): 19–25, 52–55, and (August 1935): 35–55; Thomas J. Saxon, "The United States Military Government in the Dominican Republic, 1916–1922," unpublished M.A. thesis, University of Maryland, 1964; and Military Gov-

ernor to Secretary of the Navy, "Conditions in Santo Domingo since Proclamation of Occupation," October 25, 1920, General Correspondence, Military Government of Santo Domingo, Records of the Office of the Chief of Naval Operations, Record Group 38, National Archives (hereafter cited as General Correspondence, MGSD, RG 38).

26. Quarterly reports, military governor of Santo Domingo and military representative of the United States in Haiti to the Secretary of the Navy, November 1916–October 1917, General Correspondence, MGSD, RG 38; Fuller and Cosmas, *Marines in the Dominican Republic* pp. 24–28; "Report of the Commandant U.S. Marine Corps," *Annual Reports of the Navy Department 1917* (Washington, D.C.: Government Printing Office, 1918), pp. 838–840; quarterly report, military governor of Santo Domingo to Secretary of the Navy, October 1917, General Correspondence, MGSD, RG 38; and Major C. F. Williams, "La Guardia Nacional Dominicana," *MCG*, 3 (September 1918): 195–199.

27. The most detailed accounts of the *caco* war are John C. Chapin, "The Marines' Role in the U.S. Occuption of Haiti, 1915–1922," unpublished M.A. thesis, George Washington University, 1967; Hart, "The History of the Garde d'Haiti," pp. 49–67; and Headquarters, 1st Brigade, "General Outline of the Work of the Military Occupation in Haiti," 1920, General Correspondence of Expedition Commander and 1st Brigade, 1915–1920, RG 127.

28. Chief of the *Gendarmerie d'Haiti* to all officers, "Charlemagne M. Peralte," November 26, 1919, HQ, *Gendarmerie d'Haiti,* General Correspondence, 1915–1926, RG 127.

29. Col. J. H. Russell to Maj. Gen. Cmdt. G. Barnett, October 17, 1919, copy in the Clayton B. Vogel Papers, MCPPC, and Brigadier General J. H. Russell, "A Laboratory of Government," ms., 1930 (?), pp. 7–8, John H. Russell Papers, MCPPC.

30. Wise, *A Marine Tells It to You,* pp. 301–335, and memoir of Gen. Gerald C. Thomas (1966), pp. 68–79, MCOHC.

31. Brig. Gen. J. H. Russell to Commanding Officers, 2d Regiment and 8th Regiment, "Provost Courts," September 15, 1920, General Correspondence of Expedition Commander and 1st Brigade, 1915–1920, RG 127. On American–Haitian conflict, see File 60-0 ("Investigations, 1915–1922"), HQ *Gendarmarie d'Haiti,* General Correspondence, 1915–1926, RG 127. The campaign is vividly described in Maj. (GdH) H. H. Utley, "Official Diary, Oct. 27, 1919 to July 4, 1920," Utley Papers. The basic source on the atrocity question is the collection of documents and testimony of investigating officer Major T. C. Turner and Colonel A. S. Williams, Senate Select Committee, "Inquiry into Occupation," pp. 457–509, 595–606.

32. Quarterly reports for 1918, military governor of Santo Domingo to the Secretary of the Navy, March 31, 1918; June 30, 1918; September 30, 1918; and December 31, 1918, General Correspondence, MGSD, RG 38; 2d Provisional Brigade, "Record of Proceedings of a Board of Investigation . . . to Inquire into the Moral Conditions at Santo Domingo City, Dominican Republic, Tending to Affect the Forces of Occupation Now Stationed at that Port," August 6, 1918, File 9-116 (1918), General Correspondence, MGSD, RG 38; 2d Provisional Brigade, brigade orders 1918, File 9 (1918), General Correspondence, MGSD, RG 38. Service in the Dominican Republic is summarized in Fuller and Cosmas, *Marines in the Dominican Republic,* pp. 28–45.

33. Records and correspondence, case of Lieutenant (GND) Frank Hatton and Guardias F. Chestaro, Gil Canario, and A. Bargas, File 46-17 (1918), General Correspondence, MGSD, RG 38.

34. Quarterly reports, 1918 and 1919, military governor of Santo Domingo to the Secretary of the Navy, General Correspondence, MGSD, RG 38; Brigade Commander to Military Governor, "Trip of Inspection," October 18, 1918, File 9 (1918), General Correspondence, MGSD, RG 38; RAdm. S. S. Robison to Sen. M. McCormick, January 22, 1922, Dominican Republic File (1922), Reference Section, History and Museums Division, HQMC (hereafter, H&MD); memoir of Lt. Gen. Edward A. Craig (1968), pp. 19–43, 60, MCOHC; and memoir of Maj. Gen. Omar T. Pfeiffer (1968), MCOHC, pp. 20–48.

35. Quarterly reports, military governor of Santo Domingo to the Secretary of the Navy, 1919–1920, General Correspondence, MGSD, RG 38; Col. G. C. Thorpe to Regt. Cmdr., "Engagement at Dos Rios," September 3, 1918, File 9-108 (1918), General Correspondence, MGSD, RG 38; Military governor to Brig. Cmdr., "Conduct in Exercise of Powers of Military Government," October 26, 1918, File 9-131 (1918), General Correspondence, MGSD, RG 38; Colonel G. C. Thorpe, "Dominican Service," *MCG,* 4 (December 1919): 315–326; and Lieutenant Colonel H. C. Davis, "Indoctrination of Latin-American Service," *MCG,* 5 (June 1920): 154–161.

36. Quarterly reports, 1921–1922, military governor of Santo Domingo to the Secretary of the Navy; CG, 2d Brigade to military governor, "Disciplinary Regulations for the G.N.D.," February 10, 1920, File 14-55 (1920); 2d Brigade Order 1-1921, January 2, 1921, Brigade general and special orders, File 14 (1921), all in the General Correspondence, MGSD, RG 38; and District Commander, Eastern District, to CG, 2d Brigade, "Control of Field Forces by Regimental Headquarters, 15th Regiment," January 2, 1922, and CG, 2d Brigade, to Maj. Gen. Cmdt., August 24, 1922, both in Santo Domingo File (1922), Reference Section, H&MD.

37. Testimony of Brigadier General A. W. Catlin, Senate Select Committee, "Inquiry into Occupation," pp. 649–669. The investigations and subsequent developments are summarized in Schmidt, *The United States Occupation of Haiti* (note 6 above), pp. 105–121.

38. Maj. Gen. Cmdt. J. A. Lejeune and Brig. Gen. S. D. Butler to Secretary of the Navy, October 12, 1920, and Lejeune to J. Daniels, March 31, 1930, Josephus Daniels Papers, Manuscripts Division, Library of Congress; entries of August 10, 28, and 31, 1920, and September 1, 1920, in J. David Cronon, ed., *The Cabinet Diaries of Josephus Daniels* (Lincoln: University of Nebraska Press, 1963), pp. 545, 553–555; Maj. Gen. Cmdt. to the Secretary of the Navy, "Report on the Military Situation in Haiti," October 4, 1920, Lejeune Papers; "Statement of General Barnett," October 17, 1920, and "Excerpts from the Report of the Court of Inquiry into Haitian Matters, 1920," copies in the George H. Barnett Papers, MCPPC; testimony of Brig. Gen. G. Barnett, Senate Select Committee, "Inquiry into Occupation," pp. 423–455; John H. Craige, *Cannibal Cousins* (New York: Minton, Balch, 1934), pp. 75–87; and Brig. Gen. G. Barnett to Secretary of the Navy, "Report on Affairs in the Republic of Haiti, June 1915 to June 30, 1920," October 11, 1920, ZWA-7, Subject File, 1911–1927, RG 45.

39. U.S. Senate, Select Committee on Haiti and Santo Domingo, report on inquiry conducted in accordance with Senate Resolution 112, Senate Report 79, 67th Congress, 2d Session. Entries of December 2 and 23, 1920, and January 24, 1921, Cronon, *The Cabinet Diaries of Josephus Daniels,* pp. 571, 577, 591.

40. Kelsey, "The American Intervention in Haiti and Santo Domingo" (note 1 above), p. 198.

41. Dana G. Munro, *The United States and the Caribbean Republics, 1921–1933* (Princeton, N.J.: Princeton University Press, 1974), pp. 44–56, 74–87.

42. Military Governor to Brig. Gen. H. Lee, August 4, 1922, General Correspondence, MGSD, RG 38, and Munro, *The United States and the Caribbean Republics,* pp. 55–59.

43. Brig. Gen. H. Lee to Military Governor, July 1 and August 2, 1922, and CG, 2d Brigade, to District Commanders and Commandant, PND, July 31, 1933, all in General Correspondence, MGSD, RG 38. The strength of the *Policia* was planned at 90 line officers, 20 medical officers, and 1,200 enlisted men.

44. CG, 2d Brigade, to Secretary of the Navy, July 18, 1924, Santo Domingo File (1924), Reference Section, H&MD and Lieutenant Edward A. Fellowes (chief instructor, PND), "Training Native Troops in Santo Domingo," *MCG,* 8 (December 1923): 215–233.

45. Horace Knowles, quoted in the *New York Times,* April 18, 1927.

46. Lieutenant Robert C. Kilmartin, "Indoctrination in Santo Domingo," *MCG,* 7 (December 1922): 377–386.

47. CG, 2d Brigade, to Secretary of the Navy, July 18, 1924, Santo Domingo File (1924), Reference Section, H&MD; S. Welles to Military Governor, September 12, 1922, and Military Governor to S. Welles, September 13, 1922, General Correspondence, MGSD, RG 38; CG, 2d Brigade, to Commanding Officers, 2d Brigade, and Commandant, PND, October 24, 1922, General Correspondence, MGSD, RG 38; "Inspection Report, Major General Joseph H. Pendleton, USMC," April 3–8, 1924, Pendleton Papers; and "Annual Report of the Secretary of the Navy," *Annual Report of the Navy Department, 1924* (Washington, D.C.: Government Printing Office, 1924), pp. 50–51.

48. Munro, *The United States and the Caribbean Republics,* pp. 71–115, 309–341; Raymond L. Buell, "The American Occupation of Haiti," *Foreign Policy Association Information Service Bulletin 5* (November 27–December 12, 1929), pp. 327–392; and Major General Commandant John H. Russell, "Marine Looks Back on Haiti," ms., 1934 (?), Russell Papers.

49. 1st Brigade, general and selected correspondence, 1921–1934, FOR, RG 127. These files include provost reports, monthly reports, accident and incident investigations, and administrative correspondence.

50. General correspondence of the Chief of the *Gendarmerie d'Haiti,* 1921–1923, and selected files from the general correspondence of the Commandant of the *Garde d'Haiti,* 1929–1934, FOR, RG 127; *Garde d'Haiti, Annual Report 1927* (Port-au-Prince: *Garde d'Haiti,* 1928); and *idem, Annual Report 1928* (Port-au-Prince: *Garde d'Haiti,* 1929).

51. Captain John H. Craige, *Black Bagdad* (New York: Minton, Balch, 1933); *idem, Cannibal Cousins* (New York: Minton, Balch, 1934); Faustin Wirkus and Taney Dudley, *The White King of La Gonave* (Garden City, N.Y.: Garden City Publishing Company, 1931), pp. 195–333; and memoirs of General O. P. Smith (1969), pp. 38–41; Lt. Gen. M. H. Silverthorn (1969), pp. 138–175; and Lt. Gen. P. del Valle (1966), pp. 54–62, MCOHC.

52. Schmidt, *The United States Occupation of Haiti* (note 6 above), pp. 189–206.

53. Headquarters, *Garde d'Haiti,* "Proceedings and Findings of Board to Study Plans for Haitianization submitted by U. S. Legation and President of Haiti," March 31, 1931, copy in Vogel Papers; Cmdt. (GdH) R. P. Williams to D. G. Munro, November 20, 1931, 1st Brigade, General Correspondence, 1930–1934, RG 127; Headquarters, *Garde d'Haiti,* memo, "Armament," July 11, 1933, and Brig. Gen. (GdH) T. S. Clarke, report of board to study legislation for the *Garde d'Haiti,* November 7, 1933, Vogel Papers; Headquarters, *Garde d'Haiti, Annual Report 1931* (Port-au-Prince: *Garde d'Haiti,* 1932), and *idem, Annual Report 1932* (Port-au-Prince, 1933), copies in File 1375, *Garde d'Haiti* General Correspondence, 1929–1934, FOR, RG 127; and U.S. Department of State, *Report of the President's Commission for the Study and*

Review of Conditions in the Republic of Haiti (Washington, D.C.: Government Printing Office, 1930).

CHAPTER 8. THE MARINES IN CHINA, 1905–1941

1. U.S. Department of State, circular note, August 29, 1900, *Foreign Relations of the United States, 1900* (Washington: Government Printing Office, 1902), pp. 303–304.
2. O. Edmund Clubb, *20th Century China*, 2d ed. (New York and London: Columbia University Press, 1966), pp. 36–80.
3. Jerry Israel, *Progressivism and the Open Door: America and China, 1905–1921* (Pittsburgh: University of Pittsburgh Press, 1971); Tien-yi Li, *Woodrow Wilson's China Policy, 1913–1917* (New York: Twayne, 1952); and Charles Vevier, *The United States and China, 1906–1913* (New York: Greenwood Press, 1968).
4. Louis Morton, "Army and Marines on the China Station: A Study in Military and Political Rivalry," *Pacific Historical Review*, 29 (February 1960): 51–73.
5. Kemp Tolley, *Yangtze Patrol: The U.S. Navy in China* (Annapolis: Naval Institute Press, 1971).
6. William R. Braisted, *The United States Navy in the Pacific, 1909–1922* (Austin: University of Texas Press, 1971), pp. 94–119.
7. The best summary is Lieutenant Colonel C. H. Metcalf, "The Marines in China," *MCG*, 22 (September 1938): 35–37, 53–58.
8. Brooke Astor, *A Patchwork Child* (New York: Harper and Row, 1962), pp. 48–128.
9. Paul S. Reinsch, *An American Diplomat in China* (Garden City, N.Y.: Doubleday, Page, 1922), p. 17.
10. Memoir of Brig. Gen. L. A. Dessez (1970), pp. 33–62, MCOHC.
11. Maj. L. McC. Little, "Report of Inspection," September 2, 1917, File 20224, General Correspondence of the Secretary of the Navy, 1916–1926, RG 80, NA.
12. Capt. P. W. Guilfoyle, "Report of Operations," May 11, 1922, China Files, HRS, HQMC.
13. "Activities of the U.S. Marines in the Chinese Civil War," ms., China File, 1924–1927. Reference Section, H&MD.
14. "Activities of the U.S. Marines in the Chinese Civil War," ms., China File, 1924–1927, HRS, HQMC; 2d Lieutenant R. L. Skidmore, "A Short History of the U.S. Marine Corps Expeditionary Detachment in China," April 12, 1926; extracts from the annual report of the commanding officer, Marine detachment, American legation, Peking, 1924–1927; and memoir of Maj. Gen. O. T. Pfeiffer (1968), pp. 69–88, MCOHC.
15. Russell D. Buhite, *Nelson T. Johnson and American Policy Toward China, 1925–1941* (East Lansing: Michigan State University Press, 1968).
16. Charles A. Peckham, "The Northern Expedition, the Nanking Incident, and the Protection of American Nationals," unpublished M.A. thesis, Ohio State University, 1973, pp. 11–19, 30–38.
17. Dorothy Borg, *American Policy and the Chinese Revolution, 1925–1928* (New York: Macmillan, 1947), pp. 418–431.
18. Peckham, "The Northern Expedition, the Nanking Incident, and the Protection of American Nationals," pp. 43–46.
19. Lt. Col. F. D. Kilgore to CO, 4th Mar, "Duty Performed by the Fourth Regiment in Shanghai in 1927," June 28, 1929, China Subject File, HRS, HQMC, and Kenneth W. Condit and Edwin T. Turnbladh, *Hold High the Torch: A History of the 4th Marines* (Washington, D.C.: Historical Branch, HQMC, 1960), pp. 119–134.

20. Peckham, "The Northern Expedition, the Nanking Incident, and the Protectection of American Nationals," pp. 55–73.

21. Brig. Gen. S. D. Butler to Maj. Gen. Cmdt. J. A. Lejeune, April 1, 1927, Smedley D. Butler Papers, MCPPC.

22. Brigadier General Smedley D. Butler, "American Marines in China," *Annals of the American Academy of Political and Social Science*, 146 (July 1929): 128–134, and Brig. Gen. S. D. Butler to Maj. Gen. Cmdt. J. A. Lejeune, April 5, 1927, Butler Papers.

23. Brig. Gen. S. D. Butler to Maj. Gen. Cmdt. J. A. Lejeune, April 22–May 5, 1927, Butler Papers, and memoir of Maj. Gen. L. R. Jones (1970), pp. 42–56, MCOHC.

24. Brig. Gen. S. D. Butler to Maj. Gen. Cmdt. J. A. Lejeune, May 12–July 16, 1927, Butler Papers, and Brig. Gen. S. D. Butler "Historical Report of the Occupation of Tientsin by the Third Brigade," December 31, 1928, File ZK, Subject Files, 1911–1927, RG 45.

25. Col. H. C. Davis to Maj. Gen. Cmdt. J. A. Lejeune, June 9 and 19, 1927, Butler Papers, and 4th Marines reports and operations orders, 1927–1928, FOR, RG 127.

26. Adm. M. L. Bristol to Secretary of the Navy, July 7, 1929, File ZK, Subject Files, RG 45.

27. Brig. Gen. S. D. Butler to Maj. Gen. Cmdt. J. A. Lejeune, November 2–December 27, 1927, Butler Papers; 6th Marines and 3d Brigade reports and operations orders, 1927–1928, FOR, RG 127; memoir of Lt. Gen. V. E. Megee (1967), pp. 43–58, MCOHC; and memoir of Maj. Gen. G. H. Cloud (1970), pp. 38–43, MCOHC.

28. Brig. Gen. S. D. Butler to Maj. Gen. Cmdt. J. A. Lejeune, January 31, 1928, Butler Papers.

29. Brig. Gen. S. D. Butler to Adm. M. L. Bristol, USN, December 31, 1928, File ZK, Subject Files, RG 45.

30. John V. Armonia, "The Mongol Mob," *The Western Horseman*, 24 (April 1959): 40–42, 99–100, and memoir of Brig. Gen. J. P. S. Devereux (1970), pp. 48–65, MCOHC.

31. Memoir of Lt. Gen. R. B. Luckey (1969), pp. 72–86, MCOHC; memoir of Gen. G. C. Thomas (1966), pp. 115–121, MCOHC; memoir of Gen. G. B. Erskine (1970), pp. 126–156, MCOHC; Lt. Col. A. A. Vandegrift to Col. J. Marston, August 4, 1936, A. A. Vandegrift Papers, MCPPC; HQ Marine Det. Tientsin, "Record of Events during the Tientsin Flood of 1939," n.d., China File, HRS, HQMC; Roger Willock, *Lone Star Marine* (Princeton, N.J.: Roger Willock, 1961), pp. 120–138; *The Legation Guard News* (1930–1932); *The Legation Guard News Annual* (1931–1935); *The Peiping Marine* (1939–1941); and *Tientsin Marine* (1938–1940).

32. Memoir of Gen. R. E. Hogaboom (1970), pp. 117–135, MCOHC; memoir of Maj. Gen. C. R. Allen (1969), pp. 87–133, MCOHC; memoir of Lt. Gen. J. P. Berkeley (1969), pp. 61–104, MCOHC; and the 4th Marines' newspaper, *The Walla Walla* (1929–1941), HRS, HQMC.

33. Condit and Turnbladh, *Hold High the Torch* (note 19 above), pp. 152–164, and Michael D. Reagan, "The Far Eastern Crisis of 1931–1932; Stimson, Hoover, and the Armed Forces," in Harold Stein, ed., *American Civil-Military Decisions* (Birmingham: University of Alabama Press, 1963), pp. 29–40.

34. Secretary of State Cordell Hull to the Vice President, January 8, 1938, in "American Nationals, Troops and Capital in China," Sen. Doc. 131, 75th Congress, 3d Session.

35. Secretary of the Navy C. Swanson to F. D. Roosevelt, November 10, 1934, Franklin D. Roosevelt Papers, Hyde Park, N.Y.

36. Col. C. F. B. Price (CO 4th Mar) to Col. A. A. Vandegrift, February 2, 1938, Vandegrift Papers, and Condit and Turnbladh, *Hold High the Torch,* pp. 167–176.
37. Maj. Gen. Cmdt. T. Holcomb to Maj. Gen. L. McC. Little, August 19, 1937; Maj. Gen. L. McC. Little to Maj. Gen. Cmdt. T. Holcomb, August 24, 1937; and Lt. Col. J. W. Webb to Maj. Gen L. McC. Little, September 10, 1937, all in the Louis McCarty Little Papers, MCPPC.
38. Brig. Gen. J. C. Beaumont to Maj. Gen. L. McC. Little, November 15, 1937, Little Papers.
39. Maj. Gen. Cmdt. T. Holcomb to Maj. Gen. L. McC. Little, February 3, 1938, Little Papers.
40. Maj. M. A. Edson to Miss Mary Edson and Mrs. M. A. Edson, July, 1937–May, 1939, Merritt A. Edson Papers, Manuscript Division, Library of Congress; Tolley, *Yangtze Patrol,* pp. 239–273; "Shanghai Duty, 1937–1938: How Bittersweet It Was," *USNIP* 100 (November, 1974), pp. 79–91; James H. Herzog, *Closing the Open Door: American-Japanese Diplomatic Negotiations, 1936–1941* (Annapolis: U.S. Naval Institute, 1973), pp. 1–53.
41. Capt. E. F. Carlson to Miss M. A. LeHand (FDR's private secretary), August 14, 1937–November 15, 1938, and Miss M. A. LeHand to Capt. E. F. Carlson, October 21, 1937, File PPF 4951, Roosevelt Papers, and Evans F. Carlson, *Twin Stars of China* (New York: Mead & Company, 1940).
42. Condit and Turnbladh, *Hold High the Torch,* pp. 176–193.

CHAPTER 9. NICARAGUA: END OF AN ERA, 1926–1933

1. Dana G. Munro, *The United States and the Caribbean Republics, 1921–1933* (Princeton, N.J.: Princeton University Press, 1974), pp. 116–156.
2. *Ibid.,* pp. 157–161.
3. Chief of Naval Operations memo, "Legation Guard at Managua," March 2, 1920; BuMed to Secretary of the Navy, "Condition of Marine Detachment, Managua, Nicaragua," February 4, 1920; Quartermaster Gen. C. L. McCawley to Maj. Gen. Comdt. G. Barnett, May 28, 1919; Secretary of the Navy to CO, Special Service Squadron, February 10, 1921; AmLeg Managua to Secretary of State, February 7, 1921; CO, Special Service Squadron, to CNO, December 13, 1921; and Cmdt. 15th Naval District to CNO, January 24 and 28, 1922, all in File 7418, General Correspondence of the Secretary of the Navy, 1916–1926, RG 80, NA.
4. Munro, *The United States and the Caribbean Republics,* pp. 183–186; Richard L. Millett, "The History of the Guardia Nacional de Nicaragua, 1925–1965," unpublished Ph.D. dissertation, University of New Mexico, 1966, pp. 62–85, published as *Guardians of the Dynasty: A History of the U.S. Created Guardia Nacional de Nicaragua and the Somoza Family* (Maryknoll, N.Y.: Orbis, 1977).
5. *Ibid.,* pp. 187–212. See also William Kamman, *A Search for Stability: United States Diplomacy toward Nicaragua, 1925–1933* (Notre Dame, Ind.: University of Notre Dame Press, 1968), pp. 37–68.
6. Kamman, *A Search for Stability,* pp. 69–91.
7. Munro, *The United States and the Caribbean Republics,* pp. 217–221; "Summary of Operations in Nicaragua, December 23, 1926–February 5, 1928," appendix, U.S. Senate, Committee on Foreign Relations, Hearings: "Use of United States Navy in Nicaragua," February 11–18, 1928, 70th Congress, 1st Session (Washington: Government Printing Office, 1928), pp. 2–8 (hereafter cited as "Use of United States Navy in Nicaragua").
8. Kamman, *A Search for Stability,* pp. 97–117, and E. E. Morison, *Turmoil and*

Tradition: A Study of the Life and Times of Henry L. Stimson (Boston: Houghton Mifflin, 1960), pp. 271–280.

9. Millett, "History of the Guardia Nacional de Nicaragua," pp. 130–135. For dependable histories of the Guardia, see also Major Julian C. Smith et al., "The Guardia Nacional de Nicaragua, 1927–1933," ms. history, n.d., Nicaraguan subject file, Reference Section, H&MD, and Major Julian C. Smith et al., *A Review of the Organization and Operations of the Guardia Nacional de Nicaragua*, n.d., also in the library of the Reference Section, H&MD. The American view of the occupation can be sampled in the reports, messages, and correspondence of RAdm. David F. Sellers, USN, commander, Special Service Squadron, July 1927, in the David F. Sellers Papers, Manuscripts Division, Library of Congress.

10. Neill Macaulay, *The Sandino Affair* (Chicago: Quadrangle Books, 1967), pp. 48–61, and Smith, "The Guardia Nacional de Nicaragua," pp. 31–40.

11. Macaulay, *The Sandino Affair*, pp. 62–75, and Brig Gen. L. Feland to Maj. Gen. Cmdt. J. A. Lejeune, July 8–15, 1927, Smedley D. Butler Papers, MCPPC.

12. Macaulay, *The Sandino Affair*, pp. 76–82; Capt. G. D. Hatfield, "A Brief Account of the Battle of Ocotal," ms. 1927, Nicaragua Subject File, Reference Section, H&MD; and Brig. Gen. L. Feland to Maj. Gen. J. A. Lejeune, July 18–August 13, 1927, Butler Papers.

13. Munro, *The United States and the Caribbean Republics*, pp. 228–254; Brig. Gen. L. Feland to RAdm. D. F. Sellers, April 19, 1927, Sellers Papers; and Major E. N. McClellan, "Supervising Nicaraguan Elections," *USNIP*, 59 (January 1933): 33–38. For the experience of one Marine unit, see CO, 51st Company, to CO, 5th Regt., Nopember 9, 1927, Hdqs. 2d Brigade, Miscellaneous Correspondence, 1927–1932, FOR, RG 127.

14. Sandino's activities and influence in 1927 and 1928 are best described in Macaulay, *The Sandino Affair*, pp. 83–133.

15. *Ibid.*

16. Testimony of Secretary of the Navy Curtis Wilbur and Major General Commandant John A. Lejeune, "Use of the United States Navy in Nicaragua," pp. 1–22, 47–65; Major General J. A. Lejeune, "The Nicaraguan Situation," *Leatherneck*, February–March 1928, pp. 10, 52; and Col. L. M. Gulick to Maj. Gen. Cmdt. J. A. Lejeune, October 15, 1927, Butler Papers.

17. Maj. H. H. Utley, "The Eastern Area," ms. memoir, n.d., copy in the Harold H. Utley Papers, MCPPC; Maj. H. H. Utley–Capt. M. A. Edson correspondence, August 14, 1928–February 25, 1929, Utley Papers; and Captain Merritt A. Edson, "The Coco Patrol," *MCG*, 20 (August 1936): 18–23, 38–48, and (November 1936): 40–41, 60–72.

18. Lieutenant General Vernon E. Megee, USMC (Ret.), "United States Military Intervention in Nicaragua, 1909–1932," unpublished M.A. thesis, University of Texas, 1963, pp. 125–127, 223–226; memoir of Maj. Gen. Wilburt S. Brown (1967), pp. 40–58, 119–123, MCOHC; Brigadier General John S. Letcher, USMC (Ret.), *One Marine's Story* (Verona, Va.: McClure Press, 1970), pp. 7–63; CO, Marine Det. La Moca, to CO, 5th Regt., "Patrols La Moca Area," December 3, 1927, HQ, 2d Brig., General Correspondence, 1927–1929, FOR, RG 127; and File 56, "Reports of Contacts–Engagements Northern Area, 1928," HQ, 2d Brig., General Correspondence, 1927–1929, FOR, RG 127.

19. Captain Francis P. Mulcahy, "Marine Corps Aviation in Second Nicaraguan Campaign," *USNIP*, 59 (August 1933): 1121–1132; Major Ross E. Rowell, "The Air Service in Minor Warfare," *USNIP*, 55 (October 1929): 871–877; and *idem*, "Aircraft in Bush Warfare," *MCG*, 14 (September 1929): 180–203.

20. Millett, "History of the Guardia Nacional de Nicaragua" (note 4 above), pp. 143–178.
21. Brent L. Gravatt, "The Marines and the Guardia Nacional de Nicaragua, 1927–1932," unpublished M.A. thesis, Duke University, 1973, p. 64. See also Captain Evans F. Carlson, "The Guardia Nacional de Nicaragua," *MCG,* 21 (August 1937): 7–20.
22. Kamman, *A Search for Stability* (note 5 above), pp. 143–167; memoir of Lt. Gen. Pedro A. del Valle (1966), pp. 63–69, MCOHC; HQ 2d Brig., "B-3 Periodic Operations Reports," October 21–27, 1928, HQ 2d Brig., General Correspondence, 1927–1929, FOR, RG 127; and *New York Times,* December 15 and 31, 1928.
23. Munro, *The United States and the Caribbean Republics* (note 13 above), pp. 255–279; Kamman, *A Search for Stability,* pp. 169–236, and Brig. Gen. L. Feland to Maj. Gen. Cmdt. J. A. Lejeune, January 3, 1929, and Pres. J. M. Moncada to RAdm. D. F. Sellers, December 29, 1928, both in John A. Lejeune Papers, Manuscripts Division, Library of Congress.
24. Maj. C. H. Metcalf, "An Estimate of the Situation in the Eastern Area of Nicaragua, 1929"; CO 2d Brig. to CO Special Service Squadron, "Report on the Present Conditions in Nicaragua," November 11, 1930, File 150; CO 2d Brig. to CO, Special Service Squadron, October 30, 1929; HQ, Marine Electoral Guards, 5th Regiment, "Report on the Activities of the Marine Electoral Guard Detachment During the Registrations and Elections of 1930," November 24, 1930, File 200-2; and "Investigations, 1929," File 75, all in HQ 2d Brig., General Correspondence, 1928–1930, FOR, RG 127.
25. CG 2d Brig. to CO, Special Service Squadron, March 21, 1930, File 122, and "Air Missions—1929," File 35, both in HQ 2d Brig., General Correspondence, 1928–1930, FOR, RG 127.
26. Area Commander, Northern Area, to CG 2d Brig., May 30, 1929, and CO, Northern Area, to CG 2d Brig., February 28, 1930, HQ 2d Brig., General Correspondence, 1928–1930, FOR, RG 127.
27. *JD* D. C. McDougal to Maj. Gen. Cmdt. B. H. Fuller, (?) 1930, Clayton B. Vogel Papers, MCPPC.
28. Millett, "History of the Guardia Nacional de Nicaragua," pp. 189–200; Major H. H. Hanneken, "A Discussion of the Volontario Troops in Nicaragua," *MCG,* 26 (November 1942): 120, 247–266; and HQ, GNN, Letter of Instruction to Division Commanders 1–1929, January 24, 1929, Office of the Jefe Director, Guardia Nacional de Nicaragua, General Correspondence, 1928–1932, FOR, RG 127.
29. Smith, "The Guardia Nacional de Nicaragua, 1927–1933" (note 9 above), pp. 65, 83–85; memoir of Lt. Gen. Julian C. Smith (1968), pp. 109–147, MCOHC; memoir of Lt. Gen. Edward A. Craig (1968), pp. 68–87, MCOHC; memoir of Lt. Gen. George F. Good, Jr. (1970), pp. 55–67, MCOHC; memoir of Lt. Gen. John C. McQueen (1969), pp. 15–21, MCOHC; Maj. Robert L. Denig, "Diary of a Guardia Officer," November, 1929–April, 1931, Robert L. Denig Papers, MCPPC; and Colonel H. C. Reisinger, "La Palabra del Gringo! Leadership of the Nicaraguan National Guard," *USNIP,* 61 (February 1935): 215–221.
30. Smith, "The Guardia Nacional de Nicaragua," pp. 168–190; Jefe Director memo to all officers GNN, September 1929, HQ GNN, General Correspondence, 1928–1932, FOR, RG 127, and HQ GNN, "Roster of Officers Detached from the Guardia Nacional," May 8, 1930, and Maj. Gen. Cmdt. to all officers, September 11, 1930, both Vogel Papers.
31. HQ, GNN, "Consolidated Distribution Report Showing Distribution of the

Troops of the Guardia Nacional de Nicaragua, . . ." December 17, 1929, Vogel Papers, and Burke Davis, *Marine! The Life of Chesty Puller* (Boston: Little, Brown, 1962), pp. 56–66, 76–85.

32. Macaulay, *The Sandino Affair* (note 10 above), pp. 161–185, and File "Contacts, 1930," HQ GNN, Miscellaneous Correspondence, 1927–1932, FOR, RG 127.

33. Macaulay, *The Sandino Affair,* pp. 186–218.

34. Millett, "History of the Guardia Nacional de Nicaragua" (note 4 above), pp. 273–306.

35. Maj. Gen. Cmdt. J. A. Lejeune to the Secretary of the Navy, June 23, 1928, File 1850–40, HQMC, General Correspondence, 1913–1932, RG 127; Secretary of the Navy C. F. Adams to Secretary of State H. L. Stimson, October 22, 1932, File 1975-10, HQMC, General Correspondence, 1913–1932, RG 127; and *New York Times,* April 24, 1928; October 7, 1928; December 14, 1929; January 12, 1930; and December 16, 1932.

36. Lieutenant Colonel Kenneth J. Clifford, *Progress and Purpose: A Developmental History of the United States Marine Corps, 1900–1970* (Washington: History and Museums Division, HQMC, 1973), pp. 41–43, and Jeter A. Isely and Philip A. Crowl, *The U.S. Marines and Amphibious War* (Princeton, N.J.: Princeton University Press, 1951), pp. 32–34.

37. "Professional Notes," *USNIP,* 58 (July 1932): 1067.

38. Paymaster and Quartermaster memos to the Maj. Gen. Cmdt. January 8, 1931, and Maj. Gen. Cmdt. J. A. Lejeune to Rep. W. A. Ayres, January 8, 1931, File 1975-10, HQMC, General Correspondence, 1913–1932, RG 127.

39. Major E. H. Ellis, "Bush Brigades," *MCG,* 6 (March 1921): 1–15.

40. Division of Operations and Training, "Protection of American Interests," *MCG,* 12 (September 1927): 175–183.

41. Major General S. D. Butler, "American's Armed Forces—The Navy," *Common Sense,* 4 (December 1935): 10–14.

42. Major S. M. Harrington, "The Strategy and Tactics of Small Wars," *MCG,* 6 (December 1921): 47–491, and *MCG,* 7 (March 1922): 84–93; Major H. H. Utley, "The Tactics and Techniques of Small Wars," *MCG,* 16 (May 1931): 50–53, and *MCG,* 18 (August 1933): 44–48, and (November 1933): 43–46; Headquarters Marine Corps, *Small Wars Manual U.S. Marine Corps 1940* (Washington: Government Printing Office, 1940); and Ronald Shaffer, "The 1940 Small Wars Manual and the Lessons of History," *Military Affairs,* 36 (April 1972): 46–51.

CHAPTER 10. THE CREATION OF THE ADVANCED BASE FORCE, 1900–1916

1. Harold Sprout and Margaret Sprout, *The Rise of American Naval Power, 1776–1918* (Princeton, N.J.: Princeton University Press, 1944), pp. 250–285; William R. Braisted, *The United States Navy in the Pacific, 1897–1909* (Austin: University of Texas Press, 1958), pp. 115–124, 169–180; and Seward W. Livermore, "The American Navy as a Factor in World Politics, 1903–1913," *American Historical Review,* 63 (July 1958): 863–879.

2. Daniel J. Costello, "Planning for War: A History of the General Board of the Navy, 1900–1914," unpublished Ph.D. dissertation, Fletcher School of Law and Diplomacy, 1968, pp. 1–64.

3. Costello, "Planning for War," pp. 128–173.

4. *Ibid.,* and Braisted, *The United States Navy in the Pacific, 1897–1909,* pp. 191–215.

5. Costello, "Planning for War," pp. 173–225, and Seward W. Livermore, "American Naval Base Policy in the Far East," *Pacific Historical Review,* 13 (June 1944): 113–135.

6. Braisted, *The United States Navy in the Pacific, 1897–1909,* pp. 169–180, 216–223; Richard D. Challener, *Admirals, Generals and American Foreign Policy, 1898–1914* (Princeton, N.J.: Princeton University Press, 1973), pp. 81–110, 179–198, 323–332; Louis Morton, "Interservice Cooperation and Political-Military Collaboration, 1900–38," in Harry L. Coles, ed., *Total War and Cold War* (Columbus: Ohio State University Press, 1962), pp. 131–160; and George J. Tanham, "Service Relations Sixty Years Ago," *Military Affairs,* 23 (Fall 1959): 139–148.

7. Costello, "Planning for War," pp. 226–278.

8. Col. Cmdt. C. Heywood to Rep. E. Foss, December 12, 1898, HQMC, "Letters Sent, 1884–1911," RG 127, NA.

9. Adm. G. Dewey to the Secretary of the Navy, January 14, 1909, Subject File 432, Records of the General Board, Operational Archives Branch, Naval Historical Division, Washington Navy Yard.

10. The genesis of the advanced base force is best followed in two General Board memoranda: Cmdr. R. H. Jackson, USN, "History of the Advanced Base," May 15, 1913, and *idem,* "The Naval Advanced Base," May 29, 1915, both in Subject File 408, Records of the General Board. See also Lieutenant Colonel Kenneth J. Clifford, *Progress and Purpose: A Developmental History of the United States Marine Corps, 1900–1970* (Washington: History and Museums Division, HQMC, 1973), pp. 8–21. On base defense, see Lieutenant Commander J. H. Sears, "The Coast in Warfare," *USNIP,* 27 (September 1901): 449–527, and (December 1901): 649–712.

11. Jackson, "History of the Advanced Base," GB File 408, and Clifford, *Progress and Purpose,* pp. 8, 10.

12. Brig. Gen. Cmdt. C. Heywood to Adm G. Dewey, November 22, 1900, William F. Fullam Papers, Manuscripts Division, Library of Congress.

13. General Board to Secretary of the Navy, November 1, 1901, GB File 432.

14. Brig. Gen. Cmdt. C. Heywood, memo, "General Board Recommends that the Brigadier General Commandant of the Marine Corps Be Directed to Organize and Equip an Emergency Battalion," November 16, 1901, HQMC, "Letters Sent Secretary of the Navy," RG 127, NA, and Brig. Gen. Cmdt. C. Heywood to General Board, December 17, 1901, GB File 432.

15. Secretary of the Navy W. H. Moody to Brig. Gen. Cmdt. C. Heywood, July 16, 1902, GB File 432.

16. Capt. G. C. Thorpe to Maj. H. C. Haines, April 25,1902, HQMC, "Historical Division Letters Received," RG 127; *ANJ,* August 24, 1901; and Maj. L. Karmany to C-in-C, U.S. Naval Forces on Asiatic Station, January 7, 1902, File OJ, Subject File, 1911–1927, Naval Records Collection of the Office of Naval Records and Library, RG 45.

17. Captain Dion Williams, "The Defense of Our New Naval Stations," *USNIP,* 28 (June 1902): 182–194.

18. Brig. Gen. Cmdt. G. F Elliott to Secretary of the Navy W. H. Moody, December 4, 1903, HQMC, "LSSN," RG 127, and Cmdr. J. C. Wilson, USN, to Secretary of the Navy W. H. Moody, March 5, 1903, GB File 432.

19. Maj. Gen. L. Wood to Brig. Gen. T. H. Bliss, October 25, 1904, Leonard Wood Papers, Manuscripts Division, Library of Congress; Jackson, "History of the Advanced Base," GB File 408; and *ANJ,* September 17, 1904.

20. Maj. Gen. Cmdt. C. Heywood to Secretary of the Navy W. H. Moody, July 30, 1903, HQMC, "LSSN," RG 127.

21. General Board to Secretary of the Navy, August 13, 1906, GB File 408, and GB memo, "The Naval Advanced Base," May 29, 1915, GB File 408.

22. Maj. Dion Williams, "Report on Men, Material, and Drills Required for Establishing a Naval Advanced Base," November 2, 1909, GB File 408.

23. Memos, "The Executive Order Withdrawing Marines from Cruising Ships" and "Summary of Evidence Concerning Withdrawal of Marines from Cruising Ships," both 1909, Fullam Papers.

24. Memo, Cmdr. W. L. Rogers, USN, for the President, Naval War College, "Advanced Bases," November 20, 1909; General Board to President, Naval War College, December 30, 1909; and Maj. John H. Russell, "General Principles Governing the Selection and Establishment of Advanced Naval Bases and the Composition of an Advanced Base Outfit," December, 1909, all in GB File 408.

25. Assistant Secretary of the Navy B. Winthrop to Maj. Gen. Cmdt., March 24, 1910, and General Board to Secretary of the Navy, January 31, 1910, both GB File 432.

26. Maj. Gen. Cmdt. to Assistant Secretary of the Navy B. Winthrop, April 18, 1910, GB File 432, and "Advanced Base School," appendix C, report of Board of Inspection of Navy Yard, Philadelphia, March 25–28, 1913, to Secretary of the Navy, April 19, 1913, File 1975-10, HQMC, General Correspondence, 1913–1938, RG 127.

27. Major Henry C. Davis, "Advance Base Training," *USNIP,* 37 (March 1911): 95–99, and *idem,* "Some Notes on the Training of Marines for Advance Base Work," *USNIP,* 37 (September 1911): 837–844.

28. Colonel Robert D. Heinl, Jr., "An Association Is Formed," *MCG,* 47 (April 1963): 14–17. For line dismay with Headquarters, see Lt. Col. J. A. Lejeune to Miss A. Lejeune, May 2 and July 28, 1910, John A. Lejeune Papers, Manuscript Division, Library of Congress.

29. Lieutenant Colonel E. C. Johnson and Graham A. Cosmas, *A Short History of Marine Aviation,* rev. ed. (Washington: History and Museums Division, HQMC, 1976), pp. 1–10; Lt. Col. A. A. Cunningham to Col. E. B. Miller, January 22, 1931, and James W. Jacobs, "Alfred Austell Cunningham, 1882–1939," both in Alfred A. Cunningham Papers, MCPPC; and Capt. Thomas T. Craven, USN, "History of Aviation in the United States Navy," 1920, File ZGU, Subject File, 1911–1927, RG 45.

30. President, General Board, to Secretary of the Navy, February 5, 1913; Secretary of the Navy to President, General Board, February 5, 1913; and Maj. Gen. Cmdt. to Secretary of the Navy, April 10, 1913, all File 1975-10, HQMC, General Correspondence, 1911–1938, RG 127. See also Jackson, "History of the Advanced Base" (note 10 above), GB File 408.

31. Braisted, *The United States Navy in the Pacific, 1909–1922* (note 1 above), pp. 123–140.

32. Capt. W. F. Fullam, USN, memo for Secretary of the Navy, "Establishment of Advance Base Outfit," May 1, 1913, GB File 432.

33. Commander W. W. Phelps, USN, "Naval Industrialism, Naval Commercialism and Naval Discipline," *USNIP,* 39 (June 1913): 507–550.

34. Colonel George Richards, "Discussion," *USNIP,* 39 (September 1913): 1308–1318.

35. Maj. Gen. Cmdt. to Secretary of the Navy, June 7, 1913, GB File 432, and Capt. W. F. Fullam to Secretary of the Navy, June 23, 1913, GB File 432.

36. President, General Board, to Secretary of the Navy, "Duties of Marines," July 21, 1913, GB File 432.

37. Capt. W. F. Fullam to Secretary of the Navy, June 27, 1913, Fullam Papers.

38. Maj. Gen. Cmdt. to Secretary of the Navy, August 1, 1913, File 1975-10, HQMC, General Correspondence, 1911–1938, RG 127.

39. "Hearings Before the General Board Relative to Marines and the Advanced Base Situation," September 29, 1913, GB File 432; War Department General Staff Report 10751, "Question of Duties of the Marine Corps," October 31, 1913, Correspondence Files, 1907–1916, Records of the War Department General Staff, RG 165, NA; and Capt. W. F. Fullam, USN, to Secretary of the Navy, October 16, 1913, Josephus Daniels Papers, Manuscripts Division, Library of Congress.

40. General Board memos to Secretary of the Navy, September 13–October 15, 1913, and Maj. Gen. Cmdt. to Secretary of the Navy, December 18, 1913, GB File 432, and Maj. Gen. Cmdt. to Secretary of the Navy, "Advanced Base Outfits and Their Location," September, 1913, File 1975-10, HQMC, General Correspondence, 1911–1938, RG 127.

41. Colonel Frederic M. Wise, *A Marine Tells It to You* (New York: J. H. Sears, 1929), p. 119.

42. File, "Commandant, Candidates, 1913," Daniels Papers; Lt. Col. J. A. Lejeune to Miss A. Lejeune, November 22 and 28, 1913, Lejeune Papers; and George Barnett, "Soldier and Sailor Too," Chapter 23, ms. memoir, George Barnett Papers, MCPPC.

43. President, General Board, to Secretary of the Navy, April 25, 1914, GB File 432; Maj. Gen. Cmdt. to Secretary of the Navy, December 8, 1914, GB File 432; Cmdr. W. S. Sims, USN, chief observer, to C-in-C, Atlantic Fleet, January 21, 1914, Lejeune Papers; Lt. Col. J. A. Lejeune to C-in-C, Atlantic Fleet, "Report on Maneuvers and Operations of First Advance Force Brigade," March 3, 1914, GB File 432; CO 1st Regiment to Brig. Cmdr., "Operation of First Regiment," January 30, 1914, File 1975-80, HQMC, General Correspondence, 1911–1938, RG 127; CO 2d Regiment to Brig. Cmdr., "Report of Manoeuvers and Operations," January 31, 1914, File 1975–80, HQMC, General Correspondence, 1911–1938, RG 127; and C-in-C Atlantic Fleet to Secretary of the Navy, "Report on Advance Base Expedition, Culebra, W.I., January 1914," February 16, 1914, File 1975-80, HQMC, General Correspondence, 1911–1938, RG 127.

44. Josephus Daniels, *The Wilson Era: Years of Peace, 1910–1917* (Chapel Hill: University of North Carolina Press, 1944), pp. 322–323.

45. General Board memorandum 408, "The Naval Advanced Base," May 29, 1915, GB File 408.

46. "Report of the Secretary of the Navy" and "Report of the Major General Commandant of the United States Marine Corps," *Annual Reports of the Navy Department, 1914* (Washington: Government Printing Office, 1915), pp. 53, 459, 468–469.

47. "Report of the Major General Commandant of the United States Marine Corps," *Annual Reports of the Navy Department, 1915* (Washington: Government Printing Office, 1916), pp. 755, 764–765.

48. "Report of the Major General Commandant of the United States Marine Corps," *Annual Reports of the Navy Department, 1916* (Washington: Government Printing Office, 1917), pp. 759, 768; "Statement of General Barnett. . . ," U.S. Congress, House Naval Affairs Committee, Hearings: "Estimates Submitted by the Secretary of the Navy, 1917," 64th Congress, 1st Session (Washington: Government Printing Office, 1917), pp. 299–401; Marine Corps Personnel Board to the Secretary of the Navy, "Report of Board," February 3, 1916, File 1850-40, General Correspondence, HQMC, 1911–1938, RG 127; Public Affairs Unit 4-1, *The Marine Corps Reserve: A History* (Washington: Division of Reserve, HQMC, 1966), pp. 1–7.

49. Naval War College summer conference lectures: Maj. John H. Russell, "The Preparation of War Plans for the Establishment and Defense of a Naval Advance Base," 1912; Maj. Robert H. Dunlop, "The Naval Advance Base," 1911; and *idem*, "The Temporary Naval Advance Base," 1912, all File XBAA, Record Group 8, Naval War College Historical Collection. See also Major Dion Williams, *The Naval Advanced Base* (Washington: Government Printing Office, 1912), and Lieutenant Colonel Eli K. Cole, "The Necessity to the Naval Service of an Adequate Marine Corps," *USNIP*, 40 (September–October 1914): 1395–1400.

50. Frank J. Infusino, Jr., "The United States Marine Corps and War Planning, 1900–1941," unpublished M.A. thesis, California State University–San Diego, 1973, pp. 29–54. On Ellis's career, see Lieutenant Colonel John J. Reber, "Pete Ellis: Amphibious Warfare Prophet," *USNIP*, 103 (November 1977): 53–64.

51. Col. Eli K. Cole, "Advanced Base Force," lecture, Marine Barracks, Philadelphia, June 19, 1915, File 1975-10, HQMC, General Correspondence, 1911–1938, RG 127.

52. Col. John A. Lejeune, "The Mobile Defense of Advance Base," lecture, Advance Base School, May 21, 1915, File 1975-10, HQMC, General Correspondence, 1911–1938, RG 127, reprinted in *MCG*, 1 (March 1916): 1:18.

53. Major John H. Russell, "A Plea for a Mission and Doctrine," *MCG*, 1 (June 1916): 109–122.

54. "Statement of General Barnett . . . ," U.S. Congress, House Naval Affairs Committee, Hearings: "Estimates Submitted by the Secretary of the Navy, 1916," 64th Congress, 1st Session, 3 vols. (Washington: Government Printing Office, 1916), II: 2131.

55. *Ibid.*, II: 2127–2132.

CHAPTER 11. THE WORLD WAR, 1917–1919

1. Maj. Gen. Cmdt. G. Barnett to Secretary of the Navy J. Daniels, October 21, 1915, File 2515-10, HQMC, General Correspondence, 1913–1932, RG 127.

2. Jack Shulimson, "The First to Fight: Marine Corps Expansion, 1914–18," *Prologue*, 8 (Spring 1976): 5–16, and George Barnett, "Soldier and Sailor Too," Chapter 25, ms. memoir, Barnett Papers, MCPPC. The most complete account of the Marine Corps in World War I is Major E. N. McClellan, *The United States Marine Corps in the World War* (Washington: Historical Division, HQMC: 1920; reprint, 1968).

3. "Annual Report of the Secretary of the Navy," *Annual Reports of the Navy Department 1917* (Washington: Government Printing Office, 1918), pp. 25–27, and "Report of the Major General Commandant of the United States Marine Corps," *Annual Reports of the Navy Department 1917*, pp. 835–848. For public relations and recruiting, see Robert Lindsay, *This High Name: Public Relations and the U.S. Marine Corps* (Madison: University of Wisconsin Press, 1956), pp. 23–35, and Lieutenant Colonel Gary L. Rutledge, "The Rhetoric of United States Marine Corps Enlisted Recruiting," unpublished M.A. thesis, University of Kansas, 1974, pp. 67–105.

4. McClellan, *The United States Marine Corps in the World War*, pp. 14–16, 21–24; *The Recruiters Bulletin*, April–November, 1917; *New York Times*, April 7–August 19, 1917; and J. David Cronon, ed., *The Cabinet Diaries of Josephus Daniels* (Lincoln: University of Nebraska Press, 1963), p. 157.

5. Historical Section, Army War College, *The Genesis of the American First Army* (Washington: Government Printing Office, 1938), pp. 1–3, and Brig. Gen. Joseph E. Kuhn, USA, memorandum for the Chief of Staff, "Plans for a

Possible Expeditionary Force to France," May 12, 1917, Book File, John J. Pershing Papers, Manuscripts Division, Library of Congress.

6. Secretary of War N. D. Baker to Secretary of the Navy J. Daniels, May 16, 1917, Folder 2231, G-3 GHQ AEF Correspondence, Records of the American Expeditionary Force, RG 120, NA; Adm. W. S. Benson, USN, to Maj. Gen. J. Biddle, USA, January 12, 1918, File 14503, Chief of Staff Correspondence, 1917–1921, Records of the War Department General Staff, RG 165, NA; Brig. Gen. C. L. McCawley, QMG, USMC, to Col. D. D. McCarthy, USA, May 23, 1917, File 29, Adj. Gen. AEF Correspondence File, 1917–1919, RG 120; and *New York Times*, May 20, 1917, June 25, 1917.

7. W. R. Coyle, "Parris Island in the War," *MCG*, 10 (December 1925): 187–191; Elmore A. Champie, *Brief History of Marine Corps Recruit Depot, Parris Island, South Carolina* (Washington: Historical Branch, HQMC, 1962), pp. 2–6; and Brigadier General A. W. Catlin, *With the Help of God and a Few Marines* (Garden City, N.Y.: Doubleday, Page, 1919), pp. 284–292.

8. Kemper F. Cowing, comp., *Dear Folks at Home* (Boston: Houghton Mifflin, 1919), p. 3. The enlisted man's experience in the World War I Marine Corps can be sampled in Levi E. Hemrick, *Once a Marine* (New York: Carlton Press, 1968); J. E. Rendinell and G. Pattulo, *One Man's War* (New York: J. H. Sears, 1928); Martin G. Bulberg, *A War Diary* (Chicago: Drake Press, 1927); memoir of Sgt. Harry I. Dale, 67th Company, September 10, 1918, Karl B. Bretzfelder Papers, and Pvt. Malcolm D. Aitken, 67th Company, "Letters of a Marine to His Mother and Father," 1917–1918, World War I Collection, U.S. Army Military History Institute; and memoir, GySgt. Don V. Paradis (1973), MCOHC. An excellent source on enlisted and officer training is provided by the letters of 2d Lt. Merritt A. Edson to Miss Mary Edson and Mr. and Mrs. E. A. Edson, September 20, 1917–September 26, 1918, Merritt A. Edson Papers, Manuscripts Division, Library of Congress.

9. Memoir of Maj. Gen. Robert Blake (1968), p. 4, MCOHC.

10. Captain John W. Thomason, Jr., *Fix Bayonets!* (New York: Charles Scribner's Sons, 1925), p. x.

11. For the 5th Regiment in the World War, see H. B. Field and H. G. James, *Over the Top with the 18th Co., 5th Regt. U.S. Marines* (n.p., 1919); *History of the First Battalion, 5th Regiment U.S. Marines* (n.p., 1919); *History of Second Battalion, 5th Regiment U.S. Marines* (n.p., 1919); Lieutenant Colonel Frederic M. Wise, *A Marine Tells It to You* (New York: J. H. Sears, 1929), pp. 157–253; Maj. Robert L. Denig, "Diary of a Marine Officer During the World War," Robert L. Denig Papers, MCPPC; Maj. J. D. Murray, "Memoir of World War I," ms., 1932, copy in Ben H. Fuller Papers, MCPPC; and memoir of General Lemuel C. Shepherd, Jr. (1967), pp. 295–350, MCOHC.

12. John J. Pershing, *My Experiences in the World War*, 2 vols., (New York: Frederick A. Stokes, 1931), I: 71–110; and Maj. Gen. J. F. Morrison, memo for the C/S WDGS, December 1917, File 910, Correspondence of the Chief of Staff, 1918–1921, RG 165, NA.

13. Frederick Palmer, *America in France* (New York: Dodd, Mead, 1918), pp. 97–99.

14. Denig, "Diary of a Marine Officer During the World War," p. 112.

15. Maj. Gen. Cmdt. G. Barnett to Gen. J. J. Pershing, USA, November 28, 1917, General Correspondence, Pershing Papers, and *New York Times*, October 7, 1917.

16. CG AEF to C/S AEF, July 13, 1917, File 491, Adj. Gen. AEF General Correspondence, 1917–1920, RG 120; AEF General Orders 31 (September 3,

1917) and 38 (September 17, 1917), G-3 AEF Correspondence File, RG 120; and Col. G. Van H. Moseley, AC/S G-4, memo, June 10, 1918, Adj. Gen. AEF General Correspondence, 1917–1920, RG 120.

17. McClellan, *The United States Marine Corps in the World War* (note 1 above), pp. 32–33, and Major General John A. Lejeune, *The Reminiscences of a Marine* (Philadelphia: Dorrance and Company, 1930), pp. 239–240. The 6th Regiment's service may be sampled in *A Brief History of the Sixth Regiment, United States Marines* (n.p., 1919); *History of the Third Battalion, Sixth Regiment, U.S. Marines* (Hillsdale, Mich.: Akers, Ritchie, and Hurlbut, 1919); Dr. and Mrs. W. I. Murray, comps., *History of the 96th Company 6th Marine Regiment in World War I* (privately printed, 1967); memoir of Gen. Gerald C. Thomas (1966), pp. 8–57, MCOHC; memoir of Gen. Alfred H. Noble (1968), pp. 5–17, 21–28, MCOHC; and memoir of Gen. Clifton B. Cates (1967), pp. 7–56.

18. Catlin, *With the Help of God and a Few Marines* (note 7 above), pp. 18–20.

19. Maj. Gen. Cmdt. G. Barnett to CO, Marines, AEF, November 6, 1917, and Col. F. Conner, AC/S G-3 AEF to C/S AEF, January 14, 1918, File 10171, Adj. Gen. AEF Correspondence, 1917–1920, RG 120.

20. Memoir of Maj. Gen. William A. Worton (1967), pp. 22–24, MCOHC.

21. "Marines with the Poilu," *Recruiters Bulletin,* September 1917, pp. 9, 14.

22. Memoir of Gen. G. C. Thomas, p. 16.

23. Denig, "Diary of a Marine Officer During the World War," p. 34, 55; David Bellamy (1st Lt. USMC), "A Marine at the Front," diary printed in *American History Illustrated* 5 (1971), pp. 34–35.

24. Major E. N. McClellan, "The Fourth Brigade of Marines in the Training Areas and the Operations in the Verdun Sector," *MCG,* 5 (March 1920): 81–110; Wise, *A Marine Tells It to You* (note 11 above), pp. 160–179; and Catlin, *With the Help of God and a Few Marines,* pp. 23–28. The experience of the 6th Machine Battalion is described in Major L. W. T. Waller, Jr., "Machine Guns of the Fourth Brigade," *MCG,* 5 (March 1920): 1–31.

25. "Excerpts from the Statement of the Major General Commandant, U.S. Marine Corps, Before the Committee on Naval Affairs of the House of Representatives on the Estimates of the Marine Corps, January 23, 1918," *MCG,* 3 (March 1918): 67–75, and Maj. Gen. Cmdt. F. Barnett to Sen. C. Swanson, May 22, 1918, Daniels Papers.

26. "Report of the Sub-Committee for Investigation of Conduct and Administration of Naval Affirs," *MCG,* 3 (March 1918): 76–78.

27. Adm. W. S. Benson, USN, to Maj. Gen. J. Biddle, USA, January 12, 1918, and Maj. Gen. J. Biddle, USA, to Adm. W. S. Benson, January 12, 1918, both File 14503, Correspondence of the Chief of Staff, RG 165, and Cronon, *The Cabinet Diaries of Josephus Daniels* (note 4 above), pp. 267–268, 295.

28. Cronon, *The Cabinet Diaries of Josephus Daniels.* p. 305.

29. Assistant Secretary of War B. Crowell to Assistant Secretary of the Navy F. D. Roosevelt, April 17, 1918, and Roosevelt to Crowell, April 19, 1918, File 35-199, Office of the Secretary of the Navy/Chief of Naval Operations, Confidential Correspondence, 1917–1919, General Records of the Department of the Navy, RG 80, NA.

30. Lejeune, *Reminiscences of a Marine* (note 17 above), pp. 246–248, 256–261.

31. Historical Division, Army War College, *The Genesis of the American First Army,* pp. 9–18; Pershing, *My Experiences in the World War* (note 12 above), I: 246–279, 298–316, 352–370. For maps and sector descriptions, see American Battle Monuments Commission, *American Armies and Battlefields in Europe* (Washington: Government Printing Office, 1938).

32. Colonel Oliver L. Spaulding, USA, and Colonel John W. Wright, USA, *The Second Division: American Expeditionary Force in France, 1917–1919* (New York: Hillman Press, 1937), pp. 6–28; McClellan, "The Fourth Brigade of Marines in the Training Areas and the Operations in the Verdun Sector"; Wise, *A Marine Tells It to You,* pp. 180–190; Catlin, *With the Help of God and a Few Marines,* pp. 30–60.

33. 5th Section, G/S, GHQ AEF, "Training, Marines," May 1, 1918, G-3 Correspondence, AEF RG 120. See also Lieutenant Colonel Oliver L. Spaulding, USA, "Tactics of the War with Germany," *Infantry Journal,* 17 (September 1920): 228–240.

34. CG AEF to Adj. Gen. USA, April 30, 1918, "Pershing–Harbord Letters," James G. Harbord Papers, Manuscripts Division, Library of Congress.

35. Brig. Gen. J. G. Harbord, USA, to Maj. Gen. C. R. Edwards, USA, May 11, 1918, Clarence R. Edwards Papers, Massachusetts Historical Society.

36. James G. Harbord, *Leaves from a War Diary* (New York: Dodd, Mead, 1925), p. 280, and Catlin, *With the Help of God and a Few Marines,* pp. 56–58.

37. Barrie Pitt, *1918: The Last Act* (New York: W. W. Norton, 1962), pp. 135–154.

38. The sources for the operations of the 2d Division are voluminous. The most analytical are the division history by Spaulding and Wright, *The Second Division,* and operations summaries, 2d Division, May 21–October 7, 1918, copies in the Lejeune Papers. The printed primary sources are Historical Section, Army War College, *Records of the Second Division (Regular),* 9 vols. (Fort Sam Houston, Texas, and Washington, 1924–1928), and *idem, Translations of War Diaries of German Units Opposed to the Second Division (Regular) 1918* (Washington, 1930–1932). See also Chief of Staff, 2d Division, "Brief Narrative History of the Second Division," 1919, copies in both Harbord Papers and Lejeune Papers. The most detailed study of the battle of Belleau Wood is Robert B. Asprey, *At Belleau Wood* (New York: G. P. Putnam's Sons, 1965). The view from brigade headquarters is described in Harbord, *Leaves from a War Diary,* pp. 281–296; James G. Harbord, *The American Army in France* (Boston: Little, Brown, 1936), pp. 274–300; and "Diary of the Fourth Brigade, Marine Corps, AEF . . . May 30, 1918 to June 30, 1918," copy in 4th Brigade File, Reference Section, H&MD.

39. Brig. Gen. Logan Feland, "Retreat Hell!" *MCG,* 6 (September 1921): 289–291.

40. Major E. N. McClellan, "Operations of the Fourth Brigade of Marines in Aisne Defensive," *MCG,* 5 (June 1920): 182–214; Wise, *A Marine Tells It to You,* pp. 191–206; and Asprey, *At Belleau Wood,* pp. 97–141.

41. French XXI Army Corps, Operations Order 81, June 5, 1918, in Historical Division, Army War College, *The U.S. Army in the World War, 1917–1919,* 17 vols. (Washington: Government Printing Office, 1948), IV: 143–145.

42. Major E. N. McClellan, "Capture of Hill 142, Battle of Belleau Wood, and Capture of Bouresches," *MCG,* 5 (September 1920): 277–313; Thomason, *Fix Bayonets!* (note 10 above), pp. 9–28; and Asprey, *At Belleau Wood,* pp. 142–159.

43. Maj. Frank E. Evans, Adj. 6th Marines, to Maj. Gen. Cmdt. G. Barnett, June 29, 1918, World War I File, Reference Section, H&MD; Capt. Clifton B. Cates, "Personal Observations," *Service Book in the World War,* Clifton B. Cates Papers, MCPPC; memoir of GySgt. Don V. Paradis, pp. 38–77, MCOHC; memoir of Lt. Gen. Merwin H. Silverthorn (1969), pp. 44–50, MCOHC; Floyd Gibbons, *And They Thought We Wouldn't Fight* (New York: George H. Doran, 1918), pp. 303–322; and Catlin, *With the Help of God and a*

Few Marines, pp. 106–137. For a fictionalized account of the fighting, see Thomas Boyd, *Through the Wheat* (New York: Charles Scribner's Sons, 1923).

44. Associated Press bulletins, June 6 and 7, 1918, reprinted in *MCG,* 3 (June 1918): 158–167; Lindsay, *This High Name* (note 3 above), pp. 31–33; Asprey, *At Belleau Wood,* pp. 212–216; and "You Wouldn't Dare to Tell It to the Marines Now," *Literary Digest,* 57 (June 29, 1918): 41–44.

45. Wise, *A Marine Tells It to You* (note 11 above), p. 244.

46. Major E. N. McClellan, "The Battle of Belleau Wood, *MCG,* 5 (December 1920): 370–404; Asprey, *At Belleau Wood,* pp. 201–211, 227–273; and Maj. Gen. O. Bundy, USA, to CG AEF, June 16, 1918, G-3 Reports, AEF General Correspondence, RG 120.

47. Col. B. H. Wells, USA, to Gen. T. H. Bliss, USA, June 20, 1918, G-3 Reports, AEF General Correspondence, RG 120; Maj. P. H. Clark, USA, to Gen. J. J. Pershing, June 6 and 8 and July 3, 1918, John Pershing Collection, RG 316, NA; and Gen. J. J. Pershing to Maj. Gen. H. L. Scott, USA, June 28, 1918, Hugh L. Scott Papers, Manuscripts Division, Library of Congress.

48. Intelligence Section, German IV Reserve Corps, "Interrogation," June 17, 1918, in Historical Division, Army War College, *U.S. Army in the World War, IV:* 607.

49. Asprey, *At Belleau Wood,* pp. 290–307, and HQ 2d Division, "Casualities of the Second Division," June 1, 1919, copy in Lejeune Papers.

50. Harbord, *The American Army in France* (note 38 above), pp. 319–338, and Major E. N. McClellan, "The Aisne–Marne Offensive," *MCG,* 6 (March 1921): 66–84 and (June 1921): 188–227.

51. McClellan, "The Aisne–Marne Offensive"; memoir of Maj. Gen. Robert T. Blake, pp. 13–17, MCOHC; memoir of Lt. Gen. Merwin H. Silverthorn, pp. 79–89, MCOHC; and Thomason, *Fix Bayonets!,* pp. 73–124.

52. Denig, "Diary of a Marine Officer," pp. 206–214; memoir of GySgt. Don V. Paradis, pp. 78–91, MCOHC; and 2d Lt. C. B. Cates to his family, August 1, 1918, "World War Letters of 2d Lt. C. B. Cates," Cates Papers.

53. Shulimson, "The First to Fight: Marine Corps Expansion, 1914–18" (note 2 above), pp. 15–16; Barnett, "Soldier and Sailor Too" (note 2 above), Chapter 25; and McClellan *The United States Marine Corps in the World War* (note 4 above), pp. 11, 14–15, 34–35.

54. Maj. Gen. Cmdt. G. Barnett to Maj. Gen. J. A. Lejeune, August 4, 1918, 4th Brig. Subject File, Reference Section, H&MD, and Acting Secretary of War B. Crowell to Secretary of the Navy J. Daniels, September 13, 1918, File 10050-211, WDGS General Correspondence, 1918–1921, RG 165.

55. McClellan, *The United States Marine Corps in the World War,* pp. 17–20. See also Major E. N. McClellan, "American Marines in the British Grand Fleet," *MCG,* 7 (June 1922): 147–164, and *idem,* "American Marines in Siberia During the World War," *MCG,* 5 (June 1920): 173–181.

56. Public Affairs Unit 4-1, USMCR, *The Marine Corps Reserve: A History* (Washington: Division of Reserve, HQMC, 1966), pp. 7–19.

57. Quoted in Captain Linda L. Hewitt, USMCR, *Women Marines in World War I* (Washington: History and Museums Division, HQMC, 1974), p. 38.

58. *Ibid.,* p. 41.

59. Maj. Gen. Cmdt. to CNO, "Organization of Land and Aero Squadron," July 27, 1917, and Capt. A. A. Cunningham to Maj. Gen. Cmdt., October 10, 1917, 1st Aviation Force file, Reference Section, H&MD. For general histories of Marine Corps aviation in World War I, see Lieutenant Colonel E. C. Johnson and Graham A. Cosmas, *A Short History of Marine Aviation* (Washington:

History and Museums Division, HQMC, 1976), pp. 11–25; Robert Sherrod, *History of Marine Corps Aviation in World War II* (Washington: Combat Forces Press, 1952), pp. 5–18; and McClellan, *The United States Marine Corps in the World War,* pp. 71–75.

60. Capt. A. A. Cunningham, testimony for the General Board, "Aviation," February 5, 1918; Capt. A. A. Cunningham to Maj. Gen. Cmdt. G. Barnett, February 6, 1918; General Board memo, "Dunkirk–Calais Submarine Offensive," April 5, 1918, all in Cunningham File, Reference Section, H&MD. See also Graham A. Cosmas, ed., *Marine Flyer in France: The Diary of Captain Alfred A. Cunningham* (Washington: History and Museums Division, HQMC, 1974).

61. Memoir of Lt. Gen. Karl S. Day, USMCR (1968), pp. 5–26, MCOHC.

62. Maj. A. A. Cunningham to Capt. H. B. Mims, August 1–December 19, 1919, and to Capt. R. S. Geiger, June 6–7, 1918, both Alfred A. Cunningham Papers, MCPPC, and Maj. Gen. Cmdt. F. Barnett to Director of Naval Operations (Aviation), October 16, 1918, Cunningham Papers. When the war ended, Marine aviation had 282 officers (including warrant officers) and 2,180 enlisted men, about half of whom had served overseas.

63. Major E. N. McClellan, "In the Marbache Sector," *MCG,* 6 (September 1921): pp. 253–268, and Lejeune, *Reminiscences of a Marine* (note 17 above), pp. 300–311.

64. Major E. N. McClellan, "The St. Mihiel Offensive," *MCG,* 6 (December 1921): pp. 375–397, and Lejeune, *Reminiscences of a Marine,* pp. 312–335.

65. Lejeune, *Reminiscences of a Marine,* pp. 336–344.

66. Thomason, *Fix Bayonets!* (note 10 above), pp. 133–135.

67. For the Mont Blanc battle, see Lejeune, *Reminiscences of a Marine,* pp. 345–366; Spaulding and Wright, *The Second Division* (note 32 above), pp. 161–194; memo, "Summary of Operations of the Second Division from October 1st to November 11th, 1918," January 5, 1919, copy Lejeune Papers; and Major E. N. McClellan, "The Battle of Mont Blanc Ridge," *MCG,* 7 (March 1922): 1–21 (June 1922): 206–211, and (September 1922): 287–288. The German side is described in Lt. Col. Otto Ernst GGS, "The Battle of Blanc Mont," unpublished ms., Lejeune Papers. The personal side of the fighting is captured in Thomason, *Fix Bayonets!,* pp. 140–192; Lt. C. B. Cates to his family, October 13, 1918, "World War I Letters of 2d Lt. C. B. Cates," Cates Papers; and memoir of GySgt. Don V. Paradis, pp. 128–144, MCOHC.

68. For the 4th Brigade in the Meuse–Argonne operation, see Spaulding and Wright, *The Second Division,* pp. 195–222; "Summary of Operations of Second Division from October 1st to November 11th, 1918," copy in Lejeune Papers; and Lejeune, *Reminiscences of a Marine,* pp. 367–403.

69. Memoir of Gen. C. B. Cates, p. 52, MCOHC.

70. McClellan, *The United States Marine Corps in the World War,* pp. 62–64. Service in France is described in 1st Lt. M. A. Edson to Miss M. Edson and Mr. and Mrs. E. A. Edson, October 28, 1918–November 29, 1919, Edson Papers.

71. Lieutenant Colonel Frank E. Evans, "Demobilizing the Brigades," *MCG,* 4 (December 1919): 303–314.

72. In addition to the biographical works of Catlin and Thomason, cited previously, see John W. Leonard and Fred F. Chitty, *The Story of the United States Marines* (New York: U.S. Marine Corps Publicity Bureau, 1919), and Willis J. Abbot, *Soldiers of the Sea* (New York: Dodd, Mead, 1918).

73. Major E. H. Ellis, "Liaison in the World War," *MCG,* 5 (June 1920): 135–141.

74. Secretary of War N. D. Baker to Secretary of the Navy J. Daniels, June 6, 1919, File 11112-1457, Office of the Secretary of the Navy General Correspondence, 1916–1926, RG 80; J. Daniels, *The Wilson Era, 1917–1923* (Chapel Hill: University of North Carolina Press, 1946), pp. 149–154; and J. Daniels, "Brave Deeds of the Marine Corps," *Current History,* 9 (January 1919): 116–121.

75. The Chateau-Thierry controversy of 1919 is covered in the press clippings collected in File 11112–1327, Office of the Secretary of the Navy General Correspondence, 1916–1926, RG 80. For Marine Corps–Army friction, see Maj. Gen. (Ret.) J. A. Lejeune to Maj. Gen. Cmdt. W. C. Neville, (?) 1930, Lejeune Papers; Brig. Gen. P. B. Malone, USA, to Maj. Gen. J. G. Harbord, USA, June 13, 1919, File 21676-A592, Adj. Gen. AEF General Correspondence, 1917–1920, RG 120; and Major General Robert L. Bullard, USA (Ret.), *Personalities and Reminiscences of the War* (Garden City, N.Y.: Doubleday, Page, 1925), pp. 208–209. The merger is urged in Brig. Gen. H. B. Fiske, G-5 AEF to C/S AEF, "Memorandum on Military Policy of the United States," December 24, 1918, Pershing Collection, RG 316, NA.

CHAPTER 12. AMPHIBIOUS WARFARE
AND THE FLEET MARINE FORCE, 1919–1939

1. William R. Braisted, *The United States Navy in the Pacific, 1909–1922* (Austin: University of Texas Press, 1971), pp. 409–453.

2. Louis Morton, "War Plan 'ORANGE': Evolution of a Strategy," *World Politics,* 11 (January 1959): 221–250, and *idem,* "The Origins of Pacific Strategy," *MCG,* 41 (August 1957): 36–44.

3. CNO R. E. Coontz to Maj. Gen. Cmdt., "Function of Marine Corps in War Plans," January 28, 1920, File 221-2 (1920), Secretary of the Navy/Chief of Naval Operations Confidential Correspondence, RG 80.

4. Colonel R. H. Dunlap, "Lessons for Marines from the Gallipoli Campaign," *MCG,* 6 (September 1921): 237–252.

5. Col. R. H. Dunlap to Commission on Navy Yards and Naval Stations, "Fortifications for Naval Bases in the Caribbean Sea Region," May 26, 1919, HAF 72; Col. R. H. Dunlap to Maj. Gen. Cmdt., February 28, 1919, File 1975-10, HQMC General Correspondence, 1913–1932, RG 127; Maj. A. A. Cunningham, testimony, hearings, General Board, "Development of Naval Aviation Policy," April 7, 1919, Cunningham file, Reference Section, H&MD; and War Department and Navy Department, *Joint Army and Navy Action in Coast Defense* (Washington: Government Printing Office, 1920), pp. 7, 34–35.

6. Maj. Gen. Cmdt. to CNO, September 30, 1919, File 223, Secretary of the Navy/Chief of Naval Operations Confidential Correspondence, RG 80; Maj. Gen. Cmdt. to Secretary of the Navy, December 31, 1919, "Preparedness Report," December 31, 1919, File 221, Secretary of the Navy Secret and Confidential Correspondence, RG 80; and Joint Board memo, July 30, 1920, File 33-6:4, Secretary of the Navy Secret and Confidential Correspondence, RG 80.

7. Benis M. Frank, "The Relief of General Barnett," *Records of the Columbia Historical Society of Washington* (1971–1972), pp. 679–693; memoirs of Gen. C. B. Cates (1967), pp. 64–67, Maj. Gen. W. A. Worton (1967), pp. 85–90, and Lt. Gen. E. A. Craig (1968), pp. 62–68, MCOHC; and Rep. John W. Weeks to Mrs. G. Barnett, September 2, 1920, Barnett Papers, MCPPC.

8. Bernard C. Nalty and Lieutenant Colonel Ralph F. Moody, *A Brief History of U.S. Marine Corps Officer Procurement, 1775–1969,* rev. ed. (Washington: Historical Division, HQMC, 1970), p. 6.

9. "Extracts from Testimony of the Major General Commandant Before the Sub-committee of House Committee on Appropriations on the Naval Appropriations Bill, 1922" January 21, 1921, *MCG,* 9 (March 1921): 85–111, and J. David Cronon, *The Diaries of Josephus Daniels* (Lincoln: University of Nebraska Press, 1963), pp. 500, 503. Lejeune's own account of his service as Commandant is summarized in John A. Lejeune, *The Reminiscences of a Marine* (Philadelphia: Dorrance, 1930), pp. 460–483.

10. Kenneth W. Condit and Major John H. Johnstone, *A Brief History of Marine Corps Staff Organization* (Washington: Historical Branch, HQMC, 1963), pp. 11–18; Anthony A. Frances, "History of the Marine Corps Schools," pp. 24–57, December 1945, Breckinridge Library, MCDEC; and Colonel J. C. Breckinridge, "Why Quantico?" *USNIP,* 54 (November 1928): 969–975. The Basic School for new lieutenants was moved from Quantico to Philadelphia in 1924, where it remained until World War II.

11. Maj. Gen. Cmdt. J. A. Lejeune to Brig. Gen. S. D. Butler, December 7, 1926, Butler Papers, MCPPC; Maj. Gen. Cmdt., J. A. Lejeune to Miss A. L. Lejeune, Lejeune Papers; Files 1535 (Recruiting) and 1070 (Advertising), HQMC General Correspondence, 1913–1938, RG 127; and Robert Lindsay, *This High Name: Public Relations and the U.S. Marine Corps* (Madison: University of Wisconsin Press, 1956), pp. 36–52.

12. Brig. Gen. S. D. Butler to Secretary of the Navy J. Daniels, "Marine Corps Schools at Quantico" and "Vocational and Educational Schools at Marine Barracks," 1920, Butler Papers; Brig. Gen. S. D. Butler to T. S. Butler, September 2, 1921, Butler Papers; Brig. Gen. S. D. Butler to Maj. J. C. Fegan, November 22, 1923, Butler Papers; and File 1975-70/12, HQMC General Correspondence, 1913–1938, RG 127.

13. Maj. Gen. Cmdt. J. A. Lejeune, memo for the General Board, "Future Policy of the Marine Corps as Influenced by the Conference on Limitation of Armament," February 11, 1922, File 432, Records of the General Board, and Major General J. A. Lejeune, "The Marine Corps, 1926," *USNIP,* 52 (October 1926): 1961–1969.

14. Major General J. A. Lejeune, "The United States Marine Corps, *USNIP,* 51 (October 1925): 1858–1870; *idem,* "The U.S. Marine Corps, Present and Future," *USNIP,* 54 (October 1928): 859–861; and Brigadier General Rufus H. Lane, "The Mission and Doctrine of the Marine Corps," *MCG,* 6 (September 1921): 237–252.

15. Frank J. Infusino, Jr., "The United States Marine Corps and War Planning, 1900–1921," unpublished M.A. thesis, California State University–San Diego, 1973, pp. 7–54; Col. A. T. Mason, *Special Monograph on Amphibious Warfare,* 1950 ms. history, Command File World War II, Operational Archives, NHD, pp. 4–16, 26–43; and Col. B. H. Fuller to Maj. Gen. Cmdt., "Advanced Base Plans," August 1, 1921, File 2515, HQMC General Correspondence, 1913–1938, RG 127. See also Lt. Col. Kenneth J. Clifford, *Progress and Purpose: A Developmental History of the U.S. Marine Corps, 1900–1971* (Washington: History and Museums Division, HQMC, 1973), pp. 25–39, 61–65.

16. Maj. E. H. Ellis, "Naval Bases," study for the Division of Operations and Training, 1920, Ellis File, Reference Section, H&MD.

17. Lieutenant Colonel John J. Reber, "Pete Ellis: Amphibious Warfare Prophet," *USNIP,* 103 (November 1977): 53–64.

18. Maj. E. H. Ellis, "Advanced Base Operations in Micronesia," Operation Plan 712 D, HAF 165.

19. Control Force Commander to Chief of Naval Operations, May 9, 1922, File 29419, Secretary of the Navy Correspondence, 1916–1926, RG 80, and Capt. R. Earle, USN, "Landing Operations of the Control Force," NWC lecture, December 11, 1922, RG 15, Naval War College Historical Collection (hereafter NWCHC).

20. Mason, *Special Monograph on Amphibious Warfare,* pp. 54–63, covers all the prewar landing exercises. See also "Report of the Major General Commandant of the United States Marine Corps," *Annual Report of the Navy Department* (Washington: Government Printing Office, 1926), pp. 1223–1224, and Colonel Dion Williams, "The Winter Manoeuvers of 1924," *MCG,* 9 (March 1924): pp. 1–25.

21. Brigadier General Dion Williams, "Blue Marine Expeditionary Force," *MCG,* 10 (September 1925): 76–88, and Col. R. H. Dunlap, "Overseas Expeditionary Force," NWC lecture, January 14, 1927, RG 15, NWCHC.

22. Maj. Gen. Cmdt. J. A. Lejeune to Secretary of the Navy, "Revision of Pamphlet Entitled 'Joint Army and Navy Action in Coast Defense'," August 4, 1925, Secretary of the Navy Secret and Confidential Correspondence, 1919–1926, RG 80.

23. Joint Board, *Joint Action of the Army and Navy* (Washington: Government Printing Office, 1927), p. 3. See also Joint Board to the Secretary of War and the Secretary of the Navy, "Revision of Statement of Functions of the Army and Navy," October 14, 1926, and "Further Consideration as to Joint Operations," April 5, 1927, JB Serials 325/279 and 350/289, Records of Joint Army and Navy Boards and Committees, RG 225, NA.

24. Joint Board, *Joint Overseas Expeditions* (Washington: Government Printing Office, 1933), pp. 1, 6–7.

25. Joint Board, *Joint Action of the Army and Navy* (1927), p. 12.

26. Major General E. K. Cole, "Joint Overseas Operations," *USNIP,* 55 (November 1929): 927–937, and Lieutenant Commander E. W. Broadbent, "The Fleet and the Marines," *USNIP,* 57 (March 1931): 369–372. See also Lt. Col. E. B. Miller, "Organization and Distribution of the Marine Corps to Insure Readiness for Any Emergency," May 27, 1929; Brig. Gen. Dion Williams, "The Temporary Defense of a Fleet Base," February, 1931; and Maj. Gen. Cmdt. B. H. Fuller, "The Mission of the Marine Corps," 1932, all in File 1850-30, HQMC General Correspondence, 1913–1932, RG 127.

27. "Report of the Major General Commandant of the United States Marine Corps," *Annual Report of the Navy Department 1932* (Washington: Government Printing Office, 1932), p. 1163.

28. John R. M. Wilson, "The Quaker and the Sword: Herbert Hoover's Relations with the Military," *Military Affairs,* 38 (April 1974): 41–47, and Gerald E. Wheeler, *Admiral William Veazie Pratt* (Washington: Naval History Division, 1974), pp. 315–375.

29. Maj. Gen. J. T. Myers to Col. L. McC. Little, June 30 and August 4, 1931, Little Papers, MCPPC; Maj. Gen. Cmdt. B. H. Fuller to Chairman, Executive Committee, General Board, September 8, 1931, File 432, GB Records; and Director, War Plans Division, Office of the CNO, to General Board, August 10, 1931, File 432, GB Records.

30. Chairman, General Board, to Secretary of the Navy, memo, "Examination of the Organization and Establishment of the U.S. Marine Corps," August 10, 1932, File 432, GB Records, and CNO to Secretary of the Navy, March 2, 1932, File 1850-40, HQMC General Correspondence, 1913–1938, RG 127.

31. General Board, "Report of the Board to Consider and Recommend the Reorganization of the Navy Department," March 6, 1934, File 432, GB Records.

32. Maj. Gen. Cmdt. to CNO, August 17, 1933; Director, War Plans Division, to CNO, August 23, 1933; CNO to Maj. Gen. Cmdt., September 12, 1933; Maj. Gen. Cmdt. to Col. P. M. Rixey and others, December 5, 1933, all in File 1975-10, HQMC General Correspondence, 1913–1938, RG 127. See also Major General J. H. Russell, "The Birth of the Fleet Marine Force," *USNIP,* 72 (January 1946): 49–51.

33. Col. C. F. B. Price to Brig. Gen. R. C. Berkeley, March 2, 1931, and April 17, 1931, HAF 43; Cmdt. MCS to Maj. Gen. Cmdt. October 5, 1931, HAF 43; and Maj. Gen. Cmdt. to Cmdt. MCS, "Text for Landing Operations," October 20, 1931, HAF 43.

34. "Proceedings for Conference . . . January, 1934, for the purpose of discussing, approving, and commenting on the . . . Tentative Landing Operations Manual," HAF 41; Col. E. B. Miller, "The Marine Corps in Support of the Fleet," June 1, 1933, HAF 40; and memoirs of Lt. Gen. P. A. del Valle (1966), pp. 69–81, Gen. R. E. Hogaboom (1970), pp. 103–117, and Gen. A. H. Noble (1968), pp. 49–53, all MCOHC.

35. Department of the Navy, *Tentative Landing Operations Manual* (1935), HAF 39.

36. Calvin W. Enders, "The Vinson Navy," unpublished Ph.D. dissertation, Michigan State University, 1970, pp. 41, 96, and the *Annual Report of the Navy Department, 1934–1939.*

37. Lt. W. F. Royall, USN, "Landing Operations and Equipment," August 1939, HAF 73.

38. Cmdr. A. E. Schrader, USN, "Naval Gunfire in Support of a Landing," May 10, 1929, HAF 61; Lt. Walter C. Ansell, "Naval Gun Fire in Support of a Landing," *MCG,* 17 (May, 1932), pp. 23–26; Cmdr. C. G. Richardson, USN, "Naval Gunfire Support of Landing Operations," 1938–1939, HAF 64.

39. For general histories of interwar Marine aviation, see Lieutenant Colonel E. C. Johnson and Graham A. Cosmas, *A Short History of Marine Aviation* (Washington: History and Museums Division, HQMC, 1976), pp. 27–82, and Robert Sherrod, *History of Marine Corps Aviation in World War II* (Washington: Combat Forces Press, 1952), pp. 19–33.

40. *Ibid.* See also Roger Willock, *Unaccustomed to Fear: A Biography of the Late General Roy S. Geiger, USMC* (Princeton, N.J.: R. Willock, 1969), pp. 103–177; memoirs of Gen. F. C. Schilt (1969), pp. 42–47, 80, and Lt. Gen. L. A. Woods (1968), pp. 25–65, MCOHC; Major E. H. Brainard, "Marine Corps Aviation," *MCG,* 13 (March 1928): 25–26; Colonel Harold C. Reisinger, "Flying Reserve of the Leathernecks," *USNIP,* 59 (October 1933): 1466–1472; and General Vernon E. Megee, "The Evolution of Marine Aviation," *MCG,* 49 (August 1965): 20–26.

41. *Tentative Landing Operations Manual,* paragraphs 2–401 through 2–426.

42. *A Text on the Employment of Marine Corps Aviation* (Quantico, Va.: MCS, 1935); Headquarters Marine Corps, *Marine Corps Aviation General* (Washington: Government Printing Office, 1940); and memoir of Gen. V. E. Megee (1967), pp. 97–100, MCOHC.

43. For diplomatic background, see Thaddeus V. Tuleja, *Statesmen and Admirals: Quest for a Far Eastern Naval Policy* (New York: W. W. Norton, 1963).

44. C. R. Train, memo for the President, "Appointment of Major General Commandant for the Marine Corps," July 21, 1930, File 18E Presidential Cabinet Files, Herbert Hoover Library; Sen H. Black to J. A. Lejeune, February 26, 1935, and November 23, 1935, Lejeune Papers; J. A. Lejeune to Sen. H.

Black, March 1, 1935, Lejeune Papers; J. A. Lejeune to Sen. P. Trammell, February 14, 1935, Lejeune Papers; *New York Times* July 13, 1934, and March 3–5, 1935; Col. J. C. Fegan to Maj. Gen. L. McC. Little, August 6, 1936, Little Papers; and Maj. Gen. Cmdt. J. H. Russell to M. H. McIntyre, November 5, 1936, and HQMC, memo for Lt. Col. J. F. Roosevelt, USMCR, November 12, 1937, both File OF 18-E, Roosevelt Papers, Roosevelt Library, Hyde Park, N.Y.

45. Maj. Gen. Cmdt. to CNO, "Recommended Revision of Joint Action of Army and Navy, 1935," May 11, 1936, and Acting Secretary of the Navy W. H. Standley to Maj. Gen. Cmdt., May 18, 1936, both HAF 38.

46. Brig. Gen. D. D. Porter, A&I, to all commanders, January 3, 1935, File 1365-37, HQMC General Correspondence, 1913–1938, RG 127.

47. "Testimony of Maj. Gen. Cmdt. John H. Russell *et al.,*" U.S. Congress, House, 74th Congress, 2d Session, Hearings: "Navy Department Appropriation Bill, 1937" (Washington: Government Printing Office, 1936), pp. 627–686.

48. Maj. Gen. Cmdt. to CG, Dept. of the Pacific, June 20, 1936, and Director, Division of Operations and Training, to Maj. Gen. Cmdt., July 20, 1938, File 1975-10, HQMC General Correspondence, 1913–1938, RG 127.

49. "General Statement of Thomas Holcomb, Major General Commandant of the Marine Corps, at the Budget Hearings on the Marine Corps Personnel Plan," May 27, 1937, File 1975-10, HQMC General Correspondence, 1913–1938, RG 127, and Maj. Gen. Cmdt. T. Holcomb to Maj. Gen. L. McC. Little, June 18, 1937, Louis McC. Little Papers, MCPPC.

50. Brig. Gen. L. McC. Little to Maj. Gen. Cmdt. J. H. Russell, August 9, 1935; Maj. Gen. Cmdt. J H. Russell to Brig Gen. L McC. Little, August 7, 1935; Maj. Gen. L. McC. Little, address to The Basic School, February 12, 1936; and Maj. Gen. L. McC. Little, address to the Marine Corps Schools, March 12, 1936, all Little Papers.

51. Memoirs of Lt. Gen. R. O. Bare (1968), pp. 32–46; Gen. C. B. Cates (1967), pp. 91–97; Lt. Gen. J. C. Burger (1969), pp. 75–80; and Lt. Gen. M. H. Silverthorn (1969), pp. 207–241, all MCOHC. See also A. A. Vandegrift, *Once a Marine* (New York: W. W. Norton, 1964), pp. 78–80.

52. The best studies for the FLEXes are HQ 1st Marine Brigade FMF, "Notes on the Organization and Activities of the Fleet Marine Force in Connection with Landing Operations," 1938, File 1975-10, HQMC General Correspondence, 1913–1938, RG 127, and Lt. Col. B. W. Gally, "A History of U.S. Fleet Landing Exercises," ms., July 3, 1939, HAF 73.

53. Col. E. P. Moses C/S FMF to Col. J. Marston, November 20, 1935, Little Papers.

54. HQ 1st Marine Brigade FMF, "Notes on the Organization and Activities of the Fleet Marine Force," pp. 4–8. On naval gunfire, see Lt. Cmdr. David L. Nutter, USN, "Gunfire Support in Fleet Landing Exercises," September 1939, HAF 73.

55. HQ 1st Marine Brigade FMF, "Notes on the Organization and Activities of the Fleet Marine Force," pp. 8–10.

56. *Ibid,* pp. 10–12; RAdm. M. H. Simmons to Maj. Gen. L. McC. Little, March 30, 1937, Little Papers; Cmdt. MCS to Commander, U.S. Fleet, May 22, 1937, HAF 158; Maj. K. E. Rockey to Cmdr. Battle Force, March 6, 1937, HAF 158; and Lt. E. M. Eller, USN, "Analysis of Naval Gunfire at San Clemente 1937," HAF 109.

57. Memoir of Lt. Gen. J. P. Berkeley (1969), pp. 138–140, MCOHC.

58. HQ 1st Marine Brigade FMF, "Notes on the Organization and Activities of the Fleet Marine Force," pp. 12–16; Gally, "A History of U.S. Fleet Landing

Exercises"; and Maj. Gen. L. McC. Little to Maj. Gen. Cmdt. T. Holcomb, April 7, 1938, and Col. S. A. Woods to Maj. Gen. L. McC. Little, March 5, 1938, Little Papers.

59. Clifford, *Progress and Purpose* (note 15 above), pp. 48–57.

60. "Conference Concerning Various Types of Landing Crafts, Their Capabilities and Limitations," 1943, HAF 49, proceedings of an MCS-sponsored USMC–USN conference.

61. Col. Victor J. Croizat, "The Marine's Amphibian," *MCG,* 37 (June 1953): 40–49. For the work of both Higgins and Roebling, see also the memoir of Lt. Gen. V. H. Krulak (1970), pp. 48–58, MCOHC.

62. Brigadier General William P. Upshur, "The U.S. Marine Corps Reserve," *USNIP,* 65 (April 1939): 487–493, and Public Affairs Unit 4-1 USMCR, *The Marine Corps Reserve* (Washington: Division of Reserve, HQMC, 1966), pp. 20–58.

63. Chairman, General Board, to Secretary of the Navy, memo, "Are We Ready?" August 31, 1939, File 425, GB Records.

CHAPTER 13. WORLD WAR II: DEFEATING JAPAN IN THE SOUTH PACIFIC, 1939–1944

1. Stetson Conn and Byron Fairchild, *The United States Army in World War II: The Framework of Hemispheric Defense* (Washington: Government Printing Office, 1960), pp. 3–155; Louis Morton, "Germany First: The Basic Concept of Allied Strategy in World War II," in Kent R. Greenfield, ed., *Command Decisions* (Washington: Government Printing Office, 1960), pp. 11–47; and T. B. Kittredge, "United States Defense Policy and Strategy, 1941," *U.S. News and World Report,* December 3, 1954, pp. 53–139.

2. Chairman, General Board, to Secretary of the Navy, "Are We Ready?—II," July 1, 1940, File 425, GB Records, Operational Archives, NHD.

3. Conn and Fairchild, *The Framework of Hemispheric Defense,* p. 50.

4. Vice Admiral George C. Dyer, USN (ret.), *The Amphibians Came to Conquer: The Story of Richmond Kelly Turner,* 2 vols. (Washington: Government Printing Office, 1971), I: 208–213.

5. "Report of the Board to Study Matters Concerning Regular and Reserve Personnel of the Navy and Marine Corps," November 1940, Command File World War II, Operational Archives, NHD; Archibald D. Turnbill and Clifford L. Lord, *History of United States Naval Aviation* (New Haven: Yale University Press, 1949), pp. 310–314; and Robert Sherrod, *History of Marine Corps Aviation in World War II* (Washington: Combat Forces Press, 1952), pp. 32–33.

6. Charles L. Updegraph, Jr., *Special Marine Corps Units of World War II* (Washington: Historical Division, HQMC, 1972); and memoir of Brig. Gen. R. N. Jordhahl (1970), pp. 75–139, MCOHC.

7. CNO to F. D. Roosevelt, September 19, 1940, and F. D. Roosevelt to Director, Bureau of the Budget, October 4, 1940, File 18-E, White House Office Files, Franklin D. Roosevelt Papers.

8. Major General Commandant to CNO, "Strength of the Marine Corps," March 27, 1941, and CNO to the Secretary of the Navy, "Strength of the Marine Corps," April 7, 1941, File 18-E, Roosevelt Papers, and Public Affairs Unit 4-1, *The Marine Corps Reserve: A History* (Washington: Division of Reserve, HQMC, 1966), pp. 59–61.

9. HQMC, "Proposed Peace and War Strength of the Marine Corps to Support a Two Ocean Navy," April 18, 1941, File 432, GB Records, and Frank O. Hough, Verle E. Ludwig, and Henry I. Shaw, Jr., *History of U.S. Marine*

Corps Operations in World War II, Vol. 1: *Pearl Harbor to Guadalcanal,* 5 vols. (Washington: Government Printing Office, 1958), p. 56.

10. Kenneth W. Condit, John H. Johnstone, and Ella W. Nargele, *A Brief History of Headquarters Marine Corps Staff Organization,* rev. ed. (Washington: Historical Division, HQMC, 1971), pp. 16–17; Historical Section, HQMC, "Marine Corps Administrative History," October 1946, ms., Reference Section, H&MD, pp. 5, 126–154; and Robert Lindsay, *This High Name: Public Relations and the U.S. Marine Corps* (Madison: The University of Wisconsin Press, 1956), pp. 50–51.

11. Kenneth W. Condit, Gerald Diamond, and Edwin T. Turnbladh, "Marine Corps Ground Training in World War II," 1956, ms., history. Reference Section, H&MD, pp. 14–39, 98–99; Elmore A. Champie, *Brief History of Marine Corps Recruit Depot, Parris Island, South Carolina* (Washington: Historical Division, HQMC, 1962), pp. 8–9; and memoir of Maj. Gen. L. R. Jones (1970), pp. 82–99, MCOHC.

12. George McMillan, *The Old Breed: A History of the First Marine Division in World War II* (Washington: Infantry Journal Press, 1949), pp. 1–4.

13. Memo to the President, January 13, 1941, File 18-E, Office Files, Roosevelt Papers.

14. McMillan, *The Old Breed,* p. 11.

15. Elmore A. Champie, *Brief History of the Marine Corps Base and Recruit Depot, San Diego, California* (Washington: Historical Branch, HQMC, 1962), p. 15.

16. Chairman, General Board, to Secretary of the Navy, "Are We Ready?—III," June 14, 1941, File 425, GB Records.

17. CINCLant, FLEX 6 report, June 13, 1940, Correspondence of the Office of the Chief of Naval Operations, RG 38.

18. Jeter A. Isely and Philip A. Crowl, *The U.S. Marines and Amphibious War* (Princeton, N.J.: Princeton University Press, 1951), pp. 58–67.

19. Joint Landing Force Board, "Study of the Conduct of Training Landing Forces for Joint Amphibious Operations during World War II . . . ," pp. A3–A16, May 1953, Command File World War II, Operational Archives, NHD.

20. Operations Division memos, "Amphibious Training," April 3–10, 1942, OPD 353, Operations Division Correspondence, 1942–1945, RG 165, and Kent R. Greenfield, Robert R. Palmer, and Bell I. Wiley, *United States Army in World War II: The Army Ground Forces: The Organization of Ground Combat Troops* (Washington: Government Printing Office, 1947), pp. 85–92.

21. Quoted in Richard M. Leighton and Robert W. Coakley, *United States Army in World War II: Global Logistics and Strategy, 1940–1943* (Washington: Government Printing Office, 1955), p. 65.

22. Norman V. Cooper, "The Military Career of Gen. Holland M. Smith USMC," unpublished Ph.D. dissertation, University of Alabama, 1974, pp. 41–43, 78, 89, 137–167.

23. Joint Landing Forces Board, "Study of the Conduct of Training Forces for Joint Amphibious Operations during World War II . . . ," May 1953.

24. Louis Morton, *United States Army in World War II: The War in the Pacific: Strategy and Command: The First Two Years* (Washington: Government Printing Office, 1962), pp. 44–127.

25. Hough, Ludwig, and Shaw, *Pearl Harbor to Guadalcanal* (note 9 above), p. 56.

26. *Ibid.,* pp. 70–75.

27. Lieutenant Colonel R. D. Heinl, Jr., *The Defense of Wake* (Washington: Historical Section, HQMC, 1947).

28. Hough, Ludwig, and Shaw, *Pearl Harbor to Guadalcanal,* pp. 155–202.

29. Morton, *The War in the Pacific,* pp. 98–224; Samuel Eliot Morison, *History of United States Naval Operations in World War II: The Rising Sun in the*

Pacific, 1931–April 1942 (Boston: Little, Brown, 1948), pp. 149–398; Leighton and Coakley, *Global Logistics and Strategy, 1940–1943,* pp. 166–192; and Ernest J. King and Walter M. Whitehead, *Fleet Admiral King: A Naval Record* (New York: Norton, 1952), pp. 353–354, 381–389.

30. Hough, Ludwig, and Shaw, *Pearl Harbor to Guadalcanal,* pp. 84–92.
31. Rear Admiral Julius A. Furer, USN (ret.), *Administration of the Navy Department in World War II* (Washington: Naval History Division, 1959), pp. 564–566, and *New York Times,* February 24, 1942; April 1, 1942; and September 19, 1942.
32. Martin L. Myers, *Yardbird Myers* (Philadelphia: Dorrance, 1944), pp. 41–53, and Robert Leckie, *Helmet for My Pillow* (New York: Random House, 1957), pp. 3–22.
33. Leckie, *Helmet for My Pillow,* pp. 17–18.
34. Myers, *Yardbird Myers,* pp. 229–230.
35. Condit, Diamond, and Turnbladh, "Marine Corps Ground Training in World War II" (note 11 above), pp. 158–175, 196–215.
36. General V. E. Megee, "The Evolution of Marine Aviation," *MCG,* 49 (September 1965): 55–60, and Board to Reexamine . . . [Twining Board], "An Evaluation of Air Operations Affecting the U.S. Marine Corps in World War II," Section II, ms., study HQMC, 1945, Breckinridge Library, MCDEC.
37. Staff of the Ninth Marines, *The Ninth Marines* (Washington: Infantry Journal Press, 1946), pp. 32–33; Robert A. Aurther and Kenneth Cohlmia, *The Third Marine Division* (Washington: Infantry Journal Press, 1948), pp. 7–33; Brigadier General John S. Letcher, USMC (ret.), *One Marine's Story* (Verona, Va.: McClure Press, 1970), pp. 200–212; and General A. A. Vandegrift and Robert Asprey, *Once a Marine* (New York: Norton, 1964), pp. 98–101.
38. Morton, *The War in the Pacific,* pp. 289–304, and King and Whitehead, *Fleet Admiral King,* pp. 381–389.
39. Samuel Eliot Morison, *History of United States Naval Operations in World War II: The Struggle for Guadalcanal* (Boston: Little, Brown, 1949), pp. 3–16; Dyer, *The Amphibians Came to Conquer* (note 4 above), I: 229–318; and Hough, Ludwig, and Shaw, *Pearl Harbor to Guadalcanal,* pp. 235–247.
40. Hough, Ludwig, and Shaw, *Pearl Harbor to Guadalcanal,* pp. 247–253, and Vandegrift and Asprey, *Once a Marine,* pp. 106–122.
41. *Ibid.* For the Guadalcanal campaign, see also John L. Zimmerman, *The Guadalcanal Campaign* (Washington: Historical Division, HQMC, 1949); Macmillan, *The Old Breed* (note 12 above), pp. 17–142; and Brigadier General Samuel B. Griffith II, USMC (ret.), *The Battle for Guadalcanal* (Philadelphia: Lippincott, 1963).
42. H. L. Merillat, *The Island* (Boston: Houghton Mifflin, 1944), p. 20.
43. Hough, Ludwig, and Shaw, *From Pearl Harbor to Guadalcanal,* pp. 254–273, and Dyer, *The Amphibians Came to Conquer,* I: 329–353.
44. Morison, *The Struggle for Guadalcanal,* pp. 17–64, 78–107, 146–171, 199–224, 373.
45. Sherrod, *History of Marine Corps Aviation in World War II* (note 5 above), pp. 75–129, and Twining Board, "An Evaluation of Air Operations Affecting the U.S. Marine Corps in World War II," Section III, pp. 8–20.
46. Hough, Ludwig, and Shaw, *Pearl Harbor to Guadalcanal,* pp. 274–321.
47. T. Grady Gallant, *On Valor's Side* (Garden City, N.Y.: Doubleday, 1963), p. 207.
48. For the 1st Division on Guadalcanal, see especially *ibid.,* pp. 207–362; Leckie, *Helmet for My Pillow* (note 31 above), pp. 59–140; John Hersey, *Into the Valley* (New York: Knopf, 1943); Richard W. Tregaskis, *Guadalcanal Diary*

(Garden City, N.Y.: Blue Ribbon Books, 1943); and War Department, *Fighting on Guadalcanal* (Washington: Government Printing Office, 1943).

49. Hough, Ludwig, and Shaw, *Pearl Harbor to Guadalcanal*, pp. 322–358.

50. *Ibid.*, pp. 359–374.

51. Vandegrift and Asprey, *Once a Marine*, pp. 182–185; Dyer, *The Amphibians Came to Conquer*, I: 448–452; and memoirs of Maj. Gen. O. T. Pfeiffer (1968), pp. 211–219, and Gen. G. C. Thomas (1966), pp. 428–430, 441, MCOHC.

52. JCS memo 81 with appendices, "Distribution and Composition of U.S. Amphibious Forces," September 5, 1942, File CCS 320, Records of the JCS, RG 218.

53. Navy Department and JCS memoranda, "Authorized Strength for the Marine Corps," August 19–September 7, 1942, ABC 370.01, Strategy and Policy Group/Operations Division, Records of the War Department General Staff, RG 165.

54. Lt. Gen. Cmdt. T. Holcomb to Maj. Gen. A. A. Vandegrift, December 13 and 15, 1942, A. A. Vandegrift Papers, MCPPC, and Vandegrift and Asprey, *Once a Marine*, pp. 209–218, 222–231.

55. Furer, *Administration of the Navy Department in World War II* (note 31 above), pp. 568–571.

56. *Ibid.*, pp. 566–568.

57. Lieutenant Colonel Pat Meid, *Marine Corps Women's Reserve in World War II*, rev. ed. (Washington: Historical Branch, HQMC, 1968).

58. Henry I. Shaw, Jr., and Ralph W. Donnelly, *Blacks in the Marine Corps* (Washington: History and Museums Division, HQMC, 1975), pp. 1–46.

59. Historical Section, HQMC, "Marine Corps Administrative History" (note 10 above), pp. 38–43, 105, and Furer, *Administration of the Navy Department in World War II*, pp. 586–595.

60. Historical Section, HQMC, "Marine Corps Administrative History," pp. 404–414, 440–449.

61. Morton, *The War in the Pacific* (note 24 above), pp. 376–386.

62. *Ibid.*, pp. 387–415.

63. Bernard Fergusson, *The Watery Maze: The Story of Combined Operations* (New York: Holt, Rinehart and Winston, 1961), pp. 70–72, 109–118; Dyer, *The Amphibians Came to Conquer* (note 4 above), I: 499–501; and James C. Fahey, ed., *The Ships and Aircraft of the United States Fleet,* Victory Edition (New York: Ships and Aircraft, 1945), pp. 78–79.

64. Henry I. Shaw, Jr., and Major Douglas T. Kane, *History of U.S. Marine Corps Operations in World War II*, Vol. II: *Isolation of Rabaul* (Washington: Historical Branch, HQMC, 1963), pp. 32–37, 441–477.

65. *Ibid.*, pp. 10–12, 28–31, 35–37.

66. *Ibid.*, pp. 41–163; Dyer, *The Amphibians Came to Conquer*, I: 481–596; Samuel Eliot Morison, *History of United States Naval Operations in World War II: Breaking the Bismarck Barrier* (Boston: Little, Brown, 1950), pp. 138–253; and Major John N. Rentz, *Marines in the Central Solomons* (Washington: Historical Branch, HQMC, 1952). Marine casualties in the central Solomons were 192 KIA, 534 WIA.

67. Rentz, *Marines in the Central Solomons*, pp. 140–149.

68. Shaw and Kane, *Isolation of Rabaul*, pp. 167–183. See also Major John N. Rentz, *Bougainville and the Northern Solomons* (Washington: Historical Branch, HQMC, 1948).

69. Shaw and Kane, *Isolation of Rabaul*, pp. 207–224, and Morison, *Breaking the Bismarck Barrier*, pp. 279–349.

70. Rentz, *Bougainville and the Northern Solomons*, pp. 24–46.

71. Letcher, *One Marine's Story* (note 37 above), p. 259, and Major Frank O. Hough, *The Island War* (Philadelphia: Lippincott, 1947), p. 123.

72. The Bougainville fighting is personalized in Staff of the Ninth Marines, *The Ninth Marines* (note 37 above), pp. 41–52; John R. Monks, Jr., *A Ribbon and a Star* (New York: Henry Holt and Company, 1945); and Aurthur and Cohlmia, *The Third Marine Division* (note 37 above), pp. 58–135.

73. Rentz, *Bougainville and the Northern Solomons,* pp. 59–91; Twining Board, "An Evaluation of Air Operations Affecting the U.S. Marine Corps in World War II" (note 36 above), Section III, pp. 21–35; and Charles R. Smith, *A Brief History of the 12th Marines* (Washington: Historical Division, HQMC, 1972), pp. 8–16. Marine combat casualties on Bougainville numbered 1,841.

74. Morton, *The War in the Pacific* (note 24 above), pp. 470–472, 512–520, 533–558, and Shaw and Kane, *Isolation of Rabaul,* pp. 297–306.

75. Shaw and Kane, *Isolation of Rabaul,* pp. 313–318, and Lieutenant Colonel Frank O. Hough and Major John A. Crown, *The Campaign on New Britain* (Washington: Historical Branch, HQMC, 1952), pp. 21–35.

76. Leckie, *Helmet for My Pillow* (note 31 above), p. 200.

77. Hough and Crown, *The Campaign on New Britain,* pp. 21–28.

78. *Ibid.,* pp. 48–81, 89–112, and MacMillan, *The Old Breed,* (note 12 above), pp. 161–227.

79. Hough and Crown, *The Campaign on New Britain,* pp. 113–171, and Maj. Gen. W. H. Rupertus to Lt. Gen. Cmdt. A. A. Vandegrift, March 24, 1944, Vandegrift Papers.

80. Morton, *The War in the Pacific,* pp. 586–587.

81. Isely and Crowl, *The U.S. Marines and Amphibious War* (note 18 above), pp. 190–191.

CHAPTER 14.   WORLD WAR II: AMPHIBIOUS DRIVE
ACROSS THE CENTRAL PACIFIC, 1943–1945

1. Louis Morton, *United States Army in World War II: The War in the Pacific: Strategy and Command: The First Two Years* (Washington: Government Printing Office, 1962), pp. 376–386.

2. *Ibid.,* pp. 387–399, 434–460.

3. *Ibid.,* pp. 460–472, 521–527.

4. *Ibid.,* pp. 586–605. See also Admiral Ernest J. King and Walter M. Whitehead: *Fleet Admiral King: A Naval Record* (New York: Norton, 1952), pp. 479–482.

5. Lt. Gen. Cmdt. T. Holcomb to Lt. Gen. A. A. Vandegrift, November 23, 1943, Vandegrift Papers, MCPPC, and memoir of Maj. Gen. O. T. Pfeiffer (1968), pp. 240–242; memoir of Maj. Gen. W. W. Rogers (1969), pp. 55–66; and memoir of Lt. Gen. M. H. Silverthorn (1969), pp. 254–288, all MCOHC.

6. General A. A. Vandegrift, *Once a Marine* (New York: Norton, 1964), 237–243; memoir of Gen. G. C. Thomas (1966), pp. 526–560, MCOHC; Kenneth W. Condit, Gerald Diamond, and Edwin T. Turnbladh, *Marine Corps Ground Training in World War II,* ms. history, 1956, Reference Section, H&MD; and Kenneth W. Condit, Major John H. Johnstone, and Ella W. Nargele, *A Brief History of Headquarters Marine Corps Staff Organization,* rev. ed. (Washington: Historical Division, HQMC, 1971), pp. 21–24.

7. Robert Lindsay, *This High Name: Public Relations and the U.S. Marine Corps* (Madison: University of Wisconsin Press, 1956), pp. 53–69, and Benis M. Frank, *Denig's Demons and How They Grew: The Story of Marine Corps*

Combat Correspondents, Photographers and Artists (Washington: Marine Corps Combat Correspondents and Photographers Association, Inc., 1967). See also Jim Lucas, *Combat Correspondent* (New York: Reynal and Hitchcock, 1944).

8. Morton, *The War in the Pacific,* pp. 473–501; Robert W. Coakley and Richard M. Leighton, *United States Army in World War II: The War Department: Global Logistics and Strategy, 1943–1945* (Washington: Government Printing Office, 1968), pp. 391–416, 422–424; and E. B. Potter, *Nimitz* (Annapolis: Naval Institute Press, 1976), pp. 235–256.

9. Norman V. Cooper, "The Military Career of Gen. Holland M. Smith USMC," unpublished Ph.D. dissertation, Auburn University, 1974, p. 205.

10. Thomas A. Buell, *The Quiet Warrior: A Biography of Admiral Raymond A. Spruance* (Boston: Little, Brown, 1974), pp. 177–178; Vice Admiral George C. Dyer, USN (ret.), *The Amphibians Came to Conquer: The Story of Admiral Richmond Kelly Turner,* 2 vols. (Washington: Naval History Division, 1971), II: 597–624; and Cooper, "The Military Career of Gen. Holland M. Smith USMC," pp. 192–224.

11. Lt. Gen. T. Holcomb to Maj. Gen. H. M. Smith, October 22, 1943, and Lt. Gen. A. A. Vandegrift to Brig. Gen. E. C. Long, January 21, 1944, Vandegrift Papers.

12. Cooper, "The Military Career of Gen. Holland M. Smith USMC," pp. 179–189; Brig. Gen. O. T. Pfeiffer to Col. G. B. Erskine, October 23, 1943, Vandegrift Papers; memoir of Gen. G. B. Erskine (1970), pp. 183–188, 193, 203–204, 335, 375, MCOHC; Commander AmphibForPacFlt to AmphibForPacFlt, "Amphibious Force Landing Exercises—February 21–March 9, 1943, and March 10–27, 1943," April 19, 1943, HAF 77.

13. Samuel Eliot Morison, *History of United States Naval Operations in World War II: Aleutians, Gilberts and Marshalls* (Boston: Little, Brown, 1957), pp. 69–99.

14. Philip A. Crowl and Edmund G. Love, *United States Army in World War II: The War in the Pacific: Seizure of the Gilberts and Marshalls* (Washington: Government Printing Office, 1955), pp. 60–74.

15. Henry I. Shaw, Jr., Bernard C. Nalty, and Edwin T. Turnbladh, *History of U.S. Marine Corps Operations in World War II,* Vol. III: *Central Pacific Drive* (Washington: Government Printing Office, 1966), pp. 28–45.

16. Memoir of Adm. H. W. Hill, USN (1967), pp. 289–384, MCOHC; Buell, *The Quiet Warrior,* pp. 184–185; and Dyer, *The Amphibians Came to Conquer,* II: 705–715.

17. Shaw, Nalty, and Turnbladh, *Central Pacific Drive,* pp. 35–45.

18. In addition to earlier citations, see Captain James R. Stockman, *The Battle for Tarawa* (Washington: Historical Branch, HQMC, 1947); Robert Sherrod, *Tarawa* (New York: Duell, Sloan, and Pearce, 1944); Captain Earl J. Wilson et al., *Betio Beachhead* (New York: Putnam's, 1945); and Richard W. Johnston, *Follow Me! The Story of the Second Marine Division in World War II* (New York: Random House, 1948), pp. 99–156.

19. Stockman, *The Battle for Tarawa,* p. 40.

20. Captain Richard G. Hubler, "Death," in Captain Patrick O'Sheel and Staff Sergeant Gene Cook, eds., *Semper Fidelis* (New York: Sloan, 1947), pp. 166–167.

21. Maj. Gen. J. C. Smith to Lt. Gen. A. A. Vandegrift, December 13, 1943, and Lt. Gen. A. A. Vandegrift to Maj. Gen. H. M. Smith, December 3, 1943, both Vandegrift Papers; Cooper, "The Military Career of Gen. Holland M. Smith," pp. 238–254; and Jeter Isely and Philip A. Crowl, *The U.S. Marines and*

Amphibious War (Princeton, N.J.: Princeton University Press, 1951), pp. 248–252.

22. Crowl and Love, *Seizure of the Gilberts and Marshalls,* pp. 75–126.
23. Maj. Gen. H. M. Smith to Lt. Gen. A. A. Vandegrift, January 6, 1944; Lt. Gen. A. A. Vandegrift to Maj. Gen. H. M. Smith, January 15, 1944; Lt. Gen. A. A. Vandegrift to Maj. Gen. J. C. Smith, March 15, 1944, all Vandegrift Papers; memoir of Lt. Gen. J. C. Smith (1968), pp. 295–301, MCOHC; Vandegrift, *Once a Marine,* pp. 232–236, 243–244; and Potter, *Nimitz,* pp. 260–264.
24. Morison, *Aleutians, Gilberts and Marshalls,* pp. 201–224; Potter, *Nimitz,* pp. 264–266; and Buell, *The Quiet Warrior,* pp. 210–214.
25. Crowl and Love, *Seizure of the Gilberts and Marshalls,* pp. 206–218, and Shaw, Nalty, and Turnbladh, *Central Pacific Drive,* pp. 117–141.
26. Lieutenant Colonel Robert D. Heinl, Jr., and Lieutenant Colonel John A. Crown, *The Marshalls: Increasing the Tempo* (Washington: Historical Branch, HQMC, 1954), pp. 64–107; and Captain Carl W. Proehl, ed., *The Fourth Marine Division in World War II* (Washington: Infantry Journal Press, 1946), pp. 25–27.
27. Shaw, Nalty, and Turnbladh, *Central Pacific Drive,* pp. 181–195.
28. Crowl and Love, *Seizure of the Marshalls and Gilberts,* pp. 333–365; Heinl and Crown, *The Marshalls,* pp. 117–151; and First Lieutenant Bevan G. Cass, ed., *History of the Sixth Marine Division* (Washington: Infantry Journal Press, 1948), pp. 8–11.
29. Isely and Crowl, *The U.S. Marines and Amphibious War,* pp. 270–278, 291–301.
30. *Ibid.,* pp. 284–291; memoir of Adm. H. W. Hill, pp. 420–450, MCOHC; and Cooper, "The Military Career of Gen. Holland M. Smith," pp. 277–287.
31. Robert Sherrod, *History of Marine Corps Aviation in World War II* (Washington: Combat Forces Press, 1952), pp. 230–246.
32. Lt. Gen. A. A. Vandegrift to Gen. T. Holcomb, June 6, 1944, Vandegrift Papers.
33. Lt. Gen. A. A. Vandegrift to Lt. Gen. H. M. Smith, April 26, 1944, Vandegrift Papers; Vandegrift, *Once a Marine,* pp. 255–258; and Vincent Davis, *Postwar Defense Policy and the U.S. Navy, 1943–1946* (Chapel Hill: University of North Carolina Press, 1962), pp. 48–67.
34. Historical Section, HQMC, "Marine Corps Administrative History," October 1946, ms. history, pp. 257–267, 440–449, and George W. Garand and Truman R. Strobridge, *History of U.S. Marine Corps Operations in World War II,* Vol. IV: *Western Pacific Operations* (Washington: Historical Division, HQMC, 1971), pp. 24–30.
35. "Table of Organization F-100 Marine Division," May 5, 1944, in Shaw, Nalty, and Turnbladh, *Central Pacific Drive,* pp. 168–619, and Historical Branch, HQMC, "A Brief History of the Development of the Fire Team and the Marine Corps," ms., August 31, 1955.
36. Historical Section, HQMC, "Marine Corps Administrative History," pp. 425–439, and Charles L. Updegraph, Jr., *U.S. Marine Corps Special Units of World War II* (Washington: Historical Division, HQMC, 1972).
37. Historical Section, HQMC, "Marine Corps Administrative History," pp. 325–339; Colonel Donald W. Weller, "Salvo-Splash! The Development of Naval Gunfire Support in World War II," *USNIP,* 80 (August 1954): 839–849, and 80 (September 1954): 1011–1021; Lieutenant Colonel Robert D. Heinl, Jr., "Naval Gunfire Training in the Pacific," *MCG,* 32 (June 1948): 10–15; and *idem,* "Minority Report on (J) ASCO," *MCG,* 31 (July 1947): 28–32.

38. Sherrod, *History of Marine Corps Aviation in World War II*, 324–333; Vande-grift, *Once a Marine*, pp. 246–247; General V. E. Megee, "The Evolution of Marine Aviation," *MCG*, 49 (September 1965): 55–60; and memoir of Gen. V. E. Megee (1967), I: 118–120 and II: 7, 18, 37, MCOHC.

39. Report, Board to Reexamine . . . [Twining Board], "An Evaluation of Air Operations Affecting the U.S. Marine Corps in World War II," 1945, HQMC, pp. 36–68, copy Breckinridge Library, MCDEC; General V. E. Megee, "The Evolution of Marine Aviation," *MCG*, 49 (September 1965): 55–60; memoir of Gen. V. E. Megee (1967) II: 9–29, MCOHC; and Lieutenant Colonel Keith B. McCutcheon, "Close Air Support SOP," *MCG*, 29 (August 1945): 48–50.

40. Philip A. Crowl, *U.S. Army in World War II: The War in the Pacific: Cam-paign in the Marianas* (Washington: Government Printing Office, 1960), pp. 6–20; Samuel Eliot Morison, *History of U.S. Naval Operations in World War II: New Guinea and the Marianas* (Boston: Little, Brown, 1953), pp. 3–10; and Potter, *Nimitz* (note 8 above), pp. 279–292.

41. Crowl, *Campaign in the Marianas*, pp. 21–30, and Morison, *New Guinea and the Marianas*, pp. 10–14.

42. Shaw, Nalty, and Turnbladh, *Central Pacific Drive*, pp. 263–291; Crowl, *Cam-paign in the Marianas*, pp. 71–117; and Major Carl H. Hoffman, *Saipan: The Beginning of the End* (Washington: Historical Division, HQMC), pp. 45–99.

43. Morison, *New Guinea and the Marianas*, pp. 256–304.

44. Shaw, Nalty, and Turnbladh, *Central Pacific Drive*, pp. 305–331; Crowl, *Cam-paign in the Marianas*, pp. 163–233; Hoffman, *Saipan*, pp. 126–207; Johnston, *Follow Me!* (note 18 above), pp. 196–206; and Proehl, *The Fourth Marine Division in World War II* (note 26 above), pp. 58–98.

45. Crowl, *Campaign in the Marianas*, pp. 191–201.

46. Shaw, Nalty, and Turnbladh, *Central Pacific Drive*, pp. 332–352.

47. Isely and Crowl, *The U.S. Marines and Amphibious War* (note 21 above), pp. 325–342, and memoir of Adm. H. W. Hill, I: 451–466, MCOHC.

48. Memoir of Maj. Gen. L. R. Jones (1970), pp. 134–135, MCOHC.

49. Cooper, "The Military Career of Gen. Holland M. Smith" (note 9 above), pp. 325–330, 340–341; Buell, *The Quiet Warrior* (note 10 above), pp. 281–287; Potter, *Nimitz*, pp. 305–309; and memoirs of Maj. Gen. O. T. Pfeiffer (1968), pp. 258–287, and Lt. Gen. J. C. McQueen (1969), pp. 86–93, both MCOHC. The basic correspondence on the "Smith versus Smith" controversy is collected in Department of the Navy, "Saipan controversy," November 1948, Holland M. Smith File, Reference Section, H&MD. This file includes copies of the Nimitz–King–Marshall correspondence on the incident and reports from all the affected officers on Saipan. Another source is the correspondence in the Vandegrift Papers, especially Lt. Gen. A. A. Vandegrift to Lt. Gen. H. M. Smith, July 22, 1944; Lt. Gen. H. M. Smith to Lt. Gen. A. A. Vandegrift, July 15, 1944; Adm. C. W. Nimitz to Lt. Gen. A. A. Vandegrift, October 31, 1944; Lt. Gen. A. A. Vandegrift to Adm. C. W. Nimitz, November 17, 1944; and Lt. Col. E. R. Hagenah to Lt. Gen. A. A. Vandegrift, November 3, 1944.

50. Shaw, Nalty, and Turnbladh, *Central Pacific Drive*, pp. 355–376.

51. *Ibid.*, pp. 377–428: Isely and Crowl, *U.S. Marines and Amphibious War*, pp. 351–371; and Major Carl W. Hoffman, *The Seizure of Tinian* (Washington: Historical Division, HQMC, 1951).

52. Shaw, Nalty, and Turnbladh, *Central Pacific Drive*, pp. 431–456, and Morison, *New Guinea and the Marianas*, pp. 371–382.

53. Shaw, Nalty, and Turnbladh, *Central Pacific Drive*, pp. 457–502, and Major O. R. Lodge, *The Recapture of Guam* (Washington: Historical Branch,

HQMC, 1954), pp. 37–73. See also Crowl, *Campaign in the Marianas,* pp. 339–376.

54. Lodge, *The Recapture of Guam,* pp. 74–105.

55. Shaw, Nalty, and Turnbladh, *Central Pacific Drive,* pp. 503–567, and Crowl, *Campaign in the Marianas,* pp. 377–437. For troop experience, see First Lieutenant Robert A. Aurthur and First Lieutenant K. Cohlmia, *The Third Marine Division* (Washington: Infantry Journal Press, 1948), pp. 143–162, and Cass, *History of the Sixth Marine Division* (note 28 above), pp. 13–29.

56. Robert R. Smith, *The United States Army in World War II: The War in the Pacific: The Approach to the Philippines* (Washington: Government Printing Office, 1953), pp. 450–456, and Garand and Strobridge, *Western Pacific Operations* (note 34 above), pp. 51–66.

57. Major Frank O. Hough, *The Assault on Peleliu* (Washington: Historical Division, HQMC, 1950), pp. 10–35.

58. *Ibid.;* George McMillan, *The Old Breed: A History of the First Marine Division in World War II* (Washington: Infantry Journal Press, 1949), pp. 228–270; and memoirs of Lt. Gen. M. H. Silverthorn (1969), pp. 299–319, and Gen. O. P. Smith (1969), pp. 124–145, MCOHC.

59. Hough, *Assault on Peleliu,* pp. 36–58; Garand and Strobridge, *Western Pacific Operations,* pp. 106–131; and McMillan, *The Old Breed,* pp. 271–297. See also George K. Hunt, *Coral Comes High* (New York: 1946).

60. Hough, *Assault on Peleliu,* 59–103.

61. *Ibid.,* pp. 104–170; McMillan, *The Old Breed,* pp. 321–343; and Garand and Strobridge, *Western Pacific Operations,* pp. 219–253.

62. Garand and Strobridge, *Western Pacific Operations,* pp. 291–233; Sherrod, *Marine Corps Aviation in World War II* (note 31 above) pp. 262–276; and Major Charles W. Boggs, Jr., *Marine Aviation in the Philippines* (Washington: Historical Division, HQMC, 1951), pp. 1–18.

63. Boggs, *Marine Aviation in the Philippines,* pp. 19–30.

64. *Ibid.,* pp. 31–45, and Garand and Strobridge, *Western Pacific Operations,* pp. 327–333.

65. Boggs, *Marine Aviation in the Philippines,* pp. 47–73.

66. *Ibid.,* pp. 73–106; Garand and Strobridge, *Western Pacific Operations,* pp. 334–357; and Robert R. Smith, *United States Army in World War II: The War in the Pacific: Triumph in the Philippines* (Washington: Government Printing Office, 1963), pp. 211–236, 449–579.

67. Boggs, *Marine Aviation in the Philippines,* pp. 107–135.

68. Garand and Strobridge, *Western Pacific Operations,* pp. 462–481, and Samuel Eliot Morison, *History of United States Naval Operations in World War II: Victory in the Pacific* (Boston: Little, Brown, 1960), pp. 3–19.

69. Lieutenant Colonel Whitman S. Bartley, *Iwo Jima: Amphibious Epic* (Washington: Historical Branch, HQMC, 1954), pp. 4–18.

70. *Ibid.,* pp. 19–50, and Garand and Strobridge, *Western Pacific Operations,* pp. 462–481.

71. T. Grady Gallant, *The Friendly Dead* (Garden City, N.Y.: Doubleday, 1964), pp. 32–33, 55. For D-Day, see Bartley, *Iwo Jima,* pp. 51–68. For the character of the fighting on Iwo, see especially Captain Raymond Henri et al., *The U.S. Marines on Iwo Jima* (New York: Dial Press, 1945); Richard F. Newcomb, *Iwo Jima* (New York: Holt, Rinehart and Winston, 1965); Aurthur and Cohlmia, *The Third Marine Division* (note 55 above), pp. 222–322; Proehl, *The Fourth Marine Division in World War II* (note 26 above), pp. 147–206; and Howard M. Conner, *The Spearhead: The World War II*

History of the 5th Marine Division (Washington: Infantry Journal Press, 1950), pp. 43–124.

72. Garand and Strobridge, *Western Pacific Operations,* pp. 502–527.

73. Lt. Gen. A. A. Vandegrift to Lt. Gen. H. M. Smith, March 6, 1945, Vandegrift Papers, and Walter Millis, ed., *The Forrestal Diaries* (New York: Viking Press, 1951), p. 30. For the assault on Suribachi, see Garand and Strobridge, *Western Pacific Operations,* pp. 528–546, and the memoir of Richard Wheeler, *The Bloody Battle for Suribachi* (New York: Thomas Y. Crowell, 1965).

74. Bernard Nalty, *The United States Marines on Iwo Jima: The Battle and the Flag Raising,* rev. ed. (Washington: Historical Branch, HQMC, 1970).

75. Capt. Arthur N. Hill, "Battalion on Iwo," *MCG,* 29 (November 1945): 27–29, 57–59.

76. Allen R. Matthews, *The Assault* (New York: Simon and Schuster, 1947), pp. 8–9.

77. Bartley, *Iwo Jima,* pp. 99–179.

78. Garand and Strobridge, *Western Pacific Operations,* pp. 684–712; *Life,* March 5 and 12, 1945, and April 9, 1945; *Newsweek,* March 12 and 19, 1945, and April 2, 1945; *Time,* March 12, 1945; and Newcomb, *Iwo Jima,* pp. 233–241.

79. Bartley, *Iwo Jima,* pp. 194–210; Garand and Strobridge, *Western Pacific Operations,* pp. 713–728; Potter, *Nimitz* (note 8 above), pp. 358–368; Dyer, *The Amphibians Came to Conquer* (note 10 above), II: 1040–1051; memoir of Adm H. W. Hill, I: 582–661, MCOHC; Cooper, "The Military Career of Gen. Holland M. Smith" (note 9 above), pp. 409–438; and Vandegrift, *Once a Marine* (note 6 above), pp. 280–285.

80. Benis M. Frank and Henry I. Shaw, Jr., *History of U.S. Marine Corps Operations in World War II,* Vol. V: *Victory and Occupation* (Washington: Historical Branch, HQMC, 1968), pp. 3–13; Samuel Eliot Morison, *History of United States Naval Operations in World War II: Victory in the Pacific* (Boston: Little, Brown, 1960), pp. 79–107; Roy E. Appleman, James M. Burns, Russell A. Gugeler, and John Stevens, *United States Army in World War II: The War in the Pacific: Okinawa: The Last Battle* (Washington: Historical Division, Department of the Army, 1948), pp. 1–21; and Major Charles S. Nichols, Jr., and Henry I. Shaw, Jr., *Okinawa: Victory in the Pacific* (Washington: Historical Branch, HQMC, 1955).

81. Frank and Shaw, *Victory and Occupation,* pp. 57–98.

82. *Ibid.,* pp. 109–141.

83. Morison, *Victory in the Pacific,* pp. 92–93, 181–198, 282, and Appleman et al,. *Okinawa,* pp. 84–102, 249–257.

84. Nichols and Shaw, *Okinawa,* pp. 87–118. For the Marine experience on Okinawa, see also McMillan, *The Old Breed* (note 58 above), pp. 357–424, and Cass, *History of the Sixth Marine Division* (note 28 above), pp. 59–175.

85. Appleman, et al., *Okinawa,* pp. 258–264, and Frank and Shaw, *Victory and Occupation,* pp. 188–197.

86. Nichols and Shaw, *Okinawa,* pp. 142–207.

87. *Ibid.,* pp. 207–217, and Appleman, et al., *Okinawa,* pp. 383–402.

88. Sherrod, *History of Marine Corps Aviation in World War II* (note 31 above), pp. 384–414.

89. Frank and Shaw, *Victory and Occupation,* pp. 325–394.

90. Morison, *Victory in the Pacific,* pp. 273; Potter, *Nimitz,* pp. 373–376; and Vandegrift, *Once a Marine,* pp. 387–392.

91. Frank and Shaw, *Victory and Occupation,* pp. 410–441.

92. Social Science Research Council and the Bureau of the Census, *The Statistical*

History of the United States from Colonial Times to the Present (Stamford, Conn.: Fairfield Publishers, 1965), p. 735, and Historical Reference Memo Reserve Section, H&MD, "USMC Casualties and Strengths," March 15, 1976.

93. This final section is based on Frank and Shaw, *Victory and Occupation,* pp. 677–730, and Isely and Crowl, *The U.S. Marines and Amphibious War* (note 21 above), pp. 580–590.

CHAPTER 15. WINNING THE RIGHT AND MEANS TO FIGHT, 1945–1950

1. John Lewis Gaddis, *The United States and the Origins of the Cold War, 1941–1947* (New York and London: Columbia University Press, 1972), pp. 1–31, 198–281.

2. Michael S. Sherry, *Preparing for the Next War: American Plans for Postwar Defense, 1941–45* (New Haven: Yale University Press, 1977) pp. 191–232; Perry McCoy Smith, *The Air Force Plans for Peace, 1943–1945* (Baltimore: Johns Hopkins Press, 1970), pp. 39–53, 104–116; and Vincent Davis, *Postwar Defense Policy and the U.S. Navy, 1943–1946* (Chapel Hill: University of North Carolina Press, 1962), pp. 207–270.

3. A. A. Vandegrift, *Once a Marine* (New York: Norton, 1964), pp. 295–296, 300; *New York Times,* January 11, 1946, and February 11 and 20, 1946; and HQMC, "Administrative History Supplement: History of the Various Activities of the U.S. Marine Corps . . . 1 September 1945 to 1 October 1946," 2 vols., ms. history, Command Post File, Operational Archives, NHD.

4. Gen. Cmdt. A. A. Vandegrift to Gen. T. Holcomb, April 22, 1946, Vandegrift Papers; HQMC, "Administrative History of the United States Marine Corps for the Period from 1 October 1946 to 1 July 1947," 2 vols., ms. history, Command Post File, Operational Archives, NHD; and memoirs of Gen. G. C. Thomas (1966), pp. 672–678, Gen. G. B. Erskine (1970), pp. 435–439, Gen. V. E. Megee (1967), II: pp. 106–109, and Lt. Gen. W. J. Van Ryzin (1976), pp. 106–116, all MCOHC.

5. Gen. Cmdt. A. A. Vandegrift to Lt. Gen. R. S. Geiger, August 10, 1945, Vandegrift Papers.

6. Benis M. Frank and Henry I. Shaw, Jr., *History of U.S. Marine Corps Operations in World War II,* Vol. V: *Victory and Occupation* (Washington: Historical Branch, HQMC, 1968), pp. 475–518.

7. Maj. Gen. K. E. Rockey to Gen. Cmdt. A. A. Vandegrift, October 13, 1945, Vandegrift Papers; Frank and Shaw, *Victory and Occupation,* pp. 537–570; and Henry I. Shaw, Jr., *The United States Marines in North China, 1945–1949,* rev. ed. (Washington: Historical Branch, HQMC, 1962).

8. Frank and Shaw, *Victory and Occupation,* pp. 571–593, and Shaw, *The United States Marines in North China,* pp. A-1–B-2.

9. Maj. Gen. K. E. Rockey to Gen. Cmdt. A. A. Vandegrift, April 9, 1946, Vandegrift Papers, and Frank and Shaw, *Victory and Occupation,* pp. 594–634.

10. *Ibid.,* pp. 635–650.

11. HQMC, "Navy Subsidiary Postwar Plan—Marine Corps, No. 1," November 1, 1945, HAF, Breckinridge Library, MCDEC; Gen. A. A. Vandegrift to CNO C. A. Nimitz, "United States Contingent to Security Forces of the United Nations Organization," January 28, 1946, Merritt A. Edson Papers; and *New York Times,* February 15, 1946.

12. CNO to JCS, "Missions of the Land, Sea and Air Forces," March 6, 1946,

JCS 1478/9, CCS 370, Records of the Joint Chiefs of Staff, RG 218, and David A. Greenberg, "The U.S. Navy and the Problem of Oil in a Future War: The Outline of a Strategic Dilemma, 1945–1950, *Naval War College Review,* 39 (Summer 1976): 53–64.

13. C/S USA, "Missions of the Land, Sea and Air Forces," March 16, 1946, JCS 1478/11, CCS 370, RG 218.

14. CMC to CNO, "Comments on JCS 1478/10 and JCS 1478/11," JCS 1478/12, CCS 370, RG 218, and CMC to CNO, "Mission of the Land, Naval and Air Forces," April 19, 1946, JCS 1478/16, CCS 370, RG 218.

15. HQMC, "Navy Subsidiary Post-war Plan, Marine Corps No. 2," August 1, 1946, HAF; Gen. A. A. Vandegrift to CNO C. A. Nimitz, August 28, 1946, Vandegrift Papers; and JPS, "Strategic Estimate and Deployment in the Pacific," August 30, 1946, JPS 757/9, CCS 323.361, RG 218.

16. Lt. Gen. R. S. Geiger to Gen. A. A. Vandegrift, August 21, 1946, quoted in Lieutenant Colonel Kenneth J. Clifford, USMCR, *Progress and Purpose: A Development History of the U.S. Marine Corps, 1900–1970* (Washington: History and Museums Division, HQMC, 1973), p. 71, and CNO to CMC, "Future Amphibious Operations," September 23, 1946, CNO-CMC Subject File, Reference Section, H&MD. See also Lynn Montross, *Cavalry of the Sky* (New York: Harper and Brothers, 1954), pp. 42–47.

17. Special Board, Marine Corps Schools, "Summary of Findings and Recommendations Respecting Future Amphibious Operations," December 16, 1946, and CMC to CNO, "Future Amphibious Operations," December 19, 1946, both CMC-CNO Correspondence; memoirs of Brig. Gen. E. C. Dyer (1968), pp. 191–200, and Brig. Gen. S. R. Shaw (1970), pp. 120–123, MCOHC; and Montross, *Cavalry of the Sky,* pp. 48–66.

18. Op-05 to Op-03, "Future Amphibious Operations," March 21, 1947, and DCNO (Air) to DCNO (Operations), April 15, 1947, CNO-CMC Subject File, and memoir of Brig. Gen. E. C. Dyer, pp. 195–200, MCOHC.

19. *Ibid.*

20. Lieutenant Colonel Eugene W. Rawlings, *The Marines and Helicopters, 1946–1962* (Washington: History and Museums Division, HQMC, 1976), pp. 19–29; memoir of Lt. Gen. V. H. Krulak (1970), II: pp. 114–118, MCOHC; and Montross, *Cavalry of the Sky,* pp. 78–87.

21. Rawlings, *The Marines and Helicopters,* pp. 31–40; memoirs of Gen. V. E. Megee (1967) II: 129–131, and Brig. Gen. F. P. Henderson (1974), pp. 157–159, MCOHC; and Chief BuAero to CNO, "Amphibious Warfare Assault Helicopter," December 24, 1947, CMC-CNO Subject File.

22. Demetrios Caraley, *The Politics of Military Unification* (New York and London: Columbia University Press, 1966), and Gordon W. Keiser, "The U.S. Marine Corps and Unification: 1944–1947," unpublished M.A. thesis, Tufts University, 1971.

23. Caraley, *The Politics of Military Unification,* pp. 23–56.

24. Vandegrift, *Once a Marine* (note 3 above), p. 304.

25. Keiser, "The U.S. Marine Corps and Unification," pp. 44–45. The Marine Corps experience is also described in Lt. Col. James D. Hittle, "The Marine Corps and Its Struggle for Survival, 1946–1947," ms. history, May 1948, H&MD; 1st Lt. Arthur Ochs Sulzberger, USMCR, "Unification and the Marine Corps," ms. history, 1953, H&MD; and Colonel R. D. Heinl, Jr., "The Right to Fight," *USNIP,* 88 (September 1962): 23–39. For participant accounts, see memoirs of Gen. G. C. Thomas (1966), pp. 777–852; Lt. Gen. V. H. Krulak, pp. 104–119; Brig. Gen. E. C. Dyer, pp. 202–208; and Brig. Gen. S. R. Shaw (1970), pp. 123–154, all MCOHC.

26. Caraley, *The Politics of Military Unification,* pp. 57–122.
27. Keiser, "The U.S. Marine Corps and Unification," pp. 60–63, and Vandegrift, *Once a Marine,* pp. 312–316.
28. Caraley, *The Politics of Military Unification,* pp. 125–131.
29. "Statement of General Alexander A. Vandegrift, U.S.M.C., Before the Senate Naval Affairs Committee at Hearings on S.2044," May 10, 1946, copy in "Unification" File, Reference Section, H&MD.
30. Caraley, *The Politics of Military Unification,* pp. 140–152.
31. Brigadier General Frank A. Armstrong, December 11, 1946, quoted in Caraley, *The Politics of Military Unification,* p. 151.
32. Keiser, "The U.S. Marine Corps and Unification," pp. 64–88, and Hittle, "The Marine Corps and Its Struggle for Survival," pp. 1–8. For the Army position, see "Statement of General Eisenhower Concerning Mission of Marine Corps," appended to December 3, 1946, entries, Forrestal Diaries, Operational Archives, NHD.
33. Keiser, "The U.S. Marine Corps and Unification," pp. 119–125.
34. *Ibid.,* pp. 128–136; Hittle, "The Marine Corps and Its Struggle for Survival," pp. 14–23; and House Report 961 on H.4212, 80th Congress, 1st Session, July 16, 1947.
35. House Report 961 on H.4212, 80th Congress, 1st Session, July 16, 1947; Keiser, "The U.S. Marine Corps and Unification," pp. 138–147; and Section 206 (c), National Security Act of 1947, PL 253, 80th Congress, 1st Session, July 26, 1947, 61 Stat. 495.
36. Gen. A. A. Vandegrift to Lt. Gen. H. Schmidt, May 22, 1947, Vandegrift Papers; Lt. Col. James D. Hittle, "The Marine Corps and the National Security Act," *MCG* 31 (October, 1947), pp. 57–59.
37. Joint Emergency War Plans Committee, "Emergency War Plans Halfmoon/ Fleetwood/Doublestar," May 1948, and "Off Tackle," May 1949, JCS 1844, CCS 381, RG 218.
38. General Board Study 425 (Serial 315), "National Security and Navy Contributions Thereto for the Next Ten Years," June 25, 1948, Records of the General Board, Operational Archives, NHD.
39. CNO to JCS, "Use of Fleet Marine Force Units," January 28, 1948, JCS 1829/1, RG 218; Gen. A. A. Vandegrift, "The Marine Corps in 1948," *USNIP* 74 (February, 1948), pp. 135–143; *New York Times,* April 16 and July 14, 1947, and Jnaury 3 and October 5, 1948.
40. Memoir of Gen. C. B. Cates (1967), pp. 206–210, MCOHC; A. A. Vandegrift, *Once a Marine,* pp. 330–331.
41. Reports of CMC to Secretary of the Navy for FYs 1948, 1949, and 1950, Post-1946 Command File, Operational Archives, NHD; Gen. Cmdt. C. B. Cates, "The Marine Corps and Its Functions," June 14, 1949, and "Opening Remarks, CMC's Conference for Commanding Generals," November 29, 1949, both CMC Speech File, 1949–1951, Clifton B. Cates Papers, MCPPC; memoir of Gen. G. B. Erskine (1970), pp. 440–460, MCOHC; and *New York Times,* June 16 and 18, 1948, December 2, 1948, October 18 and 30, 1949, and November 5, 1949.
42. CMC report to Secretary of the Navy for FY 1950, Post-1946 Command File, Operational Archives, NHD, and *New York Times,* January 10 and 16, 1950, and June 16, 1950.
43. Rawlings, *The Marines and Helicopters, 1946–1962* (note 20 above), pp. 31–40; Lieutenant Colonel William R. Fails, *Marines and Helicopters, 1962–1973* (Washington: History and Museums Division, HQMC, 1978), pp. 199–

204; Montross, *Cavalry of the Sky* (note 16 above), pp. 94–105; and memoir of Gen. V. E. Megee, II: pp. 100–136, MCOHC.

44. HQMC, "Digest of General Statement," January 30, 1950, "Strength and Distribution" File, 1950–1956, Reference Section, H&MD; and Public Affairs Unit 4-1, *The Marine Corps Reserve: A History* (Washington: Division of Reserve, HQMC, 1966), pp. 101–138.

45. Henry I. Shaw, Jr., and Ralph W. Donnelly, *Blacks in the Marine Corps* (Washington: History and Museums Division, 1975), pp. 47–48.

46. Kenneth W. Condit, Major John H. Johnstone, and Ella W. Nargele, *A Brief History of Headquarters Marine Corps Staff Organization,* rev. ed. (Washington: Historical Division, HQMC, 1971), pp. 24–30; and memoirs of Gen. G. C. Thomas, pp. 19, 919–921, and Maj. Gen. C. R. Allen (1969), pp. 305–306, MCOHC.

47. For the Corps and defense politics, 1948–1950, see Colonel R. D. Heinl, Jr., "The Right to Fight," *USNIP,* 88 (September 1962): 23–39; Sulzberger, "Unification and the Marine Corps," 1953 (note 25 above); and memoir of Gen. C. B. Cates, pp. 213–240, MCOHC. For interservice positions, see Paolo Coletta, "The Defense Unification Battle: The Navy 1947–1950," *Prologue,* 7 (Spring 1975): 6–17; Herman S. Wolk, "The Defense Unification Battle, 1947–1950: The Air Force," *loc. cit.,* pp. 18–26; and Richard F. Haynes, "The Defense Unification Battle, 1947–1950: The Army," *loc. cit.,* pp. 27–31.

48. CMC to Secretary of the Navy, December 11, 1947; CNO to Secretary of the Navy, December 15, 1947; and Secretary of the Navy to CMC, December 17, 1947, all reprinted in Senate Armed Services Committee, Hearings on S.677 "Marine Corps Strength and Joint Chiefs of Staff Representation," 82d Congress, 1st Session, pp. 147–149, and memoir of Brig. Gen. S. R. Shaw, pp. 161–163, MCOHC.

49. OSD and JCS, redraft of ExO 9877, "Functions of the Armed Forces," January 20, 1948, JCS 1478/20, CCS 370, RG 218.

50. OSD and JCS, "Functions of the Armed Forces and the Joint Chiefs of Staff," March 26, 1948, JCS 1478/21 and 22, CCS 370, RG 218, and JCS, "Functions of the Armed Forces and the Joint Chiefs of Staff," JCS 1478/23, CCS 370, RG 218.

51. CMC to Secretary of the Navy, "Restrictions on the Composition and Organization of the Marine Corps," May 3, 1948, Decimal File 045.3, Office of the C/S, USA, 1948, Records of the Army Staff, RG 319.

52. JCS, "Functions of the Armed Forces and the Joint Chiefs of Staff," August 21, 1948, JCS 1478/26, CCS 370, RG 218; JCS, minutes of meetings to consider FY 1950 budget, October 2–5, 1948, Section 10, CCS 370, RG 218; Office of the Chief of Army Field Forces, "Report of Army Advisory Panel on Joint Amphibious Operations," January 18, 1949, "Attacks on Marine Corps" File, Office of the CNO (Op 23), Operational Archives, NHD; and memoir of Lt. Gen. M. H. Silverthorn (1969), pp. 432–440, MCOHC.

53. Norman V. Cooper, "The Military Career of Gen. Holland M. Smith USMC," unpublished Ph.D. dissertation, Auburn University, 1974, pp. 452–470, and H. M. Smith, *Coral and Brass* (New York: Scribner's, 1949).

54. Transcript, telcon, Brig. Gen. M. A. Edson and Brig. Gen. A. A. Robinson, Division of Plans and Policies, HQMC, November 17, 1948, File 106, Edson Papers; Richard Tregaskis, "The Marine Corps Fights for Its Life," *Saturday Evening Post,* 20 (February 5, 1949): 20–21, 104–105; Merritt A. Edson, "Power-Hungry Men in Uniform," *Collier's,* 124 (August 27, 1949): 16–17, 65; and memoir of Gen. O. P. Smith, pp. 181–186, MCOHC.

55. Sulzberger, "Unification and the Marine Corps"; Heinl, "The Right to Fight"; Lieutenant Colonel James D. Hittle, "Sea Power and a National General Staff," *USNIP,* 75 (October 1949): 1091–1103; Arthur O. Sulzberger, "Concept for Catastrophe," *USNIP,* 79 (April 1953): 399–407; Appendix G, Commission on Organization of the Executive Branch of the Government, *Report* (Washington: Government Printing Office, 1949); House Committee on Armed Services, Hearing, "To Reorganize Fiscal Management in the National Military Establishment," 81st Congress, 1st Session, 1949; Senate Committee on Armed Services, Hearings, "National Security Act of 1949," 81st Congress, 1st Session, 1949; memo, Gen. O. N. Bradley, USA, May 10, 1948, Decimal File 045.3, Office of the C/S USA, RG 319; Gen. D. D. Eisenhower, memo for the Secretary of Defense, March 30, 1949, and Secretary of Defense L. H. Johnson to Secretary of the Navy, April 5, 1949, Louis H. Johnson File, Dwight D. Eisenhower Papers, Eisenhower Library; Secretary of the Navy to Distribution List, "Review of Developments under the National Security Act of 1947," October 28, 1948, Edson Papers; and Chairman, General Board, to Acting Secretary of the Navy, "Unification: The Navy's Future Course," July 27, 1949, General Board Records.

56. Statements of Gen. C. B. Cates, Gen. O. N. Bradley, USA, and Brig. Gen. V. E. Megee (assistant director, USMC aviation) in House Armed Services Committee, Hearings, "Unification and Strategy," 81st Congress, 2d Session, 1949; House Armed Services Committee, House Document 600, *Unification and Strategy,* 81st Congress, 2d Session, 1949; "Summary of the Marine Corps Position," *MCG,* 33 (December 1949): 17–19; and memoir of Brig. Gen. S. R. Shaw, pp. 184–204, MCOHC. See also Paul Y. Hammond, "Super Carriers and B-36 Bombers: Appropriations, Strategy and Politics" in Harold Stein, ed., *American Civil-Military Decisions* (Birmingham: University of Alabama Press, 1963), pp. 467–564.

57. *Congressional Record,* 81st Congress, 1st Session, 1949, pp. A660–A661, 1043, A1615–A1616, A3200, A4202–A4203, A4534–A4535, A5632–A5635, A6645–A6648, 8719, 9305–9309, 6781–6788, 10345–10349, 14781; Hammond, "Super Carriers and B-36 Bombers," in Stein, ed., *American Civil-Military Decisions,* pp. 546–554; and Edward A. Kolodziej, *The Uncommon Defense and Congress, 1945–1963* (Columbus: Ohio State University Press, 1966), pp. 89–123.

58. Memoir, Gen. G. C. Thomas, pp. 839–840; Robert Sherrod, "Get the Marines," January 13, 1950, unpublished ms., "Unification" File; and "The Report of the Secretaries of State and Defense on United States Objectives and Programs for National Security: NSC 68," April 7, 1950, reprinted in *Naval War College Review,* 27 (May–June 1975): 51–108.

CHAPTER 16. THE KOREAN WAR: FIGHTING ON TWO FRONTS, 1950–1953

1. Roy E. Appleman, *The United States Army in the Korean War: South to the Naktong, North to the Yalu* (Washington: Office of the Chief of Military History, 1961), pp. 1–35, and James F. Schnabel, *United States Army in the Korean War: Policy and Direction: The First Year* (Washington: Office of the Chief of Military History, 1972), pp. 1–40. The American military experience in Korea is authoritatively described in General Matthew B. Ridgway, USA (ret.), *The Korean War* (Garden City, N.Y.: Doubleday, 1967); General J. Lawton Collins, USA (ret.), *War in Peacetime* (Boston: Houghton Mifflin, 1969); Commander Malcolm W. Cagle and Commander Frank A.

Manson, USN, *The Sea War in Korea* (Annapolis: U.S. Naval Institute, 1957): James A. Field, Jr., *History of United States Naval Operations: Korea* (Washington: Naval History Division, 1962); and Robert F. Futrell, *The United States Air Force in Korea, 1950–1953* (New York: Duell, Sloan and Pearce, 1961). On Marine Corps operations, the basic source is Lynn Montross et al., *U.S. Marine Operations in Korea, 1950–1953,* 5 vols. (Washington: Historical Division, HQMC, 1954–1972), hereafter cited by individual volume.

2. Glenn D. Paige, *The Korean Decision* (New York: Free Press, 1968), and Dean Acheson, *The Korean War* (New York: Norton, 1971), pp. 1–31.

3. Schnabel, *Policy and Direction: The First Year,* pp. 80–99.

4. *Ibid.,* pp. 46–60; Cagle and Manson, *Sea War in Korea,* pp. 30–33; and Futrell, *United States Air Force in Korea,* pp. 4–7.

5. Appleman, *South to the Naktong, North to the Yalu,* pp. 109–247.

6. Gen. Cmdt. C. B. Cates, "Record of Events, 25 June–17 August, 1950," 1950, Clifton B. Cates Papers, MCPPC; Schnabel, *Policy and Direction: The First Year,* pp. 159–160; and Colonel Robert D. Heinl, Jr., *Victory at High Tide* (Philadelphia: Lippincott, 1968), pp. 14–17.

7. Cates, "Record of Events, 1950"; Schnabel, *Policy and Direction: The First Year,* pp. 160–164; Heinl, *Victory at High Tide,* pp. 18–24; and memoir of Gen. L. C. Shepherd, Jr. (1967), pp. 133–144, MCOHC.

8. Cates, "Record of Events, 1950"; *New York Times,* August 8, 1951; Cagle and Manson, *The Sea War in Korea,* pp. 47–51; Futrell, *The United States Air Force in Korea,* pp. 48–50, 112–116; and Collins, *War in Peacetime,* pp. 114–117.

9. Lynn Montross and Captain Nicholas Canzona, *U.S. Marine Operations in Korea: The Pusan Perimeter* (Washington: Historical Branch, HQMC, 1954), pp. 49–54, and Andrew Geer, *The New Breed: The Story of the U.S. Marines in Korea* (New York: Harper, 1952), pp. 1–11.

10. Captain Ernest H. Giusti, "Minute Men—1950 Model," *MCG,* 35 (September 1951): 22–31, and *idem, Mobilization of the Marine Corps Reserve in the Korean Conflict, 1950–1951* (Washington: Historical Branch, HQMC, 1951). The Giusti article, like many others about Korea that appeared in the *Marine Corps Gazette,* is part of a bound collection sponsored by the Marine Corps Association, *Our First Year in Korea* (Quantico, Va.: MCG, 1954). The basic official source for Marine Corps strength figures is HQMC, "Strength and Distribution," June 11, 1950, and "Marine Corps Personnel in Korea," May 28, 1953 in "Strength and Distribution" File, Reference Section, H&MD.

11. Appleman, *South to the Naktong, North to the Yalu,* 262–270.

12. Montross and Canzona, *The Pusan Perimeter,* pp. 87–156, and Geer, *The New Breed,* pp. 12–55. See also the memoir of Lt. Gen. Edward A. Craig, (1968), pp. 159–195, MCOHC.

13. Montross and Canzona, *The Pusan Perimeter,* pp. 173–206, and Geer, *The New Breed,* pp. 56–88.

14. Appleman, *South to the Naktong, North to the Yalu,* pp. 376–396, 454–487; Montross and Canzona, *The Pusan Perimeter,* pp. 207–244; and Geer, *The New Breed,* pp. 89–102.

15. Schnabel, *Policy and Direction: The First Year,* pp. 139–154; Cagle and Manson, *Sea War in Korea,* pp. 75–90; and Heinl, *Victory at High Tide,* pp. 18–38.

16. Maj. Gen. O. P. Smith, "Log," entries August 18–22, 1950, and *idem,* "Aide-Memoire—Korea, 1950–51," pp. 40–129, O. P. Smith Papers, MCPPC; memoirs of Gen. O. P. Smith (1969), pp. 193–215, and Lt. Gen. A. L. Bowser

(1970), pp. 176–225, MCOHC; and Lynn Montross and Captain Nicholas A. Canzona, *U.S. Marine Operations in Korea: The Inchon–Seoul Campaign* (Washington: Historical Branch, HQMC, 1955), pp. 53–72.

17. Heinl, *Victory at High Tide,* p. 42 ,and Collins, *War in Peacetime,* p. 118–127.

18. Heinl, *Victory at High Tide,* p. 45.

19. Montross and Canzona, *Inchon–Seoul Campaign,* pp. 73–124, and Geer, *The New Breed,* pp. 122–128.

20. Montross and Canzona, *Inchon–Seoul Campaign,* pp. 125–185, and Heinl, *Victory at High Tide,* pp. 121–150.

21. Montross and Canzona, *Inchon–Seoul Campaign,* pp. 187–292, and Heinl, *Victory at High Tide,* pp. 151–251.

22. Schnabel, *Policy and Direction: The First Year,* pp. 173–214.

23. Lynn Montross and Captain Nicholas A. Canzona, *U.S. Marine Operations in Korea: The Chosin Reservoir Campaign* (Washington: Historical Branch, HQMC, 1957), pp. 21–42.

24. *Ibid.,* pp. 43–124.

25. Smith, "Aide-Memoir, Korea, 1950–1951," pp. 446–577, Smith Papers; Montross and Canzona, *The Chosin Reservoir,* pp. 125–150; and Maj. Gen. O. P. Smith to Gen. Cmdt. C. B. Cates, November 15, 1950, Smith Papers.

26. Schnabel, *Policy and Direction: The First Year,* pp. 233–293, and Montross and Canzona, *The Chosin Reservoir Campaign,* pp. 125–150.

27. Montross and Canzona, *The Chosin Reservoir Campaign,* pp. 151–220, and Geer, *The New Breed,* pp. 270–326. See also Robert Leckie, *The March to Glory* (New York: World, 1960). An important analysis of the campaign is Smith, "Aide-Memoir, Korea, 1950–1951," pp. 727–1119.

28. Montross and Canzona, *The Chosin Reservoir Campaign,* pp. 249–303, and Geer, *The New Breed,* pp. 326–359.

29. For a professional analysis of the campaign, see Smith, "Aide-Memoir, Korea, 1950–1951," pp. 1162–1219; memoirs of Gen. O. P. Smith, pp. 215–259; and Lt. Gen. A. L. Bowser, pp. 235–250, MCOHC; Historical Division, HQMC, "Comments and Recommendations of the 1st Marine Division on the Chosin Reservoir Campaign," 1951, ms., Breckinridge Library, MCDEC; First Lieutenant Nicholas A. Canzona, "Reflections on Korea," *MCG,* 35 (November 1951): 56–65; and Col. S. L. A. Marshall, USAR, "Infantry Operations and Weapons Use in Korea," Report ORO-R-13, Operations Research Office, Johns Hopkins University, 1951.

  For favorable comment on the 1st Marine Division, see memoir of Gen. L. C. Shepherd, pp. 464–465, MCOHC; Smith, "Aide-Memoir, Korea, 1950–1951," pp. 974–978; entry for January 12, 1951, Smith, "Log" (note 16 above); Marguerite Higgins, *War in Korea* (Garden City, N.Y.: Doubleday, 1951); Keyes Beech, *Tokyo and Points East* (Garden City, Doubleday, 1954); and Maj. Gen. F. E. Lowe, USAR, "1st Marine Division in Korea," April 30, 1951, President's Secretary's Files, Truman Papers, Truman Library.

30. Entries for July 26–August 11, 1950, Cates, "Record of Events, 1950" (note 6 above); memo, Op-003, Office of the CNO, "Increase Naval Forces," July 13, 1951, Sherman Papers; *New York Times,* August 7, 8, 18, and 28, 1950; *Washington Post,* August 28, 1950; *U.S. News,* August 18, 1950; and *Congressional Record,* 81st Congress, 2d Session, pp. A5343, A6038. For the view from Headquarters, see especially memoir of Gen. G. C. Thomas (1966), pp. 841–852, MCOHC.

31. G. L. McDonough to H. S. Truman, August 21, 1950, and H. S. Truman to G. L. McDonough, August 29, 1950, copies in "McDonough Letter File," OF 1285-C, Truman Papers, and reprinted in the *Congressional Record,* 81st

Congress, 2d Session, p. A6323. For an explanation of the letter, see Maj. Gen. H. H. Vaughan, USAR (Truman's military aide), to W. H. Kyle, September 9, 1950, "McDonough Letter File."

32. H. S. Truman to Gen. Cmdt. C. B. Cates, September 6, 1950, OF 18-E, Truman Papers and Cates Papers. The four boxes of White House mail remain in OF 1285-C, "McDonough Letter Files." The reaction may be followed in "Truman vs. USMC Controversy" File, Reference Section, H&MD. See also Drew Pearson, "Washington Merry-Go-Round," *Washington Post,* September 11, 1950; *New York Times,* September 6–10; and *Congressional Record,* 81st Congress, 2d Session, pp. A6392, A6382, A6433, and 14165.

33. *Congressional Record,* 81st Congress, 1st Session, pp. 14384, 14399; *Congressional Record,* 81st Congress, 2d Session, pp. A363, 662; "Statement of Brig. Gen. Melvin J. Maas USMCR, president MCROA, September 5, 1950," copy in "Unification" Subject File; *U.S. News,* September 8, 15, and 18, 1950, and November 3, 1950; and Paul H. Douglas, *In the Fullness of Time* (New York: Harcourt Brace Jovanovich, 1972), pp. 346–348. For defense planning, see Schnabel, *Policy and Direction: The First Year,* pp. 274–293, 315–330, and Edward A. Kolodziej, *The Uncommon Defense and Congress, 1945–1963* (Columbus: Ohio State University Press, 1966), pp. 124–150.

34. Joseph C. Harsch to Dorothy Ford Mayhew, January 25, 1951, and Director of Public Information, HQMC, to CMC, March 29, 1951, with related news stories and memos, Brandt–Harsch File, Cates Papers; entries for January 14, 1951, March 21, 1951, and April 2–4, 1951, Smith "Log"; and Policy Analysis Division, HQMC, memo to CMC, "S.677–Douglas Bill," April 7, 1951, "S.677" File, Reference Section, H&MD.

35. Maj. Gen. Frank E. Lowe, USAR, to H. S. Truman, "Report of Mission, 2 August 1950–23 April 1950," April 30, 1951, Frank E. Lowe File, Truman Papers.

36. U.S. Senate, Committee on the Armed Services, Hearings: "Marine Corps Strength and Joint Chiefs Representation," April 13, 17, and 21, 1951, 82d Congress, 1st Session, Senate Report 308, May 2, 1951; and *New York Times,* May 2 and 5, 1951.

37. U.S. House of Representatives, Committee on the Armed Services, Hearings: "Fixing the Personnel Strength of the United States Marine Corps, Adding the Commandant of the Marine Corps as a Member of the Joint Chiefs of Staff," May 23–25, 1951, and June 25–26, 1951, and House Report 666, 82d Congress, 1st Session.

38. Testimony of Gen. Cmdt. C. B. Cates, House Hearings: "Marine Corps Strength," pp. 900–914; C. Vinson to M. Mansfield, May 8, 1951, and Mansfield to Vinson, May 7, 1951, S.677 bill jacket, archives of the House Armed Services Committee, NA; Acting Secretary of Defense R. A. Lovett to C. Vinson, May 22, 1951; memoir of Gen. G. C. Thomas, pp. 921–925, MCOHC; Hanson W. Baldwin columns in the *New York Times,* July 2, 1951 and August 31, 1951; and 1st Lt. Arthur Ochs Sulzberger, "Unification and the Marine Corps," 1933, ms. "Unification" File.

39. Ridgway, *The Korean War,* pp. 79–106 (note 1 above), and Lynn Montross, Major Hubard D. Kuokka, and Major Norman W. Hicks, *U.S. Marine Operations in Korea: The East-Central Front* (Washington: Historical Branch, HQMC, 1962), pp. 1–58.

40. Lynn Montross, "All in a Day's Work: Engineers and Shore Party in Korea," *MCG,* 36 (September 1952): 24–31; *idem,* "March of the Iron Cavalry: Marine Tanks in Korea," *MCG,* 36 (October 1952): 46–54; Kenneth W. Condit, "Marine Artillery in Korea," *MCG,* 36 (November 1952): 26–33; Lynn

Montross, "They Make Men Whole Again: The Medical Battalion and Chaplains in Korea," *MCG,* 36 (December 1952): 42–49; and Kenneth W. Condit, "Marine Supply in Korea," *MCG,* 37 (January 1953): 48–55.

41. Montross, Kuokka, and Hicks, *The East-Central Front,* pp. 76–78, 95–97; memoir of General G. C. Thomas, pp. 886–889, MCOHC; Futrell, *United States Air Force in Korea* (note 1 above), pp. 426–434; and Cagle and Manson, *Sea War in Korea* (note 1 above), pp. 222–280.

42. Montross, Kuokka, and Hicks, *The East-Central Front,* pp. 59–97, and Ridgway, *The Korean War,* pp. 107–123.

43. Montross, Kuokka, and Hicks, *The East-Central Front,* pp. 99–126.

44. *Ibid.,* pp. 127–161, 173–198; memoir of Gen. G. C. Thomas, pp. 853–897, MCOHC; and Major G. P. Averill, "Final Objective," *MCG,* 40 (August 1956): 10–16.

45. Montross, Kuokka, and Hicks, *The East-Central Front,* pp. 88–90, 107–108, 135–138, 142–145, 169–171, 185–186. See also Lieutenant Colonel A. Philips and Major H. D. Kuokka, "1st MAW in Korea," *MCG,* 41 (May 1957): 42–47, and 41 (June 1957): 20–26.

46. Lieutenant Colonel Eugene W. Rawlins, *Marines and Helicopters, 1946–1962* (Washington: History and Museums Division, HQMC, 1976), pp. 40–44, and Lynn Montross, *Cavalry of the Sky* (New York: Harper, 1954), pp. 109–155.

47. Montross, *Cavalry of the Sky,* pp. 156–179.

48. Conference Report, "Fixing the Personnel Strength of the United States Marine Corps and Establishing the Relationship of the Commandant of the Marine Corps to the Joint Chiefs of Staff," June 19, 1952, House Report 2199, 82d Congress, 2d Session; Carl Vinson to R. Terrill, April 8, 1952, bill jacket on S.677, archives of the House Armed Services Committee; *Congressional Record,* 82d Congress, 2d Session, pp. A2173, A2199, A2985, A3007, A3011, A3185, 5346, 7591; *New York Times,* May 17 and 20, 1952, and June 19, 20 and 29, 1952; and memoir of Gen. G. C. Thomas, pp. 921–925, MCOHC.

49. CMC to All Commanding Officers, "Status of U.S. Marine Corps within the Department of the Navy," September 21, 1953, "Roles and Missions" File, and Policy Analysis Division, HQMC, "Aide Memoire for the Commandant: Marine Corps–Navy Relationships," 1952, and "The 82d Congress Reaffirms the Status of the US Marine Corps as a Service," 1952, both "Unification" File.

50. CMC to Secretary of the Navy, September 1, 1951, and September 18, 1952, Command File, OA/NHD; HQMC, "Marine Corps Personnel in Korea," May 28, 1953, "Strength and Distribution" File; HDR-1, "Strength of the Marine Corps," December 11, 1969; and *Time,* July 23, 1951.

51. Kenneth W. Condit, Major John H. Johnstone, and Ella W. Nargele, *A Brief History of Headquarters Marine Corps Staff Organization* (Washington: Historical Division, HQMC, 1971), pp. 29–30; and memoir of Gen. Shepherd, pp. 476–483, MCOHC.

52. Henry I. Shaw, Jr., and Ralph W. Donnelly, *Blacks in the Marine Corps* (Washington: History and Museums Division, HQMC, 1975), pp. 59–64.

53. Lieutenant Colonel Kenneth J. Clifford, *Progress and Purpose: A Developmental History of the U.S. Marine Corps, 1900–1970* (Washington: History and Museums Division, HQMC, 1973), pp. 84–85, 91–93.

54. Rawlins, *Marines and Helicopters,* 46–47, 52–58.

55. *Ibid.,* pp. 48–51, 59–61, and *New York Times,* May 28, 1951, and November 15, 1951.

56. James A. MacDonald, "The Problems of U.S. Marine Corps Prisoners of War in Korea," M. A. thesis, University of Maryland, 1962, and Lieutenant Colonel

Pat Meid and Major James M. Yingling, *U.S. Marine Operations in Korea, 1950–1953: Operations in West Korea* (Washington: Historical Division, HQMC, 1972), pp. 399–443. See also Albert F. Biderman, *March to Calumny* (New York: Macmillan, 1963). Of 221 known Marine POWs, 194 returned from captivity.

57. Walter G. Hermes, *United States Army in the Korean War: Truce Tent and Fighting Front* (Washington: Office of the Chief of Military History, 1966), pp. 52–134.

58. Montross, Kuokka, and Hicks, *The East-Central Front* (note 39 above), pp. 199–246.

59. *Ibid.,* pp. 247–256, and Meid and Yingling, *Operations in West Korea,* pp. 1–17.

60. Meid and Yingling, *Operations in West Korea,* pp. 51–215.

61. *Ibid.,* p. 575; memoir of Gen. E. A. Pollock (1973), pp. 218–257, MCOHC; Major Norman W. Hicks, "U.S. Marine Operations in Korea, 1952–1953, with Special Emphasis on Outpost Warfare," M.A. thesis, University of Maryland, 1962; Lieutenant Colonel R. J. Batterson, Jr., "Random Notes on Korea," *MCG,* 39 (November 1955): 28–34; and First Lieutenant Peter Braestrup, "Back to the Trenches," *MCG,* 39 (March 1955): 32–35.

62. Meid and Yingling, *Operations in West Korea,* pp. 234–244; Lieutenant Colonel A. Phillips and Major H. D. Kuokka, "1st MAW in Korea," *MCG,* 41 (June 1957): 20–26; and Futrell, *United States Air Force in Korea,* pp. 439–508. When the war ended, the 1st MAW had suffered 258 killed and missing in action, 174 wounded in action, and 436 aircraft losses.

63. Meid and Yingling, *Operations in West Korea,* pp. 263–311. For life on the MLR in 1953, see Martin Russ, *The Last Parallel* (New York: Rinehart, 1957).

CHAPTER 17. BUILDING THE FORCE IN READINESS: YEARS OF TRIAL AND ACCOMPLISHMENT, 1953–1965

1. Douglas Kinnard, *President Eisenhower and Strategy Management* (Lexington: The University Press of Kentucky, 1977), and Glenn H. Snyder, "The 'New Look' of 1953," in Warner R. Schilling, Paul Y. Hammond, and Glenn H. Snyder, *Strategy, Politics, and Defense Budgets* (New York: Columbia University Press, 1962), pp. 279–524.

2. U.S. House of Representatives, Subcommittee of the Committee on Appropriations, Hearings: "Navy Appropriations FY 1954," 83d Congress, 1st Session (1953), pp. 5–11, 29–105, 369–370, 431–436; U.S. Senate, Subcommittee of the Committee on Appropriations, Hearings: Navy Appropriations FY 1954," 83d Congress, 1st Session (1953), pp. 93–96, 1026–1028, 1806–1815; *Annual Report of the Commandant of the Marine Corps to the Secretary of the Navy for FY 1954,* H&MD; memoir of Gen. L. C. Shepherd (1967), pp. 484–486, MCOHC; and *New York Times,* September 12, 1953, and December 19, 1953.

3. Policy Analysis Division, HQMC, "A History of Marine Corps Roles and Missions, 1775–1970," "Roles and Missions" Subject File, Reference Section, H&MD; memoirs of Gen. G. C. Thomas (1966), pp. 933–942, and Lt. Gen. R. B. Luckey (1969), pp. 210–212, MCOHC; *ANJ,* May 8, 1954; and Green Letter 2-56, January 20, 1956, Gen. Wallace M. Greene, Jr., Papers, MCPPC. Green Letters, initiated in the 1950s, are personal newsletters on policy from the Commandant to all other Marine general officers.

4. U.S. Senate, Subcommittee of the Committee on Appropriations, Hearings:

"Department of Defense Appropriations FY 1955," 83d Congress, 2d Session (1954), pp. 595–596; U.S. House of Representatives, Subcommittee of the Committee on Appropriations, Hearings: "Department of the Navy Appropriations FY 1955," 83d Congress, 2d Session (1954), pp. 1–10, 71–85; U.S. House of Representatives, Subcommittee of the Committee on Appropriations, Hearings: "Department of the Navy Appropriations FY 1956," 84th Congress, 1st Session (1955), pp. 15–135, 345–350; *Annual Report of the Commandant to the Secretary of the Navy FY 1955* H&MD; *New York Times,* January 18, 1955, June 18, 21, and 30, 1955, July 1, 15, and 18, 1955, August 3, 1955, and September 30, 1955; and Edward A. Kolodziej, *The Uncommon Defense and Congress, 1945–1963* (Columbus: Ohio State University Press, 1966), pp. 180–225.

5. U.S. House of Representatives, Subcommittee of the Committee on Appropriations, Hearings: "Department of the Navy Appropriations FY 1957," 84th Congress, 2d Session (1956), pp. 100–165; and *Annual Report of the Commandant to the Secretary of the Navy FY 1956,* H&MD.

6. Extract, "Notes on the Commandant's Weekly Conference, 21 April 1953," and Col. D. M. Shoup to CMC, "Fiscal Division, U.S. Marine Corps," March 16, 1953, both General David M. Shoup Papers, Hoover Institution of War, Peace, and Revolution; memoir of Maj. Gen. C. R. Allen (1969), pp. 315–345, MCOHC; *New York Times,* January 15, 1955; and *ANJ,* July 22, 1961.

7. Kenneth W. Condit, Major John H. Johnstone, and Ella W. Nargele, *A Brief History of Headquarters Marine Corps Staff Organization* (Washington: Historical Division, HQMC, 1971), pp. 30–32; Lieutenant General E. A. Pollock, "How the New Management Program Works in the Marine Corps' Largest Command," *Armed Forces Management* 3 (March 1957), pp. 15–16; *New York Times,* December 11, 1957; Brigadier General W. P. Battell, "EDP and Marine Corps Supply," *Armed Forces Management* 5 (July 1959), pp. 27–29.

8. Memoir of Lt. Gen. J. P. Berkeley (1969), pp. 348–389, MCOHC; Bernard C. Nalty and Lieutenant Colonel Ralph F. Moody, *A Brief History of U.S. Marine Corps Officer Procurement, 1775–1969* (Washington: Historical Division, HQMC, 1970), pp. 19–21; *New York Times,* September 29, 1956, and February 28, 1959; and *ANJ,* August 15, 1959. General Berkeley, G-1 HQMC, 1955–1959, described both officer and enlisted problems, as did Commandant R. McC. Pate in his testimony, U.S. Senate, Subcommittee of the Committee on the Armed Services, Hearings: "Military Pay," 85th Congress, 1st and 2d Sessions (1958), pp. 359–410.

9. "Military Pay" Hearings; Lieutenant Colonel R. D. Heinl, Jr., "NCOs—A Challenge from Within," *MCG,* 38 (November 1954): 43–52; *ANJ,* November 23, 1957; and Bernard C. Nalty et al., *United States Marine Corps Ranks and Grades, 1775–1969* (Washington: Historical Division, HQMC, 1970), pp. 39–43.

10. Lieutenant Colonel Eugene W. Rawlings, *Marines and Helicopters* (Washington: History and Museums Division, HQMC, 1976), pp. 61–65; "Proceedings," Marine Corps Aviation Board, February 4, 1955, Lt. Gen. Keith B. McCutcheon Papers, MCPPC; CNO to CMC, "Marine Aviation," January 12, 1955, encl. 31 to Aviation Board "Proceedings"; and memoir of Lt. Gen. W. J. Van Ryzin (1975), pp. 152–159, MCOHC.

11. Rawlins, *Marines and Helicopters,* pp. 65–69, and Landing Force Bulletin 17, "Concept of Future Amphibious Operations," December 13, 1955, HAF 453, Breckinridge, Library, MCDEC.

12. HQMC, "Report of the Fleet Marine Force Organization and Composition Board," January 7, 1957, HAF, Breckinridge Library, and memoir of Gen.

R. E. Hogaboom (1970), pp. 328–329. The board findings were summarized in a series of articles in the *Marine Corps Gazette,* 4 (April 1957): 26–30; 4 (May 1957): 10–12; 4 (June 1957): 8–12; and 4 (July 1957): 20–24.

13. Memoir of Gen. V. E. Megee (1967), pp. 218–221, MCOHC.

14. The basic evidence on the Ribbon Creek incident is summarized in "Findings, Court of Inquiry, and 1st Endorsement Commanding General, Marine Corps Recruit Depot, Parris Island," April 24, 1956, copy in "Ribbon Creek" Subject File, Reference Section, H&MD. Other sources are U.S. House of Representatives, Committee on the Armed Services, Hearings: "Report of the Commandant on Parris Island Incident," 84th Congress, 2d Session (1956), pp. 7153–7191; the extensive press coverage in "Ribbon Creek" Subject File; and Brigadier General William B. McKean, USMC (ret.) *Ribbon Creek* (New York: Dial Press, 1958). More balanced is the memoir of Lt. Gen. Joseph C. Burger (1969), pp. 287–302, MCOHC. The most complete single set of documents is the Ribbon Creek collection in the Greene Papers.

15. CMC to Secretary of the Navy, 2d Endorsement on Ribbon Creek Court of Inquiry, April 30, 1956, in Hearings: "Parris Island Incident," pp. 7155–7157; testimony of General Pate and Representative Vinson in Hearings: "Parris Island Incident," May 1, 1956, pp. 7154–7155, 7157–7160, 7164–7167; *New York Times,* April 10–16, 1956; and *Time,* April 23, 1956, and May 14, 1956.

16. Testimony of General Pate, Hearings: "Parris Island Incident," pp. 7154–7155, 7158–7159; "Findings, Court of Inquiry and 1st Endorsement Commanding General, Marine Corps Recruit Depot, Parris Island," reprinted in Hearings: "Parris Island Incident," pp. 7167–7180; memoirs of Lt. Gen. Burger and Gen. R. E. Hogaboom (1970), pp. 325–328, MCOHC; and *New York Times,* April 14–16, 1956.

17. Green Letter 15–56, June 14, 1956, and "Policy of Commandant Governing Recruit Training," May 1, 1956, copies in Greene Papers, and *New York Times,* May 1–8, 1956.

18. Hearings: "Ribbon Creek Incident," pp. 7180–7191; *New York Times,* May 11, 1956; and "Ribbon Creek Incident" documents in USMC Subject File OF-3-B-17, Central Files, Presidential Papers, Dwight D. Eisenhower Papers.

19. *New York Times,* June 10, 1956, and File, "Remarks of Marines on Recruit Training," 1956, Shoup Papers.

20. *New York Times,* July 14–August 5, 1956, and McKean, *Ribbon Creek,* pp. 274–402, 410–500.

21. *New York Times,* August 5–October 9, 1956, and February 19, 1959.

22. Maj. Gen. D. M. Shoup to Brig. Gen. W. M. Greene, Jr, August 14, 1956, Shoup Papers, and Green Letter 8–57, February 27, 1957, with enclosure "Reactions of Recruits to Recruit Training," December 1956, copies in Greene Papers.

23. Green Letter 4–57, "Extract of Remarks by Commandant of the Marine Corps to Senior Staff, HQMC," January 15, 1957, copy in Greene Papers; Brig. Gen. V. H. Krulak to Gen. R. McC. Pate, November 4, 1957, copy in "Roles and Missions" Subject File, Reference Section, H&MD; *New York Times,* October 13 and 30, 1956, November 13–19, 1956, February 7–26, 1957, March 9–15, 1957, July 22, 1957, and April 9–10, 1958. See also G. L. Rockwell, "Who Wants Panty-Waist Marines?" *American Mercury,* 84 (April 1957): 117–122; W. V. Kennedy, "Marine Corps Brutality," *America,* 98 (March 1, 1958): 621; R. L. Allen, "Making of a Marine," *Ladies Home Journal,* 76 (February 1959): 172; J. H. Baird, "Correspondent Finds Training Tough at Parris Island but Not Cruel," *Army Navy Air Force Register*

(*ANAFR*) 78 (February 16, 1957): 5, 7; and W. Phillips, "Inspection of Marine Drill Instructors," *New York Times Magazine,* February 12, 1957, pp. 12–13.

24. Kinnard, *President Eisenhower and Strategy Management* (note 1 above), pp. 37–122; Kolodziej, *The Uncommon Defense and Congress* (note 4 above), pp. 253–324; and Special Studies Report II of the Rockefeller Brothers Fund, *International Security: The Military Aspect* (New York: Doubleday, 1958). For an overview of Marine Corps policies and programs, see Headquarters Marine Corps, *Annual Reports of the Commandant to the Secretary of the Navy, FY 1957–FY 1959,* H&MD.

25. Green Letter 4–57, January 14, 1957, Greene Papers; HQMC, "Commandant's Position on Marine Corps Strength," March, 1958 "Strength and Distribution," File, Reference Section, H&MD; interview with General R. McC. Pate, "New Marine Cut Dangerous," *ANAFR,* 78 (October 1957): 3, 12; Major General R. E. Hogaboom, "Combat Staying Power Will Be Reduced by Personnel Cuts," *ANAFR,* 78 (November 16, 1958): 12–13; Green Letter 24–59, November 9, 1959, Greene Papers; U.S. Senate, Subcommittee of the Committee on Appropriations, Hearings: "Department of Defense Appropriations FY 1958," 85th Congress, 1st Session (1957), pp. 261–268; U.S. House of Representatives, Subcommittee of the Committee on Appropriations, Hearings: "Department of Defense Appropriations FY 1961," 86th Congress, 1st Session (1959), pp. 488, 491–492; G-1 HQMC, memo, "Proposed FY 1960 Manpower Guidelines," May 28, 1958, "Strength and Distribution" File, Reference Section, H&MD; and Lt. Gen. W. M. Greene, Jr., to Sen. S. Symington, June 6, 1960, Greene Papers.

26. U.S. Senate, Subcommittee of the Committee on Appropriations, Hearings: "Department of Defense Appropriations FY 1960," 86th Congress, 1st Session (1959), pp. 181–187; U.S. House of Representatives, Subcommittee of the Committee on Appropriations, Hearings: "Department of Defense Appropriations FY 1960," 86th Congress, 1st Session (1959), pp. 488, 491, 436–449; U.S. House of Representatives, Subcommittee of the Committee on Appropriations, Hearings: "Department of Defense Appropriations FY 1961," 86th Congress, 2d Session (1960), pp. 68–70, 133–134, 472–473; and *Annual Reports of the Commandant to the Secretary of the Navy for FY 1957–1959,* H&MD.

27. *Annual Report of the Commandant to the Secretary of the Navy for FY 1959,* H&MD; Rawlins, *Marines and Helicopters* (note 10 above), pp. 87–89; Senate Subcommittee Hearings, "Defense Appropriations FY 1958," pp. 607, 616, 639, 788, 803–809; House Subcommittee Hearings, "Defense Appropriations FY 1960," pp. 403, 421, 434, 450, 482, 488–490, 497; Major General J. P. Berkeley, "The Marine Corps Revolution in Transportation," *National Defense Transportation Journal,* 15 (November–December 1959): 33, 79–80, 95; and *ANAFR,* July 29, 1961.

28. For a summary of Marine aviation trends, 1952–1967, see "Marine Aviation," proceedings, General Officers Symposium, 1963, Operational Archives, H&MD.

29. House Subcommittee Hearings, "Defense Appropriations FY 1961," Part 2, pp. 183–184, and Part 5, p. 146, and Lieutenant Colonel Kenneth J. Clifford, *Progress and Purpose: A Developmental History of the United States Marine Corps, 1900–1970* (Washington: History and Museums Division, HQMC, 1973), pp. 88–90.

30. Memo, "The Marine Corps Board Biennial Review of the Fleet Marine Force Structure and Composition," 1959, copy in Greene Papers; Berkeley, "The

Marine Corps Revolution in Transportation"; House Subcommittee Hearings, "Defense Department Appropriations FY 1960," Part 1, pp. 451–481, 492, 501, and Part 5, pp. 260–270; and House Subcommittee Hearings, "Defense Department Appropriations FY 1961," Part 2, pp. 46–47, 97–102 and 144.

31. *Annual Reports of the Commandant to the Secretary of the Navy for FY 1958, FY 1959, and FY 1960,* H&MD.

32. Lt. Gen. E. A. Pollock to Maj. Gen. D. M. Shoup, October 15 and 31, 1957, and Maj. Gen. D. M. Shoup to Maj. Gen. F. M. McAlister, November 18, 1957, all Shoup Papers; Maj. Gen. E. W. Snedeker to Brig. Gen. W. M. Greene, Jr., June 20, 1958, and Green Letter 24–58, "Personnel Instability," September 19, 1958, both Greene Papers; Maj. Gen. J. P. Berkeley to Lt. Gen. W. M. Greene, Jr., August 28, 1961, Greene Papers; and *Annual Report of the Commandant to the Secretary of the Navy for FY 1961,* H&MD.

33. Public Affairs Unit 4-1, *The Marine Corps Reserve: A History* (Washington: Division of Reserve, HQMC, 1966), pp. 181–218, and House Subcommittee Hearings, "Defense Department Appropriations FY 1960," pp. 416–463, 477–478.

34. COM 6th FLT to CNO, OPNAV Report 5750-5, "History of the Sixth Fleet," 1959, Command File, Operational Archives H&MD.

35. Jack Shulimson, *Marines in Lebanon 1958* (Washington: Historical Branch, HQMC, 1966), pp. 1–10. See also participant accounts by Brigadier General Sidney S. Wade, "Operation Bluebat," *MCG,* 43 (July 1959): 10–23; Colonel Harry A. Hadd, "Orders Firm But Flexible," *USNIP,* 88 (October 1962): 81–89; and Robert McClintock (U.S. Ambassador to Lebanon, 1958), "The American Landing in Lebanon," *USNIP,* 88 (October 1962): 65–72, 74–77, 79.

36. Shulimson, *Marines in Lebanon,* pp. 11–15.

37. *Ibid.,* pp. 16–36.

38. Summaries of Pate's testimony, Green Letters 14–58 (May 7, 1959) and 17–58 (July 7, 1958), copies in Greene Papers; Kinnard, *President Eisenhower and Strategy Management* (note 1 above), pp. 89–93; and John C. Ries, *The Management of Defense* (Baltimore: Johns Hopkins Press, 1964), pp. 167–192.

39. U.S. Senate, Committee on Armed Services, Hearings: "Department of Defense Reorganization Act of 1958," 85th Congress, 2d Session (1958), and U.S. House of Representatives, Committee on Armed Services, Hearings: "Reorganization of the Department of Defense," 85th Congress, 2d Session (1958).

40. Senate Committee on Armed Services, "Department of Defense Reorganization Act," pp. 193–198, 352–357, 368–377; "Marine Corps Board Study on Effects of Department of Defense Reorganization Act of 1958," Green Letter 12–59, March 20, 1959, copy in Greene Papers; and George B. Kistiakowsky, *A Scientist in the White House* (Cambridge, Mass.: Harvard University Press, 1976), pp. 126–127, 404.

41. Acting Secretary of Defense T. S. Gates to the President, "Designation, Appointment and Assignment—General Officers," September 24, 1959, and Secretary of the Navy W. B. Franke to Acting Secretary of Defense T. S. Gates, September 21, 1959, Marine Corps File (1959), OF 3-B-17, White House Central Files, Eisenhower Papers, and memoir of Gen. R. E. Hogaboom (note 16 above), pp. 334–339.

42. Memoir of Gen. R. E. Hogaboom, pp. 334–339; memoir of Gen. David M. Shoup (1972), pp. 19–25, oral history collection, Eisenhower Library; and *New York Times,* August 13 and 28, 1959, September 10, 11, and 26, 1959, and November 10, 1959.

43. Green Letter 1–60, "CMC Remarks of 4 January 1960," January 4, 1960, copy in Greene Papers, and memoirs of Lt. Gen. C. H. Hayes (1970), pp. 224–225, and Lt. Gen. L. J. Fields (1971), pp. 239–241, MCOHC.

44. MCBul 5720, "Remarks by Commandant of the Marine Corps to Staff," January 4, 1961, Greene Papers; *Annual Report of the Commandant to the Secretary of the Navy FY 1961,* H&MD; *New York Times,* January 19, 1960, February 9, 1960, and June 11, 1960; *ARNAFJ,* August 13, 1960; and Lt. Gen. W. M. Greene, Jr. to G. F. Eliot, July 22, 1960, Greene Papers.

45. Memoir of Lt. Gen. Hayes, pp. 221; Theodore Sorenson, *Kennedy* (New York: Harper and Row, 1965), pp. 606–608; *ARNAFJ,* June 3, 1961; *New York Times,* May 26, 1961, and July 26 and 27, 1961; Brig. Gen. R. E. Cushman, Jr., to Lt. Gen. W. M. Greene, Jr., November 18, 1960, Greene Papers; Lawrence J. Korb, *The Joint Chiefs of Staff* (Bloomington: Indiana University Press, 1976), pp. 111–121; and David Halberstam, *The Best and the Brightest* (New York: Random House, 1969), pp. 66–67.

46. Policy Analysis Division, HQMC, "A History of Marine Corps Roles and Missions," 1970, pp. 17–18; *New York Times,* July 26 and 27, 1961; and U.S. Senate, Committee on Appropriations, Hearings: "Department of Defense Appropriations FY 1963," 87th Congress, 2d Session (1962), pp. 242–245, 378, 514–518. For background see Kolodziej, *The Uncommon Defense and Congress* (note 4 above), pp. 325–429, and Alain C. Enthoven and K. Wayne Smith, *How Much Is Enough? Shaping the Defense Program, 1961–1969* (New York: Harper and Row, 1971), pp. 1–72.

47. U.S. House of Representatives, Committee on Armed Forces, Hearings: "Military Posture and Appropriations FY 1964," 88th Congress, 1st Session (1963), p. 449.

48. CMC ltr. A03B15, "Policy on Deployment and Employment of Marine Corps Forces," September 25, 1963, copy in McCutcheon Papers.

49. Comptroller General of the United States, *Review of Supply Management Activities United States Marine Corps* (Washington: GAO, 1960), copy in Shoup Papers.

50. "Fiscal Highlights," proceedings, General Officers Symposium 1963, copy in Greene Papers; Comptroller General of the United States, *Overprocurement of Ammunition by the United States Marine Corps* (Washington: GAO, 1964), *idem, Procurement of Spare Parts and Assemblies in Excess of Current Needs by the United States Marine Corps* (Washington: GAO, 1965), *idem, Readiness of Combat and Combat Support Equipment Assigned to the 2d Marine Division and Force Troops, Camp Lejeune* (Washington: GAO, 1965), copies in Executive FG 125-5, White House Central File, Lyndon B. Johnson Papers, Johnson Library, Austin, Texas; U.S. House of Representatives, Subcommittee of the Committee on Appropriations, Hearings: "Department of Defense Appropriations FY 1965," 88th Congress, 2d Session (1964), pp. 379–385; and memoir of Lt. Gen. Van Ryzin (note 10 above), pp. 188–195.

51. MCO 3340.3, "Employment of Marine Air-Ground Task Forces in Amphibious Operations," April 20, 1962, McCutcheon Papers; CMC ltr A03B15, "Policy on Deployment and Employment of Marine Corps Forces," September 25, 1963, McCutcheon Papers; MCO 003410.1B, "Marine Corps Cold War Plan—1965," June 10, 1964, McCutcheon Papers; and Green Letter 8–65, "A Long-Range Marine Corps Concept," May 3, 1965, Greene Papers.

52. Testimony of Gen. D. M. Shoup, House Armed Services Committee Hearings: "Defense Appropriations FY 1964," p. 909.

53. "Problems Relating to Counterinsurgency," proceedings, General Officers Symposium, 1962; CMC ltr A03B15, "Policy on Deployment and Employment of

Marine Corps Forces"; MCO 003410.1B, "Marine Corps Cold War Plan—
1965." June 10, 1964; and memoir of Lt. Gen. V. H. Krulak (1970), pp. 188–
189, 206, MCOHC. The Corps position that counterinsurgency was counterguerrilla warfare may be sampled in two publications that received favorable
official scrutiny in the early 1960s: the official U.S. Marine Corps, *Operations
Against Guerilla Forces,* FMFM 8–2 (1962, rev. 1965), and the semiofficial
Lieutenant Colonel T. H. Greene, ed., *The Guerrilla—And How to Fight Him*
(New York: Praeger, 1962). For additional background, see Douglas S.
Blaufarb, *The Counterinsurgency Era* (New York: Free Press, 1977) pp. 52–
88.

54. "Chief of Staff's Remarks," proceedings, General Officers Symposium, 1962,
OA/HMD, and "Relationships Resulting from General Orders No. 5 and 19,"
proceedings, General Officers Symposium, 1965.
55. *New York Times,* October 28 and 29, 1961.
56. This incident may be followed in "Muzzling File, 1961" and "CMC Press
Conference File" in the Shoup Papers, as well as *Congressional Record,* 87th
Congress, 1st Session (1962), pp. 1903–1914, and Green Letter 1–63, "Remarks of the Commandant of the Marine Corps to Staff," January 3, 1963,
Greene Papers.
57. "Problems Relating to Naval Gunfire Support and Amphibious Shipping," proceedings, General Officers Symposium 1962.
58. "Logistics," proceedings, General Officers Symposium, 1964, OA/HMD; House
Armed Services Committee Hearings: "Defense Appropriations FY 1964,"
pp. 445, 981; and Subcommittee of the Committee on Appropriations, Hearings: "Defense Appropriations FY 1965," Part 3, pp. 350–364.
59. House Armed Service Committee Hearings: "Defense Appropriations FY
1964," pp. 447–450, and DC/S (Air), "Harrier AV-6B Program," n.d.
[1969?], McCutcheon Papers.
60. Rawlins, *Marines and Helicopters* (note 10 above), pp. 82–86, and House
Armed Services Committee Hearings: "Defense Appropriations FY 1964," pp.
941–943, 976, 991. For Army airmobile doctrine and development, see Lieutenant General John J. Tolson, USA, *Vietnam Studies: Airmobility, 1961–
1971* (Washington: Department of the Army, 1973), pp. 3–24.
61. *Annual Reports of the Commandant to the Secretary of the Navy, FY 1962–
FY 1964.*
62. *Annual Reports of the Commandant to the Secretary of the Navy for FY 1962–
FY 1964;* "Commanding General Fleet Marine Force, Atlantic Remarks,"
proceedings, General Officers Symposium, 1964; memoir of Lt. Gen. J. P.
Berkeley (1969), pp. 412–470, MCOHC; and Lieutenant Colonel James P.
Soper, "Observations: STEEL PIKE and SILVER LANCE," *USNIP,* 91 (November 1965): 46–58.
63. "Commanding General Fleet Marine Force, Atlantic," GOS, 1964.
64. Captain Robert H. Whitlow, *U.S. Marines in Vietnam: The Advisory and
Combat Assistance Era, 1954–1964* (Washington: History and Museums Division, HQMC, 1977), pp. 86–95.
65. *Ibid.,* pp. 16–85, 99–165.
66. For the Cuban Missile Crisis, see especially Roger Hilsman, *To Move a Nation*
(New York: Dell, 1964), pp. 159–229; Graham Allison, *Essence of Decision*
(Boston: Little, Brown), and Herbert S. Dinerstein, *The Making of a Missile
Crisis, October 1962* (Baltimore: Johns Hopkins Press, 1976). For a definitive account of military plans and deployments, see HQ CINCLANT, "Historical Account of Cuban Crisis—1962," ms. history, April 1963, Operational
Archives, H&MD.

67. HQ CINCLANT, "Historical Account of Cuban Crisis—1962."

68. "HQMC Role—Cuban Deployments," proceedings, General Officers Symposium, 1963; House Armed Services Committee Hearings, "Defense Appropriations FY 1964," pp. 908–909, 959, 966, 998–999, 1007–1008; and House Subcommittee of the Committee on Appropriations Hearings, "Defense Appropriations FY 1964," pp. 1–85.

69. For the political context of the Dominican intervention, see Abraham F. Lowenthal, *The Dominican Intervention* (Cambridge, Mass.: Harvard University Press, 1972), and Jerome Slater, *Intervention and Negotiation: The United States and the Dominican Intervention* (New York: Harper and Row, 1972).

70. Major Jack K. Ringler and Henry I. Shaw, Jr., *U.S. Marine Corps Operations in the Dominican Republic, April–June, 1965* (Washington: Historical Division, HQMC, 1970), pp. 13–29. See also Major General R. McC. Tompkins, "Ubique," *MCG,* 49 (September 1965): 32–39.

71. Tad Szulc, *Dominican Diary* (New York: Delacorte, 1965), p. 123.

72. Ringler and Shaw, *Marine Operations in the Dominican Republic,* pp. 29–43, and "Chief of Staff's Overview," proceedings, General Officers Symposium, 1965.

73. Testimony of Gen. W. M. Greene, Jr., U.S. House of Representatives, Subcommittee of the Committee on Appropriations, Hearings: "Department of Defense Appropriations FY 1964," 88th Congress, 2d Session (1964), p. 542. See also General W. M. Greene, Jr., "Our Posture Is the Most Favorable in the History of Our Corps," *Armed Forces Management,* 12 (November 1965): 56–58.

74. "Operations, Training, Readiness, and Readiness Reporting," proceedings, General Officers Symposium, 1965.

CHAPTER 18. THE LONGEST WAR:
THE MARINES IN VIETNAM, 1965–1975

1. General Lewis W. Walt, *Strange War, Strange Strategy* (New York: Funk and Wagnalls, 1970), p. 5.

2. Charles Coe, *Young Man in Vietnam* (New York: Four Winds Press, 1968), pp. 33, 46.

3. Among the authoritative works on Vietnam, see Joseph Buttinger, *Vietnam: A Dragon Embattled,* 2 vols. (New York: Praeger, 1967); Bernard B. Fall, *The Two Vietnams,* rev. ed. (New York: Praeger, 1964); Department of the Army Pamphlet 550-40, *Area Handbook for Vietnam,* rev. ed. (Washington: Government Printing Office, 1964); and Douglas Pike, *Viet Cong* (Cambridge, Mass.: MIT Press, 1966).

4. For the history of the American commitment in Vietnam, see especially Chester L. Cooper, *The Lost Crusade: America in Vietnam* (New York: Dodd, Mead, 1970); Gunther Lewy, *America in Vietnam* (New York: Oxford University Press, 1978); and Leslie H. Gelb with Richard K. Betts, *The Irony of Vietnam: The System Worked* (Washington: Brookings Institution, 1979). For military analyses, see Commander in Chief Pacific and Commander U.S. Military Assistance Command Vietnam, *Report on the War in Vietnam* (Washington: GPO, 1969); Colonel Dave R. Palmer, USA, *Summons of the Trumpet: U.S.-Vietnam in Perspective* (San Rafael, Calif.: Presidio Press, 1978); and General William C. Westmoreland, USA (ret.), *A Soldier Reports* (Garden City, N.Y.: Doubleday, 1976). On President Johnson and the war, see especially Doris Kearns, *Lyndon Johnson and the American Dream* (New York: Harper and Row, 1976).

The process of broadening the American military commitment and the assumptions upon which that policy was based may be followed in *The Pentagon Papers: The Defense Department History of United States Decision-making on Vietnam: The Senator Gravel Edition,* 5 vols. (Boston: Little, Brown, 1975), particularly Vol IV. For the role of the Marine Corps before 1965, see Captain Robert H. Whitlow, *U.S. Marines in Vietnam: The Advisory and Combat Assistance Era, 1954–1964* (Washington: History and Museums Division, HQMC, 1977). The most comprehensive treatment of the Corps and the war in one volume is Brigadier General Edwin H. Simmons, USMC (ret.) et al., *The Marines in Vietnam, 1954–1973: An Anthology and Annotated Bibliography* (Washington: History and Museums Division, HQMC, 1974), a collection of articles taken largely from *USNIP* and *MCG.*

5. Lt. Col. John J. Cahill and Jack Shulimson, "History of U.S. Marine Corps Operations in Vietnam, January–June 1965, ms. history, H&MD, pp. 25–55; and CG FMF PAC to CINCPAC, May 29, 1964, and CG FMF PAC to CINCPAC, memo, "Contingencies in Vietnam," September 24, 1964, Lt. Gen. Victor H. Krulak Papers, MCPPC.

6. Marine deployments and operations in 1965 are described in Jack Shulimson and Major Charles M. Johnson, *U.S. Marines in Vietnam, 1965: The Landing and the Buildup* (Washington: History and Museums Division, HQMC, 1978), and Brigadier General Edwin H. Simmons, "Marine Corps Operations in Vietnam, 1965–1966," in Simmons et al., *The Marines in Vietnam,* pp. 27–59. I have also used earlier studies, especially Historical Division, HQMC, "U.S. Marines in Vietnam," ms. history, 1970, in seven parts with appendices, and HQ FMF PAC, "Operations of the III Marine Amphibious Force Vietnam," monthly and seminannual reports, 1965–1971, 13 vols., H&MD. For policy-making, see "Phase I in the Build-up of U.S. Forces, March–July 1965," in *Pentagon Papers: Gravel Edition,* III: 433–485. Actually, only one of 9th MEB's two battalions landed; the second battalion flew to Da Nang from Okinawa.

7. CG FMF PAC to CINCPAC, May 14, 1956; CG FMF PAC, "A Strategic Concept for the Republic of Vietnam," June 1965; CG FMF PAC to CMC, July 7, 1965; Lt. Gen. V. H. Krulak to Maj. Gen. L. W. Walt, July 26, 1965; and Lt. Gen. V. H. Krulak to Secretary of Defense R. S. McNamara, November 11, 1965, Krulak Papers. For Westmoreland's position, see "Phase I in the Build-up of U.S. Forces," *Pentagon Papers: Gravel Edition,* III: 462–485, and Westmoreland, *A Soldier Reports,* pp. 144–155, 164–167.

8. Interview with Lt. Gen. V. H. Krulak, June 22, 1970, MCOHC; memoir of Maj. Gen. R. H. Barrow (1973), pp. 3–9, MCOHC; Col. J. R. Chaisson (G-3 III MAF) to Mrs. Chaisson, February 5, 1966, Lt. Gen. John R. Chaisson Papers, Hoover Institution for War, Peace and Revolution; Westmoreland, *A Soldier Reports,* pp. 164–167, 202–203; and Shulimson and Johnson, *U.S. Marines in Vietnam 1965,* pp. 36–49.

9. Memoir of Maj. Gen Barrow, pp. 20–23, and interview with Lt. Gen. J. R. Chaisson, April 3, 1972, pp. 22–28, MCOHC; CG FMF PAC to CINCPAC, April 27, 1965, Krulak Papers; and Shulimson and Johnson, *U.S. Marines in Vietnam 1965,* pp. 193–203.

10. Shulimson and Johnson, *U.S. Marines in Vietnam 1965,* pp. 149–163, and Lieutenant General Keith B. McCutcheon, "Marine Aviation in Vietnam, 1962–1970," in Simmons et al., *The Marines in Vietnam,* pp. 162–180.

11. For logistics, see Lt. Col. Ralph F. Moody, Maj. Thomas E. Donnelly, and Capt. Moyers S. Shore III, "Backing Up the Troops," Chapter 22, Part VII of "U.S. Marines in Vietnam," ms. history, 1970; Shulimson and Johnson, *U.S. Marines in Vietnam 1965,* pp. 181–190; Colonel James B. Soper, "A View of

FMF PAC Logistics in the Western Pacific, 1965–1971," in Simmons et al., *The Marines in Vietnam,* pp. 200–217; Vice Admiral Edwin B. Hooper, USN (ret.), *Mobility, Support, Endurance: A Story of Naval Operational Logistics in the Vietnam War, 1965–1968* (Washington: Naval History Division, 1972); and Committee on Government Operations, U.S. House of Representatives, "Military Supply Systems: Lessons from the Vietnam Experience," House Report 91-1586, 91st Congress, 2d Session (Washington: Government Printing Office, 1970).

12. Captain Russel H. Stolfi, *U.S. Marine Corps Civic Action in Vietnam, March 1965–March 1966* (Washington: Historical Branch, HQMC, 1968), and Shulimson and Johnson, *U.S. Marines in Vietnam 1965,* pp. 115–146.

13. Gordon Baxter, *13/13 Vietnam: Search and Destroy* (Cleveland: World Publishing, 1967), p. 87.

14. For the CAP program in both strategic and personal terms, see F. J. West, Jr., *The Village* (New York: Harper and Row, 1972), and the bitter, retrospective view of both Marine and GVN failures in Lieutenant Colonel William R. Corson, USMC (ret.), *The Betrayal* (New York: Norton, 1968).

15. Brig. Gen. W. E. DePuy, USA (J-3 MACV) to COMUSMACV, "Situation in I Corps," November 15, 1965, General W. E. DePuy Papers; memoir of Gen. W. E. DePuy, USA (1979) and memoir of Lt. Gen. S. R. Larsen, USA (1976), Military History Institute, Carlisle Barracks, Pa.; and Westmoreland, *A Soldier Reports,* pp. 164–167.

16. Lt. Gen. V. H. Krulak to Secretary of Defense R. S. McNamara, May 9, 1966, and Lt. Gen. V. H. Krulak to Maj. Gen. L. W. Walt, July 11, 1966, Krulak Papers, and Walt, *Strange War, Strange Strategy* (note 1 above), pp. 78–112.

17. Shulimson and Johnson, *U.S. Marines in Vietnam 1965,* pp. 69–111.

18. "U.S. Ground Strategy and Force Deployments, 1965–1968: Phase II," in *Pentagon Papers: Gravel Edition,* IV: 290–387.

19. Jack Shulimson, *U.S. Marines in Vietnam 1966: An Expanding War* (Washington: History and Museums Division, HQMC, 1980), pp. 11–24, 54–81, 112–119.

20. *Ibid.,* pp. 37–53, and Col. J. R. Chaisson to Mrs. Chaisson, March 13–May 25, 1966, Chaisson Papers.

21. Shulimson, *U.S. Marines in Vietnam 1966,* pp. 130–154, and Captain William D. Parker, *U.S. Marine Corps Civil Affairs in I Corps Republic of Vietnam April 1966–April 1967* (Washington: Historical Division, HQMC, 1970). See also NAVMC 2616, *Unit Leaders Personal Response Handbook* (HQMC, 1967).

22. Shulimson, *U.S. Marines in Vietnam 1966,* pp. 82–111, and memoir of Maj. Gen. Wood B. Kyle (1969), pp. 180–216, MCOHC. For operations in the 1st Marine Division, see memoir of Lt. Gen. L. J. Fields (1971), pp. 245–267, MCOHC, and Edward Hymoff, comp., *First Marine Division: Vietnam* (New York: M. W. Lads, 1967). For the character of the fighting in I Corps, see especially Captain Francis J. West, Jr., *Small Unit Action in Vietnam Summer 1966* (New York: Arno Press, 1967).

23. Shulimson, *U.S. Marines in Vietnam 1966,* p. 194; Brigadier General Edwin H. Simmons, "Marine Corps Operations in Vietnam, 1965–1966" in Simmons et al., *The Marines in Vietnam, 1954–1973* (note 4 above), pp. 58–59; and debrief of Brig. Gen. J. H. Chaisson, November 8, 1966, Chaisson memoirs, MCOHC.

24. "Chief of Staff's Overview," "Report CMCS," and "G-1 Briefing," proceedings of the General Officers Symposium, 1967; testimony of Gen. W. M. Greene, Hearings: "Defense Appropriations FY 1967," House Armed Services Com-

mittee, 89th Congress, 2d Session (Washington: GPO, 1966), Part 1, pp. 600–601, 692–694, and testimony of Brig. Gen. R. G. Davis (G-1 HQMC) in *ibid.,* Part 2, 164–174; and testimony of Maj. Gen. R. G. Davis, Hearings: "Defense Appropriations FY 1968," Subcommittee of the House Committee on Appropriations, 90th Congress, 1st Session (Washington: Government Printing Office, 1967) Part 1, pp. 170–218.

25. "Aviation," proceedings of the General Officers Symposium, 1967, pp. 12–13.

26. *Ibid.,* and Lieutenant Colonel William R. Fails, *Marines and Helicopters, 1962–1973* (Washington: History and Museums Division, HQMC, 1978), pp. 129–148.

27. "Personnel and "G-1 Briefing," proceedings of the General Officers Symposium, 1967.

28. "Report CG FMF LANT," proceedings of the General Officers Symposium 1967. For a readiness assessment, see testimony of Lt. Gen. L. F. Chapman, Jr., (C/S HQMC) to the special subcommittee on national defense posture, House Armed Services Committee, October 12, 1967, Green Letter 15–67, Greene Papers.

29. "Logistics" and "Material Readiness," proceedings of the General Officers Symposium, 1967, and testimony of Maj. Gen. W. J. Van Ryzin (DC/S G-4), Hearings: "Defense Appropriations FY 1967," House Armed Services Committee, 89th Congress, 2d Session (Washington: Government Printing Office, 1967), Part 3, pp. 444–455, and Hearings: "Defense Appropriations FY 1968," subcommittee of the House Committee on Appropriations, 90th Congress, 1st Session (Washington: Government Printing Office, 1968), Part 4, pp. 328–584.

30. Testimony of Gen. W. M. Greene, Jr., Maj. Gen. R. G. Davis, and Brig. Gen. E. E. Anderson, Hearings: "Defense Appropriations FY 1968," subcommittee of the House Committee on Appropriations, 90th Congress, 1st Session (Washington: Government Printing Office, 1967) Part 1, p. 217, Part 2, pp. 903–904, and Part 3, p. 341; and Westmoreland, *A Soldier Reports* (note 4 above), pp. 202–203.

31. "Aviation," proceedings of the General Officers Symposium, 1967; "Loss of Jet Aircraft Theatens Marines," *JAF,* June 24, 1967; and Green Letter 11–67, July 20, 1967, Greene Papers.

32. Fails, *Marines and Helicopters,* pp. 109–126, and Lt. Gen. V. H. Krulak to Gen. W. C. Westmoreland, USA, May 15, 1967, Krulak Papers.

33. Gen. W. M. Greene, Jr., to W. D. Moyers, July 19, 1966; S. Markman to W. M. Watson, February 7, 1968; Rep. J. Brooks to W. M. Watson, November 13, 1967; Lt. Gen. L. W. Walt to L. B. Johnson, December 7, 1967; and Gen. E. G. Wheeler, USA, to L. B. Johnson, November 29, 1967, all File 125-5, White House Confidential Files, Lyndon B. Johnson Papers, Johnson Library, University of Texas at Austin. See also *New York Times,* September 28, 1967, and November 28, 1967.

34. Michael Herr, *Dispatches* (New York: Knopf, 1977), p. 102.

35. This analysis is based upon CG FMF PAC, "Fleet Marine Force Pacific Operations," proceedings of the General Officers Symposium, 1967; Lt. Gen. V. H. Krulak to Gen. W. M. Greene, Jr., September 8, 1967, Krulak Papers; debriefing of Brig. Gen. J. A. Chaisson, November 8, 1966, and August 1, 1967, Chaisson memoirs, MCOHC; Shulimson, *U.S. Marines in Vietnam 1966* (note 19 above), pp. 186–194; and Lt. Col. Lane Rogers and Maj. Gary Telfer, "U.S. Marines in Vietnam 1967," ms. history, Section 1, Chapter 1, H&MD.

36. Moody, Donnelly, and Shore, "Backing Up the Troops: Aviation," Part VII of "U.S. Marines in Vietnam," 1970 (note 11 above), Chapter 20; Shulimson,

U.S. Marines in Vietnam 1966, pp. 155–161; Rogers and Telfer, "U.S. Marines in Vietnam 1967," Section 2, Chapter 11; and McCutcheon, "Marine Aviation in Vietnam," in Simmons et al., *The Marines in Vietnam,* pp. 180–193.

37. Memoir of Lt. Gen. W. K. Jones (1973), pp. 5–14, MCOHC; Warren A. Trest, "Single Manager for Air in SVN," ms. history, July 1968, CHECO No. 64, Office of Air Force History; General William W. Momyer, USAF (ret.), *Air Power in Three Wars* (Washington: Office of Air Force History, 1978), pp. 65–110; and Gen. William W. Momyer, USAF, end-of-tour report, "Observations of the Vietnam War, July 66–July 68," 1968, Simpson Historical Research Center, Maxwell AFB, Alabama.

38. CG III MAF to COMUSMACV, February 24, 1968; CG 1st MAW to CMC, April 22, 1968; CMC draft ltr to L. B. Johnson, August (?), 1968; HQMC talking paper, "Air Control in Vietnam," July 8, 1968; and CMC memo to JCS, "Operational Control of III MAF Aviation Assets," June 14, 1968, all in "Single Management" Subject File, H&MD. See also Lt. Col. Gary W. Parker, "The Single Management Issue," ms. history, 1979, H&MD, and Westmoreland, *A Soldier Reports,* pp. 342–345.

39. Lt. Gen. K. B. McCutcheon to Maj. Gen. H. S. Hill, August 22, 1970, and to CMC, August 16, 1970, "Single Management" file, and Moody, Donnelly, and Shore, "Backing Up the Troops: Aviation," pp. 20:56–20:65.

40. Rogers and Telfer, "U.S. Marines in Vietnam 1967," Chapters 2, 5, 6, 8, and 9, and memoir of Maj. Gen. R. L. Murray (1975), pp. 4–15, MCOHC. See also Lieutenant Colonel Willard Pearson, USA, *Vietnam Studies: The War in the Northern Provinces, 1966–1968* (Washington: Department of the Army, 1975).

41. Quoted in "Siege at Con Thien," *Newsweek,* October 9, 1967. On the use of supporting arms, see Moody, Donnelly, and Shore, "Backing Up the Troops: Artillery and Naval Gunfire," Chapter 21, Part VII, "U.S. Marines in Vietnam." For fictionalized personal accounts of the DMZ war, see Charles R. Anderson, *The Grunts* (San Rafael, Calif.: Presidio Press, 1976), and William Turner Huggett, *Body Count* (New York: Putnam's, 1973).

42. Rogers and Telfer, "U.S. Marines in Vietnam 1967," Chapters 3, 4, and 7, and memoir of Lt. Gen. D. J. Robertson (1973, 1976), pp. 1–36, MCOHC. For personal accounts of the war in Quang Nam province, see Philip Caputo, *A Rumor of War* (New York: Holt, Rinehart and Winston, 1977), and James Webb, *Fields of Fire* (Englewood Cliffs, N.J.: Prentice-Hall, 1978).

43. Rogers and Telfer, "U.S. Marines in Vietnam 1967," Chapter 10, and Douglas S. Blaufarb, *The Counter-Insurgency Era: U.S. Doctrine and Performance* (New York: Free Press, 1977), pp. 243–278.

44. Captain Moyers S. Shore II, *The Battle for Khe Sanh* (Washington: Historical Branch, HQMC, 1969), and memoir of Maj. Gen. R. McC. Tompkins (1973), pp. 15–37, 44–48, MCOHC. See also Pearson, *The War in the Northern Provinces,* pp. 32–37, 73–80, and Bernard C. Nalty, *Air Power and the Fight for Khe Sanh* (Washington: Office of Air Force History, 1973).

45. For an overview of the Tet offensive and its aftermath in I Corps, see Major Thomas Donnelly and Captain Moyers S. Shore II, "Ho Chi Minh's Gamble," Part VI of "U.S. Marines in Vietnam," 1970; "III MAF," proceedings of the General Officers Symposium, 1968; Major Miles D. Waldron, USA and SP5 Richard W. Beavers, USA, "The Critical Year 1968: The XXIV Corps Team," ms. history, 1969, copy in H&MD; and Brigadier General Edwin H. Simmons, "Marine Corps Operations in Vietnam, 1968," in Simmons et al., *The Marines in Vietnam,* pp. 90–120.

46. Donnelly and Shore, "Ho Chi Minh's Gamble," Chapter 17, and transcript,

"Hue City," discussion by Lt. Col. E. C. Cheatham, Maj. G. R. Christmas, Maj. M. P. Downs, and Maj. C. L. Meadows, July 23, 1973, MCOHC.

47. Herbert Y. Schandler, *The Unmaking of a President: Lyndon Johnson and Vietnam* (Princeton, N.J.: Princeton University Press, 1977), pp. 74–319.

48. Waldron and Beavers, "The Critical Year 1968: The XXIV Corps Team," Part II; "Pacific Operations," proceedings of the General Officers Symposium, 1969; and Simmons, "Marine Corps Operations in Vietnam, 1969," pp. 109–120.

49. HQ FMF PAC, monthly operational summaries, January–June 1969, "Operations of U.S. Marines Forces Vietnam, 1969," 2 vols. H&MD; and memoirs of Gen. R. G. Davis (1977), pp. 65–70, Maj. Gen. R. T. Dwyer (1977), pp. 17–45, and Maj. Gen. R. H. Barrow (1973), pp. 28–32, 46–58, all MCOHC.

50. Testimony of Gen. L. F. Chapman, Jr., Hearings: "Department of Defense Appropriations FY 1971," Subcommittee of the Committee on Appropriations, House of Representatives, 91st Congress, 3d Session (Washington: Government Printing Office, 1970), Part 1, pp. 739–744, 798–803, and "Joint Planning," proceedings of the General Officers Symposium, 1969.

51. Proceedings of the General Officers Symposium, 1969, OH/MHD.

52. "Joint Planning," "The Five Year Defense Program," and "Fiscal," proceedings of the General Officers Symposium, 1970; "Joint Planning," proceedings of the General Officers Symposium, 1972; and "CMC Introductory Remarks" and "POM FY-75," proceedings of the General Officers Symposium, 1973.

53. "Summary of Discussion/Conclusions on Manpower Topics," General Officers Symposium, 1969; "Manpower" and "Personnel," proceedings of the General Officers Symposium, 1972; testimony of Maj. Gen. J. M. Platt (G-1, HQMC), Hearings: "Department of Defense Appropriations FY 1970," Subcommittee of the House Committee on Appropriations, 91st Congress, 1st Session (Washington: Government Printing Office, 1969), Part 1, pp. 288–326; testimony of Maj. Gen. E. E. Anderson (deputy director of personnel, HQMC) and Maj. Gen. E. B. Wheeler (G-1, HQMC), Hearings: "Department of Defense Appropriations FY 1972," Subcommittee of the House Committee on Appropriations, 92d Congress, 1st Session (Washington: Government Printing Office, 1971), Part 3, pp. 71–110, 169, 904–938.

54. "Narcotics, Dangerous Drugs and Marijuana," proceedings of the General Officers Symposium, 1968, and "Manpower" and "Attitudinal Survey in Human Affairs," proceedings of the General Officers Symposium, 1972.

55. "Dissent/Racial Problems," proceedings of the General Officers Symposium, 1969; statement of Gen. L. F. Chapman, Jr. and ALMAR 65 (1969), Hearings: "Department of Defense Appropriations FY 1970," Subcommittee of the House Committee on Appropriations, Part 6, pp. 259–262; "Report on Inquiry in the Reported Conditions in the Brig, Marine Corps Base, Camp Pendleton" and "Full Committee Consideration of S.59, H.R. 12535, H.R. 661 and Resume of Report of the Special Subcommittee to Probe Disturbances on Military Bases," House Armed Services Committee Report 91-34, 91st Congress, 1st Session, 1969; and Henry I. Shaw, Jr., and Ralph W. Donnelly, *Blacks in the Marine Corps* (Washington: History and Museums Division, 1975), pp. 69–83.

56. HQ FMF PAC, "Operations of U.S. Marine Forces Vietnam, 1969," 2 vols., H&MD; and memoir of Lt. Gen. W. J. Van Ryzin (1975), pp. 1–16, 220–227, MCOHC. For an overview, see Brig. Gen. E. H. Simmons, "Marine Corps Operations in Vietnam, 1969–1972," in Simmons et al., *The Marines in Vietnam*, pp. 11, 122–149.

57. HQ FMF PAC, "Operations of U.S. Marine Forces Vietnam, 1970," 2 vols., H&MD; memoir of Lt. Gen. O. R. Simpson (1973), pp. 2–65, MCOHC.

58. Graham Cosmas, "U.S. Marines in Vietnam, 1970–1971," ms. history, 1978,

H&MD. See especially F. J. West, Jr., "Area Security," August 1969, RAND P-3979-1, and "The Enclave: Some U.S. Military Efforts in Ly Tin District, Quang Tin Province 1966–1968," RAND 5941-ARPA; and Bruce C. Allnut, "Marine Combined Action Capabilities: The Vietnam Experience," December 1969, interim technical report for ONR by Human Science Research, Inc., Chaisson Papers.

59. 1st MarDiv/3d MAB CG's Information Notebook, April 1971, appended to 3d MAB Command Chronology, H&MD; and ADC 1st MarDiv orientation talk to company grade officers (January 1971), appended to the memoir of Brig. Gen. E. H. Simmons, MCOHC.

60. Cosmas, "U.S. Marines in Vietnam, 1970–1971," Chapter 14; Major W. Hays Parks, "Crimes in Hostilities," *MCG*, 60 (August 1976): 16–22, and 60 (September 1976): 33–39; Dr. Thomas C. Bond, "Fragging: A Study," *Army*, 27 (April 1977): pp. 45–47; memoirs of Lt. Gen. W. K. Jones (1973), pp. 39–59, and Maj. Gen. W. F. Simlik (1976), pp. 1–12, MCOHC; and Lewy, *America in Vietnam* (note 4 above), pp. 350–356, 456. For a benign picture of pacification operations, see The Staff of *The Leatherneck, Ambassadors in Green* (Washington, D.C.: The Leatherneck Association, 1971).

61. HQ FMF PAC, "Operations of U.S. Marine Forces in Vietnam," 1971, H&MD; and Cosmas, "U.S. Marines in Vietnam, 1970–1971," ms. history, 1978, H&MD.

62. Colonel Sydney H. Batchelder, Jr., and Major D. A. Quinlan, "Operation Eagle Pull," *MCG*, 60 (May 1976): 47–60, and Brigadier General Richard E. Carey and Major D. A. Quinlan, "Frequent Wind," *MCG*, 60 (February 1976): 16–24; 60 (March 1976): 35–45; and 60 (April 1976): 35–45.

63. Colonel J. M. Johnson, Jr., Lieutenant Colonel R. W. Austin, and Major D. A. Quinlan, "Individual Heroism Overcame Awkward Command Relationships, Confusion, and Bad Information Off the Cambodian Coast," *MCG*, 61 (October 1977): 24–34.

CHAPTER 19. THE ONCE AND FUTURE CORPS, THE 1970s

1. Martin Binkin and Jeffrey Record, *Where Does the Marine Corps Go From Here?* (Washington: Brookings Institution, 1976); Robert A. Taft with William S. Lind, "A Modern Military Strategy for the United States," rev. ed. 1978, pp. 82–85, H&MD; John M. Collins, *American and Soviet Military Trends* (Washington: Georgetown University, 1978), pp. 208, 231, 298; William S. Lind and Jeffrey Record, "Twilight for the Corps," *USNIP*, 104 (July 1978): 39–43; Major General Fred C. Haynes, USMC (ret.), "The Marines Through 1999," *USNIP*, 104 (September 1978): 24–33; "What's Wrong with the Marines?" *U.S. News and World Report*, May 12, 1975.

2. General R. E. Cushman, Jr., "To the Limit of Our Vision—and Back," *USNIP*, 100 (May 1974): 106–121; statements of Gen. R. E. Cushman, Jr., on Marine Corps posture FY 1975–1977 before the House Armed Services Committee, issued by the HASC; statement of Maj. Gen. F. W. Vaught (director of plans, programs, and management) for FY 1976 before the House Armed Services Committee, issued by the HASC; James D. Hessman, "The Marine Corps Faces East," *Sea Power*, 18 (April 1975): 22–26; and testimony of Lt. Gen. Andrew W. O'Donnell, Deputy Chief of Staff for Plans and Policies, in Hearings: "NATO Standardization, Interoperability and Readiness," Committee on Armed Services, House of Representatives, 92d Congress, 2d Session (Washington: Government Printing Office, 1978), pp. 413–421, 441–453.

3. Brigadier General Edwin H. Simmons, USMC (ret.), "The Marines: Now and

in the Future," *USNIP,* 101 (May 1975): 102–117; Francis J. West, Jr., "Marines for the Future," *USNIP,* 104 (February 1978): 34–42; Lieutenant Colonel John Grinalds, *Structuring the Marine Corps for the 1980s and 1990s* (Washington: National Defense University, 1978); Congressional Budget Office, *U.S. Projection Forces: Requirements, Scenarios, and Options* (Washington: Government Printing Office, 1978); and George C. Wilson, "Marines to Form Rapid Reaction Force," *Washington Post,* December 6, 1979.

4. "Statement of General Louis H. Wilson, Commandant of the Marine Corps, before the Subcommittee on Seapower, U.S. House of Representatives, on USMC Amphibious Requirements," 1977, HASC; Vice Admiral Robert S. Salzer, USN (ret.), "The Navy's Clouded Amphibious Mission," *USNIP,* 104 (February 1978): 24–33; and Lieutenant Colonel Arthur T. McDermott and Lieutenant Colonel Fred H. Kruck, "LHA-1," *MCG,* 58 (March 1974): 23–28.

5. Binkin and Record, *Where Does the Marine Corps Go From Here?* pp. 42–48.

6. Interview with Lt. Gen. Thomas H. Miller, Jr., D/CS (Aviation), *MCG,* 63 (May 1979): 50–57; memo, UnderSecretary of the Navy R. J. Woolsey to Secretary of Defense, "DON Fighter/Light Attack Options," December 10, 1977, reprinted in *AFJI,* 116 (March 1978): 42–44; George C. Wilson, "Marines Fighting for Air," *Washington Post,* September 2, 1977; Lieutenant General Thomas H. Miller, Jr., "The Impact of the FY-79 Budget on Marine Aviation," *MCG,* 62 (May 1978): 27–29; and "OSD POM-79 Issues," General Officers Symposium, 1977.

7. Lieutenant Colonel F. J. Breth, "All Marines Have a Stake in Close Air Support," *MCG,* 62 (May 1978): 30–39; and Brigadier General Noah C. New, "Night Close Air Support," *MCG,* 59 (May 1975): 31–36.

8. Lieutenant Colonel R. Sancho, "Helicopters Can Survive the Real Threat of the Modern Battlefield," *MCG,* 62 (May 1978): 42–48.

9. Brigadier General Noah C. New, "Investment in the Future," *MCG,* 58 (March 1974): 15–22; Lieutenant Colonel Donald Q. Layne and Lieutenant Colonel Conrad A. Jorgenson, "Combat Intelligence," *MCG,* 58 (March 1974): 29–36; Major R. Edwards and Major L. Weeks, "Using Laser Technology on the Modern Battlefield," *MCG,* 62 (March 1978): 35–40; and First Lieutenant Kathleen Ryan, "Intelligence Processing and the Great Technology Race," *MCG,* 62 (March 1978): 41–44.

10. Major Louis C. Gapenski, "Ground Weaponry," *MCG,* 58 (March 1974): 43–48; Lieutenant Colonel Richard H. Moore, Major Larry L. Weeks, and Captain Dennis A. Morga, "Why the Marine Corps Is Adopting a New Howitzer," *MCG,* 63 (April 1979): 51–59; Major F. T. Klabough, "Mobile Protected Weapons Systems May Be a Substitute for Tanks," *MCG,* 62 (March 1978): 31–34; and testimony and prepared statement of Brig. Gen. Kenneth L. Robinson (director of material division, I&L Dept., HQMC), Hearings: "Military Posture and Defense Appropriations FY 1978," House Committee on Armed Services, 95th Congress, 1st Session (Washington: Government Printing Office, 1977), Part 2, pp. 313–334.

11. Major K. T. Brunsvold, "Will the LVA Ride on Air Cushion or Water Wings?" *MCG,* 62 (March 1978): 45–50.

12. ECP 1-4, *Fleet Marine Corps Organization 1979* (Quantico, Va.: MCDEC, 1979); Haynes, "The Marines Through 1999" (note 1 above); "CMC Reports to Congress: 'We Are Ready. Spirit Is High'," *MCG,* 61 (April 1977): 18–30; and Lieutenant Colonel J. E. Stanton, "Realistic Combat Training for the FMF," *MCG,* 62 (April 1978): 33–35. On logistics organization, see Colonel Paul E. Wilson, USMC (ret.), "Developing a Better Combat Service Support System for the Marine Corps," *MCG,* 62 (January 1978): 39–46.

13. For varied aspects of the recruiting problems of 1973–1977, see Commandant

of the Marine Corps, "Report on Marine Corps Manpower Quality and Force Structure," December 31, 1975, reprinted as House Armed Services Committee Report 94–59, 94th Congress, 1st Session (Washington: Government Printing Office, 1976); Binkin and Record, *Where Does the Marine Corps Go From Here?*, pp. 57–65; Lieutenant Colonel William Gilfillan II and Lieutenant J. R. Brown, Jr., "Recruiting an All-Volunteer Force," *MCG,* 61 (November 1977): 81–84; Brigadier General Bernard E. Trainor, "The Personnel Campaign Issue Is No Longer in Doubt, *MCG,* 62 (January 1978): 22–38; Lieutenant Colonel Peter J. Rowe, "Madison Avenue Marines," *MCG,* 63 (February 1979): 24–35.

14. Subcommittee on Military Personnel, House Committee on Armed Forces, *Marine Corps Recruit Training and Recruiting Programs,* House Armed Services Committee Report 94-65, 94th Congress, 2d Session (Washington: Government Printing Office, 1976); and Subcommittee on Military Personnel, House Armed Services Committee, Hearings: "Marine Corps Recruit Training and Recruiting Programs," 94th Congress, 2d Session (Washington: Government Printing Office, 1976).

15. Gen. Louis H. Wilson, "Emphasis on Professionalism for a New Generation of Marines," *Sea Power,* 19 (January 1976): 24–29, and Walter V. Robinson, "The Marines' Toughest Fight Long Battle Respectability," *Boston Globe,* June 6, 1976.

16. "Comments on the Corps by the Commandant," *MCG,* 63 (August 1979): 7.

Essay on Sources

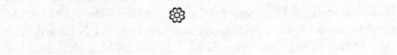

Since this book is amply footnoted by chapter, this essay discusses only the collection of official and private documents and the major printed sources of information on the Corps available to any researcher of Marine Corps history.

PRIMARY SOURCES

Organizational Records   The basic collection of Marine Corps documents is Records of the United States Marine Corps, Record Group 127, National Archives of the United States, which covers the history of the Corps from its creation in 1798 through World War II. Physically, the records are at the National Archives building in downtown Washington, D.C., and the federal records center at Suitland, Maryland. Some of the World War II organizational records and the documents of Headquarters staff sections, posts and stations, and units of the Fleet Marine Force since World War II remain in the hands of the Operational Archives Branch of the Marine Corps History and Museums Division at the Marine Corps Historical Center at the Washington Navy Yard, the staff divisions of Headquarters Marine Corps, and the headquarters of Marine Corps posts and stations.

Within Record Group 127, the most significant group of documents is the correspondence, issuances, and other records of the Office of the Commandant, 1798–1939, which also includes important collections of recruiting, operations, training, intelligence, and Marine Corps history.

In the last-named category, one finds critical documents on Marine activities in the Philippines and China (1899–1901) and Marine Corps history between 1899 and the outbreak of World War II. For the internal management of the Corps during the 1798–1949 period, one should also consult the correspondence of the Adjutant and Inspector's Department, which handled personnel matters for the Commandant and supervised the compliance with official orders. Also part of Record Group 127 are the records of the Paymaster's Department (1808–1939) and the Quartermaster's Department (1811–1942). The same record group includes scattered records from Marine ships detachments and field organizations to World War II. The most important collections for Marine overseas organizations are the records of the Marine legation guard in Peking, the Marine units deployed to Cuba (1898–1912), the Marine brigade in Haiti and the Gendarmerie d'Haiti (1915–1934), and the Marine brigade in Nicaragua and the Guardia Nacional de Nicaragua (1927–1932); the records of selected Marine detachments, organizations, and squadrons during the interwar period; and the records of Marine defense battalions during World War II. All these records are described in Maizie Johnson, comp., *Records of the United States Marine Corps* (Washington: The National Archives, 1970), supplemented by the announcements of accessions by the National Archives and Records Service.

The National Archives also holds collections of Marine Corps maps and photographs. Both are identified as Record Group 127 in their respective National Archives divisions. The cartographic records are divided into three basic subcollections: maps of Marine Corps bases, maps of geographic areas that interested Marine Corps planners up to World War II, and maps of Marine Corps operations in France in World War I. The photographic records are still photographs accessioned from the Marine Corps that portray Marine subjects through World War II. The History and Museums Division, however, still retains custody of many still photographs and the basic archives of Marine Corps motion pictures, as well as its own map collection.

Record Group 127 does not exhaust the relevant Marine collections in the National Archives. Although there is some duplication in the records, one should consult the correspondence of the Secretary of the Navy with the Commandant of the Marine Corps and other Marine officers (1804–1886) in the General Records of the Department of the Navy, Record Group 80. In the same record group are additional Marine materials in the General File, Office of the Secretary of the Navy (1897–1926); the Confidential Correspondence of the Secretary of the Navy and the Chief of Naval Operations (1917–1919); and the Confidential Correspondence, Chief of Naval Operations Planning Division to the Secretary of the Navy (1919–1926). In addition, one should consult the Records of the Office of the Chief of Naval Operations (Record Group 38) for the records of the Military Government of Santo Domingo (1916–1924). Of special importance are the collected documents of the Naval Records Collection of the Office of Naval Records and Library (Record Group 45), which covers a variety of naval subjects up to World War II. In this collection, one finds the correspondence of the Board of Navy Commissioners to the Secretary of the Navy, 1815–1842, and a variety of special subject files that deal with Marine activities. Among the latter are files "VR" (governmental relations: USMC), "OJ" (joint military and naval operations), "OH" (shore operations and landing parties), "VA" (Navy Department organization and administration), "NL" (naval personnel), "WA7" and "ZWA7" (Haiti and Santo Domingo), and "ZK" (Marines in China). In creating Record Group 45, naval historians organized a special collection of unpublished histories, labeled the "Z" File, which includes material on Navy–Marine Corps activities, many written by participants. The holdings of the "Z" File are described in Operational Archives Branch, Naval Historical Division, *Checklist: Unpublished Naval Histories in the "Z" File, Record Group 45 1911–1927* (Washington: Naval Historical Division, 1971).

Naval records outside the custody of the National Archives also yield substantial information on the history of the Marine Corps. At the Operational Archives Branch of the Naval Historical Division, Washington Navy Yard, I consulted the records of the General Board (1900–1947), selected documents from the Command File for the post–World War II period, the diaries of Secretary of the Navy and Secretary of Defense James V. Forrestal, the papers of Chief of Naval Operations Forrest Sherman, the records of the Immediate Office of the Chief of Naval Operations (1942–1950), the office files of the Deputy Chief of Naval Operations (Air) (1942–1950); and the Central Security-Classified Records of the Office of the Chief of Naval Operations (1942–1947). The Naval Historical Division also retains custody of a large collection of unpublished histories related to World War II that are described in Naval Historical Division, *Guide to the United States Naval Administrative Histories of World War II* (Washington: Naval Historical Division, 1976) and *World War II Histories and Historical Reports in the U.S. Naval History Division* (Washington, D.C.: Naval Historical Division, 1972). Another significant source of documentation are the copies of correspondence, reports, memoranda, newspaper clippings, photographs, and studies collected in the subject and biographical files of the Reference Section, History Branch, History and Museums Division of the Marine Corps, also located at the Marine Corps Historical Center.

To support their officer education programs, the senior colleges of the Navy and Marine Corps created both libraries and archives of research materials relevant to their students' interests and the program of instruction. Many of the documents are copies from the official records, but others are special lectures, plans, essays, research reports, and operational studies created by the colleges themselves. The Naval War College at Newport, Rhode Island, maintains the Naval War College Historical Collection as both a research collection and a college archive. In the general records of the Naval War College (Record Group 8), Marine-related materials on amphibious operations and related organization matters are concentrated in Files "XLFG" and "XBAA" with other assorted materials in the guest lecture files (Record Group 15) and other files in RG 8. A similar collection of Marine Corps materials may be found in the James C. Breckinridge Library, Education Center, Marine Corps Development and Education Command, Quantico, Virginia. In addition to rare books and other instructional materials, the Breckinridge Library maintains two file cases of materials called the "Historical Amphibious File." This collection of documents is indexed largely by subject matter and covers Marine Corps interest in amphibious operations—its own and others—throughout the twentieth century. It is an important, accessible source on the development of amphibious doctrine and the Marine Corps educational system.

At important points in its history, the Marine Corps became a matter of interest to agencies outside the Department of the Navy, and in the course of this study I consulted the additional collections in the National Archives: Records of the Secretary of War (Record Group 107); Records of the War Department General Staff (Record Group 165); and Records of the American Expeditionary Forces, 1917–1923 (Record Group 120); and the central decimal file of the Joint Chiefs of Staff, Records of the Joint Chiefs of Staff (Record Group 218). For the period of unification and organization of the Department of Defense, 1945–1952, I was granted access to the bill jackets and related correspondence of the Committee on Armed Services, U.S. House of Representatives, by the committee chairman.

Individual Papers The single largest collection of the private papers of Marine Corps officers and enlisted men is held at the Marine Corps Historical Center, Washington Navy Yard. Generally, the papers fall into two categories: individual collections that cover all or most of the careers of prominent officers and group collections that cover important subjects in Marine Corps history, which tend to be modern wars, amphibious development, and aviation. For the pre-twentieth-century Corps, I found the papers of the following officers especially useful: Colonel Samuel Miller (1775–1855) on the post–War of 1812 period; Major Levi Twiggs (1793–1847) on the same period; Colonel Thomas Y. Fields (1825–1905) for the middle third of the nineteenth century; Lieutenant Colonel John L. Broome (1824–1898) for much of the nineteenth century, but especially on the Civil War; Lieutenant Colonel McLane Tilton (1836–1914) from the Civil War until 1897; and Brigadier General Henry Clay Cochrane (1842–1913), an especially valuable collection of diaries and personal letters that covers all of Cochrane's career (1863–1905). For Marines whose careers spanned the dawn of the imperial years to World War II, I found the papers of the following officers most useful: Major General Wilburt S. Brown (1900–1968) on World War I, Nicaragua, and World War II; Major General Smedley D. Butler (1881–1940) on virtually every important Marine operation from Guantanamo Bay (1898) to China (1927–1929) and for the charismatic leader's views of a bureaucratizing Corps; Brigadier General Robert L. Denig (1884–1979) on World War I and Nicaragua; Major General Louis McCarty Little (1878–1949) on Haiti and the development of the Fleet Marine Force in the 1930s; Brigadier General George C. Reid (1876–1961); Major General Joseph H. Pendleton (1860–1942) on the development of the expeditionary Marine Corps; Major General George Barnett (1859–1930) on most of his service (1883–1923), but particularly on Haiti, early amphibious operations, and his tenure as Commandant; Lieutenant Colonel Harold H. Utley (1885–1951) on Haiti and Nicaragua; Major General Clayton B. Vogel (1882–1964) on his entire career, which spanned 1904–1946; Brigadier General L. W. T. Waller, Jr. (1886–1967), primarily on World War I and Haiti; and Lieutenant Colonel Alfred A. Cunningham (1882–1939) on the early development of Marine aviation. For World War II and the postwar period, see the papers of the following officers: General Thomas Holcomb (1879–1965), whose papers are best for the 1930s and the early years of World War II; General Clifton B. Cates (1893–1970) from World War I through his service as Commandant; General A. A. Vandegrift (1887–1973) on colonial service through his service as Commandant; General Holland M. Smith (1882–1967), whose papers are especially important on World War II; General O. P. Smith (1893–1977) on World War II and Korea; General Keith B. McCutcheon (1915–1971) on the development of Marine aviation from World War II through Vietnam; General Wallace M. Greene, Jr. (1907–   ) on Marine Corps affairs from China in the 1930s through his service as Commandant (1964–1968); and Lieutenant General Victor H. Krulak (1913–   ), for the 1960s and Vietnam.

Other repositories hold Marine personal papers of historical significance. The Manuscript Division of the Library of Congress holds the collections of Major General John A. Lejeune (1867–1942), which cover the general's service from the early 1900s through his commanancy (1920–1929); Major General Merritt A. Edson (1897–1955), especially useful on World War II and the unification controversy; and Major General William E. Riley (1897–1970). The Department of Archives of Auburn University, Auburn, Alabama, holds the papers of General Franklin M. Hart (1894–1967); Brigadier General Joseph L. Stewart (1915–   ); and copies of the papers and memorabilia of General Holland M. Smith. The Southern Historical Collection at the University of North Carolina–Chapel Hill maintains the papers of Major General William P. Upshur (1881–1943). The Hoover Institution of War, Peace, and Revolution at Stanford, California, holds the papers of General David M. Shoup (1904–   ), which are good on World War II, the 1950s, and Shoup's service as Commandant (1960–1963), and the correspondence of Lieutenant General John R. Chaisson (1916–1972), especially important for the Vietnam War. The library of East Carolina University, Greenville, North Carolina, holds the papers of Brigadier General Paul A. Putnam (1903–   ) and Lieutenant General William K. Jones (1916–   ), while the U.S. Army Military History Institute has the papers of Major Frederick H. Delano (1876–1944).

As part of its monograph series, the History and Museums Division has contributed to the number of printed memoirs with James P. Jones and Edward F. Keuchel, eds., *Civil War Marine* [Lieutenant Frank L. Church]: *A Diary of the Red River Expedition, 1864* (Washington: History and Museums Division, HQMC, 1975), and Graham A. Cosmas, ed., *Marine Flyer in France: The Diary of Captain Alfred A. Cunningham* (Washington: History and Museums Division, HQMC, 1974).

Outside of autobiographies and novels describing wartime service from World War I through Vietnam, there are few historical accounts by Marine enlisted men. To some degree, officer papers in the twentieth century compensate for the lack of evidence, for several important officers started their careers as enlisted men. Of the materials held by the Marine Corps Historical Center, I depended on the following for insights into the enlisted experience: the journal of Private Frank Keeler (1898), Charles V. Daugherty, "Five Years in the Marine Corps," 4 vols., on service 1901–1905; and Private Walter Bronson's diary of a cruise, 1871–1873. An important source for World War I are the letters, papers, and memorabilia of Marine veterans of the 2d Division, AEF, collected by the World War I Project of the U.S. Army Military History Institute.

For Marine Corps private papers, see Charles Anthony Wood, comp., *Marine Corps Personal Papers Collection Catalog* (Washington: History and Museums Division, HQMC, 1974), supplemented by *Fortitudine,* the quarterly newsletter of the History and Museums Division.

To add another dimension to the personal perspectives provided by private papers, any researcher on the Marine Corps should consult the large collection of oral history transcripts collected by the History and Museums Division and housed at the Marine Corps Historical Center. A second set of interviews is maintained at Breckinridge Library, Education Command, Marine Corps Development and Education Center. The collection is described in Benis M. Frank, ed., *Marine Corps Oral History Collection Catalog,* 2d ed. (Washington: History and Museums Division, HQMC, 1979). The usefulness of the transcripts, of course, varies with the interests of the researcher, the acuity of the interviewee, and the skill of the interviewer. For this book I found important information and insights in the oral history memoirs of the following officers: Major General Chester R. Allen, Major General Alan J. Armstrong, Lieutenant General Robert O. Bare, Major General Robert H. Barrow, Lieutenant General James P. Berkeley, Major General Ion M. Bethel, Major General Robert T. Blake, Lieutenant General Alpha L. Bowser, Major General Wilbert S. Brown, Lieutenant General Joseph C. Burger, General Clifton B. Cates, Lieutenant General Edward A. Craig, Lieutenant General Thomas J. Cushman, General Raymond G. Davis, Lieutenant General Karl S. Day, Lieutenant General Pedro A. del Valle, Brigadier General Lester A. Dessez, Brigadier General James P. Devereux, Brigadier General Edward C. Dyer, General Graves B. Erskine, Lieutenant General Lewis J. Fields, Lieutenant General George F. Good, Jr., Lieutenant General Charles H. Hayes, General Robert E. Hogaboom, Major General Louis R. Jones, Lieutenant General Victor H. Krulak, Major General Melvin L. Krulewitch, Lieutenant General Robert B. Luckey, Major General John H. Masters, Lieutenant General John C. McQueen, General Vernon E. Megee, Lieutenant General John C. Munn, Lieutenant General Herman Nickerson, Jr., General Alfred H. Noble, Major General DeWitt Peck, Major General Omar T. Pfeiffer, General Edwin A. Pollock, Lieutenant General Donn J. Robertson, General Ray A. Robertson, General Christian F. Schilt, Jr., Lieutenant General Alan Shapley, Brigadier General Samuel R. Shaw, General Lemuel C. Shepherd, Jr., Lieutenant General Merwin H. Silverthorn, Lieutenant General Julian C. Smith, General Oliver P. Smith, Brigadier General Edwin H. Simmons, Lieutenant General Edward W. Snedeker, Brigadier General Joseph L. Stewart, General Gerald C. Thomas, Major General Rathvon McC. Tompkins, Lieutenant General William J. Van Ryzin, Lieutenant General Louis E. Woods, Lieutenant General Thomas A. Wornham, Major General William A. Worton, and Major General Carl A. Youngdale. For the Vietnam War, researchers may also consult the interviews described in Benis M. Frank, comp., *Marine Corps Operations in Vietnam: Field Interviews* (Washington: History and Museums Division, 1975). In addition, the Marine Corps oral history collection holds a few interviews with enlisted men whose service spans the war with Spain to Vietnam.

Outside of Marine personal papers and memoirs held by the History and Museums Division, there are numerous other documents of relevance to Marine Corps history. An important source is the files of American Presidents since Herbert Hoover. The Cabinet Series, Presidential Papers at the Herbert Hoover Presidential Library (West Branch, Iowa) have six folders of Marine Corps files, four of which deal with Corps personal and policy matters. The collections of the Franklin D. Roosevelt Library (Hyde Park, New York) include two files of correspondence with Marines dating from Roosevelt's service as Assistant Secretary of the Navy (1913–1920) and the Office Files, Secretary's Files, and Presidential Personal Files (1933–1945). The main source in FDR's papers is OF-18E and PPF 4951, the correspondence with Evans Carlson. At the Harry S. Truman Library (Independence, Missouri), one finds about two linear feet of Marine Corps material in Official File 1284-C, which largely deals with unification, the Korean War, and the Truman "slur" at the Marines in 1950. The Truman Library also has the papers of Secretary of the Navy Francis P. Matthews (1949–1953), which include some documents of interest. At the Dwight D. Eisenhower Library (Abilene, Kansas), the holdings include three files under "Marine Corps" headings in the White House Central File, Official File. Although the Eisenhower papers are sketchy, those in the John F. Kennedy Library are even more sparse, limited to two files labeled "Marine Corps" in the White House Subject Files. In the Lyndon B. Johnson Library (Austin, Texas) File 125-5 (Marine Corps) Federal Government, White House Central File contains correspondence on limited Marine Corps matters and Marine participation in the Vietnam War.

Of the other collections of civilian and military officers that bear upon Marine Corps matters, I found the most useful to be: three and one-half boxes of documents and correspondence entitled "United States

Marine Corps" for the tenure of Josephus Daniels as Secretary of the Navy (1913–1921) in the Manuscript Division of the Library of Congress; the private papers of General John J. Pershing and Major General James G. Harbord, U.S. Army, for World War I in the same archive; the papers of Rear Admiral Stephen B. Luce, Rear Admiral William F. Fullam, Rear Admiral David F. Sellers, and Rear Admiral William S. Sims in the Naval Historical Foundation Collection at the Library of Congress. Of special importance for the history of the amphibious war in the central Pacific is the two-volume oral history memoir of Admiral Harry W. Hill, held in Navy archives and the Marine Corps oral history collection.

Printed Primary Sources Because the early years of the Marine Corps were shared with the American sailing navy, four important collections of naval documents contain Marine-related material. They are William Bell Clark and William D. Morgan et al., eds. and comp., *Naval Documents of the American Revolution,* 7 vols. to date (Washington: Government Printing Office, 1964–   ); Office of Naval Records and Library, U.S. Navy Department, *Naval Documents Related to the Quasi-War Between the United States and France,* 7 vols. (Washington: Government Printing Office, 1935–1938); Office of Naval Records and Library, U.S. Navy Department, *Naval Documents Related to the United States Wars with the Barbary Pirates,* 6 vols. (Washington: Government Printing Office, 1939–1944); U.S. Congress, *American State Papers, Class IV, Naval Affairs, 1789–1836,* 4 vols. (Washington: Gales and Seaton, 1834–1861). Of other printed collections of documents of interest to historians of the Marine Corps, see the reports of the Secretary of War and the Commanding General, United States Army, during the Mexican War; U.S. War Department, *The War of the Rebellion: A Compilation of the Official Records of the Union and Confederate Armies in the War of the Rebellion,* 130 vols. (Washington: Government Printing Office, 1880–1901); U.S. War Department, *Correspondence Relating to the War with Spain . . . Including the Insurrection in the Philippine Islands and the China Relief Expedition,* 2 vols. (Washington: Government Printing Office, 1902); Historical Division, U.S. Department of the Army, *United States in the World War, 1917–1919,* 17 vols. (Washington: Government Printing Office, 1948); and Army War College, U.S. Department of the Army, *Records of the Second Division (Regular),* 9 vols. (Washington and Fort Sam Houston, Texas: Second Division Historical Section, 1930–1932).

The published proceedings and reports of the U.S. Congress provide important material on the Marine Corps since 1798. The proceedings of the full House and Senate began with the *Annals of Congress* in 1789 and went through several other forms and titles before becoming the *Congressional Record* in 1873. Beyond the debates and appended material in the *Congressional Record,* one should look to the published reports and hearings of the following Congressional committees: the Senate and House naval affairs committees (until 1947), the Senate and House armed services committees (after 1947), and the subcommittees on defense spending of the Senate and House Committees on Appropriations. Marine Corps matters were also occasionally the subject of special investigating committees of either house or special joint committees. Access to Marine-related materials starts with the various indices to Congressional documents.

For the executive branch the basic documents are the Annual Reports of the Secretary of the Navy, which include basic policy statements, operational narratives, and personnel and materiel data in both subject and budget form. The Secretary of the Navy's report included the annual report of the Commandant of the Marine Corps. Until the 1920s the annual reports were bound and published both as executive department documents and as part of the Congressional Serial Set. Since World War II the Secretary's and Commandant's reports normally appear only as appendices to their testimony before Congressional committees, although each submits extensive materials to both the Office of the Secretary of Defense and the Joint Chiefs of Staff as background material to their reports and posture statements. The library of the Marine Corps Historical Center is an excellent source for these reports and supporting documents.

Marines have not published their own memoirs or collections of letters in any great number, and the quality of these primary sources is varied. Most of them emphasize wartime service. The most satisfactory memoir is Major General John A. Lejeune, *The Reminiscences of a Marine* (Philadelphia: Dorrance and Company, 1930). The next best memoir is still unpublished: Major General George Barnett, "Soldier and Sailor Too," a manuscript in the Barnett Papers. Of the other existing memoirs, the following are worth reading, but not with suspended disbelief: Major General Smedley D. Butler as told to Lowell Thomas, *Old Gimlet Eye: the Adventures of Smedley D. Butler* (New York: Farrar and Rinehart, 1933); Brigadier General Albertus W. Catlin, *With the Help of God and a Few Marines* (Garden City, N.Y.: Doubleday, Page, 1919); Lieutenant General Pedro A. del Valle, *Semper Fidelis* (Hawthorne, Calif.: Christian Book Club of America, 1976); Major General Melvin L. Krulewitch, *Now That You Mention It* (New York: Quadrangle, 1973); Brigadier General John L. Letcher, *One Marine's Story* (Verona,

Va.: McClure Press, 1970); Major General Fred S. Robillard, *As Robie Remembers* (Bridgeport, Conn.: Wright Investors' Service, 1969); Colonel Mitchell Paige, *A Marine Named Mitch* (New York: Vantage Press, 1975); General Holland M. Smith with Percy Finch, *Coral and Brass* (New York: Scribner's, 1949); John Philip Sousa, *Marching Along* (Boston: Hale, Cushman, and Flint, 1928); General A. A. Vandegrift with Robert B. Asprey, *Once a Marine* (New York: Norton, 1964); and Colonel Frederic M. Wise with Meigs O. Frost, *A Marine Tells It to You* (New York: Sears, 1929).

Journals and Newspapers As a source of participant accounts and contemporaneous information (and speculation) about Marine Corps matters, journals and newspapers provide useful information on individual experiences and the officer and enlisted subcultures of the Corps. For officer writing, the primary source is the *Marine Corps Gazette*, published at Quantico, Virginia, continuously since its creation in 1916 by the Marine Corps Association. For the enlisted men, the basic publication is *Leatherneck*, which began as a newspaper in 1917 and changed to a magazine in 1921. Of shorter lifetime was *The Marines Magazine* (1915–1920), which changed to the *The Marines Magazine and Indian* (1920–1922) in order to cater to the veterans of the AEF's 2d Division, but expired. Another important source is the *The Recruiter's Bulletin* (1914–1921). Since World War I, Marine tactical organizations (usually brigades and divisions) and Marine Corps bases have published their own newspapers; the Marine Corps Historical Center is the locale for the largest collection of such materials as well as commercially published "cruise books," which normally portray the experiences of recruit training units and deployed battalions and aviation squadrons. Outside of official and semiofficial Marine Corps publications, the principal sources of journal and newspaper information are: articles and photographic essays in the *Proceedings* of the U.S. Naval Institute, continuously published at Annapolis, Maryland, since 1874; the *Army and Navy Journal*, first published in 1862, and the *Army and Navy Register*, first published in 1879, both of which went through various title changes after World War II and eventually merged in 1962 and now publish under the title *Armed Forces Journal International*; and *Navy Times*, published since 1951.

SECONDARY SOURCES

Bibliographies The main source of guidance to the literature of the Marine Corps is the series of bibliographies published by the History and Museums Division, Headquarters Marine Corps. The basic bibliography is *An Annotated Reading List of United Marine Corps History*, rev. ed. (1971). The division (or its predecessors) has also published annotated bibliographies on Marine participation in the American Revolution (1972), the naval war with France (1963), the Barbary wars (1963), the Indian wars (1963), the war with Mexico (1963), the Civil War (1968), the Korean expedition of 1871 (n.d.), expeditions to Panama (n.d.), the war with Spain (1962), the Boxer Rebellion (1961), the expeditions to Santo Domingo, Haiti, and Nicaragua (n.d.), World War I (1967), World War II (1965), and the Korean War (1970). The Vietnam conflict is covered in Brigadier General Edwin H. Simmons, USMC (ret.), et al., *The Marines in Vietnam, 1954–1973: An Anthology and Annotated Bibliography* (Washington: History and Museums Division, HQMC, 1974). The division has also published special subject bibliographies on the Marines and guerrilla warfare (1962), artillery (1970), naval gunfire support (1971), defense organization (n.d.), close air support (1968), and American fiction (1964). For a private attempt to cover much the same body of material, see Captain John B. Moran, USMCR (ret.), comp., *Creating a Legend* (Chicago: Moran/Andrews, Inc., 1973).

To survey the literature on American naval history, see especially Naval Historical Division, *United States Naval History: A Bibliography*, 6th ed. (Washington: Government Printing Office, 1972); Myron J. Smith, Jr., ed. and comp., *American Naval Bibliography*, 5 vols. (Metuchen, N.J.: The Scarecrow Press, 1972–1974), which covers naval history from the Revolution to 1941; and Robert Greenhalgh Albion, ed. and comp., *Naval and Maritime History: An Annotated Bibliography*, 4th ed. (Mystic, Conn.: The Marine Historical Association, Inc., 1972).

General Histories For more than a hundred years, the writing of Marine Corps history has been shaped by internal organizational interest, political controversy, and a perceived public interest in the Corps, the last normally coinciding with the heroics of Marines in wartime. Like most of the writing on military institutions, Marine Corps histories have improved in their scholarly quality, but reflect a bias toward operational narratives and a distaste for either external relationships or internal difficulties. Marine Corps historical writing, which has been largely dominated by Marine enthusiasts in and out of uniform, has had a distinct utilitarian quality, that is, to build loyalty and dedication on the part of serving Marines, create public sympathy and support, present Corps's perspectives on policy issues past and present, and honor the service of former Marines. These characteristics are not unique to the Corps.

The first general history appeared during the reform movement of the 1870s, which itself had grown as a response to rumors of the Corps's abolition. Using documents provided by Captain Richard S. Collum, professional author M. Almey Aldrich wrote *History of the U.S. Marine Corps* (Boston: H. L. Shepard, 1875), a book so marred by errors that Collum himself wrote *History of the United States Marine Corps* (Philadelphia: R. L. Hamersly and Company, 1890), which Collum revised and published again with the same publisher in 1903. Although Aldrich and Collum are stronger on published documents and registers of officers than on analysis, both must be consulted on the nineteenth-century Corps. Not surprisingly, the ships guards' removal crisis produced another history: Julius Caesar Burrows, "History of the Marine Corps," Senate Document 719, 60th Congress, 2d Session (Washington: Government Printing Office, 1909), which depended largely upon Aldrich and Collum and amounted to little but a digest of the earlier works.

World War I brought a new interest in Marine Corps history. Two wartime histories were designed for a popular audience and made little original contribution to Marine Corps history except that they brought it through the World War. These histories are Willis J. Abbot, *Soldiers of the Sea* (New York: Dodd, Mead and Company, 1918), and John W. Leonard and Fred F. Chitty, *The Story of the United States Marines* (New York: U.S. Marine Corps Publicity Bureau, 1919). All of the authors were civilian popular writers. The war, however, produced more important, lasting contributions to Marine Corps history, primarily the emergence of Major General John A. Lejeune as Commandant and Lejeune's decision to create a historical section at Headquarters Marine Corps. Lejeune's choice for an official historian was Major Edwin N. McClellan, an industrious and dedicated officer and amateur historian whose history of the Corps in World War I remains the definitive study. McClellan decided to write a general history and eventually produced "History of the United States Marine Corps," 2 vols., 1925–1932, which benefited from the author's research in original documents but suffered from his uneven citation of sources and failure to synthesize and analyze the evidence. McClellan's history was never published but received limited circulation to both Marine and public libraries in mimeograph form. McClellan, whose service at Headquarters was periodically interrupted by field assignments, did not bring his manuscript into the twentieth century.

McClellan's work, however, provided the raw material for the next general history, Lieutenant Colonel Clyde H. Metcalf, *A History of the United States Marine Corps* (New York: G. P. Putnam's Sons, 1939), which was part of a series of histories of the American armed forces.

One of McClellan's successors as head of the small historical section, Metcalf produced a history characterized by sound analysis, good style, and some original scholarship, and Metcalf profited from the work of a contemporary, Captain Harry A. Ellsworth, who wrote (or compiled) *One Hundred Eighty Landings of United States Marines, 1800–1934* (Washington: Historical Section, HQMC, 1934), which was originally published in mimeograph form and then reissued in 1974 by the History and Museums Division.

World War II and the Korean War, mixed with the alarms of the Cold War and the controversies over defense organization, produced another surge of historical writing. Although the efforts of the official historians focused primarily upon administrative and operational monographs about both wars, authors close to the Corps produced three new short popular histories: George Phinney Hunt, *The Story of the U.S. Marines* (New York: Random House, 1951); Lieutenant Colonel Philip N. Pierce and Lieutenant Colonel Frank O. Hough, *The Compact History of the United States Marine Corps* (New York: Hawthorne Books, 1960); and Lynn Montross, *The United States Marines: A Pictorial History* (New York: Rinehart and Company, 1959). The chief contribution of the period came from Colonel Robert D. Heinl, Jr., also a head of the historical section, which had now become a Headquarters division. An unabashed Corps loyalist, indefatigable historian, and pungent stylist, Heinl wrote the most comprehensive history since Metcalf's, published after much controversy as *Soldiers of the Sea: The U.S. Marine Corps, 1775–1962* (Annapolis, Md.: U.S. Naval Institute, 1962). A book noted for its outspoken criticism of American politicians, generals, and admirals and their alleged efforts to abolish the Corps or curb its growth, *Soldiers of the Sea* might have been revised had not its author died suddenly in 1979.

Despite the supposed lack of interest in subjects military and historical that marked the 1960s and 1970s, historians of the Marine Corps continued to produce general histories, most of which were intended for a broad readership both inside and outside the Corps. The most significant work, notable for its focus and original research, was Lieutenant Colonel Kenneth J. Clifford, *Progress and Purpose: A Developmental History of the U.S. Marine Corps, 1900–1970* (Washington: History and Museums Division, 1973), a study written by a Reserve officer who was also a professional historian. Under the direction of Captain William D. Parker, another Reservist with academic training and the principal author, Marine official historians also produced *A Concise History of the United States Marine Corps, 1775–1969* (Washington: Historical Division, HQMC, 1970), an expanded version with photographs and appendices of an earlier short history published in 1961 and 1964 in pamphlet form. To replace earlier short histories, Brigadier General Edwin H. Simmons, in 1971 appointed director of the expanded and strengthened History and Museums Division, wrote a new general history characterized by clarity and special insight into Corps history since World War II. This history appeared in two versions: *The United States Marines* (London: Leo J. Cooper, Ltd., 1974) and *The United States Marines: The First Two Hundred Years, 1775–1976* (New York: Viking, 1974). Simmons's work profited not only from the author's extensive knowledge of Marine Corps history but from the growing number of monographs produced by his division and the inspired cartography of Lieutenant Colonel Charles Waterhouse, a Reserve officer and professional illustrator whose art work has been a signal achievement of Marine Corps history in 1970s.

Of the other popular treatments, two deserve mention. The first, Colonel James A. Donovan, Jr., *The United States Marine Corps* (New York: Frederick A. Praeger, 1967), sought to explain the Corps through its history and current organization, subculture, and military missions. Written by a longtime journalist and Corps admirer, J. Robert Moskin's *The U.S. Marine Corps Story* (New York: McGraw-Hill, 1977) emphasized Marine heroics in combat.*

Official Histories The vast majority of monographic history about the Marine Corps has been written by historians, uniformed and civilian, in the employ of the Marine Corps as permanent or temporary members of the History and Museums Division, Headquarters Marine Corps, or its predecessor organizations. Although it is true that the work of official historians is subject to much collective review by other official historians and (often) senior officers who are not professional historians, it is not necessarily true that such a process produces "court" or self-serving histories. Official historians do enjoy direct access to classified materials and to key military personalities, but such access is not difficult for other historians who have the energy and persistence to cultivate personal contacts and use the existing law to secure declassification of critical documents. My own experience with official history in this and other research projects convinces me that the only material purposely excluded was prejudicial only to individual reputations and normally skewed to protect individual rights. Of greater significance is the question of defining historical projects, which reflects organizational con-

---

* Marine Corps historians from Aldrich to Montross are discussed in the "Historians of the Corps" series in *Fortitudine,* quarterly newsletter of the History and Museums Division, in issues from Vol. II (Summer 1973) to Vol. 5 (Summer 1975).

cerns, not those of individual historians. Born in operational history, Marine Corps official history in the last twenty years has broadened in conception to the point where it is the monographic foundation upon which any general history must rest.

In terms of categories, official history (most of it published, but some still in manuscript form) falls into three groups: wartime operational history, special subjects, and unit history. The grouping is by no means neat, and studies in all three categories should be examined in comparative terms.

Nevertheless, official Marine Corps history has made its strongest contribution in describing wartime Marine operations. The pioneer study is Major Edwin N. McClellan, *The United States Marine Corps in the World War* (Washington: Historical Section, HQMC, 1920; reprint, 1968). The World War II series, *History of U.S. Marine Corps Operations in World War II*, produced five volumes:

- Lieutenant Colonel Frank O. Hough, Major Verle E. Ludwig, and Henry I. Shaw, Jr., *Pearl Harbor to Guadalcanal* (Washington: Historical Branch, HQMC, 1958).
- Henry I. Shaw, Jr., and Major Douglas T. Kane, *Isolation of Rabaul* (Washington: Historical Branch, HQMC, 1963).
- Henry I. Shaw, Jr., Bernard C. Nalty, and Edwin T. Turnbladh, *Central Pacific Drive* (Washington: Historical Branch, HQMC, 1966).
- George W. Garand and Truman R. Strobridge, *Western Pacific Operations* (Washington: Historical Division, HQMC, 1968).
- Benis M. Frank and Henry I. Shaw, Jr., *Victory and Occupation* (Washington: Historical Branch, HQMC, 1968).

The World War II volumes profit, in addition, from a series of fifteen campaign monographs written between 1947 and 1955 by officers assigned to the Historical Branch, G-3 Division, Headquarters Marine Corps. At the same time they eliminate the errors of the earlier studies and include additional U.S. and Japanese material. (The books in the earlier monograph series are listed in the History and Museums Division bibliographies.)

The five volumes of the *U.S. Marine Corps Operations in Korea, 1950–1953* maintained the same high standard set in the World War II histories, largely owing to the leadership of Lynn Montross. These books are:

- Lynn Montross and Captain Nicholas A. Canzona, *The Pusan Perimeter* (Washington: Historical Branch, HQMC, 1954).

- Lynn Montross and Captain Nicholas A. Canzona, *The Inchon–Seoul Operation* (Washington: Historical Branch, HQMC, 1955).
- Lynn Montross and Captain Nicholas A. Canzona, *The Chosin Reservoir Campaign* (Washington: Historical Branch, HQMC, 1957).
- Lynn Montross, Major Hubard D. Kuokka, and Major Norman W. Hicks, *The East-Central Front* (Washington: Historical Branch, HQMC, 1961).
- Lieutenant Colonel Pat Meid and Major James M. Yingling, *Operations in West Korea* (Washington: Historical Division, HQMC, 1972).

For Vietnam the History and Museums Division plans a series of between eight and fourteen volumes that will cover all phases of the war from the early advisory years to the final collapse of the Republic of Vietnam. Of the projected *U.S. Marines in Vietnam* series, two volumes have thus far appeared: Captain Robert H. Whitlow, *The Advisory and Combat Assistance Era, 1954–1964* (Washington: History and Museums Division, HQMC, 1977), and Jack Shulimson and Major Charles M. Johnson, *The Landing and the Buildup, 1965* (Washington: History and Museums Division, HQMC, 1978). In addition, the Historical Division holds a multivolume earlier manuscript, "U.S. Marine Corps in Vietnam," written in 1970 by official historians. It has also published special studies of value: Captain Russel H. Stolfi, *U.S. Marine Corps Civic Action Effort in Vietnam, March 1965–March 1966* (Washington: Historical Division, HQMC, 1968); Captain William D. Parker, *U.S. Marine Corps Civil Affairs in I Corps, Republic of South Vietnam, April 1966–April 1967* (Washington: Historical Division, HQMC, 1970); Captain Francis J. West, Jr., *Small Unit Action in Vietnam, Summer 1966* (Washington: Historical Division, HQMC, 1967); and Captain Moyers S. Shore II, *The Battle of Khe Sanh* (Washington: Historical Division, HQMC, 1969).

The official histories of Marine Corps participation in America's major modern wars do not exhaust the operational history bibliography. The other histories range from elaborate, exhaustive studies to brief "historical reference pamphlets." In the former category rests Charles R. Smith, *Marines in the Revolution: A History of the Continental Marines in the American Revolution, 1775–1783* (Washington: History and Museums Division, HQMC, 1975), a study so well-researched and enhanced with published documents that it should be the last word written on the subject. It includes illustrations by Charles Waterhouse. In the mid-range of research and length are several studies: Captain Stephen M. Fuller and Graham A. Cosmas, *Marines in the Dominican Republic,*

1916–1924 (Washington: History and Museums Division, HQMC, 1974); Jack Shulimson, *Marines in Lebanon* (Washington: Historical Division, HQMC, 1966), and the recently declassified Major Jack K. Ringler and Henry I. Shaw, Jr., *U.S. Marine Corps Operations in the Dominican Republic, April-June 1965* (Washington: Historical Division, HQMC, 1970). Other historical reference pamphlets have largely been absorbed or simply add minor supplementary material to more extensive official histories; in this category come several World War II pamphlets, studies of the Marines in postwar China and Japan, and the mobilization of the Marine Corps Reserve for the Korean War. Historical reference pamphlets on U.S. Marines in the Civil War, the Marine participation in the War with Spain, and the Marine intervention in Nicaragua (1910–1933) have been outdated by other published books and articles as well as by the availability of primary materials. Historical reference monographs on the Mexican War and the War of 1812 are under way, but no earlier pamphlets on either conflict exist.

The special subjects bibliography created by official Marine Corps historians is rapidly matching the operational histories in both quantity and quality. Written for both internal and public education, the special subjects monographs often reflect both pressing organizational concerns and episodic public interest rather than some long-term, coherent concept of the needs of complete organizational history. Nevertheless, since the 1960s the Corps's own historians have made substantial contributions to the understanding of many important aspects of Marine Corps history. All of these works are products of the History and Museums Division or its predecessors unless otherwise indicated. For this book, I found the following works of special utility:

- Bernard C. Nalty and Lieutenant Colonel Ralph F. Moody, *A Brief History of U.S. Marine Corps Officer Procurement, 1775–1969* (1970).
- Kenneth W. Condit, Major John H. Johnstone, and Ella W. Nargele, *A Brief History of Headquarters Marine Corps Staff Organization* (1971).
- Robert E. Barde, *The History of Marine Corps Competitive Marksmanship* (Washington: Marksmanship Branch, HQMC, 1961).
- Lieutenant Colonel John A. Driscoll, *The Eagle, Globe, and Anchor, 1858–1969* (1971).
- Elmore A. Champie, *A Brief History of the Marine Corps Recruit Depot, Parris Island, S.C., 1891–1962*, rev. ed. (1962).
- Elmore A. Champie, *A Brief History of the Marine Corps Base and Recruit Depot, San Diego, California, 1914–1962*, rev. ed. (1962).

- Kenneth W. Condit, Gerald Diamond, and Edwin T. Turnbladh, "Marine Corps Ground Training in World War II," ms. history, (1956).
- Lieutenant Colonel William R. Fails, *Marines and Helicopters, 1962–1973* (1978).
- Lieutenant Colonel Charles A. Fleming, Captain Robin L. Austin, and Captain Charles A. Braley III, *Quantico: Crossroads of the Marine Corps* (1979).
- Lieutenant Colonel Edward C. Johnson and Graham A. Cosmas, *Marine Corps Aviation: The Early Years, 1912–1940* (1977).
- Reserve Officers of Public Affairs Unit 4–1, *The Marine Corps: A History* (Washington: Division of Reserve, HQMC, 1966).
- Henry I. Shaw, Jr., and Ralph W. Donnelly, *Blacks in the Marine Corps* (1975).
- Bernard C. Nalty et al., *United States Marine Corps Ranks and Grades, 1775–1969* (1970).
- Lieutenant Colonel Eugene W. Rawlins, *Marines and Helicopters, 1946–1962* (1976).
- Lieutenant Colonel Pat Meid, *Marine Corps Women's Reserve in World War II*, rev. ed. (1968).
- Captain Linda L. Hewitt, *Women Marines in World War I* (1974). Historical Branch, G-3 Division, HQMC, *Marine Corps Aircraft, 1913–1965*, rev. ed. (1967).

In addition to these special studies, the researcher can use a four-volume chronology of Marine Corps history, 1775–1969, compiled by the staff of the History and Museums Division, 1965–1971.

Despite the centrality of unit history to the Marine Corps historical effort, official unit history lacks the flair and sense of truth that characterize "unofficial" Marine Corps units histories, particularly the histories of World War II and Korea. Part of the problem is that unit history is captive to official unit reports and command chronologies that either have limited historical value or represent collectively written, uncontroversial accounts of organizational activities. Because a major purpose of unit history is to build organizational *esprit,* official accounts seldom discuss unit failings, however temporary, or the effect of individual leaders. In addition, unit histories are normally used to establish lineage and command succession, hardly subjects to attract average Marine readers. Unit reports also tend to be unexciting statistical summaries, which, without some frame of reference, are almost meaningless. An example, however, of what unit history can be—a discussion of both operations and organizational politics—is Charles L. Updegraph,

Jr., *United States Marine Corps Special Units of World War II* (Washington: History and Museums Division, HQMC, 1972). Official unit histories are, nevertheless, numerous. The organizations treated thus far have been the 1st Marine Division (1974), the 3d Division (1975), the 4th Marine Division in World War II (1945, reprinted 1976), the 1st Marines (1968), the 2d Marines (1969), the 3d Marines (1968), the 4th Marines (1970), the 5th Marines (rev. 1968), the 8th Marines (1976), the 9th Marines (1967), the 11th Marines (1968), and the 12th Marines (1972). Although more professional in preparation and publication, recent aviation unit histories exhibit the same placidness; they include histories of Marine Fighter Attack Squadron 312 (1978), Marine Fighter Attack Squadron 232 (1978), and Marine Attack Squadron 311 (1978). Only Lieutenant Colonel Gary W. Parker, *A History of Medium Helicopter Squadron 161* (1978) deals with subjects beyond unit operations, largely because HMM-161 was a pioneer in vertical envelopment tactics. For ground units, the best official effort remains Kenneth W. Condit and Edwin T. Turnbladh, *Hold High the Torch: A History of the 4th Marines* (Washington: Historical Branch, HQMC, 1960).

Unofficial Unit Histories and Operational Accounts Although several battalions and a few companies of the 4th Marine Brigade (1917–1919) sponsored their own unit histories, the basic studies of the Marines in France remain McClellan's articles and official monograph and Colonel Oliver L. Spaulding, USA, and Colonel John W. Wright, USA, *The Second Division, American Expeditionary Force in France, 1917–1919* (New York: The Hillman Press, 1937), a division history written by two experienced officer-historians. A detailed account that also catches the ferocity of the war is former Marine Robert B. Asprey's *At Belleau Wood* (New York: Putnam, 1965).

World War II brought a new peak in the excellence and length of unit histories and produced a series of memorable studies of the Fleet Marine Force's finest hour. The classic division history is George McMillan, *The Old Breed: A History of the First Marine Division in World War II* (Washington: Infantry Journal Press, 1949). The other division histories are:

- Richard W. Johnston, *Follow Me: The Story of the Second Marine Division in World War II* (New York: Random House, 1948).
- Captain Carl W. Proehl, *The Fourth Marine Division in World War II* (Washington: Infantry Journal Press, 1946).
- First Lieutenant Robert A. Aurthur and First Lieutenant Kenneth Cohlmia, *The Third Marine Division* (Washington: Infantry Journal Press, 1948).

- Howard M. Conner, *The Spearhead: The World War II History of the 5th Marine Division* (Washington: Infantry Journal Press, 1950).
- First Lieutenant Bevan C. Cass et al., *History of the Sixth Marine Division* (Washington: Infantry Journal Press, 1948).

Two regimental histories of the 3d and 9th Marines bring the fighting and Marines even closer; they are First Lieutenant L. D. Burrus et al., *The Ninth Marines* (Washington: Infantry Journal Press, 1946), and John Monks, Jr., *A Ribbon and a Star* (New York: Henry Holt and Company, 1945). The most impressive corpus of unofficial writing in Marine Corps history is the set of operational histories written for commercial publication. An examination of the History and Museums Division's World War II bibliography covers the entire collection, but the most significant books for a comprehensive understanding of the Marines in World War II are:

- Robert B. Asprey, *Semper Fidelis* (New York: W. W. Norton, 1967).
- Benis M. Frank, *Okinawa: The Great Island Battle* (New York: E. P. Dutton, 1978).
- Brigadier General Samuel B. Griffith II, *The Battle for Guadalcanal* (Philadelphia: Lippincott, 1963).
- Jeter A. Isely and Philip A. Crowl, *The U.S. Marines and Amphibious War: Its Theory and Practice in the Pacific* (Princeton, N.J.: Princeton University Press, 1951).
- Robert Leckie, *Strong Men Armed: The United States Marines Against Japan* (New York: Random House, 1962).
- Samuel Eliot Morison, *The Two Ocean War* (Boston: Little, Brown and Company, 1963).
- Richard F. Newcomb, *Iwo Jima* (New York: Holt, Rinehart and Winston, 1965).
- Robert Sherrod, *History of Marine Corps Aviation in World War II* (Washington: Combat Forces Press, 1952).
- Robert Sherrod, *Tarawa* (New York: Duell, Sloan, and Pearce, 1944).
- S. E. Smith, ed., *The United States Marine Corps in World War II* (New York: Random House, 1969).

The unofficial operational histories written about the wars in Korea and Vietnam do not yet match in quantity those written about World War II, but they do include some of the best writing about Marines in action. In this category fall:

- Andrew Geer, *The New Breed: The Story of the U.S. Marines in Korea* (New York: Harper and Brothers, 1952).
- Colonel Robert D. Heinl, Jr., *Victory at High Tide: The Inchon–Seoul Campaign* (Philadelphia: Lippincott, 1968).
- Robert Leckie, *The March to Glory* (New York: World, 1960).
- Francis J. West, Jr., *The Village* (New York: Harper and Row, 1972).

Official Histories of Other Services If only for a different perspective upon Marine operational history, the researcher should not ignore the official histories of the other American armed services. The official histories of Navy, Army, and Air Force operations have been written with the same skill and access to documents as Marine Corps history. Since the bibliographies published by the History and Museums Division list the other official histories, as do other bibliographies on military history, it is unnecessary to list all of them in full. However, some general description seems appropriate, because I utilized these sources. For World War II, the Navy's extensive historical effort produced, among its many achievements, three studies critical to the analysis of Marine Corps history. These are Samuel Eliot Morison's fifteen-volume history of U.S. Navy operations, Duncan S. Ballantine's single volume on Navy logistics, and Julius A. Furer's massive volume on the administration of the Department of the Navy. The Office of the Chief of Military History, Department of the Army (now the Center of Military History) sponsored equally important volumes on the Pacific war as part of the *U.S. Army in World War II* series. At the politico-strategic level, see the volume by Louis Morton on Pacific planning through 1943, the two volumes on global strategy by Maurice Matloff and Edwin M. Snell, and the two volumes by Richard M. Leighton and Robert W. Coakley on global logistics. At the operational level OCMH published books by Louis Morton on the fall of the Philippines, by John Miller, Jr., on the campaigns in the South Pacific and Southwest Pacific theaters, by Philip A. Crowl and Edmund G. Love on the Gilberts and Marshalls operations, by Philip A. Crowl on the Marianas campaign, by Robert Ross Smith on the approach to the Philippines (the Palaus) and the reconquest of the Philippines, and by Roy E. Appleman on Okinawa. The seven-volume history of Army Air Forces operations in World War II written under the direction of Wesley Frank Craven and James Lea Cate is less useful, because Marine aviation and USAAF aviation fought separate wars after the early Solomons with the exception of the Philippine campaign.

For the Korean War the Army histories are the most numerous and helpful. James F. Schnabel's study of the war from the perspective of the JCS and General MacArthur is important, while Roy Appleman's book on the U.S. military operations in June–November 1950 and Walter G. Hermes's study of operations from late 1951 through the truce are equally significant. The Air Force operational history by Robert F. Futrell is worth reading, while naval operations are covered in separate volumes by Malcolm Cagle and Frank A. Manson (both Navy officers) and James A. Field, Jr., a professional historian working for the Naval Historical Division.

The armed services' historical divisions are well along on their studies of the Vietnam War, but the published output to date is scanty. The Air Force, which organized two contemporaneous historical-analytical projects under the titles "Corona Harvest" and CHECHO, has numerous in-house classified studies in its files and has begun to publish some of them in a special Southeast Asia monograph series. Although the Army plans an extensive Vietnam War series that may match its World War II volumes in authoritativeness, it has thus far published only a "Vietnam Studies" set of monographs, which, despite their general usefulness, suffer from parochialism and the fact that the authors are senior Vietnam-era generals and their principal staff officers. The Navy has published only one volume, a collectively authored study of the advisory period.

Biographies of Marines Potentially an area of significant historical contribution and rich in source material, the field of Marine Corps biography is as yet relatively unexploited, particularly in comparison with the body of work on Army and Navy officers. Part of the difficulty is certainly that historical divisions do not do biography because it tends to be controversial and forces an organizational consensus upon the criteria upon which individual achievements should be assessed. Biography also forces at least three implicit choices upon an author. For one, he can reveal character and deal with his subject only because he seems to have played a historically important role, normally in wartime command. Another choice is to deal with an individual as a subject for psychohistory, which so accentuates individual eccentricities and behavioral aberrance that it will exclude by definition almost every successful senior officer. The last option is to examine individual careers as a reflection of organizational goals and individual adaptations, an approach neither well understood nor well exploited by most historians. Marine Corps biography at the moment rests in the first category.

Given the charismatic nature of their subjects, it is not surprising that the two best studies to date are Burke Davis, *Marine! The Life of Lt. Gen. Lewis B. (Chesty) Puller, USMC (Ret.)* (Boston: Little, Brown,

1962), and Norman V. Cooper, "The Military Career of Gen. Holland M. Smith, USMC," unpublished Ph.D. dissertation, University of Alabama, 1974. Davis's work, however, emphasizes Puller's personal flair in the warrior role and underestimates Puller's professionalism. Cooper's study appropriately stresses Smith's real accomplishments and corrects the excesses of *Coral and Brass*. Much of the rest of Marine biography is notable only for its superficiality and limited knowledge of Corps institutional history. In this category fall Charles Lee Lewis, *Famous American Marines* (Boston: L. C. Page, 1950), noteworthy only for its author's knowledge of naval history and its coverage of eighteen Marine officers; Michael Blankfort, *The Big Yankee: The Life of Carlson of the Raiders* (Boston: Little, Brown, 1947); Col. Roger Willock, *Lone Star Marine: A Biography of the Late Colonel John W. Thomason, Jr., USMC* (Princeton, N.J.: Roger Willock, 1961); Colonel Roger Willock, *Unaccustomed to Fear: A Biography of the Late General Roy S. Geiger, USMC* (Princeton, N.J.: Roger Willock, 1968); and Gladys Zehnphennig, *Melvin J. Maas, Gallant Man of Action* (Minneapolis: T. S. Denison, 1967). Recent academic studies that rely upon both primary sources and individual interviews, however, demonstrate the potential for scholarly biography: Shirley Shiep Foster, "Lieutenant General Alpha L. Bowser, USMC, and the Korean War," unpublished M.A. thesis, San Diego State University, 1975; Richard H. Hoy, "Victor H. Krulak: A Marine's Biography," unpublished M.A. thesis, San Diego State University, 1974; and Joe A. Simon, "The Life and Career of General John Archer Lejeune," unpublished M.A. thesis, Louisiana State University, 1967.

General Reference Works and Special Studies Like any other complex, long-lived military organization, the Marine Corps has produced a long line of official orders, memoranda, field manuals, registers and lineal lists of officers, pamphlets, ordnance instructions, administrative and logistical manuals, and issuances of various sorts from Headquarters Marine Corps and its major field commands. From uniform regulations to mess hall manuals, the largest collection of these monuments to administrative regularization may be found in the library of the Marine Corps Historical Center. They are the authoritative source of detailed, technical information on Marine Corps policies and practices. These primary sources, however, have led to published reference works that assist the researcher.

In the field of personal information, one may consult the following works:

- Reginald W. Arthur, *Contact!* Vol. I. *Careers of U.S. Naval Avia-*

tors Assigned Numbers 1 to 2000 (Washington: Naval Aviators Register, 1967).

- Edward W. Callahan, ed., *List of Officers of the U.S. Navy and of the Marine Corps, 1775–1900* (New York: L. R. Hamersly, 1901).
- Lewis R. Hamersly, comp., *The Records of Living Officers of the U.S. Navy and Marine Corps*, 3d ed. (Philadelphia: J. B. Lippincott, 1878).
- Thomas H. S. Hamersly, ed., *General Register of the United States Navy and Marine Corps. . . For One Hundred Years, 1782–1882* (Washington: Thomas H. S. Hamersly, 1882).
- Karl Schuon, comp., *U.S. Marine Corps Biographical Dictionary* (New York: Franklin Watts, 1963).

In addition to the official uniform regulations, see also Major Edwin N. McClellan, *Uniforms of the American Marines, 1775 to 1829* (Washington: History and Museums Division, HQMC, 1974; orig. published, 1932); Colonel Robert H. Rankin, *Uniforms of the Sea Services* (Annapolis, Md.: U.S. Naval Institute, 1962); and Colonel Robert H. Rankin, *Uniforms of Marines* (New York: G. P. Putnam's Sons, 1970). For weapons, see Colonel Robert H. Rankin, *Small Arms of the Sea Services* (New Milford, Conn.: N. Flayderman and Company, 1972).

Also in the category of general reference works fall Jane Blakeney, *Heroes, U.S. Marines Corps, 1861–1955* (Washington: Jane Blakeney, 1957); Bureau of Personnel, Department of the Navy, *Decorations, Medals, Ribbons, and Badges of the United States Navy, Marine Corps, and Coast Guard, 1861–1948* (Washington: Government Printing Office, 1951); Karl Schuon, *Home of the Commandants*, rev. ed. (Washington: Leatherneck Association, Inc., 1974); William T. Larkins, *U.S. Marine Corps Aircraft, 1914–1959* (Concord, Calif.: Aviation History Publications, 1959); and Lloyd S. Jones, *U.S. Naval and Marine Corps Fighters, Navy/Marine Corps, 1922–1980s* (Fallbrook, Calif.: Aero Publications, 1979).

The number of nonofficial special studies of the Marine Corps is limited but includes several works useful to this book. For Marine Corps public relations, see Robert Lindsay, *This High Name: Public Relations and the U.S. Marine Corps* (Madison: University of Wisconsin Press, 1956), and Benis M. Frank, *Denig's Demons and How They Grew: The Story of Marine Corps Combat Correspondents, Photographers and Artists* (Washington: Marine Corps Combat Correspondents and Photographers Association, 1967). On the development of vertical envelopment operations, see Lynn Montross, *Cavalry of the Sky: The Story of*

U.S. Marine Combat Helicopters (New York: Harper and Brothers, 1954). Recent scholarly studies of Marine Corps subjects include:

- John C. Chapin, "The Marines' Role in the U.S. Occupation of Haiti, 1915–1922," unpublished M.A. thesis, George Washington University, 1967.
- Colonel John E. Fahey, "A History of the Marine Corps Recruit Depot, San Diego, California," unpublished M.A. thesis, University of San Diego, 1974.
- Frank J. Infusino, "The U.S. Marines and War Planning, 1900–1941," unpublished M.A. thesis, San Diego State University, 1974.
- Major Gordon W. Keiser, "The U.S. Marine Corps and Unification: 1944–1947," unpublished MA thesis, Tufts University, 1971.
- Major Norman W. Hicks, "U.S. Marine Operations in Korea, 1952–1953, with Special Emphasis on Outpost Warfare," unpublished M.A. thesis, University of Maryland, 1962.
- James A. MacDonald, "The Problems of U.S. Marine Corps Prisoners of War in Korea," unpublished M.A. thesis, University of Maryland, 1962.
- General Vernon E. Megee, "United States Military Intervention in Nicaragua, 1909–1932," unpublished M.A. thesis, University of Texas-Austin, 1963.
- Charles A. Peckham, "The Northern Expedition, the Nanking Incident, and the Protection of American Nationals," unpublished M.A. thesis, Ohio State University, 1973.
- Lieutenant Colonel Gary L. Rutledge, "The Rhetoric of United States Marine Corps Enlisted Recruitment," unpublished M.A. thesis, University of Kansas, 1974.

Doctoral dissertations on Marine Corps subjects are rarer, for Marine officers seldom receive Ph.D.s in history, political science, and sociology, and civilian academic interest in the Corps, not extensive, tends to focus on the use of Marines in Latin America. The three most significant works in the doctoral category are:

- Neill Macauley, *The Sandino Affair* (Chicago: Quadrangle Books, 1967).
- Richard L. Millett, *Guardians of the Dynasty: A History of the U.S. Created Guardia Nacional de Nicaragua and the Somoza Family* (Maryknoll, N.Y.: Orbis Books, 1977).
- Hans Schmidt, *The United States Occupation of Haiti, 1915–1934* (New Brunswick, N.J.: Rutgers University Press, 1971).

Miscellaneous This essay on sources does not describe all the possible evidence that provides special insight to Marine Corps history.

Who, for example, would ignore the fiction of John W. Thomason, Jr., and the photography of David Douglas Duncan? Who would ignore the semi-autobiographical Marine war fiction that now extends from World War I to the Vietnam conflict? Another vast source of information is the collection of documentary films the Corps made in order to explain itself and its missions; these films now reside in the motion picture archives of the History and Museums Division at the Marine Corps Historical Center. To understand the development of the Corps's self-image and public appeal over many years, one should examine Marine recruiting posters. Marine Corps art is also an important source of visual information on Marine operations, and the fine museum on the ground floor of the Marine Historical Center is now matched by a collection of restored aircraft and armored vehicles at the Marine base at Quantico, Virginia. Most Marine Corps bases have their own small collections of monuments, historical exhibits, and war trophies, as well as post and unit newspapers. Wherever Marines assemble, they bring with them their past.

Index

Abrams, General Creighton W., 587, 594
Abyssinia, 137, 149
Acheson, Secretary of State Dean G., 476
Act of 1798, 29–30, 70
Act of 1834, 68, 70, 82
Adams, Secretary of the Navy Charles Francis, 330
Adams, John, 7, 16–18, 26: President, 28, 30
Adams, President John Quincy, 64
Advanced base force, 261, 272, 275, 278–80, 283, 286, 291, 308, 322: aviation in, 277; advanced base force battalions, 139, 142; advanced base concept, 280, 282, 284, 320; development of, 274; advanced base regiments, 288, 296; reorganized, 324
Advanced bases, 271: defense of, 273; mission of, 275, 277; training, 272, 274
Advanced Base School, 276–77, 280–81, 283–85
Advanced Research Group, 524
"A few good men," 104
Agat, Guam, 417
Aguinaldo, Emilio, 151
Aircraft types: Bell AH-1G "Cobra," 601, 614; Bell UH-1 "Huey," 551, 582, 585, 614; Boeing B-29 "Superfortress," 410, 427, 432, 464; Boeing B-36, 472; Boeing B-52 "Stratofortress," 589; Boeing-Vertol CH-46A "Sea Knight," 551, 582, 601, 614; Brewster F2A "Buffalo," 334; Chance-Vought F4U "Corsair," 378, 422, 437, 466, 481, 502, 515; Chance-Vought F8U "Crusader," 535; Curtiss JN-4B "Jenny," 309; Curtiss SB2U "Vindicator," 334; DeHavilland DH-4, 310; Douglas AD "Skyraider," 466, 515; Douglas A4 "Skyhawk," 535, 550, 585–86, 613; Douglas SBD, 425; Grumman A-6A "Intruder," 550, 586, 613; Grumman F4F "Wildcat," 355, 368; Grumman F6F "Hellcat," 424, 437; Grumman F9F "Panther," 502; Hawker-Siddeley AV-8A "Harrier," 550–51, 612; McDonnell F4 "Phantom," 535, 550, 585, 611–12; McDonnell-Douglas F-18, 612–13; Mitsubishi "Zero," 368, 379; Piasecki HRP

"Flying Banana," 551; Sikorsky CH53A "Sea Stallion," 551, 582, 601, 614–15; Sikorsky HO3S-1, 456; Sikorsky HRS-1, 505; Sikorsky HR2S-1, 510, 524–25; Sikorsky HUS, 510, 525; Vought 02U-1 "Corsair," 249
Air liaison parties, 409, 425, 437
Air support radar teams (ASRTs), 586
Aisne-Marne salient, 305
Aisne River, 298
Alabama, 96–97
Albany, Georgia, 519, 546
Aldrich, M. Almy, 114, 739
Alexandria, Egypt, 105, 539
Alfred, 12, 15–16
Algiers, 27
Alliance, 18–19, 24
All-volunteer force, 618
Almond, Major General Edward M., 486, 490–91
Altimirona, Pedron, 258
American Legation, Peking, 137
American Legation, Tientsin, 137
American Samoa, 352
American War of Independence, 5, 14 23–25
Amiens, France, 297
Amphibian tank, development of, 341; see also Landing vehicle, tracked
Amphibious Assault Fuel System (AAFS), 536
Amphibious operations, 22, 331: in Mexican War, 74; in Civil War, 51; character of, in Pacific, 386
Amphibious warfare doctrine, 328–29, 332, 346, 376, 388
Amvets, 531
"An Act for Establishing a Marine Corps," 28
Anderson, General Earl E., 608, 611, 614, 618
Angaur, Palau Islands, 420
An Hoa, Vietnam, 570, 574, 589, 595
An Hoa basin, 575–76, 601–602
Annapolis, Maryland, 272, 277
Annexation of California, 74
Anping, China, 450
Antenna Valley, 589
Anthony, William, 129
Aogiri Ridge, Cape Gloucester, 385
Apamama, Gilbert Islands, 393
Apra, Guam, 130, 417
Arab-Israeli War of 1956, 532

Archibald Henderson, 284
Argonne Forest, France, 311–12
Argus, 44
Arias, Desiderio, 183, 191–92
Arizona Territory, Vietnam, 589
Arlington National Cemetery, 511
Armed Forces Reserve Acts of 1952
 and 1955, 538
Armistice, World War I, 316
Army and Navy Journal, 175–76
Army-Marine Corps relations, 411, 413,
 415, 438
Army Reform Act, 119
Arnold, Benedict, 6, 19–20
Arnold, General H. H., 389, 457
Articles of War, 29–30, 58, 66, 81
Asan, Guam, 417–18
Asa River, Okinawa, 436
A Shau Valley, Vietnam, 576, 584, 594
Asheville, 218
Ashley River, 23
Aslito airfield, Saipan, 412–13
Assunpink Creek, New Jersey, 13
Atlanta, 116
Atomic Energy Commission, 509
Australia, 352, 357, 363, 365
Azores, 309, 349, 464

Babelthuap, Palau Islands, 420
Badoeng Straits, 484
Bagaduce Peninsula, Maine, 21–22
Baghdad Pact, 539
Bahamas, 10
Bainbridge, Commodore William, 60
"Bainbridge Scale," 60, 62
Baker, First Lieutenant D. D., 80
Baker, Secretary of War Newton D.,
 290, 295
Balangiga, Philippine Islands, 153
Ba Long, Vietnam, 584
Baltimore, 33: *Baltimore* affair, 120
Baltimore, Maryland, 48
Bancroft, Secretary of the Navy George,
 73
Bank of Haiti, 179
Banks Island, Maine, 22
Barbary pirates, 27, 43, 45
Barbary Wars, 90, 738
Barnett, Colonel George, 180: Major
 General, 12th Commandant of the
 Marine Corps, 202–203, 277, 282–
 84, 286–87, 289–90, 293–96, 306,
 309, 318, 320, 321–23, 731, 736; on
 wartime Marine Corps functions, 285;
 plans to expand the Corps, 306
Barney, Captain Joshua, 48–49

Barrett, Major Charles D., 331: Major
 General, 373
Barrier Forts, 85
Barron, Commodore Samuel, 44
Barrow, Lieutenant General Robert H.,
 618, 621: General, 27th Comman-
 dant of the Marine Corps, 624
Barry, Captain John, 11, 24
Barstow, California, 480, 546
Base defense in the Pacific, 325:
 missions, 329
Basey, Philippine Islands, 153–54
Bashaw of Tripoli, 38, 44–45
Bataan, 505
Bataan Peninsula, Philippine Islands,
 356
Batista, General Fulgencio, 541
Bauer, Lieutenant Colonel Harold W.
 "Joe," 368
Bay of Pigs, Cuba, 554
Beadle, Colonel Elias R., 245, 253,
 255–56
Beals, Carleton, 248
"Bear Flag," 74
Beaumont, Brigadier General John C.,
 233
Beech, Keyes, 391
Beirut, Lebanon, 137, 540
Belén Gate, Mexico City, 77, 79
Bell Aircraft Corporation, 455
Belleau Wood, Battle of, 301–306, 312,
 316, 318
Ben Hai River, Vietnam, 534
Benson, Admiral William S., 290
Bering Sea Patrol, Marines in, 121
Berkeley, Brigadier General Randolph
 C., 331
Berman, Emile Zola, 531
Betio, 393, 395, 398–99; *see also*
 Tarawa
Biddle, Nicholas, 15
Biddle, Colonel William P., 11th
 Commandant of the Marine Corps,
 276–81
Bikini Lagoon, 452
Bismarck Archipelago, 352, 357, 362
Black Marines, 374–75, 468, 508–509,
 599–600
Bladensburg, Maryland, battle of, 48, 50
Bliss, General Tasker H., 290
Bluefields, Nicaragua, 169, 238, 242,
 259
Board of Admiralty, 22–23
Board of Navy Commissioners, 53, 55,
 60, 62, 67, 69
Board of Organization, Tactics, and
 Drill, 122; *see also* Greer Board

Bobo, Ronsalvo, 184–86
Bois de Belleau, France, 301; *see also* Belleau Wood
Bois de la Brigade de Marine, 304; *see also* Belleau Wood
Bonhomme Richard, 18
Bonin Islands, 426–27
Bordeaux, France, 16
Bordentown, New Jersey, 20
Borno, President Louis, 207, 209
Bosch, Juan, 556–57
Boston, 17, 116
Boston, Massachusetts, siege of, 5–6
Boston Navy Yard, 38
Bougainville, Solomon Islands, 363, 377, 381–82, 387
Bouresches, France, 301–302
Boxer, 535
Boxer Protocol, 212, 216, 226–27
Boxers, 156–58, 162
Boxer Uprising, 137, 155, 163–64, 212–13, 219, 262
Bradley, General Omar N., 471–72, 479, 497–98, 500
Brainard, Major E. H., 333
Branch, Secretary of the Navy John, 61
Brandywine, 65
Breese, Commander K. R., 98–99
Bremerton, Washington, 140
Brest, France, 316
British forces. *See also* Royal Marines, Royal Navy: British Expeditionary Force, 296, 345; Duke of York and Albany's Maritime Regiment of Foot, 3; Lord High Admiral's Regiment, 3; Royal Welch Fusiliers, 161
Bronson, Private Walter, 732
Brookings Institution, 608
Brooklyn, 58
Brooklyn Navy Yard, 38, 96
Brooks, Lieutenant John, 47, 50
Broome, Lieutenant James, 471: Lieutenant Colonel, 731
Brown, Secretary of Defense Harold R., 609
Brown, John, 89
Brown, Major General Wilburt S., 731
Buchanan, President James, 86
Buck, Pearl, 229
Buckner, Lieutenant General Simon Bolivar, Jr., 433, 435, 438
Bud Dajo Mountain, 426
Buenos Aires, Argentina, 84
Bull Run, Battle of, Marines in, 94–95
Buna, New Guinea, 377
"Bunker Hill," Korea, 514–15

Burger, Major General Joseph C., 529–30
Burke, Admiral Arleigh A., 520, 524
Burma, 352
Burrows, Lieutenant Colonel William Ward, 2d Commandant of the Marine Corps, 30–34, 36–38
Bush, Lieutenant William, 47, 50
Butaritari, 393
Butler, Captain Smedley D., 141, 150, 162, 174: Major, 185, 187; Brigadier General, 202, 204, 224–27, 322; Major General, 262, 316, 324–25, 731, 736; as commandant of the *Gendarmerie d'Haiti,* 188; occupies Bluefields, 168; on China duty, 228
Butler, Congressman Thomas, 141, 322
Butler Subcommittee, 143–44
Button, Corporal William R., 198

Cabo Gracias a Dios, Nicaragua, 238, 251, 259
Cabot, 15
Cabral, Buenventura, 205
Cabral, Donald Reid, 557
Cacos, 178, 183–84, 186–89, 196–99
Caco war, end of, 208
"Cactus," 365; *see also* Guadalcanal
"Cactus Air Force," 368
Cadwalader, Brigadier General John, 13–14
California, 622
California Battalion of Volunteers, 75
Ca Lu, Vietnam, 584, 591, 595
Cambodia, 566, 604
Cambodian incursion, 603
Cam Lo, Vietnam, 584
Campbell, Captain Hugh, 42
Camp Carroll, Vietnam, 584
Camp Elliott, California, 348
Camp Lejeune, North Carolina, 348, 376, 455, 465–66, 599, 625
Camp McCalla, Guantanamo Bay, Cuba, 132
Camp Pendleton, California, 348, 376, 465–66, 478, 480, 508, 521, 566, 577, 594, 599, 617, 625
Canada, 5, 7
Canal Zone, 166, 181
Canton, China, 84
Cape Gloucester, New Britain, 384–85
Caperton, Rear Admiral William B., 185–86, 191–92
Cape Torokina, Bougainville, 381–82
Cap Haïtien, Haiti, 184, 186, 208
Caracas, Venezuela, 541

Caribbean Sea, 4, 12, 27, 148, 163–64, 181, 238, 261, 276, 279–80, 282–83, 287–88, 291, 322–23, 325, 328, 336, 349, 537, 541, 554, 556, 596
Carl, Captain Marion, 368
Carlson, Captain Evans F., 234
Carmick, Lieutenant Daniel, 33, 35: Captain, 40–41, 49–50
Carney, Admiral Robert B., 520
Caroline Islands, 269, 320, 326, 389, 393, 399, 404, 409
Cartagena expedition, 4
Carter, Calvin B., 240
Casablanca Conference, 377
Castine, 191
Castner, Brigadier General Joseph, 225
Castro, Fidel, 541: Castroism, 554
Cates, Major General Clifton B., 428, 465, 470, 472: General, 19th Commandant of the Marine Corps, 477–79, 496–98, 500, 507, 528, 731
Catlin, Colonel Albertus W., 293, 298: Brigadier General, 202, 302, 736
Cavite, Philippine Islands, 130, 151–52, 154–55, 270, 272, 356
Cayes, Haiti, 209–10
Central Highlands, Vietnam, 563, 566, 672, 604
Central Intelligence Agency, 457
Central Pacific, 384, 387–89, 391–92, 404–405, 409, 421, 431–32
Central Powers, 296–97
Chadwick, French E., 126
Chaffee, Major General Adna R., 154, 161
Chaisson, Lieutenant General John R., 732
Chammorro, Emiliano, 169, 241–42, 245
Chamoun, President Camille, 539–40
Champagne, France, 312–13
Changchon, Korea, 484
Chang Tso-lin, General, 218–20
Chapei, China, 232
Chapman, Lieutenant General Leonard F., Jr., 583: General, 24th Commandant of the Marine Corps, 599–600, 604
Chapultepec Castle, Mexico City, assault on, 77–80, 109
Charleston, South Carolina, 22–23, 31, 96, 98
Château-Thierry, 299, 302, 305, 318
Chauchat machine guns, 294
Chaumont, 222–23, 332
Chefoo, China, 449

Chehab, General Fuad, 539–40
Chemin des Dames, France, 298
Chesapeake, 42, 47
Chesapeake Bay, 46
Chiang Kai-shek, Generalissimo, 220, 230, 232, 446, 449–50, 476
Chicago, 116, 124
Chien Men Gate, Peking, 157–58
Chihli Province, China, 156
China, 137, 152, 163, 225–26, 230–31, 261–62, 319, 329–30, 351, 354, 388–89, 410, 446, 458, 465, 490, 728–29, 731: American foreign policy in, 226; Marines in, 212–35; Occupation of North China, 448
China Relief Expedition, 735
Chinandega, Nicaragua, 244
Chindong-ni, Korea, 477, 484
Chinese Civil War, 450–51
Chinese Nationalists, 221, 226–30; *see also* Kuomintang: Nationalist armies, 223–24; 19th Route Army, 230–31
Chinese revolution, 216–17, 219, 221
Chinhung-ni, Korea, 492–93
Chinju, Korea, 482, 484
Chinwangtao, China, 220, 449
Choiseul, Solomon Islands, 381–82
Chosin Reservoir, Korea, 481, 491–92, 494–95, 498
"Chowder Society," the, 458, 461–63, 471
Christie tank, 341
Christy, Howard Chandler, 307
Chu Lai, Vietnam, 566, 569–70, 572, 574, 592
Chungking, China, 214
Church, Lieutenant Frank, 732
Cibao Valley, Dominican Republic, 179
Cibik's Ridge, Bougainville, 383
Cienfuegos, Cuba, 167
Civic action, 570–71, 575, 590
Civil Operations and Revolutionary Development Support (CORDS), 575
Civil War, 81, 88, 97, 101, 117, 131, 731, 735: Marines in, 90–92
Cleveland, 242
Clifford, Secretary of Defense Clark, 587
Clifford, Lieutenant Colonel Kenneth J., 740
Clinch, Lieutenant Bartholomew, 33, 35–36
Close air support, 263, 333–35, 361, 379, 381, 383, 386, 395, 407, 409, 413–14, 423, 425–26, 440–41, 456,

Close air support (*cont.*)
464, 466, 479, 482, 498, 501–502,
505, 513, 524, 527, 535, 551, 568,
572–73, 582, 586–89, 602, 611, 613
Cloverleaf Hill, Korea, 484
Cochrane, Lieutenant Henry Clay, 110,
112, 121: Major, 132; Brigadier
General, 731
Coco River, Nicaragua, 237, 248–49,
259–60
Coco River patrol, 251; *see also*
Edson, Captain Merritt A.
Colby, Secretary of State Bainbridge, 194
Cole, Major Eli K., 274, 279–80:
Lieutenant Colonel, 275; Colonel,
174, 284–85; Brigadier General, 327
Collins, Lieutenant General Joseph
Lawton, 458
Collins, Major General William R., 566
Collins Plan, 458, 462
Collum, Captain Richard S., 114, 739
Colombia, 164: Marine landing in, 166
Colon, Panama, 106, 164, 166
Columbia, 84
Columbian Exposition, 121
Combined Action Program (CAP),
571, 574, 589–90, 595, 601: Medical
(MEDCAP), 570
Combined Chiefs of Staff, 388
Combined Unit Pacification Program
(CUPP), 601
Commandants of the Marine Corps, 627
Company Officers School, Marine Corps
Schools, Quantico, 323
Confederacy, 23–24
Confederate States Marine Corps,
99–100
Confederate States Navy, 90, 99
Conger, Edwin H., 158
Congress, 35, 75, 97
Connecticut, authorization of priva-
teering by, 6
Conner, Commodore David, 61, 72–74
Connolly, Rear Admiral Richard L., 417
Conscription Acts of 1862, 1863, 93
Conservative Party (Nicaragua), 238,
240, 242, 246, 248, 253, 256
Constellation, 28–30, 33, 35, 57, 84
Con Thien, Vietnam, 588, 591
Continental Army, 5
Continental Congress, 6–11, 16, 25–26,
32: mounts naval war, 14; raises two
battalions of Marines, 7; Second
Continental Congress, 5
Continental Marines, 8–9, 13, 15, 20–
23, 25–26, 32

Continental Navy, 12, 14–15, 19, 26
"Controlled input" program, 538
Coolidge, President Calvin, 221–22,
243–44
Coontz, Admiral Robert E., 320
Cooper River, Charleston, South
Carolina, 23
Coral Sea, Battle of the, 363
Corinto, Nicaragua, 169, 237, 239, 244
Corregidor, Philippine Islands, 235,
254, 256, 359
Counterguerrilla warfare, 548
Counterinsurgency, 548, 553, 589
County Fair operations, 570–71
Coyotepe Hill, Nicaragua, 170
Craig, Brigadier General Edward A.,
479, 484
Craig, Lieutenant Isaac, 8
Crane, Stephen, 133
Creek Indians, 70
Croix de Guerre, awarded Marines, 315
Crowl, Philip A., 511
Crowninshield, Secretary of the Navy
Benjamin, 53–54
Cua Viet, Vietnam, 584
Cua Viet River, 584
Cuba, 5, 35, 128, 131, 142, 163, 168,
269, 273, 295, 307, 337, 541, 554–
56, 728: Second U.S. intervention in,
149
Cuban elections, 168
Cuban insurrection, 128
Cuban Missile Crisis, 555–56
Cukela, Lieutenant Louis, 199–200, 202
Culebra Island, 271, 281, 283, 337–38,
348: exercises, maneuvers on, 273,
282, 285–86
Cumberland, 97, 117
Cumberland Island, 41
Cunningham, Lieutenant Alfred A.,
277: Captain, 309–10, 732; Major,
321, 333, 625; Lieutenant Colonel,
731
Cushman, Brigadier General Robert E.,
Jr., 545: Lieutenant General, 590–
91; General, 25th Commandant of
the Marine Corps, 608, 611, 614,
618
Cushman-Anderson regime, 621
Cutts, Colonel Richard M., 205–206
Cuzco Well, Cuba, 133–34
Cyane, 47, 75, 84

Dagupan, Philippine Islands, 425–26
Dakeshi Ridge, Okinawa, 436
Dallas, Commodore Alexander J., 71

Daly, Private Dan, 159
Danang, Vietnam, 554, 564–65, 567, 569–72, 574, 576, 585, 589, 592–93, 599, 601–604
Daniels, Secretary of the Navy Josephus, 188, 202, 279–82, 289–90, 295, 308, 318, 322–23, 735
Dartiguenave, Sudre, 185–86, 207
Daugherty, Charles V., 732
Davis, Major Henry C., 276
Davis, Major General Raymond G., 595
Deane, 24
Deane, Silas, 16
Dearborn, Acting Secretary of the Navy Henry, 36
DeBellevue, Lieutenant F. B., 49
Decatur, Lieutenant Stephen, 43
Defense battalions, 346–47, 406, 728: formation of, 344
Degoutte, General Jean, 299, 301
Delano, Major Frederick H., 732
Delaware, 14–15
Delaware River, 6, 11, 20
del Valle, Lieutenant General Pedro A., 736
Demilitarized Zone (DMZ), Vietnam, 561, 576–77, 581, 583–84, 587–88, 595, 601: war in the, 589, 591–92
Democratic Republic of Vietnam, 553, 563–64; *see also* North Vietnam
Denby, Congressman Edwin, 291, 298
Denfeld, Admiral Louis E., 471–72
Denig, Brigadier General Robert L., 390–91, 731
Denny, Quartermaster General of the Marine Corps Frank L., 141
Department of Defense (DOD), 469, 497, 499, 511, 522, 532, 537, 541, 577–78, 580–84, 597–98, 600, 610, 612, 620: creation of, 472; policies of, 544
Department of the Navy, 30–32, 35–36, 38, 41, 53, 63, 65–66, 69–70, 76, 81, 83, 91–92, 101, 105–107, 110–12, 115, 117, 119, 126, 128–29, 135, 137, 140, 143, 160, 164, 166, 172, 176, 184, 203, 225, 227, 243, 261, 268–70, 272, 274–75, 277–78, 280, 282–84, 290, 293, 306–308, 318, 320, 344, 346, 446, 454, 457, 459, 464, 467, 469, 472, 478, 497, 499, 522, 533, 544: creation of, 28; under Jefferson, 38; under Madison, 38; 1829 study of expenditures, 66; war planning in, 270:
  Bureau of Aeronautics, 334, 455–

56, 510, 525; Bureau of Construction and Repair, 332, 340; Bureau of Navigation, 124–25, 138–39; Bureau of Ordnance, 120; Bureau of Weapons, 551
Derang's Neck, battle of, 98
Derna, assault and capture of, 44–45
Devereux, Major James P. S., 355
Devlin, First Lieutenant John S., 80
Dewey, Commodore George, 130, 150: Admiral, 142, 268, 274
Díaz, Adolfo, 169, 171, 242–46, 248, 250–51, 253
Dickerson, Secretary of the Navy Mahlon, 61
Diem, President Ngo Dinh, 554, 563
Dien Bien Phu, 584, 591–92
Dive bombing, first, 247
Dixie, 165, 167
Dodds, Dr. Harold W., 239
Dollar diplomacy, 181
Dolphin, 116, 133
Dominican Republic, 137, 178, 180, 182–83, 194–95, 199, 203–205, 207, 211, 333, 397, 554, 556, 558: guerilla war in, 200; military government in, 196; occupation of, 198–201; U.S. intervention in, 190; U.S. policy in, 191
Dong Ha, Vietnam, 576, 588, 594
Dong Ha airfield, 584
Douglas, Senator Paul H., 473, 497, 499, 550
Douglas–Mansfield Act, 498, 506–507, 518
Downes, Commodore John, 59
Doyen, Colonel Charles A., 292: Brigadier General, 294, 298
Doyle, Rear Admiral James H., 478, 485, 487
Draft Riot of 1863, 96
Dragon missile, 609, 615–17
Drake, 17
Drewry's Bluff, Virginia, 97–98, 100
DUKW (amphibious truck), 402, 416, 421
Dulaney, Major William, 78, 80
Duncan, David Douglas, 391, 753
Dunlap, Colonel Robert H., 250, 284
DuPont, Rear Admiral Samuel F., 91, 95–96
Dutch Curaçao, 35
Dutch East Indies, 388
Duvalier, François "Papa Doc," 211, 556
Dwight D. Eisenhower Library, 734

Dyer, Colonel Edward Colston, 453–55

East China Sea, 214
Eastern Area (Nicaragua), 259
East Indies, 59
East-West Trail, Bougainville, 383
Eaton, William H., 44–45
Eberstadt, Ferdinand, 457
Eberstadt Plan, 457
Ecole Militaire, 208, 210
Edson, Captain Merritt A., 251, 263,
    457–59, 463, 471: Major General,
    723
Edward, 11
Efate, New Hebrides, 359
Eisenhower, President Dwight D., 459,
    461, 463, 471, 516, 518–21, 532,
    539, 540–43
"El Chipote," Nicaragua, 247–50
Elliott, Captain George F., 133:
    Brigadier General, 10th Commandant
    of the Marine Corps, 136–40, 274,
    276; Commander, Panama Marine
    Force, 166
Ellis, Captain Earl H., 284–85: Major,
    262, 296; Lieutenant Colonel, 311,
    325–26
Ellsworth, Captain Harry A., 740
Emirau Island, 383
Empress Augusta Bay, 381
Enclave strategy in Vietnam, 567
Engebi, Marshall Islands, 402
Eniwetok Atoll, Marshall Islands, 399,
    401–403, 413
Enterprise, 35, 43
Erie, 61
Erskine, Major General Graves B., 428
Escondido River, 238
"Essen Hook," 312–13
Essex, 33, 50
Esteli, Nicaragua, 256
Eureka boat, 340
Evans, Captain Robley D., 125, 138,
    141
Executive Order 969, 139–40, 142:
    repealed, 144
Experiment, 35

Fajardo, Puerto Rico, 59
Farragut, Rear Admiral David, 97, 102:
    on ships' detachments, 83
Federalists, 28
Fegan, Major Joseph C., 324
Feland, Brigadier General Logan, 244,
    246–47, 250, 255, 311
Field Officers School, 323, 327, 330–31

Fields, Colonel Thomas Y., 731
Fiji Islands, 352, 357, 366
Finger Lakes, 6
Fire Support Coordination Centers, 428
Fire support ships, 396
First Indochina war, 561
First Marine Division Association, 531
First Naval Advisory Board, 115
First Opium War, 222
Fiske, Bradley A., 126, 275
Five Power Treaty (1922), 320
Fixed defense forces, 274
Flagg, James Montgomery, 307
"Flak jackets," 512
Flamborough Head, 18
Flanders, 299
Fleet exercises, maneuvers, 272, 278;
    see also Fleet Landing Exercise(s):
    1934 exercises, 337
Fleet Landing Exercise (FLEX) 1, 337;
    FLEX 2, 338; FLEX 3, 338–39;
    FLEX 4, 339–40; FLEX 5, 339–40;
    FLEX 6, 349; FLEX 7, 349
Fleet Marine Corps Reserve, 341–42
Fleet Marine Force, 335–37, 339, 341–
    43, 345–48, 350–51, 362, 372, 390,
    404, 409, 419, 439–40, 447, 451–
    53, 456, 458–61, 464–65, 469, 473,
    481, 499, 508, 518–20, 522–23, 525,
    533–34, 536–37, 541, 543–44, 546,
    548, 552, 577, 581, 596, 607–608,
    610, 614–15, 620, 622–25, 731:
    development of, 335; expansion of,
    351; origin of, 330; reorganization
    of, 345
Fleet Training Publication 167, 331,
    371
Fletcher, Rear Admiral Frank F., 172
Fletcher, Admiral Frank Jack, 364, 367
"Flexible Response," 545–46, 550, 556
Florida, 41
Florida Island, Solomon Islands, 364,
    366
Floyd, Major Oliver, 248
Foote, Commander Andrew H., 85
Forbidden City, Peking, 157
Ford, President Gerald R., 605, 607
Forêt de Retz, France, 305
Formosa, 388, 409, 424, 426, 432
Forney, Captain James, 110–11: Major,
    122
Forrestal, Secretary of the Navy James
    V., 430, 438, 457–60: Secretary of
    Defense, 470–71, 729
Forrestal-Eberstadt Proposals, 462
Fort Brooke, Florida, 71

Fort Capois, Haiti, 187
Fort Fisher, North Carolina, 98–100
Fort Lewis, Washington, 351
Fort McHenry, Maryland, 94
Fort Mifflin, Pennsylvania, 29
Fort Mitchell, Alabama, 70
Fort Monroe, Virginia, 89
Fort Pickens, Florida, 94
Fort Pitt, Pennsylvania, 20
Fort Rivière, Haiti, 187
Fort Sumter, South Carolina, 93
Fort Ticonderoga, New York, 6, 19
Fort Washington, Maryland, 94
Foss, Captain Joseph J., 368
Fox, Assistant Secretary of the Navy
    Gustavus V., 91
"Fragging" attacks, Vietnam, 602–603
France, 3, 5, 14, 16, 18–19, 27, 287,
    292–93, 316–18, 344
Francis Marion, 535
Frank, Benis M., 733–34
Franke, Secretary of the Navy William
    B., 543
Franklin, Benjamin, 16, 19
Franklin D. Roosevelt Library, 734
Frederick, Maryland, 49
Fremont, Lieutenant John C., 74
French Concession, Tientsin, 232
French Directory, 28
French forces: Army of the Center, 312;
    Fourth Army, 312; Sixth Army, 298–
    99; Tenth Army, 305; XXI Corps,
    299; XXIV Corps, 304; 1st Moroccan
    Division, 305; 167th Division, 301;
    Regiment de Walsh-Serrant, 18
Freya Stellung, German position, 315
Frigate Act of 1794, 27
Fullam, Lieutenant William F., 122–
    26, 138, 141: Commander, 141–42,
    275; Captain, 278–80; Rear Admiral,
    735; position on ships guards, 142
Fuller, Colonel Ben H., 277, 325: Major
    General, 15th Commandant of the
    Marine Corps, 329–30, 335
Funchilin Pass, Korea, 494
Funston, Brigadier General Frederick,
    173

Gale, Brevet Major Anthony, 4th
    Commandant of the Marine Corps, 55
Gallipoli, lessons learned from, 321
Galveston, 243
Gamble, Lieutenant John M., 50
Ganges, 33
Garapan, Saipan, 412–13

Garde d'Haiti, 208–10; see also
    Gendarmerie d'Haiti
Garrison, Secretary of War Lindley, 172
Gates, General Horatio, 19
Gates, Secretary of Defense Thomas S.,
    543
Gavutu, Solomon Islands, 364, 366
Geiger, Captain Roy S., 310: Major,
    334; Brigadier General, 368; Major
    General, 373, 405, 411, 417–18,
    420–21, 435, 438; Lieutenant
    General, 447, 453, 625
Gendarmerie d'Haiti, 189–90, 197–99,
    202, 204, 239, 257, 728; see also
    Garde d'Haiti: changes name, 208;
    formed, 188; Marines and, 188
General Board, 136, 267–77, 279–82,
    284, 309, 320, 329, 342, 345, 351,
    464: and Marine Corps advance base
    battalions, 142; reviews Marine Corps
    missions, 330
General Order 5, 507, 549
General Order 19, 549
General Purpose Amphibious Assault
    Ship (LHA), 610, 612
General Purpose Forces, 545
General Treaty of Peace and Amity, 237
Geneva Accords (1954), 521, 541
Georgia, 41
Germany, 282, 345, 353, 614; German
    forces:
        First Army, 298; High Seas Fleet,
        319; Imperial German Navy, 268;
        Seventh Army, 298
Ghormley, Vice Admiral Robert L.,
    363–64: relieved by Halsey, 367
Giap, General Vo Nguyen, 592
Gibbons, Floyd, 302–303
Gibraltar, 4
Gilbert Islands, 352, 357, 389–90, 392–
    93, 399–400, 402, 409, 411, 440
Gillespie, First Lieutenant Archibald H.,
    74–75
Gio Linh, Vietnam, 576, 584, 596
Go Noi Island, Vietnam, 589
Giron, Manuel, 256
Glasgow, 12
Glorious Revolution of 1688, 3
Gooch, Governor William, of Virginia, 4
Gooch's Marines, 4
Goodrich, Casper F., 126
Gouraud, General Henri, 312
Government Accounting Office (GAO),
    547
Government of Vietnam (GVN) (*See
    also* South Vietnam), 570–72, 574–

Government of Vietnam *(cont.)*
75, 577, 585, 590, 601–602;
Vietnamese Army (ARVN), 554,
561, 563, 566, 571–74, 576, 583,
586, 590, 593–94, 600, 603:
I Corps, 554, 560, 565–68, 570–
76, 583–87, 589–92, 595, 601,
604; II Corps, 568, 604; III Corps,
604; 1st Division, 583, 576, 604;
3d Division, 604; Popular Forces,
561, 571, 575, 601; Regional
Forces, 561; Revolutionary
Development Units, 572, 589–90;
Vietnamese Marine Regiment, 604
Governor, 95–96
Granada, Nicaragua, 169–70, 237–38,
240
Grant's Tomb, Marines at dedication of,
121
Great Britain, 229, 268–69, 287, 319–
20, 344: war with, 45
Great Cyprus Swamp, 71
Greater East Asia Co-Prosperity Sphere,
353
Great White Fleet, 138
Greene, Lieutenant Israel, 88–89
Greene, Brigadier General Wallace M.,
Jr., 529, 532: Lieutenant General,
543; General, 23d Commandant of
the Marine Corps, 558, 564, 583,
731
Greer, Commodore James A., 122–23
Greer Board, 122; *see also* Board of
Organization, Tactics, and Drill: on
ships guards, 123
Greytown, Nicaragua; 238 *see also* San
Juan del Norte
Griffin, Captain Charles, 94
Guadalcanal, Solomon Islands, 363–68,
370–71, 373, 378–80, 386–87, 390,
528
Guadalcanal, 535
Guam, 134, 136, 214, 267–69, 320,
334, 336, 354, 409–11, 417–18, 464,
586
Guam, 535
Guantanamo Bay, Cuba, 133–34, 168,
184–85, 269, 271, 277, 283, 327,
348, 541, 555, 731
Guardia Nacional de Dominicana, 197,
200–201, 204–205, 239; *see also
Policia Nacional Dominicana:*
organized, 195
Guardia Nacional de Nicaragua, 245,
248–49, 253–55, 258–59, 261, 728:
Company M, 258–60; created, 240

Guayacanas, Santo Domingo, 192
Guaymas, Mexico, 76
Guerriere, 47
Gulf of Chihli, China, 449
Gulf of Mexico, 73
Gulf of Riga, 321
Gulf of Tonkin incident, 564

Hagaru-ri, Korea, 492–94
Hagushi, Okinawa, 433
Haina, Dominican Republic, 205
Haiti, 178–79, 181, 183, 187, 191,
196–97, 200, 203, 207, 209, 258,
261, 283, 307, 322, 333, 335, 556,
728–29, 731, 738: American reform
of, 186; American treaty with, 191;
changes in, 204; guerrilla wars in,
202; occupation of ended, 210;
pacification of northern area, 187;
treaty services in, 196
Haitian constabulary, 188; *see also Garde
d'Haiti, Gendarmerie d'Haiti*
Hai Van Pass, Vietnam, 585
Halifax, Nova Scotia, 7
"Halls of Montezuma," the, 81
Halsey, Admiral William F., 367, 370–
71, 377–81, 386, 389–90, 423–24:
relieves Admiral Ghormley, 367
Hamilton, Alexander, 26, 28, 30
Hamlet security, Vietnam, 575
Hamhung, Korea, 494
Hancock, 15
Hankow, China, 214, 217, 221
Hanneken, Captain Herman H., 198
Hanoi, North Vietnam, 594
Han River, Korea, 485, 488–89, 501,
513
Hanyang, China, 217
Harbord, Brigadier General James G.,
commands Fourth Brigade, 298, 302–
303: Major General, commands 2d
Infantry Division, 305–306, 311, 318
Harper's Ferry, Virginia, 89
Harrington, Major Samuel M., 263
Harris, Brigadier General Field, 408:
Major General, 453, 510
Harris, Colonel John, 6th Commandant
of the Marine Corps, 88–89, 91–92,
94, 97
Harry S Truman Library, 734
Hart, General Franklin M., 732
Hata Men Gate, Peking, 159
Hatchee-Lustee, Florida, battle of, 71
Hatfield, Captain Gilbert D., 247
Havana, Cuba, 129, 166
Hawaii, 521, 577, 594, 622

Hawaiian Islands, 267–69, 328, 342, 357, 372, 417, 432

Hawk, anti-aircraft missile, 536, 564, 624

Hayes, President Rutherford B., 111

Hay-Herran Treaty, 165–66

Headquarters Marine Corps, 31, 37, 81, 87, 103, 111, 113, 118–19, 121, 136–37, 140, 174–76, 188, 203, 206, 233, 261–62, 275–77, 279–80, 282–87, 291, 293, 308, 317–18, 321–25, 327, 330–31, 333, 336–37, 340–41, 346–47, 362, 373–76, 390, 392, 405, 447, 451, 453, 457, 461, 464–71, 473, 480, 495, 497, 500, 506–509, 518–25, 528, 531, 533–34, 537–38, 541, 543–50, 552, 556, 558, 569, 578–82, 587, 596, 598–600, 608–609, 613, 615, 618–21, 624, 717: abolition of, 36; relations with Congress, 134; reorganization of, 372, 390:
    Adjutant and Inspector's Department, 109, 136, 174, 323; Division of Aviation, 375; Division of Plans and Policies, 375, 508; formed, 347; Division of Public Relations, 390; Division of Reserve, 374, 467; Operations and Training Division, 325–26, 333, 347; Paymaster Department, 136, 469; Quartermaster Department, 136, 375, 469; Supply Department, 469

Hebert, Congressman F. Edward, 532

Heinl, Lieutenant Colonel Robert D., Jr., 471

Helicopter landing zones, 573

Helicopters, 454, 509, 524; *see also* Aircraft types, Vertical envelopment

Hellzapoppin Ridge, Bougainville, 383

Henderson, 230, 232

Henderson, Lieutenant Archibald, 42: Captain, 44, 49; Brevet Major, 54–55, 58–60, 62–64; Colonel, 5th Commandant of the Marine Corps, 66, 69–70; Brigadier General, 71, 76, 80–81, 84–85, 87, 89, 103, 114, 127, 136, 322; asks for augmented Corps, 72; death of, 86; on drunkenness in the Corps, 82; goes to war, 71; improves enlisted Marines' situation, 65; and the Marine Corps mission, 56; on personal grooming, 69; restores order at Headquarters, 56

Henderson, Charles, 76, 79

Henderson Field, Guadalcanal, 367–69

Henry House Hill, 95

Herbert, Secretary of the Navy Hillary A., 120, 124–26

Herbert Hoover Presidential Library, 734

Herring, Lieutenant Colonel George W., 506

Heywood, Brevet Lieutenant Colonel, 107, 110, 118–20, 124–25, 129–30, 134: Brigadier General, 9th Commandant of the Marine Corps, 135, 137, 150, 155, 271–74, 280: and controversy with Theodore Roosevelt, 127; as McCawley's successor, 117; policy regarding Marine Corps mission, 164; reforms of, 119–20

Higgins, Andrew, 340–41

Hill, Colonel Charles S., 223

Hill, Rear Admiral Harry, 401: Admiral, 735

Hill, Major General William P. T., 469: Quartermaster General of the Marine Corps, 522

Hills: 142, 301–302; 600, 383; 600A, 383; 660, 385; 1000, 383

Hinche, Haiti, 197

Hindenburg, Field Marshal Paul von, 296

Hispaniola, 178, 181, 183, 196, 202–203, 239, 253, 257, 262, 269, 283, 286

Historical Amphibious File, James C. Breckinridge Library, Quantico, 730

Hittle, Lieutenant Colonel James D., 463: Father of, 462

Ho Chi Minh, 553, 563

Ho Chi Minh Trail, 564, 584, 586

Hoffman, Congressman Clare E., 462–63, 473

Hoffman Committee, 463; *see also* House Committee on Expenditures in the Executive Department

Hogaboom Board, 525–27, 536

Hogaboom, Colonel Robert E., 455: Major General, 525

Hoi An, Vietnam, 570, 589, 592

"Hoi Chanh," 575

Holcomb, General Thomas, 17th Commandant of the Marine Corps, 335–39, 347, 359, 371–74, 390, 404, 528, 731

Honduras, 149, 256

"Honest John" rocket, 526, 536

Honey Hill, battle of, 98

Hongchon, Korea, 503
Honolulu, 573
Honshu, China, 438, 448
"The Hook," 514–15
Hoover Commission, 472
Hoover, President Herbert, 210, 259, 262, 329
Hopeh Province, China, 448, 450
Hopkins, Commodore Esek, 9, 11–12, 15
Hopkins, John Burroughs, 19
Hornet, 47
Horse Marines, 229
Hotchkiss machine guns, 294
Hotel Embajador, Santo Domingo, 557
House of Representatives: Armed Services Committee, 462, 472–73, 496, 529–30, 542, 736; Committee on Appropriations, 736; Committee on Expenditures in the Executive Department, 462; Committee on Naval Affairs, 59–60, 66, 143, 322, 736; Military Affairs Committee, 140
Hovercraft, development of, 616
Howard, Colonel Samuel L., 356–57
Hsin-Ho, China, 450
Hue, Vietnam, 560, 566, 574, 592, 594
Hue Citadel, 593
Huerta, General Victoriano, 171, 173
Hungnam, Korea, 481, 491, 493, 502
Huntington, Lieutenant Colonel Robert W., 131–34, 271
Hwachon Reservoir, Korea, 503
Hyakutake, Lieutenant General Haruyoshi, 369–70

Iceland, 349–50, 353, 359, 464
Ie Shima, Ryukyu Islands, 434
Imjin River, Korea, 513
Imperial City, Peking, 157: Looting of, 162
Inchon, Korea, 478, 481–82, 484–88, 495, 513, 534
Indiana, 116, 125
Indian Wars, 70
Indochina, 351, 520–21
Indonesia, 541
International Relief Expedition, 161–63
International Settlement, Shanghai, 218, 222–23, 227, 230–35, 261: Settlement defense forces, 231
Interposition, as U.S. Policy, 148, 218
Interprise, 6
Interservice differences, 403
Iran, 609
Isherwood, Benjamin, 102

Isley, Jeter A., 511
Isthmus of Panama, 134, 163
Iwo Jima, 351, 409, 419, 427, 429, 432, 436, 438, 440, 454, 515, 560, 592
Iwo Jima, 535

Jackson, Andrew, 49–50, 66, 68, 70
Jackson, Donald L., 473
Jaluit, 399, 403
James C. Breckinridge Library 730, 733
Jamestown Line, Korea, 513–15
Japan, 121, 213, 229, 231, 268, 273, 278, 282, 319, 329, 345, 351, 353, 389, 427, 432, 446, 448, 476, 482, 512–13, 519–20, 569, 596, 604, 622: occupation of, 448
Japanese forces: *ground,* Thirty-second Army, 432, 434; *naval*: Combined Fleet, 352–54, 379, 384, 393; Eighth Fleet, 379; Mobile Fleet, 412–13; Special Naval Landing Force, 230, 232
Java, 47, 57
Jay's Treaty, 28
Jefferson, President Thomas, 27, 37–39, 43
Jerome, Colonel Clayton B., 423, 425: Major General, 515
Jesup, Brigadier General Thomas, 70–71
Jicaro, Nicaragua, 237, 248
Jicaro River, 248–49
Jiménez, Juan Isidro, 181, 183, 190–91
Jinotega, Nicaragua, 237, 247, 250, 254, 256, 258
John Adams, 60
John F. Kennedy Library, 734
Johnson, President Andrew, 102
Johnson, Secretary of Defense Louis H., 466, 471–77, 496
Johnson, President Lyndon B., 557, 563–66, 573, 578–83, 587, 591
Johnston Island, 344, 352, 354, 357, 359
Joint Action of the Army and Navy, 328, 336
Joint Army and Navy Board, 231, 269, 320–22, 325, 328, 344–45, 349
Joint Chiefs of Staff, 350, 357, 363, 371–72, 377, 384, 388, 390–91, 410, 419, 423, 426, 446, 451, 457–59, 464–66, 469–72, 476, 478–79, 496–97, 499–501, 518, 520, 522, 542–44, 547, 552, 556, 564, 566, 568, 594, 624, 730: 1478 Series

papers 458–59, 463; Joint Staff, 390, 404, 472, 522
Joint Coordinating Council, 571
Joint Landing Forces Board, 509
Joint Strategic Committee, 371
Joint War Planning Committee, 345
Jones, John Paul, 12, 17–18
Jones, Lieutenant General William K., 732
Jones, Secretary of the Navy William, 49, 53
Joy, Vice Admiral C. Turner, 477–79

Kadena airfield, Okinawa, 433
Kagman Peninsula, Saipan, 413
Kahoolawe, Hawaiian Islands, 407
Kamikazes, 424, 432, 434–35, 437, 440
Karamanli, Hamet, 44
Karch, Brigadier General Frederick J., 565
Kavieng Island, New Ireland, 362, 377, 384
Kearny Mesa, 348
Kearny, Captain Stephen, 75
Kearsarge, 97
Keeler, Private Frank, 732
Kellog, Secretary of State Frank, 221, 225, 243
Kelsey, Carl, 203–204
Kendall, Amos, 66
Kennedy, Senator John F., 545:
President, 548, 553–56, 583
Kenney, Lieutenant General George C., 423–24
Kerama Retto, Ryukyu Islands, 433
"Key West Agreement," 470, 555
Key West, Florida, 132
Khe Sanh, Vietnam, 576, 584, 588, 591–92, 594–95
Khmer Rouge, 604–605
Khrushchev, Premier Nikita A., 555–56
Kimball, Secretary of the Navy Dan, 507
Kim Il Sung, 475
Kimpo airfield, 485, 488, 490
Kimpo Peninsula, Okinawa, 513
King, Admiral Ernest J., 350–51, 357, 359, 363, 370–71, 377, 388–89, 404, 408–409, 415, 419
Knapp, Rear Admiral Harry S., 193, 200
"Know Nothings," 85
Knox, Secretary of the Navy Frank, 347
Knox, Captain William R., 200
Koh Tang Island, 605–606
Kolombangara, Solomon Islands, 363

Korea, 105–106, 137, 446, 451, 475, 479–81, 497–98, 502, 507, 512, 514, 516–17, 595, 747
Korean expedition, 738
Korean War, 477, 482, 504–505, 509–511, 518–19, 521, 523, 525, 535, 537, 607, 738, 740, 744, 748:
ceasefire of, 516
Koto-ri, Korea, 492–94
Kowloon, 84
Kriemhilde Stellung, German position, 314–15
Krulak, Lieutenant Victor H., 340:
Lieutenant Colonel, 454–56, 458–59, 463; Colonel, 505; Major General, 548; Lieutenant General, 564, 569–70, 573, 582–83, 732
Krulewitch, Major General Melvin L., 736
Kunishi Ridge, Okinawa, 437
Kuomintang Party, 218–19, 229, 232; *see also* Chinese Nationalists
Kuribayashi, Lieutenant General Tadamichi, 427–28, 430–31
Kwajalein, Marshall Islands, 399–401, 403
Kwang Fort, 106
Ky, Nguyen Cao, 573
Ky Lam, Vietnam, 574
Kyushu, Japan, 432, 438, 448

Lake Champlain, 6, 19, 46
Lake Erie, 46
Lake Managua, 237
Lake Nicaragua, 237–38
Lake Ontario, 46
La Loma Fortress, 240
La Mesa, battle of, 75
Landais, Pierre, 18
Landing craft, 326: need for better, 340; search for, 332; types of:
Landing Craft Infantry (LCI), 378, 384; Landing Craft Infantry, Gunboat (LCI)(G), 400;
Landing Craft Mechanized (LCM), 341; Landing Craft, Tank (LCT), 378; Landing Craft, Vehicle, Personnel (LCVP), 340, 345, 397, 401
Landing Force Bulletin 2, 509
Landing Force Bulletin 17, 524
Landing Force Development Center, 509
Landing Platform Helicopter (LPH), 510, 524, 534–45, 550–51, 557, 612
Landing Ship Dock (LSD), 378

Landing Ship Medium (LSM), 378, 395, 397
Landing Ship Tank (LST), 378, 384, 402, 486–87, 550, 586
Landing Vehicle Tracked (LVT), 341, 387, 395, 398, 401–402, 429
Landing Vehicle Tracked, Armored (LVT[A]), 400–402, 412
Lane, Colonel Rufus H., 193–94
Lang Vei, Vietnam, 592
Lang Vei Special Forces Camp, 592
Lansing, Secretary of State Robert, 184–85
Lantphibex 1-58, 537
Laos, 553–54, 564, 566, 577, 584, 586, 601, 603
La Paz, Mexico, 76
Larkin, Consul Thomas O., 74
La Romana, Dominican Republic, 200
Laruma River, 381
Las Trencheras, Santo Domingo, 192
Lauchheimer, Adjutant and Inspector Colonel Charles, 141, 282
Lawrence, 48
Lawrence, David, 438, 497
Leahy, Admiral William D., 336
Leatherneck, 308
Lebanon, 539, 541
Lee, Brigadier Harry, 205–206, 311
Lee, Brevet Colonel Robert E., 89
Lee, Rear Admiral S. P., 91
Lee, Second Lieutenant William, 258
Legation Quarter, Peking, 156–57, 213, 216, 219, 229
Leith, England, 18
Lejeune, John A., 250, 261–62, 277: Naval cadet, 111; Major, 165–66; Lieutenant Colonel, 281–82, 285; Colonel, 172–74, 287; Brigadier General, 296, 306; Major General, commands 2d Infantry Division, 311–12, 315–16; 13th Commandant of the Marine Corps, 202, 208, 224, 322, 326–28, 335, 732, 736, 739; described 322–23; educational reforms of, 323–24; and Marine Corps amphibious assault mission, 325
Leon, Nicaragua, 169–70, 238: Marine occupation of, 171
Letcher, Brigadier General John L., 736
Levant, 47, 84–85
Lewis machine guns, 294
Lexington, 11, 16
Leyte, Philippine Islands, 420, 423–24
Leyte Gulf, battle of, 424

Liberal Party (Cuba), 166, 168
Liberal Party (Nicaragua), 238, 241–46, 248, 253, 260
Limited Duty Officers, 523
Lincoln, General Benjamin, 23
Lingayen Gulf, 425
L'Insurgente, 35
Liscome Bay, 399
Little, Colonel Louis McCarty, 198; Major General, 336, 731
Litzenburg, Colonel Homer L., 489
Liversedge, Colonel Harry B., 380
Long, Colonel Charles G., 280
Long, Secretary of the Navy John D., 126–27, 129, 131, 134, 151, 271–72
L'Orient, France, 16
Los Angeles, expedition against, 75
Louis XVI of France, 16
Low, Consul Frederick, 106
Lowe, Major General Frank E., 495, 498
Lowry, Major H. B., 125
Lucas, Jim, 391, 399
Luce, Rear Admiral Stephen B., 124, 126, 142, 144, 735
Ludendorff, General Erich, 296, 299
Lunga River, Guadalcanal, 364, 370
Luxembourg, 316
Luzon, Philippine Islands, 151, 270, 356, 409, 423, 425–26: Marines in pacification of, 152
Lyndon B. Johnson Library, 734

Maas, Melvin J., 341, 467
Maass, General Octavo, 172
MacArthur, General Douglas, 356–57, 363–64, 369, 377–79, 381, 389–91, 409–410, 419–20, 423–24, 476–79, 482, 485–87, 489–90, 500–501, 504
MacDonald, Sir Claude, 158
MacKenzie, Commander Alexander Slidell, 59, 61
MacMurray, John V. A., 222–23, 226, 228
Macoris, Santo Domingo, 196, 199
Madero, Francisco, I., 171
Magloire, Paul, 211
Mahan, Captain Alfred Thayer, 116, 127, 268
Maine, 21–22
Maine, blown up, 129
Maissade, Haiti, 197
Majuro, Marshall Islands, 399, 403
Makin Island, Gilbert Islands, 393, 398–99, 403, 413

Malaya, 59
Maloelap, Marshall Islands, 399, 403
Mameluke sword, 89, 112
Managua, Nicaragua, 169, 238–40,
243–53, 255, 259
Manchu Court, 157, 162: dynasty, 84,
212
Manchukuo, 230
Manchuria, 213, 217–18, 229–30, 232,
319, 449
Manchurian Incident of 1931, 329
Manila, Philippine Islands, 128, 150–
51, 270, 353, 356, 425, 573
Manila Bay, 270: battle of, 130
Mannix, Captain Daniel A., 122
Mansfield, Congressman Mike, 473, 497,
550
Manzanillo, Cuba, 134
Mao Tse-tung, 449, 476, 550
Marbache sector, France, 311
Marblehead, 132–33
Marblehead Regiment, 5–6
Marcy, Secretary of War William L., 76
Marder, Murrey, 391
Mare Island, California, 96, 140
Mariana Islands, 269, 319, 384, 399,
401, 404–405 407, 409, 415, 419–
20, 426, 428, 440
Marine Air-Ground Task Force
(MAGTF), 547
Marine Band, 32, 39, 113: "The
President's Own," 37
Marine barracks: Brooklyn, 94, 131;
Cavite, 220; 8th and Eye, Washing-
ton, D.C., 624; Guam, 220;
Philadelphia, 111, 281; Portsmouth,
New Hampshire, 118
Marine Committee, Continental
Congress, 10–12
Marine Corps Act of 1834, 67
Marine Corps Air Stations: Cherry
Point, North Carolina, 466; El Toro,
California, 480, 520; Ewa, Territory
of Hawaii, 354
Marine Corps Association, 277, 737
Marine Corps Bases: Camp Lejeune,
North Carolina, 348, 376, 455, 465–
66, 599, 625; Camp Pendleton,
California, 348, 376, 465–66, 478,
480, 508, 521, 577, 594, 599, 617,
625; San Diego, California, 284;
Twenty-nine Palms, California, 519,
617
Marine Corps Equipment Board, 340–
41
Marine Corps Gazette, 263, 277, 285

Marine Corps Historical Center, 727,
730, 732–33, 736–37, 750, 753
Marine Corps Institute, 323
Marine Corps League, 497, 531:
organized, 324
Marine Corps Recruit Depot, Parris
Island, South Carolina, 290, 295,
348, 528–32, 618
Marine Corps Recruit Training
Commands, 530
Marine Corps Reserve, 308, 317, 374,
467, 480, 538, 552, 578, 581, 623–
24: in World War I, 307; Marine
Reserves (Female), 308;
reorganized, 341; mobilized, 347:
Fleet Marine Reserve, 341–42;
Organized Reserve, 342, 347, 467,
480–81, 523, 538, 552; Ready
Reserve, 538; Volunteer Reserve,
341–42, 481; Volunteer Training
Units, 467
Marine Corps Reserve Officers
Association, 341, 463, 471, 497
Marine Corps Schools, Quantico,
Virginia, 263, 323, 326, 328, 331,
336–37, 373, 453–54, 458, 466, 509
Marine Corps Supply Depots: Barstow,
California, 376; Philadelphia,
Pennsylvania, 376
Marine detachments: American
Legation, Managua, Nicaragua, 171,
243, 307; American Legation,
Peking, China, 214, 216–17, 219,
225–26, 230, 307; Pensacola Navy
Yard, Florida, 94; White Sulphur
Springs, Georgia, 234
Marine Expeditionary Brigades (MEB),
547
Marine Expeditionary Forces (MEF),
547, 550
Marine Expeditionary Units (MEU),
547
Marines, origins of, 3–4; duties of, 6
Marine Unified Material Management
System (MUMMS), 547
Marne River, France, 299, 304
Marshall, General George C., 351,
357, 391, 415, 450, 457, 459
Marshall Islands, 319–20, 325–26,
355, 389–90, 393, 399–400, 403–
404, 407, 409, 440
Marshall, Brigadier General S. L. A., 495
Martinez, Bartolomé, 240
Martinique, 345
Maryland marines, 21
Masan, Korea, 485, 501

Masaya, Nicaragua, 170
Massachusetts, 116
Massachusetts, 5–6, 22: Massachusetts
    marines, 21–22
Massachusetts Bay, 5
Matagalpa, Nicaragua, 237, 244
Matanikau River, Guadalcanal, 368–70
Matthews, Colonel Calvin B., 260
Matthews, Secretary of the Navy Francis,
    472, 734
Mayaguez, 605–606
Mayo, Rear Admiral Henry T., 203
Mazatlán, Mexico, 76
McCalla, Commander Bowman, 107,
    132–33
McCarthy, Joseph R., 462
McCawley, Major Charles (son of
    Commandant), 136: Lieutenant
    Colonel, 142
McCawley, Captain Charles G., 96, 102–
    104: Colonel, 8th Commandant of
    the Marine Corps, 107–11, 117–18,
    122–23; and alcoholism in Marine
    Corps, 111–12; and uniform
    production in Philadelphia, 113
McClellan, Major Edwin N., 739–40,
    742, 746
McCoy, Brigadier General Frank R.,
    248, 254
McCutcheon, Lieutenant Colonel Keith
    B., 423, 425: Brigadier General, 568,
    625; General, 731
McDonough, Congressman Gordon L.,
    496–97
McDougal, Colonel Douglas C., 256–57
McDowell, Major General Irvin, 94
McGuffey, William Holmes, 68
McHenry, Secretary of War James, 28–
    30
McKean, Colonel William B., 530
McKeon, Staff Sergeant Matthew C.,
    528–31
McKinley, President William, 128,
    134
McNamara, Secretary of Defense Robert
    S., 545–46, 549–51, 568, 577, 579–
    81, 584
"McNamara Line," 588
Meade, Captain R. W., 108
Medal of Honor, 97, 119, 137, 159,
    249–50, 432, 544, 595, 621
Mediterranean Sea, 466, 509, 520, 537,
    539, 552, 596, 625
Megee, Colonel Vernon E., 408–409,
    437; Brigadier General, 456; Major
    General, 515

Mekong Delta, Vietnam, 563
Mekong River, 553–54
Melville, Herman, 57
Mena, Luis, 169–70
Mercer, General Hugh, 13
Merrimack, 35
Mervine, Captain William, 75
Metcalf, Lieutenant Colonel Clyde H.,
    739–40
Metcalf, Secretary of the Navy Victor,
    139–40
Metz, France, 311
Meuse-Argonne offensive, 312, 314
Meuse River, France, 311, 314, 316
Mexican War, 70, 74, 81, 86, 735, 738
Mexico, 172
Mexico City, 80, 82
Meyer, Secretary of the Navy George L.
    von, 275–76, 278
M-14 rifle, 581
"Michel," German position, 312
Micronesia, 352
Middle East, 539, 609
Midway, battle of, 363, 368
Midway Island, 319, 344, 352, 354,
    357, 359
"Military-industrial complex," 543
Military intervention, purposes of, 163
Mille Atoll, 399, 403
Miller, Lieutenant Colonel Ellis B., 331
Miller, Adjutant Samuel, 48–50:
    Brevet Major, 54–56, 69; Brevet
    Lieutenant Colonel, 72; Colonel, 731
Mindanao, Philippine Islands, 419–20,
    423, 426
Minnesota, 97
Missile Crisis of 1962, 550
Mississippi River, 20
Mitchell, Major General Ralph J., 423
Mobile Bay, battle of, 97, 117
Mobile defense forces, 274, 283
Mole St. Nicholas, Haiti, 181, 184
Molino del Rey, Mexico, 77
Momyer, General William W., 586–87
Moncada, General José Marie, 242,
    244, 246–48, 254–57, 260
Monitor, 97
Monroe, President James, 55
Mont Blanc Ridge, France, 312–15
Monte Cristi, Santo Domingo, 179, 192
Monterey, 124
Monterey, California, 74
Montevideo, Uruguay, 84
Montford Point, North Carolina, 375
Montreal, expedition against, 7
Montross, Lynn, 511, 742

Moody, Secretary of the Navy
William H., 272
Morehead City, North Carolina, 348
Moret Field, Philippine Islands, 426
Morocco, 27, 137
Morris, Commodore Richard V., 43
Morris, Superintendent of Finance
Robert, 23, 30
Morristown, New Jersey, 14
Moses, Colonel Franklin J., 277
Motobu Peninsula, Okinawa, 434
Motoyama Plateau, Iwo Jima, 427–30
Mount Suribachi, Iwo Jima, 427–29
Mount Tapotchau, Saipan, 413
Mount Tipe Pale, Saipan, 412
"M" Series, Tables of Organization and
Equipment, 527
M-16 rifle, 581
Mukden Incident, 230
Mulcahy, Major General Francis P., 433
Mullan, Robert, 13–14
Munda, New Georgia, 379–81
Munro, Dr. Dana G., 210
Munsan-ni, Korea, 513
Murray, Lieutenant Colonel Raymond
L., 479, 489
Meyers, Captain John T., 156, 158–59,
162, 174
My Lai massacre, 603

Nagasaki, Japan, 448
Naha, Okinawa, 434, 436
Naktong Bulge, Korea, 484–85
Naktong River, Korea, 477, 484
Nam River, Korea, 484
Nanking, China, 214, 224, 232
Nanking Incident, 224
Napoleonic Wars, 42
Nashville, 165
Natchez, Mississippi, 20
National Association for the
Advancement of Colored People, 203
National Bank of Haiti, 182, 184
National City Bank of New York, 182
National Guard, 288
National Guard Association, 463
National Liberation Front, 561
National Rifle Association, 463
National Security Act of 1947, 457,
463–64, 469–70, 507, 542:
amended, 472, 542
Naval Appropriation Act, 143: of
1916, 287, 307–309
Naval Committee, Continental
Congress, 8, 10
Naval gunfire, 464, 572, 580, 611:

doctrine, 333, 407; ships, 416;
support, 332, 338, 386, 395, 414
Naval Historical Division, 729
Naval Historical Foundation Collection,
735
Naval Personnel Act of 1899, 150
Naval Regulations, 29–30, 122, 126:
of 1818, 54; of 1834, 67; of 1893,
124; of 1900, 137; of 1905, 137;
of 1909, 143
Naval Reserve Act of 1938, 342
Naval Transportation Service, 332
Naval War College, 117, 128, 268,
271, 284–85, 320, 325, 331
Naval War College Historical
Collection, 730
Navy Department Order 241, 330
Navy Reorganization Act of 1947, 469
Navy War Board, 128–29, 131
Navy War Plans Division, 325, 329
Ndeni, Solomon Islands, 365
Netherlands, the, 3
Netherlands East Indies, 352, 356–57,
362
Neville, Major Wendell C., 142:
Lieutenant Colonel, 172–73;
Colonel, 298, 305; Brigadier
General, 311, 323
Neville Board, 323
Newark, 124, 156
Newberry, Secretary of the Navy
Truman, 141
New Britain Island, 362, 377–78, 381,
383–86
New Caledonia, 352, 357, 359
New Georgia, 379–81, 387
New Guinea, 352, 357, 362–63, 377,
381, 383–84, 420
New Hebrides, 352, 357, 359
New Ireland, 362, 383–84
New London, Connecticut, 276
New Orleans, Louisiana, 21, 41, 46, 48,
97: battle of, 49
Newport, Rhode Island, 272
New Providence expedition, 13, 15
New River, North Carolina, 348, 350,
359
New Zealand, 362
Ngesebus Island, Palau Islands, 422
Niagara, 48
Nicaragua, 84, 137, 149, 165, 168,
211, 234, 237, 240, 243–44, 250–
51, 255, 263, 267, 329–30, 333,
731, 738: elections in, 248, 254–
55; end of intervention, 211; U.S.
intervention in, 170

Nicaraguan Expedition of 1912, 275
Nicholas, Major Samuel, 1st
    Commandant of the Marine Corps, 8,
    10, 13–14, 25
Nimitz, Admiral Chester A., 357, 363,
    370–71, 377, 389–92, 399, 403,
    405, 408–10, 415, 419–20, 426,
    428, 432, 435, 438: Fleet Admiral,
    451, 457–58, 470; appointed
    Commander in Chief, Pacific Fleet/
    Commander in Chief, Pacific Ocean
    Areas, 359
Nine Power Treaty (1922), 220
Nixon, Vice President Richard M.,
    541, 545, 594, 597: President, 604,
    607, 618
Nixon Doctrine, 596–97
Norfolk Navy Yard, 38, 94
Norfolk, Virginia, 9, 48, 165, 283, 348
Norstad, Major General Lauris, 458
North Atlantic Treaty Organization
    (NATO), 476, 512, 555, 607–609,
    617
Northern Area (Nicaragua), 250, 252,
    255, 257
North China, 449–51
North Korea, 481
North Korean People's Army
    (NKPA), 474–75, 477–78, 481–
    82, 485–91, 496, 501, 504, 512:
    4th Division, 484; 6th Division, 482
North Vietnam, 561, 564–65, 586
North Vietnamese Army (NVA),
    560–61, 564–66, 573, 575–77,
    583–84, 588–90, 592, 594: 2d
    Division, 589, 593
Novaleta, Philippine Islands, 151–52
Nova Scotia expedition, 7, 12
Nueva Segovia, Nicaragua, 246–49,
    254, 256
Nui Loc Son, Vietnam, 589
Numa Numa Trail, Bougainville, 383

Oahu, Territory of Hawaii, 327
O'Bannon, Lieutenant Presley N., 44–
    45
Obong-ni, Korea, 484
Occupation of Cuba, 166
Ocotal, Nicaragua, 237, 247, 249, 258,
    260; battle of, 248
Office of Naval Intelligence, 128, 268,
    273
Office of the Secretary of Defense, 544
Ohio River, 21
Okinawa, 409, 419, 427, 432–35, 437–
    38, 440, 477, 521–22, 537, 541,

544, 554, 556, 560, 564, 566, 569,
    577, 602, 604–605, 622
Okinawa, 535
Olongapo, Philippine Islands, 140,
    152, 155, 356
Olympia, 126
Omaha, 121
Open Door Policy, 148, 160, 212–13,
    216, 229, 231, 236
Operation Plan 712, "Advanced Base
    Force Operations in Micronesia,"
    325–26
Operations: BELEAGUER, 448;
    CARTWHEEL, 377–79, 384;
    CATCHPOLE, 401–402; CHROMITE,
    487; CROSSROADS, 453; DECKHOUSE
    IV, 576; DETACHMENT, 427, 432;
    DEWEY CANYON, 595; DYE MARKER,
    584, 595; EAGLE PULL, 605;
    FLINTLOCK, 399, 402; FORAGER,
    411, 415, 417, 419; FREQUENT
    WIND, 605, GALVANIC, 395–96;
    GOLDEN FLEECE, 571; HASTINGS,
    576; HICKORY, 588; ICEBERG, 432–
    33; KILLER, 502; LAM SON 719,
    603; LINEBACKER, 604; MARKET
    TIME, 568; PACKARD II, 455–56;
    PEGASUS, 594; PIRANHA, 572;
    PRAIRIE, 576; QUICK KICK, 552,
    555; RIPPER, 502–503; THUNDER,
    564–66, 568, 573, 586, 594;
    SHOESTRING, 364: *see also*
    WATCHTOWER; SHUFLY, 554;
    SILVER LANCE, 548, 553;
    STALEMATE, 419–20; STARLITE,
    572; STINGRAY, 602; STEEL PIKE I,
    553; STRANGLE, 502; SUMMIT, 506;
    TAYLOR COMMON, 595; UTAH, 576;
    WATCHTOWER, 363, 365, 367: *see
    also* SHOESTRING
Oregon, 116, 132, 151, 156
Organization of American States, 553
Oriente Province, Cuba, 168
Oroku Peninsula, Okinawa, 437
Orote Peninsula, Guam, 417
Ortez, Angel, 258
Osceola, 70
Outposts: Carson, 516; Reno, 516;
    Vegas, 516

Pacific Ocean, 137, 237, 274, 319,
    328, 357, 441
Pacification program, Vietnam, 567–75,
    583, 585, 589–90, 595, 600–602
Paige, Colonel Mitchell, 737
Palau, 455

Palau Islands, 326, 337, 424
"Palm Tree" exercises, 617
Palma, Tomás Estrada, 166–67
Palmyra Island, 344, 352, 354, 357, 359
Panama, 103, 105, 117, 136–37, 165, 273, 738: U.S. landing on, 122
Panama Canal, 181, 236, 376
Panama City, 106, 164, 166
Panamanian Secessionists, 106
Panama Railroad, 165
Panay, bombing of, 234
Panther, 131–32, 273
Paris, France, 299, 304–305
Paris Exposition, Marines in, 113
Paris-Metz highway, 299
Paris Peace Accords of 1973, 604
Parke, Captain Matthew, 17, 19, 24
Parker, Captain William D., 740
Parris Island, South Carolina, 289
Parry Island, 402
Patapsco, 35
Patch, Major General Alexander M., 370
Pate, General Randolph McCall, 21st Commandant of the Marine Corps, 527–34, 542–43
Pathet Lao forces, 553
Patterson, Secretary of War Robert, 458, 460
Paul Revere, 535
Paulding, Secretary of the Navy James K., 62
Pavuvu Island, Russell Islands, 421
Paymaster of the Marine Corps, 174, 323
Peace Establishment Act for the Marine Corps of 1817, 54, 60
Peacock, 60
Peace of Tipitapa, 245–46
Pearl Harbor, 270, 282, 334, 346, 352–54, 359, 440
Pearl River, China, 84–85
Pei Ho River, China, 156–57
Peking, China, 156, 160–61, 163, 216–17, 222, 227, 229–30, 232, 354, 449, 728: extraterritorial status in, 212; life in, 229; relief of, 159, 162; siege of, 158
Peleliu, Palua Islands, 419–20, 422–24, 428, 433, 440
Pendleton, Colonel Joseph H., 170, 193: Major General, 731
Penguin, 47
Pennsylvania Committee on Safety, 6, 8, 11, 13
Pennsylvania marines, 20

Pennsylvania militia, 13
Pennsylvania navy, 11
Penobscot expedition, 21
Penobscot River, Maine, 22
Pensacola, Florida, 280, 306
People's Liberation Army (Chinese Communist), 451, 514: Ninth Army Group, 492–93; 124th Division, 491
People's Republic of China, 596
Peralte, Charlemagne, 197–98
Perry, Commodore Oliver Hazard, 47, 57, 60, 73–74, 84
Pershing, Major General John J., 290, 292–98, 304, 306–307, 311, 314–15, 318: General, 735
Persian Gulf, 452, 464–65
"Personal Response" Program, 575
Phase Line Kansas, Korea, 503, 511
Phelps, Commander W. W., 278
Philadelphia, 43
Philadelphia, Pennsylvania, 20, 25–26, 31, 37, 276, 280, 283, 285, 292, 308, 546–47
Philadelphia Associators, 8–9, 13
Philadelphia Navy Yard, 38, 276–77
Philippine Insurrection, 135–37, 151, 155, 164, 166
Philippine Islands, 5, 128, 134–35, 137, 150, 217–18, 226, 228, 233, 268–70, 272–74, 319–20, 352–53, 356, 384, 388, 409–10, 419, 423, 426, 432, 441, 477, 541, 569, 728, 735
Philippine Sea, 410: Battle of, 412
Phnom Penh, Cambodia, 604–605
Phu Bai, Vietnam, 566, 570–71, 574, 592
Phu Loc, Vietnam, 592
Piasecki, Frank N., 455
Picardy, France, 298, 304
Pickle Meadows, California, 519
Pillow, Brigadier General Gideon, 77–78
Pillsbury, Rear Admiral J. E., 139–41
Pitt, William, the elder, 5
Piva Forks, Bougainville, 383
Piva River, Bougainville, 382
Piva Trail, Bougainville, 382–83
Plan "Bluebat," 540
Platt Amendment, 163, 166
Plymouth, 84
Pohang, Korea, 477, 501, 513
Policia Nacional Dominicana, 205–206; *see also Guardia Nacional Dominicana*
Polk, President James K., 72, 76

Pollock, General Edwin A., 528
Ponce, Puerto Rico, 130
Port-au-Prince, Haiti, 178, 183–85,
   198, 208
Porter, Colonel Andrew, 94–95
Porter, Captain David, 50: Commodore,
   59; Rear Admiral, 91–92, 98–99,
   102–103
Port Hudson, Louisiana, 98
Port Isbel, 73
Port Lyautey, Morocco, 539
Port Royal Sound, 290
Port Royal, South Carolina, 95
Portsmouth, 75, 85
Portsmouth, New Hampshire, 134
Potomac, 59
Potomac River, 48
Prairie, 172, 191
Pratt, Admiral William Veazie, 330
Preble, Commodore Edward, 43
President, 36
Price, Colonel Charles F. B., 235
Princeton, 535
Princeton, New Jersey, 13–14
Prisoners of war, Korea, 511, 513,
   515–16
Providence, 17
Public Law 416, 82d Congress, 2d
   Session, 507, 519
Puerto Cabezas, Nicaragua, 242, 246
Puerto Plata, Santo Domingo, 35, 179,
   192
Puerto Rico, 35, 128, 134, 165, 271,
   555–56
"Plug Uglies," Marine rout of, 86
Pukhang-gang River, 503
Puller, Captain Louis B., 258–60, 263:
   Colonel, 422, 487, 489, 492; Briga-
   dier General, 531
Punchbowl, the, 504, 512
Puruata Island, Bougainville, 382
Pusan, Korea, 477, 485, 488
Pusan perimeter, 478, 481–82, 495,
   505, 517
Putnam, Brigadier General Paul A., 732
Pyongtaek, Korea, 513

Quallah Battoo, Sumatra, 60
Quang Nam, Vietnam, 561, 563–65,
   572, 574, 576, 583, 589, 593–94,
   600–601, 603
Quang Ngai, Vietnam, 561, 569, 572,
   574, 576, 590
Quang Ngai City, 592
Quang Tin, Vietnam, 561, 566, 569,
   572, 574, 576, 589–90

Quang Tri, Vietnam, 561, 576, 583,
   587, 593, 595, 601, 603
Quang Tri City, 592
Quantico, Virginia, 263, 284, 291,
   295–96, 307, 322–23, 327, 333,
   337, 349, 359–60, 373, 455–56,
   465–66, 509, 621
Quartermaster General of the Marine
   Corps, 174, 323
Quasi-war with France, 28, 32, 34–38,
   43, 735, 738
Quebec, expedition against, 7
Que Son Mountains, 589
Quick, Sergeant John H., 133
Qulilali, Nicaragua, 237, 248–49, 251
Qui Nhon, Vietnam, 566
Quitman, Brigadier General John A.,
   77–80

Rabaul, New Britain, 362–64, 371,
   377, 380, 384, 389–90, 407, 423
Radford, Vice Admiral Arthur W., 458,
   461, 478–79: Admiral, 520
Raider Ridge, battle of, 368
Railroad Strike of 1877, 108
Rainbow Plans, 268–69, 344–45; *see
   also* War Plans
Raleigh, 15–16
Rama, Nicaragua, 259
Ramsay, Commodore Frank M., 124
Rancho Santa Margarita y Las Flores,
   348; *see also* Camp Pendleton
Randolph, 15
Randolph, John, 38, 46
Ranger, 16, 18
Rapid Deployment Force, 609
Rattletrap, 20
Read, Captain J. J., 126–27
Recruiters' Bulletin, The, 176
Recruiting Publicity Bureau, New York,
   288
Reid, Colonel George C., 136, 271:
   Brigadier General, 731
Reindeer, 47
Rendova, New Georgia, 379–80
Reprisal, 11, 16
Republic of Korea, army of, 475, 477,
   491, 513: 6th Division, 503; Korean
   Marine Corps (KMC), 488, 506,
   512:
      1st KMC Regiment, 503, 513
Resolute, 134
"Revolt of the Admirals," 472
Reynolds, Captain John G., 76, 78, 93:
   Major, 94–96

Rhee, President Syngman, 475, 490, 516
Rheims, France, 299
Rhine River, 316
Rhode Island, 6
Ribbon Creek, South Carolina, 528–30, 532, 534
Richards, Assistant Paymaster of the Marine Corps George, 142, 278
Richardson, Lieutenant General Robert C., Jr., 391–92, 405, 415
Richmond, Virginia, 98
Ridgway, Lieutenant General Matthew B., 501–504, 511
Riley, Major General William E., 732
Rio Grande River, 238, 242
Rixey, Colonel Presley M., Jr., 205
Robertson, Senator Edward V., 462
Robeson, Secretary of the Navy George M., 104
Robillard, Major General Fred A., 737
Rockey, Major General Keller E., 428, 448–49
Rockhill, W. W., 214
"Rockpile," the, 584
Rodgers, Commodore John, 106
Rodriquez Canal line, 50
Roebling, Donald, 341
Roi-Namur, Marshall Islands, 400–402
Roosevelt, Assistant Secretary of the Navy Franklin D., 203, 234, 382: President, 335, 344, 346, 351, 363, 367, 370, 372, 377
Roosevelt, James, 335
Roosevelt, Assistant Secretary of the Navy Theodore, 127: President, 167–68, 267; on abolition of the Marine Corps, 140; on the Canal Zone, 166; on removal of Marines from ships, 139
Roosevelt Roads, Puerto Rico, 541
Roosevelt Corollary, 163, 181
Rosenthal, Joe, 430
Ross, Major General Robert, 48
Route 1, Vietnam, 561, 571, 584, 604
Route 9, Vietnam, 576, 584, 591
Rowell, Major Ross E., 244, 248, 334: Major General, 408
Royal Flying Corps, 309–10
Royal Marines, 5, 32, 42, 84, 99, 105, 110, 127, 157–58, 492
Royal Navy, 3, 5–6, 9, 14–15, 23, 25, 27, 33, 38, 42, 46, 48, 62, 82, 161, 268, 307, 309
Rupertus, Major General William H., 384, 421

Russell, Major John H., 275, 284–85: Colonel, 198–99, 203–204, 209–10; Major General, 330; 16th Commandant of the Marine Corps, 335–36
Russell, W. W., 191–92
Russell Islands, 379–80
Russia, 229, 268, 287, 321; *see also* Soviet Union
Russian revolution, 296
Russo-Japanese War, 269
Ryukyu Islands, 426–27, 432, 434–35

Sabine, 96
Sacasa, Dr. Juan B., 260–61
Sacasa, Juan Maria, 240, 242, 246
Sachon, Korea, 484
Sacketts Harbor, New York, 47
Saigon, Vietnam, 560, 563–65, 568, 574, 590, 604–605
Saipan, 336, 409–12, 414–18, 433, 435
Salgado, Carlos, 249
Saltonstall, Captain Dudley, 22
Sam, General Vilbrun Guillaume, 183–85
Samana Bay, Santo Domingo, 179, 181, 192, 271
Samar, Philippine Islands, 152, 154–55, 425–26
Samichon River, Korea, 514
Samoa, 111, 149, 267, 357, 359, 362, 365
Sampson, Rear Admiral William T., 130–32
San Clemente, California, 338
San Cosme Gate, Mexico City, 77, 80
Sanderson, Lieutenant Lawson H. M., 333
San Diego, California, 74, 192, 222, 233, 295, 327, 333, 337–38, 349, 359, 376, 480–81, 599, 618
Sandinistas, 247–54, 256–59
Sandino, Augusto Cesar, 246–51, 253–55, 257–59
San Domingo Improvement Company, 179
San Francisco, California, 72, 283
San Francisco de Macoris, Santo Domingo, 195
San Gabriel, battle of, 75
San Isidro airfield, Santo Domingo, 558
San Jacinto, 85
San Jose, California, 76
San Juan, Puerto Rico, 130
San Juan del Norte, Nicaragua, 239
San Juan River, 238
San Pedro, California, 74

Santa Barbara, California, 74
Santa Cruz Islands, 365
Santiago, Cuba, 130, 132–33, 179
Santo Domingo, 35, 179, 191–92, 202, 258, 557–58, 738: military government in, 729
Santo Domingo City, 204
Saratoga, New York, American victory at, 16, 20
Sasebo, Japan, 448
Savannah, 75
Savannah, Georgia, 98
Savo Island, battle of, 367
Saylor's Creek, battle of, 100
Scala, Francis Marie, 113
Scapa Flow, 307, 319
Schilt, Lieutenant Christian F., 249, 625
Schmidt, Major General Harry, 400, 415, 428, 430
School of Application, 119–20, 122, 164
Scott, Major General Winfield, 74, 76
Sea-basing concept, 616
Sea of Japan, 477
Search and destroy operations, Vietnam, 567, 572
Schroeder, Seaton, 138
Seabees, 368
Sedan, France, 311, 314
Seibo Province, Dominican Republic, 196, 199
Selective Service Act, System, 288–89, 374
Selkirk, Earl of, 17
Sellers, Rear Admiral David F., 247, 253, 255, 735
Seminole Indians, 70
Senate Armed Service Committe, 462, 473, 608, 736
Senate Committee on Appropriations, 736
Senate Military Affairs Committee, 141, 458–59
Senate Naval Affairs Committee, 110, 141, 459–60, 736
Seoul, Korea, 121, 136, 477–78, 481–82, 485–86, 488–90, 495, 501, 513, 593
Serapis, 18
Service Technique de l'Agriculture et l'Enseignment Professionel, 207, 209
Seven Years' War, 4
Sevier, Captain Alexander, 48–49
Sewall, Congressman Samuel, 29
Seymour, Vice Admiral Edward, 159–60
Shanghai, China, 214, 217, 219, 221–24, 226, 228, 230–32, 234, 261, 451: second battle of, 233
Shanghai Racecourse, 232
Shanghai Volunteer Corps (SVC), 223, 225, 231, 235
Shannon, 47
Shantung Peninsula, China, 448–50
Sharp, Admiral Ulysses S. G., 567–68
Shepherd, Brigadier General Lemuel C., Jr., 385, 417: Major General, 435, 453, 465; Lieutenant General, 478, 486; General, 20th Commandant of the Marine Corps, 507–508, 519–20, 522, 524, 528
Sherman, Rear Admiral Forrest C., 453: Vice Admiral, 461, 472, 477–78; Admiral, 479, 496, 499–500, 506, 729
Sherman, Major General William T., 98
Sherrod, Robert, 399, 415, 471, 511
Ships landing parties, 138
Ship-to-shore movement, concept of, 332, 337, 339, 366, 378, 382, 402, 428–29, 433, 440; problems of, 454, 464, 616
"Short Airfield for Tactical Support" (SATS), 536, 568, 612
Shortland Islands, 381–82
Shoup, Colonel David M., 396–98: Brigadier General, 522, 530–31; General, 22d Commandant of the Marine Corps, 543–44, 546, 548–52, 556, 732
Shuri, Okinawa, 434, 436
Shuri castle, 436
Sibley, Major Burton W., 303
Sicily, 484
Sisgsbee, Captain Charles D., 129
Sikorsky, Igor, 455, 467
Simmons, Brigadier General Edwin H., 741
Simms, Brevet Captain John D., 85
Sims, Commander William S., 138, 141–42: Admiral, 308, 321, 735
"Single Management" issue, 587–88
Sino-Japanese War, 121, 232
Sloat, Commodore John D., 74
"Slot," the, 367
Small Wars Manual, 263
Smathers, George A., 473
Smith, Lieutenant Bernard L., 277
Smith, Major Holland M., 325: Major General, 350–51, 373, 392–93, 395–400, 403–404; Lieutenant General, 405, 408, 411, 414–15, 428, 430–31, 471, 731–32, 737

Smith, Brigadier General Jacob H., 153
Smith, Major John L., 368
Smith, Major General Julian C., 395, 397–98, 420
Smith, Brigadier General Oliver P., 421–53; Major General, 486–87, 489–92, 494–95, 498, 731
Smith, General P. F., 78–79
Smith, Major General Ralph C., 413, 415
Smith, Brevet Major Richard, 54, 57
Smith, Secretary of the Navy Robert, 37, 40
Smith vs. Smith controversy, 413–15; *see also* Saipan; Smith, Holland M.; Smith, Ralph C.
Snowden, Rear Admiral Thomas, 194, 198, 204
Society of Righteous and Harmonious Fists, 155; *see also* Boxers
Sohoton River, Philippine Islands, 153–54
Soissons, France, 299, 305–306, 311–12, 315
Solomon Islands, 357, 362, 364, 371, 377–78, 421, 425
Solomon Sea, 383
Solórzano, Carlos, 240
Somers, 59
Somme, the, France, 297
Somme offensive, 297
Somme-Py, France, 312, 314
Somoza, Anastasio, 260–61
Sonoma, California, 74
Soochow Creek, Shanghai, 222, 231–33
Sousa, John Philip, 113, 118, 737
Southard, Secretary of the Navy Samuel L., 60
South China Sea, 560–61
Southeast Asia Treaty Organization (SEATO), 541
South Korea, 466, 512, 516, 519–20, 596; *see also* Republic of Korea
South Pacific Ocean, 362–63, 372, 379, 384, 386, 388, 404, 407, 423, 440
South Vietnam, 553–54, 560, 563, 565, 591; *see also* Government of Vietnam
Soviet Union, 532, 555, 611; *see also* Russia
Spaatz, General Carl W., 459
Spain, 4, 553
Spanish East Florida, 41
Special Board, 453–55; *see also* Dyer, Edward C.; Krulak, Victor H.; Twining, Merrill B.

"Spreading Ink Blot" concept, Vietnam, 567
Springfield rifle, Model 1903, 176, 294
Spruance, Vice Admiral Raymond A., 392–93, 395, 398–99, 401, 403, 411, 415, 428, 432
Squires, Herbert G., 158
Staley, Lieutenant Colonel J. J., 341
Stallings, Lawrence, 317
Standard Fruit Company, 259
Stark, Admiral Harold R., 347
State Department, 128, 164, 168–69, 182–86, 189, 193–94, 201, 204, 206–207, 210, 214, 216, 220–21, 224–25, 227, 231, 235, 240, 243, 245, 248, 250, 259, 268
State marines, 21
State naval militias, 284, 308
State navies, 9
St. Etienne-à-Arnes, France, 312, 314
Stewart, Captain Charles, 47
Stewart, Brigadier General Joseph L., 732
Stimson, Secretary of State Henry, 210, 231, 244–45, 254
Stimson Mission, 244
St. Lawrence River, Canada, 7
St. Mary's Isle, 17
St. Mary's River, 41
St. Mihiel salient, France, 297, 311–12
Stockton, Commodore Robert F., 74–75
Stoddert, Benjamin, 28, 30
Strike Command, 555–56
"Struggle Movement," 574
Subic Bay, Philippine Islands, 152, 270, 272–74, 276, 278
Sudong, Korea, 491
Suez Crisis, 532, 539
Sugar Loaf Hill, Okinawa, 436
Suicide Creek, Cape Gloucester, 385
Suippes-Souain area, France, 312
Sullivan, Secretary of the Navy John L., 470, 472
Sun Yat Sen, 217–19
Swanson, Secretary of the Navy Claude, 342

Tabasco Expedition, Second, 73
Tabasco River, Mexico, 73
Tacloban, Philippine Islands, 424
Taegu, Korea, 477
Taft, Secretary of War William H., 167: President, 143–44, 168, 174, 277
Taiping Rebellion, 84
Taiwan, 466, 476–77, 541
Taku, China, 157, 160, 449

Tam Ky, Vietnam, 570, 592
Tampa Bay, 70
Tampico, Mexico, 72, 171–72
Tanambogo, Solomon Islands, 364, 366
Tanapag Plain, Philippine Islands, 414
Tangku, China, 156, 160, 450
Tangshan, China, 449
Tanks: M–26, 484; M–48, 615;
   M–60A1, 615; T–34, 484
Tan Son Nhut, Vietnam, 605
Tarawa, 515, 522; battle of, 393–99;
   see also Betio
Target Hill, 385
Tartar City, 156
Tartar Wall, 158–59, 162
Taylor, General Maxwell D., 564:
   Ambassador, 565–66
Tell It to the Marines, 317
Telpeneca, Nicaragua, 249
Tenaru River, battle of the, 368
Tennessee, 100
*Tentative Manual for Landing
   Operations,* 331–32, 334–37, 343
Terrett, Captain George H., 76, 79–80,
   82
Tet offensive, 592–95
*Text for the Employment of Marine
   Corps Aviation,* 335
Thailand, 352, 553, 586, 605
The Basic School, 618
Thermal boot, 512
Thetis Bay, 535
Thi, General Nguyen Chanh, 565, 574
Thieu, Nguyen Van, 573
38th Parallel, 475, 478, 490, 500, 502–
   503
Thomas, Charles S., 531
Thomas, Brigadier General Gerald C.,
   457–58: Major General, 504–505,
   524, 528
Thomason, Captain John W., Jr., 230,
   753
Thompson, Clark W., 467
Thompson, J. Walter, Company, 359
Thompson, Secretary of the Navy
   Smith, 55
Thua Thien, Vietnam, 561, 574, 576,
   594, 601
Thurmond, Senator Strom, 549
Tientsin, China, 121, 156–57, 159–61,
   218–19, 225, 227–28, 230, 354, 499
Tientsin-Peking railroad, 226
Tilton, Captain McLane, 106:
   Lieutenant Colonel, 731
Tingey, Captain Thomas, 49
Tinian, 409–11, 415–17

Tinian Town, 416
Tipitapa Agreement, 245, 254
Tipitapa River, Nicaragua, 244
Tojo, Premier Hideki, 353, 414
Toktong Pass, Korea, 492–93
Tokyo, Japan, 230, 478
"Tokyo Express," 367
Tompkins, Major General Rathvon
   McClure, 591
Torcy, France, 299, 301
Torokina River, Bougainville, 381–83
Torpedo School, Newport, Rhode
   Island, 119
Toul, France, 312
TOW antitank missile, 609, 614–15,
   617
"Toys for Tots," 467
Tracy, Secretary of the Navy
   Benjamin F., 116, 119, 122–23
"Transplacement" system, 537
Treaty of 1915 (with Haiti), 190
Treaty of Paris (1898), 150, 267
Tregaskis, Richard, 471
Tripoli, 27, 43
Tripoli, 43
Truce talks, Korean, 504
Trujillo, Rafael Leonidas, 211, 556
Truk, 379, 384, 393, 401, 409, 420
Truman, President Harry S, 446, 450,
   458–61, 465–66, 468, 471–74, 477–
   78, 488, 490, 495–99, 506, 512, 519
Trumbull, 24
Truxton, Captain Thomas, 33, 35–36
Tsingtao, China, 449–51
Tulagi, Solomon Islands, 363, 366, 368
Tulifinny Cross Roads, battle of, 98
Tunis, 27
Tun Tavern, 13
Turkey, 321
Turnage, Major General Allen H., 383
Turner, Nat, rebellion of, 68
Turner, Rear Admiral Richmond Kelly,
   364–67, 370–71, 379–81, 392–93,
   395–96, 399–400, 403, 408, 411–
   13, 415, 428, 432–33
Turner, Lieutenant Colonel Thomas C.,
   333
Tuxpan, Mexico, 73
Twiggs, Major Levi, 76, 78, 731
Twining, Colonel Merrill B., 453–56,
   458–59, 463, 528: Lieutenant
   General, 543
"Two Ocean Navy" Act, 345
Tyler, Adjutant and Inspector Henry B.,
   92
Tzu Hsi, Dowager Empress, 156

Udorn, Thailand, 554
Uijongbu, Korea, 490
Ulithi Atoll, 420
Umurbrogol Ridge, Peleliu, 420, 422
Underwater demolition teams (UDTs), 398, 403, 411
Unification controversy, 456, 732, 734
Union Nacional Dominicana, 203
Union Patriotique, 203
United Nations Command (UNC), 477, 501, 503–504, 511–13
United Nations Organization, 446, 451, 476, 504, 512–13, 516, 539: truce negotiations, 512–13
United States, 28, 57, 472
United States Air Force, 457, 470, 472, 500, 586: Far East Air Forces(FEAF), 477, 502, 504–505; Fifth Air Force, 502, 505, 513–15; Seventh Air Force, 586–88; Strategic Air Command, 519
United States Army, 271–72, 274, 278–80, 282, 285, 292, 318:
   units and commands:
   American Expeditionary Force, 290, 292–94, 296–97, 302, 306–307, 316–17;
      Service of Supply, AEF, 311
   Army Air Corps, 329; Army Air Corps Tactical School, 334; Army Air Forces, 389, 400, 410, 416, 419, 424, 427, 432, 446, 457; Army Air Service, 309; Army of Cuban Pacification, 167; Army of the Potomac, 93–95; Army of the South, 71–72; Military Assistance Command, Vietnam (MACV), 564–70, 572–73, 576–77, 581–82, 586–87, 590–91, 593–95, 600, 602; Southwest Pacific Area command, 357; First Army, 311–12, 314–16; Sixth Army, 384, 423–25; Eighth Army, 424, 426, 477, 479, 484–85, 489–95, 498, 501–505, 514:
      Joint Operations Center, Eighth Army, 502
   Tenth Army, 433–34, 437–38:
      Tactical Air Force, Tenth Army, 433, 437
   1st Joint Training Force, 350; 2d Joint Training Force, 350; Coast Artillery Corps, 270; Corps of Engineers, 270; I Corps, 311, 503, 564, 594; V Corps, 314–16; VIII Corps, 151–52; IX Corps, 503; X Corps, 486–87, 489–95, 500, 503,

512, 515; XIV Corps, 380, 393;
XXIV Corps, 98, 433, 435–36:
   Corps Artillery, XXIV Corps, 411, 423
XXXIV Corps, 593, 601;
Strategic Army Corps (STRAC), 543, 555; Americal Division, 370, 590; 1st Cavalry Division, 425, 478; 1st Cavalry Division (Airmobile), 582, 592; 1st Infantry Division, 292–94, 297, 305, 350; 2d Infantry Division, 94, 294, 297–99, 301, 303–306, 311–16, 482, 733; 3d Division, Army of the Potomac, 94; 3d Infantry Division, 302, 350, 494; 7th Infantry Division, 400–401, 403, 435, 439, 489, 492; 24th Infantry Division, 477, 484; 25th Infantry Division, 370, 482; 26th Infantry Division, 297; 27th Infantry Division, 389, 398, 400, 402–403, 411–15, 435, 439; 36th Infantry Division, 312, 314–15; 42d Infantry Division, 297, 383; 77th Infantry Division, 418, 433–35, 439; 80th Infantry Division, 315; 81st Infantry Division, 420–22, 439; 82d Airborne Division, 557–58; 96th Infantry Division, 435, 439; 101st Airborne Division, 592; 1st Brigade, 94; 3d Brigade, 299, 302, 304–305; 6th Separate Brigade, 153; 3d Artillery Regiment, 74; 5th Infantry, 482; 7th Infantry, 303; 9th Infantry, 153, 160–61, 163, 214, 484; 11th Infantry, 79; 11th New York, 95; 15th Infantry, 214, 218, 225–26, 228–29; 23d Infantry, 301; 31st Infantry, 231; 32d Infantry, 489; 106th Infantry, 402; 164th Infantry, 370; 321st Infantry, 422; Special Forces, 548, 572, 576; Task Force Kean, 482, 484
United States Army Military History Institute, 733
United States Congress, 141, 295
United States Marine Corps, 7: accepts inductees, 306, 374; advanced base force mission, 321; amphibious assault mission, 325, 342–43, 623; amphibious assault role, 261, 322–23, 330; anti-intellectualism in, 174; as colonial infantry, 164*ff*, 174; as a force in readiness, 509, 522, 524, 526, 542, 580, 621–23; as an instrument of foreign policy, 236; as

United States Marine Corps *(cont.)*
part of the Navy Department, 67;
as a separate service, 102–103; as
ships guards, 41–43, 47, 57–63, 66,
68, 70, 72–73, 81–82, 84, 86, 92,
94, 97–98, 102–105, 107, 117–18,
120–22, 124–27, 129–30, 137, 143–
44, 149, 152, 156, 167, 172–73,
184, 242, 277, 288, 307, 322, 336–
37, 354, 465; aviation, 329, 333,
611–14; aviation doctrine, 334;
aviation strength, 308–309; aviation
training, 361; barracks duty, 107;
casualties, 262, 304, 306, 316, 386,
398, 419, 423, 429, 438–39, 515,
517, 560, 576–77, 594, 602, 629;
clothing allowance, 31; democratizes
commissioning process, 289;
desertions, 88, 118; duties, 40, 43,
81, 321, 328; electronic techr.ology
in, 615; guarding the mails, 222–24,
327; helicopter developmenr and
operations, 510, 582; human relations
program, 599–600; institutional
development of, 37; in the Civil
War, 97–98; in the Spanish-
American War, 130–35; in
Vladivostok, 307; in World War I,
287–318; in World War II, 344–
441; marksmanship training, 150,
176, 360–61; military character of,
63; officer corps, character of, 97;
officers, sources of, 63, 109, 373;
officer turnover, 97; personnel
problems in, 577–79, 622; quality of
enlisted personnel, 39, 64, 117; race
relations in, 598; recruiting, 31, 104,
175, 373, 619, 621; reforms in,
108–110; relationship to Navy yard
commandants, 40; reputation of, 70;
research and development projects,
615; roles and missions, 41, 91, 120,
271, 463–64, 469–70, 473, 507,
518, 520, 544, 610; strength of, 32,
118, 329, 336, 448, 465, 560, 573,
577, 628:
    in 1812, 46; in 1850s, 81; in
    Civil War, 93; in period 1898–
    1908, 129, 135, 150; in 1918,
    296, 306; in 1941, 353; in 1942,
    359
"State Department troops," 261,
519, 604–605; structure of, 29;
threats to abolish, 61, 102; ties with
Navy, 114; training, 111, 290, 360–
61, 618; uniforms, 39, 66, 88–89,
112, 119
units and commands:
    Amphibious Corps, Pacific Fleet,
    372–73, 392; Commander,
    Aircraft, Solomon Islands, 378,
    380; East Coast Expeditionary
    Force, 324, 327; Fleet Marine
    Force, Atlantic, 508, 540–41, 547,
    553–54, 558, 578–79, 609; Fleet
    Marine Force, Pacific, 405–406,
    408, 415, 438, 447, 478, 486,
    537, 553–64, 566–67, 569, 572,
    588, 595, 621; Fleet Marine
    Force, Western Pacific, 451;
    Marine Aircraft Wings, Pacific,
    372
air units:
    1st Marine Aircraft Wing, 348,
    359, 368, 423, 426, 449–50,
    479, 481–82, 502, 504–505,
    507, 513, 515, 520, 522, 568,
    585–87, 590, 600–601; 2d
    Marine Aircraft Wing, 348,
    353, 424, 508, 579–80, 597;
    3d Marine Aircraft Wing, 372,
    508, 520, 597; 4th Marine
    Aircraft Wing, 552, 578; 4th
    Marine Base Defense Aircraft
    Wing, 372, 403; Marine
    Aircraft Group 1, 346; Marine
    Aircraft Group 2, 346; Marine
    Aircraft Group 11, 422; Marine
    Aircraft Group 12, 426, 490–
    91, 513; Marine Aircraft Group
    13, 359; Marine Aircraft Group
    14, 425–26; Marine Aircraft
    Group 21, 354; Marine
    Aircraft Group 22, 359;
    Marine Aircraft Group 24, 423,
    425–26; Marine Aircraft Group
    32, 423, 425–26; Marine
    Aircraft Group 33, 478, 485,
    495, 513; Marine Aircraft
    Groups, Dagupan, 425; Marine
    Aircraft Groups, Zamboanga,
    426; Day Wing, Northern
    Bombing Group, 310; 1st
    Marine Aviation Squadron, 309–
    10;1st Marine Aeronautic
    Company, 309; Marine
    Experimental Helicopter
    Squadron 1 (HMX-1), 455,
    466–67; Marine Observation
    Squadron 1 (VO-1M), 244,
    247; Marine Observation
    Squadron 4(VO-4M), 245;

Marine Observation
Squadron 6 (VO-6M), 501,
505, 513; Marine Medium
Helicopter Squadron 161
(HMM-161), 746; Marine
Transport Helicopter Squadron
161 (HMR-161), 505–506,
510, 513; Marine Fighter
Squadron 211 (VMF-211),
355; Marine Fighter Squadron
212 (VMF-212), 212, 359,
503; Marine Fighter Attack
Squadron 232 (VMFA-232),
746; Marine Attack Squadron
311 (VMA-311), 746; Marine
Fighter Attack Squadron 312
(VMFA-312), 746; Marine
Night Fighter Squadron 541
[VMF (N)-541], 424

ground units:
I Marine Amphibious Corps
(IMAC), 371–73, 378, 381–
82; III Amphibious Corps
(IIIAC), 405, 433, 435, 437–
38, 448–51; V Amphibious
Corps (VAC), 390, 392, 395,
399–400, 425, 427–31, 448:
Naval Gunfire Section, VAC,
406; I Marine Amphibious
Force (I MAF), 602, 617; I
Marine Expeditionary Force
(I MEF), 556; II Marine
Amphibious Force (II MAF),
580, 617; 2d Provisional Marine
Force, 539, 541; II Marine
Expeditionary Force (II MEF),
553–56; III Marine Amphibious
Force (III MAF), 560–61, 563,
565–77, 579–88, 590, 593–95,
597, 600–604, 617, 622: Force
Logistics Command, III MAF,
569; III Marine Expeditionary
Force, 553–54; Northern Troops
and Landing Force, 411–13,
415, 417; Southern Troops and
Landing Force, 411, 417–19;
Western Troops and Landing
Force, 420–21; 1st Marine
Division, 348–50, 359, 362,
365–68, 370, 378, 384–86, 390,
420–23, 433–37, 448–50,
465–66, 479–82, 485–92, 494–
96, 498, 501, 504–505, 507,
509, 511–14, 516–17, 518–21,
528, 537, 553, 566, 574, 576–
77, 589–90, 602–603, 746; 2d

Marine Division, 348–50, 353,
359, 362, 365, 370–71, 378,
389–90, 395–96, 398, 411–13,
416, 433, 435, 437, 464–65,
480–81, 508, 538–39, 541,
579–80, 599, 735; 3d Marine
Division, 362, 372, 378, 382–
83, 390, 411, 417–18, 428,
430, 508, 519–22, 537, 539–40,
547, 566–67, 574, 576, 583–84,
589, 591, 593–95, 600–601,
746; 4th Marine Division, 372,
400–401, 411–13, 415–17,
428–30, 552, 578, 746; 5th
Marine Division, 390, 428–29,
448, 576–77, 6th Marine
Division, 433, 434–45, 437,
448–50; Task Force Delta, 574,
576; 1st Advanced Base Brigade,
281; 1st Brigade, 185, 190, 197–
98, 202, 204, 208, 261, 337–39
345, 349, 418, 479, 481–82,
517; 1st Provisional Brigade,
353, 411, 417, 478; 2d Brigade,
193–95, 199–201, 204, 206,
233, 245–46, 248–50, 255,
257–58, 261, 337; 3d Brigade,
225, 227–28, 359, 508; 3d
Marine Amphibious Brigade,
566, 604; 3d Marine
Expeditionary Brigade, 554; 4th
Brigade, 294–96, 298–99, 301,
304, 306–307, 311–14, 318,
323, 465, 746; 4th Marine
Expeditionary Brigade, 558; 5th
Marine Brigade, 307, 316; 5th
Marine Expeditionary Brigade,
555; 9th Marine Amphibious
Brigade, 577, 588, 605; 9th
Marine Expeditionary Brigade,
564–65; Special Landing Force,
554, 566, 568, 574, 576, 588,
602; 1st Marines, 185, 349,
365–66, 384–85, 421, 487–88,
490–92, 503, 746; 1st Raider
Regiment, 380; 1st Regiment
(Fixed Defense), 280, 283,
285; 2d Marines, 185, 187,
349, 365–66, 396–97, 746; 3d
Marines, 199, 362, 382–83,
418, 508, 746–47; 4th Marines,
192, 199, 222–23, 225–28,
230–35, 261, 353–57, 383,
391, 411, 435, 437, 448–49,
746; 5th Marines, 244, 247,
249, 255, 292–93, 301, 303–

United States Marine Corps *(cont.)*
306, 311, 313–14, 324, 337, 349, 365, 384–85, 421–22, 436, 478–80, 484, 487–88, 491, 493–94, 746; 6th Marines, 224, 226, 233–34, 293, 297, 302–303, 305–306, 311–14, 324, 337, 349–50, 359, 396–98; 7th Marines, 349, 359, 362, 365, 368, 385, 421–22, 436, 480–81, 489–91, 493–94, 572; 8th Marines, 349, 359, 397, 437, 746; 9th Marines, 362, 383, 418, 571, 574, 576, 595, 746–47; 10th Marines, 226, 324, 327, 337, 359, 397; 11th Marines, 245, 250–51, 255, 349, 476, 480; 12th Marines, 226, 349, 746; 15th Marines, 201–202; 19th Marines, 362; 21st Marines, 362, 383, 418; 22d Marines, 390, 400, 411, 436; 23d Marines, 401; 24th Marines, 401; 25th Marines, 401, 429–30; 26th Marines, 577–78, 591; 27th Marines, 594; 28th Marines, 428–29; 29th Marines, 413, 434–37; 1st Battalion, 5th Marines, 292; 1st Defense Battalion, 354–55; 1st Parachute Battalion, 365; 1st Raider Battalion, 365; 2d Defense Battalion, 359; 2d Raider Battalion, 370, 393; 3d Defense Battalion, 354, 365; 4th Defense Battalion, 359; 6th Machine Gun Battalion, 293; 7th Defense Battalion, 359; 17th Company, 292; 49th Company, 292; 66th Company, 292; 67th Company, 292; 96th Company, 316; Horse Marines, 229; Joint Assault Signal Company (JASCO), 406–407; Landing Force Air Support Control Unit (LFASCU), 408, 437; Marine Corps Test Unit 1, 525; 6th Marine Expeditionary Unit, 557
United States Naval Academy, 110, 281–82
United States Naval Institute *Proceedings,* 117, 123, 278
United States Navy, 279, 472: and technical revolution, 53; Caribbean mission, 35; creation of, 28; reforms in, 117; units and commands: Commander in Chief, Pacific Fleet,
372, 391, 399, 420, 478, 605: *see also* Nimitz; Commander, Aircraft, Pacific Fleet, 405; Commander, Aircraft, South Pacific Force, 378; Asiatic Fleet, 214, 217–19, 221, 224, 227–28, 233, 235, 273, 356–57; Atlantic Fleet, 172–74, 350; Pacific Fleet, 140, 233, 349, 352, 354, 357, 363–64; Naval Forces, Far East (NFFE), 477; 2d Fleet, 520, 555; 3d Fleet, 377, 424; 5th Fleet, 392, 399, 411–12, 428, 432, 434–35; 6th Fleet, 465, 520, 537, 539–40, 552; 7th Fleet, 377, 477, 487, 554, 566, 568; Joint Task Force 7, 487–88, 490; Task Force 77, 495, 514; Amphibious Force, Atlantic Fleet, 350; Amphibious Force, Pacific Fleet, 350; Central Pacific Force, 392; III Amphibious Force, 381, 386, 420; V Amphibious Force, 392; VII Amphibious Force, 386, 424; United States Support Activities Group, Thailand, 605; Asiatic Squadron, 101, 121, 130, 267; East India Squadron, 84; European Squadron, 101; Florida Squadron (Mosquito Fleet), 72; Gulf Squadron, 101; Home Squadron, 72–74, 76–77; North Atlantic Squadron, 101, 130–31; Pacific Squadron, 73–76, 101; South Atlantic Blockading Squadron, 95–96, 98, 101; Special Service Squadron, 242, 253, 259; West Africa Squadron, 60; West India Squadron, 56, 59; Asiatic Station, 151, 153
U.S. v. *Freeman,* 69
Unity of command issue, 328
Upshur, Major General William P., 732
Upton, Colonel Emery, 111
Ushijima, General Mitsuru, 432, 434–36
Utley, Major Harold H., 251, 263: Lieutenant Colonel, 731

Valcour Island, New York, 20
Valley Forge, 535
Vandalia, 84, 111
Vandegrift, Major General Alexander Archer, 365–72: General, 18th Commandant of the Marine Corps, 372–73, 399, 404, 415, 432, 438, 447–48, 453–54, 457–63, 465, 528, 731, 737

Vandenburg, General Hoyt S., 479, 500
Van Fleet, Lieutenant General James, 503, 511
Vásquez, Horacio, 181, 204
Vaux, France, 304
Velásquez, Federico, 191, 204
Vella Lavella, Solomon Islands, 362, 380
Vengeance, 35
Veracruz, Mexico, 72, 74, 77, 171–74, 176, 275, 383
Verdun, France, 297, 311
Vernon, Admiral Edward, 4
"Vertical envelopment," 454, 456, 464, 466, 506, 510, 521, 524–25, 534, 537, 551, 572, 614
Veterans of Foreign Wars, 463, 531
Vicksburg, Mississippi, 98
Vieques, Puerto Rico, 339, 541
Vierzy, France, 306
Viet Cong (VC), 554, 559, 561, 563, 565–66, 571–75, 601: 1st Viet Cong Regiment, 572, 574; Doc Lap Battalion, 574
Viet Minh, 561
Vietnam, 541, 560–61, 566–67, 577, 579, 582–83, 585, 595, 597, 600, 604, 606, 610, 731, 743, 747
Vietnam War, 543, 547, 559, 576, 580, 582, 596, 598, 606, 619, 623, 732, 738, 749
Villere Plantation, 50
Vincennes, 60
Vincent, Stenio, 210
Vinson, Congressman Carl, 462, 473, 496–97, 499, 529–30
Vinson-Trammell Act of 1934, 336
Virginia, 97, 100
Virginia, colony of, 4
Virginia marines, 21
Virginia Military Institute, 292
V-J Day, 438–40, 447
Vladivostok, Marine landings at, 217
Vodun (voodoo), 178, 209
Vogel, Major General Clayton B., 350–51, 373, 731
V-12 Program, 373

Wade, Brigadier General Sidney S., 539–40
Wadsworth, Congressman James W., 462
Wainwright, General Jonathan, 357
Wainwright, Captain Robert D., 68
Wake Island, 319, 344, 352, 354–57, 592
Wake Island, 360

Walker, Lieutenant General Walton H., 477, 482, 484–85, 501
Waller, Major Littleton W. T., 153–54, 160, 162: Colonel, 142, 167, 173–74, 185–88, 277, 282; Brigadier General, 731
Wallingford, Lieutenant Samuel, 17
Walt, Major General Lewis W., 566–68, 570–71, 573–76: Lieutenant General, 582; General, 583, 590
Wana Ridge, Okinawa, 436
War Deparment, 31, 110–11, 160, 172, 269, 288–90, 293, 295–96, 298, 306–308, 318, 446, 456–67, 461: General Staff, 140, 166, 268–70, 280, 289, 292–93, 350, 458, 508
War of 1812, 45, 52, 54–55, 57, 63, 69–70, 82, 88
War of the Austrian Succession, 4
War of the Spanish Succession, 3–4
War Plans: BLACK, 268; ORANGE, 269, 320–22, 325–26, 343, 345; RED, 268; YELLOW, 225; *see also* Rainbow Plans
Warren, Senator Francis, 141
Warsaw Pact, 607
War with Spain, 4, 120, 128, 130, 134, 137–38, 147, 163, 176, 181, 267, 271, 284, 735, 738
War with Tripoli and Morocco, 42
Washington, 14, 185
Washington, General George, 5–7, 13–14, 27–28
Washington Conference on Naval Disarmament, 319–20
Washington, D.C., 31, 85, 621
Washington Gun Factory, 119
Washington Navy Yard, 38
Wasp, 47
Waterhouse, Lieutenant Colonel Charles, 741–42
Watson, Captain Samuel E., 58: Brevet Lieutenant Colonel, 76, 80
Watt, 24
Weldon, Felix de, 511
Welles, Secretary of the Navy Gideon, 91–94, 102
Welles, Sumner, 204–205
Wessin, General Elias Wessin y, 557
Western Carolines, 419
Western Front, 289–90
Western Pacific Ocean, 389, 410, 419, 423, 426, 452, 522
Westmoreland, General William C., 564, 566–68, 576–77, 582, 584, 590, 593–94
Whangpoo River, 222, 231

Wharton, Lieutenant Colonel Franklin, 3d Commandant of the Marine Corps, 38–40, 42, 46, 49, 54–55, 71: view of the Corp's mission, 48
What Price Glory?, 317
Whipple, Abraham, 19, 22–23
Whitehaven, England, 17
Wickes, Captain Lambert, 16
Wilhelm II, Emperor of Germany, 268
Wilkes Expedition, 60
Wilkinson, Major General James, 40
Wilkinson, Rear Admiral Theodore S., 381
Williams, Rear Admiral C. S., 219, 222–25
Williams, Captain Dion, 273: Major, 274, 284; Colonel, 327
Williams, Captain John, 41
Williams, Captain Lloyd, 301
Willing, James, 20
Wilmington, North Carolina, 98
Wilson, Earl, 391
Wilson, General Louis H., 26th Commandant of the Marine Corps, 612, 614–15, 617–18, 621–22, 624
Wilson, President Woodrow, 171, 183, 185, 193, 201, 282, 287–89, 306: and interposition, 172; and withdrawal of Marines from Dominican Republic, 203
"Wilson Plan," 183–84, 194, 196
Winder, Brigadier General William H., 48
Windward Passage, 181
Winthrop, Assistant Secretary of the Navy Beekman, 276
Wise, Captain Frederic M., 191, 303: Colonel, 737
Wolmi-do, Korea, 487–88
Women Marines, 468, 508: in World War I, 307, 374
Women Armed Services Integration Act of 1948, 468
Women's Reserve, 374
Wonsan, Korea, 490–91
Wood, Charles Anthony, 733

Wood, Major General Leonard, 139, 141, 172, 273
Woodrum Committee, 404
Woods, Colonel Louis, 368: Brigadier General, 408; Major General, 433
World War I, 150, 190, 196, 262, 282, 287–318, 465, 735
World War II, 211, 217, 263, 325–26, 343–441, 446, 452–53, 465, 481, 523, 528, 560, 607, 621, 728, 740
Worth, Brigadier General William J., 77, 79
Wotje, Marshall Islands, 399, 403
Wu Pei-fu, General, 218
Wuchang, China, 217

Yae Take, Mount, Okinawa, 434–35
Yalu River, Korea, 490–92
Yamamoto, Admiral Isoroku, 352
Yang-Tsun, battle of, China, 162
Yangtze Patrol, 219, 227–28, 231, 234–35
Yangtze River, China, 214, 217, 226, 232–34
Yangtze Valley, 213, 218, 221, 232, 451
Yap, Caroline Islands, 419
Yarmouth, 15
Yarnell, Admiral Harry E., 233
Yerba Buena, California, 74
Yokosuka, Japan, 448
Yom Kippur War of 1973, 609, 613
Yonabaru, Okinawa, 434
Yongdongpo, Korea, 488
Yontan airfield, Okinawa, 433
Yuan Shi-kai, 213, 217–18
Yudam-ni, Korea, 492–94

Zacharias, Rear Admiral Ellis M., 463
Zeilin, Captain Jacob, 94: Major, 96; Colonel, 7th Commandant of the Marine Corps, 91–93, 102–104, 108, 112
Zelaya, José Santos, 168–69
Zeledón, Benjamin, 170